RICHARD MALTBY
HOLLYWOOD CINEMA
SECOND EDITION

Blackwell
Publishing

350 Main Street, Malden, MA 02148-5018, USA
108 Cowley Road, Oxford OX4 1JF, UK
550 Swanston Street, Carlton South, Melbourne, Victoria 3053, Australia
Kurfürstendamm 57, 10707 Berlin, Germany

First edition published 1995
Second edition published 2003 by Blackwell Publishing Ltd

Library of Congress Cataloging-in-Publication Data

Maltby, Richard, 1952–
Hollywood cinema / Richard Maltby. – 2nd ed.
p. cm.
Includes bibliographical references and index.
ISBN 0-631-21614-6 (hardcover: alk. paper) – ISBN 0-631-21615-4
(pbk. : alk. paper)
1. Motion pictures – United States – History.   2. Motion picture
industry – United States – History.   I. Title.
PN1993.5.U6 M2296 2003
791.43′0973 – dc21

2002015918

A catalogue record for this title is available from the British Library.

Set in 10 on 12.5 pt Galliard
by SNP Best-set Typesetter Ltd., Hong Kong
Printed and bound in the United Kingdom
by TJ International, Padstow, Cornwall

For further information on
Blackwell Publishing, visit our website:
http://www.blackwellpublishing.com

for my family

Contents

Acknowledgments   xii
List of Boxes   xiv

Introduction   1

Part I   The Commercial Aesthetic

1   Taking Hollywood Seriously   5

  "Metropolis of Make-Believe"   5
  Art and Business   7
  The Commercial Aesthetic of *Titanic*   10
  A Classical Cinema?   14
  Hollywood and its Audiences   19
  Ratings and Franchises   22
  Hollywood's World   28
  Summary   30
  Further Reading   31

2   Entertainment 1   33

  Escape   33
  Money on the Screen   40
  The Multiple Logics of Hollywood Cinema   46
  Summary   52
  Further Reading   53

3 Entertainment 2   54

The Play of Emotions   54
Regulated Difference   59
Singin' in the Rain: How to Take Gene Kelly Seriously   66
Summary   71
Further Reading   72

4 Genre   74

Genre Criticism   83
Genre Recognition   86
The Empire of Genres: *Pat Garrett and Billy the Kid*   93
Genre and Gender   101
Summary   107
Further Reading   108

Part II   Histories

5 Industry 1: To 1948   113

Industry   113
Distribution and Exhibition   114
Exporting America   126
Divorcement   128
The Studio System   130
The Star System   141
How Stars are Made: *A Star is Born*   146
Summary   154
Further Reading   156

6 Industry 2: From 1948 to 1980   159

The Effects of Divorcement   161
Roadshows and Teenpix   165
Independents, Agents, and Television   170
Corporate Consolidation and the "New Hollywood"   173
Ratings   177
Hollywood in the Multiplex   181
Summary   186
Further Reading   187

7 Industry 3: Since 1980   189

Video and New Markets   191
The Pursuit of Synergy   205
Globalization   212

Independence 217
Summary 224
Further Reading 225

8 Technology 227

Realism and the Myth of Total Cinema 229
Sound 238
Sunny Side Up 241
Color 248
Widescreen 251
Technology and Power 255
The Triumph of the Digital 259
Summary 264
Further Reading 265

9 Politics 268

The Politics of Regulation 270
Hollywood Goes to Washington 276
Washington Goes to Hollywood 280
Representing the Political Machine 287
Controversy with Class: The Social Problem Movie 292
Ideology 300
Summary 306
Further Reading 307

Part III Conventions

10 Space 1 311

The Best View 312
Making the Picture Speak: Representation and Expression 313
The Optics of Expressive Space 319
Deep Space: Three-Dimensionality on a Flat Screen 326
Mise-en-Scène 328
Editing 332
Summary 339
Further Reading 340

11 Space 2 343

The Three "Looks" of Cinema 343
Points of View 346
Safe and Unsafe Space 353
Ordinary People 358
Summary 365
Further Reading 365

Contents

12 Performance 1   368

  The Spectacle of Movement 3pg   372
  The Movement of Narrative   375
  Acting as Impersonation   377
  The Actor's Two Bodies   380
  Star Performance 1pg   384
  Summary   390
  Further Reading   391

13 Performance 2   393

  The Method   393
  Acting as a Signifying System   398
  Valentino   401
  The Son of the Sheik   406
  Summary   410
  Further Reading   411

14 Time   413

  Time Out   414
  Film Time   419
  Movie Time   423
  Deadlines and Coincidences: *Madigan*   426
  Mise-en-Temps   429
  Tense   432
  Back to the Present: History as a Production Value   436
  The Politics of History: *Forrest Gump*   440
  The Lessons of History: *Juárez*   443
  Summary   449
  Further Reading   450

15 Narrative 1   452

  Narrative and Other Pleasures 17 pgs   452
  Show and Tell   454
  Theories of Narration   458
  Plot, Story, Narration   462
  Clarity: Transparency and Motivation   465
  Summary   469
  Further Reading   470

16 Narrative 2   471

  Regulating Meaning: The Production Code   471
  Clarity and Ambiguity in *Casablanca*   475
  Narrative Pressure   484

Summary 488
Further Reading 489

Part IV Approaches

17 Criticism 493

From Reviewing to Criticism 494
Early Theory and Criticism in America 496
From Criticism to Theory 501
Criticism in Practice: *Only Angels Have Wings* 511
Summary 521
Further Reading 523

18 Theories 526

Entering the Academy 526
Structuralism and Semiology 528
Cinema, Ideology, Apparatus 531
Psychoanalysis and Cinema 535
The Spectator   3 pgs 537
Feminist Theory 540
Poststructuralism and Cultural Studies 542
Neoformalism and Cognitivism 546
From Reception to History 549
Summary 553
Further Reading 555

Chronology 557
Glossary 578
Appendices 593
1 The Motion Picture Production Code 593
2 The Code and Rating System, 1968 598
3 The Classification and Rating System: "What the Ratings Mean" 601
Notes 603
Bibliography 644
Index 666

Acknowledgments

Since its inception, this book has been a collaborative project, and many people have helped it along its journey. Ian Craven and I began the book as a joint project, and shared the construction of its conceptual framework. Ian also wrote early versions of some sections, and the book retains much of our original plan.

This book benefited greatly from the critical assessments of Blackwell's anonymous readers, who forced me to reconsider a number of my assumptions. The issues explored here have also been examined and refined by several generations of my students. Through their questioning and debate, they have added to my understanding of Hollywood cinema in a myriad ways. If they read this, many of them will recognize an idea or a phrase that first saw the light of day in their seminar.

At a crucial moment in the book's writing, Kate Bowles brought order to an unruly text, and insisted that its author actually say what he meant. When all else failed, Kate found ways of saying it, especially in the material now in chapters 15 and 16, where she recast much of the argument. Ruth Vasey has read and corrected half-a-dozen versions of the text and improved it on every occasion. Readers who wish this book were shorter will never know how grateful they should be to Ruth for insisting that it not get any longer. To properly express my gratitude to her would take another book, so I just thank her for everything.

Friends at Exeter read and listened to some of the arguments in this book, advised and supported me through the tribulations of authorship, and just generally tolerated its production beyond the calls of collegiality. I thank, sincerely, Stuart Murray, Karen Edwards, Anthony Fothergill, Judith Higginbottom, Jo Seton, Michael Wood, Richard Bradbury, Peter Quartermaine, Ron Tamplin, and most especially Mick Gidley, for his friendship, his guidance, and his example as scholar and teacher. I am also grateful to the School of English and American Studies at Exeter for a study leave that allowed me to complete the writing. For trading ideas that have become central to this book, I happily acknowledge my gratitude to Tino Balio, David Bordwell, Mary-Beth Haralovich, Lea Jacobs, Steve Neale, Janet Staiger, and Kristin Thompson. Douglas Martin helped prepare the chronology.

Other intellectual debts are legion, as the book's voluminous notes reveal. The collaborative nature of this project is most clearly visible in those pages, near the end of the book, which record the contributions of the scholars whose ideas this book discusses, borrows, and argues with. Thanks are also due to the librarians and archivists who helped me discover the primary documents cited here: Sam Gill, Howard Prouty and the staff at the Margaret Herrick Library of the Academy of Motion Picture Arts and Sciences in Los Angeles, Maxine Fleckner-Ducey and the staff of the Wisconsin Center for Film and Theater Research in Madison, Gillian Hartnoll and the staff of the British Film Institute Library in London. In chapter 3 the lyrics of "Moses" (Roger Edens/Betty Comden/Abel Green; 1952 EMI Catalogue Partnership/EMI Robbins Catalog Inc.) are reprinted by permission of CPP/Belwin Europe, Surrey, England.

At Blackwell's, Simon Prosser kept faith with the project of the first edition for longer than he or I would care to remember, and guided it to completion. Hazel Coleman and Emma Gotch skillfully turned the manuscript into a book, and Fiona Sewell's copy-editing unobtrusively added clarity and consistency to what the book said. Ginny Stroud-Lewis's picture research and Frances Tomlinson's illustrations enhanced the book's argument as well as its appearance. My thanks to them all.

Much like its predecessor, the second edition of this book became a great labor of many hands. At Blackwell's, Susan Rabinowitz, Jayne Fargnoli, and Ken Provencher have nurtured its production and borne my many renegotiated deadlines with sanctifiable patience. Simon Eckley and Lisa Eaton have steered this edition through its production, and Fiona Sewell has discreetly improved the text for a second time. Arlene Hui found several of the pictures in this edition. Some of the new material included here was developed during my time at Sheffield Hallam University, with the help of colleagues Steve Neale, Tom Ryall, and Gerry Coubro. At Flinders, this book depended on the support of colleagues in the Department of Screen Studies and the School of Humanities, and it would never have been finished without the help of Rebecca Vaughan and Nick Prescott, who performed heroic labors in the final stages of completion, and of Wendy Hill, who kept the rest of my working life organized. Whatever faults remain here are mine.

And the most important last: Ben Maltby has shared my workspace, brought music into our house, and provided the best definition of theory I know; Ruth Vasey has shared every part of this project as well as tolerating its intrusion into the rest of our lives with grace, patience, good humor, and good sense. Of all the gin joints in all the towns in all the world, she walked into mine.

List of Boxes

1.1	Rating the movies	24
1.2	Contemporary Hollywood's audience	26
3.1	The Motion Picture Production Code of 1930	62
4.1	Types of motion picture, 1944–6	80
4.2	Types of motion picture, 1993–5	83
5.1	Movie theaters in the United States	115
5.2	Distribution and exhibition in the United States, 1945	116
5.3	The costs of running a movie theater	119
5.4	The balanced program	122
5.5	The clearance system	123
5.6	Weekly attendance in the United States	124
5.7	Features released by the majors	128
5.8	Production cost of the average feature	129
5.9	Production categories of the major companies, 1939: by budget	132
5.10	"The real boss"	136
5.11	*Casablanca*'s budget	138
5.12	Acting in Hollywood	148
6.1	Drive-ins	164
6.2	The US box-office year	185
7.1	The video market, 1980–9	193
7.2	Exhibition windows, 2000	194
7.3	Hollywood's changing market, 1980s	196
7.4	The escalating cost of the average movie, 1980–2000	198

7.5	Box-office grosses	200
7.6	Platform release	204
7.7	The Oscar effect	206
7.8	How the box-office dollar is split	210
7.9	US and international rentals, 1965–99	213
10.1	The Golden Section	317
10.2	Hal Wallis edits *Angels with Dirty Faces*	334
14.1	Models of the Hollywood story	417

Introduction

Why would anyone need to be introduced to anything so familiar, so much a part of the world's daily life, as Hollywood? My answer to this perfectly reasonable question is that however well acquainted we are with Hollywood's stars and movies, few of us actually spend much time thinking seriously about what they mean, or about how they mean what they mean. This book aims to introduce – perhaps better, to *re*introduce – its readers to Hollywood: to the cultural and commercial institution that is Hollywood, and also to the critical study of the products of that institution, the movies. As importantly, it also aims to provide its readers with the critical tools to articulate everything they already know about Hollywood, which is often far more than we realize. As chapter 1 declares in its title, my aim in this book is to take Hollywood seriously.

Several critical assumptions underlie my approach. The first is that Hollywood is different from other national cinemas or film movements primarily because of its commercial scale. Hollywood movies are determined, in the first instance, by their existence as consumable goods in a capitalist economy. Secondly, the book places the movies it discusses within the economic and historical context of their production, circulation, and consumption. Although *Hollywood Cinema* is not organized chronologically, it argues consistently that Hollywood's audiences, genres, technology, and formal properties have histories and are best understood through those histories. The examples discussed cover almost the whole of Hollywood's history, from 1915 to the present. Finally, in thinking about how Hollywood movies work, I assume that far from being passive recipients of a finished "text," the cinema audience plays an active role in the construction of a movie's meaning. Only by thinking about the way Hollywood movies are used by their audiences can we understand the ways in which movies contrive to be expressive.

This book is as concerned with the idea of Hollywood as it is with individual movies. It starts from the proposal that in order to understand how movies work, we have first to consider what they are for. Why do people go to the movies, and what place do these mass-produced fictions have in our lives? What exactly do we mean when we talk of Hollywood as a source of entertainment or escapism? What do we escape from, and where do we escape to? These questions about entertainment shape the book's discussion of the forces that have formed Hollywood as a cultural institution.

This second edition of *Hollywood Cinema* has reorganized the book's material into four parts in order to make its contents more flexible. Part I, "The Commercial Aesthetic," explores the book's central proposition, that the aesthetic systems at work in Hollywood movies cannot sensibly be separated from their underlying commercial ambitions, and that as a cultural institution, Hollywood is best understood by considering the intricacies and contradictions of what I have called its commercial aesthetic. Part II, "Histories," proposes that Hollywood's commercial aesthetic has evolved over time, and that its history can best be understood through an understanding of the industry's economic and technological operations, and through its political activities. Part III, "Conventions," examines the formal properties of Hollywood movies, and the ways in which a movie's manipulation of space, time, and movement can affect the audience's relationship to the cinema screen. It argues that the formal properties of Hollywood cinema are consistent in terms of their functional equivalents, but have also evolved through history. Part IV, "Approaches," provides an overview of the development of the critical and theoretical machinery used to disassemble and assess the products of the dream factory. In considering critical history, it suggests that the kinds of questions that have been asked about Hollywood cinema have also changed over time. The four parts can also usefully be read separately, or used in a different order.

Most of the chapters in this edition contain an extended analysis of an individual movie as an illustration of the chapter's argument. The movies analyzed have been chosen partly for their chronological coverage of Hollywood's history, and partly because they are "typical" Hollywood products rather than exceptional ones. While some movies are better known than others, that choice has been deliberate. The aim of the book is to explore the workings of Hollywood as an industrial and formal system, not to make claims for Hollywood, or any of it products, as Art.

Each chapter in this edition includes a summary of its main arguments, together with suggestions for further reading. Discussion of recent and contemporary Hollywood has been enlarged, in the chapters on industry and technology and more generally throughout the book, which also incorporates issues raised by scholarship and commentary published since the first edition. This edition includes more statistical data than previously, and is more fully illustrated. The glossary has been expanded, and the chronology and bibliography updated. Appendices on the Motion Picture Production Code and on the Code (later "Classification") and Rating system have been added.

PART I
THE COMMERCIAL AESTHETIC

CHAPTER ONE
Taking Hollywood Seriously

You can take Hollywood for granted like I did, or you can dismiss it with the contempt we reserve for what we don't understand. It can be understood too, but only dimly and in flashes. Not half a dozen men have ever been able to keep the whole equation of pictures in their heads.

F. Scott Fitzgerald[1]

"Metropolis of Make-Believe"[2]

Welcome to Hollywood, what's your dream? Everyone comes here. This is Hollywood, land of dreams. Some dreams come true, some don't, but keep on dreamin'.

Happy Man (Abdul Salaam El Razzac) in *Pretty Woman* (1990)

You can't explain Hollywood. There isn't any such place.

Rachel Field[3]

The sign said "HOLLYWOODLAND." A real estate company put it up in 1923, to advertise a housing development in Beechwood Canyon, Los Angeles. Each letter was 50 feet tall, 30 feet wide, and studded with 4,000 electric light bulbs. It cost $21,000. The "land" was taken down in 1949, but the rest of it is still there, and on its fiftieth anniversary, the sign became an historic-cultural monument. But if you go looking for Hollywood the sign won't help you find it, because the place you're looking for isn't really there. As private detective Philip Marlowe

The Hollywood sign, 1923
Courtesy of the Academy of Motion Picture Arts and Sciences

observes in Raymond Chandler's 1949 novel *The Little Sister*, "you can live a long time in Hollywood and never see the part they use in pictures."[4] You can't find the entertainment capital of the world, the "Metropolis of Make-Believe," simply by following directions to Schwab's drugstore on Sunset Boulevard.

Instead, you will find Hollywood much closer to home, in the familiar surroundings of the neighborhood movie theater, the back seat of the family car at the local drive-in, and now most often in your living room, on television, video, or digital "home cinema." With every viewing, these mundane places are transformed into Hollywood, the movies, a never-never land of wish-fulfillment, fantasy, and immediate gratification, where, as the song says, "every shop girl can be a top girl" and every office worker can fulfill her dream of being, for a while, Joan Crawford or "the wrenchingly beautiful Winona Ryder in everything she ever was cast in."[5] Hollywood is a state of mind, not a geographical entity. You can visit it in the movies, and make it part of the soap opera of your own life. But as anyone who has walked down Hollywood Boulevard after dark will tell you, you wouldn't want to live there.

This introduction to Hollywood cinema is less concerned with the art of film than with the phenomenon of cinema. Film is a material and a medium. Cinema is a social institution, and the concerns of this book are primarily with questions of culture rather than of art. There is a critical tradition that makes significant claims for Hollywood cinema as an art practice comparable to the practice of literature or painting. This tradition has many strengths. Its weakness lies in its tendency to take movies out of the context of their production and consumption as objects in an industrial and commercial process. This book argues that we can only understand Hollywood's movies by examining that context. Most introductions to film studies propose that the common technological and aesthetic properties of film allow the various forms of cinema to be treated together as a single subject for study. The more limited focus of this book concentrates exclusively on mainstream American cinema. Hollywood differs in distinct and definable ways from other national cinemas or international film movements. Two Hollywood movies separated by 80 years, such as *Way Down East* (1920) and *Titanic* (1997), have more in common with each other than either does with contemporary European art cinema, documentary, or avant-garde film. Within this book's specific focus, however, we shall look not only at how movies work formally and aesthetically, but also at their cultural function as consumable goods in a capitalist economy.

Throughout this book, I make a distinction between the terms "film" and "movie." I use **film** to refer to the physical, celluloid material on which images are registered and a soundtrack recorded, and **movie** to refer to the stream of images and sounds that we consume as both narrative and spectacle when the material is projected. This distinction between film and movie is similar to the distinction between print and literature: the material (film) and the experiential (movie) forms have different properties. Most critical writing, however, uses the two terms "film" and "movie" interchangeably. Making this distinction emphasizes that my principal concern is with the experience of Hollywood's viewers rather than the intentions of its producers.

Art and Business

> Moviemaking is a marriage between art and business.
> Jack Valenti[6]

In 1968, as film studies began to appear on the curricula of American universities, the *New Yorker*'s film critic Pauline Kael complained that students who interpreted a movie's plot as a mechanism for producing audience response were being corrected by teachers who explained it in terms of a creative artist working out a theme, "as if the conditions under which the movie is made and the market for which it is designed were irrelevant, as if the latest product from Warners or Universal should be analyzed like a lyric poem." Kael wanted to preserve Hollywood from the excesses of academicization. *Morocco* (1930), she thought, was "great trash," and "trash doesn't belong to the academic tradition." Part of the pleasure in trash was "that you don't have to take it seriously, that it was never meant to be any more than frivolous and trifling and entertaining." What draws us to movies, Kael argued, is the opening they provide "into other, forbidden or surprising, kinds of experience," "the details of crime and high living and wicked

At the end of *The Wizard of Oz* (1939), Dorothy (Judy Garland) wakes up to discover that her journey to Oz took her no further than her own back yard.
Produced by Mervyn LeRoy; distributed by MGM Pictures.

cities . . . the language of toughs and urchins . . . the dirty smile of the city girl who lured the hero away from Janet Gaynor." As the title of this chapter indicates, I want to take entertainment seriously. But in doing so, it is important to bear in mind Kael's stricture that "If we always wanted works of complexity and depth we wouldn't be going to movies about glamorous thieves and seductive women who sing in cheap cafés."[7] Taking Hollywood seriously involves acknowledging the cultural importance of the entertainment industry and examining its products for what they are, rather than evaluating them according to criteria borrowed from other critical traditions.

If Hollywood is not a suburb of Los Angeles, perhaps it is best thought of as a place in our communal imaginations, or as a gateway to a place of common imagining. In *The Wizard of Oz* (1939), when the screen turns from black-and-white to Technicolor, Dorothy (Judy Garland) tells her little dog, "I don't think we're in Kansas any more, Toto." It turns out that she is both right and wrong. The inhabitants of Oz are all familiar figures from the Midwest farm she left, and when Dorothy finally achieves her ambition to get back to Kansas, she realizes that "If I ever go looking for my heart's desire again, I won't go looking any further than my own back yard, because if you can't find it there, then you probably never lost it in the first place." This inscrutable observation encapsulates the relationship Hollywood proposes between itself and the everyday world of its audience: Oz is Kansas, but in Technicolor. It has, at the same time, the familiarity of home and the exoticism of a foreign country. In the very proposition that it gives its audiences what they want, Hollywood lays claim to benevolence, much like the Wizard of Oz himself. Hollywood – the movies – is the space in our lives where dreams come true, time after time after time.

Many people who have visited Los Angeles to look for Hollywood have written about their encounters as if they were discovering a familiar foreign land. European writers of travel books about America in the 1920s and 1930s often included a chapter detailing some of the exotic features of the place, and in due course it fell prey to the investigations of anthropologists. In 1946 Hortense Powdermaker, whose previous fieldwork had been among the Melanesian peoples of the south Pacific, spent a year among the natives of Hollywood. Her book, *Hollywood the Dream Factory: An Anthropologist Looks at the Movie-Makers*, provided the model for a stream of later journalistic and sociological investigations. In it she compared ex-cannibal chiefs and magicians to front-office executives and directors. In Hollywood's atmosphere of permanent crisis and its belief in "the breaks" as the cause of success, she found elements of magical thinking that might have been recognizable in New Guinea: "Just as the Melanesian thinks failure would result from changing the form of a spell, so men in Hollywood consider it dangerous to depart from their formulas. . . . The Melanesian placates hostile supernatural forces through a series of taboos; Hollywood attempts to appease its critics and enemies with the [Production] Code." Stressing the absence of planning on the part of studio executives ("The god is profits, and opportunism the ritual of worship"), Powdermaker found Hollywood to be a fundamentally irrational place, where a "pseudo-friendliness and show of affection cover hostility and lack of respect." The Hollywood she observed was a site of irretrievable contradictions, both "a center for creative genius" and "a place where mediocrity flourishes;" at the same time "an important industry with worldwide significance" and "an environment of trivialities."

For Powdermaker, the contradictory nature of the place revealed itself most vividly in one essential opposition: "Making movies must be either business *or* art, rather than both." For many filmmakers, she suggested, "there seems to be a continuous conflict, repeated for each picture, between making a movie which they can respect and the 'business' demands of the front office. It is assumed . . . that a movie which has the respect of the artist cannot make money." This opposition also structured her own account of Hollywood, as it has structured so many other writers' tales. Describing one of her informants, "Mr Literary," a successful writer of A-features, she suggested that:

> He regards his work at the studio as a form of play and rather enjoys it as such. He uses the word "play" because he says that he cannot take it seriously. . . . He has never worked on any movie which has even moderately satisfied him. Each time he starts with high hopes that this one will be different, but each time it is the same: so many interferences, so many changes, that the final script is not his, although he has far more influence over it than do most writers. He does not have this attitude of "play"

toward writing a novel or a short story. That is deadly earnest. Then he is concerned with working out a real problem and any interference with it he would regard as a real crisis.

Powdermaker saw the contradiction between business and art as ordinarily resolved only in failure, when business and aesthetic weakness combine to produce "the confusion, wastefulness and lack of planning . . . which is taken for granted in Hollywood."[8] Writing three decades later, Steven Bach echoed Powdermaker's criticism, suggesting that the "art versus business" conflict "has remained stubbornly resistant to resolution and remains the dominating central issue of American motion pictures to the present day." Bach's book, *Final Cut*, is an account of the production of *Heaven's Gate* (1980), a Western directed by Michael Cimino that went catastrophically over budget. Intended to be "a blockbuster with 'Art' written all over it," the movie's epic failure in fact led directly to the sale of United Artists, the company which had financed it. Bach, head of production at United Artists at the time, argues that the movie's commercial failure was inextricably interwoven with its aesthetic pretensions. Characters and story were sacrificed to the director's indulgence in "an orgy of brilliant pictorial effects." *Heaven's Gate* failed, according to Bach, not because its budget escalated to $44 million, way beyond any hope of profit, but because it failed as entertainment: it did not "engage audiences on the most basic and elemental human levels of sympathy and compassion."[9]

Bach's definition of Hollywood's entertainment purpose was little different from that of successful screenwriter Frances Marion in 1937. What the audience wanted, she argued, was to have its emotions aroused:

> it wants something that will pleasantly excite it, amuse it, wring it with suspense, fill it with self-approval, or even arouse its indignation; it cries . . . "console me, amuse me, sadden me, touch me, make me dream, laugh, shudder, weep!" and above all things, it wants to be "sent home happy." It looks to the photoplay to provide it with a substitute for actual life experience, and to function in such fashion the screen story must contain elements that are emotionally satisfying. Something approaching the ideal life is what this audience prefers to see, rather than life as it actually knows it. It wants to see interesting things which, within the limits of possibility, might happen to it; preferably things to which its own day dreams turn.[10]

The Commercial Aesthetic of *Titanic*

The desires of Hollywood's audiences have not greatly changed. *Titanic* (1997), the first movie to gross more than $1 billion, delivered all the emotions Marion enumerates, principally by focusing its spectacular disaster story through a romance, since according to director James Cameron, "only by telling it as a love story can you appreciate the loss of separation and the loss caused by death."[11] As its production ran massively behind schedule and over budget, *Titanic* was frequently compared to *Heaven's Gate*, but its release showed that unlike Cimino, Cameron was a "fiscally responsible *auteur*" whose personal vision had resulted in a commercially immensely successful product, justifying its budgetary excesses by its unprecedented profits. What Justin Wyatt and Katherine Vlesmas have called *Titanic*'s "drama of recoupment" was supplied with its "obligatory happy ending" through the movie's astonishing commercial success.[12]

Titanic's commercial and aesthetic success depended on its ability to provoke a range of emotions in a wide variety of audience groups. Only because it had what one reviewer called "enough different moves, moods, and ideas to keep everyone happy at least part of the time" could it succeed on the scale that it did.[13] That commercial success relied not on the movie's underlying aesthetic unity or coherence, but rather on the sheer diversity of its various elements, which allowed its different audiences to turn it into the experience they wished to have. *Titanic* was, at the same time, a teenage love story, a heritage movie, a special-effects spectacular, a costume drama, a "chick flick," a disaster movie, a cross-class romance, an intimate historical epic, and the most expensive movie ever made. Different audiences could view it as a celebration of selflessness and self-sacrifice, a subversive commentary on class relations, a sumptuously nostalgic display of bygone opulence, a denunciation of capitalist greed, a brilliant exercise in state-of-the-art special effects, a demonstration of the transcendent triumph of love over death, a feminist action-adventure movie, or an extended opportunity to gaze at Leonardo DiCaprio. Its commercial success, indeed, relied on its appealing across the usual audience categories, to both sexes and all ages. The movie's appeal to its most devoted fans, women under 25 – "costless liberation brought to you by a devoted, selfless, charming, funny, incredibly handsome lover [who] points you toward a long, richly eventful future and dies, beautifully, poetically and tragically" before he can disappoint you – was not necessarily the same quality that persuaded older men to see it.[14]

Titanic's commercial success relied to a great extent on repeat viewings. According to a *Newsweek* survey two months after the movie's release, 60 percent of *Titanic*'s American audience were women, and 63 percent were under 25. Forty-five percent of women under 25 who had seen the movie had seen it twice, while 76 percent of all repeat viewers planned to see it again.[15] The satisfaction these audiences found in the movie was clearly repeated on subsequent viewings, while the high number of repeat viewers (20 percent of the total audience, as against a norm of 2 percent) also meant that *Titanic* stayed longer in more theaters, giving other viewers more opportunities to see it.

Titanic's aesthetic success was dependent on its commercial success to the same extent as *Heaven's Gate*'s aesthetic failure depended on its commercial failure. If it had not demonstrated its popularity at the box-office, *Titanic* would not have won eleven Academy Awards. Neither the Oscars nor Hollywood's aesthetics are solely a matter of money, but both are inextricably bound to the industry's existence as a commercial activity. The title of part I of this book, "The Commercial Aesthetic," deliberately confronts the contradiction between art and business by insisting on addressing the ways in which Hollywood's aesthetic practices serve commercial purposes. In Hollywood, commerce and aesthetics are symbiotic, or in the industry's

The Utopian resolution of *Titanic* (1997) sees the abolition of class distinction and the marriage of commerce and aesthetics.

Produced by James Cameron and Jon Landau; distributed by Twentieth Century-Fox, Paramount Pictures; directed by James Cameron.

current terminology, synergistically intertwined. Like Rose and Jack in the fantastic, Utopian happy ending of *Titanic*, in Hollywood's most successful products commerce and aesthetics embrace each other for everyone's delight.

Like most Hollywood movies, *Titanic* contains two distinct plots, a love story and, in this case, an account of the disaster. These two plots are as connected to each other as any individual viewer requires. Chronologically, they are almost completely separate. The love story reaches its climax and resolution 100 minutes into the movie's 194-minute running time, when Rose (Kate Winslet) tells Jack (DiCaprio) that she intends to leave the ship with him. Immediately afterwards, the ship hits the iceberg and the spectacular action movie begins. This coincidence allows viewers to connect the two sequences of events if they choose to do so: Rose, who has described the *Titanic* as "a slave ship, taking me back to America in chains," rejects the luxurious repression the ship represents, and by her act of free will dooms the ship. For those viewers who choose such an interpretation, the story "moves from Rose's sexual objectification and her suicidal frame of mind (in which she turns her anger against herself) to her sexual liberation and the externalization of her aggressive impulses in the spectacle of the ship's destruction."[16]

In his book on *Titanic*, David Lubin suggests that the simultaneity of the kiss and the crash "adhere to the governing rule of historical fiction, which is that public and historically significant events are best understood by taking measure of the private and personal struggles of fictitious characters put forth as ordinary people whose lives happen to be directly affected by those events."[17] We witness the disaster from the perspective of Rose, Jack, and the other characters we have met in following their love story. In the end, the spectacle of the sinking takes on its meaning through Rose's telling of her story. Other viewers may pay less attention to the love story and take their pleasure simply in sheer vertiginous amazement at the movie's spectacle. What film historian Tom Gunning has called the cinema's "aesthetic of astonishment" has always been an integral element of Hollywood's appeal to its audiences.[18] In 1907, entertainment entrepreneur Frederick Thompson observed that his customers:

> are not in a serious mood, and do not want to encounter seriousness. They have enough seriousness in their every-day lives, and the keynote of the thing they do demand is change. Everything must be different from ordinary experience. What is presented to them must have life, action, motion, sensation, surprise, shock, swiftness or else comedy.

Thompson was not, in fact, describing cinema audiences but the clientele of his Luna Park amusement park on Coney Island. In Luna Park, which one journalist described as "an enchanted, storybook land of trellises, columns, domes, minarets, lagoons, and lofty aerial flights," Thompson sought to create "a different world – a dream world, perhaps a nightmare world – where all is bizarre and fantastic" for his visitors, and invited them not simply to observe that world, but to become participants in its spectacular attractions.[19]

Gunning has described early cinema – before 1906 – as a "cinema of attractions," engaging its viewers' attention through an exciting spectacle, in which the story, if there was one, simply provided "a frame upon which to string a demonstration of the magical possibilities of the cinema":

> Display dominates over narrative absorption, emphasizing the direct stimulation of shock or surprise at the expense of unfolding a story or creating a diegetic universe. The cinema of attractions expends little energy creating characters with psychological motivations or individual personality.[20]

Gunning takes the term "attractions" from the Russian filmmaker and theorist Sergei Eisenstein, who developed a concept of cinema as a "montage of attractions," a calculated assembly of "strong moments" of shock or surprise stimulating the audience's response.[21] The purpose of Eisenstein's didactic, political cinema was "the moulding of the audience in a desired direction," to be achieved by subjecting them "to emotional or psychological influence, verified by experience and mathematically calculated to produce specific emotional shocks in the spectator."[22] Eisenstein himself took the term "attraction" from the fairground, possibly indeed from the roller-coaster in Petrograd's Luna Park; he later described his term "montage of attractions" as being "half-industrial and half-music-hall."[23] In its earliest years, the cinema was most frequently exhibited as an attraction on a vaudeville or variety bill. The appearance of dedicated motion-picture theaters after 1905 encouraged the integration of cinema's spectacular attractions into longer sequences, held together by a story. But, as Gunning argues and as a viewing of *Titanic*'s final 94 minutes demonstrates, the cinema of attractions remains an essential part of popular cinema, not necessarily contained or disguised within narrative.

As well as being a love story and a disaster movie, *Titanic* is an emotional roller-coaster ride for its audience. Not all of the ride is made up of spectacular thrills; the first half of the movie provokes a quieter range of emotions. Its purpose is not necessarily to mold its audience's ideological beliefs in the way Eisenstein intended, although the material for such a molding exists in the thematic relationships that can be identified between characters and class, for instance, and commentators in the *Washington Post* charged Cameron with "kindergarten Marxism."[24] Cameron himself summarized the movie's more straightforward entertainment purpose: "I hope we make people feel like they've just had a good time . . . Not a good time in the sense they've seen a Batman movie, but a good time in the sense that they've had their emotions kind of checked out. The plumbing still works."[25]

As Cameron's remark suggests, audiences go to the movies to consume their own emotions. In order to consume their emotions, spectators have first to produce those emotions, in response to the movie's stimulation. Through the integration of attractions into their plots, moviemakers have to organize movies so that spectators will produce their emotions in a sequence and pattern that they find satisfying. Hollywood's **commercial aesthetic** is grounded in this objective. *Titanic*'s division into love story and action-adventure movie provides what is in fact a very simple and schematic model of this process, but its exceptional commercial success demonstrates that its admixture of attractions provided its audiences with a range of aesthetic satisfactions.

A Classical Cinema?

The very name Hollywood has colored the thought of this age. It has given to the world a new synonym for happiness because of all its products happiness is the one in which Hollywood – the motion-picture Hollywood – chiefly interests itself.

Carl Milliken, 1928[26]

Hollywood's history is as unreliable as its geography. Its products are designed to be consumed in a single viewing, and the audience's experience of an individual movie is fleeting, lasting only as long as the movie is on the screen. Theater advertisements told their patrons to see a movie "today, tomorrow and Thursday – then *Chang* will be gone forever."[27] Like other industries of fashion engaged in the production of ephemeral commodities, Hollywood views itself as in a state of constant change, and in this process it discards, reuses, or reinvents its past as its present requires. Since the 1960s, in particular, Hollywood has persistently been described as not being "what it was," and a succession of both journalistic and critical works have talked of *The Fifty-Year Decline of Hollywood, Hollywood in Transition, The New Hollywood*, or *Hollywood and After*.[28] Part II of this book will look at a number of different ways in which we can view Hollywood's history, but it is important to recognize that, beyond its technological, organizational, or stylistic changes, Hollywood's essential business has remained the same: entertaining its audience, producing the maximum pleasure for the maximum number for the maximum profit. The continuity of its economic purpose enables us to make generalizations about Hollywood over a period spanning nearly a century.

If we are to take Hollywood seriously by understanding its business, the first thing we must do is to describe the way American movies work. The most influential critical work written on Hollywood in the last twenty years has been *The Classical Hollywood Cinema: Film Style and Mode of Production to 1960*, by David Bordwell, Janet Staiger, and Kristin Thompson. In it, they delineate the formal features of what they call the **Classical Hollywood** style, and trace its evolution in tandem with the organizational history of Hollywood's production practices. They argue that the essential features of the classical style were in place as early as 1917. Since then, these features – the way that a movie organizes narrative time and space, the continuity script, the management structure, and the division of labor in production – have remained fundamentally unchanged.

Published in 1985, *The Classical Hollywood Cinema* set new standards for historical research in film studies, and also gave a new precision to ideas of "the classical" in relation to Hollywood. The French critic André Bazin (whose work is discussed on a number of occasions in the following pages) first described Hollywood as "a classical art," to be admired for the richness of its traditions and its capacity to absorb new influences creatively. He also suggested that the genius of the Hollywood system should be analyzed through a sociological approach to its production, since a crucial element of that system was the way in which it "has been able, in an extraordinarily competent way, to show American society just as it wanted to see itself."[29] The idea of a classical cinema has influenced most critical accounts of Hollywood, although it has most frequently been invoked as a background against which exceptional works could be defined and distinguished. Bordwell, Staiger, and Thompson, however, chose to investigate the formal organization of the "ordinary film," basing their account of "Classical" style on an analysis of a randomly selected sample of Hollywood movies. Their analysis of style thus addressed what Bazin had suggested was most admirable about Hollywood, with a precision that had been largely absent from previous descriptions of "classic narrative film." The authors of *The Classical Hollywood Cinema* argue that "the principles which Hollywood claims as its own rely on notions of decorum, proportion, formal harmony, respect for tradition, mimesis, self-effacing craftsmanship, and cool control of the perceiver's response – canons which critics in any medium usually call 'classical.'"[30] The idea of "the classical" implies the observance of rules of composition and aesthetic organization that produce unity, balance, and order in the resulting artwork. "Classical" works conform. They are bound by rules that set strict limits on innovation.

By contrast, this book argues that Hollywood functions according to a commercial aesthetic, one that is essentially opportunist in its economic motivation. The argument that Hollywood movies are determined, in the first instance, by their existence as commercial commodities sits uneasily with the ideas of classicism and stylistic determination. Bordwell, Staiger, and Thompson acknowledge that economic factors have strongly affected the development of the classical style, but regard stylistic factors as providing the most interesting explanation of Hollywood filmmaking. For them, a set of formal conventions of narrative construction, spectacle, verisimilitude, and continuity "constituted Hollywood's very definition of a movie itself."[31] From the critical perspective adopted in this book, these investigations of Hollywood's formal conventions can address one of the two sets of questions we can ask about the way movies work: the way in which Hollywood is, in David Bordwell's phrase, "an excessively obvious cinema."[32] There is, however, another set of issues not examined in *The Classical Hollywood Cinema*, dealing with the relationships that exist between movies and their audiences, and with external forces at work in the Hollywood system. As Bordwell, Staiger, and Thompson acknowledge, the sociological approach that Bazin advocated requires a history of Hollywood's reception – of "the changing theater situation, the history of publicity, and the role of social class, aesthetic tradition, and ideology in constituting the audience" – to accompany their history of its stylistic evolution.[33]

Answers to questions about what Hollywood is for must be sought not only in its movies but also in the social, cultural, and institutional contexts that surround it. In examining Hollywood's commercial aesthetic, we shall be concerned at one level with how viewers use movies "to learn how to dress or how to speak more elegantly or how to make a grand entrance or even what kind of coffee maker we wish to purchase, or to take off from the movie into a romantic fantasy or a trip."[34] At another level, we must consider how Hollywood movies are organized to deliver pleasure to their audiences. Take something as obvious as Hollywood's happy endings. The authors of *The Classical Hollywood Cinema* found that 60 percent of the movies they analyzed "ended with a display of the united romantic couple – the cliché happy ending, often with a 'clinch' – and many more could be said to end happily."[35] In contrast to a strictly formal analysis that sees classical movies as driven by the logical progression of their narratives, Rick Altman has argued that the obligation to arrive at a happy ending leads classical narrative to "reason backward," "retrofitting" the beginning so that it appears to lead logically to the predetermined happy ending. "The end is made to *appear* as a function of the beginning in order better to disguise the fact that the beginning is actually a function of the ending."[36] More generally, movies are engineered to produce a sequence of audience responses, "thrilling us when we should be thrilled," as a writer in *Nickelodeon* put it in 1910, "making us laugh or cry at the appointed times, and leaving us, at the end of the film, in a beatific frame of mind."[37] Screenwriting manuals and practicing screenwriters alike emphasize that scripts are engineered to maintain a level of engagement on the part of the audience. When John Sayles was hired to rewrite *Piranha* (1978), the producers told him:

> "Make sure you keep the main idea, the idea of piranhas being loose in North American waters." I said, "Okay, how often do you want an attack? About every fifteen minutes?" They said, "Yeah, but it doesn't have to be an attack. Maybe just the threat of an attack – but some sort of action sequence about that often to keep the energy going." I said, "Anything else?" They said, "Keep it fun."[38]

As a final level of our inquiry into the movies' commercial aesthetic, we must examine the institutional and ideological constraints on Hollywood. Movies have happy endings because part of their cultural function is to affirm and maintain the culture of which they are part. The industry's **Production Code**, which regulated the content and treatment of movies between 1930 and 1968, inscribed this cultural function as a convention of every Classical Hollywood product. (The Production Code is discussed in detail in chapters 3 and 16, and is reproduced in appendix 1.) The fact that 85 percent of Hollywood movies feature heterosexual romance as a main plot device should be seen in the light of this regulatory framework. If the movie theater is a site in which cultural and ideological anxieties can be aired in the relative safety of a well-regulated fiction, we might well ask why we need quite so much reassurance that heterosexual romance is supposed to end happily. Questions such as this require us to look beyond the movie theater to explain what happens on the screen. Although these questions raise a different set of issues from those explored in *The Classical Hollywood Cinema*, the two kinds of analysis complement each other.

One further question about Classical Hollywood has to do with whether it still exists. Bordwell, Staiger, and Thompson conclude their analysis in 1960, a date that they acknowledge is "somewhat arbitrary."[39] By then, Classical Hollywood's mode of production, the vertically integrated company operating a studio, had come to an end, but the style it produced persisted. Although the style altered after 1960, it had also altered before, and the style of the New Hollywood of the 1970s can best be explained, they suggest, by the same process of stylistic assimilation that had operated throughout Hollywood's history: "As the 'old' Hollywood had incorporated and refunctionalized devices from German Expressionism and Soviet montage, the 'New' Hollywood has selectively borrowed from the international art cinema."[40] In her 1999 book, *Storytelling in the New Hollywood*, Kristin Thompson argues strongly that "contemporary Hollywood's most important and typical narrative strategies . . . are in most respects the same as those in use in the studio era . . . The ideal American film still centers around a well-structured, carefully motivated series of events that the spectator can comprehend easily." She suggests that those critics who have identified a "'post-classical' cinema of rupture, fragmentation and postmodern incoherence" in the New Hollywood of the 1970s and the "high concept" style of production since 1980 overstate the extent to which movies made after the demise of the studio system deviate from the classical norms of narrative clarity and coherence.[41]

Some of the questions of emphasis raised by Thompson's argument are addressed in the discussion of post-Classical space in chapter 11. More importantly, perhaps, her argument also raises the question of how we conceptualize Hollywood's history. Thompson's own analysis emphasizes narrative, and in doing so makes a strong case for the continuity of "a tradition which has flourished for eighty years."[42] Other approaches, more concerned with economic or technological aspects of Hollywood's history, stress moments of change or discontinuity, arguing that the introduction of sound or the break-up of the studio system divide Hollywood's history into distinct periods. As part II of this book makes clear, however, different emphases produce different patterns, and it is more accurate to describe Hollywood as having several interconnected histories than to impose a single dominant perspective.

Each of these histories describes a dialog between continuity and change, which may help explain how a "classical" style can persist in a "post-Classical" cinema. The use of capital letters allows us to distinguish between the set of aesthetic norms identified by Bordwell, Staiger, and Thompson, and the historical period in which they were developed and flourished under the studio system of production. Throughout this book, I use "Classical Hollywood" to refer to a specific period of Hollywood's history from the early 1920s to the late 1950s, and as a description of the style, the mode of production, and the industrial organization under which movies were made in that period.

This book is not a history of Hollywood so much as a thematic investigation of what Hollywood is, and what Hollywood movies are. It is, however, informed by the belief that we need to understand Hollywood from a range of historical perspectives. Hollywood has at least three separate but overlapping histories. The history of production, the story of the studios and their stars, has preoccupied the majority of movie historians. Much less notice tends to be taken of movie reception, but Hollywood's audience has a history, too, and that history – the history of the box-office – has shaped the history of production, as I begin to describe in the next section. Third, Hollywood has a critical history: a history of the changes in what critics have understood Hollywood to be. Most critical histories of Hollywood are descriptive, charting its high and low points, although different critics, of course, describe that history differently. Chapters 17 and 18 discuss the history of criticism of Hollywood, and aspects of this critical history arise in several other places, such as the discussion of auteurist criticism in chapter 2.

These three overlapping accounts of Hollywood are narratives of continuity as well as change. All are in competition with Hollywood's history of itself, projected in fan magazines, star biographies, and "exposés," as well as in movies about Hollywood. Much of what passes for Hollywood's history has been written as if it were itself a Hollywood story and as if the history of entertainment were under an obligation to be entertaining. *Singin' in the Rain* (1952), for instance, provides us with a history of Hollywood's introduction of sound, in which Cosmo Brown (Donald O'Connor) discovers the principles of sound dubbing by standing in front of Kathy Selden (Debbie Reynolds) and moving his mouth while she sings. This is a much more entertaining version of history than the more accurate but more mundane account of the development of multiple channel recording and post-synchronization.

The most common explanation for the introduction of sound, that it was a last desperate gamble by an almost bankrupt Warner Bros., is likewise a Hollywood fantasy, disproven by research that has shown that the major companies' transition to sound was a much more orderly and considered process.[43] Nevertheless, this explanation is still widely reproduced, because its story of the kids from the ghetto making good with an invention the big studios had turned down fits in with the mythological history of Hollywood, the *Singin' in the Rain* history, which proposes that the history of Hollywood must conform to the conventions of its own narratives. This Hollywood was the invention of press and publicity agents. It served as a disguise for the American movie industry, the means by which public attention was diverted away from the routine, mechanical, standardized aspects of the industry's central operations toward its more attractive, glamorous periphery. That disguise has worked almost as well for many of Hollywood's critics and historians as it did for the readers of its fan magazines in the 1930s. Despite the media attention now paid to opening weekend grosses, which depict movies competing against each other in a form of sporting contest, the economic forces and business practices involved in selling entertainment remain largely concealed behind the images of Hollywood as "Metropolis of Make-Believe."

Hollywood and its Audiences

The last couple of years, I thought that a large proportion of the American public wanted to see blood or breasts. Now I think they want to see cars. Our biggest film to date, *Eat My Dust!*, just piles up one car after another.
Roger Corman, 1977[44]

Our dream was to make a movie about how movies screw up your brain about love, and then if we did a good job, we would become one of the movies that would screw up people's brains about love forever.
Nora Ephron on *Sleepless in Seattle* (1993)[45]

Although Hollywood's goal of entertainment has remained constant, the audience it has sought to entertain has changed as many times in the 80 years of Hollywood's existence as have the ways of producing and packaging movies. Since 1950, moviegoing has been a minority activity. In 1946, one third of the American public went to a movie every week. By 1983, fewer than a quarter went once a month, but that group of regular viewers accounted for 85 percent of all movie admissions.[46] In 2000, 30 percent of the American population over 12 went once a month, while 26 percent never went.[47] The industry's idea of its audience has also changed. In the late 1920s, the industry estimated that between three-quarters and four-fifths of its audience were women.[48] Although the reliability of this estimate is open to question, for most of the 1930s and 1940s there was a widespread assumption among production and distribution personnel that the large majority of movie audiences in the US and Europe were female. In 1939 a sociologist reported that "it is really that solid average citizen's wife who commands the respectful attention of the industry."[49]

From the mid-1920s to the 1940s the industry's understanding of its audience was closely interwoven with the way that it classified both its pictures and its theaters. Pictures were conceived by the industry and evaluated by the trade press as suitable for exhibition in different types of theater, which were attended by different types of audience. Exhibitors classified audiences according to a series of overlapping distinctions between "class" and "mass," "sophisticated" and "unsophisticated," "Broadway" and "Main Street," as well as distinguishing between groups of viewers by gender and age. Industry rhetoric promoted the idea of an undifferentiated audience in support of Hollywood's claims to practice a form of cultural democracy, but in actuality distributors classified theaters hierarchically from first-run picture palaces to neighborhood double-bill houses, allocating each theater a position in a movie's commercial life-span on the basis of its potential audience.

Classical Hollywood's principal mechanism for understanding its audience was through its theater managers. Theaters were assumed to have local and fairly stable audiences, with a particular make-up and characteristics known to the manager. This local knowledge was amassed through the distribution company's sales department, and then fed back to production. Decisions about the location, architecture, and entertainment policy of new theaters were based on the economic character and leisure habits of their surrounding population, and information on the operation of the major companies' theaters was forwarded to the main office in New York, to be used in the planning of future programs. Companies used this information to assess the appeal that the various component parts of their output held for different sectors of the audience and to guide their decisions about the content of future productions. In the process, audience tastes were categorized implicitly by income and class as well as explicitly by gender and age.

Classical Hollywood organized its output to provide a range of products that would appeal to the different groups of viewers it identified. Movies were assembled to contain ingredients appealing to different, generically defined areas of the audience, so that their marketing and exploitation could "position" each picture in relation to one or more of those "taste publics." Apparent changes in the generic tastes of audience groupings were often invoked to justify shifts in production policy, such as the deliberate creation of a "family" audience for a bourgeois cinema of uplift in the mid-1930s. In this way, Hollywood periodically reinvented and reconfigured its audience, typically discovering a "new" audience who had previously not attended, and devising products that would unite this audience with existing ones.

Some audiences were, however, more important than others. Surveys in the 1920s and early 1930s supported the industry assumption that women formed the dominant part of its audience, and all the evidence from the trade press and other industry sources makes clear that during those decades the motion picture industry assumed that women were its primary market, both through their own attendance and through their roles as opinion leaders, influencing the males with whom they attended. Fan magazines of the 1920s insistently promoted the image of a "new and improved" female movie fan – the flapper – a young metropolitan woman aspiring to the condition of Clara Bow or Alice White. These "Woolworth sirens," who made up "the stenographer trade" and read the fan magazines in the largest numbers, were constructed as idealized consumers, fascinated by the star system and dependent on movies to generate their needs and desires.[50]

By the mid-1930s the "flapper" had evolved into "Tillie-the-Toiler, the busy, yearning little girl who supports the box office," named by *Motion Picture Herald* editor Terry Ramsaye after a comic strip character. Tillie, he claimed, "does not want to go home from the show with any more problems than she had when she started out for the evening. Tillie wants action and satisfaction. She wants to feel, not to think and worry and reason."[51] During the 1930s, the industry's conception of its target viewer – the opinion-leader making decisions about which movie to attend on behalf of a group – changed neither age, gender, nor class. The specifically male audience, "the boys who go for the gangster stuff," was relatively small, exclusively metropolitan, and catered to by such stars as James Cagney. According to *Variety*, when a new Cagney picture opened at the Strand theater on Broadway, it would gather a 90 percent male audience in the expectation of "this player socking all and sundry including all the women in the cast." The potential audience for a Janet Gaynor–Charles Farrell musical was, however, "larger than that drawn by the gun mellers, and it's tradition that a technically mediocre talker of this type will do a lot better than a rougher feature of equal rating."[52]

In an industry dominated by men, the assumption that to be profitable its products had to appeal mainly to women had profound effects on Classical Hollywood's development of the star system and on the eventual emergence of the "woman's film," as the industry employed women screenwriters to craft mainly female-centered stories. This assumption also encouraged the development of an increasingly elaborate system designed to use movies to sell consumer goods, and stimulated the growth of the discursive apparatus of fan culture.

Industry assumptions about the composition of its audience were to some extent challenged by the methodologies introduced by George Gallup's Audience Research Institute in the 1940s. Gallup identified three key components in the composition of Hollywood's audience: age, gender, and income or class; he argued that the audience was younger, more male, and poorer than the industry had previously assumed. In its most important aspects, however, Gallup's research largely duplicated the results of the major companies' earlier procedures, confirming existing industry wisdom that, for instance, men preferred action films and women were drawn to romance, and that movies needed to contain elements that appealed to both audience groups. His findings therefore validated the conventional Hollywood practice by which the overwhelming majority of pictures combined a love story with another plot.[53]

Audience research in the 1950s began to suggest that as Hollywood's audience declined, its social composition also changed. In 1941 Gallup had suggested that the great majority of movie tickets were purchased by people on low or average incomes. Surveys in the 1950s, by contrast, indicated that people in higher socioeconomic brackets attended more frequently than did others. Not until the early 1960s, however, did the industry begin to reconsider its idea of its principal target viewer, and the process was not complete until the late 1960s. This redefinition of the primary audience for Hollywood has most often been explained as a "juvenilization of the movie audience." But the discovery that teenagers were "the best picture-goers in the country at this time – the most consistent, the best equipped with leisure time and allowance money, the most gregariously inclined, and to be sure the most romantic – " simply echoed the findings of Gallup in the 1940s and the assumptions that the major companies had made in the 1920s and 1930s.[54]

In the 1960s, the movie industry gradually came to the conclusion that its principal target viewer had changed gender. This change was most concisely captured in a strategy developed by American-International Pictures (AIP), an independent company specializing in "exploitation" pictures, which had its first major commercial success in 1957 with *I Was a Teenage Werewolf*. "The Peter Pan Syndrome," as AIP executives called it in 1968, proposed that younger children would watch anything older children would watch, and girls would watch anything boys would watch, but not vice versa. Therefore, "to catch your greatest audience you zero in on the 19-year-old male."[55]

It can be argued that this shift in the gender of Hollywood's principal target viewer was the real marker of the change from Classical to post-Classical Hollywood. It was also closely related to a major shift in the age distribution of the American population. The two decades between 1946 and 1964 saw an explosion in live births, which came to be known as the "baby boom." By 1965, four out of every ten Americans were under the age of 20. Birth rates then fell until around 1980, before rising again to levels similar to the baby boom period until 1994, when they began to fall once more. The demographics of the postwar "baby boom" described an ascending curve of live births, so that for more than a decade after 1965, there were always more 16- or 17-year-old females in the American population than there were 19-year-old males to date them at the movies. By 1972, *Variety* was regularly expressing the then-operative Hollywood wisdom that women's visits to the movies were now "dominated by their male companion's choice of screen fare."[56]

The effects of this change were most strikingly indicated in the shift in the gender balance of top-ranking box-office stars. In Classical Hollywood a roughly equal number of male and female stars appeared in exhibitors' polls of leading box-office attractions. Since the late 1960s, however, these lists have become increasingly dominated by men, to a proportion, by the late 1980s, of nine to one. A 1987 survey in which adults were asked to name their three favorite celebrities gave an indication of how this came about. It reported that 59 percent of the females polled selected a male celebrity as one of their top three favorites, but none of the men selected a female.[57] Just as the influence of the young female viewer dominated Classical Hollywood's system of representation to a far greater extent than attendance figures would have suggested was appropriate, the male domination of Hollywood cinema has continued well beyond the demographic conditions that may have originally contributed to it.

Ratings and Franchises

The change in gender of Hollywood's principal target viewer coincided with a major alteration in the industry's production policy. Although censor boards in many foreign countries had long prohibited children from attending some movies, Classical Hollywood's distributors had always resisted any proposals for similar schemes in their domestic market, asserting their commitment to providing universal entertainment for undifferentiated audiences. Instead they preferred to use the Production Code as a system of regulation to ensure that all Hollywood movies would only offer entertainment that would prove harmless to all their audiences. (The operation of the Production Code is discussed in chapter 3.) By the mid-

1960s, however, shifts in American cultural values had undermined the credibility of the Production Code, and in 1968 it was replaced by a **rating system** which classified certain movies as unsuitable for sections of the potential audience. The industry's decision to introduce a ratings system was immediately provoked by two decisions of the US Supreme Court, upholding the rights of local governments to prevent children being exposed to books or movies considered suitable only for adults. In the wake of these decisions the industry faced a flood of state and municipal legislation establishing local schemes for film classification. The introduction of a rating system administered by the industry's trade association, the Motion Picture Association of America (**MPAA**), was an attempt to outmaneuver that legislation.

The Code and Rating Administration (**CARA**) divided movies into four categories: G, suitable for general admission; M, allowing unrestricted admission, but suggesting that parents should decide whether the movie was suitable for children under 16; R, restricting attendance by requiring children under 16 to be accompanied by an adult; and X, restricting attendance to those over 16. Since 1968, the system has been modified several times. (Appendices 2 and 3 show versions from 1968 and 2002.) In 1970 the M category became GP, when the age restriction was raised to 17; in 1972 GP was renamed PG (for parental guidance suggested); and CARA itself was renamed the Classification and Rating Administration in 1977, abandoning any reference to the existence of a Code governing movie production as well as the practice of vetting scripts in advance of production. In 1984, CARA added another category, PG-13, providing a "strong caution" to parents of children under 13. In 1990, CARA renamed its X category NC-17 in an attempt to create a category for art movies restricted to the over-17s, since X was generally understood as referring to pornography. The major companies have continued to show no enthusiasm for the adults-only rating, however, particularly after the 1995 box-office failure of *Showgirls* confirmed the industry's conventional wisdom that NC-17 movies could not make money at American theaters.

The rating system has imposed few actual limitations on attendance, but it has required producers to conceive of their audiences differently, engineering their movies to achieve a particular rating – a requirement often built into a movie's finance agreements. Distributors will not handle X- or NC-17-rated movies, and movies such as *Dressed to Kill* (1980), *Angel Heart* (1987), and *South Park: Bigger, Longer and Uncut* (1999) have been re-edited to qualify for an R. The G rating has been almost equally firmly avoided, an indication of the extent to which Hollywood scaled down the production of big-budget movies aimed at the female-led "family" audience after 1968. Of 336 films rated in 1981, for example, only seven were rated G, and it has been common industry practice to insert swearing, nudity, or violence to ensure a PG or R rating.[58]

The abandonment of the Production Code for the rating system also made the movie theater an increasingly uninviting venue for women. Taken on a date to see *Taxi Driver* (1976), for instance, a woman would witness Travis Bickle (Robert De Niro) taking Betsy (Cybill Shepherd) to a porn movie, and extracts from the porn movie, as well as the culminating scenes of violence. In the two decades after 1970,

Box 1.1   Rating the movies

Since 1968, the Classification and Rating Administration (CARA) has classified Hollywood's output as a means of offering "advance information about movies so that parents can decide what movies they want their children to see or not to see."

From 1968 to 2000, CARA rated 16,320 movies. Over the whole period, 7 percent were rated G, 34 percent PG or PG-13, 56 percent R, and 3 percent X or NC-17. These figures include all movies submitted for rating, including imported foreign pictures, and thus do not simply represent Hollywood's output. The vast majority of imported features are rated R.

A 1981 study indicated that R-rated movies were significantly less likely to be successful at the box-office than either PG- or G-rated pictures. Between

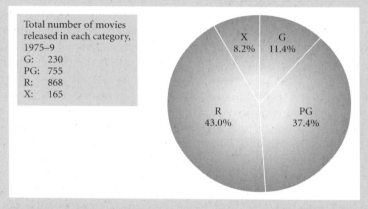

Total number of movies released in each category, 1975–9
G: 230
PG: 755
R: 868
X: 165

CARA ratings, 1975–9

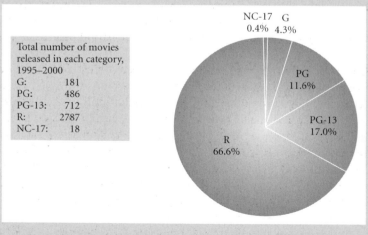

Total number of movies released in each category, 1995–2000
G: 181
PG: 486
PG-13: 712
R: 2787
NC-17: 18

CARA ratings, 1995–2000

1969 and 1979, only 13.7 percent of R-rated movies were reported by *Variety* as earning more than $1 million in domestic rentals (1969 dollars, with figures adjusted annually for inflation), while 26.7 percent of PG-rated movies and 24.2 percent of G-rated movies earned that amount. The authors concluded that "there was a constant market for a certain volume of R films, no matter how many were released: between 20 and 33 R films reached the adjusted million-dollar level each year, even though the total released varied from 83 to 276 annually."[59]

women were rarely specifically addressed as an audience, and then only by modestly budgeted pictures. Female stars no longer occupied the top positions as box-office attractions, and barely a handful of actresses were regarded as "bankable." During the 1980s, the most successful female-oriented pictures – *Tootsie* (1982), *Flashdance* (1983), *Rain Man* (1988) – tended also to be male-centered, and at best earned only half the revenue of their male- or family-oriented competitors.

By the late 1980s, however, marketing strategists in the major companies were beginning to pay attention to the "graying of the movie-going audience." In 1984, only 15 percent of the audience was over 40. In 1990, the over-40s made up 24 percent of the audience, providing a more viable target market. Fox production chief Roger Birnbaum suggested that these changes in audience composition meant that "a studio can develop a slate of pictures that doesn't just cater to one demographic." In a return to much earlier assumptions, he reported that "the demographic on women, today, is very strong."[60] The exceptional box-office performance of two 1990 movies, *Pretty Woman* and *Ghost*, indicated the commercial potential of female-oriented pictures, which the industry identified as romantic comedies and "dating movies," capable of generating repeat viewings, the key feature of post-*Star Wars* (1977) box-office success. Despite this success, industry executives in the 1990s continued to target young male viewers, believing that young women could not persuade their boyfriends to see a picture without a bankable male star. Like Classical Hollywood's long-term attachment to "Tillie-the-Toiler," post-Classical Hollywood's reluctance to revise the identity of its 19-year-old male target viewer is perhaps best understood as a basic commercial conservatism.

Post-Classical Hollywood's increasing acceptance of the "demographic vistas"[61] of audience research also acknowledged its close interrelationship with television, where the measurement of audiences and the identification of "lifestyle" groups through statistical factor analysis has become an integral aspect of both program production and economic organization. When the baby boom generation passed beyond the age of most frequent movie attendance in the late 1970s, the industry sought to narrow the gap it had previously maintained between cinema as an entertainment for the young and television as a product for older people, most obviously through the extraordinarily rapid development, between 1984 and 1990, of a secondary market for video release.

More influential on production trends in the 1990s than the over-40 audience, however, was "Generation Y," the 72 million Americans born between 1977 and

Box 1.2 Contemporary Hollywood's audience

As the baby boom generation has aged, the audience attending American movie theaters has changed its age profile. In 1990, the over-40s made up 24 percent of the audience, but by 2000, this had risen to 32 percent. Teenagers, however, remained the most frequent attenders. Half the 12–17 age group went to the movies once a month, while only 5 percent never went. The most frequent adult attenders were parents with teenage children. Males were more likely than females to be frequent attenders, but also more likely never to go to the movies.

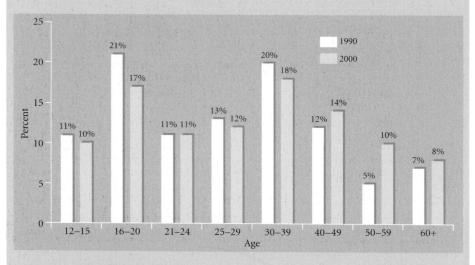

American movie theater attendance by age, 1990–2000

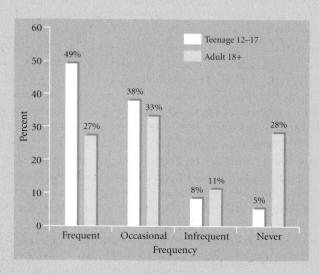

Frequency of movie theater attendance by age, 2000

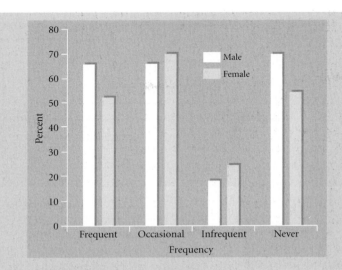

Frequency of movie theater attendance by sex, 2000

Total admissions rose by nearly 25 percent during the 1990s, and the average American went to the movies five times in 2000.[62]

(*Note*: these figures contain no information on the attendance of children under 12, since the MPAA does not include them in their survey data, despite the importance of this demographic group.)

1995, who represented a demographic bulge almost as large and arguably as socially important as their baby boom parents' generation. By 1995, children 18 years of age or younger comprised 28 percent of the overall US population, a cohort roughly equal to baby-boomers aged 31–40. Exploiting the potential of the video rental and "sell-through" markets in the late 1980s, the industry began to produce a new variant on the family movie, targeted at the diverse array of relationships among baby-boomers and their "echo boom" children which comprise the postmodern family. As film historian Robert Allen describes it, the postmodern family movie, archetypally represented by *Home Alone* (1990), identified "a set of narrative, representational, and institutional practices designed to maximize marketability" by stimulating tie-ins, licensing, and "synergistic brand extension." The target consumer for these movies, and even more clearly for what Allen calls "the movie on the lunchbox" – the raft of toys, clothes, home furnishings, and other merchandising tie-ins that accompanied them – was the pre-adolescent "echo boom" child.[63]

The economic motivations for this strategy are clear enough. In the 1990s, "family" movies, rated PG or PG-13, were three times more likely than an R-rated picture to take over $100 million at the box-office. With most video purchases being made by parents for their children, family movies also dominated video sales.

"Gosh, I'm eating junk and watching rubbish. You'd better come out and stop me!" Kevin (Macauley Culkin), Hollywood's target audience for "non-drop-off" movies in the 1990s, *Home Alone* (1990).

Produced by John Hughes; distributed by Twentieth Century-Fox.

The need for not only the movie but also its ancillary product range to appeal to this audience group shaped Hollywood's increasing use of animation and digital effects technology, by requiring family movies to have a distinctive and reproducible iconography that its producers could copyright and license. In the 1990s the Disney company was reborn as the market leader in this economy, in which movies coexist with franchises, tie-ins, and licensing as elements in a diversified product range, existing as toys and Happy Meals in advance of theatrical release, and surviving on video and as computer games long after the movies have left the shopping-mall multiplexes.

Hollywood's World

Contemporary Hollywood does not, of course, only make movies for echo-boomers; it does not have only a single demographic understanding of its audience, any more than Classical Hollywood did. Hollywood has always understood its audience through the perceptions of marketing and the evolving methodologies of market research, and at the same time the industry's notion of its audience has had to remain very generalized, because of the size of a movie's market. Hollywood movies have always been made for an international audience, and since the early 1920s, between a third and half of Hollywood's earnings have come from audiences outside the United States. Much of the cultural power of Hollywood and other artefacts of American mass culture has lain in the fact that they were designed "for universal exhibition."[64] Several times in this book I describe Holly-wood's values as Utopian. As the description of its immaterial geography suggests, Hollywood itself is a Utopia, a nowhere that has also been America to most of the rest of the world since the early twentieth century. To the citizens of Manchester, Melbourne, and Mombasa, America's most recognizable landscapes are those of the Western and the inner city neighborhood of the crime movie. Hollywood has exported an image of the United States that has become so much a part of every-day life in even distant and scarcely westernized areas as to seem, paradoxically, less an *American* product and more a part of an international mass culture in which we all share. At the center of this empire, Americans can become too possessive of their cultural capital. In his history of the American musical, Rick Altman claims that however much non-American critics may understand "the context and meaning" of a movie such as *Singin' in the Rain*, they will inevitably lack the familiarity with American culture that equips them to translate the movie's "raw thematic material into . . . the culture's master themes."[65] Altman argues that:

> The culture's master themes are not actually *in* the text, yet the text is produced in such a way as to evoke them for a particular interpretive community. Perception of the relationship is a more important cultural phenomenon than any actual relation-ship that might exist. It is through the spectator's knowledge and perception that culture and cinema interact in a reciprocal relationship.[66]

While not questioning Altman's general proposition about the relationship between cinema and culture, it is worth pointing out that because Hollywood movies have never been made only for an American audience, they have also been part of the other cultures they have visited. An Austrian audience watching *The Sound of Music* (1965) or an Australian audience watching *The Sundowners* (1960) saw their national histories Americanized. In movies like these, audiences outside the United States have viewed their own cultural pasts through a filter in which their domestic environment has been represented as exotic, while the "domestic market" addressed by the movie has not been theirs but that of North America. In such circumstances, it is hardly surprising that Hollywood should have become an imaginative home to many of its foreign audiences. In a 1989 article about the effect of new communications technologies on cultural identity, David Morley and Kevin Robins suggested that "American culture repositions frontiers – social, cul-tural, psychic, linguistic, geographical. America is now within."[67] But for much of the world, American popular culture had become part of their cultural identity before 1926, when a State Department official observed that "If it were not for the barrier we have established, there is no doubt that the American movies would be bringing us a flood of the immigrants. As it is, in vast instances, the desire to come to this country is thwarted, and the longing to emigrate is changed into a desire to imitate."[68] Two years later, a film industry representative declared that motion pictures "color the minds of those who see them," and were "demon-strably the greatest single factors in the Americanization of the world."[69] Less enthusiastically, the *Daily Express* complained that British cinemagoers "talk America, think America, and dream America. We have several million people, mostly women, who to all intent and purpose are temporary American citizens."[70] They were, of course, not American citizens at all, but citizens of Hollywood's imagined Utopian community. For many people who visit the familiar foreign territory of Hollywood in the movies and in their imagination, however, Hollywood is what they imagine America to be.

Summary

- "Hollywood" is not so much a physical place as it is a conception, a state of mind, or a place in our communal imaginations.
- This book makes a distinction between "film" (the physical material used to record images and sound) and "movie" (the stream of images and sounds experienced as a narrative or spectacle).
- This book presents a study of cinema as a capitalist cultural institution rather than a study of film as art. The symbiotic relationship between "art" and "business" in Hollywood is central to understanding its commercial aesthetic, which is essentially opportunist in its economic motivation. The commercial and aesthetic success of *Titanic*, for example, relied on the diversity of its attractions, which allow different audiences access to different pleasures, rather than on the movie's underlying aesthetic unity or coherence.
- There are at least three different kinds of histories of Hollywood: the history of production, the history of reception and the audience, and the history of critical response to Hollywood. Each of these histories competes with Hollywood's history of itself. The period of Hollywood's history from the early 1920s to the late 1950s is referred to in this book as "Classical Hollywood."
- Beyond its technological, organizational, or stylistic changes, Hollywood's essential business has remained the same: to entertain its audience and make a profit. Hollywood argues that it gives its audiences what they want, implicitly claiming to be benevolent. The Production Code used in Classical Hollywood claimed to ensure that Hollywood provided only entertainment that would not harm any of its viewers. The rating system that replaced it in 1968 makes similar claims.
- Audiences go to the movies to consume their own emotions. Movies have to be organized so that viewers will produce their emotions in a sequence and pattern that they find satisfying.
- Although Hollywood promoted the idea of an undifferentiated audience, it has always classified its audiences. In Classical Hollywood, women were understood to make up the majority of the audience. Since the 1960s, however, Hollywood has identified teenage males as its primary target audience.
- Hollywood has always produced movies for international audiences as well as for its domestic market. In doing so, it has often Americanized the national histories of other countries, while the American product seems to be part of an international mass culture.

Further Reading

Hollywoodland

Hollywood has been a rich source for journalism, popular sociology, and fiction, and some of this material is well worth reading for information on the production process. F. Scott Fitzgerald, *The Last Tycoon* (Harmondsworth: Penguin, 1974), gives a more accurate account of the operation of the studio system than many critical works and popular histories, while a fictional account of contemporary Hollywood can be found in Michael Tolkin, *The Player* (London: Faber, 1989). Two sociological studies, Leo Rosten, *Hollywood: The Movie Colony, the Movie Makers* (New York: Harcourt, Brace, 1941), and Hortense Powdermaker, *Hollywood the Dream Factory: An Anthropologist Looks at the Movie-Makers* (Boston: Little, Brown, 1950), are extremely informative. Among the more illuminating contemporary "insider" accounts are William Goldman's books *Adventures in the Screen Trade: A Personal View of Hollywood and Screenwriting* (New York: Warner Books, 1983) and *Which Lie Did I Tell?: More Adventures in the Screen Trade* (New York: Pantheon, 2000). There is a history of the Hollywood sign at www.hollywoodsign.org/index3.htm.

Heaven's Gate, Titanic, and the cinema of astonishment

Tom Gunning presents his description of early cinema in "An Aesthetic of Astonishment: Early Film and the (In)credulous Spectator," *Art and Text* 34 (Spring 1989), pp. 31–45, and discusses its implications for other forms of cinema in "The Cinema of Attractions: Early Film, its Spectator and the Avant-Garde," in *Early Cinema: Space, Frame, Narrative*, ed. Thomas Elsaesser (London: British Film Institute, 1990).

Steven Bach, *Final Cut: Dreams and Disaster in the Making of Heaven's Gate* (London: Faber, 1986), provides a detailed account of the movie's production. Not everyone regards *Heaven's Gate* as an aesthetic failure: Robin Wood, "*Heaven's Gate* Reopened," *MOVIE* 31/2 (1986), argues that it is "one of the few authentically innovative Hollywood films."

For essays on *Titanic*, see Peter Krämer, "Women First: *Titanic* (1997), Action-Adventure Films and Hollywood's Female Audience," *Historical Journal of Film, Radio and Television* 18:4 (1998), pp. 599–618, and Kevin S. Sandler and Gaylyn Studlar, eds, *Titanic: Anatomy of a Blockbuster* (New Brunswick, NJ: Rutgers University Press, 1999).

Classical Hollywood histories

Part One of David Bordwell, Janet Staiger, and Kristin Thompson, *The Classical Hollywood Cinema: Film Style and Mode of Production to 1960* (London: Routledge and Kegan Paul, 1985) provides an analysis of the formal properties of classical Hollywood style. Thomas Cripps, *Hollywood's High Noon: Moviemaking and Society before Television* (Baltimore, MD: Johns Hopkins University Press, 1997), provides a social history of Classical Hollywood. No one has yet written a history of Hollywood's reception, but *Moviegoing in America*, ed. Gregory Waller (Malden, MA: Blackwell, 2002), contains several accounts of the place of cinema in everyday American life, drawn from the trade and popular magazine press. Janet Staiger outlines a theoretical basis for such a history and provides some case studies in *Interpreting Films: Studies in the Historical Reception of American Cinema* (Princeton, NJ: Princeton University Press, 1992).

A series of books under the general title *The History of the American Cinema* is being published by Charles Scribner's Sons and the University of California Press. When complete, this is intended to be a standard reference history. Eight of a proposed ten volumes have been published at the time of writing: Charles Musser, *The Emergence of Cinema: The American Screen to 1907* (1990); Eileen Bowser, *The Transformation of Cinema: 1907–1915* (1990); Richard Koszarski, *An Evening's Entertainment: The Age of the Silent Feature Picture, 1915–1928* (1990); Donald Crafton, *The Talkies: American Cinema's Transition to Sound, 1926–1931* (1997); Tino Balio, *Grand Design: Hollywood as a Modern Business Enterprise, 1930–1939* (1993); Thomas Schatz, *Boom and Bust: American Cinema in the 1940s* (1997); David A. Cook, *Lost Illusions: American Cinema in the*

Shadow of Watergate and Vietnam, 1970–1979 (2000); and Stephen Prince, *A New Pot of Gold: Hollywood under the Electronic Rainbow, 1980–1989* (2000).

Hollywood and its audiences

Margaret Thorp, *America at the Movies* (London: Faber, 1946), is a classic study of Hollywood's relationship with its audience. Bruce A. Austin, *Immediate Seating: A Look at Movie Audiences* (Belmont, CA: Wadsworth, 1989), provides a more recent analysis, while essays on Hollywood's historical audiences can be found in *American Movie Audiences: From the Turn of the Century to the Early Sound Era* and *Identifying Hollywood's Audiences: Cultural Identity and the Movies*, both eds Melvyn Stokes and Richard Maltby (London: British Film Institute, 1999).

Ratings

The MPAA's description of its ratings categories is reproduced in appendices 2 and 3. Its account of the rating system can be found at its website, www.mpaa.org, while Jon Lewis provides a more critical view in *Hollywood vs Hardcore: How the Struggle over Censorship Saved the Modern Film Industry* (New York: New York University Press, 2000), in which he argues that the principal function of the rating system, like that of the Production Code, is to manage entry into the exhibition marketplace, in the interests of the major companies who are members of the MPAA. These ideas are discussed further in chapters 6 and 7. The recent history of ratings is discussed in Kevin Sandler, "The Naked Truth: *Showgirls* and the Fate of the X/NC-17 Rating," *Cinema Journal* 40:3 (Spring 2001), pp. 69–93.

Hollywood and the world

Kristin Thompson, *Exporting Entertainment: America in the World Film Market, 1907–1934* (London: British Film Institute, 1985), and Ruth Vasey, *The World According to Hollywood, 1918–1939* (Exeter: University of Exeter Press, 1997), explain Classical Hollywood's economic and political relationship with its foreign market. Other accounts can be found in Andrew Higson and Richard Maltby, eds, *"Film Europe" and "Film America": Cinema, Commerce and Cultural Exchange, 1925–1939* (Exeter: University of Exeter Press, 1999), and Geoffrey Nowell Smith and Stephen Ricci, eds, *Hollywood and Europe: Economics, Culture, National Identity, 1945–95* (London: British Film Institute, 1998). Toby Miller, Nitin Govil, John McMurria, and Richard Maxwell, *Global Hollywood* (London: British Film Institute, 2001), examines the contemporary industry's global market.

CHAPTER TWO
Entertainment 1

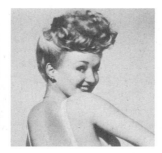

To recapture the active response of the film-fan is the first step toward intelligent appreciation of most pictures . . . One cannot profitably stop there,
but one cannot sensibly begin anywhere else.

V. F. Perkins[1]

At the most fundamental level, anything that stimulates, encourages or
otherwise generates a condition of pleasurable diversion could be called
entertainment. . . . Although life is full of constraint and disciplines, responsibilities and chores, and a host of things disagreeable, entertainment, in
contrast, encompasses activities that people enjoy and look forward
to doing. This is the basis of the demand for or the consumption of entertainment products and services . . . Entertainment – the cause – is thus
obversely defined through its effect: a satisfied and happy psychological
state.

Harold L. Vogel[2]

Escape

My mother obtained a job at the State cinema when I was ten. For me
that meant a ticket to Paradise, and regularly I worshipped at the shrine
of the gods and goddesses. I couldn't wait for the moment to come when
the velvet curtains would sweep apart, the lights dim, and a shared intimacy would settle on the hushed audience.

British movie fan, describing cinemagoing in the 1940s[3]

Truly, a great picture. A rousing, stirring picture. A romantic picture. A story that sweeps you out of your humdrum life and carries you off to sea – to fight with strong, silent Elmo Lincoln against the perils of mutiny on the high seas – to fall in love with a beautiful woman and sacrifice liberty for her sake – to make a miraculous escape from the fetid dungeon of a southern republic and become master of a colony of beach-combers, conquering them by might of fist and brain and then – to save the one woman from a terrible fate in the midst of red revolution.

Advertisement for *Under Crimson Skies* (1920)[4]

We have all grown up with Hollywood as an important but usually unconsidered part of our lives. From the games of cowboys and Indians we play as children to our first date at the movies, from the way we hold a beer glass or style our hair after our favorite movie star to the way we think about love and heroism, we could all trace Hollywood's influence on us. But usually we don't bother. For the most part we barely acknowledge the cultural influence of the movies in an apologetic tone of voice. If we are ever asked to do more than take Hollywood for granted, we are likely to say that the movies are not serious enough to be taken seriously. They are, after all, only entertainment, and the whole point about entertainment is that we are not supposed to take it seriously. Describing an experience as "entertaining" often seems to have said all that needs to be said about it. What entertainment is, and what the word "entertainment" means, seem self-evident. What makes a movie entertaining is apparently so obvious as to need no explanation. Entertainment is . . . what we find entertaining.

Although we recognize entertainment easily enough when we experience it, we generally have difficulty in defining it. The dictionary is no help, for there the word seems self-explanatory: entertainment is "that which entertains . . . amusement; a performance or show designed to give pleasure."[5] Rather than defining entertainment, we tend to describe the satisfactions we expect from it. We say that we want our entertainment to be "diverting" or "amusing," or to "hold our attention." This language circles around the object of our concern rather than taking us any closer to it, and in popular use the word seems to defy our attempts to analyze or enlarge upon its meaning. The adjectives most often attached to the noun "entertainment" are dismissive: "just," "mere," "only," "light." It is hard to imagine alternatives: what would "heavy entertainment" be like? These problems of definition are symptomatic of the place entertainment occupies in our lives. What we recognize as entertainment is something that provides a pleasurable distraction from our more important concerns – of work or politics or Art. When discussing entertainment, therefore, it seems inappropriate to apply the more rigorous intellectual criteria that we use in other areas of our lives, including those of definition.

The vexed questions of what entertainment is and why no one takes it seriously will haunt every page of this book. At the outset, it is important to recognize how distinctive the experience of entertainment is. Entertainment presents itself to us as almost wondrously benign. It offers us pleasure and makes no demands on us, except that it asks us not to think about it. It justifies itself in the very notion that it gives its audiences what we want. If we sometimes feel uneasy, even guilty, about taking entertainment seriously, we are merely responding to the forces in our culture that tell us that if we are going to devote our energies to thinking, we should be thinking about something more serious, more difficult. The forces impelling us into this attitude are twofold. One is the attitude of the entertainment industry itself, which has consistently sought to describe the cultural effects of its products as trivial, and has thus contributed to the treatment of its products as trivial. When the president of Cinemavision was asked about the cultural impact of his company's plans to distribute Hollywood movies in India and eastern Europe in 1992, he replied, "US culture is not pernicious. I'm only talking leisure, entertainment, here."[6]

The other force governing our attitudes to entertainment is the practice of criticism. I shall discuss the institutions and ideologies of criticism later in this chapter, and again in chapter 17, but for now it is enough to note that the principal cultural function of criticism is to make judgments of value, and that the most authoritative forms of criticism in our culture have not valued entertainment highly. For most of the twentieth century, critical authority saw movies as part of a mass culture it condemned as vulgar, philistine, or lacking in moral seriousness. Since about 1970, Hollywood has become an acceptable object of study (on university film studies courses, for instance), but entertainment cinema is seldom studied as entertainment. Instead, elaborate academic discourses explain that as well as being entertaining, entertainment movies deal with "history, society, psychology, gender roles, indeed, the meaning of life," and these concerns can be discussed with much the same seriousness as previous generations of critics brought to the study of literature.[7]

In their different ways, both industrial and critical discourses place entertainment in a curious cultural limbo, where it is simultaneously disregarded and protected. Because we do not have to take it seriously (or if we are taking it seriously, we treat it as something else), we also do not have to worry about it. Because it is somehow not fully part of "culture," entertainment exists in a separate, self-contained, social space, where the fact that we consider it unimportant protects it from scrutiny. Our everyday experience of moviegoing is not so different. The movie theater, the great dark room where the dream factory's dreams are sold, permits its audiences the intensity of privacy in a public space. Our eyes, our minds, and sometimes our hands are permitted to wander, perhaps into forbidden places in an exploration of self, of other, of difference. Gazing desiringly at the screen, we are aware that the great dark room is a site of Eros: at the most banal level one of our culture's places for adolescent sexual discovery, but also a place for **public fantasy**, for the public expression of ideas and actions we must each individually repress in our everyday behavior.

The price of admission to this everyday place of refuge from the everyday is our knowledge that what happens inside the great dark room is isolated from what happens outside. No matter how vividly we have experienced its imaginary landscapes and Utopian possibilities, we leave the theater reminding ourselves that what we have seen was "only a movie." That is the hidden reason why Hollywood movies have happy endings. The re-establishment of order renders the viewer's experimentation with expressive behavior a matter of no consequence, contained within the safe, unexplored, unconsidered, and trivialized space of entertainment. In that space, stories are governed not by their own developmental logic, but by the logic of a conventionalized, generic morality, which ensures that entertainment functions as a process of "recreation," by which, as the authors of the Production Code put it in 1930, "a man rebuilds himself after his work, after his labor, during which he gets the chance to rebuild himself physically . . . morally, spiritually and intellectually."[8] Others, as we shall see, have viewed this machine for the production of pleasure as much less benevolent. But for both its creators and its detractors, Hollywood's most profound significance lies in its ability to turn pleasure into a product we can buy. We need to attend closely to the industrial and economic processes involved in the manufacture and marketing of these transient images as well as to their content if we are to appreciate the full complexity of our relationship to Hollywood, and Hollywood's relationship to American culture. However we come to view Hollywood, we should begin in the place where we view it, in the great dark room.

Watching Tom Cruise in *Mission: Impossible II* (2000) on video both is and is not like the experience that earlier generations had watching Douglas Fairbanks in *The Black Pirate* (1926) in an "atmospheric theater," decorated to create the illusion that its patrons were watching the movie and listening to the 50-piece orchestra in an ancient, moonlit Italian garden. Some of the technological changes in production are obvious, but equally important are changes in the conditions in which movies are consumed. Among the new entertainment media innovated since the late nineteenth century – the still camera, the gramophone, radio, and television – cinema was the only one not designed for consumption at home. The picture palaces of the 1920s invited their audiences into the temporary occupation of a gilded mansion more lavishly decorated and staffed than the finest hotels. When New York's Roxy Theater, "The Cathedral of the Motion Picture," opened in 1927, the souvenir book commemorating the event declared that "when you enter its portals you step magically from the drab world of confusion and cares into a fairy palace . . . with all the allurements that art, science and music can offer."[9] Very little of that goes on when you put the cassette in the video-recorder and watch *Mission: Impossible II* in "the drab world of confusion" that is your living room.

If we think about what pleasures and satisfactions the movies offer their audiences, however, we can find a consistency beneath the obvious variations. A 1925 Paramount advertisement encouraged audiences to:

> Go to a motion picture . . . and let yourself go. Before you know it you are *living* the story – laughing, loving, hating, struggling, winning! All the adventure, all the romance, all the excitement you lack in your daily life are in – Pictures. They take you completely out of yourself into a wonderful new world. . . . Out of the cage of everyday existence! If only for an afternoon or an evening – escape![10]

This product, the experience of escape packed into a two-hour story in which a sympathetic character overcomes a series of obstacles to achieve his or her desire,

During the 1920s Famous Players-Lasky ran monthly advertisements promoting the activity of "going to the movies." The secret of the fascination of Paramount or Artcraft pictures, they explained, "is that they show you yourself as you really are, or as you *might be*."

has consistently provided the basis of Hollywood's appeal to its audiences. Like 1920s audiences in the palaces of fantasy, "home cinema" viewers today can become part of the high life they watch in a darkened room. For an hour or two, the happy ending can be theirs, too.

The idea of "escape" is still central to popular accounts of contemporary Hollywood, but this term, too, has received little serious critical attention. In examining what satisfactions entertainment offers its audience, Richard Dyer has suggested that the appeal of what is usually called "escapism" is better understood as "Utopian." He argues that the movies provide a Utopianism of the feelings, presenting "head on as it were, what Utopia would feel like, rather than how it is organized." Entertainment's escape is to a revised, Utopian version of the audience's own world: Utopian both in the sense that it is a place of more energy and more abundance than the "real" world, and also in the sense that its issues, problems, and conflicts are clearer and more intense than those we experience in our day-to-day reality. Dyer argues that entertainment can thus be seen to answer "real needs created by society." Importantly, however, it only responds to some needs: broadly, to the needs of its audience as individuals, rather than as members of social groups or classes. While entertainment therefore responds to real social needs, it also defines what people's legitimate social needs are understood to be. As Dyer suggests, "the ideals of entertainment imply wants that capitalism itself promises to meet."[11]

Dyer was not the first person to suggest that Hollywood provides Utopian solutions to everyday desires. In the late 1940s, two sociologists, Martha Wolfenstein and Nathan Leites, examined a group of over 60 movies with a contemporary urban setting. Their conclusions dealt not so much with the issues that might arise in a Hollywood thriller or comedy as with the way their stories unfolded and the range of events that occurred. Unconcerned with the artistic status of the movies they studied, Wolfenstein and Leites saw them as a reservoir of common, ready-made daydreams that were "not merely escapes from the routines of daily life." Because movies were shared public experiences, and therefore less embarrassing than the "more fugitive, private, home-made day-dreams" of individuals, members of their audience could more easily incorporate the movies' accounts of emotional problems into their own lives.[12] In this way, Wolfenstein and Leites suggested, the movies engaged their audience in an interplay between experience and wish. While their study was confined to a narrow period, some of their comments could just as well describe how Hollywood movies of the 1930s or the 2000s worked.

American movies, suggested Wolfenstein and Leites, do not try to reconcile their audiences to the disappointments and complications of life by dramatizing them. Characters with antisocial motives are seldom presented as sympathetic, while Hollywood's heroes and heroines are absolved from both guilt and responsibility for what they do. The destructive impulses in a plot are externalized, usually by being embodied in unsympathetic characters who are eventually defeated. What we wish for the hero and heroine is accomplished less often by their own actions than by the world around them, a world ultimately served by benevolent coincidence: "the car that gets out of control, the ticket agent who assigns the hero and heroine the same berth." Hollywood movies provide solutions to emotional problems in which "wish-fulfillments can occur without penalties. . . . The contention of American films is that we should not feel guilty for mere wishes." In keeping with this world without consequences, love in American movies rarely involves suffering, since "whenever life may look discouraging, a beautiful girl turns up at the next moment." Hollywood movies "express confidence both in the plenitude of opportunities and in the adequate strength of impulses. . . . the lost opportunity is comic rather than tragic in American films."[13]

Heroes and heroines are seldom made vulnerable by their emotions; objects of affection are easily replaced. Love tends to be reasonable and righteous, and, of course, ends happily. Defining an unhappy ending as involving the death or defection of one partner, Wolfenstein and Leites discovered that only one Hollywood movie in six had such an ending; French films, on the other hand, "show love turning out unhappily half the time." Violence and romance share many of the same properties in Hollywood. Violence may be fast moving, noisy, or technically intricate but it is unlikely to be emotionally involved. People are most likely to be murdered in Hollywood to get them out of the way when they become obstacles to the achievement of some goal. The murder victim becomes a thing, a block in the path, rather than an object of intense feelings and possible regret. In

American movies, Wolfenstein and Leites suggested, "men and women may, and often do shoot each other. They do not break each other's hearts."[14]

Such an account of Hollywood emotions might describe *Fatal Attraction* (1987) or *Basic Instinct* (1992) as well as it described *The Big Sleep* (1946) or *The Mask of Dimitrios* (1944), but it also comes close to describing Hollywood emotions as superficial, stereotyped, and dishonest. Anthropologist Hortense Powdermaker expressed a similar view in *Hollywood the Dream Factory* when she maintained that no one in Hollywood was concerned with "the reality of emotions and with truthfulness of meaning":

> Man, according to Hollywood, is either completely good, or bad. His personality is static, rarely showing any development either in growth or in regression. The villain is a black-eyed sinner who can do no good and who cannot be saved; while the hero is a glamorous being, who can do no wrong of his own volition, and who is always rewarded. Missing is a realistic concept of the human personality, a complex being who can love and hate, who has human frailties and virtues.

Only the exceptional movie showed "real human beings living in a complicated world" with any truthfulness or understanding, but audiences, she feared, had been conditioned by years of viewing not to expect anything different.[15]

Such charges against Hollywood movies persist; director Henry Jaglom, for instance, decries contemporary Hollywood movies because they "lie to you so overwhelmingly; they never talk back to people about their real lives."[16] The charges are fundamentally aesthetic ones, part of a more general accusation that Hollywood's output is banal, repetitive, and predictable – in a word charged with derogatory connotations, melodramatic. (Chapter 4 discusses melodrama as a fundamental mode of Hollywood cinema, and its history as a term of abuse.) These aesthetic complaints about Hollywood's dishonesty in representing social reality are often linked to charges that the movies either exploit their audiences or pander to their baser instincts. One of the most devastating critiques of Hollywood's escapist aesthetics was written in the late 1940s by two émigré members of the Frankfurt School for Social Research, Theodor Adorno and Max Horkheimer:

> Amusement under late capitalism is the prolongation of work. It is sought after as an escape from the mechanized work process, and to recruit strength in order to be able to cope with it again. But at the same time mechanization has such power over a man's leisure and happiness, and so profoundly determines the manufacture of amusement goods, that his experiences are inevitably after-images of the work process itself. . . . what happens at work, in the factory, or in the office can only be escaped from by approximation to it in one's leisure time. All amusement suffers from this incurable malady. Pleasure hardens into boredom because, if it is to remain pleasure, it must not demand any effort and therefore moves rigorously in the worn grooves of association. No independent thinking must be expected from the audience: the product prescribes every reaction . . . Any logical connection calling for mental effort is painstakingly avoided.[17]

Not every hostile critic of Hollywood would share Adorno and Horkheimer's political opinions, but the accusation that the "escapism" offered by the movies is shallow because it is aesthetically deficient is a critical commonplace. Writing at the same time as Adorno and Horkheimer, art critic Clement Greenberg denounced what he called "kitsch" and others called "mass culture" on the grounds that it "predigests art for the spectator and spares him effort, provides him with a shortcut to the pleasures of art that detours what is necessarily difficult in genuine art." Kitsch, claimed Greenberg, "provides vicarious experience for the insensitive with far greater immediacy than serious fiction can hope to do."[18] Such critical attitudes have lost little of their conviction in the intervening years, and continue to present an obstacle to the task of taking Hollywood seriously, since by their predetermined criteria Hollywood is not serious, except perhaps as a symptom of a social condition in need of diagnosis.

Money on the Screen

The budget is the aesthetic.
James Schamus[19]

"You know what prestige means, don't you?"
"Sure, pictures that don't make money."
Steve Canfield (Fred Astaire) and Peggy Dainton (Janis Paige)
in *Silk Stockings* (1957)

When I was at Bennington some of the English teachers who pretended an indifference to Hollywood or its products, really *hated* it. Hated it down deep as a threat to their existence.
F. Scott Fitzgerald[20]

The obstacles to our thinking critically about Hollywood have as much to do with a set of prevailing attitudes toward the movies' cultural status as with anything intrinsic to its products. Before we can begin to take Hollywood seriously we first have to reconsider our conventional expectations of it, and the tradition of criticism that has produced these attitudes. In unpacking that tradition we can start to account for our often automatic responses to Hollywood and to question both their origin and their appropriateness.

Many of our reactions to Hollywood movies are grounded in "common-sense" assumptions about the place of art, and of criticism, in our culture. Reading a daily newspaper will tell you that Art is a separate sphere, located in its own discrete section away from the concerns of "the real world" on the news pages. A newspaper's arts pages also inform us that the primary function of criticism is evaluative. Whether it is deciding which play is worth going to see, or if a novel can enter the canon of great works to be studied on university literature courses, common-sense criticism is judgmental. The privileges of Art – immunity from the laws of obscenity as well as from the demands of commerce, for instance – are valuable enough for common sense to remind us that they should not be given out indiscriminately. As part of the shared "common sense" that enables us to function on a daily basis in our culture, we acquire a set of assumptions that help us to recognize Art when we see it.

A first principle of this knowledge is that, like gold, Art must be scarce and difficult to get if it is to retain its value. Common sense tells us, perhaps a little perversely, that Art is never commonplace. We are encouraged to recognize an opposition between "High" Art and that which is merely "popular," as though aesthetic quality were inversely proportional to the scale of a work's appeal. Although the detailed criteria by which "high" culture is distinguished from "popular culture" are subject to variation, they are grounded in three familiar assumptions. To qualify as Art within the conventions of traditional western aesthetics, the thing in question must be a specific, definable object: a poem, a painting, but first of all a distinct "*work*" of art." Secondly, the "work" must express the sensibility of the artist who produced it, and thirdly, it must also require "work" from its viewer or reader before he or she can appreciate it. As Robert Allen says, by these criteria, "the greater the art, the more difficult it is for the uninitiated to understand."[21]

Some cinema, distanced from the more recognizable forms of Hollywood, can be constructed as Art, but traditional criticism has always found Hollywood more difficult to take seriously than European or Third World cinema. "The main stumbling block for film aesthetics," suggests Peter Wollen, "has not been Eisenstein, but Hollywood. There is no difficulty in talking about Eisenstein in the same breath as the poet Mayakovsky, a painter like Malevich, or a theatre director like Stanislavsky. But John Ford or Raoul Walsh?"[22]

One of the main differences between Hollywood and the most widely recognized tradition of European filmmaking has been that European films have displayed a much closer alliance to the other arts, in both their narrative and pictorial structures. While the history of the American cinema is most often constructed as a history of its genres, the history of the European film is conventionally written as a series of movements: German expressionism, Italian neo-realism, the French New Wave, for example. In their content, but even more importantly in the framework that they provide for criticism, these movements correspond to similar movements in literature or painting. We recognize a movie such as Ingmar Bergman's *Persona* (1966) as having aesthetic worth: a self-consciously expressive visual style makes it *look* like Art, and as we watch it we *work* at understanding what it is "about." Its themes express the sensibility of an individual author and are serious enough to grace a work of literature: the boundary between sanity and madness, the illusion of human personality. When critic David Cook describes Bergman as "essentially a religious artist whose films concern the fundamental questions of human existence: the meaning of suffering and pain, the inexplicability of death, the solitary nature of being, and the difficulty of locating meaning in a seemingly random and capricious universe," he is using terms that could equally well describe the thematic preoccupations of Samuel Beckett, T. S. Eliot, or Franz Kafka.[23]

As an equally archetypal work within its own tradition, *The Wizard of Oz* (1939) makes rather different claims on our attention. With the utter implausibility of its storyline, the tendency of its characters to burst into song-and-dance routines at the drop of a hat, the presence of its stars, and the artificial intensity of its color and special effects, it almost defies us to take it seriously. It seems primarily intent only on celebrating its own status as entertainment. If we start talking about what *The Wizard of Oz* is "about," we are more likely to recapitulate the plot than discover themes suitable to literary or pictorial Art. Trying to argue for an interpretation of *The Wizard of Oz* that makes it seem intellectually complex will probably make us feel uncomfortably pretentious. The movie is patently more concerned with its production values than with symbolism, suggestive ambiguity, or psychologically dense characterization. By **production values**, Hollywood publicity usually means those elements of a movie designed to appeal to an audience independently of the story: the sets, the costumes, the star performances, the "quality" of the product visible on the screen. In a more critical language, they represent areas of pleasure offered to the viewer incidental to, and separate from, the plausibility of the fiction. In contrast to the authenticity and organic unity cherished in *Persona*, *The Wizard of Oz* is characterized more by its synthetic quality, and by its opportunist aggregation of elements designed to appeal to a range of different viewers. The commercial motivation underlying its organization is apparent and inescapable.

To stress economics in an account of Hollywood runs the risk of encouraging the belief that, because all movies are made for profit, they are all equally tarred with the same brush of impurity, whether we call it commercialism or capitalism. If we are to take Hollywood's commercial aesthetic seriously, we must deal first with the fundamental incompatibility that traditional criticism has constructed between the commercial and the aesthetic. For many academic critical practices, evaluating a work aesthetically requires the exclusion of questions of money. This is one function of the art gallery. If you want to see Sandro Botticelli's painting *The Birth of Venus*, you can go to the Uffizi gallery in Florence, make your way through the other tourists and stand in front of it for a few minutes, before turning to look at all the other Botticellis in the Botticelli room. While standing there, you might find yourself contemplating the painting's fusion of a high Gothic pictorial style with its Renaissance rediscovery of classical subject matter. But *The Birth of Venus* was not originally painted to hang in a museum for the edification of tourists with a smattering of art history in their education. It was commissioned by an Italian nobleman for his private contemplation at his country villa, where he "escaped from the business, heat or plague of the town to recreate himself with the tranquility and pleasures of a rural retreat."[24] Insofar as the painting's Neo-Platonic allegory expresses a thematic purpose, that purpose belonged not to Botticelli but to his patron, Lorenzo di Pierfrancesco de' Medici. The painting expresses Botticelli's craft skills, and it is the celebration of those skills that draws crowds to the Uffizi. What Botticelli had to do with the construction of the painting's allegorical meaning is another question; at most, he was one participant in a negotiation between patron, writer, and artist. Like all commissioned art, *Venus* is the site of that negotiation, a compromise between diverse motives.

By taking *Venus* out of the grand-ducal wardrobe and putting her in the gallery, the academicians have literally transported the picture out of the material world in which it was produced and perceived, and placed it in another, altogether more sanitized and abstracted context, in which it can be studied without reference to the economics of its production.[25] Preserved in conditions designed to minimize the physical effects of the passage of time, the painting has become a definable aesthetic object and ceased to be a commodity. A financial valuation of it would have little meaning; it possesses an aesthetic value but not an exchange value, and so has become literally "priceless." Most textual criticism – whether of paintings, writing, or movies – performs a comparable act of dematerializing the text it criticizes. Questions of money have been seen as the specialized interests of economists and business historians, separate from the loftier task of analyzing texts. In talking about books, we seldom discuss the processes of a book's production or the commercial transactions involved in its transmission from author to reader. The book as a physical object is seen only a necessary vessel carrying the text's abstract ideas. Money may affect its manufacture but does not impinge on its meaning.

Extracting the text from its context can be immensely productive. It may permit very precise acts of interpretation and evaluation; it may allow real pleasure to be taken in the text. Abstraction frees the reader to encounter the text without distracting questions of origin or intended destination. But it also tends to treat the text entirely as something "found," finished and complete, its meaning intrinsic and only awaiting release. This practice does not give readers or viewers much authority in their relationship with the text, since their limited role is to rediscover that intrinsic meaning, and their competence in this role is judged according to their sensitivity to a nuance of meaning already inscribed in the text. Textual authority – the capacity to make meaning through a text – is conventionally attributed to its author, while the role of the reader is, according to Umberto Eco, to "deal interpretively with the expressions in the same way as the author deals generatively with them."[26] As readers or critics, we begin by seeking the author's voice as a name to give to the unifying thematic and stylistic patterns in the text. Believing that these textual patterns have been placed there by the author to communicate his or her ideas, we construct the book as the expression of the author's sensibility. Our competence as critical readers comes to be judged on our ability to discover the author's intentions. In our invention of an intending author, we construct a criticism that resembles a game of hide-and-seek, or else a detective

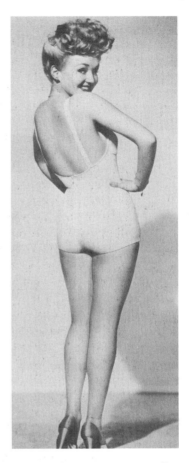

Art historians argue over the exact allegorical meaning of Sandro Botticelli's *Birth of Venus*, but their descriptions of the painting's sensuousness recognize an erotic dimension to its representation of the Neo-Platonic idea that "physical perfection is the mirror and emblem of a pure and noble spirit." In something of a similar spirit, the US military circulated this pinup image of Betty Grable during World War II, to remind American troops what they were fighting for.

mystery, in which the critic has, like Sherlock Holmes, to discover the correct interpretation which fits all the evidence and exposes all the meaning encoded by the
author within the work. The more cleverly the secret meaning of a text is buried,
the better we perform as critics if we can unearth it, and the greater the artistry
of the author in his or her act of concealment.

Few Hollywood movies respond well to this critical treatment, which often
exposes their relative thematic banality. What does most to discredit Hollywood
movies as objects of critical scrutiny, however, is the fact that they cost money and
are formally organized in the interests of profit. The very things that most emphatically define Hollywood cinema's commercial function as entertainment – musical
routines, car chases, screen kisses, the spectacular, the star presence – become the
greatest obstacles to dealing critically with the movies themselves. For many critics,
where the operation of money cannot be suppressed, Hollywood must be abandoned; it cannot function as art because it is a commodity. Publicists in the 1920s
had often described Hollywood as an "art industry," but Adorno and Horkheimer
chose the term "culture industry" as a deliberately ironic description, because they
believed the juxtaposition of the two terms to be an oxymoron, a contradiction
in terms. Dwight MacDonald's 1953 denunciation of mass culture shared their
contempt:

> It is fabricated by technicians hired by businessmen; its audiences are passive con-
> sumers, their participation limited to the choice between buying and not buying. The
> Lords of *kitsch*, in short, exploit the cultural needs of the masses in order to make a
> profit and/or to maintain their class rule. . . . Like nineteenth-century capitalism,
> Mass Culture is a dynamic, revolutionary force, breaking down the old barriers of
> class, traditions, taste, and dissolving all cultural distinction. It mixes and scrambles
> everything together, producing what might be called homogenized culture. . . . It
> thus destroys all values, since value judgments imply discriminations. Mass Culture
> is very, very democratic: it refuses to discriminate against, or between, anything or
> anybody. All is grist to its mill, and all comes out finely ground indeed. . . . It is a
> debased, trivial culture that voids both the deep realities (sex, death, failure, tragedy)
> and also the simple, spontaneous pleasures . . . the unsettling and unpredictable
> (hence unsalable) joy, tragedy, wit, change, originality and beauty of real life. The
> masses, debauched by several generations of this sort of thing, in turn come to
> demand trivial and comfortable cultural products.[27]

MacDonald's position combined an elitist cultural conservatism with political radicalism; he argued that mass culture was an instrument of political domination,
differentiated from both High and Folk Culture by being mechanical, commercial, imitative, vulgar, bureaucratic, and centralized, and appealing to its audiences'
worst instincts – all negative qualities to be denigrated against the positive values
of High or Folk Art. Both politically and culturally, this is an extremely pessimistic
position: mass culture, as represented by Hollywood, is seen to be aesthetically
banal and conservative in its inherent support for the status quo. Although this
position acknowledges the revolutionary force of mass culture, Hollywood's is not
a revolution of which it approves.

For the vulgar Romantic in us all, Hollywood is not Art because it is commercial. For the vulgar Marxist in us all, Hollywood's enslavement to the profit system means that all its products can do is blindly reproduce the dominant ideology of bourgeois capitalism. We can, however, avoid both these simplifications by analyzing Hollywood's status as a commodity, the very thing that usually frustrates a more detailed understanding of it. Far from disqualifying movies from consideration as "art" objects worthy of serious consideration, an emphasis on Hollywood in commercial terms may begin a debate about the critical assumptions that underpin our expectations of what constitutes art and culture as a whole. More than any other cinema, Hollywood makes its industrial and economic negotiations with its audience explicit. Precisely because of that, Hollywood can become the paradigm for an examination of the material relationships between texts and the audiences and critics who encounter and engage them, not just in cinema, but in other media and at other historical moments.

A starting point for a more positive response to Hollywood and its commercial aesthetics is offered by a colleague of Adorno and Horkheimer at the Frankfurt School, who had proposed a more optimistic view of the aesthetic and political possibilities of new technologies like the cinema. Far from seeing the cinema negatively as something opposed to the true values of High Art, Walter Benjamin enthused over its ability to overturn earlier hierarchies of value in art by mass producing the artistic object. Abolishing the scarcity of the art object – the uniqueness that made *The Birth of Venus* priceless – mechanical reproduction also abolished the power which that scarcity placed in the hands of its owners. An elite class was thus deprived of its traditional ability to determine artistic value. Mechanical reproduction robbed the aesthetic object of what Benjamin called its "aura" of uniqueness; the aesthetic object became more familiar and less intimidating in its reproducibility.[28] To an even greater extent than photography, cinema minimized the value of the unique original by requiring the production of large numbers of identical objects, none of which could be seen as more original, and therefore more valuable, than any of the others. The economics of Hollywood rely expressly upon this technical possibility, since any number of prints can be struck from an original master negative and exhibited simultaneously.

Benjamin was, however, concerned more with political and ideological questions than with the economics of the motion picture industry. He stressed that the mechanical reproducibility of art made important shifts in the traditional power relationships between producers and consumers, granting more authority over the use and possible meanings of an art object to the consumer. Rather than approaching the art object with reverence, the movie spectator approaches it with demands and expectations. As a result, Benjamin suggested, the mechanical reproducibility of art, as most clearly represented by the cinema, changed the relationship between art, artists, and society in fundamental ways. Nevertheless, while Benjamin applauded the radically democratic possibilities of cinema, he was no more enthusiastic about what Hollywood actually produced than were Adorno and Horkheimer.

The most frequently voiced criticism of Benjamin's argument is that he failed to acknowledge the economic power of the culture industries, which have simply demonstrated a greater inventiveness in commodifying art in new ways. The fact that you can now buy a reproduction of Van Gogh's *Sunflowers* almost anywhere in the world has done nothing to diminish the market value of the original painting to the Japanese insurance company that now owns it. The problem, however, may lie as much with the critical assumptions involved in the separation of culture and industry as it does in the objects produced by the culture industries. Hollywood movies are everything Dwight MacDonald said they were. But if we are to examine the revolutionary force that they represent, we need to do more than declare that, according to an aesthetic regime to which they have never conformed, they are vulgar and banal. Instead, we must find ways of approaching Hollywood that recognize Hollywood's commercial aesthetic for what it is.

The Multiple Logics of Hollywood Cinema

No one is capable of accurate forecasts in a business/art form where to be guided by logic is to deal in illusion.
Jack Valenti.[29]

We were witnessing a mute struggle between Von Sternberg and his actors. . . . the stars could not afford to think exclusively of the artistic merits of the final picture. . . . The director wanted to create a masterpiece of unrelenting reality; the stars had to avoid shocking their public. Yet they were conscious that, on the wings of a real masterpiece (that is, a masterpiece measured as masterpieces of the films are measured, by box-office receipts), they, as actors, might mount yet higher in the salary scale . . . on the other hand, to sacrifice ever so small a section of their public esteem for a poor picture would be mere folly.
Jan and Cora Gordon[30]

Rather than recognize Hollywood's commercial aesthetic, film criticism has frequently attempted to reconstruct its products in terms more amenable to traditional criticism. At a relatively early point in the development of an academically respectable version of film criticism, there emerged an authorial criticism that became known as the "*politique des auteurs*" because of its origins in French critical theory and the group of writers clustered around the journal *Cahiers du Cinéma*. When it was adopted by Anglo-American critics, it was half-translated by one of its early proponents, Andrew Sarris, as "the *auteur* theory." It sought to establish individual creativity as the source of value in Hollywood. Sarris argued that a "premise of the *auteur* theory is the distinguishable personality of the director as a criterion of value." The auteur theory, he claimed, "values the personality of the director precisely because of the barriers to its expression. It is as if a few brave spirits had managed to overcome the gravitational pull of the mass of movies."[31]

This celebration of individual directorial genius valorized the work of ostentatiously rebellious Hollywood figures such as Orson Welles, whose career was marked by confrontations with "the system." An expectation still active in the criticism of literature and the visual arts, of artists as figures outside and largely unaffected by their surrounding society, was transported into film criticism, reinforcing the already ingrained perceptions of an irresolvable conflict between art and business. By contrast to the elevation of individual creativity, what André Bazin called "the genius of the system," and the achievements of those who functioned competently within it, were denigrated. "What makes Hollywood so much better than anything else in the world is not only the quality of certain directors," suggested Bazin in a critique of the *politique des auteurs*, "but also the vitality and, in a certain sense, the excellence of a tradition":

> Hollywood's superiority is only incidentally technical; it lies much more in what we might call the American cinematic genius, . . . The American cinema is a classical art, but why not then admire in it what is most admirable, i.e. not only the talent of this or that filmmaker, but the genius of the system, the richness of its ever-vigorous tradition, and its fertility when it comes into contact with new elements.[32]

Michael Curtiz, the senior contract director at Warner Bros. in the 1930s and 1940s, provides a case in point. Movies like *The Adventures of Robin Hood* (1938) and *Mildred Pierce* (1945) are marked by a consistently detailed visual style, and the head of production at Warner Bros., Hal Wallis, insisted that "you couldn't mistake a Curtiz setup," because "it had a stamp as clearly marked as a Matisse."[33] **Auteurism**, however, paid more attention to a director's thematic consistency than to the craft skills for which they were employed, and cast Curtiz as a craftsman "blessed with talent but not genius."[34] Sarris categorized Curtiz as "lightly likable" and considered him an "amiable technician": "If many of the early Curtiz films are hardly worth remembering, none of the later ones are even worth seeing. . . . The director's one enduring masterpiece is, of course, *Casablanca*, the happiest of happy accidents, and the most decisive exception to the auteur theory."[35]

It is not difficult to see why industry practitioners should have been so resistant to a critical approach that suggested that a single individual – the director – should be credited with the creation of a movie. The multiplicity of people involved in a production and the multiplicity of pressures exerted upon it make the negotiations surrounding a commissioned painting seem relatively straightforward. The individual intentions of a director or writer may conflict with a corporate interest; the producer's desire to spend money on lavish production values may run up against the studio executive's commitment to staying within budget; the belief that the exploitation of sex and violence onscreen maximizes profits has to negotiate with the institutions of censorship; generic expectations may square uncomfortably with a studio style.

On the other hand, it is not difficult to see the appeal of the auteur theory, and its emergence as a response to changes in the structure of Hollywood itself. The economic crisis of the late 1960s seemed to indicate that "Old Hollywood" had lost its ability to anticipate the tastes of its audience. As early as 1954 it had been suggested the "lost audience," "mature, adult, sophisticated people who read good books and magazines, who attend lectures and concerts, who are polit-

Hal Wallis may have thought that Michael Curtiz's compositions were as distinctive as Matisse's, but he objected to paying for this "artistry." After seeing the dailies from this scene from *The Charge of the Light Brigade* (1936), Wallis dictated a three-page memo to Curtiz complaining, "It is the same old stuff with you, of shooting composition and forgetting all about the action . . . the feeling that is in the script is absolutely lost because you still want to be an artistic cameraman and you will not level down and make a motion picture story. . . . I would once like to see a shot of a compound, shooting from one end to the other, without something in front of me blocking off the sight." Wallis cut almost all of Curtiz's "artistry" from the final version of the sequence to concentrate on the action. Produced by Samuel Bischoff, Hal B. Wallis; distributed by Warner Bros.

ically and socially aware and alert," might be attracted back to the theaters by a more sophisticated cinema, or at least a cinema with greater pretensions, such as that which played in the art-house circuit.[36] The identification of an individual artist as a movie's responsible creator was a valuable element in the establishment of such a cinema, as it was in the establishment of cinema as a subject of academic study.

A critical model of the director-as-author had developed in more high-toned American reviewing during the 1960s. While this approach found little favor with the older generation whose artistry it sought to recognize, it did provide a model by which Hollywood could be discussed as art, and a new generation of directors, many of them educated in its precepts at film schools or university film courses, could see themselves in the role of artist. The "movie brat" directors who emerged during the short-lived "Hollywood Renaissance" of 1971–4 – Francis Coppola,

Martin Scorsese, Brian De Palma, Steven Spielberg, George Lucas – found obvious material benefits in the enhanced industrial status of the director, in part because they became marketable commodities, even stars, in their own right. As a critical as well as a commercial commodity, "Steven Spielberg" is as valuable a brand name as "Tom Cruise." Moreover, the much greater instability of contemporary studio management has increased both the practical authority of the director and his or her relative permanence within the system. The director now assumes many of the functions previously undertaken by a studio producer. According to Pandro S. Berman, a producer at RKO and MGM:

> My greatest contribution was to find the story material, develop it into a screenplay, cast it, and make the picture, usually using other studio personnel for all those jobs. To make a distinction between the producer I am describing and the producer of today, the producer of today is more of an agent, a packager, a promoter, or a financial man who will put things together and take them to a studio, a distribution company, or a bank and get financing. That method has had a very great effect in that the producer has abdicated his function as the creative man in the set-up. He has gone to other business activities, leaving the director as the creative influence.[37]

Variations in practice between different studios, and the variable influence of individuals, make all generalizations about the role and influence of producers, directors, actors, and technical personnel tendentious. The hierarchy of the industry was never immutable, and there were major shifts with the growth of independent production from the 1940s on. Whatever his or her title may be on any particular movie, a producer still performs the role of the project's creative administrator. By the 1980s, however, authorship in Hollywood had become a commercially beneficial fiction, indicated by the opening credits of movies that declare themselves to be "a Taylor Hackford film" or "a John Badham film," and by video re-releases of the "director's cut" of a successful movie, in what Barbara Klinger has called "a commodified version of auteurism."[38] But the multiple logics and intentions that continue to impinge on the process of production ensure that authorship remains an inadequate explanation of how movies work.[39]

In his history of Hollywood filmmaking in the studio period, Thomas Schatz has castigated auteur criticism for "stalling film history and criticism in a prolonged state of adolescent romanticism," by misdescribing the actual relations of power, creative control, and expression within Hollywood, and by denying the material and the economic at the base of production.[40] Hollywood is inescapably a film *industry*, the show *business*, the dream *factory*. As Harry Cohn, head of Columbia Studios, explained to Robert Parrish in 1949:

> Let me give you some facts of life. I release fifty-two pictures a year. I make about forty and buy the rest. Every Friday, the front door of this studio opens and I spit a movie out onto Gower Street . . . If that door opens and I spit and nothing comes out, it means a lot of people are out of work – drivers, distributors, exhibitors, projectionists, ushers, and a lot of other pricks. . . . I want one good picture a year. That's my policy. Give me a *Mr Deeds* or a *Jolson Story* or an *All the King's Men* or a *Lost Horizon* and I won't let an exhibitor have it unless he takes the bread-and-butter product, the *Boston Blackies*, the *Blondies*, the low-budget westerns, and the rest of

Harry Cohn, thinking about spitting a movie
out onto Gower Street. Courtesy BFI.

the junk we make. I like good pictures too, but nobody knows when they're going
to be good, so to get one, I have to shoot for five or six, and to shoot for five or
six, I have to keep the plant going with the program pictures.[41]

The "other pricks" Cohn mentioned included directors, writers, actors – the
people usually seen as being central to the creative process. Cohn relegated them
to areas incidental to the industrial and commercial process he described. His economic logic also made the symbiotic relationship between the "good" pictures
and "the rest of the junk we make" inescapably clear.

Every area of the Hollywood cinema is determined, in the first instance, by economic considerations. A scene at the start of *Sullivan's Travels* (1941), a "screwball" comedy set in Hollywood, makes it clear that purely aesthetic questions
cannot be separated from economic issues. Tired of making formula entertainment like *Ants in Your Plants of 1939*, successful director John L. Sullivan (Joel
McCrea) announces his desire to make *O Brother, Where Art Thou?*, a prestige
message-picture about contemporary social conditions. Studio executives Lebrand
(Robert Warwick) and Hadrian (Porter Hall) attempt to dissuade him, arguing
that message pictures lose money. Failing to put him off, they seek a compromise:

Sullivan:	I want this picture to be a commentary on modern conditions, stark realism, the problems that confront the average man.
Lebrand:	But with a little sex in it.
Sullivan:	A little, but I don't want to stress it. I want this picture to be a document. I want to hold a mirror up to life. I want this to be a picture of dignity, a true canvas of the suffering of humanity.
Lebrand:	But with a little sex in it.
Sullivan:	With a little sex in it.
Hadrian:	What about a nice musical?[42]

And so the debate continues, with Sullivan arguing for something that will "realize the potentialities of film as the sociological and artistic medium that it is," and the executives arguing for the profitability of entertainment. Partly through the power that his position as a successful director allows him, partly through sheer stubbornness, Sullivan eventually gets his way, and, disguised as a tramp, he embarks on a trip to gather material for his picture at first hand. An unlikely chain of events leads him to confront contemporary social conditions rather more forcefully than he had anticipated, as a prisoner on a chain gang. A night at a picture show, the prisoners' only form of "escape" from their imprisonment, convinces Sullivan of the importance of entertainment cinema. He eventually returns to Hollywood with a renewed commitment to musicals and comedies.

Sullivan's Travels is itself a product of the multiple logics that shape Hollywood's commercial aesthetic, as well as a discourse upon them. It rationalizes a commitment to entertainment cinema as socially responsible. It acknowledges the world of the audience's response while framing that world within its own conventions. Like Sullivan, it enacts a compromise, and ends up operating somewhere between social commentary and slapstick comedy. It satirizes Hollywood and the studio system, but endorses its capacity to bring pleasure to even the most oppressed. It portrays the misery of the chain gang with at least as much authenticity as any other Hollywood movie, and then abandons its critique of American judicial institutions as soon as Sullivan regains his identity. It is neither slavishly "escapist" nor unremittingly dedicated to the social realism toward which it intermittently gestures. Its drive toward profitability has to be balanced against any social statement it wishes to make.

As a network of competing and conflicting impulses, *Sullivan's Travels* helps to break down our more monolithic conceptions of Hollywood. We see Hollywood as divided against itself, its various agents in competition and conflict with each other. As Lebrand, Hadrian, and Sullivan debate the most appropriate social role for cinema, contradictions are raised and explored, and aspirations set against each other. The resonances of these multiple logics inform our understanding of the subsequent story at every level. At the end of the plot the contradictions are tidied up, and Sullivan returns to making *Ants in Your Plants of 1941*. We are left with an image of Hollywood as a site of conflicting voices, held together in tension by the forces that cross it. In this complex network, a movie is most usefully understood as an object crossed and shaped by many (often contradictory) intentions and logics, each transforming it more or less visibly and more or less effectively. As opposed to auteurism, which supposes and expects a movie to be narratively, thematically, and formally coherent, a view of the production process that acknowledges its multiple logics and voices will recognize that Hollywood's commercial aesthetic is too opportunistic to prize coherence, organic unity, or even the absence of contradiction among its primary virtues.

This is not, of course, to argue that Hollywood prizes incoherence, disunity, or contradiction as virtues in themselves. Like most Hollywood movies, *Sullivan's Travels* tells a perfectly comprehensible (if absurd) story, in which characters' desires motivate their actions and causes have effects. It provides a good example of what Kristin Thompson sees as "the glory of the Hollywood system," its unobtrusive craftsmanship and "its ability to allow its finest scriptwriters, directors, and other creators to weave an intricate web of character, event, time and space that can seem transparently obvious."[43] None of the technical facility of its narrative construction, however, can resolve the contradictions embedded in the movie's exploitation of poverty and glamorization of suffering. *Sullivan's Travels* retreats from the implications of its satire, abandoning its caustic critique to celebrate "the motley mountebanks, the clowns, the buffoons . . . whose efforts have lightened our burden a little." Its retreat does not, however, eradicate the critique that preceded it. As critic Robert Stam argues, the movie appears to endorse the dichotomy of art and business in Hollywood, "between serious message pictures (what Veronica Lake disparagingly calls 'deep dish movies') on the one hand, and mindless entertainment on the other . . . between *O Brother, Where Art Thou?* and *Hay Hay in the Hay Loft!*" In its own enactment of this dichotomy, however, "*Sullivan's Travels* is itself both instructive *and* pleasurable, entertaining *and* provocative, serious *and* comic."[44]

Summary

- Entertainment is hard to define, and presents itself as almost wondrously benign. It is rarely taken seriously, because in itself it encourages us not to take it seriously, and because critics and cultural authority have by and large not taken it seriously. To take entertainment seriously appears perverse, because it turns amusement into work.
- Hollywood's most profound significance lies in its ability to turn pleasure into a product we can buy. The dream factory's dreams are sold to us as a form of public fantasy that allows for the public expression of ideas and actions we must all individually repress in our everyday behavior.
- Assumptions about the relative status of "High Art" and popular culture, and critical practices that traditionally exclude questions of money from aesthetic evaluation, have presented obstacles to taking Hollywood, and its commercial aesthetic, seriously. Rather than simply view Hollywood's movies as banal, repetitive, and predictable escapism, or reconstruct them in terms acceptable to traditional criticism, this book argues that it is more productive to analyze Hollywood's product as commodities, that is, precisely in commercial terms.
- Hollywood's version of entertainment provides an escape into a revised, Utopian version of the audience's own world. Hollywood movies provide Utopian solutions to everyday problems and desires. In the Utopian realm, issues and problems are clearer, emotions more intense, and problems solved at little cost. Movies package this experience of escape in stories in which a sympathetic character overcomes a series of obstacles to achieve his or her desire.
- Auteurist criticism has provided one of the most influential critical frameworks for discussing Hollywood movies, because it ascribes intention to a single originating author, usually the director. It is not, however, an accurate description

of Hollywood's production processes, and is an inadequate explanation of the creation or functioning of movies. The approach taken in this book acknowledges the multiple logics and competing voices participating in the production of a Hollywood movie, and argues that Hollywood's commercial aesthetic is too opportunistic to prize coherence, organic unity, or the absence of contradiction among its primary virtues.

Further Reading

Entertainment

The dearth of good writing on what entertainment is and how entertainment works is itself indicative of the lack of attention given to this issue within the critical practices of film studies and cultural studies. A key essay on the subject is Richard Dyer, "Entertainment and Utopia," *MOVIE* 24 (1977), pp. 2–13, anthologized in Richard Dyer, *Only Entertainment* (London: Routledge, 1992). This chapter has also used arguments from Martha Wolfenstein and Nathan Leites, *Movies: A Psychological Study* (Glencoe, IL: Free Press, 1950).

"The genius of the system"

Thomas Schatz, *The Genius of the System: Hollywood Filmmaking in the Studio Era* (New York: Pantheon, 1988), takes his central argument from André Bazin's argument about Hollywood's virtues, and provides an historical account of how the studio system operated.

· Theodor Adorno and Max Horkheimer's critique of the culture industry can be found in *Dialectic of Enlightenment* (London: Verso, 1979). Abbreviated versions can be found in *Mass Communication and Society*, eds James Curran, Michael Gurevich, and Janet Woolacott (London: Edward Arnold, 1977), and in *The Film Studies Reader*, eds Joanne Hollows, Peter Hutchings, and Mark Jancovich (London: Arnold, 2000), which also has a shortened version of Dwight MacDonald's essay, "A Theory of Mass Culture," originally published in

Mass Culture: The Popular Arts in America, eds Bernard Rosenberg and David Manning White (New York: Free Press, 1957). Walter Benjamin's essay, "The Work of Art in the Age of Mechanical Reproduction," is widely anthologized, and is in *Illuminations*, a collection of Benjamin's writings (London: Cape, 1970).

Auteurist criticism

The *auteur* theory is discussed at several points in this book, particularly in chapters 4 and 17. Andrew Sarris's foundational essay, "Notes on the Auteur Theory in 1962," was originally published in *Film Culture* 27 (Winter 1962–3), and is anthologized in *Film Theory and Criticism: Introductory Readings*, eds Gerald Mast, Marshall Cohen, and Leo Braudy (New York: Oxford University Press, 1992). There is an abbreviated version, along with formative essays by François Truffaut, Peter Wollen, and Robin Wood, in Hollows et al. Sarris's elaboration of his argument appeared as the introduction, "Toward a Theory of Film History," in *The American Cinema: Directors and Directions, 1929–1968* (New York: Dutton, 1968). James Naremore provides a useful brief overview of the history of auteurism, and a concise defense of its critical value, in "Authorship," in *A Companion to Film Theory*, eds Toby Miller and Robert Stam (Malden, MA: Blackwell, 1999), pp. 9–24. Timothy Corrigan provides a useful perspective on the commercialization of auteurism in "Auteurs and the New Hollywood," in *The New American Cinema* (Durham, NC: Duke University Press 1998), pp. 38–63.

CHAPTER THREE

Entertainment 2

The Play of Emotions

The paradox is that because the American cinema is so commercial, because the pressure of money is so strong, everything in a film has to be the very best. That means the most expensive, but it also means the most authentic, the most honest. No half measures, everything on the edge of excess ... The amount the Americans are prepared to spend on making their films is in a way a sign of respect for the audience.

Andrzej Wajda[1]

It seems to me that seduction can only take place when one is willing.

Nina Yuvshenko (Cyd Charisse) in *Silk Stockings* (1957)

In *The Courtship of Eddie's Father* (1962) Tom Corbett (Glenn Ford) and Elizabeth Marten (Shirley Jones) have an argument over the aesthetic sensibilities of "people who cry at sad movies." When Tom disparages this behavior, Elizabeth rounds on him, demanding "why do you think people go to cry at sad movies?" The question is one of some critical significance, since Elizabeth's proposition, that the tears may be triggered by the movie but are given substance by the viewer's life outside the cinema, has implications for what we include in our critical concerns. Hollywood relies for much of its aesthetic effect on its affective qualities, on the emotional engagement of its audience with the text – on the tears, laughter, fear, and erotic arousal it provokes in its viewers. In the experience of its audience, a movie is the emotional equivalent of a roller-coaster ride at least as much as it is a thematically significant story: borrowing a term, we might call the combination a "story-ride."[2]

Hollywood companies have always pre-tested their product by showing it to preview audiences before its final editing and release, in an attempt to ensure that the movie provides a maximum of audience pleasure and therefore a maximum profit. In the 1940s this pre-testing progressed in complexity from simply asking viewers to fill in cards at the end of the movie to employing devices, such as the Televoting Machine and the Reactograph, that required preview audiences to monitor their engagement with a movie during its screening by turning a dial graded from "very dull" to "like very much."[3] Synchronized to the projector, these devices literally produced a continuous graph of audience response. In adjusting the final release version of a movie to the results of these preview tests, what was being altered was what Thomas Elsaesser terms "the rhythm of the action" rather than the action of the movie itself.[4] The endings of *Blade Runner* (1982) and *Fatal Attraction* (1987), for instance, were modified on the strength of preview audience demands for an upbeat coda in one case and vengeance in the other. Such changes modified the story or thematic structure of the movies in response to what the producers perceived as the higher commercial priority of providing an "entertaining" emotional pattern.

What exactly are we buying when we go to the movies? What does Hollywood sell us as entertainment? In a 1989 screenwriting manual, Michael Hauge argues that audiences go to the movies not to see characters laugh, cry, or get frightened, but to have those experiences themselves; movies attract us because they provide "an opportunity to experience emotion."[5] Popular evaluative criticism – the reviews of Gene Siskel and Roger Ebert, for example – concur. Much in the manner of a screenwriting manual, they emphasize the presence or absence of emotionally engaging characters about whom it is possible to "care." Siskel's comment on *Unforgiven* (1992) – "great to look at but stuffed with unimportant characters and told at a much too slow pace" – does not so much summarize the movie as articulate the essence of a commercial aesthetic, one that concurs with Steven Bach's final opinion on *Heaven's Gate* (1980), cited in chapter 1. The generation of audience emotion substitutes for "Art" in Hollywood's commercial aesthetic. Story construction and "realism" in character consistency or setting are vehicles by which that goal is achieved, but they can also be sacrificed to a movie's larger purpose of entertaining its audience in the safe public space of the cinema.

Our reasons for going to the movies may be only tangentially related to the featured picture being shown. The Paramount chain advertised itself in 1929 by telling its customers, "You don't need to know what's playing at a Publix House. It's bound to be the best show in town."[6] Surveys taken in the 1920s indicated that 68 percent of the audience went to the movies for the "event," while only 10 percent went specifically to see the featured movie. The scheduling of "continuous performances" also worked to undermine the centrality of the main feature to the experience of moviegoing, since audiences tended to enter and leave the theater at times that suited their convenience rather than that of the movie's narrative, a practice that gave us the phrase, "this is where we came in." One spectator recalled her experience of moviegoing as a child in the 1940s: "You just went in and stayed until you recognized the spot where you came in. Consequently, I was about nine or ten before I discovered that movies were *supposed* to make sense. Until then, I thought everyone was as confused as I was."[7] Advertising campaigns for even such a prestige movie as *Gone with the Wind* (1939) found it necessary to remind exhibitors to stress start and intermission times, to ensure that audiences saw the movie from beginning to end. In 1960, *Psycho*'s advertisements insisted that "No one . . . BUT NO ONE . . . will be admitted to the theater after the start of each performance."[8] As part of the academization of cinema, film criticism has centered its concern on the individual feature movie as a text, and has largely ignored the conditions under which its audiences experienced it.

The picture palaces offered entry into a luxurious environment that in itself was an "escape" from the oppressions of metropolitan life. In the 1930s, the installation of air-conditioning in American movie theaters turned the summer months from the worst-attended season to the best-attended; for many Americans, the movie theater was the only cool place available on hot summer evenings. For a substantial part of the audience, a principal attraction of the cinema has always been the dark itself, the fact that it offers a public privacy to groups who have no other legitimate access to a comfortable, unchaperoned space. The movies' preoccupation with heterosexual romance may not be unconnected to the place of the cinema as a prime site for courtship rituals in western culture. A 1933 investigation into the relationship between movies and the conduct of adolescents reported anxiously that the majority of them admitted imitating the forms of lovemaking they saw on the screen. As one 15-year-old girl explained, "What movie does not offer pointers in the art of kissing? I do not think that it is surprising that the younger generation has such a fine technique. . . . A young couple sees the art of necking portrayed on the screen every week for a month or so, and is it any wonder that they soon develop talent?" A 21-year-old male college junior explained that in his experience, movies played upon their viewers' emotions, putting them "in a particularly sensitive and weakened mood in relation to that emotion which the movie most stressed . . . so a highly charged sex movie puts many girls in an emotional state that weakens, let us say, resistance. . . . I generally pick the movies we attend with that point in mind."[9] Three decades later, at least one group of 15-year-old girls "learned the fine art of seduction by watching Faye Dunaway smolder" in *Bonnie and Clyde* (1967): "We dressed like her, walked like her, smoldered just like her."[10] For some audiences, at least, watching the screen to construct hypotheses about characters, narrative, and theme has not always been the primary purpose in attending the cinema.

To begin our consideration of the way movies entertain and the things they entertain us with, we can define entertainment as a commercial commodity, produced and consumed as part of a capitalist industrial system. In return for the price of admission to an entertainment, we expect to witness some kind of performance produced by people who make their living performing for paying audiences. We might be watching professional football, a highwire act in the circus, or operatic recitals instead of going to the movies. These activities are linked by the conditions of their consumption. In each, paying customers form themselves as an audience, to be served by specialist entertainers who are paid to perform. Hollywood's commercial aesthetic addresses us as consumers as well as spectators, and we commonly describe our encounter with cinema in monetary terms. A "good" movie is one that gives us our "money's worth," a return in pleasure for the money we have invested in the ticket price. Hollywood manufactures a non-durable consumer commodity which is the experience of "going to the movies," rather than the more discrete experience of any particular movie. We experience cinema entertainment as an alternative leisure-time experience to eating at a restaurant or spending an evening with friends in a bar or pub. Like food or drink, but unlike a book or record, the entertainment of "going to the movies" is a transient experience; when we finish consuming a movie, we have only a ticket stub to show for our transaction. What we really buy at the cinema is time; our tickets grant us access to the viewing space for a fixed duration, while we rent the apparatus of cinema.

The buying and selling of time is the central activity of the leisure industries in a capitalist economy. Leisure time is most fully understood as time that is not obligated, by either work or other social responsibilities.[11] Entertainment is one of the commodified forms that leisure can take. The notion that leisure is a prerogative of everyone, and not just the wealthy few, belongs to industrial societies. The factory system organized and disciplined the hours of work to a much greater extent than had happened in pre-industrial cultures, establishing a more rigid distinction between time spent working and time spent doing something else. From the second half of the nineteenth century onward, people living in industrial societies began to experience time-not-working – leisure time – as an empty period that needed to be occupied.

Leisure time is bought by time spent at work, where we normally act under instruction or from some sense of compulsion. In our leisure time, within economic and legal constraints, we can choose and control our activity. The metaphors used to discuss leisure time link it specifically to commercial processes; we talk of "spending time" or of "time-consuming" activities. We expect to occupy much of our leisure time as consumers of commercial commodities: sports equipment or children's toys, for example. Nevertheless, something of a nineteenth-century producer ethic remains in the sense of moral superiority that still attaches to participatory leisure activities like playing a sport or practicing a craft, as opposed to "vicarious" experiences that involve us as paying customers at professional performances. It is often suggested that the best use of leisure time is in a form of production, when we "amuse ourselves" by "making our own entertainment." This hierarchical distinction between participatory activity and "vicarious" passivity is one source of the idea that entertainment involves no work on the part of its consumer, no expenditure of energy, but only of money. Unlike folk culture, which is something you make, entertainment is something you buy.

Hollywood seduces us. The movie theater is a place where we are encouraged to accept the fantasies we see in front of us as a substitute for other realities. By its framing devices, from the entrance lobby to the dimming of the lights just before the movie starts, the building is designed to cut us off from the world outside, and propel us into the alternative world on the screen – perhaps no longer as effectively as the picture palaces of the 1920s and 1930s, but the mechanisms

Fred Astaire seduces Cyd Charisse and the audience for capitalism in *Silk Stockings* (1957).
Produced by Arthur Freed; distributed by MGM.

Gene Kelly and Donald O'Connor improvise the "Moses Supposes" routine in *Singin' in the Rain* (1952).
Produced by Arthur Freed; distributed by MGM.

and the intent are the same. From the moment the lights go down and we are transported into the other world on the screen, the movie seeks our cooperative involvement in its fantasy. Midway through *Silk Stockings* (1957), Fred Astaire, playing movie producer Steve Canfield, and Cyd Charisse, as Soviet commissar Ninotchka, perform a dance routine that could stand as a metaphor for Hollywood's relation to its audience. The scene is the culmination of Canfield's sexual and political seduction of Ninotchka, both for himself and for capitalism. As the routine develops, she is slowly and at first reluctantly pulled into Astaire's dance, until eventually they dance together. By the end of the dance, she is in love.

The process of seduction that comes with the purchase of the commodity is more visible in the musical than elsewhere in Hollywood, because musical numbers represent a world of fantasy more explicitly. The change into the world of fantasy is signaled by changes in the way characters move and behave. For them, musical numbers represent an escape from the more pressurized world of the movie narrative, just as the cinema offers its audience the same opportunity for escape from the everyday. Hollywood movies present themselves to us as effortless, both in their production and in our consumption of them. When we watch Gene Kelly and Donald O'Connor improvise the "Moses Supposes" dance routine in *Singin' in the Rain* (1952) with whatever props happen to be available, we are unlikely to think about the amount of rehearsal time required to make their performance look so spontaneous. The active participation of the audience, its involvement in its own seduction, is a primary goal of Hollywood cinema; for without this participation the audience may well not return to the movie theater. In economic terms, the consumer is both the source and object of Hollywood cinema, because unless we continue to engage Hollywood's products and take pleasure from them, production will cease.

Given the place that entertainment occupies in our culture, to study Hollywood is to perform an unnatural act, perversely to turn amusement into work. Inevitably, it involves interpreting movies "against the grain" of their declared absence of seriousness. Some critics have sought to demonstrate that movies which seem on the surface to be lighthearted, sentimental, and frivolous are covertly complex, serious, and responsible works of major artistic importance. Others have argued that the most characteristic of Hollywood movies – *The Beautiful Blonde from Bashful Bend* (1948), for example, whose very title encapsulates its industrial ambition to entertain – are symptoms of American culture and essentially interesting, as Canfield puts it to Ninotchka in *Silk Stockings*, as "a sociological study" in textual form. While not denying either possibility, this book argues that money's determining influence on production values requires us to move away from established models of artistic production and how texts produce meaning when studying Hollywood. We must try to account for Hollywood in the terms in which the movies themselves operate, and avoid critical reconstructions of Hollywood movies that overlook their commercial status. In the remainder of this chapter, I want to point to some of the defining characteristics of Hollywood entertainment as a commodity.

Regulated Difference

Griffin (Tim Robbins):	[The story] lacked certain elements that we need to market a film successfully.
June (Greta Scacchi):	What elements?
Griffin:	Suspense, laughter, violence, hope, heart, nudity, sex, happy endings. Mainly happy endings.

The Player (1992)

Hollywood movies are frequently accused of being formulaic. A marginally less hostile way of making the same point is to say that they are conventional. A movie is designed for consumption in a single act of viewing. One reason you only need to see a movie once is that movies are so like each other, and that is part of the pleasure they offer their audiences (although novelist Gore Vidal observed, recalling his experience of viewing *The Mummy* in 1932, that "since we knew that we would have only the one encounter, we learned how to concentrate totally").[12] A movie that conforms to convention activates its viewers' prior knowledge of those conventions, and reinforces that knowledge as a result of their ability to predict the movie's development or outcome. Describing the Western in terms that might apply much more generally to Hollywood's product, Robert Warshow suggested that it "is an art form for connoisseurs, where the spectator derives his pleasure from the appreciation of minor variations within the working out of a pre-established order."[13] Echoing the economic system by which the movies were manufactured, Hollywood's commercial aesthetic extends the principles of standardization, interchangeability, minor variation, and market placement that underlie the consumer industries of fashion and cosmetics into the cultural form of entertainment fiction. Steve Neale has described this system of product differentiation as "an aesthetic regime based on regulated difference, contained variety, pre-sold expectations, and the re-use of resources in labour and materials."[14] Repetition and variation are central to Hollywood's commercially motivated aim of providing the maximum pleasure for the maximum number, to ensure a maximum profit.

To talk of interchangeability and standardization is to use the terminology of industrial manufacture, not as a metaphor, but as a description of a production process. In place of the ideas of uniqueness and organic forms that are commonly applied to more traditional aesthetic objects, a Hollywood movie can be thought of as a manufactured assembly of component parts. These parts may function harmoniously, like a well-designed machine, but they are also visible as separate elements: we may dislike the story but love the costumes, think the co-star is terrible but really enjoy the bit where her grandfather tells the story about the frog – and, of course, we would watch it again anyway just for Keanu Reeves, or Gwyneth Paltrow, or even Gary Cooper. A Hollywood movie is an aggregation of familiar parts, and its individuality results from its particular combination of standardized elements. As a mode of production, aggregation relies on the interchangeability of these elements, and the connoisseur's pleasures in an aesthetic of aggregation involve a strong sense of **intertextuality**: of a movie's inheritance from, and resemblance to, other similarly styled aesthetic objects.

Historically, Hollywood's commercial aesthetic has been a regime of regulated difference in several senses. Economically, the flow of product through the production and distribution system was regulated in ways examined in chapters 5, 6, and 7. Production was also socially and morally regulated. The movies were a form of public culture, and until 1952 they were explicitly denied the freedom of expression guaranteed the press under the First Amendment. In 1915 the Supreme Court had ruled that motion pictures were "mere representations," ideas and sentiments, already published and known. The court regarded the motion picture industry not as "part of the press of the country, or as organs of public opinion," but as "a business, pure and simple."[15] This judgment established the legality of state movie censorship, and its consequences obliged the industry to make sure that their product was acceptable not only to their customers but also to the guardians of American public culture. As the president of the industry's trade association, Will Hays, told producers in 1932, "Whether we like it or not, we must face the fact that we are *not* in that class of industries whose only problem is with the customer. Our public problem is greater with those out of than those in the theater." It was not the people who frequented saloons, he reminded them, who had enforced prohibition upon the country.

To counter the threat of regulation imposed from outside by censorship, the industry devised mechanisms of self-regulation to ensure that the content of its movies proved acceptable to "the classes that write, talk, and legislate" as well as to their audiences.[16] The most important of these mechanisms was the Production Code of 1930, which had a determining effect on movie content throughout the Classical period of studio production. Much more importantly than its fabled trivial requirement that one of the four participating feet remain on the floor during a love scene (to avoid what was delicately known as the "horizontal embrace"), the Production Code contributed significantly to Hollywood's avoidance of contentious subject matter, and was a controlling force on the movies' construction of narrative and character. The agreements that underlay the Code amounted to a consensus about what constituted appropriate entertainment for an undifferentiated mass audience in America and, by default, the rest of the world.

Quite overtly at issue in the industry's internal discussions about self-regulation was a definition of the social function of entertainment, and when the industry implemented the Production Code, it acquiesced in the suggestion that entertainment had a moral obligation to its consumers, to provide them with what the Code called "correct entertainment . . . which tends to improve the race (or at least to re-create and rebuild human beings exhausted with the realities of life)." Movies were thus endowed with an affirmative cultural function that was dramatically at odds with a view of art as a vehicle of social criticism or negation. This affirmation was most clearly articulated in one of the Code's governing principles, that "No picture shall be produced which will lower the moral standards of those who see it." Through the strict moral accountancy which this law imposed on Hollywood's plots, the guilty were punished and the sympathetic were found to be innocent.

Self-regulation had other effects, however. As Will Hays was fond of saying, show business was everybody's business. In a speech his association often quoted, Hays told a group of clubwomen, "the fact is, motion pictures are yours rather than ours. It is for you indeed to say what they shall be like and how far forward they may go toward their limitless possibilities."[17] Hollywood has constantly asserted that the movies belong to their public rather than their producers. As Irving Thalberg, head of production at MGM, put it in 1930, "we do not create the types of entertainment; we merely present them":

> The motion picture does not present the audience with tastes and manners and views and morals; it reflects those they already have. . . . People see in it a reflection of their own average thoughts and attitudes. If the reflection is much lower or much higher than their own plane they reject it. . . . The motion picture is literally bound to the mental and moral level of its vast audience.[18]

The producers consciously sought to deny authorial responsibility for whatever moral or political intent was imputed to their product. In part their attitude arose from the movies' legal status as unprotected speech, but it also had to do with the perception of movies as commodities. The Production Code became the industry's guarantee that it manufactured "pure" entertainment, amusement that was not harmful to its consumers, in much the same way as the purity of meat or patent medicines was guaranteed by the US Food and Drug Administration. What constituted purity in entertainment was never defined solely by the producers themselves, however. Throughout Hollywood's history, the press, religious, educational, and civic groups, and state and national legislatures have expressed their opinions and exercised their authority over what is harmful in entertainment.

The producers' attitude also denied responsibility for the meaning of any movie. They saw themselves manufacturing a product that was used by its consumers. Responsibility for its use resided with the purchaser rather than the seller. In

Box 3.1   The Motion Picture Production Code of 1930

The Production Code was a set of guidelines for producers that stipulated what was and was not permissible in Classical Hollywood's field of representation, particularly with regard to sexual and criminal subject matter. Its main purpose was to enable movies with controversial subject matter to be brought to the screen in a form that would not encounter censorship problems at home or abroad. It also served the important function of protecting the industry from attacks by powerful sections of the community, such as church groups, social workers, and politicians.

The Code was written in early 1930 by a group of Hollywood executives and officials from their trade association, the Motion Picture Producers and Distributors of America (MPPDA). Trade paper editor Martin Quigley and Jesuit priest Daniel Lord provided some input, but the basis of its text was the MPPDA's extensive knowledge of previous censorship action that had curtailed the circulation of controversial films. The text of the Code was amended on a number of occasions, most significantly in 1934 when, mainly as a public relations exercise, a document written by Lord was added as "the Reasons Supporting the Code."

Contrary to the version of events promulgated by the MPPDA and still widely reproduced, the Code was enforced from its adoption in 1930. Producers and Code administrators spent the early 1930s negotiating its stipulations into a system of representational conventions. Now usually remembered for the intricate silliness of some of its requirements (which usually arose from the extensive and arbitrary codes of state and foreign censorship, rather than from perversity on the part of the Production Code Administration), the Code was often blamed for Hollywood's timidity and triviality. While it contributed to Hollywood's avoidance of contentious subject matter, it did so as the instrument of an industry policy about the appropriate content of commercial entertainment cinema. The Code remained a determining influence on the content of Hollywood movies for the next three decades, and constituted a particularly powerful demonstration of Classical Hollywood's determination to balance the "artistic" ambitions of producers with the commercial imperatives of wide-scale distribution. The Code was subject to increasing challenge after 1952, was completely rewritten in 1966, and was replaced with a ratings system in 1968.

If the Production Code itself was a statement of a set of principles, the implementation of those principles was a complex practical matter, involving extensive negotiation over procedure and detail. Many studio personnel viewed the Code as an instrument of restraint, prohibiting some representations and requiring that plots be morally unambiguous in their development, dialog, and conclusion. Over matters of incident and detail, however, the Code forced producers to develop techniques of ambiguity in their representations, particularly in representing sexual subject matter. As Lea Jacobs has argued, under the Code "offensive ideas could survive at the price of an instability of meaning . . . there was constant negotiation about how explicit films could be and by what means (through the image, sound, language) offensive ideas could find representation."[19] The Code's regulation of movie content can, therefore, best be understood as a generic pressure, comparable to the pressure of convention in a romantic comedy or a Western. "Sophisticated" viewers, familiar with the conventions of representation operating under the Code, learned to imagine the acts of misconduct that the Code had made unmentionable.

The text of the 1930 Production Code is reproduced in appendix 1.

keeping with the ideological assumptions surrounding the circulation of money in the cultures that have produced and consumed Hollywood movies, viewers may reasonably demand to do what they like with the movie they have paid to watch. Literary texts and paintings assert authorship as a principle of creativity. Hollywood's commercial aesthetic, on the other hand, not only advertises its products as being created by a multiplicity of personnel, but also concedes to the individual viewer the authority to decide what a movie's content means. Viewers are provided with a host of opportunities to exercise that authority to maximize their pleasure from the movie. Within limits, Hollywood movies are constructed to accommodate, rather than predetermine, their audiences' reactions, and this has involved devising systems and codes of representation that permit a range of interpretations and a degree of instability of meaning.

What cinema historian Ruth Vasey has called the producers' "principle of deniability" resulted in a particular kind of ambiguity and textual uncertainty in movies regulated by the Production Code.[20] As Colonel Jason S. Joy, the Code's first administrator, explained, to entertain its undifferentiated audience, the movies needed a system of representational conventions "from which conclusions might be drawn by the sophisticated mind, but which would mean nothing to the unsophisticated and inexperienced."[21] Once the limits of explicit "sophistication" had been established, the production industry had to find ways of appealing to both "innocent" and "sophisticated" sensibilities in the same object without transgressing the boundaries of public acceptability. This involved devising systems and codes of representation in which "innocence" was inscribed into the text while "sophisticated" viewers were able to "read into" movies whatever meanings they pleased to find, so long as producers could use the Production Code to deny that they had put them there. This requirement was perhaps most obvious in dealing with representations of sexuality, but it applied equally to Hollywood's representation of other subjects – particularly the treatment of crime, which was often merely suggested rather than detailed on the screen.

Martha Wolfenstein and Nathan Leites explored some of the consequences that this had for Hollywood's conventions of representation. Moving beyond the dismissive recognition that people in Hollywood movies only really behaved like people in Hollywood movies, they were interested in the implications of that behavior. Hollywood movies, they suggested, above all involve a play with appearances; they are, repeatedly, dramas of false appearances, in which we see the hero and heroine enacting forbidden desire, but in the end escaping any penalty for it

Rita Hayworth as the "good-bad girl" in *Gilda* (1946). In 1950 Martha Wolfenstein and Nathan Leites observed that "American ways of fusing goodness and badness in women start with a good woman and spice her up. . . . An alternative procedure is to take a girl who appears too good and make her more sexy." Their descriptions might equally apply to other American representations of female sexuality, such as *Playboy*.
Produced by Virginia Van Upp; distributed by Columbia Pictures.

because the enactment is revealed as only a false appearance. In particular, they drew attention to a character they called "the good-bad girl," who attracts the hero by an appearance of wickedness, but whom, in the end, he discovers "he can take home and introduce to Mother." Lauren Bacall as Vivian Sternwood in *The Big Sleep* (1946) or Julia Roberts as Vivian Ward in *Pretty Woman* (1990) are instances of the type, which Wolfenstein and Leites identified as specifically American. The double aspect of the character of her partner, the good-bad man, is more concerned with violence than sex, since he is likely to be suspected of crimes he did not commit:

> The theme of looking guilty but being innocent recurs persistently in various forms throughout American films. . . . A young couple may spend a night innocently alone together or pose as husband and wife, but only to get a tourist cabin or serve some equally non-sexual exigency. . . . In such scenes the audience knows that the couple are innocent, but onlookers in the film regard them as guilty. The appearances tell a falsely accusing story. There is much less than meets the eye; and it is not always easy to prove it. . . . The older drama of conscience, where the conflict is internal and the

individual suffered from feelings of guilt, has been transformed into a conflict between the individual and the world around him. Self-accusations have become accusations of others, directed against the self from outside. . . . The movie hero, warding off false accusations, suffers almost as much as if he were guilty; his feeling of relief in the end, and the freedom he wins, are in part paid for by this suffering.[22]

A number of functions are achieved by this structure of projection and denial. The forbidden desires that the viewer projects onto the characters are enacted through the false appearance of their guilt, but the unfolding of the plot demonstrates that the hero and heroine never imagined those forbidden desires. The movie's happy ending tells us that social sanctions to enforce good behavior are superfluous, since people are inherently good, and would behave impeccably if left to themselves:

> What the plot unfolds is a process of proof. Something is undone rather than done: the false appearance is negated. The hero and heroine do not become committed to any irretrievable act whose consequences they must bear. Nor do they usually undergo any character transformation, ennoblement or degradation, gain or loss of hope, acceptance of a new role of the diminution and regrets of age. They succeed in proving what they were all along. They emerge from the shadow of the false appearance.[23]

Finally, Wolfenstein and Leites's analysis points to another recurrent feature of Hollywood movies: their self-reflectivity. "The drama of false appearance" not only describes Hollywood's most recurrent plots; it also summarizes the accusation, by Hollywood's strongest critics, that movies lie to us about real life. We know that Hollywood is Tinseltown, constructed by gossip columnists, studio publicists, and special effects technicians whose profession is the manufacture of deceptive illusion – because Hollywood tells us so. It is one expression of the "art versus business" dichotomy, and its contradictions and intricacies manifest themselves most clearly in Hollywood movies about Hollywood. Hollywood's entertainment is self-explanatory, self-contained (in the safe space of the movie theater), self-justifying ("it's only entertainment"), and self-regulated. It is, then, hardly surprising that Hollywood represents itself so often in its movies.

Silk Stockings is a musical remake of an earlier comedy, *Ninotchka* (1939). It plays with questions of art and entertainment, value and pleasure. Among its subjects are the production of Hollywood cinema, the need for entertainment, and the values that entertainment endorses. On the surface the movie's values could hardly be more straightforward: it seems to present a Cold War celebration of the "American way." The evolution of the lovers' relationship allows for the presentation of a series of crude oppositions between "east" and "west." The east is cold, austere, its people subject to material deprivation and the dictates of autocratic government; the west is warm, beautiful, and the people live happy and free in material abundance. The east aspires to the values of High Art while the west is committed to the values of entertainment. Even this interpretation, however, suggests that entertainment has a political function, meeting the deep-rooted "universal" and "human" needs that can find expression in its forms. Ninotchka's "liberation" insists that these needs can be suppressed but never ultimately destroyed by the repressions of a social system antithetical to them. Hollywood can help us to liberate ourselves too; as in *Sullivan's Travels* (see chapter 2), entertainment is sanctioned as both pleasurable and humanizing.

Hollywood's multiple logics, however, ensure that the movie will equivocate in its statement of values; the movie's self-reflectivity means that *Silk Stockings* cannot take itself too seriously, so it qualifies its overtly political, even propagandist effect. The movie's representation of Hollywood is persistently ironic: movie producer Canfield wants to turn Tolstoy's *War and Peace* into a musical called *Not Tonight Josephine*. The adaptation is presented as a debasement. As well as a basis for liberation, entertainment is presented as hallucination and narcotic. However lightheartedly and affirmatively, the movie remains troubled with the Hollywood it has imagined. Although it celebrates entertainment for its own sake, it is clear that if we wish to interpret it in other terms, the movie will also cooperate with that interpretation. Hollywood movies most commonly tell their audiences two distinct but intertwined stories, both of which are structured around oppositions, and the movie works to reconcile both sets of oppositions by its conclusion. If Hollywood's movies lie to us, they do so most often by suggesting that contradictions can be resolved. We are, however, under no obligation to accept the movie's frequently facile resolution. We may instead choose to explore the movie's representation of cultural contradiction. If we do so, we are likely to discover that Hollywood's most interesting products are those in which "the story is simple but the subtexts are disturbingly complex."[24] Hollywood's commercial status as entertainment does not prohibit our critical activity, but it does challenge us to explain the relationship between a movie's existence as a commodity and also as a text invested with meaning.

Singin' in the Rain: How to Take Gene Kelly Seriously

Hollywood is more likely to be playfully complex than disturbing. Its representation of its own complexity, like its representation of sexuality, is often only there if the "sophisticated" viewer chooses to see it, and the complexity it represents is introverted. Much of Hollywood's product is about itself; the world represented in Hollywood movies is an enclosed world, no matter how exotic its back-lots may pretend to be. Perhaps the extent of Hollywood's self-reflexivity has been overlooked by critics because it is one of the ways in which Hollywood advertises its lack of seriousness: it seems at times to be *only* about itself. As we saw in chapter 1, *Singin' in the Rain* presents the history of entertainment as an entertainment. Thematically *Singin' in the Rain* is banal, but its self-reflective playfulness also makes it a complex aesthetic object.

The story could not be more familiar. Escaping from fans after a Hollywood premiere, movie star Don Lockwood (Gene Kelly) meets actress Kathy Selden (Debbie Reynolds), who tells him that movies are only cheap entertainment, nothing to do with real art. It turns out, however, that she is performing in the chorus of the party Don is going to. Don pursues her, rousing the fury of his co-star Lina Lamont (Jean Hagen). Despite everything Don does to dissuade her, Lina believes the fan magazine stories about her offscreen romance with Don. Don's romance with Kathy begins to blossom, but the studio they work for, Monumental Pictures, is plunged into crisis by the coming of sound. Studio head R. F. Simpson (Millard Mitchell) decides to remake Don and Lina's current movie, *The Dueling Cavalier*, as a musical. The only snag is Lina's thick Brooklyn accent, but after Don's best friend Cosmo Brown (Donald O'Connor) invents dubbing, the solution is found: Kathy will speak and sing for Lina. The plan works, the movie triumphs, and Don, Cosmo, and Simpson foil Lina's scheme to force Kathy to go on singing and talking for her. Don and Kathy become the onscreen and offscreen lovers the fan magazine readers thought Don and Lina were, and we leave them embracing in front of a poster for their next movie, *Singin' in the Rain*.

The movie provides its audience with two plotlines: the development of Don and Kathy's romance, and the successful innovation of the musical form itself. Both move toward the reconciliation of their initial oppositions, and the two develop in tandem. Kathy's spontaneity provides the impetus for Don and Cosmo to innovate the technological solution of dubbing, and the movie's ending celebrates the perfect union of image and sound, body and voice, in the formation of Don and Kathy's perfect couple. While the plotlines intersect and support each other, the movie is really constructed around its 13 songs, which are used to express the characters' emotional states, explain the plot, or interrupt it. At the same time as they draw attention to the players' performances, the numbers emphasize the effortlessness of performance, effacing the labor of choreography and rehearsal involved in making Kelly's dancing seem as natural as walking.

In addition to the musical numbers, there is a 15-minute "Broadway Ballet" sequence, completely detached from the plotline, showing the rise of a young dancer (Kelly) from burlesque to stardom. In the casino sequence of the "Broadway Ballet," Cyd Charisse appears in a white dress that echoes the final wedding dress costume in the earlier "Beautiful Girl" fashion number. From the casino the ballet dissolves into a fantasy sequence that makes obvious visual references to the paintings of Salvador Dali. It also repeats the motifs of wind and sky from Don's "You Were Meant for Me" number, in which he revealed the devices of the sound stage while constructing a romantic fictional space in which he could declare his love for Kathy.

Through a number of different devices, the costuming and decor of this scene set up references to other levels of *Singin' in the Rain*'s fiction. Charisse's white dress evokes the fantasy of a wedding that doesn't come true, but that fantasy is replaced by the fantasy of dance, which, like the dress, is repeated (restated, reborn, renewed) by the Kelly lookalike who revives Kelly's own spirits with the "Gotta Dance" call after Charisse has abandoned him in the ballet. All this, it should be added, goes on in a dream sequence that is a visualization of an offscreen verbal description of a scene to be shot in a movie to be put into a movie that is the subject of the movie we are watching. These Chinese boxes of cross-reference and self-consciousness are discarded as a joke: when we leave the "Broadway Melody" number to return to Simpson's office, he announces, "I can't quite visualize it.

Gene Kelly and Cyd Charisse in the fantasy sequence of *Singin' in the Rain*.
Produced by Arthur Freed; distributed by MGM.

Don Lockwood and Kathy Selden advertise the movie Gene Kelly and Debbie Reynolds are starring in.
Singin' in the Rain; produced by Arthur Freed; distributed by MGM.

I'll have to see it on film first," and Cosmo replies, "On film it'll be better yet." The same sense of a discarded or throwaway complexity is evident in the final image of the movie, where the screen dissolves from Don and Kathy's final duet to their images on a poster advertising their next Monumental Studios production: *Singin' in the Rain*, the movie we have just been watching, starring not Gene Kelly and Debbie Reynolds but Don Lockwood and Kathy Selden, the characters they play in the movie we have been watching.

The movie's own dismissal of any substance behind its complex levels of self-reflectivity makes it easy to both overlook and disregard the textual complexity of something so frivolous as *Singin' in the Rain*. As a backstage musical, it takes pleasure in exposing the technical operations of filmmaking and the manufacture of performance. The production processes of musicals rely on the separation of sound from image in order to engineer the illusion of their unity. The music in a number is pre-recorded and played back on the set during shooting, so that the physical performance is synchronized to the soundtrack. Later, sound effects, including the taps in tap-dancing, are dubbed in. The perfect integration of sound and image, and the spontaneity of their performance, is an illusion engineered by the technology of cinema.

In one sequence in *Singin' in the Rain*, we see the mechanics of pre-recording a musical number. But at the same time as it demystifies the process of production, it also remystifies it. Kathy sings "You Are My Lucky Star" with an orchestra, while Don gazes adoringly on. The movie dissolves to Lina practicing lip-synchronization, then to the set where the number is being filmed. The device by which Lina is given Kathy's voice is revealed to us. But then we see a shot that begins as the studio camera's viewpoint on Lina and Don in costume. It tracks in to a closer shot of Lina, and changes from color to black-and-white. Then it pulls back along the same axis and keeps going, to reveal that we are now in a projection room, watching rushes with Don, Cosmo, and Simpson. This change of location, and the move in and out of levels of the fiction signified by the color/black-and-white switch, is done without a cut, making its processes completely mysterious – for those members of the audience who notice it. For the majority of the audience, however, this process of demystification and remystification remains, ironically, invisible. Seduced by the perfect marriage of sound and image, most viewers simply fail to notice the absence of a cut, and remain unaware of the technical complexity of what they have been presented with. Much like the "Broadway Melody" scene-within-a-scene, the movie does not require its viewers to recognize the complexity of what they view in order to take pleasure from it, and even more clearly it does not require them to articulate that complexity or to work at comprehending it.

Throughout the movie, musical numbers are used as a means of entering and leaving a relatively flimsy and predictable plot that is itself concerned with the implausibility of the storylines on which Hollywood movies regularly rely. Our familiarity with the story ensures that neither the movie nor its audience needs to devote much attention or conviction to its development. *Singin' in the Rain* constantly discusses artifice, both overtly and in its own operation of artifice. We see performance conventions being undermined when Don and Lina insult each other while playing a love scene in the silent version. There is a dense pattern of references to the rest of "the world of entertainment": Donald O'Connor's invocation of the clown Pagliacci combined with an imitation of Chico Marx, or the references in Kelly's performance to silent movie star John Gilbert, for instance. At the same time, the movie frequently dissolves between one level of fiction and another. In the opening scene, we are presented with two versions of Don's career, his own "highbrow" account of his commitment to artistry and "dignity, always dignity," contrasted with an image and music stream that describes a progression from pool hall to smalltime vaudeville.

The movie's blatant willingness to crack open the shell of a coherent fictional world is at the center of its self-reflectivity. There is no attempt in *Singin' in the Rain* to propose that the movie's constant shifting between fictional levels demands perceptual skills beyond those of the ordinary spectator, because such a proposition would deter audiences. The movie explicitly underlines the arbitrariness and redundancy of its plotting. Cosmo invents the plot of *The Dancing Cavalier*, the backstage musical version of *The Dueling Cavalier*, in a single speech, delivered very fast:

> The hero is a modern young hoofer in a Broadway show. Right? . . . Well, one night backstage, he's reading *The Tale of Two Cities* between numbers, see? A sandbag falls on his head, and he dreams he's back in the French Revolution! This way we get in modern dancing numbers – Charleston-Charleston – but in the dream part we can use all the costume stuff – right?

Simultaneously, Cosmo reprises the plot of *Dubarry was a Lady*, a Cole Porter musical filmed in 1943, and summarizes the way the storyline of *Singin' in the*

Rain was itself devised to fit the predetermined ingredients of its songs, Kelly, and even O'Connor himself.

Singin' in the Rain makes no more attempt to justify its own plot by integrating the musical numbers into a justifiable chain of events than *The Dancing Cavalier*. The "Moses Supposes" number, for instance, is performed without any evident plot motive, and also for no evident plot audience. At the same time as it naturalizes the exuberance of the characters' use of screen space and the apparent spontaneity with which they dance with whatever props and pieces of furniture they find to hand, much of it is staged as if directed out across a proscenium arch at the movie audience. And the audience readily accommodates the multiple identities embodied in such performances. In the plot we watch Don Lockwood, but in the musical numbers we see Gene Kelly dance. These functions are unevenly distributed throughout the movie: Jean Hagen, for instance, is always in character as Lina, while Donald O'Connor seldom has any need to be Cosmo and spends most of his time in one or other performance piece. The nonsense lyrics of "Moses" verbalize a comparable contradiction:

> Moses supposes his toeses are roses,
> But Moses supposes erroneously.
> For Moses he knowses his toeses aren't roses
> As Moses supposes his toeses to be.
> Hoopty-doopty-doodle!

Hoopty-doopty-doodle, indeed! The condition of erroneous supposition in the face of knowledge is as good a description of the audience's dual position, between star and character, performance and plot, convention and novelty, as the more usually invoked idea of a "suspension of disbelief." More important than the terms of this description, however, is the ease with which characters and audience move from one fictional level to another throughout the movie.

In the movie's final scene, the romance is brought alive to the audience in the preview theater by Don's asking them to stop Kathy from running away, and then singing a love duet with her. *The Dancing Cavalier* leaves the screen of the preview theater and is acted out in the space between the audience and the screen, in a literalized version of 3D. *Singin' in the Rain* enacts the conventions that it parodies. It presents a love story between the two stars of a movie we don't see (the one in the hoarding at the end), who are also (as Kelly and Reynolds) contemporary stars. Thus their story presents a true version of the false love story the fan magazines have told about Don and Lina. Although involved in an examination of its own mechanisms of self-reflectivity, *Singin' in the Rain* is also committed to an unchallenged and conventional notion of entertainment. What appears on one level to be banal and conventional – the love story between two stars – is, on another, intricately complex. Different levels of plausibility are established for different levels of immersion within the fiction, as the movie tells the same story, of the rise from obscurity to stardom, on three different occasions, in three separate modes.

Although *Singin' in the Rain* contains much spontaneity and celebratory behavior, invoking the condition of entertainment as Utopia, it also comprises a process of repeated deferral or slippage between levels of the fiction. Even the happy ending defers, opening up the possibility of another movie becoming or substituting for the movie we have ourselves just been watching. If we have gone this far down a critical path that interprets *Singin' in the Rain* against its entertainment function by taking its playfulness seriously, we will now be aware of the rehearsal and labor that have gone into making the prop dances appear so effortlessly spontaneous. At the same time, we can be convinced by the serendipitous nature of the movie's prop dances, and recognize the engineering skills that have gone into the production of such apparent serendipity. And even if we do not suppose character spontaneity in the face of our knowledge of the movie's engineering, *Singin' in the Rain* reminds us not only that it takes "five hundred thousand kilowatts of stardust" to make *either* Debbie Reynolds *or* Kathy Selden *that* beautiful, but also that she sure does look beautiful in the moonlight. The world of entertainment celebrates its ordinariness at the same time as it celebrates its illusion, and while it brings these elements together in its conclusion – the romantic couple are united at the moment of the show's success – it makes little attempt to sustain that moment beyond simply providing a point of rest that allows the audience to leave the cinema. As Jane Feuer puts it, "The Hollywood version of Utopia is entirely solipsistic. In its endless reflexivity the musical can only offer itself, only entertainment as its picture of Utopia."[25]

Summary

- Audiences go to the movies to experience emotion themselves, and the generation of audience emotion substitutes for "Art" in Hollywood's commercial aesthetic. Narrative and realism may be a part of producing this audience emotion, but can easily be sacrificed to the larger goal of profitable entertainment.

- Hollywood manufactures a non-durable consumer commodity, which is the experience of "going to the movies" rather than the more discrete experience of any particular movie. What we really buy at the cinema is time, access to the viewing space while we rent the apparatus of cinema. The buying and selling of time is a central activity of the leisure industries in a capitalist economy.

- A movie is designed for consumption in a single act of viewing. At the same time, its play with conventions makes it an art form for connoisseurs who take pleasure in the repetition and variation of familiar forms and structures.

- A Hollywood movie can be thought of as a manufactured assembly of component parts, rendered individual by its particular combination of standardized elements.

- In acquiescing in the self-regulation of the Production Code, Hollywood's producers acknowledged the movies' moral obligation to its audiences and to the forces of social order. The obligation to supply "correct entertainment" required that the guilty were punished and the sympathetic were found to be innocent.

- Classical Hollywood producers consistently and consciously sought to deny authorial responsibility for whatever meanings audiences might choose to "read into" their movies. Hollywood's commercial aesthetic concedes to the individual viewer the authority to decide what a particular movie means, and this policy encouraged the development of forms of representation which allow for a range of interpretations and an instability of meaning. Hollywood movies frequently enact a "drama of false appearances," in which the protagonists appear guilty of a crime or sin, but are actually innocent.

- Hollywood movies often tell their audiences two distinct but intertwined stories structured around oppositions, and the movie works to reconcile both sets of oppositions by its conclusion. Frequently, however, the resolution is superficial, and the viewer is free to explore the complexities of the movie's contradictions.

- Hollywood's entertainment is self-explanatory, self-contained, self-justifying, self-regulated, and self-reflexive. Hollywood tells us about Hollywood. As *Singin' in the Rain* demonstrates, Hollywood's self-referentiality can be playfully complex, but this complexity is present only if the viewer chooses to explore it.

Further Reading

The Production Code and regulated difference

The text of the Production Code is reproduced in appendix 1. It has also been widely anthologized, for example in *The Movies in Our Midst: Documents in the Cultural History of Film in America*, ed. Gerald Mast (Chicago: University of Chicago Press, 1982), which is a valuable source of primary documents in American cinema history, including the 1915 Supreme Court decision in *Mutual Film Corp. v. Ohio Industrial Commission*. That decision is discussed in Garth Jowett, " 'A Capacity for Evil': The 1915 Supreme Court *Mutual* Decision," *Historical Journal of Film, Radio and Television* 9:1 (1989), pp. 59–78. Jowett's article is anthologized with several other important essays in *Controlling Hollywood: Censorship and Regulation in the Studio Era*, ed. Matthew Bernstein (New Brunswick, NJ: Rutgers University Press, 1999). Another valuable collection on the topic is Francis G. Couvares, ed., *Movie Censorship and American Culture* (Washington, DC: Smithsonian Institution Press, 1996).

A detailed history of the drafting of the Code can be found in Richard Maltby, "The Genesis of the Production Code," *Quarterly Review of Film and Video*, 15:4 (March 1995), pp. 5–63, and a history of the Code's origins and implementation in Richard Maltby, "The Production Code and the Hays Office," in Tino Balio, *Grand Design: Hollywood as a Modern Business Enterprise, 1930–1939*, volume 5 of *The History of the American Cinema* (New York: Scribner's, 1993), pp. 37–72. Two excellent book-length studies of the workings of self-regulation in Classical Hollywood are Lea Jacobs, *The Wages of Sin: Censorship and the Fallen Woman Film, 1928–1942* (Madison: University of Wisconsin Press, 1991), and Ruth Vasey, *The World According to Hollywood, 1918–1939* (Exeter: University of Exeter Press, 1997).

Steve Neale elaborates his concept of regulated difference in "Questions of Genre," *Screen* 31:1 (Spring 1990).

Singin' in the Rain

The true connoisseur of self-referentiality in *Singin' in the Rain* will know that the furniture in Don's mansion came from the set of the John Gilbert–Greta Garbo movie *Flesh and the Devil* (1927), while Kathy's car used to belong to Andy Hardy. In the "Broadway Ballet," Cyd Charisse's appearance is modeled on a combination of silent stars Pola Negri and Louise Brooks, Kelly's on Broadway star Harry Richman, and the gangster's on George Raft in *Scarface* (1932). References to other Hollywood musicals abound. There is also a further level of ironic self-reflexivity in the dubbing sequence. The speaking voice actually used when Kathy speaks as Lina is not Debbie Reynolds's but Jean Hagen's own voice: Hagen is dubbing Reynolds playing Kathy dubbing Lina. (When Reynolds sings as Lina, the voice is that of Betty Royce.) There are accounts of the movie's production in Hugh Fordin, *The World of Entertainment:* *Hollywood's Greatest Musicals* (New York: Avon, 1975), and Rudy Behlmer, *Behind the Scenes* (New York: Samuel French, 1982). The movie has also been well analyzed from a number of critical perspectives, in Rick Altman, *The American Film Musical* (Bloomington: Indiana University Press, 1987), Jane Feuer, *The Hollywood Musical* (London: British Film Institute, 1982), Peter Wollen, *Singin' in the Rain* (London: British Film Institute, 1992), and Steven Cohan, in *Reinventing Film Studies*, eds Christine Gledhill and Linda Williams (London: Arnold, 2000).

CHAPTER FOUR
Genre

These ambiguities, redundancies, and deficiencies recall those attributed by Dr Franz Kuhn to a certain Chinese encyclopedia entitled *Celestial Emporium of Benevolent Knowledge*. On those remote pages it is written that animals are divided into (a) those that belong to the Emperor, (b) embalmed ones, (c) those that are trained, (d) suckling pigs, (e) mermaids, (f) fabulous ones, (g) stray dogs, (h) those that are included in this classification, (i) those that tremble as if they were mad, (j) innumerable ones, (k) those drawn with a very fine camel's hair brush, (l) others, (m) those that have just broken a flower vase, (n) those that resemble flies from a distance.
Jorge Luis Borges[1]

I know Billy, and he ain't exactly predictable . . .
Pat Garrett (James Coburn) in *Pat Garrett and Billy the Kid* (1973)

Hollywood is a generic cinema, which is not the same thing as saying that it is a cinema of genres. This chapter examines the way in which critics have used the idea of **genre** to classify Hollywood's output into a number of different types and to construct a genre-based history of American films. It points out a number of problems inherent in this approach, and suggests alternative ways in which Hollywood can be understood as a generic cinema. First, however, it may be useful to look at how the idea of genre is used in other discourses about Hollywood.

Audiences, producers, and critics all discuss movies in generic terms. They may use the same terms as each other, but they often mean something very different by them. Critics place movies into generic categories as a way of dividing up the map of Hollywood cinema into smaller, more manageable, and relatively discrete areas. Their analyses often suggest a cartographer's concern with defining the exact boundary between one genre and another. Audiences and producers use generic terms much more flexibly: for example, you might describe the movie you saw last night as a comedy, a thriller, or a science fiction movie. The local video store similarly labels its offerings by type: action, horror, drama. Such everyday distinctions are descriptive and, above all, functional. If you avoid horror movies, it is useful to know that *Hannibal* (2001) falls into that category when choosing a video. This use of genre as a way of differentiating among movies assumes that there is a consensus about what constitutes a Western or a musical. As Andrew Tudor puts it, genre "is what we collectively believe it to be."[2] We know a thriller when we see one. Indeed, we know a thriller before we see one, and to some degree we also recognize that, beyond describing the obvious content of a movie, these generic categories have a broader cultural resonance. Tudor suggests that they are embedded features of our social lives, providing narrative structures and emotional landscapes that we can use to construct ourselves socially. The horror movie, for instance, allows us to experiment with the experience of fear, and gives us a vocabulary of images with which to describe and articulate the fearful.[3]

Generic categories such as "the thriller" or "the weepie" are identified by the affect or emotional reaction they produce. Other descriptions, particularly of action movies likely to appeal to a predominantly male audience, such as "the Western" or "science fiction," concern themselves primarily with content. These two methods of classification may be incompatible if the objective is to produce a single coherent system of movie genres, but for everyday purposes they indicate the ways in which categorical systems intersect and overlap, confirming that the distinctions we make do not have to be either precise or mutually exclusive. Genres are flexible, subject to a constant process of change and adaptation. Generic boundaries can never be rigidly defined, and all generic groupings are susceptible to extensive subdivision. *Oklahoma!* (1955), for instance, is both a Western and a musical, and to suggest that it should be excluded from either category on the grounds that it belongs in the other would be to use generic classification in a very reductive fashion. At the same time, within the relatively small category of musical Westerns we might want to distinguish between *Oklahoma!* and *Rose Marie* (1936) on the grounds that they are both different types of musical (*Rose Marie* is an operetta) and different types of Western (*Rose Marie* is set in Canada).

Rather than occupying discrete categories, most movies use categorical elements in combination. We are familiar with generic hyphenates: musical-comedy, comedy-adventure, Western-romance. In 1979, the *Monthly Film Bulletin* described *Nocturna* as "the first soft-porn-vampire-disco-rock movie," while in 1991 *Arachnophobia* advertised itself as a "thrillomedy": generic mutants, perhaps, but these labels do give potential viewers quite a full description of what they might expect. Audiences, too, invent their own generic categories, both by making connections and by breaking genres down into ever smaller subsets. When the British sociologist J. P. Mayer asked readers of *Picturegoer* magazine to write about their film preferences in 1946, one 24-year-old female stenographer expressed her general enjoyment of "Love and Romance" movies, and then qualified this by adding: "Boy-meets-girl romances are always refreshing to me; triangles bore me; Bette Davis' acting I admire, but continual self-sacrifice irritates me; and the mask-like new faces with which we have recently been inundated, with the possible exceptions of Van Johnson and Lauren Bacall, bewilder me."[4] Stars and story-type distinguish this viewer's preferences within the general category of romance. "Boy-meets-girl" and "triangle" stories might be regarded as sub-genres of romance; these classifications intersect with those expressed in preferences for particular stars or star types, and using this particular matrix of opinions, it would be possible to predict which 1947 romances would have been likely to appeal to this viewer. More analytically, a broad generic category such as the romance can be understood as a field containing a large collection of more or less familiar elements: stars, settings, plot events, motives, and so on. For both producers developing or promoting a movie and viewers determining their response to it, the individual genre movie achieves its uniqueness through the way that it combines these elements.

The specificity of a genre arises not from its possessing features that are exclusive to it so much as from its particular combination of features, each of which it may share with other genres. Steve Neale suggests that this overlap of elements between genres makes the definition of any genre difficult, since a genre is not simply a combination of repetition *and* difference, but a process of difference *in* repetition.[5] Genres may appear to be bound by systems of rules, but an individual genre movie inevitably transgresses those rules in differentiating itself from other movies in the same genre. The rules of a genre are thus not so much a body of textual conventions as a set of expectations shared by audiences and producers alike. Genre movies share family resemblances with each other, and audiences recognize and anticipate these familiar features. Generic consistency allows for the shorthand of convention and stereotype, but also for the interplay between confirmed expectation and novelty. The conventions of a genre exist alongside more general conventions of realism or verisimilitude (verisimilitude implies probability or plausibility, less a direct relation to the "real" than a suggestion of what is appropriate). Sometimes generic conventions transgress these broader regimes of social or **cultural verisimilitude**: when a character bursts into song while walking down a street, for instance.[6] Douglas Pye's account of genre as a context in which meaning is created suggests ways in which audience expectations and producers' commercial motivations form a common currency. The generic context is, he argues, "narrow enough for recognition of the genre to take place but wide enough to allow enormous individual variation." In any individual movie, "any one or more than one element can be brought to the foreground while others may all but disappear. Plot, character, theme, can each become central . . . characters can be fully individualized, given complex or conflicting motivation, or may be presented schematically as morality play figures, embodiments of abstract good or evil."[7]

The notion of a genre as a set of stable categories across which movies connect, or within which fluctuation occurs, is useful for both producers and critics. It also, however, presents critics and empirical audience researchers with the problem of how to sort the genres into mutually exclusive categories, despite the many constant features which they share, and the many ways in which categories dissolve into one another. A 1955 audience research study, for example, originally asked open-ended questions, somewhat like Mayer's, about preferences. This produced a "fuzziness . . . in the meaning of names given the program types by the respondents." Substituting a predetermined list of generic categories from which respondents had to select gave rise to another problem. "If we ask, 'What type of movie do you like best?' the answers depend upon the way the movie types are classified and upon the respondents' understanding of the terms we are using."[8]

When the motion picture industry has investigated its audience's generic preference it has usually done so by asking questions about "story-types." One 1942 survey by the Motion Picture Research Bureau enumerated 18 types:

Comedies:
    sophisticated comedies
    slapstick comedies
    family life comedies
    musical comedies
    "just" comedies
War pictures
Mystery, horror pictures
Historicals, biographies
Fantasies
Western pictures
Gangster and G-men pictures
Serious dramas
Love stories, romantic pictures
Socially significant pictures
Adventure, action pictures
Musicals (serious)
Child star pictures
(Wild) animal pictures

The study's author, Leo Handel, remained dissatisfied with this classification because of "the overlapping of the different types. A war picture may also be a serious drama, a historical picture, and at the same time it may contain a love story. A socially significant picture may feature a child star." He also noted that "it has been found repeatedly that it is the particular story rather than the story type that determines the interest."[9]

The preferences his survey recorded, however, give some indication of why any individual movie was likely to be a generic cocktail. Women expressed strong dislikes for mystery and horror pictures, gangster and G-men movies, war movies and Westerns. Their greatest enthusiasms were for love stories, the category most strongly disliked by men, whose strongest preference was for war movies. Hollywood's logic was to combine the two, a logic repeatedly expressed in movie advertisements that, for instance, summarized the Korean war movie *The Bridges at Toko-Ri* (1954) as "Tomorrow, the deadliest mission . . . tonight, the greatest love!" The advertising copy for *Twelve O'Clock High* (1949), about World War II pilots, promised "a story of twelve men as their women never knew them." It might have been addressing the reservations of women who felt that war pictures lacked "human interest" because they dwelt too extensively on their scenes of fighting at the expense of providing thorough characterizations. Even more blatantly, perhaps, the poster for *Destroyer* (1943) declared "Her only rival is his ship! . . . You feel toward a ship as you do toward a woman when you marry her . . . You take her for better or you take her for worse . . . and you don't leave her when the going gets tough!"

The production industry began classifying its product according to "story-type" from an early stage. In 1905 the Kleine Optical Company listed its offerings under the headings of comic, mysterious, scenic, personalities, and three types of story: historical, dramatic, and narrative.[10] In the mid-1940s, in the process of passing all Hollywood's feature movies through the Production Code, the industry's trade association classified them into a heterogeneous matrix that divided its six major categories into 57 subdivisions. The largest single category was melodrama, which accounted for between a quarter and a third of all production. Westerns, comedies (which included musical comedies), and drama each made up about 20 percent of annual production, with the rest falling into a small crime category and a larger miscellaneous group. The subdivisions within drama and melodrama overlapped considerably: each group had action, comedy, social problem, romantic, war, musical, psychological, and murder-mystery as sub-categories. But Hollywood never prioritized genre as such. Like that of other fashion industries, Hollywood production was cyclical, always seeking to replicate its recent commercial successes, in what Andrew Tudor has described as a commercial version of the survival of the fittest, in which "financially successful films encourage further variations on their proven themes, thus generating a broadly cyclical pattern of successes which then decline into variously unsuccessful repetitions of the initial formula."[11] For instance, what the Production Code Administration classified as the "Farce-murder-mystery" was a one-season wonder: although eleven were made in 1944, only two were made in the following season, and none the year after. Some cycles might last for several seasons, and perhaps come to form subsets within a larger generic grouping: Biblical and Roman epics in the early 1950s, for instance. Cinema historian Barbara Klinger has called these subsets "local genres": categories that "functioned as a recognized and influential means of classifying films" for an historically specific period.[12]

On occasion, critics have elevated what the production industry understood as a cycle to the status of a genre. The "gangster film," for instance, was initially the product of a single **production season** (1930–1) and, at least within the industry's operating definitions, comprised no more than 23 pictures; nonetheless, it has attracted critical attention as a genre, and most critical accounts have suggested that *Little Caesar* (1930), *The Public Enemy* (1931), and *Scarface* (1932) "forged a new generic tradition," in which they also constituted "a point of classical development."[13] Tino Balio has argued that, rather than working within genres, Hollywood's Class A pictures during the 1930s followed what he identifies as a number of "production trends." Ranked in order of their cost, duration, and box-office performance, these production groupings were: prestige pictures, musicals, woman's films, comedies, social problem pictures, and horror movies.[14] Some of these terms correspond to critically established genres while others, including the most important category of the prestige picture, fall across or outside academically recognized genre boundaries. In much the same way, the contemporary industry divides movies aimed at the family market into "drop-off" and "non-drop-off" movies, depending on whether they expect parents to watch the movie with their children or simply leave them at the theater.

For producers, then, generic distinction offers a layered system of classification, which they use in an opportunistic way that does not assume that one generic category excludes others. These classification categories are being constantly revised, so that there is always more than one system in operation at any one time, and inevitably contradictions in classification arise. Nevertheless, the advantages to producers of the principle of classifying movies by type are clear. Firstly, they offer a financial guarantee: generic movies are in a sense always pre-sold to their audiences because viewers possess an image and an experience of the genre before they actually engage any particular instance of it. Some genres, moreover, have predictably higher earning capacities than others. Until the 1960s, science fiction movies were expected to perform noticeably less well at the box-office than other movies with comparable stars and spectacle. An analysis of theatrical receipts during the 1970s suggested that had changed, and that science fiction now carried a generic premium higher than horror or comedy.[15] Secondly, genre movies promise that their fictional events will unfold with a measure of certainty for the audience and that expected satisfactions will be provided. By offering this fore-knowledge, a generic cinema encourages that sense of pleasurable mastery and control that we have associated with entertainment. Andrew Britton describes his experience of watching *Hell Night* (1981) with an audience of teenage horror-movie aficionados:

> It became obvious at a very early stage that every spectator knew exactly what the film was going to do at every point, even down to the order in which it would dispose of its various characters, and the screening was accompanied by something in the nature of a running commentary in which each dramatic move was excitedly broadcast some minutes before it was actually made. The film's total predictability did not create boredom or disappointment. On the contrary, the predictability was clearly the main source of pleasure, and the only occasion for disappointment would have been a modulation of the formula, not a repetition of it.[16]

This audience demand for predictability meshes harmoniously with the economic advantages to the industry that come with the standardization of production. In this context, genre serves as a central component of Hollywood's aesthetic regime of regulated difference, and also regulates the act of consumption. Every teenager in the audience for *Hell Night* was consuming a known quantity, and Britton describes the ritualized aspects of the viewing experience as well as of the movie itself.[17] Low-budget production emphasizes the formulaic and predictable, as an oft-told story about Bryan Foy illustrates. Foy ran B-feature production at Warner

Box 4.1 Types of motion picture, 1944–6

In 1947, the Motion Picture Association of America published a tabulation of "the types and kinds of feature-length films approved during 1944, 1945, and 1946 by the Production Code Administration."[18]

Melodrama:	109	128	151	388
Action	26	19	33	78
Adventure	3	7	6	16
Comedy	21	22	12	55
Juvenile	6	6	4	16
Detective-mystery	7	9	9	25
Murder-mystery	33	40	47	120
Social problem	7	11	9	27
Romantic	0	2	5	7
War	4	4	0	8
Musical	1	0	2	3
Psychological-mystery	1	0	0	1
Psychological	0	8	8	16
Crime	0	0	5	5
Murder	0	0	7	7
Mystery	0	0	2	2
Fantasy	0	0	2	2
Drama:	83	75	100	258
Romantic	6	13	13	32
Biographical	5	1	2	8
Social problem	39	24	37	100
Musical	8	5	8	21
Comedy	9	11	25	45
Action	5	2	7	14
War	4	14	2	20
Psychological	4	4	4	12
Religious	3	0	0	3
Historical	0	1	1	2
Murder-mystery	0	0	1	1
Western:	85	73	88	246
Action	71	63	68	202
Musical	4	8	13	25
Mystery	10	2	7	19
Comedy:	104	58	53	215
Romantic	42	25	31	98
Musical	56	31	16	103
Juvenile	6	2	4	12
Fantasy	0	0	1	1
Murder-mystery	0	0	1	1
Crime:	5	9	6	20
Action	5	6	6	17

Prison	0	2	0	2
Social problem	0	1	0	1
Miscellaneous:	56	47	27	130
Fantasy	1	5	2	8
Fantasy-musical	0	1	0	1
Comedy-fantasy	1	2	0	3
Comedy-fantasy-musical	0	1	0	1
Farce-comedy	20	19	15	54
Farce-murder-mystery	11	2	0	13
Horror	13	11	2	26
Horror-psychological	2	0	1	3
Documentary	4	3	0	7
Musical-crime-drama	0	1	0	1
Drama	0	2	0	2
Travelog	1	0	0	1
Folklore	0	0	1	1
Folklore-travelog	0	0	1	1
Cartoon-musical-fantasy	0	0	1	1
Musical romance	0	0	4	4
Farce-horror	1	0	0	1
Cartoon	1	0	0	1
Historical	1	0	0	1
Total	442	390	425	1,257

The first chart shows the relative distribution of the major categories identified by the Production Code Administration (PCA). The second shows the relative distribution of different content types, using the PCA's sub-categories for classification.

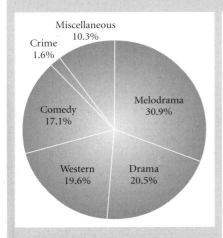

Types of motion picture by MPAA major category, 1944–6

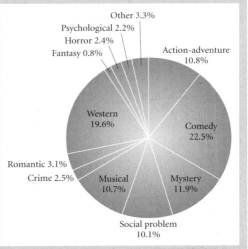

Types of motion picture by content, 1944–6

Bros. in the late 1930s and was known as the "keeper of the Bs." He is supposed to have kept a pile of about 20 scripts on his desk. Each time his unit completed a movie, its script would go to the bottom of the pile. Over a period of about a year, it would gradually work its way back up to the top. Then it would be dusted off and given to the scriptwriter to rewrite: a crime story would become a Western, the sex of the leading characters would be changed, the location moved.[19] In due course, the new script would return to the bottom of the pile to be recycled in the same way. Whether or not the story is apocryphal (and Foy did once boast that he had made the same movie 11 times), it illustrates the cost-effectiveness of Hollywood's system of constructing familiar fictions that fulfilled their audiences' requirement that movies be "just like . . . but completely different from" each other. The more recent tendency to produce sequels (*Friday the 13th* reached part 10 as *Jason X* (2001)) is an even less disguised practice, since in many cases the sequels could more accurately be described as remakes. The director of *Halloween* (1978), John Carpenter, acknowledged that "basically, sequels mean the same film." People, he claimed, "want to see the same movie again."[20]

Foy's activities were, however, as much concerned with providing novelty as predictability, balancing recognizable features with elements of difference and variation. In addition to being like other movies which have in the past satisfied the audience, a movie also needs to have certain features that set it apart: "angles" or "edges" around which to promote and distinguish it as something new. The higher the budget, the more likely that its recognizable elements will be provided by its stars, and the novelty by its plot and setting; lower-budget movies may rely more heavily on conventions of plot and genre, but the same principle of regulated difference applies.

Hollywood's mode of promotion is similarly organized around the play between likeness and novelty. One way of summarizing a movie, used by writers "pitching" a story idea to a producer as well as by reviewers, is to describe it as a hybrid of two other pictures. A juxtaposition such as "*Out of Africa* meets *Pretty Woman*" (proposed by a character in *The Player*, 1992) conjures up a field of reference recognizable in the moment, but probably not over a longer period of time. Generic conventions offer more durable frames of reference, but they also accommodate change: the variations in plot, characterization, or setting in each imitation inflect the audience's generic expectations by introducing new elements or transgressing old ones. Each new movie extends the repertoire of conventions understood by producers, exhibitors, and ticket-buyers at any given historical point. This means that, as Steve Neale puts it, "the elements and conventions of a genre are always *in* play rather than being, simply, *re*-played; and any generic corpus is always being expanded."[21]

The boundaries of a genre can always be extended not only to admit new movies, but also to incorporate the surrounding discourses of advertising, marketing, publicity, press and other media reviewing, reporting, gossip, and the "word-of-mouth" opinions of other viewers. These all contribute to the expectations and knowledge of the audience prior to the commercially crucial moment when they purchase their tickets at the box-office. Including these discourses magnifies the problems in studying the movies, but it is essential that we pay

Box 4.2 Types of motion picture, 1993–5

A survey of the top 100 box-office champions in 1993, 1994, and 1995 categorized them into ten types.

Action/Adventure	38
Children/Family	38
Comedy	62
Drama	52
Foreign	2
Horror	5
Musical	1
Mystery/Suspense	17
Sci-fi/Fantasy	18
Western	8
Total	241

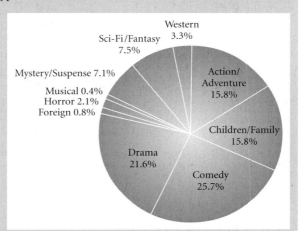

Types of motion picture, 1993–5

While there are some very obvious differences from the distribution of types 50 years earlier, such as the demise of the Western and the musical, there are also some noticeable similarities, in the proportion of production resources committed to comedy and to action/adventure movies. It is, however, important to stress that in both surveys, the classification was subjective, and the basis on which they were made is not available for scrutiny.[22]

attention to Hollywood's generic fluidity if we are to progress from examining individual movies as isolated objects to considering the relationships among movies as elements in a system of production and consumption.

Genre Criticism

Criticism has understood genre in Hollywood quite differently from the industry itself, ignoring most of the industry's own categories and introducing alternatives of its own. In much the same way as auteur criticism found itself drawn to "rebel" directors such as Orson Welles, an ideologically oriented genre criticism has found itself involved in what Barbara Klinger has called "the critical identification of a series of 'rebel' texts within the Hollywood empire," distinguishing certain categories of movies such as film noir, fifties melodrama, and seventies horror movies as "progressive" or "subversive."[23] But as Klinger argues, to pursue "radical" or "progressive" categories of Hollywood production is to hunt for a chimera, since the politics of a genre are by no means immutably fixed. Some Westerns, for instance, are more racist than others, but few avoid the subject of racism altogether, any more than they avoid at least some gunplay.

Genre criticism also shares with auteurism a concern to delineate Hollywood cinema by defining subsets within the whole, but the map of Hollywood that it seeks to draw is concerned less with identifying individual creativity than with examining the kind of world in which the horror movie or the Western or the musical could make sense.[24] James Twitchell has suggested that genre criticism's concern with broader cultural and historical meanings requires an approach more akin to ethnology or anthropology, in which stories are analyzed "as if no one individual telling really mattered," since the search is for what is stable and repeated in them. In such an analysis, considerations of authorship or originality are, he maintains, "quite beside the point," since the critic's main concern is with trying to understand why some images and narratives "have been crucial enough to pass along."[25] In practice, however, many critics have used genre as a starting point for a discussion of authorship in Hollywood: perhaps the most frequent instances are critical essays examining John Ford's contribution to the Western.

Twitchell's comments describe an underlying tendency in genre criticism to see the persistence of some genres as evidence that they represent a modern equivalent of folklore or mythology, stories in which contemporary social conflicts and contradictions can be explored. Writing about horror movies, Carol Clover has suggested that the swapping of themes and motifs between movies, their use of archetypal characters and situations in sequels, remakes, and imitations, are like oral narrative. In both there is "no original, no real or right text, but only variants; a world in which, therefore, the meaning of the individual example lies outside itself."[26] Robert Warshow makes a similar point about the therapeutic function of the Western's ritualized forms, which "preserve for us the pleasures of a complete and self-contained drama . . . in a time when other, more consciously serious art forms are increasingly complex, uncertain, and ill-defined."[27] These perceptions explain why genre criticism has drawn so heavily on what we can broadly term "structuralist" methods of analysis, and has argued that the recurrent structures of a genre distill social rather than individual meanings. In *Sixguns and Society*, for instance, Will Wright identifies the common plot patterns in a group of Westerns, and then suggests that each of the variant plots has a "mythical" significance, encapsulating a set of "concepts and attitudes implicit in the structure of American institutions." Like other structuralist approaches, Wright's analytical scheme borrows from the analysis of **myth** in "primitive" cultures by the French anthropologist Claude Lévi-Strauss, and in part from the Formalist analysis originally developed in Vladimir Propp's study of Russian fairy tales.[28]

Generic distinction is of most value when it can be used to distinguish between types of object that share fundamental similarities. We do not, for instance, need a system of generic distinctions to establish the difference between a refrigerator and a camel.[29] The capacity to distinguish between types of object becomes more important as the objects concerned become more like each other – a camel and a dromedary, perhaps. Douglas Pye has noted that the use of genre terms like "Western" or "thriller" focuses attention on the first part of what is in fact "a double-barrelled name, with the second term suppressed." That second term, "film" or "movie," identifies a larger generic category, the Hollywood movie, of which they are variations. Pye's point is that notwithstanding the differences between these genres, they share larger similarities, which is precisely why we need the tools of generic analysis to distinguish between them.[30] This gives rise to the recurring paradox of generic analysis: the attention that is paid to defining the boundaries of a genre, despite the fact that generic classification of similar objects can seldom be exclusive. Not only do genres contain sub-genres, but the mechanism of generic criticism supplies different sets of criteria for making distinctions, and these sets tend to be overlapping rather than mutually exclusive. In looking for the consistencies by which to establish stable and discrete systems of classification, genre criticism seeks to establish patterns of repetition between movies, and regards these as of more importance than differences of surface detail. Thomas Sobchack, for instance, argues that "the basic underlying coordinates of a genre are maintained time after time. . . . Any particular film of any definable group is only recognizable as part of that group if it is, in fact, an imitation of that which came before."[31] This critical definition of genre also distinguishes between movies that fall into specific genres and "non-genre films,"[32] in contrast to the industry's view that all of its output fell within one category or another.

Genre criticism usually identifies up to eight genres in Hollywood feature film production. The Western, the comedy, the musical, and the war movie are four uncontested categories. Different critics will then argue the relative independent merits of at least one of the thriller and the crime or gangster movie, and list the horror movie and science fiction as either one or two additional genres.[33] Each of these genres is usually seen as stable enough to possess a history of its own, existing outside the flow of industry history. The history of a genre is commonly described as an evolution from growth to maturity to decay, or a development from the experimental to the classical to the elaborated to the self-referential, "from straightforward storytelling to self-conscious formalism."[34] As both Alan Williams and Tag Gallagher have suggested in relation to the Western, the genre accorded the greatest stability and the most longevity until 1975, such critically imposed accounts lack an awareness of the historical specificity of the genres they describe, and do not take sufficiently into account either the range of variation within any given grouping at a particular moment, or the sensitivity of contemporary audiences to generic nuance.[35]

These genre histories, however, do not so much provide an accurate chronological account as delineate a body of work, a canon of texts, to be compared with each other. In creating a canon, genre criticism practices a form of discrimination similar to that I associated with auteurism in chapter 2. The imposition of an internal historical structure in which movies as texts influence each other actually eliminates the need to consider external questions of industry, economics, and audience in favor of a search for recurrent textual structures, whether these are narrative, thematic, or visual. Perhaps the clearest instance of strain between critical and industrial notions of genre concerns the group of movies produced in the decade after World War II which are usually called film noir. The term was first used by French film critics to identify "a new mood of cynicism, pessimism and darkness that had crept into American cinema"[36] in the postwar period. Film noir was entirely a critical classification, rather than an industry or an audience definition, something which does not invalidate it as a category, but clearly does privilege the critical recognition of common textual features (such as lighting or the characterization of the female lead) over other contexts and assumptions. The movies now usually identified as film noir probably occupied more than a dozen different categories in the Production Code Administration's classification of 57 types.[37]

Genre Recognition

Even where a critically established genre boundary more or less coincides with industrial parameters, as is the case with the Western, genre criticism reconstructs a slightly different history from that generated by other modes of research. Most accounts of the Western regard Edwin S. Porter's *The Great Train Robbery* in 1903 as constituting its birth. Recent historical research, however, suggests that such an identification came only several years later, and that contemporary audiences recognized *The Great Train Robbery* as a melodramatic combination of the "chase film," the "railway genre," and the "crime film." The Western had emerged by 1910, its great appeal to American producers lying in its being an identifiably American product that could not be successfully imitated by their European competitors. This both strengthened their hold on their home market and improved their sales abroad. Not until the Italian film industry began producing "spaghetti Westerns" in the 1960s were European audiences, let alone American ones, prepared to accept foreign substitutes for the real American product.[38]

Discussions of genre recognition have most commonly been conducted around the Western, because it provides a clearer or more convincing demonstration of the case than most other types. Almost every frame of a Western movie identifies it as such by the objects within it, whether these generic signifiers be setting, characters, costumes, or accoutrements. The image shown on p. 87, for instance, is dense with the Western's **iconography** or system of recurring visual motifs. These provide a shorthand system enabling a knowledgeable viewer to glean a great deal of information about the characters and the situation simply from the way the characters are dressed, the tools they use, and the settings in which the action takes place, and this level of meaning provides viewers with another means of gaining pleasure from the movie. An iconographic approach to genre allows us to establish quite precisely what we might expect to find in a Western. The presence of familiar objects repeatedly confirms what kind of movie we are watching and, together with the recognition of recurrent plot situations, reinforces our expectations of how the story will develop.[39] As part of the attempt to come to terms with visual discourse in cinema, early genre criticism concentrated on genres marked by their iconographic richness.

Matthew Garth (Montgomery Clift) asserts his independence from patriarchal Tom Dunson (John Wayne) in *Red River* (1948). The audience's knowledge of Western iconography tells us a great deal about what is happening in scenes like this.
Produced by Howard Hawks; distributed by Monterey Pictures. United Artists.

Along with their iconography, Westerns are equally easily identified by the actors who appear regularly in them – not just John Wayne or Clint Eastwood, but also character actors in smaller roles, such as Slim Pickens, Andy Devine, or Jack Elam – and by their recurrent situations: gunfights, saloon brawls, the final scene in which the hero bids farewell to the woman he is leaving behind. While the representational conventions of these familiar icons and situations have changed over time, so that a silent Western such as *The Iron Horse* (1924) looks very different from *Unforgiven* (1992), the situations, iconography, and characterizations recur with sufficient consistency to override historical distinctions and establish the Western as a consistent, transhistorical phenomenon.

The Western is not, of course, the only genre to possess such features. In looking at the crime film, for instance, we could identify an iconography and produce a list of recurring situations. We might, however, find more ambiguities at the visual level. For example, we can be sure that the image overleaf, of Edward G. Robinson and Humphrey Bogart about to shoot it out, must come from the climax of the movie, in which the hero confronts the principal villain. But we are unlikely to know simply from the iconography which of them is the hero and which the villain, any more than we can tell whether Al Pacino or Robert De Niro is playing the cop in *Heat* (1995) simply from their appearance. Such ambiguities are an inherent part of both the recurrent plots and thematics of the crime movie: this image comes from a 1936 Warner Bros. movie, *Bullets or Ballots*, in which Robinson plays a cop masquerading as a racketeer. The movie's advertising made use of Robinson's persona as a gangster with lines like "Little Caesar's Back in Town!," while its thematic concern, like those of many crime films, examined the relationship between law, justice, and morality.

It would be more difficult to come up with a consistent iconographic scheme for the horror movie or for the musical. On the other hand, just as the lighting in the image from *Bullets or Ballots* suggests that this is a crime movie because its play with shadow and strong areas of black and white tells us that this is an image of the city at night, so we recognize the image on p. 89 as unmistakably coming from a musical because only in a musical could all these people have any convincing reason for adopting the same pose at the same time. We can recognize gestures, and speak of there being gestural codes, although it is more difficult to attach precise meanings to them than to the iconographic elements we have discussed in relation to the Western. In Westerns, too, we find hierarchies of

Edward G. Robinson confronts Humphrey Bogart in *Bullets or Ballots* (1936). The lighting tells us that this is the city at night, but which of the two actors is the villain?

Produced by Louis F. Edelman; distributed by Warner Bros. Aquarius Picture Library.

West Side Story (1961). Only in a musical could all these people gesture in the same way at the same time.

Produced by Robert Wise; distributed by United Artists. Mirisch-7/United Artists.

gestural coding: the gunfighter's narrowed eyes, the hero's purposeful stride, or the familiar choreography of the saloon brawl feature in different movies to broadly the same effect. Not all genres, however, have systems of gestural coding that are exclusive to them, any more than they necessarily have specific lighting or iconographic codes.

Nonetheless, most genre critics argue that movies within a genre will share recurrent situations and consistent narrative patterns. For example, in a structuralist study of "the stalker film," a late-1970s sub-genre of the horror movie, Vera Dika outlines a specific sequence of plot functions that identifies them as a group. Their plots have "a two-part temporal structure," the first part of which presents a past event, structured as follows:

The members of a young community are guilty of a wrongful action.
The killer sees an injury, fault, or death.
The killer experiences a loss.
The killer kills the guilty members of the young community.

The second section of the movie, set in the present, also comprises a sequence of narrative events, ordered according to a strict pattern:

An event commemorates the past action.
The killer's destructive impulse is reactivated.
A seer warns the young community.
The young community takes no heed.
The killer stalks the young community.
The killer kills members of the young community.
The heroine sees the murders.

The advertising material for *Bullets or Ballots* exploited Edward G. Robinson's gangster persona, even though he actually played an undercover cop in the movie.

> The heroine sees the killer.
> The heroine does battle with the killer.
> The heroine subdues the killer.
> The heroine survives but is not free.[40]

As *Hell Night*'s audience demonstrated, viewers recognize genres through plot structures like these, as well as through advertising, iconography, and gestural codes. Often such indicators overlap; in the practice of a genre-based criticism this is almost bound to be the case.

Rick Altman has distinguished between what he calls the "semantic" approach to genre – a cataloguing of common traits, characters, attitudes, locations, sets, or shots – and a "syntactic" approach that defines a genre in terms of the structural relationships between those elements that carry its thematic or social meaning.[41]

Just as the semantic approach has been most often applied to the iconography of the Western, the structure of the Western has frequently been the subject of syntactic analysis. In John Cawelti's analysis, for instance, the Western takes place on the frontier between savagery and civilization, where the hero confronts his uncivilized double.[42] Another instance of the fruitful application of a structural approach to what Altman calls "the genre's fundamental syntax" is Jim Kitses's highly suggestive tabulation of "the shifting ideological play" in what he identifies as the genre's central opposition between civilization and the wilderness:

The Wilderness	Civilization
The individual:	*The community:*
freedom	restriction
honor	institutions
self-knowledge	illusion
integrity	compromise
self-interest	social responsibility
solipsism	democracy
Nature:	*Culture:*
purity	corruption
experience	knowledge
empiricism	legalism
pragmatism	idealism
brutalization	refinement
savagery	humanity
The west:	*The east:*
America	Europe
the frontier	America
equality	class
agrarianism	industrialism
tradition	change
the past	the future[43]

Westerns contrast the west with the east, nature with culture, the individual with the community, but in describing these oppositions, the positive term in each of Kitses's pairings is sometimes in the wilderness and sometimes in civilization. This tabulation indicates that comparable situations and characters – semantic units, in Altman's terms – can be inflected with a wide variety of thematic significances, depending upon which of these oppositions is given most weight. Kitses's tabulation clearly and concisely illustrates the potential thematic and ideological richness of a genre form.

A criticism that combines these various semantic and syntactic approaches to genre study can also look for the persistence of particular features in a genre, making it possible to trace fluctuations in their occurrence over time. This provides a means by which genre movies can be interpreted as rich sources of historical evidence. Film noir, for instance, has often been examined as a fluctuation in the more persistent genre of the crime movie, and its specific characteristics can be related to the historical circumstances of the period 1945–55. Similarly, an account of the Western might look at the ways in which the revisions of its conventions address the changing historical needs of its audience. Taking American history as its subject matter, the Western provides an opportunity to trace the changing construction of that history by the present. In its discussion of men taming a wilderness and transforming it into a garden, the Western has taken to itself a central aspect of American mythology: the civilizing spirit of American individualism. It has also become an arena in which Americans examine the relationship between individuals and society, and the tension between individual and community priorities. Along with iconographic conventions, the emphases within that ideological tension have shifted over time. Brian Henderson, for instance, has suggested that:

> The emotional impact of *The Searchers* can hardly come from the issue of the kinship status and marriageability of an Indian in white society in 1956. . . . It becomes explicable only if we substitute black for red and read a film about red–white relations in 1868–1873 as a film about black–white relations in 1956.[44]

Henderson's is a common critical strategy, in part designed to elevate the text's status by demonstrating its cultural significance. By such a process critics can legitimize their own activity, finding ways to demonstrate that, when viewed from the "right" perspective, the texts they study are far more important than the familiar and predictable objects they might on the surface appear. Such interpretive strategies exclude movies as well as including them, however. As Neale argues, in their quest to establish the social and aesthetic significance of their objects of study, genre histories may choose to "by-pass routine productions and films which simply do not fit the models and theories with which they are principally concerned," offering accounts of particular genres as far more consistent and far less opportunistic than was in fact the case.[45] The Western has not consistently staged the conflict between savagery and civilization, and critical accounts of the genre emphasizing frontier mythology have omitted or marginalized significant periods of its history which do not fit this paradigm.

Genres, then, can be thought of as fields inhabited by thematic, iconographic, narrative, and political propensities, as instances and instruments of Hollywood's system of regulated difference. Their emphasis shifts over time, and from individual movie to movie. They are also subject to a range of industrial, aesthetic, cultural, and technical factors. At any time, an individual movie may be seen as crystallizing the forms and meanings of the genre as a whole – *My Darling Clementine* (1946), for instance, is sometimes cast in this role for the Western – but historical shifts in ideological and stylistic fashion make it difficult to speak for long about any single movie as definitive of its genre. One way of appreciating Hollywood's complex reflection of, and influence on, American culture is by looking at how such everyday phenomena as the family, romance, heroism, femininity, or childhood have been represented in different genres at different times. Generic features make it possible for us to account for the connections we make between one movie and another, not so much in terms of their similarities, or their resemblance to the imaginary composite which "typifies" a particular category, but in terms of the differences between them, and the extent to which they play with existing conventions.

The Empire of Genres: *Pat Garrett and Billy the Kid*

The Westerner could not fulfill himself if the moment did not finally come when he can shoot his enemy down. But because that moment is so thoroughly the expression of his being, it must be kept pure. . . . The Westerner is the last gentleman, and the movies which over and over again tell his story are probably the last art form in which the concept of honor retains its strength. . . . Really, it is not violence at all which is the "point" of the Western movie, but a certain image of man, a style, which expresses itself most clearly in violence. Watch a child with his toy guns and you will see: what most interests him is not (as we so much fear) the fantasy of hurting others, but to work out how a man might look when he shoots or is shot. A hero is one who looks like a hero.

Robert Warshow[46]

Much that has been written about the Western film has been written . . . by men who cherish the fantasies embodied in these films and who, therefore, resent any effort at dispelling those fantasies.

Jon Tuska[47]

The Western exhibits a number of different kinds of what Andrew Tudor has called "genre imperialism." One survey of the genre suggests that between 1926 and 1967, Westerns comprised a quarter of all Hollywood's output, and on the basis of that statistic claims that it is not only the largest but also the most significant of Hollywood's genres.[48] Critic Robert Ray has argued that the genre is in a sense even larger than that, because "many of Classic Hollywood's genre movies" are best understood as "thinly camouflaged Westerns," concerned with the conflict between individualism and community. For Ray, the ability to reconcile this irreconcilable opposition makes the Western the thematic paradigm for Hollywood's commitment to "the avoidance of choice."[49] Douglas Pye also argues for the centrality of the Western to genre analysis, suggesting that its thematic richness comes from "the peculiar impurity of its inheritance," by which the archetypal imagery of romantic narrative could be blended with American history.[50] The genre imperialism exhibited here is similar to that of critics such as Will Wright, who see the persistence of genre, and of the Western in particular, as evidence that its formulae operate as particularly effective agencies for the circulation of cultural as well as purely cinematic meaning.

For contemporary audiences, this poses a difficulty, since the decline of the Western since the mid-1970s has been so absolute. Central to the operation of any genre movie, including the Western, is the cumulative expectation and knowledge of the audience. Over time, this frame of reference grows ever more dense and extensive, although we should bear in mind that viewers forget as well as remember, and that the whole field of generic knowledge is unlikely to be available to any given audience, even of aficionados.[51] Loss of knowledge is particularly important in this case as Hollywood's production of Westerns declined precipitously after 1970, with barely a handful being made during the 1980s. Hollywood's apparent abandonment of what had been its most common genre raised questions about the critical arguments that claimed that the Western was central to the expression of an American mythology. Had the mythology changed, so that the Western was no longer relevant? Or had the mythology migrated elsewhere, to other genres, and if so, had it changed its meaning in the process? Or had Hollywood somehow stopped articulating American mythology? Whatever set of circumstances had brought about the change, it shows that even so self-generating and apparently transhistorical a genre as the Western is subject to historical forces.

Pat Garrett and Billy the Kid is a Western made at the end of the line of continuous production in 1973, directed by one of the genre's last celebrated auteurs, Sam Peckinpah. As a retelling of one of the genre's most oft-told tales, it is a particularly good example of the ways in which a generic movie can set in play a complex dynamic of confirmation and revision of audience expectations. Its own case is given an added complexity by the fact that two quite distinct versions of the movie exist: one initially released by MGM in 1973 and a somewhat longer version, released for the first time in 1989, which was claimed to be much closer to the director's preferred final cut. Auteurist criticism would certainly regard the latter as more "original," but the existence of multiple versions really demonstrates the presence of conflicting intentions among the movie's producers. Multiple variants of movies have always been part of Hollywood's production logic and the idea of an "original" is in significant contradiction to the norms of American film industry practice.

The case of *Pat Garrett and Billy the Kid* is, therefore, only unusual in the amount of attention paid to the variations, a situation that came about because of the claims made for Peckinpah as an author whose "work" had been vandalized by the studio.[52] One critic went so far as to suggest that the "arbitrary and piecemeal" recut was ordered because the head of the studio, James T. Aubrey, "hated Peckinpah, and was bent on sabotaging his work."[53] While the movie's production and post-production processes were marred by intense acrimony, the studio executives were motivated by release schedules and the need to produce a commercially successful version, and found Peckinpah's 140-minute cut too long.[54] Their one addition was to prolong the scene of Sheriff Baker's (Slim Pickens) death, so that Bob Dylan's song "Knockin' on Heaven's Door" could be played over it. Although this scene has been described as being "as moving as anything in Peckinpah's work," its presence in the movie owes more to the commercial considerations of emphasizing Dylan's contribution to the movie as an additional appeal to the audience.[55]

Like most Westerns, *Pat Garrett and Billy the Kid* is easily identifiable in terms of its setting and subject matter. It establishes itself as a retelling of a familiar episode from Western history, the pursuit and killing of William Bonney by Pat

Garrett. Expectations raised by the title are confirmed in the image track: a moving camera rapidly establishes the familiar Western iconography of landscape, architecture, costumes, and props. At the same time, we are alerted to stylistic emphases that give new inflections to these familiar forms. The most forceful of these are the shots of the live chickens being used by Billy and his fellow outlaws for target practice. We see their destruction in extreme close-up, and this encounter with "realism" in the presentation of violence is likely to influence our attitudes to the rest of the movie. The audience will probably be aware of Peckinpah's reputation for using explicit violence to revise Western conventions in the name of an enhanced realism. The use of setting and costume, too, indicates that the movie is making claims to historical verisimilitude: this is, it implies, the "true" story of Billy the Kid. Both the expansiveness and timelessness of the "mythic" West will be replaced with an increasing sense of "historical" claustrophobia; here both time and space are running out. Mythical struggles give way to crudely political and economic ones. In their first encounter, Garrett announces in very simple terms the motivation of the action that will follow: "the electorate want you gone, Billy." Their subsequent exchange summarizes the shifting values that they represent and that will be contested through the story. "How does it feel," asks Billy, to have "sold out" to the Santa Fe Ring? "It feels like times have changed," Garrett replies. "Times maybe, but not me," is Billy's response.

The central dramatic tension in the movie, established here and encapsulated in its very title, recapitulates what is perhaps the Western's key structuring opposition, between the individualist values embodied by the outlaw and the values of community represented by the lawman. Some critics have suggested that this opposition explains the persistence of the genre itself, because it answers a specifically American cultural anxiety about the need to preserve both sets of ideals, and stages the dramatic conflict between them at the historical moment when America was formed as a modern nation. In Classical Westerns like *Stagecoach* (1939) and *My Darling Clementine*, the official hero and the outlaw hero overcome their differences in a larger battle to protect civilization from a greater savagery.[56] In revisionist Westerns, however, that greater savage threat no longer exists, and the value systems of sheriff and outlaw are placed in a seemingly inevitable opposition. In *The Man Who Shot Liberty Valance* (1962, and, like *Stagecoach* and *My Darling Clementine*, directed by John Ford) the death of the individualist hero (John Wayne) is the price paid for the democratic populism (perfectly embodied by James Stewart) that replaces him. In *Pat Garrett and Billy the Kid*, the values of the West will be replaced only by something more meager, as civilization is associated not with community, but with the corruption and corporate self-interest of the Santa Fe Ring who hire Garrett.

We should, however, be wary of suggesting too firmly that the generic evolution of the Western has seen "the blessings of civilization" subjected to increasingly hostile scrutiny. Tag Gallagher has pointed out how tenuous and selective such evolutionary arguments tend to be, and in counterpoint has suggested that because of changes in the conventions of representation across American culture as a whole, "the films of the sixties had to work harder, had to be more strident and dissonant, in order to try to express the same notions as earlier films." In support of his argument that Western heroes changed less in the 1960s than other critics have suggested, he offers an unconventional interpretation of Henry Fonda's performance as Wyatt Earp in *My Darling Clementine* that might also describe James Coburn's performance as Garrett:

> charm hides a self-righteous prig, and a marshal's badge and noble sentiments hide a "near-psychotic lust for violent revenge" even from Earp himself, but this upstanding Wyatt is all the more ambivalently complex a character for the sublimation of his hypocrisy and violence. . . . Wyatt clearly loves lording it over people without using his gun . . . there is no recognition in the film of Wyatt as "hero of the community": Ford cuts directly from the battle's last death to Wyatt's solitary farewell to Clementine outside of town. Nor is there any "reward" of a wedding.[57]

Gallagher's analysis might perhaps have been less convincing if the later movies did not exist to demonstrate the possibility of such interpretations, but it demonstrates that critics and audiences as well as filmmakers can make revisionist interpretations of the Classical.

For André Bazin, the Western had dramatized an epic and very public battle between "the forces of evil" and the "knights of the true cause." He saw the genre addressing basic human realities through the mythologization of a particular phase of American history.[58] The Western is an epic that works determinedly toward its final chapter. Its antagonists will eventually meet to dramatize this trial of strength through the spectacle of a shootout in the main street. The morality-play character of the shootout exemplifies perhaps best of all what Robert Warshow saw as the moral "openness" of the Western, "giving to the figure of the Westerner an apparent moral clarity which corresponds to the clarity of his physical image against his bare landscape."[59] With moral terms more relative and positions more compromised, however, the Western universe depicted in *Pat Garrett* operates on an altogether cloudier and more domestic level. The bulk of the movie is presented as a private drama between former friends. Garrett is obsessively unwilling even to discuss the rights and wrongs of his actions, let alone to seek their ratification through their display in the public spectacle of the shootout. As the shared value system of a Western "code" disintegrates, the traditional roles of sheriff and outlaw become confused and compromised.

Garrett is no longer the archetypal independent hero described by Warshow, reluctantly acting on behalf of the community to preserve its fragile civilization from the forces seeking to destroy it. He is rather the paid employee of a corporate interest group, hired for a dangerous job and expendable. Although from the outside he retains something of the character attributed to the Westerner as "last gentleman" by Warshow, and certainly displays the "moral ambiguity which darkens his image and saves him from absurdity," he is no longer able to "defend the purity of his own image."[60] He is a long way from the godlike figures wielding near-magical powers inherited by the Classical Western from American folklore and romantic narrative. Declaring itself to be an historically more accurate account of the events it depicts, the movie also asserts that the mythology of frontier heroism was always a deception. For all his maintenance of their physical decorum, Garrett does not possess the conviction of earlier lawmen. Nor does he enjoy the support of the community itself. His silences, so long a trait of the Western sheriff, now indicate not so much a moral status as the impossibility of his claiming any authority for what he does. As he arrives at a fuller understanding of the contradictions in which he is caught, stranded between a past he has rejected and a future of which he can be no part, Garrett becomes increasingly introspective. These contradictions are not resolved with the death of Billy. When Garrett rides out of Fort Sumner, a small child runs into the frame to throw stones at him. The action ironically echoes the ending of *Shane* (1953), in which Joey (Brandon de Wilde) runs after the hero he idolizes (Alan Ladd), calling for him to come back.

Billy (Kris Kristofferson) is also a revised character, no longer embodying the primitivism and savagery that must be overcome by the force of law. Instead, the outlaw now represents the positive values that "lawful" society is itself destroying. It is the landowner Chisum's men who kill and torture for pleasure, and the character whose behavior comes closest to the psychopathic is not any of the outlaws but rather the fundamentalist sheriff Ollinger (R. G. Armstrong). The movie does not, however, sentimentalize the outlaw as a doomed figure. Billy may be an anachronism, but he is scarcely a victim. His reluctance to use violence certainly matches that of the traditional Western hero, but he can also act violently and

Billy (Kris Kristofferson) and Garrett (James Coburn) play poker, watched by Ollinger (R. G. Armstrong), in *Pat Garrett and Billy the Kid* (1973).
Produced by Gordon Carroll; distributed by MGM. Aquarius Picture Library.

outside the "code" when circumstances require it, shooting Alamoosa Bill (Jack Elam) before the count in their duel is complete.

A number of formal aspects of the movie echo these shifts in value and characterization. Barbed wire fences cut suggestively across a number of Classical Western compositions. The land is presented less as a symbolic scene for the realization of heroic potential than as property from which Billy, like everyone else, is to be excluded. As the land is closed, the protagonists are forced into domestic spaces, where detail is emphasized at the expense of physical action. Outlaws wear spectacles, trading posts stock "fine quality tomatoes" in "airtights," colors are muted. Spaces are deprived of their mythic functions: any space can now become the scene of the violence once confined to the prairie and the main street. Tracked not to the summit of a mountain but to a domestic interior, Billy is finally shot dead in the kitchen of an aging cowboy.

If the movie dissents from the Western's tendency to endorse the role of capitalism in the settlement of the West, its revision of the genre's conventional representation of women appears much less radical. Traditionally, the genre gives women little significant presence or responsibility. Where they do figure in the Western it is usually to signify value systems that the hero is to endorse or ultimately refuse (the school marm, the saloon girl). As director Budd Boetticher observed, "What counts is what the heroine provokes, or rather what she represents. She is the one, or rather the love or fear she inspires in the hero, or else the concern he feels for her, who makes him act the way he does."[61] Western men can be redeemed by eastern women, but western women are seldom offered the same opportunity. Doc Holliday's (Victor Mature) descent in *My Darling Clementine* is evidenced by his involvement with Chihuahua (Linda Darnell), whose quasi-Mexican name and overt profession as a saloon entertainer ensure that their relationship is doomed, and that she, like him, will meet her conventionally inevitable end. Traces of those roles are evident in *Pat Garrett*: none of its central characters is a woman, or does anything for women or because of women.

Relationships between men occupy the center of a story that revolves, as Terence Butler has put it, around "the enforcement of law versus the fraternal loyalty of male friendship."[62] It is the male rather than the female body that is displayed and celebrated. Billy luxuriates in his already mythical status, and his body is repeatedly frozen in static postures in the image. Garrett, by contrast, is consistently framed in motion. Depicted from the outset as a fastidious dresser, he grows increasingly obsessed with his own image, aware that he will enter myth as Billy's executioner. Their shared narcissism revises Robert Warshow's observation that it is not violence which is the "point" of the Western so much as "a certain image of man, a style, which expresses itself most clearly in violence." Warshow's Westerner lives in a world of restrained violence: "There is little cruelty in Western movies and little sentimentality; our eyes are not focussed on the sufferings of the defeated but on the deportment of the hero."[63] Here violence is less restrained and less orderly in its occurrence, and shorn of any semblance of heroism, instead presented as "a symptom of individual defeat and loss of freedom."[64] The tidy rituals of the shootout are replaced by a series of haphazard ambushes, the outcomes of which are resolved not by skill but by sheer firepower.

Lawmen and outlaws carry rifles or shotguns, not six-shooters. With the significant exception of the killing of Billy himself, most deaths are bloody. Only the final gunplay reiterates the traditional stylization of the Western death, but the movie concludes not with a gunfight but with an execution, or, as some commentators have seen it, with the "crucifixion" that resolves the majority of Peckinpah's Westerns. The brutalization of the body that accompanies the death of male characters throughout much of Peckinpah's work is conspicuously absent in the treatment of the death of Billy. Garrett, on the other hand, is from the movie's outset unable to escape his own self-destruction. The longer version of the movie opens with Garrett's own death, in 1909, at the hands of the same corrupt powers who hired him to kill Billy. This scene is intricately interwoven with the scene of Billy's gang shooting chickens in Fort Sumner in 1881. Images of the gang firing are intercut with Garrett's death, as if, across time, they were shooting him. Finally, Garrett joins in the chicken shoot, and is seen to fire at himself. It is an action he repeats after he kills Billy, when he fires a second shot at his own image in the mirror. In Stephen Prince's analysis, Garret is "a man doubly dead," who loses his humanity "through the choices he makes, the friends he betrays, and the comrades he kills." The movie strips "the Western genre of its fundamental, underlying myth of beneficent historical progress, and the violence here does not offer a ritual of cleansing and purgation. It registers personal dehumanization and social corruption in a parable of historical and existential loss."[65]

Pat Garrett and Billy the Kid is a complex object, both commercially and aesthetically. Our perception of its complexities depends on our awareness of the conventions that are being displaced or revised. As a revisionist Western, the movie is particularly self-conscious about the self-referentiality that is an implicit part of genre cinema, and therefore of Hollywood. This self-consciousness is most noticeable in the performances of Coburn and Kristofferson. Their dialog, their delivery, and even the way they move convey a foreknowledge both of what will happen in the plot, and of the narrative tradition that has predestined those events. There is little suspense: Pat, Billy, and the audience all understand the inevitability of Billy's death. The wider structures of the movie also incline toward such self-consciousness. Rather than Billy, Garrett stands at the center of the story, concentrating our interest on the figure who will make Billy a myth by finally destroying him as a man. Peckinpah's movie thus emerges not simply as an attempt to demythologize the genre or move it toward a greater realism, but also as an attempt to revise mythology in the light of contemporary circumstances. As such it offers a particularly bleak account of American experience in the 1970s.

As the quotations from Warshow suggest, the genre's conventional narrative is essentially one of ideological self-confidence. Defeat in Vietnam, the erosion of faith in domestic politics after Watergate, the oil crisis of the mid-1970s, and the long-term decline of the American economy all questioned the self-confidence at the core of the expansionist ideology represented in the Classical Western. The revisionism of *Pat Garrett and Billy the Kid* is an instance of the questioning of that self-confidence, but its self-consciousness also indicates the extent to which it, and other similar movies made in the same period, exposed the conventions by which the genre had operated. This excessive self-consciousness also contributed to the subsequent decline of the Western, as it became impossible to conceal the genre's conventions or render them transparent again. Criticism may well have played a part here, too. A writer, director, or producer working in the 1980s would have had to be extraordinarily cine-illiterate not to know that the Western was where Hollywood discussed American history and staged conflicts between alternative versions of heroism. The few Westerns made between the mid-1970s and the mid-1990s all displayed an extreme generic self-consciousness, an awareness of their status within a generic tradition that some critics and some of its practitioners have chosen to elevate to the status of art.

At the same time, with so few Westerns made, audiences lost familiarity with their generic conventions. Movies could make fewer assumptions about their viewers' competence in the genre, and thus found themselves handicapped both by their self-consciousness and by the need to elaborate the genre's first principles for a new audience. It is perhaps hardly surprising that the few Westerns made in the 1980s and 1990s were all very long movies – *Heaven's Gate* (1980) ran for 219 minutes in its original version, and *Wyatt Earp* (1994) for 189 minutes. It is also an indication of the extent to which the Western has ceased to function fluently as a vehicle for American culture to tell itself the stories it needs to hear. Instead, the genre has acquired sufficient cultural respectability for Clint Eastwood's *Unforgiven* (1992) to become the first Western to win the Oscar for Best Picture since *Cimarron* in 1931. Contemporary Westerns are one-sided, serious affairs. Their heroes are outlaws on their way to defeat at the hands of a villainous corporate power. Instead of mythologizing individualism as a civilizing force through images of white men transforming a wilderness into a garden, in *Dances with Wolves* (1990) and *The Last of the Mohicans* (1991) civilization's malaise is registered through a celebration of the "natural" nobility of its savage opposite, the Indian. The oppositions in Kitses's table no longer have the resonance they once had; the play (in both senses) has gone out of the genre, and migrated, in the main, to science fiction and horror movies. Carol Clover, for example, produces a brilliantly perverse account of the generic migration of the "settler-versus-Indian" story to rape-revenge movies such as *I Spit on Your Grave* (1977):

> by making the representative of urban interests (what would normally be taken as the white male elite) a woman, and the representatives of the country (what would in the western have been Native Americans) white males, these movies exactly reverse the usual system of victim sympathies. That is, with a member of the gender underclass (a woman) representing the economic overclass (the urban rich) and members of the gender overclass (males) representing the economic underclass (the rural poor), a feminist politics of rape has been deployed in the service of class and racial guilt. Raped and battered, the haves can rise to annihilate the have-nots – all in the name of feminism.[66]

The argument sometimes made that *The Hills Have Eyes* (1977) and *Aliens* (1986) are disguised Westerns is perhaps rooted too much in nostalgia for the apparently lost certainties of the Western's particular account of melodramatic male action. More importantly, representing the central opposition in the Western's narrative between civilization and savagery in traditional generic terms has become near-impossible given contemporary evaluations of the relation between nature and culture: the Indian as murdering, raping, ignoble savage is no longer a marketable commodity. The Western's conventional thematics are, as a result, severely restricted. Narratives dealing with civilization's conflict with the savage Other have migrated to other generic fields, where women can be given more to do, and where, since the alien Other is purely a creature of the imagination, no one will complain about cultural distortion, or argue that aliens are peaceful hunter-gatherers, leading a sustainable existence in a stable eco-system. In space, no one can hear you scream about misrepresentation.

Genre and Gender

> Although mass media can scarcely be characterized as in any sense less self-conscious or analytic than criticism and theory about them, the fact that the discourse *within* horror cinema and the discourse *about* it diverge on some crucial points would seem to suggest that the folks who make horror movies and the folks who write about them are, if not hearing different drummers, then reading different passages of Freud.
>
> Carol J. Clover[67]

Given that the Hollywood genre about which most criticism has been written has little place for women, it is not surprising that genre criticism can hardly be described as gender neutral. Looking at the list of critically recognized genres reveals an extreme gender imbalance that perhaps reflects the simple fact that at the period when genre criticism took shape in the 1960s, most of the critics practicing it, and in the process legitimating their own tastes in popular culture, were men. Implicit in the preferences of much genre criticism is a valorization of patriarchal and masculine concerns, by which certain genres have been accorded an increased cultural status through a recognition of their larger thematic concerns, while the status of other genres in this critical hierarchy is demonstrated by their hardly being named or described.

In the generic mapping of Hollywood, the glaring omission is that of romance, which features as the principal or secondary plot in 90 percent of Hollywood's output. Meanwhile, missing from our list on p. 77 is that category often identified as "melodrama," which in contemporary critical discourse usually refers to stories of family trauma, pathos, and heightened emotionalism. From the mid-1970s the term was often used as an alternative generic label for "the woman's film." The designation of a category of Hollywood movies for women was a more or less deliberate attempt to redress the gender imbalance within the genre categories then receiving critical attention. The two terms then became fixed in their meaning. Melodrama has become synonymous with a group of movies preoccupied with the domestic, the sentimental, and heightened emotions: women's films, "weepies," soap operas, stories of family conflict and maternal sacrifice. In much the same way as early genre criticism of the Western identified John Ford's *Stagecoach* as "the ideal example of the maturity of a style brought to classic perfection,"[68] the "ideal type" of melodrama was represented by a group of movies directed by Douglas Sirk in the 1950s, such as *All That Heaven Allows* (1955), in which wealthy widow Cary Scott (Jane Wyman) scandalizes the New England town of Stoningham by having an affair with her gardener, Ron Kirby (Rock Hudson). Along with this linkage has gone a critical assumption that the group of movies identified were regarded as "Hollywood's lowliest form, the woman's weepie."[69]

As Christine Gledhill has pointed out, however, this dismissive and pejorative use both of "melodrama" and of the "woman's film" reflected the preferences of a predominantly male group of critics, rather than the practices of the industry. Jackie Byars suggests that in a way very similar to the creation of film noir as a category, "a genre was born . . . the theoretical genre of 'melodrama' was now formed in the mold of a group of Hollywood family melodramas produced by a few talented directors obsessed with stylistic manipulation."[70] Byars goes on to observe that constructing melodrama in these terms "obscured the existence of other melodramatic genres, the melodramatic aspects of other genres like the Western, the historical variations within individual melodramatic genres, and the relationships between kinds of melodramatic genres." As she suggests, "melodrama" would more helpfully describe one of Hollywood's fundamental aesthetic strategies, the defining features of which would include a presentation of sensational events, a moral didacticism, and a determined attempt to provoke a sequence of emotional responses in the audience. Linda Williams has elaborated Byars's argument, proposing that melodrama should be recognized as "the fundamental mode" of Classical Hollywood cinema: "if melodrama was misclassified as a sentimental genre for women, it is partly because other melodramatic genres such as the western and gangster films . . . had already been constructed . . . in relation to supposedly masculine cultural values."[71]

One consequence of the critical misrecognition of melodrama as Hollywood's fundamental mode has been a marginalization of the role of emotion in viewing. Rather than acknowledging "the complex tensions between different emotions as well as the relation of thought to emotion," critical analyses of melodrama have more often dismissed viewers' emotions as both excessive and monopathic, the result of the feminized spectator's over-identification with the melodrama's protagonist causing her to mimic the single emotional note struck by the character. Instead of this oversimplification, Williams proposes that criticism needs to undertake "the serious study of how complexly we can be 'moved.'" In making this argument about the centrality of melodrama to Hollywood's aesthetic practice, she also disputes "the notion that the classical Hollywood narrative subordinates spectacle, emotion, and attraction to the logic of personal causality and cause and effect":

we have only to look at what's playing at the local multiplex to realize that the familiar Hollywood feature of prolonged climactic action is, and . . . has always been, a melodramatic spectacle . . . no matter how goal-driven or embedded within narrative it may be. . . . Big "sensation" scenes, whether of prolonged "feminine" pathos or prolonged "masculine" action, or mixtures of both, do not interrupt the logical cause-effect progress of a narrative toward conclusion. More often, it is these spectacles of pathos and action that are served by the narrative.[72]

Melodrama was a term of product classification used within the industry, and its predominant trade meaning seems to have been almost diametrically opposite to that to which criticism has put it. "Ask the next person you meet casually how he defines a melodramatic story," wrote a critic in 1906, "and he will probably tell you that it is a hodge-podge of extravagant adventures, full of blood and thunder, clashing swords and hair's-breadth escapes."[73] From then until at least 1960, the trade's understanding of "melodrama" continued to embrace this sense, deriving from the tradition of spectacular stage melodrama, full of "trap doors, bridges to be blown up, walls to be scaled, instruments of torture for the persecuted hero-ines," and the like.[74] The trade press, for instance, described *White Heat* (1950), *Body and Soul* (1947), and *Psycho* (1960) as melodramas, not *Stella Dallas* (1937), *Back Street* (1931 and 1941), or *Imitation of Life* (1934 and 1959). As far as the industry was concerned, James Cagney, not Joan Crawford, made melodramas, and directors of action movies and thrillers such as Alfred Hitchcock, Fritz Lang, Raoul Walsh, and Samuel Fuller were identified in the trade press as masters of melodrama.[75] In the 1940s the industry labeled about a third of its product as melodrama, and it clearly expected these pictures to appeal predominantly to the men in the audience.[76]

Within the trade's usage, "melodrama" was certainly not an elevated term. The "woman's film," on the other hand, had a relatively prestigious status in Classical Hollywood. Most woman's films, which would be identified as "melodramas" by the conventions of recent criticism, were placed by the industry in its other general category, of "drama." As an industry term, "woman's film" embraced a range of sub-groupings that included romantic dramas, "fallen women" films, Cinderella romances, and working-girl movies.[77] Given that Classical Hollywood assumed that the majority of its audience was female, it is hardly surprising that these "dramas" were generally of higher budget and status than the "melodramas" designed with a more masculine appeal.[78] Far from being a despised or denigrated production category, the "woman's film" was one of Hollywood's "quality" products.

This discrepancy between the language of the trade and that used by critics demonstrates with particular poignancy the difficulties in establishing an appropriate generic terminology. Although it would be possible to argue that much genre criticism, like much auteur criticism, has avoided Hollywood's history rather than explained it, that criticism has nevertheless provided many important insights into Hollywood as a cultural institution. The critical classification of melodrama also provides a useful example of the way in which, since the 1960s, critical assumptions have had a bearing on how post-Classical Hollywood has understood itself. The term has largely dropped out of currency within the trade, which has come to accept the derogatory overtones that critics incorrectly argued it always possessed. When "melodrama" is used now to describe a movie like *The Prince of Tides* (1991), it implies something similar to its now established critical meaning, equating it with the woman's film.[79]

That point is central to the second reason for considering the case of melodrama. Because criticism has constructed histories for Hollywood – generic and authorial histories, for instance – that are in important respects different from Hollywood's economic history, it is at times necessary to consider these histories in tandem. It is not a simple matter of saying that one is right and the other wrong; histories are seldom that absolute. Feminist criticism of the 1970s and 1980s not surprisingly recognized Classical Hollywood cinema's endorsement of patriarchal values. But one of the strategies it developed to both analyze and resist that endorsement, the creation of the "woman's film" as a genre, addressed the endorsement of patriarchal values in existing criticism at least as much as it addressed that endorsement in the practices of Hollywood itself. It both contributed to and hindered the analysis of Hollywood's representation of women. The valuable work done as part of that strategy cannot be ignored, but the discrepancies between the history produced by that strategy and other histories of Hollywood must be noted. In his essay "Mass Culture as Woman: Modernism's Other," Andreas Huyssen explores the extent to which popular culture has been accorded pejorative feminine characteristics as a means of discrediting it from critical attention. From the start of the twentieth century, Huyssen argues, political, psychological, and aesthetic discourses have "consistently and obsessively" gendered "mass culture and the masses as feminine, while high culture, whether traditional or modern, clearly remains the privileged realm of male activities." The gender imbalance of genre analysis represents an attempt on the part of critics, almost exclusively white and male, to identify some aspects of popular culture as part of that "real, authentic culture" which the aesthetics of Modernism have seen as "the prerogative of men."[80] In this respect, critical practice has differed significantly from Hollywood's own bluntly commercial project. For however it may have represented women, Hollywood emphatically did not exclude them either from its movies or from the audience it sought to attract.

Recognizing these historical circumstances may allow criticism to explore the contradictions of Hollywood genres and its generic hybrids, rather than attempt to resolve those contradictions in the defense of an individual movie's internal coherence. When, in the early 1970s, critics first made the case for studying the domestic melodramas directed by Douglas Sirk, their arguments emphasized Sirk's subversive purposes in offering "a devastating indictment of the entire society's world view."[81] For once, a Hollywood director responded positively to the needs of critics to find ideologically acceptable hidden meanings. The posters for *Written on the Wind* (1956) had described it as the story of a Texas oil family's "ugly secret that thrust their private lives into public view!", but Sirk called it "a piece of social criticism, of the rich and the spoiled and of the American family." Declaring that "irony doesn't go down well with the American public,"[82] he compared the ironic happy endings of his movies to the plays of Euripides, written in Athens in the fifth century BC:

There, in Athens, you feel an audience that is just as happy-go-lucky as the American audience, an audience that doesn't want to know that they could fail. There's always an exit. So you have to paste on a happy end. . . . This is what I call the Euripidean manner. And at the end there is no solution of the antitheses, just the *deus ex machina*, which today is called the "happy end."[83]

Sirk's comments gave support to critical arguments that saw his movies as **Brechtian** critiques of both the society they depict and their own generic conventions. As Christine Gledhill has pointed out, however, these arguments required their proponents to patronize the movies' original audiences: "Irony and parody operate between two secure points: the position which we who perceive the irony occupy and that which, held at a distance, it critiques. The 'radical reading' of the 70s belonged to the critics, made at the expense of the naïve involvement of American 'popular' audiences in the 1950s."[84] These "readings" proposed that the distance between the movie's sentimental plot and its ironic style had not been visible to the original audience. In Paul Willemen's analysis, irony was a property of the movie as a text, and the problem of the audience was dealt with by suggesting that "there appears to be a discrepancy between the audience Sirk is aiming at and the audience which he knows will come to see his films."[85] The implications for a politics of gender in critical references to Sirk's "mastery" of the "woman's film" were even more bluntly revealed in Jean-Loup Bourget's assertion that "by systematically using the cliché-image he [Sirk] creates a distance not between the film and the audience (women ply their handkerchiefs at Sirk's films), but between the film and the director."[86]

Such criticism distinguished Sirk the subversive auteur from the genre he was working in by assuming the gullibility of the public, adopting a position that came dangerously close to the contempt for the mass audience to which Huyssen drew attention. Movies such as *All That Heaven Allows* or *Written on the Wind*, however, provoke a multiplicity of interpretations, often in contradiction to each other, and most movies can provoke complex interpretations for reasons other than their own internal complexity. A movie may articulate contradictions powerfully without resolving them: in *All That Heaven Allows*, Cary's emotional and sexual liberation is achieved only when she subordinates her own desires to Ron's; the movie ends with the couple reunited, but only after Ron has been badly injured so that Cary becomes his nursemaid, not his lover.[87] A movie may simply be powerfully inarticulate, expressing the dramatic or ideological conflict at its center not through dialog but in the form of spectacle, through decor, color, gesture, and composition, and through its ability to provoke an intense emotional response on the part of its audience. Or else a movie may derive its complexity from the number of contradictory viewpoints that it asks its audience to hold at the same time, something that generic hybrids do very frequently. Laura Mulvey has pointed out that ideological contradiction is "not a hidden, unconscious thread" in domestic melodrama, detectable only by special critical processes. Instead, contradiction is melodrama's "overt mainspring . . . the 1950s melodrama works by touching on sensitive areas of sexual repression and frustration," re-presenting contradic-

The ironic happy ending of *All That Heaven Allows* (1955). Cary (Jane Wyman) can care for Ron (Rock Hudson) as a nurse, not a lover.

Produced by Ross Hunter; distributed by Universal-International Pictures.

tions in an aesthetic form.[88] The women Bourget disparages may have gone to "weepies" like *All That Heaven Allows* not only to escape from reality but also to lament it.[89]

Situating a movie within the historical framework of its original reception can change the critic's perception of its relation to genre. Barbara Klinger has suggested that *Written on the Wind* and other domestic melodramas of the 1950s can be seen as part of a general industry trend toward more "adult" entertainment, "defined by a combination of sensationalistic and serious social subject matters."[90] In 1956 *Variety* suggested that along with blockbusters, "unusual, off-beat films with adult themes that television could not handle" allowed the industry to retain one section of its audience. The production of such "adult" movies was facilitated by revisions in the Production Code in the same year, permitting the treatment of drug addiction, abortion, and prostitution. Studios adapted novels and plays that already had "adult" profiles, and the cultural kudos of their original authors gave the movies prestige as well as notoriety. The "adult" movie category, which involved a combination of sensationalism, "adult" subject matter, and a style emphasizing excess and psychodrama, cut across conventional generic boundaries: Klinger suggests that in the mid-1950s it included not only adaptations of Tennessee Williams's plays like *Baby Doll* (1956), Nelson Algren's novel about drug addiction *The Man with the Golden Arm* (1955), or Grace Metalious's *Peyton Place* (1957), but also *The Searchers*, more conventionally seen as a pillar of the Western, but "adult" in its sensationalist treatment of the theme of miscegenation. Certainly *Written on the Wind* fits into this cycle very well. Studio pre-release publicity described the movie as "a searing adult drama that at one time might have been considered too explosive to handle. Today, however, it takes its place among important Hollywood products that have dared to treat unconventional themes in a sensitive, realistic fashion."[91] While contemporary reviewers disagreed as to its relative sensitivity or sensationalism, many of its press reviews concurred with the opinion that "This adult drama, a penetrating exploration of morals and Freudianism, of four people tossed into an emotional whirlpool by cross-relationships, a drama of vast dimension and delicacy, is further proof that Hollywood has really grown up."[92]

Genre criticism has provided an important counter-position to auteurism, and its intertextual approach provides one of the most useful points of access to Hollywood's commercial aesthetic. But genre criticism has often itself made ahistorical assumptions about its object of study. Looking at the ways in which a movie like *Written on the Wind* was situated for its potential audience complicates an analysis that requires that audience to be no more than "women plying their handkerchiefs," victimized by a text subverting generic conventions too cleverly for them to recognize. Instead, *WOW*, as it was often referred to in its publicity, can be placed within a matrix of alternative definitions, allowing its audiences and critics to interpret its complexities in a variety of generic contexts. The movie's visual appearance, the focus of many later critical claims for its subversiveness, was promoted as part of its spectacle on its first release. Articles publicizing the movie drew female spectators' attention to its decor as a source of inspiration for their own home decoration.[93] Barbara Klinger's historical examination of *Written on the Wind* helps to explain the way that generic conventions negotiate with and contradict each other across a single Hollywood movie. Such analysis may fragment a critically constructed genre such as "melodrama" into something much closer to the production industry's cycles, but it also extends our understanding of Hollywood as a generic cinema.

Summary

- Critics place movies in generic categories as a way of dividing up the map of Hollywood cinema into smaller, more manageable, and relatively discrete areas, while audiences and producers use generic terms more loosely and flexibly. But however defined, genres literally constitute only generalized categories whose boundaries cannot be rigidly delineated. Most movies use elements of various generic categories in combination. Hollywood is a generic cinema rather than a cinema of genres.
- Classifying movies by type is advantageous to producers in financial terms: genre movies are in a sense always "pre-sold." Audiences enjoy anticipating and recognizing familiar generic features.
- Generic consistency allows for the shorthand of convention and stereotype, but also for the interplay between confirmed expectation and novelty. In addition to being like other movies which have satisfied audiences in the past, a movie

also needs certain features that set it apart, and allow it to be promoted as "new."

- Genre criticism uses classifications different from those of the industry itself, derived in part from a tendency to regard some genres as an equivalent of folklore, and in part from a search for "progressive" or "subversive" categories. It provides an important counter-position to auteurism, and draws heavily on structuralist methods of analysis.

- A movie's iconography – its system of recurring visual motifs – provides a shorthand system for a knowledgeable viewer to glean a great deal of information about characters and situation. Early genre criticism concentrated on genres marked by their iconographic richness.

- The Western is usually seen as taking American history as its subject matter, and as an arena in which Americans examine the relationship between individual and society. The Western has declined as a genre, in part because of the extreme self-consciousness of revisionist versions of the genre's narratives, such as *Pat Garrett and Billy the Kid*, and in part because it has ceased to function fluently as a vehicle for American culture to tell itself the stories it needs to hear. Stories of civilization's conflict with savagery have migrated to other generic fields such as science fiction and horror movies.

- Genre criticism manifests an extreme gender imbalance: implicit in the preferences of much genre criticism is a valorization of patriarchal and masculine concerns. Certain genres, such as the modern gangster picture, have thus been accorded an increased cultural status, while others, most obviously romance and domestic drama, have been paid less critical attention.

- Melodrama is best understood not as a sentimental genre aimed primarily at a female audience, but as "the fundamental mode" of Classical Hollywood cinema. Action movies are as much melodramas as are stories of "feminine" pathos.

Further Reading

Ideas of genre

Initially proposed as an alternative to auteurism, the idea of genre has taken firm root in academic and popular discussions of Hollywood without the aid of a very sophisticated theoretical elaboration. Formative elaborations of the idea include Jim Kitses, *Horizons West: Anthony Mann, Budd Boetticher, Sam Peckinpah: Studies of Authorship within the Western* (London: Thames and Hudson, 1969); Colin MacArthur, *Underworld USA* (London: Secker and Warburg, 1972); John G. Cawelti, *The Six-Gun Mystique* (Bowling Green, KY: Bowling Green Popular University Press, 1970); Will Wright, *Sixguns and Society: A Structural Study of the Western* (Berkeley, CA: University of California

Press, 1975); and Thomas Schatz, *Hollywood Genres: Formulas, Filmmaking, and the Studio System* (New York: Random House, 1981). See also the essays collected in *Film Genre Reader*, ed. Barry Keith Grant (Austin: University of Texas Press, 1986).

Several publications in the late 1990s have revived debates around genre, interrogating the relationship between the critical concept and industry practice, and arguing for a fundamental reassessment of ideas of genre and the generic in Hollywood. While not all these works agree with the ideas expressed in this chapter, they share a common set of concerns: Steve Neale, *Genre and Hollywood* (London: Routledge, 2000); Rick Altman, *Film/Genre* (London: British Film Institute, 1999); Nick Browne, ed., *Refiguring American Film Genres: Theory and History* (Berkeley, CA: University of California Press, 1998); Christine Gledhill, "Rethinking Genre," in *Reinventing Film Studies*, eds Christine Gledhill and Linda Williams (London: Arnold, 2000).

Works on individual genres

Westerns

An almost unavoidable starting point is Robert Warshow's widely anthologized essay, "Movie Chronicle: The Westerner," in *Film Theory and Criticism*, eds Gerald Mast and Marshall Cohen, 3rd edn (New York: Oxford University Press, 1985), pp. 434–50. Richard Slotkin, *Gunfighter Nation: The Myth of the Frontier in Twentieth-Century America* (New York: Harper, 1992), provides a wide-ranging argument about the persistent relevance of the Western myth. Peter Stanfield, *Hollywood, Westerns and the 1930s: The Lost Trail* (Exeter: University of Exeter Press, 2001), offers a significant corrective to the dominant focus on the frontier. See also Edward Buscombe, ed., *The BFI Companion to the Western* (London: André Deutsch, 1988); Ian Cameron and Douglas Pye, eds, *The Movie Book of the Western* (London: Studio Vista, 1996); Jim Kitses and Gregg Rickman, eds, *The Western Reader* (New York: Limelight, 1998); and Edward Buscombe and Roberta E. Pearson, eds, *Back in the Saddle Again: New Essays on the Western* (London: British Film Institute, 1998).

On Peckinpah, see Stephen Prince, *Savage Cinema: Sam Peckinpah and the Rise of Ultraviolent Movies* (Austin: University of Texas Press, 1998); Bernard F. Dukore, *Sam Peckinpah's Feature Films* (Urbana: University of Illinois Press, 1999); Paul Seydor, *Peckinpah: The Western Films: A Reconsideration* (Urbana: University of Chicago Press, 1980); Michael Bliss, *Justified Lives: Morality and Narrative in the Films of Sam Peckinpah* (Carbondale: Southern Illinois University Press, 1993); and a biography, David Weddle, *Sam Peckinpah: "If They Move . . . Kill 'Em"* (London: Faber, 1996).

Women's films and melodrama

Christine Gledhill, ed., *Home Is Where the Heart Is: Studies in Melodrama and the Woman's Film* (London: British Film Institute, 1987), is a collection of influential essays on the relationship between melodrama and women's films. Some of the same material appears in Marcia Landy, ed., *Imitations of Life: A Reader on Film and Television Melodrama* (Detroit: Wayne State University Press, 1991). Both Jackie Byars, *All That Hollywood Allows: Re-Reading Gender in 1950s Melodrama* (Chapel Hill: University of North Carolina Press, 1991), and Barbara Klinger, *Melodrama and Meaning: History, Culture, and the Films of Douglas Sirk* (Bloomington: Indiana University Press, 1994), raise significant questions about the critical construction of melodrama as a genre. Linda Williams's essay, "Melodrama Revised," in *Refiguring American Film Genres*, argues that melodrama should be understood as the fundamental mode of the movies.

Crime movies and film noir

James Naremore, *More than Night: Film Noir in its Contexts* (Berkeley, CA: University of California Press, 1998), provides an excellent account of the critical origins and history of film noir, combined with insightful analysis of a range of movies. Two useful collections of writing on film noir are Joan Copjec, ed., *Shades of Noir* (London: Verso, 1993), and Ian Cameron, ed., *The Movie Book of Film Noir* (London: Studio Vista, 1992). See also Alain Silver and James Ursini, eds, *Film Noir Reader* and *Film Noir Reader 2* (New York: Limelight, 1996 and 1999).

On crime movies in general, see Philip Hardy, ed., *The BFI Companion to Crime* (London: Cassell, 1997), and Jonathan Munby, *Public Enemies, Public Heroes: Screening the Gangster from Little Caesar to Touch of Evil* (Chicago: University of Chicago Press, 1999).

Action-adventure movies

On recent action-adventure movies, see Peter Krämer, "Would You Take Your Child to See This Film? The Cultural and Social Work of the Family-Adventure Movie," in *Contemporary Hollywood Cinema*, eds Steve Neale and Murray Smith (London: Routledge, 1998); Yvonne Tasker, *Spectacular Bodies: Gender, Genre and the Action Cinema* (London: Routledge, 1993); Geoff King,

Spectacular Narratives: Hollywood in the Age of the Blockbuster (London: Tauris, 2000); and José Arroyo, ed., Action/Spectacle Cinema: A Sight and Sound Reader (London: British Film Institute, 2000).

Horror

David J. Skal, The Monster Show: A Cultural History of Horror (New York: Penguin, 1994), and Andrew Tudor, Monsters and Mad Scientists: A Cultural History of the Horror Movie (Oxford: Blackwell, 1989), provide historical accounts of the genre. See also Noël Carroll, The Philosophy of Horror, or Paradoxes of the Heart (London: Routledge, 1990); Jonathan Lake Crane, Terror and Everyday Life: Singular Moments in the History of the Horror Film (Thousand Oaks, CA: Sage, 1994); and Ken Gelder, ed., The Horror Reader (London: Routledge, 2000).

For feminist readings, see Carol J. Clover, Men, Women and Chainsaws: Gender in the Modern Horror Film (London: British Film Institute, 1992), and Rhona J. Berenstein, Attack of the Leading Ladies: Gender, Sexuality, and Spectatorship in Classic Horror Cinema (New York: Columbia University Press, 1996).

On post-Classical Hollywood horror, see William Paul, Laughing Screaming: Modern Hollywood Horror and Comedy (New York: Columbia University Press, 1994), and Gregory A. Waller, ed., American Horrors: Essays on the Modern American Horror Film (Urbana: University of Illinois Press, 1987).

Comedy

For an overview, see Andrew S. Horton, Comedy/Cinema/Theory (Berkeley, CA: University of California Press, 1991). For particular periods of Hollywood comedy, see Mark Winokur, American Laughter: Immigrants, Ethnicity, and 1930s Hollywood Film Comedy (London: Macmillan, 1996); Alan Dale, Comedy Is a Man in Trouble: Slapstick in American Movies (Minneapolis: University of Minnesota Press, 2000); Kristine Brunovska Karnick and Henry Jenkins, eds, Classical Hollywood Comedy (London: Routledge, 1995); Stanley Cavell, Pursuits of Happiness: The Hollywood Comedy of Remarriage (Cambridge, MA: Harvard University Press, 1981); and Ed Sikov, Laughing Hysterically: American Screen Comedy of the 1950s (New York: Columbia University Press, 1994).

Other genres

On musicals, see Rick Altman, The American Film Musical (Bloomington: Indiana University Press, 1987); Altman, ed., Genre: The Musical (London: Routledge and Kegan Paul, 1981); and Jane Feuer, The Hollywood Musical (London: British Film Institute, 1982). On science fiction, see Vivian Sobchack, Screening Space: The American Science Fiction Film (New York: Ungar, 1991). On road movies, see Steven Cohan and Ina Rae Hark, eds, The Road Movie Book (London: Routledge, 1997). On exploitation movies, see Eric Schaefer, "Bold! Daring! Shocking! True!": A History of Exploitation Films, 1919–1959 (Durham, NC: Duke University Press, 1999).

PART II
HISTORIES

CHAPTER FIVE
Industry 1:
To 1948

Industry

The modern industrial enterprise – the archetype of today's giant corporation – resulted from the integration of the processes of mass production with those of mass distribution within a single business firm. The first "big
businesses" in American history were those that united the types of distributing organization created by the mass marketer with the types of factory
organization developed to manage the new processes of mass production. . . . The visible hand of managerial direction had replaced the invisible hand of market forces in coordinating the flow of goods . . . a firm was
able to coordinate supply more closely with demand, to use its working
force and capital equipment more intensively, and thus to lower its unit
costs.

Alfred D. Chandler, Jr[1]

We sell tickets to theaters, not movies.
Marcus Loew[2]

Hollywood's commercial aesthetic recognizes that to make money, you have to
spend money, and that the reputation of a movie is enhanced by the conspicuous
display of its production budget. Movies now advertise their budgets and box-
office receipts as part of their general appeal, but the spectacle of "putting money
on the screen" has always preoccupied Hollywood producers. Despite the indus-

try's often apparently cavalier attitude to spending, it is in fact as constrained as any other business by the need to save time and money, to reduce unnecessary excess and risk, and to stabilize and regulate the flow of production. From the 1920s to the 1950s, the studio system was a way of organizing production to suit these economic preconditions, and the stability of that system generated the familiar style, the immediately recognizable patterns of camera movement, editing, narrative, and genre, that identify a Hollywood movie. As a description of the American film industry's organization, the "studio system" is, however, something of a misnomer, in that it overemphasizes the role of production in the economics of the industry as a whole. What characterized the functioning of the motion picture industry during the period of the studio system was not the existence of the studios as production centers, but the dominance of the major companies as distributor-exhibitors.

Distribution and Exhibition

In 1939, "Hollywood's greatest year," 33,687 people were employed in movie production. But the industry as a whole employed 177,420 people. For every actor, writer, electrician, or carpenter working in Los Angeles, there were five distribution company salespeople, theater managers, projectionists, ushers, and box-office clerks staffing the 15,000 cinemas in the United States.[3] The industry often claimed to be the fourth largest in America, a claim based on the total amount of capital invested in it. In 1940 this investment exceeded $2 billion, more than was invested in automobile production or the chemical industry. But 94 percent of this investment was in the real estate of movie theaters, and only 5 percent in the plant and facilities used in production. The industry's major concern was the successful commercial management of this real estate, turning a better profit than could be produced by putting the buildings to some other commercial use. During the 1930s, when on average Americans went to the movies once every two weeks, movie theaters took in two-thirds of all the money spent in places of entertainment. By other measures of economic size, however, the industry was nowhere near as prominent as it claimed; smaller, in terms of its total sales, than hotels, restaurants, or the liquor or tobacco industries. As Douglas Gomery has suggested, "despite all the glamour and hype, the movie industry could never be considered more than a moderately successful industry, one affected by the usual booms and busts of twentieth-century US capitalism."[4] Even this cautious assessment may actually overrate its success: at the end of the silent period the average return for capital invested in the industry was estimated to be as low as 2 percent.[5] Technical advances like sound, or the absence of alternative choices for expenditure during World War II, produced short-term windfall profits, but the cost of the industry's real estate kept its overall long-term profitability quite low.

On the other hand, the value of its real estate holdings provided the industry with a good deal of economic stability, and attached it closely to the banking system. When the major companies expanded in the 1920s, building new studios

Box 5.1 Movie theaters in the United States

After rising to a peak of over 23,000 in 1929, the number of theaters fell sharply during the Depression, but recovered during the World War II boom in attendance. The steady closure of "four-wall" theaters in the postwar years was compensated by the spread of drive-in theaters catering to the teenage and young adult audience. In the 1970s, increasing numbers of theaters housed multiple screens, showing two or more movies to different (and smaller) audiences in the same building, which was most likely to be in a shopping mall. The growth of multiplexes, with between 8 and 15 screens, and megaplexes with 16 or more screens, has doubled the number of screens since 1980, but the number of buildings in which movies are shown has continued to shrink as each theater complex grows larger.[6]

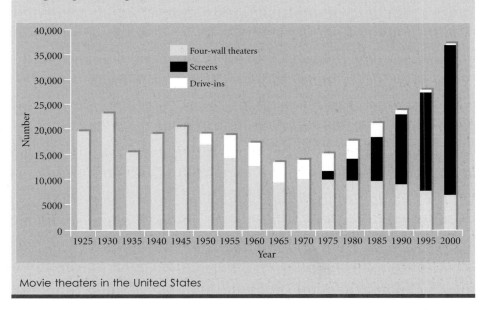

Movie theaters in the United States

and picture palaces, these developments were financed on Wall Street, where brokers and bankers looked to reap what one company called "the Golden Harvest of the Silver Screen."[7] The major companies' enormous purchases of real estate made them both attractive and secure investments in the boom market of the late 1920s. When the Depression demonstrated that the industry had expanded too far too quickly, the Wall Street firms that had financed this expansion recalled their loans and effectively secured control over the major companies. This change in ultimate ownership, however, produced no dramatic shift in industry policy or behavior, and this fact in itself suggests that, however much Hollywood's publicity claimed that no business was like the "show business," in practice the American film industry was an industry much like others, developing similar organizational structures for similar aims.

Box 5.2 Distribution and exhibition in the United States, 1945

In 1945, the 19,013 theaters in the US had approximately 11 million seats between them. The major companies owned 22 percent of the country's seating capacity, almost entirely in theaters seating over 1,000 spectators, showing the most recent movies at the highest prices. At the other end of the market, over half the theaters in the country had fewer than 500 seats, and the great majority of these theaters were independently owned and operated.

In 1941 the Motion Picture Producers and Distributors of America, Inc. (MPPDA), estimated that 8,488 towns in the US had motion picture theaters. There were a total of 450 first-run theaters in the 95 cities with populations of over 100,000. Seventy percent of theaters were in towns of under 50,000 population, but seating capacity and exhibition revenue was concentrated in the urban centers. There was one seat for every 12.5 members of the US population in 1941.[9]

Population of town	Towns with theaters	No. of theaters	No. of seats	Average seats per theater
Over 500,000	14	2,301	2,374,108	1,031
200,000–500,000	29	1,099	962,770	877
100,000–200,000	49	743	685,674	923
50,000–100,000	107	898	808,872	901
20,000–50,000	304	1,278	1,072,839	841
10,000–20,000	550	1,405	991,773	706
5,000–10,000	937	1,715	1,016,366	593
2,500–5,000	1,398	1,967	924,676	470
1,000–2,500	2,736	3,075	1,021,051	332
Under 1,000	2,364	2,470	613,713	248
Total	8,488	16,951	10,451,442	617

There were 31 distribution centers in the United States, located at:

Albany	Detroit	Omaha
Atlanta	Indianapolis	Philadelphia
Boston	Kansas City	Pittsburgh
Buffalo	Los Angeles	Portland
Charlotte	Memphis	St Louis
Chicago	Milwaukee	Salt Lake City
Cincinnati	Minneapolis	San Francisco
Cleveland	New Haven	Seattle
Dallas	New Orleans	Washington
Denver	New York	
Des Moines	Oklahoma City	

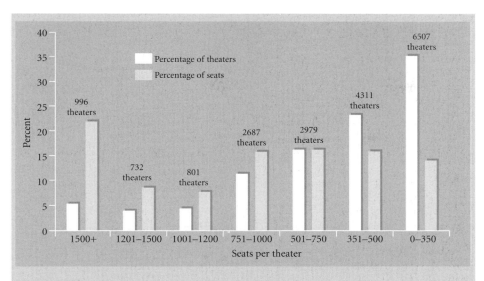

Theaters in the US, 1945[10]

Source: Douglas Gomery, *The Hollywood Studio System* (London: Macmillan, 1986), p. 13.

State	No. of theaters	Total seats	Average capacity	Admissions (millions)	Admissions ($m)
New York	1,241	1,249,898	1,008	430.75	193.40
Texas	1,224	683,960	559	188.82	Not available
Pennsylvania	1,134	844,198	774	260.26	89.11
California	1,060	892,116	842	246.63	114.73
Illinois	903	686,193	760	212.95	83.80

The four states of New York, California, Pennsylvania, and Illinois contained 25 percent of the nation's movie theaters, but took in 39 percent of all exhibition revenues. New York was by far the largest single exhibition market. Texas had nearly as many theaters, but most of them served much smaller populations and had far fewer seats on average.[11]

Before Hollywood had been established as a production center, the most powerful American motion picture interests sought to combine, in order to monopolize the industry and determine its profitability. The first attempt at such a combination was the Motion Picture Patents Company, established in 1908. It failed because it tried to dominate the industry by controlling the production of movies but, as was already clear by 1915, the other two branches of the industry, **distribution** and **exhibition**, provided more effective ways of dominating the industry as a whole. Until 1903, film manufacturers sold prints outright to exhibitors, which meant that each exhibitor owned a small collection of prints that he might use until they were physically worn out. While this arrangement worked well enough for traveling exhibitors putting on tent shows or playing the vaudeville circuits, permanent movie theaters needed a more elaborate system of film distribution. The creation of film exchanges, where an exhibitor could rent pictures rather than buy them, made possible the development of dedicated motion picture theaters. The first "nickel-Odeons" were often no more than converted stores or saloons charging five cents to enter – hence the name. By 1910, however, exhibitors had begun to construct increasingly grandiose, purpose-built theaters to accommodate the demands of middle-class audiences for better facilities, and from then on, in the words of one entrepreneur, "theaters replaced shooting galleries, temples replaced theaters, and cathedrals replaced temples."[8]

During the 1910s, companies also began to integrate the mass production of movies in purpose-built studios in Los Angeles with systems of mass distribution, the first stage in the evolution of **vertical integration** within the industry. A vertically integrated company is involved in all three branches of its business: manufacture, wholesaling, and retailing. A vertically integrated food company, for instance, owns the plantations where its crops are grown, the canning factories where they are processed, the trucks that deliver the cans, and the grocery stores in which they are sold. The involvement in all branches of an industry obviously gives the vertically integrated company a much greater degree of control over its terms of trade than a company involved in only one branch of the business can exercise. A small number of vertically integrated companies, all pursuing the same business strategies, can between them dominate an industry. The history of American business since the beginning of the twentieth century has been predominantly a history of the growth of vertically integrated corporations, and with it the growth of **oligopoly** control: monopoly power exercised by a small group of individual companies.

This pattern emerged in the motion picture industry in the years immediately after World War I, when the largest producer-distributor, Adolph Zukor's Famous Players-Lasky, developed a theater chain. In retaliation First National Pictures, the largest exhibition consortium, began producing movies. During the 1920s a series of mergers produced three, then four, vertically integrated companies which dominated the industry: Paramount, which included Famous Players; Warner Bros., which expanded greatly in the late 1920s and took over First National; Loews, Inc., the parent company of MGM; Fox, which became Twentieth Century-Fox in 1935. By the late 1920s the scale of investment required meant that only the largest of concerns could contemplate setting up a vertically integrated company to compete with these four. The Radio Corporation of America (RCA), the dominant presence in the radio industry, succeeded in doing so in 1928 when RKO (Radio-Keith-Orpheum) was created out of the amalgamation of a number of smaller distribution and exhibition organizations. Even so, RKO was always the smallest and least profitable of the majors, and the only one to go permanently out of business, when Howard Hughes stripped its assets in 1955. Although the other four companies have all been taken over or merged with other concerns, they have remained dominant forces within the industry. From the late 1920s to the mid-1950s, however, the "Big Five," as they were known, dominated the

Box 5.3 The costs of running a movie theater

The California Theater was a large, second-run neighborhood theater, seating around 800 patrons, and changing its program at least twice a week. The high cost of theater orchestras was one of the principal incentives behind the introduction of sound.[12]

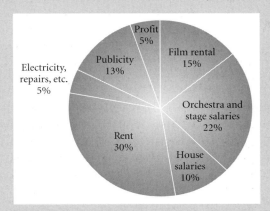

The California Theater, 1927

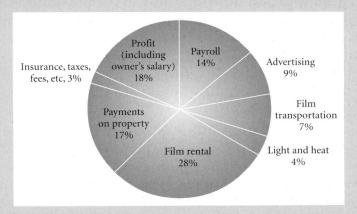

The Star Theater, early 1930s

The Star Theater was the only theater in Milford, Michigan, 40 miles from Detroit. It had 250 seats, and showed mainly late-run "specials" and program pictures to its small-town and farming audience, who paid 25 cents admission. In the early 1930s the Star Theater's total weekly expenses were $144, and its average weekly income was $175, giving its owner-manager-janitor $31 per week.

Although the California Theater paid far more to rent its movies than the Star's $50 per week, film rental comprised only 15 percent of its budget, half the share at the lower-run theater.[13]

Interior of a picture palace.
Courtesy BFI.

industry not through their control of production but through their ownership of the most desirable and profitable movie theaters. Between them they owned no more than 15 percent of the theaters in the United States, but that included almost all the large metropolitan theaters, which charged the highest admission prices and took in almost 70 percent of the total American box-office income.

The picture palaces of the 1920s were perhaps the movie industry's most conspicuous sites of excess, where the display in the auditorium rivaled the display on the screen. The pastiche ornamental styles of these theaters were accumulated from a jumble of earlier cultures, but their opulence had its own economic rationale and they were highly profitable business operations. Hollywood's extravagance was as democratic as it was vulgar: the inventive grandeur of the picture palaces proclaimed their availability to anyone who had the price of admission. Run according to the same commercial strategies as the rapidly expanding chain store business, they offered the clerks and shopgirls of American cities luxury at prices they could afford. William Fox declared the motion picture to be "a distinctly American institution" because "movies breathe the spirit in which the country was founded, freedom and equality." One group of Americans was, however, excluded. The rich might rub elbows with the poor in a theater, but African-Americans were at best seated in a segregated section, usually the balcony. In many Southern states the theaters themselves were legally segregated as late as the 1960s, and throughout the country, black audiences were largely restricted to their own neighborhood theaters, the vast majority of which were owned by white businessmen.

Only in the largest American cities did the Big Five directly compete with each other for theater audiences; elsewhere, because they owned theaters in different parts of the country from each other, their theaters normally exhibited movies made by other companies as well as their own. Metro-Goldwyn-Mayer's (MGM) parent company Loew's, Inc. made money in its theaters by showing the best product of Paramount, Warner Bros., and RKO as well as MGM, and thus benefited from the success of its offspring's rivals. Whichever studio actually produced a hit movie, it would be profitable for all the vertically integrated companies. The Big Five's economic power came from their theaters, and a movie denied access to these theaters was unlikely to make a profit. Three other companies – Columbia, Universal, and United Artists, known as the "Little Three" – owned no theaters, but were involved in production and distribution on a slightly smaller scale than that of the Big Five. As Harry Cohn explained in chapter 2, the majority of the movies produced by Columbia and Universal were mid- or low-budget features. United Artists was formed in 1919 by Douglas Fairbanks, Charlie Chaplin, D.W. Griffith, and Mary Pickford to distribute their own movies and later those of other independent producers such as Samuel Goldwyn. Most independent production, however, was undertaken by the "Poverty Row" companies such as Republic, Monogram, and Tiffany, which met the demand for B-feature product to fill the bottom half of a movie theater's double bill. In the 1930s most theaters changed their program twice a week or more, and outside city centers the main feature was presented as part of a package that might also contain a newsreel, a cartoon or travelog, a B-feature, a game of Screeno, trailers for forthcoming attractions, popcorn, and ice cream. This stable packaging meant that it was perfectly possible to have a good night out at the movies without liking the main feature.

The Big Five and the Little Three came to be known as the "majors," and they operated together as an effective cartel controlling the industry. At the height of the studio system in the 1930s and 1940s, Los Angeles-based companies accounted for 90 percent of all American film production, and for 60 percent of all world film production. Although Poverty Row companies made between 100 and 200 movies a year, the majority of Hollywood's production was undertaken by the eight majors. Between them, the majors took in 95 percent of all monies paid by exhibitors for film rental in the United States. As distributors, the majors determined which movies were shown in which theaters. They classified every movie theater in America and allotted them different positions in a system, known as **"clearance,"** that determined the order in which theaters in the same area or **"zone"** could show a picture. The normal pattern of release was for a movie to open at first-run houses in New York or Los Angeles, and shortly thereafter in

Box 5.4   The balanced program

Although film studies has concentrated almost exclusively on the feature movie, Classical Hollywood produced a much wider range of product, and audiences spent nearly as much of their time watching other types of pictures as they spent watching the main feature. The mixture of items on a program displayed a reminder of cinema's exhibition origins in vaudeville. A typical early 1930s neighborhood theater bill might look like this:

Item	Minutes
Fox Movietone Newsreel	8
Cartoon	7
Live musical interlude on organ	5
Comedy short	10
Universal Newspaper newsreel	8
Feature presentation	70–90
Comedy short	10
Trailers	10

The program was continuous, and newspaper advertisements seldom displayed the feature's starting times. As one usher complained in 1934, "The majority of the patrons do not desire to be in the theater on the starting times, but seem to come in during the program."[14]

As well as features, the major studios produced short subjects, one- or two-reel movies lasting between 5 and 25 minutes. The most popular shorts – and the most readily available today – were animated cartoons, but short subjects also regularly featured travelogs, vaudeville, music or dance performances, personality portraits, fashion parades, and comedies. During the 1931–2 production season, for example, MGM produced 46 two-reel comedies, including eight featuring Stanley Laurel and Oliver Hardy and eight in the *Our Gang* series. Travelogs, cartoons, and sports pictures brought the studio's total short subject output to 93 items, in addition to 104 issues of the Hearst Movietone newsreel. The exhibition practice of double-billing two features, which began in the Depression, reduced the demand for short subjects while increasing the demand for programmers – movies that could play on either half of a double-bill – and B-features. Saturday afternoon children's matinee programs combined a program of short subjects, including adventure serials, with a B movie, usually a Western. By the end of the 1930s the largest cities had specialized theaters screening only newsreels.

other metropolitan areas such as Chicago and Boston. After that it would be released to second-run cinemas, then third-run, and so on down the scale until it eventually reached the neighborhood theaters in America's small towns and rural areas several months after its premiere. Later-run theaters charged lower admission prices, but the distributor's advertising campaigns were designed to encourage audiences to consume movies as soon after their initial release as possible, while they were still "new." This maximized the distribution company's income by encouraging patrons to pay the highest prices to see a movie at a first-run house, which was in any case most likely to be owned by one of the Big Five.

Box 5.5 The clearance system

Zone

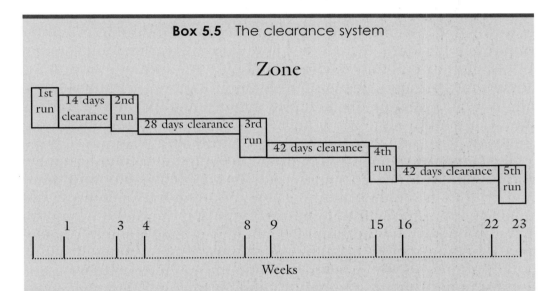

The exhibition release pattern of a Classical Hollywood movie in the United States ran like clockwork, according to a timetable determined by the clearance system. The major distributors divided the country into 30 territories, with each territory subdivided into up to a dozen zones. Within each zone, every theater was designated according to the order in which it would be given access to a movie. The movie would first play in the downtown movie theaters, which were most likely to be owned by the major companies themselves. These first-run theaters charged premium ticket prices for showing the most recent movies in the most opulent surroundings. After the movie had played at the first-run houses, there would then be a period of "clearance" in the zone before it would open in second-run theaters. These were likely to be in neighborhood business districts, and charged lower ticket prices. Later-run theaters were located farther out from the population center of the zone. Although an A-feature earned over three-quarters of its box-office income in first- and second-run exhibition, it would still be playing the later-run theaters in some zones a year after its initial release.

In addition to this system of clearance, the majors also imposed a practice known as **block-booking** on smaller exhibitors. Under this arrangement, theaters were not permitted to hire individual movies, but had to accept them in blocks, sometimes as large as 50, but more commonly in packages of five or six. A block of this size might attach several lower-budget movies with less popular stars to an expensive production. The system worked in the distributor's interest by ensuring a wider distribution for lower-budget movies and preventing independent exhibitors from buying only the most successful product. Distributors argued that block-booking also benefited exhibitors by minimizing sales costs, so that it was still sufficiently profitable for the distributor to bother doing business with the smallest exhibitors.

As the domineering behavior of the distributors indicated, the central structuring tension within the industry did not lie in the competition between the major companies. Rather, it was in the incessant disputation between the powerful, ver-

Box 5.6   Weekly attendance in the United States

As a social practice, going to the movies reached its peak in the late 1920s, just prior to the Wall Street Crash, and then again at the end of World War II, when audience levels had recovered from their fall during the Depression of the 1930s. Attendance fell steadily in the postwar period until 1965, when it stabilized at about a quarter of its wartime peak. Since 1985, attendance has climbed by 35 percent.

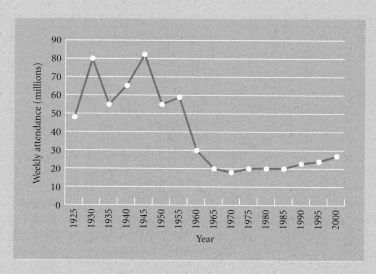

Weekly attendance in the United States

tically integrated corporations and the large number of small, independent, or "unaffiliated" exhibitors, the 10,000 "Mom and Pop" theaters seating under 500 patrons and changing their programs at least three times a week. Although these outlets were of relatively minor economic importance to the majors, renting movies for as little as $7 a booking and totaling under 20 percent of the majors' distribution income, they were centrally important to the industry's presentation of the motion picture as a universal mass entertainment. Because almost every American lived within easy traveling distance of at least one movie theater, the industry felt able to justify its claim that movies were not a luxury item for their consumers but "a great social necessity, an integral part of human life in the whole civilized world."[15] During World War II, the government acknowledged this argument by granting movies the status of an "essential industry," facilitating access to rationed goods and exemptions from military service for industry personnel. At other times, the industry used the same argument in resisting attempts to impose additional taxes on it.

Although it is best known for its administration of self-censorship, the industry's trade association, the **MPPDA**, was established in 1922 to prevent government interference in the operations of the major companies, and the most important part of its work involved safeguarding their political interests by countering attempts to impose a strict application of the US anti-trust laws to the industry. According to its by-laws, the association was created "to foster the common interests of those engaged in the motion picture industry in the United States."[16] In practice, its restricted membership was dominated by the major companies, and it operated as an instrument of cartelization, by which the majors' non-competitive pricing and distribution policies were justified as "business self-regulation." Although the majors often operated in collusion, their relationship during the studio era has been aptly described by Douglas Gomery as being "like a chronically quarrelsome but closely knit family."[17] Will Hays, president of the MPPDA from 1922 to 1945, often arbitrated on these disputes and, as importantly, acted to ameliorate the majors' worst excesses in dictating terms to independent exhibitors.

Like the small exhibitors, few of Hollywood's workers were likely to have felt part of a family. Labor relations in the production industry were notoriously poor, the result of the studios' reliance on a casual workforce in a city infamous for its hostility to trade unions. The Academy of Motion Picture Arts and Sciences had its origins in an attempt to establish company unions in the late 1920s. Studio managements put up a vigorous and often violent resistance to unionization in Hollywood in the 1930s and 1940s, exploiting jurisdictional disputes and accusations of Communist influence among unions. For a period in the late 1930s, studios paid extortion money to the corrupt Hollywood leadership of the International Alliance of Theatrical and Stage Employees (IATSE) to secure a subdued and strike-free labor force. From March to October 1945, 10,500 studio craft workers in the Conference of Studio Unions (CSU) went on a prolonged and bitter strike which ended only after fierce picket-line battles at Warner Bros. and Paramount studios. The unresolved dispute flared again in September 1946 when CSU workers were locked out of the studios, with more violence on picket lines, mass arrests, and the eventual defeat of the CSU. These labor disputes were a precursor to the House Un-American Activities Committee's investigations into "Communist influence in the motion picture industry." Labor unions were a principal target of those investigations and the blacklisting of industry workers that followed. In the late 1940s IATSE's Hollywood representative, Roy Brewer, was a leading figure in the anti-Communist "cleansing" of the industry. Brewer subsequently became a production executive, and IATSE has dominated Hollywood labor since 1950.[18]

Exporting America

If the United States abolished its diplomatic and consular services, kept its ships in harbor and its tourists at home, and retired from the world's markets, its citizens, its problems, its towns and countryside, its roads, motor cars, counting houses and saloons would still be familiar in the uttermost corners of the world . . . The film is to America what the flag was once to Britain. By its means Uncle Sam may hope some day, if he is not checked in time, to Americanize the world.

New York Morning Post, 1923[19]

Hollywood was an international industry, not just an American one. It achieved its domination of the world's movie screens during World War I, and consolidated its hold during the 1920s with the aggressive marketing of a product that seemed to have universal appeal.[20] By the late 1920s, American movies occupied as much as 80 percent of the screen time in those countries that had not established quotas on American imports to protect their own film production industries. The foreign market brought the American film industry approximately 35 percent of its total income in the late 1920s and 1930s, of which nearly two-thirds came from Europe.[21] The scale of the American domestic market, which had about half the world's cinemas, provided the major companies with a bedrock of economic security: they expected a movie at least to break even on its exhibition in the United States and Canada, and so they could look on foreign earnings as clear profit. As a result, American companies could sell their movies to exhibitors in Britain or Argentina at lower prices than domestic producers could afford, while the American market was also effectively closed to non-American product. For a German or French exhibitor, Hollywood's economic miracle was that it spent much more on the movies it made than domestic producers could, but sold them much cheaper, so that even in their own domestic market, European, Australian, or Latin American film producers did not compete on equal terms with Hollywood. This sales strategy was part of a deliberate American policy of weakening the international competition. A more visible aspect of the same policy was Hollywood's enthusiasm for luring European directors and stars to work in Los Angeles.

Hollywood's production values, encapsulated in the million-dollar movie you could watch for a few pennies or centavos or lei, projected a powerful image of American material abundance. Trade no longer followed the flag, argued Will Hays in the 1920s. Instead, "trade follows the film."[22] Movies, declared one of his officials, were "demonstrably the greatest single factor in the Americaniza- tion of the world and as such fairly may be called the most important and signif- icant of America's exported products."[23] An analyst at the State Department confirmed this sentiment when he commented in 1926 that "the peoples of many countries now consider America as the arbiter of manners, fashion, sports customs and standards of living."[24] The moviegoing habit was a familiar, domestic ritual around the world. American movies and their stars were a significant part of mil- lions of non-American people's daily experience and personal identity. Holly- wood's influence was literally domesticated in the 1930s, for example, when British working-class parents named their children Shirley, Marlene, Norma, or Gary.[25] European nationalists feared that the movies were bringing about what one British politician called "the annexation of this country by the United States of America."[26]

In the postwar period, the foreign market became an even more important source of income to Hollywood. By the early 1960s foreign sales generated about half of the majors' revenues, and, with minor fluctuations, the division between domestic and foreign income has remained roughly equal ever since.[27] With the foreign market so important a part of the industry's income, an "international" element in Hollywood's production became even more attractive than it had been before the war, but instead of bringing European stars to Hollywood, American production migrated abroad. The attractions of this policy included not only exotic locations and European co-stars, but also lower labor costs and subsidies from European government legislation designed to protect domestic production industries from American competition. With the aid of the Motion Picture Export Association, as the Foreign Department of the MPPDA became in 1945, American companies became adept at maneuvering around this legisla- tion by having their movies produced by subsidiary organizations classified as "British," "Italian," or "German." **Runaway production**, as this practice was known, reached its height during the late 1960s, when nearly half the features made by American companies were produced abroad. Thereafter, rising foreign wage rates and the devaluation of the dollar reduced the attraction of overseas production, but the influence of the foreign exhibition market continued to be felt.[28] Since the 1930s, sales departments had told producers that action-oriented movies did better business abroad, particularly in non-English-speaking markets, than "walk and talk" pictures, as movies reliant on dialog to develop their story were known.[29] For essentially unchanged reasons, the overseas market has been particularly important to the profitability of the movies of Sylvester Stal- lone and Arnold Schwarzenegger. More than any other star, Schwarzenegger per- sonified Hollywood's orientation toward a global market in the 1990s. Nicholas Kent called him "a walking, talking brand-name" who, unlike Stallone, success- fully diversified his appeal by making comedies as well as action-adventure movies.[30]

Box 5.7 Features released by the majors

The eight major companies each produced about one movie a week during the 1930s, but the volume of feature production dropped dramatically during World War II as average budgets doubled. Numbers continued to drop steadily until 1975, when they leveled off at about 100 per year. The video boom has seen a steady expansion in both numbers and average budgets since 1985.[31]

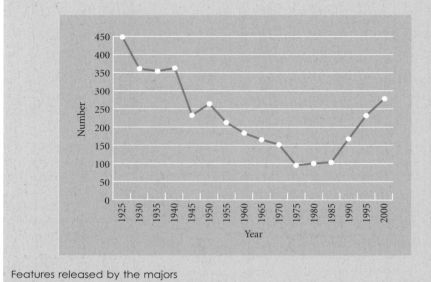

Features released by the majors

Divorcement

Although 1946 was Hollywood's most successful year at the box-office, the industry went into a precipitate decline over the next ten years. In 1953, only half as many people in the US were going to the movies as had gone seven years earlier. The primary cause of this industry recession was, perversely, the prosperity of the postwar American economy that produced the migration to the suburbs and the baby boom. At the same time, the industry underwent drastic structural changes in its organization. In 1948, the US Supreme Court finally ruled that the majors' control of distribution and first-run exhibition constituted an illegal monopoly, and ordered the separation of exhibition from production-distribution. This decision (known as the **Paramount case** decision) signaled the end of the "studio system" of production, and with it the beginning of the end of the Classical Hollywood cinema. It was not, of course, the end of Hollywood, but the Supreme Court's decision undercut the economies of scale that provided the ratio-

Box 5.8 Production cost of the average feature

The costs of production have risen steadily, but when adjusted for inflation, they reveal a different picture. The largest jump in production costs occurred during World War II, and, as the graphs here and in box 5.7 show, it coincided with a sharp fall in the number of movies produced by the major companies. A similar amount of money was spent on production, but it was spent on the production of fewer movies. In the second half of the 1980s, the average Hollywood budget rose by **40** percent, reflecting the increase in the size of the overall world market brought about by the development of video as an additional system of release. During the 1990s, it rose by a further 55 percent.[33]

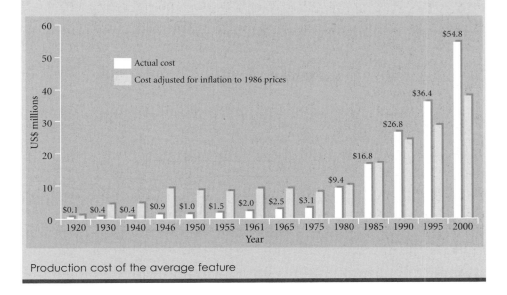

Production cost of the average feature

nale for the system of production Harry Cohn described so vividly in chapter 2. **Divorcement**, as the separation of exhibition was known, meant that the producers and distributors were no longer guaranteed a market for all their products, but had instead to sell each movie on its individual merits. In an entertainment market that was also shrinking because of the growth of television, producers concentrated on a smaller number of productions designed to play for long spells at early-run theaters. By 1959 the majors were producing fewer than 200 movies a year, compared with nearly 300 a decade earlier.[32] In the early 1950s, the major companies reorganized their operations, concentrating their market power in their distribution activities.

The studios cut their permanent payrolls, and came to operate increasingly as providers of facilities for independent production companies constructed around an individual writer, director, or star. The enormous growth of television from the mid-1950s is often erroneously cited as the cause of the decline of the studio system. In fact, television in many respects perpetuated a studio system of production. Although the Paramount decision effectively prevented the majors moving into television broadcasting, by the mid-1950s the studios had entered television production and rapidly colonized it. They moved the center of television production from New York to Los Angeles, and established stock companies to produce television serials like *Father Knows Best* (1954–9) and *Gunsmoke* (1955–75). By 1963, 70 percent of American prime-time television programming was coming from Hollywood, and the major companies were earning 30 percent of their revenues from telefilm production.[34] The made-for-TV movie in the mid-1960s was a commercially logical development, but it began to confuse the boundaries between different kinds of Hollywood production, just as watching movies on television had already begun to confuse boundaries around the consumption of Hollywood.

The Studio System

God has always smiled on Southern California; a special halo has always encircled this island on the land. Consider, for example, the extraordinary good luck in having the motion-picture industry concentrated in Los Angeles. The leading industry in Los Angeles from 1920 to 1940, motion pictures were made to fit the economic requirements and physical limitations of the region like a glove. Here was one industry, perhaps the only one in America, that required no raw materials, for which discriminatory freight rates were meaningless, and which, at the same time, possessed an enormous pay-roll. Employing from thirty to forty thousand workers, the industry in 1939 spent about $190,000,000 in the manufacture of films and of this total $89,884,841 was spent in salaries, $41,096,226, wages, and only $31,118,277 was spent on such items as film, fuel and energy, and miscellaneous items . . . . Like the region itself, this key industry is premised upon improvisation, a matter of make-believe, a synthesis of air and wind and water . . . . What could be more desirable than a monopolistic non-seasonal industry with 50,000,000 customers, an industry without soot or grime, without blast furnaces or dynamos, an industry whose production shows peaks but few valleys?

Carey McWilliams[36]

In marked contrast to the central position that movie production is accorded in popular memory and critical studies alike, an economic analysis downgrades it to a subsidiary role in the American motion picture industry. That analysis explains the way that production was organized into the studio system. For a major company, committed to the distribution of a full range of product, the studio system was economically the most rational way to provide the regulated stability of production and the economies of scale required by any major manufacturing operation – the means by which Harry Cohn could spit a movie out onto Gower Street every week. Despite this level of regulation, one of the motion picture industry's favorite myths about itself is that it is always in crisis. Leo Rosten observed in 1941 that:

> There are few places in our economy where fluctuations in earnings and security can be as violent and unpredictable as they are in Hollywood. . . . "You're only as good as your last picture" is a by-word in the movie colony . . . This is scarcely a climate conducive to psychological serenity or efficient digestion. . . . The movie colony gets a curious satisfaction out of drumming these facts home – to itself.[37]

In part this melodramatic view of Hollywood production as a quixotic and unstable business resulted from thinking only about individual productions, individual careers, and the amount that needed to be invested in each movie without any guarantee that it would produce a commensurate return. Compared with other industries, the motion picture business turned out few products, even in the studio period. The individual Hollywood product was extremely expensive, and carried a much larger share of the company's financial well-being than, say, an individual automobile did for General Motors. Moreover, the success or failure of these products was firmly attached to the popularity of individual personalities. As the number of movies being made fell after 1960, the sense of risk attached to each production, and each production decision, increased.

This vision of the riskiness of film production is substantially mitigated if the concerns of the industry as a whole are taken into account. Under the studio system, Hollywood sustained a level of production sufficient to supply the level of demand in the existing market, but to some extent the executives who ran the major companies from New York regarded production as an inconvenient necessity, at best only marginally profitable. It has been suggested that the studio system was, for most of its life, never truly economically efficient, since it encouraged overproduction, so that too many feature films were produced to earn to their maximum potential.[38] It was expected that nine Hollywood-produced movies out of ten would turn a profit, but only a small one, while the larger profits were gathered in distribution and first-run exhibition. Although primarily designed to maximize the profitability of the whole industry, the studio system ensured that production itself was a very high-cost activity, not simply because "money on the screen" was assumed to be a necessary part of the entertainment package, but also because the high costs and the general impression of instability and crisis deterred any potential competitors. According to business historian Alfred Chandler, the tactic of internalizing transactions between production and distribution divisions within a single business entity was an inherent feature of the "modern business enterprise": "Such administrative coordination in turn created formidable barriers to entry. High-volume throughput and stock-turnover reduced unit costs. Advertising and the provision of service maintained customer loyalty. Rival firms were rarely able to compete until they had built comparable marketing organizations of their own."[39]

Economic historians investigating Classical Hollywood's production and distribution practices argue that contrary to Hollywood's mythology, the industry was run by rational economic agents making commercial decisions according to rec-

> **Box 5.9** Production categories of the major companies, 1939: by budget
>
> ### A-features
>
> *Superspecials*
> - Budget $1m +
> - Prestige pictures or big-budget musicals
> - Top stars
> - Expensive production values
> - Up to 2.5 hours' running time
> - Roadshow exhibition
>
> *Specials*
> - The bulk of the class-A line
> - Pre-sold properties
> - Popular stars
> - Following main production trends
> - Regular running times
> - Budget $200,000–500,000
> - "Grind" or continuous performance exhibition
>
> *Programmers*
> - Could play either half of a double bill
> - Lowest budgets of class-A production
> - Original stories
> - Minor stars
> - Running times as low as 50 minutes
>
> *B features*
> - Fifty percent or more of major studios' output after 1934
> - Budget $50,000–100,000
> - No stars
> - Rented to exhibitors on a flat fee, not percentage
> - Also produced by Poverty Row studios – up to 300 per year

ognizable business criteria. John Sedgwick and Michael Pokorny suggest that the majors' annual production schedule can be viewed as an investment portfolio, with each production seen as an individual asset incurring some level of risk and generating some rate of return. The great majority of a studio's features – the Specials, programmers, and B-features – were designed to fill the screen time of the parent company's theaters with company product and service the secondary markets of lower-run theaters throughout the country. Rates of return on these movies were relatively stable, as was the risk involved in producing them, but while low- to medium-budget pictures were unlikely to make significant losses, they generated only about half of a studio's profits. Risk, profit, and competition between the majors were concentrated on the production of a relatively small number of high-budget "superspecials"' designed to play for extended periods in the company's own first-run theaters and also to gain access to the screens of rival corporations.[40] These pictures were most likely to become commercial hits, but in any season only a handful of pictures – no more than 2.5 per cent of those in release, and far fewer than the industry's total output of high-budget pictures – earned more than five times the average box-office take.[41] While some high-budget pictures would generate higher box-office revenues, they also carried a substantially higher risk of commercial failure than medium- or low-budget movies.[42]

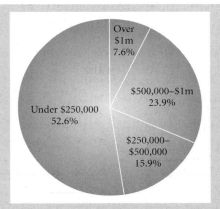

Production budgets, 1938

The major studios classified their productions by their budgets as well as by their content, and this classification also determined how they would be rented to exhibitors. In 1939, for example, MGM produced four "superspecials," each rented to exhibitors for 40 percent of their box-office gross, 20 "specials," for 30 or 35 percent of the gross, and 25 B-features, which were rented for fixed dollar amounts. Some of these B-features would also turn up as the top half of a double feature program in lower-run theaters.

In 1938, six major companies (MGM, Twentieth Century-Fox, Warner Bros., RKO, Universal, and Columbia) produced a total of 251 movies between them. Nineteen had budgets of over $1 million, 60 cost between $500,000 and $1 million, and another 40 cost between $250,000 and $500,000. More than half – the programmers and B-features – cost under $250,000.

Intriguingly, this analysis suggests a much closer degree of continuity between Classical Hollywood's production economics and those of the blockbuster syndrome which came to dominate the industry after the Paramount decision.

An incidental advantage of the high cost of production was that it allowed a proportion of the profits to be diverted away from the investors and shareholders toward the individual talents responsible for production, through the high salaries paid to stars, production heads, and successful writers and directors. Twentieth Century-Fox argued that since Shirley Temple earned the company something over $20 million in the 1930s, it was not unreasonable to pay her $5,000 a week. In the 1930s and 1940s half the cost of movie production was spent on salaries, setting standards of pay and conditions that potential competitors would find hard to match, and thus helping to preserve the monopoly of the major companies. The highest salaries, however, went not to stars but to studio executives. In 1938, at least 217 people in the movie business were paid an annual salary of more than $75,000; of the nation's 25 highest salaries, 19 went to people employed in the

Louis B. Mayer, MGM studio head, 1925.

Courtesy BFI.

Darryl Zanuck, probably one of the two most influential producers in the history of the American cinema.

Courtesy BFI.

film industry, including the highest, $1.2 million paid to Louis B. Mayer, head of MGM. The only American industry that spent a higher percentage of its annual volume of business on executive salaries was cement manufacturing.[43]

In 1932, *Fortune* magazine described the MGM studios in Culver City as presenting:

> the appearance less of a factory than of a demented university with a campus made out of beaverboard and canvas. It contains twenty-two sound stages, a park that can be photographed as anything from a football field to the gardens at Versailles, $2,000,000 worth of antique furniture, a greenhouse consecrated to the raising of ferns, twenty-two projection rooms, a commissary where $6,000-a-week actors can lunch on Long Island oysters for fifty cents, and a Polish immigrant who sometimes makes $500,000 a year and once spent the weekend with the Hoovers at the White House.[44]

In this environment, frequently described by visiting writers as somewhere between the chaotic and the surreal, MGM produced between 40 and 50 pictures a year, and the other studios did the same. A studio was normally presided over by two executives, the head of the studio and the head of production. The exact distinction between these two roles was never absolute, and no two studios were completely alike in their practice. At Twentieth Century-Fox, for instance, the two roles were combined in the single figure of Darryl Zanuck. As the studio's head of production from 1935 until 1956, and the company's president from 1962 to

1971, Zanuck was one of the most influential figures in the history of Hollywood production, but as yet he has been paid little critical attention. Apart from Zanuck, the most stable management teams were at MGM and Warner Bros., and these two companies are the most frequently cited models of studio operation, if only because Louis B. Mayer and Jack Warner were the most notorious studio executives. Leo Rosten was referring to these figures when he observed that:

> each studio has a personality; each studio's product shows special emphases and values. And in the final analysis, the sum total of a studio's personality, the aggregate pattern of its choices and its tastes, may be traced to its producers. For it is the producers who establish the preferences, the prejudices, and the predispositions of the organization, and, therefore, of the movies which it turns out.[45]

The product of those studios led by the same head of production for long periods showed a more consistent studio style than did the output of studios like RKO and Paramount, which regularly changed their production heads during bouts of economic instability or political infighting.

One explanation of why Hollywood has not been taken seriously has lain in the assumption that "the fourth largest industry in America" was run by buffoons. There has never been any shortage of anecdotes caricaturing the studio heads as philistines or philanderers. Mayer, it is said, looked on all his stars as his children, wanted them to bring their problems to him, and, notoriously, cried on cue if they ever became recalcitrant over the details of their contracts or the parts he chose for them. After a visit to Fascist Italy in the early 1930s, Harry Cohn, whose nicknames included "His Crudeness," had his office at Columbia redecorated to look like Benito Mussolini's. Sam Goldwyn's abuses of the language were renowned, even if most of them were invented by writers. There was an apparently endless supply of stories about producers. Leo Rosten recalled:

> the producer to whom a writer, in telling a story, used the word "frustrated." The producer requested an explanation, and the writer resorted to this analogy: "Take a book-keeper, a little man earning twenty-five bucks a week. He dreams of getting a big, beautiful boat and sailing to the South Seas. But he can't fulfill his dreams – so he's frustrated." To which the producer cried: "I like that! Put a boat in the picture."[46]

Lurking not far below the surface of such caricatures was both a class prejudice against the movie audience and a racism that drew exaggerated attention to the number of first- or second-generation Jewish immigrants working in the industry. Although several convincing explanations have been offered as to why entertainment industries might have proved particularly attractive to Jewish immigrant entrepreneurs, the extent of Jewish "domination" of the motion picture industry has always been overstated, whether positively or negatively, because of the cult of personality. Zanuck, for instance, was born in Wahoo, Nebraska, the child of a Swiss Methodist and a third-generation American of English stock, but he was frequently identified as Jewish. Responding to accusations of "Jewish control of the movies," a 1941 news story asserted that "Jews number only a bare 33% among film executives … not more than 10% of financial control (the control which really fixes policies) of the movies can be said to be in Jewish hands."[47] The mythologizing of the Hollywood moguls, whether as vulgar alien immigrants unable to master the language or as creators of "an empire of their own," has consistently tended to obscure their abilities as entrepreneurs and businessmen.

To a criticism that seeks to divorce art from economics, the movie moguls were no better than bullying philistines, and epitomized all that is wrong with Hollywood. They were, however, the men who decided which movies did and did not get made, and who made innumerable decisions about those that did. Against the caricatures we might cite Jesse Lasky's paean of self-praise as being no less accurate:

> The producer must be a prophet and a general, a diplomat and a peacemaker, a miser and a spendthrift. He must have vision tempered by hindsight, daring governed by caution, the patience of a saint and the iron of a Cromwell … his decisions must be sure, swift, and immediate, as well as subject to change, because conditions change continuously in the motion picture industry. … The producer's resources must be such that no contingency can stop him from finding [a] star, soothing the director like a super-Talleyrand, or, in all-night conferences in shirt sleeves and heavy cigar smoke, "doctoring the scripts by his own creative power." … In his hands lies the supervision of every element that goes to make up the finished product. These elements are both tangible and intangible, the control of human beings and real properties as well as the control of the artistic temperament, the shaping of creative forces and the knowledge of the public needs for entertainment.[48]

Like Hortense Powdermaker, Lasky emphasized the conflicting, even contradictory roles of the producer, but did so in a positive spirit more closely aligned to F. Scott Fitzgerald's definition of a first-class intelligence as displaying "the ability

---

Box 5.10 "The real boss"

The cold, cruel fact is that the real boss of the studio picture production is the sales department, in convention at a different city each year, when the film sales clans gather from all the thirty-four key cities of the land to decide just what kind of pictures they can sell during the coming year … The erudite and cultivated gang from the exchanges, filled with higher culture and a keen psychological insight into what you and the rest of the picture patrons are thinking or going to think during the next twelve months, make that decision solemnly, and with the calm restraint of a dog fight … The program of so many Westerns, so many rough-stuff melos, so many comedies with real snappy kick in them, so many this, that and the other … is banged out, and … the studio chief, perhaps a little sorrowful and subdued, goes back to Hollywood and studies his typewritten list of fifty-two features and twenty-six "shorts" with a somewhat jaundiced eye. Sighing (sometimes), he gathers his studio cabinet and delivers the ukase of the real bosses.[50]

to hold two opposed ideas in the mind at the same time and still retain the ability to function."[49] The division of responsibility between the studio head and the head of production varied: both Mayer and Jack Warner, for instance, were quite heavily involved in, respectively, Republican and Democratic party politics in California, and much less involved in day-to-day production decisions than Zanuck. The studio head was, however, the conduit for communication between the studio and the New York offices of the studio's parent distribution and exhibition company. It was in New York that the basic decisions about a studio's production were made: how many movies to produce in a season, and at what budget; what their release schedule was to be. The job of the studio head was then to ensure the delivery of movies according to that budget and schedule. He was likely to approve the initial idea for the project, assign writers and director, approve the approximate budget, and supervise casting and the hiring of other personnel. He might also approve the final version of the script and check the movie's progress through production by viewing **dailies** (the first printing from the day's exposed negative stock, also called **rushes**) and supervising the final stages of editing, although many of these tasks might be left to the head of production.

One of the best accounts of a head of production's activities is F. Scott Fitzgerald's description of Monroe Stahr's work in *The Last Tycoon*.[51] Fitzgerald clearly modeled Stahr on Irving Thalberg, head of production at MGM during the early 1930s, and saw the heads of production, the "half a dozen men" who were "able to keep the whole equation of pictures in their heads," as the real "stars" of Hollywood. Less enthusiastically, director Frank Capra complained in 1939 that "about six producers today pass upon ninety percent of the scripts and cut and edit about ninety percent of the pictures."[52]

At the executive level below the head of production were line producers, who were almost as frequently disparaged as the moguls themselves. Several Hollywood adages emphasized the executives' nepotism in such observations as "the son-in-law also rises," and Ogden Nash's epithet about Universal's founder and president:

> Carl Laemmle
> has a very big family.

Sons-in-law and "Uncle Carl's" relations were most likely to rise to the rank of producer, and hence attract the vitriol of writers and directors about "front-office interference." In 1938, the Screen Directors Guild, struggling both for union recognition by the studios and for the establishment of minimum working conditions, argued for a change in the existing system of production to eliminate "the involved, complicated, and expensive system of supervision which separates the director and writer from the responsible executive producers." Directors were not questioning the need for executive supervision, they declared, nor were they telling the producing companies how to run their businesses. They did not condemn all producers, only "the army of the inept, who have been promoted to positions of authority for which they are unqualified, inexperienced, and utterly lacking in creative ability." According to the directors, such producers had "little respect for the medium, less respect for their audiences and excuse their lack of imagination by ridiculing it in others."[53] Critical arguments that assign creativity to individual talents and crass commercialism to "the system" echo the directors' perspective.

But however vociferously writers or directors complained, and whatever they subsequently told their interviewers or ghost-writers about the crass philistinism of their producers, many of them nevertheless aspired to become producers, since the producer oversaw and controlled the whole production, integrating the contributions of other personnel and balancing creative and financial considerations. What the directors were objecting to was the adaptation to Hollywood of a decentralized management system first introduced in American industry by General Motors in the 1920s, and itself evidence of the studios' assertion of their existence as industry rather than art form. The head of production assigned a producer to each movie, and the producer then supervised the processes of writing, shooting,

---

Box 5.11 *Casablanca's* budget

At just under $900,000, *Casablanca*'s budget was typical for an A-feature in 1942, although it might have cost as much as $1,400,000 if it had been made at MGM instead of the notoriously frugal Warner Bros. *Casablanca*'s director, Michael Curtiz, was paid over twice as much as any of the movie's stars, and the studio spent more on outside talent hired at weekly rates just for the movie than it did on the salaries of its contract players. Salaries made up 85 percent of the movie's direct costs, with performers' salaries accounting for less than half of that. Much of the cost of set construction, props, costume, and the like were absorbed in the 35 percent charge attached to the budget for the overheads in running the studio.[54]

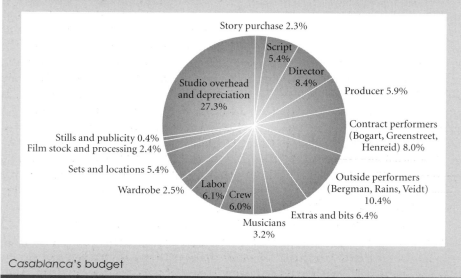

Casablanca's budget

and editing. The major studios each had a staff of about six "line producers," each responsible for six or eight productions a year. Typically, a **producer** worked on three or four movies, in different stages of production, at a time. Since the producer was more closely involved in the production of a movie at all its stages, he or she (usually he – no more than a handful of women producers or directors worked in Hollywood studios) was in a position to exercise more control over the development of a movie's story, script, and editing than any other individual, although whether he or she either chose to exercise that control or was effective at doing so was another matter. Producers might or might not be good at what they did, and that consideration might or might not be related to how actively they were involved in productions. Historian Thomas Schatz has argued that studio producers are "the most misunderstood and undervalued figures in American film history," in part because their oversight of the whole production process meant that they were less constrained by a narrow definition of their responsibilities than were directors, writers, or other production personnel.

Directors had a more circumscribed role in the studio system than critical concepts of directorial authorship would imply. Frank Capra, then president of the Screen Directors Guild, observed in 1939 that "there are only half a dozen directors in Hollywood who are allowed to shoot as they please and who have any supervision over their editing." Within the studio system, a director was not necessarily involved in either the writing or the editing of the movie, and it was quite normal practice for him or her to be given a script only a few days before he or she was due to start shooting. Since the economic logic of production usually required shooting out of sequence, it was perhaps not surprising that Capra went on to suggest "that 80 per cent of the directors today shoot scenes exactly as they are told to shoot them without any changes whatsoever, and that 90 per cent of them have no voice in the story or in the editing."[55] Although a movie rarely had as many directors as the six or more who worked on *Gone with the Wind* (1939), it was common for action sequences to be shot by a second unit, and quite normal for additional scenes or retakes to be directed by other people. A director, however, might reasonably expect to have some influence over at least the final stages of writing and the early stages of editing. His or her main job was to translate the script into a movie, and he or she was in effective control of the project while it was shooting. A director, according to George Cukor, "should shoot the scene before the producer sees it," and one of the reasons that Cukor withdrew from *Gone with the Wind* was that producer David O. Selznick insisted on dictating the spatial organization of each scene.[56] The justification for claims of directorial authorship in Hollywood stem from the director's supervisory control of the movie's visual appearance and its performances. Many of Hollywood's industrial practices qualified the extent to which this control was exercised, however: producer–director and even producer–director–writer teams were quite common features of Hollywood's collaborative processes.

The influence of the writer on the final product was at least as circumscribed as that of the director. It was normal studio practice to employ several writers on a given movie, often working independently of each other at the same time. Writers were seen as technical staff, many of them employed for particular specialist skills.

A writer's contribution to a script might, for instance, be limited to structuring a sub-plot or adding half a dozen gag lines. To an extent the studios traded in literary reputations, employing the likes of William Faulkner or Aldous Huxley for the cachet their names added to a movie as a production value rather than for their literary expertise. Many novelists found the experience of working in Hollywood intensely unsatisfying, in large part because of the industrial constraints of scriptwriting. Unlike a novel, a movie script is an incomplete form, merely an outline of dialog and action. Given the multiplicity of hands through which it passes before production, it is seldom likely to be entirely the work of a single individual or the expression of a single personality – and as Joe Gillis (William Holden), the cynical scriptwriter in *Sunset Boulevard* (1950), observes, "people don't know that someone actually *writes* the picture. They think the actors make it up as they go along." The discipline of writing for the movies may have been as unattractive to many novelists as the banality of the work they were often required to produce. Critics have often cited F. Scott Fitzgerald as the most prominent example of a major literary talent destroyed by Hollywood. Fitzgerald's own accounts were, however, much more sympathetic to the industrial system that employed him mainly to inject a few lines of classy dialog into scripts on

Cast and crew on the sound stage of *Only Angels Have Wings* (1939).
Courtesy BFI.

which his name never appeared. Many of the most successful Hollywood screen-writers, including Ben Hecht, Charles MacArthur, and Jules Furthman, had been journalists, a profession in which their writing was also liable to be reworked by others.

More minor influential roles in production were occupied by figures whose work was limited to a particular aspect of the movie. The **director of photography** was responsible for lighting the set, and possibly for camera placement if the director he or she was working with was primarily concerned with securing the actors' performances. Directors of photography were rarely engaged on a movie for any longer than the period of shooting. The **art director** was most involved at the pre-production stage, designing sets and supervising their construction.[57] Like other creative personnel, art directors were normally employed on long-term contracts, and this might give them the opportunity to exert an influence on the studio's house style. Editing was the only area of production other than writing in which there were more than a handful of women employed. The work of the **editor** was perhaps the most self-effacing in the studio system, because Hollywood's aesthetics chose not to draw attention to editing procedures, and movies were in the main edited according to a fairly inflexible set of conventions, which are discussed in more detail in chapters 10 and 11. Working largely independently of the other production personnel, the editor began assembling the movie from the daily rushes, producing an initial **rough cut** shortly after the shooting stopped. This rough cut was then refined under the supervision of the producer and sometimes the director, until a final version received the approval of the head of production. Music was usually added at a late stage in the editing, with the composer producing pieces of background music to timed sequences; movies were seldom edited to fit musical scores that were already fully formed.

Apart from stars and supporting actors, production involved a much larger group of personnel in skilled labor. Camera, sound, and lighting "crews," electricians, carpenters, set decorators, makeup artists, hairdressers, wardrobe mistresses, continuity people, propmen, stand-ins, stunt men, and extras all exerted very little direct influence over the movie's finished form. Like the doctors, secretaries, dialog coaches, caterers, transportation staff, and auditors, not to mention the staffs of the laboratories, these people all came under the general control of the production manager and the assistant directors who organized the logistics of production.

The Star System

Hollywood did not require its audience to possess a knowledge of its industrial processes in order to enjoy or understand its products. All its viewers were, however, familiar with the stars, whose public lives provided a glimpse into the melodramatic world of the dream factory. As well as being the most visible part of the industry, the star system was central to the standardization of movie product, and to its interrelations with other consumption industries and advertising. Under the studio system, stars had only a limited amount of power, in no way commensurate with their power to attract audiences at the box-office. Most stars were employed on long, fixed-term contracts with a single studio, and had relatively little control over the roles they were cast in or the movies they made. If they refused a part, their contract might be suspended without pay as punishment.[58] Once chosen for a part, however, they could exert some influence over their characterization, and hence over the whole structure of the movies in which they appeared. With the decline of the studio system, the power of the star was enhanced. Stars like Clint Eastwood and Robert De Niro set up their own production companies (Malpaso, Tribeca), using their economic power to control the movies in which they appeared, often producing and sometimes directing them themselves.

The real influence of the stars lay not with their employers, but with the paying public. Far more than the type of movie, stars were the commodities that most consistently drew audiences to the movies. A "star vehicle," a movie constructed around the appeal of one or more particular stars and sold on that basis, was bound to have a set of conventional ingredients, much like a genre. An Elvis Presley movie, for instance, offered its star several opportunities to sing, a number of girls for him to choose his romantic partner from, and a plot in which he would be misunderstood by older characters. The repetition of these standard ingredients created an audience expectation of these elements. Similarly, a star's repetition of performance elements over a number of movies would lead to the consolidation of that performance as a set of gestures and behavior patterns recognizable to the audience, who could then predict what the star was likely to do in any movie he or she appeared in. The studio system was committed to the deliberate manufacture of stars as a mechanism for selling movie tickets, and as a result generated publicity about the stars' offscreen lives designed to complement and play upon their screen images. At its height, the publicity machine was a peripheral industry in its own right. There were about 20 fan magazines in the United States in the late 1930s, each with circulations between 200,000 and one million. *Photoplay*, *Modern Screen*, and *Shadowland* regularly reached the most devoted quarter of the weekly movie audience. "Gossip" was a requirement of the industry, and seemed to circulate around it with an almost material force. Many stars and studio heads fervently believed that the main gossip columnists exercised very real power over public taste and opinion, and therefore had to be courted and feted at every possible opportunity.

The publicity surrounding the star system told its audience that stars were basically like them. When the male star of *The Hurricane* (1937), Jon Hall, was sent on a promotional tour of the United States, his publicity agent made a point of telling his interviewers that Hall only owned one suit. He was presented as "just a typical American boy who happens to be working for his living in pictures instead of hardware." As the boy next door, his persona imitated James Stewart's. Stewart's promotional material in the late 1930s featured remarks "overheard in the lobby," including: "He's a real American type, the kind I'd like to have around the house"; and "Reminds me of how my Frankie makes love, so modest like."

In 1939, Margaret Thorp noted that a female star "need not be extravagantly beautiful" if she was "individual":

> The ranking box-office favorites must be good to look at certainly but they are not required to be creatures of classic perfection. In many ways it is an advantage for a star not to be too beautiful. She stands then closer to the average and that is what the fans want, an ideal they can emulate, a creature not too bright and good, one whose heights they might actually scale themselves, given a little energy and a little luck. That is Janet Gaynor's great appeal: her home-town personality, the little blonde from the typewriter or the kitchen or the ribbon counter who has exchanged her imitation lapin coat for sables, her hall bedroom for a Beverly Hills villa, her Woolworth jewelry for real diamonds. The glamorous star today is as natural as possible. She does not pluck her eyebrows and paint in new ones; she develops the natural line. She does not tint her hair to exotic hues. She does not try to be a fairy-tale princess but an average American girl raised to the nth power. "Vivid" is the adjective she works for hardest.[59]

Thorp's idea of the average "raised to the nth power" was intricately interwoven with Hollywood's "escapist" appeal. At the height of its operation, the star system provided every member of the audience with an ideal version of the self, with sufficient variations among types for considerable nuance in the individual viewer's choice. Tyrone Power was like Robert Taylor, for instance – he was, in fact, Twentieth Century-Fox's version of MGM's Robert Taylor. The choice between Ronald Colman, Brian Aherne, and David Niven was similarly a consumer choice among different but comparable branded goods. Leo Rosten produced a description of the operation of studio publicity by charting all the romantic attachments of Tyrone Power during the production season 1937–8, when the gossip columns and fan magazines solemnly reported him to be enamored of Loretta Young, Sonja Henie, Janet Gaynor, Simone Simon, and Arleen Whelan:

> Scarcely a week went by without hints of the infatuation existing between the versatile Mr Power and one or another of these charming maidens, each of whom, during this fecund period, was also reported to be profoundly jealous of at least two of the others. Wonderful to relate, it turns out that Mr Power and the Misses Young, Henie, Gaynor, Simon, and Whelan were all employees of the same ingenious studio, Twentieth Century-Fox!

Tracing the sentimental attachments of each of Power's paramours, Rosten further discovered that all of them had been romantically linked to Cesar Romero, four to Richard Green, and two to Michael Brooke, who were also all employees of the same studio. A similar exercise conducted on Warner Bros. star George Brent produced the same result: his affections were shared among three of Warners' leading ladies, except for a brief involvement with Fox's Loretta Young while he was on loan to that studio for an appearance in *The Rains Came* (1939):

> The moral to be drawn from this whole quaint analysis is simple: the romances, scandals, and inter-personal complications of Hollywood often involve *the same individ-*

uals week in and week out; and this leads to a somewhat lopsided impression of love and heartbreak in Hollywood. All is not true that appears in the gossip columns – to put it charitably.[60]

Nevertheless, it was important to the functioning of the star system that these archetypes were also connected to the audience's world. Fan magazines regularly ran articles such as "Who is Your Husband's Favorite Actress? And What Are You Going to Do About It?," which featured such advice as: "Many a quiet, stay-at-home man goes crazy over Harlow. If your husband comes out of the theater raving about Jean's radiant loveliness and bare shoulders, you should do something about it. And you had better not waste much time."[61] More pointedly, Margaret Thorp observed:

> There is social and psychological significance in the fact that 70 per cent of Gary Cooper's fan mail comes from women who write that their husbands do not appreciate them. Their ideal is still the ideal husband of the Victorian era who told his wife at breakfast each morning how much she meant to him, but that husband is not a type which the post-war American man has any interest in emulating. He prefers to conceal his deeper emotions at breakfast, and during the rest of the day as well. His wife, consequently, has to spend her afternoons at the movies.[62]

Equally important, however, was the other half of the paradox, by which fans were discouraged from envying the stars. The fan magazines regularly ran pieces such as "So You'd Like to Be a Star" in which Myrna Loy told:

> all of you little Marys and Sues and Sarahs who wish you could be movie stars, who see them through rainbow-colored glasses . . . that my work is nine parts drudgery and one part thrill and glamour. There is nothing I know of that is quite so exhausting . . . I'd give away two years of my life to be able to get together with girl friends and talk about my marriage and new house which are, naturally, the most thrilling topics in my life. If I could be the plain Myrna Williams I am at heart, instead of forever figuring out what Myrna Loy dare and dare not say, I'd talk about Arthur and our romance and marriage and new home.[63]

In the late 1930s fan magazines identified Loy as "the Movies' Model 'Mrs,'" declaring that she had "established a reputation as the perfect wife" to Leslie Howard, William Powell, Clark Gable, and Warner Baxter onscreen, and to producer Arthur Hornblow Jr in "real life." In one piece of studio publicity, she explained that she had acquired her philosophy for marital conduct from the roles she played: "mystery, Myrna insists, is the greatest weapon woman has in the love game. Men enjoy the chase. They are apt to weary when they have achieved their capture. The wise wife, therefore, does not allow romance to degenerate into familiarity."[64] After her divorce in 1942, Loy featured in an article on "Why the Perfect Wife's Marriage Failed": "These are things Myrna Loy might have told you about her breakup with Arthur Hornblow Jr. They are things that make you wonder if romance is, after all, the right basis for marriage."[65] Through this paradoxical representation of stars as characters to be envied and pitied, emulated but not imitated, the fan magazines sustained a discourse on romance, marriage, and sexuality that paralleled the movies' own concerns. In addition, they supported a subsidiary industry of advertising through star endorsements.

The star system provided one of the principal means by which Hollywood offered audiences guarantees of predictability, while the plots within which the star persona was embedded offered a balancing experience of novelty. The audience's recognition of a star, in both the movie and its publicity, led viewers to expect a certain kind of performance, and as a result a certain kind of experience. Movie posters would typically create expectations about the kinds of performance that the star might offer, often literally foregrounding the star's image against a background of scenes from the movie. When an advert promised that in *Dark Victory* (1939), "Bette Davis brings you her Crowning Triumph," audiences could anticipate the known qualities of a Davis performance (one British fan described her as being "adept at mannerisms . . . clipped phrases and highly dramatic movements"), organized within the novelty of an unfamiliar story.[66] Such advertising established the star's performance as a separable element of the movie's aggregate package of potential pleasures, one that the audience could enjoy as a production value independently of the rest of the movie.

While audiences may have thought of individual stars as talented actors, idealized versions of the boy or girl next door, role models or creatures of fantasy, distribution executives saw commodities: the market would bear two or three vehicles for each major star every year, and exhibitors would often buy product in advance on the strength of no more information than the star's name. To Twentieth Century-Fox, a "Betty Grable" was a musical starring the actress, who probably earned more money for her studio than any other female star in the Classical period. To the other companies, a "Betty Grable" was a product to be acquired or simulated – by Betty Hutton, Esther Williams, or Rita Hayworth. Frank McConnell suggests that the star vehicle existed to display "its leading players in as many of their famous postures as possible."[67] It provided its viewers with the familiarity of recognition when they were offered "Mr and Mrs Miniver . . . together again! Greer Garson and Walter Pidgeon give their best performance in their best picture, *Madame Curie*" (1943).[68]

Since stars were themselves examples of the principles of interchangeability, minor variation, and market placement that underlay the consumer industries of fashion and cosmetics, it was appropriate that their commercial function was not restricted simply to selling the movies in which they appeared. From very early on in its history, Hollywood recognized and accepted its role as a powerful sales agent for what advertising counselor Christine Frederick called "consumptionism."[69] In the late 1910s Cecil B. de Mille responded to pressure from his company's sales department for "modern photoplays" like *Why Change Your Wife?*, displaying the latest styles in fashions and home decor. Stars became, as Irving Thalberg put it, "examples of style," conscious experimenters with roles, identities, and appearances, using their bodies as the sites of their experiments. They were to a large extent interchangeable: speaking in 1929, Thalberg commented that "it is no accident that Clara Bow with her representation of the flapper of today, is a star. If it hadn't been her, it would have been some other girl of exactly her type."[70] More fixed, perhaps, was the conception of the consumer at whom all these experiments were aimed:

> Out there, working as a clerk in a store and living in an apartment with a friend, was *one girl* – single, nineteen years old, Anglo-Saxon, somewhat favoring Janet Gaynor. The thousands of Hollywood-assisted designers, publicity men, sales heads, beauty consultants and merchandisers had internalized her so long ago that her psychic life had become their psychic life. They empathized with her shyness, her social awkwardness, her fear of offending. They understood her slight weight problem and her chagrin at being a trifle too tall. They could tell you what sort of man she hoped to marry and how she spent her leisure time.[71]

If trade followed the films, stars were its guides, coaching their fans in the use of new consumer products. Jean Harlow, for instance, advised readers of *Modern Screen* in 1933 to care for their stockings "the Hollywood way – with Lux! Never rub, never use ordinary soap or hot water. Stockings *do* look so much lovelier washed the Lux way."[72] By the 1930s Hollywood was so heavily embroiled in the promotion of fashions, furnishings, and cosmetics that it had become the biggest single influence on women's fashion throughout the world. Fans copied the dress and makeup styles of their favorite stars either from style photographs in women's magazines and Sunday supplements or from the movies themselves, where they could see "the dress in action," as one fan magazine put it. From the early 1930s, studios were also involved in publicity **tie-ins** or tie-ups with other manufacturers. MGM stars drank Coca-Cola between takes for "the pause that refreshes" in a tie-up worth $500,000 to the studio, while Warner Bros. movies featured the General Electric and General Motors products that their stars also advertised in magazines.[73] **Product placement,** as the practice of inserting brand-name goods into movies is known, has remained an established Hollywood practice: *2001: A Space Odyssey* (1968) advertised a Pan Am space shuttle, *Back to the Future Part II* (1989) featured Toyotas, Texaco, Miller beer, and Nike shoes, while *Cast Away* (2000) was, among other things, a two-hour promotional movie for Federal Express.[74]

How Stars are Made: *A Star is Born* (1937)

It's useless to wait. It's useless to insist. You're wasting your time. Recommendations won't get you anywhere. This place was not meant for you. Do not enter. Do not embarrass yourself or attendant asking to visit the sets. This is forbidden.

Sign at the entrance to Universal Studios, 1936, as reported by Blaise Cendrars[75]

One of Hollywood's most telling characteristics is that, while appearing to draw attention to the mechanisms of its industrial processes, it masks one level of its operations by selectively highlighting another. Hollywood circulates accounts of its process of production, but these accounts obscure the profit motive that drives them by substituting a discourse on loss: "The Price they Pay for Fame," how "In Hollywood, Health, Friends, Beauty, even Life Itself, are Sacrificed on the Altar of Terrible Ambition."[76] Hollywood's most frequent version of this story is *A Star is Born*. First produced as *What Price Hollywood?* in 1932, the 1937 version was remade as a musical with Judy Garland in 1954, and again in 1976 with Barbra Streisand, when its setting was transferred to the rock music business. The 1937 version with Janet Gaynor, however, crystallizes Hollywood's self-representations, in which stardom is the central condition, the site at which ordinariness acquires charisma and acknowledges the cost of success. Its two central ingredients are the effortless chance discovery of the female star (the same thing happens in *Singin' in the Rain* (1952)) and "The Price they Pay for Fame," the dark side of this version of the American dream:

> Maybe after all it is enough – just a few short days, or years in the burning searchlight of motion picture fame. . . . Perhaps what comes after doesn't really matter. . . . Fame is the consolation prize which is given when everything else has been sacrificed. It is a killing pace, this winning and holding success on the silver screen. Not many of the glittering figures of filmland have withstood it for more than a few years. There have been far too many who have dropped by the wayside, health gone, beauty gone, money gone, youth gone before its time.[77]

The dream and the price of fame are staple features of Classical Hollywood's movies about itself, in which the function and meaning of Hollywood are mythologized as a complex relationship of desire and disavowal between the fan and her ideal. In its fictions, Hollywood peoples itself with heroes and heroines (handsome male leads, beautiful "rising" female stars), villains (tyrannical studio bosses, moneymen, jealous second-leads), and other malcontents (drunken screenwriters and aging starlets) all endlessly engaged in contests for power and celebrity, enacting the industry's mythology of constant crisis. Economic uncertainty drives the narrative, whether it tells of a young hopeful's struggles on the road to stardom or the attempted comeback of a once great director. Often the producer's last desperate gamble to prevent the imminent collapse of the whole studio gives a break to the kid who turns out to be just what the public have been waiting for. Although *Singin' in the Rain* represents a comic celebration of Hollywood, the industry's vision of itself is frequently as bleak as that of its most mordant critics. *The Big Knife* (1956) begins with a scene in which a vindictive gossip columnist threatens to destroy a star's career when he refuses to comment on the state of his marriage, and ends with the star's suicide after he refuses to be implicated in the murder of a bit player. In *Sunset Boulevard* (1950) a studio writer is murdered by a crazed silent movie goddess. *The Bad and the Beautiful* (1952) depicts the ruthless rise and precipitate fall of an archetypal "boy genius" producer.

Box 5.12   Acting in Hollywood

Stars were at the top of the hierarchy of actors' labor in Classical Hollywood: in 1941 Leo Rosten estimated that there were 80 stars out of a total of about 1,250 actors in Hollywood.[78] Stars were the studios' most costly investments in talent, but they performed a distinct and highly profitable function in drawing audiences into theaters and regulating the industry's product. The majority of studio contracts were for character actors and bit players. Although these "supporting players" were generally acknowledged to be the most talented performers in the system, they were most often cast according to narrowly defined "types." By far the largest group of actors in Hollywood were screen extras, who were paid minimal day wages.

While much publicity was given to the size of stars' salaries, the Screen Actors Guild estimated that only 4 percent of the actors who worked in Hollywood in 1933 earned more than $50,000, while 12 percent earned between $5,000 and $10,000 and 71 percent earned less than $5,000.[79] In 1939, 55 percent of actors earned under $6,000, 14 percent earned $6,000–10,000, 24 percent earned $10,000–40,000, and 7 percent earned over $40,000.[80] In 1940, there were 6,534 extras in the Screen Actors Guild, but only about 3,000 of them actually worked in movies that year, and only 633 earned more than $1,000 from motion picture production in the year.[81]

The oversupply of talent represented by the large pool of unemployed actors ensured that the studios exercised largely unregulated control over conditions of employment. "The promise of moving up in the star system hierarchy kept hopefuls in line, while the fear of plummeting to the bottom was used to keep employed actors from challenging their employers and complaining about exploitative labor practices."[82] Actors and other studio workers were, for example, regularly:

> required to work almost every Saturday night and often into the early hours of Sunday morning. If a studio closed for a holiday during the week, the actor often would be required to work the following Sunday without pay to make up for the holiday. Meal periods came at the producers' convenience . . . Actors often worked well past midnight and then were ordered to report back for work at 7 a.m. Actors were not paid for overtime and no premium was paid for work on Saturdays, Sundays and holidays nor for night work.[83]

Working conditions for extras were often dangerous as well as arduous, as this report suggests:

> Forty women received the call to report at 5:30 p.m. to the set for "Riff Raff" which J. Walter Ruben was directing for Metro-Goldwyn-Mayer. The call from Central Casting Corp. had specified "light rain." . . . A few minutes after 10:00 p.m., the women were ordered into the rain for the first time. The set was equipped with overhead sprinklers, three fire hoses, and three wind machines. The latter created such a terrific gale that a number of women were forcibly knocked

down and bruised in each take. One woman was knocked unconscious while another, who took the full force of the stream of water from the hose on her back, was paralyzed from her hips down for several hours. Four women were temporarily blinded when the water hit them full force in the eyes.[84]

Studios owned their actors. Ginger Rogers's 1933 contract with Warner Bros. gave the studio exclusive right to "photograph and/or otherwise produce, reproduce, transmit, exhibit, distribute, and exploit in connection with [a] photoplay any and all of the artist's acts, poses, plays and appearances of any and all kinds." Most actors had no rights over how their images or their names were exploited. The studio could use the actor's image in advertising or sell that image to other advertisers. Bette Davis's 1943 contract with Warner Bros. stipulated that the studio had "sole and exclusive" right:

to use or make use of and control her name and/or her professional name and to use and/or distribute her pictures, photographs or other reproductions of her physical likeness for advertising, commercial or publicity purposes, whether or not in connection with the acts, poses, plays and appearances of the Artist or the advertisement or publicity of the photoplays produced hereunder.

The studio could also publish material under Davis's name in "trade papers and newspaper column stories and items, feature stories and items, motion picture production news, radio breaks" at the "sole discretion of the Producer."[85] According to Milton Sperling:

studio loyalty was a factor of your life. If you were a Warner employee, or a Fox employee, or a Metro employee, that was your home, your country . . . You played baseball against the other studios. You had T-shirts with your studio's name on them. It was just like being a subject, and a patriotic subject at that.[86]

While Hollywood's audiences negotiated the contradictions exposed by the fan magazines, Margaret Thorp illustrated an equally contradictory attitude within the industry toward "the Cinderella legend" of stardom. The studios, she said, published discouraging statistics about the number of people who came to Hollywood to break into the movies, and the difficulty of finding work even as a waitress:

They explain how much difficult technique and hard training must be added to beauty and natural talent. They talk about the fearful cost. *But* – they keep on telling the Cinderella story over and over again, lovingly, in the biography of every other star. How Joan Crawford was once a shop girl; Janet Gaynor a clerk in a shoe store; James Cagney a thirteen-dollar-a-week elevator boy; Clark Gable not so many years ago an unnoticed extra; that the highest paid of scenario writers, Frances Marion, began as a twenty-five-dollar-a-week stenographer. The moral is always that she stuck it out against odds; she would not be discouraged.[87]

The 1937 version of *A Star is Born* enacts this contradiction. The movie begins in a small backwoods town in North Dakota, where Esther Blodgett (Gaynor) spends her every spare moment in the movie theater, swooning over the stars and dreaming of joining them in Hollywood. Her particular favorite is Norman Maine. This fantasy life, nurtured by a constant reading of fan magazines, is ridiculed by the other members of her family. But Esther's dreams of stardom are encouraged by her grandmother (May Robson), who gives her money and puts her on the midnight train to California. Arriving in Hollywood, her first brush with stardom is far from propitious; she is silenced by a worse-for-drink Norman Maine (Frederic March) at a Hollywood Bowl concert. Later, taking a fill-in job as waitress at a party hosted by studio head Oliver Niles (Adolphe Menjou), Esther meets Maine in person. Attracted to her, Maine organizes a screen test ("she has the sincerity and honestness that makes great actresses") and she is soon contracted to Niles's studio. Scarcely has Libby (Lionel Stander) of the publicity department completed the studio "bio" that turns her into Vicki Lester, "Cinderella of the Rockies," than she gets a chance to play opposite Maine in his next picture. Hailed as an overnight success, she embarks upon a romance with her co-star. When Norman agrees to stop drinking, the couple are married and settle down in Beverly Hills. Esther's early dreams of "being somebody" seem completely fulfilled; the fantasy of consumption depicted by the fan magazines has become a reality.

An idyllic sequence set in the gardens of Esther's Beverly Hills mansion, reminiscent of fan magazine pictorial features on the homes of the stars, is only the lull before a storm. As Vicki's career builds, Norman's goes into sharp decline. Left alone as his wife works on picture after picture, he begins drinking again. When Vicki's success is recognized with an Academy Award for Best Actress, he disrupts the presentation ceremony. Esther finally decides that he needs medical help to quit drinking. Following a spell in a sanitarium, Norman recovers, but is driven back to drink when he is humiliated in public by Libby. After a further binge and an appearance in night-court, he is remanded into Vicki's care. Now deeply concerned about his health, she tells Niles that she must give up her career to care for her husband. Already deep in depression, Norman overhears the conversation, and drowns himself. Unable to cope with the trauma of Norman's funeral, Esther plans to abandon Hollywood forever. But just as she is leaving, her grandmother reappears and persuades her to stay. The movie ends with a scene depicting enthusiastic crowds gathered for the premiere of Esther's comeback picture.

A Star is Born is a melodrama, its characters subject to unseen forces apparently beyond their control in a world where whims of fashion and taste make careers and destroy lives. Hollywood is a community peopled by figures with a single character trait: the villainous Libby; the paternalistic Niles; the poor-but-honest assistant director McGuire (Andy Devine). Characters are prone to inflated gestures that declare their obvious significance, as when Norman and Vicki watch themselves kissing onscreen in huge close-up. As in any melodrama, coincidence plays a central role. When Esther arrives in Hollywood, a woman at the Central Casting Corporation where extras seek work explains to her, and to all the young hopefuls in the audience, that her chances of becoming a star are 100,000 to one. "But maybe," replies the indomitable Esther, "I'm that one." And, because she is in the right place at the right time, she gets her break. At the same time as the movie announces that stardom is an impossible dream, it also asserts that any audience member with Esther's dedication can become a star. Questions of talent and training are, significantly, obscured. Esther's talent is democratized as the skill she displays in imitating Greta Garbo, Katherine Hepburn, and Mae West, a skill shared by countless audience members. Although the movie repeatedly tells the audience of her hard work, we never really see Vicki performing, and we are given no opportunity to judge her abilities. Her appearance in *The Enchanted Hour* is reduced to a single screen kiss with Norman in which her face is entirely obscured, and we see nothing of her Oscar-winning performance as the "unforgettable Anna" in *Dream Without End*. Esther's rise to stardom is extraordinarily rapid and unstoppable, a deliberation on American possibility itself. Norman's decline is equally inevitable, and the trajectories of their careers form a symmetry centered on the movie's intensely contradictory image of Hollywood, playing off the mythology of a "beckoning Eldorado" where dreams come true against the suffering of the stars for whom fame proves both artificial and ephemeral.

It is not simply the frequency with which *A Star is Born* has been produced that makes its particular mythology so central to understanding Hollywood's relationship with its audience. Its love affair between a rising and a falling star is also a recurrent story in the publicity surrounding Hollywood. For instance, it is reproduced in almost identical form in a fan magazine version of the story of Ruby Keeler and Al Jolson:

> Five years ago it was the great Al Jolson and "who was that little chorus girl he married? . . ." Even before talkies Al was the greatest entertainer in the world. He made more money than any of the then-great. Came talkies and he was the one great star . . . And just the other day he answered the 'phone and told me Ruby Keeler was out. Isn't it amazing that now this slip of a girl, not much over twenty . . . is now the star of the family and Al Jolson – the great Jolson – makes appointments for her and languishes away a California afternoon while she rehearses and has fittings at her studio?[88]

This eclipsing of the male head of the household had repercussions which extended beyond the lives of the one in 100,000 women who might be discovered by Hollywood. The lesson was echoed repeatedly in the fan magazines in articles with titles like "Are Women Stars the Home Wreckers of Hollywood?":

> We do NOT believe that any man can stand, for long, the ignominy of trotting about in the refracted aura of his wife. . . . Men can bear to be all or they can bear to be nothing, but they cannot bear to be – *incidental*. . . . There seems to be only one way that is the safe way – the old, old way of the Missus being the Missus and the husband going into the arena to wrestle for the glory and the gold. When the wives are the stars, they wreck the homes and the marriages. When the husbands are the stars, the homes are built upon a rock that endures."[89]

Stars may have served as their audiences' surrogate explorers in a world of glamor and romance, but the traveler's tales they told the fan magazines were far more often of conquest, adventure, and catastrophe than of settlement and contentment.

For a movie that represents Hollywood as a paradigm for the myth of success, *A Star is Born* looks anything but Utopian. Despite the resources of early Technicolor, the movie's somberly lit images leave its playing spaces persistently shadowy and insecure. The primary colors of Hollywood are distinguished from the dark grays, browns, and cold blues of Esther's hometown, but the movie's foreboding visual style is deliberately at odds with what we see of *The Enchanted Hour* and the other products of Niles's studio. The story itself also works to qualify Esther's early fantasies. From the very outset, life in the movie colony is associated with artificiality and illusion. An early montage sequence shows figures at leisure around a swimming pool, apparently enjoying stars' lifestyle. As the camera pans, we see that we are looking at a movie set, and the sun-worshipers are playing for another camera. We discover that stars are made, not born: we witness the fabrication of Esther's own star image in all its mechanistic detail, as she is processed into a marketable commodity. As her life-story is cynically reconstructed to play to the fantasies of her potential audience, the transformation of her identity is accompanied by a loss of personal control. Given a new face, a new walk, a new voice, and a new name, she is reconstructed as the studio "property" Vicki Lester.[90] In a telling irony, Niles tells her that she has been signed for her authenticity, because "tastes are going back to the natural."

The movie's ambivalence toward Hollywood is suggested in its self-consciousness about its own fiction, beginning and ending with images of its own shooting script. It is also embodied in the opposed figures of Libby and Niles. The studio publicist is singled out as the architect of falsification. The movie is punctuated by inserts of front-page stories distorting the lives of the stars: "Night-court drama as star pleads for husband's freedom"; "Ex-star perishes in tragic accident." In search of "angles," Libby robs the stars of their private lives. Esther and Norman narrowly escape the ballyhoo with which Libby threatens to overwhelm their wedding, but their escape is only temporary and their marriage a trigger for further column-inches of gossip: "Which famous male star has stopped gargling the grog and is now taking a non-alcoholic honeymoon?" At their Beverly Hills mansion, Norman tells Esther that they will leave the studio outside the gates of their new home, only to be interrupted immediately by Libby and the studio photographer. Enjoying power without responsibility, Libby relishes and abuses his parasitical position, becoming more vicious as the movie progresses. His contempt for Norman lasts beyond Norman's suicide, as Libby tells a barman, "first drink of water he had in 20 years, and he had to get it by accident. . . . How do you wire congratulations to the Pacific Ocean?"

Significantly, Libby works in a subsidiary industry, and his motives are contrasted with those of the industry proper. Set against his parasitical malevolence is the paternalist figure of Niles, head of the studio, whose only concern is the best interest of his stars. Louis B. Mayer, father-in-law to *A Star is Born*'s producer David O. Selznick, might well have recognized himself in Adolphe Menjou's performance, even if few of his stars would have agreed. Niles is presented as a paragon of virtue, and Vicki is rewarded for subjecting herself to the autocratic control of the star system by earning Niles's support. Prepared to take a loss at the box-office out of loyalty to Maine, he is also willing to offer him work as a way to build his confidence on leaving the sanitarium. This differing representation of the publicist and the studio head reiterates the double image of Hollywood as both dream and nightmare that structures the remainder of the movie. Esther is certainly "reconstructed" to serve the studio's economic self-interest, but also for a larger motive, in which her authentic self-realization is linked to a notion of public service. Esther's star quality lies in making "ordinariness" special, and according to the movie the manufacture of such a contradiction performs a vital role in American culture.

At the start of the movie, Esther's grandmother self-consciously links the idea of Hollywood to the foundation myths of American national identity, and her granddaughter's destiny to the archetypal American experience of the frontier:

> When I wanted something better I came across those plains in a prairie schooner with your grandfather. . . . we were going to make a new country, besides, we wanted to see our dreams come true. . . . There'll always be a new wilderness to conquer. . . . Maybe Hollywood's your wilderness now, from all I hear it sounds like it.

As the agents of a benign destiny, she and Niles share a rhetoric, revolving around the price "in heartbreak" that Esther may have to pay for her success. When Esther prepares to leave Hollywood after Norman's death, her grandmother returns *ex machina* to remind her of her Faustian contract:

> It seems to me that you got more than you bargained for, more fame, more success, even more happiness . . . maybe more unhappiness . . . but you did make a bargain, and now you're whining over it . . . I don't think I'd feel so very proud of myself if I were you, Esther.

After she has enabled Esther to conquer her wilderness and fulfill her specifically American destiny, her grandmother extends her emancipatory power to the movie audience as a whole. At Esther's comeback premiere, she tells a world-wide radio audience:

> Maybe some of you people listening in dream about going to Hollywood, and maybe some of you get pretty discouraged – well, when you do, you just think about me. It took me seventy . . . sixty years to get here, but here I am and here I mean to stay.

Delivered in near direct address outward from the screen, this message incorporates the movie's audience as part of Hollywood, with a role to play in the maintenance of its cultural power and with a lesson to learn from Esther's experience. The movie finally becomes a discussion of the mutual obligations of audiences and stars, and it offers two distinct representations of the audience as well as two versions of Hollywood stardom. As Niles explains, stars are created by audiences, not studio promotion. Stars are representatives of the audience, as much their "property" as the studio's. Audiences validate stars' images through the box-office; the volume of Esther's fan mail provides the key evidence of her acceptability. Because the labor of acting is not shown in the representation of stardom, the ways in which stars are different from their audiences are concealed. Instead, the audience is embodied in Esther/Vicki and celebrated as the industry's ultimate guarantor and harshest judge. Niles tells Norman that "every 25 cents they pay for a theater ticket buys them the right to be a critic."

The audience's loyalty is not guaranteed, however. Crowds cheer outside premieres but they also riot outside churches where private funerals are taking place. Their judgment can be fickle as well as harsh, and there is always the danger that their considerable power will be misguided by the publicists. Their desertion of Norman brings about his collapse and death. In pointing its moral, the movie suggests that stars should keep in touch with audiences, avoid abusing their positions of prestige and power, guard against excess, and not succumb to the publicity myths generated about them. Audiences, on the other hand, should be more skeptical of studio "hype," and exercise their power at the box-office with care, without expecting standards of behavior from the stars that they themselves could not meet. In such ways *A Star is Born* delivers a firm directive to the audience as to its function in the reproduction of Hollywood. The audience should no more consider deserting the stars in the hour of their greatest need than the stars should consider abandoning their audiences when the going gets tough.

Ronald Haver has suggested that *A Star is Born* is "the closest thing we have to an ideal of the movies: what they meant to the people who worked in them and to the people who went to see them."[91] Although the movie is less Utopian than that, its discourse on stardom and the audience indicates that Hollywood's mode of production has always been a tangible force on the way that its movies contain and produce meaning. The audience's knowledge of that mode of production and the industrial system behind it has also provided a source of pleasure to many of its consumers. The conventions by which a viewer is guided through a movie presume an accumulated knowledge of what Hollywood is that extends beyond the boundaries of any individual movie fiction. In this commercial relationship between the audience and the industry, the individual movie is a transient object, an instance in the viewer's longer-term consumption of Hollywood.

Summary

- The 1910s saw the beginning of vertical integration in Hollywood – that is, a company's ownership of and involvement in all branches of the motion picture business: production, distribution, and exhibition. During the period of the "studio system" (1920s to 1950s), the commercial strength of the major companies derived from their status as distributor-exhibitors, rather than from their domination of production. Together, the majors exercised oligopoly control over the industry.

- In 1922, the industry established a trade association, the Motion Picture Producers and Distributors of America, Inc. (MPPDA), to streamline its trade practices and to represent the industry's commercial and political interests both at home and abroad. The MPPDA also administered the industry's system of self-regulation over movie content, as part of its public relations activities.

- American movies achieved domination of the world's movie screens during World War I, and consolidated this domination during the 1920s. By the late 1920s, the foreign market brought the industry approximately 35 percent of its total income. Hollywood's foreign influence was recognized as an important instrument for promoting the sale of American goods abroad.

- Although the motion picture industry has maintained a myth that it is always in financial and artistic crisis, economic historians argue that the industry has been run by rational economic agents making commercial decisions on the basis of standard business criteria. The studio system was economically the most rational way to provide the regulated stability of production and the economies of scale required by the major companies. Maintaining production as a very high-cost activity deterred potential competitors from challenging the majors' control of the industry, as well as providing the expensive spectacle considered to be an essential part of the entertainment package.

- The "studio system" came to an end in 1948 when the US Supreme Court ruled that the majors had an illegal monopoly over the industry, and ordered that production and distribution be separated from exhibition. This ruling, known as the Paramount case decision, marked the beginning of the end of Classical Hollywood production. Subsequently the majors concentrated their industrial power in distribution, acting primarily as bankers and as providers of facilities for independent production companies.

- During the studio period, writers and directors had circumscribed influence upon the final product, and certainly much less influence than the producer, who exercised control over almost all aspects of a movie's development. Stars too had limited power: most were employed on long, fixed-term contracts with a single studio and had little control over their appearance in movies.

- The typical product of the studio system was a "star vehicle," a movie constructed around the appeal of one or more particular stars and sold on that basis. Stars were the commodities that most consistently drew audiences to the movies, and the star system in the studio period provided every member of the audience with an ideal version of herself or himself.

Further Reading

The early industry

In addition to *The Classical Hollywood Cinema* and the volumes in the *History of American Cinema* series by Charles Musser and Eileen Bowser (see the "Classical Hollywood histories" section of chapter 1's "Further Reading" for bibliographical details), see Richard Abel, *The Red Rooster Scare: Making Cinema American, 1900–1910* (Berkeley, CA: University of California Press, 1999).

Distribution and exhibition

Douglas Gomery, *Shared Pleasures: A History of Movie Presentation in the United States* (London: British Film Institute, 1992), examines the important and often neglected exhibition sector, and includes a discussion of theaters for black audiences. Maggie Valentine, *The Show Starts on the Sidewalk: An Architectural History of the Movie Theater* (New Haven: Yale University Press, 1994) provides a good introduction to this aspect of exhibition history. There is as yet no comprehensive history of movie distribution, but Tino Balio, ed., *The American Film Industry*, 1st edn 1976, revised edn (Madison: University of Wisconsin Press, 1985), provides an excellent account of the operations of the majors as vertically integrated companies. Two good historical overviews of the Classical industry are Douglas Gomery, *The Hollywood Studio System* (London: Macmillan, 1986), which has a chapter on the economic history of each of the major Hollywood studios, and John Izod, *Hollywood and the Box Office 1895–1986* (London: Macmillan, 1988). Two useful collections of essays on aspects of the industry are Gorham Kinden, ed., *The American Movie Industry: The Business of Motion Pictures* (Carbondale: Southern Illinois University Press, 1982), and Paul Kerr, ed., *The Hollywood Film Industry* (London: Routledge and Kegan Paul, 1986).

The best sources of statistics on the industry are the annuals *Film Daily Yearbook* (New York: Jack Alicoate) and *Motion Picture Almanac*, later *International Motion Picture Almanac* (New York: Quigley). Joel W. Finler, *The Hollywood Story: Everything You Always Wanted to Know about the American Movie Business but Didn't Know Where to Look* (London: Octopus Books, 1988), is a useful source of financial and statistical information.

The studio system

Thomas Schatz, *The Genius of the System: Hollywood Filmmaking in the Studio Era* (New York: Pantheon, 1988), is the best history of production during the studio period. The volumes by Schatz, Tino Balio, Donald Crafton, and Richard Koszarski in the *History of the American Cinema* series are also valuable sources, as are Janet Staiger's contributions to *The Classical Hollywood Cinema*.

Older histories of individual studios tend to rely for most of their information on reminiscence and anecdote and, like the great majority of Hollywood biographies, should be handled with care, and not assumed to be accurate. More recent works, making use of studio records, are much more reliable. Some good examples are Tino Balio, *United Artists: The Company Built by the Stars* (Madison: University of Wisconsin Press, 1976); Nick Roddick, *A New Deal in Entertainment: Warner Brothers in the 1930s* (London: British Film Institute, 1983); and Bernard F. Dick, *City of Dreams: The Making and Remaking of Universal Pictures* (Lexington: University Press of Kentucky, 1997). Rudy Behlmer, ed., *Inside Warner Bros. (1935–1951)* (London: Weidenfeld and Nicolson, 1986), is a collection of production documents that provides valuable insights into the operation of a studio.

Classical Hollywood's publicity machine is described and illustrated in Robert S. Sennett, *Hollywood Hoopla: Creating Stars and Selling Movies in the Golden Age of Hollywood* (New York: Billboard Books, 1998). Mark S. Miller describes another aspect of promotion in "Helping Exhibitors: Pressbooks at Warner Bros. in the late 1930s," *Film History* 6:2 (Summer 1994), pp. 188–96.

Mike Nielsen and Gene Mailes, *Hollywood's Other Blacklist: Union Struggles in the Studio System* (London: British Film Institute, 1995), offers a first-hand account of the union movement in Hollywood as well as an historical overview of the events and issues. Denise Hartsough, "Crime Pays: The Studios' Labor Deals in the 1930s," in *The Studio System*, ed. Janet Staiger (New Brunswick, NJ: Rutgers University Press, 1994), describes the studios' relationship with the unions in the 1930s. Gerald Horne, *Class Struggle in Hollywood, 1930–1950: Moguls, Mobsters, Stars, Reds and Trade Unionists* (Austin: University of Texas Press, 2001), has a detailed account of the strikes of the 1940s. More recent aspects of Hollywood's labor history are discussed in Lois S. Gray and Ronald L. Seeber, eds, *Under the Stars: Essays on Labor Relations in Arts and Entertainment* (Ithaca, NY: Cornell University Press, 1996).

The moguls

F. Scott Fitzgerald's fictionalized account of a studio head's work in *The Last Tycoon* (Harmondsworth: Penguin, 1974) remains the most accessible explanation of what the most powerful and important figures in the studio system did. Leo Rosten, *Hollywood: The Movie Colony, the Movie Makers* (New York: Harcourt, Brace, 1941), has an excellent description of the day-to-day activities of a producer on pp. 231–8. George F. Custen, *Twentieth Century's Fox: Darryl F. Zanuck and the Culture of Hollywood* (New York: Basic Books, 1997), provides an assessment of Darryl Zanuck's career as, "with Irving Thalberg, the most important and most influential producer in the history of the American cinema." In his book about Warner Bros. in the 1930s, Roddick makes a similar argument for the studio's head of production, Hal Wallis, being its dominant creative presence.

In *Hollywood and Anti-Semitism: A Cultural History* (Cambridge: Cambridge University Press, 2001), Steven Carr argues that the mythology of Jewish control of the industry – what he calls "the Hollywood Question" – has been a determining influence on the writing of Hollywood's history. For an influential example of this mythologizing, based on anecdote rather than corporate history, see Neal Gabler, *An Empire of Their Own: How the Jews Invented Hollywood* (New York: Crown, 1988). Lary May presents a more persuasive argument about the significance of Jewish influence on movie production in *Screening Out the Past: The Birth of*

Mass Culture and the Motion Picture Industry (New York: Oxford University Press, 1980).

Writers and scandals

Richard Fine, *West of Eden: Writers in Hollywood, 1928–1940* (Washington, DC: Smithsonian Institution Press, 1993), describes the position of writers in the studio system. Tom Dardis, *Some Time in the Sun: The Hollywood Years of Fitzgerald, Faulkner, Nathanael West, Aldous Huxley, and James Agee* (London: André Deutsch, 1976), and Ian Hamilton, *Writers in Hollywood* (London: Heinemann, 1990), reproduce most of the best-known anecdotes about the studios' employment of major literary figures.

For discussions of women in Classical Hollywood production, see Cari Beauchamp, *Without Lying Down: Frances Marion and the Powerful Women of Early Hollywood* (Berkeley, CA: University of California Press, 1997), and Lizzie Francke, *Script Girls: Women Screenwriters in Hollywood* (London: British Film Institute, 1994).

For accounts of Hollywood's scandals untroubled by any obligation to historical accuracy, the best source is Kenneth Anger, *Hollywood Babylon* (San Francisco, CA: Straight Arrow, 1975) and *Hollywood Babylon II* (London: Arrow, 1984). A more reliable guide can be found in Adrienne L. McLean and David A. Cook, eds, *Headline Hollywood: A Century of Film Scandal* (New Brunswick, NJ: Rutgers University Press, 2001).

Stardom

Much has been written about the phenomenon of stardom, and there is an abundance of biographies and autobiographies of most Hollywood celebrities, most of them of little real value for understanding the star system. Richard Dyer's books *Stars* (London: British Film Institute, 1979) and *Heavenly Bodies: Film Stars and Society* (London: Macmillan, 1987) are substantial studies, and Christine Gledhill, ed., *Stardom: Industry of Desire* (London: Routledge, 1991), provides a good collection of essays on various aspects of the star system. Richard deCordova, *Picture Personalities: The Emergence of the Star System in America* (Urbana: University of Illinois Press, 1990), is an excellent account of the development of movie stardom. Danae Clark, *Negotiating Hollywood: The Cultural Politics of Actors' Labor* (Minneapolis: University of Minnesota Press, 1995), and Sean P. Holmes, "The Hollywood Star System and the Regulation of Actors' Labor, 1916–1934," *Film History* 12:1 (2000), pp. 97–114, describe the working conditions of actors in early and Classical Hollywood. Jackie Stacey, *Star Gazing: Hollywood Cinema and Female Spectatorship* (London: Routledge, 1994), explores the relationship between audiences and stars.

CHAPTER SIX
Industry 2:
1948 to 1980

Ownership of entertainment distribution capability is like ownership of a toll road or bridge. No matter how good or bad the software product (i.e., movie, record, book, magazine, tv show, or whatever) is, it must pass over or cross through a distribution pipeline in order to reach the consumer. And like at any toll road or bridge that cannot be circumvented, the distributor is a local monopolist who can extract a relatively high fee for use of his facility.

Harold L. Vogel[1]

I gotta have a lot of money. I gotta have a lot of money to juice the guys I gotta juice, so I can get a lot of money, so I can juice the guys I gotta juice.

Marty Augustine (Mark Rydell) in *The Long Goodbye* (1973)

The Supreme Court's decision in the Paramount case signaled the end of the Classical Hollywood system by undermining its economic rationale. The major companies' oligopoly power had resided in their domination of both distribution and first-run exhibition. Divorcement separated these interests, forcing the majors to find ways of orchestrating the industry's profitability through their control of distribution alone. At the same time, moviegoing ceased to be a regular habit for most of the American population. By 1953, only half as many people in the US were going to the movies as had done seven years earlier. A 1957 survey found that only 15 percent of the American public attended the cinema as often as once a week, and this group of frequent attenders – three-quarters of them under 30 – accounted for nearly two-thirds of total admissions. As the American middle class moved to the suburbs, audiences gradually abandoned the city-center picture palaces and neighborhood theaters of the 1930s, first for drive-in theaters, and after 1970 for the shopping mall multiplexes that replaced them.

The industrial system that came to replace Classical Hollywood was shaped by large-scale social, economic, and technological changes that were barely discernible when the Paramount decrees came into force. Just as the development of Classical Hollywood's system of vertical integration was more clearly visible with the hindsight provided by the view from the mature system, so it is now possible to see Hollywood's postwar history as a long process of development toward the American cinema we recognize today, in which Hollywood is a fully integrated part of a much larger and more diversified entertainment industry. The industry's reorganization was a long, slow process, and the period of transition from one system to another lasted more than 20 years, as Hollywood adjusted to shifting leisure habits and devised new production, financing, and marketing regimes. No longer the dominant mass entertainment form, movies became a specialized form of participatory activity in a larger field of recreational behavior.

By 1970, the "**blockbuster** syndrome" was shaping industry assumptions about the profitability of its products. A 1972 *Variety* analysis indicated that in 1971, 52 percent of the total box-office income had been earned by only 14 movies, and as few as one-third of the 185 pictures released had broken even.[2] The industry came to accept that a seismic shift had occurred in the market, concentrating prof-itability on a very small number of movies. The guiding principles of the indus-try's practice grew from this and other analyses of the blockbuster syndrome, in which it was to be expected that seven movies out of every ten would lose money, two would break even, and one would make sufficiently large profits to cover the distributor's losses on the other nine. The majors' new corporate managements devised production and distribution strategies to manage the increased risks of post-Classical Hollywood's new economics. Counter-intuitively, perhaps, these strategies included a sharp reduction in the volume of production and an escala-tion in the cost of production and marketing, which has continued unabated since 1970.

Between 1968 and 1971, the industry experienced a financial crisis generated by an overinvestment in feature production. This crisis signaled the end of the Classical Hollywood system of industrial production, and its replacement by a much more fragmented system in which movies were assembled through a complex of short-term contractual agreements orchestrated by an entrepreneurial packager. "Studios" ceased to be centers of production, becoming instead sources of finance and distribution. By the mid-1970s the post-Paramount attitude of regarding each production as a one-off event had reached a point where none of the majors any longer possessed a recognizable identity either in its personnel or in its product. For a brief period in the early 1970s, however, the collapse of the old order was understood as having given rise to a new American cinema created by the first generation of film-school trained auteurs for a more critically informed and adult audience. The illusion that power in the Hollywood system had shifted from the major companies to the creative talent lasted for most of the 1970s, but the tax incentives that had funded the auteurist cinema of the "Hollywood Renaissance" were withdrawn in 1976, and production funding for aesthetically adventurous but uncommercial movies evaporated. During the 1970s the box-office recovered on the strength of blockbusters aimed primarily at a young male audience, and by 1980 it was apparent that the legacy of the crisis of the late 1960s was not greater freedom for the individual filmmaker, but a distribution system that sought stability through the intensive marketing of a small number of high-budget movies.

The Effects of Divorcement

The year 1946 was the industry's most profitable, with the largest audiences ever. Most industry leaders expected the postwar industry to go from strength to strength, but instead, from 1947, it went into quite sudden, precipitous decline. Moviegoing had accounted for 25 percent of Americans' expenditure on recreation during the war, but as more options became available in the postwar years, that proportion fell rapidly to 12.3 percent in 1950. By 1962, admissions had fallen to barely a quarter of their 1946 level, although because ticket prices were inflated, box-office gross fell by only half. As historian Tino Balio has explained, "Hollywood upscaled its top product in the face of waning consumer demand and raised the price of admission."[3] Contrary to the intentions of the Paramount decrees, the majors retained their near-monopoly over distribution, and actually increased their share of box-office income, from 30 percent in 1948 to 48 percent in 1963. To retain their control over distribution and prevent a fall in the cost of film **rentals**, the majors reduced the number of pictures they released, forcing exhibitors to compete harder for product.

The divorcement of theaters would have been enough to bring about the abandonment of the studio system by itself, since that system's heavy investment in the overheads of studio plant and contract lists was economically viable only so long as the profitability of the bulk of its product was guaranteed. The slow, reluctant decline of the studios was obscured by the companies' continuing successful operations as distributors of independently produced films. Because the Paramount decrees drastically altered the basis on which movies were sold for exhibition, the decline was inevitable once they took effect.

In the period immediately after divorcement, Hollywood retrenched, cutting back severely on production: B-pictures, shorts, cartoons, and newsreels were dropped, and the studios concentrated their efforts on fewer A-pictures. The studios gradually phased out the standardized production of the moderate- to low-budget, formulaic movies that had sustained the industry by dependably meeting the fixed expense of studio overhead and the screen-time demands of exhibitors. No longer guaranteed a market for all their products, producers and distributors alike were forced to sell each movie on its individual merits. Production values and costs rose to ensure sales, with an ever-increasing emphasis on the "prestige" pro-

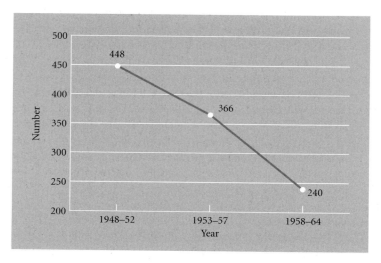

Pictures released by the major companies, 1948–64

duction. MGM's *Mogambo* in 1953 was far from being the most extravagant of the studio's products for that year, but it featured three of their highest-salaried contract stars – Clark Gable, Ava Gardner and Grace Kelly. A-feature budgets of over $1m, rare in the 1940s, became the norm after 1953 as talent and finance were concentrated on a smaller number of productions intended to play for long spells in early-run theaters.

This change meant dropping term contracts with creative personnel and reducing production at the studios. In 1947, 742 actors were under contract to the major studios; by 1956, only 229 were, most of them at MGM or Universal. In 1958, *Variety* observed that "it is generally believed that the entire theatrical output of Hollywood can now be made in one studio, such as Metro's or Warner's."[4] The major studios increasingly became packagers, financiers, and distributors of independently produced feature films. RKO, always the weakest of the Big Five, had its assets stripped by Howard Hughes, and was closed down in 1955.

The primary cause of this industry recession was not, as is often suggested, television, but, somewhat perversely, the prosperity of the American economy that produced the migration to the suburbs and the baby boom. Television was the most visible superficial symptom of the profound change in postwar entertainment patterns, but the real cause of the movies' decline lay in the economic and socio-cultural transformation of blue- and white-collar Americans into the "leisured masses." During the war, wages had doubled and savings had tripled. In the immediate postwar years, people cashed in their savings, spending them on long-unavailable consumer durables. Sponsored by government loans, home ownership increased by nearly 50 percent between 1945 and 1950, and by another 50 percent between 1950 and 1960, as the American middle class fled the cities to new suburbs. During the 1950s, 18 million Americans moved to the suburbs, and by 1960 one-quarter of the entire population lived in new suburban areas. Sixty percent of American families owned the homes they lived in, 75 percent owned a car and a washing machine, and 87 percent owned a television set. Never, as one commentator put it, "had so many people, anywhere, been so well off."[5]

As fast as the newly affluent Americans bought consumer goods, they also acquired children, raising birth rates to record levels during the "baby boom" of 1945–64. Disposable personal income rose by 35 percent at the same time as the length of the working week fell from 48 to 40 hours. With more money to spend and more leisure time in which to spend it, middle- and working-class Americans could devote larger blocks of time to recreation than had been possible before. The traditional six-day working week had encouraged the careful budgeting of leisure time, making an evening at the movies an ideal solution to consumers' short-term needs for inexpensive entertainment. The new postwar five-day work week and paid vacations created more opportunities for other, more time-intensive activities such as gardening, "do-it-yourself," and sports. Television suited this new lifestyle by providing easily available passive entertainment at all times. Suburban development gave a boost to all forms of "home entertainment" and domestic hobbies, but no new consumer commodity has ever sold so fast or penetrated the available market so thoroughly as television did in the US in the 1950s. It was the perfect commodity for the moment; like the recliner chair, television was a consumer durable that "did" something; like the radio only better, television brought entertainment into the home, and in doing so it reinforced the value that suburbanites put on the nuclear home as the protected center of their existence.

Although the smaller independent exhibitors had apparently won their case in the Supreme Court, the policy decisions taken by the majors ensured that these exhibitors were, in fact, the principal victims of the Paramount decision. Starved of product by the majors' policies of phasing out B-features and medium-budget pictures, faced with competition from television, and deserted because of migration to the new suburbs, the "Mom and Pop" theaters in inner cities, neighborhoods, and rural areas closed in droves, while the majors' now separate production-distribution and exhibition operations remained relatively healthy. Between 1947 and 1963, 48 percent of four-wall theaters closed, at the rate of about two a day. In 1956, of the 19,000 theaters operating in the US, 5,200 were operating at a loss and 5,700 were breaking even; 56 percent were failing to make a profit. The vast majority of those that closed, and a majority of those doing poorly, were small, late-run houses catering mainly to family audiences in neighborhood or rural areas. Those audiences had disappeared, while the small theaters that relied on showing two or three different programs a week to a small but regular audience were afflicted by the chronic product shortage. Unable to afford the cost of conversion to the new projection methods, these theaters were deprived of the most profitable part of the industry's product, while audiences who wished to see *How to Marry a Millionaire* (1953) were lured away from the neighborhoods by advertising campaigns which stressed the novelties only available in the more expensive theaters. At the same time, drive-in cinemas, catering to a younger

Box 6.1   Drive-ins

The first drive-in was opened in New Jersey in 1933, but there were fewer than 25 in the country in 1945. By 1948 there were 800, by 1950 there were 2,000, by 1956 there were 4,000. By 1952, 4 million patrons per week attended drive-ins, and 25 percent of box-office grosses came from them. By 1958 nearly one-third of the cinemas in the country were drive-ins, and their capacity more than made up for the number of seats lost through other closures.

In many ways, drive-ins represented a return to older, pre-Classical Hollywood exhibition strategies, attracting a noticeably different, more informal audience from those attending the downtown theaters. Publicity designed to appeal to working-class families often emphasized that audiences did not need to dress up to go to the drive-in, which promoted themselves as "the answer to the sitter problem, and to the downtown parking problem . . . the answer to the young family's night out."[6] As Mary Morley Cohen argues, drive-ins allowed viewers to be "at home" in the partial privacy of their own automobile, "to relax and ignore the conventions and constraints of public behavior."[7] Drive-in viewers could smoke, eat, talk, and most important for their family clientele, they could bring the children, usually for no extra cost:

> The obligatory playground was always prominently placed directly under the screen. The idea was that parents could watch the film and monitor the children at the same time. Its location also meant that the rest of the audience was constantly reminded that children were present. ... The emphasis on children . . . created a spectacle of innocence, youth and old-fashioned family values.

As well as a playground, a deluxe drive-in accommodating 2,000 or more cars would contain a cafeteria with snack bar, and laundry facilities so that families could finish household chores while watching the movies. Some offered shuffleboard, horseshoes, miniature golf, wading pools, baby bottle warmers, firework exhibitions, facilities for the family cat or dog, free pony rides, or petting zoos. Drive-ins also sold about five times as much candy, popcorn, and soft drinks as the average "hard-top." Some operators calculated that for every dollar spent on admission, another dollar was spent at the concession stand, and teenagers were the highest spenders, as well as the most reliable sector of the audience.

Although drive-ins attempted to project a family image, local authorities and distributors viewed them unsympathetically. City officials often imposed curfews, on the grounds that they had "a demoralizing influence leading to promiscuous relationships,"[8] and encouraged juvenile delinquency. Major distributors were reluctant to allow drive-ins access to their product, at least in first-run, in the belief that it lowered the status and the earnings potential of the movie. Despite their popularity with a section of the "lost" audience, drive-ins never overcame distributor opposition, or their widespread reputation as teenage "passion pits."

and more mobile audience, were opening at almost exactly the same rate as four-wall houses were closing down.

The Paramount decrees prevented the major theater chains from any substantial expansion, effectively prohibiting them from acquiring or building new theaters in the suburbs. Faced with declining attendance figures, reduced cash flow and rampant theater closings, few independent theater chains could afford to expand. Drive-ins were the quickest and cheapest way to develop new theaters in the suburbs, incurring only the costs of land acquisition and development, and the construction of a screen, projection booth, and sound system. The drive-in – "the neighborhood theater of the future," according to exhibitor Robert Lippert – was the most obvious indication that urban downtown areas were ceasing to be the center of social and cultural activity for most Americans.[9] Suburbanization doomed the downtown deluxe movie theater, which had been "the lifeblood of the motion picture industry for decades."[10]

Roadshows and Teenpix

Only days before the Paramount decrees came into effect in December 1949, Paramount released a movie that was at the same time a return to the prewar studio system's "superspecial" roadshow picture, and a portent of the "blockbuster" phenomenon that came to dominate Hollywood's economic and aesthetic practice. *Samson and Delilah*, a $3.5-million Technicolor Biblical epic produced and directed by Cecil B. de Mille, seemed quite out of keeping with the dominant styles and strategies of the late 1940s, harking back instead to de Mille's exotic spectacles of the 1920s. Its huge domestic and international success, however, signaled the industry's future direction. Earning as much as *Gone with the Wind* had done on its initial release and more than twice as much as any other movie released in 1949, *Samson and Delilah* spawned a cycle of extravagant Biblical spectaculars that dominated the box-office during the 1950s: *David and Bathsheba* (1951), *Quo Vadis?* (1952), *The Robe* (1953), *The Ten Commandments* (1956), *Ben-Hur* (1959). In part addressed to the 60 percent of Americans who affirmed the American Way of Life through church membership, the Biblical blockbusters united their epic subject matter with the new widescreen technologies, demonstrating the majors' pre-eminent strengths as production-distribution companies for the international market; by the early 1960s, the majors were earning over 40 percent of their distribution income from foreign sales.[11]

These movies were the centerpieces of the most profitable distribution strategy of the 1950s and 1960s, the **roadshow**, which replaced the exhibition practice of continuous performance with a limited number of showings (usually two a day), reserved seating ("hard tickets") at higher than normal prices, and long engagements, usually at only one large theater in each market. Roadshow pictures were Hollywood's most extravagant demonstration that movies were greater and grander than television, and the industry's most explicit attempt to turn moviegoing into a special occasion. Apart from Biblical pictures, roadshows were most

The Robe (1953), the first movie in CinemaScope, was also one of a cycle of biblical epics made in the 1950s, offering to engulf its audience in its story of "Love, Faith, and Overwhelming Spectacle."

often historical epics or musicals, but they were defined by their large budgets, long running times, multiple-star casts, lavish production values, and big-screen technology. The commercial success of CinemaScope pictures in the early 1950s confirmed the belief that big-budget movies were more profitable than smaller productions, particularly as far as distributors were concerned. In 1968 *Variety* reported that of the 25 movies that had earned over $15 million in rentals, 17 had had a "hard-ticket" premiere. Ultra-high-budget movies were not only more profitable, but also more reliably profitable than other pictures: one-third of the roadshow pictures earned over $10 million in rentals in the 1960s, compared to only 1 percent of all releases.

Roadshow movies formed a relatively small part of Hollywood's output, with each major releasing no more than one or two a year during the 1960s. Other high-budget prestige productions were released on "**exclusive engagements**," for continuous performances in a limited number of theaters, before going into "general release," where they would play in several theaters in each market at the same time. This pattern later became known as **platform release.** The combination of these production and exhibition strategies concentrated earnings and

Julie Andrews brings the hills, and the box-office, to life in *The Sound of Music* (1965).
Produced by Robert Wise; distributed by Twentieth Century-Fox.

profits in fewer movies, as the blockbuster phenomenon developed. Before 1960, only 20 movies had grossed over $10 million in the domestic market; by 1970, more than 80 had.[12] For the successful, the profits were enormous, far greater than those made under the old studio system. In 1965, *The Sound of Music*, which was made for $8 million, earned $72 million in the US and Canada alone. Unsuccessful blockbusters were comparably damaging: the commercial failure of *Mutiny on the Bounty* (1962) was largely responsible for MGM's corporate loss of $17 million in 1963. For distributors, however, the relatively small number of big successes outweighed the losses on the majority of releases. Of a group of 20 features produced by the Mirisch brothers for United Artists (UA) between 1958 and 1963, only five – *Some Like It Hot* (1959), *The Apartment* (1960), *The Magnificent Seven* (1960), *Irma La Douce* (1963), and *The Great Escape* (1963) – earned profits, and the group as a whole lost $8.7 million on a total rental income of $92 million. UA, however, absorbed the loss within their distribution fees of $32 million, and remained comfortably in surplus after their distribution costs had been paid.[13]

As both production and audiences declined, a number of smaller urban theaters turned to non-Hollywood product as a means of sustaining their business. The postwar revival of European film production and the shortage of American product stimulated this trend. By 1949, about 250 theaters were regularly playing foreign films, while an occasional critically acclaimed release like *The Bicycle Thief* (1949) achieved wider circulation. By 1952, as many as 1,500 American theaters had some policy of booking "art" movies, while nearly 500 "art houses" in major cities and college towns consciously fostered a specialized audience. *The Bicycle Thief* was one of many foreign movies to experience difficulties with the Production Code and local censorship: as one critic observed in 1951, "sex in frank, liberal doses helps a foreign film earn a profit."[14] The Supreme Court's decision to reverse its 1915 ruling and award movies the Constitutional protection of free speech under the First Amendment came in a case heard in 1952 over the attempt to ban Roberto Rossellini's *The Miracle* (1948) in New York on the grounds that it was "sacrilegious."

The growth of the art-house circuit provided perhaps the clearest indication that the industry recognized its audiences as increasingly segmented. It also signaled that at least part of "the lost audience" – "the hundred million people physically and financially able to attend theaters" – could be lured back to the cinema with the right product, which, according to a 1959 survey, meant "a realistic treatment of a social problem."[15] UA experimented with releasing independent producer Stanley Kramer's social problem movies *Champion* and *Home of the Brave* (both 1949) through art houses before giving them a broader release, and repeated the strategy with *Marty* in 1955; more generally, the success of the art houses' appeal to adult-only audiences stimulated Hollywood's willingness to combine serious social subjects with varying degrees of sensational appeal in "adult" dramas. (See chapter 4 for more discussion.)

The "adult" movie was one sign that Hollywood was gradually recognizing that the mass audience had fragmented. The industry seemed, however, reluctant to acknowledge what every audience survey revealed: that, as critic Gilbert Seldes observed in 1950, "the real paying audience is made up of younger people . . . The movies live on children from the ages of ten to nineteen, who go steadily and frequently and almost automatically to the pictures." Once they reached their twenties, people went to the movies less and less often, while more than half the American population over 30 "do not bother to see more than one picture a month; after fifty, more than half see virtually no pictures at all." The industry's vaunted four billion paid admissions a year was actually made up of "a probable thirty million separate moviegoers, chiefly young people, many of whom go several times a week." As few as 15 million individuals "actually see the basic staple commodity of Hollywood, the A feature-picture."[16]

What changed in the 1950s, however, was not so much that Hollywood recognized a long-established truth about the composition of its audience as that the "seven golden years" of adolescence were identified for the first time as a specific market for the manufacture and merchandising of consumer goods. Although the word "teen-age" had been in circulation since the 1920s, the idea that the period of life between childhood and adulthood had its own peculiar characteristics was a cultural innovation of the postwar years. Before then, "teen-agers" were not differentiated from young adults as consumers, but by 1959, the teenage consumer market was estimated to be worth $10 billion a year.[17]

Much of this market was for cheap consumable goods that identified teenagers as a subculture. Its defining commodity was music: to a much greater extent than any previous form of popular music, rock 'n' roll appealed specifically to one generation and was heartily rejected by their elders, not least because of its blatant transgression of racial and class boundaries. The first major rock 'n' roll hit single, the Crew Cuts' *Sh-Boom*, was released in 1954. In 1955, teenage audiences made James Dean a cult star. In 1956, independent producer Sam Katzman made the first rock 'n' roll **exploitation** movie by building a picture around the title music from *Blackboard Jungle* (1955), an "adult" movie about juvenile delinquency which was reported to be the favorite movie of high-school students. Marketed at teenagers to the pointed exclusion of their elders, *Rock Around the Clock* demonstrated that teenage audiences could sustain a box-office hit, and it was followed almost immediately by half a dozen rock 'n' roll pictures. By the end of 1956, *Variety* noted that:

> the demand for teenage pictures . . . is coming from all quarters – from small theaters as well as large circuits, from rural towns as well as big cities. The cry to assuage [the] teenage market is so great that some observers are already expressing the fear that the only outlet for mature films will be the art house. . . . The exploitation pix and rock 'n' rollers, while not drawing the audience "we want," are nevertheless bringing crowds to pay windows.[18]

"Exploitation pictures" had previously filled an exhibition niche beneath the respectability of the majors, presenting subjects prohibited by the Production Code such as sex hygiene, prostitution, and drug use in a style that combined sensationalism, a purportedly "educational" manner, and a very low budget. In the mid-1950s the term came to be more loosely applied to the output of independent companies such as American International Pictures (AIP) and Allied Artists, which sought to fill the product shortage for the 8,000 theaters still showing double bills. Unlike B-features, these movies had to sell on their own appeal rather than as additions to an A-feature, and their distributors resorted to exploitation strategies in marketing them specifically at the teenage audience. Two of the earliest movies in the cycle, Universal's *Running Wild* and Katzman's *Teenage Crime Wave* (both 1955), advertised themselves as "The Stark Brutal Truth about Today's Lost Generation!" and "The Terrifying Story of Our Teenagers Gone Wrong!"

Inevitably, this approach raised concerns about the movies' role in provoking juvenile delinquency, but despite their titles *Hot Rod Girl* (1956), *Untamed Youth* (1957), *Young and Wild* (1958), *High School Hellcats* (1958), and *High School Confidential* (1958) were far more circumspect in their content than the majors' "adult" movies had become, particularly after the 1956 revisions to the Production Code. As *Motion Picture Herald* explained to exhibitors in 1957, AIP's policy was to provide "satisfactory screen material for the teenage audience without estranging their elders or their juniors . . . AIP product . . . must not ever under any conditions seem to have been especially chosen for them, conditioned to their years, or equipped with special messages."[19] Comparing their product to major productions like *Peyton Place* and *No Down Payment* (both 1957), AIP's Samuel Z. Arkoff declared that the monsters in AIP's horror movies "do not smoke, drink or lust."[20] "Our stories," insisted company head James H. Nicholson,

> are pure fantasy with no attempt at realism. Because of this it is difficult to see how anyone could take our pictures so seriously that psychological damage could occur . . . In our concept of each of our monsters, we strive for unbelievability. Teenagers, who comprise our largest audience, recognize this and laugh at the caricatures we represent, rather than shrink in terror. Adults, more serious-minded perhaps, often miss the point of the joke.[21]

AIP's teenpix represented one element in the growth of independent production in the postwar period. The majors' reconstruction of their business created a range of new opportunities for independent producers to enter the market. There was a steady rise in the number of independent producers, from 40 in 1945 to 93 in 1947 to 165 in 1957. In 1949, 20 percent of the movies released by the majors were produced by independent production companies; by 1957, that proportion had tripled to 58 percent. By then only Universal had no involvement with independent production. The growth of independent production companies did not, however, increase the overall level of production, and the majors retained control over the industry by securing both producers' access to exhibition and exhibitors' access to product.

Independents, Agents, and Television

The gradual abandonment of the studio system of production effectively redefined the term "studio." From the mid-1950s, "studio" identified a company involved in the production and distribution of pictures. Increasingly, "studios" provided financing, studio space, and most importantly distribution deals to "independent" production companies. Independent producers had no corporate ties to distributors, and might be contracted to produce a single picture or an annual slate. Most independent producers were former studio employees, freed from long-term studio contracts and seeking the tax advantages that came from operating their own companies.

Independent production was initially hailed as "a kind of cure-all for what ails Hollywood, both artistically and commercially," and as "a source of new freedom, new talent, and new ideas," allowing for more individual expression than had been permitted under the studio hierarchies.[22] In reality, however, independent producers were only as free as their distribution deal let them be, and few had any more creative autonomy than an established studio producer had under the Classical system. Most producers would be more accurately classified as "semi-independent," since the precondition of their movies' production was a guarantee of distribution, under terms defined by the major distributor. Effectively, the majors assimilated independent production as an alternative to the studio system, and UA, which had always operated as a distributor of independently produced movies, became the prototype for the post-Paramount "studio."

Under the management of Arthur Krim and Robert Benjamin, UA was responsible for the most vigorous development of independent production methods. As Tino Balio argues, UA "established the parameters of the relationship between the distributor-financier and the producer," and formulated the main line of development for the post-Classical industry.[23] Krim and Benjamin offered independent producers complete production financing, creative control over their own work, and a share of the profits for distribution rights. Unburdened by the overhead costs of studio facilities borne by the other majors, UA also allowed producers to work wherever they liked, and thus take advantage of foreign subsidies and tax benefits. The company secured its reputation for supporting creative talent by backing producer-director Otto Preminger's challenges to the Production Code over *The Moon is Blue* (1953) and *The Man with the Golden Arm* (1955), and financing off-beat productions such as *Marty*, an adaptation of a television play about a romance between a Bronx butcher and a schoolteacher, which won four Oscars, including best picture in 1956. By 1967, these strategies had turned UA into the largest producer-distributor in Hollywood.

In a period of falling audiences and increasing production costs, the value of successful stars rose. So did their bargaining power, since movies would not secure financing without a name of proven box-office worth. The majors developed semi-autonomous production units that offered producers and stars a much greater element of creative authority, as well as a share of the often elusive profits. In a famous early example, James Stewart's contract for starring in *Winchester '73* (1950) gave him 50 percent of the movie's profits. Its unexpected success meant that Stewart earned $600,000 for this performance.

When the studios dismantled the studio system, they gave up their role of developing and nurturing talent. This role, and the power that accrued to it, passed to the talent agents, and agencies such as William Morris and the Music Corporation of America (MCA) took over the traditional studio function of "packaging" a movie's basic "properties" – the script, one or two stars, perhaps the director – and selling the package to a studio, which acted primarily as a banker supplying financing and a landlord renting studio facilities to the production company. By the late 1960s, as much as two-thirds of Hollywood's production output was "pre-packaged" in this way, and both the practice and the terminology of packaging stressed what I have called the aggregated character of Hollywood's commercial aesthetic (see chapter 3). Writer Joan Didion argued that packaging the deal had itself become a Hollywood art form, described in aesthetic terms: " 'A very imaginative deal,' they say, or, 'He writes the most creative deals in the business.' . . . The action is everything . . . the picture itself is in many ways only the action's by-product."[24] Packaging certainly altered the distribution of power within Hollywood production, greatly enhancing the influence and authority of talent agencies, but its procedures were in practice not very different from the way that a studio head of production would assemble a team to produce a star vehicle in the studio system.

Blockbuster distribution patterns flattened out the multiple exhibition tiers of the clearance system into a two-tier system of roadshows or exclusive engagements and general release, with a third, much later tier of television screenings. The parts of the exhibition system most affected by both blockbusters and television were the later subsequent-run theaters, in which the majors had always had least financial interest. Television was not the initial cause of the decline in attendance. When box-office receipts began to fall in 1947, there were fewer television sets in the US than there were cinemas. By 1950, when a third of the weekly audience had stopped going to the movies, there were still only a handful of television stations and only four million families owned sets. By 1955, when television services began to be really profitable, the box in the family home reinforced older people's decisions to stay home, and those decisions continued to undermine the economics of subsequent-run exhibition.

In addition to its effect on exhibition patterns, the Paramount decision was pivotal to the relationship between the film and television industries. The government's anti-trust suit against the majors stimulated anxieties that they might also attempt to control television, unless they were resisted by regulation. From the mid-1940s onward the Federal Communication Commission (FCC) restricted the majors' involvement in broadcasting, and in particular hindered the development of pay TV, which the film industry had recognized as a potential additional mode of exhibition.[25] The FCC's resistance ensured that, during the 1950s and 1960s, only the production sector of the movie industry became integrally involved in television, while experiments with subscription and theater television gradually withered away. The steady decline in movie audiences pitted exhibitors against television as an outlet, but for the studios themselves television production replaced in both volume and quality the formulaic output of programmers, B-features, and shorts that had serviced the economies of scale in plant and personnel and justified the studio system.[26] In several cases, including Columbia's Screen Gems, the subsidiary company responsible for the production of shorts was converted into the television subsidiary.

While the majors were deprived of the opportunity to control television distribution by government regulation, historian Michelle Hilmes has argued that during the 1950s and 1960s the production industry "appears to have been able to have its cake and eat it too," using television as an additional exhibition site for its otherwise obsolete and commercially valueless product, dominating the television series market, and developing an alternative economic strategy for feature film production and distribution to the Classical production schedule of a weekly release from each of the major studios.[27] By the mid-1950s, the center of television production had moved from New York to Los Angeles, where the major studios joined independent telefilm companies and talent agencies as key providers of prime-time programming in what historian Christopher Anderson has called "the consolidation of American television."[28] Filmed material replaced live programming as the dominant television form because it was durable, and therefore capable of earning profits on subsequent-run syndication. By 1960, the major Hollywood studios were producing 40 percent of network programs, while 80 percent of that year's prime-time schedule was generated in Hollywood.[29] In 1959, *Broadcasting* magazine observed that instead of television being "the dreaded destroyer" the movie production industry had feared, it had "turned out to be the good provider."[30]

Independent exhibitors also wanted to prevent the majors from using broadcasting as an alternative form of exhibition. Until 1953, neither the scale of network coverage nor the number of television sets in use was sufficient to support high-priced programming, and the production industry's initial attitude to releasing their product to the new medium was summarized by Barney Balaban in 1953: "television can have Paramount product when it can pay for it."[31] When television had achieved sufficient market penetration to justify high-cost programming, the networks were themselves reluctant to "weaken TV as a medium" by becoming "just a new system of distribution" for Hollywood.[32] While the networks downplayed their use of theatrical movies, the majors sold their pre-1948 films to individual stations, either directly or indirectly. When, in 1961, major features were released to the networks relatively soon after their first theatrical run, their success cemented the victory of filmed programming over live TV, and promoted demand for new hardware in the form of color television sets.[33]

While the two industries negotiated mutually beneficial and interdependent relationships through the development of filmed television, the networks' oligopoly power ensured that they controlled the terms of these relationships, and the major film companies' attempts to create alternative means of distribution through pay-cable continued to meet government resistance into the late 1970s. The majors were, indeed, far from being the most adept players in establishing television operations, in part because they continued to see television production as a way of preserving the studio system. The independent producers and talent agencies that diversified into program packaging and distribution innovated and prospered, most visibly with MCA's purchase of Universal in 1962.

As the major companies demanded increasingly high prices for sales to television in the mid-1960s, the networks began to develop alternative formats: the made-for-TV movie in the late 1960s, and later the mini-series. Movies premiering on television could be produced for less than the charge for screening a blockbuster, and drew comparable or better ratings. By 1970 made-for-television movies had become a mainstay of network programming.[34] As importantly, the networks' move into production contributed significantly to the crisis of overproduction at the end of the 1960s.

Corporate Consolidation and the "New Hollywood"

Being young and single is the overriding demographic pre-condition for being a frequent and enthusiastic moviegoer.
Variety, 1968[35]

The period after World War II saw a general consolidation of American business, as many companies merged to form a relatively small number of conglomerates, large corporations with diverse interests in unrelated fields. During the 1960s most of the major motion picture companies merged with or were taken over by conglomerates attracted by their undervalued stock, their film libraries, and their real estate, and the years from 1966 to 1969 in particular saw an upheaval in company ownership more substantial even than that of the early 1930s. Initially, the conglomerates taking over the major companies were widely diversified corporations. Gulf and Western, which took over Paramount in 1966, began as a producer of automobile bumpers before spreading into zinc mining, sugar, cigars, and real estate during the 1960s as its total assets grew to 250 times their size at the start of the decade. Transamerica Corporation, which took over UA in 1967, was an insurance and financial services company. Its president, John R. Beckett, envisioned the creation of a "multi-market corporation" containing "diversified but interrelated interests" primarily in the service sector of the economy, and functioning much as General Electric operated in the industrial sector. As well as economies of scale, Beckett and other corporate managers argued that conglomerates brought the advantages of "synergy," the enhanced effects produced by operating two organizations together rather than separately, or as Beckett defined it, "the art of making two and two make five."[36]

The precedent for the longer-term development of media corporations was, however, set by Lew Wasserman's establishment of MCA-Universal. The Music Corporation of America was a talent agency that expanded into Hollywood in 1945. Wasserman was the agent who negotiated James Stewart's profit-participation contract on *Winchester '73*, and during the 1950s MCA became the leading "packager" of product for both movies and television, while Wasserman became one of the most powerful executives in Hollywood. As part of a program of diversification, MCA moved into television production in the 1950s, acquired Paramount's film library in 1958, and began a take-over of the ailing Universal Pictures in 1959, which was completed in 1962. At the same time, under the threat of government anti-trust action, MCA divested itself of its talent agency business, but by 1965, when "the octopus" (as MCA was known) absorbed Decca Records, Wasserman had established the company as the prototypical media corporation of the post-Paramount era.

By 1965, the major studios were firmly established as the principal suppliers of programming for the US television networks, as live programs were almost completely phased out in favor of filmed product. Although Hollywood exerted a substantial influence over the forms of television programming, the networks were, as the distributors of that programming, the dominant partners in the relationship. By 1966, the networks had realized that feature films, even if they had not been box-office hits, were the best audience draw on television, and as a result increased the amount of money they were prepared to pay for them. The average price for two showings of a feature rose from $150,000 in 1961 to $400,000 in 1965 and $800,000 in 1968, when the networks were scheduling movies every night of the week.

As the networks granted feature films a central position in their programming, estimates of the value of the majors' film libraries rose to between two and three times the market price of their stock, making them ripe for take-over. Like Universal, several of the majors were ailing by the late 1960s, with aging management teams failing to make the most of the opportunities provided by television and in need of the restructuring provided by their new corporate leadership. Kinney National, which took over Warner Bros./Seven Arts in 1969, was a New York-based conglomerate engaged primarily in car rental, parking lots, construction, and funeral homes. Under Steven Ross it also moved into publishing, merchandising tie-ins, and creative talent management, concentrating its entertainment industry interests in Warner Communication Inc. (WCI) in 1972. WCI established the pattern by which film production and distribution companies became components in multi-media conglomerates geared to the marketing of a product across a number of interlocking media. The company's multiple profit centers in different media reinforced each other, keeping revenues and profits within the corporation. The merger with other media concerns, particularly the record industry, was in a sense only an extrapolation of the majors' post-Paramount commitment to a power-base in distribution – more generally in software publishing – rather than in production. An early instance of these synergistic product relations came from WCI's purchase of the rights to film the 1969 Woodstock music festival, which yielded a successful album on its subsidiary Atlantic Records, as well as the seventh highest-grossing movie of 1970.

In the late 1960s the industry entered a cycle of overproduction that precipitated a financial crisis between 1969 and 1971. Although this crisis is usually represented as the result of the industry's "directionless floundering" in search of a successful formula to attract an audience with which it had lost touch, it in fact had more to do with the industry simply spending too much money on production to make profits.[37] The two top box-office movies for 1969 were the road-show musical *Funny Girl* and *The Love Bug*, a Disney comedy. Both earned less than half the box-office take of the most successful movie of 1968, *The Graduate*. While such figures were taken as evidence that tastes were fragmenting, they really indicated that too many movies were competing for the box-office dollar, and that income was, as a result, spread more thinly.

In the early 1960s Hollywood's feature film output had dropped to about 130 a year; in 1969, it rose to 225. New entrants into production and distribution – CBS, ABC, and National General – increased the supply of films and bid aggressively for talent and properties, contributing to the escalation of budgets to a level insupportable by theatrical demand. At the same time the networks, having acquired enough product to meet their needs for four seasons, suddenly stopped buying movies in 1968, leaving the theatrical market oversupplied with product. Bankers estimated that the industry was spending approximately twice as much on production as the market could return, and the major companies registered corporate losses of $200 million in 1969. Companies had, in effect, financed a significant number of pictures that had no realistic likelihood of recovering their investment. Some of these were products of what Arthur Krim called "the new wave of picture making – daring, innovative, imaginative" that the majors sponsored in 1969 "when it appeared that all traditional picture making was outmoded and audiences – mainly youthful – were ready to support only the off beat." By the time the majority of the pictures were completed, however, "this premise had been proven erroneous."[38] On the other hand, many unsuccessful products were more conventional fare, and Krim argued that both traditional generic material and auteur cinema had been produced in too large quantities and at budgets too high to be profitable.

The most overt signs of overproduction were several very costly failed road-show pictures attempting to repeat the success of *The Sound of Music*. Fox, in particular, incurred massive losses in 1969 and 1970, but in the restructuring that followed the crisis, only Disney and MCA escaped without deficits. The three new companies closed, and Fox and Columbia were potential candidates for receivership. Darryl Zanuck, the last of the studio-era moguls, was forced out of Fox, and most companies changed their management. Under pressure from their corporate parents and bankers, the majors retrenched, closing branch offices, combining studio facilities, arranging joint foreign distribution, and, for a while, cutting their production budgets.

Roadshow exhibition was a casualty of the industry recession as the majors concentrated their marketing effort on the most frequent attenders, but the blockbuster phenomenon persisted, becoming the central strategy in the reshaping of the industry during the 1970s. *Love Story*, 1971's top-grossing film, earned more money in domestic rentals than the next three highest-earners combined. The successes of such movies as *The Godfather* (1972), *The Poseidon Adventure* (1972), and *The Exorcist* (1973) confirmed that the industry's profits would remain concentrated in a handful of enormously successful movies in each production season. Three-quarters of the movies released failed to recoup their costs at the box-office, but for the major companies, increasingly operating as distributors and financiers in a system of "vertical disintegration," television provided a compensatory degree of stability absent from the theatrical market.

The period of instability coincides with the "Hollywood Renaissance," which is usually seen as the period in which a group of new and mainly young directors took the opportunity provided by the industry's corporate uncertainty to produce a number of stylistically innovative and thematically challenging movies. Like the teenpix of the previous decade, the most successful movies of the late 1960s – *Bonnie and Clyde* (1967), *The Graduate* (1967), *Easy Rider* (1969) – were relatively low-budget productions targeted at a younger audience. For the babyboomers then reaching critical mass as an audience, these movies provided identification figures in rebellion against some form of authority. In search of the profitable youth movie and uncertain where to find it, most of the majors made small-scale – and therefore low-risk – investments in new, mainly young, production talent, such as Francis Ford Coppola's American Zoetrope company, and themselves backed a few small-budget first features by young directors, which were uniformly unsuccessful. The few "anti-establishment" successes of the period were made by older or more established directors, but the Hollywood Renaissance did epitomize a generational shift in Hollywood management. The economic crisis was most frequently explained as a consequence of having too many old men controlling production. Between 1966 and 1973 all the majors acquired new, much younger production heads, most of them drawn from outside the immediate confines of Hollywood. The public search for young auteurs concealed a more enduring palace revolution giving power to a younger generation of executives whose previous careers were most likely to have been in television, talent agencies, or "creative management," such as James Aubrey, Ted Ashley, or David Begelman. These figures, rather than the "movie brat" auteurs, guided the direction of the New Hollywood, but the full impact of their decision-making was not evident until the late 1970s, and the illusion that an auteurist American cinema might provide serious social and political comment through mainstream movies persisted throughout the 1970s.[39]

Ratings

In many respects the history of late 1960s and early 1970s resembles that of the early 1930s, suggesting that periods of economic instability in Hollywood appear also to be periods of relative instability in the movies' codes of representation, providing opportunities for experimentation and formal innovation. As in the early 1930s, a revision of the industry's procedures for content regulation led to significant changes in representational codes. The Production Code had been subject to increasing challenge throughout the 1960s, and on his appointment as President of the Motion Picture Association of America (MPAA) in 1966, Jack Valenti decided to overhaul the increasingly moribund system. A temporary solution was found later that year in a revision of the Code which created the designation "Suggested for Mature Audiences" (SMA), to be attached to the advertising and promotional material of adult-oriented movies. Even so, in 1967 MGM chose to release *Blow-Up* without a Code seal rather than cut it, and its commercial success further undermined the Production Code Administration's (PCA) effectiveness. The number of movies designated "for mature audiences" rose to nearly a quarter of the majors' releases in 1967, and in the 12 months before the adoption of the MPAA rating system in November 1968, nearly 60 percent of the majors' releases were given this rating. At the same time, local protests, prosecutions, and restrictions on the exhibition of particular movies had increased steadily during the 1960s. Because this legal action was directed at theater owners rather than at the distributors, the MPAA's proposal of an age-based classification system was strongly supported by the National Association of Theater Owners (**NATO**). (The text of the 1968 Code is in appendix 2.)

The period following the introduction of classification was inevitably one of uncertainty, as the boundaries of classification and the economic implications of different ratings were established. The most contentious issue presented by classification was the commercial viability of the "X" category. Movies classified "X" were not given a seal, and were therefore not covered by the MPAA's commitment to provide legal support to all movies under the seal. By the end of 1969, 47 percent of exhibitors declared that they would not play an "X," and several newspapers refused to advertise them.[40] Within the MPAA, this was taken to mean that the boundary between "R" and "X" had been inappropriately set, and in early 1970 it was realigned by increasing the indicated age restriction from 16 to 17, allowing for a broadening of what could be included in the "R" category: *M*A*S*H, Zabriskie Point*, and *The Boys in the Band* (all 1970) were early beneficiaries of the broader "R." The concomitant effect, however, was to confirm the opinion that "X" was defined as "a dumping ground for movies which warrant no official notice from the industry or consideration from general audiences," an opinion effectively confirmed by CARA director Eugene Dougherty's comment that "when we broadened the R category, we hoped no serious film-makers would want to go beyond the limits of the R."[41] The experiments of *Myra Breckinridge* and *Beyond the Valley of the Dolls* (both 1970) were not repeated, and the majors had effectively abandoned the "X" category to the hard core pornography market by mid-1971, when the Rating Administration responded to public criticism from religious groups about its excessively permissive standards by becoming more restrictive. In 1972, Stephen Farber observed that the "stigmas attached to the X rating" required filmmakers to cut their films to achieve an "R" if they were to "achieve nationwide release and reach an intelligent diversified audience."[42] Whatever the MPAA's Declaration of Principle had claimed about the rating system's objective of encouraging "artistic expression by expanding creative freedom," in practice the pressures to avoid an "X" were as firm a constraint as the Production Code had been.

The constraint was, however, different in nature. Designed as a means of labeling movies according to the degree of explicitness in their representation of sex, violence, or language, the rating system became a marketing device, inciting such representations up to the limits of the permissible. The introduction of ratings accelerated the trend that critic Linda Williams dates from the release of *Psycho* (1960), "when the experience of going to a mainstream film began to be constituted as a sexualized thrill: a sort of sado-masochistic roller-coaster ride whose pleasure lay in the refusal completely to re-establish equilibrium."[43] Historian Jon Lewis has argued that the importance of the rating system was that it "reestablished a system by which the studios might continue to produce and distribute films under a set of mutually agreed-upon guidelines . . . it gave the studios control over entry into the entertainment marketplace."[44] By the mid-1970s, the rating system was bringing about a two-tiered system of production, in which studios aimed either to make cross-generational PG blockbusters like *Jaws* (1975), or else tailored their product for specific segments of the market: children and the "family audience," (G), or adults (R).

The immediate effect, however, was that independent distributors were briefly able to gain wider access to the domestic exhibition market, taking a 30 percent share of it in 1970. For a short period in the early 1970s, pornography achieved a degree of cultural legitimation. In 1970 *Variety* reported that over 600 theaters in New York City were showing "skin flicks," and registered the profitability of X-rated movies for their exhibitors and independent distributors alike. In 1973, the hard core *Devil in Miss Jones* earned the seventh-highest box-office gross in the US, and *Deep Throat* the eleventh. This development was, however, contained by a 1973 Supreme Court decision upholding state and local censorship standards, which effectively gave state or city governments authority to ban the theatrical exhibition of sexually explicit movies on the grounds that they offended local community standards.

The short-lived wide circulation and profitability of hard core pornography was one indication of the instability and unpredictability of the market in the early 1970s. While this unpredictability fueled the Hollywood Renaissance and the auteur-led cinema of the 1970s, it also indicated that the industry was failing fully to exploit the commercial potential of the blockbuster system by producing movies that appealed across the broad spectrum of audience taste. While *Last Tango in Paris* (1972) gained its reputation and its revenues from a marketing campaign that exploited its sexual explicitness, it was a lone exception to the rapid decline of the art-house sector. In spite of the apparent diversity of taste exhibited by the American audience in the early 1970s and audience research indicating a strong correlation between moviegoing and higher education, *Variety* reported that no foreign-language movie had grossed over $1 million in the US in 1972, and that there were only six subtitled movies in the 200 top-grossing pictures for the year.

The rating system permitted the majors to produce and distribute the kind of overtly sensationalist material they had previously left to independents like AIP. *The Godfather* (1972) was perhaps the most spectacular individual example, credited at the time with single-handedly restoring box-office prosperity and securing an American auteur cinema, but the shift in content to exploitation genres was more obviously signaled by *The Exorcist*, which attached a blockbuster budget and production values to a conventionally low-budget genre movie, inaugurating a cycle of big-budget horror movies that included *The Omen* and *Carrie* (both 1976).

This shift in content registered the industrial origins of many of the new directors, who had first worked on exploitation movies for independent companies like AIP or Roger Corman's New World. Corman, in particular, has been seen as something like the godfather of a new generation of American filmmakers who rose to prominence at this period. Many of the directors who attained critical prominence in the rest of the decade – Francis Ford Coppola, Martin Scorsese, Peter Bogdanovich, Jonathan Demme, Jonathan Kaplan, Irving Kershner – worked for Corman early in their careers, as did Jack Nicholson. Corman's own success was, like that of AIP, in large part dependent on the omissions and miscalculations of the majors, through his exploitation of otherwise unrequited demand, whether that was for biker movies or importing Ingmar Bergman. His working methods were not a solution to Hollywood's economic problems, because they did not provide the majors with substantial enough product. In looking to Corman protégés, however, the majors tacitly acknowledged a significant shift in the nature of the traditional Hollywood movie. During the 1970s, the industry, led by the film-school generation, would frequently produce big-budget versions of 1950s exploitation cinema – gangster movies, teen hot-rod movies, science fiction, horror, monster movies.

To a significant extent, the period of experimentation and formal innovation in the early 1970s was subsidized by the most unlikely of collaborators: President Richard Nixon. In the wake of the 1969–71 recession, the industry had lobbied successfully for assistance from the federal government, in the form of beneficial taxation provisions. From 1971, tax shelters and investment tax credits became a major means of securing production finance, sustaining the production schedules of several studios and probably keeping Columbia from bankruptcy. In the following five years, tax shelter financing added $150 million to the majors' production budgets, effectively financing 20 percent of the movies produced between 1973 and 1976. Tax shelter financing also reduced the immediate effect of the blockbuster syndrome: because investors were guaranteed the benefits of tax deferrals of two-and-a-half times their investment, they were less concerned than other investors might be with the profitability of the movies they helped produce. The existence of this form of financing, which minimized the risks of investing in production, combined with the apparent unpredictability of blockbuster success and the prestige of auteurism to sustain the directorial careers of figures such as Sam Peckinpah and Robert Altman for much of the 1970s, despite the poor commercial record of their movies. While some of the iconoclastic movies of the period made modest profits, they were frequently remembered as having been much more commercially successful than they were.

The mid-1970s saw the peak of the American art cinema: *Chinatown, The Conversation* (both 1974), *Night Moves, Nashville* (both 1975), *Taxi Driver* (1976). This period of experimentation, however, concluded shortly after *One Flew Over the Cuckoo's Nest* became the biggest critical and commercial hit of 1976. Federal legislation closed tax shelter financing in that year, reducing the appeal of projects that were not clearly commercial, although foreign tax shelter provision continued to ensure that this remained a significant element in movie financing. Auteur cinema lost much of its industry appeal when projects such as Bogdanovich's *At Long Last Love* (1975), Hal Ashby's *Bound for Glory* (1976), William Friedkin's *Sorcerer* (1977), and Scorsese's *New York, New York* (1977) failed. The excess and near-catastrophe of Coppola's *Apocalypse Now* (1979) and the disaster of Michael Cimino's *Heaven's Gate* (1980, discussed in chapter 1) effectively closed the major studios' doors to a number of the most prominent auteurs of the new Hollywood. After *Popeye* (1980), Altman made only one more movie for a major studio, *O.C. and Stiggs* (1983), which MGM chose not to release for four years. Since then he has worked entirely in other media or for independents. The careers of Ashby, Bogdanovich, Friedkin, and Bob Rafelson all followed similar trajectories, while Coppola and Scorsese found themselves obliged to respond to a more commercial marketplace. As historian David Cook observes, auteurism

> became a marketing tool that coincided neatly with the rise of college-level film education among the industry's most heavily courted audience segment. From the cinema of rebellion . . . America's youth transferred its allegiance to the "personal" cinema of the seventies auteurs without realizing how corporate and impersonal it had become.[45]

The auteurist cinema of the 1970s addressed a young, well-educated target audience, but in the main those movies failed to capture the less-educated younger audience. In many respects, the prototype for the type of movie that would reliably appeal to this audience was the most consistently successful movie series of the 1960s, the James Bond pictures produced by Cubby Broccoli and Harry Saltzman for UA. By the third Bond movie, *Goldfinger* (1964), the producers had fully developed both the conventions and the financial regime of the series. Financed at relatively low budgets by UA and using their British production base to access film subsidies, the Bond movies were action adventure stories designed to appeal to international audiences through their multiple-nationality casts and exotic locales. Their plots were constructed as a series of what Broccoli called "bumps," or self-contained action sequences occurring at regular intervals through the picture, and other features, including the "Bond girls," the gadgets, and the elaborate set for the villain's lair, were elements in the formula. So was the series' comic self-consciousness, which assuaged the *Playboy* sexuality of the movies and established the game-playing nature of the audience's engagement with each new episode. By 1965, a substantial merchandizing campaign, from toys to toiletries, reinforced the trademark properties of the "007" logo, while the movies themselves were saturation-booked into each market.[46] The formula was durable enough to withstand several recastings of the Bond character, as well as providing the template for subsequent, if less durable, action adventure "franchise" movies such as the *Indiana Jones* series.

Hollywood in the Multiplex

The unpredictability of the alchemy that takes place when the right product meets the right audience does not mean that entertainment is an inherently shaky business. It's a gamble, but as in gambling there are consistent winners. Hits are what make the entertainment business run.

Michael Wolf[47]

The crucial fact is just this: nobody knows what makes a hit or when it will happen.

Arthur De Vany and W. David Walls[48]

In the five years after 1969 the industry returned to equilibrium, with only the theatrical exhibition sector not prospering. It was, however, a new equilibrium with a production and distribution regime that would have been barely recognizable to the moguls. "Studios" were no longer in the business of routinely making movies: in 1975, Paramount produced only five of the 25 movies it distributed. Movie finance no longer came from the reinvestment of box-office income and established credit arrangements with commercial banks, as it had in the past, but from tax shelters and credits, advance sales to television and cable networks, advance exhibitor guarantees and merchandizing. Perhaps most obviously of all, the number of movies released by the majors had fallen back to as few as 120 a year. The major distributors no longer felt under an obligation to supply exhibitors with product all year round, but instead concentrated their own releases on the most popular periods of the year: summer, the holiday season from Thanksgiving to New Year, and Easter. The majors' strategy of restricting the supply of product combined with the blockbuster syndrome to enable them to demand a greater share of box-office income from exhibitors, so that the proportion of box-office receipts going to distributors rose from around 30 percent at the beginning of the 1970s to between 40 and 45 percent at their end.[49]

At a time when the number of screens was increasing rapidly as a result of the construction of shopping mall multiplex theaters, the majors' new corporate management was discovering how to control the market, and the distribution of profits, by restricting the supply of products and using marketing to drive up demand. To an extent, in synchronizing production and marketing the industry was doing no more than very belatedly conforming to normal business practice, but the majors' concern with marketing and risk minimization was itself only possible under a changed industry leadership composed of lawyers, bankers, agents, and business executives who saw filmmaking "primarily as an investment strategy, not unlike commodities trading, which combined the risks of high-stakes speculation with a virtually limitless potential for corporate tax-sheltering."[50] These strategies of "risk-aversion" effectively substituted for the commercial security provided to the vertically integrated majors through their ownership of theaters in the Classical system.

The ownership changes of the late 1960s left the industry in fairly stable structural shape through the 1970s, when the companies affiliated with conglomerates – Paramount, Warner Bros. Universal, UA – maintained a bigger market share than those – Columbia, MGM, TCF – that were not. Advertising and promotion costs increased enormously, creating a situation in which a few hits would draw the available business. If several strong movies were released at the same time, other pictures would attract very little business. The majors offset the risks of production by cutting operating costs, adopting defensive marketing tactics and pre-selling pictures to foreign distributors. In the mid-1970s they began to capitalize on the value of ancillary markets by negotiating television sales in advance of production, so that these revenues could be taken into account in calculating budgets. Stabilized distribution economics and a more mobile corporate management were the most substantial legacies of the crisis of the late 1960s, rather than any greater freedom for the individual filmmaker. Contrary to most accounts of the theatrical market's unpredictability, analyst Martin Dale argues that the "demand curve" for movies in the US domestic market has remained fairly stable since the 1960s, with about ten movies grossing over $100 million (in 1995 prices), another ten grossing over $50 million, and a further 40 grossing over $20 million.[51]

In this context, in which the majors accepted the blockbuster syndrome as a fact of life, their defensive strategies made economic sense. Reducing the volume of production and increasing costs – by 450 percent during the 1970s – greatly increased the strength of the distributors' negotiating position with exhibitors, since they controlled access to scarce, high-cost commodities. Production costs, which had nearly tripled during the 1960s, increased from an average of $1.9 million in 1972 to $8.9 million in 1979. The majors secured substantially better terms for themselves, forcing exhibitors to accept paying guarantees and extracting an increasing share of the box-office revenue from them.

As well as content, the majors began to adopt the distribution and exhibition strategies of the independents. **Saturation booking** – releasing a movie simultaneously to a large number of theaters – was a distribution strategy initially associated with exploitation movies, designed to produce a quick return from audiences titillated by sensationalist press advertising, for movies unlikely to build a reputation through word-of-mouth. In 1954, for instance, Warner Bros. distributed *Them!* to 2,000 theaters within one month, upgrading many drive-ins to first-run status for the exercise. In 1960, UA used the saturation technique on a regional basis, linked to extensive television and radio advertising, for its release of *The*

In its pattern of distribution as well as in its emphasis on spectacle, *Jaws* (1975) indicated the future direction of Hollywood's development.

Produced by David Brown, Richard F. Zanuck; distributed by Universal Pictures.

Magnificent Seven, and repeated the practice for the James Bond series and also for *A Hard Day's Night* in 1964, considering it particularly effective for movies with a ready-made audience.

In the summer of 1975, saturation booking was combined with a national television advertising campaign for the release of *Jaws*, which opened simultaneously on 464 screens and became the first movie to earn over $100 million in rentals. Partly as a result of the movie's phenomenal commercial success, the pattern of wide initial release became standard industry practice over the next decade. By 1990, it was not uncommon for a movie to open simultaneously in 2,000 theaters, necessitating the provision of ten times as many prints as might have been made of an A-feature released in 1940. This distribution practice increased print and advertising costs, and by the late 1970s expenditure on publicity occasionally exceeded the cost of production. *Alien* (1979) cost $10.8 million to produce and $15.7 million to market.

Wide release further flattened the tiers of the exhibition system, giving more theaters first-run status and emphasizing the importance to the distributors of early box-office returns. It also confirmed the fact that the principal site of American moviegoing had been relocated, in line with the radical transformation in American retailing brought about by the building of suburban shopping centers in the 1960s and shopping malls in the 1970s.[52] A new wave of theater-building began in the late 1970s, led by General Cinema and American Multi-Cinema, effectively replacing the downtown movie palaces. The new theaters were built in shopping malls, and had multiple screens. The first twin-screen theater was built in a Kansas City shopping mall in 1963, but the real development of multiplex theaters took place in the 1980s, as the number of screens in the US increased from 16,901 in 1979 to 23,689 in 1990 – more than there had been since the height of audience attendance in the late 1920s. During the 1980s several new companies – United Artists Communications, Plitt Theaters, Cineplex Odeon – developed national theater chains to join those established in the 1970s. Television advertising for movies made economic sense only if the picture was widely and conveniently available. Multiplexes provided the most effective means of distributing mass-advertised pictures for immediate consumption by their primary audience, because they allowed for frequent reconfigurations of the number of seats available for each movie in order to maximize the use of space. A prestige movie might open on four or five screens at one site, reducing that number as attendance waned.

Initially, it was thought that multiplexes would increase the variety of movies in circulation by using spare screens for revivals or foreign pictures outside peak attendance times. In fact, however, the multiplex has narrowed the range of pictures available by shortening the commercial life-cycle of movies in theatrical release. Where a Classical Hollywood movie might take as long as two years to work through a complete exhibition cycle from first-run to the lowest neighborhood theater, the contemporary event movie has a theatrical box-office life of as little as two months, and even that life is dependent on its success on its opening weekend. The system is designed to maximize income for the exhibitor and distributor, and is dependent on a constant oversupply to ensure that the best-performing product is most widely available at any given moment.

Wide release facilitated the evolution of the blockbuster into the **event movie**, a product designed to maximize audience attendance by drawing in not only the regular 14-to-25-year-old audience, but also that section of the audience who attend the cinema two or three times a year, often as a family, at Thanksgiving, at Christmas, and during the summer holidays. The calendar of the viewing year has gradually shifted since the early 1970s, when movies were still being released regularly throughout the year. The summer season now accounts for nearly half the annual domestic box-office. The other peak vacation times also draw on the most reliable sector of the audience, teens out of school.[53] The companies' emphasis on event movies as their principal source of revenue concentrated earnings and profits on a very small number of movies. In 1977, for instance, the top six movies in the North American market earned one-third of the total rental received by distributors. To an even greater extent than was the case in the studio system, figures such as these appear to make the movie business an immensely risky one. For production executives it is. Where Louis B. Mayer had ruled MGM from 1924 to 1951, the studio had six studio heads between 1968 and 1979. In the 1980s, Twentieth Century-Fox and Columbia each had five different studio heads. This is, however, also clearly a self-perpetuating circumstance, since the majors' adoption of strategies to respond to the blockbuster syndrome reproduce the situation to which they see themselves responding.

The majors' production of 100–25 movies per year did not meet demand, and the shortfall was covered by the output of independent producers and distributors. In the year June 1975–June 1976, 300 independent movies were released, amounting to two-thirds of US production, but generating only 10–15 percent of box-office rentals. Although the majors began to lower their distribution fees, or offer other inducements to attract independent producers with finished

Box 6.2   The US box-office year

The box-office year is conventionally divided into five seasons, and 2001 was typical of the pattern of attendance across the year since 1970. Winter, lasting from the beginning of the year to mid-March, is a period of steady attendance among regular moviegoers. In Spring, cinemagoing peaks over Easter and then falls off to a pre-summer low. Summer, from Memorial Day to Labor Day, sees 36 percent of the year's business in three months, while the "autumn plateau" before Thanksgiving is the quietest season of the year. Attendance picks up for Thanksgiving, plummets to a pre-Christmas low in early December, and then peaks over the Christmas–New Year holiday period, with the Holiday season seeing the same amount of business as Winter, Spring, or Fall in half the time.

The five seasons

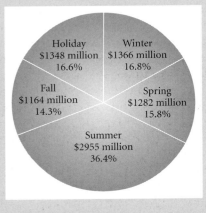

Attendance, 2001

product, they were nevertheless effectively transferring risk to the independents. Their combined strategies of limited product supply and wide release concentrated income on a small group of movies which they controlled and from which they profited, leaving the less profitable margins of the production industry to be supplied by independent producers at their own risk. Although the majors distributed only one-third of all movies released, those movies continued to take 90 percent of the box-office revenues. Between 1972 and 1978 box-office grosses increased by 67 percent, but the distributors' share of that gross increased by 143 percent.

Success on this scale forced the major companies to diversify their operations further. Fox, one of the least diversified of the majors in the late 1970s, could not rationally invest the huge profits from *Star Wars* (1977) in increased production; instead it broadened its activities by adding soft drink, resort, and video businesses to its portfolio. For the most diversified conglomerates like Gulf and Western and Transamerica, their entertainment businesses represented little more than 10 percent of their total operations. Diversified parent companies could also ride out the losses of a bad year much more successfully than a distribution company with no other, more stable businesses in its portfolio. Ever-rising costs drove all but the majors out of the industry: by the end of the 1970s smaller distributors like AIP and Allied Artists had either merged with other companies or closed.

Summary

- After 1948, as a result of the Justice Department's "divorcement" of exhibition from production and distribution, Hollywood reduced its levels of production. It cut its number of contract personnel, dropped the production of B-pictures and shorts, and reduced the number of A-pictures released, forcing the exhibitors to compete for product. Each movie had to be sold on its merits, which led to a massive rise in production values and costs.
- At the same time, postwar migration to the suburbs and the widespread adoption of television combined to bring about a decline in cinema audiences. The most profitable cinematic distribution strategy of the 1950s and 1960s was the "roadshow," movies characterized by large budgets, long running times, multiple-star casts, lavish production values, and big-screen technology, which provided a clear contrast to the smaller-scale attractions of television.
- Cinema audiences were increasingly segmented. As many smaller neighborhood theaters closed, drive-in theaters catering to the new suburban population opened. The exhibition of foreign movies in small urban theaters ("art houses") appealed to "adult" audiences, while teenagers were drawn to movies made and marketed specifically for their tastes.
- As the studio system was abandoned, "studios" increasingly provided financing, studio space, and distribution deals to "independent" production companies. The role of developing and nurturing talent was passed to talent agents, and agencies took over the function of packaging and selling movies to a studio.

The "blockbuster syndrome," by which income and profits were concentrated on a small number of movies while the majority lost money, came to dominate the industry's commercial practice.

- Between 1966 and 1969 most major motion picture companies merged with or were taken over by conglomerates that were attracted by their undervalued stock, film libraries, and real estate assets. The late 1960s saw a cycle of over-production, and overspending on production, that precipitated a financial crisis between 1969 and 1971.

- This period of financial instability coincided with the "Hollywood Renaissance," a period in which a group of new and mainly young directors produced stylistically innovative, thematically challenging, but only occasionally commercially successful movies. The more enduring change, however, came from the installation of a new, younger generation of executives who guided the direction of the New Hollywood, devising production and distribution strategies to manage the increased risks of post-Classical Hollywood's new economics. These strategies included a sharp reduction in the volume of production and an escalation in the cost of production and marketing.

- Subject to increasing challenge during the 1960s, the Production Code was replaced in 1968 by an age-based rating system administered by the MPAA's Code (later Classification) and Rating Administration.

- In the late 1970s new cinemas with multiple screens began to be incorporated into shopping malls. The multiplex narrowed the range of pictures available by shortening the commercial life-cycle of movies in theatrical release as the majors adopted saturation booking after 1975. The majors' combined strategies of limited product supply and wide release intensified the blockbuster phenomenon, and strengthened their negotiating position with exhibitors. Increasingly, the majors left the less profitable margins of the production industry to be supplied by independent producers at their own risk.

Further Reading

Hollywood after Paramount

Thomas Schatz, *Boom and Bust: American Cinema in the 1940s* (New York: Scribner's, 1997), provides a clear summary of the Paramount case and its immediate effects. Tino Balio, *United Artists: The Company that Changed the Film Industry* (Madison: University of Wisconsin Press, 1987), provides a detailed history of the company from 1950 to 1980. See also the essays in part 4 of Tino Balio, ed., *The American Film Industry*, 1st edn 1976, revised edn (Madison: University of Wisconsin Press, 1985).

Thomas Doherty, *Teenagers and Teenpics: The Juvenilization of American Movies in the 1950s*

(Boston: Unwin Hyman, 1988), surveys the growth of the teenage market in the 1950s. Gregory A. Waller, ed., *Moviegoing in America* (Malden, MA: Blackwell, 2002), contains several articles on drive-ins and contemporary cinemagoing, as well as excellent coverage of the Classical period. Douglas Gomery, *Shared Pleasures: A History of Movie Presentation in the United States* (London: British Film Institute, 1992), provides an historical account of developments in exhibition in the period covered in this chapter.

Michele Hilmes, *Hollywood and Broadcasting: From Radio to Cable* (Urbana: University of Illinois Press, 1990), provides an historical survey of the relationship between the motion picture, radio, and television industries. This overview can be well supplemented by the essays in Tino Balio, ed., *Hollywood in the Age of Television* (Boston: Unwin Hyman, 1990), and by Christopher Anderson, *Hollywood TV: The Studio System in the Fifties* (Austin: University of Texas Press, 1994), which explains the majors' role in television production.

The "New Hollywood"

David A. Cook, *Lost Illusions: American Cinema in the Shadow of Watergate and Vietnam, 1970–1979* (New York: Scribner's, 2000), in the *History of the American Cinema* series, provides a detailed account of the industry's history in the aftermath of the crisis of 1969–71. A shorter overview can be found in Thomas Schatz, "The New Hollywood," in *Film Theory Goes to the Movies*, eds Jim Collins, Hilary Radner, and Ava Preacher Collins (New York: Routledge, 1993), while Peter Biskind, *Easy Riders, Raging Bulls: How the Sex-Drugs-and-Rock 'n' Roll Generation Saved Hollywood*, (New York: Simon and Schuster, 1998), provides a more anecdotal history. See also Jon Lewis, *Whom God Wishes to Destroy: Francis Coppola and the New Hollywood* (Durham, NC: Duke University Press, 1995); Jim Hillier, *The New Hollywood* (London: Studio Vista, 1993); and Michael Pye and Lynda Myles, *The Movie Brats: How the Film Generation Took Over Hollywood* (London: Faber, 1979). On ratings, see Jon Lewis, *Hollywood vs Hardcore: How the Struggle over Censorship Saved the Modern Film Industry* (New York: New York University Press, 2000), and Stephen Farber, *The Movie Rating Game* (Washington, DC: Public Affairs Press, 1972). Of a number of "insider's accounts," one of the most informative is William Goldman, *Adventures in the Screen Trade: A Personal View of Hollywood and Screenwriting* (New York: Warner Books, 1983). Goldman has continued his commentary in two later books, *The Big Picture: Who Killed Hollywood? and Other Essays* (New York: Applause, 2000), and *Which Lie Did I Tell?: More Adventures in the Screen Trade* (New York: Pantheon, 2000).

CHAPTER SEVEN

Industry 3:
Since 1980

Sometime in the last two decades entertainment executives realized that trying to move into profitability on the initial theatrical release of a film was somewhere between impossible and suicidal. A film began to be looked at as an anchor product that gives birth to other businesses. . . . increasingly, without multiple revenue streams there would ultimately be no profit, and no profit means no long-term business.

Michael J. Wolf[1]

Since 1980 the movie industry's revenues have been growing at an astonishingly high compound annual growth rate of around 9 percent. The initial growth was caused by the development of video, followed in the 1990s by the expansion of the overseas market. This high growth rate ensured strong competition within the industry and persistent interest from other enterprises in buying into it. The competition manifested itself most obviously in the exponential escalation of the cost of production and marketing from 1985, and had the effect of steadily pushing down the major companies' profit margins from an average of 15 percent in the 1970s to between 5 and 6 percent in the late 1980s. While the American domestic box-office grew by 45 percent between 1991 and 1998, the average costs of production and marketing rose by 104 percent, and despite the huge expansion of its markets, the profitability of the movie industry has remained uncertain.

As historian Janet Wasko argues, however, the feature film business no longer exists in its own right.[2] Since the revival of the American theatrical market in the 1970s, the industry has seen a succession of new markets develop: American home video and pay-TV from the early 1980s, the European theatrical market from 1985, new geographical markets in Asia and eastern Europe since 1990, digital distribution via DVDs and the Internet since the late 1990s. The growth of ancillary markets in video and television has meant that while 54 percent of total movie revenues came from the domestic box-office in 1978, less than 20 percent has come from that source since 1995.[3] Movie production has become, in significant part, the creation of "filmed entertainment" software, to be viewed through several different windows and transported to several different platforms maintained by the other divisions of diversified media corporations. In only the first of these windows, theatrical exhibition, does a movie now appear on film; all its subsequent formats are electronic. Both the economic and aesthetic boundaries of contemporary Hollywood are difficult to define, but they differ considerably from the economics of a single industry, which, with whatever additions, the motion picture industry remained until 1948.

Where Classical Hollywood produced a full range of products used in the presentation of an evening's movie entertainment, including shorts and newsreels, the major Hollywood corporations are now involved in the production and distribution of a chain of interrelated cultural products: books, television shows, records, toys, games, videos, T-shirts, magazines, as well as tie-ins and merchandizing arrangements with the entire panoply of producers of consumer goods. The converged entertainment industries – the copyright industries (movies, television, music, books, and software) – now make up the second-largest net export sector of the US economy, generating $79.65 billion in overseas sales and exports in 1999, and dominating the global market to an extent comparable only to the position of Hollywood at the height of the late silent era. The company names survive, but are now incorporated into larger entities: AOL-Time Warner; Disney-ABC; News Corporation/Fox; Viacom/Paramount; Sony-Columbia.

Since 1975, movies have become increasingly commodified, both in themselves as objects forming part of a chain of goods, and as "multipliers" for the sale of other products. *Star Wars* (1977) took over $500 million at the box-office in 1977, but the sales of ancillary goods far exceeded that figure, as well as extending the life of the product and guaranteeing the success of its sequels. In the early 1980s, world-wide sales of *Star Wars* goods were estimated to be worth $1.5 billion a year, while *Batman* (1989) made $1 billion from merchandizing, four times its box-office earnings. *Jurassic Park* (1993) went so far as to advertise its own merchandizing within the movie: at one point, the camera tracks past the Jurassic Park gift shop, showing a line of T-shirts, lunch boxes, and other souvenirs identical to the ones available for purchase in the lobby of the theater. In these aspects of their aesthetic organization, movies have increasingly adopted the heavily commodified aesthetic of broadcasting, by which the viewer is, as Michele Hilmes argues, led "away from the text itself into those commercial frames that surround it."[4]

Contemporary movies rely heavily on advance audience analysis to identify market opportunities not only for their own advertising, but also for that of their collaborators in licensing and merchandizing. In 1999, the total retail value of the licensed product market was estimated to be more than $70 billion a year, and the most successful movie series existed most prominently as brands or **franchises**, in which, as historian Robert Allen has argued, each new movie in the series "becomes the narrative and iconographic field through which old licenses are renewed and from which new licenses can be harvested – the malleable materials of fantasy from which other fantasies can be fashioned."[5]

Video and New Markets

Entertainment is one of the purest marketplaces in the world. If people don't like a movie or record they won't see it or buy it. The fact that the American entertainment industry has been so successful on a worldwide basis speaks to the quality and attractiveness of what we're creating.
Robert Shaye[6]

Although divorcement had forced the majors to cut their direct ties with theatrical exhibition, they were not prevented from being heavily involved in other ways of circulating their product, through video, cable television, and associated merchandizing of an expanding range of "software," from books-of-the-film and soundtrack CDs to toys and computer games. In the early 1980s, the economic logic that emerged from this diversification downplayed the importance of cinema exhibition as a whole. Rather, a conglomerate such as Warner Communications Inc. (WCI) saw its goal as being to "bring movies conveniently and economically into the home," so that it could "reach the enormous market that rarely, if ever, attends movie theaters."[7] Along with Gulf and Western (Paramount), Disney, and MCA (Universal), WCI dominated production and distribution during the 1980s. A second tier of companies, with fluctuating shares of the market, was similarly connected to ancillary markets: MGM/UA, Columbia (owned for most of the decade by Coca-Cola), and Twentieth Century-Fox. Although the ownership, management, and profitability of these seven companies changed quite frequently during the decade, their common underlying strategy of diversification combined with multi-media distribution of software was firmly established. One tier down the production hierarchy were the mini-majors, companies such as Orion, Cannon, and Dino De Laurentis, financing movies by pre-selling their distribution rights before production began. These companies flourished in the mid-1980s, then overexpanded through diversification and an excess of product. Cannon collapsed in 1986, De Laurentis in 1988, and Orion in 1992. Servicing the low-budget sectors of the market were the descendants of Poverty Row companies, including American International Pictures, Crown International, and New Line.[8]

In the latter half of the 1980s, encouraged by the Reagan administration's relaxed attitude to business regulation, several of the majors returned to theater ownership. In 1986 Columbia purchased some theaters in New York; within a year, MCA, Paramount, and WCI had bought or acquired stakes in important theater chains throughout the country, acquiring more than 3,500 of the 22,000 screens in the US, or approximately the same percentage as they had owned in

1938. Although first-run theatrical release continues to provide the vital evidence of product quality that will attract the interest of later "distribution windows,"[9] the distributors' return to ownership in the exhibition sector was not an attempt to recreate the vertical integration of Classical Hollywood. Rather, they were simply securing an additional element in a new strategy of what industry analyst Harold Vogel has called "entertainment industry consolidation."[10] As the governing economic logic of the industry, vertical integration has given way to horizontal integration of the New Hollywood's tightly diversified media conglomerates, which favor the circulation of movies strategically open to multiple readings and multi-media reiteration. By the end of the 1980s, theatrical release accounted for only 30 percent of the studios' total receipts, while ancillary markets made up the other 70 percent. *Batman*, released in 1989, earned $250 million in the first five months of its theatrical release. When Warners released it on video, it earned another $400 million.[11]

Such figures reflected the doubling of the total world market between 1984 and 1989, an expansion primarily brought about by the development of video as an additional system of release. This expansion fueled the apparently inexorable rise in the cost of production as well. The extravagant budgets of the 1980s were also part of a cyclical economic pattern that has affected the film industry since the early 1960s, in which a number of spectacular successes push production costs to new heights until overproduction results in a sharp downturn in profits. Because its effect is concentrated on so few products, what is in fact a stabilization of the market appears to be the catastrophic failure of one or two movies: *Cleopatra* in 1963 and *Heaven's Gate* in 1980 are perhaps the two most notable examples. While *Cleopatra*'s losses had some, albeit brief, restraining effect on budgets as well as on the costume epic cycle, the *Heaven's Gate* disaster did not lead the industry to rein in production costs: by September 1982 there were 20 movies in production with budgets over $20 million.

The development of video as a highly profitable subsequent release system fundamentally altered the economic structure of the movie industry and its marketing practices. Initially fearing the effects of a distribution system that they did not control, the industry reacted to video with the same apparent hostility it had shown to television in the early 1950s. Jack Valenti declared that it was a parasite likely to kill moviegoing, and in 1976, Universal and Disney brought a lawsuit against Sony claiming that its Betamax machine encouraged infringement of copyright and arguing that its manufacture should be prohibited. By 1984, however, when the Supreme Court ruled in Sony's favor that home recording constituted "fair use," the production industry had recognized the profits to be made by developing video as a subsequent release market and reached an accommodation with the makers of the hardware.

Video-cassette recorders (VCRs) found their way into American homes even more rapidly than television sets had done 30 years before. The hardware manufacturers recognized that, like record players and music centers, VCRs demanded software. While part of the VCR's function was initially understood as "time-shifting" the viewing of favorite TV programs, a vast market for home consumption of movies rapidly emerged during the 1980s. At the start of the decade fewer

Box 7.1 The video market, 1980–9

Sony introduced home video technology in 1975, but it did not move out of the "videophile" phase and into the mass market until 1984. Where it had taken television 15 years to reach 50 percent of US households, the VCR achieved that level of market penetration in just 12, with 80 percent of that penetration occurring between 1983 and 1987. By 1990, the video-cassette recorder had found a place in two-thirds of American homes, with the average family buying three or four pre-recorded videos a year – usually the previous year's big box-office hits. Eighty percent of the video business was, however, in rentals rather than sales and by 1990, renting a picture from the local video store and watching it at home had become the most common way of consuming movies in the US.[12]

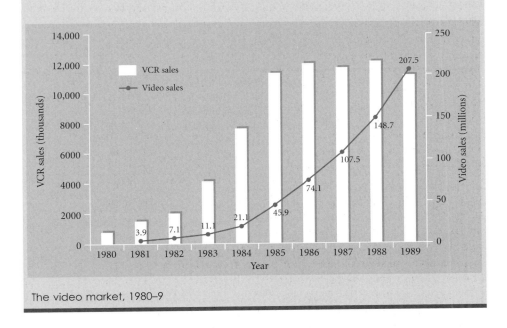

The video market, 1980–9

than 2 percent of US households owned a VCR. At its end, nearly 70 percent did, and American families were spending $10 billion a year on pre-recorded videos. By 1986, the majors earned more revenue in the domestic market from home video than they did from theatrical release. In the same period, the number of subscribers to pay cable grew from 9 million to 42 million. The $8.4 billion taken in video rentals in 1990 was nearly twice as much as the total box-office gross, although both the video and pay-TV markets relied on the "shop window" of the theatrical market to identify hit products. As late as 1980, the domestic box-office represented 80 percent of studio revenue, but by 1992 it returned no more than 25 percent.

The majors initially expected the video market to behave as previous audiences had, viewing each movie once only. Accordingly, they priced their video releases for sale to video rental outlets rather than to consumers, and experimented unsuccessfully with systems of pay-per-view that kept their control over the product. By 1990, however, a two-tier system had emerged, in which movies were released for video rental several months after their theatrical release, and were then released at lower prices for "sell-through" to individual consumers several months later. In the early 1990s video rentals reached a plateau, but video sell-through sales continued to grow at a rate of 20 percent a year, and in 1992 the value of video sell-through sales exceeded the domestic theatrical box-office for the first time. The clearance time between releases to each "window" have steadily narrowed; in particular, the time-lag between US domestic theatrical release and release into the major foreign markets shrank considerably during the 1990s.

The availability of new delivery systems in the 1980s was one factor encouraging a new wave of mergers as both film and television companies sought to gain control of the new technologies. By 1980, several of the majors had integrated

---

Box 7.2 Exhibition windows, 2000

A typical Hollywood movie has a domestic theatrical life of six months or less, and is released to parts of the international market two or three months after the American opening. It will be available on video, DVD, and US pay-per-view television as its theatrical run is tailing off, will be on pay-TV nine months after its theatrical release, and will premiere on network television six to nine months after that. Each foreign market follows a similar pattern of sequential release into each less profitable market window, and the time-lag between each window is becoming steadily shorter. On video and syndicated television, a movie has an unlimited afterlife.

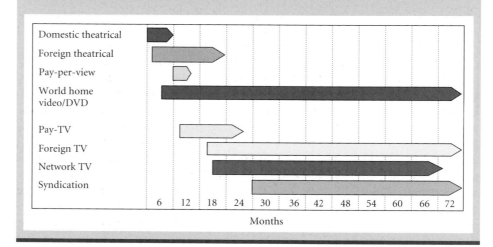

their business into a broader entertainment market embracing movies and publishing within the corporate framework of large, diverse conglomerates such as Gulf and Western or Warner Communications Inc., each of which also operated a range of businesses unrelated to the movies. The mergers and divestments of the 1980s were part of a broader merger movement across the US economy, and were in large part driven by the desire to exploit the emerging new technologies in ancillary markets. These mergers reshaped the majors as key components in more closely integrated and tightly diversified corporations which focused their activities on entertainment and communications media. In 1985 Rupert Murdoch's News Corporation acquired Twentieth Century-Fox (TCF) and Metromedia Television, the largest group of independent stations in the country, as the first move in creating a fourth US television network, in itself a platform for a global television, publishing, and entertainment corporation. The expansion of News Corp., and of Bertelsmann in Germany, set off further mergers. Blaming the commercial failure of its technically superior Betamax system on the shortage of movie titles available in its format, Sony bought CBS records in 1986 and Columbia Pictures in 1989 in order to be able to market a software library alongside its own new equipment in future. In 1990 Sony's rival Matsushita, the world's largest consumer electronics company, bought MCA in search of hardware–software synergies. Responding with an alternative version of synergy based on the remarketing of talent through a range of media, Warner Communications merged with Time Inc., which owned Home Box Office, the largest pay cable television service in the United States, to create Time Warner Inc., the world's largest media conglomerate.

The integration of television and film interests continued in the 1990s. In 1994 Paramount Communications, the only studio other than Disney not to change hands during the 1980s, was acquired by cable company Viacom, Inc.; in 1995 Disney acquired the ABC network, and in 1996 Time Warner, in response, took over Turner Broadcasting as the base for a potential fifth American network. News Corporation has continued to expand, particularly into the Asian market. The 1996 Telecommunications Act, which permitted telephone companies to provide programming content for their systems, encouraged the economic convergence of the software, computer, and telecommunications industries, in order to facilitate the technological convergence of old and new media. By the turn of the millennium the *Wall Street Journal*'s 1989 prediction that the conjoined entertainment and information industries – the copyright industries – would be dominated by a few giant concerns, each "controlling a vast empire of media and entertainment properties that amounts to a global distribution system for advertising and promotion dollars," seemed well on the way to achievement.[13] In January 2000, America Online (AOL), the biggest Internet service provider in the world, merged with Time Warner, the world's largest entertainment conglomerate, in the biggest merger (worth $534 billion) in financial history. In December 2000, the French conglomerate Vivendi took over Seagrams and Universal to form Vivendi Universal as a "consumer-focused, performance-driven, values-based global media and communications industry."[14] Only the subsequent collapse in the stock market value of "dot.com" companies delayed a further round of imitative mergers among the other major companies, and exposed some significant weaknesses in the new conglomerates' financial structure.

Since the mid-1980s, distribution via video, pay-TV, and free-to-air television has come to operate as a far more profitable tiered subsequent-release system than Classical Hollywood's clearance system had ever been. Classical Hollywood's economics had concentrated profitability in first-run exhibition, and as late as 1975, 60 percent of domestic box-office revenues came from 1,000 first-run theaters.[15] Fifteen years later, an entirely different economic system was in place. Once the major companies recognized the size of the video market, they took over video distribution to secure the bulk of revenue from this source. The majority of a movie's income to the distributor now comes from subsequent release, and while initial US domestic box-office receipts are the crucial signal for a movie's overall earning capacity – the industry rule-of-thumb is that if a picture's domestic gross receipts equal its **negative cost**, it will make a profit – the changes in distribution and circulation patterns have profoundly altered the industry's conception of its product. While the principal audience for movies has been in the home since 1960, video has massively increased the industry's earning capacity from home consumption.

From the mid-1980s, the growth of additional markets in video sales and pay-TV added a new, electronic life to both old and new movies. They also affected the nature of the movie product: how well a movie could service ancillary markets

Box 7.3 Hollywood's changing market, 1980s

As late as 1980, theatrical exhibition provided two-thirds of Hollywood's feature movie revenue. During the 1980s the number of VCRs in the US rose from under two million to 62 million, or two-thirds of all households, and the sales of pre-recorded videos increased from three million units in 1980 to 220

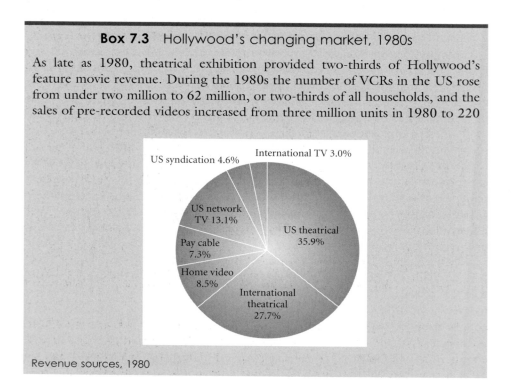

Revenue sources, 1980

million in 1990. Once the size of this market became evident, the major companies took over the distribution of videos, securing the substantial majority of income from this source. In the same period, the number of subscribers to pay cable grew from 9 million to 42 million. The changes since 1990 have been much less dramatic, consolidating those of the previous decade, and seeing a significant growth in the international market.[16]

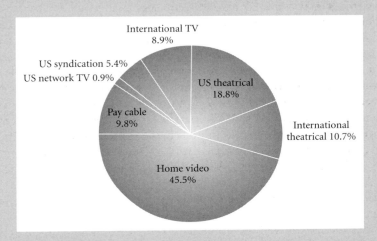

Revenue sources, 1990

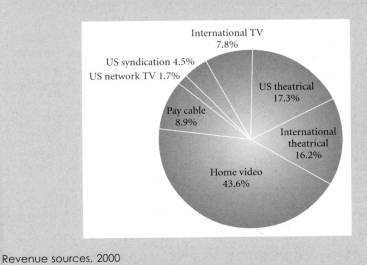

Revenue sources, 2000

became an increasingly important question as budgets escalated during the 1980s. Sequels, which were even more effectively "pre-sold" than adaptations of successful stage plays or novels, accounted for 10 percent of Hollywood's output. Video also provided a financial cushion for movies that failed at the theatrical box-office: the science fiction adventure *Willow*, produced by George Lucas in 1988, cost $55 million and grossed only $28 million in American theaters. But it earned an additional $18 million in video sales, and $15 million in television sales. Combined with its foreign earnings of $42 million in theaters and $22 million in video and television sales, its earnings from ancillary markets ensured its profitability.[17] By 1993, when video game revenues exceeded the theatrical box-office, a movie's "gameability" – the possibility of its being reconfigured as a video game – had become a factor in assessing its likely profitability.[18]

These ancillary profits fueled the continuing increase in production costs and budgets. During the second half of the 1980s, and allowing for inflation, the average Hollywood budget rose by 40 percent. In 1990, a major movie might be budgeted at $25 million, with additional marketing and distribution costs of $20 million. With overheads and interest charges, the studio that financed it would have to recoup more than $50 million to break even. Within the industry, cost inflation was blamed on the availability of outside money, particularly as it was introduced in the complex financing packages utilized for high-concept blockbusters by independent producers such as Carolco, and on the greatly increased power of agents to demand ever-higher payments to a small number of stars whose presence in a movie was believed to underwrite the escalating budgets. Despite occasional exhortations to cut costs – most famously Jeffrey Katzenberg's leaked 1990 memo to Disney staff arguing that the studio should return to producing smaller character-driven movies – budgets rose even more rapidly during the 1990s, since the underlying economic logic of the blockbuster syndrome demonstrated its effectiveness every time a special-effects-driven, uncomplicated, high-budget "event" movie broke a new box-office record.[19]

Hollywood's development of ancillary markets does not, however, present an entirely healthy industrial or economic history. Much of the potential profitability from the new markets was absorbed by the apparently uncontrollable escalation of production costs, directing revenues to the handful of stars and celebrity directors whose agents were able to dictate their market value to the majors. In Stephen Prince's analysis, the history of Hollywood since 1980 has been one of "delayed and deferred crisis," in which "new markets and technologies helped the industry stave off the insoluble economic contradictions that it faced."[20] Because the industry was chronically hit-driven, it inevitably produced more product than could

---

Box 7.4 The escalating cost of the average movie, 1980–2000

Since 1980, the production and marketing costs of the average movie produced by the major companies has risen exponentially. In the second half of the 1980s, the average Hollywood budget rose by 40 percent, and during the 1990s, budgets rose by another 60 percent in real terms. Marketing budgets rose even faster, doubling in real terms during the 1990s. In 1999 the major film companies spent a total of $2.55 billion on advertising. Only the automobile and retail industries spent more.

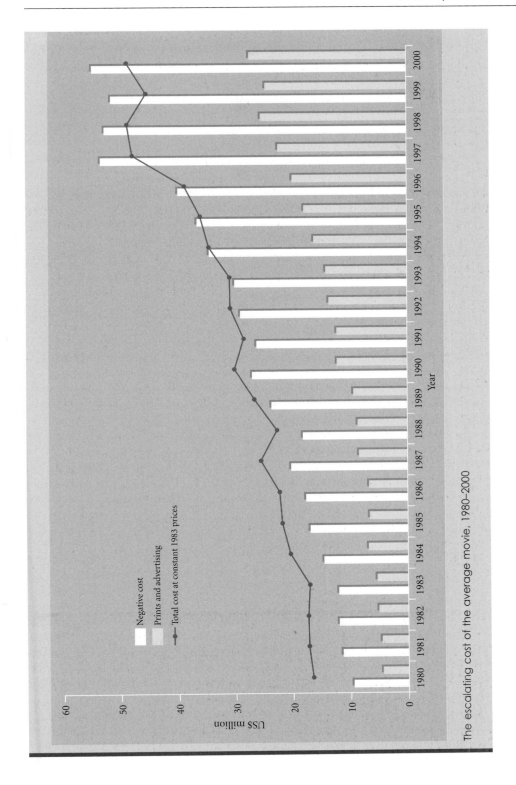

The escalating cost of the average movie, 1980–2000

Box 7.5   Box-office grosses[21]

The event movie has a short but exciting life at the box-office. The life of a non-event movie, as we might call a failed blockbuster, is shorter. The graphs here show the first part of the life-cycle of a successful event movie (*The Mummy Returns*, 2001), and a notable box-office failure (*Book of Shadows: Blair Witch 2*, 2000). Both movies opened very widely, on more than 3,300 screens. Failing to emulate the success of *The Blair Witch Project* (1999), *Book*

The Mummy Returns (2001); produced by Sean Daniel, James Jacks; distributed by Alphaville Films; directed by Stephen Sommers.

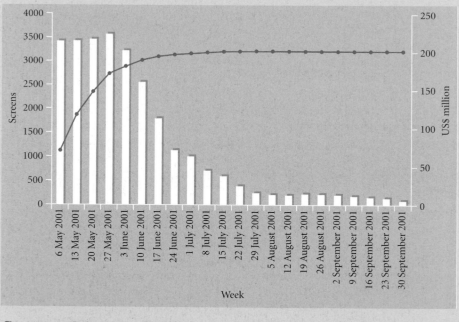

The Mummy Returns box-office gross

of Shadows died very quickly. By the third week of its release, it had made 95 percent of its eventual box-office gross, and was rapidly withdrawn from circulation. The earning pattern of *The Mummy Returns* was, however, not so different. By its third week, it had earned 72 percent of its eventual gross; by its fifth week, it had earned 90 percent; and after two months in release, even though it was still playing on over 1,000 screens, it had earned 97 percent of its eventual gross. The striking similarity of the pattern of earnings for movies released in this manner, regardless of their success, indicates why the industry pays so much attention to a movie's opening weekend grosses as a predictor of its eventual commercial performance. During the 1990s, an industry rule-of-thumb suggested that a movie's total domestic box office earnings would be three-and-a-half times its opening weekend gross. In 2001, the disappointing performances of several major summer releases, including *Pearl Harbor*, revised this ratio down to two-and-a-half times the opening weekend gross. It is, of course, also true that these patterns represent self-fulfilling prophecies on the part of the distributors.

Economic analyses of contemporary Hollywood's production and distribution practice argue that, contrary to persistent mythology, the industry is run in an economically efficient manner. According to economic historians John Sedgwick and Michael Pokorny, the unpredictability of audience behavior, and therefore of revenue, results from the difference between viewers' expectations of any given movie prior to viewing it, and their evaluation of the movie after seeing it. This pattern of consumer experience is, they note, unlike the normal

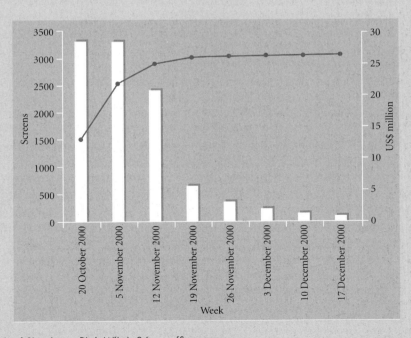

Book of Shadows: Blair Witch 2 box-office gross

one in which "rigorously standardised products meet precisely a set of ex ante expectations built upon repeated consumption."[22]Audiences seek to guarantee their expectations by viewing pictures with familiar elements that have satisfied them on previous occasions, such as stars and story types, but they also require novelty.

Economists Arthur De Vany and W. David Walls argue that the contemporary distribution and exhibition industry's flexible contractual arrangements over rental prices and the supply of theatrical outlets are highly adapted to optimize the economic opportunities provided by the particular uncertainties of the business.[23]These uncertainties, they argue, center on the inherent unpredictability of audience taste: audiences make hits "not by revealing preferences they already have, but by discovering what they like."[24] De Vany and Walls provide a descriptive economic model of how the process the industry calls "word-of-mouth" operates: consumers transmit information to other consumers, and "demand develops dynamically over time as the audience sequentially discovers and reveals its demand."[25] The industry's mechanisms of distribution and exhibition must be capable of adapting the supply of product to exploit these opportunities, because "as soon as individual differences emerge among the films, these differences can grow at exponential speed. . . . A broad opening at many cinemas can produce high and rapidly growing audiences; but it can also lead to swift failure if the large early crowd relays negative information."[26]

cumulatively be profitable, oversupplying the market for any given product type. Perhaps most worrying of all, domestic theatrical admissions remained static during the 1980s, and rose only 20 percent during the 1990s. Admissions have grown at a rate significantly lower than that of the underlying growth of US population, so that while movies may circulate more pervasively through the culture, a declining proportion of the population is going to movie theaters to see them.

Vogel argues that while successful event movies may continue to lure audiences to theaters:

> admissions to pictures requiring less immediate responsiveness probably are being replaced by home screenings that on average generate much less revenue per view . . . what is gained in one market may be at least partially lost in another; that is, in the aggregate, ancillary-market cash flow is often largely substitutional . . . the contributions from new ancillary revenue sources, especially those from pay cable and home video, have merely offset the sharply diminished profitability of theatrical production and release.[27]

While industry revenues have grown rapidly since 1984, the majors' operating margins, and therefore their profits, have grown at a far slower rate, in part because production and releasing costs have risen even more rapidly than revenues, because of weak cost constraints and increased competition. In Vogel's analysis, new media revenues have been more important as a prop to the declining profitability of theatrical exhibition than as a source of improved aggregate industry profitability.

One consequence of the emergence of video and pay-TV as a subsequent-release system has been the further flattening of the theatrical exhibition system into what is effectively a single tier. The growth of multiplex and megaplex theaters has meant that the number of screens has increased substantially, particularly since 1990, but at the same time older and smaller single-screen theaters have closed. By the mid-1980s, the major theater chains controlled 35 percent of the 22,000 screens in the US, but those 7,500 screens were the best located and most modern, and took in 80 percent of the box-office. Between 1980 and 2000, the number of screens in the US more than doubled from 17,590 to 37,396, but the number of theaters housing them almost halved from 13,100 to 7,421. The increased number of screens does not, however, translate into an increase in the overall attendance level or a growth in seating capacity. Multiplexes have an average of 200 seats per screen, one-third the capacity of single-screen theaters in 1960, and at the end of the century the overall seating capacity of US movie theaters was only half that of 1960. (See box 5.1.)

Saturation booking, now called **wide release**, became not so much the domi-nant release strategy as, effectively, the only release strategy during the 1990s. In 1989, *Driving Miss Daisy* was platform released to four theaters in New York and Los Angeles, before opening on 277 screens after four weeks and 895 after six weeks. Three months after its opening, it was still playing on 1,668 screens, and its total 36-week domestic release brought in a box-office gross of $107 million. A decade later, such long release patterns had disappeared, and audiences no longer had the opportunity to discover a **sleeper**, a picture initially assumed to have limited appeal which gains a much larger audience through word-of-mouth recommendation. The contemporary system prefers to identify such movies in advance, through the festival circuit, and then provide a very short platform – seldom more than a couple of weeks – to establish audience recognition, before releasing the movie to hundreds of theaters. While the precise pattern of any indi-vidual movie's circulation varies with the particular demographic group identified as its primary target audience, the dominance of wide release is absolute: in 1995, the 153 movies which were released to more than 800 screens earned over 95 percent of all theatrical revenues.[29]

The theatrical exhibition life of an individual movie has been greatly shortened by the wide release multiplex pattern, as the illustrations in box 7.5 demonstrate. A variety of factors has led to what Paramount executive Arthur Cohen called the "nightmare algebra" of contemporary Hollywood, "that you have to grab half your gross in your first two weeks."[30] Marketing has become heavily dependent on television advertising, with the majors spending over half their escalating mar-keting budgets on short, concentrated bursts of TV ads just before and during a movie's opening week. The majors' contracts with exhibitors give distributors a larger proportion of the box-office gross in a movie's first two weeks of release, encouraging the distributor to move product rapidly through the exhibition "pipeline" to maximize profit. The vastly increased profitability of subsequent release through video means that the distributor makes more money by with-

Box 7.6 Platform release[28]

In a platform release, a movie first opens in a small number of key theaters, and then expands into more exhibition outlets over a number of weeks, as word-of-mouth grows. While an "event" movie will earn 90 percent of revenue in five weeks, a successful platform release like *O Brother, Where Art Thou?* may take four months to earn the same proportion of its total revenue. Although it played on fewer screens and grossed only a quarter of the total earned by *The Mummy Returns*, it had a much longer theatrical life. Like *The Mummy Returns*, its total domestic box-office gross was almost exactly twice its budget.

O Brother, Where Art Thou? (2000); produced by Ethan Coen; distributed by Buena Vista Pictures; directed by Joel Coen.

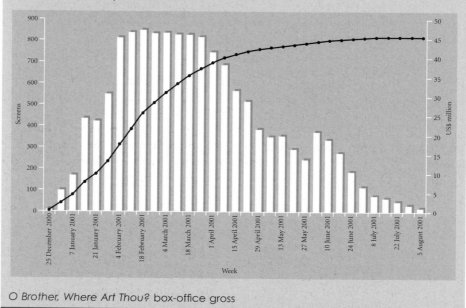

O Brother, Where Art Thou? box-office gross

drawing a movie from the theatrical market once its earnings have reached a plateau, and subsequently releasing it to a series of overlapping but different audiences on video, pay-TV, and network television. These subsequent markets ensure that while the theatrical life of a movie is much shorter than previously, its overall life as a product is considerably extended. In the case of a "franchise" movie, its product life begins well in advance of its release – 40 percent of tie-in toys are sold before the movie opens – and continues much longer, in the millions of video copies in consumers' homes, and as a tangible asset in the distributor's film library, which is now acknowledged to be the most important component of a major company's assets. As the total market for entertainment expanded after 1980, the value of film libraries was repeatedly revised upward. By 2000, the majors' libraries were valued at about $8 billion, 20 times the value placed on them in 1980.

The Pursuit of Synergy

The true value of the film business is not the profits generated by the film, but the synergies that movies provide with other areas. These include television production, theme parks, consumer products, soundtracks, books, video games and interactive entertainment. All of these areas have lower costs, lower risks and higher returns. Feature films provide the key to this magic kingdom.

Martin Dale[31]

If you don't have synergy, you have nothing but new products. . . . If you have synergy, it goes on and on.

Michael Eisner[32]

Nobody knows anything.

William Goldman[33]

In the 1980s, Hollywood had to reposition itself in relation to what historian Robert Allen calls the new, "shifting, decentered constellation of markets for its products," a situation that was radically different from the market only ten years previously, and one in which the domestic theatrical market was in itself much less important as a proportion of both revenue and profitability. The core theatrical audience – the 10 million "avid" moviegoers who attended at least once a week and bought 40 percent of all tickets – were overwhelmingly teenagers and single young adults. The great majority of video sales, on the other hand, were to a different audience: the "twenty-something" and "thirty-something" baby-boomers and their "echo-boom" children, who together made up the "family" audience at which Hollywood marketed its "cross-generational," "non-drop-off" family movies. The need for movies and their ancillary product range to appeal to the echo-boom children of "Generation Y" shaped Hollywood's increasing use of animation and digital effects technology. To maximize their earnings from the toys, clothes, home furnishings, and other merchandising tie-ins required family movies to have a distinctive and reproducible iconography that its producers could copyright and license, preferably without incurring financial obligations to movie stars. As Disney has long understood, animated animals, whether drawn or trained, have no legal interests in conflict with those of their copyright-holders.

No longer the culturally dominant form or the economic center of mass entertainment, the industry found its new hope in the model provided by *Star Wars*, in which the movie became the lead product in a complex of media and lifestyle goods. Between 1978 and 1983, the volume of licensed merchandise sales tripled. The change was most marked in the toy industry: in 1980, 10 percent of all toys sold were based on licensed characters, but by 1987, 60 percent were. Not all licensing was based on movies, but *Star Wars*, in particular, provided a model for the way in which character images increasingly merged with toys, inviting children to re-enact scenes from the movie.[35] The camera's tracking past the Jurassic Park gift shop was not accidental: the movie was constructed under an obligation to provide a range of merchandising and marketing opportunities or "hooks." As Steve McBeth, vice-president of consumer products for Disney, said of the little rubber replica of the Flounder from *The Little Mermaid* (1989) in a McDonald's Happy Meal, "it extends the entertainment experience for the child – it's a way of letting the fun of the movie continue."[36] "Extending the entertainment experience" is a description of what we might otherwise call commercial intertextuality. On its circulation as a movie, *Jurassic Park* was accompanied by a thousand pieces of officially licensed merchandise, while the vehicles used in its sequel, *The Lost World* (1997), were designed in conjunction with the Hasbro toy company to ensure the "playability" of their toy replicas.[37] The two movies took in a total of $1.5 billion at the box-office world-wide, and

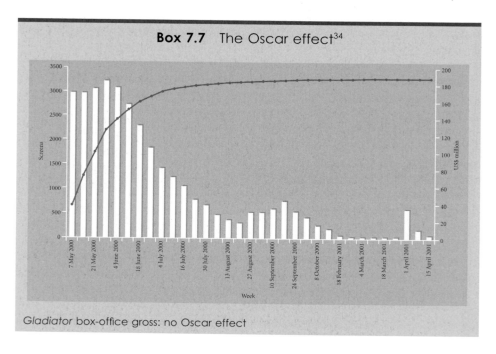

Box 7.7 The Oscar effect[34]

Gladiator box-office gross: no Oscar effect

Some movies' earnings are very significantly affected by Academy Award nominations and Oscars, while it makes little difference to others. In 2000, *American Beauty* won five Oscars including Best Picture, reviving its box-office performance to the extent that it grossed nearly as much in the four months after it was nominated as it had done in the five months of its initial release. In 2001, *Gladiator* won five Oscars including Best Picture, but this performance brought it no more than two weeks' additional life at the box-office. Academy Awards are far more likely to benefit smaller-budget movies aimed at an adult audience than spectacle-laden blockbusters.

American Beauty (1999); produced by Bruce Cohen, Dan Jinks; distributed by Dream-Works SKG; directed by Sam Mendes.

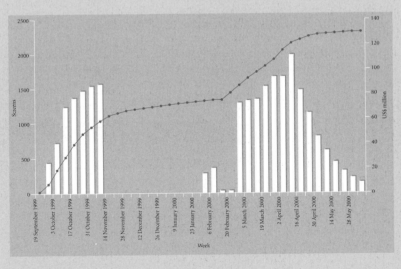

American Beauty box-office gross: the Oscar effect

generated sales of licensed toys, video games, and other merchandise worth a similar sum. Together with video sales and other revenue, including the spin-off television series *The Land Before Time*, *Jurassic Park*'s multiple revenue streams had created sales of over $5 billion before the release of the third movie in the series in 2001.

The Classical industry generally declined to permit advertising in its products or its exhibition sites, but almost every ultra-high-budget movie produced in contemporary Hollywood is, among other things, an advertising space for the placement of consumer products. Advertisers defend the practice because portraying "someone using a product in real life" makes both the product and the fictional situation appear more authentic. According to producer Al Ruddy, "you can't have Mel Gibson picking up a pack of 'Ajax' cigarettes and drinking 'Aqua' beer, because people won't believe it."[38] The Teenage Mutant Ninja Turtles, for example, ate Domino's Pizza to make both themselves and, in a different sense, the pizza more "credible."[39] Domino's Pizza paid for participating in this commercial realism, just as General Motors, Pepsi-Cola, Havoline Oil, Budweiser, Heinz, Levi's, and more than 70 other products paid to participate in the capitalist realism of *Days of Thunder* (1990), because product placement delivers a demographically desirable audience to advertisers at very low cost.

The extent to which these new markets and commercial relationships have altered both the industry and its products is a matter for continuing debate. Allen argues that the reconfiguration of the marketplace means that "the Hollywood cinema – the institutional, cultural, and textual apparatus we have known since the 1910s – is dead." The majors "are no longer in the film business or the television business or, arguably, even the entertainment business, but in the business of synergistic brand extension":

> When Hollywood was in the cinema business and moviegoing in the local picture palace was habitual, the release of any new film drew upon the cinema's institutional capacity for enchantment, and individual films were "promoted" by their participation in the cinema. Today, however, films have to constitute themselves as events on an ad hoc basis, and they need as much help as they can get from promotional tie-ins to stand tall as movie "events" at least for a couple of weeks.[40]

In the last two decades of the twentieth century, Hollywood's boundaries certainly became more difficult to define, as its commercial operations became increasingly intertwined with those of other enterprises – not merely television, but toys, theme parks, and food franchises. In 1996, Disney signed a ten-year licensing agreement with McDonald's, under which the fast food chain paid the distributor $100 million a year for exclusive licensing of all Disney's features. Through this arrangement, McDonald's became the world's largest distributor of toys, while Disney characters supplied the promotably inedible part of a Happy Meal.[41] Lucasfilms and PepsiCo reached a similar agreement. Such promotional tie-ins commonly double the amount of money spent marketing a movie, once the food retailer's promotional budget is included. Sony committed $50 million to the launch of *Godzilla* in the summer of 1998, but its marketing partners spent three times that amount in cross-promoting their products linked to the movie, with the fast food chain Taco Bell alone spending $60 million.[42] Relying on the cross-promotional marketing campaigns of its licensees, merchandisers, and retailers, LucasFilms kept the marketing budget for *Star Wars Episode 1 – The Phantom Menace* (1999) to a mere $14 million.

Disney has been the prototype for brand synergy. Chairman Michael Eisner explained in the company's 1995 Annual Report:

> We are fundamentally an operating company, operating the Disney brand all over the world, maintaining it, improving it, promoting it and advertising it with taste. Our time must be spent insuring that the Brand never slides, that we innovate the Brand, experiment and play with it, but never diminish it.[43]

Together with Frank G. Wells and Jeffrey Katzenberg, Eisner revived Disney in the second half of the 1980s, developing the company through increasing production, successfully relaunching its animation franchise, and exploiting its under-utilized ancillary markets, and then broadening its range of products through acquisitions and mergers.

The multiple logics of synergy drove a further cycle of industry mergers at the end of cinema's first century, creating companies that conformed to entertainment industry analyst Michael Wolf's description of what successful performance in the entertainment industry now required:

> only entities with a broad financial base and access to costly talent can front the money it takes to gamble that an audience will find and then like what it presents. To spread their risk and to enhance their distribution, entertainment companies are typically forced to own a combination of assets that might include a motion picture studio, a TV network, cable networks, a book-publishing company, a magazine division, TV stations, retail stores, theme parks, and merchandize.

Without multiple revenue streams, Wolf argues, there will ultimately be no profit in the entertainment economy: "in the long run, entertainment companies . . . will thrive only to the extent that they can transform hits into megabrands."[44]

Each of the six major studios distributes a slate of between ten and twenty pictures a year, with an average production and marketing budget (in 2000) of $82.1 million per picture.[45] Movie production and distribution remains, as it has been since at least 1948, a very high-risk commercial activity, in which at least six out of ten pictures fail to return their costs, while another one or two break even. At the same time, the blockbuster phenomenon's concentration of earnings on a handful of pictures requires studios to gamble high stakes on potential block-busters. The single phenomenal success – a world box-office gross of $100 million in 1990, or $300 million in 2000 – acts as a "tentpole" supporting the rest of the production slate, particularly for sales to subsequent markets such as pay-TV. However carefully it observes the rules, there is no guarantee that in any partic-ular year a studio will distribute one of the top five pictures, and each of the majors' share of the theatrical market tends to vary dramatically each year. While the ultra-high budget picture strategy operates on an entirely justifiable commercial logic, it is not a logic that produces inherent commercial stability for any of the companies investing $1 billion in only a dozen products. Diversification is, therefore, an attendant logic. Because it is impossible to achieve profitability on a movie's theatrical release alone, the majors have come to view each big movie as an "anchor" product creating revenue "downstream" in other businesses:

> A studio could sell its movie to network television, cable, foreign distributors, and foreign broadcasters. It could release a sound-track album. It could sell toys for both kids and adults. It could build theme-park rides. It could tie it into a fast-food promotion. It could create sequels II, III, and IV.[46]

Box 7.8 How the box-office dollar is split

The "house nut" is a fixed sum agreed by the distributor and exhibitor to cover the operating costs of the theatre. After that deduction, the box-office **gross** is divided between distributor and exhibitor, usually 90:10. The distributor takes a distribution fee of 30–5 percent of the distributor's gross (or "rentals" gross), and also deducts the costs of prints and advertising, and other expenses, such as taxes, transportation, and MPAA fees. This leaves less than a third of the box-office dollar to cover a movie's negative costs.

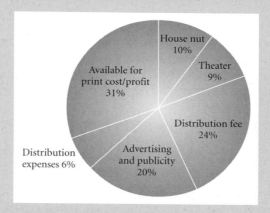

How the box-office dollar is split

Contemporary Hollywood's accounting is notorious for its "creativity," particularly its capacity for bookkeeping that demonstrates that a hugely successful movie has somehow failed to make a profit. While independent producers, in particular, may view the studios' accounting practices as little better than licensed larceny, these practices have their basis in the distributors' costs. The distribution fee covers the costs of the distribution apparatus, and more importantly provides the means by which the distributor will make enough on very successful movies to cover losses on the majority.[47]

Some of these revenue streams applied to all movies, others only to the "event" movie, the "franchise," or the "megabrand." These products – *Batman, Jurassic Park, Harry Potter* – apparently provided the logic for mergers, since the integrated media company maximized the possibilities for "synergistic brand extension" and for retaining the profits from downstream commercial activities within the parent company that had originated the product. Synergy was not, however, an inherent outcome of mergers: the comment of one insider about the lack of effective interaction between components of Time Warner, "At Time Warner, synergy means they all charge each other retail,"[48] actually reveals a more endemic condition. While the media mergers have most commonly been accounted for in terms of the synergies they produce, synergy is actually a rationalization of what is in reality a largely defensive commercial practice aimed at spreading the necessary risk of ultra-high-budget movie production into the lower-cost businesses downstream. As economist Richard Caves has argued, "Observers of the media conglomerates' post-merger behavior generally detect no significant synergies."[49] Certainly, neither Sony nor Matsushita found any substantial software–hardware synergies in their purchases of media companies, and in 1995, only five years after buying MCA, Matsushita sold it to the Seagram Company. Caves argues that "the basic traits of creative industries cast a pall of skepticism over the growth of entertainment conglomerates," and that "the synergies they pursue are probably illusory . . . They at best offer defensive value when they unite media content with distribution channels. To create greater value from their integration of functions demands complex collaboration in the development of creative inputs, which requires a water-and-oil mixture of creative talents with bureaucratic planners."[50]

The creation of "megabrands" therefore in a sense provides a public justification for the integration of the various components of the media corporation, most visible, perhaps, in their theme parks displaying ride versions of their most successful movies. The value of the megabrand is, however, always up for debate and revaluation, particularly in the light of the low profit margins of movie production. The multi-media conglomerates continue to look askance at the instabilities and unpredictabilities of production, by comparison to the much more secure operations of a delivery system that can take profits through distribution without incurring the risks in developing new content. Synergy may evolve to a point where it once again separates production and distribution, but as Wolf argues, not only is the hit-driven nature of the industry unlikely to change, but other consumer businesses will increasingly be drawn into the entertainment economy and become more and more subject to its "volatile but inescapable cycle." In particular, the Internet, on which "business and entertainment finally converge . . . will provide one more reason for the integration of entertainment content and practices into every other consumer business."[51]

According to this analysis, then, the integrated entertainment marketplace is most receptive to multi-media franchises, and once the majors created a corporate structure designed to maximize the benefits of synergy, they found themselves inevitably obliged to develop products capable of "synergistic brand extension." Not all of these objects had to be movies – *Lara Croft: Tomb Raider* (2001), for example, was a brand created around a computer game – but the effects-driven, ultra-high-budget movie has proven to be the product most likely to lead a franchise, because of Hollywood's status among the media and because the movies' budgeting on single products is far higher than any other form of production in the entertainment industry. The conundrum, however, remains that the apparently inexorable inflation of the costs of both talent and effects-driven spectacle continues to push the production costs of franchise movies to points at which only the most spectacular success can make the movies themselves sources of profit.

Franchises also appear to have a fairly limited shelf life, and none of the post-1978 examples have survived beyond a fourth recycling, or matched the durability of the Bond or *Star Wars* ones. By the late 1990s the franchises that had fueled the post-1985 mergers – *Indiana Jones, Batman* – had exhausted their market, and were in need of replacement. The reasons are fairly straightforward: sequels are less profitable than originals. They cost more to produce than the initial franchise movie because the participants, particularly the stars, expect a larger share of the income from the franchise. They earn less because it is the exceptional box-office performance of the original that initiates the franchise. Subsequent sequels show diminishing profitability for distributors: although *Lethal Weapon 4* (1998), for example, grossed $270 million world-wide, most of its profit went to the movie's stars, particularly Mel Gibson. Peter Bart's book *The Gross*, which chronicles the summer of 1998, describes the persistent feeling of dissatisfaction among studio executives that, while industry revenues continued to rise, and a number of movies grossed over $150 million, none had been phenomenal successes, and none had created a new brand. Most obviously, *Godzilla* (1998), while far from unsuccessful at the box-office, failed to launch the franchise that would have created a brand identity for Sony/Columbia comparable to that given to Warners by *Batman* or to Universal by *Jurassic Park*.

Globalization

It's hard to tell what constitutes a "Hollywood" movie any more, apart from the fact that it has a bigger budget than anyone else can remotely afford.
Philip McCarthy[52]

We have created a product that by, say, putting the name of Warner Brothers on it is a stamp of credibility. But that could be an Arnon Milchan film, directed by Paul Verhoeven, starring Gérard Depardieu and Anthony Hopkins, and shot in France and Italy, and made with foreign money.
John Ptak[53]

American movies that do not travel are getting more difficult to make.
Steven J. Ross[54]

Classical Hollywood brought the world to California, where it blended the exotic ingredients provided by imported production personnel into its conventional products. Sometimes the mixture worked perfectly, in the Hollywood careers of directors Ernst Lubitsch or Douglas Sirk, for instance. Sometimes, as in the brief American career of their compatriot G. W. Pabst (discussed in chapter 10), it did not. The American movies of European stars like Garbo were often more successful in Europe than in the US, but whatever the national origins of their production personnel, Classical Hollywood's products were unmistakably identified as American when they were exported abroad.

Post-Paramount Hollywood, on the other hand, has been a more self-consciously "international" cinema, partly because of the increasing economic importance of the global market for its products and partly because the end of the studio system literally removed the physical constraints that required "Hollywood" movies to be produced in the Los Angeles studios of the major companies. This has not slowed the rate at which Hollywood sucks in talent from around the world, and a pattern is well established whereby both directors and actors, having a level of success in their countries, migrate to Hollywood in search of opportunities not provided by their domestic industries. This aspect of Hollywood's internationalization and international dispersal was, for example, particularly evident in the 2002 Oscar nominations, when half of the 20 actor nominations went to non-Americans.

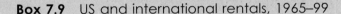

Box 7.9 US and international rentals, 1965–99

The international box-office has accounted for slightly under half of the major companies' total income from theatrical rentals since the 1960s. In the late 1970s, the American theatrical market recovered significantly more than overseas markets, while the international market grew strongly in the 1990s.

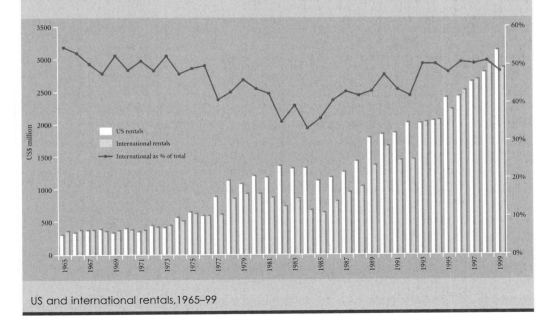

US and international rentals, 1965–99

In the immediate aftermath of World War II, European governments' policies restricting currency exports encouraged the majors to invest in production overseas, and the increasing importance of the international market, which in 1953 exceeded the size of the domestic market for the first time, required the production of movies that would appeal across all the major world markets. The action-packed, simply plotted blockbuster was the form that most easily and profitably crossed national borders: "make it simple and keep it moving" was understood to be the international formula.[55] Runaway production provided exotic locations, local color, and opportunities for the majors to take advantage of subsidies designed to promote "national cinemas," or circumvent laws restricting the export of profits. Since 1960, more than a third of "Hollywood" movies have been made outside the US, and American investment in international production has increased rapidly since 1977, while production finance also increasingly involves overseas backers.

The principal factor determining a production's location has been financial. While for some productions the lower cost of production personnel or facilities has been of crucial importance, the single largest impetus for runaway production has been the dollar's exchange rate with foreign currencies. A strong US dollar encourages production to migrate from California, as happened in the 1990s when the Canadian and Australian dollars lost 20 percent of their value against the US dollar. A weak US dollar reduces the attraction of exotic locations and cheap foreign crews, and sees productions return to the US, but it also increases the value of foreign earnings. The phenomenon of runaway production intermittently provokes fears that Los Angeles is gradually becoming "a center of entertainment design and management" rather than of production itself.[56] At the height of a bout of runaway production in 2001, for example, employment levels in the California motion picture and television industries fell by 12 percent. These fears were, to an extent, compounded by the growing foreign ownership of the major companies. Such sentiments were, however, mild echoes of the anxieties expressed in other countries where the desire for a national cinema of cultural expression conflicted with the desire for American money to sustain a strong production base. Hollywood remained largely untouched by such concerns, because its status as a "national" American cinema was never formulated in the relatively narrow terms employed elsewhere.

The internationalization of production to a significant extent reflected the steadily increasing economic importance of the international market. By the 1990s, entertainment had become the second largest American export category after military hardware, and since 1990 many of Hollywood's most expensive products, star- and effects-driven event movies, have earned more of their income overseas than in the domestic market. Globalization was a central component in the development of transnational multi-media corporations. The Time Warner "synthesis" was the result of a common recognition that globalization was "a fact of life. No serious competitor could hope for any long-term success unless, building on a secure home base, it achieved a major presence in all the world's important markets."[57]

The global entertainment market has expanded steadily since 1975, and there is no sign of that expansion stopping in the near future. In 1980 Europe had one-third as many screens per capita as there were in the US, and most of these were old. As part of a concerted policy by the American majors and their European partners to rebuild and renovate cinemas, 500 new multiplex screens were built in Britain during the 1980s, and there was a similar expansion elsewhere in Europe and in Japan, which is now the largest single national market for American movies outside the US. The overseas non-theatrical market grew in the late 1980s as a result of the deregulation of state broadcasting and the growth of cable, and most of all through the spread of video as a second-run exhibition window. By 1989 video was the largest source of Hollywood's overseas revenue. The deregulation of much European television resulted in an enormous increase in the number of commercial television stations and satellite services. By 1989, western European television reached a larger market (320 million people, 125 million households) than US television (250 million people, 90 million households). A movie may now make as much as 90 percent of its revenue outside the US.

Convergence and globalization have resulted in the American film industry no longer necessarily being owned by Americans, although its product has, if anything, become more exclusively American in perspective. The fears of a "Japanese invasion" of American culture expressed at the time of the Sony and Matsushita take-overs have since evaporated. Globalization and the new markets have made the majors increasingly stable, whoever actually owns them. Through the development of new markets and synergies, their combined revenues have been growing at a remarkably steady rate of 9 percent per annum since 1980, from $4 billion in 1980 to $15 billion in 1995.[58] Economically, their most effective strategy has been the ultra-high-budget film, and the rewards of the international market have been a major factor in the escalation of production budgets since 1980. Ultra-high budgets also act as effective barriers to entry into the profits from synergy, securing the majors' control of the most profitable sectors. The existence of stable secondary markets has made the risk-taking involved acceptable, by providing a financial cushion for movies that fail at the theatrical box-office: while the commercial failure of *Heaven's Gate*, at a cost of $44 million, brought about the sale of United Artists in 1980, *Waterworld*, produced in 1995 for an alleged cost of $200 million, grossed only $80 million in the US, but earned $170 million overseas, and eventually recouped its costs in secondary markets.

The "globalization" of Hollywood has been created almost as much by the actions of its potential competition as it has by any deliberate policies on the part of the major companies themselves. While American movies have enjoyed constant revenues in Europe since 1960, the audience for European cinema has collapsed: in the half-century after the end of World War II, the box-office revenues of European-produced cinema fell to one-ninth their value in 1945. Europe exports only in niche "cultural" fields, and while most critics attribute the economic decline of European cinema to Hollywood's "unfair" advantages of scale, industry analyst Martin Dale argues that European cinema "has turned its back on popular traditions, and decided to focus on 'culture.'"[59] This is, he argues, a direct

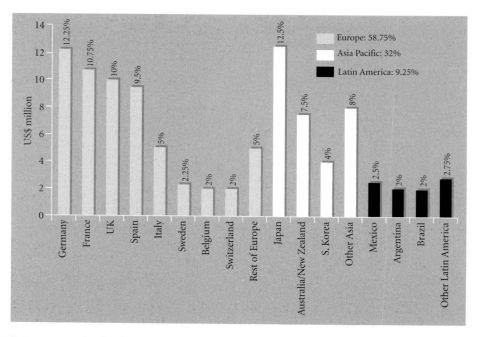

Major sources of Hollywood's international theatrical revenue, 1992

consequence of the various European state subsidies for film production, which have all encouraged a definition of "national cinema" in terms of an elite or bourgeois culture rather than a popular generic cinema operating in direct competition with Hollywood. This change occurred in Britain and Germany in the 1960s and early 1970s, in Italy in the late 1970s and early 1980s, and in France during the 1980s. Hollywood's increased proportion of these markets, Dale argues, came less from any intrinsic qualities, good or bad, of the American product than from the collapse of domestic competition.[60]

One consequence of this shift in European production toward "culture cinema" has been that some of the European capital previously used in the production of popular European cinema has become available for investment in "Hollywood." In 2000, for example, nearly 20 percent of the $15 billion spent on Hollywood production was German investment money, based on tax subsidies.[61] Three-quarters of the money invested in film production by Europe's media groups was invested in American production in the mid-1990s, with only a quarter going to European production. The practice of packaging foreign investments was initially developed by independent producers such as Dino De Laurentis or Carolco seeking a means of entry into high-budget production, but the majors' defensive strategies of spreading risks also encouraged them to seek overseas investments and international co-production. Production companies such as Mutual Film have developed to direct the resources of foreign distributors into the financing of "Hollywood" movies. In 1998, for example, Mutual produced *Hard Rain*, directed by expatriate Dane Mikael Saloman, and financed by a consortium of theatrical distributors, exhibitors, and television companies in France, Britain, Germany, Holland, Denmark, and Japan.[62] Increasingly, cable, satellite, and new media distributors are replacing banks as the principal source of foreign funds for Hollywood production.[63]

"Hollywood"'s movies have thus become increasingly international in three crucial aspects: their sources of finance; their creative personnel; and their revenues. These three factors do not, of course, balance each other out, although there is some evidence that, for instance, Hollywood movies directed by German directors such as Wolfgang Petersen and Roland Emmerich are popular in Germany. Dale suggests that "Europeans working in Hollywood . . . provide popular culture through the back door" for European distributors, particularly in action movies starring Europeans or ex-Europeans such as Arnold Schwarzenegger or Jean-Claude Van Damme.[64] Such an appeal to a particular local market is not, of course, provided by a local source of capital, but the sources of funding for Hollywood movies are as diverse as its production sites.

The globalization of the entertainment and copyright industries partakes of the same fundamental forces as the globalization of other sectors of the economy: the development of large consumer markets for consumable and consumer goods in areas of the world previously considered either too poor or otherwise inaccessible to capitalism. For many of the same reasons for which the entertainment industries educated the working classes of the First World in habits of consumption in the first half of the twentieth century, the entertainment and copyright industries are taking a leading role in the larger process of globalization as markets are expanded in Russia, China, India, and Latin America. Michael Wolf anticipates that:

> the costs of a global presence are so high, and the local conditions so varied, that the trend will be more toward relationships and partnerships that distribute risk while balancing the strengths and resources of global brands with the advantages of local experts. Just as Coca-Cola built its worldwide business through local partnerships, entertainment companies will create global businesses based on strong local alliances.[65]

While these markets will necessarily be serviced in large part by local product, this will be in conjunction with the circulation of very high-budget product aimed increasingly at the international market, a product that will continue to be identified as coming from "Hollywood."

Independence

If you don't have a distributor, you're independent. If you have a distributor, none of us are independent.

Chris Eyre[66]

Independent is just a word that the eight established companies decided to apply to their competition when they designated themselves as majors.

Robert Shaye[67]

production and then contract to a minimal form at other times. The complexity of post-Classical Hollywood's contractual arrangements is visible in its movies' credits: a typical movie will be "presented" by its distributor and financiers, and "produced" by one or more other companies, often "in association with" several others. All of these companies are independent of the studio-as-major distributor, in the sense that they are also contractually free to collaborate with other companies and in other combinations.

The fragmentary nature of the production industry's organizational practices provides a significant space for "independent" creative activity, but there is considerable latitude over how the independence of an "independent" production can be defined. In his history of American independent cinema, Greg Merritt produces an operational distinction between independent and semi-independent movies. Merritt defines an independent production as "any motion picture financed and produced completely autonomous of *all* studios, regardless of size," whereas "a semi-indie" is not produced directly by a major studio, but does have a distribution guarantee before production begins, and may be made by a smaller company such as Miramax or Gramercy.[71] Such a definition suggests that in practice, independence is almost invariably qualified. As Chris Eyre's quotation at the head of this section indicates, if "independence" is defined as financial independence from the major distributors, a production company can only secure aesthetic autonomy at the expense of access to the exhibition market. If a distribution contract is the necessary condition of a movie's financing, the "independent" production company is bound by the conditions of its contractual relationship with the distributor. Power is certainly no less concentrated in post-Classical Hollywood than it was in the earlier system.

Independent production has become increasingly important to the way that the major companies compile their release schedules. As well as bringing partially completed projects to the majors for a production-finance-distribution (PFD) deal, independent producers provide completed movies for distribution, allowing the majors a greater degree of flexibility in their release schedule than is available from projects they finance themselves. These **pickup** deals, which accounted for around one-third of box-office revenues in the 1980s, involve a much lower and more predictable level of risk for the distributors than is entailed in initiating a project, since the distributor does not have to bear any of the development costs or commit resources to producing similar products. Moreover, the distributors' minimal investment in this product allows them to maintain a degree of distance from it, should any movie prove either unprofitable or excessively controversial. The element of deniability that was built into the conventions of Classical Hollywood production has been transferred, like much else in the transition to post-Classical Hollywood, to the contractual relationship between distributor and independent producer. If the movie makes money or wins awards, the distributor can take credit for the film's success and quality; if it is unsuccessful or offensive, then simply withdrawing it from distribution, preferably before much money is committed to its promotion, effectively makes the movie disappear and minimizes negative public relations exposure.[72]

In the late 1980s, independent distributors had a 15 percent share of the domestic theatrical market, and through the promotion of events such as the Sundance Festival, low-budget independent movies had gained enough commercial and critical attention to be presented as an alternative American cinema to the mainstream high-concept production of Hollywood. The most successful independent distributors, New Line and Miramax, secured their market share by developing movies that "crossed over" the boundaries of the art-house market to a larger audience.[73] New Line's profits from its distribution of the *Teenage Mutant Ninja Turtles* and *Nightmare on Elm Street* franchises and Jim Carrey comedies underwrote their distribution of more obviously "independent" and less commercial movies. Miramax's cross-over success with *sex, lies and videotape* (1989) promoted a widespread belief in an emerging American independent production sector in the early 1990s, but it also significantly raised the earnings threshold required for an independent movie to be considered a success.

Miramax consciously adopted a policy of stimulating media-induced controversies over some of their releases, publicly criticizing the rating system as being prejudiced against independent production, and using the sensationalist techniques of exploitation marketing to draw cross-over audiences to "art-house" product. Their consistent success established Miramax as the leading brand-name for American independent product. The extent to which this brand was commercially compatible with the majors was made evident in 1993, when Disney bought Miramax and Ted Turner bought New Line, which in 1996 became a component of Time Warner. During the early 1990s, each of the majors either acquired a successful independent distributor or developed one or more subsidiary distribution companies as an additional "label" for their products, in imitation of their music companies. While these former independents operate as semi-autonomous divisions, some of their product and marketing techniques have sat uncomfortably with the family image of the parent company, and access to the market has occasionally been hobbled by corporate taste, with Turner's disapproval of *Crash* (1996) being the most notorious example. Miramax, however, has attained cultural respectability by winning a parade of Academy Awards and nominations, and has succeeded in retaining its appeal to a niche market for "quality" product, while at the same time fitting into Disney's overall strategy of becoming "the largest producer of intellectual property in the world."[74]

By bidding aggressively for distribution rights and increasing the price paid for product, the "major independents" increasingly polarized and restricted the market for independent movies, expanding marketing budgets and making the independent sector increasingly hit-driven.[75] While in 1990 an independent distributor might have successfully circulated 20 prints of a low-budget movie to take $2 million over the course of a year, the wide-release practices that now dominate even the "specialty" market require platform-released movies to "go wide" to at least 200 screens within a few weeks, or else disappear.[76] The overall effect of these changes has been to reduce the available market for independent cinema, to further blur the distinction between the majors and independents, and to drive a number of production and distribution companies unaffiliated with the majors out of the market. The last of the significant independent distributors, October Films, was acquired by Universal in 1997.

"Independent," is, then, a highly qualified term in contemporary Hollywood. Rather than describing a production or distribution practice, it is better understood as a generic term signifying a production trend, a product type directed at a niche audience, and defined and marketed as distinct from and to a large extent in opposition to – in several senses riskier than – Hollywood's mainstream product. Economically, however, "independent production" has become effectively integrated into the activities of the majors, and if we apply Merritt's definition, true independent distribution "is now at its lowest level since the Code era."[77] Chuck Kleinhans argues that the majors use low-budget independent movies as "an inexpensive, low-risk source for an increasingly differentiated market":

> Rather than investing its own money in initial production, the industry sponsors . . . a highly speculative system in which about three hundred independent films a year are winnowed down to about thirty that are released nationally, and about ten that are profitable or at least come close to returning their investment.[78]

This activity remains marginal to the industry's highly speculative mode of operation, however. One of its additional functions is as a training ground for new talent, while another is to identify niche markets for the majors to exploit with a cycle or the movie equivalent of a cover version: "less imaginative, less politically committed, and less interesting than the original," but with the potential to break out of the niche market it is aimed at because of its higher budget and stars: *Reality Bites* (1994), for example, was a star vehicle tailored to the niche Generation X market identified by *Slacker* (1991).[79] In commercial terms, the ideal "indepen-

Matt Damon and Robin Williams in *Good Will Hunting* (1997): for its distributor, the ideal "cross-over" independent movie.
Produced by Lawrence Bender; distributed by Miramax Films; directed by Gus Van Sant.

dent" movie such as *Good Will Hunting* (1997) projects an off-beat quality to a mainstream audience, and earns a box-office gross of ten or twelve times its production cost.

As was always the case, Hollywood's production types are most significantly distinguished by their budget categories, which to a large extent determine their content and treatment. Until 1995, Hollywood's production could be categorized as being of three kinds. Apart from ultra-high-budget high-concept, the distribution and exhibition machinery was maintained by moderately priced star vehicles financed and distributed by the majors. Independent low-budget or "boutique" productions, which might hope to achieve cult movie status, complemented these routine features, offering something between European art-house cinema and the mainstream star vehicle and delivering an attention to theme, character relationships, and social relevance. Either of these two production modes might be aimed primarily at a single audience "quadrant" such as the "women over 24" who made *Driving Miss Daisy* a hit. Since 1995 the distinction between these two types has eroded, and it may be more accurate to distinguish Hollywood's output as belonging to only two categories: big-budget international movies and smaller-budget movies with less dependence on the international market. This latter category is highly diverse, encompassing a range of products from movies starring Samuel L. Jackson, Martin Lawrence, or American TV stars with limited global appeal to what James Ulmer describes as "the *Sling Blade* syndrome: a very specific movie about weird problems blue collar people suffer in middle America" that "nobody watches overseas."[80] It is, perhaps, only unified by the fact that its lack of international appeal gives it, arguably, the status of an American national cinema, in a sense that has not previously applied in the same way to Hollywood's product.

Hollywood's attention, however, remains primarily focused on the global market, into which the major companies are expanding horizontally, across a spectrum of delivery platforms, at the same time as they minimize the risks of production through partnerships and arrangements with "independent" producers. As applied to contemporary Hollywood's organization, "synergy" describes a "creative" horizontal relationship between practices and products, between hardware and software, between media, and between interpretations. This is now the governing economic logic of New Hollywood's tightly diversified media conglomerates, and the likely future developments in the new technologies of distribution will only add further layers to this process. If the activities of the major companies now bear little resemblance to the studios whose names and histories they still trade on, this will not prevent the identity of the future industry they create from remaining "Hollywood." As one executive observed in 1983:

> When television started in the 1950s, there was a strong view that that was the end of Hollywood. When cable came, we thought that would kill our sales to the networks. None of these things happened. Every time the market expands, the combination is greater than before. After all, it should be immaterial to Hollywood how people see its product so long as they pay.[81]

As Hollywood has outlived film, so it may also outlive cinema as a cultural form.

Summary

- Hollywood's postwar history can be seen as a long process of development toward the American cinema we recognize today, in which Hollywood is a fully integrated part of a much larger and more diversified entertainment industry. Vertical integration has been replaced by the horizontal integration of New Hollywood's tightly diversified media conglomerates, for which movies are one version of a product existing in several media forms.

- In the 1980s, the development of new systems for delivering movies to audiences, including home video, cable, and satellite, encouraged a wave of industrial mergers as film and television companies sought to gain control of new technologies and new markets. Profits from "subsequent release," licensing, and ancillary markets increased in proportion to theatrical cinema revenues. By 1986 the majors earned more in the domestic market from home video alone than they did from theatrical release.

- Wide release became effectively the dominant strategy during the 1990s. This greatly shortened the theatrical life of individual movies, but the subsequent release to overlapping but different audiences on video, pay-TV, and network television ensured that the overall economic life of a movie was considerably extended. Hit movies increasingly became the lead product in a complex of synergistic media and lifestyle goods.

- The end of the studio system removed the physical constraints that required "Hollywood" movies to be produced in the Los Angeles studios of the major companies. Since 1960 more than a third of "Hollywood" movies have been made outside the US, with financial advantage becoming the principal factor determining the location of production.

- The global entertainment market has expanded steadily since 1975, and this expansion has been a central component in the development of transnational multi-media corporations. By the 1990s entertainment had become the second largest American export category after military hardware. Since 1990 many of Hollywood's most expensive products have earned more of their income in the international than in the domestic market. Hollywood's movies have become increasingly international in their sources of finance, their creative personnel, and their revenues.

- The products that service Hollywood's global market most profitably are predominantly "event" movies, franchises, or "high-concept" movies, which have easily comprehended storylines and consist of previously tested, reliable ingredients, particularly for the global market.

- "Independent" is a highly qualified term in contemporary Hollywood. It signifies a type of product and a market category, defined as distinct from and to a large extent in opposition to Hollywood's mainstream product. In economic terms, however, "independent production" has effectively become integrated into the activities of the major distributors.

- Until 1995, Hollywood's production could be separated into three categories: ultra-high-budget movies; moderately priced star vehicles financed and distributed by the majors; and independent low-budget or "boutique" productions. Since 1995 the distinction between the last two types has been eroded, and it may be more accurate to distinguish between only two categories: big-budget international movies and smaller-budget movies with less dependence on the international market.

Further Reading

Hollywood since 1980

Stephen Prince, *A New Pot of Gold: Hollywood under the Electronic Rainbow, 1980–1989* (New York: Scribner's, 2000) provides an excellent overview of a decade of great change in Hollywood's industrial organization and activity. Justin Wyatt analyzes the dominant production trend in *High Concept: Movies and Marketing in Hollywood* (Austin: University of Texas Press, 1994), from both an industrial and an aesthetic perspective. Two anthologies of essays on contemporary Hollywood which pay close attention to industrial and economic issues are Steve Neale and Murray Smith, eds, *Contemporary Hollywood Cinema* (London: Routledge, 1998), and Jon Lewis, ed., *The New American Cinema* (Durham, NC: Duke University Press, 1998).

The contemporary industry is analyzed by Martin Dale, *The Movie Game: The Film Business in Britain, Europe and America* (London: Cassell, 1997); Harold L. Vogel, *Entertainment Industry Economics: A Guide for Financial Analysis*, 5th edn (Cambridge: Cambridge University Press, 2001); Michael J. Wolf, *The Entertainment Economy: How Mega-Media Forces Are Transforming Our Lives* (London: Penguin, 1999); and Barry R. Litman, *The Motion Picture Mega-Industry* (Boston: Allyn and Bacon, 1998).

These accounts can be supplemented by a number of more technically oriented books examining industry business practices: Schuyler M. Moore, *The Biz: The Basic Business, Legal and Financial Aspects of the Film Industry* (Los Angeles: Silman-James Press, 2000); Bill Daniels, David Leedy, and Steven D. Sills, *Movie Money: Understanding Hollywood's (Creative) Accounting Practices* (Los Angeles: Silman-James Press, 1998); and John W. Cones, *Film Finance and Distribution: A Dictionary of Terms* (Los Angeles: Silman-James Press, 1992).

Peter Bart, *The Gross: The Hits, the Flops – the Summer that Ate Hollywood* (New York: St Martin's

Press, 1999), provides an informed journalistic account of one year's production. For other informative "insider accounts," see Mark Litwak, *Reel Power: The Struggle for Influence and Success in the New Hollywood* (London: Sidgwick and Jackson, 1987); Jason E. Squire, ed., *The Movie Business Book*, 2nd edn (New York: Simon and Schuster, 1992); and Nicholas Kent, *Naked Hollywood: Money, Power and the Movies* (London: BBC Books, 1991).

The Motion Picture Association of America website provides an annual economic review of the industry, with a great deal of valuable statistical information: www.mpaa.org.

New markets

Robert Allen, "Home Alone Together: Hollywood and the Family Film," in *Identifying Hollywood's Audiences: Cultural Identity and the Movies*, eds Melvyn Stokes and Richard Maltby (London: British Film Institute, 1999), examines the emergence of the family as the principal consumers of Hollywood's video and ancillary markets. Janet Wasko, *Hollywood in the Information Age: Beyond the Silver Screen* (London: Polity, 1994), considers the impact of new technologies on the configuration of the industry. Essays in *Film Policy: International, National and Regional Perspectives*, ed. Albert Moran (London: Routledge, 1996), and Toby Miller, Nitin Govil, John McMurria, and Richard Maxwell, *Global Hollywood* (London: British Film Institute, 2001), consider the increasing effects of the global market on Hollywood's organization and product.

Independent production and distribution

For histories of independent American cinema, see Emanuel Levy, *Cinema of Outsiders: The Rise of*

American Independent Film (New York: New York University Press, 1999); Greg Merritt, *Celluloid Mavericks: A History of American Independent Film* (New York: Thunder's Mouth Press, 2000); John Pierson, *Spike, Mike, Slackers and Dykes: A Guided Tour Across a Decade of Independent American Cinema* (London: Faber, 1996); David Rosen, with Peter Hamilton, *Off-Hollywood: The Making and Marketing of Independent Films* (New York: Grove, Weidenfeld, 1990); and Jim Hillier, ed., *American Independent Cinema: A Sight and Sound Reader* (London: British Film Institute, 2001).

CHAPTER EIGHT
Technology

We must not destroy all truth in the theater by too frequent use of conventions; but neither must we destroy the theatrical illusion by too great fidelity to fact. And by theatrical illusion I mean the pleasure in search of which people go to the theater – that theatrical pleasure, partly composed indeed of the illusion that they are seeing a reality, but mingled with a feeling of personal safety and a sincere conviction that they are assisting only at an illusion. That sense of security must never be destroyed. If by dint of realism or artifice you succeed in making your spectator forget absolutely that he is witnessing a mere spectacle, he ceases to be amused . . . Therefore, try to produce an apparent truth; but let it be true only in seeming.

Constant Coquelin, 1880[1]

No-one ever bought a ticket to watch technology.
Syd Silverman[2]

Many of the scientific discoveries and inventions that gave rise to the cinema as we know it were designed for other purposes. To make photographs that moved required several inventions, but the most complex creation was a material that could be impregnated with chemicals sensitive to light, and was thin and flexible enough to be wound through a camera. That material was celluloid, first used as a substitute for ivory in the manufacture of billiard balls and false teeth, and later to make detachable collars for men's shirts. Rather than being a technological innovator, the movie industry has routinely adapted the inventions of others, deploying technology – like genre – in the service of its system of regulated difference. In intermittently offering a "new and improved" product, Hollywood has used technology to renovate and on occasion to reinvent itself in what Philip Hayward and Tana Wollen have called "a continuing dynamic, a drive towards product upgrading in order to retain and revive audiences."[3] Novelty has been provided sometimes through technical innovations such as sound or widescreen. More consistently but less obtrusively, technology has supplied an element of predictability through standardization.

Technology has influenced what movies look and sound like in their small details as well as in the major changes occasioned by the introduction of color or electronic recording. Each studio's distinctive visual style in the late 1930s, for instance, was as much composed of myriad "background" decisions about film stocks and lighting systems as it was by the studio's contract roster of stars or writers. The rich, pearly-gray tones in which MGM's stars were photographed came from the studio's decisions about how it exposed and processed its film, and the higher contrasts and starker blacks and whites of Warner pictures came from different decisions about the same technical questions.[4] Alongside production factors lay Hollywood's relationship with exhibition technology. From air-conditioning to DVDs or the "total sensory involvement" of recent large-format projection systems, technical developments have periodically revised the viewing experience. Sound, for instance, radically changed the interior architecture of movie theaters. Picture palaces were designed to sound like concert halls or churches, the appropriate acoustical settings for the large orchestras that accompanied silent movies. The talkies needed more intimate spaces with much less echo, and the Moderne theaters of the 1930s were engineered to minimize sound reverberation and maximize the intelligibility of dialog.[5]

Because the determining effect of technological change on Hollywood is a subject of some controversy among cinema historians and critics, we must look not only at the various technologies, large and small, but also at the different ways in which the history of cinema technology has been understood. Most histories of cinema begin with a technical history, an account of the movies' invention in the 1890s. This reminds us that although the cinema became a form of expression and mass communication in the twentieth century, the sources of its technology lie in the scientific exploration and the thought of an earlier period. With their cogs, sprocket teeth, and gearing systems designed to produce the interrupted motion that holds a single frame of film still in front of the lens for a fraction of a second, and then moves on to the next frame, film cameras and projectors are complex mechanical objects not unlike spring-powered clocks or machine guns. They depend on a mechanical technology, and these "machines of the visible" are, as William K. Dickson, principal inventor of the Kinetoscope, put it, "the crown and flower of nineteenth-century magic" rather than pieces of twentieth-century technology.[6] Although cinema uses electricity, it is a mistake to think of it as an electrical medium. Its earliest forms made no use of electrical power; cameras and projectors were hand-driven or "cranked" rather than powered by an electric motor, and illuminated by gas, not electric light. Even by the late 1920s, when the sound cinema of the picture palaces incorporated all the major features of cinema technology, it was essentially synthesizing nineteenth-century inventions: mechanical sound recording (pioneered by Thomas Edison during the 1870s), an efficient film transport mechanism (produced by Edison and others in the 1890s), the electric light (also generally agreed to have been invented by Edison around 1878), and the electric motor (demonstrated by Michael Faraday in 1821 and perfected by Zenobe Theophise in Vienna in 1873).

Although few histories of the cinema pay much attention to the development of sound technology, the cinematic apparatus is a machine of the audible as well as the visible, and more fundamental changes have taken place in the technology of electrical sound recording and transmission than in the optics and chemistry of image processing.[7] Many of cinema's technical pioneers were involved in the development of both sound and image reproduction. Thomas Edison developed the Kinetoscope with the intention of adding images to his phonograph sound recording system. Charles Pathé, who pioneered the phonograph in Europe, industrialized cinema and provided the model for its successful commercial exploitation. Between 1908 and 1911 the Cameraphone system, recording the sound of a vaudeville performance on a phonograph disc synchronized with a film image, enjoyed a brief commercial success. More recent developments out of sound recording have given us television and video-recording, and the shifting relation between image and sound technology continues to play a significant role in digital technology's redefinition of Hollywood's commercial aesthetic.

Realism and the Myth of Total Cinema

Doug Quaid: How real does it seem?
Bob McLean: As real as any memory in your head. I'm telling you, Doug, your brain will not know the difference. And that's guaranteed or your money back.
The salesman for Recall Inc., selling "the memory of your ideal vacation, cheaper, safer and better than the real thing," in *Total Recall* (1990)

The history of Hollywood's technological development is one of opportunism driven by economic motives. Many critical accounts, however, suggest that the invention of cinema, and its subsequent technological development, responded to a pre-existing aesthetic and cultural need to achieve the objective, unmediated reproduction of reality. The most influential expression of this position has been that of the French critic, André Bazin. In a 1946 article, "The Myth of Total Cinema," he suggested that:

the guiding myth . . . inspiring the invention of the cinema, is the accomplishment of that which dominated in a more or less vague fashion all the mechanical reproduction of reality in the nineteenth century, namely an integral realism, a recreation of the world in its own image, an image unburdened by the freedom of interpretation of the artist or the irreversibility of time.[8]

"The crown and flower of nineteenth-century magic," the early motion picture camera (this illustration dates from 1915) was a complex, but hand-driven, mechanical device. Unexposed film was stored on a reel in the box on the upper left, and passed through the shutter gate by a system of sprocket wheels, to be rewound in the lower box. The crank handle, with which the operator wound the film through the camera, can be seen on the lower right. Only when sound movies demanded an exact consistency in the rate at which the films passed through the camera did an electric motor replace "hand cranking."

Source: Bernard E. Jones, *The Cinematograph Book* (London: Cassell, 1915).

Bazin gave technological innovation as such a secondary role in the development of cinema, seeing "basic technical discoveries" as "fortunate accidents" brought about by the "preconceived ideas of the inventors." In his account, ideas preceded inventions, and often had to wait for technology to "catch up" before they could be realized. Inventors were "prophets" not technicians, who as long ago as the 1880s visualized a "total cinema" that could produce a "total and complete representation of reality, . . . the reconstruction of a perfect illusion of the outside world in sound, color, and relief."[9] In emphasizing that vision over material forces, Bazin's explanation was idealist. It was also teleological: he thought the goal of "total cinema" was as predetermined as if it were "a fetus in its inventors' imaginations." "The basis of cinema since its origins . . . is a quest for realism of the image. A realism, one could say, implied by the automatic generation of the image, and which aims to confer upon this image as many common properties of natural perception as possible."[10] Like all history, Bazin's account was written retrospectively, looking for causes in the past to explain the present. He emphasized those events that best supported his evolutionary argument, and constructed them into a continuous narrative that recounted cinema's technological development as a far more coherent process than it could have appeared to any of its innovators or "prophets."

Bazin did not claim that cinema would eventually achieve an undetectable simulation of reality, but rather that the drive behind successive technical developments such as synchronized sound and deep-focus cinematography was to give the viewer "as perfect an illusion of reality as possible within the limits of the logical demands of cinematographic narrative and of the current limits of technique."[11] Other theorists resisted sound and color photography as impediments to cinema's development as an art deriving its power from its unreality, but Bazin argued that the particular aesthetic of the cinema lay in the contradiction between its goal of perfect illusion and the inevitable failure of its achievement. "Perception," he held, "is a synthesis whose elements react against each other," and he illustrated his case by pointing out that stereoscopic filming in 3-D created an effective impression of objects in space – things seemed to be projected out of the screen toward the audience – but that these objects were "in the form of intangible phantoms" the audience could see but not touch. "The internal contradiction of this depth which one cannot touch gives an impression of irreality that is even more perceptible than that of flat cinema in black and white."[12] The aesthetic possibilities of cinema would, he thought, continue to evolve through such contradictions, as technical developments simultaneously added to and disturbed cinema's realism.[13]

What did Bazin mean by **realism**? It is a term with a multiplicity of meanings and a complex history of its own, on which an enormous amount of intellectual energy has been expended. It has a particularly troublesome relation to the study of cinema, and we shall return to its use in different critical contexts at several points in this book. Much of what Bazin proposes about realism in the cinema is a sophisticated version of commonly held assumptions about why the movies should be regarded as somehow inherently more "realist" than other, less **mimetic** media. For that reason, as well as because his propositions form the starting point for almost every discussion of the subject, Bazin represents an obvious place to begin our consideration of this thorny territory.

Bazin's complex interweaving of ideas about perception and ideas about space may also indicate that, whether they are fully articulated or not, our commonplace ideas about realism are more complex than we might at first imagine. In our everyday use of the term "realistic," we invoke realism to evaluate the extent to which a representation or a narrative is like some previously established reality – or, in a commonly used critical phrase, the extent of its "adequacy to the real." When, for instance, we describe a plot coincidence in a movie as unrealistic, we mean that coincidences like that don't happen in real life. Importantly, however, we need to know already what the "reality" or "real life" we are referring to is, before we can assess the "realism" of a representation in this sense.

This is in large part why definitions of realism seem so circular. Literary critic Raymond Williams has suggested that the purpose of realism in art is "to show things as they really are."[14] John Ellis maintains that "'Realism' denotes the expectation that a particular representation should present a 'realistic portrayal' of character and event," and then points out that beneath this tautology lie several other tautologies dealing with different ways in which "realism" can be "realistic": it "should have a surface accuracy; it should conform to notions of what we expect to happen; it should explain itself adequately to us as audience; it should conform to particular notions of psychology and character motivation."[15] But no account of realism progresses very far before it recognizes that realism, like all other approaches to art, relies on a system of conventions of representation. Terry Lovell explains that "Because the work of art is constructed out of different materials from the world it represents, the extent to which that representation is 'like' the thing represented must be strictly limited."[16] A photograph of a table is a photograph, not a table. To look at a photograph and see a table is to look through the system of representation, and choose to ignore its presence. Unless we are only talking about *trompe l'oeil* or special effects, however, we are not fooled about what we see: we do not believe the photograph to be a table. When we choose to ignore the representation we choose, in effect, to accept a representational convention as if it were transparent.[17] But as Lovell argues, it is not necessary to the success of realism in art that viewers should mistake the art object for what it represents. Viewers are "much more aware than conventionalist critics suppose, or than they themselves can articulate, of the rules which govern this type of representation. The critics' or the viewers' naïve complaint that such and such is 'not realistic' frequently masks a complaint that the rules have been broken."[18]

To an even greater extent than the photographic image, recorded sound is ordinarily assumed to be mimetic, mechanically neutral in its reproduction of the external world. Even critics who insist on the conventional nature of photographic representation regard sound as much less mediated: "provided that the recording is well done . . . nothing distinguishes a gunshot heard in a film from a gunshot heard in the street."[19] But as James Lastra observes, "anyone who has ever attempted to post-sync a gunshot for a film can tell you that there are dozens of acceptable substitutes – many of them more acceptable than an actual gunshot." What matters is the viewer's ability to identify the source of the sound, and for this to happen, synchronization of sound and image is far more important than the fidelity of the recording. As Lastra argues, "Decades of tin-sheet thunder and coconut shell hooves . . . prove that fidelity to source is not a *property* of film sound, but an *effect* of synchronization."[20] Walter Murch, the sound designer on *Apocalypse Now* (1979), created part of the sound made by the helicopters in their attack on a Vietnamese village from the recording of a chain twirling against a paper bag, while the sounds of a television set and a film projector were blended to produce the hum of Luke Skywalker's light saber in *Star Wars* (1977). Since the introduction of Dolby noise reduction systems in the late 1970s, soundtracks have become increasingly complex in their mixing of multiple layers of sound, and the great majority of a movie's soundtrack, including the dialog, is re-recorded during the post-production phase, using a process known as Automatic Dialog Replacement. Contemporary Hollywood soundtracks are designed and constructed, rather than simply recorded. As film historian John Belton observes, "sound mixing no longer observes the integrity of any pre-existent reality; it builds its own to match earlier recorded visual information. . . . The building of the sound track, using the image rather than the pro-filmic event as a guide, now becomes a final stage in the 'realisation' of the image."[21]

Sound recording, then, just as much as the photographic image, is better understood as sound *representation* rather than sound *reproduction*. The observable phenomenon that any brief, explosive sound can stand in for a gunshot is a reminder of the distance between representation and external reality, and of the extent of an audience's enthusiastic cooperation in bridging that distance. Amy Lawrence argues that the audience's awareness of the cinematic apparatus and its "ability to deceive" is fundamental to its appeal:

> When a phonograph listener of 1898 gazed at a flat wax disc and murmured to himself, "That's Caruso," he was participating in a sophisticated form of make-believe. This type of "play" openly demonstrates the listener/viewer's facility at a skill essential to subjectivity: the ability to construct "reality" or realism out of the most brazen artifice.[22]

But at the same time that we recognize that what we invoke in the name of "realism" is a system of convention – it is what in chapter 4 I called cultural verisimilitude – we must also acknowledge the power of the term itself. The goal of realism is an illusion. Art cannot "show things as they really are," because the "real" in realism is understood to be exactly that which is unmediated by representation. Since it is outside representation, the "real" cannot be represented: representations can be only more or less inadequate imitations or substitutions for it. Precisely because it remains an absolute, untarnished by the compromises of representation, the "real" retains a tremendous power as a point of reference to be invoked in the rhetoric of criticism. For theorists like André Bazin, the fact that a "total and complete representation of reality" was unattainable did not prevent its inventors and creators pursuing the quest for realism.

Bazin understood cinema to be fundamentally a photographic process, one that objectively recorded and revealed the concrete empirical reality of objects in space. In Bazin's sense, the object of realism was not to fool the eye but "to give significant expression to the world both concretely and in its essence." The significance of cinema in this general aesthetic project was not that it did this more accurately than other means – that would be part of what he called the pseudo-realism of deception – but that it worked by mechanical reproduction. The fact of mechanical reproduction gave photography its credibility, and made it "objective" in a way that painting could never be. In French, "*objectif*" not only means "objective"; it is also the word for "lens." Bazin called cinema "objectivity in time."[23] He identified a fundamental distinction between those filmmakers "who put their faith in the image, and those who put their faith in reality." By "the image," he explained, he meant "everything that the representation on the screen adds to the object there represented." Against this tendency to embellish, he championed the aesthetic in which "the image is evaluated not according to what it adds to reality but what it reveals of it."[24]

What the realist image crucially revealed was the continuity of space and time and what Bazin called "the ambiguity of reality."[25] The idea of the ambiguity of reality is central to Bazin's thought: a movie ought to imitate this, and provide audiences with the opportunity for multiple, even conflicting, acts of interpretation. As Dudley Andrew suggests, this is almost a moral argument: "the spectator *should* be forced to wrestle with the meanings of a filmed event because he *should* wrestle with the meanings of events in empirical reality in his daily life. Reality and realism both insist on the human mind wrestling with facts that are at once concrete and ambiguous."[26]

The major events in Bazin's account of cinema's technological development included the arrival of sound and deep-focus photography, which he saw as coming about not as a solution to a "technical problem," but out of "a search for a style." Bazin celebrated Orson Welles, among others, for taking cinema closer and closer toward this complete illusion of reality, by using deep-focus to create dramatic effects "for which we had formerly relied on montage." What Bazin saw as important about deep-focus photography was that it allowed the viewer a continuous gaze over a continuous space, rather than fragmenting the viewer's perception of that space through editing. His objection to narrative editing was that it presupposed that a piece of reality or an event has only one sense at any given moment, and that by specifying the meaning of the raw material, editing conflicted with our normal, ambiguous relationship to empirical reality. There was, he maintained, "a deeper psychological reality, which must be preserved in realistic cinema: the freedom of the spectator to choose his own interpretation of the object or event."[27] In this way deep-focus had "reintroduced ambiguity into the structure of the image."[28]

For Bazin, ambiguity was inherent in human perception: viewing an event, we recognize that our perception of it is only partial, and that the event remains available for perceptions and interpretations different from our own. "If perceptual space and time are rendered with honesty, a narrative will lie obscured within the ambiguities of recalcitrant sense data. If, on the other hand, narrative space and time are the object of a film, perceptual space and time will have to be systematically fragmented and manipulated."[29] Bazin understood cinematic realism as ultimately a matter of the cinema's fidelity to the psychology of human perception, rather than involving a physical imitation of the way we see objects. To achieve that fidelity, however, required a constant technical improvement in the imitation of our perception of space and time. Some examples may help to explain this. In

1898, a traveling exhibitor commented that in a film of the Spanish–American War he showed "the pictures of the battleships in action were so real that every time a shot was fired the women would duck their heads to let the thirteen-inch shells pass over."[30] Later, more sophisticated audiences would have had no difficulty in recognizing that particular cinematic illusion, but they would in turn experience a similar moment of vertigo when their perception of cinematic space and time became uncertain in other ways.

The plot of *Total Recall* (1990) revolves around a Bazinian sense of perceptual realism, for both its central character and the audience. In 2084 Douglas Quaid (Arnold Schwarzenegger) is a construction worker who buys himself "the memory of a lifetime," a fantasy vacation trip to Mars in which he will play the role of a secret agent. When the memory implantation procedure goes wrong, he discovers that he is really an agent called Hauser who is being hunted by an interplanetary conspiracy, and he escapes to Mars to avoid assassination. In the middle of his adventure a doctor appears, claiming that none of it is actually happening, and that Quaid is still really in the vacation parlor. "What you're experiencing," he explains, "is a free-form delusion based on our memory tapes, but you're inventing it as you go along . . . and we can't snap you out of it." What Quaid (and the audience) have experienced so far is "a paranoid episode triggered by acute neurochemical trauma," he says. Both Quaid and the audience are faced with an existential crisis about the ontological status of what they are perceiving: what cues could we use to tell delusion apart from reality? The only certainty for the audience is that we know we cannot distinguish between the reality of Earth in 2084 and Quaid's paranoid fantasy about Mars. The two *look* completely interchangeable, as perceptually real as each other. Quaid's decision to remain inside the fantasy, and the audience's compliance with that decision, make it impossible for either him or us to tell the difference between real perceptions and imagined ones – just as the salesman promised when he promoted the holiday: "By the time the trip is over, you get the girl, kill the bad guys and save the entire planet."[31]

The technology involved in manufacturing *Total Recall*'s perceptual illusions is vastly more complex than that involved in the 1898 film (and the technology the movie imagines is more complex still), but the blurring of perceptual categories is comparable. Technological innovators have most often invoked the rhetoric of greater realism to sell their product. Early filmmakers described their images as "life-like," and Vitaphone insisted that sound made characters in movies "act and talk like living people." Cinerama proclaimed that it "creates all the illusion of reality . . . you see things the way you do in real life."[32] A producer of 3-D movies declared that he planned to exploit the three-dimensional effect by throwing things at the audience "until they start throwing them back," while in 1953, Twentieth Century-Fox claimed that CinemaScope "simulates [the] third-dimension to the extent that objects and things appear to be part of the audience."[33] More technical explanations of CinemaScope suggested that it activated the viewer's peripheral vision and required lateral eye movement. Together these ocular effects replaced the feeling of watching a framed picture with the sensation of viewing an

Morphing technology in *The Matrix* (1999) puts in question the credibility of the photographic image.

Produced by Joel Silver; distributed by Silver Pictures, Village Roadshow Productions; directed by Andy Wachowski, Larry Wachowski.

actual space: "Scope places the spectator in an environment and creates a feeling of participation."[34] Along with more exotic systems such as Smell-o-Vision, used in the 1960 movie *Scent of Mystery*, or Sensurround, which used low-frequency sound to simulate the sensations of an earthquake tremor in *Earthquake* (1974), all these devices were designed to provide not so much a greater realism as a greater illusion of audience involvement with the spectacle of the screen, requiring an ever-greater elaboration of that illusionist spectacle. John Belton observes that:

> the advent of sound, color, and widescreen was identified not only with realism but with spectacle. The attention of the audience was drawn to the novelty of the apparatus itself. The "greater realism" produced by the new technology was understood, it would seem, as a kind of excess, which was in turn packaged as spectacle.[35]

This habit of packaging spectacle had little appeal for Bazin, whose insistence on the ambiguity of reality meant that he preferred some outcomes of technological change to others. The special effects technology so abundant in *Total Recall*, for example, would count very much as an enhancement of "the image," not in any sense a revelation of reality.[36] But the technology of "morphing" used in *Terminator 2: Judgment Day* (1991), in which the image is altered through computer manipulation so that one object can be transformed into another in a continuous shot, questions Bazin's basic assumption that "the objective nature of photography confers on it a quality of credibility absent from all other picture making."[37] The computerized revision of the image – literally a re-vision – makes the distinction between reality and the image ever more difficult to maintain: the plot of *The Matrix* (1999) elaborates on *Total Recall's* conceit, grafting the spectator's inability to distinguish between filmed event and computer-generated image onto the characters' position within the fiction. Like the audience,

Neo (Keanu Reeves) does not know whether what he is looking at is "real" or not.

Computer-generated images (CGI) have produced the visual equivalent of this narrative effect, apparently seamlessly integrating fantastical objects like the giant statues of the kings of Gondor into the New Zealand landscape, transforming it into the imaginary geography of Middle Earth in *Lord of the Rings: The Fellowship of the Ring* (2001). CGI permits more elaborate and sophisticated special effects than earlier technologies, but in these applications they do not fundamentally revise the older technologies' aesthetic conventions of assimilating spectacular, artificially produced illusion into a photographically "realistic" stream of images. Digital technology's capacity to manipulate the image, however, raises issues about the ontology of the moving image, whether that manipulation takes a blatant form like morphing or more simply involves the digital removal of unwanted objects from a shot. The digital image is ambiguous in a sense not considered by Bazin, because it is no longer necessarily dependent on the camera's capacity to copy a **pro-filmic** source, or authorized by reference to anything external to itself: "the connection of images to solid substance has become tenuous . . . images are no longer guaranteed as visual truth."[38] As media theorist Henry Jenkins argues, digital images ignore photography's indexical relation to reality,

> translating images into pixels which can be transformed, reworked, and redesigned like text in a word-processing program. The line blurs between animation (which involves creating images where none existed previously) and editing (which involves recutting or rearranging fragments of events which occurred before the camera).[39]

As Jenkins observes, in such an environment seeing is no longer believing.

While the power of digital technology to manipulate the image will no doubt increase exponentially in the future, it is nevertheless all too easy to exaggerate the extent to which it troubles the cinema's image-system. Since the early 1980s, computer graphics artists have been attempting to create "imaginary people." According to Robin Baker, the ambition underlying this project involves conquering reality and establishing "the supremacy of the synthetic over the real."[40] Baker's argument echoes the cultural preoccupations of movies such as *Blade Runner* (1982), set in a future society in which only the most sophisticated combination of technological and psychoanalytical investigation can tell an android apart from a person. A casual viewing of the "virtual actors" in *Final Fantasy: The Spirits Within* (2001) suggests, however, that CGI animation is still some distance from this ambition. Alternatively, CGI animation may pursue a different visual aesthetic from that of photographic realism, developing what Michelle Pierson has called a "synthetic hyperrealism" that does not limit itself to the imitation of an earlier technology's aesthetic.[41] The success of CGI-animated movies from *Toy Story* (1995) to *Shrek* (2001) demonstrates the existence of a solid commercial base for such an aesthetic in the family market, although the commercial failure of *Final Fantasy* indicates that for other audiences this aesthetic has not yet transferred from its origins in computer games.

Sound

The introduction of sound from 1927 provides one of the clearest examples of the complex ways in which technological changes contribute to a reformulation of Hollywood cinema. Sound had important aesthetic consequences for Hollywood, and a considerable impact on the cultural experience of filmgoing in the late 1920s and 1930s.

If there were such things as silent movies, there was never such a thing as silent cinema, because cinemas have never been silent. The eighteenth- and nineteenth-century precursors of cinema entertainment such as the Phantasmagoria and the Diorama were multi-media events, in which sounds complemented and enhanced the images. What we call silent cinema was in fact a performance event in which one part of the performance, the image stream, was pre-recorded, while the rest, the sound accompaniment, was live. The most literal enactments of this phenomenon took place in the first decade of the century, when the Humanophone Company's actors stood behind the screen reciting dialog in synchronization with the images. Even more common were narrators, who stood beside the screen providing a commentary on the screen action. Cinema performances also commonly included elements of audience participation, and sing-alongs to illustrated songs were a common feature of moviegoing well into the 1940s, when the illustrated song was replaced with an animated version, in which the audience sang along with the bouncing ball indicating the correct tempo. "Silent" cinema also provided opportunities for other forms of audience participation: commentary or other kinds of interaction with the events on the screen.

The Humanophone was intended to achieve synchronicity; it was a performative substitute for the mechanical synchronization of sound and image that Thomas Edison had originally envisaged in his Kinetophone of 1895. Edison was by no means alone in his attempts to develop such a system, and the first 30 years of cinema history are full of more-or-less successful attempts to solve the mechanical problems involved in sychronization. The technology used to innovate synchronized sound in the late 1920s had been developed some years before it was actually put to use; the timing of its introduction had more to do with the economics of distribution and exhibition than with technical capacity.

From early in cinema's history, exhibitors used the quality of their sound accompaniment as a way of distinguishing their theaters from each other: higher-quality theaters had higher-quality sound provision, in the form of either a larger orchestra or a more elaborate organ. Audiences came to expect that the live sound performance that accompanied the pre-recorded images would be synchronized "with the spirit of the picture," as a 1912 trade paper put it.[42] Musicians used classical orchestral music, opera, and popular tunes to reinforce the storyline's development of character and theme and heighten its emotional affect on the audience. Before 1920, studios had adopted the practice of producing and distributing music scores to accompany their major productions, while increasingly complex mechanical organs or "automatic orchestras" provided theaters with a range of sound effects and musical tones. The Marr and Colton Symphonic Registrator, for example, allowed the organist to produce a range of musical effects such as "Love (Mother)," "Love (Passion)," "Love (Romantic)," "Jealousy," "Suspense," "Happiness," and "Hate" with a single key.[43]

Because the sound accompaniment was live, it was susceptible to variation. The trade press often criticized obtrusive or badly timed musical accompaniment for interfering with the audience's ability to attend to the story. In some venues, however, such as the movie theaters catering to African-American audiences, which employed jazz-based "race orchestras," the relationship between sound and image was one of deliberate counterpoint, as the orchestras played music "against the grain" of the movie, ignoring the narrative and the sheet music library, undermining or satirizing the white cultural forms of the movie, and providing black spectators with "a lively demonstration of ethnic difference and invention, quite separate from the entertainment on the screen."[44]

At the other end of the exhibition spectrum, the most ornate picture palaces also presented a performance that combined live sound with pre-recorded images. In a presentation cinema in the 1920s a show would be one-third live, two-thirds motion picture, and last 150 minutes, with the movie cut to fit the program if necessary. Stage shows were designed to appeal to a middle-class audience still attached to traditions of vaudeville. A typical program would contain:

Overture by orchestra (25–100 players)	5 minutes
Stage show	15–30 minutes
Newsreel	5–10 minutes
Shorts	10–20 minutes
Feature	60–80 minutes

As this program reveals, the spectacular and ornate picture palaces of the 1920s were very labor-intensive enterprises: movie theaters were the largest employers of live musicians in the country. The underlying explanation for the introduction of mechanically synchronized sound can be found in the cost of performers' labor. Even in a second-run cinema like the California Theater, nearly a quarter of the total running costs went on orchestra and stage salaries (see box 5.3). Warner Bros.' intention in innovating sound was to offer cinema owners a substitute for the live performers in the orchestra and stage show. Their initial project was to provide synchronized musical soundtracks and Vitaphone shorts as a substitute for the stage prologs. The wholesale move to "all-talking" dialog pictures was, if not exactly an accident, certainly not the first objective in the addition of mechanically synchronized sound. *The Jazz Singer* (1927) was really a "silent" movie with a mechanically synchronized soundtrack which also contained four songs by its star, Al Jolson, the most popular jazz vocalist of the period.

Although *The Jazz Singer* was not, in fact, the unprecedented box-office success that it is usually described as being, it did establish the viability of lip-synchronization, and triggered the wiring of American movie theaters for sound. Jolson's more successful second movie, *The Singing Fool* (1928), established the musical as the first dominant sound genre, not only because singing demonstrated synchronization in the most vivid way, but also because the musical embodied the

At last, "PICTURES that TALK like LIVING PEOPLE!"

Vitaphone Talking Pictures are electrifying audiences the country over!

For *Vitaphone* brings to you the greatest of the world's great entertainers ...

Screen stars! Stage stars! Opera stars! Famous orchestras! Master musicians!

Vitaphone recreates them *ALL* before your eyes. You see and hear them act, talk, sing and play—like human beings in the flesh!

Do not confuse *Vitaphone* with mere "sound effects."

Vitaphone is the *ONE* proved successful talking picture—exclusive product of Warner Bros.

Remember this—if it's not Warner Bros. *Vitaphone*, it's *NOT* the real, life-like talking picture.

Vitaphone climaxes all previous entertainment achievements. See and hear this marvel of the age—*Vitaphone*.

Early advertisements for Vitaphone pictures emphasized how "real" and "lifelike" this new technology was. The sound-on-disc system played the soundtrack back on a separate gramophone that was kept synchronized to the projector. The system was always liable to mechanical failure, and was rapidly abandoned in favor of the sound-on-film system, in which the soundtrack was imprinted on the film as a series of light pulses.
Courtesy BFI.

commercial connection between the motion picture, radio, and phonograph industries in audio-visual performances by singers who had previously only been heard by the majority of their audience. The other major companies adopted the Western Electric sound-on-film system in 1928, while the Radio Corporation of America created Radio-Keith-Orpheum (RKO) to exploit its rival Photophone system. For a brief period before the Wall Street stock market crash of October 1929, it seemed likely that some of the major companies would merge with each other and with broadcasting companies to create a small number of media conglomerates.

Sound replaced live shows with vaudeville shorts, and presentation cinema had become all-movie by 1930, putting thousands of musicians out of work. The soundtrack marked the end of the cinema as a multi-media show with live performance, giving way to the cinema as a single-medium event. Audiences no longer visited a multi-media show that was primarily staged on their side of the screen. Instead, they went to the cinema to see what happened on the screen. Movies no longer came to the theater as semi-manufactured goods, but as final products. The new technology also put an end to local variations in presentation. Because the soundtrack was physically printed on the film, sound movies were much less malleable than silent movies had been, and the exhibitor's ability to alter the movie was reduced to a minimum.

The picture palaces of the 1920s had been designed for large-scale orchestral music, with similar reverberating acoustics to those that would be found in large concert halls. They were, therefore, very badly designed for making speech comprehensible, making everything sound as if it was taking place in huge spaces. While the picture palaces were really killed off by the economic effects of the Depression, their unsuitability for dialog reproduction was a contributing factor. By 1932, almost all the once vast army of picture palace ushers had been dismissed, and the few who remained were employed in crowd control, rather than crowd assistance.

Sunny Side Up

The introduction of sound had an immediate effect on film aesthetics. The microphones available in the first five years of sound were omnidirectional and sensitive to ambient noise. As a result it was necessary to work indoors on sets, since location shooting was almost impossible because of variations in the levels of ambient sound recorded. Sound mixing was not possible until 1933, so direct sound and music were not mixed prior to then, unless the playback system was used: playing a pre-recorded music track on set.

Sunny Side Up, the first musical starring the immensely popular romantic couple Janet Gaynor and Charles Farrell, set new box-office records for the Fox company on its release in October 1929, earning $3.5 million in domestic rentals.[45] The movie, which was also shot in the Grandeur large-screen process and boasted sequences in color, demonstrates that the sound "revolution" proposed no simple break with the cinema of the past.[46] Rather, the industry looked in the first instance for sound equivalents of the devices of silent cinema in order to preserve the basic strategies of the existing film style. Like other early musicals, *Sunny Side Up* shows Hollywood's hesitancy over how best to take advantage of the new technology, as well as a sense of relish about the possibilities created by the "sound-on-film" system that literally fused sound and picture on the same film strip, guaranteeing the synchronization of recorded speech with projected image. With the expressive techniques of late silent cinema intersecting with those of the early "talkie" throughout the movie, *Sunny Side Up* suggests that sound renewed as well as revised the dominant aesthetics of Hollywood movies.

It is often suggested that the "talkies" provoked aesthetic conservatism in other aspects of cinematic form. The cumbersome recording equipment and the microphones' sensitivity to camera noise are alleged to have imprisoned the camera in fixed soundproof booths, bringing the increasingly mobile camera of the late 1920s to a standstill. Such accounts scarcely prepare us for this movie's opening, which uses camera movement not only to set the scene for the introduction of its central characters, but also as a way of displaying the elaborate setting and staging of action as a spectacle in its own right. The soundtrack augments a camera movement as fluent as those achieved by the most mature of the late silents, showing just how quickly Hollywood had found ways of recovering the visual flexibility that the technical requirements of sound had threatened to inhibit.[47]

A superimposed title sets the time and place ("New York, July the Fourth, with the Four Million"), and fades to reveal the opening image. We see a close-up of a water hydrant around which children are laughing and playing, then the camera **cranes** up and **tracks** forward to frame a game of street baseball. It then executes a series of cranes and **pans** to examine the occupants of a street-side tenement building through their open windows. In one room a child cries as his hair is cut beneath a pudding bowl, while another child practices the violin; in another room a young man takes refuge from his furious wife beneath a bed. After showing the audience these vignettes of tenement life, the camera cranes down and right to follow a courting couple as they pass down the street, abandoning them to frame a social worker attempting to sell copies of the *Birth Control Review* to a woman surrounded by children, and then tracking forward to introduce the first of the movie's central characters. This single shot lasts 2 minutes and 25 seconds.

The movie as a whole does not sustain the bravura display of its opening sequence, but it routinely tracks and pans to reframe action and cover character movement. As in silent cinema, camera movement is also used to aid narrative exposition. Near the beginning we move from one party scene to another by tracking-in on a bottle of home-made beer to end one scene, fading to an **intertitle** ("Southampton, Long Island, with the 400"), and then to a track-out from a bottle of champagne to begin the next scene. The movie efficiently contrasts the two lifestyles through the formal symmetry of its camera movements. Far more noticeable than any loss of camera mobility is the reduced range of optical effects (**dissolves**, **wipes**, and **fades**) and the much slower cutting rate of the movie in comparison to both late silent and subsequent sound movies. Nevertheless, retaining the fluidity of point of view and the sense of variable duration achieved

An early sound stage, with the camera temporarily enclosed in a soundproof booth. By 1933, recording equipment had improved sufficiently to allow the mixing of a separate music track with the dialog without a loss of sound quality. This development allowed the return of extradiegetic background music, which had, of course, always accompanied silent movies, setting the mood of each scene in a similar way to the use of color tints in the image.

Courtesy BFI.

by silent cinema remained a key goal for transitional movies such as *Sunny Side Up*.

Aiming to package the excess of its sound effects as production values, the movie seeks quite self-consciously to demonstrate the new pleasures available to its spectator-auditors. In one sequence Jack (Charles Farrell), the romantic male lead, gazes at a framed photograph of Molly (Janet Gaynor), the object of his affections, and begins to sing "If I Had a Talking Picture of You." As he does so, Molly's picture comes to life and sings back to him. Sound has made the picture "speak," adding a new dimension to a familiar experience. For the picture to talk, it must also move, and *Sunny Side Up* presents the new relationship between sound and image as one of complementarity, unity, and synchronization. Throughout the opening sequence, a continuous "mix" of significant sound recorded by several strategically placed microphones accompanies the mobile camera, with each "framing" of activity in the street or the tenement accompanied by an equivalent concentration on the soundtrack: we hear the children's songs and the boy playing the violin as the camera reaches them. Even before we reach the central characters, the possibilities of synchronized speech and other special effects are being relished. The soundtrack registers the cultural diversity of the street, playing accent off against accent (Irish, Swedish, and Italian voices are clearly discernible) and blending ambient sound (barrel organ music, the foghorns of ships in the nearby Hudson river, traffic noise) with the play of voices.

Once the physical problems of synchronization had been solved, perhaps the greatest technical difficulty facing early sound cinema lay in working out how to match visual and auditory perspective, so that sound was synchronized with its apparent source not only temporally but also spatially. If it was to conform to Hollywood's "invisible" style, dialog had to sound as if it was being produced from an appropriate point within the image. Volume and the degree of reverberation could be mixed to suggest the apparent distance of the speaker from the auditory equivalent of the camera's viewpoint. Close-ups needed louder sound with less reverberation, longer shots needed fainter sound and greater reverberation to suggest the remoteness of the sound source from the point of the camera's observation. Standards emerged quite slowly, however.

Sound engineers debated whether the perspective fidelity of a recording made with a single microphone placed near the camera's line of sight was preferable to the greater intelligibility that might result from using multiple microphones. One technician argued against mixing because "the resultant blend of sound may not be said to represent any given point of audition, but is the sound which would be heard by a man with five or six very long ears, said ears extending in various directions."[48] On the whole, however, the matching of sound perspective to the image in each shot was subordinated to a combination of maximizing the intelligibility of the dialog and keeping the volume level of the soundtrack constant.[49] If variations in aural timbre became too marked, they would draw attention to the shift in camera position between cuts. To accommodate the need for a consistency in sound levels, the image lost some of its priority. If the transitions between aural perspectives fell within tolerable limits, sound perspective could follow the image. If they threatened to draw attention to themselves, the spatial synchronization of sound and image was sacrificed in the interests of clarity. At the first Southampton party in *Sunny Side Up*, we hear the central characters' conversation much more clearly than that of other guests who are standing closer to the camera. On other occasions, sound claims priority, resulting in simpler stagings and a more restricted range of camera set-ups. Dialog scenes are mainly presented in **establishing shots** showing speakers speaking before the camera, demonstrating the visible synchronization of lip movement and vocal sound and turning the speech act into the movie's principal spectacle of technology. Even the most minimal of separations between sound and image are avoided: the movie shows a marked reluctance to cut from the master group shot to close-ups, and there are very few **cut-aways** to non-speaking figures in dialog scenes. This very formal staging slows the narrative's tempo drastically.

Until 1930, studios using sound-on-disc recording systems experimented with a technique of multiple-camera shooting similar to that subsequently used in television studios. Each scene was played straight through, giving a continuous sound-

The crew filming a scene in *Mr Smith Goes to Washington* (1939) with a camera crane. In the center of the picture, the boom microphone records the principal characters' dialog. Courtesy BFI.

track. Shots from the various cameras, arranged round the edge of the set, could then be intercut without losing sound continuity. Since sound discs could not be edited, the soundtrack determined the length of a scene, and the image track was edited to fit it. The inflexibility of this method, combined with its restrictions on camera placement and movement, encouraged the industry to find a more workable compromise between its preferred style and the requirements of the new technology. Far from being incompatible with sound technology, the mobile camera, used in combination with multiple microphones as in the opening shot of *Sunny Side Up*, was in fact one solution to the problem of matching sound and visual perspectives. *Sunny Side Up* also uses background sound to establish offscreen space and create a sense of the surrounding environment. In one scene, we hear distant band music slowly growing louder while the couple converse in a tenement room. We infer that an Independence Day parade is approaching, and in due course the scene cuts outside to show it. Two simultaneous events in discontinuous space have been represented without using any of silent cinema's conventional devices such as **cross-cutting**. On the whole, however, other sources of sound are deliberately restricted, partly because of the limitations of the technology available for mixing soundtracks during editing, but also because of early uncertainty about the audience's ability to interpret sound conventions confidently.

In order to avoid ambiguity about sound sources by anchoring sound to the image, almost everything audible in *Sunny Side Up*, including the music in numbers, is **diegetic**: it appears to originate from within the fictional world described on the screen. There is very little **non-diegetic** sound, that is, sound not explained in terms of any perceived source, such as mood music, although some of the songs do have minimal orchestral support from an offscreen source. The preference for identifiable sounds helps explain the movie's curious storyline, in which characters burst into song accompanied by conveniently located orchestras or else happen to find themselves pulled into stage shows that provide an opportunity for song-and-dance routines. No opportunity is lost to motivate an impromptu song: Molly is established early on as a character given to expressing her innermost feelings lyrically, with the songs used to chart the ups and downs of her romance with Jack.

Sound also enhances the movie's comic dimensions. Although there are plenty of sight-gags, the movie takes pleasure in the new possibilities of verbal comedy, with the script providing endless opportunities for the rapid-fire dialog and virtuoso vocal display associated with the "zany" comedy of the Marx Brothers and other ex-vaudeville teams. Eddie (Frank Richardson) and Bee (Marjorie White) provide a constant flow of comic repartee that balances the more melancholic sequences. Their low-life dialog is contrasted with the upper-class diction of the Southampton colony inhabited by Jack, his family, and friends. As the figure who mediates between her surrounding company of poor-but-honest eccentrics and the less spontaneous world of Southampton, Molly is capable of improvising performances across a range of linguistic registers, allowing Janet Gaynor's skills of impersonation and mimicry free rein. The effect that sound had on performance styles is evident in the way that she uses her voice rather than her body to express herself.

Some historians have argued that sound's influence also changed the cultural role of American movies. Robert Ray and others have suggested that "talking pictures" made Hollywood more culturally specific than it had been when silent cinema met no language barrier in addressing its global audience: "Overnight, merely by the addition of voices, Hollywood movies became more American. The movies crackled with the localized inflections that drew an aural map of the United States: Cagney's New Yorkese complementing Cooper's Western laconicism, Hepburn's high-toned Connecticut broad ah's matching Jean Arthur's Texas drawl."[50] Ray also suggests that sound threw Hollywood back upon more specifically American mythologies as a basis for its story-telling. These movies preached an American "exceptionalism" that guaranteed success and fulfillment in a land of opportunity as a reward for integrity, hard work, and optimism. Thanks to the resources of the American environment and the abundance available to all in an egalitarian society based on infinitely expanding resources, there was no reason why every American's narrative should not have a happy ending – or so the mythology suggested.

This argument oversimplifies the industry's relations with its foreign market, and with the domestic political forces that regulated the content of motion pictures. Silent movies were a universally available form not, as the industry sometimes claimed, because they were in any sense an "international language" capable of communicating ideas and values across national and linguistic boundaries, but because they were so easily altered to the circumstances of their exhibition by censors, distributors, or even individual exhibitors. Through the use of intertitles Hollywood characters could speak any language or dialect; in Lithuania they spoke three languages at once, since historical and political circumstances required the intertitles to be rendered in German and Russian as well as the local language.[51] The malleability of silent movies contributed significantly to the development of a world market for cinema, dominated by Hollywood.

Sound greatly restricted this malleability, fixing dialog and eliminating much of the ambiguity of silent movies. The duration of a sound movie was much less flexible: no longer could exhibitors project movies at faster speeds than they had been photographed at in order to shorten their running time, as had been common in the late silent period. Nor could local censor boards cut parts of scenes without the movie losing synchronization. The industry agreed to adopt the Production Code in 1930 in large part because it recognized that the inflexibility of sound meant that the industry could be held much more accountable for the detailed meanings of its movies than had been the case with silent film. The purpose of the Production Code was, as MGM's head of production Irving Thalberg put it, to find ways in which talking pictures could "speak delicately and exactly" about the subject matter in the Broadway plays and modern novels the studios wanted to adapt, without offending "the folks who represent the intelligentsia in the country towns and small cities," who might not go to the movies but whose involvement in civic life gave them power over what it was acceptable to exhibit.[52] *Sunny Side Up*'s final spectacular routine, "Turn on the Heat," for instance, was censored as too risqué in some places.

When Hollywood's American identity became audible, European elites expressed alarm every time they encountered a shopworker affecting an American accent. In a British Parliamentary debate in 1937, a Conservative MP suggested that the movies were achieving "the annexation of this country by the United States of America. . . . Personally I have very little opportunity of visiting the pictures, and, if I do get an opportunity, I do not use it, because I dread having to spend an hour or two suffering from a mixture of glucose, chewing gum, leaden bullets and nasal noises."[53] But for those who did visit the pictures, the Utopianism of Hollywood was intensified by the distance between foreign audiences and the particulars of American social organization that movies depicted. James Cagney's accent lost its specific class coding and became generalized as American, not to be distinguished from, say, William Powell's.[54] George Orwell shrewdly suggested that American English "gained a footing in England . . . most of all, because one can adopt an American word without crossing a class barrier."[55] The movies offered European working-class audiences an escape into an imagined Utopian society in which the inflexibility of class distinction either did not exist or was not recognizable. By contrast, in every European production the coming of sound brought accents into play as unavoidable signifiers of social class. After 1929, Hollywood seemed to address its audience more clearly as a single, unified entity and to produce that same unity in its fictions. In America, sound made Hollywood more overtly an "official" cultural form, enhancing its potential for unification by more completely standardizing the movie experience for its many different domestic audiences. In the rest of the world, however, the American culture that Hollywood offered was an alternative to national culture, and could be adopted as a gesture of local resistance to "official" culture.

Color

Just as "silent" movies always had sound accompaniment of some kind, from very early on pictures had been in color. In the 1920s, as many as 80–90 percent of silent movies had been printed on tinted film, associating color with mood rather than with naturalism.[56] The introduction of sound largely put an end to this process, initially because the dyes used in tinting the film reduced the quality of sound reproduction. Although this technical problem could have been overcome, the aesthetic regime of sound movies discouraged the symbolic use of color tints. This change can be seen as a move toward a greater realism, but it can also be seen as an uncertainty in how to use color in relation to sound. Color, like widescreen, might have been developed in the early 1930s, but the uncertain fortunes of the major companies during the Depression deterred them from adopting it except for very occasional spectacular effect. For the best part of two decades until well into the 1950s, color was promoted as a spectacular production value in its own right, and fewer than one movie in ten was made in color until the late 1940s.

The production of color film was initially the preserve of one company, Technicolor, which had a virtual monopoly over the color system used by the major studios until 1948, largely because of its agreements with Eastman Kodak. Technicolor's three-strip system recorded separate red, blue, and green images on different negatives, and required the use of a special camera, which the studios could only lease, not buy. Technicolor also controlled the supply and processing of film stock and the number of color films in production, rationing them out among the major companies and even demanding approval of subject matter. The studios had to hire Technicolor cameramen and color consultants to work with the studios' art directors and set designers. The bulky beam-splitter Technicolor camera restricted movement, and the Technicolor stock's need for comparatively even lighting schemes deterred other kinds of visual experimentation. Through these means, Technicolor exercised a good deal of control over the aesthetic uses to which color was put, and over Hollywood's creation of the illusion of reality through color.

Technicolor's color consultants keyed color reproduction to skin tones and forcibly discouraged the use of filters or unconventional effects. Above all, a movie's color was coordinated around the visual presentation of its female star, who "must be given undisputed priority as to the color of make-up, hair and costume which will best complement her complexion and her figure. If her complexion limits the colors she can wear successfully, this in turn restricts the background colors which will complement her complexion and her costumes to best advantage."[57] Technicolor exposed the "unnaturalness" of styles of makeup devised for black-and-white photography. It required a different technique: as Max Factor, who devised a new range of makeup for Technicolor, explained, "We are no longer striving for a purely artificial contrast but seeking to imitate and enhance the subject's natural coloring."[58] The making-over of Janet Gaynor in *A Star is Born* (1937) illustrates the considerable technology of cosmetic artifice directed toward the rendering of Hollywood's female stars as sites of "natural beauty." As Steve Neale puts it, female movie stars, already positioned as "socially sanctioned objects of erotic looking," functioned "both as a source of the spectacle of color in practice and as a reference point for the use and promotion of color in theory."[59] Hollywood's female stars were both natural and glamorous, and the technology that produced them was meant, like Hollywood's other technologies, to be both present and invisible. It fulfilled this contradiction by claiming to add art to reality: Technicolor advertised itself as "natural color" that had nevertheless "painted" a new world for movie fans.[60]

Technicolor's chief consultant, Natalie Kalmus, explained in 1938 that color photography had brought an "enhanced realism" into being, which "enables us to portray life and nature as it really is": "A motion picture, however, will be merely an accurate record of certain events unless we guide this realism into the realms of art. To accomplish this it becomes necessary to augment the mechanical processes with the inspirational work of the artist."[61] This "inspirational work" meant planning the use of color to fit the mood of each scene and augment its dramatic value – a more elaborate version of the symbolic use of color in tinting silent movies. Lansing C. Holden, color designer on *A Star is Born*, explained that "Color should be used like music, to heighten the emotional impact of a scene."[62] The realism invoked here was contradictory. The spectacle of "natural" color had the potential to distract from a movie's narrative and its other spectacles, but Technicolor's aesthetic regime deployed color design in a subordinate role in which it enhanced both story-telling and the pleasures of looking at the female star. When Technicolor introduced a more sensitive film stock in 1939, cinematographer Ernest Haller declared that it would allow a cameraman to use the same "little tricks of precision lighting he has used in monochrome to glamorize his stars"; the result would be "that color is going to be more flattering than ever to the women!"[63]

While color remained the exception rather than the rule, and therefore a spectacle in itself, it inevitably clashed to some extent with other conventions of Hollywood's particular understanding of realism, or what I have called cultural verisimilitude. One solution to the problem of motivating color was to reserve its use for fantasy movies: *The Wizard of Oz* (1939), in which dreary black-and-white Kansas gives way to the phantasmagoric colors of Oz, is a very clear-

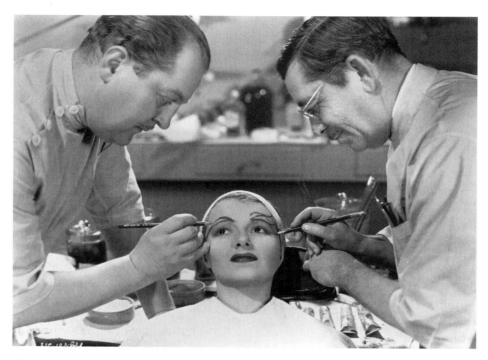

After being given "that Crawford smear" and "that Dietrich naaych," Janet Gaynor still looks surprised during her color makeup test in *A Star is Born* (1937).

Produced by David O. Selznick; distributed by Selznick International Pictures, United Artists. Courtesy of the Academy of Motion Picture Arts and Sciences.

cut example of this.[64] In the 1940s, a color movie was most likely to be a musical; Hollywood represented itself in color, while the rest of the world was in black-and-white.

Color only lost these connotations when it became the norm, which was not until the mid-1960s. The number of color movies produced rose slowly but steadily during the 1940s, and much faster in the 1950s when Eastman Kodak introduced Eastmancolor, a single-film (or "monopak") color process that did not need a special camera.[65] Like widescreen technologies, color differentiated movies from television, but at the end of the 1950s just half of Hollywood's output was in color. It was only when television converted to color in the 1960s that Hollywood abandoned black-and-white. As late as 1960, a routine Hollywood product such as *Ocean's 11* displayed a high degree of color coordination, precisely matching tones of salmon pinks, sea greens, and pearl grays between furnishings and characters' costumes. Since then, although the aesthetic regime of coordinated color used for symbolic purposes that Natalie Kalmus described remains in place, color has also been naturalized by audience expectation. Evident restrictions or distortions of a movie's color range, such as occurs in *Three Kings* (1999) and *Traffic* (2000), remain relatively rare.

Widescreen

The introduction of widescreen systems provides an example of the interrelationship between technological and economic forces in determining the appearance and the realism of Hollywood movies. The screen changed shape in the early 1950s not because producers were pursuing a more impressive simulation of reality for its own sake, but because of the catastrophic decline of movie audiences. For large parts of the audience, newly moved to the suburbs with their young families, moviegoing stopped being a regular weekly or twice-weekly experience. With profits falling even more drastically, the production industry had to repackage its product very rapidly, and sell it on a different basis. A movie had to become much more of a special event to draw its audience.

From 1952 onward, the industry experimented with a number of enhancements to a movie's sound and image to lure the audience back, by giving them, literally, a bigger picture. The first widescreen process, Cinerama, involved a very extensive (and expensive) conversion for existing cinemas, building new booths for each of the three projectors it used, installing a much bigger screen, and reducing the number of seats. A handful of picture palaces in major cities converted, and played the few movies made in Cinerama in extended runs of as long as two years. The most successful Cinerama movies were travelogs, reminiscent of early cinema's initial production of "scenics" and "topicals" rather than dramatic stories. Reviewers compared the behavior of audiences leaning sideways in their seats or ducking to avoid passing spray to the responses of the earliest cinema viewers, but they also remarked that "the very size and sweep of the Cinerama screen would seem to render it impractical for story-telling techniques now employed in film."[66] Although Cinerama was profitable in the few locations in which it was installed, installation cost far too much for it to become an industry standard. By contrast, 3-D systems were much cheaper for exhibitors to install, but were technically far from perfect. Moreover, audiences disliked the glasses they had to wear to see the 3-D effect, and rapidly tired of the gimmick of having things thrown at them in a series of low-budget adventure and horror movies. Twentieth Century-Fox (TCF) devised CinemaScope as a system that would also augment a movie's sound and image, but in a way that would enhance the kinds of fictional movie Hollywood made, attract the lost audience back on a regular basis, and prove economically acceptable to the great majority of exhibitors.

Widescreen was the most drastic shift in what the screen *looked* like in the history of cinema. It required alterations in the internal architecture of movie theaters almost as large as those required by sound. Widescreen processes literally changed the shape of the image, almost doubling its width from the previous standard **aspect ratio** (image height:image width) of 1:1.33 to 1:2.6 in Cinerama or 1:2.35 in CinemaScope. The basic optical technology behind the widescreen processes of the early 1950s was not, however, new. The CinemaScope anamorphic lens system, which compressed an image horizontally in photographing it, and "stretched" it out again in projection, had been invented in the 1920s, but unlike the technology of sound reproduction, no large corporate interests under-

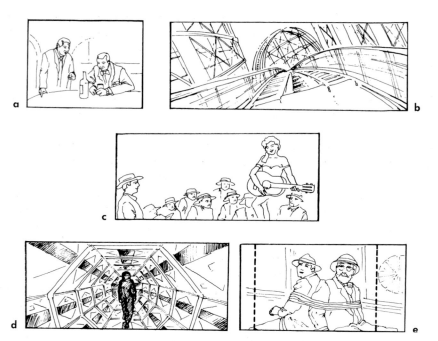

The standard aspect ratio of 1:1.33 of Classical Hollywood (a) was known as the Academy ratio (aspect ratios are expressed as image height:image width). This was the ratio of silent film, but when sound was introduced, the optical soundtrack running down one side of the frame produced a squarer picture. This posed problems in projection, and in 1932 the Academy of Motion Picture Arts and Sciences established a standard image size which gave a 1:1.33 ratio but also left room for the optical soundtrack. This shape was revised in the 1950s. Cinerama (1:2.6) was the most extreme widescreen system (b), its curved screen filling the viewer's vision. During the 1950s, directors were encouraged to compose for the whole width of the CinemaScope frame (initially 1:2.55, but later reduced to 1:2.35 (c)), so that viewers would scan the frame horizontally as they watched. But as sales to television became more important to movie finances, less extreme widescreen systems replaced CinemaScope. Panavision, the most common widescreen process since the 1960s, has an aspect ratio of 1:2.25 (d). In 1960, the Society of Motion Picture Engineers (SMPE) adopted a revised standard aspect ratio of 1:1.85 (e). Because of the importance of sales to television, movie images are now normally composed to accommodate television screenings, with the significant visual information being contained within the "safe action area" of television's aspect ratio (e), which is close to the original Academy ratio.

wrote its development. CinemaScope was not, however, a piece of 1920s technology that had sat on the shelf for 25 years, waiting for a suitable set of economic circumstances. It relied on postwar technological developments in film stock, sound recording, computer lens design, and the materials used in making cinema screens, assembled together by TCF's research and development department.[67] To persuade exhibitors to accept CinemaScope, TCF had to guarantee a supply of pictures in the format, and that involved persuading other major companies to adopt it. They also had to cut down the package they had initially developed. Like Cinerama, CinemaScope was designed for stereophonic sound, but the costs of installing stereo and fitting the new metallic screens deterred small independent exhibitors, and these requirements were eventually dropped to ensure the widespread adoption of the system.

CinemaScope was sold to exhibitors and audiences alike on its scale, its technological novelty, and its added realism. Studios were concentrating production resources on fewer, more expensive movies because of the decline in audiences, and CinemaScope allowed them to represent this in terms of the grandeur of the projects they were producing. A trade paper advert in December 1953 declared that "CinemaScope demands a bigger story, more action." As a result, Darryl Zanuck had adapted not one but "two great Broadway stage plays" to produce *How to Marry a Millionaire* (1953). "Exhibitors know that the public wants to see only great pictures, and since CinemaScope requires bigger and better pictures, this system represents to the theater man the answer to the box office drop."[68] The system's association with scale, and most importantly the immediate success of its first releases, established CinemaScope as a drawing power in its own right. In 1954, TCF announced a switch in their production strategy, from stars to "subject matter," movies that would emphasize the advantages of CinemaScope.

André Bazin recognized that widescreen had been innovated because of the economic crisis in the industry, but he nevertheless saw it as further evidence that "this industrial art, prey to economic accident, has only known, fundamentally, technical advances which moved in the same direction as its aesthetic advances,"[69] not least because widescreen images had a greater depth of focus than the Academy ratio. Bazin's attitude to deep-focus, his theory of technological progress, and his preference for an observational cinema all encouraged him to view the arrival of widescreen cinema in the early 1950s as an important advance in the cinema's potential for realism, even though his enthusiasm was somewhat tempered by his viewing of the first CinemaScope movie, a Biblical epic called *The Robe* (1953).

The way in which CinemaScope was marketed as an intensified experience was sharply at odds with Bazin's preference for technological developments that encouraged an observational cinema. If no one was exactly going to the movies to see technology, they were at least going because of the scale that technology implied. The experience that CinemaScope offered was often expressed in terms of a greater feeling of audience participation: "You're the same as in the front row of a legitimate theater."[70] The industry's promotional connection between the movies and "the legitimate theater" relocated some of the cultural assumptions attached to the moviegoing experience, as well as strengthening the major exhibition chains by differentiating their product from the conventional format movies shown in neighborhood subsequent-run theaters. CinemaScope's success, however, meant that this commercial advantage was relatively short-lived: by 1956, only three years after its launch, 80 percent of American theaters were equipped to show widescreen movies.[71] The added realism that CinemaScope provided lay not so much in its simulation of reality as in the enhancement of fiction in terms of Hollywood's already established narrative and spectacular logic. Cinerama presented the reality of a rollercoaster ride or a flight through the Grand Canyon, but CinemaScope "reaffirmed a vision of the cinema as dramatic fiction, a form of illusion that was apparent as such to the spectator. . . . CinemaScope could provide a more realistic presentation of a fiction, and in so doing increase the power of the fiction."[72]

Although the histories of sound, Technicolor, and CinemaScope are usually presented as accounts of innovation, they also indicate the tendency of cinema technology to move toward standardization. In order to gain audience acceptance, a new technology has to offer its novel appeal within the existing, predictable framework of Hollywood's formal conventions. Equally, technical innovations have needed to be compatible with existing equipment. Seen from this perspective, the history of film technology follows a pattern less of accumulated progress toward a predetermined goal than of assimilation into an existing aesthetic and institutional system. If a given technology could not be integrated into the cinema's industrial and aesthetic system as a whole, it would either be abandoned or further modified to contain its difference. Technicolor, for example, went into rapid decline in the face of widescreen, which was incompatible with the three-strip Technicolor cameras. Meanwhile, Kodak developed the "monopak" Eastmancolor system, which was compatible with CinemaScope and rapidly became the industry standard color film. The extent to which these two technological innovations of the early 1950s sustained each other helps to explain the eagerness with which they were adopted by the industry.

Technological assimilation also explains how innovations are adapted and overhauled as circumstances change. As the history of widescreen formats since 1950 demonstrates, few innovations have been truly permanent. By the late 1960s CinemaScope had all but disappeared in favor of the less extreme widescreen system, Panavision, which had an aspect ratio of 1 : 2.25, while in 1960 the Society of Motion Picture Engineers adopted a new standard aspect ratio of 1 : 1.85. As subsequent sales to television became an increasingly recognized and important element of film budgeting, movies shot in widescreen formats were also composed with the television screen in mind. Camera manufacturers produced viewfinders that marked the television frame inside the widescreen frame, allowing cinematographers to ensure that the essential object in each shot fell inside what was called the **safe action area** of the composition.[73] In 1992, distribution companies reversed the trend, and began reissuing some videos in widescreen format; naturally, they charged their purchasers more for this more complete version that actually only occupied half the picture on their television screens.[74]

Behind the standardization of audience expectation lies an economic motive common to all systems of mass production or distribution: the benefits in efficiency of economies of scale. This is most obviously seen in the standardization of such basic mechanical elements as the width or **gauge** of film itself (normally 35 mm), the speed at which the film travels through the camera and projector (24 frames per second for sound film), and the way in which sound is recorded onto film stock.[75] Such mechanical, chemical, and optical standardization ensures the consistency of the audience's movie experience at a fundamental level likely to be disrupted only by avant-garde filmmakers. Once we recognize the similarities between these technological forms of standardization and those produced by genre or the star system, we can consider other ways in which technology works to standardize our experience of "going to the movies," such as the optics of camera lenses discussed in chapter 10.

Technology and Power

Although André Bazin recognized the place of economics in cinema's technological development, he gave the main roles in his history to individuals: either to the inventors of cinema or to the individual artists (usually directors) who put it to good aesthetic use. Any historical account that focuses on invention is likely to emphasize the ingeniousness and creativity of individuals – the "geniuses" of the nineteenth century who invented cinema's basic technology. Rather less is usually made of subsequent inventors, largely because the major shifts in the appearance of cinema have resulted from an accumulation of relatively minor technological developments produced almost anonymously in corporate research laboratories. A more consciously economic account of technical development distinguishes between the three stages by which a technological change is introduced. **Invention** requires only a limited financial commitment to fund experimentation and the development of a prototype. In the second stage, **innovation**, the invention is adapted to meet the requirements of a market, a process involving much greater expenditure in developing the market. The final stage, **diffusion**, occurs when the product is adopted as an industry standard, and the whole industry invests in its exploitation.[76] As the case of widescreen makes clear, the innovation and diffusion of a new technology are far more significant to both the economics and the aesthetics of cinema than the invention itself.

Recognizing the institutional place of technology allows us to see its history not as making steady progress toward an ideal mode of representation, but as a series of more erratic shifts, hesitations, and reversals, more in keeping with the multiple logics that shape Hollywood production. Any given technological innovation, such as the introduction of sound, is likely to have contradictory aesthetic effects. Innovations in one area may well produce setbacks in others, so that the history of technology is most properly seen as dialectical, constructed out of the clashes between contradictory forces.

In an overview of the history of cinema technology, Peter Wollen suggests that these contradictions are usually simplified into an account organized around a number of "great moments" or "breakthroughs," leading logically to the present, although different accounts will regard that present as displaying either a greater realism or the improved illusions of special effects.[77] Wollen observes that the "breakthroughs" around which these histories are organized emphasize the technological shifts that reinvigorated the commercial viability of Hollywood and reinforced the existing power-relations of the film industry. As an experimental filmmaker, Wollen suspects that the very construction of technological histories has important political consequences in this regard: "the innovations that restricted access to filmmaking, that demanded enormous capital investment and caused real set-backs, have attracted attention, while the steady development of stock – chemical rather than optical or electronic – has never been comprehensively chronicled."[78] In suggesting the outline of alternative technological histories, Wollen draws attention to some technical innovations and developments considered too minor to feature in the grand teleological accounts. He concentrates on the consistent improvement of the recording media themselves. Changes in film stock and magnetic tape produce the most subtle (often even unnoticeable) rather than the most spectacular effects.

During the 1930s, the accumulation of a series of relatively minor changes in film stock and processing, and in lighting and lens technology, made possible the apparent "breakthrough" of deep-focus cinematography in *Citizen Kane* in 1941. In a valuable account of both these technical changes and the aesthetic impulses behind the development of deep-focus, Patrick J. Ogle traces the gradual development of the style in the late 1930s as well as its full-blown emergence in the combined work of Welles and his cinematographer Gregg Toland.[79] Rather than regarding deep-focus as the result of a commitment to realism and attributing the style to Welles's innovations, Ogle describes a series of incremental technological developments that allowed an aesthetic initiative to take advantage of them. He places what is usually thought of as a personal film style within its technological and institutional context.

Ogle's analysis demonstrates the ways in which an examination of apparently minor or peripheral technical changes may revise the established dicta of Hollywood's history. Peter Wollen's argument is, however, more directly concerned with the political ramifications of technological change. In his account, new technology often generates resistance on aesthetic grounds, as filmmakers struggle against the new technology in order to master it and make it serviceable for the Hollywood style. While the effect of major technological changes has been to exclude people who did not have substantial financial backing from an involvement in film production, Wollen follows Walter Benjamin (discussed in chapter 2) in suggesting that smaller, more gradual developments in optical and chemical technology have had the reverse effect, democratizing film production by making possible first 16-mm, then 8-mm filming, low-cost video and the camcorder, and, most recently, the possibilities of digital recording and circulation via the Internet.[80]

Video represented the most substantial collision of interests between the cinema industry and another major media industry since the development of broadcast radio and the creation of sound movies in the 1920s. As chapter 7 illustrated, the industry's response to video in many ways repeated its reaction to radio and to television, but video and subsequent technologies have expanded audience choice over both what movies it consumes and how it consumes them, in ways that neither of the movies' other "rivals" did. Video has also drastically revised Hollywood's relations with its viewers.[81] The habits of domestic viewing are more casual and intermittent than those of the cinema audience; attention is less firmly maintained, distraction and commentary are a more important and constant part of the viewing experience. Occasional middle-aged cinemagoers note with displeasure the extent to which these viewing habits have been taken into the shop-

Walter Parks Thatcher (George Coulouris) confronts Mr Bernstein (Everett Sloane) and Charles Foster Kane (Orson Welles) in the deep-focus space of *Citizen Kane* (1941).
Produced by Orson Welles; distributed by RKO Pictures. RKO.

ping-mall multiplex by the majority teenage audience, and fondly recall the passivity of the "better behaved" audiences they remember themselves to have been. An alternative analysis might see this more interactive behavior as a form of "making your own entertainment" out of the movie on offer, and later in the book I shall argue that this is, in fact, the dominant mode of consumption of the Hollywood text, and the one for which it was designed.

In its attitudes to technological development, the production industry perhaps most clearly reveals the extent to which it should be seen as a service industry. All the major technological developments discussed in this chapter, as well as the great majority of the minor ones, were introduced to the industry from outside. The studios themselves undertook very little technological research, leaving the development of optical and chemical technology to others. Production departments were not geared or equipped for these kinds of research. Rather, studio personnel such as Gregg Toland applied improved technology to develop innovative techniques like deep-focus, or engineered the specialized equipment needed for more mobile camera styles such as the crab dolly in the mid-1940s and the Steadicam in the late 1970s.

These relatively minor studio-produced innovations did not create the spectacular disturbances to Hollywood's aesthetics that came with Technicolor or widescreen, and it is perhaps not surprising that little attention is paid to them in most histories of film technology. But some small developments, such as labor-saving editing devices, have had discreet but profound effects on the appearance and experience of cinema. Comparing *Dracula*, made in 1930, with *G-Men*, made five years later, it is very noticeable that the latter cuts much more frequently. The average number of shots in a typical Hollywood movie nearly doubled in those five years, from around 400 in 1930 to around 700 in 1935.[82] Editing sound introduced a number of technical problems not encountered by editors of the silent image track alone. The most persistent of these was the need to keep sound and image in synchronization. Early sound movies contained significantly fewer cuts than had been normal in the late silent period, and *Sunny Side Up*'s disinclination to cut from establishing shot to close-up is typical of the temporary effect of this new technology. Cutting frequencies only increased after several minor technical developments, such as numbering the edges of film stock, to more easily keep track of it, and the appearance of the sound Moviola editing machine, made editing sound and keeping synchronization significantly easier.

If this was an instance of a breakthrough (sound) producing a setback eventually modified by minor technical adjustments to return to an aesthetic norm, then the other noticeable change in the frequency with which movies were cut involved the application of an external technology. Cutting rates increased in the 1960s, in part because using a magnetic soundtrack the same physical size as the film made sound editing much quicker and simpler, and in part because clear adhesive tape came into use as an alternative means of joining two pieces of edited film together. Previously, the editor would have to go through the laborious process of physically sticking the join with film cement. This was not only time-consuming, but also meant the loss of two frames every time a cut was adjusted. Using adhesive tape meant that the editor could stick the pieces of film together much faster and more easily, making it economical on studio personnel's time to cut more often and to experiment more with editing. More recently, digital editing has further enhanced the ease with which shots can be assembled, and this, combined with the influence of music video's non-linear aesthetics, has encouraged increased cutting rates and a more widespread use of discontinuous and disjunctive editing practices.

The industry itself seldom draws attention to changes such as these, however significant their cumulative effects on Hollywood's image system might be. The much more visible "breakthroughs" represent only the tip of the iceberg that is Hollywood's technological history. But whether introducing large or small changes, technological innovation has been motivated less by the desire for progress toward an ever more perfect reproduction of reality than by a practical impulse to put technology to work within the larger economic and signifying systems of the American cinema, in the service of maintaining novelty within predictability, variation within a stable mode of production, and a hierarchy of industrial organization.

The Triumph of the Digital

The first major technological innovations of post-Classical Hollywood cinema were in the quality of the soundtrack, and since the late 1970s developments in sound technology have constructed the contemporary movie theater as a complex acoustic space providing audiences with a previously unavailable range of pleasures. Since the opening shot of *Star Wars* (1977), Hollywood has exploited the sonic architecture of the theatrical space, building increasingly densely layered, three-dimensional soundtracks using multiple-channel "surround" sound, and reducing the stress placed on the illusory coherence of visual and sound space. Technological and commercial synergies between the movie and music industries have promoted the status of the soundtrack, while audiences used to high-quality sound reproduction at home have also come to require it from movie theaters. Digital sound systems, first introduced in 1992, permit the creation of extremely powerful and detailed soundtracks with very little distortion at high volume, so that the sound "architects" of action movies, in particular, can construct the soundtrack as a sensuous experience. The audience can literally be "hit" with sound, experiencing the movie with a far greater degree of physical involvement than was previously possible. As the soundtrack has become more intricate, more complex, and straightforwardly louder, the audience has become less a participant in the performance, and more simply an auditor. The movie theater has become less of a space of social interaction and more of a three-dimensional extension of the screen's two-dimensional image in which the audience is surrounded by sound. As Robert Stam suggests, in this "immersive" cinema, "The spectator is 'in' the image rather than confronted by it. Sensation predominates over narrative and sound over image, while verisimilitude is no longer a goal; rather, it is the technology-dependent production of vertiginous, prosthetic delirium."[83]

Digital technology has introduced and will continue to introduce even more profound changes to the cinematic experience. Film is an obsolete medium, the dying vestige of a nineteenth-century technology, rapidly being abandoned in favor of electronic and digital forms of image capture, storage, and transmission. The commercial motion picture industry has lagged significantly behind domestic and amateur use of moving pictures, where video-recording replaced 8-mm film by the late 1980s, and digital video began to replace video-tape around the turn of the millennium. By 2001, some Hollywood movies were being shot with digital cameras, and George Lucas declared that *Star Wars: Episode III* would only be available in digital form when it was released in 2005. Some production personnel proclaimed the superior quality of digital imagery, as well as stressing that the digital image was not vulnerable to physical damage or deterioration as photochemically produced images were. Other industry figures, however, suggested that one crucial factor likely to delay its widespread adoption was that, unlike video, the move from film to digital production created no new business opportunity, but merely saved production and distribution costs. In this context, at least, digital image recording can be seen as a minor technological change, comparable to earlier changes in film stock. The huge reductions in recording and processing costs are of much less significance to a major commercial production than they are in the domestic market, for instance.

The more profound effects of digital technology are being felt in the distribution of motion pictures and in the renegotiation of commercial relations between distributors and exhibitors that it occasions. In 2001, it was estimated that digital distribution to theaters for digital projection would save the major distributors $800 million a year in print and freight costs, but the total cost of installing digital projection in all the screens in the US would be $20 billion.[84] As with the conversion to sound and widescreen, the crucial issue was economic rather than technological, and the principal concern was with how a transition from film to "e-cinema" would be financed. For producer-distributors, the advantages of digital distribution were potentially even larger if they distributed directly to the consumer's "home theater," but the benefits to the distributors worked to the clear disadvantage of exhibitors, who would lose the competitive advantage provided to them by first access to the product. By 2001, there was a widespread belief that the theatrical market had seriously overexpanded in the 1990s, with some estimates suggesting that one-third of US screens were surplus to demand. A cycle of exhibition chain bankruptcies also indicated that the exhibition industry was not well placed to finance an extensive retooling – although we should remember that the introduction of both sound and widescreen also occurred during downturns in exhibition.

Digital distribution has also raised other issues for the industry and its consumers, including fundamental questions about property rights. The distribution and exhibition technology of film established the expectation that movies, and the experiences they provided, were rented by exhibitors and consumers rather than purchased outright. This distinction was maintained in the fine print on video boxes, which restricted the rights of purchasers to show the movie they had bought to private home use. Video "piracy," concentrated predominantly in marginal markets, presented a relatively contained problem to the industry, but the greatly increased flexibility of digital media raised questions about the rights that consumers might have to use a movie in ways other than those originally intended by its distributors, by, for instance, re-editing or otherwise digitally manipulating it. The industry's concerns with digital "piracy" of movies echoed those expressed on the appearance of the video-recorder, and have threatened to delay the diffusion of digital distribution, projection, and television broadcasting. As with the introduction of sound and widescreen, however, the publicly expressed concerns over copyright protection have concealed internal negotiations over how the new technology could best be deployed to secure the maximum economic advantage for the major companies, in this case through the standardization of digital distribution formats and copyright protection systems.

From the late 1990s, the major companies actively promoted the Digital Video Disk (DVD) as another tier to the home market, selling initially on its enhanced picture and sound quality and subsequently through the promotion of supplementary material, such as commentaries, out-takes, and alternative scenes. For some directors and other production personnel, the DVD has also provided an opportunity to revise the theatrical release version, once again undermining the concept of a single "original" version of a movie, and, indeed, the idea of the movie as finished product. In its promotion of "special collector's editions" and "director's cuts," the video distribution industry has adopted the music industry's concept of the "dance mix," which provides different versions of a product for different formats and different users. The DVD of *Moulin Rouge* (2001), for example, offers viewers the opportunity to choose from a number of different camera angles during some of the dance sequences, going beyond any notion of a director's cut to what the head of research for Philips electronics once called "the punter's cut."[85]

The DVD's additional material offers viewers forms of licensed "interactive" engagement with the movie or movie-related material. DVDs of movies aimed at the child market have also contained games and links to Internet sites, for instance. Industry marketing has also promoted the idea that additional material could provide connoisseur viewers with "insider knowledge" of production techniques and the creative process. Such material is, however, aimed at constructing the viewer as an expert rather than as a critic, emphasizing the "magic" of the production process rather than demystifying it. The industry sought to construct its up-market domestic viewers as cinephiles, "mesmerised by the machines of reproduction that deliver the cinematic illusion" and, indeed, as equally engaged with the hardware of their home theater equipment and with the software used on it.[86]

Some viewers, however, sought to expand their interactive options beyond those intended by the industry. Minimally, digital technology enhances video's capacity to alter or interrupt a movie's temporal flow by skipping, rewinding, or pausing it at will. More drastically, viewers can re-edit movies, sample scenes, or combine footage from several movies together, using software readily available for home computers. The most celebrated instance is the so-called "Phantom Edit," a re-cut version of *Star Wars: Episode 1 – The Phantom Menace* (1999) produced on a desk-top computer by a freelance editor disappointed with the released version. The industry might view such activities as abusing the invitation to "interactive" engagement with the movie in its digital form, but such objections run counter both to the industry's historical attitude of denying responsibility for its audiences' use of its products, and to the inherent interactive properties of digital "information." More importantly, perhaps, attempts to restrict viewers' rights over the use of digital versions of movies in order to secure profits promise a period of instability and acrimonious exchanges between the major software companies and hardware manufacturers seeking to keep the cycle of electronic and screen-based consumer goods as short as possible. Such conflicts of interest occasionally became explicit and public. In February 2002, for example, nine of the major high-tech companies, including Microsoft, IBM, and Intel, declared their opposition to proposed movie-industry-sponsored legislation requiring copy-protection technology to be built into hardware, proposing instead the development of "voluntary multi-industry standards" as a more effective market solution.[87]

Digital technology thus threatens not only to set the distribution and exhibition branches of the motion picture industry at odds with each other, but also to disrupt the common interests around which the convergence of hardware and software companies have been constructed. As fundamentally at stake in the new digital technology, in a way not previously encountered, are issues of ownership and the rights attached to it. As Klinger argues, cinema can now be "contained in small boxes, placed on a shelf, left on the coffee table or thrown on the floor." Movies have been transformed into home furnishings responding to the concerns and rituals of domestic space: "This previously physically remote, transitory, and public medium has thus attained the solidity and semi-permanent status of a household object, intimately and infinitely subject to manipulation in the private sphere."[88] In the process, control over the object, and what it can be used for, appears to have been transferred, for the first time, from the distributor to the consumer.

The distributors' ideal business model remains video on demand, which would use the Internet to deliver digital movies on a rental basis, and the majors have tentatively experimented with such services. For the time being, however, this remains an unfulfilled promise, partly because of the excessive demand it would place on the Internet as a distribution system, partly because an effective business model for its implementation has not yet been developed, and partly because it is far from clear that consumers will be willing to rent when they can own. The movie industry's insecurities about digital distribution were massively increased by the music industry's struggles from 1999 to 2001 with Napster peer-to-peer file-sharing software, which effectively provided free access to an enormous digital music catalog. The music industry's court victory declared Napster's technology in breach of US copyright law, but this provided little more than a temporary stay until a more refined technology circumvented the issue, while both industries sought a business model that would balance the profits of copyright holders against the interests of private users, and at the same time make it easier for consumers to buy music and movies via digital distribution than to "steal" them.

By 2001, as much as 80 percent of a movie's revenue came from sales after theatrical release. This relatively new dependence on secondary sales markets, and the synergies and relationships that have been rapidly developed to exploit these markets, were at risk from unauthorized digital distribution. For the majors, one threat of the new technology was that consumers could also become unauthorized distributors, but what was fundamentally challenged by digital recording was the process of transient access around which the industry constructed its principal business model. The same resistance to consumer ownership was visible in lawsuits brought by the majors questioning the legality of personal video-recorders, which allow consumers to record broadcast programming on the basis of a series title or actor's name. The majors contended that the storage, sorting, and automated recording features of personal video-recorders "encourage consumers to assemble libraries of copyrighted material," damaging the market for pre-recorded DVDs and videos. While the basis for the argument seemed slight, it clearly signaled the majors' belief that they should continue to control consumers' access to their product in order to preserve their intellectual property rights, rather than allowing consumers themselves to control their own access.

All these strategies seem unlikely to be successful. While the rollout of digital projection will, in all probability, be relatively slow, with physical film distribution likely to continue well into the future as the principal means of access to cinema for most of the world outside the US, the impact of digital distribution is unavoidable, driven as it is by the convergence of consumer hardware and digital processing. The economic logic of digital distribution is to extend the exhibition practice of saturation release to encompass the simultaneous release of a movie in all its distribution forms: theatrical exhibition, DVD and video, and digitally through the Internet, in part to minimize losses through piracy, but also to recoup production and marketing costs more rapidly. Such a development, which would drastically revise the industry's existing business model, would clearly damage first-run theatrical exhibition's competitive advantage, and so discourages exhibitors from adopting the new technology.

The most probable longer-term solution will be a version of the business model that operates in the computer industry, which has succeeded in persuading consumers to buy high-cost hardware and software with built-in immediate obsolescence. The life-span of home consumer entertainment formats is likely to continue to fall, as it has done over the last two decades, and with each new consumer hardware upgrade, consumers will have to repurchase their libraries. Rapid technological transformation may leave many contemporary texts and artifacts inaccessible because the hardware they require has ceased to operate; we can expect an increase in the number of "dead media" rather than a decrease. The industry, meanwhile, will have the opportunity to again revise, repackage, and remaster its history, in the way that it has done with both video and DVD. Digitally encoded "content" will be transferred from one medium to another, occasionally requiring renewal to accommodate upgrades in hardware or software.

Digital technology contains apocalyptic possibilities for cinema, in which "the end of cinema" is envisaged in its dissolution into "the larger bitstream of the audio-visual media," in a multimedia environment in which no medium is distinct from any other.[89] An alternative but not necessarily incompatible hypothesis views the state of cinema at the beginning of the twenty-first century as comparable to that at the beginning of the twentieth century, as one among a wide spectrum of "simulation devices," with a range of potential uses. Digital technology holds out the promise of low-cost, high-quality audio-visual production for a much larger group of producers, and democratic exchange in "a new kind of international communication . . . that is more reciprocal and multi-centered than the old Hollywood-dominated international system."[90] The history of Hollywood's engagement with technology should, however, lead us to doubt the Utopian promise of infinite availability. Convergence, both technological and economic, makes it supremely unlikely that a model of democratic production and distribution will prevail, at least as a mainstream cultural activity. In any case, the Utopian promise of infinite availability ignores the problem of choice in an apparently increasingly time-poor culture. For many, the actual if unacknowledged function of the video-recorder has been to watch television for them, so that they could do something else without feeling that they were missing the possibility of viewing. Digital technology will, surely, generate subcultures of fans and enthusiasts customizing and reconfiguring the products of popular culture in innovative and quirky ways, but the fan edit, the house mix, slash fiction, and other forms of amateur postmodern pastiche are unlikely to achieve more than the most local circulation. These activities will not supersede or replace the mainstream circulation of high-budget audio-visual commodities. And no matter how virtual its occupation of the Los Angeles basin becomes, those commodities will continue to be produced and distributed by an economic institution called Hollywood.

Summary

- The history of Hollywood's technological development is one of opportunism driven by economic motives. Rather than being a technological innovator, the movie industry has routinely adapted the inventions of others, assimilating them into Hollywood's existing aesthetic and institutional system.
- The mechanical technology of the cinema is the product of the nineteenth century, and the cinema of the early twentieth century was the product of a synthesis of various nineteenth-century technologies.
- Many critical accounts, including that of André Bazin, suggest that the invention of cinema was a response to a pre-existing aesthetic and cultural need to achieve the objective, unmediated reproduction of reality. "Realism" is actually a system of representational conventions.
- According to Bazin, cinema has the ability to achieve objectivity in recording concrete empirical reality because of its basis in a mechanical recording apparatus (photography). The major events in Bazin's account of cinema's technological development toward the "real" included sound and deep-focus photography. Recent technological innovations such as computer-generated images, however, raise issues about the ontology of the moving image, and suggest the need to revise some of Bazin's assumptions about the objectivity of cinematography.
- The technology involved in presenting synchronized sound had existed for some years before it was extensively used in the cinema. Its adoption in 1927 was influenced more by economic considerations than by technical capacity. Prerecorded sound marked the end of the cinema as a multi-media form, and of local variations in presentation. The musical was the first dominant genre after the introduction of sound.
- Until well into the 1950s color was promoted as a spectacular production value in its own right. Early color production was dominated by the Technicolor company, and a movie's color was coordinated around the visual presentation of the female star. Before color became standard it remained a spectacle within a movie, and clashed with other conventions of Hollywood's understanding of realism. One solution to this problem was to reserve the use of color for fantasy movies and musicals; Hollywood thus represented itself in color and the rest of the world in black-and-white.
- Widescreen technology, the most drastic shift in the appearance of the screen in the history of cinema, was introduced in the early 1950s in an attempt to regain declining audiences. Cinerama (1:2.6) proved too expensive in implementation to become industry standard; 3-D systems were cheaper but tech-

nically problematic. CinemaScope $(1:2.35)$ was sold to exhibitors and audiences on the basis of its scale, novelty, and realism. By the late 1960s the less extreme Panavision $(1:2.25)$ had become the more commonly used widescreen system.

- The history of cinema technology is not one of steady progress toward an ideal mode of representation, but a series of erratic shifts in keeping with the multiple logics of Hollywood production. Major shifts in the appearance of cinema have often resulted from an accumulation of minor, anonymous technological advances, rather than from the heroic creativity of individuals.
- Film is an obsolete medium, rapidly being discarded in favor of electronic and digital forms of image capture, storage, and transmission. Nevertheless, the move from film to digital production creates no new business opportunity, and conversion to digital projection (like that to sound and widescreen) is very expensive.
- Although digital technology has the potential to enhance the quality of the cinematic image, the most significant changes it will introduce are to the industry's distribution system and business model, revising the relationship between distributors and exhibitors and encouraging direct sales to consumers. Because digital information is inherently interactive, the new technology also encourages viewers to seek other forms of pleasure in altering or manipulating digital movies. Such activities will not, however, threaten Hollywood's commercial dominance.

Further Reading

Technology and the movies

The best general introduction to a discussion of technology and the movies is Steve Neale, *Cinema and Technology: Image, Sound, Colour* (London: Macmillan, 1985). A broader overview is provided by Brian Winston in *Media Technology and Society: A History from the Telegraph to the Internet* (London: Routledge, 1998). Barry Salt, *Film Style and Technology: History and Analysis*, 1st edn 1983, 2nd edn (London: Starword, 1992), explores the implementation of production technologies and their effect on style. So, from a different perspective, does David Bordwell in Part Six of Bordwell, Janet Staiger, and Kristin Thompson, *The Classical Hollywood Cinema: Film Style and Mode of Production to 1960* (London: Routledge and Kegan Paul, 1985). Michael Allen, "From *Bwana Devil* to *Batman Forever*: Technology in Contemporary Hollywood Cinema," in *Contemporary Hollywood Cinema*, eds Steve Neale and Murray Smith (London: Routledge, 1998), provides an overview of technological change since 1950. See also Peter Wollen, "Cinema and Technology: A Historical Overview," in his *Readings and Writings: Semiotic Counter-Strategies* (London: Verso, 1982).

Bazin and realism

André Bazin's most important essays, including "The Myth of Total Cinema," "The Ontology of the Photographic Image," and "An Aesthetic of Reality," are collected in his *What is Cinema? Vol. 1*, trans. Hugh Gray (Berkeley, CA: University of California Press, 1967), and *What is Cinema? Vol. 2*, trans. Hugh Gray (Berkeley, CA: University of California Press, 1971). For a general discussion of realism and cinema, see Terry Lovell, *Pictures of Reality* (London: British Film Institute, 1980). On *Total Recall*, see Fred Glass, "Totally Recalling Arnold: Sex and Violence in the New Bad Future," *Film Quarterly* 44:1 (Fall 1990), pp. 2–13.

For discussions of deep-focus, see David Bordwell, *On the History of Film Style* (Cambridge, MA: Harvard University Press, 1997); Patrick J. Ogle, "Technological and Aesthetic Influences upon the Development of Deep Focus Cinematography in the United States," in *Screen Reader 1: Cinema/Ideology/Politics*, ed. John Ellis (London: Society for Education in Film and Television, 1977), pp. 81–108; Robert L. Carringer, *The Making of Citizen Kane* (Berkeley, CA: University of California Press, 1985).

Sound

Donald Crafton provides an authoritative history of the introduction of sound in *The Talkies: American Cinema's Transition to Sound, 1926–1931* (New York: Scribner's, 1997). James Lastra, *Sound Technology and the American Cinema: Reception, Representation, Modernity* (New York: Columbia University Press, 2000), combines a history of sound technology to 1940 with a theoretical consideration of sound's relationship with the image. A more anecdotal history can be found in Scott Eyman, *The Speed of Sound: Hollywood and the Talkie Revolution* (New York: Simon and Schuster, 1997).

Two valuable collections of essays on aspects of sound technology are Rick Altman, ed., *Sound Theory, Sound Practice* (New York: Routledge, 1992), and Elizabeth Weis and John Belton, eds, *Film Sound: Theory and Practice* (New York: Columbia University Press, 1985). See also Michel Chion, *Audio-Vision: Sound on Screen*, trans. Claudia Gorbman (New York: Columbia University Press, 1994). On aspects of speech, see two books by Sarah Kozloff: *Invisible Storytellers: Voice-Over Narration in American Fiction Film* (Berkeley, CA: University of California Press, 1988); and *Overhearing Film Dialogue* (Berkeley, CA: University of California Press, 2000).

On sound and music in silent cinema, see Martin Miller Marks, *Music and the Silent Film: Contexts and Case Studies* (New York: Oxford University Press, 1997), and Mary Carbine, "'The Finest Outside the Loop': Motion Picture Exhibition in Chicago's Black Metropolis, 1905–1928," *Camera Obscura* 23 (May 1990), pp. 9–41. More generally on film music, see Claudia Gorbman, *Unheard Melodies: Narrative Film Music* (Bloomington: Indiana University Press, 1987); Royal S. Brown, *Overtones and Undertones: Reading Film Music* (Berkeley, CA: University of California Press, 1994); Russell Lack, *Twenty Four Frames Under: A Buried History of Film Music* (London: Quartet, 1997); and Jonathan Romney and Adrian Wooton, eds, *Celluloid Jukebox: Popular Music and the Movies Since the 50s* (London: British Film Institute, 1995).

Color

Bruce Block, *The Visual Story: Seeing the Structure of Film, TV, and New Media* (Boston: Focal Press, 2001), provides a practical analysis of the use of color in cinema. Two discussions of the introduction of color into Hollywood are Edward Branigan, "Color and Cinema: Problems in the Writing of History," in *The Hollywood Film Industry*, ed. Paul Kerr (London: Routledge and Kegan Paul, 1986), pp. 120–47, and Gorham A. Kindem, "Hollywood's Conversion to Color: The Technological, Economic and Aesthetic Factors," *Journal of the University Film Association* 31:2 (Spring 1979), pp. 29–36. For a history of Technicolor, see Fred E. Barsten, *Glorious Technicolor* (London: A. S. Barnes, 1980).

Widescreen

John Belton, *Widescreen Cinema* (Cambridge, MA: Harvard University Press, 1992), is an excellent historical account of the development and implementation of widescreen. See also the articles in a special issue of the *Velvet Light Trap* 21 (Summer 1985) on widescreen; Steve Neale, "Widescreen Composition in the Age of Television," in Neale and Smith; and John Belton, "CinemaScope and Historical Methodology," *Cinema Journal* 28:1 (Fall 1988), pp. 22–44. On 3-D, see William Paul, "The Aesthetics of Emergence," *Film History* 5:3 (Summer 1993), pp. 321–55.

New technologies

Work on new technologies dates rapidly. A good reference point is Philip Hayward and Tana Wollen, eds, *Future Visions: New Technologies of the Screen* (London: British Film Institute, 1993), while the theoretical implications of new media technologies are well discussed in Henry Jenkins, "The Work of Theory in the Age of Digital Transformation," in *A Companion to Film Theory*, eds Toby Miller and Robert Stam (Malden, MA: Blackwell, 1999), pp. 234–61. Lev Manovich discusses historical continuities between cinema and new media in *The Language of New Media* (Boston: MIT Press, 2001). See also Martin Lister, ed., *The Photographic Image in Digital Culture* (London: Routledge, 1995); Bruce M. Owen, *The Internet Challenge to Television* (Cambridge, MA: Harvard University Press, 1999); and the collection of work on media in transition at http://media-in-transition.mit.edu.

On special effects, see Christopher Finch, *Special Effects: Creating Movie Magic* (New York: Abbeville, 1984); Mark Cotta Vaz and Patricia Rose Duignan, *Industrial Light + Magic: Into the Digital Realm* (New York: Ballantine, 1996); and articles in *Cinefex*.

CHAPTER NINE
Politics

Hollywood is too deeply embedded in America's culture to be isolated from its politics.

Ronald Brownstein[1]

A conservative director may work with a liberal writer, or vice versa, and both, even if they are trying to impose their politics on their films (which often they're not), may be overruled by the producer who is only trying to make a buck and thus expresses ideology in a different way, not as a personal preference or artistic vision, but as mediated by mainstream institutions like banks and studios, which transmit ideology in the guise of market decisions: this idea will sell, that one won't. The very question "Will it play in Peoria?" masks a multitude of ideological sins. . . . Hollywood is a business, and movies avoid antagonizing significant blocks of viewers; they have no incentive to be politically clear.

Peter Biskind[2]

Despite its promise of "escape" from the everyday world, Hollywood remains a social institution, and its movies describe recognizable social situations in their plots and themes. Hollywood's engagement with "the other America out there in reality" is, however, most often indirect. In *America in the Movies,* Michael Wood notes the presence of two newspaper headlines in *For Me and My Gal* (1942), a Gene Kelly–Judy Garland musical set in World War I. At one point, Harry Palmer (Kelly) is holding a newspaper headlined "Germans Near Paris," but he is not reading the story. Later, he is asleep under a paper headlined "Lusitania Sunk." Wood sees in these unnoticed events a paradigm of the way entertainment works: "the world of death and war and menace and disaster is really there, gets a mention, but then is rendered irrelevant by the story or the star or the music." Movies, he argues, dramatize "our semi-secret concerns" in a story, allowing them a "brief, thinly disguised parade": "Entertainment is not, as we often think, a full-scale flight from our problems, not a means of forgetting them completely, but rather a rearrangement of our problems into shapes which tame them, which disperse them to the margins of our attention."[3]

Hollywood movies contain themes of social relevance not so much because their viewers need to have those issues dramatized as because that thematic material establishes a point of contact between the movies' Utopian sensibility and the surrounding social environment of its audience. *My Man Godfrey* (1936) invited its middle-class audiences to imagine what the Depression would be like if it took place on a studio back-lot where events were played out according to the conventions of a screwball comedy. *West Side Story* (1961) and *Do the Right Thing* (1989) invited their audiences to imagine what racial conflict would look like if it happened according to the conventions of the musical or the teenpic. *Mississippi Burning* (1988), which I discuss in more detail below, invited its audience to imagine institutionalized racism as if it could be solved by the conventions of a detective story, while *Air Force One* (1997) invited its audiences to imagine that "Harrison Ford is the President of the United States," combating a terrorist attack according to the conventions of an action movie.[4]

It would be wrong to conclude from this that Hollywood's politics are inevitably trivial, but they are always mediated by the systems of convention that I have been discussing throughout this book. As Danny Madigan (Austin O'Brien) discovers when his magic movie ticket takes him through the screen in *The Last Action Hero* (1993), Hollywood is not so much a distorted mirror of American society as a parallel universe, in which the conditions of existence are subtly – or not so subtly – different. This universe is, however, recognizably like our own, in that it shares many of the same social, cultural, and political conventions. To understand cause and effect within a movie, we rely on our culturally acquired knowledge of human behavior, social organization, and moral principles. In the casual, everyday sense in which we identify one movie as more "realistic" than another, "realism" implies that its conventions more closely resemble those we pessimistically assume to operate in the world outside the cinema. Happy endings are as notoriously "unrealistic" as they are emotionally satisfying.

Hollywood's politics are always mediated and almost never, in that everyday sense, "realistic," but that is not to say that they are irrelevant. If it is to sustain its appeal, Hollywood's parallel universe has to demonstrate its relevance to the lives of its viewers, to the very lives from which it allows them to escape. The movies' relation to the preoccupations of ordinary life may be, as Wood suggests, one of wish, echo, transposition, displacement, inversion, compensation, reinforcement, example, or warning. But they also affect the circulation of those preoccupations in ordinary life by providing us with structures of thought and feeling, "pictures of probability," and shapes that we can give to experiences outside the movie theater. These structures, shapes, and pictures explain why movies matter so much to us, even when we seldom give them a second thought.[5] They are the most ingrained aspect of Hollywood's politics.

The Politics of Regulation

Entertainment is the most political issue in America. . . .
It's very hard to grasp
what America understands as "political"
because this notion all too often
exists only in its negation,
as the absence of the political.
Wim Wenders[6]

Although the use of the term "political" in this discussion certainly includes overt forms of party-political activity, it obviously extends some way beyond their boundaries. The politics of Hollywood's representations embrace its treatment of social organization in the broadest sense, taking in large issues such as race, class, nationality, and sexuality, refracting them in various different circumstances, and routinely repressing or emphasizing different aspects at different times, for different reasons. The industry's own representatives have, however, always routinely denied that Hollywood is a political entity. In 1938 Will Hays declared that:

In a period in which propaganda has largely reduced the artistic and entertainment validity of the screen in many other countries, it is pleasant to report that American motion pictures continue to be free from any but the highest possible entertainment purpose. The industry has resisted and must continue to resist the lure of propaganda in that sinister sense persistently urged upon it by extremist groups. . . . The distinction between motion pictures with a message and self-serving propaganda is one determinable only through the process of common sense. . . . Entertainment is the commodity for which the public pays at the box-office. Propaganda disguised as entertainment would be neither honest salesmanship nor honest showmanship.[7]

Regardless of this attempt to declare that entertainment was free from propaganda, the industry was the subject of constant government and legislative attention. In any given year between 1925 and 1940, an average of more than 250 bills affecting the industry (almost invariably adversely) were presented in the state legislatures, while each session of the US Congress saw the introduction of bills intended to tax theater admissions, establish federal censorship, or prohibit industry trade practices such as block-booking. Between 1934 and 1941 there were five major investigations of the industry by committees of Congress, the last of which investigated charges "that the motion picture and the radio have been extensively used for propaganda purposes designed to influence the public mind in the direction of participation in the European war."[8]

In its foreign markets the industry also faced censorship and quota restrictions on the number of Hollywood movies that could be exhibited, as well as bearing the brunt of cultural complaints about the Americanization of other national cultures. As a major domestic and export enterprise, the motion picture industry had similar interests at stake in the country's political and economic policies to those of other large commercial concerns, and like other businesses, this "harmless" and "apolitical" industry maintained a substantial and expensive lobby in Washington, assiduously courting the State Department to gain its support in disputes with foreign countries over questions of tariffs and quotas. In this specific sense, Hollywood cinema was very much a political institution, with an active engagement in state, federal, and international affairs. But the overwhelming majority of its political activity was defensive in nature, undertaken for the primary purpose of sustaining the profitability of the industry's enterprises.

In 1936, MGM decided to abandon a planned adaptation of *It Can't Happen Here*, a novel by Sinclair Lewis about a Fascist take-over of the United States. The company was accused of bowing to political pressure from the Republican party and the German and Italian governments. Lewis claimed that "an extremely important and critical question concerning free speech and free opinion in the United States" was at stake,[9] and the case is often cited as one demonstration of the "almost contemptible timidity" of Hollywood's foreign policy in making concessions in order to continue doing business with European dictatorships.[10] There is certainly no question about the industry being run by conservatives, but MGM's decision was motivated by economic considerations rather than political ones. The movie was bound not to be profitable because its political content would exclude it from many foreign markets – not simply the German and Italian markets but also those over which they could exert diplomatic pressure, including Britain and France. This, then, was a matter of commercial aesthetics. In an editorial in *Motion Picture Herald*, Terry Ramsaye explained the distinction the industry made between one of Lewis's books and a movie:

> If a reader of his works, for instance, take violent exception to the content, that reader is merely annoyed with Mr Lewis. He is not outraged at Doubleday, Doran and Company, and at the whole art of the printed word. But the motion picture spectator, when he is annoyed, is annoyed with "the damned movies" and likely as not the theater where he saw the annoying picture. . . . If his publishers were continuously on a battlefront defending the book business from attempts at punitive taxation, from measures of censorship, from measures addressed at nationalization of their industry, they would perhaps at times weigh the possible effect of product of political implication and influence.[11]

At the root of Hollywood's denial that its representations engaged in politics was a politically self-interested calculation about the industry's public image. Many people in the 1920s and 1930s believed that the movies had demonstrated their enormous potential as instruments of propaganda in inciting popular support for American entry into World War I, and much of the academic writing on cinema in this period was by liberal social scientists concerned with the effects of exploitative media on the conduct and beliefs of those exposed to them. Particular movies

Posters advertising the Ku Klux Klan as heroes of *The Birth of a Nation* (1915).
Epic (courtesy Kobal).

added momentum to this debate. In 1915 D. W. Griffith's *The Birth of a Nation* provoked extensive and sometimes violent protests at its viciously racist representation of the South under Reconstruction. The movie's capacity to "grind and pound and pulverize your emotions," to stir its audiences to "a perfect frenzy,"[12] greatly intensified liberal anxieties at what reformer Jane Addams called its "pernicious caricature of the negro race."[13]

The Birth of a Nation bears some significant responsibility for the rebirth of the Ku Klux Klan: advertising and publicity stunts for the movie's openings stressed the Klan's role as the movie's heroes. The number of lynchings of African-Americans by white mobs increased dramatically in the few years after its release. The outcry over the movie ensured, among other things, that from then on the industry was far more circumspect in its representation of African-Americans: with few exceptions, they were confined to the stereotypes of servitude. This reticence, however, resulted from the industry's excessive deference to the Southern box-office, expressed, for instance, in the reservations Colonel Jason Joy, head of the Studio Relations Committee, had over the script for *I Am a Fugitive from a Chain Gang* (1932):

> While it may be true that the [chain gang] systems are wrong, I very much doubt if it is our business as an entertainment force to clear it up, and thereby possibly get into trouble with the Southern States who, as our Southern representative puts it, can stand any criticism so long as it isn't directed at themselves.

He wondered whether it was wise "from a business standpoint for our medium of entertainment . . . to incur the anger of any large section." Joy subsequently suggested minimizing the number of black prisoners shown on the chain gang, so as to make its setting less "unmistakably Southern," exemplifying Thomas Cripps's observation that Hollywood's pre-war "aversion to the racial contradictions in American life reduced African Americans to absent, alibied for, dependent victims of marketing strategies aimed at a profitable universality."[14]

Debates over the censorship of the movies, like those over the regulation of other forms of popular culture, were actually debates over the nature of social control. Although they focused on the content or structure of the entertainment form, their real concern was with its effects on consumers. This was most commonly expressed as an anxiety about the influence of entertainment on children, specifically on the criminal behavior of adolescent males and the sexual behavior of adolescent females. These concerns partially concealed deeper, class-based anxieties about the extent to which the viewing conditions in movie theaters provided opportunities for the mixing of classes. In addition, since the first motion picture censorship ordinance came into force in Chicago in 1907, public debate revolved around the question of whether a commercially motivated industry was morally fit to control the manufacture of social recreation. As chapter 3 explained, it was in this context that the Supreme Court determined that movies were not to be granted freedom of speech under the First Amendment of the Constitution, because while they might be "vivid, useful, and entertaining," they were also "capable of evil, having power for it, the greater because of their attractiveness and manner of exhibition."[15] By categorizing the movies as potentially harmful entertainment, the 1915 Supreme Court ruling imposed an obligation on the industry to produce demonstrably harmless entertainment that needed no further, externally imposed censorship. Its decision established the legal status of the cinema until the court reconsidered the question in 1952 and granted movies First Amendment protection, but the effect of the 1915 ruling has persisted, encouraging the industry to avoid political controversy in its products.

The First Amendment did not, however, protect the movies from political scrutiny. In the 1950s, public debates over the effects of mass culture focused on widespread concerns about juvenile delinquency. Underlying these concerns was a more amorphous public perception that pernicious outside forces directed from media centers in Hollywood, New York, or even Moscow were permeating every home and threatening "to destroy the decency and morality which are the bulwarks of society" by promoting values contrary to those of many parents.[16] A Senate Subcommittee chaired by Senator Estes Kefauver undertook a highly publicized investigation into the industries of mass culture and the effects of their products, concluding that stricter systems of self-regulation should run in parallel with state and local regulatory bodies.

Such anxieties, and such solutions, have recurred cyclically in recent American history, and figured prominently in the "culture wars" of the Reagan and Bush presidencies, when a similar vision of American culture besieged by the forces of chaos was promulgated by a constellation of socially and politically conservative interest groups. Since 1980, the American political right has seen Hollywood as "a godless industry whose products were corrosive to the spiritual health and values of the nation."[17] The Oscar-winning *American Beauty* (1999), for example, was widely denounced by American political conservatives as a deliberate attack on "family values." *Focus on the Family*, a Christian website, summarized its objections:

> A neighbor couple is gay. . . . parental role models are atrocious. . . . Respect for elders is non-existent here, not that these despicable adults deserve it. . . . just about everything in *American Beauty* – from drugs and sex to hatred and death – is sick, ugly and repulsive.[18]

The interpretation rendered *American Beauty* – which its publicity promoted as a dark, quirky comedy – a culturally and politically subversive object. Entertainment's implicit claim to be apolitical leaves it constantly vulnerable to an interpretation challenging that claim, and disputes over a movie's meaning are always potentially political disputes, since they may also be disputes over the political context in which the movie is viewed and discussed.

In September 2000, the Federal Trade Commission's report that the motion picture industry routinely marketed R-rated movies at children under 17 triggered a sequence of Congressional hearings and turned media responsibility into a minor theme of that year's presidential elections, as both political parties invoked the threat of federal regulation of the entertainment industries. The industry responded with a program of voluntary reforms which succeeded in defusing the immediate political situation and avoiding the need for legislation. Both the concerns expressed in this sequence of events and their outcome were typical of the way in which the movie industry and its products have been politicized, and equally typical of the way in which the industry, through its trade association, has sought to represent itself as a socially responsible purveyor of apolitical entertainment.

When the major companies established the Motion Picture Producers and Distributors of America, Inc. (MPPDA), as its trade association in 1922, their principal purpose was to safeguard the political interests of the emerging oligopoly, and the association's central task was to counter the threat of any legislation or court action that might impose a strict application of the anti-trust laws to the industry. The public means to achieve this was through a demonstration of the industry's respectability, and so the declared purpose of their organization was "to establish and maintain the highest possible moral and artistic standards of motion picture production."[19] As well as being the most respectable man their money could buy, the MPPDA's president, Will Hays, was one of the most able political organizers in the country. He had masterminded the Republican election campaign of 1920 that brought Warren Harding to the White House. Hays's skills and influence were invaluable in securing government cooperation with the industry, and maintaining a network of political contacts throughout the country that protected the industry from the flood of hostile local legislation. Although the MPPDA was always careful to differentiate the "self-regulation" of its advisory activities from "political censorship," Hays recognized that the most effective means of containing the threat posed to the industry by external censorship was to render it unnecessary. This could be achieved by ensuring that the entertainment his member companies produced was "pure," comparable to the pure meat guaranteed by the Federal Food and Drug Administration, according to an analogy widely used at the time. Although the great majority of controversies over what was or was not harmful revolved around the representation of sex or violence, implicit in the definition of "pure entertainment" was the idea that it was "entertainment unadulterated, unsullied by any infiltration of 'propaganda.'"[20]

Under Hays's leadership, the industry therefore strove to maintain a neutrality in the representation of party politics. Newsreels, for instance, balanced the amount of coverage given to the two parties so carefully, according to the *Motion Picture Herald*, that "in the 1932 campaign a tally showed a difference of only six feet in the footage given to the Republicans and Democrats."[21] The *Herald*'s publisher, Martin Quigley, was one of the godfathers of the Production Code in the early 1930s. Primarily out of a concern to preserve the political neutrality of the exhibition site, the movie theater, he insisted that entertainment ought to be entirely free of political or propagandist content. In 1938, during a public controversy over *Blockade*, a movie set in the Spanish Civil War and denounced as Communist propaganda by a number of Catholic groups, Quigley proposed an amendment to the Production Code, that: "No motion picture shall be produced which shall advocate or create sympathy for political theories alien to, and subversive of, American institutions, nor any picture which perverts or tends to pervert the theater screen from its avowed purpose of entertainment to the function of political controversy."[22] The amendment was not accepted because it was not felt necessary. The industry presumed that the producers, their audiences, and the civic groups that sought to exercise a parental concern over American public culture shared a common view about "what is right and what is wrong" – politically as well as morally.

The industry's insistence that its entertainment was apolitical was part and parcel of the way that it displaced responsibility for the interpretation of a movie's content onto its audience. Despite the frequent use of the word "controversial" as a promotional value, producers chose overwhelmingly to avoid subjects of genuine political controversy. The promotional material for *It Happened in Springfield* (1946) even went so far as to praise its story for neatly sidestepping the controversial issue of racism.[23] In preparing *The Public Enemy* for production in 1931, Darryl Zanuck, then head of production at Warner Bros., concocted the movie's "environmentalist" explanation of the causes of crime as the product of poor social conditions in order to evade discussing the more urgent, substantial, and politically sensitive question of the repeal of Prohibition.[24] Even "social conscience" pictures like *I Am a Fugitive from a Chain Gang* maintained a respectful distance from specific questions of political intervention. In defending *I Am a*

Fugitive before state censor boards, the MPPDA argued that "it is not a preachment against the chain gang system in general, but a strongly individualized story of one man's personal experiences arising from one particular miscarriage of justice."[25] Jack Warner later claimed the movie as "the first sermon I had ever put on film," but the movie's commitment to social reform was more a matter of the studio publicity department's opportunism than principle.[26] Nick Roddick has argued that social conscience movies such as *I Am a Fugitive* contained the conflict they apparently staged between an individual and the law within "the context of a *fundamentally* just society which offered the individual, even under the most extreme circumstances, the chance to reestablish himself . . . through hard work."[27] Such movies therefore remained within the industry's consensual definition of entertainment, by which Hollywood could promote itself as offering an affirmative vision of national community, and affirm the movie theater in which that vision was experienced as being a safe and apolitical space. Beyond that, it was invariably argued that "political" movies were in any case "box-office poison." At the time of the 1941 Senate investigation, Leo Rosten noted that *Abe Lincoln in Illinois* (1940), *Our Town* (1940), *The Long Voyage Home* (1940), *Juárez* (1939), *Confessions of a Nazi Spy* (1939), *Escape* (1940), and *The Mortal Storm* (1940) had all "either lost money or made a disappointing profit. . . . In nineteen separate surveys made by Dr George Gallup, it was found that only New York audiences seem to want pictures with political content involving Hitler and the Nazis."[28]

Hollywood Goes to Washington

Given these circumstances, the fact that the industry ever turned to political subjects is evidence of the extent to which no single logic has entirely shaped production decisions in Hollywood. The quest for topicality has often drawn it to political subjects, albeit those capable of being represented without violating the industry's political neutrality. Sometimes this has been achieved by taking a period interest in past political crises still felt to affect the present (*Guilty by Suspicion*, 1990, *JFK*, 1991). On other occasions, such as *Falling Down*'s (1993) "tale of urban reality" depicting "the adventures of an ordinary man at war with the everyday world," it has involved negotiating more immediate political realities in an attempt to capture the zeitgeist.[29] Such movies usually achieve neutrality by using their political subject matter as a background for a story that conforms to a familiar generic norm. The Russian Revolution of 1917 served as a backdrop for a love story between Douglas Fairbanks Jr and Nancy Carroll in *Scarlet Dawn* in 1932; in 1982 the same event served the same purpose for Warren Beatty and Diane Keaton in *Reds*. Plots develop against the logic of their political content in order to remain within the broader logic of their status as apolitical entertainment. *Grand Canyon* (1991) begins as if it is going to be a movie about the decay of America's inner cities, but it becomes a movie about individual and family regeneration.

Jefferson Smith (James Stewart) defending his American principles against corruption in the form of Senator Joseph Paine (Claude Rains), in a perfect reproduction of the Senate chamber in *Mr Smith Goes to Washington* (1939).
Produced by Frank Capra; distributed by Columbia Pictures.

This pragmatic response to the assumed preferences of the audience is not in itself sinister, simply evidence of the industry's expectation that political subject matter must be dramatized in some way to make it palatable for the audience. In his survey of American political movies, Terry Christensen suggests that movies have been hampered in their representation of politics by a reluctance to articulate any but the most general and consensual political ideas. Excluding ideological conflict as a source of political motivation reduces all political motives to self-interest: "the bad guys act out of greed or ambition, and the good guys act to stop the bad guys." To avoid offending anyone's political beliefs, politics is trivialized, reduced to the "need for occasional individual action to regulate an essentially good, smoothly functioning process by pointing out flaws in the form of bad individuals and sometimes bad organizations like gangs, machines and corporations."[30] In such movies politics may be little more than the framework for a generically familiar plot, but as the reception of *Mr Smith Goes to Washington* (1939) makes clear, even these stories retain a power to offend in a political context.

James Stewart plays Jefferson Smith, a Boy-Scout leader from a small Midwestern town who is appointed to the Senate by a group of corrupt politicians on the death of the incumbent senator. They assume that he is so naïve, and so in awe of Joseph Paine (Claude Rains), the senior senator from his state, that he will not realize that Paine and the party machine are using a Senate bill to push through a crooked land deal. Throughout the movie Stewart's star image coincides with the political image of innocent idealism that the movie is endorsing. Smith's first action in Washington, for example, is to go on a tour of the Capitol buildings and to read, reverently, the inscriptions on the recently opened Lincoln memorial. As the plot progresses, however, Smith discovers that he has been duped and made a scapegoat. On the point of being expelled from the Senate, Smith delivers a long, filibustering speech about political principles, quoting extensively from the Declaration of Independence and the Constitution. This expression of American first principles provokes a magical transformation, in which Paine breaks down and confesses his part in the conspiracy, exonerating Smith and declaring his own unworthiness to serve the people.

The movie's production history reveals the way in which Hollywood's interest in representing party politics grew in part from its response to criticism that the Production Code was politically repressive. In January 1938 MGM and Paramount asked the Production Code Administration (PCA) for their opinion of a manuscript by Lewis Ransom Foster called "The Gentleman from Montana," a fictionalized account of the early career of Senator Burton K. Wheeler. PCA Director Joseph Breen discouraged them from pursuing the project because its "portrayal of the United States Senate as a body of politicians, who, if not deliberately crooked, are completely controlled by lobbyists with special interests" produced a "generally unflattering portrayal of our system of government, which might well lead to such a picture being considered, both here, and more particularly abroad, as a covert attack on the democratic form of government."[31]

Breen saw the PCA as "participants in the processes of production" along with producers, directors, and writers. Part of his role was to represent a national consensus on political issues as well as moral ones. He therefore saw nothing sinister in his rejecting material that characterized "a member of the United States Senate as a 'heavy'; or . . . in which police officials are shown to be dishonest; or . . . in which lawyers, or doctors, or bankers, *are indicted as a class*." He defended his rejection of a script that portrayed "the unfair treatment of the blacks by the whites . . . an alleged attack by a black man on a white woman, [and] an attempted lynching of a negro" because "it deals with such an inflammatory subject":

> Surely the organized motion picture industry is performing a useful public service when spokesmen for the Association insist that screen material involving racial conflicts between whites and blacks be handled in such a way as to avoid fanning the flame of race prejudice. The film *Fury* proves conclusively that there is a way to handle satisfactorily and with tremendous dramatic power the heinous crime of lynching without including the racial angle.[32]

The studios, he claimed, expected him to give them "sound guidance on matters of political censorship."

By 1938, however, Breen's success in keeping controversy from the screen was itself becoming controversial in the face of allegations that "self-regulation . . . has degenerated into political censorship." With the industry facing an anti-trust suit, its chief Washington lobbyist argued that the rejection of a movie "on the ground that it was politically 'dangerous'" would provide exactly the kind of evidence of monopoly behavior that the Department of Justice might use against them.[33] So when producer-director Frank Capra revived "The Gentleman from Montana" as *Mr Smith Goes to Washington* in January 1939 and submitted a script to the PCA, Breen's attitude had changed:

> I think if we could emphasize the thought, which is now present in the script, that the Senate is made up of a group of fine, upstanding citizens, who labor long and tirelessly for the best interests of the nation, and that Fletcher and his two Congressmen are not typical of the character of the men of Congress, no serious offense will be taken from this particular story. . . . It is a grand yarn that will do a great deal of good for all those who see it and, in my judgment, it is particularly fortunate that this kind of story is to be made at this time.

Most analyses of the movie have followed a contemporary review in seeing in it a reflection of the shift in American social values in the late 1930s, from the concerns of the Depression to new wartime ideas of nationalism that invoked an idealized American political tradition – what Breen called "the rich and glorious heritage which is ours and which comes when you have a government 'of the people, by the people, and for the people.'"[34] At the time of its release, however, the movie was viewed very differently, at least by some of its audience. Capra meticulously reconstructed the Senate chamber on a Columbia sound stage and hired the ex-superintendent of the Senate as a technical advisor to ensure that the movie accurately represented Congressional procedure. When it was premiered in Washington, however, the senators of the 78th Congress were grievously upset not by such details, but by its "cynical approach to the political scene," which many of them regarded as an "insult."[35] They were outraged at its apparent allegation that they themselves did not embody the fundamental American political principles the movie trumpeted, and even more outraged at the suggestion that they needed to be reminded of those principles by a Boy-Scout leader or an equally upstart movie. Senators expressed strong opposition to the scenes on the Senate floor depicting senators "as smugly acquiescent in the perpetration of the fraud." The Washington press corps expressed their anger at being represented, once again, by "an amiable drunk."[36] Press coverage of the reaction widely recorded the rumor that senators would take their revenge by engineering the passage of a bill to prohibit block-booking. More threateningly, Burton Wheeler, the Montana senator who had been misrepresented by James Stewart, was the chairman of the Senate Committee on Interstate Commerce, responsible for the 1941 investigation into propaganda and monopoly in the movies. With such power at its disposal, the Congress of the United States was perhaps the most extreme among interest groups capable of exerting political pressure in ways that might prove damaging to the industry. Despite its commercial success, then, the case of *Mr Smith* may explain why the industry was so concerned that its representation be politic rather than political.

Washington Goes to Hollywood

If you have something worthwhile to say, dress it in the glittering robes of entertainment and you will find a ready market . . . without entertainment no propaganda film is worth a dime.
Darryl Zanuck, 1943[37]

It is time for us to be courageous, but we must also be sensible, and not too courageous with other people's money.
Darryl Zanuck, 1950[38]

Is democracy so feeble that it can be subverted merely by a look or a line, an inflection, a gesture?
Humphrey Bogart, 1947[39]

Most accounts of the politicization of Hollywood begin with the 1934 campaign for the governorship of California, in which the Democratic candidate was the socialist novelist Upton Sinclair. As part of his EPIC (End Poverty in California) campaign, Sinclair announced his intention of taxing the movie industry, provoking studio executives into threatening to migrate en masse to Florida. They also provided propaganda newsreels for the Republican campaign, and levied contributions from their employees to save California from "Russianization."[40] This conscription stirred a reaction among studio personnel, already involved in attempts to unionize several branches of the production industry, and the bitterness created by the moguls' actions consolidated the left in Hollywood. From 1890, Los Angeles had been "the last citadel of the open shop," its hostility to unionism being one of the features that had attracted the movie industry there in the first place. According to Carey McWilliams, the mass political movements that emerged in southern California in the mid-1930s were "the inevitable expression of political aspirations that had been maturing for a quarter of a century and which, during this period, had been brutally and systematically suppressed."[41] Sinclair's campaign, indeed, was itself evidence of the absence of an established Democratic political machine in the state. Compounded by the conditions of the Depression, that absence encouraged extremism in the politics of the film community.

Although studios discouraged actors from taking political positions to avoid alienating any of their fans, Hollywood became a significant center of progressive political activity in the late 1930s. Three of the country's most important organizations in the alliance of liberals and radicals known as the Popular Front were based in Los Angeles: the Hollywood Anti-Nazi League, the Motion Picture Artists' Committee, and the Motion Picture Democratic Committee.[42] These organizations, together with many others, would be labeled as Communist fronts in the late 1940s, and their members attacked as "fellow travelers." The Communist party was indeed the most active force in Hollywood's progressive politics until 1939, but Hollywood's Popular Front organizations were a conscious coalition of liberal and radical political opinions, broadly supportive of the New Deal and concerned particularly to draw attention to the threat of Fascism in Europe. Very little of this politics ever surfaced in the movies, however: *Mr Smith Goes to Washington*, for instance, bears few signs of having been written by a Communist party member.[43] Gore Vidal summarizes:

> It is true, of course, that some of the movie writers *were* Communists but, as they all agreed in later years, you couldn't get anything of a political nature into any film. . . . On the other hand, it is worth at least a doctoral thesis for some scholar to count how often in films of the thirties and forties a portrait of Franklin Roosevelt can be found, usually hanging on a post-office wall; and then try to discover who put it there: the writer, the director, the producer – the set designer?[44]

The threat of Fascism led some producers to a partial reassessment of Hollywood's social role. Harry Warner signed his name to a public statement arguing that, above and beyond their primary commercial obligation to the box-office, "the men and women who make a nation's entertainment have . . . an ever present duty to educate, to stimulate, and demonstrate the fundamentals of free government, free speech, religious tolerance, freedom of press, freedom of assembly, and the greatest possible happiness for the greatest possible number."[45] Warner's attitude was most visible in his own studio's movies, such as *Juárez* and *Confessions of a Nazi Spy*. As Hollywood's foreign markets contracted after the outbreak of war in Europe, the studios took an increasingly interventionist line, and were far more assertive in defending themselves against the isolationist senators investigating propaganda in 1941. Warner defended the company's right to "portray on the screen current happenings of our times," and argued that these films were similar to the "pictures on current affairs" that the studio had always made; that other media were paying much more attention to the war and "the Nazi menace"; and that Warners' representation was, therefore, consensual. It was true, he said:

> that Warner Bros. has tried to cooperate with the national defense program. . . . It is true that we have made a series of shorts portraying the lives of American heroes. To do this, we needed no urging from the government and we would be ashamed if the government would have to make such requests of us. We have produced these pictures voluntarily and proudly. . . . You may correctly charge me with being anti-Nazi. But no-one can charge me with being anti-American.[46]

He insisted that *Sergeant York* (1941) was "a factual portrayal of one of the great heroes of the last war . . . If that is propaganda, we plead guilty."[47] "If you charge us with being anti-Nazi you are right," declared Darryl Zanuck, "and if you accuse us of producing films in the interest of preparedness and national defense you are also right."[48]

The two major political parties had begun to recognize Hollywood's potential as a source of funds and celebrity endorsements in the 1940 presidential election campaign, but Hollywood's political standing changed fundamentally during World War II. In 1942 the government established a Bureau of Motion Pictures in the Office of War Information (OWI), staffed in the main by former journalists of liberal and progressive opinions. The bureau issued a *Government Information Manual for the Motion Picture Industry*, "the clearest possible statement of New Deal, liberal views on how Hollywood should fight the war."[49] Among other questions, it asked producers to consider:

> Will this picture help win the war?
> What war information problem does it seek to clarify, dramatize or interpret?
> If it is an "escape" picture, will it harm the war effort by creating a false picture of America, her allies, or the world we live in?
> Does it merely use the war as the basis for a profitable picture, contributing nothing of real significance to the war effort and possibly lessening the effect of other pictures of more importance?
> . . . Does the picture tell the truth or will the young people of today have reason to say they were misled by propaganda?[50]

The bureau never acquired an authority within the industry to match that of the Production Code Administration, but it did give a degree of legitimacy to Hollywood's expression of political ideas. Some of those expressions – the endorsement of the USSR as America's ally in *Mission to Moscow* (1943), for example – would return to haunt their makers in the early years of the Cold War.

The OWI discouraged studios from dealing with domestic problems, advocating that they "write out" difficult characters or situations. In the same way as the Production Code prohibited movies from showing systematic corruption, the OWI only allowed the depiction of social problems if the movie showed them being solved. The historians of the OWI's involvement in Hollywood conclude that wartime movies showed social problems to be individual, ephemeral, and easily solved, a treatment that contributed to "the impoverishment of dialogue about American society."[51] Some changes did, however, result from the OWI's support of what Thomas Cripps calls Hollywood's "conscience-liberalism,"[52] a broad commitment to racial and social equality unattached to any specific political program. The OWI's director Elmer Davis proposed that "the easiest way to inject a propaganda idea into most people's minds is to let it go in through the medium of an entertainment picture when they do not realize that they are being propagandized": by, for instance, "casually and naturally" introducing propaganda messages into "ordinary dialogue, business and scenes,"[53] in the way that Gore Vidal suggests Roosevelt's portrait was exhibited. Casting women and black extras in uniform in crowd scenes emphasized both the pervasiveness of the war and a sense of equal participation. Cripps argues that the war was "a moment of high opportunity" for African-Americans, and if these "small deliberate acts" seem relatively inconsequential, they were also irreversible.[54] The surface verisimilitude of Hollywood's depiction of contemporary America changed during the war. African-Americans were no longer represented primarily by their absence.

Hollywood's occasional mild liberal advocacy continued after the war, encouraged by the commercial success of two 1947 movies about anti-semitism, *Crossfire* and *Gentleman's Agreement*. A liberal consensus was also evident in the widespread support in the film community for Henry Wallace's Progressive party in the 1948 election, despite the intrusion, the previous year, of the House Committee on Un-American Activities (HUAC) investigating "Communist Infiltration of the Motion Picture Industry." The committee included in its membership some of the most extreme right-wingers in the Congress, intent on discrediting the New Deal and wartime administration of President Roosevelt by alleging that its policymakers were Communist sympathizers. The purpose of its investigation of Hollywood was to suggest that card-carrying members of the Communist party had written, produced, or directed "subversive" movies with the connivance of government officials. The committee held hearings in Washington in November 1947, when it rapidly became clear that there was no evidence to support these paranoid claims. Since HUAC's interest in Hollywood was primarily for its publicity value, however, the behavior of the ten "unfriendly witnesses" who refused to testify to their political affiliations and denounced the committee in vitriolic terms served its purpose almost as well. Testimony like that of Jack Warner, that the "intellectual" writers were the most avid supporters of the Soviet Union, and that "some of these lines have innuendoes and double meanings, and things like that, and you have to take eight or ten Harvard law degrees to find out what they mean," also suited the committee's attempts to induce paranoia.[55] They could assert, without needing proof, that the Communists had done and were doing things to the movies, and they were so smart that Joe Public didn't even know he was being brainwashed.

The "Hollywood Ten" were cited for contempt of Congress and subsequently imprisoned. Although studio heads had argued against the committee's proposal to blacklist "subversive" writers on both moral and practical grounds, they fired the Ten because, they claimed, their "actions, attitude, public statements and general conduct" had brought them "into disrepute with large sections of the public, have offended the community, have prejudiced this corporation . . . and the motion picture industry in general."[56] The committee did not return to its investigations of the movies until 1951, by which time the political atmosphere had worsened. The Communist victory in the civil war in China, the outbreak of war in Korea, the successful testing of an atomic bomb by the Soviet Union, and the federal government's institution of a loyalty program had created a climate of fear and reaction, in which it was no longer necessary for HUAC to provide evidence that left-wing opinions were subversive.[57] Between 1951 and 1954 HUAC called several hundred witnesses from the industry, demanding that they testify to their past political allegiances and demonstrate their present rectitude by naming their former associates in the Communist party or "front" organizations. The 200 people who refused to cooperate were blacklisted from further work in the industry. A larger number, who failed to clear their names against unsubstantiated allegations about their political beliefs or activity, found themselves on a "graylist" for "fellow travelers." Careers were destroyed by little more than rumors, and many blacklisted personnel were forced to leave Hollywood or work under assumed names.

Terry Molloy (Marlon Brando) and Crime Commission investigator Glover (Leif Erickson) in
On the Waterfront (1954).
Produced by Sam Spiegel; directed by Columbia Pictures.

The history of "the Inquisition in Hollywood" has most often been told as a
melodrama of villains and victims, with roles pivoting around the clear moral
choice of whether to "name names" before HUAC. The moral dilemmas of the
informer appeared in a number of dramas in the mid-1950s, most notably in *On
the Waterfront* (1954), a crime melodrama set and shot in the New Jersey dock-
yards, in which Terry Molloy (Marlon Brando) is eventually persuaded to testify
to the Crime Commission investigating waterfront corruption. Scripted and
directed by "friendly witnesses" who had "named names" to save their careers,
the movie received the industry's approval, as shown by its eight Oscars in 1955.[58]
Hollywood's acquiescence in the anti-Communist witchhunts undoubtedly
reflected the industry's timidity as well as its consistent desire to avoid political
controversy, but it was also in keeping with national sentiment. Movie producers
behaved no worse (if also no better) than university administrators, business executives, or union leaders; it was merely that some of the Hollywood victims of the
anti-Communist witchhunts were more prominent public figures.

Devastating as the experience of the blacklist was to the individuals it affected,
it failed to destroy Hollywood's liberal consensus. In one sense the destruction of

the Popular Front ultimately strengthened the influence of the left in Hollywood by steering it toward the political mainstream of the Democratic party, and also by branding the right with responsibility for the purge. The Inquisition was "a victory from which the conservatives never quite recovered." Throughout the 1950s, the Democratic and Republican parties competed on roughly equal terms for the allegiance of Hollywood notables, but Hollywood's prominent Republicans were older, and the right's failure to secure support in the movie colony indicated that

> for the generations that succeeded those maimed by the investigations, it was the inquisitors, not their victims, who bore the shame. As the 1960s progressed and the Vietnam War called into question the entire Cold War edifice, the blacklistees were resurrected in Hollywood as well-meaning progressives hounded for their prescience by the forces of ignorance, reaction and hysteria. Their ruined careers were raised like bloody shirts as monuments to the danger of reflexive anticommunism.[59]

In other aspects of Hollywood's politics it was also clear that even in the reactionary climate of the early Cold War the ground gained by liberals during World War II would not be surrendered. In its ruling on the Paramount anti-trust case in 1948 the Supreme Court declared that it now regarded movies as "included in the press whose freedom is guaranteed by the First Amendment," an opinion it confirmed in 1952 when it declared that it was unconstitutional for the New York censor board to ban the Italian movie *The Miracle* (1950) because they considered it "sacrilegious." The MPPDA – after 1945 the Motion Picture Association of America (MPAA) – joined forces with the National Association for the Advancement of Colored People to challenge the legitimacy of racist municipal censorship in the Southern states. Beginning in 1949, a cycle of movies applied the liberal formulas of *Crossfire* and *Gentleman's Agreement* to the issue of racial prejudice: *Home of the Brave, Lost Boundaries, Pinky, Intruder in the Dust* (all 1949), *No Way Out* (1950). The cycle, which continued throughout the next decade, preached an unmistakable message of integrationism. A lone African-American protagonist – archetypically Sidney Poitier – is set down in a small town or a hospital, where he teaches the white community tolerance by example. These movies betray the virtues and faults of Hollywood's political simplicity. The Poitier hero's excessive decency reduces the issue of prejudice to no more than a matter of skin pigmentation, but as Stanley Kramer, producer of *Home of the Brave, The Defiant Ones* (1958), and *Guess Who's Coming to Dinner* (1967) observed, it also obliges the viewer to regard race as the *only* reason for discrimination. Thomas Cripps points out, too, that these movies' formula for discussing racism through the admission of a single, iconic African-American character into a white circle anticipated and perhaps even influenced the shape that racial integration would actually take, in confrontations over the admission of a lone African-American figure to a school, a university, or a lunch counter, and then in the pattern adopted by American businesses of engaging "token Negroes."[60]

The social commentary in Hollywood's movies was neither frequent nor radical, and it was no more free of the effects of the multiple logics of production than

Bill McKay (Robert Redford) in *The Candidate* (1972): the idealized image of the political idealist.

Produced by Walter Coblenz; distributed by Warner Bros.

tification with its star, the movie itself relies on exactly the politics of image and personality that its central character denounces. Completely disregarding the fact that Henry Fonda is delivering the line, Russell declares that "Men without faces tend to get elected President, and power or personal responsibility tend to fill in the features." In effect, the movie finds a way to practice exactly what it rejects: it provides a representation of party politics exclusively in terms of images, without ever actually discussing issues or espousing a cause.[69]

In several subsequent movies, Hollywood has represented the political by repeating *The Best Man*'s concentration on the divide between image and issue as a strategy for avoiding issues of political substance. *The Candidate* (1972) follows the progress of Bill McKay (Robert Redford) from idealistic radical lawyer to newly elected senator, deploring the way his campaign managers maneuver him away from discussing the issues of the campaign. Like *The Best Man*, *The Candidate* employs the stylistic devices of documentary – and the presence of several professional politicians and television newsreaders – to assert the accuracy of its representation of the political process.[70] But the movie inevitably becomes caught in its own conundrum about the politics of image. Although apparently intended as a political instrument – Redford, director Michael Ritchie, and scriptwriter Jeremy

Larner wanted it shown to delegates at the 1972 Democratic national convention – *The Candidate* itself remains trapped within the web of irony it constructs for its central character. Its description of the electoral process is caustic in its cynicism, but at the same time, the movie relishes its opportunities for glamorously backlit close-ups of its star, Redford. The movie asserts that politics has no place for sincerity, but it relies on the sincerity of Redford's performance to convey its theme. Thus it becomes primarily concerned not with the political attitudes of its characters, but with those of its producers.

In *Mr Smith Goes to Washington*, James Stewart's performance mannerisms, and in particular his hesitant vocal delivery, become signs of Jefferson Smith's sincerity, "his emotion at being called to embody the democratic ideal," while Senator Paine's eloquence signifies that he is false to the democracy he supposedly represents.[71] *Mr Smith* is a star vehicle, so that Stewart's star persona matches and reinforces his character as his character conforms to that persona. Stewart's idealistic sincerity is inseparable from that of Jefferson Smith or the movie. By contrast, *The Candidate*'s irony creates a distance between Robert Redford's performance and the character of Bill McKay. Throughout the movie questions are raised about McKay's honesty and integrity, and the extent to which he has been corrupted by a political machine. The political sincerity of Robert Redford, on the other hand, is not in doubt. It is indeed demonstrated by his willingness, as both star and producer of the movie, to put his own image on the screen as the image to be questioned. The sincerity of Redford's motives in criticizing the political process are established by the movie's questioning of his character, but the ironic distance which is created between performer and role leaves the movie itself without a platform for any alternative political position. A promotional stunt for the movie demonstrated its hollow representation of political vacuity: on a parodic whistlestop tour through Florida, Redford told the crowds he assembled, "I have absolutely nothing to say."[72] The final layer of irony involved in the movie's sincere articulation of political insincerity is the revelation that it was *The Candidate* that allegedly inspired J. Danforth Quayle, vice-president to George Bush from 1988 to 1992, to enter politics. The same irony attaches itself to *Bob Roberts* (1992), which, according to its director, documents "how politics has exploded with an obsession on image rather than substance, and how the media is compliant with that," but also unavoidably participates in the process it deplores.[73]

Terry Christensen concludes his study of American political movies by arguing that above all, these movies "tell us that politics is corrupt." The most radical and pessimistic, those that present an image of politics as "evil and corrupting, best avoided by decent people," may reinforce the system they condemn by confirming the prejudices and entrenching the political alienation and apathy of their audiences. "After all, if it takes Warren Beatty, Jane Fonda or Robert Redford to beat the system, what chance do the rest of us have? And if even they can't beat it, how can we?"[74] There is, however, an element of blaming the messenger for the message in this account. Ronald Brownstein argues that it is not Hollywood but politicians, their consultants, the disengaged public, and the "inexorable demands of television for abbreviated debate" that have trivialized American politics by encouraging national politicians to become "actors playing a broadly scripted part

The personality as political symbol: Dave Kovic (Kevin Kline) pretending to be president in *Dave* (1993).

Produced by Ivan Reitman, Lauren Shuler-Donner; distributed by Warner Bros.

– virile young hero (John F. Kennedy), ascetic moral leader (Jimmy Carter), benevolent father (Ronald Reagan), read-my-lips tough guy (George Bush)":

> At a time when public debate revolves around personalities who stand as political symbols, it is inevitable that causes will deploy as spokespeople stars who are themselves symbols – of intelligence, empathy, bravery, compassion, desire. . . . We have all lowered the level of discussion to a point where stars can more easily participate.[75]

This apparently symbiotic relationship between political and entertainment celebrity shapes the version of politics staged in *Dave* (1993), in which Kevin Kline plays Dave Kovic, the manager of an employment agency who is persuaded to impersonate President Bill Mitchell (also played by Kline) after Mitchell suffers a stroke. In many respects *Dave* is a self-conscious reconstruction of *Mr Smith Goes to Washington*: at one level it is concerned with what would happen if an ordinary person who just looked like the president became the president. But at the same time as *Dave*'s representation of politics replays the sentimental populism of *Mr Smith* (in place of Mitchell's program of cutting welfare, Dave proposes policies that will "help people"), the movie is far more self-referential in its treatment of political celebrity. *Dave* is populated with celebrities playing themselves: several senators and congressmen give simulated interviews on CNN; comedians and political pundits appear on TV talk shows; Oliver Stone, director of *JFK*, is seen on TV propounding a conspiracy theory about President Mitchell's stroke. These appearances, however, work not to guarantee *Dave*'s realism so much as to comment ironically on its fiction. The authenticity of Dave Kovic's performance as president is attested to by his public celebrity appearance with Arnold

Schwarzenegger, who is playing Arnold Schwarzenegger the celebrity. But when Dave visits a Washington factory and is photographed using automated lifting arms like those in *Aliens* (1986), the movie makes a conscious reference to the celebrity presence in *Dave* of Sigourney Weaver, who is playing not Sigourney Weaver but Ellen Mitchell, the president's wife.

In its post-Classical playfulness, *Dave* assumes that a state of complete flux exists between the fictions of politics and the fictions of Hollywood, and on that premise, it might as well have a feel-good happy ending as not. Dave resolves the plot by confessing to all of President Mitchell's misdeeds, bringing down the villainous chief of staff Bob Armstrong (Frank Langella) with him, and then staging a second, apparently fatal stroke. Thus he succeeds in handing over power to the vice-president, whom we know to be an honorable politician, partly because the movie tells us so and partly because we recognize Ben Kingsley, the actor playing the part, as Mahatma Gandhi from *Gandhi* (1982). Dave, inspired by his experience as president, decides to run for election to his local council, and the movie ends with him in a romantic clinch with the president's widow. Unlike *The Candidate* or *The Best Man*, *Dave* makes no attempt to be coherent about the political issues it touches on. Its politics are purely a matter of images, and it is happily unconcerned about its own implication that these images have no political content.

Describing itself as "a comedy about truth, justice and other special effects," *Wag the Dog* (1997) was one of several political movies of the late 1990s to satirize the relationship between electoral politics and the media. Two weeks before the election, news of a sexual scandal involving the president threatens to ruin his campaign for re-election. With the aid of Hollywood producer Stanley Motss (Dustin Hoffman), political spin-doctor Conrad Brean (Robert De Niro) concocts a simulated war with Albania to distract the media and the electorate from the scandal. While offering itself as a comic Hollywood fantasy about Hollywood's ability to manipulate politics and audiences, the movie also raises questions about both the political manipulation of the media and the media's construction of politics as show business. Within weeks of the movie's release, President Clinton was embroiled in the sexual scandal that dominated news coverage of his second term.

Wag the Dog's reception ironically illustrates the extent to which producers' intentions exert only a limited influence over a movie's interpretation. The premise of the novel on which it was based was that the previous president, George Bush, had instigated the Gulf War of 1991 as a media event to secure his re-election.[76] Despite this, and the fact that its producers, including Hoffman and De Niro, were prominent Clinton supporters, the movie's distributors advertised the parallels between it and the Clinton scandal, gaining media attention that benefited the movie's box-office by tens of millions of dollars. *Wag the Dog* offered a critique of the media's responsibility for the decline of American politics, but the coincidence of its release with the Clinton scandal and US military action against Iraq, Sudan, and Yugoslavia provided an opportunity for the movie to be widely used in the media as an interpretive framework for the actual events.[77] During 1998 and 1999, *Wag the Dog* was appropriated by the Iraqi and Yugoslav governments

Stanley Motss (Dustin Hoffman) and Tracy Lime (Kirsten Dunst) construct political reality in *Wag the Dog* (1997).

Produced by Robert De Niro, Barry Levinson, Jane Losenthal; distributed by New Line Cinema; directed by Barry Levinson.

to provide an explanation for US military action against them. During the NATO campaign against Yugoslavia in defense of the Albanian population of Kosovo, the *New York Times* reported that one Yugoslav official claimed that the Kosovar refugees were "actors . . . getting paid $5.50 a day by NATO."[78]

In September 2001, the terrorist threat invoked as the excuse for *Wag the Dog*'s phony war was enacted in the attacks on the World Trade Center and the Pentagon, rendering the movie's satirical observations that "war is show business" no less relevant but much less comic. One of the most frequently cited contexts for immediately situating the events of September 11, 2001, was the disaster movie, a phenomenon that in itself raised cultural concerns about "the triumph of entertainment" over an understanding of political actuality.[79] If, as several cultural critics observed, an incidental casualty of those events was the ironic, cynical view of politics that *Wag the Dog* itself presented and that its reception then compounded, one of the first ironies lost in the aftermath was that the federal government was reported as enacting part of the movie's scenario by "secretly soliciting terrorist scenarios from top Hollywood filmmakers and writers."[80]

Controversy with Class: The Social Problem Movie

"Let's give 'em controversy with class. Shock America, Darryl."
Spyros Skouras[81]

I suppose I see myself as a serious artist, and it felt right to do something of historical import. . . . It's really the story of how two guys from totally different backgrounds work out their relationship in the process of solving a problem – in this instance the violation of civil rights, and murder. I suppose it's the difference between a right-wing Republican and a fairly liberal Democrat – though we never discussed politics.

Gene Hackman on *Mississippi Burning*[82]

To make a film about racism, Hollywood uses the buddy movie.

Gavin Smith[83]

Despite repeated assertions that entertainment should shun "the lure of propaganda" and be without political position or effect, Hollywood has persistently produced movies that blur distinctions between entertainment and politics. Social problem movies of the kind Will Hays termed "motion pictures with a message" have formed a recurrent category of Hollywood production, despite the controversies they have regularly triggered and their often unimpressive record at the box-office. They are part of Hollywood's claim to cultural integrity, and their numbers have increased since 1950. Once television became the primary provider of the affirmative cultural vision of America as a national community, Hollywood could engage controversial material on a more routine basis than the studios had attempted before. Only a few movies such as *The Candidate* and *Bob Roberts* have depicted the American political apparatus explicitly, but many more have discussed political questions and strategies more obliquely.

In part this simply reflects Hollywood's enduring concern for topicality, but it is also part of a refined political logic that has preserved Hollywood from outside interference. Although these movies have often drawn adverse government or interest group attention to the industry, Hollywood has generally viewed their production as a necessary element in its defensive political strategy for safeguarding its freedom of movement and the profitability of its enterprises. There are contradictory impulses behind the social problem movie, involving both the recognition and the disavowal of Hollywood's power. By indicating its ability to deal responsibly with issues of political import to American audiences, Hollywood has sought to acknowledge the political influence attributed to its movies by social scientists and lobby groups, and also to show that such power is indeed safe in its own hands. As I have suggested in chapter 3, the movie moguls recognized early that if handled appropriately, overtly "concerned" cinema could lend prestige to its producers, by demonstrating a serious-minded concern for a wide range of social problems.

Appropriate handling involved integrating a politically controversial theme with the forms of entertainment preferred inside the cinema. Where the industry itself has understood this fusion in terms of "dramatic potentials" and "angles," the metaphor most regularly employed by criticism to describe the process has been one of sugaring the didactic political pill with the more pleasurable elements of genre and star performances, and above all by individualizing the issue depicted. In adapting *Dust Be My Destiny* (1939), Jerome Odlum's novel about vagrancy among young people in the Depression, Hal Wallis instructed his scriptwriters to take out all the "sociological references." The script outline declared itself to be "the story of two people – not a group. It is an individual problem – not a national one."[84]

By contrast to most of Hollywood's output, social problem movies represent their settings as dystopian rather than Utopian. In particular, community is almost invariably absent from them, replaced by the worst excesses of individualistic behavior in a war of each against all: "Do it to him before he does it to you," as Terry Molloy explains to Edie Doyle (Eva Marie Saint) in *On the Waterfront*. One of the distinctive generic features of social problem movies is a denial that the movie takes place in "America." When Father Barry (Karl Malden) tells the dockers that no other union in the country would stand for the conditions they work under, he is told "the waterfront's tougher, Father, like it ain't part of America." Characters make similar observations in *Bad Day at Black Rock* (1955) – "it just seems to me that there aren't many towns like this in America, but one town like it is enough" – and *Storm Warning* (1951), both movies dealing with a community's attempts to conceal a racist murder. *I Am a Fugitive from a Chain Gang* had all references to its setting in Georgia removed. A montage sequence in which James Allen (Paul Muni) travels across America looking for work includes a map marking his journey, but as he heads South it fades away, suggesting that he has now entered a space that cannot be found on an American map. When Hollywood was not romancing the South it frequently demonized it, casting it as America's geographical Other in movies as diverse as *The Long Hot Summer* (1957), *In the Heat of the Night* (1967), *Deliverance* (1972), and *Southern Comfort* (1981).[85]

Mississippi Burning, a detective movie dealing with the murder of three civil rights activists during the voter-registration campaigns that preceded the 1964 presidential elections, reinstated this vision of the South against the "good old boy" version of the New South portrayed in *Smokey and the Bandit* (1977) and its sequels. At first sight, Joe Breen's injunctions against Hollywood's raising the "racial angle" in *Fury* might seem light years away from the focus of *Mississippi Burning*. The politics of racism are central to the movie, not a background to more familiar generic elements. The movie is a fictionalized account of the events following the murders of civil rights activists James Chaney, Andrew Goodman, and Michael Schwerner, which had focused national attention on the role of the Ku Klux Klan in Southern state politics. In the publicity surrounding the movie's release its director, Alan Parker, suggested that he was drawn to *Mississippi Burning* by its "potential for social and political comment."[86] *Mississippi Burning* constructs the South as a backwoods Other to the more liberal America that its protagonists, FBI agents Ward (Willem Dafoe) and Anderson (Gene Hackman), are presumed to share with the audience. Mayor Tilman (Lee Ermey) tells Anderson, "the simple fact is . . . we've got two cultures down here, the white culture and the colored culture . . . the rest of America don't mean jack shit, you're in Mississippi now." The voices of racism therefore identify themselves as being un-American, while Ward expresses the movie's moral after the suicide of Mayor Tilman: "anyone is guilty who watches this happen and pretends it's not."

Mississippi Burning (1988): only in Hollywood could FBI agents Anderson (Gene Hackman) and Ward (Willem Dafoe) be the heroes of a detective story about racism.
Produced by Robert F. Colesberry, Frederick Zollo; distributed by Orion Pictures.

Parker's sense of the movie as a contribution to the struggle for civil rights indicates the extent to which Hollywood in the late 1980s, as in the late 1930s, faced as much pressure to display politicized images as to avoid them. Like its manufacture of other genres, Hollywood's production of social problem movies was cyclical, but this cycle has probably been more directly affected by external political conditions than any other, flourishing best in a liberal climate. Like the late 1950s, the late 1980s saw the emergence of such a climate in Hollywood, although its manifestations in more explicit political arenas were more delayed. If *Rambo: First Blood Part II* (1985) represented the apotheosis of what Andrew Britton called "the politics of Reaganite entertainment,"[87] its revision of the Vietnam war was answered within a year by *Platoon*'s account of Vietnam as a war in which Americans fought Americans, and both sides lost. By 1987, there were signs of an emergent liberal discourse reassessing the politics of the previous decade – *Wall Street*'s (1987) critique of Gordon Gecko's (Michael Douglas) philosophy of "greed is good," for instance.

In this context, *Mississippi Burning* can be seen as a liberal revision of the nostalgia for the time before Vietnam, visited by so many 1980s movies. Its commemoration of the civil rights campaign of the early 1960s and the "Great Society" liberal reform program undertaken during the Kennedy and Johnson presidencies provided an alternative to conservative idealizations of the 1950s suburban white middle-class family. The movie also declared the relevance of the civil rights campaign to its contemporary audience. Parker argued that the movie "is not intended to be a history lesson. . . . It's not about racism 24 years ago, it's about racism now, the racism that is everywhere and in all of us."[88] In its depiction of race relations *Mississippi Burning* has a firm sense of "what is right and what is wrong," and wears its conscience-liberalism on its sleeve. Its protagonists disagree only at the level of tactics, and these disagreements are framed within a political attitude that the audience is presumed to share. Some critics saw the movie's modification of historical fact as an attempt "to create a better story for a racially-mixed audience," and to construct the liberal consensus it claimed to address.

On its release, however, the movie proved as controversial as any of the earlier pictures mentioned in this chapter. It was condemned by several African-American civic leaders and denounced by *Time* magazine as "a cinematic lynching of the truth."[89] Negative criticism focused not only on its alleged inaccuracies of period detail and historical fact (a standard critique of the period picture as history, discussed in more detail in chapter 14) but also on its portrayal of African-Americans as passive objects of irrational white prejudice and violence. According to Robert Stam,

> it turns the historical enemy in the 1960s – the racist FBI which devoted most of its energies to harassing and sabotaging the civil rights movement – into the heroes, while turning the historical heroes – the thousands of blacks who marched, suffered, and died – into passive victim-observers waiting for white official "rescue."[90]

As more than one critic observed, a movie about racism that has no central African-American character has at its center an absence, "a deafening silence."[91]

The producers' response to this criticism indicated that Hollywood's strategies of denial have changed relatively little. Parker defended the movie by insisting on its good intentions, at the same time as he drew attention to the inevitable commercial constraints imposed on it:

> Our film cannot be the definitive film of the black Civil Rights struggle. Our heroes are still white. And in truth, the film would probably never have made if they weren't. This is a reflection of our society not the Film Industry. But with all of its possible flaws and shortcomings I hope our film can help to provoke thought and allow other films to be made because the struggle still continues.

In the movie's "Production Notes," Parker acknowledged the compromises necessary to construct it as a Hollywood product: it had to have attractive locations and omit scenes that slow the action; for legal reasons it could not name the murder victims. But he also argued that the movie's treatment of African-Americans as passive victims was historically accurate: "I did my homework on that and in Nashoba County in 1964 where the incident took place, there were no aggressive blacks."[92] This defense displays an opportunism that matches its good intentions: accused of historical inaccuracy, the movie defends itself as fiction; accused of failing to address contemporary requirements, it defends itself on grounds of historical accuracy. This position is caught exactly in the movie's final title: "This film was inspired by actual events which took place in the South during the 1960s. The characters, however, are fictitious and do not depict real people either living or dead."[93]

Even within the consensus it addresses, however, a movie's politics must be understood not only from its overt political statements, but also from the concessions it makes to its commercial obligations. Like *All the President's Men* (1976) and *The Best Man*, *Mississippi Burning* is constrained by the dramatic conventions within which it operates. These conventions ensure that the very form of the movie works to reinforce our expectation that solutions exist to the problems it presents. Its first obligation to its audience is to entertain them. Institutionalized racism is not in itself entertaining, any more than is the movie's message that it can be overcome. *Mississippi Burning* must find other ways of entertaining its audience, less through its story than through the way the story is revealed: action, spectacle, subplots, character relations, music, and cinematography provide the audience's entertainment. The movie's generic conventions place the political and moral questions it raises within the familiar, overlapping contexts of the detective story and the Western. Along with these generic elements, the structure of retrospect that orders the fiction offers the audience an escape from the traumatic issues raised by the movie into the relative safety of familiar conventions. Set not in 1989 but in 1964, the movie implies that the disorders represented have been ameliorated if not entirely overcome in the present. Nevertheless, Jessup County, Mississippi, exists within the "fundamentally just society" that Nick Roddick evoked in his account of *I Am a Fugitive from a Chain Gang*, or that Joseph Breen identified in *Fury's* depiction of Hollywood's version of lynching as a social problem unrelated to issues of race.[94] As in the two 1930s movies, very little of that larger, more just society actually finds representation in the movie, and our knowledge of subsequent events might lead us to less optimistic conclusions outside the cinema. As a narrative movie, however, *Mississippi Burning* holds out the promise of resolution and closure, and with it the expectation that the audience will leave the theater with an optimistic sense that good has once again triumphed over evil.

The detective story structure dramatizes the relationship between racism, authority, and social order, as Anderson and Ward's federal authority is brought into conflict with the local forces of law and order. In this context, Anderson and Ward operate less as embodiments of political principle than as agents of narrative closure. Our pleasure in the movie as entertainment assumes that they will solve the murders, convict the killers, and enable the plot to reach a point of resolution. Their political affiliations are subordinate to this formal responsibility to the entertainment audience. Somewhat less evidently, the movie evokes Western conventions: Anderson and Ward ride into a town on the edge of civilization at the beginning of the movie, establish order, and ride out at the end, with Anderson even bestowing on Mrs Pell (Frances McDormand) the Westerner's kiss to the woman he must leave behind. Echoes of the Western occur in individual scenes: Anderson greets the residents of Shiloh with a "Howdy," and two of his exchanges of violence with the Klan members take place in the barber's shop. In Western terms, Anderson is the self-confident, renegade outlaw hero to Ward's self-righteous, repressed official hero. When Ward warns Anderson, "Just don't lose sight of whose rights we're violating," their debate over the rule of law takes place in terms that Tom Doniphon (John Wayne) and Ransom Stoddard (James Stewart) would have recognized in *The Man Who Shot Liberty Valance* (1962).[95]

Like Stoddard, Ward eventually convinces himself that he has to embrace lawlessness in order to defeat the unregulated power of the movie's villains.[96]

Tension between the two men fuels the drama, which is repeatedly diverted from the process of investigation to consider their differing motives and strategies. They disagree about personal methods and about the political nature of their investigation. Anderson sees it as a simple missing-persons case, while Ward ("a Kennedy boy") regards their inquiries as an active intervention into the political life of the South, part of a positive drive toward changing attitudes and reforming the culture. They pursue their hunt for clues in different ways. Ward employs marine reservists to drag a swamp for the bodies, and drafts in hundreds of FBI agents in an outright display of federal power and official political will. Anderson, himself a Mississippian, makes leisurely inquiries based on his local knowledge, then explodes into a violence that disturbingly echoes the behavior of the racists he is hunting. The political dilemma for the audience is posed in terms of personal behavior. What should our position as audience members be? Are Anderson's tactics justified by the situation they face? Do these tactics reproduce racist attitudes? Are Ward's liberal protestations and commitment to "procedure" impediments to an effective defeat of the Ku Klux Klan? These questions are posed for the audience not as abstract political or ethical problems, but through the more generic issue of finding the evidence to solve the murder, while the political friction between the two investigators is staged as a temperamental discord.

As the movie drives toward its conclusion, Anderson and Ward find themselves agreeing more and more, learning from each other, and defending each other against threats from outsiders. But their cooperation is not between equals. The greater industrial status of one performer over another ensures that, despite Ward being Anderson's superior, Willem Dafoe concedes the investigative initiative to the bigger star, Gene Hackman. Anderson, not Ward, produces the hard evidence that convicts the Klan murderers and allows the movie to reach its resolution. After Mrs Pell is assaulted Ward agrees to "new rules – we nail them any way we can, even your way." From then on he moves to the sidelines of the action, and his principal function becomes the articulation of white guilt. Anderson solves the case by brute intimidation: one Klan member is subjected to a mock lynching, while Mayor Tilman is threatened with castration by a caricatured African-American man of violence (Badja Djola) specially imported by Anderson from Chicago. "As usual in Hollywood, vigilantism wins."[97] There is more than a little of the vigilante in Anderson, and the movie owes as much to what Robert Ray terms the "right cycles" of *Death Wish* (1974), *Dirty Harry* (1971), and even *The French Connection* (1971) as it does to earlier, more manifestly liberal depictions of the South, *In the Heat of the Night* and *The Chase* (1966).[98]

While *The Best Man* – made in the year in which *Mississippi Burning* is set – advocated the preservation of principles at all costs, the sacrifice of those principles in the accomplishment of political goals is here seen as acceptable. The movie's political ambivalence thus comes down, in the end, to the viewer's understanding of Anderson's motives, and therefore to her or his interpretation of the ambivalent qualities of Gene Hackman's central performance. This performance seems designed to raise questions about his character's sincerity, rather than to answer them. His relationship with Mrs Pell remains ambiguous: are his advances toward her a sign of romantic affection or is he simply using her to elicit the information that will help convict her husband? His political attitudes are little clearer. At the beginning of the movie, he sings a Klan song with as much relish as he later brings to telling Mayor Tilman that he likes baseball because "it's the only game where a black man can wave a stick at a white man without starting a riot." But he has no confessional scene, in which he unequivocally states his motives, either to Ward or to the audience. The closest he comes is when Ward asks him where all this hatred comes from. Anderson tells a story about his father, a poor white farmer, poisoning an African-American neighbor's mule simply to keep him in comparative poverty. When Ward asks, "Where does that leave you?," Anderson answers, "With an old man so filled with hate, he didn't realize that it was being poor that was killing him." Parker argued that the scene was present to offer an economic explanation of racism, that a "black underclass had always been there as a pathetic comforter to the poor whites – there was always someone worse off than they were."[99] But if the speech airs the movie's conscience-liberalism, it does not clarify Anderson's own attitude. Hackman's performance may be a tour de force in conveying the divided loyalties and ambiguity of Anderson's position, but what makes it "great acting" is also what contributes to the ambivalence surrounding Anderson's motivation, and that motivation is finally left to the audience to evaluate.

Hollywood still routinely insists that committed movies such as *Mississippi Burning* are about characters caught up in political events rather than politicized statements in their own right. What political charge they may possess is thus an expression of the audience's political convictions, rather than those of the producers. Such movies, in other words, still see themselves as reflecting what Irving Thalberg called popular "tastes and manners and views and morals."[100] The ambivalence centered on Hackman's performance affects other aspects of the movie's interplay between authenticity and commitment. The movie's use of documentary scenes and television-style interviews opens up a space for political commentary that is never directly engaged. Its most extravagant occasions of spectacle are the African-American churches, schools, and houses it burns at frequent intervals, with sufficient visual flair for the movie to win an Oscar for Best Cinematography.[101] Its ambivalence – its inability to resolve the issues it raises as readily as it can resolve its storyline – is evident in its final scenes. The optimistic graveside spirituals sung at the burial of the murdered African-American activist (Christopher White) are followed by a slow track across the cemetery to a desecrated tombstone, on which the only words legible are "1964, not forgotten." The image declares the continuing relevance of the movie's thematic concerns, which are still unresolved. But the morale-raising gospel music resumes over credits that last almost 10 minutes, so that as a commodity the movie ends on a point of elevation. Both by what it includes and by its exclusions, hesitations, and absences, the movie remains equivocal, not about the rights and wrongs of racism so much as about how a movie can make its discourse about racism entertaining, and about what an entertainment movie can say about racism.

Ideology

I shall define an ideology as a possible relation between individual consciousness and its social ground. It is a largely coherent system of images, ideas, values, feelings, and actions by which, and through which, persons experience their societies at various times.

Edward Branigan[102]

The more impossible and unthinkable wars become,
worldwide ones in particular,
the more evident worldwide entertainment will appear
as the "continuation of politics by other means."

Wim Wenders[103]

At several points in this book I have suggested that entertainment is Utopian. Movies offer their audiences a sense of escape or displacement from their immediate surroundings into a more nearly ideal environment. Paradoxically, however, the Utopian world is always partially familiar. Descriptions of Utopian space and social organization almost always involve a tension between elements we recognize from our present situation and elements that have been altered in some way. In the details of this tension, we can discover the central political concern of a particular Utopian point of view. Richard Dyer relates the compensations offered by entertainment to specific inadequacies in society: in response to scarcity, exhaustion, dreariness, manipulation, and fragmentation, the movies represent abundance, energy, intensity, transparency, and community. He points out, however, that although "we are talking about real needs created by real inadequacies . . . they are not the only needs and inadequacies of the society." Absent from the list of tensions or absences addressed by this Utopian sensibility is any mention of class, race, or patriarchy:

> The ideals of entertainment imply wants that capitalism itself promises to meet. Thus abundance becomes consumerism, energy and intensity personal freedom and individualism, and transparency freedom of speech. . . . The categories of the sensibility point to gaps or inadequacies in capitalism, but only those gaps or inadequacies that capitalism proposes itself to deal with. At our worst sense of it, entertainment provides alternatives *to* capitalism which will be met *by* capitalism.[104]

The politics of Hollywood, then, lie as much in the gaps in its representation as in what it chooses to represent. To examine Hollywood as a political institution we must look beyond the ways in which it engages with the politics of Washington. We must examine the terms of its inclusions and exclusions, and the frameworks within which those choices are made. We must look, that is, at ideology.

In fact, we have been discussing ideology in Hollywood already; for example, in the analysis of *Mr Smith Goes to Washington*. Most of the criticism in this book, indeed, could properly be considered ideological criticism, in that it is concerned with understanding how movies function as forms of social expression. Like a number of the other terms we have examined, "ideology" is imprinted with its own difficult history. Writing about "the exhaustion of political ideas" in 1960, American sociologist Daniel Bell declared that "the ideologies . . . which emerged from the nineteenth century . . . have lost their power to persuade" in the face of "such calamities as the Moscow Trials, the Nazi–Soviet pact, the concentration camps," and "such social changes as the modification of capitalism, [and] the rise of the Welfare State." Bell understood ideologies to be singular and distinct entities: the "Communist ideology," for instance. This account of ideology saw it as a dogmatic and inflexible system of beliefs, a dangerous secular form of political faith, adhered to by its followers independently of its empirical "truth."[105]

Bell's account of ideology is close to the most common, common-sensical meaning of the word, in which ideology involves thinking by rote, according to a prescribed mode of thought. It is the opposite of common sense, the antithesis of empirical thinking. In this usage, there is always a pejorative overtone to the word: it refers to a coherent and unified set of political beliefs mistakenly held by people other than ourselves. This common-sense usage of ideology also defines it as being explicitly political: ideology politicizes experiences such as entertainment which common sense tells us are not political at all. Thus while *they* have an ideology, which is explicitly political, *we* have a way of life, in which we recognize that some things are political, and some things are not, and in which we can distinguish, for instance, between propaganda and entertainment. This account of ideology suggests that it is something to be avoided or overthrown. In Bell's terms ideology ends when there is consensus, when "serious minds" agree, when "they" come to believe the same things "we" believe.

This version of ideology, in which the word is a term of abuse used by the victors, will be of little use to us. As critics of culture we must recognize that our consensus, our common sense, and our way of life are as ideological as anybody else's. As Catherine Belsey suggests, this is to understand that "ideology is not an optional extra, deliberately adopted by self-conscious individuals ('Conservative ideology,' for instance), but the very condition of our experience of the world, *un*conscious precisely in that it is unquestioned, taken for granted."[106] For any society, the maintenance of its people's belief in its political and economic system and in its cultural values is a matter of primary importance. Ideology performs this maintenance work, manufacturing and securing consent to the existing social formation. For the most part, this activity passes unnoticed, like the maintenance work of painting bridges. Because the bridge-painting is continuous, and because the painters always paint the bridge the same color, the results of their work are never particularly noticeable. In the same way, ideology works to make a society's institutions, customs, practices, beliefs, vocabulary – the existing social formation – appear normal, "natural," and immutable to us. This naturalizing function of ideology explains why it is so much easier to recognize other people's ideology than it is to identify our own. The farther away from the consensus you are, the easier it is to recognize ideology at work. It is not necessary to occupy an oppositional position to recognize ideology at work, but doing so makes the work of ideology in the everyday much more apparent. This is one reason why the most fully articulated theories of ideology have been developed by Marxist political theory in examining the tradition of western liberal democracy.

In this definition, ideology is not a separate entity, existing independently of culture or society. Rather, the terms "culture," "society," and "ideology" overlap each other. Ideology pervades culture; culture is both a site and an instrument of ideology. As a *system* of beliefs and practices, ideology has no material form, but it has material effects in the way that a society translates its beliefs into political or cultural practices. This is to understand ideology not as a specific *list* of beliefs or ideas, but as a *process* by which beliefs become conventions, norms, and standards, by which ideas and institutions become and continue to be seen as natural, normal, and conventional, to such an extent that they are not really seen at all. Like the conventional systems for representing space, time, and movement in Hollywood discussed in part III, ideology works by rendering complex structures transparent to viewers or users through familiarity. Ideology is not, therefore, simply a matter of conscious, intentional expression. Ideology is also attitudes, habits, feelings, and assumptions, and, as the French Marxist theorist Louis Althusser suggested, it is experienced less as ideas than as images and most of all as structures: structures of thought, structures of story-telling, structures of experience. In Althusser's terms, ideology is a matter of "the *lived* relation" between people and their world: "Ideology is *inscribed in* discourse in the sense that it is literally written or spoken *in it*; it is not a separate element which exists independently in some free-floating realm of 'ideas' and is subsequently embodied in words, but a way of thinking, speaking, experiencing."[107] It is, indeed, a way of life, but a way of life perceived and analyzed through a political consciousness. In this definition, entertainment, far from being completely outside ideology, becomes the ideal location for the process of ideology – the maintenance of consent – to take place.

Despite the fact that we are usually unconscious of it, our experience of ideology is always layered, operating at several levels at the same time. For example, *Casablanca* (1942, and discussed in detail in chapter 16) has an explicit ideological project: to persuade its audience that World War II required America's committed entry into world affairs. It is, however, also possible to identify a whole catalog of other ideological processes in the movie, in which existing cultural assumptions about race, ethnicity, gender roles, sexuality, the family, and heroism are expressed and enacted. For instance, we encounter monogamy not as an idea in the movie, but as a plot device. When Rick (Humphrey Bogart) fixes the roulette game so that Annina (Joy Page) does not have to risk losing her husband's trust, we attach the nobility of his gesture to his renunciation of Ilsa (Ingrid Bergman) and then more generally to his rediscovery of principle and the need for sacrifice. An ideology of gender roles and sexual behavior structures the story, and in doing so reinforces a social convention. As we have seen, although its producers would not have identified this plot element as ideological, the Production Code explicitly recognized its role in ensuring that Hollywood movies maintained cultural conventions.

This example may also indicate why it is often so difficult to pin down the effect of the work of ideology. Much of the sociological study of the media has been concerned with quantifying its effects, and it might have been possible in 1943 for the OWI to investigate how effective *Casablanca* was in its overt ideological project by surveying audience attitudes to American isolation before and after viewing the movie. A comparable question about the ideology of gender roles would be much more difficult to construct: "To what extent have you been dissuaded from committing adultery by watching *Casablanca*?" However preposterous this question sounds, most inquiries into the "effects" of violence in the media have asked questions of this type. Such simple questions, looking for single causes of single effects, fail completely to recognize the main work of ideology, which is not to change attitudes or behavior, but to confirm and reinforce them by reminding us of their familiarity.

Using the term "ideology" instead of "way of life" or "common sense" implies a critique of the social system under discussion, or at least a degree of critical distance from it. Louis Althusser has argued that ideology constantly addresses individuals with an ideal version of their way of life, leading them to "work by themselves" to "freely accept their subjection."[108] The maintenance activity of ideology is thus an act of perpetual partial deception, as Catherine Belsey argues:

> Ideology obscures the real conditions of existence by presenting partial truths. It is a set of omissions, gaps rather than lies, smoothing over contradictions, appearing to provide answers to questions which in reality it evades, and masquerading as coherence in the interests of the social relations generated by and necessary to the reproduction of the existing mode of production.[109]

Belsey points out, however, that ideology "is in no sense a set of deliberate distortions foisted upon a helpless working class by a corrupt and cynical bourgeoisie. If there are groups of sinister men in shirt-sleeves purveying illusions to the public these are not the real makers of ideology."[110] Ideology is not, in that sense, a conscious creation, and there is no position outside it from which it may be manipulated. "The study of ideology," suggests literary theorist Terry Eagleton, "is among other things an inquiry into the way in which people may come to invest in their own unhappiness. It is because being oppressed sometimes brings with it some slim bonuses that we are occasionally prepared to put up with it."[111] Richard Dyer's set of relations between the categories of the Utopian sensibility and the inadequacies of society presents an instance of the way in which people may come to invest in their own unhappiness: entertainment is one of Eagleton's "slim bonuses." Ideological analysis of this entertainment therefore seeks to bring to consciousness the concealed politics of its operation.

Representations of the political in *Mr Smith Goes to Washington* or *The Best Man* conform very closely to Althusser's definition of ideology as "images," "concepts," and "structures": the images of James Stewart and Henry Fonda invoke the concepts of American political fundamentalism that the movies endorse. The dominant critical interpretation of *Mr Smith* has concentrated on what Frank Nugent called a "celebration of the spirit, rather than the form, of American government"; in other words, not on those representations of political procedure to which the senators objected, but on the ideology of the movie's images, the way that they might be examined as "an index to the popular mind," and the way that they represented Joe Breen's "rich and glorious heritage . . . which comes when you have a government 'of the people, by the people, and for the people.'" From this perspective, the main ideological burden, both in terms of the movie and in supporting the wider institution of Hollywood as star system, is carried by the image of Stewart, rather than by any specific discourse on corruption within the American political machine.[112]

Ideological analysis argues that Hollywood movies represent the political just as emphatically when they appear to be harmless and apolitical entertainment. An analysis of Hollywood's politics must consider their mode of representation, treating the movies themselves as instances of ideology rather than as imitations or simulations of the political from somewhere outside politics. This line of argument views the consumption of movies itself as a significant ideological activity, since the movies exemplify what Althusser calls the "lived relations" between the viewer and his or her world. We can expect to find ideology, then, not so much in Hollywood's themes as in its processes, in the ways in which images and stories are produced and consumed. To find the politics of the cinema we must examine the interaction between the movie and the viewer, in the space between the audience and the screen.

Most ideological analysis of Hollywood, and indeed most academic film criticism (including that practiced in this book), is written from a political position significantly to the left of the consensus Hollywood conventionally addresses. One of the anxieties frequently manifested by that criticism is that its attention to the forces of political repression, such as Hollywood, may become complicit with those forces. Strategies of subversive reading offer a way to resolve these anxieties positively, as a critical "rewriting" of the text "against its grain." It is hardly surprising that the movies that have fared worst from such analysis have been those that have dealt with explicit political subject matter within the conventions of Hollywood, where their politics are too close to the surface to need much decipherment. Where the repressed subtext of an overtly reactionary movie may turn out to be progressive, the repressed subtext of Hollywood's well-intentioned conscience-liberalism almost invariably turns out to be reactionary. My own accounts of *The Best Man* and *The Candidate* exhibit this tendency, and *Mississippi Burning* offers plenty of fissures for a critical deconstruction of its liberal ideological presumptions. The movie seems, however, to acknowledge this property in the knowingness of its narration, which underlines its status as a site of conflicting logics and discourses. Rather than requiring us to "work against the grain" of the text and take it by surprise in our criticism, *Mississippi Burning* almost invites its audience to question its own politics. This knowingness, which is most visible in the wry humor of Hackman's performance, is a strategy for self-preservation, affording the movie some distance from the controversy it provokes. As a comedy, *Dave* can carry this strategy of self-referentiality and knowingness even further, exposing itself as a political fiction, declaring in its closing credits that any reference to actual persons or buildings is coincidental and unintended – despite most of the movie being set in the White House and the credits listing a string of roles as having been played by "Himself" and "Herself." *Dave* carries the clear implication that the only place in which an ordinary person could become the president is in a fictional movie, just as *Mississippi Burning* carries the implication that the only place the FBI can become the heroes of the civil rights struggle is in a fictional movie.

From a viewpoint outside the consensus that *Mississippi Burning* addresses, it can hardly appear as anything other than a white liberal equivocation. Without denying the Hollywood opportunism evident in Parker's defense of the movie, it is nevertheless important to acknowledge that no movie could adequately respond to criticism from outside the ideological consensus it addresses. From such a position, the politics of any movie will always appear imperfect. For example, the critical enthusiasm that initially greeted the commercial success of black director Spike Lee's "guerrilla filmmaking"[113] has been tempered by suggestions that *Do the Right Thing* and *Jungle Fever* (1991) fail, as Hollywood movies do, to analyze the causes of the racism they depict.[114] Mark Reid criticizes Spike Lee's use of black idioms in *Do the Right Thing* for seducing its audience into "accepting a simulated form of blackness" as an adequate "filmic representation of urban black 'reality.'" According to Reid's analysis, the attention focused on Lee has meant that "the ongoing work of independent black filmmakers and video artists is ignored, and the variety of black voices is smothered by the masculinist and often homophobic black images that reign in major studio-produced black films." In a persuasive rebuttal of such arguments, Malcolm Turvey points out that

> an argument that insists that a black film-maker *should* adequately represent "the oppressed" or "the underclass," that he *should* include "the woman's point of view," that he *should* always and everywhere address homophobia . . . produces an image or fantasy of black film-makers that severely limits and above all controls *who* may be a "black film-maker" and what black film-makers may produce . . . the demand that [Lee] and others like him be the perfect, radical *real* black film-maker is an impossible and dangerous one.

Turvey's comments address what he calls "the burden of desire" placed not only on *Malcolm X* (1993, and also directed by Lee), but on any movie or producer identified as articulating a political position against the expectations of Hollywood entertainment cinema.[115]

At several points in this discussion, I have returned the often hermetically sealed frame of ideological analysis to the brutishly commercial context of Hollywood's industrial assumptions. Hollywood's politics are so equivocal because Hollywood's commercial interests are best satisfied by maximizing its audiences and allowing for the unpredictable satisfactions of specific audience members. In that sense any movie is an infinitely open text, a showcase of endless incidental pleasures encouraging, rather than repressing, consumer choice. The political process in the cinema is finally constructed by the audience's engagement, as consumers, with movie texts designed to accommodate their consumers' desires for meaning and likely to allow those meanings to be discovered wherever viewers (including critics) choose to look.

Summary

- Despite its promise of "escape" from the everyday world, Hollywood remains a social institution, and its movies describe recognizable social situations in their plots and themes. Hollywood's engagement with "the other America out there in reality" is most often indirect; issues of class, nationality, and sexuality are more likely to be embodied in characters and action than to be expressed as themes.

- Although the industry's representatives have always denied that Hollywood is a political entity, the industry has often constituted an object of ideological anxiety, both at home and abroad. This has been expressed in censorship, quota legislation and other legislative controls, and complaints about the Americanization of other national cultures.

- Debates over the censorship of the movies, like those over the regulation of other forms of popular culture, were actually debates over the exercise of social control. Although they focused on the content of the entertainment form, their real concern was with its effects on consumers. This was most commonly expressed in fears about the influence of entertainment on children and adolescents, but these apprehensions also concealed ethnic- and class-based anxieties about the effects on social behavior that might result from the democratic mixing of the audience.

- A 1915 Supreme Court ruling which denied the cinema First Amendment protection encouraged the industry to avoid political controversy in its products, but this position also made commercial sense, as it protected the industry from the disapprobation of politically influential sections of the community. Hollywood's cautious political stance was institutionalized by regulatory mechanisms introduced by its trade association (the MPPDA).

- Despite Hollywood's refusal to engage in serious political discourse, since World War II it has tended to subscribe to "conscience-liberalism," a broad commitment to racial and social equality unattached to any specific political program. This is not to suggest that all Hollywood movies were liberal or free from racism, but rather to argue that when Hollywood movies overtly asserted a political position they declared to be political, that position belonged to the liberal center.

- Hollywood's acquiescence in the anti-Communist witchhunts of the 1950s reflected the industry's timidity as well as its consistent desire to avoid political controversy, but it failed to destroy Hollywood's liberal consensus.

- Postwar Hollywood's attitude to politics has continued to combine a pragmatic concern for political influence to secure its business interests with a desire not to damage the profitability of its product with undue controversy. Since 1960, however, its representation of politics has reinforced the disillusionment of its audiences with the political process, and the incidence of "social problem" movies has increased.

- *Mississippi Burning* is an example of Hollywood's approach to a contemporary political and social problem. An analysis of the movie reveals the ways in which its "conscience-liberal" message is consistently rendered subservient to the movie's essential entertainment purpose, which is expressed less through the story (concerning institutionalized racism) than through action, spectacle, sub-plots, character relations, music, and cinematography.

- To examine Hollywood as a political institution we must look beyond the ways in which it engages with the politics of Washington to consider its ideology: the terms of its validations and condemnations, its inclusions and exclusions, its enthusiasms and its silences. Ideological analysis of entertainment seeks to bring to consciousness the power relations and politics implicit in its representations.

- Ideology pervades culture; culture is both a site and an instrument of ideology. Far from being completely outside ideology, entertainment is an ideal location for the process of ideology – the maintenance of consent to the existing social formation – to take place.

- Hollywood's politics are equivocal because Hollywood's commercial interests are best satisfied by maximizing its audiences and allowing for the satisfactions of as many specific audience members as possible.

Further Reading

Hollywood and politics

On Hollywood and politics in the 1930s, see Giuliana Muscio, *Hollywood's New Deal* (Philadelphia: Temple University Press, 1997), and Saverio Giovacchini, *Hollywood Modernism: Film and Politics in the Age of the New Deal* (Philadelphia: Temple University Press, 2001).

The politics of Hollywood's craft unions are analyzed in Nancy Lynn Schwartz, *The Hollywood Writers' Wars* (New York: Knopf, 1982); David F. Prindle, *The Politics of Glamour: Ideology and Democracy in the Screen Actors Guild* (Madison: University of Wisconsin Press, 1988); and Stephen Vaughn, *Ronald Reagan in Hollywood: Movies and Politics* (Cambridge: Cambridge University Press, 1994).

Greg M. Smith, "Blocking *Blockade*: Partisan Protest, Popular Debate, and Encapsulated Texts," *Cinema Journal* 36:1 (Fall 1996), pp. 18–38, describes the controversy surrounding a Hollywood movie about the Spanish Civil War in 1938. The politics of Hollywood's role in World War II is described in Clayton R. Koppes and Gregory D.

Black, *Hollywood Goes to War: How Politics, Profits and Propaganda Shaped World War II Movies* (New York: Macmillan, 1987).

On the traumas of the investigation of the industry by the House Committee on Un-American Activities, see Larry Ceplair and Steven Englund, *The Inquisition in Hollywood: Politics in the Film Community, 1930–1960* (Berkeley, CA: University of California Press, 1983), and Victor S. Navasky, *Naming Names* (New York: Viking Press, 1980).

For more recent interactions between Hollywood and politics, see Ronald Brownstein, *The Power and the Glitter: The Hollywood–Washington Connection* (New York: Pantheon, 1990). For a conservative view of Hollywood as a left-wing conspiracy, see Michael Medved, *Hollywood vs. America: Popular Culture and the War on Traditional Values* (New York: HarperCollins, 1992). Medved's argument is a conspiracy theory: that Hollywood is run by an elite coterie of cynical sophisticates, whose perverse values are at odds with those of "Middle America." Medved's book has been influential on many subsequent conservative attacks on Hollywood.

Political interpretations of movies

Brian Neve, *Film and Politics in America: A Social Tradition* (London: Routledge, 1992), and Terry Christensen, *Reel Politics: American Political Movies from Birth of a Nation to Platoon* (New York: Blackwell, 1987), provide overviews of Hollywood's political moviemaking.

Richard Maltby, *Harmless Entertainment: Hollywood and the Ideology of Consensus* (Metuchen, NJ: Scarecrow, 1983), argues for the dominance of the liberal perspective in Hollywood's postwar output. Peter Biskind, *Seeing is Believing: How Hollywood Taught Us to Stop Worrying and Love the Fifties* (London: Pluto Press, 1983), provides an extended analysis of the consensus of corporate-liberal pluralism in Hollywood's movies of the 1950s, and its preoccupation with therapy and social control.

Alan Nadel, *Flatlining on the Field of Dreams: Cultural Narratives in the Films of President Reagan's America* (New Brunswick, NJ: Rutgers University Press, 1997), and William J. Palmer, *The Films of the Eighties: A Social History* (Carbondale: Southern Illinois University Press, 1993), provide detailed analyses of some of the key movies of "President Reagan's America."

On *Mr Smith Goes to Washington*, see Charles Wolfe, "*Mr Smith Goes to Washington*: Democratic Forums and Representational Forms," in *Close Viewings: An Anthology of New Film Criticism*, ed. Peter Lehman (Tallahassee: Florida State University Press, 1990), and Eric Smoodin, "'Compulsory' Viewing for Every Citizen: *Mr. Smith* and the Rhetoric of Reception," *Cinema Journal*, 35:2 (Winter 1999), pp. 3–23.

On *Wag the Dog*, see James Castonguay, "Hollywood Goes to Washington: Scandal, Politics, and Contemporary Media Culture," in *Headline Hollywood: A Century of Film Scandal*, eds Adrienne L. McClean and David A. Cook (New Brunswick, NJ: Rutgers University Press, 2001). Two articles on the urban and ethnic politics of *Falling Down*

are Jude Davies, "Gender, Ethnicity and Cultural Crisis in *Falling Down* and *Groundhog Day*," *Screen* 36:3 (Autumn 1995), pp. 214–32, and John Gabriel, "What Do You Do when Minority Means You? *Falling Down* and the Construction of 'Whiteness,'" *Screen* 37:2 (Summer 1996), pp. 129–52.

Hollywood, race, and ethnicity

On the reception of *Birth of a Nation*, see the documents in *Focus on The Birth of a Nation*, ed. Fred Silva (Englewood Cliffs, NJ: Prentice-Hall, 1971), and in *The Birth of a Nation*, ed. Robert Lang (New Brunswick, NJ: Rutgers University Press, 1994), and Michael Rogin, *Ronald Reagan, the Movie and Other Episodes in Political Demonology* (Berkeley, CA: University of California Press, 1987).

Two books by Thomas Cripps, *Slow Fade to Black: The Negro in American Film, 1900–1942* (New York: Oxford University Press, 1977), and *Making Movies Black: The Hollywood Message Movie from World War II to the Civil Rights Era* (New York: Oxford University Press, 1993), provide excellent accounts of Hollywood's relationship to and representation of African-Americans. The essays in two books edited by Daniel Bernardi, *The Birth of Whiteness: Race and the Emergence of US Cinema* (New Brunswick, NJ: Rutgers University Press, 1996), and *Classic Hollywood, Classic Whiteness* (Minneapolis: University of Minnesota Press, 2001), and the essays in *Unspeakable Images: Ethnicity and the American Cinema*, ed. Lester D. Friedman (Urbana: University of Illinois Press, 1991), provide a range of approaches to the analysis of Hollywood's representations of ethnicity. On the representation of Native Americans, see Peter C. Rollins and John E. O'Connor, eds, *Hollywood's Indian: The Portrayal of the Native American in Film* (Lexington: University Press of Kentucky, 1998).

PART III
CONVENTIONS

CHAPTER TEN
Space 1

*[handwritten: mise-en-scène!
the most meaningful
PRODUCTION DESIGN ♥]*

The cinema exists in the space between the audience and the screen.
Jean-Luc Godard
In a place like Stoningham you can't ignore convention.
Cary Scott (Jane Wyman) in *All That Heaven Allows* (1955)

In the first two parts of this book we have considered some of the ways in which the economic organization of the motion picture industry determines the aesthetic conventions of the movies it produces. It is now time to consider the more formal properties of Hollywood's commercial aesthetic. The flat image on the theater screen represents a three-dimensional space, which the audience can enter imaginatively, unimpeded by the two-dimensionality of the screen. The space that Hollywood provides for its characters and audiences is, however, highly conventionalized, and this chapter and the next examine the conventions by which Hollywood space is constructed, while the following chapters in this part explore conventions of performance, time, and narrative. Just as generic convention requires the cooperative participation of the viewer, so Hollywood's spatial representations can only transform images into meaningful components of a spectacle or a story if audiences have the necessary experience to enter into the expected conventional relationship with the fiction. Although the specifics of these conventions have changed through history, their underlying goals have remained more or less consistent: "what we look *at* is guided by our assumptions and expectations about what to look *for*."[1] For the most part, contemporary Hollywood

[handwritten right margin: through meaning → there is psychology behind the space]

[handwritten: (frame)]

[handwritten bottom: → it depends on the viewer what they interpret from what's on the screen]

movies still seek to direct us toward content – story and star performance – to the same extent as Hollywood movies in the 1920s did, and despite a number of superficial differences, they do so according to a very similar set of principles.

The Best View

Watching the movie from a comfortable seat in a darkened auditorium, we are gradually robbed of the sensory coordinates that we use to locate ourselves in the world outside the theater. The movie theater constructs us as spectators, heightening our sense of vision and focusing our attention; in ideal viewing conditions our only sense that we ourselves occupy space comes from watching the screen. Once the movie starts, it positions us physically and imaginatively as invisible spectators of the scenes we are shown. We are present to witness what happens, but unless one of the characters addresses the camera directly, we remain absent as far as they are concerned. Our usual relation to the characters is that of a participant observer, often literally looking over their shoulders, included within the pictorial space projected on the screen but not part of it, involved with the action but not impeding it, missing nothing. Hollywood's representation of space is usually organized to secure our attention to what is going on in that space. In return, it offers us the chance to oversee and overhear the action from a succession of ideal viewpoints.

Hollywood space rewards us for looking at it by constantly addressing and satisfying our expectations in looking. We can take pleasure in looking simply because, in the benevolent space of a Hollywood movie, we repeatedly see what we want to look at. A few months after Disneyland opened, the head gardener asked Walt Disney's permission to fence off one of the flower beds, because visitors were walking on it to take photographs of the fairy castle. Instead, Disney ordered him to build a path with a sign saying, "This way for the best view of the castle." Hollywood's space is Utopian: in giving us the best view, it provides us with a pleasurable experience quite distinct from our more fragmented and less complete view of the world outside the movie. Hollywood's system of spatial construction, usually called the **continuity system**, constructs the space in which its action unfolds as a smooth and continuous flow across shots. Within this system the camera remains relatively unobtrusive, seldom drawing attention to its mediating presence. Few shots are held long enough for the audience to take conscious notice of the camera's position in the screen space, and each shot is presented as if "triggered" by the events unfolding in the fiction, as the camera reframes to accommodate figure movement, for instance.

The continuity system also discourages filmmakers from juxtaposing shots that will jar with each other or draw the viewer's attention to the cut. The graphic balancing of each shot with the one before and the one after makes it easier for the audience to understand the camera (or more exactly the movie's image stream) as an invisible presence in the screen space. Even at relatively conspicuous moments, when the camera draws the audience's attention to the microphone hidden in the flower vase by tracking in on it, we view the camera's movement and its act of looking as transparent. We look *through* the camera, and rather than pay attention to the camera's moving viewpoint, we look for the significant action or detail that it reveals. The **transparency** of the camera's look is often understood as contributing substantially to the particular kind of realism that Hollywood offers. This chapter suggests a slightly different emphasis and concentrates on the way that the continuity system provides a **safe space** for the development of a story, for the pleasure of spectacle, and most importantly for the secure placement of the audience in relation to the fictional world represented in the movie. Our sense of security within the continuity system is indicated by how little viewers normally notice editing, because cuts are placed where they will be as unobtrusive and as informative as possible. Because we expect the movie to explain itself to us, we assume that two juxtaposed shots show us a connected space, and each unemphatic cut confirms our ability to move freely around the space of a scene in search of the ideal viewpoint. The rules that organize that space and make it as transparently comprehensible as possible also make it a safe place for the audience to be.

Making the Picture Speak: Representation and Expression

Midway through *Singin' in the Rain* (1952), Gene Kelly makes a piece of Hollywood space. The plot has reached the point where he must tell Debbie Reynolds that he loves her but he is, as he says, "such a ham" that he chooses to dramatize his desire in a song-and-dance routine. Playing a Hollywood star, Kelly can only declare his love by singing "You Are My Lucky Star" in the proper setting. He ushers Reynolds onto an empty studio stage and literally constructs the romantic space he needs with the technological resources he finds there: lighting effects, a step ladder, a wind machine. With the aid of "five hundred thousand kilowatts of stardust," the audience comes not only to witness but also to share the emotional intensity of the relationship between the two of them.

The scene is a particularly revealing example of a process in which Hollywood constantly engages: alternating the viewer's relationship to the fiction between one based on watching and one based on imaginative or emotional participation. Often this alternation is achieved by transporting the audience from one kind of space into another. We move from a space that we understand as representing the actual space in which the action of a scene takes place, to a space that expresses something about what is happening or being said within it, and back again. Part of what the audience does while watching a movie is to recognize the movie's narration as a process of continual displacement between these two categories of represented and expressive cinematic space.

Represented space is the area that exists in front of the camera lens and is recorded by it. It is the recognizable space in which actors stand, in which props are placed, and in which things happen. Unlike the writer's pen, the camera cannot simply conjure objects into existence. Whatever the camera records has to exist in material form; that existence involves its occupation of represented space. Even

313

everything has purpose, even the smallest things, but they help tell a story

imaginary creatures like the Wookies and robots of *Star Wars* (1977) had to be realized – constructed, costumed, and made to move in front of the camera – rather than simply being described as their literary equivalents might be. As special effects work has come to make increasing use of computer-generated images, the need to construct cinematic illusions physically has diminished: Jar Jar Binks in *Star Wars: Episode 1 – The Phantom Menace* (1999) was a completely computer-generated character. Nevertheless, he had to be positioned in represented space by other characters' looks and actions, in order to construct the illusion of his existence in the same space as them.

At the beginning of the "You Are My Lucky Star" sequence in *Singin' in the Rain*, Kelly and Reynolds occupy represented space in a very obvious sense: we see them walking through the studio lot and into the sound stage, and we recognize these spaces as having a literal or material existence, which anyone could occupy. As the sequence proceeds, however, Kelly gradually transforms this represented space into a more **expressive** one, endowed with meaning beyond the literal. We move from a space that signifies its own depth and continuity to a space that signifies the direct experience of "being in love." The empty sound stage has been transformed into a site for romance, and in this expressive space the intimacies of the courtship can safely be represented as a bravura display of song, dance, and special effects. In accepting this suspension of literal representation, we also accept the different texture and composition of space during the sequence. As soon as Kelly finishes constructing his space, he can put what he wants to say into words. In the glow of the studio lights, he declares, "You sure look lovely in the moonlight, Kathy," and in the shot that follows, she does. When we see him draw in his breath, hear the musical accompaniment pause slightly, and spot the camera craning down onto him, we recognize the cue for a song. For the rest of the sequence, the screen offers the couple a space in which to dance. As they dance, the camera dances with them, demonstrating its acquiescence in Kelly's expressive world. The couple's ability to fill space harmoniously indicates that their courtship is complete, and the sequence as a whole illustrates how the audience of Hollywood cinema can be persuaded to abandon its secure perspective on a represented space in order to build up an understanding of character, predict future movement in the storyline, or allow an expressive action to take place.

Although the disruption of represented space by a musical number is perhaps an extreme example, the audience's perception shifts between represented and expressive space repeatedly in even the most run-of-the-mill movies. Represented space is three-dimensional; expressive space often combines the sculptural three-dimensionality of the space in the image with the graphic two-dimensionality of the image itself. In a scene from *Double Indemnity* (1944), one shot positions Phyllis Dietrichson (Barbara Stanwyck) graphically between her lover (Fred MacMurray) and her husband (Tom Powers), whom they are plotting to kill. In the represented space she is sitting on the other side of the room, but the composition places her in an expressively more significant relation to the action. Her position creates a tension in the scene. Will the husband detect their plot against him? In other words, will he recognize the significance of the composition of which he is part? Significantly, the play between graphic composition and three-

314

Don Lockwood (Gene Kelly) constructs expressive space out of an empty sound stage in *Singin' in the Rain* (1952).

Produced by Arthur Freed; distributed by MGM.

Phyllis Dietrichson (Barbara Stanwyck) graphically positioned between lover and husband in *Double Indemnity* (1944).

Produced by Joseph Sistrom; distributed by Paramount Pictures.

In this image from *Imitation of Life* (1959), the audience knows that Sarah Jane (Susan Kohner) is embarking on an impossible relationship, because she is graphically separated from the man by the screen of the louvre door. Unaware of her place in the composition, Sarah Jane does not yet know the affair is doomed.

Produced by Ross Hunter; distributed by Universal-International Pictures.

The dark foreground in this still from *All That Heaven Allows* (1955) suggests that Cary Scott (Jane Wyman) will not easily escape from the trap of domestic respectability her children (William Reynolds and Gloria Talbot) want to keep her in. Later, Cary and her son Ned will find themselves separated by the screen behind Cary's left shoulder.

Produced by Ross Hunter; distributed by Universal-International Pictures.

dimensional space is available only to the audience, not to the characters, who cannot see the composition in which they are placed. Likewise, in the image from *Imitation of Life* (1959), the position from which the viewer looks is one of privileged knowledge: the two figures remain unaware that they are separated by the louvre door that splits the screen. In *All That Heaven Allows* (1955), there is a heavily ironic use of the graphic properties of expressive space in one confrontation between Cary (Jane Wyman) and her son Ned (William Reynolds) over her relationship with Ron (Rock Hudson). Ned has threatened to leave home unless Cary gives Ron up. About to leave the house, he is positioned in the frame so that a fire-screen divides him off from Cary and the camera. From the camera's viewpoint, when Ned declares, "Mother, we can't let this come between us," the screen has already separated them irreparably. Standing where they are, of course, neither Ned nor Cary can see the irony in their expressive occupation of space; the knowledge provided by expressive space is only available to the audience.

One distinction between the three-dimensional scene and the two-dimensional image is that the image is **framed**. The composition of an image takes place in relation first of all to its borders and its frame, something you can verify every time you put a still camera to your eye and then adjust your position to make a better composition. Many of the early aesthetic debates about the cinema posed the question of two- or three-dimensionality in terms of whether the cinema frame should be seen as a window opening onto a world which extended into the offscreen space beyond the limits of the frame, or as a border, much like that of a painting, in which composition was a crucial determinant of meaning.[2] In practice, Hollywood cinema uses the frame in both ways, encouraging us to accept a sense of the continuity of offscreen space, while simultaneously focusing our attention on specific points in the space actually represented onscreen. Because we presume that we are looking at the best view of the action, we also assume that the represented space we view is charged with particular significance because of its framing. One consequence of this is that by comparison to actual social space outside the movies, the composed space within the frame is condensed: characters are positioned in relation to each other according to the requirements of the composition, not according to the social conventions that might apply to the situation they are in. Usually, this means that the frame places them much closer together than they would be in "real life."

Hollywood's rules of composition for the single shot are borrowed from the conventions of painting and photography. One of many geometrical principles of composition observed in western art since before the Renaissance, for example, suggests that compositions will be balanced if the main objects of attention are positioned on the lines that observe the principle of the Golden Section or Golden Mean.

The idea of frontality is also derived from Renaissance painting, and indirectly from Greek and Roman theater. It assumes that characters will be grouped according to their compositional relation to the camera rather than their spatial relation to each other; figures tend to stand in lines or semi-circles, facing the camera rather than each other. David Bordwell has argued that Classical Hollywood cinema also uses:

Box 10.1   The Golden Section

The Golden Section is a mathematical principle of composition and architectural construction used since the time of the ancient Egyptians. It divides a line into sections, so that the ratio of the large piece to the whole line is the same (1.618:1) as the ratio of the small piece to the large piece. Compositions that position their main objects of attention on these lines look balanced.

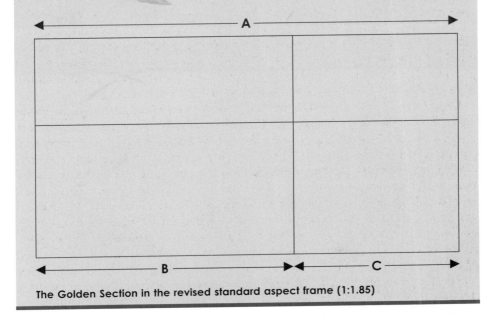

The Golden Section in the revised standard aspect frame (1:1.85)

a privileged zone of screen space resembling a T: the upper one-third and central vertical third of the screen constitute the "center" of the shot. This center determines the composition of long shots, medium shots and close-ups, as well as the grouping of figures. . . . Classical filmmaking thus considers edge-framing taboo; frontally positioned figures or objects, however unimportant, are seldom sliced off by either vertical edge.[3]

The composition of an individual shot in a Hollywood movie is never as intricate as that of a Renaissance painting, in part because the composition of any one shot must be considered in combination with the other shots in the sequence, and in part because the composition of the moving image is itself dynamic. Frequently, a movie will make use of this by beginning a shot with an unbalanced composition that demands an action to fill the empty field. In the saloon scene from *My Darling Clementine* (1946), our gaze is drawn to the vacant space in the foreground by the diagonal line of the bar counter. We wait for the Clanton gang to walk into the frame. Composition anticipates the movie's action and creates audience expectation.

Wyatt Earp (Henry Fonda) and Sam (J. Farrell McDonald) wait for the empty space at the bar to be filled by the Clanton gang in *My Darling Clementine* (1946).
Producer: Samuel G. Engel; distributed by Twentieth Century-Fox.

The composition of a shot often establishes meaningful tensions and anticipations within the frame, encouraging the viewer to respond to the representation of space. This response is, however, seldom consciously articulated. Instead, the audience's recognition of compositional stress is normally displaced into an insight about a character or the plot situation. A self-conscious disruption of the norms of composition can produce a space expressive of discomfort, as in the image here from *Shampoo* (1975). The awkward composition and uncomfortable postures in which the characters are caught express the unstable relationship between them. Their inability to fill the frame comfortably embodies their lack of equilibrium; their emotional separation from each other is made visible in the composition by the vertical lines between them. The image from *Written on the Wind* (1956) operates according to similar principles. Throughout the movie, Kyle Hadley (Robert Stack) is in the way of other characters, his antisocial behavior making him a disconcerting and unwelcome liability to them. As an expression of this, he is constantly caught in uncomfortable compositions in which he either intrudes on the arrangement of other characters or is rendered spatially insecure by standing in awkward places – with a picture behind his head, or in front of a window, through which he seems likely to fall.

In these examples, the framing of the composition produces meanings separate from those located in either dialog or action. Characters in Hollywood movies have a pressing need to establish themselves spatially, to dominate the composition or to keep a secure hold on their place in it, in order to maintain their narrative centrality. Throughout *Shampoo*, George Rounby's (Warren Beatty) failure to make choices is expressed in spatial terms through his inability to move purposefully in any given direction long enough to establish a course of action. Dialog underlines the many images of George's restless but ineffectual motion: his girlfriend Jill (Goldie Hawn) tells him, "You never stop moving. You never go anywhere." Spatial indecision usually incurs a narrative penalty in Hollywood

George Rounby (Warren Beatty) argues with his girlfriend Jill (Goldie Hawn) in *Shampoo* (1975). The instability of their relationship is expressed in the awkward composition of the shot.

Produced by Warren Beatty; distributed by Columbia Pictures.

The spatially insecure Kyle Hadley (Robert Stack) in *Written on the Wind* (1956).

Produced by Albert Zugsmith; distributed by Universal-International Pictures.

movies. George is finally abandoned in a featureless landscape after the last of his several lovers has left him for another man.

The Optics of Expressive Space

In chapter 8, I argued that Hollywood's application of technology works to standardize our experience of "going to the movies" in much the same way as generic conventions do. The part of our movie experience in which this is perhaps most true, but at the same time least noticeable, is in our perception of space and perspective relations within a movie's image stream. Hollywood's use of camera lenses makes going to the cinema a predictable optical experience, and plays a key role in controlling our perception of movie fictions and their meanings.

The human eye is a far more complex optical instrument than a camera lens, and in a purely technical sense André Bazin's ideal goal of a "total" cinema capable of identically reproducing the perceived and sensed world is not within the capacity of optical technology. Our stereoscopic vision, the result of the brain's ability to combine the two distinct images from each of our eyes into a single picture, allows us to see in perspective and to judge the shape, size, and distance of an object from the way it is located in the space around us. Flat surfaces such as cinema screens or painting canvases cannot reproduce stereoscopic images: superimposing two images taken from different points on top of each other produces only a blur. One of the enduring legacies of Renaissance painting was the establishment of a perspective system that imitated the effect of stereoscopic vision through a series of "depth cues." Before the Renaissance, European artists commonly represented the size of people and objects not according to how far away they were supposed to be from the painter at the time of painting the picture, but according to their relative importance. More consequential personages were literally represented as being of greater stature. Renaissance painting, however, perfected a system of representation that replicated the perspective relations between objects when viewed from a single point, as if looking at a landscape through a window. This system is known as **monocular perspective**: the perspective produced when viewing the world through a single lens. Seventeenth-century Dutch painters such as Johannes Vermeer painted with the aid of a camera obscura, a box with a lens in one side that projected an image in monocular perspective. This mode of representing the world dominated the central tradition of western European art from the Renaissance until the early twentieth century.

Although monocular perspective is only a convention of representation (Japanese painting, for example, employs a principle of multiple perspectives, in which different objects in a single painting are seen from different viewpoints), the nineteenth-century inventors of photography worked within its optical tradition. A camera is simply a camera obscura with a film or plate on which the image is permanently recorded. It was in large part the ease and efficiency with which cameras could represent views in monocular perspective that led to expectations of its realist aesthetic, since photography's mechanical reproduction was far more densely detailed than could be achieved by drawing or painting. "From today," declared French painter Paul Delaroche in 1839, after the first public demonstration of the Daguerreotype, "painting is dead," and photography is often indirectly credited with encouraging the Cubists' experimentations with styles of painting that rejected monocular perspective in the early twentieth century. Photography fixed the conventions of monocular perspective as a set of optical principles and mathematical formulae for the design of camera lenses. Early cinema lenses relied on the optical systems devised for still photography, reproducing depth relationships between objects according to the conventions of monocular perspective. These conventions have become so firmly fixed by the development of photographic technology that their conventional nature is almost always invisible to us. We expect images to conform to the perspective relations we regard as normal, and we find them more difficult to comprehend if they do not. Unless its perspective relations are ostentatiously distorted, we tend to regard the photographed image as a transparent representation of the space it contains. Steve Neale has argued that photography constituted "an enormous social investment" in the system of monocular perspective and its image of the world. This was also, he suggests, an investment "in the centrality of the eye, in the category and identity of the individual . . . and in an ideology of the *visibility* of the world." Photography made perspective reality, and literally put reality into perspective.[4]

One of the attractions of widescreen is that it resembles the shape of the human field of vision more closely than the Academy ratio. Cinerama was advertised as virtually filling the cone of human vision, which is about 165 degrees horizontally and 60 degrees vertically. No optical technology can duplicate all the properties of the human eye, however. In particular, our eyes have an intricate mechanism for differential focusing that no camera lens can reproduce. Although we have a very wide cone of vision, we keep only a very small proportion of it – as little as 2 degrees – in exact focus at any given moment, while objects in the rest of our vision become increasingly blurred the closer they are to the periphery of what we can see. We compensate for this limited field of exact vision by constantly moving our eyes about. The much simpler optics of a camera lens cannot reproduce this behavior. Instead, the lens keeps all objects in the same plane – that is, the same distance from the camera – in focus at the same time. How deep that plane is depends on how wide the lens's angle of view is, and how large the aperture of the lens is. The smaller the aperture, the greater the depth of the plane in focus, or **depth of field**. Since the aperture also controls the amount of light passing through the lens, the smaller the aperture, the more light is needed to expose the film.

The camera lenses that most closely approximate to our perception of depth and spatial relations have an angle of view of about 37.5 degrees vertically and, in the Academy ratio, about 50 degrees horizontally. These are known as "standard" or "normal" lenses. With widescreen the horizontal angle of view is greater, although perspective relations remain constant. Other lenses, with wider or narrower angles of view, produce apparent distortions in our perception of spatial relations. Wide-angle or "short" lenses (so called because they have a short **focal length**) and telephoto or "long" lenses change our sense of depth and perspective and alter the apparent depth relationships between objects within the space. Using different lenses, a camera can produce quite different representations of spatial and object relations without physically moving.

The simplest way of demonstrating how different lenses represent spatial relations is by comparing three images in which one object – in this case a human figure – is kept the same size by moving the camera closer to the figure for the wide-angle lens, and further away for the telephoto. The differences in the way each lens represents space are then quite apparent. The wide-angle lens reveals

Depth of field is the term used to describe the amount of an image that is in sharp focus. It is controlled by the aperture of the camera lens: the smaller the aperture, the greater the depth of field, but also the more light is needed to illuminate the scene.

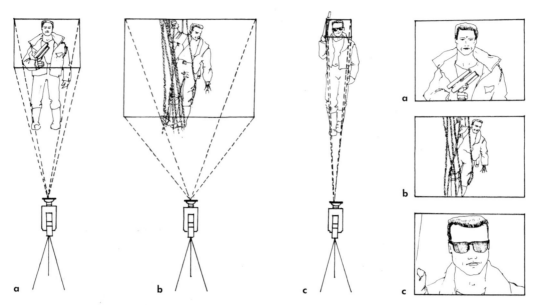

Different lenses' representation of spatial relations.

The choice of camera lens determines the appearance of the image in a number of ways. If the camera stays at the same distance from the subject, a wide-angle lens (b) will show more of the figure than a standard lens (a), while a telephoto lens (c) will provide a close-up.

a great deal of the background, with almost all of it in focus. With its much more concentrated angle of view, the telephoto lens shows much less of the background, and its restricted depth of field concentrates the viewer's attention on the figure. While the wide-angle shot draws us into the space of the image and emphasizes movement within it, particularly toward and away from the camera, the telephoto shot tends to distance us from the subjects in the shot, and minimizes the significance of movement toward and away from the camera.

Optical technology can give us only an approximation of the way we see things in space, not an imitation of our vision. This approximation is also a way of ordering and representing space, and the significantly different ways in which different lenses present space can be used for dramatic and expressive purposes. Hollywood's conventions, however, ensure that in the vast majority of movies, audiences remain as little aware of the choice of lens as they are of cutting rates. A movie such as *Rio Bravo* (1959) relies on the use of standard lenses to provide a consistent and easily comprehensible space in which the audience can feel a comfortable sense of engagement with the characters, while Alfred Hitchcock used standard lenses throughout *Psycho* (1960) because he wanted the camera to give the audience the sense that they were viewing the movie's action "as if they were seeing it with their own eyes."[5] The system is not absolutely dependent on a tech-

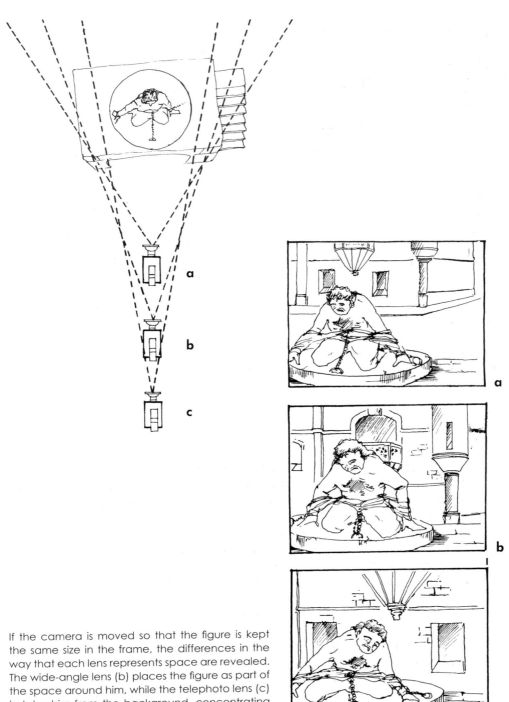

If the camera is moved so that the figure is kept the same size in the frame, the differences in the way that each lens represents space are revealed. The wide-angle lens (b) places the figure as part of the space around him, while the telephoto lens (c) isolates him from the background, concentrating the viewer's attention on him.

John T. Chance (John Wayne) and Pat Wheeler (Ward Bond) in the normal space of *Rio Bravo* (1959).

Produced by Howard Hawks; distributed by Armada.

nical choice, however. The audience's sense of spatial representation will tolerate some variation without undue attention being drawn to the mechanics of the image's production. It is normal Hollywood practice to use slightly wider-angle lenses for establishing shots, standard lenses for medium shots, and longer lenses for close-ups, to separate the character's face from the background, and concentrate audience attention on his or her reactions and motivation. As with Hollywood's other conventional systems such as sound perspective (discussed in chapter 8), the continuity of space offered by the use of standard lenses is provisional rather than absolute, and will accommodate some variation in the interest of maintaining the audience's attention on the movie's narration. It is, in fact, very rare for a movie to be shot exclusively with a standard lens, as *Psycho* was.

Choosing a lens that falls outside the standard range can draw attention to itself as a stylistic device. The consistent use of long telephoto lenses gives the audience a much less secure sense of space. In *The Long Goodbye* (1973), for example, Philip Marlowe (Elliott Gould) has little purchase on the spaces in which he finds himself, often becoming lost among other people in the general confusion of the movie's images. Likewise, the audience has difficulty judging where people are in relation to each other, and is as a result less able to assess how they may behave or what will happen next. Telephoto shots represent a more discontinuous space than standard lenses, and because their images are more difficult to "match" against another, the audience is also likely to be more aware of the abruptness of cuts between shots.

The consistent use of wide-angle lenses produces an even more confusing and discontinuous sense of screen space. In *Touch of Evil* (1958), for instance, a sense

Philip Marlowe (Elliot Gould) isolated in space by a telephoto lens in *The Long Goodbye* (1973).
Produced by Jerry Bick; distributed by E-K Corporation. United Artists/Lions Gate.

of menace and threat is aroused by almost every image, partly as a result of the spatial distortion that the wide-angle lens produces. Perspective relations between objects are exaggerated to the extent that it sometimes becomes impossible to judge distance with any certainty. Characters move with threatening rapidity through the image space, and we are confronted quite literally with the distorted logic of the world they inhabit, a nightmare world of exaggerated and twisted space which is plainly organized according to rules quite different from our own. Director Orson Welles places figures against each other in individual frames and guides our attention not so much through the use of editing as through performances and the placement of objects in the frame. The wide-angle lens is therefore crucial in determining our understanding of substantial portions of the movie.

Both *The Long Goodbye* and *Touch of Evil* exhibit visual styles outside the norms of Hollywood's standardized representation of spatial relations, and conventional criticism recognizes these stylistic traits as markers of the work of an auteur director. This brief account of *Touch of Evil* connects its visual style both to the decision-making of the director, and to thematic consistency. A similar argument might be made in the case of *The Long Goodbye* for director Robert Altman's use of the telephoto lens to demolish coherent screen space and direct our attention to his actors, if necessary at the expense of the narrative. Comparable stylistic choices are much less noticeable in movies that remain within the broad conventions of spatial and perspectival representation. Just as Welles makes use of high- and low-angle shots in *Touch of Evil* to intensify the distorting effects of the wide-angle lens, so director Howard Hawks maximizes the normative representation of space in *Rio Bravo* by shooting as consistently as possible from an eye-level camera position, benevolently allowing the viewer a much more comfortable relationship with the fiction.

Police chief Hank Quinlan (Orson Welles) interrogates Uncle Joe Grandi (Akim Tamiroff) in the threatening, distorted space of *Touch of Evil* (1958).
Produced by Albert Zugsmith; distributed by Universal Pictures.

Deep Space: Three-Dimensionality on a Flat Screen

I think I'm in a frame . . . All I can see is the frame. I'm going in there to look at the picture.

Jeff Markham (Robert Mitchum) in *Out of the Past* (1947)

As the discussion of expressive space has shown, the screen space of an individual shot is neither strictly three-dimensional nor two-dimensional, but constantly shifts between them, as our attention shifts between the graphic and the architectural or sculptural features of the image. The way a set is lit can emphasize its depth or draw attention to the existence of the frame by constructing another frame within it. Extreme lighting effects, such as those common in film noir, can present the frame predominantly as a graphic composition, in which the lines and shapes of the image are more communicative than the image's depth relations.[6] Color can serve similar functions. Through what the Society of Motion Picture Engineers called "color normalcy" it can contribute unobtrusively to the verisimilitude of the image. It can express a specific narrative meaning, for instance by drawing attention to a character's change in demeanor, as when Cary signals a change in her sexual identity by putting on a red dress in *All That Heaven Allows*. Or it can render the image unnatural, drawing attention to the image as image, or to tensions within the action that cannot be expressed through dialog. *All That Heaven Allows* contains a particularly vivid example of color used to excess, when Cary's daughter Kay (Gloria Talbott) confronts her mother over her relationship with Ron in a bedroom apparently lit through a multicolored glass window. The intensity of the color signals the unnatural intensity of the scene's emotional exchange.

When we look at the screen, our eyes are drawn to movement, and we are most likely to understand movement in the image as being movement through space. If we did not invest the screen with depth, we would find it very difficult to watch movies at all, particularly if we expected them to construct themselves as stories. Writing in 1923, French art critic Elie Faure registered his deliberate rejection of narration in favor of the purely graphic qualities of the cinematic image:

> The revelation of what the cinema of the future can be came to me one day: I retain an exact memory of it, of the sudden commotion I experienced when I observed, in a flash, the magnificence there was in the relationship of a piece of black clothing to the gray wall of an inn. From that moment on I paid no more attention to the martyrdom of the poor woman who was condemned, in order to save her husband from dishonor, to give herself to the lascivious banker who had previously murdered her mother and debauched her child.[7]

Faure's rejection of narration led him to stress the formal qualities of film as a mobile, two-dimensional image. His predictions of a future cinema that explored the play of light, color, and tone, approaching the condition of music at the expense of any discernible story content, were fulfilled by the work of avant-garde filmmakers such as Man Ray and Moholy-Nagy in the 1920s and 1930s and Jonas Mekas and Malcolm Le Grice in the 1960s and later.[8]

Against this High Modernist aesthetic of form we do not simply have to argue a populist preference for being told stories. There is no cinematic equivalent to the simple sentence, "A man walked down the street," because any cinematic image must add considerably to the bare, abstract statement, amplifying it by showing a particular man walking in a particular way down a particular street. An unwillingness to recognize the film image as a representation of a three-dimensional space is the equivalent of only recognizing the words on the pages of a literary text as shapes in black ink on a white background. Total belief in the three-dimensionality of the image is just as unhelpful as total disbelief. If cinema ever achieved the perfect illusion of reality that Bazin envisioned for it in "The Myth of Total Cinema" (discussed in chapter 8), it would disappear, at least in the form that we now recognize it. Story-telling – the highly artificial arrangement of information, including spatial information – would become impossible, and our attention would be arbitrarily distributed among central and insignificant details, much as it is in real life. Alternatively, our experience would be similar to that of the first cinema audiences, who reportedly ducked under their seats for fear they were about to be run over by an approaching locomotive. Cinerama sold itself successfully on a similar kind of audience participation in the screen space:

> You won't be gazing at a movie screen – you'll find yourself swept right into the picture, surrounded by sight and sound. . . . Everything that happens on the curved Cinerama screen is happening to you. And without moving from your seat, you share,

personally, in the most remarkable new kind of emotional experience ever brought to the theater.[9]

The rollercoaster ride at the beginning of *This is Cinerama* (1952) often convinced viewers of its representation of three-dimensional reality strongly enough to make them sway, recoil, or even be sick. But as critics observed at the time, so persuasively spectacular an illusion hindered the construction of a drama. A viewer worrying about motion sickness is hardly in the best frame of mind to catch the nuances of dialog or the details of a plot. For much the same reason, the Imax large-screen system has proven equally intractable to the demands of fiction. The space in a movie must provide the opportunity for spectacle *and* narrative. It must be simultaneously two- and three-dimensional, graphic and architectural. Screen space differs from the space we inhabit outside the theater because it represents three-dimensionality with a two-dimensional image; its capacity to express *and* to represent, to signify *and* to narrate originates in the play between the surface of the image and the depth it represents. Much of Hollywood's benevolence toward its audience (or, as some critics would put it, its exercise of control over their perception) consists in the way that it reassures viewers that they have *comprehended* each image as both a three-dimensional space and the two-dimensional composition in which that space is always framed, and that they have understood it as both represented and expressive space.

Mise-en-Scène

In a movie designed for a single viewing, the representation of space must be both comprehensible and significant. It must provide the audience with a sense of the relation between characters, and between events unfolding in the fiction. Familiar elements in the organization of space may even help to make incoherent storylines accessible and acceptable. The image should not be so intricate as to distract our interest from the intended focus of action, and it should create an expectation that leads smoothly from one shot to the next. This arrangement of screen space as a meaningful organization of elements is known as **mise-en-scène**: literally, the "putting into a scene" or staging of a fiction. It is through mise-en-scène that represented space becomes expressive. Classical Hollywood mise-en-scène balances and fills the frame, avoiding both distracting detail and empty spots in the composition, and using conventional compositional principles to focus attention on the main line of action.

We should think of mise-en-scène not as a list of devices or techniques, such as set design, lighting, or camera placement, but as a form of textual economy, comparable to the financial and generic economies we have already considered, and thus as another site at which the multiple logics of Hollywood cinema encounter each other. Mise-en-scène makes the image, in Will Wright's phrase, "maximally meaningful."[10] An efficient mise-en-scène serves the needs of both the producers and the consumers of the fiction, maintaining the viewer's involvement in the

In *Rebel Without a Cause* (1955), characters are only too aware of the expressively architectural space that separates them.
Produced by David Weisbart; distributed by Warner Bros.

transparent & comprehensible

action by allowing for understanding and interpretation without impeding its progress with intrusive explanation. The audience must be able to recognize the conventions of mise-en-scène, but because the meaning produced by mise-en-scène is displaced into the viewer's perception of a movie's narrative, spectacle, or performance, the audience does not need to be able to articulate its conventions. Mise-en-scène fills out the meaning of otherwise neutral spaces in the interests of the audience's wider dramatic involvement. It also limits or closes down the potential meanings that even the simplest stream of images can suggest, by encouraging some meanings for its audience and discouraging others. When the system is functioning smoothly we have the sense of witnessing events unfolding in an extended three-dimensional space, in which we are nevertheless able to interpret specific details because of the way in which particular elements are highlighted for us. Hollywood space is thus something that we both look *at* and look *into*.

In talking about the composition of the image, I have already been discussing one major aspect of mise-en-scène, by which an action is framed to enhance the viewer's understanding of its significance. Sometimes the camera's viewpoint gives the audience knowledge the characters do not share, as in the example from *Imitation of Life*, above (p. 315). In other instances, such as *Rebel Without a Cause* (1955), characters are as aware as the audience of the thematic significance of spatial arenas, and of the crucial importance of transitional spaces such as doors and staircases.[11] By drawing attention to everyday objects or architectural features, mise-en-scène can imbue them with narrative significance. In *The Searchers* (1956), a doorway becomes a powerful sign of Ethan Edwards's (John Wayne) exclusion from the community, when at the end of the movie he is framed by the doorway of a homestead he cannot bring himself to enter. Throughout the movie he has been unable to pass through any doorway shot from inside looking out, a visual expression of his inability to enter the institutions of society. Elsewhere, doors can be much more ambiguous instruments of spatial organization: the closing of a door separates different arenas, while an open door provides the expectation of an

stuff will be smoother." The movie, *A Modern Hero* (1934), was Pabst's only American production, and Pabst was fired, probably "for not buckling under to the system."[13]

At its most mechanical, the division of labor in the studio system would encourage a director to provide **coverage** of a scene by photographing the whole action in a master shot including all the characters, then rephotographing it several times with closer shots of each character, in order to provide the editors with enough material to construct the scene as they, or the producer, saw fit. For some directors, including John Ford, the practice of "cutting in the camera" that Hal Wallis objected to was a means of maintaining authorial control over the mise-en-scène. Other directors, most famously Alfred Hitchcock, planned their movies shot by shot on **storyboards**, deliberately making the process of shooting itself as mechanical an act of recording a predetermined set of images as possible. Storyboards are widely used in the preparation of contemporary Hollywood movies, particularly for complex action sequences or scenes involving special effects. Whether it is seen as directorial style or a list of techniques and devices, mise-en-scène is obviously inseparable from the process of editing individual shots into a flow of images. Although editing is often regarded as a separate element in the production process, it is appropriate to consider it here as a part of our discussion of mise-en-scène and Hollywood's presentation of space.

Editing

Hollywood's commercial aesthetics rely on editing. As well as the obvious appeal of frequent changes in the image, there are sound economic reasons for its practice of comparatively frequent cuts and short takes. **Long takes** with a mobile camera, such as the opening shot of *Sunny Side Up* (1929), are technically the most difficult shots to coordinate; breaking the action into small segments makes it easier to produce footage at a predictable rate. Directors in the dream factory of the 1930s were expected to shoot between 12 and 20 **set-ups** per day, producing two-and-a-half minutes of film that would end up in the rough cut of the movie. In practice, the output of individual directors varied considerably, as did the demands of production executives at each studio. Warner Bros., famous for its economic production style, was a more natural home for a Mervyn LeRoy, a director capable of shooting as much as six minutes of finished film in one day, than for William Wyler, whose predilection for intricate camera movements invariably slowed down output.[14] As Hal Wallis's complaint to G. W. Pabst makes clear, a cinema constructed by editing also ensured that control over the appearance of the final product remained with producers. Wallis normally oversaw the final editing of major Warner Bros. productions, watching the rough cut of the movie and dictating the changes he required. His detailed cutting notes on *Angels with Dirty Faces* (1938), for instance, run to eight pages. Contracts providing the director with rights over the "final cut" have always been the rarest accolade of a company's confidence in him or her.

In combination with framing and composition, editing works to make space representative and expressive, informative of the present and predictive of the future. It modulates audience interest from the general to the particular, and emphasizes significant details. Hollywood's editing codes have been among the most consistent of its practices over time, relatively little affected by changes in technology. Some writers would argue that audiences have gradually become visually more sophisticated, so that they need rather less guidance through the geography of a scene than their parents or grandparents. Since 1980, the stylistic influences of television commercials and music videos have accustomed audiences to more disjunctive patterns of editing. The fact that movies are subsequently released on video has also encouraged the increased use of close-ups and simpler patterns of staging better suited to small screens, while the development of digital editing has further contributed to an increase in the frequency of cutting. A contemporary Hollywood movie is more likely to cut from a long shot to a close-up, or to use a cut instead of a dissolve to indicate a temporal ellipsis. Whether these changes are enough to mark the end of Hollywood's Classical style, or merely its adaptation, is a subject of some debate, and is discussed in the next chapter.

Before considering that question, however, it will be useful to establish some terms for describing the different scales of shot. We can discuss **shot scale** in terms of the most commonly represented object, the human body. An extreme long shot presents a landscape in which figures are barely visible: a horseman on a distant horizon, perhaps. In a **long shot (LS)**, people fill half or three-quarters of the height of the screen, but the shot will emphasize the setting the figures are in. Such a shot will often be used at the beginning of a scene, to show the space in which the scene will take place. Then it is known as an establishing shot. In a **full shot**, the height of the frame is filled with the human figure, while a **medium long shot** covers the body from mid-calf or knees up. In the Academy frame, this shot balances the figure against its surroundings, presenting characters as the principal focus of attention, but giving them space to move and interact within the shot. French critics have called this shot (especially a two-shot, featuring two characters) the **plan Americain**, because of the frequency of its use in Hollywood; in English it is occasionally called a "Hollywood shot." A **medium shot (MS)**, cutting characters off at about the waist, offers similar possibilities for character interaction. A **close shot** takes in the character from the chest up, focusing attention on her face and expression when she is delivering or reacting to dialog. The range from the long shot to the close shot encompasses the vast majority of shots used in Classical Hollywood cinema. **Close-ups (CU)** were comparatively rare, used mainly as an emphatic device.

The initials "LS," "MS," or "CU" on a shooting script provide only a rule-of-thumb guide to the way a scene is to be shot. They are never absolute designations, merely points on a sliding scale, descriptive of relative distances between the subject of the shot and the viewer. Beginning with an establishing long shot that sets up the arena in which the scene will be played out and the relative positions of the characters, a typical scene will cut to medium shots to play out the characters' interactions in space. Dialog scenes usually progress to closer shots of

---

Box 10.2 Hal Wallis edits *Angels with Dirty Faces*

As head of production at Warner Bros., Hal Wallis would watch studio editor Owen Marks's cut of all the studio's movies, and provide detailed suggestions about what changes he required. The extract below is from his notes on the final sequences of *Angels with Dirty Faces*, and as they make clear, Wallis normally took out a lot more than he put back in. A good deal of Warners' famous fast-pacing was due to Wallis's preferences for the staging of action:

Rocky Sullivan (James Cagney) walks to his death with Father Jerry (Pat O'Brien) in *Angels with Dirty Faces* (1938).

Produced by Samuel Bischoff; distributed by First International Pictures. Courtesy of the Academy of Motion Picture Arts and Sciences.

Take Cagney down two flights of steps, then cut outside to the men starting to break in the door, then cut to Cagney already back up the steps where he's shooting at them at the door. Don't take him all the way down the first time.

Take out the tear gas the first time. Don't show one until we see a cop drop it in.

Take out the man on the circular staircase and the two or three cuts that go with it. After the tear gas, come right to Cagney emptying his gun.

Right after the second machine blast at the window, go to the cop saying "Sullivan, are you coming out or must we smoke you out?"

After they shoot the tear gas in the last time, cut to the car with O'Brien coming up.

Put in the cut of the waterbucket and the tear gas hitting it.

Trim on the first floor thing when O'Brien starts up, and after the second cut of Cagney emptying the gun, pick O'Brien up at the top of the flight of stairs. Lose one cut of Cagney and one flight.

Take a foot or two off the long shot of the street after the man says "but stand by."

Take out the sound of the tin can when Cagney stumbles.

Trim on the doors before Cagney and O'Brien open them.

After he says "Back, back" to the cops, go back to a long shot and show the cops pulling back and the two of them standing there, then go to a shot of Cagney and O'Brien where he says "Duck, Jerry."

Take out the inset implicating the higher up.

Take out the line "Save a reserved seat for me."

Put in the close shot where Cagney says "No," when O'Brien looks at him.

Add three or four feet to Cagney's closeup just before he breaks.

Take two or three feet off the radiator shot.

Put the radiator shot in first and then the cop struggling with him.

Take out the doctors.

Put in the straight closeup of O'Brien instead of that light change on him.

Take out the high shot in the "last mile" walk.[15]

each of the characters, normally taken from over the other character's shoulder. The procedure operates unobtrusively, to encourage an equivalent focusing of audience interest on the action, not the editing. We are gradually drawn into a space made safe and familiar to us because of the familiar way it is presented to us. The smoothness of this progress is emphasized: a Classical Hollywood movie will almost never cut directly from long shot to close-up because of the jarring effect it would produce. Inside this safe space, we can direct our attention to engaging emotionally with the characters, confident that the movie's image stream will avoid any sudden shocks that might abruptly disrupt our involvement in the action.

Unless it was seeking a particular dramatic effect, Classical Hollywood's cutting between images was intended to appear as fluid as possible. The obvious reason for this had to do with cinema's capacity to alter its viewpoint, compared to our own relatively static positioning. When we want to vary our viewpoint we have to move ourselves physically from one place to another. In cinematic terms, we perform a tracking shot and, since we lack ability to cut from one viewpoint to another, we might describe waking experience as one long tracking shot. Because editing is so unnatural to our own perception, it ought to be particularly discomforting to us; and the anecdotal histories of early cinema are full of stories of producers worrying that if audiences were presented with a close-up, they would demand to know what had happened to the rest of the actor. Continuity editing works to overcome this disruptive effect by making the transition from one shot to another as comfortable as possible, covering our perception of the shot change by emphasizing the continuity of action across the cut. Cuts are positioned at the

Framing heights for the human figure.

This exterior long shot (a) from *It Happened One Night* (1934) places Ellie Andrews (Claudette Colbert) and Peter Warne (Clark Gable) in their setting. An interior long shot (b) is often an establishing shot, showing the space in which the scene will take place. From there the scene can cut to a medium two-shot (c) of both characters, a close medium two-shot (d), or a medium shot (e), close shot (f), or close-up (g) of either player.

Produced by Frank Capra; distributed by Columbia Pictures.

least noticeable moment – when they are covered by a character's movement, for instance – but at the same time, a cut is also motivated by what André Bazin called "the material or dramatic logic of the scene . . . by allowing a better view and then by putting the emphasis where it belongs."[16] Motivating the cut in both these ways helps persuade the audience that the space represented on the screen at any given moment is the most important segment of a larger story space, which we can also access when it becomes significant. Reframing the shot by panning, tilting, or tracking the camera to accommodate figure movement has the same reassuring effect: the movie will show us what we need to see.

Another convention of camera placement and editing provides a particularly clear example of how the presentation of space has to conform to a conventional system in order that the audience can overlook it and concentrate on something else. In filming a scene between two characters, we can draw an imaginary line that connects them. So long as the camera stays on one side of this **center line** or **line of action**, the characters will stay in the same relation to each other in the screen space. In the example from *Casablanca* on p. 338, so long as the camera stays in front of Captain Renault (Claude Rains) and Rick Blaine (Humphrey Bogart), Renault will appear on the left of the frame in every image, and Rick on the right. If they are kept in these relative positions by the camera's placement, the movie can cut between any two images taken from below the line without disturbing the audience. It can, for example, cut to a close-up of either character without making the audience wonder where the other character is. If, however, the camera crosses behind them, Renault appears on the right of the screen, facing in the other direction. Unless this change of direction is strongly motivated (in this case by the aircraft taking off), viewers are likely to lose their secure sense of spatial position, and be distracted from following the conversation. The center line or **180-degree rule** maintains audience comprehension of figures' relative situations in represented space by granting the spectator a relatively stable viewpoint on the action. It applies with equal force but greater complexity in scenes involving three or more characters, but as with many of Hollywood's conventions, we only really notice the operation of this "rule" when it is broken.

Audience comprehension is further aided by a convention governing the direction of the characters' gaze, known as **eyeline matching**. When a character looks offscreen in one shot, we expect the next shot to show us what the character is looking at. Following characters' eyelines thus allows us to connect the spaces in separate shots. Manuals of continuity editing observe that "the most natural cut is the cut on the look," because "the eyes are the most powerful direction pointer that a human being has to attract or to direct interest":

In the same way that the focal length of the lens and the angle of the camera can place the viewer in a definite relationship with the subjects on the screen, the eyeline of a subject clearly determines spatial relations in the scene space. Viewers are particularly sensitive to incongruities in the sight lines between subjects who are looking at each other and in most situations can easily detect when the eye match is slightly off.[17]

The center line; eyeline matching; shot/reverse shot.

Rick Blaine (Humphrey Bogart) and Captain Renault (Claude Rains) illustrate spatial conventions in *Casablanca* (1942). The "180-degree rule" draws a line between the two characters. So long as the camera stays on one side of the line (as in a, b, and c), Rains will remain on the left side of the frame looking to the right, and Bogart will stay on the right side of the frame, looking to his left. If the camera crosses this line, however, their screen positions are reversed, and the audience's comprehension of the space is confused (d). If the characters' eyelines remain matched, viewers can connect the spaces in separate shots. Conversation scenes such as this are most often presented in a sequence of shot/reverse shot, with the camera looking over the shoulder of each character in turn (e).

Produced by Hal B. Wallis; distributed by Warner Bros.

Eyeline matching provides a means of cueing the cuts between a succession of shots which we then understand as the "looks" of characters in the fiction. Since what we see in each shot adds to our construction of the character whose gaze we share, this convention provides us with subjective information about the character without robbing us of our sense of physical placement. The matching of imaginary lines between gazes helps to guide us between quite disparate spaces and to generate a sense of the story's action taking place in a three-dimensional, continuous dramatic space. Through these conventions, the **blocking** or physical placement of characters in a scene can be constantly reframed around shifting ideal viewpoints without disturbing the audience's sense of spatial continuity.

These conventions, recognized but not consciously attended to by audiences, steer us through Hollywood's representation of space in the majority of its scenes. It seems appropriate to describe these conventions as benevolent, because they make our perception of the movie's images more comfortable – more safe – and therefore allow us to concentrate on what is being presented. Nevertheless, the conventions can be breached for practical reasons or expressive effect. They have also changed over time, as a result of technological change affecting the possibilities of spatial expression. The more widespread use of telephoto and zoom lenses from the mid-1960s, for example, revised many conventions of spatial presentation. The more abrupt editing strategies of contemporary Hollywood still require a set of spatial conventions to maintain the audience's attention on what is being represented in the screen space, rather than on the manner of its representation. Like other aspects of the New Hollywood, however, these changes amount to variations on a set of conventions rather than fundamental alterations in the practice of representation.

Summary

- Just as Hollywood's generic conventions require the cooperative participation of the viewer, so the conventions of spatial representation can only transform images into meaningful components of story or spectacle with the cooperation of viewers.
- Hollywood's representation of space works to secure our attention and offers us a succession of ideal viewpoints from which to observe the action. It rewards us for looking at the screen by constantly addressing and satisfying our expectations. One of the ways in which Hollywood's space is Utopian is that it gives us the best view of the action on screen.
- Hollywood's continuity system of spatial construction constructs space as a smooth and continuous flow across shots. In this system the camera usually remains unobtrusive. The continuity system provides a safe space for the development of a story, for the pleasure of spectacle, and for the secure placement of the audience in relation to the fictional world.
- The audience recognizes movie narration as a process of continual displacement between represented space – the area that exists in front of the camera

and is recorded by it – and expressive space – space which is endowed with meaning beyond the literal, and which signifies a particular feeling or experience. Represented space is three-dimensional; expressive space often combines the sculptural three-dimensionality of the space in the image with the graphic two-dimensionality of the image itself.

- The cinematic apparatus cannot reproduce the human eye's breadth of vision, or its perception of depth and spatial relations. By using a variety of lenses (standard, wide angle, telephoto) the movie camera can, however, produce quite different representations of spatial and object relations without physically moving.

- The arrangement of screen space is known as mise-en-scène, literally "putting into a scene" or staging of a fiction. It is through mise-en-scène that represented space becomes maximally meaningful.

- In combination with framing and composition, editing also works to make space representative and expressive. Editing can be informative about the present and past and predictive of the future. It modulates and maintains audience interest, and emphasizes details of the action.

- The continuity system observes a number of conventions which are fundamental to its construction of screen space. The "center line" or 180-degree rule insists that the camera stay on one side of a line between two characters, and grants the spectator a relatively stable viewpoint on the action. By presenting a succession of shots as the "looks" of characters in the fiction, "eyeline matching" allows the viewer to connect space in separate shots, and provides us with subjective information about characters without robbing us of our sense of physical placement.

Further Reading

Viewing spaces

The story of the fleeing audience is often told about the first screening of the Lumière brothers' "actuality" film, *L'Arrivée d'un Train en Gare de la Ciotat* (1895), which showed a train pulling in at a railway platform and passengers descending from its carriages. It may well be apocryphal, as Tom Gunning suggests in "Primitive Cinema: A Frame-Up? Or the Trick's on Us," in *Early Cinema: Space, Frame, Narrative*, ed. Thomas Elsaesser (London: British Film Institute, 1990), and in the same collection, Dai Vaughn, "Let There be Lumière," discusses its significance. The history of the story is traced in Stephen Bottomore, "The Panicking Audience: Early Cinema and the 'Train' Effect," *Historical Journal of Film, Radio and Television* 19:2 (June 1999), pp. 177–216.

It is often suggested that the experience of watching movies in familiar domestic surroundings, where the video or television is in competition with a range of other activities and interruptions, proposes a different relationship to the screen than the rapt attention given in the cinema. We remain fully aware of our occupation of real space, and in some cases consciously use this awareness in self-protection against certain extreme forms of affectivity with which Hollywood threatens us, for example in the horror movie. The disjunction between the two viewing conditions may not be as radical as is often claimed, however: the theater audience in practice remains conscious of its surroundings, while the home audience commonly recreates theater conditions in miniature, assembling in a group, turning off the lights, and so on. Barbara Klinger explores aspects of this issue in

"The New Media Aristocrats: Home Theater and the Domestic Film Experience," *Velvet Light Trap* 42 (Fall 1998), pp. 4–19.

The continuity system

The continuity system is not unique to Hollywood. It is the dominant system of spatial representation in mainstream western cinema and television. Since it evolved across several national cinemas in the period before World War I, Hollywood cannot really be credited with its creation. But Hollywood was and is its greatest exemplar and exponent, and has taken the benevolence of spatial representation in the continuity system farther than other national cinemas.

Some of the most useful works for understanding the operations of the continuity system are guides written for practitioners, such as Daniel Arijon, *Grammar of the Film Language* (Los Angeles: Silman-James Press, 1976); Steven D. Katz, *Film Directing Shot by Shot: Visualizing from Concept to Screen* (Los Angeles: Michael Wiese Productions, 1991); and Bruce Block, *The Visual Story: Seeing the Structure of Film, TV, and New Media* (Boston: Focal Press, 2001). Block is particularly useful on lenses, perspectival relations, and composition. Patrick Tucker, *Secrets of Screen Acting* (New York: Routledge, 1994), has a useful chapter (chapter 3) on "The Frame" and screen space.

David Bordwell reports that in the 100 movies he, Janet Staiger, and Kristin Thompson subjected to shot-by-shot analysis, "less than 2 per cent of the shot-changes violated spatial continuity [the 180-degree rule], and one-fifth of the movies contained not a single violation. No wonder," he adds, "that, of all Hollywood stylistic practices, continuity editing has been considered a set of firm rules." Bordwell discusses Classical Hollywood style in part 1 of Bordwell, Staiger, and Thompson, *The Classical Hollywood Cinema: Film Style and Mode of Production to 1960* (London: Routledge and Kegan Paul, 1985). See also Barry Salt, *Film Style and Technology: History and Analysis*, 1st edn 1983, 2nd edn (London: Starword, 1992).

On editing, see Karel Reisz and Gavin Millar, *The Technique of Film Editing* (New York: Hastings, 1973); Ken Dancynger, *The Technique of Film and Video Editing* (Boston: Focal Press, 1993); and Walter Murch, *In the Blink of an Eye: A Perspective on Film Editing* (Los Angeles: Silman-James Press, 1995).

A discussion of alternative modes of spatial representation can be found in David Bordwell and Kristin Thompson, *Film Art: An Introduction*, 6th edn (New York: McGraw-Hill, 2001), pp. 278–87.

Mise-en-scène

Critiques of what I have called the benevolence of Hollywood space can be found in André Bazin, "The Evolution of the Language of Cinema," in his *What Is Cinema? Vol. 1*, trans. Hugh Gray (Berkeley, CA: University of California Press, 1967), and in Daniel Dayan, "The Tutor-Code of Classical Cinema," in *Movies and Methods*, ed. Bill Nichols (Berkeley, CA: University of California Press, 1976), pp. 438–51. As well as Bazin's writings on mise-en-scène, see V. F. Perkins, *Film as Film: Understanding and Judging Movies* (Harmondsworth: Penguin, 1972). Ben Brewster and Lea Jacobs discuss the evolution of Classical staging in part 4 of *Theatre to Cinema: Stage Pictorialism and the Early Feature Film* (Oxford: Oxford University Press, 1997). Vance Kepley Jr offers a model analysis of Classical mise-en-scène in "Spatial Articulation in the Classical Cinema: A Scene from *His Girl Friday*," *Wide Angle* 5:3 (1983), pp. 50–8. David Bordwell explores the varieties of deep-focus mise-en-scène in *On the History of Film Style* (Cambridge, MA: Harvard University Press, 1997).

Cinematography, art direction, architectural and graphic space

On Classical Hollywood cinematography, see John Alton, *Painting with Light* (1st edn 1949, reprint edn Berkeley, CA: University of California Press, 1995), and the documentary *Visions of Light: The Art of Cinematography* (Image Entertainment, 1993), which provides an excellent visual introduction to Hollywood cinematography.

Charles Affron and Mirella Jona Affron, *Sets in Motion: Art Direction and Film Narrative* (New Brunswick, NJ: Rutgers University Press, 1995), explores the function of set design in Hollywood. Léon Barsacq, *Caligari's Children and Other Grand Illusions: A History of Film Design* (New

casual observation of audiences, however, suggests that viewers retain a considerable range of options in engaging with a Hollywood movie. How often have you listened to the conversation of fellow audience members on leaving the cinema and felt that they were discussing a different movie from the one you had just seen? By looking more closely at our taken-for-granted notion of simply "watching a movie," we can begin to uncover an account of cinema spectatorship that suggests a far more active collaboration with the cinema, one much closer to James Clifford's description of participant observation as the "dialectic of experience and interpretation" provided by the "continuous tacking between the 'inside' and 'outside' of events." This model of viewer engagement allows us to describe a more subtle and complex series of interactions between audiences and the movies they watch than one permitted by theories of the passive spectator.

In a more precise sense than we usually employ, it is never true to suggest that we simply look at cinema. Our attention to the image only intermittently stops, as Elie Faure's did, at the surface of the screen. Rather, we alternate between investing the image with depth and volume to make sense of figure movement and action, and recognizing the screen as a flat plane which shows us the graphic relations between the elements of its image. The curious status of cinematic space as neither strictly two-dimensional nor three-dimensional ensures that our attention to the screen takes the form of a play of looks *at*, *into*, and *through* the screen space. Hollywood uses the mobility of our viewpoint on the action to hold our attention. The camera's shifting gaze lets us examine different perspectives within the frame, allowing us not only to explore space, but also to understand its meanings through identifications of and with characters. In this way, Hollywood encourages in us the sense that we can enter space and participate along with characters in the action played out within it.

Three different kinds of looking are in play in this mobile viewing: the audience's look at the screen; the camera's look at characters or action; and the characters' looks at each other. The audience's look is the least frequently used by the movie itself, although voice-over narrations sometimes draw attention to our act of looking: "the picture you are about to see. . . ." In addition, the audience's look at the screen can resist the camera's suggestions or the subjective looks of the characters, and can explore the screen according to its own interests, particularly if the scene is composed in deep-focus. But for most of the time our attention is directed insistently toward the action within the playing space. The camera's look promises to cover the action, allowing us to lose a sense of looking at the screen and to participate imaginatively in the action. The environments the characters occupy seem appropriate and meaningful to the actions going on in them, and their contribution to the significance and legibility of the scene is almost unnoticed.

Some analysts have argued that Hollywood's use of the camera is governed by the justification of the camera's look, and therefore the audience's look, as apparently originating within the playing space. This argument derives from an analysis of one of Hollywood's most frequent formal figures, the **shot/reverse shot**, in which two consecutive shots depict complementary spaces. The most common instance of this figure occurs in dialog scenes presented in over-the-shoulder close

a

b

Hollywood's most conventional way of presenting a conversation is in a matched pair of over-the-shoulder shots of the participants. The graphic continuity of the two shots is crucial to the smoothness with which the movie can cut between them. The viewer's attention is most likely to be focused on the characters' eyes, which appear in the same part of the frame in both shots. In these shots from *Rio Bravo* (1959), our attention is concentrated on Feathers (Angie Dickinson), around whom the cut pivots. Because viewers tend to watch reactions rather than actions, a convention of performance and editing stages a character's reactions fractionally in advance of the action that supposedly provokes it, in order to give the audience time to react to both the action and the reaction. The character subjectivity revealed to us in these shots is that of the character whose face we see, not the character whose look we share.

Produced by Howard Hawks; distributed by Armada.

medium shots, where the looks of the characters at each other and the graphic similarity between the shots help the viewer infer that the spaces in the two shots are contiguous. French critic Daniel Dayan has argued that this figure is crucial to Hollywood's rhetoric of "realism" in that it constantly offers an explanation for the source of each shot as emanating from the shot that preceded it. Dayan suggests that editing constantly fragments the audience's look, abruptly shifting us from place to place, and thus "regularly and systematically raises the question . . . 'who is watching this?'" Dayan's answer is that in the shot/reverse shot figure, the question of whose look is shown in the first shot is answered by the second, reverse shot, and its look is, in turn, explained by cutting back to the first shot. Dayan describes this operation as a process of **suturing**, by which the viewer perceives gaps in the space represented, only to have these gaps filled. The succession of views represented by the image stream is explained as having its own source. Camera looks are apparently motivated internally by the movie itself rather than externally by some agency of production, and Dayan argues that through this suture Hollywood cinema masks both its formal and ideological operations: "the code effectively disappears and the ideological effect of the film is thereby secured . . . Unable to see the workings of the code, the spectator is at its mercy."[3]

Such an interpretation helps to explain how the audience can situate its own look as originating within the fiction, but it both overemphasizes the centrality and oversimplifies the operation of the shot/reverse shot figure in Hollywood's practice. In *Secrets of Screen Acting*, Patrick Tucker provides a simpler alternative explanation for the extensive use of this editing pattern. He suggests that in dialog scenes, we look at the listener rather than the speaker, since we can tell from the sound of the voice more or less what is on the face of the speaker, but we need to watch the listener to know what she is thinking or feeling.[4] Bruce Block argues that graphic continuity in the shot/reverse shot figure is crucial to the "invisibility" of the cut between the two shots.[5]

Not every shot in Hollywood cinema can be understood as the subjective look of a character, and viewing a Hollywood movie involves a play between the three looks of character, camera, and audience.[6] They may function together, as Dayan suggests, with audience and camera looks disguised as character looks, but they can also be driven apart to emphasize the camera's mediating function, the subjective looks of characters at each other, or the audience's role as spectator. In long takes, such as the opening shot of *Touch of Evil* (1958) (discussed in more detail in the next chapter), the audience becomes uncomfortably aware of the duration of the shot and the movie's refusal to cut.

Points of View

Johnny Friendly (Lee J. Cobb):	You ratted on us, Terry!
Terry Molloy (Marlon Brando):	From where you stand maybe, but I'm standing over here now.

On the Waterfront (1954)

Meaning in Hollywood movies is often a matter of the position from which events are viewed, and how we are positioned to interpret them. Much film theory has maintained that the key function of point of view is to produce **identifications**, arguing that our primary identification with the camera (we have to look where the camera looks; the camera is the eye/I) is displaced in Classical Hollywood cinema, onto the characters that the camera shows us, encouraging us to make a range of secondary identifications with characters within the fiction. The equation of looks is understood as an equation of knowledge and experience: we feel as though we are experiencing the events of the story at first hand, because we are shown them from the same point of view as a character. The very notion of point of view seems to imply a kind of sharing of position, a mutuality of vision. Discussion of point of view is, however, often confused by the way that the camera produces *literal* viewpoints. If we are to avoid equating the camera's literal perspective with the fictional perspectives of either a movie's narration or its characters, and collapsing narration into camerawork, it is important to make a clear distinction between what we mean by viewpoint and point of view. The **viewpoint** of a shot is a matter of its position in space: its angle, level, height, and distance from its subject. **Point of view**, on the other hand, is a position of knowledge in relation to the fiction, a matter of its relative subjectivity or omniscience. Characters in a scene therefore have both viewpoints and points of view. They occupy physical positions in the playing space and direct their glances toward objects or characters within it, and they also possess degrees of knowledge, attitudes, prejudices relevant to their situations in the fiction. Shots from particular viewpoints may encourage the audience to construct characters' points of view, but differences between the optics of lenses and the human eye mean that the camera cannot literally show characters' viewpoints, even by taking up their exact position in the represented space. Character vision and character knowledge can never be made entirely identical.

Hollywood cinema prefers to keep camera viewpoint and character viewpoint separate, principally to preserve its own narrational role. While the camera's viewpoint might encourage the viewer to side with a character, it seldom literally takes the place of that character. If, in a dialog scene between two people, the camera were to usurp the literal position of each character, both characters would address the viewer head-on. Such an arrangement restricts the viewer's ability to identify or empathize with either character. The shots quite forcibly remind us of the limitations of either viewpoint. Instead, the continuity system's over-the-shoulder shot/reverse shot figure provides us with a more intricate sense of character subjectivity, and allows us to acquire knowledge through our perception of expressive space. By adopting viewpoints adjacent to those of the characters, we can witness their subjectivities as they express their points of view through speech, reaction, or gesture, and we can move among these subjectivities to establish our own, more omniscient point of view. As David Bordwell has suggested, the omnipresence of the camera's look suggests the omniscience of the narration.[7]

About 20 minutes after the start of *Stagecoach* (1939), the passengers halt at Dry Fork for a meal. The scene that follows explores the social division that

a

b

c

d

e

f

g

Viewpoint and point of view in *Stagecoach* (1939).

Shot (a) establishes the scene, and puts Mrs Mallory (Louise Platt) at its visual center, so that the camera's views will pivot around her viewpoint. Shot (b) is taken from a position close to where she is sitting, and shots (c) and (e) show her looking with disapproval at Dallas (Claire Trevor). But though we share her viewpoint in shots (d), (f), and (g), we do not share her point of view about Dallas, and as the story unfolds, our judgment about Dallas's worth is proved correct.

Produced by Walter Wanger; distributed by Walter Wanger Production.

separates the cavalry officer's wife, Mrs Mallory (Louise Platt), from the prostitute Dallas (Claire Trevor), who has been run out of the town of Tonto by the Ladies' Law and Order League. Mrs Mallory sits at the head of the table, and the gauche outlaw Ringo (John Wayne) invites Dallas to sit next to her. The crucial act in the scene is an exchange of looks between the two women. In a shot from down the table we see Mrs Mallory looking at Dallas, and then cut to a viewpoint adjacent to hers, showing Dallas, who recognizes her social inferiority and looks down, not meeting Mrs Mallory's gaze. We understand the significance of this moment (Dallas concurs in Mrs Mallory's judgment of her), but in approximating Mrs Mallory's viewpoint (necessary in order to see the gaze not met), we do not concur in her point of view. The story later confirms our hypothesis that Dallas is worthy of more respect than Mrs Mallory's superficial dismissal suggests.

Classical Hollywood occasionally restricted the audience's viewpoint, but seldom for long, and usually in order to produce a specific effect by withholding information from the audience. Hollywood's most sustained attempt to restrict the audience's viewpoint to that of a character was *The Lady in the Lake* (1946), an adaptation of a detective novel by Raymond Chandler. The movie attempted to imitate the novel's first-person narration by having the camera occupy the viewpoint of its detective hero, Philip Marlowe. For most of the movie Robert Montgomery, the actor playing Marlowe, only appeared when Marlowe stood in front of a mirror, and the movie aimed to offer its audience the pleasure of investigating the series of crimes at first hand. Neither audiences nor critics deemed it a satisfying experiment, primarily because it so heavily restricted the expressive use of space offered by editing.[8] As Bordwell argues, cinematic attempts to fabricate the first-person narration possible in the novel are doomed to failure so long as they seek to identify camera viewpoint with either literal viewpoint or fictive point of view, and Hollywood's predominant practice is to use "the omnipresence of classical narration to move fluidly from one character to another."[9]

These experiments and variations from the norm point to the extent to which the continuity system's construction of screen space creates hierarchies of knowledge among characters, and between characters and the audience. In their analysis of Hollywood movies in 1946, Martha Wolfenstein and Nathan Leites stressed the frequency with which plots turned on false appearances, and drew attention to the importance of "the character who sees things mistakenly," a character they identified as "the comic onlooker," "who habitually sees illicit implications in the innocent behavior of hero and heroine." In crime movies a comparable role may fall to the police, falsely accusing the hero of a crime. In either case, the role of mistaken interpreter is crucially important to the audience's activity in the theater, since the misinterpretation "conjures up a pleasurable aura of illicit possibilities around harmless acts." Like the audience, this character interprets the action and forms hypotheses about what it means and what will happen next. The misinterpretation provides a guarantee of the reliability of our interpretation:

> The comic onlooker makes us feel effortlessly omniscient. We in the audience know the true state of affairs; we know that what we see is all there is ... The comic onlooker mistakenly believes that what he sees is only a fragment of a larger whole,

Characters seldom return the viewer's gaze and look back into the camera at the audience. One instance in which this does happen is in Hitchcock's *Rear Window* (1954), at the moment when murderer Lars Thorwald (Raymond Burr) realizes that L. B. Jeffries (James Stewart) has been spying on him and knows his secret. Thorwald stares across the courtyard directly into the camera, and his return of our look both implicates the audience in Jeffries's voyeurism and terrifies us with the realization that this movie character is staring not at another character in the same movie, but directly at us as we sit in the theater. A more benign version of this fantasy is enacted in *The Purple Rose of Cairo* (1984), when a movie's leading man comes through the screen into the theater to pursue a romance with one of his fans.

Produced by Alfred Hitchcock; distributed by Paramount Pictures.

the rest of which he attempts to reconstruct. We are able to laugh at his superfluous mental exertions. Without making any such effort we know everything since the film obligingly shows us everything there is. . . . The significant events which he imagines are happening just out of sight exist only in his imagination.[10]

The subjectivity of a character is almost always nested within a more omniscient view, and within the continuity system a subjective viewpoint is established not by one shot, but by at least two and usually three. Shot 1 shows a character looking; shot 2 reveals what the character is looking at from a position close to but not identical with his or her viewpoint; shot 3, which usually reiterates shot 1, confirms that shot 2 was subjective but that we are now back with the omniscient view of the narration. Even in its most diagrammatic instances, such as its use by Alfred Hitchcock, shot 2 rarely originates exactly from the place described by shot 1, in case another character should return the gaze and look directly into the camera. Instead, it originates from a position close enough to the viewpoint of shot 1 to signal its fictive status as standing in for that viewpoint. Such shots are often called "point of view shots," but that term confuses the discussion by eliding the distinction between literal and fictional views. A shot intended to represent a

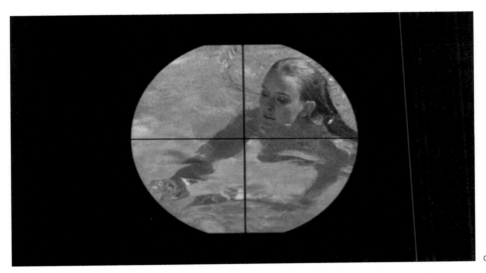

The target-shaped mask in this image from *Dirty Harry* (1971) stands in for the viewpoint of the assassin.

Produced by Don Siegel; distributed by Warner Bros.

character's viewpoint must be marked by some convention. At the beginning of *Dirty Harry* (1971), for instance, a black mask in the shape of a target sight is superimposed over the image of a woman swimming in a rooftop pool, to represent the view of an assassin through the sight of his rifle, although the camera is placed at a considerable distance from him. In such a case, the "point of view" shot is simply motivating a closer look in order to reveal a detail less obtrusively than an unmotivated camera movement might do.

For viewers to interpret character subjectivity, they need paired shots of what the character sees and the character's reaction to it. This structure is particularly important when it is used to reveal the look of one character at another. This is one of Hollywood's most consistent ways of establishing characters' desires, with

a

b

The camera's height in this shot (a) of Ron (Rock Hudson) indicates Cary's (Jane Wyman) point of view of him, not her physical viewpoint (b).

Produced by Ross Hunter; distributed by Universal-International Pictures.

the eroticized look of male characters at female characters (and, less frequently, vice versa) being the most recognizable example.

In an early scene in *All That Heaven Allows* (1955), Cary (Jane Wyman) must decide whether or not she can put social etiquette aside and go with Ron (Rock Hudson) to visit his tree nursery. The majority of the scene is played out in unemphatic medium shots, but as soon as Wyman makes the decision to go, the camera cuts to a new view of Hudson. Instead of seeing him from the comfortable perspective of the third-person observer interested in but detached from events, we suddenly glimpse Hudson from a new position that we recognize as Wyman's point of view: a low-angle shot, into which he looms slightly menacingly. We understand from this that she sees him as something exciting but also threatening. This shot offers us information about a new plot development, disrupting the space established by the previous two or three shots. We may have some difficulty in articulating this change, since its effect is almost more physical than intellectual, inducing a mild sense of disruption and loss of place. Spatial presentation operates at this level in Hollywood fictions; the mild sense of displacement produced by the change of view is itself displaced into an act of interpretation at the level of character, action, or story.

Using the mechanisms I have been describing, Hollywood movies guide their audiences through an extensive and apparently continuous spatial network, giving us a sense of actually occupying the movie alongside the characters. The resulting experience, of fluctuating between spectatorship and apparent participation, and between the points of view of different characters, is a marker of our engagement as viewers. It is a far less passive condition than the common-sense impression of moviegoing has implied. We can, for instance, detect some of the power relations being structured through a movie by looking at the distribution of viewpoints among the characters, and at what knowledge is attributed to characters and what is retained by the movie's omniscient narration.

Spatial presentation is rarely stressed in Hollywood, making it difficult for us to appreciate its significance, but its role in the communication between a visual entertainment medium and its audiences is a crucial one. We can achieve a much richer understanding of any Hollywood movie by examining its visual presentation than we will obtain if we presume that its meaning is located solely in plot and dialog.

Safe and Unsafe Space

The workings of patriarchy, and the mould of feminine unconscious it produces, have left women largely without a voice, gagged and deprived of outlets (of a kind supplied, for instance, either by male art or popular culture) in spite of the crucial social and ideological functions women are called on to perform. In the absence of any coherent culture of oppression, a simple fact of recognition has aesthetic and political importance. There is a dizzy satisfaction in witnessing the way that sexual difference under patriarchy is fraught, explosive, and erupts dramatically into violence within its own private stamping ground, the family. . . . Hollywood films made with a female audience in mind tell a story of contradiction, not of reconciliation.

Laura Mulvey[11]

Much of what I have suggested about the way that Hollywood cinema creates a safe and stable space for the audience to experience the movie would apply equally well to any period of Hollywood's history. The fundamental principles of the continuity system were established by 1920, and while Bordwell, Staiger, and Thompson's monumental account of *The Classical Hollywood Cinema* concludes its analysis of film style in 1960, its authors argue quite firmly that "most American commercial cinema has continued the classical tradition . . . the classical premises of time and space remain powerfully in force."[12] Like technological developments, changes in Hollywood's techniques of spatial representation can be considered as merely the exchange of "functional equivalents" within a stylistic system in which the "enduring principles" remain constant. The model of film style that Bordwell, Staiger, and Thompson advance assumes that "the most distinct changes take place at the level of stylistic devices," while the historical continuity of the Classical Hollywood style is established at a more general level. For example, the general conventions of Classical Hollywood style might begin a scene by drawing back from a significant object. In 1917, this would most likely have been accomplished through an iris, in 1925 through a cut, and in 1935 through a camera movement. The three historically variable devices are alternative variants of the stylistic practice.[13]

Despite its fundamental continuity, Hollywood space has a history, demarcated by technological changes and aesthetic innovations. Widescreen technology changed the shape of the cinema screen; it also changed Hollywood's presentation of space by increasing the quantity and depth of space represented in every shot. In the process, it created a series of technical and aesthetic problems in constructing stories to fit the space of CinemaScope. On the other hand, selling movies to television compromised the scale of widescreen space by requiring that the essential action in any shot be contained in the "safe action area." This compositional practice necessarily implied that within the Panavision frame, the represented space outside television's frame was redundant, industrially disabled from contributing to Hollywood's expressive space to the same extent as the space within the smaller frame. The expressive qualities of Hollywood's space were diminished by the more restricted graphic potential of this new waste space.

A critical history of Hollywood space might also link changes in spatial representation to shifts in subject matter, star images, or economic conditions, or to periods of thematic experimentation or ideological uncertainty. The "restless and unstable" space of film noir, for instance, with its unconventional lighting plots and composition, provides an appropriately unsettling environment for those movies' interrogation of some of Hollywood's more benign conventions: "no character can speak authoritatively from a space that is being continually cut into ribbons of light."[14] It is, however, possible to argue that in or about June 1960, Hollywood space changed. Thirty-five minutes into the projection of *Psycho*, its central character, Marion Crane (played by the movie's most prominent star, Janet Leigh), is savagely, meaninglessly murdered by an unidentifiable figure with a butcher knife. Horror has escaped from its Gothic castle. *Psycho* brings it home to small-town California, to the intimate spaces of the family and the bathroom. *Psycho*'s shower scene destroys Hollywood's conventions of safe space with unique brutality and abruptness. The description by *Psycho*'s director, Alfred Hitchcock, of the murder in the screenplay read: "The slashing. An impression of a knife slashing, as if tearing at the very screen, ripping the film."[15] The image itself is dismembered: the murder scene lasts under a minute, but contains 78 separate shots. The soundtrack's shrieking violins stab repeatedly at the viewer's eardrums. Until it happens, the audience has been so engrossed in Marion's story and so secure in their conventional anticipation of her eventual salvation that, as Robin Wood puts it, "we can scarcely believe it is happening; when it is over, and she is dead, we are left shocked, with nothing to cling to, the apparent center of the film entirely dissolved."[16] Our sense of the screen as a safe space to look at is destroyed with Marion's life on the first occasion we watch *Psycho*. From then on, not just in this movie but in every movie, we look on the screen more warily, in the knowledge that our comforting ability to predict what will happen in a space or a story can be arbitrarily violated.

It is, of course, an exaggeration to date the creation of **unsafe space** in Hollywood so precisely around the release of *Psycho*, but the movie did carry the destabilization of space practiced by film noir and other 1950s thrillers to new heights of malevolence. This impression was widely recorded by critics at the time. One described the atmosphere surrounding its screening as "deeply charged with apprehension." The audience was constantly aware that something awful was about to happen: "indeed, it had the solidarity of a convention assembled on the

Mrs Bates tears the screen in *Psycho* (1960); screen space was never completely safe again.
Produced by Alfred Hitchcock; distributed by Shamley Productions.

common understanding of some unspoken *entente terrible.*"[17] Against the benign character of Hollywood's safe space, in which the devices of invisible editing, eyeline matches, and shot/reverse shot patterns secure the viewer's mapping of a movie's spatial and narrative topography, the unsafe space of post-*Psycho* "nightmare movies" is actively malign, victimizing its audience. Hitchcock enthusiastically explained his apparently personal delight in manipulating the audience: when asked by critic Penelope Houston what "the deepest logic of your films" was, he replied "to put the audience through it." *Psycho*, he said, was like taking the audience "through the haunted house at the fairground or the roller-coaster." In another interview, he justified his policy of insisting that audiences not be allowed to enter screenings of *Psycho* after the start of each performance by explaining that, in the game he played with the audience, his task was to try "to outwit them."[18] Even more tellingly, perhaps, he told screenwriter Ernest Lehman that he thought of the audience as being "like a giant organ that you and I are playing. At one moment we play *this* note on them and get *this* reaction, and then we play *that* chord and they react *that* way."[19]

In this context, however, we are less concerned with exploring the psychology of the auteur or with a psychoanalytic interpretation of the movie-as-text than with the relationships that the new, unsafe space created between the audience and the screen. Where a shot/reverse shot figure in safe space secures a character's viewpoint, in unsafe space the same device tells us that the character cannot see what she is looking for, and that we cannot, either. The climax of *Cop* (1988), for example, takes place in a school gymnasium, where Lloyd Hopkins (James Woods) is hunting serial killer Bobby Franco (Steven Lambert). For several minutes the sequence is constructed of alternate shots of Hopkins moving around the gym, looking and listening, and views of what he sees: the empty gym, with Franco nowhere in sight but always liable to intrude into the space of each shot. Typically, unsafe space empowers malign characters, capable of moving through screen space in a manner incomprehensible or invisible to the audience, and threatening both sympathetic characters and viewers with their sudden, unpredictable appearance. The "stalker" or "slasher" movies of the 1970s analyzed by Vera Dika (discussed in chapter 4) make extensive use of this device: a spatial convention of the cycle is that the frame can be violently penetrated by a murderous implement, at any moment and from any angle. The movies' sadistic game is to catch their audience unawares, to stab screen space when they least expect it. In these scenarios, the audience is associated with the fictional victims, even when the camera's viewpoint is that of the monster as it attacks. Restricting the camera's viewpoint in this way, as many movies have done in imitation of *Jaws* (1975) and *Halloween* (1978) – *Alien 3* (1992) provides a good example in its chase scenes – refuses the audience a sight of the monster itself and forces them to imagine the appearance of the threat.

Unsafe space disorients the viewer, emphasizing the power of a movie's image track to control the viewer's look. As well as depriving the viewer of the power of sight by not showing things, it can also make the audience look at whatever is presented to them. Much of the art of horror, according to Carol Clover, "lies in catching the spectatorial eye unawares – penetrating it before it has a chance to close its lid."[20] Movies may assault their audiences physically, stabbing them in the eye with flashes of light, rapid, disjointed cutting, or sudden movement. Many 1980s horror movies delighted in the special effects technology of rubber prosthetics controlled by servo-motors to produce ever more excessive distortions of the human body, ever more liable to violate their audience's sensibilities. In one sequence in *The Thing* (1982), an alien capable of assuming the physical shape of any creature it takes over erupts into a grotesquely distorted amalgam of its victims that few viewers can watch without flinching. The shape-changer demonstrates that even the space occupied by a recognizably human or animal body is no longer safe to look at. Movies such as *The Thing* offer their audiences an experience in the exaggeration of anxiety, threatening them with a malign reorganization of space and rendering the act of looking itself dangerous and liable to punishment. The logical conclusion of what we might call this cinema of the unwatchable spectacle occurs at the climax of *Raiders of the Lost Ark* (1981), when Indiana Jones (Harrison Ford) tells Marion Ravenswood (Karen Allen) that the only way to survive the scene in which the ark is opened – the movie's most elaborate spectacle – is not to look at it.

Audiences have devised alternative defensive strategies for coping with their victimization in unsafe space, most prominent among them the anticipatory laughter Andrew Britton found so distasteful when watching *Hell Night* (1981).[21] Carol Clover argues that such screenings take the form of a game, substantially detached from the consumption of a movie's plot, in which the movie aims to catch the audience by surprise or "gross it out."[22] *Scream* (1996) and its sequels incorporate the conventions of these screening games into the events of the movie, allowing the movie's characters to respond to its events as if they were watching the movie, rather than being contained within its fiction.

The pleasure of viewing unsafe space is perverse in that it involves taking pleasure in associating with the victim, and audience behavior suggests that the most conventional form that this takes involves converting the masochistic pleasure of identifying with the victim into the sadistic pleasures of anticipating and enjoying the victim's experience. Conventionally, our culture genders sadism as a masculine pleasure, and when unsafe space is concentrated into generic form in the horror movie, empirical evidence confirms that its majority audience appeal is to young males.[23] As Tania Modleski remarks of *Psycho,* in the plots of slasher movies, "men's fears become women's fate."[24] Carol Clover has, however, argued persuasively that "sadistic voyeurism" is too simple a description of the complex processes of identification going on between the female victim and the male viewer of contemporary horror, pointing out that male audiences "cheer the killer on as he assaults his victims, then reverse their sympathies to cheer the survivor on as she assaults the killer," who is usually "a male in gender distress." Ironically disposing of simple applications of gendered sadistic voyeurism to these movies, Clover declares, "woe to the viewer of *Friday the Thirteenth I* who identifies with the male killer only to discover that he is a middle-aged woman." The male audience in these movies, she argues, identifies with the female survivor, whom she calls the Final Girl, the heroic self-rescuer whose body is female but whose "smartness, competence in mechanical and other practical matters, and sexual reluctance set her apart from the other girls and ally her, ironically, with the very boys she fears or rejects, not to speak of the killer himself." Horror is the principal generic location of unsafe space, and in Clover's view the primary aim of horror cinema is "to play to masochistic fears and desires in its audiences – fears and desires that are repeatedly figured as 'feminine.' . . . sadism, by definition, plays at best a supporting role."[25]

Whatever interpretation is placed on the way that male audiences identify with female protagonists, it is also important to register that these overtly masochistic identifications take place more intensely in unsafe space than they do in the safe space of Classical Hollywood. It seems hardly coincidental that the diffusion of unsafe space into Hollywood movies occurred at a time when the industry was reorienting its strategies of appeal toward its audience, abandoning its earlier attachment to a primary audience it had always assumed was female, and developing the marketing strategies discussed in chapter 1 as the "Peter Pan Syndrome." Even such exactly formal devices as the destabilized shot/reverse shot structure can be related to the economic core of Hollywood's commercial aesthetic. The shift in recreational practice from the habit of "going to *the* movies" to the much more differentiated activity of "going to see *a* movie" may have contributed to the economic viability of unsafe space, because "the risk of alienating the spectator from a single movie is economically considerably less than the risk of alienating him/her from the movies per se." *Psycho* itself had this effect, attracting a high proportion of teenagers and young adults for whom it became, according to Robert Kapsis, "a major social event not to be missed," but alienating many of Hitchcock's older fans, particularly women.[26]

Ordinary People

If Classical Hollywood projected a safe space for its audience's fantasies, we might very well regard unsafe space as post-Classical. Certainly it has become a common feature of Hollywood movies since 1960. The stylistic experimentations of the Hollywood Renaissance at the end of the 1960s were a response to the industry's changing sense of its audience as well as to the ideological uncertainties of the period. Some of the most prominent movies of those years presented a destabilization of Hollywood space through the use of a wider range of lenses and a more discontinuous editing style. If the early 1970s saw many of the certainties of Classical Hollywood re-examined, a good number of them were re-established in the latter part of the decade, and it may be more appropriate to describe a movie such as *Ordinary People* (1980) as a piece of late Classical Hollywood filmmaking, rather than the product of a post-Classical sensibility. The movie's attachment to conventions of the horror genre, however, gave it an ideological as well as a stylistic inheritance from the 1970s. Using *Ordinary People* as an occasion to examine Hollywood's changing historical representations of space allows us to consider not only this movie's politics, but also those of the genres to which it alludes.

Marking the directorial debut of Robert Redford, *Ordinary People* attracted much critical analysis at the time of its release. Industry commentary constructed it as an indication of Hollywood's renewed commitment to a more socially conscious mode for the new decade, an opinion confirmed by its four Academy Awards. In a wealthy Chicago suburb, Calvin Jarrett (Donald Sutherland), his wife Beth (Mary Tyler Moore), and younger son Conrad (Timothy Hutton) attempt to come to terms with the accidental death by drowning of elder son Buck (Scott Doebler). Conrad, recently released from hospital after a suicide attempt, reluctantly agrees to counseling with psychiatrist Dr Berger (Judd Hirsch). Intent on not being reminded of what has happened, Beth refuses to show Conrad the love she had bestowed on his brother. Calvin attempts contact with both Beth and Conrad, but his efforts prove ineffectual. Conrad forms a friendship with Jeanine (Elizabeth McGovern), but their first date is ruined by a group of boisterous schoolfellows. Disappointed by his friends and elders, and in turn disappointing to them, Conrad becomes increasingly lonely and introspective. In desperation he turns to Dr Berger, and in a moment of catharsis purges himself of his feelings of guilt at his brother's death. He achieves a new point of stability, and is reunited with Jeanine, but just as Conrad finds himself, his parents experience further crisis. Beth is unable to surrender to her own confused emotions, and insists on her right not to be disturbed by any sense of her own implication in the family's tragedy. Calvin is unable to hold the family together. As the movie ends, Beth leaves while father and son try to find some comfort together.

Ordinary People was one of several movies in the early 1980s that returned the attention of American audiences to their immediate domestic surroundings and to the fate of the middle-class family after the cultural upheavals of the previous decade. Its thematic focus on the affluent but troubled was a marked change from

Hollywood's representation of more working-class milieus in the 1970s, and its tightly constructed plot also signaled a shift away from the more expansive structures of that decade's road and odyssey pictures. With their evident concerns with the home, family, and community, domestic melodramas became as prominent a feature of the Hollywood landscape in the first half of the 1980s as they had been in the 1950s. They were also endorsed by the industry via the Academy Awards: *Kramer vs Kramer* (1979) won five Oscars, *On Golden Pond* (1981) three, *Tender Mercies* (1982) two, and *Terms of Endearment* (1983) five. Against the more militaristic strain of much of the most commercially successful product of the period (*An Officer and a Gentleman*, 1982; *Rambo: First Blood Part II*, 1985), these movies represented Hollywood's appeal to both an older audience and an established tradition of social commentary. In interviews, Redford described *Ordinary People* as a polemic on behalf of understanding and as having the serious, necessary, and difficult purpose of articulating the trauma of middle Americans after almost 20 years of neglect by movies and political culture alike:

> The middle-class is tremendously neglected . . . in order for something to be dramatic, it has to be about the very, very poor or the very, very rich, as Scott Fitzgerald said. I have always been more interested in that part of America that really makes it go . . . The idea that there is something wrong with the middle-class has never hit the middle-class fully, so that the neuroses that exist are something that have never been attended to. It's now starting.[27]

A much less sympathetic version of that argument has been offered by historians Michael Ryan and Douglas Kellner, who argue that although these new melodramas indicated an audience need for representations of emotional and familial security in a time of economic and social instability, they were also a symptom of "the increasing self-concern of an ascendant white upper middle class that no longer wants to be bothered with questions of poverty or inequality."[28]

Critical responses to the movie were also less inclined to endorse its therapeutic function. By 1980, a body of critical opinion recognized that when *All That Heaven Allows* gave its heroine a voice, it spoke against the dominant social discourses of patriarchy in 1955. A contemporary movie that deprived the central female protagonist of a voice, however, offended critical understandings of how patriarchy should be represented. Andrew Britton saw the movie as belonging to a cycle of family melodramas centered on father–son relationships, whose "Reaganite" function was to refurbish ideas about patriarchy in light of feminist critiques. Describing the movie as being, "like the vast majority of contemporary Hollywood films . . . an unabashed apology for patriarchy," Britton jointly summarized the plot of *Kramer vs Kramer* and *Ordinary People*:

> the patriarchal family is threatened with dissolution by the mother's dereliction of duty . . . the films move towards the formation of an all-male family from which she is expelled. . . . the woman, the value of whose independence has already been undermined, is denied as well even her traditional sphere of competence, and is left, as the endings of both films make very clear, with absolutely nowhere to go.[29]

Britton's interpretation was echoed by Robin Wood, who saw the movie as a paradigm for Hollywood's understanding of gender relations in the 1980s:

> If the woman can't accept her subordination, she must be expelled from the narrative altogether, like Mary Tyler Moore in *Ordinary People* . . . leaving the father to develop his relationship with his beautiful offspring untrammeled by female complications. *Ordinary People* makes particularly clear the brutality to the woman of the Oedipal trajectory our culture continues to construct: from the moment in the narrative when our young hero takes the decisive step of identification with the father/acquisition of his own woman, the mother becomes superfluous to Oedipal/patriarchal concerns, a mere burdensome redundancy.[30]

These ideological interpretations of the movie concerned themselves exclusively with plot and character, viewing its expressive use of space as sufficiently transparent to require no comment. *Ordinary People*, however, breaks with the stylistic impulses of much Hollywood cinema of the 1970s, reconstructing a Classical style that provides the audience with a secure sense of placement in the fiction, no matter how dislocated its characters may become. In *Ordinary People* doubt, anxiety, and ambiguity are the prerogative of Conrad and Calvin, and these experiences are shared by the audience insofar as they come to identify with these characters. But in contrast to their dislocation and panic, the movie's mise-en-scène remains calm and utilitarian, offering its viewers a firmly focused overview of plot events and their meanings.[31] Dialog scenes are presented in graphically matched shots taken from complementary set-ups, with the editing balanced according to Bazin's "material or dramatic logic of the scene." The movie adheres firmly to conventions of eyeline matching, the 180-degree rule, and the connective possibilities of diegetic and non-diegetic sound, in a mise-en-scène that firmly asserts the benevolence of a Hollywood space given over to elaborating character psychology.

These emphases are visible from the opening sequence, a textbook instance of Hollywood's preferred construction of screen space. A series of shots of progressively shorter scale locates the environment in which the plot will unfold, and leads us to the movie's central character. An empty image of blue sky gives way to a string of picturesquely composed images of a peaceful and affluent Chicago suburb, gradually taking us closer to the soundtrack's source, a school choir in rehearsal. The camera's panning movements across the choir are resolved on a pale-faced youth whom we identify as the movie's likely protagonist – at which point the movie cuts suddenly to the same youth jarred awake from a nightmare. This cut is an example of the way in which a device used with increasing arbitrariness in movies of the 1970s, the **"impact" edit**, is given a contained narrational function. The impact edit in *Ordinary People* still produces the violent disruption of spatial continuity that it did in *Easy Rider* (1969), but that disruption is now attributed to the character as an indicator of Conrad's sudden shifts in mood and stability. It thus comes to signify subjectivity rather than the disjunction of Classical narration or the director's sense of style. Even this degree of disruption is reduced as the plot progresses. As Conrad regains his stability, the flashbacks to his brother's drowning become less and less disruptive of continuity. Scenes of the boating accident become memories, not dreams that come upon him unawares, and rather than being disjointed individual shots they gain a continuity of their own. By the same means they cease to unsettle the audience, and instead provide us with a means of understanding Conrad. The disjunctive effect of cuts between scenes also diminishes as the movie progresses, because the graphic matching of the two shots is progressively more balanced, and because many of the early scenes emphasize the abruptness of the cut by beginning with a percussive sound effect, while later scenes often carry the sound of one scene across the cut to smooth the transition between spaces.

Ordinary People's mise-en-scène echoes this gradual shift, drawing out the expressive possibilities of represented space in an understated way, so that the meaning produced by spatial representation is displaced onto character and event. Spaces become contexts for different stages of the plot and acquire connotations. As the movie unwinds and characters start to move across the initially empty spaces of the opening sequence, we come to recognize that those peaceful and ordered two-dimensional framings mask a more turbulent three-dimensional scene, in which action and event extend beyond the frame's attempts to lend them a balanced composition. The movie sacrifices the clarity, symmetry, and harmony represented by the opening images for a series of more ambiguous and unbalanced but also more expressive framings that admit movement and history and provide the story with the possibility of resolution.

This change is indicated most clearly in the interview sequences between Conrad and Berger. As they establish a relationship and Conrad learns to lose "control" and absolve himself of guilt for his brother's death, the unemphatic lighting in Berger's office becomes darker and more expressive. The architectural mise-en-scène of the movie's early scenes in the Jarrett home gives way to a more expressive image stream that provides an arena for the movie's psychological climax. When Conrad makes the verbal slip that leads him to realize that his problems result from his failure to forgive himself for surviving the accident that killed Buck, he stands up and walks to the window of Berger's office, where he is bathed in alternating red and green light from a neon sign outside. Although the sign and the nighttime setting offer a realistic motivation for the darkness of the final interview, this use of excessive color constructs expressive space through the same devices as 1950s domestic melodrama used.

Ordinary People also gradually constructs a hierarchy of points of view that establishes the viewer in a privileged position, sharing the insights of characters but often knowing more than those characters do. We follow Beth and Calvin on their golf holiday in Houston and know about their arguments before Conrad does; we know that Conrad has quit his swim team long before his parents do. In keeping with our privileged knowledge, the camera's look is motivated by an engagement with the action, and transitions into subjective points of view are cued in advance. Perhaps most importantly for an understanding of the ideological issues raised by Britton and Wood, *Ordinary People* limits the number of points

For Conrad Jarrett (Timothy Hutton), his psychiatrist's office becomes an increasingly expressive space in *Ordinary People* (1980).
Produced by Ronald L. Schwary; distributed by Paramount Pictures.

of view through which we can organize our interpretation of character and ideology. In this respect, the movie's politics are impeccably patriarchal: Jeanine never acquires enough status to be given a point of view, but more importantly, Beth is persistently denied the right to subjectivity throughout the movie. When Cary shatters a Wedgwood jug in *All That Heaven Allows*, she, Ron, and the audience all share the same recognition that the jug has become a symbol of her relationship with Ron. When Beth breaks a plate in *Ordinary People*, the significance of the action is clearly signaled to the audience, but we have no way of knowing whether Beth shares our understanding of its meaning.

Only Calvin and Conrad can motivate the flashbacks that provide the audience with some access to their thought processes, just as only Calvin and Conrad experience the talking cure of psychoanalysis. Beth is given no chance to gain our sympathy by sharing her memories with us. She has only one scene to herself, when she enters the room of her dead son and is surprised out of her reverie by Conrad's sudden appearance behind her. This scene explicitly invokes the conventions of the "stalker" movie, with Beth as victim and Conrad as monster.[32] Beth is alone, and images of her isolation are intercut with shots of Conrad entering the house and climbing the stairs. The scene of Beth's reverie is silent, presented as a series of cuts between close shots of her blank, haunted expression and panning shots from nearly her viewpoint of the trophies and photographs on the walls. With no more information than is provided by the editing, viewers must construct whatever emotional meaning they can from the scene. Conrad's appearance abruptly curtails Beth's reverie before we have learnt its significance, but our prior sight of his arrival – and our knowledge that despite invoking the spatial conventions of

When Calvin (Donald Sutherland) tries to take a photograph of Beth and Conrad in *Ordinary People*, he discovers that he cannot make them occupy the same frame together comfortably.
Produced by Ronald L. Schwary; distributed by Paramount Pictures.

horror, he is the movie's hero – ensure that we are startled more by the vehemence of Beth's reaction to his intrusion than by his interruption.

From almost the start of the movie, Beth is regularly isolated in space, constantly trying to escape every two-shot in which she is caught with Conrad. This becomes explicit in a scene in which Calvin takes a family photograph. He tries to frame his wife and son in the same image, but fails because his clumsiness with the camera prevents him getting the "really good picture of the two of you" that he wants. Calvin's failure only repeats the movie's persistent compositional strategy. In an early scene over dinner, Calvin and Conrad talk to each other in the dining room across alternating close-ups taken close to the center line. The matched shots emphasize their alliance, while Beth is photographed from behind both of them, distanced from them and trapped in the kitchen, framed in a composition that uses the doorway to graphically box her in. Beth is frequently vulnerable to such graphic boxes. Another occurs when Calvin returns from his meeting with Dr Berger and insists on questioning her about her behavior at Buck's funeral. The composition of the full shot over Calvin's shoulder cuts her off at the knees and traps her in the narrow space of the garage doorway, where she is forced against her will to listen to his account of the funeral. While she is trapped in this way, he is privileged with a medium close shot matching his over-the-shoulder shot. In the scene around the family Christmas tree, Calvin ends up forcibly holding Beth so she cannot escape from the medium two-shot that represents another composed image of the family harmony to which he wants to cling. But when he offers his analysis of her – "You are beautiful, and you are unpre-

Beth (Mary Tyler Moore) is isolated in space, framed by the kitchen doorway in *Ordinary People*.
Produced by Ronald L. Schwary; distributed by Paramount Pictures.

dictable, but you're so cautious. You're determined, Beth, but you know something, you're not strong, and I don't know if you're really giving" – she is framed immobile in the doorway, denied entry into his space. As the movie drives toward reconciliation and conclusion, Beth is excluded and our attention is concentrated on Calvin and Conrad.

An analysis of mise-en-scène, point of view, and spatial representation in *Ordinary People* does not show the movie to have an ideology inherently different from that suggested by Britton and Wood, but it can explain how that ideology operates in the movie, rather than simply asserting its presence. That explanation can, in turn, complicate our critical response to the movie. It is possible to argue that the political significance of *Ordinary People*'s formal organization lies in its attempt to restage the domestic melodrama of female oppression in a classical space. Against a straightforwardly didactic reading of the plot as patriarchal, an interpretation of *Ordinary People* that pays attention to its construction of domestic space registers Beth as the movie's persistent victim, deprived of the representational rights accorded to the rest of her family. Such an interpretation would equate Beth with Cary in *All That Heaven Allows*, boxed in by the TV set her children give her for Christmas and by the lover reduced to the status of a child at the end of the movie. Like Cary, Beth seeks her own space, in which she may speak with her own voice. Like Cary, and like the central female protagonists in most noir movies, she is consistently denied that space, and hence offered no opportunity to speak, in a movie that places the greatest of value on the curative power of the act of speech.

Summary

- As viewers, we have two kinds of perceptions of cinematic space. On the one hand we invest the image with depth and volume to make sense of figure movement and action; on the other hand, we recognize the screen as a flat plane which shows us the graphic relations between the elements of its image. The status of cinematic space as neither strictly two-dimensional nor three-dimensional ensures that our attention to the screen takes the form of a play of looks at, into, and through the screen space.

- It is useful to distinguish between viewpoint and point of view. The viewpoint of a shot is a matter of its position in space: its angle, level, height, and distance from its subject. Point of view, however, is a position of knowledge in relation to the fiction. Characters in a scene therefore have both viewpoints and points of view.

- Despite its fundamental continuity, Hollywood space has a history, which has been influenced by technological changes and aesthetic innovations. Changes in spatial representation might also be linked to shifts in subject matter, star image, economic conditions, thematic experimentation, or periods of ideological uncertainty.

- Unsafe space disorients the viewer, emphasizing the power of a movie's image track to control the viewer's look. As well as depriving the viewer of the power of sight by not showing things, it can also make the audience look at whatever is presented to them.

- Unsafe space is a phenomenon of post-Classical Hollywood, and its most influential early occurrence was in *Psycho* (1960). The pleasure of viewing unsafe space is perverse in that it involves taking pleasure in associating with the victim, and audience behavior suggests that the most conventional form this takes involves converting the masochistic pleasure of identifying with the victim into the sadistic pleasures of anticipating and enjoying the victim's experience.

- Movies that exploit the conventions of unsafe space offer their viewers an experience in the exaggeration of anxiety, threatening them with a malign organization of space and rendering the act of looking itself dangerous and liable to punishment. In its more extreme versions, such as *The Thing* (1982), unsafe space presents its audiences with an experience we might call the cinema of the unwatchable spectacle.

Further Reading

Point of view and identification

Douglas Pye provides a critical history of the term "point of view" and detailed examples of its use in close analysis of movies in "Movies and Point of View," *MOVIE* 36 (2000), pp. 2–34.

Other critics have borrowed the term "focalization" from Gerard Genette's analysis of literary narrative in *Narrative Discourse: An Essay in Method*, trans. Jane E. Lewin (Ithaca, NY: Cornell University Press, 1980), to describe what I am calling point of view. Edward Branigan, in "The Point of View Shot," in *Movies and Methods. Vol. II*, ed. Bill Nichols (Berkeley, CA: University of California Press, 1985), pp. 672–91, and in *Point of View in the Cinema: A Theory of Narration and Subjectivity in Classical Film* (New York: Mouton, 1984), takes another term from Genette in discussing the "filmic voice" that "speaks" the points of view of characters in much the same way as a narrator establishes subsidiary points of view in a novel. I prefer to retain the spatial metaphor for a process that works through the representation of space. Noël Carroll discusses point of view in "Toward a Theory of Point-of-View Editing: Communication, Emotion and the Movies," in *Theorizing the Moving Image* (Cambridge: Cambridge University Press, 1996), pp. 125–38. See also George M. Wilson, *Narration in Light: Studies in Cinematic Point of View* (Baltimore, MD: Johns Hopkins University Press, 1986).

Laura Mulvey's article, "Visual Pleasure and Narrative Cinema," identifies the three looks of audience, camera, and character discussed in this chapter, but develops her argument in a quite different direction from that followed here. Mulvey's article, first published in *Screen* 16:3 (Autumn 1975), had great influence on subsequent feminist and psychoanalytic film criticism, and has been widely anthologized, including in her own collection of essays, *Visual and Other Pleasures* (Bloomington: Indiana University Press, 1989). It is also discussed in chapter 18.

A psychoanalytic theory of identification is most fully elaborated in Christian Metz, *The Imaginary Signifier: Psychoanalysis and the Cinema*, trans. Celia Britton, Annwyl Williams, Ben Brewster, and Alfred Guzzetti (Bloomington: Indiana University Press, 1982), pp. 49–52. It has, however, been disputed, notably by Noël Carroll, who argues (in Carroll, *Mystifying Movies: Fads and Fallacies in Contemporary Film Theory* (New York: Columbia University Press, 1988), p. 40):

> If I truly identified with the camera, I suppose that I would experience the entire visual array of the projection as coextensive with my visual field. Yet, when I look at a film image, I only focus on part of it, usually upon what is represented in the foreground . . .

often the camera's field of view is broader than mine; my field of vision is not coextensive with its field of vision.

Alternative understandings of identification between viewers and characters are explored in Murray Smith, "Altered States: Character and Emotional Response in the Cinema," *Cinema Journal* 33:4 (Summer 1994), pp. 34–56, and in the essays in *Passionate Views: Film, Cognition and Emotion*, eds Carl Plantinga and Greg M. Smith (Baltimore, MD: Johns Hopkins University Press, 1999). Murray Smith enlarges on his ideas in *Engaging Characters: Fiction, Emotion, and the Cinema* (Oxford: Oxford University Press, 1995).

Safe space

David Bordwell discusses the security of Classical Hollywood space in part 1 of Bordwell, Janet Staiger, and Kristin Thompson, *The Classical Hollywood Cinema: Film Style and Mode of Production to 1960* (London: Routledge and Kegan Paul, 1985). Kristin Thompson, *Storytelling in the New Hollywood: Understanding the Classical Narrative Technique* (Cambridge, MA: Harvard University Press, 1999), argues strongly for the continuity between Classical Hollywood's stylistic practices and those of American cinema since the 1970s.

The scene from *Stagecoach* is analyzed in detail in Nick Browne, "The Spectator-in-the-Text: The Rhetoric of *Stagecoach*," in *Narrative, Apparatus, Ideology: A Film Theory Reader*, ed. Philip Rosen (New York: Columbia University Press, 1986), pp. 102–19. Browne's argument is elaborated further in his *The Rhetoric of Filmic Narration* (Ann Arbor: University of Michigan Press, 1982).

Film noir, *Psycho*, and unsafe space

Psycho has been widely recognized as being of pivotal significance for the horror movie, and for larger cultural concerns. It is well summarized by Robin Wood in *Hollywood from Vietnam to Reagan* (New York: Columbia University Press, 1986), pp. 150–1:

> *Psycho* is clearly a seminal work, definitively establishing two concepts crucial to the

genre's subsequent development: the monster as human psychotic/schizophrenic and the revelation of horror as existing at the heart of the family. . . . Since *Psycho*, and especially in the '70s, the definition of normality has become increasingly uncertain, questionable, open to attack; accordingly, the monster becomes increasingly complex.

Psycho's pivotal position between Classical and post-Classical Hollywood is discussed in Linda Williams, "Discipline and Fun: *Psycho* and Postmodern Cinema," in *Reinventing Film Studies*, eds Christine Gledhill and Linda Williams (London: Arnold, 2000).

On space in film noir, see chapter 5 of James Naremore, *More than Night: Film Noir in its Contexts* (Berkeley, CA: University of California Press, 1998); Alain Silver and James Ursini, *The Noir Style* (New York: Aurum, 1999); Vivian Sobchack, "Lounge Time: Postwar Crises and the Chronotope of Film Noir," in *Reconfiguring Film Genres: Theory and History*, ed. Nick Browne (Berkeley, CA: University of California Press, 1998), pp. 129–70; and several of the analytical essays in *The Movie Book of Film Noir*, ed. Ian Cameron (London: Studio Vista, 1992). On the unsafe spaces of horror movies, see Carol J. Clover, *Men, Women and Chainsaws: Gender in the Modern Horror Film* (London: British Film Institute, 1992); Jonathan Lake Crane, *Terror and Everyday Life: Singular Moments in the History of the Horror Film* (Thousand Oaks, CA: Sage, 1994); and essays in *The Horror Reader*, ed. Ken Gelder (London: Routledge, 2000). On horror movies' gendered appeal, see Brigid Cherry, "Refusing to Refuse to Look: Female Viewers of the Horror Movie," in *Identifying Hollywood's Audiences: Cultural Identity and the Movies*, eds Melvyn Stokes and Richard Maltby (London: British Film Institute, 1999), pp. 186–203, and Isabel Cristina Pinedo, *Recreational Terror: Women and the Pleasures of Horror Film Viewing* (Albany: State University of New York Press, 1997).

CHAPTER TWELVE
Performance 1

Perhaps Hollywood movies give us pleasure and a sense of identification simply because they enable us to recognize and adapt to the "acted" quality of everyday life: they place us safely outside dramatic events, a position from which we can observe people lying, concealing emotions, or staging performances for one another.

James Naremore[1]

We set an actor in front of us, asked him to imagine a dramatic situation that did not involve any physical movement, then we all tried to understand what state he was in. Of course, this was impossible, which was the point of the exercise.

Peter Brook[2]

In the early 1920s, one of the founders of Soviet cinema, Lev Kuleshov, may have edited together a sequence of shots that has since become probably the most discussed piece of lost film in cinema history. According to Kuleshov's pupil, Vsevolod Pudovkin, Kuleshov cut together a close-up of the actor Ivan Mosjoukine's face with three other shots: a bowl of soup, a child playing with a toy bear, and a woman lying in a coffin. The shot of Mosjoukine's expressionless face was the same in all three sequences, but when they were shown to audiences, "the public raved about the acting of the artist. They pointed out the heavy pensiveness of his mood over the forgotten soup . . . the deep sorrow with which he looked on the dead woman . . . the light, happy smile with which he surveyed the girl at play. But we knew that in all three cases the face was exactly the same."[3] The footage of the Kuleshov experiment, as it has become known, has long disappeared, but the claims based on its results were fundamental to the montage-based theories of Soviet cinema in the 1920s, and to much subsequent theorizing about how cinema, and in particular cinema acting, constructs meaning.

Pudovkin's argument was that "the film is not *shot*, but *built*, built up from the separate strips of celluloid that are its raw material."[4] He maintained that the juxtaposition of the close-up of Mosjoukine and each of the other shots generated a precise and predictable meaning in the mind of the spectator that was present in neither shot by itself. Spectators, however, understood the meaning to be the result of the actor's performance: a performance apparently created entirely by editing. The resulting theory of the production of cinematic meaning corresponded to both the ideological and aesthetic preferences of early Soviet society. Editing constructed meaning **dialectically**: the juxtaposition of two shots – thesis and antithesis – produced the synthesis of the spectator's recognition of sorrow or happiness. Pudovkin's theory of montage emphasized the power of the cinematic machine, under the control of the director and editor, to create meaning with the reliability of a factory assembly line. Much of the cinema's appeal as an instrument of ideological education and persuasion lay in this mechanical predictability: the correct assembly of a sequence would invariably result in the correct interpretation of the sequence by every spectator, since "the camera compels the spectator to see as the director wishes." Pudovkin did not regard the spectator as entirely passive, however, arguing that cinema required "an exceptional concentration of attention" from its viewers. The task of the director, the creative intelligence guiding the construction of the image stream, was to direct the spectator's attention.[5] "With correct montage, even if one takes the performance of an actor directed at something quite different, it will still reach the viewer in the way intended by the editor, because the viewer himself will complete the sequence and see that which is suggested to him by the montage."[6]

We rely on Kuleshov and Pudovkin themselves for the accounts we have of the Kuleshov experiments, and several critics have noted the imprecisions in their descriptions. Attempts to duplicate the experiment have failed to reproduce the claimed results. Whether or not the "Kuleshov effect" ever existed as it was described, it has had a substantial influence on subsequent theorizing about both the passivity of the spectator and the power of editing to create performative meaning. The readiness with which this account of the relationship between spectator and text has for so long been accepted contrasts noticeably with Peter Brook's description, at the beginning of this chapter, of a much less successful theatrical experiment in communicating meaning without movement: "Of course, this was impossible, which was the point of the exercise." Kuleshov's faith in the mechanical effectiveness with which the cinema produces audience emotion is in stark contrast with critic Frank McConnell's assertion that the spectator's ability to register and respond to an emotion speaks not to the power of the machine, but to "a crucial, archetypal aspect of all film personality: that struggle of the human to show itself *within* the mechanical." The screen performer, he argues, "is burdened with the necessity of realizing his role – which is to say, his physical reality –

through a medium which resists the full reality of that presence." McConnell describes screen performance as "a warfare between personality and mechanism." His concern is with what he sees as the "existential paradox" of cinema, "the real presence of human figures and faces who, although they are never really there as we watch the screen, are nevertheless the best and only reason anyone has for looking at the screen at all."[7]

As McConnell observes, movie criticism has found it difficult to discuss the role of the actor. Almost every analysis of acting in the cinema begins by commenting on the paucity of the vocabulary available for the critical examination of performance. The explanation for this paucity is surprisingly simple: acting is difficult to analyze because it is not understood as a systematic or standardized practice. Acting is usually understood in more individual terms, as the particular practice of particular actors. Most writers either give an impressionistic account of what it felt like to witness the performance ("a tight, brittle, monstrously subdued performance")[8] or else list in detail the gestures and intonations the performer uses (John Wayne expresses amusement "by the following performance: his eyes look slightly left, slightly heavenward, there is a faint smile on his face, he moves his right leg and upper body just a little, keeping his arms behind his back").[9] However detailed such notations become, they fail to catch the nuance of performance because acting is **analogical**, a mode of communication that works in terms of proportion, gradation, and inflection rather than the clear-cut distinctions and differences of **digital** sign systems. The constant, subtle changes of expression and intonation that comprise a performance are easily comprehended within the context of a movie, but are notoriously difficult either to describe or to analyze in words. Instead, description and analysis both fall back on what James Naremore, in his book *Acting in the Cinema*, calls "fuzzy adjectival language."[10] The great bulk of writing about film acting is evaluative, concerned almost exclusively with declaring how good or bad a particular performance is, although the criteria by which these judgments are made are often very vague. In this chapter and the next I will try to provide some terms by which movie acting can be described and different types of performance distinguished from each other. These chapters are, however, only partially concerned with acting, and we must consider a number of other senses of the term "performance" as well.

However unreliable they might be, accounts of the Kuleshov experiment suggest the extent to which a cinematic performance is never constructed by an actor alone. Perhaps the most obvious way in which cinematic acting differs from theatrical acting is that a cinematic performance is discontinuous, fragmented into the individual shots which are the movie's constituent parts, and reassembled in the editing room. Pudovkin was right to stress how far a movie performance is built, not shot. For an actor to "build" a movie performance is, however, more difficult than it is in the theater, because the individual fragments of that performance will normally be recorded out of order. In *Film Acting*, Pudovkin argued that:

> The discontinuity of the actor's work . . . demands from the film actor firstly a knowledge of how consciously to exploit the possibilities of vari-angled shooting for the

purposes of his work on the external shaping of his role, and, secondly, clear consideration of its creative place in the edited composition of the whole film, in order that he may understand and bring out the most comprehensive and profound bases of his acting.[11]

The constructed nature of a movie emphasizes the extent to which a movie performance is not only the work of the actor, however. Several different bodies may be used to construct a single performance: voices are dubbed, stunt artists are used for dangerous action sequences, and sometimes hand models and body doubles provide body parts to substitute for the actors. As an extreme example, in *Psycho* (1960), the performance of Mrs Bates is constructed from the bodies of three actors and the voices of three more.[12] A movie performance is also constructed out of the performance of the camera, the editing, and the mise-en-scène.

A movie is a performance and not a text. If movies were texts, we could write about them with much more critical confidence than we do. All attempts to reduce movies to texts, whether through analogies between film and language, shots and words, or through formal analysis, ultimately fail to resolve the interpretive complexities of performance signs and thus also fail to resolve the dialectic of cinema's warfare between personality and mechanism, or the paradox that McConnell identifies in cinema's peculiar power to create "the presence of absence, a 'reality' which is not there" by projecting light onto the screen.[13] This absent presence is perhaps most obviously realized in the incidental music that accompanies a movie's performance. The music is a form of commentary on the action, but it is present neither in the represented space of the movie nor for the actor at the moment of his or her performance. Since it lacks an identifiable point of origin, the viewer cannot attribute its commentary to anyone other than himself or herself. The audience hears it, but since it is not present in the movie's **diegesis**, the characters cannot hear it. Yet, as well as teaching the audience how to interpret the action and the characters' behavior and emotions, these "unheard melodies" "support the physical and emotional work of the actor, justifying and rendering plausible gestures that might seem "large, excessive, vacuous, or grafted-on as an afterthought" without the musical support and interpretation.[14] The music is itself, of course, a performance, and for "silent" cinema audiences, the musical performance constituted the live part of a multi-media presentation. In sound cinema, the disembodied, sourceless music functions to unite the viewer emotionally with the absent performer.

Cinema criticism has borrowed its discourses of performance from theater. Some of those discourses have referred to acting, some to the star system, and others to the vocabulary of performance itself. In a commercial sense, a movie "performs" at the box-office, where the quality of its performance is strictly related to its profitability. A screening is also called a performance of the movie; perhaps this is the most mechanical sense of a movie's performance, since apart from the audience, the only thing performing during a movie's performance is the projector. The cinema's "performance," its capacity to create the illusion of movement through space and time, is, therefore, dependent on the efficient performance of a well-engineered machine. This sense of cinema's mechanical performance was most vividly evoked by Soviet filmmaker Dziga Vertov's description of the camera's "Kino Eye," a mechanical eye which is "more perfect than the human eye for examining the chaos of visual phenomena that resemble space."[15]

The Spectacle of Movement

The spectacle of movement was the cinema's first "production value." For the first time the world was revealed in motion, and the impression of lifelike movement amazed and excited its earliest viewers. An advertisement for the first exhibition of Edison's Vitascope in New York in 1896 promised that the audience would see the "Perfect Reproduction of Noted Feminine Figures and Their Every Movement."[16] Early "actuality" films were often primarily demonstrations of cinema's ability to record movement, in single shots of waves breaking on a shore, processions, or horse races. Reviewing the Vitascope exhibition, the *New York Herald* critic was most impressed by R. W. Paul's film of *Rough Sea at Dover*:

> Far out in the dim perspective one could see a diminutive roller start. It came down the stage, apparently, increasing in volume, and throwing up little jets of snow-white foam, rolling faster and faster, and hugging the old sea wall, until it burst and flung in shredded masses far into the air. The thing was altogether so realistic and the reproduction so absolutely accurate that it fairly astounded the beholder. It was the closest copy of nature any work of man has ever yet achieved.[17]

Film historian Tom Gunning has argued that these early films were organized "less as a way of telling stories than as a way of presenting a series of views to an audience, fascinating because of their illusory power . . . and exoticism." Gunning calls this conception the **"cinema of attractions,"** taking his term from the "attractions" on display to the audience of a vaudeville or variety theater. He suggests that while an alternative set of spectator relations came to predominate in narrative-oriented cinema after 1906, the cinema of attractions remained "a component of narrative films, more evident in some genres (e.g. the musical) than in others."[18] The word "cinema" itself is derived from the Greek word for motion, *kinema*, and Hollywood's tendency to call its products motion pictures or movies rather than films is an indication of its commitment to the spectacle of the moving image. Chapter 15 will argue that a Hollywood movie can usefully be understood as a series of attractions organized into sequence by a story.

American fiction movies have stressed movement from the outset, with early chase films providing the first synthesis of narrative and the attractions of spectacular movement. Slapstick comedy incorporated frenetic chases, stage melodramas were "opened out" with climactic races against time, and Westerns developed a new rhetoric of dramatic exposition with their extended action sequences across expansive outdoor spaces. Hollywood cinema has never lost this initial excitement in, and celebration of, the spectacular attraction of sheer movement, quite separate from the construction of the movie's story. *Grand Prix* (1966), *Days of Thunder* (1990), and *Driven* (2001), all set in the world of motor racing, feature several extended action sequences each in which cars drive around race tracks. In every case, the sequences give far more attention to the spectacle of speed than to the narrative activity of telling us who is winning the race. Sports movies in general follow a convention of showing the highlights of their action in slow motion, presenting the cinematic performance of motion as spectacle in as pure a manner as *Rough Sea at Dover*, and giving us the chance to dwell on our delight in the representation of movement for its own sake. *Jurassic Park* (1993) and its sequels spent millions of dollars on fabricating the lifelike movement of long-extinct animals.

In addition to early cinema's reliance on the movement of objects within a fixed frame, however, we can identify two further kinds of movement in Hollywood movies: the movement of the camera itself, and the movement produced in the editing process. These three kinds of movement usually work in combination. The car chase in *Bullitt* (1968), for example, suspends narrative development for 10 minutes while Steve McQueen pursues a pair of assassins through the streets of San Francisco in a spectacular high-speed car chase. The sequence makes effective use of a shot similar to that of the rollercoaster ride in *This is Cinerama* (1952). The camera shoots through the windshield of McQueen's car as it hurtles down the steep inclines of San Francisco's streets, bouncing furiously every time he crosses an intersection. Audiences, too, bounce up and down energetically in their seats, their sympathetic motion physically expressing their willingness to cooperate with the movie in anticipating, perceiving, and reacting to movement within the image. These viewpoint shots, showing us forward movement seen through the fixed frame of the car windshield, provide an analog for the viewer's position in the theater, sitting in a fixed seat looking at a static screen, on which images move without the viewer having to move to see them. These shots are intercut with two other representations of movement: panning shots of the two cars speeding past taken from static camera positions, and shots taken from vehicles moving at the same speed as the cars, in which the cars themselves remain fairly stable in the frame, while the background speeds by. The full effect of the spectacle comes from the intercutting of these viewpoints, as the audience's position alternates between being inside and outside the action, while the sequence as a whole emphasizes the general impression of speed for its own sake, rather than developing the narrational possibilities of the scene. In this scene, just as much as in the dialog scenes analyzed in the previous chapter, the audience's involvement is produced by the editing of the sequence placing us as participant observers, alternately within and outside the space of the action.

Hollywood's delight in movement for its own sake ensures that nearly every movie has at least one sequence which displays action or physical expertise as a production value, interrupting narrative and challenging its dominance. Again, musical sequences provide some of the clearest examples. Midway through *Singin' in the Rain* (1952), Donald O'Connor gives an exuberant performance in a number called "Make 'Em Laugh," a demonstration of the art of laughter-making and a polemic on its behalf, reveling in bodily movement. Like most musical performances it follows a cue for a song, and features a lively, up-tempo lyric that escalates into a dance routine and a series of comic pratfalls. These devices mark it as taking place outside the narrative constraints of the movie. Staged on a movie studio set, its obvious theatricality provides O'Connor with a safe space in which the normal rules of physical mobility are suspended, so that he can move in any way he chooses, completely controlling his environment and the props within it. Safe spaces for performance, where the human body is the center of the spectacle, are often marked by theatrical devices. In this scene the back wall of the set is painted as a corridor receding in perspective, but O'Connor exposes the illusion by running up the wall to perform a back-flip. The first couple of times he walks into solid objects we may worry about his being injured, but we soon recognize that in this performance space he cannot be hurt. By the end of the performance we watch him leap through a brick wall and still find it funny.

As the sequence snowballs, O'Connor's movements become increasingly assertive and energetic: eccentric dance-steps, tumbles, and back-flips. Camera movement and editing are kept to a minimum: both simply recompose space to support O'Connor's performance. The camera keeps a fairly constant distance from the performance, positioning O'Connor clearly and centrally, showing the whole of his body and allowing him room to move, but concealing the physical effort involved in sustaining the routine. As important as shot scale is minimal cutting: a single long take covers most of the routine, with panning movements reframing the space to cover O'Connor's actions. Musical sequences and comedy routines are often constructed like this, with the duration of the shots emphasizing the complexities of a sustained performance. In this case, shot duration intensifies our attention to O'Connor's antics and our sense of his skill.

This sequence suspends some of the causal logics that usually structure a Hollywood movie. O'Connor's routine is an **autonomous spectacle**, offering the audience a source of pleasure independent of the narrative – an "attraction," in Tom Gunning's terms. Inviting us to share in O'Connor's obvious delight in movement for its own sake, the sequence compensates for interrupting the plot by ostentatiously celebrating its own surplus energy. Our appreciation of the performer's skill concentrates our attention on O'Connor, and the expertise with which he performs his gymnastic feats, while his character, Cosmo, effectively disappears from the scene. The effect of movement in a performance routine contrasts markedly with the restrictions placed upon characters trapped within more solidly narrative spaces. Characters caught up in a particular narrative situation may be entirely deprived of the assertive power of movement. As *High Noon* (1952) approaches its climax, the townspeople who have refused to help Marshall Kane (Gary Cooper) are caught in static poses as they wait uneasily for events to unfold. Their immobility is emphasized by the movie's cutting pointedly between them and the image of a clock in Kane's office, where the only movement visible in the sequence is the mechanical swinging of the clock's pendulum.

The Movement of Narrative

Nearly all editing points in narrative film are devised to set up a framework
of expectations in a series of shots. The result is narrative motion.
Steven D. Katz[19]

As well as offering spectacular interludes, physical movement within the frame is
a principal source of story information and the basis of many of our perceptions
about characters. Likewise, camera movement is usually used to emphasize the
narrative significance of an action rather than the spectacular pleasures of its
representation. The camera moves to accommodate the movement of characters
across represented space, panning to follow a character as he or she walks across
a room, for instance. Narrative motion is rarely produced through camera movement alone, however. It is completed in the editing process, so that cuts cover
significant transitions and combine viewpoints. If the character goes through a
doorway, the movie will cut to a new angle from the adjoining room. Expressive
camera movement can also operate in a conventional fashion. At the death of
Sheriff Baker (Slim Pickens) in *Pat Garrett and Billy the Kid* (1973), the camera
draws back to a long shot, both to frame Baker and his wife (Katy Jurado) in the
landscape and to draw a veil over the precise moment of death. The movement
accords Baker the closest thing to heroic dignity available in the movie.

One of Hollywood's conventional modes of reframing is "frame cutting": just
as a figure is moving out of the frame, the screen image cuts to the adjacent space,
giving the audience the sense that the space represented on the screen at any given
moment is the most important segment of a larger environment. Frame cutting
also makes the cut smooth and speeds up the flow of the action. The continuity
system encourages cutting on action, as the flow of the movement from one shot
to the other diverts the viewer's attention away from the change in camera angle.
Minimizing the viewer's attention to the presence of the camera is also achieved
by camera movements that reframe the action. Such movements imitate our
human tendency to move our eyes and head to keep the object of interest in the
center of vision, and seem less distracting than a static camera in which figure
movement in the fixed frame unbalances the composition.[20]

Like editing, lens choice, and other elements of mise-en-scène, camera movement generally follows what André Bazin called "the material or dramatic logic of
the scene,"[21] directing audience attention without drawing attention to itself. That
apparently transparent logic is, however, highly mediated. Classical editing technique does not, for instance, cut when the camera is moving. Even when following a character walking from one room to another, the image will pause briefly at
the end of one panning movement, cut to the other side of the doorway, and only
after the cut from static frame to static frame will the camera pick up the movement again. A movie like *Nashville* (1975), in which this convention of not cutting
on camera movement is systematically breached, produces a strong sense of
disorientation and unease in most audiences. Since the mid-1980s, however, the

stylistic tendency of music video sequences to cut at much higher rates than narrative features or television have accustomed audiences to more disjunctive patterns of editing than were previously accepted.

When camera movement is not motivated by character movement, the change of viewpoint may give the audience a new point of view on the action in the scene. The combination of points of view can offer the audience knowledge that characters do not share. Alfred Hitchcock's movies, always on the point of playfully exposing Hollywood's conventions, often dwell on the relationship between viewpoint and point of view, and occasionally do so through the use of elaborate camera movement. In one scene in *Notorious* (1946), Alicia (Ingrid Bergman) is trying to steal a key from her husband, Alexander Sebastian (Claude Rains). Almost caught in the act, she hides the key in her clenched fist. The camera's repeated movements in on their hands keep the audience's attention concentrated on where the key is, while Sebastian remains oblivious to what the scene is really "about." In the ballroom scene that follows, the same point is made in a more extreme fashion. A high-angle long shot from the top of a staircase surveys the room in which Alicia and Sebastian are greeting their guests. In an elaborate crane movement, the camera descends the stairs and continues insistently to track in on Alicia, coming to rest on a tight close-up of the key being turned in her hand. At one level, this camera movement unmotivated by character focuses the narrative. But in drawing attention to itself, this ostentatious visual gesture also becomes the sign of a stylistic **excess** identifying the presence of a movie's auteur – in this case a kind of mischievousness on Hitchcock's part, as he insistently draws attention to the very thing that Alicia is trying to hide.

The opening sequence in *Touch of Evil* (1958) is staged as a long mobile shot involving several complex tracking and craning movements. Lasting for over three minutes, it covers all of the initiating action of the movie. The shot's very complexity draws attention to the presence of the camera. Viewers who notice the absence of cuts are likely to register the camera's bravura display and wonder at how difficult the shot must have been to stage. Even viewers who do not consciously register that the sequence is presented in a single shot become oppressively aware of the passage of time as the shot continues. Like the two scenes in *Notorious*, the shot produces a hierarchy of knowledge: the audience knows that a bomb has been planted in the car we intermittently follow, but its occupants and the couple walking beside it (Charlton Heston and Janet Leigh) do not. The longer the take goes on, therefore, the more uncomfortable the audience becomes, both dreading and longing for the explosion that will allow the movie to cut away from the oppressive viewpoint of the single camera position.

Long takes make the audience aware that they have no control over the passing of time. Much of the opening shot in *Touch of Evil* takes the form of a backward tracking movement, producing an effect rather like riding backwards on a train: you can't see where you're going or what's in front of you. Despite the expansiveness of its movement, it provides the audience with a single viewpoint, and as a result it supplies a very restricted amount of story information. The shot forces us to wait, watch, and grow more nervous as the movie deliberately refuses us the luxury of escaping back into a more comfortable, edited narrative time or a safer vantage point. The long take's effect is, however, determined by its context. While a musical's use of the long take may allow the audience to celebrate the performers' skill, suspense movies are usually much less benign, turning the audience themselves into victims of the movie's manipulations.

Visual style is not usually so conspicuous an element in a movie's performance. In *Touch of Evil* we notice the emphasis on the camera as an active agent in the manipulation of the audience precisely because we are used to the more anonymous and self-effacing strategies associated with Hollywood camerawork. Long takes or extravagant camera gestures stress the existence of an instrumental, manipulative presence possessing more knowledge (of where the camera is going in both literal and metaphorical terms) than the viewer. It is, therefore, not surprising that the examples we have discussed are often cited as the directorial signatures of two of Hollywood's pre-eminent auteurs. The distinctive visual styles of both Hitchcock and Welles typically deploy a mobile camera to declare a controlling narrating presence. In 1948 Hitchcock directed *Rope*, a movie consisting of only a dozen shots, each lasting about ten minutes or the length of a reel of film. At the end of each shot the camera settles on a static object, such as the lid of a trunk, so that the next shot can begin from that point, as if the whole movie were taken in a single shot. To compensate for the absence of editing, the camera has to keep moving to adjust composition. In the performance of the movies he directed as well as in his public persona, Hitchcock – "the Master of Suspense" – turned his audiences into victims by emphasizing their powerlessness to influence the action on the screen. Auteurist criticism has often recognized visual style as a sign of the presence of an intending narrator – here "Hitchcock" or "Welles" – and has described this manipulation of the audience's position in terms of individual artistry. The claustrophobic effect of the opening shot of *Touch of Evil* is, however, mitigated by the fact that the credits are superimposed over it. Auteurist critics have denounced this decision, made by the movie's producers against Welles's objections, as philistine, and in 2000 Universal released a version of the movie "restored to Welles' vision," with the credits removed and a different soundtrack over the opening shot.[22] It is, however, possible to suggest a more sympathetic account of the producers' action. By providing a distraction from the intensity of the long take, the credits make it more comfortable to watch, offering a kind of cutting within the image. We may not applaud this motive, but we should recognize it as purposeful, not merely insensitive, an instance of the lengths to which Hollywood's commercial aesthetic will go to keep its customers satisfied. It also suggests the practical restrictions on an auteurist reading of even the most self-consciously authored movie.

Acting as Impersonation

I don't understand this Method stuff. I remember Laurence Olivier asking Dustin Hoffman why he stayed up all night. Dustin, looking really beat, really bad, said it was to get into the scene being filmed that day, in which he was supposed to have been up all night. Olivier said, "My boy, if you'd learn to act you wouldn't have to stay up all night."

Robert Mitchum[23]

Actors with only one dimension do not often become stars. Actors who create surprise, embody contradiction, impel the spectator to hold two conflicting ideas in the head at the same time, stand a better chance.

Robert Sklar[24]

Hollywood appropriates performance styles from a variety of theatrical traditions: from vaudeville, from circus and pantomime as in the "Make 'Em Laugh" number from *Singin' in the Rain*, and elsewhere from burlesque, radio, and television. In part this simply reflects Hollywood's industrial practice of exploiting talent already trained in other theatrical disciplines, but it also suggests that different performance styles are necessary in different generic contexts. The presentation of performance as autonomous spectacle is not confined to musicals, of course. Comedies have gag-sequences, war movies have action sequences, thrillers their final chase. Alongside the notion of performance as action, however, Hollywood also draws on the different definition of performance associated with the concept of acting, a practice that enjoys a higher cultural status than the performance tradition represented by O'Connor's routine. The relative cultural status of Hollywood movies is in large part governed by the kind of performance they sponsor: some of Hollywood's most respectable movies, from *Cavalcade* (1933) to *Who's Afraid of Virginia Woolf?* (1966), have been versions of critically acclaimed stage plays, while few physical comedies, musicals, or action adventures have won Academy Awards for Best Picture or Best Performance. The higher status of acting is in part derived from the superior cultural prestige of **legitimate theater** by comparison to vaudeville, and in part from its aspirations to "truth" or verisimilitude in the imitation of character.

Although acting performance can draw attention to itself and function as a separate spectacle, it more routinely aspires toward transparency, in the same way as codes of editing and camerawork seek to render themselves invisible. This "invisible" style of acting imitates the expressions and emotions of the everyday world, with the aim of creating a sense of character for the audience without making them consciously aware of how that sense is created. Criticism often judges the quality of these performances in the rather vague terms of assessing their "sincerity" or their "truth." Acting manuals invoke an idea of "truth" in performance almost as often as they invoke the rhetoric of realism, although they seldom explain exactly what they mean by suggesting that "your job as an actor is to convince the audience of the truth of what is happening to you," or "the aim of acting in a picture is to be as real as the rock you sit on or the tree you lean against."[25] As these quotations suggest, it is not only criticism that lacks a clear descriptive terminology for discussing what acting entails; by comparison with other aspects of the production process, acting remains a largely untheorized, intuitive activity, summarized in one recent manual for the aspiring screen actor as "whatever works."[26]

Almost every account of what acting attempts to achieve describes its objective as the imitation of "real life." In 1900, dramatic critic Bronson Howard defined "the art of acting" as being "the art of seeming to move, speak, and appear on the stage as the character assumed moves, speaks, and appears in real life, under the circumstances indicated in the play. In that word 'seeming,'" he added, "lie nearly all the difficulties, the intricacies, the technicalities of acting."[27] Audiences share the expectation of realism: as theater historian David Mayer explains, "we expect that a cinema actor, with facial nuances, small suggestive gestures, and vocal modulations such as those we might use in our daily lives, will try to confirm the corporeality and actuality of the environment that he or she inhabits. The actor makes fiction into reality."[28] Even in a movie in which unpredictable or implausible events occur – a screwball comedy, for instance – characters need to have convincing motives for their actions, and these are most readily supplied by patterns of behavior and psychology that we recognize from the everyday world. In Frank McConnell's terms, acting is the site of the human in the machine of cinema. McConnell sees movie acting as being radically different from stage acting, not in its technical skills but in the actor's relation to space and the audience. While the craft of the stage actor is to assimilate himself or herself to a predetermined role that becomes realized in his or her physical presence on the stage, the movie performer never shares a common space with the audience, and thus the dynamics of their relationship are different. The stage actor has to persuade the audience to "see through" his or her presence to the character. The movie actor has first of all to assert his or her own coherent physical presence against the artifice and mechanisms of cinema's capacity to fragment and deconstruct time, space, and the body.

Editing can transport the viewer from a long shot's distant view of the actor's body in a landscape to the almost physically impossible intimacy of an extreme close-up. Actors must vary the scale of their performances in accordance with the distance between them and the audience in any given shot, modulating the size of their gestures and their vocal level from shot to shot in the same scene, if necessary. The close-up's intimate scrutiny – what makes the screen, in Bette Davis's phrase, "a fantastic medium for the reality of little things" – may require the subtlest level of expression at the same time as it may require the actor to do more than she would on the stage, since her only acting instrument is her face. Shooting a Western called *Bandido* (1956), director Richard Fleischer needed a reaction shot of Robert Mitchum, a notoriously minimalist actor. After the first take, when Fleischer protested that Mitchum had not reacted, Mitchum responded that he had just not noticed the underemphatic reaction. The shot was retaken, with Mitchum playing the scene as Fleischer wanted but insisting that Fleischer would end up using the first take. When he saw the scene in the editing room, Fleischer acknowledged that Mitchum had been right.

The variations in the scale of performance required between shots add one more element of fragmentation to the actor's task. Manuals such as Patrick Tucker's *Secrets of Screen Acting* emphasize that, contrary to the common wisdom that acting for the screen requires more natural behavior than is needed on the stage, the camera's presence makes screen performance intensely artificial, counter-

Charlton Heston's eagle's profile inhabits the fictional character of *Ben-Hur* (1959); like Moses and Michelangelo, Ben-Hur has become Charlton Heston.
Produced by Sam Zimbalist; distributed by MGM.

intuitive, and anything but natural, a matter of "techniques rather than feelings." To show a character scrutinizing himself in a mirror, the mirror must be angled so that the camera, not the actor, can see the reflection: "the actor has to pretend to be seeing himself."[29] The circumstances of production ensure that actors cannot experience their performances as coherent, but they must use their unnatural techniques to create the plausible illusion of a unified personality.

The Actor's Two Bodies

From the audience's point of view, the work of the actor matters less than the effects it has. Acting is the principal means by which audiences can attribute traits to characters and elaborate their individual psychologies. Hollywood movies also exploit the actor's performance at another level. The audience experiences the presence of the performer as well as – in the same body as – the presence of the character. The bodily presence of the performer is at the same time a distraction from the fiction and one of the principal means by which viewers invest in the existence of characters as if they were real people. Watching the sex scenes in *Basic Instinct* (1992), the audience wonders how close Michael Douglas and Sharon Stone came to intercourse during the filming at the same time as we make deductions about the story from our knowledge that Nick Curran and Catherine Tramell (the characters Douglas and Stone play) now have a passionate sexual relationship. In less spectacular or less prurient moments, a movie's storyline minimizes the discrepancy between what the body of the actor and the body of the character do, so that our recognition of the real body of Charlton Heston allows us to grant credence to the fictional existence of Michelangelo in *The Agony and the Ecstasy* (1965), or Ben-Hur in the movie of that name (1959), or Moses in *The Ten Commandments* (1956). French critic Michel Mourlet famously described Heston as:

an axiom of the cinema. . . . By himself alone he constitutes a tragedy, and his presence in any films whatsoever suffices to create beauty. The contained violence expressed by the sombre phosphorescence of his eyes, his eagle's profile, the haughty arch of his eyebrows, his prominent cheek-bones, the bitter and hard curve of his mouth, the fabulous power of his torso; this is what he possesses and what not even the worst director can degrade.[30]

Heston exists independently of any of the characters he plays, but as Mourlet's enthusiastic prose suggests, the effect of Heston's presence on the screen is no less a function of the movie's formal organization than the characters are. Watching Heston play Moses, we are aware of the dual presence of both Heston and Moses; Hollywood's commercial aesthetic encourages performance styles that produce this dual presence, and allow the two halves of a performance to play against, or play with, each other. In a manner similar to the way a viewer's perception shifts easily between represented and expressive space, our impressions of an actor's presence and his or her "disappearance" into character readily alternate with each other.

In a cinema as goal-oriented as Hollywood, where the hero's desire – for money, love, power, adventure – drives the dramatic action, character serves as the principal means of plot motivation as well as the chief source of plausibility. Thrillers and comedies both work by putting convincing characters in improbable situations and watching how they behave. We can describe these acting performances, in which characters are bound up in the plot's progression, as being **integrated** into the narration, and contrast them with the more **autonomous performances** of routines like Donald O'Connor's. This distinction between autonomous and integrated performances will help us to distinguish the characteristics of Hollywood's various performance styles. In his book *Acting in the Cinema*, James Naremore makes a related distinction between presentational and representational modes of acting. Presentational styles acknowledge the co-presence of performer and audience, usually through a conventionalized form of direct address such as a Shakespearean aside. Representational styles, on the other hand, offer the audience the illusion that they – or the cinematic apparatus that records the action – are invisible to the performers. As Naremore notes, "the impenetrable barrier of the screen favors representational playing styles," but there is also a substantial element of the presentational in the constant by-play between star performance and role.[31]

Frank McConnell has suggested a similar opposition, more concerned with a typology of performers than with a typology of performance. On the one hand he identifies performers such as Charlie Chaplin and Humphrey Bogart who appear bound by the same laws as other characters, tied into the process of the narration with no opportunity to cease being characters. On the other hand there are those performers whom McConnell aptly describes as being in a "state of grace," living independently of other characters and by different rules. As instances he cites Buster Keaton and James Cagney; we might add Donald O'Connor in *Singin' in the Rain*. Keaton moves through a world of threatening objects sublimely unaware of the danger they represent or even of the presence of other characters for most of the time. Cagney's "state of grace," however, is more akin to O'Connor's safe space, generated by his intense nervous energy, which allows him to dominate the spaces he is in by his unrivaled ability to move around in them.[32] McConnell's analysis is useful because it describes performance in terms of complementary and contrasting functions, rather than seeking to identify a single mode of screen performance as typical of Hollywood cinema.

One definition of good acting – the one articulated by Laurence Olivier in the quotation that heads this section – assumes that acting skill should be measured by the distance between the actor's characteristics and those of the character he or she is impersonating. This argument is frequently accompanied by the claim that since the technical resources of cinema appear to do the actors' work for them, a movie performance can hardly be compared to "real" acting in the "legitimate" theater. It is often suggested that the studio system limited star performers by typecasting them into set roles, restricting the range of their acting and leading to charges that many stars – John Wayne is frequently mentioned – could not "act," since they always "played themselves." Many of these arguments are simply expressions of the perceived low cultural status of the movies, and they ignore the fact that versatility was considered a cardinal actorly virtue only during the relatively brief period between 1920 and the 1960s, when repertory theaters employed stock companies of actors performing in a dozen different plays in a season. An actor's versatility has never been held in such high esteem in the American theatrical tradition as it has in Europe. All American acting, argues Steve Vineberg, "assumes what would be sacrilege to a classically trained English or French actor: that the actor and not the text is the most important element in a play or movie."[33] Star acting simultaneously provides audiences with autonomous and integrated performances. The star is present as a production value and as a known bundle of personality traits, and therefore performs his or her star persona in a movie autonomously. At the same time the star is an actor "disappearing" into his or her role.

There is, however, a paradoxical element in the idea of the actor's disappearance. In every performance, two identities – actor and character – inhabit the same body, and in the **naturalist** style of acting I have so far been calling "invisible," the technical skill of the actor consists in eliding the difference between the two identities, in disembodying himself or herself to embody the role. But if the actor disappears, the performance becomes invisible; as Vineberg puts it, "you don't see the process at all."[34] In this description, acting resembles makeup: "successful make-up is invisible to the audience; only its effect is noticeable."[35] This "invisible" technical skill is, paradoxically, most apparently exhibited when the character is physically different from the actor: Dustin Hoffman's performances as Dorothy Michaels in *Tootsie* (1982) and the autistic Raymond in *Rain Man* (1988) are examples; so, in a different register, are Lon Chaney's performances as Blizzard, the legless ruler of San Francisco's underworld, in *The Penalty* (1920), or the knife-throwing circus star Alonzo the Armless in *The Unknown* (1927). As Foster Hirsch has noted, part of what the audience does during such performances is to see "if we can detect the actor himself peering through his character's facade."[36] Hollywood's acting manuals were much concerned with this question of how visible the performer should be. In 1922, Inez and Helen Klumph suggested that the actor should "obliterate himself, as much as he possibly can":

> The audience must be kept from thinking, "How pretty Pauline Frederick looks there," or "How good looking Elliott Dexter is." If they think of the actor, they cannot be carried along by the story, or be caught up by the suspense that helps to build up the climax. They aren't going to be afraid the heroine won't be saved; they're going to sit comfortably back in their seats and know that of course Gloria Swanson won't be killed![37]

Lillian Albertson, on the other hand, argued in 1947 that the audience's synthesis of the competing presences of actor and character was more complex. Denying that the actor needed to "live the part," she asked:

> Do you think Robert Montgomery felt any pressing desire to cut off Rosalind Russell's charming head in *Night Must Fall* – or even Dame May Whitty's? But he gave you the creeps just the same, didn't he? . . . an audience is never quite that emotionally involved. Even in the presence of the greatest acting they always retain a little objectivity. The very presence of an audience is bound to impinge on the consciousness and keep them from forgetting entirely that it is, after all, *acting.*[38]

Albertson's observations touch on a long debate within performance theory about the relationship between the two identities of actor and character. Constant Coquelin, the French *comédien* for whom Edmond Rostand wrote the play *Cyrano de Bergerac* in 1897, argued that the actor must have a double personality: a first self as the player who conceives the performance, and a second self as the "instrument" through which the performance is created: "The first self works upon the second self till it is transformed, and thence an ideal personage is evolved – in short, until from himself he has made his work of art."[39]

Coquelin's own concern, along with that of most writers on acting, was with how the actor negotiated what he called the "paradox of dual consciousness," the co-presence of two identities in one body. This negotiation is as complex for the audience as it is for the performer. However successfully the actor manages to create the illusion of character, the audience is not prevented from recognizing the illusion for what it is.[40] Actors work inside a set of performance conventions that viewers recognize as representing an absence of performance and producing a transparent effect of "the real." As with the other conventional systems of transparency, the viewer must recognize the performance convention and at the same time see through it to register the effect. Otherwise, we could not tell acting apart from being, or identify a "sincere" performance. A movie's plot will often require the viewer to judge whether a character is being sincere or not: whether Bridget O'Shaughnessy (Mary Astor) is lying to Sam Spade (Humphrey Bogart) in *The Maltese Falcon* (1941), for instance.[41] As competent viewers, we must distinguish between two simultaneous performances: that of the character and that of the actress, and we end up complimenting Astor on her sincere performance of the character's insincerity. The audience enjoys the actress's performance as well as the role, while she exhibits not only the role, but also her technical prowess: that is, she exhibits herself.

The audience manages the co-presence of the actor's two bodies in much the same way as we navigate the multiple viewpoints we are offered in a movie, alternating unproblematically between a perception of the screen as a two-dimension graphic arrangement and a three-dimensional space, and between a view from outside the diegetic space of the fiction and a view from within it. Our commitment to the fiction is always provisional: no matter how "realistic" the action, we are not concerned that the actor has disappeared so far into the character that Robert Montgomery will really kill Rosalind Russell. Equally, knowing that the car did not drive over the cliff-edge the last time we saw *North by Northwest* (1959) does not stop heartbeats racing when we watch the movie a second or third time, just as it did on the first occasion. Watching a movie requires us to maintain two contradictory ideas at the same time: we remain aware of the movie's artifice, and we also voluntarily, but always provisionally, disregard that awareness. In performing our role as participant observers of the movie, we can choose our levels of engagement with the fiction, and just as we can shift between multiple viewpoints, we can alter our forms of engagement, temporarily abandoning our emotional involvement with characters and their narrative fate to revel in the attractions of the movie's spectacular performance. Both these forms of audience pleasure, however, rely on the actors' performance as both figures within the fiction and presences beyond it.

Star Performance

A star has two things an actor doesn't have: charisma and the ability to sell tickets. Eddie Murphy will sell tickets around the world to a movie that is not a very good movie. That is a movie star.

Ned Tanen[42]

Star performances place the most explicit emphasis on the person of the actor. The commercial imperatives of the star system require that stars are always visible through their characters: in *The Eiger Sanction* (1974), it is not just the fictional Jonathan Hemlock hanging over an Alpine precipice, it is also Clint Eastwood who cuts the rope that is keeping him (both of them) from dropping hundreds of feet to certain death. The star is always himself or herself, only thinly disguised as a character: as the adverts announce, "Clint Eastwood IS *Dirty Harry*." As Naremore notes, "a substantial body of intelligent critical writing has described the performances of the classic stars as if they were little more than fictional extensions of the actor's true personalities," and the instance he cites, Edward Wagenknecht's description of Lillian Gish in *True Heart Susie* (1919), is typical: "The part and the actress are one. In a very deep and very true sense, she is the profoundest kind of actress: that is to say she does not 'act' at all; she *is*."[43] "Being"

Charlotte Vale, transformed into the glamorous Bette Davis in *Now Voyager* (1942).

Produced by Hal B. Wallis; distributed by Warner Bros.

Clark Gable *is* Rhett Butler in *Gone with the Wind* (1939).

Produced by David O. Selznick; distributed by Selznick International Pictures. Selznick/MGM.

Dean Martin renounces his off-screen persona in *Rio Bravo* (1959).

Produced by Howard Hawks; distributed by Armada.

is often offered as an almost technical description of Classical Hollywood's predominant acting style, and in these terms, a star's performance can resolve the tension of two identities in one body in a more complete manner than any "actorly" performance could reasonably hope to achieve.[44] An established star is, literally, a body of expectations, and these bodies function as very economical narrative devices. A great deal of information is conveyed about characters simply because they are played by Harrison Ford or Bette Davis. Audiences know in advance what Charlotte Vale will sound like in *Now Voyager* (1942), how she will walk across a room or stub out a cigarette, and thus we can predict not only how Davis will act – that is, perform – but also how Charlotte is likely to act – that is, behave – in any likely dramatic situation. Both the suspense and the surprise in *What Lies Beneath* (2000) depend on audience expectations about how a character played by Harrison Ford will behave. Conversely, many analyses of film acting are really discussions of the behavior of a fictional character, rather than an analysis of how that character is embodied.

Classical Hollywood's star system engineered a correspondence between star and role that was archetypally embodied in Clark Gable's casting as Rhett Butler in *Gone with the Wind* (1939). At the time of the movie's production, and ever since, it has seemed impossible to imagine the part being played by anyone else.[45] The common recognition that a role "might have been written" for a particular actor did no more than acknowledge the actualities of Hollywood industrial practice, by which scripts were written specifically to exhibit the already established traits and mannerisms of their stars. The fact that a star's persona circulated in the media as part of the promotion of specific movies allowed for a considerable interaction between the star's performance and offscreen persona, and in many respects substituted for versatility in the roles a star undertook. Many star careers have been constructed around the play of variation centered on a star's public persona.

Offscreen and onscreen, Dean Martin enacted the role of an amiable heavy drinker. In *Rio Bravo* (1959), Martin plays a drunken ex-gunfighter. In one scene he resolves to stop drinking, and pours a shot of whisky back into its bottle. His off-screen persona adds a resonance to the gesture that extends beyond its significance in the story, and his character is not so much a function of the fiction as evidence of Martin's presence in the role.

In Marilyn Monroe's case the play of variation lay in the combination of an innocence expressed by her voice and gestures and a sexual promise expressed by her body, making her sexually alluring and vulnerable at the same time, and allowing for a constant play between aspects of her fictional character and her offscreen persona. In *Gentlemen Prefer Blondes* (1953) she plays a manipulative gold-digger who, despite her best intentions, is too dumb to succeed in exploiting her millionaire fiancé. While she spends much of the movie berating Jane Russell for always falling in love with men without money ("I keep telling her, it's just as easy to fall in love with a rich man as a poor man"), she doesn't know what a letter of credit is when her fiancé gives her one. When he explains that it is "like money," she tells him, "Be sure and write me every day. I'll be so lonesome." If her performance is an attempt to provide a credible impersonation of the fictional character, it is completely unconvincing, but the playing with type is not intended to convince so much as amuse. Monroe and Russell's competition for the audience's attention turns their performances into a contest on an industrial level between the two stars as stars, but this has very little to do with the characters they are playing.

In the production of a star vehicle, the character is adapted to fit the star. A frequently used mechanism centers the plot on a character who eventually displays the skills that the audience already knows the performer possesses. A convincing performance is thus one in which the character becomes the star persona as the movie progresses: Gary Cooper in *Meet John Doe* (1941), Janet Gaynor in *A Star is Born* (1937), Bette Davis in *The Letter* (1940), or "the heroines of all Jane Fonda movies [who] begin as apolitical airheads, undergo sartorial and intellectual transformation, and end up as Jane Fonda."[46] Barbara Klinger describes the process by which a movie reveals its star's persona through the progress of the plot as being "a kind of dramatic striptease" that reveals "the 'real' image of the star behind the disguise of the character in question."[47] In *Bicentennial Man* (1999), Andrew the robot spends the entire movie trying, as he puts it, to "make something of myself," and eventually succeeds in becoming – literally – Robin Williams.

Cathy Klaprat has traced Bette Davis's early career as a sequence of experimental efforts by her studio to develop a star persona for her. Using fan mail, sneak previews, exhibitor preferences, and box-office grosses as guides, Warner Bros. built her persona around the performances that produced the most favorable audience reaction. Davis's success in *Of Human Bondage* (made on a loan-out to RKO in 1934) established "the correct match between narrative role and actor," and led to repetitions of the role of "deadly seductress" in her next two movies, *Bordertown* (1935) and *Dangerous* (1935), as well as a representation of Davis "herself" as being "fiery, independent . . . definitely not domesticated . . . hard-boiled and ruthless, determined to get what she wants" in the fan magazines.[48]

Once Davis's persona had been sufficiently firmly fixed in the public imagination, however, it opened up opportunities for "offcasting" in roles opposite from those of her established image: as the good woman in *The Great Lie* (1941), for example, which advertised itself by announcing that "*contrary* to the former Davis pattern Bette Davis' new film does not find her killing anyone or acting nasty." The marketing logic of offcasting was simple. Davis was contracted to appear in three movies a year. Audiences might well tire of seeing three similar performances, but with offcasting the studio could invoke audience expectations while offering something different at the same time. Movie adverts repeatedly offered audiences the chance to see a star "as you've never seen her before." Offcasting was one way of extending a star's box-office potential through a form of product variation. It also enhanced the star's image as a great performer:

> Portraying only one type of character made the star vulnerable to charges that she wasn't acting but "just being herself." . . . However, once the studio offcast the star it could claim, "There are as many Bette Davises as there are Bette Davis-starring pictures! That's part of Miss Davis' greatness: the ability to make each character she plays stand by itself, a distinct and memorable triumph of screen acting."[49]

Negotiations such as these involving Monroe and Davis are the common currency in which the star system conveys information through convention and audience expectation, rather than through a more realist-inspired characterization. The frequency with which this happens suggests the extent to which a mythological knowledge of Hollywood, derived from fan magazines, gossip columns, or talk shows, is assumed by the film industry. There could be no more graphic demonstration of the way that Hollywood addresses its audience as competent consumers of its fictions. Criticisms of typecasting misunderstand the industrial function of a star performance, where the audience must first recognize Julia Roberts as Julia Roberts, and then transform their engagement with Roberts's presence into an investment in the character she plays and the story being told. Hollywood's commercial aesthetic places a higher priority on the star's recognizable performance as himself or herself than on the psychological plausibility of the character the star portrays or the coherence of the plot. Describing his performance in *The Great Gatsby* (1974), Robert Redford once commented, "I could have played the part very well, but I was paid all those millions of dollars to present Bob Redford."[50]

The industrial requirements of a star performance can also determine the outcome of a plot. Questions raised at the level of the plot can be resolved at the level of performance, as the audience's attention is displaced away from the issues at stake in the fiction onto the way in which the stars exhibit themselves under the pressure of those issues. On occasion this has proved useful to a cinema wishing to exploit political subject matter without abandoning its commitment to entertainment. In *All the President's Men* (1976), two junior reporters on a Washington newspaper uncover a story of political corruption that will eventually bring down a president. Although Robert Redford, who produced the movie, wanted to cast two unknowns in the central roles, he was unable to raise finance

Junior reporters Bob Woodward and Carl Bernstein given the authority of stars Robert Redford and Dustin Hoffman in *All the President's Men* (1976).
Produced by Walter Coblenz; distributed by Warner Bros.

for the project unless the parts were played by stars; in the event, by Dustin Hoffman and himself. The movie is much preoccupied with the documentary accuracy of its representation. A good deal of it is played out on a set that precisely copies the *Washington Post* office, even down to transporting the contents of the actual office's wastepaper bins. Ultimately, however, the movie succumbs to the industrial logic of the star system, abandoning its documentary aesthetic. In a key scene toward the end of the movie, the investigation is about to stall unless Redford's character can extract some information from his contact in the White House, Deep Throat (Hal Holbrook). Deep Throat begins by refusing to do more than confirm information gleaned from other sources, as he has throughout the movie. But this is not enough, because the movie is already two hours long and must achieve a resolution. Redford, producer and star, exerts his industrial muscle. "Cut out the chickenshit and tell me what I need to know," he demands. For no convincing fictional reason, Deep Throat concedes, and reveals all Redford needs to know in order to expose the president. He succumbs not so much to the moral rectitude of the character Redford plays as to Redford's charismatic force as a star – to Redford's presentation of "Bob Redford," rather than to his representation of the reporter Bob Woodward. The resolution, along with the audience's attention, is displaced from the movie's fiction to its status as a commodity.

To summarize: any individual performative act in a Hollywood movie can be seen as operating somewhere between the poles of integration into the narrative and autonomy from it. Taking these as base terms, we can construct a table of oppositions that provides a structuring frame onto which individual performances can be mapped:

Autonomous performance	Integrated performance
Attraction	Narration
Action	Acting
Presentation	Representation
Visibility	Invisibility
Display	Disguise
Spectacle	Narrative
Excess	Plausibility
Technical skill	Character psychology
Low status	High status

Few Hollywood performances are so schematic as to fall entirely into one category, however. Different tendencies are emphasized at particular moments, or else are characteristic of particular performers, and most Hollywood movies are organized to accommodate both kinds of performance, and to shift, at different moments, between them. Sometimes the functions are split between performers in a single movie, as in the straight and crazy pairing of numerous screen comedy teams (Dean Martin and Jerry Lewis, for instance). Hollywood's most common strategy, however, is to synthesize them, simultaneously generating the pleasures of spectacular display and those of a more realist characterization. Even the most integrated performance contains an element of display; even the most autonomous routine contributes something to our understanding of a character's motivation.

Allowing for some variation in the relative authority given to the performances of stars and character actors, movies generally establish a broadly uniform acting style, by such simple means as having characters adopt convincingly similar accents.[51] The requirements of narrative economy, however, commonly mean that the smaller the part, the more its performance will resort to conventional signs of character type, broad gesture, and caricature. In *Acting in the Cinema*, Naremore uses the term **"ostensiveness"** to designate the degree to which a performance is marked out as a performance for its audience, aligning it with the quality that actor Sam Waterston has called "visibility."[52] To maintain plausibility, performances within a movie must operate with roughly equal degrees of ostensiveness. While this uniformity may make performance conventions invisible to a contemporary audience, these conventions change over time to renew the effect of the real in performance. As historians of screen acting have often demonstrated, acting styles once read as natural subsequently often seem contrived, highly coded, and artificial. Equally, with the passage of time and the completion of a career, a star's presence tends to overwhelm the presence of character in his or her performances: in *The Shootist* (1976) we witness not so much the death from cancer of J. B. Books, famous fictional lawman, as that of John Wayne, whose last performance this was.

Summary

- Movie criticism has found it difficult to discuss the role of the actor, and the vocabulary for critically examining performance remains limited. One explanation for this is that acting is analogical, a mode of communication that works in terms of proportion, gradation, and inflection rather than the clear-cut distinctions and differences of digital sign systems.

- Movies and movie performances are "built" rather than "shot." Unlike theatrical acting, a cinematic performance is discontinuous, fragmented into the individual shots which are the movie's constituent parts, and reassembled in the editing room.

- A movie is a performance and not a text. All attempts to reduce movies to texts, whether through analogies between film and language, shots and words, or through formal analysis, ultimately fail to resolve the interpretive complexities of performance.

- The spectacle of movement was the cinema's first "production value." For the first time the world was revealed in motion, and the impression of lifelike movement amazed and excited its earliest viewers. Taking his terminology from vaudeville, film historian Tom Gunning has described early cinema as a "cinema of attractions," which he suggests has remained a component in Hollywood's subsequent production.

- Movement is present in Hollywood movies not only in the sense of the movement of objects within a fixed frame, but also in the movement of the camera itself, and the movement produced in the editing process. These three kinds of movement usually work in combination with other elements of mise-en-scène to direct audience attention without drawing attention to themselves.

- Nearly every Hollywood movie has at least one sequence which displays movement as a production value, interrupting the narrative of the movie, and challenging its dominance. Chase sequences and dance numbers are clear examples of these "autonomous spectacles," a source of pleasure offered to the audience independent of the narrative. We can distinguish between such *autonomous* performances and performances which are *integrated* into the narrative of a movie, but Hollywood movies are organized to accommodate both kinds of performance and to shift, at different moments, between the two.

- In keeping with Hollywood's conventions of representation, acting performance routinely aspires to transparency, creating a sense of character without making the audience aware of how this is achieved. While Hollywood appropriates performance styles from a variety of theatrical traditions, providing different performance styles for different generic contexts, acting has a higher status than other styles, deriving from the superior cultural prestige of legitimate theater. Acting remains, however, a largely untheorized, intuitive activity.

- Contrary to the common wisdom that acting for the screen requires more natural behavior than is needed on the stage, the camera's presence makes screen performance intensely artificial, counter-intuitive, and anything but natural, a matter of "techniques rather than feelings." The circumstances of

production ensure that actors cannot experience their performances as coherent, but they must use their unnatural techniques to create the plausible illusion of a unified personality.

- Hollywood's commercial aesthetic places a higher priority on the star's recognizable performance as himself or herself than on the psychological plausibility of the character the star portrays or the coherence of the plot. In the production of a star vehicle, the character is adapted to fit the star.

Further Reading

The Kuleshov experiments

Accounts of the Kuleshov experiments can be found in Vsevolod Pudovkin, "On Film Technique," in *Film Technique and Film Acting: The Cinema Writings of V. I. Pudovkin*, trans. Ivor Montagu (New York: Bonanza, 1949), and Lev Kuleshov, "Art of the Cinema," in *Kuleshov on Film: Writings by Lev Kuleshov*, ed. and trans. Ronald Levaco (Berkeley, CA: University of California Press, 1974). Another of Kuleshov's experiments demonstrated the cinema's Frankenstein-like power to construct a body from disparate parts: "I photographed a girl sitting before her mirror, making up her eyes and eye-lashes, rouging her lips, lacing her shoes. Solely by means of montage we showed a living girl, but one who did not actually exist, because we had filmed the lips of one woman, the legs of another, the back of a third, the eyes of a fourth. We cemented these shots, fixing a certain relationship among them, and we obtained an entirely new personage, using nothing but completely real material." Quoted in Jay Leyda, *Kino: A History of the Russian and Soviet Film*, 3rd edn (Princeton, NJ: Princeton University Press, 1983), p. 165. A feminist critique of this experiment would emphasize the way that it fragments and fetishizes the female body. In *Film as Film: Understanding and Judging Movies* (Harmondsworth: Penguin, 1972), p. 106, V. F. Perkins points out some of the imprecisions in Pudovkin's and Kuleshov's accounts. A description of an attempt to restage the experiment is in Stephen Prince and Wayne E. Hensley, "The Kuleshov Effect: Recreating the Classic Experiment," *Cinema Journal* 31:2 (Winter 1992), pp. 59–75.

"Cinema of attractions"

Tom Gunning defines the cinema of attractions as directly soliciting:

> spectator attention, inciting visual curiosity, and supplying pleasure through an exciting spectacle – a unique event, whether fictional or documentary, that is of interest in itself. ... Theatrical display dominates over narrative absorption, emphasizing the direct stimulation of shock or surprise at the expense of unfolding a story or creating a diegetic universe. The cinema of attractions expends little energy creating characters with psychological motivations or individual personality. Making use of both fictional and non-fictional attractions, its energy moves outward towards an acknowledged spectator rather than inward towards the character-based situations essential to classical narrative.

Tom Gunning, "The Cinema of Attractions: Early Film, its Spectators and the Avant-Garde," in *Early Cinema: Space, Frame, Narrative*, ed. Thomas Elsaesser (London: British Film Institute, 1990), pp. 58–9.

Stars and acting

Cynthia Baron describes the performance practices and training of Classical Hollywood in "Crafting Film Performances: Acting in the Hollywood Studio Era," in *Screen Acting*, eds Alan Lovell and

Peter Krämer (London: Routledge, 1999), pp. 31–45.

The best analysis of acting in Hollywood is James Naremore, *Acting in the Cinema* (Berkeley, CA: University of California Press, 1988). See also several of the essays in Lovell and Krämer, and Foster Hirsch, *Acting Hollywood Style* (New York: Abrams, 1991). Patrick Tucker, *Secrets of Screen Acting* (London: Routledge, 1994), is a good technical account. Two other collections of essays are Jeremy G. Butler, ed., *Star Texts: Image and Performance in Film and Television* (Detroit: Wayne State University Press, 1991), and Carole Zucker, ed., *Making Visible the Invisible: An Anthology of Original Essays on Film Acting* (Metuchen, NJ: Scarecrow, 1990). See also the works about method acting cited in chapter 13.

Frank McConnell's discussion of acting is in the final chapter, "Adam Awakening: Personality, Persona and Person in Film," of his *The Spoken Seen: Film and the Romantic Imagination* (Baltimore, MD: Johns Hopkins University Press, 1975).

For analyses of some specific performances, see the essays in Christine Gledhill, ed., *Stardom: Industry of Desire* (London: Routledge, 1991); Virginia Wright Wexman, *Creating the Couple: Love, Marriage, and Hollywood Performance,* (Princeton, NJ: Princeton University Press, 1993); Charles Affron, *Star Acting: Gish, Garbo, Davies*

(New York: Dutton, 1977); Dennis Bingham, *Acting Male: Masculinities in the Films of James Stewart, Jack Nicholson and Clint Eastwood* (New Brunswick, NJ: Rutgers University Press, 1994); and Richard Dyer, *Stars* (London: British Film Institute, 1979).

On star casting, see Cathy Klaprat, "The Star as Market Strategy: Bette Davis in Another Light," in *The American Film Industry*, ed. Tino Balio, 1st edn 1976, revised edn (Madison: University of Wisconsin Press, 1985), and Maria LaPlace, "Producing and Consuming the Woman's Film: Discursive Struggle in *Now Voyager*," in *Home Is Where the Heart Is: Studies in Melodrama and the Woman's Film*, ed. Christine Gledhill (London: British Film Institute, 1987). Robert Sklar in *City Boys: Cagney, Bogart, Garfield* (Princeton, NJ: Princeton University Press, 1992) takes a much less favorable view of Warner Bros.' handling of their stars, suggesting that typecasting stars in their personas had more to do with the pressures of the studio production schedule: "There were just too many stories to develop, too many pictures to cast, too many productions to watch over, too much product to move into theaters – and not enough good parts to go around. It was easier to pigeonhole or typecast performers, to slot them into familiar genre categories, to use them as often as possible in repetitive roles" (p. 76).

CHAPTER THIRTEEN

Performance 2

The Method

In America, there is an opinion prevalent among actors, managers and the public at large to the effect that all work done on the stage should be the result of temperament rather than study; that if any study is given, it should be entirely personal, and should come from the actor's observation of his own emotions. More than this, they declare, is injurious, and will make one mechanical and elocutionary.

Genevieve Stebbins[1]

Acting is the expression of a neurotic impulse.
Marlon Brando[2]

Although they took place less than a year apart, it is hard to imagine a style of screen performance more distant from Donald O'Connor's routine in *Singin' in the Rain* than Marlon Brando's performance as Stanley Kowalski in *A Streetcar Named Desire* (1951). The performance style known as Method acting took shape during the 1930s in the work of New York's Group Theater, where Lee Strasberg taught his version of the theories of Russian director Constantin Stanislavski. Although other actor trainers such as Stella Adler disputed Strasberg's interpretation, the "Stanislavski system" emerged as a dominant force on the American stage immediately after World War II, when it was principally associated with a group lay in the adaptability of its performers to an already established text, again registering a degree of cultural prestige in the literary and theatrical forms. Although in one sense Method actors seemed constantly to work on the edge of disappearance into their roles, the mannerisms of the Method were often as visible as those of the comedian-comic. Where Donald O'Connor was admired for escaping from his role into a routine, Brando and James Dean were lauded for their skill in confining themselves to an expressive range plausible in terms of their characters' psychology. Generally this involved distinctive patterns of body movement and vocal delivery, featuring a highly indirect and equivocal mode of addressing the audience, in contrast to the near-direct address of the comedian-comic. Brando's performances, in particular, were distinctively paced, slowed down by hesitations, measured pauses, and contemplative offscreen gazes. No movie with Brando, suggests Foster Hirsch, could be "action-packed."[10]

Brando's performance as Stanley Kowalski in *A Streetcar Named Desire* employs the conventions of Method acting in a way that underlines their dissent from the rhetoric of what was then the dominant version of naturalist acting style. At the same time, the movie also suggests how the Method's representational emphasis allowed its techniques to be absorbed by the Classical Hollywood cinema, renovating rather than overturning mainstream style. The movie's director, Elia Kazan, described the intended effect of the Method as being to provide "a surface realism and strong feelings underneath,"[11] and insisted that:

> *Streetcar* is the first non-sentimental picture we have made over here. It's a landmark. Its issues are not oversimplified, and you're not in there "rooting for somebody" – all that old shit the motion picture industry is built upon. There is no hero, no heroine; the people are people, some dross, some gold, with faults and virtues – and for a while you are muddled about them, the way you would be in life.[12]

Brando had achieved theatrical stardom when he played in the Broadway production of Tennessee Williams's play in 1947, and the movie followed the original as closely as the Production Code would allow. The neurotic Blanche DuBois (Vivien Leigh) arrives in New Orleans to stay with her sister Stella (Kim Hunter), and is gradually destroyed by the brutal behavior of Stella's husband Stanley. From the outset, Brando's acting functions to register Stanley's complexity and contradictions. His machismo and latent aggression are set against his childishness, his assertiveness contrasts with his vulnerability, the conviction of his body language plays against the inarticulacy of his speech. A dense network of signs is orchestrated to communicate a spontaneity and authenticity defined by its disturbance of performance conventions. His speech is vernacular, heavily accented, and often mumbled. He is incessantly chewing gum, and his facial expressions change abruptly, breaking into sudden grins or puzzled stares. His posture appears comfortably at ease one moment, tense and intimidating the next, and he has a collection of apparently involuntary behavioral tics. The muscularity of his body signals the physical threat he poses to Blanche. He paces constantly and is prone to sudden explosive action, at one point hurling a radio set through a window. According to James Scott:

Stanley Kowalski's (Marlon Brando) "animal aggressiveness" in *A Streetcar Named Desire* (1951).
Produced by Charles K. Feldman; distributed by Warner Bros.

> In *Streetcar* Brando evidently built his performance around his sense of Stanley Kowalski's animal aggressiveness. Sometimes this is innocently canine, as when his incessant scratching of back and belly remind us of a dog going after fleas. But the Kowalski character is also destructive, as we are told in Brando's use of the mouth: he chews fruit with loud crunching noises, munches up potato chips with the same relentless jaw muscles, washes beer around in his mouth and then swallows it with physically noticeable gulps.[13]

But for all its excessiveness, as in Stanley's increasingly hyperbolic exchange with Blanche immediately before her collapse, the combination of these signs allows the viewer to build up a sense of Stanley's character in all its inconsistency through an apparently seamless flow of "natural" behavior.

To a cinema peopled by recognizable types performing generically prescribed functions and by stars occupying roles tailored to their known personalities, the Method was very disruptive, reducing the security previously afforded the viewer by characterization and performance style. It ascribed multiple, even contradictory, traits to characters, making it more difficult for viewers to predict their behavior. In *A Streetcar Named Desire*, Brando's performance so details Stanley's character that the future direction of the plot is very much in doubt. Only a prior knowledge of the play-text can counter the uncertainty generated by Brando's performance. The audience's uncertainty about the plot's development, however, gives them further encouragement to place the performance at the center of their attention.

Acting as a Signifying System

Stylistic innovations in performance almost invariably lay claim to a greater degree of realism than the mainstream style they are challenging. The Method, with its emphasis on the psychological investigation of both character and actor, was certainly no exception to this rule. But invoking "realism" as a description of a performance style – as in actress Maureen Stapleton's description of the Method's aim as being "to be true, to be real, to be true to the part"[14] – is just as much a rhetorical gesture as the claims of color, widescreen, and other technological innovations to bring "greater realism" to the screen. The Method's rhetoric appeared to make large moral and mystical claims for "the power of truth in acting,"[15] but its ascendancy in the postwar decade had much to do with the appropriateness of its performance style to both the dramas and the cultural concerns of the time. In many respects the "realism" of Method acting in the 1950s, like that of widescreen technology, can be thought of as a kind of excess, packaged as spectacle – an "attraction" in itself – and in *East of Eden* and *Rebel Without a Cause* (both 1955) the excesses of James Dean's performance style served to fill the excess space of the CinemaScope frame.

The Method also addressed postwar American culture's preoccupation with psychoanalysis. Its construction of character in psychoanalytic terms corresponded to the psychological themes of postwar American drama and, increasingly, of Hollywood. According to Thomas Atkins, the most effective Method roles – which are almost invariably male – are "characters with a subtle anxiety within them but with little external power to cope with it . . . divided parts based on the unresolved tension between an outer social mask and an inner reality of frustration that usually has a sexual basis." Because of the pressure of this conflict, they appear constantly "on the verge of breaking down, falling to pieces, or becoming violent."[16] Steve Vineberg suggests that the Method's popularity in the 1950s was mainly a consequence of the fact that "the rebel without a cause was the exclusive turf of Method actors."[17] Certainly, its emphasis on emotional meaning over other aspects of character succeeded in investing male performance with a degree of emotional expressiveness not seen since silent melodrama, and emphatically reasserted the connection between the display of emotion and "good acting." Richard Dyer argues that while the Method could be used to express any psychological state, "in practice it was used especially to express disturbance, repression, anguish, etc., partly in line with a belief that such feelings . . . are more 'authentic' than stability and open expression."[18] Dyer also suggests that disturbance and anguish were the characteristics usually attributed to men, while repression was depicted as a female quality. James Naremore specifies the most common form of Method anguish:

> Whether the character is a laborer, an upwardly mobile son of a wage-earning family, or an affluent teenager, he has the same problem: an uneasiness with official language and no words for his love or rage. At the same time, he brims over with sensitivity and feeling, the intensity of his emotion giving him a slightly neurotic aspect."[19]

Method performances in the 1950s thus combined psychoanalysis and melodrama, and concentrated audiences' attention on the male psyche of Brando, Dean, and the characters they enacted.

Much more explicitly than the performance styles of Classical Hollywood's star vehicles, the Method registered the distinction between actor and character, and exposed a fundamental tension between two opposed impulses in acting performance: naturalism and expressionism. The Method's concern with psychological realism attached it to the dominant tradition of naturalism in American acting, but Method performances were very visibly performances, collections of expressive gestures and techniques. Writing in 1966 in a manual *On Method Acting*, Edward Dwight Easty advised actors learning the Method to:

> Always remember that for an actor to give the appearance of reality, he cannot pretend or make believe he is thinking. . . . His thoughts must be real thoughts in order to produce real and believable actions. Remember, too, the audience never knows the thoughts which go on in the actor's mind and any which produce real behavior can and should be utilized.[20]

Easty's terminology catches the ambivalences of performance: his actor must communicate the action of thinking, and thus he or she must really think and not just pretend. The audience, however, will not recognize thought, or even thinking, so much as a series of gestural signs which convey the impression of thinking: the head angled down, a hand to the forehead, eyes focused on vacant space. These gestures, of course, are conventional, already known by the audience, and are realistic to the extent that they are recognizable as gestures in the everyday world. Although the actor must be convinced of the psychological "truth" of his or her character's actions, he or she must become a spectacle of sign and gesture to communicate that psychological verisimilitude. What matters, as Patrick Tucker puts it, "is whether the moment was truthful and effective for an audience, not what the actor felt when it was shot."[21]

Easty's version of the Method occupies an extreme position in a long-established debate about acting. In *The Paradox of Acting*, written in 1773, the French philosopher Denis Diderot argued that the actor ought not to feel the character's emotion during a performance, but should instead concentrate on the technical devices by which he produces the effects of that emotion for the audience – on what Inez and Helen Klumph later called "the mechanics of emotion."[22] Diderot's approach encouraged a more rigidly conventionalized style of performance, in which the meaning of gestures could be codified with much the same precision as language possessed, and emotion could be objectified as a public gesture.

During the nineteenth century a number of authors produced manuals of rhetorical gesture and "dramatic expression," in which actors could learn the appropriate pose to communicate pity, despondency, or pride.[23] Probably the most influential of these writers was a Parisian elocutionist, François Delsarte, whose analysis of what he called the "semeiotic" function of gesture was a major element in the training methods used in American theater schools at the end of the century, as well as in "recitation books" and courses in public speaking. Delsarte defined "semeiotics" as "the science of signs, and so the science of gesture." With semeiotics, he suggested, one could study the "organic form" of a gesture, and infer the sentiment that produced it. His conception of semeiotics differed significantly from the later semiology of the Swiss linguist, Ferdinand de Saussure, whose theories have a much wider currency in contemporary criticism, and are discussed in chapter 18.[24] Both pantomime and melodrama employ the idea of a vocabulary of gesture, but the Delsartean proposition that facial and bodily gesture can be understood as a language was countered by a more naturalistic impulse. When electric stage lighting replaced gaslight at the end of the nineteenth century, the more powerful illumination created the impression of a "fourth wall" of light preventing the brightly lit actors from seeing the audience in the darkened auditorium, encouraging them to direct their performances at the other actors rather than presenting those performances to the audience. At the same time, the "naturalistic" dramas of Henrik Ibsen, Anton Chekhov, and George Bernard Shaw showed a concern with the inner psychological reality of their characters that required a quieter, more prosaic performance style, and made the semiotic conception of acting ("signal acting") appear overblown, flamboyant, and "melodramatic" in its most pejorative sense.

Delsarte's system was far more nuanced than his later detractors suggested. Providing an elaborate analysis of facial and bodily gesture, it was designed to be combined with the study of character, observations from life, and what Genevieve Stebbins called "*interior memory*, – that unconscious storehouse where inherited tendencies, traits, and aptitudes are also found."[25] Although these ideas make Delsarte's system more compatible with Stanislavski than is usually suggested, theater historian Benjamin McArthur points out that we should not "read back into this pre-Stanislavski era a psychological realism obsessed with sub-texts which did not yet exist. The early days of naturalistic acting merely involved a subduing of gesture and a less-cadenced speech."[26] More importantly, Delsarte's system made it clear that acting is a semiotic activity: the audience comprehends emotions by recognizing their signs. Psychological theories of acting, of which the Method is the most famous, concentrate on the means by which an actor produces signs of emotion. Semiotic theories such as Delsarte's remind us that an audience does not intuit a character's emotion but recognizes it through a process of signification. As with any process of signification, there must be a consensus between actor and audience about the relationship between the emotion signified and the signifier the actor uses. Even the most internally motivated Method actor must use a range of gestures that the audience will understand.

Much of the debate within dramatic theory about the actor's expression of emotion took very little notice of the audience's reception of those emotions, and remained a largely internal debate among actors and their teachers about how acting performance should be constructed. As the most influential exponent of the new naturalist style of the late nineteenth century, Stanislavski remained central to these debates in the twentieth century. His name appears on three textbooks on performance, but only the first of them, *An Actor Prepares*, was published during his lifetime. *An Actor Prepares* stressed the importance of spontaneity, improvisation, and introspection in the training of actors and the construction of performances. Published in America in 1936, it provided the inspiration and the theoretical basis for the Method as formulated by Strasberg in the Group Theater and the Actors Studio, but Stanislavski's later books, published after his death in 1938, contradicted much of Strasberg's practice by placing much less emphasis on psychological preparation and much more on the external elements of performance. Stanislavski's various interpreters have argued that "the Stanislavski system" constitutes the most fully developed theoretical basis for acting and its teaching, although few of them agree on what that basis is. Whether it derived its principles from Stanislavski or not, a naturalistic performance style – one that emphasized emotional verisimilitude and the actor's use of his or her own personality in constructing a role – dominated American drama on stage and in cinema throughout the century. Strasberg acknowledged as much in his observation that "The simplest examples of Stanislavski's ideas are actors such as Gary Cooper, John Wayne and Spencer Tracy. They try not to act but to be themselves, to respond or react. They refuse to do or say anything they feel not to be consonant with their own characters."[27] We could add a great many other names to Strasberg's list, but rather than claim Barbara Stanwyck, for example, as an "untrained Method actor," it would be more accurate to see the Method as a variant on the mainstream naturalist tradition rather than a revolutionary change in American acting techniques.

Valentino

A Heart Breaker! A Record Breaker! . . . An eye feast of virile action, colorful settings and glowing climaxes.
Advertisement for *The Son of the Sheik* (1926)[28]

As well as providing the main motive force for a movie's narration through the elaboration of character, Hollywood's performance styles have offered their audiences idealized versions of human behavior. At times, these ideal types of masculinity and femininity have confronted cultural norms, as Brando's combination of sexual aggression and neurotic vulnerability did in the early 1950s. Moral conservatives have consistently found more to object to in Hollywood's performances than in its stories. Rudolph Valentino, with whom Brando has sometimes been

EXTREME DESPAIR.

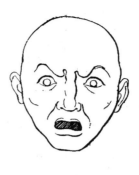

SURPRISE MIXED WITH FRIGHT.

COMPOUND MOVEMENT OF PAIN.

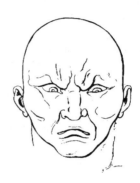

VIOLENT MOVEMENT.

Late nineteenth-century acting manuals codified gestures and expressions, and described in detail how an actor could learn to arrange his or her face, hands, and body to communicate the desired emotion to the audience. In *The Actor's Art: A Practical Treatise on Stage Declamation, Public Speaking and Deportment, for the Use of Artists, Students and Amateurs*, published in 1882, Gustave Garcia declared that acting "can be taught, like grammar, by means of a series of rules." The pictures reproduced here illustrate the "semeiotic" project of classifying "each movement of the face or action of the body according to the sentiments or passion that is to be expressed." In the expression of violent emotions, the features of the face "become disordered and take all sorts of directions, upwards, downwards, and lateral." Garcia's codification of gesture allowed him to prescribe the "attitudes and actions" an actor should perform to communicate a particular emotion to the audience. While later and more naturalistic performance styles would question the prescriptive quality of Garcia's project, his basic proposition – that the actions of an actor communicate the thoughts of the character he or she is playing to the audience through a recognizable set of gestures – remains central to the audience's understanding of performance in Hollywood movies.

Source: Gustave Garcia, *The Actor's Art* (London: Pettitt, 1882).

compared, provided one of the movies' earliest and most significant questionings of the dominant representation of gender in the wider American culture.

Acting has always been a disreputable profession. In puritanical cultures, "playing" is what children do, not a job of work, while to pretend to be someone you are not is, outside the theater, most often the behavior of a criminal. In 1642 the English Parliament decreed that "all Stage-Players, and Players of Enterludes, and common Players, are hereby declared to be, and are, and shall be taken to be Rogues, and punishable."[29] If the act of performance is associated with deception and dissimulation, the spectacle of performance has also been understood to carry moral dangers. At best it is identified as a site of voyeurism: in the safe space of the theater, the audience vicariously experiences the actors' passionate exhibition. At worst, it is held responsible for stimulating desire and leading to imitation. In 1762, the New Hampshire House of Representatives banned an acting company on the grounds that the theater had a "peculiar influence on the minds of young people, and greatly endanger[s] their morals by giving them a taste for intriguing, amusement, and pleasure."[30] As early as 1908, newspaper reports and advocates of censorship argued that the movies produced a cycle of addiction and crime: children watched movies in which criminal acts were committed, and then imitated the crimes to steal the money they needed to attend the movies. More often, however, the moralists' concern has been with sexual rather than criminal behavior. In European and American culture the theater has long been seen as a site of sexual license, and its performers viewed with a mixture of envy and disapproval.[31] In their well-publicized "private" lives, actors have provided their audiences with another form of voyeuristic satisfaction. Audiences could vicariously violate cultural taboos by consuming accounts of the players' unconventional behavior, and enjoy imagining what the liberation from social restrictions would feel like, without themselves having to suffer the consequences.[32]

The actor's position in society began to change in the last quarter of the nineteenth century, as players' organizations made self-conscious attempts to improve their social status and new popular magazines developed a culture of celebrity. The movies inherited the star system, as well as some stars, from the stage: Valentino's predecessors included America's first "matinee idol," Henry Montague, a theatrical star of the 1870s whose sudden death at the height of his popularity was, like Valentino's, the occasion for a frenzy of public mourning on the part of his female fans. Matinees were afternoon performances, overwhelmingly attended by women, who used them as opportunities for an emotional expression otherwise denied them by social convention: "at the matinee, surrounded by other women, she could give vent to her desire to shout, blow kisses, even swoon at the sight of her idol making love to the lucky woman on the stage."[33] By 1912 the movies of Maurice Costello and Francis X. Bushman, America's "Most Handsome Man," were providing their audiences with similar opportunities for emotional satisfaction.

A star system began to take shape in the movies after 1907, as movies with actors came to be differentiated from other types, and individual actors were identified as "picture personalities" whose movie characters were created from the performer's own personality: Mary Pickford's "Little Mary," for example.[34] By

1914 the personality had evolved into the star. More attention was paid to the players' existence outside their movie appearances, and their private lives became increasingly a matter of public knowledge. During the 1910s, industry-controlled publicity emphasized the stars' health and moral virtue, implicitly contrasting the movies with the more questionable behavior of theater people. But a series of heavily publicized scandals in the early 1920s – Mary Pickford's divorce and remarriage to Douglas Fairbanks, the star Wallace Reid's death from heroin addiction, the unsolved murder of director William Desmond Taylor, and, most notoriously, the trial of comedian Fatty Arbuckle for the manslaughter of "starlet" Virginia Rappe – gave the tabloid press all the opportunities they needed to assert that behind the images constructed by Hollywood's publicists lay a secret world of social unconventionality and moral turpitude.

More blatantly than any previous male star, Valentino was presented in his movies as an object of desire, an erotic body to be exhibited and gazed at. In most of his movies Valentino's beautiful body was undressed, and in many of them it was beaten or whipped, perhaps to punish its beauty. The oscillation between sadism and masochism – in his movies, Valentino often threatens the women who desire him with sexual violence – is only one of several ambivalences in his presentation as a figure of both power and weakness, alternately (sometimes simultaneously) master and victim of the desiring gaze. This ambivalence about Valentino's sexual role extended, inevitably, to his star persona: he was rumored to be homosexual, impotent, dependent on domineering women, a "tango pirate" and gigolo who had lived off women, and at the same time a bigamist whose second wife, Natasha Rambova, gave him a platinum "slave bracelet" but kept their marriage unconsummated because of her lesbian relationship with Alla Nazinova.[35] The enigma of Valentino's sexuality lay at least as much in the desiring audience as in their object of desire, however, and none of Valentino's own attempts to demonstrate his virility through publicity shots of him boxing or fencing had any effect in countering the assertion that he was a "Pink Powder Puff."[36]

Valentino's image needs to be placed in its historical setting. In the 1920s women's sexual desire became, for the first time in American culture, a subject of public discussion, as a "new feminism" concerned with women's personal expression and satisfaction substituted for the overtly political feminism that had achieved women's suffrage in 1920. The language and preoccupations of modern psychology began to appear in social commentary, where the emancipation of female desire was most often seen as a threat to family, civilization, and American masculinity. "If it is true that man once shaped woman to be the creature of his desires and needs," wrote Lurine Pruette in 1927, "then it is true that woman is now remodeling man."[37] The movies, which sociologist E. A. Ross believed were making the young more "sex-wise, sex-excited, and sex-absorbed" than any previous generation,[38] were identified as a prime site of this cultural revolution, and the anxieties it provoked were focused most intensely on the body of Valentino, who seemed to personify the extent to which the "woman-made man" differed from the established ideals of American masculinity. Even more disturbing than his androgynous dancer's body was his "exoticism." Valentino, the "Latin Lover,"

The Son of the Sheik (1926): Rudolph Valentino's desiring gaze at Yasmin (Vilma Banky). Produced by John W. Considine Jr; distributed by United Artists. United Artists (courtesy Kobal).

invoked a set of racist stereotypes about the excessive, predatory sexuality of the ethnic or racial Other at precisely the historical moment when the United States was restricting immigration in a climate of xenophobia and nativism. Valentino threatened the norms of "100 percent American" masculinity because despite "his small eyes, his flat nose and his large mouth," and his failure "to measure up to the standards of male beauty usually accepted in this country,"[39] women, both on the screen and in the "Valentino traps" of the movies, desired to look at him. Male commentators who feared that female desire would lead to a "mongrelization" of the Anglo-Saxon race were unappeased by – or more likely simply did not hear – the comments of female fans that their relationship with the screen was more complex, that, as one put it, "we are speaking of actors and their acting and not of intermarriage with them." It was true, wrote another:

> that our feminine hearts go pit-a-pat when we see Valentino up on the screen. . . . But when the lights go up on every day life once more, how perfectly splendid it is for American women to have one hundred percent, plain, American husbands, who treat them as pals and equals and love them for saving pennies for the children's future, instead of spending them on sunken marble baths.[40]

Issues of race are part of the fabric of Valentino's movies, most evidently in his most famous role as *The Sheik* (1921), where the movie's plot both exploits aspects of his star image and tries to defuse hostility to that image by qualifying it. The exotic figure of sexual aggression ("When an Arab sees a woman he wants, he takes her," announced the movie's advertising) turns out in the plot to be the son of English and Spanish nobility, and once his secret is known, his behavior becomes much more restrained. His subsequent movies often provided him with some version of a doubled characterization, in which he would have to renounce "Valentino" to win the love of a deserving woman.[41] These movies negotiated the contradictions of his persona within their stories, but since those contradictions embodied cultural concerns much larger than Valentino or even the movies, a plot-line could hardly resolve them. Although it repeated this narrative pattern, Valentino's last movie, *The Son of the Sheik*, took a more ironic attitude to his star persona. Since the movie was released immediately after his sudden death in August 1926, the ironies of this interpretation were overridden in the "notorious necrophilic excesses" of his public mourning.[42]

The Son of the Sheik (1926)

The Son of the Sheik is one of Hollywood's last silent movies. Within a few months of its release, "talkies" would begin to alter Hollywood's performance styles and its organization of camera movement. Without the resource of synchronized dialog, silent film depended on movement as a source of signification and meaning for audiences. Characterization and story relied on gesture and action, and audience attention was sustained by a mobile image, in which camera movement and editing played as important a performative role as the actors. As the discussion of *Sunny Side Up* (1929) in chapter 8 suggested, however, the arrival of sound also confirmed stylistic changes that were already under way, and although *The Son of the Sheik* frequently revels in the rhetoric and expressive techniques of much earlier cinema, some of its performance strategies anticipate the arrival of the talkies.

As a typical star vehicle, *The Son of the Sheik* organizes its mise-en-scène to emphasize the performances of its leading players. Valentino plays two roles, the eponymous hero "young" Ahmed, and his father from the earlier movie, Ahmed Ben Hassan. The movie showcases Valentino's personal repertoire of gestures – what James Naremore has called the star's "idiolect"[43] – and it adds a further fascination with performance in those scenes in which, through processing work and doubling, Ahmed and his father apparently play together. Agnes Ayres, who had portrayed the heroine in *The Sheik*, reappears as Ahmed's mother, Diana, while the new heroine, Yasmin, is played by MGM's new Hungarian "discovery," Vilma Banky. Pre-release publicity drew attention to this casting and the movie plays with cultural memories of *The Sheik*, using footage from it in one flashback sequence.

The movie's storyline is focused strictly on its single plot. Ahmed, a desert sheik, encounters and falls in love with a dancing girl, Yasmin. At their first rendezvous, Ahmed is taken prisoner and held to ransom by Yasmin's scheming father, André (George Fawcett), and his henchmen, led by the villainous Ghabah (Montague Love). After being tortured, Ahmed is rescued by his servant, Ramadan (Karl Dane), and returned to a friend's house. Believing that Yasmin had been a party to his kidnap, Ahmed determines on revenge and abducts Yasmin to his desert encampment, where he threatens her with physical and sexual violence and she tries to kill him. Ahmed's father arrives, and Ahmed is persuaded to release the girl. Ramadan escorts Yasmin to her camp and learns of her innocence. He and Ahmed pursue her back to the town of Touggourt, where she is dancing in the casbah. Yasmin and Ahmed finally declare their love for each other, but at the last moment she is abducted by Ghabah. Ahmed is joined by his father, and after a lengthy fight sequence, he kills Ghabah and rescues Yasmin. They ride off together into the desert.

Devoid of the sub- or parallel plots common in later Classical Hollywood stories, the action is presented as a series of clearly motivated movements and counter-movements, captures and rescues, chases and escapes, allowing ample opportunity for autonomous set-piece displays of Valentino's idiolect: swashbuckling fight sequences, horseback races-to-the-rescue, torrid love scenes. Between such sequences, there are moments of more introspective performance, particularly in scenes between Ahmed and Yasmin and between Ahmed and his father. The autonomous, presentational performance of separable action sequences is balanced against the more integrated, representational performances of scenes between major characters. These shifts are not as explicit as in a musical, but a similar rhythm alternating action with family melodrama is established across the movie.

Although Hollywood seeks to balance performances in order to create an untroubling consistency, within these limits it also varies that uniformity to create further levels of pleasurable play and demarcate the relative status of particular characters. Acting style varies across the movie, from the understatement of Valentino at his most statuesque, gazing significantly offscreen, to the gestural excess of Ramadan's wide-eyed stares and face-pulling and Ghabah's endless grimacing and snarling. The performances of major characters and the morally virtuous pull toward a greater naturalism, while second leads, villains, and minor characters are marked by a Delsartean declamatory excess. Yasmin's father is a compendium of actorly poses, grimaces, and inflated gestures, while Ghabah's outlaw band frequently squabble and fight in accelerated motion. This variation of volume, intensity, and ostensiveness suggests the way in which Hollywood uses performance as an agency of narrative clarity. The moral authority granted Valentino by the story is reinforced by codes of greater authenticity at the level of performance.

Such strategies also have ideological implications. In *The Son of the Sheik* distinctions in acting style are mapped onto the representation of race, in which the daughter of a Frenchman must be rescued from the lascivious Moor for Ahmed's legitimate desire. The movie's racism is visible in the contrast between Valentino's performance as Ahmed ("English born, Sahara bred, undisputed ruler in this sea of sand," an **intertitle** informs us) and Montague Love's performance as Ghabah ("The Moor, whose crimes outnumber the sands"). By this maneuver Valentino is cast on the heroic side of the racial divide, "playing the white man" through the transparent codes of naturalism, while Love is consigned to a near-animal excess of ostensiveness. The contrast is even stronger between Ahmed's family and the opposing "family" of Ghabah. Agnes Ayres's performance as Diana is the most

Ahmed (Valentino) stripped and beaten for his beauty by the villainous Ghabah (Montague Love) in *The Son of the Sheik*.
Produced by John W. Considine Jr; distributed by United Artists. Courtesy BFI.

understated in the movie, while Ghabah's followers are a gaggle of grotesques, described by an intertitle as "a vagrant troupe, entertainers by profession, thieves by preference," and reduced from the outset to parody and stereotype. The racial distinction employed in the contrast between "sophisticated" and "primitive" performance styles is also registered visually by differences in makeup: Valentino's face is a white screen, while Ghabah and his crew have the exaggerated features of painted masks.

The Son of the Sheik was made during a period of transition, and to an extent the major players seem caught between the more declamatory modes of the silent cinema and the increasingly naturalist emphases that would find fuller fruition in the sound era. Vilma Banky's performance anticipates much of the mainstream style of later cinema, making use of expressive objects to reduce the burden placed on face and body. A ring, first given her by Ahmed and then thrown away, becomes the means by which she registers loss and regret, simply through a close-up in which she touches her now ringless finger. Such detail contrasts with the broad gestures of minor characters: Ramadan indicates the imminent arrival of Ahmed's father by outlining the shape of his beard on his own face. At times, however, all the performers fall back on the formalized sign languages of body movement and gesture. On arriving at his desert villa, Ahmed's father registers anger at his son's disappearance by clenching his fist determinedly. Yasmin poses balletically as Ahmed carries her around the interior of a desert tent.[44] Even Valentino can never entirely resist the posturing or face-pulling characteristic of the most exteriorized of expressive techniques. His contempt for Yasmin is signaled by the narrowing of his eyes when he spots her bartering for a necklace in a Touggourt casbah. He stands, feet apart, arms folded across his chest, refusing her gaze. This unequivocal delivery contrasts with an acting style that elsewhere displays a greater hesitancy and spontaneity, and has to be interpreted through the subtlest of facial gestures.

It has been argued that the development of pantomimic styles was part of an attempt to reduce the number of intertitles needed by silent Hollywood. In this respect, performance style fulfilled one realist goal at the same time as it introduced other new areas of artificiality. In a similar vein, many critics thought that the advent of sound brought a return to the more artificial conventions and mannerism of stage acting, at least for a while. Exaggerated elements of performance persist in contemporary acting styles: think of Arnold Schwarzenegger's use of facial expressions, or Sylvester Stallone's pantomimic version of the Method in *Cliffhanger* (1993). At one level the excesses of exaggeration signal the fact of performance within a predominantly realist style. At another level, a set of familiarly communicative gestures, postures, and expressions contributes to the commercial aesthetic's economical presentation of character and narrative.

Screen performance can, however, never really be considered in isolation, but as a reciprocal orchestration of bodily and gestural codes with those of mise-en-scène, camera placement, editing, and soundtrack. In *The Son of the Sheik* figure placement at times emphasizes presentation, displaying a marked tendency toward stage-like frontality in the way that static figures turn outward toward the camera while their faces are twisted toward each other, producing an effect often referred to as "rubbernecking." The presentational effect of direct address is simulated by the occasional equation of camera viewpoint and character point of view, as when Ahmed advances threateningly on Yasmin in his tent, and the audience is offered a "head-on" track-in on her, until her eyes fill the screen in extreme close-up. The disproportionately long action sequences also show a continued commitment to the "cinema of attractions," rooted less in the traditions of psychological realism than in the presentational modes of more popular theatrical entertainment. In general, however, *The Son of the Sheik* uses camera movement prosaically, to help maintain an unimpeded view of action and aid the processes of characterization that were once the sole preserve of bodily designation.

Combining the work of actors, cameramen, and editors, Hollywood maintains a loose equation between shot scale and degree of ostensiveness. Extravagant action sequences are filmed in long shot, but performances are scaled down in closer shots to pick up nuances of facial expression and build a greater intimacy between characters and audiences. Conversations are regularly presented in shot/reverse shot structures that provide all the accessibility of the more primitive frontal style without its artificiality. The close-up helps to do this by eliminating the actors' bodies. Other scenes reduce body motion to an absolute minimum, as characters indicate crisis not by gesturing excitedly, but scarcely using their bodies at all, their presences animated by editing or by the sheer concentration afforded by the close-up. *The Son of the Sheik* exploits this most intensely in the erotic charge it develops between Ahmed and Yasmin, something achieved through a series of **reverse-angle** close-ups which do away with the need for more tangible signs of their passion.

Strasberg chose the "Method" as a label for a practice that "emphasized elements that [Stanislavski] had not emphasized and disregarded elements which he might have considered of greater importance." Strasberg's own account of his practice is in *A Dream of Passion: The Development of the Method* (Boston: Little, 1987). For Strasberg's particular understanding of Stanislavski's system, see Sharon Marie Carnicke, "Lee Strasberg's Paradox of the Actor," in *Screen Acting*, eds Alan Lovell and Peter Krämer (London: Routledge, 1999), pp. 75–87. The Method as an acting practice is also described in Edward Dwight Easty, *On Method Acting*, 1st edn 1966 (New York: Ballantine, 1989). Two books provide biographical histories of the Actors Studio and its members: Foster Hirsch, *A Method to their Madness: The History of the Actors Studio* (New York: Norton, 1984), and Steve Vineberg, *Method Actors: Three Generations of an American Acting Style* (New York: Macmillan, 1991). For a contextualization of the Method as a performance style in the 1950s, see Steven Cohan, *Masked Men: Masculinity and the Movies in the Fifties* (Bloomington: Indiana University Press, 1997).

There is an account of the difficulties that *A Streetcar Named Desire* had with the Production Code Administration and the Catholic Legion of Decency in Leonard J. Leff and Jerrold R. Simmons, *The Dame in the Kimono: Hollywood, Censorship, and the Production Code from the 1920s to the 1960s* (New York: Grove, Weidenfeld, 1990), pp. 172–7.

Delsarte

Delsarte's work is described in Genevieve Stebbins, *Delsarte's System of Expression* (New York: Edgar S.

Werner, 1902; reprinted New York: Dance Horizons, 1977), and in George Taylor, "Francois Delsarte: A Codification of Nineteenth Century Acting," *Theatre Research International* 24:1 (Spring 1999), pp. 71–81.

Silent performance

On Valentino, see Miriam Hansen, "Pleasure, Ambivalence, Identification: Valentino and Female Spectatorship," *Cinema Journal* 25:4 (Summer 1986), reprinted in *Stardom: Industry of Desire*, ed. Christine Gledhill (London: Routledge, 1991), pp. 259–82, and three essays by Gaylyn Studlar: "Discourses of Gender and Ethnicity: The Construction and De(con)struction of Rudolph Valentino as Other," *Film Criticism* 13:2 (1989), pp. 18–35; "The Perils of Pleasure? Fan Magazine Discourse as Women's Commodified Culture in the 1920s," *Wide Angle* 13:1 (January 1991), pp. 6–33; and "Valentino, 'Optic Intoxication,' and Dance Madness," in *Screening the Male: Exploring Masculinities in Hollywood Cinema* (London: Routledge, 1993), eds Steven Cohan and Ina Rae Hark, pp. 23–45. Hansen enlarges her analysis in *Babel and Babylon: Spectatorship in American Silent Film* (Cambridge, MA: Harvard University Press, 1991), and Studlar synthesizes her argument in *This Mad Masquerade: Stardom and Masculinity in the Jazz Age* (New York: Columbia University Press, 1996).

Giannino Malossi, ed., *Latin Lover: The Passionate South* (Milan: Edizioni Charta, 1996), provides a context for Valentino's archetype. See also the chapter on Valentino in Jeanine Basinger, *Silent Stars* (Hanover, NH: Wesleyan University Press, 2000).

CHAPTER FOURTEEN
Time

Obviously, the photoplay has points of distinct superiority over the stage drama. Its weakness, no less, is its transiency. Where nothing stands still, nothing endures.... The circulation of a popular picture is immediate and world-wide ... but this vast diffusion is paid for by a corresponding brevity.

Joseph P. Kennedy[1]

As the song in *Casablanca* (1942) tells us, we must remember that one of the fundamental things that applies in cinema is that time goes by. The projection of moving images in a temporal sequence is the most obvious feature distinguishing cinema from earlier art forms. We recognize narrative motivation and dramatic effect largely through the representation of space, but we experience cinema's representation of space by perceiving film's movement through time. Movies manipulate our experience of time with particular rigor, but audiences are skilled in recognizing the conventions by which these temporal shifts are signaled. In the course of the most unremarkable movie, audiences may need to comprehend the significance of acceleration and delay, parallel time-frames, and the mechanisms of temporal continuity and its violation.

Time Out

Cinema is life, with the boring bits cut out.
Alfred Hitchcock

An interviewer once asked director Howard Hawks what his next movie was about. "Well," he replied, "it's about two hours long." Apart from demonstrating Hawks's notorious disdain for answering critical questions about his work, this remark makes an obvious but important point about the nature of movies: they take time, and they do so in a particular way. Our perception of time and of the way we normally occupy it fluctuates constantly. Our sense of history, too, is formed by the idea that some passages of time are more significant than others. Movies, on the other hand, occupy time with mechanical consistency. *The Matrix* (1999) takes 131 minutes to screen, whenever and wherever it is shown. The price of admission to the movie theater is, effectively, the price of renting a seat for a couple of hours while you watch the movie. Cinema offers us nothing tangible, just the opportunity to spend time in a particular way, to take time "out" from the continuum of the rest of our lives.

The buying and selling of time is the central activity of the leisure industry in a capitalist economy. This process of commodification itself has a history. When the culture of consumption spread from the propertied classes down through the social system in the late nineteenth and early twentieth centuries, the form in which leisure activities occupied time became more mechanical. While books allowed readers to organize their own time and pace their own activity, records, radio, and movies all required their consumers to conform to the mechanical and temporal requirements of the medium. Exhibition practice emphasized a transience that distinguished movies from more durable cultural commodities. When we buy a book or a picture we possess the physical object in addition to experiencing the act of consumption. Possessing the object allows us to repeat the experience, or use the book for any other purpose we choose: to prop up a table leg, or to fill up a bookshelf with titles chosen to impress our friends with our good taste. The entertainment experience of cinema leaves us with no second, durable consumer commodity. If we want to repeat the experience we must return to the movie theater.

At first glance, the appearance of video-tape and later technologies like DVD would seem to blur these distinctions, but a more considered view suggests that these alternative versions emphasize how specific the experience of cinema – of viewing a movie in the shared public space of a movie theater – is. Since the mid-1980s it has been possible to come home from the local shopping mall or high street with a copy of a recent Hollywood movie – as easily as buying a paperback book or a CD. They each cost about the same, and the delay between theatrical and video release is comparable to that between hardback and paperback publication dates. This ought not to surprise us; the distribution and merchandizing of these different forms of "software," all competing for a share of our leisure expenditure, have clearly learned from each other. Indeed, the marketing of video for home consumption took some time to settle into a stable format, having initially set its retail prices at much higher levels and expected to do almost all its business through low-cost rentals in a form of consumption that substituted a transient experience in the home for the visit to the movie theater. (See chapter 7.)

Gradually, however, the industry recognized that an opportunity also existed to sell copies of movies to viewers who would collect them in much the same way as they owned collections of books or records. On video, movies became household objects, far more readily available than they had ever been before, and also subject to much more flexible patterns of consumption than those permitted by the cinema's fixed schedule of performances. One of the pleasures of owning a movie is being able to view and repeat-view parts of it with almost the same ease as we read and re-read a book. As an incidental bonus to the industry's finding another way to sell its products, video has undoubtedly made the study of Hollywood a good deal easier. Indeed, the industry has gradually learned to repackage and recommodify its products to appeal to movie collectors as connoisseurs. During the 1990s, "special edition" videos often provided a "director's cut" or a documentary on the making of the movie, while laser discs frequently included a "Collector's Supplement" with "inside" production information, storyboards, script versions, and special effects. DVDs have increased the repackaging of movies for connoisseurs incrementally: the 2001 deluxe Special Edition DVD of *Se7en* (1995) includes four commentary tracks, offering the aficionado behind-the-scenes information on the movie's stars, story, picture, and sound. To fully consume the DVD requires watching *Se7en* at least five times.

As the technologies of audio-visual home entertainment evolve, it becomes clearer that the difference between the cinematic experience and that of watching the same film on video-tape at home is not to be found in a purist notion of the superiority of celluloid, of image size or resolution, but in the transience and non-repeatability of the experience of consumption in the movie theater. It is possible, now, to walk into any video store and find a copy of *Singin' in the Rain* (1952) or *The Public Enemy* (1931). At the time of their initial production and release, most moviegoers had one week, or even less, in which to see them, and then, like a restaurant meal, they were gone, with only traces in the audience's memories to mark their passing. That condition of consumption, more than any other, has marked their manufacture and the forms that they have taken.

Critics of mass culture such as Theodor Adorno and Max Horkheimer (discussed in chapter 2) stressed the extent to which the mechanical occupation of time by the leisure forms of capitalism approximated and imitated the work process. Movies sought to disguise this imitation, by superimposing an alternative, narrative sense of time on the mechanical organization of time produced by the technology of film. A movie offers its audience a sense of temporal displacement, which viewers often register if, having gone into a cinema in daylight, they come out into darkness, and experience for a moment the shock of time having passed, in some sense, without them. One of the pleasures of cinema comes from escaping the confines imposed by the uniform passage of time outside the movies, into a world where time moves according to its own internal logic, in obedience to the continuity of the story.

This is, of course, no coincidence. Stories must be carefully plotted to fit into the block of time available for each screening. Contemporary screenwriting manuals declare emphatically that "proper structure occurs when the right events occur in the right sequence to elicit maximum emotional involvement in the . . . audience . . . good plot structure means that the right thing is happening at the right time."[2] To this end, they suggest that a movie screenplay should have three acts. Act 1, the **setup**, establishes the plot situation in the first quarter of the movie. Act 2, the **confrontation**, builds it during the next half. Act 3, the **resolution**, brings the story to its conclusion in the final quarter. Within this rigid structure, smaller rigidities exist. Declaring that "the standard screenplay is approximately 120 pages long," and that "one page of screenplay equals one minute of screen time," Syd Field argues that a script's first ten pages must establish who the main character is, what the story is about (what its premise is), and what circumstances it takes place in (what the dramatic situation is). In *Chinatown* (1974), for instance, we encounter Jake Gittes (Jack Nicholson), a private detective specializing in divorce work in 1930s Los Angeles, and Mrs Mulwray (Diane Ladd), who wants to hire him to find out whether her husband is having an affair. At the end of act 1, between pages 25 and 27, there is a **plot point**, an event or incident that "hooks into the story and spins it around into another direction."[3] In *Chinatown*, after Jake has discovered Mulwray in a "love nest" and the story has appeared in the newspapers, the plot point is the appearance of the *real* Mrs Mulwray (Faye Dunaway); Jake must spend act 2 trying to find out who set him up, and why. Act 2 also has a plot point at its end, between pages 85 and 90, which again redirects the plot into the sequence of events that will lead to its conclusion. Field insists that "all good screenplays" fit this pattern, and encourages his readers to watch movies with a stopwatch to identify the plot points that occur 25 and 85 minutes into the movie's running time.[4]

Other writers have proposed that Hollywood stories commonly operate according to different but equally rigid structures. In *Story*, Robert McKee describes the three-act structure as "the necessary minimum for a full-length work of narrative," and then elaborates variations which add subplots or additional acts.[5] In *Storytelling in the New Hollywood*, Kristin Thompson argues that most Hollywood movies have four acts, of approximately equal duration, dividing the movie into quarters: the setup, the complicating action, the development, and the climax. Acts are separated by events she calls "turning points," and each act conventionally lasts for between 20 and 30 minutes. Shorter movies – B-movies lasting only 70 minutes, for example – are likely to have only three acts, while epics running for more than two-and-a-half hours will in all probability have five acts.[6]

The rigidity of these structures suggests the formulaic nature of Hollywood narration: Field unequivocally asserts that time in the movies is constrained by the need for linear continuity and the achievement of goals. He defines dramatic structure as "a linear arrangement of related incidents, episodes or events leading to a dramatic resolution," and insists on the importance of strong, conclusive, and preferably "up" endings: "There are better ways to end your screenplays than have

---

Box 14.1 Models of the Hollywood story

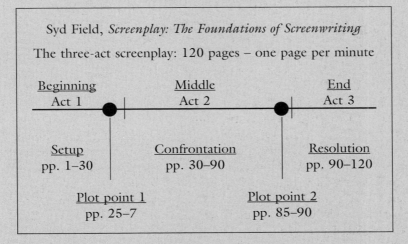

Syd Field, *Screenplay: The Foundations of Screenwriting*

The three-act screenplay: 120 pages – one page per minute

Beginning	Middle	End
Act 1	Act 2	Act 3

Setup	Confrontation	Resolution
pp. 1–30	pp. 30–90	pp. 90–120

Plot point 1	Plot point 2
pp. 25–7	pp. 85–90

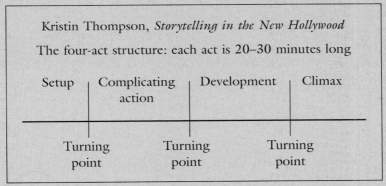

Kristin Thompson, *Storytelling in the New Hollywood*

The four-act structure: each act is 20–30 minutes long

Setup	Complicating action	Development	Climax

Turning point	Turning point	Turning point

Since the 1970s, a long portion of a movie has been called an "act." The most common structure that screenwriting manuals propose for a Hollywood movie has a three-act structure, with climaxes occurring one-quarter and three-quarters of the way through the movie's running time. Kristin Thompson argues, however, that plots are more often composed of roughly equal parts, each lasting 20–30 minutes.

---

your character shot, captured, die, or be murdered."[7] The assertion of Hollywood's commercial aesthetic could hardly be clearer. Although a screenplay's suitability for production may be evaluated according to a schema such as Field's, the commercial aesthetic also requires that it conceal its structure of acts and plot points behind the novelty of its plot events. A convention of romantic comedies, for example, is that the lovers "meet cute": that is, they encounter each other in improbable circumstances. If the meeting is cute enough – on the back seat of a

Gentlemen Prefer Blondes (1953): Marilyn Monroe and Jane Russell perform out of time. Produced by Sol C. Siegel; distributed by Twentieth Century-Fox.

bus in *It Happened One Night* (1934) or, repeatedly, through a radio talk-show in *Sleepless in Seattle* (1993) – the audience's pleasure at the skillful variation of convention overrides any concern with the predictability of the event.

Even in Hollywood's rigid sense of temporal continuity, the play with conventions means that narrative progression can be interrupted by alternative forms of entertainment. There is always room for the incidental pleasures of spectacle and performance. Take the opening sequence of *Gentlemen Prefer Blondes* (1953, directed by Howard Hawks). Immediately after the Twentieth Century-Fox fanfare and before any credits appear, the image on the screen is revealed to be a set of curtains, which part far enough to allow Jane Russell and Marilyn Monroe, dressed in identical red floor-length dresses slit virtually to the waist in both directions, to step through. On a dark green staircase they sing "We're Just Two Little Girls From Little Rock." This minimal stage background sets their performance not only outside the diegetic world established by the movie's fiction, but also outside narrative time, before the credit sequence starts. The primary source of audience enjoyment in the scene is the pleasure we gain from watching Marilyn Monroe and Jane Russell perform for an offscreen audience; our reward is spectacular, rather than narrational. The sequence draws its viewers out of their ordinary external relation to the passage of time, because the sequence itself has no identifiable temporal context: viewing it, we have no idea when or where it happens. As a result there are no visible constraints upon how long it may last. In fact, like the movie that is "about two hours long," it lasts for as long as its producers believe it can sustain the audience's interest. And at that point, almost at the end of the song, the movie cuts to a shot of a night-club audience, locating the sequence for the first time within a narrative framework. The James Bond series established a convention of opening with a spectacular pre-credit sequence with little direct connection to the main story that followed the credits, and this convention has been widely adopted by action movies since 1980. The 12-minute opening South American sequence of *Raiders of the Lost Ark* (1981) introduces us to the character of Indiana Jones (Harrison Ford) and sets a tone for the action that follows, but it is just as self-contained and detached from what follows as Russell and Monroe's performance.

As the excessive precision of Syd Field's rules of screenplay construction suggest, Hollywood movies structure time to meet the needs of their audiences, and they define those needs in the process of meeting them. One often-repeated story about Harry Cohn, the acerbic head of production at Columbia, tells of his behavior at a preview of one of his studio's prestige productions. The production personnel gathered round him after the screening, eager for his good opinion. It was fine, he declared, except that it was exactly 19 minutes too long. Their astonishment at the precision and speed of his analysis was immediately blunted by his declaration that "exactly nineteen minutes ago, my ass started to itch and right there I know the audience would feel the same."[8] The aesthetic assumption behind the story, which circulated widely as a piece of industry lore, is that the requirements of narrative must be constrained within the limits of the audience's anticipated temporal tolerance. This principle applies not only to time out within the movies, such as the musical numbers, but crucially to the logics governing the typical duration of an entire movie, as time out from its audiences' routine. Hollywood movies are not all "about two hours long," and the expected duration of a movie has varied significantly over Hollywood's history: few 1930s movies were longer than 100 minutes, few 1990s movies were under two hours long. But in any given period, the overwhelming majority of movies share a similar running time, roughly corresponding to an ideal duration which most closely meets the needs of production efficiency, the economics of exhibition, and the comfortable limits of audience tolerance.

Film Time

Any expressive form lives only in its own present – the one it itself creates.
Clifford Geertz[9]

The distinction between film and movie made in chapter 1 and used throughout this book also clarifies Hollywood's articulation of different types of time. **Film**

time, the amount of time a movie requires of its audience, is a matter of fixed duration, determined by the length of the film and the set speed at which it passes through the projector. *Once Upon a Time in America* (1984) runs for 3 hours and 48 minutes. **Movie time**, the time represented within the fiction, is much more flexible. The movie time of *Once Upon a Time in America* begins in 1922 and ends in 1968, and involves flashbacks and flashforwards, ellipses, parallel narratives, and sequences in slow motion.

In mechanical terms, a film camera moves a strip of film at a uniform rate past an aperture – a lens – through which light passes. Sprocket holes at the sides of the film engage with the teeth of the camera's sprocket wheels; the film is pulled forward, stops briefly in front of the lens to be exposed, and is then pulled on again, at a uniform rate, usually 24 times per second. If you then hold a strip of film up to the light you see the result of this process: a long string of almost identical still images. These images are then animated by being projected. Each frame is stopped in front of the projector gate and the projector light shows the image. Between the illumination of each frame, a baffle blocks out the light while the motor winds the film on to the next frame.

The illusion of continuous motion celebrated in a Hollywood movie is therefore actually based on the regularly interrupted movement of the film through the projector. Significantly, the major mechanical complication involved in the development of the motion picture camera lay in inventing a reliable device for coordinating the interrupted motion of the film past the camera lens and projector gate. If the film did not stop exactly in the same place 24 times a second, while being exposed or projected, the movie would appear on the screen as an indecipherable blur. Moreover, the film must be projected at the same speed as it was shot to produce the conventional illusion of movement. Most silent movies were shot at a camera speed of about 18 frames per second, and if they are projected at the normal sound camera speed of 24 frames per second, the represented movement is speeded up by a third, making it appear quick and jerky. The effect disappears when the film is projected at the same speed as it was shot.[10] **Slow-motion** effects are produced by passing the film through the camera at a faster rate than normal, so that the film takes longer to project than the duration of the action it records.

Variations between camera speed and projector speed reveal the extent to which the cinema's illusion of movement is dependent, first, on the film's rigidly mechanical occupation of time. The illusion of movement depends, second, on a process of human perception, by which we recognize a sequence of rapidly viewed still images as being in continuous motion. Until recently, this perceptual quirk was explained by the theory of **persistence of vision**. This theory is at least as old as the classical Greeks, but it was formalized in 1824 by Peter Mark Roget (better known for his *Thesaurus*), who suggested that every time we look at something, a brief residual image is stored on the retina of the eye. You notice the effect if you stare at a bright light, and then close your eyes. A negative image of the light remains for a while, temporarily burned onto the retina. Roget's theory of persistence of vision suggested that this phenomenon occurs constantly, but over very short durations, so that in watching sequences of still images, each individual image is retained until the next one appears to replace it. More recent research into the psychology of perception, however, suggests that the process is much more complicated, and that seeing – and hearing – are positive mental activities, not involuntary physical processes. Rather than the illusion of movement being created by a deception of the eye, the brain constructs a continuous image from the sequence of stills, filling in the missing parts. The viewer, not the projector, creates the illusion of movement. If you project a strip of film in an empty cinema, it is only a sequence of consecutive still pictures. Film needs an audience to become a movie, and the psychological explanation of the perception of motion is important to a discussion of the interactive relationship between Hollywood and its audiences.[11]

At a number of levels, the basic apparatus of cinema insists on the ephemerality of film, graphically demonstrated at the end of *Two Lane Blacktop* (1972). The final shot of the movie appears to be being projected more and more slowly, at first giving the viewer time to register each separate image as a still picture. Eventually, a completely still frame seems to be held in the projector gate, heating up until the celluloid melts and catches fire. We are given the impression that the film has, literally, brought the movie to an end. If a sense of this material evanescence has underpinned much critical dismissal of cinema, the fact that the base material itself moves may have also contributed to a sense that the movies were somehow never still enough long enough for critics to gain a purchase on them. For instance, the detailed analysis of spatial relations in a scene almost invariably requires the critic to look at individual still frames, studying them for much longer than is possible during projection. While this is comparable to the close textual analysis of a literary work, it involves a disruption of the movie's experiential form.

Hollywood's own commercial practices confirm that close criticism (which has often called itself "reading") is a perverse activity based on the critical misconception of a movie as a fixed "text."[12] Classical Hollywood's accountants assumed that a movie would earn all its income within two years of its initial release, after which it was taken off the company's books. Any further earnings were treated as windfall profits. Until television and then video demonstrated the commercial importance of a film company's library, the production industry made little effort to preserve what were regarded as last season's no longer fashionable goods. A movie might be remade – with added ingredients in the form of new stars, color, or widescreen – but it was unlikely to be re-released, at least into the first-run market.[13] It was not uncommon for companies to destroy prints in order to recover the small amounts of silver in their emulsion. Hollywood movies thus offered themselves as doubly ephemeral, designed neither in content nor in material to persist as part of an artistic tradition, but to be consumed, exhausted, en route to further acts of consumption. In 1928 a San Francisco theater announced that, despite *The Way of All Flesh* being "the wonder engagement of all time . . . it cannot stay forever!," since Friday would see the arrival of *The Big Parade*.[14]

Even when a movie is preserved, abstracted from its original theatrical viewing conditions, and placed in a research archive, the notion that this represents the survival of a fixed, stable "text" corresponds poorly with the actual distribution and exhibition practices of the industry. In the silent period in particular, the movie was a highly malleable object: as well as the variable performance element provided by the musical accompaniment to silent movies, the prints themselves were regularly cut by distributors, local censor boards, and individual exhibitors for a variety of reasons. Because of the poor quality of duplicate negatives in the early 1920s, silent movies were sometimes shot on two cameras to produce one negative for the domestic market and one for export use. The export version of a movie such as *The Four Horsemen of the Apocalypse* (1921) was, therefore, slightly but significantly different from the American domestic release version.[15]

Although the precise nature of this malleability changed with the introduction of sound, it is still the case that different versions of the same movie emerge as Hollywood tailors its products to different exhibition circumstances – for a television showing, for example, which requires a movie's running time (that is, what I am calling film time) to adapt to a predetermined time-slot in the schedule and accommodate interruptions for advertising time. More recent technologies for home viewing have proliferated multiple versions: video rental chains such as Blockbuster often require distributors to supply them with "softer" versions of R-rated movies, with reduced levels of sex or violence. "Special editions" released to video, on the other hand, include previously unavailable spatial material such as the extra portion of the screen in a widescreen version, extra footage previously excluded – literally, extra time. In 1992, *Dances with Wolves* (1990) was released to video in four versions: in widescreen and standard formats, with and without an additional hour's footage. The 2001 Collector's Edition DVD of *Hannibal* (2001) promised "over 6 hours of entertainment," including 15 deleted and extended scenes, an alternative ending, and an optional commentary by director Ridley Scott.

Perhaps more than any other factor, the movies' transient and unstable existence has accounted for the low cultural status they have been accorded for most of their history. Artifacts that have "stood the test of time" are valued not simply for their material longevity, but also because they have claimed a place as part of a tradition or heritage, valued for its intrinsic and supposedly universal values. This process of cultural abstraction is celebrated in John Keats's "Ode on a Grecian Urn." The poem describes an object kept in the British Museum, and discusses the way that cultural artifacts become museum pieces, preserved in a temporal limbo quite separate from the places and circumstances of their production. Keats celebrates the fact of the urn's survival through the uncertainties of history, to the point when, from the safety of the museum, its aesthetic certainties will continue to address viewers indefinitely:

> When old age shall this generation waste,
> Thou shalt remain, in midst of other woe
> Than ours, a friend to man, to whom thou say'st,
> "Beauty is truth, truth beauty", – that is all
> Ye know on earth, and all ye need to know.

This transcendent aesthetic value is connected to the form of the frieze on the urn. In describing the scenes on the frieze, the poet gives the actions they depict a significance that transcends history precisely because they are frozen in time, and can never be completed:

> Bold lover, never, never can'st thou kiss,
> Though winning near the goal – yet do not grieve;
> She cannot fade, though thou hast not thy bliss,
> For ever wilt thou love, and she be fair!

Unprojected, a movie would be reduced to a sequence of still frames, static spectacles that would share many of the temporal properties Keats attributes to the urn. As with the urn, a viewer might decipher scenes and character types by identifying the conventional iconography of star and genre, but such iconographic recognitions cannot provide a precise narrative framework within which to locate the character of the exchanges taking place. Nor, crucially for the movie's organization of time, can the unprojected film strip provide any information about duration, pace, or performance.[16] The image requires the animation produced by its projection to restore its full dramatic and expressive activity.

Movie Time

Time, though invisible and abstract, has many concrete ways of assisting or damaging the motion picture narration.
Eugene Vale[17]

It could mean that that point in time inherently contains some sort of cosmic significance, almost as if it were the temporal junction point for the entire space-time continuum. On the other hand it could just be an amazing coincidence.
Doc (Christopher Lloyd) in *Back to the Future Part II* (1989)

Both film time and movie time are matters of duration, of different senses of how the passage of time is being measured. Film time is rigid and mechanical, while movie time – the time represented within the narrative – is much more flexible. Very early cinema engaged its audiences with the novelty and spectacle of movement, occupying time in the uncomplicated manner provided by the literal recording of an event. As the exhibition industry expanded in the mid-1900s, the demand for product rose rapidly, and by 1907 there was a marked shift toward the production of dramatic fictions. Unlike topical or actuality films, manufacturers could produce a constant supply of story films from a purpose-built studio at a predictable cost, and release them on a regular schedule. The industry's wholesale switch to story-film production was instigated by manufacturers seeking to take advantage of the economies of scale provided by mass production rather than by audience demand, but demand combined with industrial production to develop longer, more complex narrative forms. As one cinema manager reported,

"Bullet time" in *The Matrix* (1999).

Produced by Joel Silver; distributed by Silver Pictures, Village Roadshow Productions; directed by Andy Wachowski, Larry Wachowski.

> The people want a story . . . When we started we used to give just flashes – an engine chasing to a fire, a base runner sliding home, a charge of cavalry. Now, for instance, if we want to work in a horse race it has to be a scene in the life of the jockey, who is the hero of the piece – we've got to give them a story; they won't take anything else – a story with plenty of action . . . More story, larger story, better story with plenty of action – that is our tendency.[18]

The fiction film emerged as the dominant form because it was the most effective means of packaging the ingredients audiences required from cinema as a form of mass entertainment. The development of forms that could sustain audience interest for longer durations in turn required technical apparatuses and discursive conventions that could make more complex stories comprehensible, and from this process the rhetoric of Classical Hollywood cinema gradually emerged.

Like the other formal properties of a Hollywood product, movie time operates according to established but permeable conventions. Movie time is usually longer and more complex than film time, involving time lapses or ellipses, where Alfred Hitchcock's "boring bits" have been cut out. Very occasionally movie narratives represent a continuous time: *Rope* (1948), for instance, tells a story that supposedly takes place in a period of just 80 minutes, exactly matching the film's projection time. At the other extreme, in *2001: A Space Odyssey* (1968) movie time covers two million years in the film's two-hour duration. In theory, movie time could also be shorter than film time. This happens most visibly in slow-motion sequences, where there is spectacular action – the final battle in *The Wild Bunch* (1969), the winning touchdown in *The Longest Yard* (1974), "bullet time" in *The Matrix* – and in a different sense it also happens during flashbacks that are presented as a character's act of memory; but no Hollywood movie has sustained this principle of organization for its entire length.

Within movie time (which you will often see referred to as narrative time), we must make a further distinction between the duration of the story and the duration of the plot. The duration of the story of *2001* is two million years, but the movie dramatizes only a few brief periods in this long span. Story duration encompasses the entire period covered by a narrative, including events merely referred to in dialog or inferred by the viewer. Plot duration, on the other hand, includes only those periods of time directly presented on the screen, and across the entirety of a narrative plot duration will normally be much shorter than story duration. Within any one scene, however, plot and story durations will often appear to be the same. In *Madigan* (1968), for example, film time is 101 minutes; plot duration is roughly 48 hours, from Friday morning to Sunday morning; story duration is considerably longer, going back several years, to previous encounters between characters.

Typically, film time dominates the temporal hierarchy. The rule that one page of screenplay equals one minute is a calculation in film time, and the iron laws of the three-act structure and plot-point positioning are devices by which movie time must be fitted to the commercial aesthetic of film time, which determines that a movie is "about two hours long." Hollywood cannot, therefore, tell stories that will be longer or shorter than about two hours in the telling. One of the perennial complaints about movie adaptations of novels is that the movie leaves so much of the original out – although the complainants seldom explain where they expect the missing parts to fit. In *The Technique of Screenplay Writing*, Eugene Vale suggests that a Hollywood movie has, on average, 30 scenes: that is, 30 discrete sections of its plot, each occurring in a separate place or time from the scene before. Movies thus tell stories that shape themselves into about 30 separate events, each of which can show its section of the story in three or four minutes of film time. Thirty is, of course, only an average, and screenwriting manuals will dispute whether the scene or the sequence is the most important unit in screenplay construction. Syd Field defines a sequence as being a block of dramatic action unified by a single idea. A sequence may be a single scene, or even a single shot, but it may also be a series of scenes tied together by its unifying idea, and Field cites the wedding that opens *The Godfather* (1972) as one sequence, although it covers several hours of story time.[19] But whether a movie has 12 sequences (*Dog Day Afternoon*, 1975) or 31 scenes (*The Palm Beach Story*, 1942), there are limits to the range of variation. A movie cannot have 200 scenes or only a single sequence without straining the conventional experience of its audience, and therefore Hollywood cannot conventionally tell stories requiring those forms of organization.

Movies are always racing against time: "you've got thirty pages to set up your story, and . . . within the first ten pages, you must establish the *main character*, set up the dramatic *premise*, and establish the *situation*."[20] Field's imperatives sound like the deadlines so often imposed on movie characters. Just as the hero must rescue the heroine before the bomb explodes, so the story must be over before film time runs out. Deadline-setting, digression, and coincidence help to disguise this commercial and industrial imperative: movie time imposes fictional pressures on the characters' actions, so that the audience can overlook the external pressures of film time. You are not meant to be checking your watch for the plot point in the second act 85 minutes into the movie, because in the ideal

Hollywood movie, the time it takes to project the movie's film should perfectly match the time it takes for the story to unfold.

Deadlines and Coincidences: *Madigan* (1968)

Hollywood movies conventionally open "*in medias res*," in the middle of the story, so that we are plunged "into an already moving chain of cause and effect."[21] Action movies tend to begin their plots closer to the end of their stories than other genres, so that they need to spend less time in the exposition of their cause-and-effect chain. The audience's knowledge that the movie's story will resolve itself just when it is time for them to go home allows for some play in the arrangement of an audience's temporal experience of a movie. The plot may, for instance, declare at the outset when it will end. *Madigan* opens with the simple title "Friday," when two detectives, Dan Madigan (Richard Widmark) and Rocco Bonaro (Harry Guardino), attempt to pick up a suspect, Barney Benesch (Steve Ihnat), for questioning. Instead, he escapes with their pistols and is later found to be wanted for murder. Police Commissioner Russell (Henry Fonda) gives the detectives 72 hours to bring Benesch in. The audience knows immediately that time will be a conscious preoccupation for the movie, and this is emphasized throughout by the mise-en-scène: calendars are frequently visible on office walls, and the plot's movement toward its climax is punctuated by titles announcing the arrival of "Saturday" and "Sunday."

Setting a deadline makes it possible to read the relative temporal position of any given scene, and makes the movie's sense of pace meaningful. The urgency with which characters function becomes an index of how close the movie is to its closure. The detectives are constantly on the move, grabbing sleep where they can. The pressure imposed on them by Russell's deadline leaves little time for such luxury, and their attempts to withdraw even briefly from the action are usually interrupted by reminders that time is at a premium. "Can't you move this thing any faster?" Madigan asks Bonaro as they race to an appointment; elsewhere, after they have answered a false tip-off, he announces that he has "a lousy feeling that time is running out."

The race against time can also be lost if events move too quickly. Just as the movie must end before the last reel of film winds through the projector, it also must not end before then. Protagonists of suspense movies can never go to the police, for fear they may solve the mystery too quickly. But the plot, of course, must contrive some fictional reason to cover this implausibility. As a movie disguises its acceleration through deadline-setting, it will also introduce digressions to mask any delay or deceleration of its story. The most common strategy of delay involves the use of multiple plotlines. In *Madigan*, Benesch's escape establishes the main manhunt plotline, but the detectives cannot simply recapture him as he makes his break across the rooftops, or the movie would be concluded too quickly and with very little satisfaction. Instead, tension is generated around this main strand of action first by introducing subsidiary plots, and then by alternating between them. Sub-plots and minor characters have a number of functions in Hollywood dramaturgy: "they make excellent vehicles for comedy relief, crisis relief, and time-lapse cutaways. When the major story line becomes too tense, the action can always be cut away to the antics of the characters in the subplot."[22] As well as providing the audience with these incidental pleasures, this strategy places further pressure on the main characters by delaying the progress of the main plot and restricting the film time in which it must find resolution. The proliferation of sub-plots also covers over ellipses in the main plot, clarifying its advance.

Madigan develops four subsidiary plots, each with its own structure of deadlines and pressure:

1   The infidelity plot, in which Russell is having an affair with a married woman (Susan Clark), raising the question of whether she will stay with him or return home, and whether she will provoke a shift in his politics, principles, or sense of duty.

2   The brutality plot, in which a black clergyman, Dr Taylor (Raymond St Jacques), has made accusations about police brutality toward his arrested son, which Russell must investigate.

3   The corruption plot, in which Chief Inspector Charles Kane (James Whitmore) is discovered to be taking bribes from a local racketeer to protect his son, raising the question of how Commissioner Russell will decide to respond.

4   The domestic plot, in which Madigan's marriage comes under stress because of the demands made on his time by his work, raising the question of whether the marriage will survive, or whether he will take up again with a former girlfriend, Jonesy (Sheree North).

The alternation between plotlines hides the extent to which *Madigan* orders events in a firmly progressive sequence driven by its concentrated plot duration. The events that set the five plot-chains going are established early, but we join the stories relatively late on, at points where resolution already seems imminent. A clear causal sequence of action is made possible by beginning nearer to the end than the beginning, allowing viewers to concentrate on action likely to produce resolution rather than any further elaboration of causes. Exposition is kept to a minimum. Dialog is restricted to providing the necessary information, hooking scenes together, and performance is minimally distracting: Russell explains the corruption plot to his lover in a single toneless sentence, "Charlie Kane has done me in," and the movie cuts to the next scene. Despite its surface representation of the randomness of its milieu, causal connections drive both the sequence of events and the audience's attention in *Madigan*.[23] Events are given enough time for their staging and interpretation, but no more. Film time is distributed according to a temporal economy that concentrates the audience's attention on movie time. Characters cooperate with this economy by anticipating outcomes or creating future appointments that they then struggle to meet or avoid: Madigan must attend the captains' ball with his wife; Russell must investigate the accusations of brutality by Monday; another racketeer, Midget Castiglione (Michael Dunn), must produce information about Benesch's whereabouts before Benesch finds him. In this way, every scene advances at least one of the plots.

Madigan produces a sense of gradual acceleration both by the use of increasingly swift cutting rates, and by narrowing the focus of our interests as the subsidiary plots are successively resolved, with the main plot surviving longest:

1   In the infidelity plot, Russell's lover makes it clear that she will go back to her husband and children when they return to New York.
2   In the brutality plot, Kane confirms to Russell that Dr Taylor's son was not assaulted by his arresting officers, implying that Russell will back his men against the false accusations.
3   In the corruption plot, Russell confronts Kane with his corruption and Kane offers his resignation, but it is refused with a strong implication that he can be cleared.
4   In the domestic plot, despite a drunken spree that almost leads to her seduction, Julia reasserts her love for her husband.
5   In the manhunt plot, Madigan and Bonaro finally corner Benesch in an apartment, where both Benesch and Madigan are shot. Madigan dies on the way to hospital.

In all of these plots, the movie responds to the pressure to condense events with a heavy use of coincidence. Such coincidences are essential to Hollywood's temporal economy. They have become so thoroughly naturalized that they bypass our incredulous resistance to their likelihood, pushing the action on without needing elaborate explanation. Characters in Hollywood movies frequently acknowledge the role of coincidence in their lives, however, sharing a knowing complicity with the audience over this aspect of Hollywood's reconstruction of time. As Rick Blaine (Humphrey Bogart) says in *Casablanca*, "of all the gin joints in all the towns in all the world, she has to walk into mine." If she hadn't, there would be no story, in the sense that if the movie spent a credible amount of time waiting for its principals to reunite, there would be no time left for the rest of the tale.

The management of film time is a central function of a movie's narration. Detective movies employ a narrative of investigation, constructed around the timed release of plot information so that detective and audience explicitly share in the activities of hypothesis-forming and testing. In *The Big Sleep* (1946), for instance, the private detective Philip Marlowe (Humphrey Bogart) is in a sense employed by the audience to explain the plot, just as much as he is employed by General Sternwood (Charles Waldren) to protect his daughters from blackmail. Contemporary dramas and action movies such as *Falling Down* (1993) and *The Matrix* borrow their story structures as well as much of their imagery from video or computer games, moving their central character from one scene's confrontational level to the next. Story-telling is not the only way that movies can manage the passage of film time, however. Physical comedy like that of Jerry Lewis or Steve Martin, or the team comedy of the Marx Brothers, breaks the plot up with gags and set-

piece routines. Action movies such as *Lethal Weapon 2* (1989) devote more attention, and sometimes more time, to spectacle than to story, in much the same way
as musicals use story premises as little more than an excuse for extended song-
and-dance numbers which revel in their interruption of plot progression.

Alfred Hitchcock's remark that cinema is "life with the boring bits cut out"
points to a fundamental principle of a movie's temporal organization: elision. In
the movies, time lasts as long as necessary and no longer. This is why it seems
much easier for characters in movies to get taxis than it does for the rest of us: we
would not find it particularly entertaining to sit watching characters trying to hail
a taxi for ten minutes when nothing else was happening. If a man in Chicago wants
to go to Miami, and has the money, the time, and a good reason for his journey,
there is very little entertainment value in our watching him go to the airport, buy
his tickets, get on the plane, read the airline magazine, and so on. Vale advises
screenplay writers that they can cut much of their exposition by losing it in the
time lapses between scenes. The audience, he suggests, will assume that every
intention ("I'm going to Miami on the next plane!") will be fulfilled unless an
obstacle is placed in its path. The execution of an intention only becomes interesting if there is a possibility of its frustration ("We can't let him reach Miami
alive!"). As this hyperbolic but all too typical example indicates, Vale's suggestion
about temporal economy has a determining influence on what kinds of event can
happen in a movie's plot: as he puts it, "in order to be permitted to show the execution of an intention, we must create an opposing difficulty." Following such
rules of construction, movies come to tell only those stories in which a sympathetic character overcomes a series of increasingly difficult obstacles to achieve a
compelling desire:

> If a man and a woman with perfect affinity and no obvious difficulties meet each
> other, there is no doubt that they will attain their goal. The picture would have to
> show their marriage in the next shot, since we have no doubt of the fulfillment of
> their intention. All love scenes in between are without any interest. In order to show
> these love scenes, we must give the spectator a knowledge of some difficulties to
> prevent him from concluding to the goal.[24]

The process of constructing a coherent sequence without the boring bits relies on
a series of conventions similar to those by which Hollywood constructs its spatial
framework. Like mise-en-scène, these conventions are both obvious and virtually
invisible to us – we recognize their operation, but find it hard to articulate them
as such, instead displacing our awareness of them onto analysis of character
motivation or narrative development. It therefore seems appropriate to label this
parallel construction of movie time **mise-en-temps**.

Mise-en-Temps

Movies take much longer to shoot than they do to project. On a good day in the
Classical Hollywood production system, a film crew would hope to record four

minutes of a movie's final footage in eight or ten hours' work, although two-and-a-half minutes was nearer the norm. In the compilation of a movie, each separately filmed shot is subsequently edited together into a narrative continuum, and in such a system of production there is no compelling logic for shooting a movie in plot order. In fact, Hollywood's commercial aesthetic generally militates against this. It is usually more economical to shoot all the scenes using one location or one performer at the same time, regardless of plot sequence. Thus the movie will finally be assembled out of radically discontinuous temporal fragments. In a literal sense, therefore, film makes time in the editing process, creating narrative time out of this process of assemblage, subsuming all other sorts of time to its needs.

In the same way as a system of spatial conventions converts potentially incoherent, partial views into a recognizable and expressive representation of space, the fragments of time recorded in each shot are assembled into a linear sequence to supply a comprehensible temporal experience. As audience members, we cannot alter this fixed sequential order in the way movies tell us stories. We can only keep our place in the story and understand the events unfolding before us by remembering the details we learned earlier on. If we watch a movie more than once, now knowing which clues to look out for, we may notice details that we ignored the first time around. Hollywood cannot, however, rely on its audience paying to see a movie twice, and it must therefore make sure that the most significant clues, relationships, or hidden character motivations announce themselves in some way.[25]

The inflexibility of film time encourages movies to arrange themselves as a series of reiterated explanations – another aspect of the benign nature of Hollywood's conventions. A movie will state and restate character relationships, for example, "to sum up the situation for the benefit of those viewers who may have missed the beginning of the picture," or at least to ensure that the audience is not confused.[26] Significantly, these formal strategies, which evolved when Hollywood's audiences were watching movies exclusively in movie theaters, have become so integrated into Hollywood's narrative aesthetic that they persist even in the age of video. Although video allows the viewer to disrupt the normal relationship between film and movie time by skipping, interrupting, or repeating film time, this increasingly interactive relationship with Hollywood's output generally occurs on second or subsequent viewings, and is therefore premised on the viewer's prior knowledge of the story. These variant viewings are, moreover, usually solitary activities, in which the viewer pursues his or her exclusive preferences, as opposed to the shared initial consumption of the story.

Hollywood's construction of time is more difficult to analyze than its construction of space, because temporal effects are less visible. We can see what a cut or dissolve does to space, but we must interpret its effect on the passage of time more indirectly. Perhaps the best way to identify Hollywood's elusive temporal strategies is to confront them at a moment when they are unusually exposed. Thrillers and action movies push Hollywood's temporal logic to extremes, and the generation of suspense involves a particularly assertive control over the audience's sense of time. *North by Northwest* (1959) plays a temporal game with the audience to see just how much of this manipulation they will tolerate. Not only is the plot absurd, but there is often either too much or too little time for the audience and the characters. In the Prairie Stop sequence, the audience's expectations of narrative time are flouted when Roger Thornhill's (Cary Grant) contact does not arrive, and we and Thornhill are left with time on our hands, loitering in a bleak, featureless landscape with no details to occupy our sight and no visible hiding places for clues. For an uncomfortable length of time we seem to have life with the boring bits left in, while the movie withholds the next piece of action – the attack on Thornhill by the crop-dusting plane which has been circling in the distance, but to which our attention has not been unduly alerted.

North by Northwest's malign treatment of the audience in this scene is revealing precisely because it is not typical. The movies of its director, Alfred Hitchcock, achieve their distinctiveness in large part because they work on the edges of Hollywood's conventions. As I suggested in chapter 11, Hitchcock's influence has revised those conventions of temporal and spatial representation in ways that encourage a more antagonistic relationship between movie and audience. But just as Classical Hollywood mise-en-scène seeks to avoid distracting visual information in the way it organizes an image, Classical Hollywood mise-en-temps works to avoid the very time in which that distraction might take place. This avoidance of "dead time" has the effect of concentrating our attention on the significant action. In keeping with Vale's advice on elision, journeys are often presented by juxtaposing the departure with the arrival in a sequence that tells us not only that a character has gone from one place to another, but also that nothing consequential has happened en route. Many events can be covered by narrative devices other than staging, by voice-over expositions, or by being reported by one character to another. Mise-en-temps is therefore another form of Hollywood's textual economy – excising the irrelevant and maximizing our attention to the relevant, showing us all we need to see and getting the most from what we do see.

A second function of mise-en-temps is to preserve continuity within a scene assembled out of material shot weeks or months apart. If noticed by a viewer, errors in continuity – variations in the length of a character's cigarette, or changes in their clothing, for example – can be disastrous to the fiction, because they reveal so sharply the discontinuous fragments of external time from which the sequence is constructed. A system of conventions disguises this temporal discontinuity. The use of non-diegetic background music, for instance, smoothes over the potential rupture between two discontinuous images. This bridging effect may be reinforced by elements of visual harmony in the two shots, such as matched compositions or camera movements. For instance, the camera might tilt up to the sky at the end of one scene, and begin the next scene with a tilt down from the sky, concealing a dissolve. Optical effects such as this have quite specific conventional meanings in their presentation of time. A dissolve from one image into another indicates a brief passage of time, shorter than that suggested by a fade to black and then a fade up to the next scene. A wipe, on the other hand, suggests less the passage of time than a spatial move from one location to another, in continuous time. More explicit devices occur in subtitles, or the intertitles of silent movies that declare "Two Years Later" or even "Meanwhile Back at the Ranch." The caption "mean-

a   b

Rick (Humphrey Bogart) and Ilsa (Ingrid Bergman) are oblivious to the passage of time as the background dissolves in the Paris flashback in *Casablanca* (1942).
Produced by Hal B. Wallis; distributed by Warner Bros.

while" effectively brings an event that has occurred (presumably while we were watching the parallel event) into the present.

Paradoxically, Hollywood may also establish continuity precisely by fore-grounding temporal rupture in its mise-en-temps. In a **flashback** scene in *Casablanca*, Rick (Humphrey Bogart) and Ilsa (Ingrid Bergman) are shown driving down the Champs Elysées in a tight two-shot, with the Arc de Triomphe in the background behind them. Then the image in the background dissolves to a view of a country road, while the foreground image of Bogart and Bergman remains uncut. The shot is a conventional piece of studio-filmed back-projection, but the use of dissolves in back-projection is rare, because of the disturbing effect it has on the scene's temporal sense. Within the one image, two different kinds of time occur: more time goes by in the background than in the car. As we have come to expect, this semantic contradiction in the temporal organization of the material from which the scene is composed is properly resolved at the higher level of the fiction that viewers construct from that material, since what matters is what such literal discontinuities contribute to our understanding of character and situation. We interpret the romance between Bogart and Bergman as making them for the moment oblivious to the grand narrative of historical time, which passes behind them.

Tense

For film to produce the illusion of movement, the projected image must be con-stantly and rapidly changed, with each image seen not in its singularity, but as part of a continuum that the viewer experiences as a constant present. At whatever point in a movie's story an event takes place, the audience always experiences it as being in the here and now of a **continuous present**. Movies are therefore characterized by a sense of immediacy that persists even during a second viewing, when the plot's future is already known. Movies very rarely confine themselves to present action, with no reference to past motivations or future deadlines, however. In searching for the cinematic equivalent of the past tense, movies encounter a difficulty which is crucial for our understanding of Hollywood's organization of time. While a literary narrative is predominantly engaged in an act of telling, a cinematic narrative is an act of showing. As you can only tell something that has already happened, you can only show something that is happening as you show it. A movie audience has to "cook" its own story from the plot ingredients the movie offers, performing for itself the role that the narrator of a literary fiction undertakes. The sentence "The man walked down the street" is unfilmable not only because of its lack of spatial specificity, but also because film cannot visualize the past tense. Representing the future tense, rather than a future event staged in the continuous present, presents a further problem. The future can be discussed, or inferred ("We have 14 days to save the Universe!"), but it cannot be visualized without being translated into the present tense.

Hollywood must therefore find other ways to signal temporal change within the movie, and thus establish a chronology of events in the story. Such devices cannot function as subtly as changes of tense in spoken language, and are therefore likely to exist as highly visible markers: the changing date on a calendar, the changing time on a clock. In *Written on the Wind* (1956), the credit sequence stages the climax of the movie, ending with the camera tracking in to a tight close-up of a desk calendar. As the pages of the calendar start to blow backwards, the image dissolves to another shot of a similar calendar in a different setting. When the pages have stopped blowing, the camera tracks out to its new setting, and the movie's action, from then on organized in chronological sequence, begins. The effect of the shot is to take the audience back into the past so that it can experience that past as the present. In one sense it is a literalization of the act of narration – the equivalent of declaring, "to explain these events, we must go back to . . ." – but the effect of the shot does not reproduce the sense of temporal distance from the events described that the past tense in written or spoken language provides. During the sequence itself, film time advances while time in the movie's narration moves backward.

Hollywood often uses obvious narrational clues to establish temporal shifts, in particular with characters narrating **voice-overs** in the past (perfect) tense. At the start of *Double Indemnity* (1944) Walter Neff (Fred MacMurray) sets the plot in motion by confessing a crime into a recording machine. As he speaks into the microphone, the movie dissolves "back" to the events he is describing, and the voice-over runs on over images of his arrival at the house of the woman with whom he will commit murder. The viewer's comprehension of time in this sequence is complex and the tense involved contradictory. Just listening to the soundtrack reproduces the perfect (past) tense of a written narration: Neff, situated in the auditor's present, narrates events in the past tense. The images, however, all occur in the continuous present of film time. At one point in the sequence, this temporal contradiction is given spatial expression in a split between viewpoint and point of view. MacMurray is physically placed in the represented space of the scene,

Walter Neff (Fred MacMurray) confesses the story of *Double Indemnity* (1944) to a phonograph.

Produced by Joseph Sistrom; distributed by Paramount Pictures.

at the same time as he is describing his view of Barbara Stanwyck's legs in the narration. The shots we see of Stanwyck, however, are taken from a different position: they represent MacMurray's point of view, but not his viewpoint, since he is not in a position actually to see Stanwyck descend the staircase. Recognizing this sequence as being simultaneously a memory and an imaginative reconstruction of the scene, we elide the distinction between viewpoint and point of view and displace both the temporal and spatial contradictions into an interpretation of character psychology.

The voice-over points up differences in the knowledge available to the narrator and the audience: the narrator demonstrates her or his knowledge of the whole story, including the end, by setting it in the past, whereas the audience experiences the past tense as a present uncertainty while the story unfolds.[27] The device may be laid bare, in a Formalist sense, by having the first-person narrator discovered in the act of narration at the end. In *Double Indemnity*, Neff discovers that Keyes (Edward G. Robinson), the man for whom he has been recording his confession, has actually been present to hear the last part of it. At the end of *The Postman Always Rings Twice* (1946, and, like *Double Indemnity*, based on a novel by James M. Cain), the narration is similarly brought into the present as the audience discovers that Frank Chambers (John Garfield) has been telling the story not to us, but to a priest in the condemned cell just before his execution. *Sunset Boulevard* (1950) goes one step beyond this, since its narrator, scriptwriter Joe Gillis (William Holden), is already dead at the start of the movie, which tells the story of the events leading up to his murder.

In his conversations with François Truffaut, Alfred Hitchcock suggested another example where the order in which information is revealed to the audience conditions their response to the scene:

> We are now having a very innocent little chat. Let us suppose that there is a bomb underneath this table between us. Nothing happens, and then all of a sudden, "Boom!" There is an explosion. The public is *surprised*, but prior to this surprise, it has seen an absolutely ordinary scene, of no special consequence. Now, let us take a *suspense* situation. The bomb is underneath the table and the public *knows* it, probably because they have seen the anarchist place it there. The public is *aware* that the bomb is going to explode at one o'clock and there is a clock in the decor. The public can see that it is a quarter to one. In these conditions the same innocuous conversation becomes fascinating because the public is participating in the scene. The audience is longing to warn the characters on the screen: "You shouldn't be talking about such trivial matters. There is a bomb beneath you and it's about to explode!"[28]

Hitchcock's hypothetical example demonstrates how suspense is generated by the mise-en-temps of a deadline. Even if the bomb is not visible, the memory of its earlier arrival governs the audience's response to the present scene. In Hollywood, bombs are not planted in order to be forgotten. The linear causality of Hollywood plotting ensures that, once a bomb is planted, a movie will progress inexorably toward either its discovery or its explosion. In the continuous present that we experience outside the cinema, the future is unknown. But in the continuous present of movie time, audiences recognize the conventions of causality and coincidence, which make it possible, in examples like Hitchcock's, for them to be simultaneously innocent of and aware of the movie's narrative future.

Cinematic tenses, therefore, resemble our extra-cinematic experience of temporal continuity, but also allow us to have multiple temporal perspectives on the events we witness, by taking time "out" from the narrative. When Barbara Stanwyck comes downstairs in *Double Indemnity*, for instance, the movie encourages the audience to pause in their decoding of the narrative to take pleasure in the spectacle of Stanwyck's legs. That the formal "time-out" qualities of a musical number, car chase, or saloon brawl can be encapsulated in this momentary diversion – no more than a double-take, barely calling attention to itself – is an important reminder that Hollywood's ability to interrupt itself is not restricted to exceptional situations, but is an absolutely routine part of its provision of spectacular pleasure. In this example, the splitting of audience attention between narrative and spectacle occurs as a division between soundtrack and image. More generally, we can now describe "time out" within a movie as a cinematic tense operating outside the normal narrative continuum of past–present–future, just as entertainment cinema itself occupies "time out" in its audiences' lives from their extra-cinema experience of the constant, relentless passage of time.

were explicitly stated by one of its writers, Wolfgang Reinhardt, in a memo on one of the early script treatments. A good writer "with a sense of political correlations" could, he suggested,

> point up in a dramatic and *entertaining* fashion the analogy between conditions prevalent then and happenings of today. The dialog, as far as it is political and ideological, must consist of familiar phrases from today's newspapers; every child must be able to realize that Napoleon, in his Mexican intervention, is none other than Mussolini plus Hitler in their Spanish adventure.[57]

The script went through an extensive evolution that blunted its political sentiment in compromises with its generic status as historical romance and star vehicle. But its producer Henry Blanke maintained that the movie's representation of Juárez as a "Mexican Lincoln" explained "the ideology of a Democracy" to its audiences, and supported United States foreign policy doctrine in uniting the American continents against European totalitarianism. *Juárez*'s publicity campaign encouraged schools to stage debates about the meaning of democracy, and public-speaking contests about the parallels between the events in the movie and the aggressive foreign policies of the totalitarian states. The study guide to *Juárez* suggested that the movie reflected "a series of present day events," and that "the theme of the picture, *that democracy can make no condescensions* [sic] *to the most benevolent authoritarianism*, is significant to the present day world."[58] Within the movie itself, the contemporary relevance of its version of history is most overtly expressed in the speech Juárez makes to a group of European ambassadors when he refuses their pleas for him not to execute Maximilian:

> Your Excellencies make use of a jargon which was designed to conceal the principle that motivates your European civilization: a civilization which permits the oppression of the weak by the strong; wherein each great power in turn inflicts its will upon some weaker union. . . . By what right, senores, do the great powers of Europe invade the lands of simple people . . . kill all who do not make them welcome . . . destroy their fields . . . and take the fruit of their toil from those who survive . . . ? Is it a crime against God, then, that the skin of some men is of a different color from others . . . that they do not wear shoes upon their feet . . . that they know nothing of factories and commerce . . . that there are neither bankers nor speculators in their land . . . ?[59]

In Hollywood as elsewhere, however, the lessons of history are always subject to revision in accordance with the needs of the present. *Juárez* was re-released in the very different political climate of 1954, when the formerly European villains had become Cold War allies. So the speech, and its motivation of the plot, were omitted, together with all other references to European imperialism. *Juárez*'s revision of history, and its own subsequent revision, makes perhaps the overriding point about Hollywood and historical accuracy, the same point made by *Forrest Gump*'s 1994 version of the 1960s: whether at the level of costume or of ideology, it is most often the inaccuracies or reworkings of history in Hollywood movies that make the movies themselves such informative historical documents.

Summary

- Our perception of time and of the way we normally occupy it fluctuates constantly; movies, by contrast, occupy time with mechanical consistency: any specific movie will take the same amount of time to screen, no matter where or when it is shown. Movies manipulate our *experience* of time, but audiences are skilled in recognizing the conventions by which these temporal shifts are signaled.

- The fiction feature movie emerged as the dominant form of cinema because it was the most effective means of packaging the ingredients audiences required from cinema as a form of mass entertainment.

- Stories must be carefully plotted to fit into the block of time available for each screening. Screenwriting manuals suggest that Hollywood stories should have "acts" and "turning points" strictly structured according to time elapsed, and the rigidity of these structures suggests the formulaic natures of Hollywood narration. Nevertheless, Hollywood's commercial aesthetic also requires that it conceal its structure of acts and plot points behind novel plot events, and there is always room for the pleasures of spectacle and performance.

- Hollywood movies structure time to meet the needs of their audiences, in terms of both the duration of the entire movie as "time out" from the audience's routine, and instances of "time out" within movies – the suspension of narrative for autonomous spectacle such as musical numbers.

- "Film time" refers to the running time of the movie – a matter of fixed duration; "movie time" refers to the time represented within the fiction, and is much more flexible.

- Movie time imposes fictional pressures on characters' actions, so that the audience can overlook the external pressures of film time. In the ideal Hollywood movie, the length of the film should perfectly match the length of time it takes for the story to unfold. The audience's knowledge that a movie's story will resolve itself just when it is time to go home allows for play – deadlines, digressions, or sub-plots, for example – in the arrangement of the audience's temporal experience. Movies are always racing against time, and coincidences are an essential aspect of Hollywood's temporal economy.

- Hollywood relies on a series of temporal conventions – called here mise-en-temps – to construct coherent movie time. Like those of mise-en-scène, these conventions are both obvious and virtually invisible. Classical Hollywood mise-en-temps is another form of Hollywood's textual economy: it seeks to avoid "dead time" – time in which audience distraction might occur; concentrates our attention on significant action; and preserves continuity within a scene assembled out of material shot weeks or months apart.

- At whatever point in a movie's story an event takes place, the audience always experiences it as being in the here and now of a continuous present. This produces difficulties in showing past or future events. Devices such as shots of calendars or clocks, and character voice-overs, are used to elide these difficulties and establish temporal shifts. Such cinematic substitutes for the tenses of language allow us to have multiple temporal perspectives on events we witness.

- Hollywood uses history – the past – as a production value. Historical events in period movies motivate and justify spectacle. It is, however, the inaccuracies and reworkings of history in Hollywood movies that make the movies themselves such informative historical documents – less about the events they represent than about the period in which those events are reinterpreted on screen.

Further Reading

Screenwriting manuals

Screenwriting manuals are a useful source of information about the narrative and temporal conventions of Hollywood movies, in large part because they present these conventions as a system of rules, such as "don't cause false anticipation by making bit parts more interesting than necessary" (Robert McKee, *Story: Substance, Structure, Style and the Principles of Screenwriting* (London: Methuen, 1998), p. 381), for the aspiring writer to observe. Screenwriting manuals were being published as early as 1915, but the number of such books has increased rapidly with the popularity of university screenwriting courses. Syd Field's *Screenplay: The Foundations of Screenwriting* (New York: Dell, 1979) has been an influential model; McKee's *Story* is a current example.

Michael Tolkin, *The Player* (London: Faber, 1988), is an acerbic account of Hollywood in the 1980s, and like F. Scott Fitzgerald's *The Last Tycoon* (Harmondsworth: Penguin, 1974), it provides an accessible point of entry to the operations of the contemporary production industry. Tolkin describes the reaction of his central character, studio executive Griffin Mill, to screenplays constructed according to formulae such as Field's:

> Some [writers] tried to condense their ideas to twenty-five words, as they'd learned in some screenwriting class taught by someone who'd made a science out of yesterday's formula. They'd talk about the "arc of the story." They'd use little code words and phrases like *paradigm* and *first-act bump*. They were exact. "At minute twenty-three

she finds out . . ." What does she find out? That this movie won't get made.

Four pages later, Mill is discussing "plot points" (pp. 13, 17).

Story, plot, segmentation

The distinction between plot and story duration is discussed by David Bordwell in chapter 6 of *Narration in the Fiction Film* (London: Methuen, 1985). Bordwell's terminology differs somewhat from that used in this book: as well as employing the Formalist terms of *fabula* and *syuzhet* for story and plot (discussed in the next chapter), he also identifies what I have called film time as "screen duration" or "projection time." The differences in terminology are, however, less important than the concurrence of ideas, although Bordwell might not agree with the suggestion made here that the distinction between film time and movie time is of a different categorical order to that between plot and story duration.

Screenwriting manuals offer different definitions of "scene" and "sequence," although they generally agree that "a change of scene is marked by a change of place or a lapse of time." Critics and theorists of cinema since Pudovkin and Eisenstein have also discussed the units into which a movie can be segmented, a question which touches on the idea of identifying the fundamental units of cinematic narrative. One of the most elaborate attempts was the "*grande syntagmatique*" of French theorist Christian Metz, in *Film Language: A Semiotics of the Cinema*, trans. Michael Taylor (New York: Oxford

University Press, 1974), where he identified eight main types of narrative segment. Metz's categorization, however, needed so many qualifications in its application that as an instrument of analysis it proved both unwieldy and restrictive. The more empirical categories deployed by Field, Vale, and other functional analysts of Hollywood structures turn out to be as useful as more elaborate structuralist models. Kristin Thompson, *Storytelling in the New Hollywood: Understanding the Classical Narrative Technique* (Cambridge, MA: Harvard University Press, 1999), provides detailed analyses of the plot structure of several recent Hollywood movies.

Continuity

A number of books and websites revel in identifying continuity errors in movies. The Internet Movie Database (www.imdb.com), for instance, identifies in its "Goofs" section continuity errors as well as anachronisms, "plot holes," "revealing mistakes" showing how action sequences are staged, and occasions on which crew or equipment are visible. Such attention to detail in spotting lapses in the fabric of the fiction's illusion of reality can, perhaps, be viewed as another form of spectatorial pleasure available to the connoisseur viewer.

Hollywood and history

A number of books enthusiastically take Hollywood to task for its historical inaccuracies, with varying degrees of seriousness. Two examples are Mark C. Carnes, ed., *Past Imperfect: History According to the Movies* (London: Cassell, 1996), and Robert Brent Toplin, *History by Hollywood: The Use and Abuse of the American Past* (Urbana: University of Illinois Press, 1996). George F. Custen, *Bio/Pics: How Hollywood Constructed Public Fiction* (New Brunswick, NJ: Rutgers University Press, 1992), provides an excellent analysis of why Hollywood's history took the forms it did. Robert A. Rosenstone, *Visions of the Past: The Challenge of Film to Our Idea of History* (Cambridge, MA: Harvard University Press, 1995), considers some of the implications of historical cinema, using examples from Hollywood and elsewhere. Brian Taves surveys Hollywood's historical product in *The Romance of Adventure: The Genre of Historical Adventure Movies* (Jackson: University Press of Mississippi, 1993).

The disputes over *Forrest Gump*'s manipulation and interpretation of history provide the material for a case study of Hollywood's use of history; it is well examined in Jennifer Hyland Wang, "'A Struggle of Contending Stories': Race, Gender and Political Memory in *Forrest Gump*," *Cinema Journal* 39:3 (Spring 2000), pp. 92–115, and in Robert Burgoyne's *Film Nation: Hollywood Looks at US History* (Minneapolis: University of Minnesota Press, 1997), which also contains essays on two historical movies directed by Oliver Stone, *Born on the Fourth of July* (1989) and *JFK* (1991). *Thirteen Days* (2000) offers another recent instance of Hollywood's treatment of historical subject matter.

CHAPTER FIFTEEN
Narrative 1

Narrative is a perceptual activity that organizes data into a special pattern which represents and explains experience. More specifically, narrative is a way of organizing spatial and temporal data into a cause–effect chain of events with a beginning, middle, and end that embodies a judgement about the nature of the events as well as demonstrates how it is possible to know, and hence to narrate, the events.

Edward Branigan[1]

Narrative and Other Pleasures

Let's start from the beginning again, Jeff. Tell me everything you saw, and what you think it means.

Lisa (Grace Kelly) in *Rear Window* (1954)

Most critical writing on Hollywood assumes that the primary purpose of a movie is to tell a story. When we remember a movie, we normally recall it as a sequence of events rather than a sequence of camera angles. We do, in other words, what Lisa asks Jeff (James Stewart) to do in *Rear Window*: tell ourselves what we saw, and interpret it. The result is a story. Many everyday accounts of movies such as reviews treat a movie and its story as if they were interchangeable: we expect a movie adaptation to tell the same story as its source novel, for instance. More elaborate critical formulations also maintain that narrative has the dominant role in

Rear Window (1954): Lisa (Grace Kelly) asks Jeff (James Stewart) to tell her everything he saw, and what he thinks it means.
Produced by Alfred Hitchcock; distributed by Paramount Pictures.

Hollywood. Jane Gaines has argued that a model of Classical Hollywood narrative cinema – "the protagonist-driven story film, valued for the way it achieves closure by neatly resolving all of the enigmas it raises as well as for the way it creates this perfect symmetry by means of ingenious aesthetic economies" – has dominated film studies since the 1970s.[2] David Bordwell suggests that in Hollywood cinema, "a specific sort of narrative causality operates as the **dominant**, making temporal and spatial systems vehicles for it."[3] The common sense of everyday experience and the common wisdom of critical consensus would, then, expect to begin a discussion of Hollywood with an examination of its story-telling. Why have I left its consideration until this late stage?

Put simply, my argument is that in Hollywood, narrative functions as part of the provision of pleasure in cinema entertainment, not as the point of it. Story-telling helps ensure that the movie can be consumed as a coherent event, but it holds no privileged place among the pleasures a movie offers. The story is the part of the movie that holds its component parts together, sequences them, and provides an explanation or justification for that sequencing. At the most familiar level, we may enjoy the chase scenes in an action movie, the songs in a musical, or the performance of a favorite star while remaining disengaged from the overly familiar or repetitive plotline. It is every bit as hard to imagine a movie without spectacle or performance, without special effects or a star, as it is to imagine a movie without a story. This has important implications for a critical practice that understands the moviegoer not as the passive subject of the movie-as-text, but as actively constructing his or her own satisfaction by choosing to concentrate on some aspects of a movie and avoiding others.

Many theorists of narrative would agree with Edward Branigan that the construction of narrative is one of the strategies we use to make the world intelligible to us. As "a fundamental way of organizing data," narrative becomes a necessary feature of our consumption of movies as well as being basic to our consciousness of everyday events.[4] For some theorists, this position leads to the idea that as a principle of organization, narrative transcends the formal differences between the media through which it is expressed. **Narratology**, as the general study of narrative is called, assumes that narrative can be studied as a comparative phenomenon across different media forms. Literary critic Seymour Chatman, for instance, defines narrative discourse as "a connected sequence of narrative statements, where 'statement' is quite independent of the particular expressive medium." He holds that the "transposability" of a story "is the strongest reason for arguing that narratives are indeed structures independent of any medium."[5]

Like critical arguments about realism, however, most arguments about narrative in cinema are derived from literary models, and there are sometimes problems in translation. The word "narrative" itself is both a noun and an adjective. It is often ambiguous in its meaning, describing both the activity of story-telling and the story that is told. It is commonly used interchangeably to refer to a process (a "narrative strategy") and to the object that results from that process (a "melodramatic narrative"), and in both everyday and critical usage its meaning floats between these various senses. This sense of play in the meaning of narrative makes it at the same time a useful and a difficult term. In order to understand the role of narrative in Hollywood, we must (not for the first time in this book) establish some clear-cut distinctions between terms that are often seen as being interchangeable: plot, story, narration, narrative. First, however, we must consider how a movie narrates.

Show and Tell

A character who acts, speaks, observes or has thoughts is not strictly telling or presenting anything to us for the reason that spectators, or readers, are not characters in the world. Characters may "tell" the story to us in a broad sense, but only through "living in" their world and speaking to other characters.

Edward Branigan[6]

In a movie you don't tell people things, you show people things.
William Goldman[7]

What constitutes the story in a visual medium? A minimal definition of a story requires it to have a before and after, to register change over time. Contrary to popular wisdom, every picture does not tell a story. Instead, every picture, or at least every still photograph, *needs* a story to be constructed around it, to place it in a temporal context and provide it with a before and after, a story in which it is a significant moment. This is what John Keats's poem, discussed in the previous chapter, does for the Grecian urn. It could be argued that when a filmstrip is projected so that the sequence of pictures creates the illusion of movement, change over time becomes manifest and the minimal before-and-after definition of a story is met. But most analyses of narratives require something else, something that distinguishes narrative from the mere movement of the breaking waves in the "cinema of attractions" that entertained the movies' earliest audiences. For novelist E. M. Forster, the crucial distinction was between chronology and causality. The statement, "the king died and then the queen died," was not a narrative, but "the king died and then the queen died of grief" was.[8] The expression of causality requires a position of knowledge outside the events described: the speaker of the second sentence must know the relationship between the two events. In stories that are literally told – in words – this position is a temporal one, articulated by the conventional use of the perfect tense or the "objective" third-person narration of historians. History books routinely describe events in ways that could not have been known by contemporary witnesses: for example the statement, "the Thirty Years War began in 1618," could not have been known to be true in 1618.[9] In the previous chapter, I argued that movies exist in the continuous present. So how might such a distinction operate in a movie?

The discussion of *The Son of the Sheik* (1926) in chapter 14 referred to a title that is intercut with close-ups of Valentino apparently lost in thought: "Like all youths, he loved a dancing girl. Like all dancing girls, she tricked him." This sounds like the observation of a figure familiar from the analysis of the novel and history textbooks alike: the omniscient narrator, positioned outside the diegetic world of the movie's events and thus able to comment on, generalize from, and interpret those events. A number of critics have argued that the written narratives of "classic realism" are composed of a hierarchy of different discourses. What each character says is enclosed within inverted commas and framed by the commentary of the omniscient narrator (" 'I am telling the truth,' he said, knowing that his lie would be believed"). This commentary is, according to Colin MacCabe, "privileged as the bearer of *the* truth, and therefore functions as a metalanguage by which to judge the truth or falsity of the other discourses."[10]

Hollywood's silent movies frequently feature the commentary of an omniscient narrator, and the function and formal conventions of a silent movie's intertitles echo those found in a realist novel. Dialog is marked by inverted commas, while the narration uses either the perfect tense (as in *The Son of the Sheik*) or the historical present: in *The Conquering Power* (1921), a title informs us that "Woman has this in common with the angels – all suffering creatures are under her protection" – a remark comparable in its use of tense, as well as its ideological reverberations, with the opening of Jane Austen's novel *Pride and Prejudice*: "It is a truth universally acknowledged, that a single man in possession of a good fortune, must be in want of a wife."[11] These generalized moral commentaries may alert us to the presence of a narrator, whom we may even identify: Sarah Kozloff suggests that in his silent films, D. W. Griffith "habitually took advantage of his titles to judge his characters, make personal asides, or draw parallels between the screen action and current events – in short, to open up a direct line of communication between himself and his audience and to suggest a personal tone of voice."[12] In a silent movie, the narrating intertitles are visibly detached from the diegetic world. Our sight of them interrupts our viewing the action, and in watching a silent movie, a viewer constantly switches between the two discrete activities of viewing the images and reading the intertitles. The titles fix the meaning of the images, in much the same way as captions may fix the meaning of photographic images.[13] In *The Son of the Sheik*, the title tells us what Ahmed is thinking. This is perhaps the one situation in which it is accurate to speak of a viewer "reading" a movie.

With the coming of sound, Hollywood lost the mechanism of generalized moral commentary so readily provided by intertitles. The omniscient narrator ceased to be disembodied, and was instead obliged to speak with an individual voice: the voice of radio announcer Lou Marcelle in the opening narration of *Casablanca* (1942), for instance. *Casablanca* is typical of Hollywood sound movies in restricting overt acts of narration to the beginning of a movie, after which they give way to the movie's screen world. In the opening sequence of *The Pirate* (1948), the first shot we see is of the cover of a book called *The Pirate*. A voice we may recognize as Judy Garland's starts to recite its introduction, while hands turn the pages of brightly colored drawings. Gradually the camera pulls back to reveal Manuela (Garland) among a group of young women in a studio version of the eighteenth-century Caribbean, and they interrupt Manuela's recitation by mocking her romantic notions about piracy. As the movie slips into its dramatization we find ourselves no longer being told about the book *The Pirate*; we are in the screen world of the movie *The Pirate*. Its events have come to life in our present, and while the narration can move around freely within that world, it cannot enter and leave it with the ease that a literary form, like an intertitle, possesses.

The distinction here is one I introduced in the discussion of tense in the previous chapter, between modes of narrative that *tell* their audiences what happened, and modes of narrative that *show* them what happens. The distinction between showing and telling is as old as narrative theory itself. In the *Republic*, Plato distinguishes between "one kind of poetry and fable which entirely consists of imitation: this is tragedy and comedy," and "another kind consisting of the poet's own report."[14] While some forms such as epic poetry might contain both kinds, Plato's distinction between mimesis, in which the poet "makes a speech pretending to be someone else," and diegesis, in which "the poet speaks in his own person," was one between performance and report.[15] In the *Poetics*, Aristotle explains that a poet "may imitate by narration . . . or he may present all his characters as living and moving before us."[16] Some theorists of literary narrative have used this distinction between mimesis and diegesis to define narrative as a strictly verbal activity in which film cannot engage. Quoting a description of landscape from a short story, Slomith Rimmon-Kenan comments: "In a play or a film, all this would be shown directly. In narrative fiction, it has to be said in language." She continues:

The opening movement into the world of *The Pirate* (1948).

Produced by Arthur Freed; distributed by MGM.

on stage there are characters (actors) who act, make gestures and speak, in a way analogous to people's behavior in reality. In narrative, on the other hand, all actions and gestures are rendered in words, and consequently . . . "an imitation of an action" becomes a more problematic concept. . . . no text of narrative fiction can show or imitate the action it conveys, since all such texts are made of language, and language signifies without imitating. All that a narrative can do is create an illusion, an effect, a semblance of *mimesis*, but it does so through *diegesis* (in the Platonic sense).[17]

Rimmon-Kenan is concerned to exclude drama and cinema from her analysis of linguistic narrative, but her use of the terms "narrative fiction" and "narrative" to refer exclusively to verbal forms leaves critics of the performing arts seriously short of terminology. Within Rimmon-Kenan's frame of reference, the crucial distinction is, she argues, "not between telling and showing, but between different degrees and kinds of telling." Equally, there are distinctions to be made within cinema not between showing and telling, but between different kinds of showing. That proposition, however, insists with Rimmon-Kenan that between written and cinematic forms of narration there is a crucial distinction between telling, a verbal activity requiring temporal distance between its object (what is told) and the performance of telling, and showing, a visual and therefore spatial activity requiring the temporal co-presence of the object shown and the performance of showing.

Theories of Narration

The theories of Plato and Aristotle have been repeatedly reinterpreted in the two millennia since their formulation, and both mimesis and diegesis have acquired broader meanings than the specific, Platonic sense. Because most narrative theories regard narrative as a way of organizing data, they frequently elide the Platonic distinction between mimesis and diegesis into something less fundamental. David Bordwell, for instance, employs the terms to distinguish between two bodies of narrative theory:

> *Diegetic* theories conceive of narration as consisting either literally or analogically of verbal activity: a telling. . . . *Mimetic* theories conceive of narration as the presentation of a spectacle: a showing . . . since the difference applies only to "mode" of imitation, either theory may be applied to any medium. You can hold a mimetic theory of the novel if you believe the narrational methods of fiction to resemble those of drama, and you can hold a diegetic theory of painting if you posit visual spectacle to be analogous to linguistic transmission.[18]

For Bordwell, the distinction between showing and telling becomes a way of distinguishing theories about narration, not a fundamental distinction between ways of narrating. In *Telling Stories*, Steven Cohan and Linda Shires initially acknowledge a distinction between narrative and drama, only to circumvent it:

> narrative resembles drama but with one important difference: a play presents an action – Hamlet's duel with Laertes, say – directly, and a narrative does so indirectly, through the words which recount or describe the action. That narrative recounts and drama enacts persuades some critics to propose a strict definition of narrative as a purely verbal medium. Other critics believe that the term "narrative"

applies to the visual medium of storytelling as well. In a film, for instance, the camera recounts – because it records – events no less than a novel does.[19]

Cohan and Shires's account hangs on a metaphor: in saying "the camera recounts," they describe the camera as performing a verbal activity. In Bordwell's terms, they offer a diegetic theory of film narrative, in which showing an action is subsumed within the dominant activity of telling a story. Movies, however, are a "show" business. What they actually do is what the movie *The Pirate* does: an opening act of telling is subsumed within the dominant activity of showing the audience the action. This is not to suggest that a movie's images are any more "natural" or "objective" than words – far from it – but it is to argue that the conventions of cinematic narrative, and the way narrative information is conveyed in a movie, are radically different from those employed in verbal forms. If this seems to labor an obvious point, it is because the inheritance from literary criticism so often leads analysts of movies to make the metaphorical leap into treating a movie "as a sort of linguistic event, as the narrator's speech even when there is none."[20]

The verbal form allows its reader to contemplate the significance of an account's choice of words: what difference it makes, for instance, to describe the heroine's red hair as "russet tresses." A movie's showing is at once more concrete and less exactly interpretive: the choice is a matter not of how something is described but of what is seen. The audience is most likely to be aware of the image's frame as a component of meaning when it is active – when, for instance, it pans away from the clandestine lovers' embrace to the villain who is watching them from behind the shrubbery. In several scenes in *Traffic* (2000), we become aware of the frame as a component of narrative meaning when two of the movie's otherwise unconnected plots overlap as the camera follows Javier (Benico Del Toro) into a Tijuana street or the San Ysidro border post, encounters Helena (Catherine Zeta-Jones) and follows her into the next part of her story. Framing is, however, always selective, even when it is simply showing a fixed space, as in Donald O'Connor's "Make 'Em Laugh" routine (discussed in chapter 12), for example. Because framing is always selective, it is always an active component of meaning. A movie's choice of camera angle, lens, lighting, shot scale, and editing pattern is analogous to a novel's choice of words in that these components of framing determine the way that the viewer is guided through the movie. But they are only analogous to word choice, not equivalent to it. The slippage occurs because we conventionally understand narrative to require language: "tell me what you saw," demands Lisa in *Rear Window*. The construction of a story seems inherently to involve a translation into the verbal, and the act of translation is so commonplace that we seldom notice it.

In the last chapter I discussed the temporal complexities of the opening of *Double Indemnity* (1944), which, like *The Pirate*, begins with an onscreen narrator and then dissolves into showing the events he began to describe. Although we return to Walter Neff's office to witness his continued narration several times in the course of the movie, our experience of being shown the events is evidently very different from having them recounted to us by Neff, as they are in the novel. Neff is a character in the scenes we witness, and except when we hear

459

his voice-over narration, we have no more privileged insight into his motivation than we do that of any of the other characters. Neff only tells us those parts of the story that he literally recites. Perhaps most decisively, we must be shown Neff telling us: we see him enter his office at night, settle in a chair, put a wax cylinder in the dictaphone, light a cigarette, and begin. Movies *can* tell us things, and most movies do, in titles like "Old Fort Sumner, New Mexico, 1881," in *Pat Garrett and Billy the Kid* (1973), or "Most of what follows is true," in *Butch Cassidy and the Sundance Kid* (1969). But overwhelmingly, sound movies have abandoned the alternation between showing and telling provided by intertitles, and choose to show their audiences the actions and events that make up their narratives.

Diegetic theories of narrative have found the movies' practice of showing events to be particularly troublesome, and have frequently tried to escape the difficulties this creates by making a metaphorical equation between "the camera" and a literary narrator. In one formulation of this metaphor, Colin MacCabe asserts that like the "metalanguage" of classic realist fiction, the camera "shows us what happens – it tells the truth against which we can measure the discourses [of the various characters]."[21] As an instance of his argument, MacCabe describes the final scene of *Klute* (1971), in which the image shows John Klute (Donald Sutherland) and Bree Daniels (Jane Fonda) packing to leave New York together, while on the soundtrack we hear Bree telling her psychiatrist that she doubts that the relationship will last. Although sound and image present discordant evidence, in MacCabe's interpretation, "the camera . . . tells the truth." *Klute*'s ending is "happy," not ambiguous, because "the reality of the image" "tells" him that what Bree "really wants to do is to settle down in the mid-West with John Klute."[22]

It is possible to argue with this interpretation on a number of levels,[23] but MacCabe's assertion is interesting because it involves a deliberate limitation of possible meanings which, according to Dudley Andrew, is an important function of cinematic narrative. In *Concepts in Film Theory* Andrew argues that narrative is "above all . . . a logic for delimiting meaning." In the cinema as much as in everyday life, our ability to construct, comprehend, and interpret stories is crucial to the way we organize the excess of information with which we are surrounded. Andrew regards cinema as a medium in which there is an excess of signification, producing too many meanings, and suggests that viewers construct narratives in order to transform this excess into a more limited but more coherent body of meanings.[24] This is what MacCabe's interpretation does. Like any other interpretation, it actually depends on a number of choices made by the viewer about which evidence to privilege in constructing the story. Each choice, as Andrew suggests, fixes meaning in much the same way as the intertitle in *The Son of the Sheik* fixes the meaning of Ahmed's expression.

If it is not true that "every picture tells a story," it is rather more true that "the camera never lies," because "seeing is believing." The audience trusts the images it sees, because the camera cannot show something that is not, in some sense, there. A movie's images cannot be unreliable in the ways that a verbal narrator

Audiences actively constructing meaning

can be. Bree and Klute do leave her apartment together. We have very little choice but to accept what we are shown, since we cannot choose to believe half of an image and not the other half. Like *Forrest Gump* (1994, discussed in the previous chapter), *Zelig* (1983) requires its viewers to overcome their knowledge that Woody Allen, playing "the human chameleon" Leonard Zelig, only appears in documentary footage with Adolf Hitler and Franklin Roosevelt through special effects. In a documentary about Hitler, these images would be fraudulent. But in a fictional movie about Leonard Zelig, if we do not accept them, we give ourselves no opportunity to enjoy the movie's parody of documentary style.

While the words we read or hear in a movie may be subsequently established as untruthful, the images we see may be partial but are almost never false. Sarah Kozloff cites the case of *Evil Under the Sun* (1982), a murder mystery in which each of the suspects recounts his or her alibi in a voice-over flashback. In their speeches, the two murderers lie, but when Hercule Poirot (Peter Ustinov) recounts what really happened, in another voice-over flashback at the climax, we see the same shots as were shown in the murderers' flashbacks, but now re-edited to include additional material. "The shots that the audience saw originally were *not* false, they were just partial and anchored by verbal lies."[25] Only once has a movie shown its audience a sequence in flashback that the plot later establishes did not happen. Perhaps not surprisingly, this one instance was in a movie directed by Alfred Hitchcock: *Stage Fright* (1950), in which Jonathan Cooper (Richard Todd) recounts a voice-over flashback in which "the scenic presentation colludes with the narrator's false account of events," convincing both the heroine and the audience of his innocence.[26] The "lying flashback" is not revealed as such until the end of the movie, and the device was widely condemned by critics outraged at being deceived and accusing Hitchcock of lying to them.[27]

The hostility to this practice gives some indication of the force of a conventional assumption about Hollywood's framing. A writer in *American Cinematographer* argued in 1935 that the camera's "omniscient eye . . . stimulates, through correct choice of subject matter and set-up, the sense within the percipient of 'being at the most vital part of the experience – at the most advantageous point of perception' throughout the movie."[28] David Bordwell reformulates the idea of the camera as an ideal, invisible observer as "the tendency of the classical film to render narrational omniscience as spatial *omnipresence*."[29] This formulation captures both the possibilities and the limitations of Hollywood's powers of narrative. Inside the screen world of *The Pirate* or any other movie, the narration can change its viewpoint at will, cutting freely between different camera positions within a scene and between scenes in different locations. But it has no spatial equivalent to the temporal distance of a literary narrator from the events he or she narrates. The closest a movie comes to that omniscience is in its musical accompaniment, the element in a movie most conspicuously located outside the diegetic world. Composer George Antheil neatly summarizes the narrative role of music: "The characters in a film drama never know what is going to happen to them, but the music always knows."[30]

Plot, Story, Narration

Just as I have suggested that "film" and "movie" can be seen as distinct terms, it is helpful to use the terms "plot," "story," and "narration" to refer to the different aspects of the process I am describing. In making a distinction between plot and story, I am following the practice adapted by Bordwell and Thompson from Russian Formalist criticism. The **plot** is the order in which events are represented in the movie, for which the Formalists used the word **syuzhet**: "the structured set of all causal events as we see and hear them presented."[31] The **story**, on the other hand, is the reconstruction of the events in their chronological order, through which we can establish the chain of causality which links them, designated the **fabula** by the Formalists. The Formalists' concern with the role of the author in literary production led them to argue that the author started with the fabula/story and out of it constructed the syuzhet/plot. Bordwell and Thompson's "neoformalist" film criticism, however, regards the story as being retrospectively constructed by the viewer as a means of explaining the causal relations between plot events. The viewer's position is analogous to that of the detective, who pieces together the original sequence of events from clues picked up in a different order, and rearranges them into a coherent sequence that links them and explains their meaning. Like the detective, whose account is often verified by the protagonists at the end of the investigation, a viewer may have to account for his or her understanding of the story when, for instance, discussing the movie on leaving the theater. Since the viewer constructs the story, an even more apt metaphor for the activity of the audience than the idea of detection is the work of an investigative reporter.

The distinction between plot and story also helps to define the term **narration**. Edward Branigan suggests that "narration is the overall regulation and distribution of knowledge which determines *how* and when the spectator acquires knowledge, that is, how the spectator is able to know what he or she comes to know in a narrative." Where plot and story can both be understood as objects – sequences of events – narration is a process: the process by which a plot is arranged to permit the telling of a story. One part of this process is undertaken by the movie's producers, when they arrange the sequence of events and actions within the plot, distribute cues encouraging viewers to form hypotheses about the connection between events, and position devices that either confirm those hypotheses or introduce ambiguities. The procedures of mise-en-scène and editing become the means by which viewers are guided through the plot. Although the devices of narration are constructed on the sound stage and in the editing room, the process of narration is only completed in the movie theater, when viewers use their knowledge of convention and the plot information provided for them to construct the story in their own minds.

The ambiguous senses of the term **narrative** – which is often used as a synonym for all three of the other terms – only become useful if we understand the term as identifying the play between senses of plot, story, and narration in our experience of viewing a movie. The distinction between narrative and narration is of greater significance to movie criticism than to literary criticism. Because cinematic fictions unfold in the continuous present, they are often taken to be self-narrated. This is perhaps the most potent source of cinema's so-called "reality effect": the idea that a Hollywood movie promotes the illusion that its viewers are watching an unmediated reality. It is hard to know how literally critics expect us to take their statements about cinema's ability "to convince viewers that it is one and the same with the physical world." Taken at their face value, such comments propose an idea of the viewer as extraordinarily naïve, apparently capable of forgetting his or her physical circumstances and surrendering his or her identity to the flow of images. Such an "ideal spectator" may be a critical convenience, but it does not have much to do with what real viewers actually do in movie theaters.

On the other hand, Hollywood's conventional systems of spatial and temporal representation encourage audiences to treat what they see *as if it were real*: to see space as three-dimensional, characters as having psychological motivations akin to our own, and so on. That is to say, Hollywood's conventions of representation help the audience to bring their conventional perceptions of the everyday world – from a perception of the hardness of a brick wall to the perception of a motivation for jealousy – to bear on the events they witness on the screen. In the idea that audiences see what they see in the movies as if it were real, the "as if" is crucial. This is a conditional state, conditional on a movie's performance not in imitating reality but in sustaining audience pleasure. Individual viewers or whole audiences can and often do withdraw their voluntary support for a movie's plausibility if an alternative source of pleasure – such as pondering the hydraulics of Becky's (Dana Wynter) strapless gingham dress in *Invasion of the Body Snatchers* (1956), for example – suggests itself.

Narration sustains a movie's plausible performance by arranging plot events according to a principle of cause and effect, with a minimum of redundancy and a maximum of coherence. The operation of causality enjoys a privileged place in most aesthetic accounts of Hollywood cinema. David Bordwell's analysis of the Hollywood style, for example, suggests that:

> psychological causality, presented through defined characters acting to achieve announced goals, gives the classical film its characteristic progression. . . . The conventions of the well-made play – strong opening exposition, battles of wits, thrusts and counter-thrusts, extreme reversals of fortunes, and rapid denouement – all reappear in Hollywood dramaturgy, and all are defined in relation to cause and effect. The film progresses like a staircase: "Each scene should make a definite impression, accomplish one thing, and advance the narrative a step nearer the climax." Action triggers reaction: each step has an effect which in turn becomes a new cause.[34]

In prioritizing the causality of the narrative system over what he sees as the possibly disruptive effects of the temporal and spatial systems, Bordwell's analysis emphasizes those conventions and devices that establish causality, linearity, and clarity. From this perspective, the typical Hollywood movie appears as a coherent, unified, story-telling whole:

> Coincidence and haphazardly linked events are believed to flaw the film's unity and disturb the spectator. Tight causality yields not only consequence but continuity, making the film progress "smoothly, easily, with no jars, no waits, no delays." . . . The ending becomes the culmination of the spectator's absorption, as all the causal gaps get filled. The fundamental plenitude and linearity of Hollywood narrative culminate in metaphors of knitting, linking, and filling.[35]

Screenwriting manuals also usually set out the aesthetic consequences of an adherence to causal logics, in terms that our own viewing experience may readily confirm. In *A Practical Manual of Screenplay Writing*, Lewis Herman, for example, argues that:

> story holes engender vague dissatisfaction in the audience with the story as a whole. A well planned, well plotted, holeless story leaves the audience with the feeling that they have witnessed a completely unified, satisfying tale of events that could have happened to anyone, even themselves.
>
> Everything in any story must be completely understandable to the audience, at least after the denouement. . . . Care must be taken that every hole is plugged; that every loose string is tied together; that every absence is fully explained; that every entrance and exit is fully motivated, and that they are not made for some obviously contrived reason; that every coincidence is sufficiently motivated to make it credible; that there is no conflict between what has gone on before, what is going on currently, and what will happen in the future; that there is complete consistency between present dialogue and past action – that no baffling question marks are left over at the end of the picture to detract from the audience's appreciation of it.[36]

Herman's rhetorical ambition to produce the perfectly closed text is, however, at odds with the norms of audience experience. While it explains some of Hollywood's most persistent traits, such as its emphasis on continuity, it is nonetheless the case that in any Hollywood movie we certainly find coincidences, inconsistencies, gaps, and delays. Moreover, so total a commitment to causal explanation of character-and-event-relations takes little account of the competing logics which also inform the commercial Hollywood movie. Describing the trailer he made for *Casablanca*, Arthur Silver explained, "We sold the adventure. We sold the action, the romance, and the stars," while the plot "was left vague."[37] Silver was describing what we might call the "exploitation values" of the movie: the ingredients central to a movie's promotion, by which it is identified and sold as a commodity. A movie's exploitation values overlap with, but are not necessarily the same as, its production values. They correspond to what Barbara Klinger has called the "consumable identity" of a movie, which draws the audience past the box-office into the cinema.

During a movie's performance this pre-existing identity may distract viewers into selecting some other aspect of the movie than its story to entertain us: mise-en-scène, star biography or behavior, or the conspicuous display of budget and technical wizardry. These digressions are not so much evidence of a malfunction within the aesthetic system as the manifest signs of the movie's existence as a commercial entity, offering its viewers a variety of pleasures. Both during a viewing and afterward, movies provide frameworks for what Klinger calls "momentary guided exits from the text . . . set off by promotional narratives that address how a scene was done, the star's marital history or status as a romantic icon, what other films a director has made." Hollywood, she suggests, is less concerned with producing coherent interpretations of a movie than with promoting "multiple avenues of access" to it, so that it will "resonate as extensively as possible in the social sphere in order to maximize its audience."[38] Collectors' edition videos and DVDs package this material, in increasing quantities, as part of the object they sell.

In contrast with Bordwell, therefore, I would argue that the movie neither exists primarily as coherent narrative, nor is necessarily dominated by narrative. Narrative operates alongside other spatial and temporal articulations, as part of the complex means whereby Hollywood fulfills its industrial obligation to entertain for profit. Formalist criticism also ultimately withdraws from the suggestion that every hole can be plugged and every string tied together, choosing instead to suggest that stories do have excess material that escapes the unifying narrative structure, revealing the hidden psychic or ideological processes at work in the text. According to this account, narrative is the attempt to contain this excess, an attempt that is paradoxically bound to fail. In her analysis of an "ordinary film," *Terror by Night* (1946), Kristin Thompson suggests that while Classical Hollywood narrative lends the movie the *appearance* of single-minded linear progression, very little of the constant stream of information the audience is given actually leads them toward the conclusion of the movie's mystery story: "much of it, in fact, may be deflecting us into digressions."[39] This account, too, leaves open the possibility of incidental pleasures available to the audience outside the inexorable progression of the "completely unified, satisfying tale of events."

Clarity: Transparency and Motivation

I am sure that you will agree that the very worst fault a picture can have is lack of clarity. If an audience doesn't know what is going on, and is worried by its own conclusion, inevitably dramatic values suffer greatly.
David Selznick[40]

Paradoxically, the more exactly we describe the narration, the more fragmented it becomes.
Edward Branigan[41]

Hollywood's commitment to establishing causal relations between the elements of a movie ensures that the audience's experience of its story will usually be one of clarity. A Hollywood movie appears transparent. Its spatial and temporal conventions work to efface themselves through their very familiarity, producing an apparently unimpeded access to the events of the plot and their meaning in the story. Devices such as "invisible" editing draw no attention to their contribution

Clint Eastwood rides into Lago at the start of *High Plains Drifter* (1973).
Produced by Robert Daley; distributed by the Malpaso Company.

to the movie's narration. At the same time, the movie's obligation to the continuous present enhances its sense of presence and immediacy, so that it becomes
almost impossible to "see" the movie as an assembly of rhetorical and descriptive
strategies *producing* an effect of transparency.

In fact, transparency is produced as much by the moviegoer as the moviemaker,
and is as much an effect of watching and interpreting as it is of showing and telling.
In the Hollywood movie, material is placed at our disposal by all manner of
stylistic devices, but the movie assumes our competence in dealing with these
materials through its reliance on spatial, temporal, generic, and performative
conventions. The audience must work within those conventions if it wishes to
give priority to its attention to a movie's story. At any moment in any movie
narrative, several of these conventional fields of information will be operating
together: at the opening of *High Plains Drifter* (1973) we watch Clint Eastwood
playing a character with no name ride into the town of Lago, as we listen to
suspenseful music, knowing that we are watching a Western directed by Clint
Eastwood. Provided that we understand *why* a particular element or device is
present in such a scene, and *how* a particular device is being deployed, it can contribute positively to our pleasure in the movie, as well as to our comprehension
of it.

In making sense out of the assembly of devices active in any given scene or
sequence of scenes, the audience seeks a sense of **motivation**, a logical justification for its inclusion in the narrative. Formalism distinguishes between four kinds
of motivation within the typical Hollywood movie: compositional, realistic, intertextual, and artistic. **Compositional motivation** explains the presence of a device
as part of the causal sequence required for story comprehension: something
happens because it causes something else to happen. **Realistic motivation** justifies the presence because it enhances a movie's surface verisimilitude: an object is
there because it makes the movie look more authentic, something happens because

it helps the audience to accept a sequence of plot events as plausible, or because it provides a level of consistency for character. **Intertextual motivation** appeals directly to the audience's familiarity with convention: an event happens in this movie because events like that usually happen in movies of this kind. **Artistic motivation** explains that a particular feature is present simply for its own sake: something is there for non-narrative reasons, such as providing spectacle or appealing to notions of "showmanship" or authorial style. Usually these kinds of motivation operate collaboratively. In *High Plains Drifter*, compositional motivation explains the character's arrival at the saloon; realistic motivation justifies his costuming; intertextual motivation helps the audience come to terms with the sudden, violent shootout which follows; and artistic motivation helps us to make sense of the self-conscious playing, framing, and editing of the scene in terms of our knowledge of its authorship as "a Clint Eastwood movie."

If we acknowledge the multiple logics of Hollywood production, however, we need to broaden the concept of artistic motivation to cover not only those features of a movie that can be explained in terms of an individual director's "artistic license," but also those that can be explained in terms of legal, moral, technical, political, industrial, and cultural factors. Subdividing the category of artistic motivation produces a more diversified sense of the range of activities open to the audience as they watch even the most typical Hollywood movie.

Formalism suggests that the viewer's search for motivation encourages him or her to use all available information to make *narrative* sense of the events depicted. Even realism in this model tends to be understood as *narrative* realism. Formalism's privileging of compositional motivation in general, and of psychological causality in particular, also suggests that we take the coherence and credibility of behavior within a movie as an indication of its merits as a whole. At stake is the internal coherence of the movie as an object, and formalist accounts usually suggest a strong sense of hierarchy among the pleasures that a movie offers its audience. For example, the final blending of a character's behavior with the persona of the star playing the character could be seen as supporting a Formalist argument that other pleasures are ultimately subordinate to the story. But this takes no account of the agency of the viewer, who might choose to reject the consistency of the character in favor of the pleasurable activities of watching the star's performance, right up to the movie's conclusion. Movies often subordinate character consistency to other objectives, such as an obligation to display their highly paid stars in their most emblematic and desirable positions. For fans of a particular star, the continuity of the star's persona across individual performances matters more than subordinating the star to the dictates of character. Richard Dyer argues that if you like Gary Cooper or Doris Day, "precisely what you value about them is that they are always 'themselves' – no matter how different their roles, they bear witness to the continuousness of their own selves."[42] In recognizing and admiring the star's favorite mannerisms, fans achieve a transparency of access to the star's "real" personality rather than using transparency to support their belief in the narrative.

"Comedian" comedies built around a comic personality make the tension between star and character especially evident, and undermine the dominance of

467

causal motivation. Comedians such as Bob Hope and Woody Allen first constructed their comic personas outside the cinema, in vaudeville or night-clubs, and brought to their movies a style of performance that involved a direct address to their audience. This mode of direct address makes it uncertain whether the character or the performer is speaking: is it Alvy Singer or Woody Allen who is telling us jokes at the beginning and end of *Annie Hall* (1977)? In *The Road to Bali* (1952), does Bob Hope or Harold Gridley tell us, "He's [Bing Crosby – or George Cochrane?] going to sing, folks. Now's the time to go out and get the popcorn"?[43]

A "screwball" comedy such as *Bringing Up Baby* (1938) is built around a comic loss of the coherence usually provided by compositional motivation. Professor David Huxley (Cary Grant) continually tries to escape from the chaotic and implausible succession of events in which he is caught up, and get back to the saner, more tranquil world of an altogether more ordinary narrative. But as Susan Vance (Katherine Hepburn) tells him, he has made too much of a spectacle of himself to be allowed back into any simple, believable story. *Bringing Up Baby* demonstrates very little by way of a credible plot logic. It proceeds at breakneck speed, fabricating not narrative progress but what Stanley Cavell calls "purposiveness without purpose" in which "the attempt at flight is forever transforming itself into a process of pursuit."[44] Its effect depends upon the very precise timing and overlapping of dialog and the subjection of the audience to the pressure generated by this rapid-fire exchange. David's every attempt at the fabrication of a chain of causally related actions is sabotaged by the misunderstandings of other characters, utterly unbelievable coincidences, and an absolute refusal to recognize Cary Grant's industrial status as the movie's major star. The movie's sustained implausibility obliges David to make a spectacle of himself even as he tries to reassert a more orderly storyline. In a restaurant, he finds himself trying to conceal the fact that he has accidentally torn Susan's dress and exposed her underwear by hitting her on the bottom with his top hat. After losing his clothes he is forced to explain to Susan's Aunt Elizabeth (May Robson) that he is wearing Susan's negligee "because I just went gay all of a sudden." Despite his best attempts to preserve the agenda with which the movie has furnished him, David is doomed to succumb to the competing plot logic represented by Susan, even though their romance culminates in the destruction of his brontosaurus.[45]

Hollywood regularly uses compositional motivation to serve the exhibition of its stars: in the Western, the reluctant hero is finally forced by narrative circumstance to accept that he must buckle on his gun and display his physical prowess; in the backstage musical the ingénue star eventually gets the lucky break that lets her sing and dance as the audience always knew she would. Hollywood narration must negotiate the pleasurable interruptions of performance or spectacle, before reasserting itself in order to bring them (and consumption) to an end. The two elements of story-telling and spectacle are held in an essential tension, and the movie exists as a series of minor victories of one logic over the other. Narration is therefore crucial to the organization of the audience's pleasure, but this is far from saying that story-telling in itself is the primary source of that pleasure, or the main instrument by which it is provided.

Summary

- In contrast to the assumption made by most critical writing on Hollywood that the primary purpose of a movie is to tell a story, this book argues that in Hollywood, narrative functions as part of the provision of pleasure in cinema entertainment, not as the point of it. The story is the part of the movie that holds its component parts together, sequences them, and provides an explanation or justification for that sequencing.

- Movies seldom *tell* their audiences a story; instead they *show* the actions and events from which viewers can construct the story. The conventions of cinematic narration are very different from those employed in verbal forms of story-telling.

- Cinematic narration can change its viewpoint at will, to cut freely between different camera positions within a scene and between scenes in different locations. It has, however, no spatial equivalent to the temporal distance of a literary narrator from the events he or she narrates. The closest a movie comes to that omniscience is in its musical accompaniment, the element in a movie most conspicuously located outside the diegetic world.

- The plot is the order in which events are represented in the movie, for which the Formalists used the word "syuzhet." The story, on the other hand, is the reconstruction of the events in their chronological order, through which we can establish the chain of causality which links them, which the Formalists called the "fabula." Narration is the process by which a plot is arranged to permit the telling of a story.

- Because cinematic fictions unfold in the continuous present, they are often taken to be self-narrated. This is perhaps the most potent source of cinema's so-called "reality effect": the idea that a Hollywood movie promotes the illusion that its viewers are watching an unmediated reality.

- The typical Hollywood movie seeks to appear as a transparent, coherent, unified, story-telling whole, linking plot events in a sequence of cause and effect. Devices such as "invisible" editing draw no attention to their contribution to the movie's narration. Nevertheless, movies invariably contain coincidences, inconsistencies, gaps, and delays, which are signs of the competing logics which also inform Hollywood's commercial aesthetic.

- Formalism's contention that other pleasures are ultimately subordinate to those presented by the story takes no account of the agency of the viewer, who may privilege other aspects of the moviegoing experience, such as watching the performance of a particular star. Movies themselves also subordinate narrative and character consistency to other objectives, such as displaying stars, or instances of autonomous spectacle.

- In making sense out of the assembly of devices active in any given scene or sequence of scenes, the audience seeks a sense of motivation, a logical justification for its inclusion in the narrative. Usually the four kinds of motivation identified by Formalist criticism – compositional, realistic, intertextual, and artistic – operate collaboratively.

Further Reading

Narrative analysis

While this chapter takes a broadly Formalist approach to the analysis of narrative, its perspective is not exactly aligned with any theoretical position. David Bordwell, *Narration in the Fiction Film* (London: Methuen, 1985), provides a comprehensive analysis of Classical Hollywood's narrative practice, which complements his account in Bordwell, Janet Staiger, and Kristin Thompson, *The Classical Hollywood Cinema: Film Style and Mode of Production to 1960* (London: Routledge and Kegan Paul, 1985). Edward Branigan, *Narrative Comprehension and Film* (London: Routledge, 1992), is another major work in the area, seeking to develop a general theory of narrative from an examination of cinema, rather than applying literary models of narrative to cinema. Branigan's work builds on that of Seymour Chatman in *Story and Discourse: Narrative Structure in Fiction and Film* (Ithaca, NY: Cornell University Press, 1978) and *Coming to Terms: The Rhetoric of Narrative in Fiction and Film* (Ithaca, NY: Cornell University Press, 1990).

A useful overview of discussions of narrative in cinema can be found in part 3, "Film-narratology," of Robert Stam, Robert Burgoyne, and Sandy Flitterman-Lewis, *New Vocabularies in Film Semiotics: Structuralism, Post-Structuralism and Beyond* (London: Routledge, 1992). Specific aspects of Hollywood narration are examined in Sarah Kozloff, *Invisible Storytellers: Voice-Over Narration in American Fiction Film* (Berkeley, CA: University of California Press, 1988), and Maureen Turim, *Flashbacks in Film: Memory and History* (New York: Routledge, 1989). Roy Armes, *Action and Image: Dramatic Structure in Cinema* (Manchester: Manchester University Press, 1994), provides an analysis of cinematic narrative emphasizing the points of contact between cinematic and stage drama.

Neoformalism

Kristin Thompson provides an explanation of neoformalist film analysis in *Breaking the Glass Armor: Neoformalist Film Analysis* (Princeton, NJ: Princeton University Press, 1988). Rick Altman offers a critique of neoformalism in "Dickens, Griffith, and Film Theory Today," in *Classical Hollywood Narrative: The Paradigm Wars*, ed. Jane Gaines (Durham, NC: Duke University Press, 1992), pp. 9–47. George Wilson provides another in "On Film Narrative and Narrative Meaning," in *Film Theory and Philosophy*, eds Richard Allen and Murray Smith (Oxford: Oxford University Press, 1997), pp. 220–38.

Barbara Klinger, "Digressions at the Cinema: Reception and Mass Culture," *Cinema Journal* 28:4 (Summer 1989), pp. 3–19, raises some significant questions about the centrality of narrative to the activity of viewing and consuming cinema.

CHAPTER SIXTEEN

Narrative 2

Regulating Meaning: The Production Code

spectacle

The previous chapter described how narration organizes the viewer's knowledge of a movie's story to provide a coherent experience, and explored the relationship between narrative and other pleasures on offer in a Hollywood movie. This chapter elaborates on the idea that in addition to providing the opportunity for Hollywood to make a spectacle of itself, narrative also allows a movie to control the range of possible meanings that its sound and image streams might generate. We have already encountered something of this process of control in our discussion of mise-en-scène, which was understood as orchestrating visual meaning to facilitate the audience's comprehension of story-telling. Mise-en-scène can never entirely stabilize narrative meaning, however, and the Hollywood cinema involves many further levels of regulation. Principal among these is the regulation of the erotic, both in the specific sense of the representation of sexuality, and in the more generalized notion that the very act of looking at cinema depends on the **scopophilic** instinct: that is, the eroticized love of looking upon which spectacle plays, and which it satisfies, often through the display of the human body. We can understand Hollywood's mechanisms of regulation as a form of intertextual motivation: consistent modes of treatment arose from strategies developed to deal with the representation of "sensitive" or "dangerous" subjects.

Hollywood's need to regulate the erotic was most obviously articulated in the Motion Picture **Production Code** of 1930. The Code's stipulations explicitly stated the ways in which narrative might be used to contain the sexually or ideologically disruptive power of the image. The three "general principles" of the Production Code were:

> No picture shall be produced which will lower the moral standards of those who see it. Hence the sympathy of the audience should never be thrown to the side of crime, wrongdoing, evil or sin.
>   Correct standards of life shall be presented on the screen, subject only to necessary dramatic contrasts.
>   Law, natural or human, should not be ridiculed, nor shall sympathy be created for its violation.[1]

The Code's authors were sensitive not only to the problem of difficult subject matter, but to the impact of moviegoing in general upon the industry's diverse audiences. As Father Daniel Lord, who helped to draft the Code, put it in 1930, "In general, the mobility, popularity, accessibility, emotional appeal, vividness, straightforward presentation of fact in the film make for more intimate contact with a larger audience and for greater emotional appeal. Hence the larger moral responsibilities of the motion pictures."[2] This argument is characteristic of what might be called a "fear of entertainment," in which cinema's production of pleasure through the projection and fulfillment of desire is thought to be innately threatening to the moral health of both the individual and the community.[3] Screenwriting manuals insist that Hollywood stories be structured around a protagonist's pursuit of his or her object of desire, and that the audience's emotional engagement with the movie be sustained through their bond with the protagonist. In Lord's argument, Hollywood risked stimulating superfluous, excessive desire in the unnecessary cause of mere entertainment, and it was, therefore, all the more important that such desires be rendered harmless through suitable systems of regulation. We can recognize the legacy of this argument that entertainment as a process has inevitable negative consequences, regardless of its content, in contemporary anxieties about the effects of television, or the playing of video and computer games.

Although the Production Code was written under the assumption that spectators were only passive receivers of movies, the movies themselves were constructed to accommodate, rather than predetermine, the variety of their audiences' reactions. The economic logic for that construction came out of what Umberto Eco has called "the heavy industry of dreams in a capitalistic society."[4] As I suggested in chapter 3, fulfilling the commercial aesthetic goal of producing the maximum pleasure for the maximum number for the maximum profit involved producers ceding responsibility for determining the meaning of a movie to its consumers. This in turn involved developing representational conventions that would allow for a range of interpretations and encourage a degree of instability of meaning, so that "sophisticated" viewers might draw conclusions about character and narrative that were not available to more inexperienced or innocent spectators.

Preferring that all of its products be available to all of its potential audience, the industry chose not to adopt a rating system which would have segregated "innocent" and "sophisticated" viewers by age. Instead, it used the mechanism of the Production Code to assert that all its products were free from harmful content or corrupting influence, and to deny the producers' responsibility for any "sophisticated" interpretation that some viewers might choose to "read into" a movie. So long as the story remained comprehensible at the "innocent" level, innocence was protected, because "innocent" viewers were not educated into sophistication by being forced into some half-understood suggestive interpretation. Much of the work of self-regulation in the 1930s and 1940s lay in the maintenance of this system of conventions, which operated, however perversely, as an enabling mechanism at the same time as it was a repressive one. As Production Code Administration director Joseph Breen persistently argued, the Code was not so much a system of censorship as an alternative to one: a system by which socially sensitive subjects could be represented on the screen, with their censurable content coded and codified so as to avoid censorship.

Sexuality was the primary site of private pleasure to be simultaneously concealed and disclosed in public. Those charged with administering the Code worked in cooperation with the studios to devise complex strategies of ambiguity in order to address more than one audience at the same time. As Ruth Vasey has argued, the early sound period in which the Production Code was developed was of central importance to this process.[5] In a letter to Will Hays during the production of *The Smiling Lieutenant* (1931), a Code administrator detailed his successes in making changes to the script:

> The scenes in which Franzi, who wants to put off Niki, says, "First tea – then dinner – and then, maybe – maybe breakfast," and the succeeding action which fades in to show them having breakfast together, indicating that Niki persuaded her to spend the night with him, will be changed as follows: Franzi, after saying "First tea, etc.," will definitely *leave the apartment* and go away, breaking the sequence. The camera will then fade in on a tea set, indicating that they are having tea together at a later time, then on supper dishes, indicating that they are having a supper together, and then to the scene on the balcony where they are having breakfast. This will, of course, delicately indicate that Franzi is Niki's mistress, but the time element removes most of the worry and adds a delicacy of treatment in my opinion.
>
> The scenes in which Franzi is shown gathering her negligee, stockings and a handkerchief from under Niki's pillow, etc., which serve only to pound home the fact that she was his mistress, will be altered to show her gathering up her music, her violin, etc., things which first brought them together. This will remove the personal property, the body connection, of the scene, and be far less offensive. In fact it should leave them rather in doubt of their connection.[6]

On the one hand the Production Code strove to eliminate any moral ambiguity in a movie's narrative progression by imposing a rigidly deterministic plotline that ascribed every character a position on a fixed moral spectrum. But at the same time, precisely the same forces obliged movies to construct strategies of ambiguity around the details of action which they were not permitted to present explicitly. On September 18, 1931, Darryl Zanuck, then head of production at Warner Bros., wrote a memo to his scriptwriters dealing with the script treatment of an illegal operation in *Alias the Doctor*:

> We should stress the point that the operation is not an abortion, but at the same time the audience will guess that it is an abortion but in all dialogue and everything, it must be treated as merely an operation, and at the climax when Carl is found with the girl, he is not arrested for performing an abortion, but is arrested for illegally operating because of the fact that he is not yet a graduated doctor.[7]

Two months later, Colonel Jason Joy, head of the Studio Relations Committee, wrote to him pointing out that the inclusion of an abortion was prohibited by the Production Code and would make the movie "utterly unusable in censorship territories." Zanuck replied that he was "amazed and bewildered" at Joy's suggestion: "We make mention of an operation, but this has nothing whatsoever to do with an abortion." When Joy insisted that "abortion . . . will be the inference which the audience and the censors will draw from the picture," and that "the mere insertion of a medical term for the operation to indicate that it was not an abortion will not be sufficient to escape the fact," Zanuck blustered defensively:

> If it is impossible for us to tell a story of a boy who has a love affair with a girl – gets tired of the girl – avoids her, and then in a drunken argument causes an accident to occur to her, then illegally operates to save her life and instead causes her death, we might just as well quit making motion pictures. . . . The trouble, if I may be permitted to say so in this case, is whoever has been handling this script with you is reading between the lines and reading in conditions which cannot possibly prove to be facts.[8]

The knowing double entendre, whose greatest exponent was Mae West, "the finest woman who ever walked the streets," was a step toward a satisfactory economic solution to the problem of censoring sexuality. In providing pictures that, as the trade paper *Film Daily* put it, "won't embarrass Father when he takes the children to his local picture house," it accommodated both the sophisticated and the "innocent" viewer at the same time. Through the 1930s, Hollywood developed the double entendre to the point reached by Zanuck in this argument, where the responsibility for the sophisticated interpretation could be displaced entirely onto the sophisticated viewer ("whoever has been handling this script with you is reading between the lines and reading in conditions which cannot possibly prove to be facts"). Late 1930s movies achieved a particular "innocence" by presenting a deadpan level of performance that acted as a foil to the secondary "sophisticated" narrative constructed within the imagination of the viewer. In screwball comedies and Fred Astaire and Ginger Rogers musicals, characters remained innocent of the suggestiveness that typically underpinned their social relations. The more the movie world diverged from what audiences knew went on in the real world, the more the movies took on a comic sophistication of their own. They gained a wit, a knowingness that audiences could take pleasure in, because it revealed and rewarded their own sophistication.

Screwball comedies such as *Bringing Up Baby* (1938) require that we disregard their considerable implausibility, and tease us into reading beneath their surfaces through innuendo and symbolization. But because the comic and erotic effects of these movies are so dependent on what each individual viewer recognizes as lying beyond the rapid-fire dialog and the disintegration of plot logic, their meanings become impossible either to determine in any absolute sense, or to regulate. Stanley Cavell describes the position of the viewer who is encouraged to make an interpretation of *Bringing Up Baby* that the movie, at another level, denies:

> While an explicit discussion, anyway an open recognition, of the film's obsessive sexual references is indispensable to saying what I find the film to be about, I am persistently reluctant to make it very explicit. Apart from more or less interesting risks of embarrassment (for example, of seeming too perverse or being too obvious), there are causes for this reluctance having to do with what I understand the point of the sexual gaze to be. It is part of the force of this work that we shall not know how far to press its references.[9]

An audience willing to play a game of double entendre could find hidden, "subversive," or "repressed" meanings in almost any movie by supplying "from its own imagination the specific acts of so-called misconduct which the Production Code has made unmentionable."[10] They might in the process supply more plausible motivations for the behavior of characters in scenes that had been designed, according to Elliott Paul, to "give full play to the vices of the audience, and still have a technical out" as far as the Production Code was concerned.[11] In the case of adaptations from novels, the repressed of the text might often be the original story, the "unsuitable" or "objectionable" elements of which had been removed in the process of adapting it to the screen.[12] Looked at in this way, regulatory motivation raises questions about the extent to which Hollywood movies were and are characteristically "transparent," and suggests that narration in Hollywood movies has had as much to do with promoting indeterminacy as with maintaining clarity.

Clarity and Ambiguity in *Casablanca*

> Whatever a spectator *first* believes may be enough to drive the story forward. Just as essential plot details are usually repeated several times to promote clarity, so a variety of motivations circulating in the text may be useful options in filling out, and making definite, causal sequences. . . . This allows the story to be made "unique" in many different ways to many spectators . . . it would be better to think of narration not as a single process, but as several processes moving on different levels, proposing and abolishing contradictions with varying degrees of explicitness and success.
>
> Edward Branigan[13]

> I've heard a lot of stories in my time. They went along with the sound of a tinny piano playing in the parlor downstairs. "Mister, I met a man once," they'd always begin.
>
> Rick Blaine (Humphrey Bogart) in *Casablanca*

Casablanca (1942) is regularly cited as exemplifying the ways in which the Hollywood movie constructs and explains its storylines. The movie's idiosyncrasies, however, also indicate the flexibility of Hollywood's narrative conventions. *Casablanca* has, it seems, been all things to all critics: while much of the popular criticism of the movie has described it as perfectly blending "a turbulent love story and harrowing intrigue," Umberto Eco has, with equal affection, insisted that it is "a hodgepodge of sensational scenes strung together implausibly," its plot and its characters "psychologically incredible." It endures, he argues, because of its "glorious ricketiness."[14] In part because of its continuing popularity as "America's most beloved movie," in part because of the frequent claims for its typicality – Eco suggests that *Casablanca* "is not *one* movie. It is 'movies'" – *Casablanca* makes a particularly suitable case for the examination of the practice of Hollywood narrative.[15]

Normally, argues Edward Branigan, "the classical narrative does not give the appearance of ambiguity, nor does it encourage multiple interpretation, but rather, like the chameleon, it is adaptable, resilient and accommodating. It will try to be what the spectator believes it to be."[16] Like *Titanic* (1997, discussed in chapter 1), *Casablanca* is at least two movies at once, and in that respect it is quite typical of Hollywood's product, in which the heterosexual romance is counterpointed by an alternative plot. In *Casablanca* a romance and an adventure–war story coexist as separable commodities, and although it is possible to reconcile them into a unified whole, it is not necessary to do so. Different viewers can, as Branigan suggests, construct different stories from the variety of motivations the plot provides, and the accommodating "classical, chameleon narrative . . . will congratulate the spectator for his or her particular selection by intimating that that selection is uniquely correct."[17]

Casablanca begins with a voice-over describing the refugee trail from Europe to America, arriving at Casablanca, which is controlled by the Vichy French government. Then the movie announces its initiating action. Letters of transit allowing their bearers to leave Casablanca unhindered have been stolen from their German couriers. Meanwhile, Gestapo Major Strasser (Conrad Veidt) arrives in Casablanca in pursuit of escaping Resistance leader Victor Laszlo (Paul Henreid). Ugarte (Peter Lorre) arrives at the Café Americain run by expatriate American Rick Blaine (Humphrey Bogart) and persuades him to conceal the letters of transit, which Ugarte intends to sell to Laszlo. Moments later, Ugarte is arrested by the local chief of police, Captain Renault (Claude Rains).

Renault introduces Rick to Strasser, but Blaine refuses to be drawn on his opinions or beliefs. "Your business is politics," he tells Strasser, "mine is running a saloon." Laszlo arrives at the café with Ilsa Lund (Ingrid Bergman). She and the café's piano-player Sam (Dooley Wilson) recognize each other, and despite his alarm at seeing her, he reluctantly agrees to play "As Time Goes By" "for old time's sake." The music brings Rick over for the first of a string of tense encounters with Ilsa, but the revelation of their past is delayed by Strasser's ordering Laszlo to meet him at Renault's office the next day. Later that night, Rick gets drunk while remembering his love affair with Ilsa in Paris, which was interrupted by the German invasion. When Ilsa comes to the café to explain why she did not leave Paris with him, Rick refuses to forgive her, and she leaves.

Next morning, Strasser and Renault tell Laszlo that he will never leave Casablanca. Meanwhile, Rick meets Ilsa in the market, and attempts an apology, but now she refuses him, telling him that she and Laszlo are married. Ferrari (Sydney Greenstreet), the "leader of all illegal activities in Casablanca," tells the Laszlos that even he cannot obtain exit visas for both of them, but suggests that they ask Rick about the letters of transit. That evening, all the protagonists assemble at the café. Rick's discarded lover Yvonne (Madeleine LeBeau) arrives in the company of a German, who fights with a French officer. Rick stops it, telling them to "lay off politics, or get out." His neutrality is weakening, however. He rigs his own roulette table for a young Bulgarian couple to enable them to purchase exit visas from Renault. Laszlo offers to buy the letters of transit, but Rick refuses to sell, telling Laszlo to ask Ilsa for an explanation. When German officers in the café start singing the "Wacht am Rhein," Rick consents to Laszlo leading the band and other customers in a stirring rendition of the Marseillaise. Infuriated by this affront, Strasser orders Renault to close the café.

On their second night in Casablanca, Victor goes to a meeting of the local resistance, while Ilsa visits Rick in an attempt to obtain the letters of transit. Becoming desperate, she threatens him at gunpoint, but breaks down. They are reconciled, and she explains that she abandoned him in Paris because she had just discovered that Laszlo, her husband, was alive and on the run from the Germans. He accepts her explanation and she tells him that she cannot leave him again, and that he will "have to think for both of us, for all of us." Events now accelerate. Laszlo returns from the meeting to the café. Before he is arrested he asks Rick to take Ilsa to America. Promising to frame Victor with the letters of transit, Rick persuades Renault to release him, but then forces Renault to take the Laszlos to the airport at gunpoint. At the airport Rick sends Ilsa away with Laszlo and shoots Strasser. He and Renault plan to leave Casablanca together, to continue the fight against Germany.

As this summary suggests, there is more talk than action in *Casablanca* and the movie repeatedly stresses the immobility of its central characters. Casablanca is a staging post that few can leave, and the movie rarely strays from the confines of Rick's café. Plot and story times are clearly explained, and events for the most part occur in their chronological order. The passage of time is registered by transitions from daytime to night-time sequences and the daily departure of the Lisbon plane. Parallel and sub-plots abound in the movie, however, introducing areas of meaning that are far less integrated into the narrative than the summary suggests. Although the credit sequence in which Bogart, Bergman, and Henreid are given joint billing tells us that the Rick–Ilsa–Laszlo plotline will be the emotional center of the movie, much of *Casablanca*'s early development remains incidental to this familiar "triangle" plot. Rick's appearance is delayed until contextual material has established the milieu, discussed the plight of refugees from occupied Europe, and set up the letters of transit as the trigger to the causal chain of events which motivates the majority of the action. Even when the movie's trio of stars has moved to the center of our attention, *Casablanca* suspends its storyline for autonomous performances such as the Marseillaise scene.

Setting the scene of the story also elaborates the psychology and ideological beliefs of the movie's central character, Rick: reluctant hero, non-combatant, and isolationist, insistently aloof from the dramatic crises around him, but unable to return to America for reasons that are never explained. His reluctance to act (he is first introduced playing chess against himself) initially displaces the responsibility for narrative progress onto a circle of subsidiary characters, all of whom seem intensely goal-oriented and desperate to change the story's initial situation. The movie's delays intensify our desire for Rick's eventual intervention as a fulfillment of his "true" character, which Renault reveals when he points out that Rick had fought for the Loyalist cause during the Spanish Civil War. Rick's cynicism and instinct for self-preservation provide far more resistance to his taking on narrative responsibility than any external obstacles. The delay that occurs while Rick struggles with his conscience creates a correspondingly greater level of satisfaction when he finally decides to act in keeping with Bogart's star image. *Casablanca* needs its hero: only when Rick commits himself to effecting a resolution can the central plot assert its priority and pull the movie toward closure. To put it another way, only when the production values of its credit sequence come into synchronization with the priorities of its storyline can the audience's act of consumption be concluded.

Casablanca is a remarkably "knowing" movie. Not only does it verbally acknowledge its dependence on coincidence ("of all the gin joints in all the towns in all the world, she has to walk into mine"), it also suspends plot chronology to justify that dependence by inserting supplementary information which will make it plausible. Placed at the precise moment when we require information about Rick and Ilsa's earlier relationship, the Paris flashback confirms the hypotheses we constructed from the worried looks between Sam and Ilsa and the interlocked gazes of Ilsa and Rick in the bar. When we return from the flashback in time for Ilsa's appearance, Rick's hostility seems justified on the basis of what has "just" occurred. It takes a further flashback of sorts, although not a visual one, to engineer Rick's conversion to the cause of both the Resistance and the progression of *Casablanca*'s narrative. This time the narration itself grants Ilsa the time to explain why she abandoned him, and as she tells her story the camera shows her to us, supplying the evidence by which we judge her truthfulness. But even with Rick convinced, motivated, and narratively engaged, the plot continues to withhold information from us about his plans. This concealment increases the moral force of his responsible action in asserting fidelity and self-sacrifice in the name of a greater cause at the movie's end: "Ilsa, I'm no good at being noble, but it doesn't take much to see that the problems of three little people don't amount to a hill of beans in this crazy world."

Like the narratives of many Hollywood movies, *Casablanca* is dependent for its coherence on its own system of internal pressures, not on the accuracy of its external references. *Casablanca*'s letters of transit are an archetypal instance of what Alfred Hitchcock called the "MacGuffin" of a movie plot. Hitchcock defined the term as the device, the gimmick, if you will, or the papers the spies are after. . . . the "MacGuffin" is the term we use to cover all that sort of thing: to steal plans or documents, or discover a secret, it doesn't matter what it is. And the logicians are wrong in trying to figure out the truth of a MacGuffin, since it's beside the point. The only thing that really matters is that in the picture the plans, documents, or secrets must seem to be of vital importance to the characters. To me, the narrator, they're of no importance whatever.[18]

The whole of *Casablanca*'s plot hinges on the implausible presumption that the permission to leave Casablanca granted by the letters cannot be rescinded, even if they are in the hands of "an enemy of the Reich." It also relies on the Nazis' observance of the city's neutrality in their pursuit of Victor Laszlo, on no grounds other than those Laszlo himself offers Strasser, that "Any violation of neutrality would reflect on Captain Renault." "Suspension of disbelief" somehow seems too mild a term to describe the audience's required relationship to such fictions, but the Maguffin's implausibility is also part of the movie's guarantee of its status as entertainment: we are in Hollywood's version of wartime Casablanca, not the actual Vichy-run city where "men like Victor Laszlo were being arrested by the police of the administrators the U.S. supported in North Africa."[19]

Although *Casablanca* is more sympathetic to the Free French than US foreign policy actually was at the time of its release, the movie is committed to clarity in the sense that its storyline articulates a propagandist message which seems utterly unambiguous to present-day audiences. Its drama of personal relations is, however, much less clear, and causal connection much harder to establish. Very early on in *Casablanca* we come to understand that the movie will be centrally concerned with the relationship between Rick and Ilsa, without really knowing any details of that relationship. We must formulate hypotheses about, for example, the reactions of Rick and Ilsa to each other and Ilsa's reaction to Renault's enigmatic description of Rick: "He's the kind of man that, well, if I were a woman, and I were not around, I should be in love with Rick." Above all, the sustained close-ups of Bergman's expressionless face declare themselves to be pregnant with significance, without specifying exactly what is being signified: viewers are invited to supply their own interpretations, or else simply to contemplate her luminously photogenic features.

Casablanca's "chameleon narrative" is most evident in an ellipsis at the center of the movie's romance, when the lovers are reconciled in Rick's apartment. As they kiss, the image dissolves to a shot of the airport tower, and then back to the apartment, with Rick standing looking out of the window. He turns to Ilsa, sitting on a sofa, and asks, "And then?" She resumes her story of events in Paris as if there has been no interruption.[20] The audience must guess the length of the ellipsis, and what, if anything, happened in it. Lacking any incontrovertible evidence in the scene itself, each viewer must decide whether their regenerative romance has been consummated or not on the basis of his or her interpretation of convention. Is the tower a phallic symbol, is that a post-coital cigarette Bogart is smoking? Or has Rick's decision to provide the young Bulgarian couple with money to pay for their exit visas so that Annina (Joy Page) will not have to do "a

In most of the close-ups of Ilsa (Ingrid Bergman) in *Casablanca* (1942), her face is expressionless, but her eyes are moist.

Produced by Hal B. Wallis; distributed by Warner Bros.

bad thing" with Renault established his commitment to marital fidelity? The movie provides equally persuasive evidence for either interpretation, and returns self-consciously to the ellipsis in an exchange between Rick and Laszlo in its final scene:

Rick: You said you knew about Ilsa and me?
Victor: Yes.
Rick: You didn't know she was at my place last night when you were . . . she came there for the letters of transit. Isn't that true, Ilsa?
Ilsa: Yes.
Rick: She tried everything to get them and nothing worked. She did her best to convince me that she was still in love with me. That was all over long ago; for your sake she pretended it wasn't and I let her pretend.
Victor: I understand.

What that means is anybody's guess, but like Stanley Cavell's embarrassed concern with the sexual references in *Bringing Up Baby*, the issue at stake in this instance is more substantial than a merely prurient concern with whether these two characters had sex or not.[21] In an important demonstration of Hollywood's contradictory refusal to enforce interpretive closure at the same time as it provides plot

"If you only knew how much I loved you . . . how much I still love you" . . . "And then?" What happens in the ellipsis between these two scenes in *Casablanca* is a matter for each member of the audience to decide.

Produced by Hal B. Wallis, Warner Bros.

resolution, the movie neither confirms nor denies either interpretation. Indeed, it goes beyond this ambiguity to provide supporting evidence for both outcomes, while effectively refusing to take responsibility for the story some viewers may choose to construct. This is a particularly fruitful example of the principle of deniability in action. In the early years of the Production Code's existence, its administrators constantly negotiated with producers over just how explicit movies could be in representing "offensive ideas," and what means could be used to represent them. The convention emerged that such material could remain in a movie only if its meaning was destabilized in its representation.[22] At this later stage of the Code's operation, the ground rules of "delicate indication" had been tacitly established between producers and regulators, replacing the earlier, more overt discussions of the desirability of the double entendre. The changes that Joseph Breen proposed making to *Casablanca*'s script illustrate this mutually cooperative understanding:

viewers to attribute their own activity to some other party, whether they choose to identify that party as actor, auteur, or text. Such stories appeal so strongly and intensify our pleasure in the text because they offer us a sophisticated version of our innocent assumptions about where movies come from.

Classical Hollywood movies have determinate narrative structures. Convention, whether in the form of generic predictability or the Production Code, dictates order, morality, and outcome. In the journey that a knowledgeable audience takes through a Hollywood narrative, they always know where they are going, and they never know the route. Imagining that it is "being made up as they go along" is the intertextually innocent response to this combination of a determinate outcome and an unpredictable progression. The "sophisticated" viewing of a movie, on the other hand, can be an act of fatalistic resistance to the inevitability of its moralistic ending. In the early days of the Production Code, reformers often castigated the industry for having "invented the perfect formula – five reels of transgression followed by one reel of retribution."[26] But as the implementation of the Code developed, it insisted on an ever-more coherent narrative, and audiences "viewing against the grain" found themselves also viewing against what David Bordwell has called the "stair-step" construction of narrative causation, in which each story event has an effect which causes the next event.[27] "Sophisticated" or perverse viewing strategies survived within Hollywood cinema because compositionally coherent story-telling was overlaid with, or even constructed from, plot implausibility, character inconsistency, and melodramatic coincidence. These devices provided audiences – and later, critics – with opportunities to escape from the conventional moral constraints of the movie-as-text and to allow the repressed of the text to return in some parallel imagined version, no less implausible than the one on the screen. But for the "sophisticated" audience, the "escape" from Hollywood convention is only temporary, a momentary optimism that the narrative will end somewhere other than where it always does, with transgression just for once triumphant.

Narrative Pressure

What do we "consume" when we go the cinema? We consume a story, certainly, but not a story that could be recounted by a friend or summarized in prose to the same effect. Our experience of film is tied more to the specific telling of the story than to the abstract result of that telling, the story told. Our pleasure, in short, follows from our engagement in the film as process.

Richard deCordova[28]

I didn't allow any dull moments to develop in my films. I was always afraid that the audience might get ahead of me and say to themselves: "That guy is going to get killed in a minute." Therefore, I had to go faster than them.

Raoul Walsh[29]

The broadly Formalist accounts of Hollywood story-telling that I have considered so far make up the dominant paradigm in which narrative in Hollywood cinema is discussed. The possibilities of an alternative account, more centered on the viewer's position, have been less fully explored, but a starting point is provided by an essay by Thomas Elsaesser entitled "Narrative Cinema and Audience-Oriented Aesthetics."[30] Elsaesser examines the aesthetics of Hollywood not simply as a narrative cinema, but as a particular response to the temporal and sensory regime of the movie theater. The psychological terms of this discussion provide a more complete framework for considering what we have previously suggested about Hollywood cinema's benevolence to its audiences. According to Elsaesser, the primary material of cinema is not celluloid but the viewing situation itself: "in the cinema we are subjected to a particularly intense organization of time, experienced within a formal structure which is closed, but in a sense also circular: we are 'captured' in order to be 'released,' willingly undergoing a fixed term of imprisonment."[31]

This almost physical explanation of Hollywood narrative sees the cinematic experience as potentially anxiety-provoking, as the viewer is rendered uncomfortable by the restrictions imposed by the viewing situation. Anyone who has had to sit through a movie he or she absolutely loathed will recognize the discomfort that can be imposed by the experience. (In an extreme example within a movie, in *A Clockwork Orange*, 1971, Alec (Malcolm McDowell) is forced to watch movies with his eyelids taped open and his head clamped facing the screen as part of an aversion therapy program.)[32] The pressure that the cinema's organization of experience places upon the viewer is an important element in the sensory experience we purchase when we enter the movie theater. The viewer must sit still in a darkened space for a fixed period of time. With no opportunity for the expression of physical motor energies, he or she must rely on the screen to provide an outlet for psychic energy, through a process of transformation.

According to Elsaesser, transformation occurs at a variety of levels in the process of the interaction between the viewer and the events on the screen. Segments of action or charged emotional exchanges on the screen engage the viewer's psychic energy, provoking an emotional response. The viewer transforms that emotional response into a consistent interpretation of the screen events, providing the coherence that the screen events themselves lack, by filling in the gaps between events in a manner akin to the way he or she fills in the gaps between the movie's successive still images. The viewer then transforms events into plot, and plot into story:

> The fact that the spectator is pinned to his seat and has only the screen to look at, causes impulses to arise which demand to be compensated, transferred and managed, and it is on this level that style, ideational content, causality, narrative sequence, plot, themes, point of view, identification, emotional participation enter into the viewing situation: whatever else they are, they are also ways in which the film manipulates, controls and directs the defenses and impulses mobilized by motor-paralysis.[33]

At its most basic level, this provides an explanation of Hollywood's enthusiasm for action, as a vicarious substitute for the movement the viewer is denied. Early cinema presented movement as a spectacle in itself, and the exhilaration of movement remains one of the pleasures of the Hollywood movie. But narrative also offered possibilities that the "cinema of attractions" could not by itself fulfill. As it developed from 1912 to 1917, the feature-length movie transformed the performance and spectacle of early cinema into a variety of goal-oriented activities. In an economic sense, the feature extended the act of purchase; by persuading the spectator to buy longer periods of time, exhibitors could charge higher entrance fees at the box-office. Narrative added another commodity, the story, that the movie could sell. The story also fitted the psychic requirements of the viewing situation. Unlike the cinema of attractions, a story has a clearly marked beginning and end that match the sense of closure and enclosure characterizing the cinematic experience. Narrative, however, is not a necessity for cinema or an aesthetic goal in itself. Narrative is a convention which aids in the industrial standardization of Hollywood entertainment. Narrative is the dominant form of cinema not because the movies acquired an established aesthetic from the realist novel, or for reasons to do with the aims and desires of filmmakers or questions of commercial competitiveness, but because it provided the most effective means of satisfying the inherent psychological needs established by the viewing situation itself.

This argument addresses one of the most frequent critiques of Hollywood: that its stories are psychologically unrealistic, mechanically conventional, "melodramatic," implausible, excessively dependent on coincidence, or otherwise fail to fulfill Lewis Herman's objective of the "holeless story," discussed in the previous chapter. An interviewer once complained to Alfred Hitchcock about the implausibility of one of his plots. Why, he asked, did the characters not simply go to the police? Because, replied Hitchcock, then the movie would be over. In that answer we can see not only the workings of an industrial logic that dictates the duration of a movie, but also the logic of a narrative system that functions less in terms of a psychological realism among the characters than in terms of the construction and release of the pressure exerted on both characters and audience.

The possibility of exerting this pressure allows movies to construct stories in ways quite different to those of literature. Faced with a scriptwriter's complaint that he was making a character behave illogically, *Casablanca*'s director Michael Curtiz allegedly responded, "Don't worry what's logical. I make it so fast no one notices."[34] Action movies like *Die Hard* (1988) or *White Heat* (1950) are bound together not so much by characterization or causal explanation as by the pace at which they move. Driven by the momentum of the image stream, *White Heat*'s audience race to keep up with Cody Jarrett (James Cagney) as he places everyone around him under intense physical and psychological stress. We grow restless during the movie's longueurs when the FBI agents tell each other what is going on. Cody Jarrett is provided with a personality disorder, but only the most psychoanalytically committed of critics could take his Oedipus complex seriously.[35] Rather, *White Heat* is typical of action movies in which the central protagonist is defined dynamically as "the focus of perpetual agitation and motion," reflecting and catalyzing "the pressures and constraints which the psychic matrix mobilizes in the spectator."[36] Elsaesser points out the recurrence of "plots of pursuits, quests, treks and themes centered on the ambition to arrive, make it, get to the top, or avenge, control," which require characters to respond to pressure, struggle against deadlines, or solve a puzzle. Elsaesser's persuasive account of the persistence of these patterns is worth quoting at length:

> The narrative tradition developed by Hollywood is based on strongly profiled, "typical" plots: geometrical in shape (linear, though occasionally circular or tangential), consecutive, generated by an alternating rhythm of conflict, climax, resolution. . . . These dramatic configurations engineered through plot and protagonists are evidently important structural constants in the American cinema . . . precisely because of the high degree of schematization the plots provide a possible way of regulating psychic pressure. . . . This would help to account for the inordinate emphasis of the Hollywood tradition on action, violence, eroticism, the predominance of energy-intensive heroes, the graphs of maximum investment of vitality, phallic models of identity and self-assertion, instinctual drive-patterns, the accentuation of voyeuristic and fantasizing tendencies and projections, as well as the value placed on the spectacular, the exotic, the adventurous. Being quite possibly subliminal ways of charting a course of energy expenditure/management, these plots compensate very directly, and from a psychological point of view very efficiently, motor inhibitions and allow for massive discharges of anxiety feelings through the arousal of less primary but dramatically or intellectually validated tensions and "suspense" which is then managed by the plots and the action.[37]

Elsaesser's account provides a fuller articulation of the notion, nervously anticipated by the authors of the Production Code, that the peculiar physical characteristics of cinema produce effects that are inevitably erotic, scopophilic, and potentially transgressive, and that their careful management is a cultural necessity. In part, this management involves the use of narrative to regulate Hollywood's pleasures by restricting what can be said or shown to what can be delicately, ambiguously, and above all deniably indicated. If entertainment is to function smoothly within the general requirements of the organization of work and leisure under capitalism, it must open the Pandora's box of pleasure, but then reseal it by the end of the movie, confining the expression and satisfaction of desire to the safe space of licensed public fantasy. That is why narrative closure appears to be so heavily stressed in the Hollywood movie. At one level it asserts the determinist morality of the Production Code. At another, it licenses the movies as a site for the expression of desire, by emphasizing their artificiality and the extent to which they are governed by the external forces of the viewing situation, rather than being spontaneously generated by the logic of their own narratives.

Just as we construct a history around the still picture, a movie can only exist as a selected portion of a temporal continuum, and a specific location within potentially infinite offscreen surroundings. In this sense, narrative closure is less secure than it appears. *Casablanca*, for example, concludes with an opening rather than a closing statement: "Louis, I think this is the beginning of a beautiful friendship." The story is "to be continued" even though the plot is over. This is characteristic of Hollywood's ambivalence toward closure: put the camera on the other side of the mesa toward which Henry Fonda rides at the end of *My Darling Clementine* (1946) and you have the opening shot of another Western. Even the complete destruction of *Jurassic Park* (1993) does not prevent the creation of first one sequel, then another. The residual feeling of a narrative process extending beyond the confines of the particular plot events in any movie is an important element in the economic patterns of movie consumption preferred by Hollywood cinema. *Casablanca* typically presents a crisis in the lives of its characters, but it is important for the audience to accept that these characters have existences before and after this crisis in order for us to feel that the story is in any way significant. It is a means by which the cinema can both complete the individual narrative and at the same time renew the audience's enthusiasm for the repeat experience of narration as process. Narrative closure releases the viewer from the movie in full awareness that the story never really ends, and thus arouses, satisfies, and, crucially, reawakens the desire to be entertained.

Summary

- One function of narrative is to limit and regulate the range of meanings that a movie's stream of sound and image may potentially generate. At the same time, Hollywood movies are chameleon-like, accommodating the variety of their audiences' reactions and seeking to reward each viewer's interpretive choices.
- Classical Hollywood attempted to stabilize the meanings, especially the erotic meanings, overtly produced by movies by regulating narrative strategies. The Production Code, which operated as an alternative to governmental censorship, stipulated ways in which narrative could be used to contain the sexually or ideologically disruptive power of the image. But because the Code was designed to find ways to render sensitive material capable of being generally exhibited, it was an enabling mechanism at the same time as it was a repressive one.
- The double entendre, developed in Hollywood movies throughout the 1930s, was one form of satisfactory solution to the problem of censoring sexuality, allowing a "sophisticated" audience to find hidden "subversive" or "repressed" meanings in scenes which were still "innocent" enough not to violate the Production Code. Such forms of regulation suggest that narration in Hollywood movies sought to promote indeterminacy as much as to maintain clarity.
- *Casablanca* exemplifies Hollywood's methods of constructing narratives. It is dependent for its coherence on its own system of internal pressures, rather than on the accuracy of its external references. The narrative of *Casablanca* is structured in such a way that the movie, while providing plot resolution, neither confirms nor denies either of two entirely plausible interpretations.
- Narrative provides the most effective means of satisfying the inherent psychological needs established by the viewing situation itself. The cinema's attachment to structured and often formulaic narratives can partly be explained by the fact that narrative serves to guide the audience, in an organized way, through the time interval occupied by the movie event.

- Classical Hollywood movies have determinate narrative structures: convention dictates order, morality, and outcome. Despite this, "sophisticated" viewing strategies survive within Hollywood because story-telling is interwoven with implausibility, inconsistency, and coincidence. Through these devices audiences and critics can temporarily "escape" from Hollywood's deterministic moral conventions into a parallel imagined version of the movie, no less implausible than the one on the screen.

- Narrative closure allows for the exploration of pleasure and desire within the safe space of licensed public fantasy which the cinema provides. Closure is not, however, necessarily absolute. The sense that characters have lives beyond the closing credits, that the story continues even though the plot is over, is an important element in the economic patterns of movie consumption preferred by Hollywood cinema, as it renews the audience's enthusiasm to re-experience the process of narration.

[handwritten margin note: Reason that goes beyond narrative + character coherence]

Further Reading

Regulation and ambiguity

There are several book-length studies of the Production Code. The best accounts are provided in Ruth Vasey, *The World According to Hollywood, 1918–1939* (Exeter: University of Exeter Press, 1997), and Lea Jacobs, *The Wages of Sin: Censorship and the Fallen Woman Film, 1928–1942* (Madison: University of Wisconsin Press, 1991), and in the essays in *Movie Censorship and American Culture*, ed. Francis G. Couvares (Washington, DC: Smithsonian Institution Press, 1996), and *Controlling Hollywood: Censorship and Regulation in the Studio Era*, ed. Matthew Bernstein (New Brunswick, NJ: Rutgers University Press, 1999). I elaborate my argument about the Production Code's contribution to the ambiguities and indeterminacies of *Casablanca* in Richard Maltby, "'A Brief Romantic Interlude': Dick and Jane Go to Three-and-a-Half Seconds of the Classical Hollywood Cinema," in *Post-Theory: Reconstructing Film Studies*, eds David Bordwell and Noel Carroll (Madison: University of Wisconsin Press, 1996), pp. 434–59.

Strategies of ambiguity continue to flourish. In March 1991 the British Board of Film Classification concluded 18 months of deliberation and gave Nagisa Oshima's *Empire of the Senses* (*Ai No Corrida*) an 18 certificate without asking the distributor (the British Film Institute) to make "a single cut." The scene that caused most difficulty in this decision was a "very, very brief" shot of the central female character touching a boy's penis. "The final solution was an ingenious optical distortion so that, as one BFI spokeswoman put it, 'We know everything happens . . . you see what she's doing but you don't fully see what she's doing'" (Farrah Anwar, "The Empire Strikes Back," *Guardian*, March 28, 1991). In 1999, in order to obtain an R rating for *Eyes Wide Shut*, Warner Bros. superimposed several computer-generated figures to conceal the action in the movie's orgy scene. As Jon Lewis suggests in *Hollywood vs Hardcore: How the Struggle over Censorship Saved the Modern Film Industry* (New York: New York University Press, 2000), these figures "seem only to be standing in for the CARA board, watching the film as we watch it, putting their entire torsos in our way as we try to see what it is they can see that we can't" (p. 297).

Casablanca

Much has been written about *Casablanca* as an archetypal Hollywood movie. One of the most perceptive and entertaining analyses is Umberto Eco, "*Casablanca*: Cult Movies and Intertextual Collage," in his *Travels in Hyperreality* (London: Picador, 1987). For accounts of the movie's ideological project, see Robert B. Ray, *A Certain*

Tendency of the Hollywood Cinema, 1930–1980 (Princeton, NJ: Princeton University Press, 1985), and Richard Maltby, *Harmless Entertainment: Hollywood and the Ideology of Consensus* (Metuchen, NJ: Scarecrow, 1983). For a useful historical contextualization of the movie's ideological project, see Richard Raskin, "*Casablanca* and United States Foreign Policy," *Film History* 4:2 (1990), pp. 153–64.

The fiftieth anniversary of *Casablanca*'s production saw the appearance of several accounts of it. The most comprehensive is Aljean Harmetz, *Round Up the Usual Suspects: The Making of Casablanca – Bogart, Bergman, and World War II* (New York: Hyperion, 1992); see also Frank Miller, *Casablanca: As Time Goes By* (London: Virgin Books, 1993), and Harlan Lebo, *Casablanca: Behind the Scenes* (New York: Simon and Schuster, 1992).

Casablanca has been also the site of a multiplicity of alternative narratives, from the unproduced play on which it was based, *Everybody Goes to Rick's* ("revived" as *Rick's Bar, Casablanca* in London in 1991), to the unmade versions starring Ronald Reagan or George Raft or Ann Sheridan, to two television series in 1955 and 1983, to Woody Allen's *Play It Again, Sam* (1972), which enacts the ritual relationship between cult spectator and movie when film critic Allen Feliz (Woody Allen) renounces his best friend's wife (Diane Keaton) at an airport by reciting Rick's "hill of beans" speech and adding, "That's from *Casablanca*. I've waited my whole life just to say it," to Robert Coover's "You Must Remember This," in *A Night at the Movies or, You Must Remember This* (London: Paladin, 1989), a piece of *Playboy* postmodernism that inserts four sex acts into the elided encounter between Rick and Ilsa.

PART IV
APPROACHES

CHAPTER SEVENTEEN
Criticism

Criticism is neither a science nor a fine art, but it resembles both. Like them, it depends upon cognitive skills; it requires imagination and taste; and it consists of institutionally-sanctioned problem-solving activities. Criticism is, I think, best considered a practical art, somewhat like quilting or furniture-making. Because its primary product is a piece of language, it is also a rhetorical art.

David Bordwell[1]

It is intriguing and useful to listen to the sacred rhetoric of the cinema groups and intellectual critics, but very little of it gets up on the screen in the next picture.

Jerry Lewis[2]

The critical discourses that surround Hollywood play an important role in defining our understanding of it. Criticism is not something detached from the movie industry. Instead, Hollywood requires criticism to help it fix its social and cultural identity. Despite Jerry Lewis's observation, even academic criticism forms part of the sense-making apparatus that allows cinema to be meaningful in society. Pam Cook argues that cinema is "kept alive not just through systems of production, distribution and exhibition, but also through the circulation of debates which provide the cultural context in which it can flourish."[3] The circulation of debate has been an important sub-industry for Hollywood cinema, one in which its cultural status has been established and its significance contested. Some critical approaches to Hollywood, such as the idea of the director as auteur, have permeated the industry's understanding of its own processes, altering the history of movie production itself.

From Reviewing to Criticism

The vast majority of people are in need of guidance in the matter of photoplays. It is no longer a question of giving them what they want. It is a question of so directing their tastes that they will want what is best. And they can come to know what is best only through that organ of universal enlightenment, the public press.

Frances Taylor Patterson, 1920[4]

The species of movie criticism that we encounter most frequently is the review, a short account of a newly released movie in a newspaper or in the television program guide. Reviews outline the plot, identify the stars and perhaps the director, and offer an opinion about whether the movie is worth paying to see. Reduced to its minimal form, it is encapsulated in the one-liner reviews and star ratings of *Halliwell's Film Guide* and its imitators, in which *Desperately Seeking Susan* (1985), for instance, is awarded one star and assessed as a "mildly diverting romantic mystery which could have been both funnier and more thrilling."[5] The review is a form of consumer criticism, often taken by reviewers themselves, and sometimes other critics, to be the function of all criticism. Donald C. Willis, for instance, regards the critic's main concern as being "to determine if and why a film is good or bad or partly good and partly bad."[6] More loquaciously, in a newspaper review of anthologies of the reviews of C. A. Lejeune and Dilys Powell, Michael Church opined that "true criticism is a rare substance, presupposing both knowledge and love, and requiring that head and heart speak with one voice. It has to entertain – otherwise it won't be read – but it must never lose sight of its primary function (Is this book/film/show worth the reader's time and money?)."[7]

The evaluative criticism being so extravagantly praised here is ultimately concerned with value for money, and is commonly delivered in the "entertaining" terms that it often disparages in the movies it assesses. This premise leads it, on the whole, to accept Hollywood on its own terms. Leslie Halliwell again provides a case in point. "Hollywood at its best," he suggests, "was the purveyor of an expensive and elegant craft which at times touched art, though seldom throughout a whole film." Even during its "golden age," however, "the worthwhile movies were the tip of the iceberg: probably eighty per cent of what was produced was ghastly rubbish." Halliwell represents Hollywood as the provider of a service, entertainment, which is in need of no further analysis. To that extent his critical judgments on a movie contribute to the endorsement of the production system, regardless of whether any individual judgment is positive or negative. At points, review discourse is openly hostile to other kinds of criticism. In describing "the Decline and Fall of the Movie," Halliwell blames, among others, "verbose and pompous critics who were determined to turn it into serious art."[8]

Reviewing can be seen as a secondary, supplementary activity supporting the motion picture industry as a whole, a part of the machinery of publicity that the industry propagates. Aspects of journalistic reviewing attach themselves to the publicity operations served by fan, celebrity, and cinephile magazines such as *Premiere*, and websites and television shows combining clips from new releases, celebrity interviews, and "inside news" from Hollywood. These forms of reviewing have evolved from the activities of gossip columnists such as the notorious and nationally syndicated Louella Parsons and Hedda Hopper during the Classical period. In the 1930s and 1940s the press books that studio publicity departments supplied to exhibitors for each movie included complete reviews that could be printed in the local paper. Not surprisingly they were invariably unstinting in their praise, and unquestioning in their promulgation of entertainment as self-evidently valuable. Although often carried on with a more subtle gloss, the enthusiastic festival report or the deferential celebrity interview still present the industry's publicity on the industry's terms. More generally, most journalistic reviewing has made its judgments according to criteria established by the industry, rating movies for their "entertainment value" or on the strength of their central performances.

At the other extreme of sophistication from the advertisement-as-review produced by studio publicity, some reviewers have elevated evaluative criticism to the status of a "practical art." For many years after the original publication in 1937 of an anthology of British and American reviewing, *Garbo and the Night Watchmen*, this kind of writing on the movies constituted the only major body of criticism of Hollywood cinema and the only critical material to be offered the longevity of publication in book form.[9]

Journalism and publicity provided the basis for several other discourses on cinema, including the star biographies that performed a similar function to fan magazines in circulating the persona of the star. Embryonic movie criticism with a more industrial, technical, and commercial emphasis developed from the 1930s around professional trade publications. With the exception of the *Hollywood Reporter*, which for much of its history was as much a gossip sheet as it was a newspaper, the trade papers were aimed primarily at the exhibition sector, and their reporting of industry affairs is a salutary corrective to the emphasis on production in the body of anecdotal accounts that for so long passed as film history. Although *Variety* is the best-known of the "trades," *Motion Picture Herald* has perhaps a greater claim to be regarded as the industry's journal of record, for the completeness of its account of the industry's economic and political affairs, until it ceased publication in 1972. Professional journals such as the *Journal of the Society of Motion Picture Engineers* and *American Cinematographer* circulated much less widely, mainly among members of the craft guilds that sponsored them. As well as information on guild or union matters they also included material on new technologies and new techniques being developed on the lots.[10] These journals played an important role in disseminating standards of practice among cinematographers and other technicians, and also sought to promote the prestige of particular crafts both inside and outside the industry. At a crucial point in its development, the emerging academic subject of film studies resisted the industrial discourses contained in both the trade papers and the professional journals in favor of critical practices drawn from elsewhere in the Academy. In that process, the opportunity for a sustained critical engagement with the industry's professional practice and history was lost, or at least long postponed.

The kind of criticism we have examined so far is seldom informed by much theoretical consideration. The trade papers and professional journals were publications of the moment, concerned with the day-to-day practicalities of their industry. Reviews in *Variety* primarily offered an assessment of a new movie's box-office potential. The ideological assumptions underlying these assessments were seldom explicitly articulated, and when they were, the terms used were little different from those that Will Hays himself might have employed. In 1938 Martin Quigley, publisher of *Motion Picture Herald*, expressed his belief that "the sole, exclusive business of the motion picture theatre of entertainment is entertainment." On these grounds he warned the producers of *The Life of Emile Zola* (1937) against promoting the movie as if it were "a learned and scholarly inquiry into the life and times of Zola." As an evening's entertainment about an idealized character, he suggested, the movie was excellent; but to consider it serious biography or history was absurd.[11]

Reviewing as it is practiced today remains consciously impressionistic, guarding against excesses of seriousness and absurdity, with the reviewer and his or her readership gradually constructing a relationship by which readers come to trust the reviewer's opinion or else know the extent of their divergence from it. Readers, reviewers, and their publishers all invest in the personal basis on which the reviewer forms his or her opinion; the "head and heart speaking with one voice" that Michael Church describes. Undoubtedly, such writings can provide us with valuable insights into movies, and critics such as Pauline Kael use consistent procedures and criteria in making their evaluations. A more general reluctance to employ a consciously adopted, systematic method in asking and answering questions about movies means that the use-value of this criticism may well come down to a matter of whether the critic's value-judgments accord with those of his or her readership, however. If criticism wishes to escape the limitations of unrestrained subjectivity and an obligation to evaluate, it needs to be informed by a consistent and systematic method which asks different questions from those of an impressionistic reviewer, and comes to different conclusions. In the attempt to elaborate such a criticism, many writers on cinema have appealed to a concept of **theory**.

Early Theory and Criticism in America

> The cinematic critic ought to take his mission in life seriously. He ought to learn all there is to be learned about his profession, cultivating a knowledge of all the other arts from which the photoplay borrows.
> Frances Taylor Patterson, 1920[12]

The word "theory" has its origins in a Greek root, *thea*, meaning sight. It shares a common linguistic point of origin with "theater," and a common point of derivation with ideas of both spectacle and speculation. To formulate a theory is thus to articulate a point of view. An adequate history of film theory, giving even minimal space to the points of view of its most important figures, would require at least a full-length book. Although the shelves of university libraries testify to the burgeoning "theory industry" of the 1970s and 1980s, a great deal of significant film theory was written during the cinema's first 60 years. The fact that it had comparatively little influence on either criticism or the practice of film production in America is no reason to ignore it, since much early theory has come to be seen as important both in itself, and as a starting point for our contemporary discussions.

The earliest film theorists, such as the American poet Vachel Lindsay, were primarily concerned with staking out the artistic ground that film might occupy. They consciously sought to elevate movies to the level of Art, which would allow them to be evaluated according to traditional critical principles. Usually they did this by comparing motion pictures with the arts of music or theater, and in most cases their comparisons were metaphorical, lyrical, and lacking in much of the precision normally associated with the term "theory." An exception was perhaps the most important of the early theorists, the psychologist and philosopher Hugo Münsterberg, who undertook the first rigorous inquiry into the nature of film in his book *The Photoplay: A Psychological Study*, first published in 1916. Münsterberg's theorizing was primarily concerned with the audience's reception of narrative cinema, and his account of the correlation between cinematic properties and the viewer's psychological processes bears comparison with Thomas Elsaesser's "audience-oriented aesthetics," discussed in chapter 16. Like his contemporaries, Münsterberg also addressed the question of whether cinema was an independent art, but unlike many of them he did so from within a broadly grounded, philosophically based aesthetics. He argued that cinema's claim to aesthetic validity lay in the fact that it transformed reality into an object of the viewer's imagination; a claim he justified through the argument that the "photoplay" only exists in the mind of the viewer, and is constituted in the act of its consumption. His writing, however, had much less impact than it deserved: the coincidence of his own death in 1917 and the anti-German propaganda of World War I obscured his reputation not only as a film theorist but also as a psychologist.

Similar considerations were also to limit the influence, in America at least, of the first important group of practitioner-theorists of film, the Russian Constructivist filmmakers, of whom the most prominent was Sergei Eisenstein. Eisenstein's importance as a filmmaker, and his stress on editing and montage as cinema's central creative act, have ensured the continued currency of his ideas. Their origins in Soviet revolutionary cinema kept them in only limited circulation, however, particularly in the United States, where Eisenstein's influence was largely restricted to a handful of left-wing critics writing for magazines such as *New Theatre and Film* in the 1930s. Elsewhere in the west, Eisenstein's cinema was for a long time dismissed as propaganda, and his theories, insofar as they were considered at all, were regarded as explanations of a propagandist activity. The extent of Hollywood's lack of attention to Eisenstein is indicated by the specific Hollywood meaning of the word "montage," the central term in Eisenstein's theory. A Hollywood "montage sequence" was a highly stylized inserted sequence, such as that depicting the Wall Street Crash in *The Roaring Twenties* (1939), generally involving fast cutting and a variety of optical effects, conveying a condensed impression of an event or the passage of time. Hollywood credited the principles of its montage not to Eisenstein, but to an emigré Serb, Slavko Vorkapich, whose "Principles Underlying Effective Cinematography" echoed aspects of Eisenstein's writings. During the 1930s Vorkapich was employed by a number of Hollywood studios as a specialist creating what were first known as "Vorkapich shots" and later "montage sequences," which were as close as Hollywood came to a stylistic imitation of Eisenstein.[13]

The German aesthetician Rudolph Arnheim's important work of film theory *Film als Kunst* was first published in 1932, but not translated into English (as *Film as Art*) until 1957. The core of Arnheim's theoretical position was that film art lay in the tension between the medium's necessary representation of reality, and the equally inevitable inadequacies of that representation. Artistic expression took place because of and through the limitations of film's ability to reproduce reality perfectly. While this position was not unique to Arnheim, he used it to draw a particularly conservative set of conclusions, suggesting that cinema had reached the height of its expressive powers in the final years of silent cinema. Arnheim saw the introduction of sound as a regression for film art, because in increasing the extent of film's representation of reality, it decreased the medium's possibilities for artistic expression. It was an argument he later repeated in relation to other technological innovations, such as color and 3-D.

Intellectual engagement with cinema on aesthetic terms declined noticeably from the mid-1930s in the United States, as many intellectuals who had flirted with the cinema as art during the 1920s withdrew their interest from a medium then under strenuous attack as mercenary and mediocre. The conservative revision of cultural assumptions that accompanied the early Depression retarded the development of film criticism considerably, and until the 1960s no American filmmaker was accorded the degree of intellectual respect that Chaplin in particular had received in the 1920s. Curiously, the figure who came closest to that position, especially in the 1930s, was not John Ford or Irving Thalberg or even Orson Welles, but Walt Disney. This was in part because Disney's animated movies lay outside the world of photographic representation altogether, and in part because, in works such as *Fantasia* (1940), Disney displayed a manifest aspiration to something other than naturalist realism.

From the mid-1930s to the mid-1960s, the dominant aesthetic theory of film was broadly realist. Its most articulate advocate, André Bazin, incorporated Hollywood's general aesthetic intentions into the system of his own realist aesthetics (discussed in chapter 8). For example, he understood the adoption of deep-focus in Hollywood as a positive endorsement of realist aesthetic goals. There is little evidence, however, that such theoretically motivated explorations of cinema aesthetics had any significant effect on what actually happened in Hollywood studios.

At the same time, a good deal of academic energy in the United States was devoted to the investigation of a quite different set of concerns about the movies: their effect on society and on the attitudes of individual spectators. From the beginning of cinema this had been an area of immediate, practical concern, which manifested itself most obviously in censorship legislation. With the rapid growth of sociology and psychology departments in American universities from the 1920s, a large number of studies of mass communication began to appear. Early works in this field drew their inspiration from the general opinion that the propaganda produced by both sides in World War I, and particularly that produced by the Allies, had been extremely effective in influencing attitudes on the Home Front. Investigations into the propagandist effect of the mass media continued until well after World War II, influenced by an awareness of first Russian and then Nazi propaganda, and then by the wartime need for the allies themselves to produce effective propaganda.

This sociological approach asked very different questions about the movies from those posed by aesthetic film theory. Sociology offered itself as a scientific inquiry into social organization based quite consciously on investigative models drawn from the natural and physical sciences. Applied to the movies, this new discipline had little to do with ideas of cinema as art, and was hardly interested in asking questions about the forms and structures of the movies themselves. Instead, it was concerned with what institutions such as the cinema could reveal about the habits and the obsessions of the societies in which they existed. Much of this work was highly critical of what it saw as the damaging effect of Hollywood on American society, and particularly on its youth. The first large-scale sociological and psychological examination of the movies' effects, the Payne Fund Studies (1933), were widely interpreted as concluding that those effects were almost entirely pernicious, and that the movies therefore required very close scrutiny. Although they were later derided for the inadequacy of their research methods, the Payne Fund Studies were generally accepted as scientifically valid at the time of their publication, and they had a considerable influence on debates about regulating the movies, and more generally on the drift of sound cinema into comparative intellectual disrepute. The broad methodologies of empirical inquiry they undertook have also continued as the basis for most subsequent research into the effects of cinema and television.

Another aspect of this sociological approach was a body of work studying the sociology of moviegoing and Hollywood itself. Important works in this field were Margaret Thorp's *America at the Movies* (1946), Leo Rosten's *Hollywood: The Movie Colony, the Movie Makers* (1941) (these remain two of the best accounts of Hollywood cinema during the studio period), and Hortense Powdermaker's *Hollywood the Dream Factory* (1950). For historians of American culture, it is unfortunate that these works emphasized the sociology of movie production rather than that of viewers. Our lack of reliable information about movie audiences, particularly during the studio era, remains one of the greatest gaps in our knowledge of the Hollywood cinema, one that current historical research is seeking to fill.

During the 1940s, the sociological tradition of inquiry gradually absorbed influences from the study of psychology, especially in the period immediately after World War II. During the war the American military put substantial resources into psychological investigations of their troops, some of them concerned with the effectiveness of propaganda on individual soldiers. The publication of this research was partially responsible for the growth of a hybrid form of study into American (and other) culture, which was part sociology, part anthropology, and part psychology. Geoffrey Gorer's *The Americans* (1948) and David Riesman's *The Lonely Crowd* (1950) are important examples of what Gorer called "psychocultural studies," and both treated movies as revealing and exemplifying the conscious and unconscious concerns of American society.

At a time when Hollywood was itself preoccupied – especially in film noir – with the psychology and psychoanalysis of its characters, there was an immediate appropriateness to this type of inquiry into the movies' function in society. A number of books examining cinema from this perspective appeared in the late 1940s and early 1950s. Perhaps the most influential dealt not with Hollywood, but with German cinema in the 1920s: Siegfried Kracauer's *From Caligari to Hitler: A Psychological History of the German Film.* Kracauer also wrote about Hollywood, and one of his students, Barbara Deming, produced a work in the same vein: *Running Away From Myself: A Dream Portrait of America Drawn from the Films of the Forties* (written in 1950 although not published as a book until 1969). Another important work in this area was Martha Wolfenstein and Nathan Leites's *Movies: A Psychological Study* (1950, discussed in chapter 3). Like Deming, Wolfenstein and Leites drew out the largely unconscious inferences of Hollywood's plot material. In a far more whimsical and witty way, so did Parker Tyler, for whom Hollywood was "the industrialization of the mechanical work's daylight dream."[14] His two books, *The Hollywood Hallucination* (1944) and *Magic and Myth of the Movies* (1947), delighted in exploring Hollywood's construction of popular mythology, as well as its "displacements" of sex, without the tone of concerned responsibility that the academics brought to the task.

Although this cultural criticism examined movie content and paid little attention to questions of form, its concerns anticipated the ideologically oriented analysis of the 1970s and 1980s. It assumed that the intellectual value in studying movies lay in their significance as a phenomenon of mass culture rather than in any intrinsic aesthetic values they might have. Although after 1950 American audiences could see more foreign (mainly European) movies, which were often recognized as having legitimate artistic pretensions, Hollywood itself remained a primary target for the critiques of "mass culture" that appeared in the 1950s, whether they came from liberal humanists alarmed by what they saw as a decline in cultural values, or the disaffected Marxist social critics of the Frankfurt School, who saw the politically oppositional role of Art being destroyed by its absorption into a capitalist system of production and consumption.

The movies' return to intellectual respectability began in the 1960s, and happened for a number of interrelated reasons. One was that they had been replaced as the aestheticians' bête noire by television. Another was that the substantial growth in universities on both sides of the Atlantic during this period made possible the introduction of new subjects, particularly in humanities departments. A third was the increasing visibility of the European art cinema, providing thematically dense, formally self-conscious material in the best traditions of European modernism, well suited for inclusion on university courses teaching critical skills. The increasing availability of English translations of theoretical works also offered a framework for a more rigorous kind of film criticism than had previously existed in America. Bazin was translated into English in 1967; Walter Benjamin's important essay "The Work of Art in the Age of Mechanical Reproduction" (discussed in chapter 2), written in 1936, was first published in English in 1968; while major works in the Russian Formalist tradition had begun appearing in translation a few years earlier. The work of Roland Barthes (discussed in the next chapter) was published in English from 1970 onwards.

From Criticism to Theory

Sometimes the inadequate criticism of current plays is due to the more or less antagonistic attitude the critic adopts toward the motion picture. . . . Often his criticism is not analysis, but vituperation and abuse.
Frances Taylor Patterson, 1920[15]

Early in this book, we looked at two important critical methodologies: auteurism and genre-based criticism. The first purpose of both these approaches is to organize the large, undifferentiated corpus of "the Hollywood cinema" into smaller, related, and comprehensible groups of movies. From there both identify common features within a group, and they may then go on either to draw some aesthetic or ideological judgement about the group as a whole, or to comment on one movie in relation to the group. Although these critical approaches "avoid the dangers of impressionistic connoisseurship which haunt the unsystematic critic," neither of them constitutes a theory as such.[16] As Dudley Andrew argues, auteurism deploys theoretical principles to evaluate particular movies and rank directors in a hierarchy of worth, rather than to achieve a systematic understanding of cinema as a general phenomenon. Andrew distinguishes between theory and criticism by suggesting that theory is concerned with the properties of cinema as a whole. Criticism can put theory into practice, but its primary object of investigation is the individual movie, a group of movies, or the study of particular techniques. Despite its undoubted explanatory power, criticism alone could not establish the movies as a legitimate object of academic study. For the activity of criticism to gain acceptance as an academic discipline (that is, for movie criticism to become film studies), it had to develop a set of theoretical concerns recognized by the academy's established institutional criteria. Only with these concerns in place could study of the movies proceed to the higher ground of the established humanities or social sciences.

The importation of European thought helped to give the emerging subject of film studies a degree of cultural and academic legitimacy that the movies themselves did not possess. The polemical assertion of the possibility of individual authorship in Hollywood was initially developed in the French film journal *Cahiers du Cinéma* as a strategy – *la politique des auteurs* – for attacking existing bourgeois orthodoxies of cultural value and bringing new forms of personal filmmaking into being. Its proponents – François Truffaut, Jean-Luc Godard, Claude

Chabrol, Eric Rohmer – became the leading figures in the French New Wave cinema of the 1960s. As a strategy, auteurism retained its iconoclastic challenge to traditional notions of aesthetic quality when it was translated into Anglo-American critical practice, through its assertion of the aesthetic merit of some popular culture and its valorization of some Hollywood directors as individual artists. Its most influential American proponent was Andrew Sarris, who promulgated the "auteur theory" as a system of classifying and evaluating Hollywood cinema, and a means by which the aesthetic history of Hollywood could be written as an account of successive individual artistic achievements, deliberately detached from the material circumstances of their production and consumption. Like the French critics, Sarris championed an unabashedly Romantic conception of individual creativity, in which an artwork was valuable to the extent that an artist had expressed his or her personality through it.

Although auteurism was strongly contested by critics whose values it rejected, its adoption as a critical approach was crucial to the elevation of cinema to academic respectability. Auteurism provided a basis for the detailed examination of individual Hollywood movies, and this allowed the study of cinema to find accommodation in university literature departments, since its model of authorship fitted easily into the dominant patterns of Anglo-American literary studies. Extending literature's organizing principle of authorship to cinema opened up the enormous and previously unexplored body of twentieth-century cinematic narrative to academic study, and provided a familiar means by which that study could be organized. In Britain, this association produced a body of criticism that combined close textual analysis of mise-en-scène with an assertion of the moral seriousness of the movies under discussion, particularly in the work of writers for the journal *MOVIE*, such as Robin Wood and V. F. Perkins.

The evaluative critical paradigms initially borrowed from Leavisite or New Critical methods of literary studies, however, rapidly revealed the difficulties inherent in their application to cinema. These methods were broadly formalist in their critical procedures, evaluating works according to internal criteria such as coherence and complexity. Their formalism made it possible to disregard the historical circumstances of Hollywood's production processes, but it also detached the "author" as a particular set of textual practices from the biographical personage who directed the movies under analysis. The strain this caused was nowhere more evident than in interviews with the auteurs in question, where inquiries about their stylistic preferences and thematic preoccupations were often met by an irrelevant anecdote or a contemptuous dismissal of the question.

The political and intellectual turmoil of the late 1960s saw ideological objections raised to both the individualist emphasis of auteurism and its celebration of Hollywood. The body of critical theory that spread from France in the wake of the student protests and strikes of May 1968 exposed the internal inconsistencies of auteurism and offered some radical alternatives, which replaced the study of the author with studies of signification and ideology. Critical attention was focused not on the creativity of the individual genius, but on the "text" as a site for the production of meaning. Rather than coherence, this politically informed criticism looked for ideologically significant oppositions structuring a text at a deeper level than its thematic and stylistic consistencies. This approach heavily influenced the London-based *Screen*, the dominant English-language journal of film theory in the 1970s, which in turn bore markedly on the academic study of cinema in the USA. While the political persuasion of almost all the theoretical criticism produced in the 1970s was clearly on the left, concerned with championing the "progressive text" that denied the easy pleasures of Hollywood, many writers retained a residual attachment to Hollywood cinema that drew them back, repeatedly, to its critical assessment. The movies of Sarris's "pantheon" directors – Ford, Hitchcock, Sternberg, Welles – remained central objects of this critical endeavor.

No single term provides an exact description of the work produced around these journals, but we can group the wide range of theoretical discourses brought to bear on the Hollywood cinema in the 1960s and 1970s as broadly **structuralist** in orientation, because rather than attending to the apparent characteristics of a movie – usually in isolation – they sought to identify the wider structures within which a particular movie was produced and against which it was "read." Deriving from the **semiology** (literally, the study of signs) of Swiss linguist Ferdinand de Saussure, structuralism directed intellectual attention to the organizing principles and relationships underlying human behavior, institutions, or texts. As an intellectual movement, structuralism originated in the proposition, made by anthropologist Claude Lévi-Strauss, that kinship relations and primitive myths were structured like language, and could be studied by using Saussure's principles of linguistic analysis.[17] Structuralism maintained that the elements within a structure did not possess meaning as independent units, but gained their meaning through their relations to other elements. Meaning is, for instance, often constructed through binary oppositions: "good" means something only in relation to "bad"; "raw" and "cooked" signify opposing states.

Applications of the structuralist approach proliferated in European thought in the 1960s, and cultural theorists such as Roland Barthes and Umberto Eco argued that cultural events could be understood by examining the structure that underlay them as if it were a language. In another important instance, discussed more fully in the next chapter, French psychoanalyst Jacques Lacan claimed that the unconscious was not an amorphous repository of repressed feelings, but rather a network of associative patterns "structured like a language." Applied to cinema, structuralism produced a variety of analytical methods. It might have been logical to expect the structuralist approach to provide a firmer theoretical framework for genre studies, which had obviously related concerns. But in the first instance, as Anglo-American criticism awaited the translation of the major texts of French structuralism, its approach was more influential in revising notions of authorship.

An attempt to avoid the Romantic excesses of the auteur theory was developed by a number of critics in the late 1960s and early 1970s, and given the cumbersome name **auteur-structuralism**. This work recognized the advantages of the auteur approach as a way of classifying Hollywood cinema, but resisted the idea of autonomous creativity as a supreme value. Combining a system of classification by director/author with a text-based inquiry into the structuring principles of any given work, it breathed new life into a set of debates about the status of the director. What most clearly differentiated auteur-structuralism from auteurist studies

Alfred Hitchcock promoting himself in the trailer for *Psycho* (1960).

was not its mode of analysis so much as its project of detaching the common structural features of a body of movies "signed" by the same name from the cult of
personality encouraged by auteurism. Movies marked by the sign "Directed by
Alfred Hitchcock," for example, could be shown to possess recurring structures,
but auteur-structuralists relieved themselves of the burden of having to demonstrate that Alfred Hitchcock had intentionally placed them there. "Hitchcock"
became a body of structuring principles that could be divined from a critical examination of films, and bore no necessary relation to the small, fat, male body of
Alfred Hitchcock the person, which routinely appeared in each of these movies.
The author became, in one formulation, the "author-code," one among several
organizing principles of coherence in a text.

This proposition alleviated many of the problems created by the homages of
auteurism, and established the critic's interpretive independence from the intentions of the director, but it produced as many contradictions of its own. Beginning from the assumption of individual creativity as the basis for its system of
classification, it then leaned toward the other half of its hyphenate in denying any
credit to that individual for the structural consistencies it identified, even when it
accorded aesthetic value to them. Auteur-structuralism associated the structure it
identified in a movie with its director, "not because he has played the role of artist,
expressing himself or his vision in the film, but because it is through the force of

his preoccupations that an unconscious, unintended meaning can be decoded in the film, usually to the surprise of the individual involved."[18]

In trying to avoid an approach based on a director's intentions or agency, auteur-structuralism thus found itself propelled toward the uncertain waters of a psychoanalytic explanation of directorial consistency. Peter Wollen quoted Jean Renoir as having observed that a director spends his whole life making one film, and Wollen saw the critic's task as being to reconstruct this "one film" out of the whole body of a director's work.[19] In describing the movies of an auteur in terms much closer to genre criticism, auteur-structuralism proposed that the auteur's "one film" constituted a myth, in the precise sense in which the structuralist anthropologist Lévi-Strauss used the term. The recurrent thematic consistencies or binary oppositions from which this myth could be distilled were usually attached both to the unconscious preoccupations of the director, and to those of the wider social group for which he or she was taken to speak. Where auteurism celebrated an individual's genius, auteur-structuralism seemed, at times, to come dangerously close to celebrating his or her unconscious as symptomatic of the equally unconscious preoccupations of the culture surrounding his or her work. Ultimately, the "one film" constructed by auteur-structuralists revealed social rather than individual meaning.[20]

More productively, another version of auteur-structuralism simply declared its lack of interest in explaining how any given set of structures had come into being, limiting its activity to observing those structures in a common body of texts. This approach demonstrated a more consistent and rigorous attitude to the activity of textual criticism, but in the process it abandoned any relationship between the text and history. It could explain neither how the texts themselves came into being as the result of a particular mode of production in Hollywood, nor what the wider relationship between those texts and the culture for which they were produced might have been. Instead, the system of production was seen simply as an obstacle to critical comprehension: "A great many features of films analyzed have to be dismissed as indecipherable because of 'noise' from the producer, the cameraman or even the actors."[21] In Wollen's account of the means by which the critic could unscramble meaning from this background of noise, metaphors of psychoanalysis compete with metaphors of detection: what was proposed was a careful treatment of textual evidence leading to a correct induction.

In any of its versions, auteur-structuralism was a stressful marriage between an individualist organizing principle and an interpretive strategy that denied individual agency. Nevertheless, the structuralist approach provided the necessary theoretical support for criticism to distance itself from the insufficiently rigorous practices of journalistic writing, producing a form of textual analysis that would meet the criteria of the academy. As a method by which the detailed study of movies could be validated in terms borrowed from literary criticism, and as a pedagogic instrument by which the skills of "practical criticism" could be imparted on film studies courses, structuralism displayed its institutional usefulness in establishing film studies as a discipline. In practice, auteurist criticism proved much more successful in dealing with thematic meaning, derived from verbal sources in the text, than with the significance and the signifying practices of Hollywood movies' image streams. Auteurism and auteur-structuralism have both produced important and valuable bodies of critical knowledge, but they cannot provide complete or satisfactory methods for understanding Hollywood cinema, primarily because their concern with the internal organization of a movie can supply only very partial answers to the historical and ideological questions of the cinema's relation to the culture within which it is produced and to which it is addressed.

Debates about authorship evaporated in the 1970s, more because poststructuralist criticism bypassed them than because the idea of directorial authorship was recognized as being an historically inaccurate account of Hollywood production. Criticism, however, continues to need an authority for the text, a figure with whom the critic can engage and argue, and whom they can reassess. If the auteur theory is surely dead, so are the debates over "the death of the author" initiated by Roland Barthes and Michel Foucault at the outset of poststructuralism.[22] Hardly any academic critic would now call himself or herself an auterist, and the critical study of cinematic authors is not now a central activity of film criticism, in the sense that auteurist examinations of the thematic preoccupations of James Cameron or the stylistic consistency of Ron Howard are unlikely topics for academic research. Nevertheless, the great majority of academic criticism continues to be written as if the director could be named as the author of the text – for instance, in the normal critical practice of citing movies as "Sean Cunningham's *Friday the 13th*," or attaching the director's name in parentheses after the title: "*City Slickers* (Ron Underwood)."[23] As Robert Stam argues, "auteurism no longer triggers polemics partly because it has *won*. Auteurism is now widely practiced even by those who have reservations about the 'theory.'"[24] As an organizing principle, auteurism persists in museum and festival programming, university courses and book publishing, while what Timothy Corrigan has called "the commerce of auteurism" is in widespread use throughout the industry.[25]

Paradoxically, at almost exactly the same time as authorship was displaced from the central debates of film studies in the 1970s, it obtained a much stronger purchase in industrial discourse than ever before, as the directors of the New Hollywood – the first generation to have been taught to study cinema – claimed the status and authority of authorship. The auteur became a marketing strategy during the 1970s, to the extent that historian Gerald Mast could proclaim in 1981 that the American cinema had become a "director's cinema," and the director "one of the film's stars."[26] Reports of the author's triumph, however, turned out to have been as exaggerated as the simultaneous reports of his or her death. Corrigan and Justin Wyatt both argue convincingly that the major companies' willingness to embrace an auteur cinema was little more than an adaptation of their established practices from contracting talent and marketing product. In the comparatively uncertain 1970s, studio executives could also blame a movie's commercial failure on an auteur's excess, as happened most spectacularly in the case of "Michael Cimino's *Heaven's Gate*" (see chapter 1).[27]

More broadly, contemporary marketing policies use the auteur as a trademark, aiming to establish "a relationship between audience and movie whereby an intentional and authorial agency governs, as a kind of brand-name vision whose aesthetic meanings and values have already been determined." Much like auteur-structuralism, Corrigan's account of commercial auteurism describes a version of the "author code" that resembles a set of generic conventions. Much of the pleasure in viewing *Schindler's List* (1993) primarily as a "Spielberg movie," he argues, is "the pleasure of refusing an evaluative relation to it . . . in being able to already know, not read, the meaning of the film as a product of the public image of its creator. An auteur film today seems to aspire more and more to a critical tautology, capable of being understood and consumed without being seen."[28]

The place of the auteur in contemporary criticism is thus paradoxical. What Michael Budd calls "the romantic discourse of authorship, which removes a text from its economic and social context and places it in an ideal realm of personal expression," has simultaneously lost its place in academic critical practice and been taken up by the culture industry as the ideal strategy for marketing a "boutique cinema" to an up-market audience.[29] The industry promotes a commodified, designer notion of authorial intention to the extent that it willingly releases a "director's cut" as a marketing strategy to recirculate movies in secondary markets, and a promotional industry utilizes the instruments of popular criticism to sustain the cult status of directors. Academic criticism, meanwhile, has abandoned "the romantic individualist baggage of auteurism," and acknowledges the interplay between institution, convention and personality in the production of a movie, but many critics would endorse James Naremore's argument that "a fine-grained understanding of both film style and the general culture" cannot be produced without the historical study of individuals.[30] Revealingly, perhaps, much of the most informative work published on individual directors in Classical Hollywood since 1985 has been in the form of biographies rather than critical studies.

The theoretical discrediting of authorship as an interpretive paradigm has, therefore, done little to damage its commercial and critical success, because the concept of authorship fulfils a number of ideological purposes and provides audiences with additional opportunities for interpretive pleasure. The cinematic author may now be understood, in theory, as the name of a sign, a matrix of textual devices, or "merely a term in the process of reading and spectating," but critical practice continues to treat it as if it were a person.[31] In her book on "Hitchcock and feminist theory," for instance, Tania Modleski declares her intention of treating "Hitchcock's work as the expression of cultural authority and practices existing to some extent outside the artist's control."[32] Hitchcock is, however, an active presence in Modleski's text, placing the camera, arousing sympathy for characters in the spectator, offering opinions on the sanity or otherwise of "his" characters, and even imagining himself bisexual.[33]

In Modleski's book, as in most writing on Hitchcock, the term "Hitchcock" functions as a synonym for "Hitchcock's films" or the "Hitchcock text." The relationship between the term and the person of the director is seldom discussed in poststructuralist criticism, but as Virginia Wright Wexman suggests, the canonic status of several "Hitchcock" texts from the 1950s and early 1960s attests to "the continuing vitality of the auteur theory."[34] Psychoanalytic theorist Slavoj Žižek, for instance, responds to reproaches that his analysis elevates Hitchcock into "a God-like demi-urge who masters even the smallest details of his work" by suggesting that this is merely a critical strategy, in which "Hitchcock functions as the

Scottie Ferguson (James Stewart) questions Madeleine Elster (Kim Novak) in *Vertigo* (1958). Produced by Alfred Hitchcock; distributed by Paramount Pictures.

'subject supposed to know.'" For Žižek, the strategy is justified because it is theoretically productive.[35] "Hitchcock" here becomes no more than an element in a theoretical procedure, while the critic-analyst assumes the authority to speak in the name of the author. The critic claims the authority of the author for his or her interpretation, and simultaneously attributes responsibility for that interpretation to a textual source. In his essay on *Vertigo* (1958), for example, William Rothman claims that although "the *Vertigo* that emerges . . . in this essay is not the film as viewers ordinarily experience it," his reading accounts for that ordinary experience, explaining it as "the experience that fails to acknowledge Hitchcock and hence misses *his* meaning" (emphasis added).[36] Although Modleski dismisses Rothman's claims for Hitchcock's "masterful" control over the spectator and calls for feminist critics to resist being "absorbed by male authority and male texts . . . and withhold the authorial acknowledgment the texts exact," she nevertheless concludes her book by identifying herself as one of "Hitchcock's daughters," sharing a "monstrous father" with Patricia Hitchcock and other female viewers.[37]

Hitchcock is evidently an exceptional case, and one reason for the canonic status of so many of the movies he directed may well be the extent to which these movies bear the distinctive marks of an authorial and self-referential presence that encourages the terminological slippage between Hitchcock and "Hitchcock." The canonic status of Hitchcock the auteur-enunciator also depends on the aesthetic distance between these movies and Classical Hollywood narrative, and the extent to which "his films constantly denaturalize themselves, calling attention to the components of film production, in order to point up the 'enunciated', discursive, constructed quality of film story."[38] But the Hitchcock persona seems to alter with each critic. Ann West suggests a far more hesitant figure than William Rothman's

Among its other pleasures, *Vertigo* offers its viewers a sightseeing tour of the landmarks of San Francisco.
Produced by Alfred Hitchcock; distributed by Paramount Pictures.

"master": for her, Hitchcock "seems to have been gently calling attention to the idea of plot as contrivance."[39]

Poststructuralism's lack of interest in historical questions has allowed critics to largely ignore the extent to which the figure of "Hitchcock" was a deliberate commercial creation. Before Hitchcock the author there was Hitchcock the marketing strategy, promoting the visibly self-conscious presence of Alfred Hitchcock in the movies he directed and pioneering "the business of being an auteur."[40] This marketing strategy continued after Hitchcock's death, transmuted into critical accounts of self-reflexivity but more materially present in the commercial activity surrounding the re-release, in the early 1980s, of five previously unavailable Hitchcock movies, including *Rear Window* (1954) and *Vertigo*. For the Hitchcock estate, these movies quite literally constituted capital that accumulated both commercial and aesthetic value because they were withheld from circulation. In their scarcity they acquired something of the aura of art, contributing to the fetishization of Hitchcock "as a lost figure of high culture."[41] Their re-release capitalized on "Hitchcock's" critical reputation, and the volumes of criticism that followed represented an investment in Hitchcock's canonic status by both the exhibition industry and the critical industry of academic interpretation. *Vertigo*'s second appearance released a range of meanings unavailable to its audiences in 1958, but it is also true that some elements of its appeal to its original audiences, including its function as a tour guide to San Francisco, have been ignored by later analysts.[42]

At the same time as this capitalization on Hitchcock's creative persona is typical of Hollywood's commercial opportunism, it also makes these movies exceptions to the norms of Hollywood, precisely because of the emphasis placed on the name of their author. The analysis presented here has suggested that part of the pleasure of movies lies in their apparent *lack* of an authorial voice, which makes it possible for their consumers to value them for whatever they care to take: for Grace Kelly's dresses in *Rear Window*, for the way Robert Mitchum drives one-handed around parking lots in *The Friends of Eddie Coyle* (1973), or for Susan Sarandon's T-shirt, jeans, and "unruly red hair" behind the wheel in *Thelma and Louise* (1991).[43] In that sense any movie could be seen as an infinitely open "text," a showcase of endless incidental pleasures encouraging, rather than repressing, consumer choice. Poststructuralist criticism enacts this consumer choice, selecting aspects of the text for its ruminations, and justifying its choice by the proposal that, as Žižek says of Hitchcock, "*everything has meaning* in his films, the seemingly simplest plot conceals unexpected philosophical delicacies."[44] Frederic Jameson, for example, finds a "peculiar and obsessive" pattern in the serrated grooves of the furrowed cornfield and Mount Rushmore carvings in *North by Northwest* (1959),[45] while Lucretia Knapp seeks to redirect attention to the "relatively unexplored" issue of lesbianism in Hitchcock: "A lesbian perspective opens up the possibility of reading the ambiguities in a film like *Marnie*, seeing what is in a film in a different way and therefore constructing a different text than the heterosexual eye might observe." At the same time, however, Knapp asserts her critical position against what she takes to be a dominant one. The female space and female voices in *Marnie*, she suggests, "have been repressed or overlooked" by Raymond Bellour, "who sees in the film nothing but a male oedipal drama." In preferring her own analysis to Bellour's, Knapp cites authorial authority: "The explicitly Freudian text [that Bellour uncovers] is almost too obvious, as if Bellour's discovery is no more than Hitchcock's trap."[46]

Poststructuralist criticism has therefore come to practice what I described in chapter 16 as the sophisticated viewer's fatalistic act of resistance to the inevitability of a movie's moralistic ending. It converts that viewer's momentary optimism that for once the narrative will end with transgression triumphant into a critical "re-reading" of the text. Interpretations of this kind have come to constitute what David Bordwell has called the current practice of "ordinary criticism," the equivalent in humanities disciplines of what Thomas Kuhn called "normal science": the application of established problem-solving routines to expand and fill out a realm of knowledge.[47] As Paul Willemen has noted, however, such criticism frequently tends to reach "the familiar conclusion that the 'text' under analysis is full of contradictory tensions, requires active readers and produces a variety of pleasures."[48] This re-reading is all too often achieved at the expense of the audience. According to Žižek:

> If . . . the pleasure of the modernist interpretation consists in the effect of recognition which "gentrifies" the disquieting uncanniness of its object ("Aha, now I see the point of this apparent mess!"), the aim of the postmodernist treatment is to estrange its very initial homeliness: "You think what you see is a simple melodrama even your senile granny would have no difficulties in following? Yet without taking into account . . . /the difference between symptom and *sinthom*; the structure of the Borromean knot; the fact that Woman is one of the Names-of-the-Father; etc., etc./ you've totally missed the point!"[49]

Although Žižek's poststructuralist criticism studies objects available for universal consumption, the practice by which their meanings are determined has become more elitist than ever. While the distinction between high and low culture has ceased to be tenable at the level of the aesthetic object under examination, much academic criticism has nevertheless sought to maintain a distinction at the level of reception. The Hitchcock who is Žižek's "subject supposed to know" is almost certainly unrecognizable to the moviegoer ignorant of the difference between symptom and *sinthom*. That, perhaps, measures the distance that criticism has traveled from Eric Rohmer's declaration in 1957 that the goal of *Cahiers du Cinéma* was to "enrich" its readers' reflections on the movies they saw.[50]

Criticism in Practice: *Only Angels Have Wings*

The only way to keep a work reasonably fresh upon many repeated viewings is to look for different things in it each time – more subtle and complex things, seen in new ways.

Kristin Thompson[51]

Not that you're trying to make every scene a great scene, but you try not to annoy the audience. If I can make about five good scenes and not annoy the audience, it's an awfully good picture.

Howard Hawks[52]

One way to examine the various functions, purposes, and pleasures of auteurist critical approaches to Hollywood is to compare their responses to a single movie or group of movies. What follows is an account of criticism as it has been directed toward the work of one Hollywood director, Howard Hawks, and to just one of the movies directed by him, *Only Angels Have Wings* (1939). Historian Robert Sklar has suggested that Hawks was "the most successful independent director in Hollywood," working at every major studio, where he managed to flout budget restrictions, ignore production schedules, undermine studio rules, and subvert the established screen personas of the stars with whom he worked.[53] Hawks survived in Hollywood long enough to become the subject of a wide range of different critical approaches, although his reputation and those of his movies have seen considerable fluctuation. He directed his first movie, *The Road to Glory*, in 1927 and his last, *Rio Lobo*, in 1970. He died in 1977.

There is, however, another reason for selecting *Only Angels Have Wings*, one that returns us to the starting point of this book in asking the question, "How do we take Hollywood seriously?" In this context, the question is a sign of film studies' preoccupation with its self-justification and legitimation, constantly seeking to demonstrate its claims to "seriousness" against the surface of the material it studies. On its surface, which is by far the most important part of a Hollywood text, *Only Angels Have Wings* does not aid the critic determined to take it seriously. Set vaguely in the Latin American port of Barranca, recognizable only as the Columbia studio back-lot, it also features papier-mâché Andes mountains,

The critically embarrassing Napoleon the donkey in *Only Angels Have Wings* (1939).
Produced by Howard Hawks; distributed by Columbia Pictures.

a number of very obvious model planes, and, to the profound embarrassment of any earnest critic, Napoleon the donkey. To those already persuaded by Hollywood or Hawks, *Only Angels Have Wings* appears to be a deeply moving work. To those insufficiently persuaded, the movie, and the very idea of taking it seriously, are only absurd. I want, therefore, to discuss the ways in which critics have evaluated and valued *Only Angels Have Wings*, in order to examine the critical projects in which they were engaged.

Hawks's well-established industrial reputation as a capable action director is indicated by the steady pattern of his output throughout his career. His early critical reputation, on the other hand, rested on the writings of the group of French film critics associated with *Cahiers du Cinéma* in the 1950s. Jacques Rivette, for instance, maintained that

> Hawks epitomizes the highest qualities of the American cinema: he is the only American director who knows how to draw a *moral*. His marvelous blend of action and morality is probably the secret of his genius. . . . There seems to be a law behind Hawks' action and editing, but it is a *biological* law like that governing any living being: each shot has a functional beauty, like a neck or an ankle. The smooth orderly succession of shots has a rhythm like the pulsing of blood, and the whole film is like a beautiful body, kept alive by deep, resilient breathing . . . even if he is occasionally drawn to the ridiculous or the absurd, Hawks first of all concentrates on the smell and feel of reality, giving reality an unusual and indeed long hidden grandeur and nobility; how Hawks gives the modern sensibility a classical conscience. The father of *Red River* and *Only Angels Have Wings* is none other than Corneille.[54]

Hawks's reputation among Anglo-American reviewer critics was, however, rather more as a skilled craftsman than as a latter-day Corneille. Most were initially less enthusiastic. Peter John Dyer found *Only Angels Have Wings* "childish, banal, phony and enjoyable," its story "frankly terrible":

> Inside the big cliché are the small ones: the equation of maturity with an acceptance of sudden death; the heroine playing Liszt in the lounge at one a.m.; the stiff upper lip inventory of the dead pilot's belongings; the pseudo tough byplay accompanying the lighting of a cigarette or the flipping of a double headed coin; the probing for the bullet in the hero's shoulder; the nursemaid relationship between him and the old friend too blind to fly.[55]

Manny Farber, one of the best examples of the reviewer as critic, saw Hawks as "a bravado specialist who always makes pictures about a Group," and *Angels* as "a White Cargo melodrama that is often intricately silly." Farber's commentary anticipates Umberto Eco's celebration of *Casablanca*'s "glorious ricketiness," in which "all the archetypes burst out shamelessly" and "the clichés are talking among themselves, celebrating a reunion."[56] In direct contrast to Rivette, Farber suggested that no artist "is less suited to a discussion of profound themes than Hawks, whose attraction to strutting braggarts, boyishly cynical dialogue, and melodramatic fiction always rests on his poetic sense of action."[57]

A conscious attempt to read Hawks's work as the sign of an authorial presence developed in the United States in the 1960s. In 1961 Andrew Sarris, beginning to shift the discourse of reviewing toward a more systematic director-based criticism, wrote that in *Only Angels Have Wings*, "the themes of responsibility and expiation are applied to men striving to perform the impossible for purely gratuitous reasons." The movie was

> the most romantic film of Hawks's career, and its pessimistic mood was the director's last gesture to the spirit of the Thirties reflected in the doomed cinema of [Jean] Renoir and [Michel] Carné. . . . In the violent world of Howard Hawks, one has to be good to survive honorably and at least on this level, Hawksian heroes follow the canons of Sophoclean tragedy enunciated by Aristotle more closely than do Blanche du Bois, Willy Loman, and the tormented protagonists of Eugene O'Neill.[58]

By 1968, when Sarris published what was to become perhaps the central statement of Anglo-American auteurism, *The American Cinema: Directors and Directions, 1929–1968*, Hawks's place in Sarris's pantheon was assured.

As if answering Sarris's call for a program of more detailed study of the major Hollywood directors, Robin Wood's book on Hawks, first published in 1968, provided the English-speaking world with its first full-length study of his work, and an archetypal statement of authorial criticism. Wood's innovation was to examine the Hawksian "oeuvre" as a whole rather than merely responding pragmatically to individual movies. He developed his analysis by grouping the movies together not by genre but by the thematic concerns they evidenced. For film studies the procedure was radical and productive, but in entirely erasing questions of economics, industry, and technology, it represented only a small step forward in understanding the movies as specifically "Hollywood" forms. The book contained a number of strained parallels between the movies and the novels of Joseph Conrad

Bonnie Lee (Jean Arthur) and Jeff Carter (Cary Grant) join the colorful Barrancans in a song of defiance against darkness and chaos in *Only Angels Have Wings*.
Produced by Howard Hawks; distributed by Columbia Pictures.

and others. According to Wood, *Only Angels Have Wings* was one of Hawks's greatest works, because it was one of the most unified: it was "a completely achieved masterpiece, and a remarkably *inclusive* film, drawing together the main thematic threads of Hawks's work in a single complex web."[59] What were seen as clichés by Dyer and Farber became for Wood the building blocks of an original aesthetic statement: "That Hawks does not feel himself superior to material many may find 'corny,' 'melodramatic' or 'banal' is not a sign of inferior intelligence or sensibility. He responds, directly and spontaneously, to all that is valid in the genre, assimilates it and transforms it into a means of personal expression."[60]

For Wood the movie as artwork was a deeply emotional experience, in which both the artist's and the characters' sensibilities were exposed to the spectator:

> No one who has seen the film will forget Jeff's singing (with Bonnie's participation) of the "Peanut Vendor," as the culmination of the sequence of Bonnie's initiation into, and acceptance of, the fliers' code. Joe has been dead perhaps an hour. We haven't forgotten, and we know that they haven't. But Joe's death has ceased to be the issue: the song becomes a shout of defiance in the face of the darkness surrounding human life and the chaos of the universe.[61]

In Wood's interpretation, artist and characters speak in a language that is transparent and expressive, uncluttered by the uncertainties of communication and the instability of meaning so central to post-Saussurean thought. At the same time, for all its dependence on the conventions and practices of Hollywood studio cinema, Wood took the movie to be both "realist" and intensely relevant to our contemporary experience:

The directness – the vital, spontaneous frankness – with which the characters confront and attack each other is enormously affecting, because this urgency of contact derives from their constant (not necessarily conscious) sense of the imminence of death, of the surrounding darkness, a *physical* intuition that prompts them to live, *now*, to the maximum. It is partly this that makes Hawks's films, in fact, so modern: in the world of the hydrogen bomb, one doesn't have to be an Andes mailplane flier to feel that one may be dead tomorrow.[62]

Wood's arguments remain often fascinating and convincing, but within the study there are also signs of doubt about the validity of the basic critical activity. Although Wood values above all a "freshness" and "total lack of self consciousness" in Hawks, his own writing betrays a self-consciousness missing from the reviews and the early writing of Sarris. He apologizes for his tone, concerned that anyone reading his book, "with its talk of fugues, of stylistic and structural rigour, of moral seriousness, will be totally unprepared for the consistently relaxed, delightful, utterly unpretentious film that *Rio Bravo* is. In fact, when it first came out, almost nobody noticed that it was in any sense a serious work of art."[63] Writing of a scene in *Red Line 7000* (1965), he self-consciously identifies the limits of structural criticism: "the beauty of the scene . . . arises not from any content that can be intellectualized and removed from the images, but from the very precise timing of the acting and the editing, form, gesture, expression, intonation, exchanged glance. That is why (the reader had best be warned now) Hawks is ultimately unanalyzable."[64]

Hardly had the auteurist case been made before its methodology came under criticism. Peter Wollen's *Signs and Meaning in the Cinema*, published the same year as Wood's book, offered a sustained assault on "traditional" auteurist critical practices and included a re-reading of Hawks from a structuralist perspective. Instead of talking about Hawks as the author/producer of the movies bearing his name, Wollen regarded Hawks as the "sum of the attitudes manifest in the movies' recurrent structural oppositions." Drawing on the structuralist approach of Claude Lévi-Strauss, he set about detaching the production of meaning in the movies from any individual's intention and saw it as a fundamentally social phenomenon, addressing the ideologies in which the movie was immersed, as they were represented by these sets of oppositions. The "objective stratum of meaning" Wollen found in Hawks's movies was ideologically rather than authorially determined, and as a result Hawks could only really be understood as a critical construct, an invisible narrational function guiding our response and playing with our subjectivity.[65] Along with this methodological critique went a catalogue of thematic objections: "Hawks sees the all-male community as an ultimate; obviously it is very retrograde. His Spartan heroes are, in fact, cruelly stunted."[66]

Wollen's re-reading of Hawks eventually produced a rejoinder from Wood, who took offense at Wollen's reading of the movies as implicitly, if not explicitly, patriarchal and misogynist. Wood found Wollen's account of supposedly "typical" Hawskian dialog between men and women to be a "destructive parody" of "the specific complexities and qualifications brought by context" to particular dialogs and male–female relationships.[67] Wood saw the attempt to reduce the movies to a single structural pattern as a reduction of the range of available meanings in the movies, and questioned the legitimacy of a structural method more intent on discovering deep-rooted core oppositions than examining the nuances of performance and mise-en-scène. This insistence on the reductionism of the structural approach was to become a keynote in many of the debates that followed; it remains, for instance, the essence of V. F. Perkins's critique of neoformalism.[68] This critical dispute opposed methods as well as evaluations: Wollen's structures against Wood's interpretations; Wollen's oppositions against Wood's unities; Wollen's examination of ideology against Wood's concern with the stature of Hawks as an artist.

Subsequent criticism took other directions. Ideological criticism brought a new concern for the structuring of gender relations in cinema. Early feminist criticism found crucial ambiguities that troubled the movies' relation to dominant ideology. Molly Haskell saw Hawks as both a product and a critic of sexual puritanism and male supremacy: "In the group experience of filmmaking, he lives out the homo-erotic themes of American life, literature and his own films."[69] Although centered on male groups involved in traditionally "masculine" generic pursuits such as investigating crimes or big-game hunting, many of Hawks's movies also qualified their endorsement of patriarchy by exposing male fears of women and deconstructing masculinity. Haskell, however, did not regard this as a redeeming quality. For her, Hawks was "like the young boy who, recoiling from his mother's kiss, refuses to acknowledge his debt of birth to her and who simultaneously fears revealing his own feelings of love and dependency."[70] In this context *Only Angels Have Wings* was hardly Hawks's central achievement:

> Jean Arthur provides an alternative to the all male world of stoical camaraderie on the one hand, and to the destructive femininity represented by Rita Hayworth on the other, but what an alternative! A man dies trying to land a plane in a storm for a date with her, she breaks down in defiance of the prevailing stiff upper lip ethic, and thereafter she hangs around like a puppy dog waiting for Cary Grant to fall in love with her.[71]

Broadening the terms of this discussion of individual character to encompass the movies' ideological function, Richard Dyer produced a rather different reading:

> What seems to me to be happening in the narrative of these films is that there is a contempt for female characteristics yet an obligation to have female characters. This problem is resolved in the person of the woman who becomes a man (almost) . . . "Femininity" is primarily a social construction and, moreover, a construction made by men. Yet it is a construction men often find it hard to cope with – it is the category into which they project more fundamental fears about gender, which one can conceive psychoanalytically in terms of castration or socio-historically in terms of men's power over women and simultaneous dependence on them. Hawks' films like most films legitimate this fear. They say, in effect, that women, especially "feminine" women, really should be feared by men; in other words, they take what is a projection from men and claim that it really emanates from women.[72]

Haskell and Dyer reached different conclusions about Hawks's progressiveness by reading the movies at two different levels with two different critical practices. More generally, debates about the relative appropriateness of authorial criticism and structuralist approaches continued behind and between the criticisms we have identified here in relation to one movie. Each new contribution to those ongoing debates drew upon earlier work, challenging or revising it, or introducing new critical methodologies. John Belton's work, for example, focused principally on questions of visual style, mise-en-scène, and performance, finding evidence of directorial authority in the "intuitive and organic . . . coherence and integrity" of Hawks's work.[73] By the late 1970s, such traditional approaches could be sustained only with considerable effort under the impact of the new criticisms. Gerald Mast's study of Hawks as "storyteller" described a curious combination of Wood's author and Wollen's narrative function. Although a celebration of Hawks, Mast's book also drew on Wollen's work on the structuring oppositions of the movies, some-times making for a revealing confrontation between logically opposed critical discourses:

> The stories expose several of our culture's familiar moral and psychological opposi-tions as either false or facile abstractions. It is perhaps in the nature of our language and our culture to organize meaning paradigmatically; a word or a value can be known only in contrast with its opposite: male and female, adult and child, human and animal, and so forth. Although such polarities may be both linguistically and cul-turally necessary, Hawks exposes their artificiality by collapsing these abstract dichotomies into specific human actions which reveal that the tidy verbal oppositions are neither so tidy nor so valid as the existence of the words suggests.[74]

Mast's work was published in 1982, as was Leland Poague's book *Howard Hawks*. Apart from Todd McCarthy's 1997 biography and an anthology of essays mainly written before 1980, edited by Jim Hillier and Peter Wollen (1996), these remain the most recent book-length contributions of any merit to the study of what was once almost unproblematically called "Hawks's oeuvre."[75] That in itself is indica-tive of the status of auteur studies in contemporary critical practice: the auteur position is far from abandoned, but it is certainly marginalized by debates that have centered on abstract questions of spectator position and ideologies of repre-sentation. Hawks's movies are more likely to have been recently assessed in terms of their representation of masculinity, for instance, than in terms of their visual style or thematic concerns. Both Robin Wood and Peter Wollen have returned to their earlier work and found no great need to change their position. For Wollen, "the structuralist methodology of the 60s still seems appropriate for writing about Hawks," while for Wood, Hawks's work retains "its ambiguous relationship to the dominant Hollywood ideology," for example in its refusal of "the role which the woman traditionally fills" in Hollywood. Hawks's cinema represents "an inex-haustibly fascinating and suggestive intervention, which raises the most funda-mental questions about the nature of our culture and the ideological assumptions that structure it."[76]

Unlike Hitchcock, however, Hawks has not been "canonized" or productively reconfigured as a space where discourses intersect. Poststructuralist criticism has made few attempts to dissect or deconstruct the "beautiful body" that Jacques Rivette described – perhaps because the body too closely typified Classical Hollywood's lack of formal self-consciousness. As cinema criticism has moved away from its initial need to justify its own existence by finding artists in need of discovery, however, it has become possible to recognize the existence of Hollywood as a mode of production. Bolstered by such (literally) weighty tomes as *The Classical Hollywood Cinema*, film studies departments can now confidently run courses in the study of Hollywood as a culture industry and system of representation without feeling obliged to defend its reputation as Art.

Yet *Only Angels Have Wings* continues to present the same critical problem: how to take it seriously? In 1975 Donald Willis argued that it was difficult for a critic to justify a claim that the movie's value lay more in the performances of Cary Grant and Jean Arthur than in the story or its themes: "It may seem condescending to say that a work that has been praised for its depth should instead be praised (and just as highly) for its surface excitement, but I don't think it is."[77] For an evaluative criticism of Hollywood, Willis's concerns remain: is it more condescending to assess a Hollywood movie "on its own terms" as no more than a success or failure of surface excitement, or to argue for the critically inventive project of discovering profundity? Whether or not *Only Angels Have Wings* is identified as "Hawksian," the question, symbolized perhaps by Napoleon the donkey, will not disappear.

This review of critical responses to *Only Angels Have Wings* makes clear that while in one sense the movie has remained constant, any critical notion of it as an autonomous object is clearly a fiction. Questions of its Conradian high moral sense, central to its initial recognition in the 1960s, can no longer be posed with much conviction. What, then, might be asked of *Only Angels Have Wings* from within the critical-historical paradigm being advocated in this book? Many of the issues raised by previous critical accounts retain their relevance: the representation of masculinity, femininity, and heroism, for instance, can benefit from a more specific historical contextualization than they have commonly been given. Historian Robert Ray has analyzed *Only Angels Have Wings* as a prototype of the motifs that dominated Hollywood's portrayal of combat during World War II:

> the male group directed by a strong leader, the outsider who must prove himself by courageous individual action, the necessity for stoicism in the face of danger and death, the premium placed on professionalism, and the threat posed by women. . . . The group of flyers in *Angels* became the model for the patrols or platoons of the wartime movies – patrols cut off from the main body of the army . . . or assigned to a particularly dangerous mission behind enemy lines . . . The war movies employed these small, isolated groups as a device for viewing a world war that, without this focusing, would have seemed only an enormous, impersonal machine.[78]

Ray's analysis, which reiterates and quotes those of Peter John Dyer and Manny Farber, does not engage with those critical positions that argue for the movie's moral seriousness. Rather, he argues that Hawks's techniques of compression and

Jeff (Gary Grant), Gent Shelton (John Carroll), and Joe Souther (Noah Beery Jr), prototype for the platoon of Hollywood's wartime combat movies.
Produced by Howard Hawks; distributed by Columbia Pictures.

indirect statement reduced what he sees as Hollywood's dominant thematic paradigm – the avoidance of choice between the opposed values represented by individualism and community – to its most basic elements: "By using *Angels*' reductive version of the Classic Hollywood pattern as the model for its combat films, therefore, the industry proposed to its audience that reality be ignored for the duration of World War II." The conscious artificiality and melodrama of *Only Angels Have Wings* made it, in Ray's analysis, "the inevitable model for the combat films whose propagandistic project was to reaffirm the American myth that, even in wartime, essential choices could be avoided."[79]

A different set of historical issues of representation, and its relation to politics, can be examined through the movie's portrait of Barranca and its inhabitants. Ruth Vasey has argued that *Only Angels Have Wings* presents a typical instance of Hollywood's solution to the problem of representing "the foreign" by the use of a mythical locale. The device of the "mythical kingdom" allowed the industry to deny that its invocation of cultural stereotypes was an offense to foreign countries, since no actual country was being represented. Nevertheless, these representations were often the subject of heated exchanges between foreign embassies, the Motion Picture Producers and Distributors of America, and the State Department. Barranca is such a mythical location constructed out of the most recognizable, and hence most offensive, of cultural stereotypes. It could not possibly have been identified as an actual place without provoking a diplomatic incident. For Vasey, Barranca is "a South American diplomat's nightmare . . . literally rendered as a banana republic," described in a title as a "port of call for the South American banana boats." As she describes it, the movie opens on:

a crowded wharf bustling with peasants, children, dogs, donkeys, ducks and loads of bananas. Bonnie Lee (Jean Arthur) descends from a boat to experience the local color and discovers the natives, who for some reason are holding an impromptu song and dance in the middle of an operating port, to be charming and musical. Nevertheless, she is outraged when approached by two young men (Allyn Joslyn and Noah Beery, Jr.), until she discovers that they are Americans. She exclaims, "Why, I thought you were a couple of – !" (Perhaps "Barrancans" would have sounded too ridiculous). "It sure sounds good to hear something that doesn't sound like pig-latin," she tells them. The party is nearly mown down by a quaint-looking vehicle mounted on rails, driven by hat-waving locals, blasting its horn, and pursued by cheering children. . . . her companions take her through more throngs of banana-toting natives to meet Dutchy, the "postmaster and leading banker of Barranca."[80]

The element of artifice and self-parody in this setting has not always been recognized, for instance in Robin Wood's claim that the movie's opening shots "vividly create . . . the South American town in which the film is set."[81] While being nowhere in particular and thus a Utopian setting for romance (the set was actually built next to the Shangri-La of Columbia's 1937 Utopian fantasy *Lost Horizon*), Barranca is generically South American in a manner that proclaims the ethnic, cultural, and economic superiority of the United States.[82] Although the plot displays no overt interest in questions of hemispheric power relations, it centers on the attempts of Jeff (Cary Grant) to secure contracts for South American airmail routes, the same strategy used by American carriers such as TWA in their contemporaneous corporate colonialism of South American commercial airspace. The movie's politics are on its surface, visible "on the level of performance and decor . . . in the easy sexuality of the local girls, and in the ubiquitous bananas."[83]

Vasey's analysis offers a recontextualization of both the movie and much of its criticism, attaching them to a substantive ideology by which *Only Angels Have Wings* is in several senses an imperial adventure. Perhaps this offers a way to re-engage Wood's parallels with Conrad, but rather than develop that theme, I would simply note one other area for exploration, in the repression and censorship within the movie. Critics who have commented on the relative emotional inarticulacy of the characters have described it variously as being anything from stoic to adolescent. What might be involved in the movie's stunted emotional exchanges (on the whole quite typical of Hollywood), however, is a mechanism of transformation by repression, by which the audience is obliged to articulate the emotions not fully articulated by the characters. Through such a device, the movie offers its audience opportunities for the discovery of emotional resonances drawn from their own lives and concerns. What is, in one sense, being represented (at the same time as it is being manipulated) is the emotional state of the audience. The characters' emotional commonplaces are counterpointed by the exotic settings, but in its representation of masculinity and femininity the movie declares Hollywood's democracy of sentiment: film stars and exotic characters share the emotional characteristics of their audience. As a fan wrote in *Motion Picture* magazine in 1936, "these glamorous people are just simple human beings like ourselves."[84]

It would be wrong to conclude this chapter without recognizing the limitations of Hollywood's expressive range. In their several guises as ideological projects Hollywood movies represent and legitimize the already dominant power. Dismissing them, whether as entertainment, ideology, or art, does not make that cultural function disappear, and its persistence and power provide an important justification for analysis of the movies. The dominant ideology, however, is only dominant; it never succeeds in being totalizing. The critical procedures discussed in this book provide us with opportunities to identify the spaces in the texts we examine, the sites at which they reveal their mechanisms, and the cultural forces behind them. By examining these sites we can come to comprehend the ideological and aesthetic work of Hollywood, and, as importantly, that of its audiences.

Academic criticism has often sought to establish the importance of its own activity in the claimed importance of its object; that is no less true of the claim that cinema is an agent of subject positioning or a symptom of ideological constitution than it is of the claim that *Only Angels Have Wings* is a work of high moral seriousness. Much of the discomfort experienced in critical attempts to find a respectable approach to Hollywood results from the hesitation in acknowledging that although the industries of culture are of central importance to the daily life of all western and most other societies, they are not important because of any inherent profundity they may possess. On the contrary, their lack of profundity is a condition of their status as entertainment. *Only Angels Have Wings* is "about" the response to death, heroic stoicism, imperialism, racism, and contempt for femininity, but it is not profoundly about those things. It is shallowly, sentimentally, and inarticulately about them. It is about the surfaces of these themes and commonplace attitudes and assumptions about them, and it is about them on its own surface. But this does not diminish Hollywood's importance. For if we are to study a culture, then its sentiments, its commonplace attitudes, its silences, and its hesitations are a vital part of that study. A criticism that takes Hollywood seriously can look less to the discovery of profound meanings or concealed purposes in its texts, and more to the equally difficult task of articulating the silences and equivocations, the plenitudes, excesses, and banalities of their surfaces. It is there, on the surface, that we may find answers to some of the American cinema's most mysterious and important questions: what can explain the success of Hollywood's cultural imperialism, and why do people like to cry at sad movies?

Summary

- While film theory is properly concerned with the properties of cinema as a whole, criticism's primary object of investigation is the individual movie, a group of movies, or the study of particular techniques.
- Criticism plays an important role in defining the ways in which we understand the functions and meanings of Hollywood movies. Some critical approaches, such as the idea of the director as auteur, have informed the industry's own assumptions about the nature of its business.

- The review is an evaluative form of consumer criticism in which an opinion is offered about whether a movie is worth paying to see. Review discourse accepts Hollywood on its own terms, implicitly endorsing its production system, and is often hostile to other kinds of criticism. It may be seen as supporting the motion picture industry, and as part of its publicity machine, making judgments according to criteria established by the industry, such as "entertainment value."

- Different kinds of theoretical approaches ask different kinds of questions about movies. Early film theorists consciously sought to elevate movies to the level of Art, so that they could be evaluated according to conventional critical principles. By contrast, between the 1930s and the 1960s aesthetic approaches were characterized by a preoccupation with realism. Sociological and psychological studies examined the sociology of moviegoing and Hollywood itself, and asked what the cinema could reveal about the habits and obsessions of the societies in which it existed. Much of this work was highly critical of what it saw as the damaging effect of Hollywood on American society.

- Auteurism privileges the "authorship" of a movie as an individual artistic achievement, and largely dismisses the material circumstances of a movie's production and consumption. Despite its limitations, auteurism was crucial to the elevation of cinema to academic respectability, and it persists as an organizing principle in such arenas as museum and festival programming, university courses, and book publishing. Within the industry, the auteur became a marketing strategy during the 1970s.

- The wide range of theoretical discourses brought to bear on the Hollywood cinema in the 1960s and 1970s may be grouped as broadly structuralist in orientation, because they sought to identify the wider structures within which particular movies were produced and against which they were "read." Structuralism directed intellectual attention to the organizing principles underlying human behavior, institutions, and texts, and was influential in revising notions of authorship.

- Part of the pleasure of movies lies in their apparent lack of an authorial voice, which makes it possible for their consumers to value them for whatever they care to take from them. Viewed in this way, movies are infinitely open texts, showcases of endless incidental pleasures which encourage rather than repress consumer choice. Poststructuralist criticism enacts this consumer choice in its selection of aspects of the movies for analysis and its proposal that *everything* within a movie is potentially meaningful.

- As cinema criticism has moved away from its initial need to justify its own existence by discovering unrecognized "artists," it has become possible to recognize the existence of Hollywood as a mode of production. Film studies departments can now operate within the academy by studying Hollywood and its production as a culture industry and as a system of representation, without having to defend its reputation as Art.

- A criticism that takes Hollywood seriously should aim not so much to discover profound meanings or concealed purposes in its movies as to explore the ambiguities, contradictions, silences, and equivocations on their surfaces, and consider how these features express aspects of the culture to which the movies belong.

Further Reading

Reviews and publicity

The rating system that *Halliwell's Film and Video Guide 2000* (Leslie Halliwell, ed. John Walker, 15th edn (London: HarperCollins, 1999), p. vii) uses for classifying movies is typical of the unstructured evaluation found in most reviewing:

> Four stars indicate a film outstanding in many ways, a milestone in cinema history, remarkable for acting, direction, writing, photography or some other aspect of technique. Three stars indicate a very high standard of professional excellence or high historical interest. Or, if you like, three strong reasons for admiring it. Two stars indicate a good level of competence and a generally entertaining film. One star indicates a film not very satisfactory as a whole; it could be a failed giant or a second feature with a few interesting ideas among the dross. No stars at all indicates a totally routine production or worse; such films may be watchable but they are at least equally missable.

A number of magazines and websites combine industry news and gossip with reviewing: *Premiere* and *Empire* magazines; Ain't It Cool News (www.aintitcoolnews.com). Outlets nominally aimed at the industry, such as *James Ulmer's Hollywood Hot List: The Complete Guide to Star Ranking* (New York: St Martin's Press, 2000), provide soundbite-sized digests of Hollywood's public self-presentation.

Early criticism and theory

There are several anthologies of contemporary criticism of Classical Hollywood: Alistair Cooke, ed., *Garbo and the Night Watchmen*, 1st pub. 1937 (London: Secker and Warburg, 1971); Stanley Kauffmann, ed., *American Film Criticism from the Beginnings to Citizen Kane* (New York: Liveright, 1972); Stanley Hochman, ed., *From Quasimodo to*

Scarlett O'Hara: A National Board of Review Anthology, 1920–1940 (New York: Ungar, 1982); Herbert Kline, ed., *New Theatre and Film, 1934–1937* (New York: Harcourt Brace Jovanovich, 1985). Collections of the writings of individual critics include James Agee, *Agee on Film* (New York: Beacon, 1958); Manny Farber, *Negative Space: Manny Farber on the Movies* (London: Studio Vista, 1971); Harry Alan Potamkin, *The Compound Cinema*, ed. Lewis Jacobs (New York: Teachers College Press, 1977).

Two recent histories of American movie criticism are Greg Taylor, *Artists in the Audience: Cults, Camp, and American Film Criticism* (Princeton, NJ: Princeton University Press, 1999), and Raymond J. Haberski, Jr, *"It's Only a Movie": Films and Critics in American Culture* (Lexington: University Press of Kentucky, 2001). See also Edward Murray, *Nine American Film Critics: A Study of Theory and Practice* (New York: Ungar, 1975).

Significant works of early film theory concerned primarily with Hollywood include Vachel Lindsay, *The Art of the Moving Picture*, 1st pub. 1915 (New York: Liveright, 1970); Hugo Münsterberg, *The Photoplay: A Psychological Study*, 1st pub. 1916, reprint (New York: Dover, 1970); Gilbert Seldes, *The Seven Lively Arts* (New York: Sagamore Press, 1924); Rudolf Arnheim, *Film as Art* (Berkeley, CA: University of California Press, 1957); Rudolf Arnheim, *Film Essays and Criticism*, trans. Brenda Benthien (Madison: University of Wisconsin Press, 1997).

Dudley Andrew, *The Major Film Theories: An Introduction* (New York: Oxford University Press, 1976), remains the best concise introduction to the field.

Sociology and censorship

One of the most perceptive of the early sociological investigations of American cinema is Jane Addams, *The Spirit of Youth and the City Streets* (New York: Macmillan, 1909). Extracts of this and other early expressions of this concern are reprinted in *The Movies in Our Midst: Documents in the Cultural History of Film in America*, ed. Gerald Mast (Chicago: University of Chicago Press, 1982). See also J. J. Phelan, *Motion Pictures as a Phase of Commercialized Amusement in Toledo, Ohio*, 1st pub. 1919, reprinted in *Film History* 13:3 (2001).

The 12 Payne Fund Studies were published in eight volumes by Macmillan in 1933. Denunciations of the studies were largely orchestrated by the Motion Picture Producers and Distributors of America (MPPDA), which sponsored the production of Raymond Moley's attack on them, *Are We Movie Made?* (New York: Macy-Masius, 1938), in 1938, and the more considered philosophical dismissal by Mortimer Adler, *Art and Prudence: A Study in Practical Philosophy* (New York: Longman, 1937). A more balanced account of the studies can be found in Shearon Lowery and Melvin L. DeFleur, *Milestones in Mass Communication Research: Media Effects* (New York: Longman, 1983). A full account of the research program is provided by Garth Jowett, Ian C. Jarvie, and Kathryn H. Fuller, *Children and the Movies: Media Influence and the Payne Fund Controversy* (Cambridge: Cambridge University Press, 1996).

For summaries of audience research, see Leo A. Handel, *Hollywood Looks at its Audience: A Report of Film Audience Research* (Urbana: University of Illinois Press, 1950); Bruce A. Austin, *Immediate Seating: A Look at Movie Audiences* (Belmont, CA: Wadsworth, 1989); Melvyn Stokes and Richard Maltby, eds, *American Movie Audiences: From the Turn of the Century to the Early Sound Era* (London: British Film Institute, 1999); Melvyn Stokes and Richard Maltby, eds, *Identifying Hollywood's Audiences: Cultural Identity and the Movies* (London: British Film Institute, 1999).

1940s psychocultural criticism

Among the writings of the 1940s aiming to interpret American culture through the movies were Geoffrey Gorer, *The Americans: A Study in National Character* (London: Cresset, 1948); David Riesman, *The Lonely Crowd: A Study of the Changing American Character* (New Haven: Yale University Press, 1950); Siegfried Kracauer, *From Caligari to Hitler: A Psychological History of the German Film* (Princeton, NJ: Princeton University Press, 1947); Barbara Deming, *Running Away from Myself: A Dream Portrait of America Drawn*

from the Films of the Forties (New York: Grossman, 1969); Martha Wolfenstein and Nathan Leites, *Movies: A Psychological Study* (Glencoe, IL: Free Press, 1950); Parker Tyler, *The Hollywood Hallucination* (New York: Simon and Schuster, 1944); Parker Tyler, *Magic and Myth of the Movies* (New York: Simon and Schuster, 1947); Bernard Rosenberg and David Manning White, eds, *Mass Culture: The Popular Arts in America* (New York: Free Press, 1957); Theodor Adorno and Max Horkheimer, *Dialectic of Enlightenment* (London: Verso, 1979). For a general discussion of the relationship of this literature to the movies, see Richard Maltby, "Film Noir: The Politics of the Maladjusted Text," *Journal of American Studies* 18:1 (1984), pp. 49–71.

Auteurism

Key expressions of auteurism as a critical principle include Andrew Sarris, "Toward a Theory of Film History," in his *The American Cinema: Directors and Directions, 1929–1968* (New York: Dutton, 1968); essays by the New Wave critics collected in *Cahiers du Cinéma: The 1950s*, ed. Jim Hillier (Cambridge: Cambridge University Press, 1986); John Caughie, ed., *Theories of Authorship* (London: British Film Institute, 1981); Peter Wollen, *Signs and Meaning in the Cinema*, 1st pub. 1968, revised edn (London: Secker and Warburg, 1972).

Recent overviews of auteurism are James Naremore, "Authorship and the Cultural Politics of Film Criticism," *Film Quarterly* 44:1 (Fall 1990), pp. 14–23; Stephen Crofts, "Authorship and Hollywood," in *The Oxford Guide to Film Studies*, eds John Hill and Pamela Church Gibson (Oxford: Oxford University Press, 1998), pp. 310–24; James Naremore, "Authorship," in *A Companion to Film Theory*, eds Toby Miller and Robert Stam (Malden, MA: Blackwell, 1999), pp. 9–24; Timothy Corrigan, "Auteurs and the New Hollywood," in *The New American Cinema*, ed. Jon Lewis (Durham, NC: Duke University Press, 1998), pp. 38–63. For a taxonomic examination of the possible bases for claims for authorship in mainstream Hollywood, see Berys Gaut, "Film Authorship and Collaboration," in *Film Theory and Philosophy*, eds Richard Allen and Murray Smith (Oxford: Oxford University Press, 1997), pp. 149–72.

The conscious marketing of Hitchcock's persona is the subject of Robert E. Kapsis, *Hitchcock: The*

Making of a Reputation (Chicago: University of Chicago Press, 1992). Recent major biographies of significant figures in Classical Hollywood include Joseph McBride, *Frank Capra: The Catastrophe of Success* (London: Faber, 1992), and Bernard Eisenschitz, *Nicholas Ray: An American Journey*, trans. Tom Milne (London: Faber, 1993). Tom Gunning, *The Films of Fritz Lang: Allegories of Vision and Modernity* (London: British Film Institute, 2000), is an eloquent demonstration of the critical strength of auteur studies.

On Hawks, see Jim Hillier and Peter Wollen, eds, *Howard Hawks: American Artist* (London: British Film Institute, 1996); Robin Wood, *Howard Hawks*, 2nd edn (London: British Film Institute, 1981); Gerald Mast, *Howard Hawks, Storyteller* (New York: Oxford University Press, 1982); Joseph McBride, ed., *Focus on Howard Hawks* (Englewood Cliffs, NJ: Prentice-Hall, 1972); Todd McCarthy, *Howard Hawks: The Grey Fox of Hollywood* (New York: Grove Press, 1997).

CHAPTER EIGHTEEN
Theories

We should countenance as film theory any line of inquiry dedicated to producing generalizations pertaining to, or general explanations of, filmic phenomena, or devoted to isolating, tracking, and/or accounting for any
mechanisms, devices, patterns and regularities in the field of cinema. . . .
this inquiry may transpire at many different levels of generality and abstraction and may take as its objects things as different as cutting practices and
industrial contexts.

Nöel Carroll[1]

Analysis tends to find what it is looking for.
Robert Stam[2]

Entering the Academy

A dedication to legitimising and professionalising cinema and its study . . .
involves the processes of academicisation of knowledge.

Toby Miller[3]

As an activity distinct from criticism, film theory is a generalizing practice concerned with the basic signifying procedures and underlying conventions of cinema,
which at its broadest would seek to account for the aesthetic, psychological, and
social dimensions of cinema. The history of attempts to theorize cinema since 1960
has been of a steady diminution of scale, from the ambitious prospectus of a single

Grand Theory that would simultaneously explain the language, apparatus, and reception of cinema to far more modest, localized approaches to particular aspects of "the whole equation of pictures."

Before 1960, theories of cinema sought to achieve a comprehensive understanding of what Dudley Andrew has called the "cinematic capability."[4] Their aim was to identify cinema as a field of aesthetic experience, and to consider it as a system of hierarchically related questions which their theory would then address. In 1963, Jean Mitry published *Ésthétique et Psychologie du Cinéma*, in which he described encyclopedically the questions that had preoccupied film theory since its inception, and outlined the major positions taken on those questions.[5] Reviewing Mitry's book, Christian Metz argued that it could be seen as the culmination of a first phase of film theory, and that a second, less idealist, and more scientific phase, more limited but more precise in its investigations, should now begin. This second phase of theory, to which Metz's own work was foundational, has been a garden of forking paths, in which critics have pursued some lines of inquiry and ignored other routes, which may still wait to be explored. This chapter seeks to trace the main current of academic theorization of cinema since the mid-1960s, and considers why particular directions were taken. The explanation is as often a matter of context as of the power of an argument, and the prevailing context for the efflorescence of film theory has been its entry into the academy as a discipline in universities in Europe, the United States, and elsewhere.

The growth of universities after 1960 provided opportunities for the broadening and loosening of the academic curriculum, allowing for the introduction of new fields of study, particularly in the humanities. Cinema was an obvious candidate, once a way was found to overcome the critical disdain in which it was held. Film theory was instrumental in legitimating the academic study of cinema through its insistence on the intellectual complexity of its own activity (rather than, necessarily, the intellectual complexity of the objects about which it theorized). The struggle to legitimate cinema studies as an academic activity was a real one, contested in curriculum and appointment committees in universities across the world, and formed part – often a leading part – of a more general interdisciplinary revision of humanities programs. For radical scholars in the 1960s and 1970s, cinema study provided an opportunity to introduce subjects that challenged the conventional curriculum in both their content and their method: cinema presented "an open set of texts where new theories appeared even newer, and where there were as yet no traditional ways of dealing with the subject."[6] Studying cinema was popular among the expanding student population of the 1970s and 1980s. Film theory made cinema studies sufficiently complex and difficult to justify it as an academic activity in the humanities, by providing the means by which movies could be analyzed as texts according to the protocols of the usual institutional landlords, departments of literature. Initially, at least, theory also distanced academic cinema studies from any concern with the economic and industrial issues that have framed much of this book's consideration of Hollywood.

Within the academy, cinema studies has been a radical presence, challenging established canons of value and taste. Much of its radical energy came from its firm occupation of ground on the political left, and its alliance with other emergent areas of academic work in women's studies, gay, lesbian, ethnic, and cultural studies. At the same time, the development of an obscure and difficult theoretical explanation for the operation of entertainment itself represented a retreat from the political confrontations of the late 1960s into a much safer academic radicalism. The film theory of the 1970s and 1980s was grandly pessimistic, as if cinema had to bear the burden for the defeats and failed promises of the 1960s. In one perverse sense, cinema studies was the beneficiary of the hostile political climate of the 1980s. Its popularity as a field of undergraduate study ensured its continued existence in the skewed market economies of universities in President Reagan's America and Thatcher's Britain.

The cultural radicalism that film theory's heady mix of Marx, Freud, and Hollywood undoubtedly carried in 1969 gradually became institutionalized and diffused as the broader political climate grew less tolerant under the conservative regimes of the 1980s. The political energies of film theory were transferred to other forms of oppositional activity, most importantly to the politics of identity as the triad of race, gender, and sexuality replaced Marxism's singular emphasis on class as the determinant of social conflict. They were also internalized: inside the academy, as Henry Louis Gates Jr observed in 1989, literary and cultural studies could turn the analysis of texts

> into a marionette theater of the political, to which we bring all the passions of our real world commitments. . . . Academic critics write essays, "readings" of literature, where the bad guys (you know, racism or patriarchy) lose, where the forces of oppression are subverted by the boundless powers of irony and allegory that no prison can contain, and we glow with hard-won triumph. We pay homage to the marginalized and demonized, and it feels as if we've righted an actual injustice.[7]

As cinema studies turned inward, like other academic subjects, it also turned to internal acrimony over its direction. Its formative radicalism was still visible in the disputants' accusation that their opponents represented a mainstream orthodoxy that they were challenging, but perhaps the overly heated exchanges in which film theorists indulged in the 1990s were signs that the disputants at least felt sufficiently secure of their place in the academy to devote their energies to disagreeing with each other.

Structuralism and Semiology

Everything is present in film: hence the obviousness of film, and hence also its opacity. . . . A film is difficult to explain because it is easy to understand.
Christian Metz[8]

The body of work we know as "film theory" emerged from the interaction of three intellectual traditions in France in the 1960s: structuralism, Marxism, and psychoanalysis. The enthusiasms of auteurism had provided a platform for the more evidently and unapologetically academic project of understanding cinema from within the analytical framework of one or more of these intellectual traditions, which between them seemed to provide the most relevant context for that understanding. Each of the three traditions was itself the site of innovative and empowering theoretical work in the 1960s, and together they offered a way to re-examine and challenge conventional explanations of a wide range of social and cultural phenomena at a moment of European cultural crisis.

The aftermath of World War II and the postwar process of decolonization occasioned a period of profound uncertainty and self-doubt among European intellectuals, leading them to question the master narratives of social, scientific, and cultural progress that had justified European imperialism in the name of civilization. This loss of faith was encapsulated in Theodor Adorno's aphorism that "to write poetry after Auschwitz is barbaric."[9] As an intellectual force, structuralism arose from Claude Lévi-Strauss's rejection of the hierarchy of civilizations inherent in biological models of anthropology (see chapter 17). Instead, he turned to the structural linguistics initially developed by Ferdinand de Saussure in the early twentieth century, applying Saussure's principles of analysis to his own examination of myth. Lévi-Strauss activated the "science of signs" that Saussure had outlined as a conceptual possibility in his *Course in General Linguistics*:

A science that studies the life of signs within society is conceivable; it would be a part of social psychology and consequently of general psychology; I shall call it *semiology* (from Greek *semeion* "sign"). Semiology would show what constitutes signs, what laws govern them. Since the science does not yet exist, no one can say what it would be; but it has a right to existence, a place staked out in advance. Linguistics is only a part of the general science of semiology; the laws discovered by semiology will be applicable to linguistics, and the latter will circumscribe a well-defined area within the mass of anthropological facts.[10]

Saussure's work provided the foundation for the study of language as a system, but the rigorous study of non-verbal sign systems that he proposed remained dormant for the first half of the twentieth century. At approximately the same time as Saussure, the American philosopher Charles Sanders Peirce developed a "speculative grammar" of signs, which he called semiotics. In keeping with the European domination of theoretical work in the humanities, Saussure's work proved far more influential than Peirce's.[11] The *Course in General Linguistics* (published posthumously in 1915) was first translated into English in 1959, and the influence of semiology on film theory and criticism began to be strongly felt in the late 1960s, through the influence of the French writers Roland Barthes and Christian Metz. Together with Italian theorist Umberto Eco, Barthes played a leading role in the promotion of semiology as a method for analyzing the production of meaning in culture, communication, and behavior. Barthes's own work varied between comparatively playful analyses of advertisements, striptease, and "The World of Wrestling," and dense pieces of theoretical writing, such as his essay "Myth Today."[12] Like Eco, Barthes wrote about cinema, but it was not a major focus of his work. Barthes's impact on film studies was more indirect, through his proposition of a theoretical method that looked for meaning in the underlying structures of a text and for the traces of these structures in the signs or symbols on its surface.

For a period in the 1960s and 1970s, semiology appeared to offer the basis for a science of culture, a means of analyzing cultural and symbolic systems with the precision that structural linguistics had brought to the study of language. For cinema, it promised a structuralist methodology potentially able to take account of cinema's complex orchestration of verbal and non-verbal signals. In the work of Christian Metz, semiology began to formalize attention to the expressive systems of cinema, such as mise-en-scène, performance, and soundtrack. Unlike Barthes's and Eco's, Metz's writings were almost exclusively concerned with cinema, and particularly with the cinema as a "specific signifying practice." Rather than simply invoking the commonly used metaphor of "the language of cinema," Metz set out to explore systematically the proposition that cinema operated like a language, with its own equivalent of syntactical rules and structures. His early work, presented in *Film Language*, proposed a typology of the different ways in which time and space could be organized through editing. His "Grand Syntagmatique," with its eight principal categories and further subdivisions, encountered much detailed criticism, however, and has since been largely discarded. Metz nevertheless exercised a substantial influence over the direction that the critical study of cinema has subsequently taken, through the proposition that a movie should be understood as a "textual system," a matrix of codes and conventional structures.

Cine-semiology failed to deliver on its most grandiose promises because its fundamental proposition, that cinema is constituted like a language, proved unusable. Saussure's essential insight into the arbitrary relationship between signifier and signified in language did not apply to cinema's analogical system of representation, and cine-semiology consequently displaced its inquiry onto the study of some aspect of cinema, usually narrative, rather than its basic procedures. As a discipline in itself, cine-semiology studied the devices of cinematic communication rather than technology, industrial organization, or audience response. Inevitably, however, the critics and theorists who employed the terminology of semiology (code, system, message, text, structure) sought to connect the two fields. In the late 1960s, when the new theoretical insights derived from semiology and the structuralist approach interacted with the energetic political radicalism of the New Left, these tools were deployed in the ideological analysis of cinematic texts and of the apparatus of cinema. That analysis combined an understanding of ideology derived from the work of French Marxist philosopher Louis Althusser with a semiology increasingly influenced by the linguistically informed psychoanalytic theories of Jacques Lacan. It understood cinema to be an ideological apparatus that constructed "the spectator" as the subject of its totalizing system.[13]

Cinema, Ideology, Apparatus

> When films are texts rather than movies they become worthy of the same
> serious attention normally given to literature.
> Robert Stam[14]

The events of 1968 – the political uprisings in France in May, the Soviet invasion of Czechoslovakia in August, the outbreak of political violence in Northern Ireland, the assassinations of Martin Luther King and Robert Kennedy, and the ongoing protests against the Vietnam war – provided a powerful impetus for the political analysis of culture and cultural forms. At the end of his essay "The Work of Art in the Age of Mechanical Production," Walter Benjamin had condemned Fascism's aestheticization of politics and called for the politicization of art (see chapter 2). After 1968, this call was primarily understood by film theorists as requiring an examination of cinema as a "quasi-autonomous realm of political struggle": the aim was to make and analyze cinema politically, rather than to make or analyze a cinema of overt political content.[15] The most influential call for such a politically oriented criticism, "Cinema/Ideology/Criticism" by Jean-Louis Comolli and Jean Narboni, appeared originally as an editorial in *Cahiers du Cinéma* in October 1969. Comolli and Narboni argued for a criticism explicitly grounded in Louis Althusser's concept of ideology as the expression of the imaginary relation of individuals to the real conditions of their existence, a conception that recognized the ideological in cinema at every level from style to content to technology itself (Althusser's concept of ideology is discussed in chapter 9).[16]

Comolli and Narboni argued that previous theories of cinema that had emphasized its realism were "eminently reactionary." The "reality" that the camera supposedly recorded, they proposed, "is nothing but an expression of the prevailing ideology. . . . What the camera in fact records is the vague, unformulated, untheorized, unthought-out world of the dominant ideology . . . reproducing things not as they really are but as they appear when refracted through the ideology."[17] Cinema, they suggested, "is one of the languages through which the world communicates itself with itself," and as a result "the film is ideology presenting itself to itself, talking to itself, learning about itself." From this they concluded that as a sub-set of the ideology it endorses, cinema has its own ideology in "the cinema's so-called 'depiction of reality,'" which was present in "every stage in the process of production: subjects, 'styles,' forms, meanings, narrative traditions; all underline the general ideological discourse." The purpose of their article was to establish a system of categories by which critics could distinguish between movies that "allow the ideology a free, unhampered passage," and those that "attempt to make it turn back, intercept it and make it visible by revealing its mechanisms."[18]

Their system of classification involved first a distinction between fiction and "live cinema" (documentary), and then within each of these a distinction between form and content. These well-established critical distinctions provided them with four categories of fiction film:

(a) The vast majority of films, whose form and content both carry and endorse the dominant ideology unthinkingly.

(b) A small number of films which attempt to subvert the dominant ideology through both their content and formal strategies that breach the conventions of "realist" cinema.

(c) Movies whose content is not explicitly political, but whose formal radicalism renders them subversive.

(d) The reverse of category (c): movies whose explicitly political content is contained within the realm of dominant ideology by their conventional form.

Comolli and Narboni expressed their aesthetic and political preferences when they declared that movies in categories (b) and (c) "constitute the essential in cinema," and should be the chief subject of critical work. This preference for formal experimentation in the name of ideological subversion was one that much of the criticism that called itself film theory pursued for the next decade and more. The canon of politically "progressive" work established by that criticism included little of Hollywood.

The most innovative and influential part of Comolli and Narboni's argument, however, entirely cut across the structure of the schema they advanced, and established at least some space for considering Hollywood. They created a fifth category that was logically incompatible with the other four. It comprised

(e) films which seem at first sight to belong firmly within the ideology and to be completely under its sway, but which turn out to be so only in an ambiguous manner. . . . The films we are talking about throw up obstacles in the way of the ideology, causing it to swerve and get off course.

Movies in this category expressed the ambiguities and contradictions of the dominant ideology: "An internal criticism is taking place which cracks the film apart at the seams. If one reads the film obliquely, looking for symptoms; if one looks beyond its apparent formal coherence, one can see that it is riddled with cracks."[19]

This category contradicted the framework established by the remainder of the article, but it was a crucial move in establishing a basis for ideological criticism. It redirected critical attention away from a concern with the internal unity of a work toward a set of analytical procedures that could examine a text for symptoms of the ideology it carried. This shift from "work" to "text" – the title of a highly influential Roland Barthes essay – installed the critic as an agent in the production of meaning. While Barthes defined a "work" as a finished product with a single, pre-ordained authorial meaning, the "text" was "a multi-dimensional space in which a variety of writings, none of them original, blend and clash"; while the "work" was an object of passive consumption, "the Text is experienced only in an activity of production," as if it were a musical score performed by the act of critical reading.[20] The "death of the author" enhanced the authority of the critic, who was no longer limited to the mere task of explication. Instead, the critic's task was to interrogate the text. In a pun perhaps more telling than its author recognized, Barthes observed that "nowadays, only the critic executes the work."[21] As Dudley Andrew observed, in the film theory emerging from these propositions

Meaning, significance, and value are never thought to be discovered, intuited, or otherwise attained naturally. Everything results from a mechanics of work: the work of ideology, the work of the psyche, the work of a certain language designed to bring psyche and society into coincidence, and the work of technology enabling that language to so operate.[22]

In relation to Hollywood in particular, the critic's labor to produce meaning contrasted with the movies' own effacement of the work involved in their production. Applying Barthes's propositions, Comolli and Narboni argued that when the critic applied the right investigative methodology from the right perspective to a category (e) movie, "The ideology . . . becomes subordinate to the text. It no longer has an independent existence: it is *presented* by the film. This is the case in many Hollywood films for example, which while being completely integrated in the system and the ideology end up by partially dismantling the system from within."[23] In many respects the raison d'être for this category was a rationalization of pleasure, in that it provided the means for recuperating Hollywood movies of apparent ideological disrepute: as Richard Dyer suggested, part of the initial appeal of psychoanalysis "lay in its promise to explain why socialists and feminists liked things they thought they ought not to."[24] More substantially, the approach that Comolli and Narboni argued for opened up possibilities for ideological analyses of Hollywood, and was in many respects highly productive. Analyses of *Young Mr Lincoln* (1939) and *Morocco* (1930) by the editors of *Cahiers* provided a model that remained extremely influential in the textual analysis of individual movies and in the articulation of film theory for well over a decade. The critic assumed the role of diagnostician, examining not so much the text's sign system as its symptoms, the evidence of its ideological condition. The aim of this diagnosis was to make texts "say what they have to say *within* what they leave unsaid, to reveal their constituent lacks . . . [and their] *structuring absences . . .* the unsaid included in the said and necessary to its constitution."[25] The medical metaphor for interpretation already indicated the influence of psychoanalysis on film theory; the obligation to analyze cinema ideologically was the motivating force behind the development of psychoanalytic and feminist film theory in the 1970s.

In addition to "symptomatic readings" investigating the ideological functioning of a range of Hollywood "texts," Comolli and Narboni's proposition that cinema possessed its own ideology of realism led film theorists to argue that that bourgeois ideology was built into the cinematic apparatus itself. Concerned with the wider "use-value" of film theory, critics following Comolli and Narboni's call drew on both Althusser's structuralist Marxism and Jacques Lacan's revision of Freud to provide a political momentum to cinema study and a social dimension to the work of criticism. The ideological operation of a movie had to be examined not only at the level of *representation* (how does a given movie construct a version of the "real"?) but also at the level of *affect* (how does a particular movie engage our psychic lives, and whose interests does that engagement serve?). From Althusser, critics such as Stephen Heath took the argument that "ideological state apparatuses," such as the church and the education system, addressed individuals as "subjects." Althusser's argument interwove the legal, grammatical, and psychological meanings of the word "subject." The grammatical subject ("I") was free, "a centre of initiatives, author of and responsible for its actions." The legal subject, however, was "a subjected being, who submits to a higher authority, and is therefore stripped of all freedom except that of freely accepting his submission." The apparatuses of ideology, Althusser suggested, addressed legal subjects as if they were grammatical subjects, leading them to misconstrue their subjection as freedom.[26] The "viewing subject" constituted by the cinematic apparatus was understood to be equally misinformed about his or her position.

Jean-Louis Baudry initially defined the "apparatus" of cinema as a network formed by the relation between the projector, the screen, and the spectator, and later expanded this definition to incorporate the spectator's metapsychology. **Apparatus theory** engaged and shifted debates about realism, since it credited the **cinematic apparatus** with delivering an impression of reality so charged as to be more than real, an effect Baudry described as the "fantasmatization of objective reality."[27] The cinema's impression of reality, according to Baudry, was so powerful that it immersed the spectator in its illusory representation, giving the spectator"

the illusion of being omniscient and omnipresent. The delusions of grandeur of the spectator mirrored those of the "free" subject of bourgeois society. The code of perspective, furthermore, produced the illusion of its own absence; it "innocently" denied its status as representation and passed off the image as if it were actually the world.[28]

Baudry emphasized some of the same circumstances of viewing as Thomas Elsaesser raised in his discussion of cinematic narrative: the spectator's motor inhibition, for instance (see chapter 16). Unlike Elsaesser, however, Baudry compared the movie screen to the "dream screen," the blank background on which, according to some psychoanalysts, dreams seem to be projected. Baudry suggested that cinema, like the dream, was an expression of a nostalgic desire to return to earlier stages of psychosexual development, redefining popular understandings of the movies providing "wish-fulfillment" as a form of psychological regression.[29]

The engulfing, "womblike" sensation of cinema's "reality-effect" restaged childlike experiences of unrestraint and libidinous expression, and the "real" that cinema's impression of reality addressed was understood as defined by unconscious rather than conscious mental activity. Metaphors of "projection" favored by the discourse of psychoanalysis helped to secure the analogies involved, and a long history of popular association between cinema and dream lent these ideas considerable persuasive force. The analogy between dream and viewing was crucial to the application of psychoanalysis to cinema. On the strength of this analogy, the rhetorical power of psychoanalysis was appropriated by film study as if it had the authority of an established science.

Psychoanalysis and Cinema

The critic is responsible to a degree for articulating those voices dominated, displaced, or silenced by the textuality of texts . . . finding and exposing things that may otherwise be hidden beneath piety, heedlessness, or routine.

Edward Said[30]

The construction of a psychoanalytically-based paradigm for understanding the ideological functioning of Hollywood movies was both intellectually complex and controversial, and much of the subsequent history of film theory and criticism has been preoccupied with contesting or revising the psychoanalytic inheritance. Providing film scholars with a common medium of discourse for much of the 1970s, psychoanalytic approaches fragmented and proliferated through the 1980s, in part as a consequence of the insights that they themselves provided into the complex and multivalent character of movie–audience relations. General propositions about how the study of cinema appropriated psychoanalysis are difficult to formulate, as different theorists drew on the work of differing clinical authorities, particularly Freud and Lacan, and gave attention to cinema at a variety of different levels. As its borrowings from Marxism and semiology engaged with its preoccupation with the workings of the unconscious mind, however, **cine-psychoanalysis** slowly coalesced around versions of apparatus theory and the practice of symptomatic criticism. Its concerns extended the agendas of semiology, and it has often been identified as a "second-phase" semiology, concerned with the "subject-effects" produced by the cinematic apparatus rather than with film language or structure. Its preoccupation with issues of gender and sexuality also created new questions and whole new critical sub-industries.[31] By the early 1990s, "psychoanalytic film theory" and "contemporary film theory" had became more or less synonymous terms.

Psychoanalysis was understood primarily as a cultural theory, and at the heart of cine-psychoanalysis there remained an insistence that movie analysis should be a politically sensitive activity that could contribute to a transformation of wider social relations. Their appeal to psychoanalysis ensured that "the political" would be redefined in more personal terms, however. The concern with the affective dimension of the movies led cine-psychoanalysis in search of analogies for the experience of moviegoing in dream, daydream, fantasy, and other kinds of psychic phenomena. Cine-psychoanalysis sought to attach these analogies to a theory of ideology in order to explain how we experience ourselves as subjects in cinema. Closely linked to this concern was an analysis of pleasure, a remarkably neglected area in the study of Hollywood given that its provision remains a central function of entertainment.

Followers of Lacan argued that the usefulness of psychoanalysis as an explanation of culture stemmed from Lacan's emphasis on the mediations of language in the unconscious. The persistence of psychoanalytic interpretations of culture for much of the twentieth century suggests, however, that its attraction may have more to do with what a psychoanalytic framework allows critics to do, rather than what it explains. Freud's concept of the unconscious as a repository of deeper meaning concealed by the processes of repression has been perhaps the most powerful influence on artistic theory and practice since 1900. Many of the earliest applications of psychoanalysis to critical study were hopelessly literal, often directed at the psychobiography of the author, but the idea that dreams contain unconscious material susceptible to expression only in symbolic form constituted an immensely powerful new critical procedure when it was applied to artistic production. The promotional publicity for a 1991 book on *Hitchcock and Homosexuality*, for example, claimed that it used "orthodox psychoanalysis" to offer insights to "anyone wanting to learn how to arrive at hidden meanings in films."[32]

Cine-psychoanalysis stated its claims in more oblique and elaborate language than this, but its practitioners regarded it as a powerful instrument for diagnosing a movie. Lacan's reformulation of Freud in linguistic terms provided the means by which critics could generalize the unconscious beyond the site of the individual. This led to the idea that analysis could reveal a text's unconscious, examining the repressed material that surfaced in the details of its narrative, form, or style. Not only could a text be interpreted as a symptom of its author's, its characters', or its culture's condition, but the concern of psychoanalysis with repressed meaning granted critics a license to examine texts as much for what they displaced, condensed, or censored as for what they said. Storylines could be considered in terms of their Oedipal trajectories, or characters construed as "patients" driven by unconscious motivations and drives. In a final move, the supposed "author" of a movie could be redefined as a point of "enunciation," from which the process of cinematic fantasy and desire emanates. Just as psychoanalysis could disinter the latent structural content of a dream from the confusing manifest content of the dream's surface narrative content, cine-psychoanalysis could interpret recurrent plot motifs or stylistic traits as symptoms of deep-seated anxiety and neurosis made manifest unknowingly in the organization of movie aesthetics.[33]

Work on the "apparatus" as dream-state lead readily to a consideration of textual style or technique as analogous to the processes by which the dreamer produces unconscious fantasy. To cine-psychoanalysts, montage and editing seemed akin to Freud's description of the dream-work processes of displacement and condensation, through which unconscious desire is transformed into the manifest content of the dream. For Christian Metz, the spectator's recognition of this "externalization" accounts for much of the joy of moviegoing: "The spectator, during the projection, puts himself into a state of lessened alertness (he is at a show; nothing can happen to him); in performing the social act of 'going to the cinema,' he is motivated in advance to lower his ego defenses a notch and not to reject what he would reject elsewhere."[34]

Cine-psychoanalysis understood aspects of mise-en-scène and point of view as "eroticized" elements, representing and playing upon their viewers' "scopophilic" desire, and triggering fantasies of gratifying engagement with the movie and its protagonists. In a much-quoted passage from his essay "The Imaginary Signifier," Metz proposed that the cinematic institution is not just the cinema industry (which works to fill cinemas, not to empty them), it is also the mental machinery – another industry – which spectators "accustomed to the cinema" have internalized historically and which has adapted them to the consumption of films. The institution is outside us and inside us, indistinctly collective and intimate, sociological and psychoanalytic.[35]

Cine-psychoanalysis promised to make an enduring contribution to the understandings of Hollywood's ideological operations by exploring the relationship between the "economies of desire" set in play by a movie and the capitalist economy that financed it. In practice, however, psychoanalytic criticism took little interest in the industrial conditions under which cinema was produced and consumed.

The Spectator

The psychoanalytic conception of the cinema spectator is the matrix from which all other descriptions in the field flow. But this is a very particular kind of viewer . . . psychoanalytic film theory discusses film spectatorship in terms of the circulation of desire. . . . [It] sees the viewer not as a person, a flesh-and-blood individual, but as an artificial construct, produced and activated by the cinematic apparatus.

Sandy Flitterman-Lewis[36]

The most enduring contribution of cine-psychoanalysis to movie criticism was its formulation of a theory of film spectatorship. Christian Metz had moved on from his work in early semiotics to examine the relationship between cinematic signs and their spectators, concluding that audiences acquire the competences necessary for understanding movies not only from their exposure to convention over a period of time, but also because they recognize structures they already "know" from their own psychosexual pasts in the apparatus of cinema. Invoking the psychoanalysis of Jacques Lacan's "mirror stage," Metz theorized that cinema engages us by recalling decisive moments in our development as subjects. For Lacan, the "mirror stage" was a crucial element in childhood development, in which the child acquires its sense of autonomous identity when it encounters its own mirror image and identifies with its reflection. Like the mirror, the cinema screen confers a sense of perceptual mastery on its spectator, but according to Metz that sense of mastery is based on a misapprehension, as the spectator falsely identifies with the cinematic apparatus.[37]

The figure of the spectator is central to cine-psychoanalysis, but this spectator bears little resemblance to the audience studied by sociologists or market researchers, or to the viewer proposed by Formalist theory, who consciously constructs hypotheses about narrative development. The spectator of psychoanalytic film theory is not a person, but a conceptual "space." Like a seat in the movie theater, this subject position is "empty," in the sense that anyone can occupy it.

Just as every seat in a well-designed movie theater will provide a comparably clear view of the screen, so the experience of each spectator is identical, since the subject position that is "the spectator" is constructed by the cinematic apparatus. Subjected to a movie, the empty space of the spectator becomes "productive" as the spectator identifies both with the act of looking and with the apparatus that stages the spectacle. Metz constructed an elaborate diagram of a movie's projection to propose that cinema constructs the spectator as an apparently unified subject:

> There are two cones in the auditorium: one ending on the screen and starting both in the projection box and in the spectator's vision insofar as it is projective, and one starting from the screen and "deposited" in the spectator's perception insofar as it is introjective (on the retina, a second screen). When I say that "I see" the film, I mean thereby a unique mixture of two contrary currents: the film is what I receive, and it is also what I release, since it does not pre-exist my entering the auditorium and I only need close my eyes to suppress it. Releasing it, I am the projector, receiving it, I am the screen; in both these figures together, I am the camera, which points and yet which records.[38]

Metz's spatial representation of spectator–movie relations as mutually productive suggested that the ideological importance of this structure lies in cinema's resecuring the viewer's self-hood while mystifying its own role in the process. Hollywood's cinematic apparatus simultaneously proffers us attractive illusions of ourselves as unified and autonomous identities and positions us as its ideological subjects. By masking its own point of enunciation as the spectator's point of access to the fiction, the movie deludes us into imagining that its discourse is in fact our own. Metz therefore saw the viewer's "primary" identification in cinema as being not with the characters in a movie, but with "the (invisible) seeing agency which *puts forward* the story and shows it to us": that is, with the movie itself as a discourse. "Insofar as it abolishes all traces of the subject of enunciation, the traditional film succeeds in giving the spectator the impression that he is himself that subject, but in a state of emptiness and absence, of pure visual capacity."[39]

This may all seem very remote from this book's discussions of moviegoing, consumption, and the economic logics of the Hollywood movies. At least for non-believers, cine-psychoanalysis constructs a complex and highly indirect theoretical edifice on the basis of a suggestive but also questionable analogy between viewing and dreaming. Seldom does it attempt to justify its project: that is, to explain why we should psychoanalyze cinema. Its critics argue that its reasoning by analogy becomes hermetically self-fulfilling, in the sense that the cinema it constructs can be understood only in the terms proposed by its analogy to the dream.[40] Arguing that psychoanalytic theory was originally intended "to conceptualize irrational behavior," Nöel Carroll questions why it should be deployed to explain behavior, like attending and understanding movies, that could equally be explained by "conscious or merely tacit intentions, beliefs, and reasonings."[41] Richard Allen suggests that it has often been arbitrary in its blending of incompatible psychoanalytic concepts, and has too frequently "made sweeping empirical claims on wholly metaphysical grounds."[42] Whatever else cine-psychoanalysis has achieved, however, it has helped to illustrate the profound difficulties involved in accounting for the taken-for-granted pleasures that are inherent in moviegoing. The enduring importance of psychoanalytic investigations into cinema lies not in their conclusions about its psychic "regime" (is movie-watching akin to voyeurism?) or the unconscious preoccupations of this or that practitioner (is Alfred Hitchcock a sadist or a misogynist?), but rather in the example they offer of a symptomatic criticism making the assumption that surface meanings can only be understood as indicators of deeper realities waiting to be uncovered by the discerning analyst.

Despite its aspirations to deal with questions of spectatorship, cine-psychoanalysis ultimately operated as a text-centered theory. Work on the "apparatus," film style, or subject positioning rarely left space for an account of the actual, socialized subject who might take up what Daniel Dayan called the "empty spot predefined" by the address of a movie.[43] Nor did cine-psychoanalysis consider the status of the spectator as part of a wider viewing collective such as an audience. Analogies between cinema and dream led Christian Metz to define the cinema experience as "privatized," despite the evidence that many different forms of cinema event – cult cinema, for instance – involve a sharing of experience between audience members. Finally, cine-psychoanalysis seldom recognized any historical dimension to questions of spectatorship, and very few analysts were prepared to suggest how the psychic structures invoked by Baudry, Metz, and others might have changed over time. Rather, in an echo of André Bazin's formulation of movie history as a continuing struggle for an ever-fuller effect of the real (see chapter 8), Metz saw movies as satisfying a transhistorical desire for contact and presence, with moving pictures as only one example of a far longer line of projection apparatuses that stretched back to ancient times.

The origins of cine-psychoanalysis within the New Left of the late 1960s ensured that the deeper reality it uncovered would be understood politically as the operation of a dominant ideology, in which mainstream cultural forms such as cinema were seen to operate in the service of ruling interests, to mystify its consumers and inhibit the consciousness-raising that could lead to liberation. To established theories of ideological subordination, psychoanalysis contributed an account of how this process might be made pleasurable, and how subjects might be relied upon to cooperate with their own containment. While insisting on the primacy of ideological struggle, cine-psychoanalysis sought to identify the operation of ideology at the most basic levels of cinema, and thus reiterated the disempowerment of the moviegoer that its account of cinema described. Jean-Louis Baudry's location of the operation of ideology in the very mechanics of film projection leaves little space for political contradiction within cinema. The concept of the spectator as predetermined by the ideological operations of the cinematic apparatus, and constituted at the level of unconscious fantasy, also proposes an extreme account of cinema as a manipulative practice.

Whatever else it signified, writing of this kind was indicative of a profound political paranoia, far in excess of any governing the protective politics of the Hollywood film industry. Albeit supported by a very much more sophisticated methodology, cine-psychoanalysis's account of what cinema did to its spectators resembled nothing so much as the conspiratorial fantasies of the HUAC investigators in 1947. Rather than the "eight or ten Harvard law degrees" that Jack Warner had suggested (see chapter 9), you now needed years of theoretical study to find out what the "innuendoes and double meanings" meant. In part the very "unprovability" of the theses of cine-psychoanalysis (how could one test an assertion about the operation of the cinematic unconscious empirically?) could only serve to feed this paranoia. Despite, or perhaps because of, the depth of its paranoid assumptions, a psychoanalytically grounded model of cinema provided the dominant framework within which academic criticism approached Hollywood in the dozen years between the mid-1970s and the mid-1980s. Because these years saw the consolidation of film studies as an academic discipline, cine-psychoanalysis has been a determining influence on the priorities that the discipline has established for itself. Film studies has often led other humanities subjects in its adoption of theory, to the extent that in many academic settings, the study of cinema has been justified because of the theory that has underpinned it rather than through any claims about the intrinsic value of the movies themselves. At the same time, many of the fundamental assumptions of "Grand Theory's" attempts to explain cinema as a total phenomenon have become subject to increasing question. More recent moves in the history of movie criticism suggest that cine-psychoanalysis may, in the long run, prove to have been important mostly for what it has provoked.

With its concern for issues of desire, gratification, and sublimation, psychoanalysis offered one starting point for an understanding of pleasure in western culture. It could pose some very basic questions about why people go to the movies, and how that event is organized to maximize enjoyment. With its attention to gender relations, psychoanalysis could provide insights into the differing pleasures of masculine and feminine subjects. In the context of wider struggles around sexual liberation, feminism, and gay politics in the early 1970s, cine-psychoanalysts appropriated this body of theory to formulate understandings of the differing viewing pleasures of male and female moviegoers.

Feminist Theory

> Ultimately, the meaning of woman is sexual difference . . . the woman as icon, displayed for the gaze and enjoyment of men, the active controllers of the look, always threatens to evoke the anxiety it originally signified . . . Going far beyond highlighting a woman's to-be-looked-at-ness, cinema builds the way she is to be looked at into the spectacle itself. . . . cinematic codes create a gaze, a world, and an object, thereby producing an illusion cut to the measure of desire.
>
> Laura Mulvey[44]

Perhaps the most significant work to develop from Comolli and Narboni's proposition was a body of feminist criticism that suggested that within mainstream cinema the gaze of the camera, and the position of the spectator, were inherently masculine. The most influential contribution to this argument was Laura Mulvey's 1975 article "Visual Pleasure and Narrative Cinema," in which she appropriated the psychoanalytic approach of apparatus theory "as a political weapon," to demonstrate "the way the unconscious of patriarchal society has structured film form."[45] Mulvey's article, which may well be the single most widely anthologized essay in film theory, triggered an avalanche of theoretical writing addressing questions of gendered spectatorship and the relations of patriarchal power "inscribed" in the movie text.

One important aspect of Hollywood's "magic," Mulvey argued, was its "skilled and satisfying manipulation of visual pleasure." Hollywood "coded the erotic into the language of the dominant patriarchal order," so that an active male spectator gazed at a passive female object. Mulvey proposed that the cinematic pleasure in looking was gendered: within the cinematic fiction, "woman is posited as image, man as bearer of the look." Although the spectacle of femininity appears at first to disrupt the narrative, "the split between spectacle and narrative supports the man's role as the active one forwarding the story, making things happen." In addition, a movie's male protagonist "emerges as the representative of power in a further sense: as the bearer of the look of the spectator," deploying it to neutralize and contain the disruptive spectacle represented by the woman. This containment takes the form either of a narrative sadism, in which the woman is investigated and either punished or saved (film noir, for example), or of fetishism, in which the glamorized image of the woman (Marlene Dietrich in *Morocco*) is presented as a "perfect product," in "direct erotic rapport with the spectator."[46] By orchestrating the "three looks" of spectator, camera, and character, the cinematic apparatus naturalized a masculine gaze in the service of patriarchal ideology, leaving the female spectator without a gaze of her own.

Mulvey's analysis relied on a body of psychoanalytic speculation whose relevance to cinema was only asserted. It also depended on the claim that a link could be made by analogy between the look of some (but not all) characters in the fiction and the look of the spectator (all spectators) in the movie theater. This link allowed her to support an account of the spectator's subject position with evidence drawn from the plots of movies. Despite these logical weaknesses, Mulvey's article provided the foundation for feminist film theory's discussion of both Hollywood's representation of gender, and alternatives to it. The article itself called for the destruction of visual pleasure, "a total negation of the ease and plenitude of the narrative fiction film," and much energy was subsequently devoted to debates about how an alternative feminist film practice might represent the female body differently.[47] Feminist analysis nevertheless also returned repeatedly to the principal site of ideological contestation, to reconsider the limitations on both female expression and the female viewer proposed by Mulvey's original formulation. If patriarchal ideology was structured into the apparatus of mainstream cinema so that the female spectator had no choice but "to identify either with Marilyn Monroe or with the man behind hitting the back of my seat with his knees," then a feminist analysis was bound to place all Hollywood movies in the unredeemable category (a).[48] Avenues of critical exploration that looked for signs of "female enunciation" in the work of the few women directors in Hollywood (particularly

Dorothy Arzner, the only woman working regularly as a major studio director in the 1930s) were at odds with the theoretical claim that the apparatus of cinema constructed subject positions. As Mary Ann Doane argued, however, that theoretical position compounded the patriarchal repression of the feminine that it described, since it traced "another way in which the woman is inscribed as absent, lacking, a gap, both on the level of cinematic representation and on the level of its theorization."[49]

The solution to this theoretical impasse, for feminist criticism as well as for other politically committed ideological analyses of Hollywood, was the extension of the symptomatic criticism that Comolli and Narboni proposed for their category (e). "Reading against the grain" of a Classical Hollywood movie became a widely adopted and productive strategy for textual analysis. As with category (e), movies could be examined for their gaps and fissures, in which the workings of ideology were exposed. In this kind of interpretation, declared the editors of a 1984 collection of feminist essays, "the critic is less concerned with the truth or falsity of the image of woman than with gaining an understanding of the textual contradictions that are symptomatic of the repression of women in patriarchal culture."[50] The idea of "the contradictory text" proved enormously fruitful in developing the ideological analysis of Hollywood. Contemporary feminist analyses continue to acknowledge Mulvey's formulations for providing a significant insight into the inscription of femininity in Hollywood movies, but they also present a more nuanced, less monolithic case. Despite the structuring presence of patriarchy, women's discourses are seen to permeate such "contradictory" Hollywood texts as *Pretty Woman* (1990) and *The Little Mermaid* (1989), so that the real concerns of women are expressed in fragmented or "subtextual" ways. Susan White suggests that contemporary feminist criticism sees "most cultural products as a complex weave of oppression, rebellion, play with existing structure, recuperation, and transformation."[51]

Poststructuralism and Cultural Studies

What permits the endless variety of meanings to be generated from a film are in large part the critical practices themselves . . . The ambiguity sought by the New Critic, the polysemy praised by the structuralist, and the indeterminacy posited by the post-structuralist are largely the product of the institution's interpretive habits.

David Bordwell[52]

Attempts to deal with the frustrating "unprovability" of cine-psychoanalysis became evident from the early 1980s. As structuralist models seemed to reach points of exhaustion, a host of new "poststructural" methods began to make inroads into the critical edifice of cine-psychoanalysis, most importantly through a rejection of the totalizing claim that the spectator was determined by the apparatus and the text. Feminist criticism led the way in arguing for a range of ideological positions from which a suitably equipped spectator could read against the grain to produce a "subversive reading."

Poststructuralism can best be understood as a reaction to structuralism's attempts to establish broad, incorporative theoretical procedures. Rather than being a theory in itself, poststructuralism proposed a mode of inquiry concerned with what had been left out of, or repressed by, structuralism's totalizing systems. It argued for a "decentering" of the attention paid to the structures of a text, and a deconstruction of textual meaning. Although poststructuralism involved a rejection of the structuralist claim to scientific status, it also evolved out of structuralism's concerns and shared several of its fundamental assumptions. Cine-psychoanalysis was itself in part a poststructuralist theory. Jacques Lacan is usually considered a poststructuralist, and the concerns of cine-psychoanalysis with repressed meaning and with the fissures of a text were typically poststructuralist preoccupations. The origins of cine-psychoanalysis in apparatus theory, however, indicate its attachment to structuralist Grand Theory. Overall, cine-psychoanalysis demonstrates the difficulty of establishing categorical distinctions between structuralism and its successors. Rejecting the claim to science allowed poststructuralist critics to abandon the requirement to prove theoretical precepts. Rather, they came to rely on different bodies of assumptions held within a number of distinct critical communities. In imitation of other established disciplines, distinct "schools" of critical thought, with increasingly diverse interests, emerged in film studies.

The pattern of development charted by feminist film theory shared many features with other analyses of Hollywood's ideology. The idea that it was possible to "read" Hollywood movies for their ideological subtexts and structuring absences, to make them say "not only what this says but what it doesn't say because it doesn't want to say it,"[53] amounted to what David Bordwell has called a "search warrant" for the investigation of repressed meanings.[54] "Reading obliquely" or "against the grain" offered the possibility of discovering the textual fissures of a category (e) movie; the argument that such textual analysis revealed the movie's "unconscious" meant that the analysis neither expected nor required external corroboration from, for instance, the movie's producers. It also justified the psychoanalytic metaphors that often structured this critical approach. In the article that served as a prototype for these investigations, the editors of *Cahiers du Cinéma* asserted that *Young Mr Lincoln* operated under a "double repression – politics and eroticism."[55] These two preoccupations remained dominant in subsequent analyses of Hollywood. Where politically committed auteurist criticism had been under an obligation to discover the overtly radical in a director's work (an obligation it often found difficult to meet), the ideological criticism of category (e) movies could identify unconscious "rebel" texts within the Hollywood empire. For example, Charles Eckert's analysis of *Marked Woman* (1937), a gangster melodrama about prostitution in New York, contended persuasively that the movie is "rooted in class conflict." Its class oppositions are, however, displaced onto a number of surrogate conflicts: the characters' ethical dilemmas, and the regional oppositions of city and country. The "muddled logic" with which these are expressed reflects "a struggle between desires to articulate and to repress class conflicts. . . . There are, in addition, tonal overlays (toughness, sentimentality) which cover the film like a skin, masking the real and substitute conflicts alike, and enticing the audience into solipsism and false emotion."[56]

Analyses such as Eckert's demonstrated the extent to which ideological criticism could reassess a movie's cultural function. More often, however, textual analysis sought to identify "progressive" or "subversive" features in individual Hollywood movies or in genres, with the implicit intention of redeeming the text in question, at least as an object of study. Critics paid particular attention to groups of movies deemed to be in some sense marginal to Classical Hollywood – film noir, women's films, family melodrama, exploitation and B-movies – giving rise to what Barbara Klinger has identified as the "progressive genre." The distinguishing features of these movies, she suggests, are a pessimistic world view, a thematic demolition of the values attached to such social institutions as the law and the family, a narrative structure that exposes contradictions rather than represses them, and a tendency to stylistic self-consciousness and formal excess.[57] Claims for the existence of "progressive genres" made clear that the abiding legacy film criticism inherited from Comolli and Narboni was the opposition between category (a) and category (e) movies. As Klinger argues, the critical investment in designating and elucidating progressive genres required a fixed conception of classical narrative – the "classic realist text" discussed in chapter 15 – against which it could define progressive practice and identify "the inventions and departures of the progressive text."[58] Most of these analyses emphasized the formal or stylistic differences of the progressive text, to the extent that specific formal features – "expressionist" lighting, a "refusal" of narrative closure – were understood as embodying the progressive position. Such arguments tended to validate formal and stylistic subversion at the expense of overt ideological statement; this means of identifying subversion served the dual purpose of displaying the critic's skills in "reading" the text's repressed meanings and demonstrating the political relevance of the critic's activity.

These ideological analyses frequently exhibited a contradiction implicit in Comolli and Narboni's essay, however. On one side, dominant ideology was understood as being structured into the cinematic apparatus and the subject position of the spectator. On the other, it was possible for texts and textual strategies to subvert or expose the dominant ideology or its "unconscious." The apparent contradiction between these two positions raises the question of whether the ideology of a movie can be located in its formal structures, its content, or its interpretation. In practice it is impossible to maintain the distinctions between categories (a) and (e) other than through the purely empirical criterion of the level of skill involved in the interpretation. In the three decades since Comolli and Narboni's original formulation, deconstructive criticism has demonstrated that any text is sufficiently fissured to expose its ideological operations if read closely enough. A criticism that looks for ideology only in the text, in order to judge the movie as progressive, reactionary, or contradictory, sets itself a number of interrelated problems, however. The problem of how the critic explains his or her own apparent ability to either penetrate or evade ideological constitution is closely tied to the notion that the text is innately determining and authoritative in a way that everyone but the critic fails to perceive.

By the mid-1980s it was more appropriate to talk of film theories than Film Theory. At the same time, however, the various approaches came to share a canon of "texts" now generally acknowledged to be central to the field of film studies. Through the canon, different methodologies communicate about (rather than with) each other; and the role of the canon is to permit this common body of cross-reference. Yet the poststructuralist Balkanization of the short-lived empire of Grand Theory has produced a situation in which canonic texts proliferate interpretations and accommodate multiple meanings that are, if not exactly mutually unintelligible, certainly under no obligation to speak to each other. As Deborah Linderman writes of her account of *Vertigo* (1958): "my remarks . . . resonate both with [Robin] Wood's and [Tania] Modleski's, but although I traverse some of the same features of the text as they do, my analysis is very differently elaborated."[59] The critical capacity to discover a limitless plurality of meanings within a movie is one important element in the movie's qualification for the canon. The more it can be read and re-read to fuel critical argument, and the more it can sustain multiple but not necessarily conflicting meanings, the better. As David Bordwell's comment at the head of this section suggests, however, the source of these multiple meanings lies in the questions the critic asks and the methods by which she or he tries to answer them. In this environment the reader of criticism becomes another kind of consumer, exercising choice among a range of critical styles and conclusions.

Althusser's powerfully pessimistic conception of ideology proved too debilitating for gay, lesbian, ethnic, and other minority groups seeking to assert their cultural identities through their engagement, theoretical or otherwise, with popular culture. It was replaced by Antonio Gramsci's more dynamic concept of hegemony, which viewed the distribution of political power as never fully secure and provided space for protest or negotiation.[60] Michel Foucault's more diffuse model of power proved even more useful to the proponents of cultural studies.[61] Moving from apparatus theory's insistence on the cinema's constitution of the spectator as a viewing position, feminist criticism had demonstrated the possibility of an alternative or subversive interpretative position. Cultural studies pluralized this in Stuart Hall's concept of dominant, oppositional, and negotiated "readings" of a text, shifting the site of meaning from the text to the reading, and valorizing plural acts of interpretation.[62] As a critical practice, cultural studies extended the concept and analysis of "text" to encompass the much broader terrain of culture, which was understood as being the site where subjectivity is constructed and meaning is produced through the interactions of social institutions, texts, and spectators.

Cultural studies can be seen as a strategy to maintain film theory's ideological critique of dominant culture, while avoiding the totalizing constraints of cine-psychoanalysis's insistence on the ideological determination of the subject by the text and its apparatus. It formulated the spectator as the subject of both textual discourses and external social practices, and sought to ask questions about how social subjects actively used popular culture to participate in the formation of their own identities. Nevertheless, cultural studies followed cine-psychoanalysis in rejecting empirical audience studies based on social science models of inquiry, eventually opting for more subjective methodologies that claimed to be "ethnographic" in their approach. While cultural studies was, in the hands of its more extreme practitioners, vulnerable to the accusation that it merely celebrated consumption as a form of resistance, it also equipped previously marginalized groups with the means to declare and specify their politically productive occupation of a viewing and interpretive identity; the body of queer theory and criticism developed since 1990 is perhaps the most substantial evidence of its productivity.

Neoformalism and Cognitivism

The neoformalist critic assumes that spectators are able to think for themselves, and that criticism is simply a tool for helping them to do it better in the area of the arts, by widening the range of their viewing abilities.
Kristin Thompson[63]

In the mid-1980s, as poststructuralism questioned the grand edifice of Film Theory from within, it also came under siege from without. The obfuscations and jargon-laden language of semiotics and cine-psychoanalysis had often been attacked by journalist critics and historians, but these attacks seldom possessed any degree of theoretical sophistication and were easily dismissed. By 1985 this situation had changed, as an alternative theoretical paradigm challenged many of the fundamental assumptions of cine-psychoanalysis. The new paradigm, **neoformalism**, took its inspiration and many of its theoretical premises from the work of a group of Russian literary critics of the 1920s known as the **Formalists**. These premises were integrated with an understanding of viewing activity informed by the branches of psychology concerned with perception and cognition rather than with psychoanalysis. Like cine-psychoanalysis, neoformalism understood cinema as a system, but as an essentially rational rather than irrational one. "Contrary to psychoanalytic criticism," wrote Kristin Thompson, "I assume that film viewing is composed mostly of nonconscious, preconscious and conscious activities. Indeed we may define the viewer as a hypothetical entity who responds actively to cues within the film on the basis of automatic perceptual processes and on the basis of experience."[64]

The claims for neoformalism were argued in David Bordwell's 1985 book, *Narration in the Fiction Film*, and put into critical practice there and in *The Classical Hollywood Cinema*, co-written by Bordwell, Janet Staiger, and Kristin Thompson and also published in 1985. The first part of Thompson's 1988 book, *Breaking the Glass Armor*, provides a concise and accessible account of neoformalism's premises, and its arguments with psychoanalytical approaches.[65] I have referred frequently to the work of these scholars throughout this book's account of Hollywood, and the principal tenets of neoformalism are outlined in chapter 15. Bordwell's critique of cine-psychoanalysis, amplified by that of Nöel Carroll, has also informed the arguments earlier in this chapter. Much of my account of Hollywood concurs with a neoformalist approach, differing mainly in emphasis. Some of these differences have already surfaced: where neoformalism understands Hollywood to be primarily concerned with narrating stories, I have situated narration as one among a range of pleasures that a movie offers its audience, and not necessarily the most important. My account of the viewer as actively recognizing cues and constructing hypotheses from the movie accords with a neoformalist analysis, but the viewer I describe is more often distracted from the narrative, or perhaps more independent of a movie's linear temporal progression. These are, however, differences in emphasis rather than incompatibilities. My larger disagreements with neoformalism have to do with my pursuit of a different object of inquiry.

Neoformalism is an aesthetic theory, and as such it is concerned with the aesthetic processes of cinema, and film as an aesthetic system. My object of inquiry is in some ways narrower and in others broader. In chapter 1 I distinguished Hollywood from other cinemas on grounds that were not primarily aesthetic, but rather industrial and economic, and it is worth repeating now that this book's specific concern is with Hollywood, not with film as a medium or cinema as a formal category. At the same time, my concern to understand Hollywood as a cultural phenomenon has frequently taken my discussion outside the limits of purely aesthetic inquiry into questions of ideology and power. Neoformalism positions such questions as part of the "background" to its principal concern, which is to analyze the formal relationships within an artwork.

Neoformalism, and Bordwell's work in particular, has attracted much more vituperative criticism than this. Precisely because neoformalism provided itself with an alternative theoretical base from which to question cine-psychoanalysis, it was first of all seen as a challenge to "contemporary film theory." As cine-psychoanalysis fragmented, neoformalism was rapidly promoted into an orthodoxy less by its advocates than by some of its opponents, who preferred to see themselves dissenting from an orthodox doctrine rather than practicing one. Critiques of neoformalism have in the main focused on its self-declared limitations. In the conclusion to *Narration in the Fiction Film*, Bordwell suggests that his "partial theory of narrative in fictional cinema" makes no attempt to address "issues such as sexuality or fantasy" or to answer "broader cultural, economic, or ideological questions about the filmmaking institution."[66] Those who see neoformalism as a new orthodoxy, however, fear that its disinclination to consider such questions implies that the questions themselves are in danger of disappearing from the critical agenda. To them, neoformalism is insufficiently radical. Bill Nichols, for instance, sees in its appropriation of cognitive theory a claim to scientific accuracy and objectivity, but a claim made at the expense of any consideration of history or subjectivity in a system "that treats narrative as data or information for genderless, classless, stateless 'processors,'" rather than "gendered, historically situated subjects whose very being is at stake within the arena of history."[67] Critiques of Bordwell in *MOVIE* have similarly seen neoformalism as seeking to make criticism a scientific practice. V. F. Perkins argues forcefully that interpretation must not be understood as an attempted proof, but as "a description of aspects of the film with suggested understandings of some of the ways they are patterned." "The interesting meanings of films," he argues, are not discovered by a critical practice that extracts from them "statements which are hidden but otherwise resemble messages . . . They consist rather in attitudes, assessments, viewpoints – balances of judgment on the facts and behavior portrayed."[68]

These arguments recapitulate the debates around structuralism's claim to science in the early 1970s, and also invoke more enduring debates about the provision of a scientific or theoretical basis for work in the humanities. The claim to science – a claim that, importantly, neoformalism does not make for itself – has primarily been a rhetorical one, defining the opposite pole to that of complete critical subjectivity. Critical theories are best not considered as attempts at scientific theory, since they lack some of the essential features of such theory: they cannot, for instance, be subject to experimental disproof. A critical methodology may, however, be judged by such criteria as clarity, rigor, consistency, its use of evidence, and a knowledge of its limitations. Neoformalism's project of "a historical poetics of cinema" is not an attempt to reformulate an all-inclusive Grand Theory, precisely because of the self-imposed limitations that its antagonists have understood as its weaknesses. As Thompson describes it, it is a "modest approach," seeking only to explain the realm of the aesthetic and its relation to the world.[69] In this less intimidating form, it can readily coexist with other approaches, particularly those seeking answers to questions concerning the cultural and ideological function of cinema. As Barbara Klinger suggests, textual analysis does not necessarily have to claim that the text determines or constitutes its spectator. It can restrict its activity to describing the textual features and forces that influence a viewer's act of reception.[70]

The particular path taken by film theory since the 1960s has meant that some possible avenues of inquiry were ignored and some routes remain unexplored. Semiology, the science of signs, has not yet examined deeply the basic properties of the moving sound-image, and the history of cinematic style is a project so far principally undertaken by neoformalists, while there are few, if any signs of a rapprochement with the methodologies of social science. Neoformalism's emphasis on the spectator's conscious activity led to its engagement with cognitive psychology and analytical philosophy in what its advocates called "a stance toward film research" identified as cognitivism. According to David Bordwell and Nöel Carroll, a cognitivist analysis "seeks to explain human thought, emotion, and action by appeal to processes of mental representation, naturalistic processes, and (some sense of) rational agency."[71] While this stance has provided an opportunity to develop theoretical accounts of cinema based on psychological, philosophical, and linguistic models other than those of Freud, Marx, and Saussure, its robust critique of psychoanalytic theory has inevitably provoked an equally hostile response that its conceptual framework is "regressive" and "radically incommensurate with a politics of multiculturalism and social representation."[72]

Film theory has become much more complicated since 1960. While it no longer aims for a total theory of cinema, it instead operates under the expectation that the field requires an understanding of a range of disciplines and bodies of theoretical knowledge, and there is much disagreement about which disciplines and bodies of knowledge should be given pride of place. What is clear, however, is that the dominant theoretical paradigm with which cinema studies was installed in the academy no longer exercises the authoritative power over the terms of debate it once did, and that theorizing about cinema remains an unsettled and disputatious terrain. A belief in the prospect of "Grand Theory" is no longer sustainable.

Instead, paraphrasing the titles of some recent anthologies, the field of theoretical cinema studies is viewed as being in the process of reconstruction, refiguration, or reinvention.[73] What may emerge from this reformulation is an understanding of cinematic theory as a field of activity, occurring, as Nöel Carroll proposes, at "different levels of generality and abstraction . . . without being subsumed into a single general theory."[74] Such an outcome would, however, require the practitioners of different methodologies to acknowledge that civil conversation is more beneficial than the contentiousness that has so far marked exchanges between divergent theoretical positions.

From Reception to History

By placing a film within multifarious intertextual and historical frames – the elements that define its situation in a complex discursive and social milieu – the film's variable, even contradictory, ideological meanings come into focus. . . . the researcher uncovers different historical "truths" about a film as she/he analyses how it has been deployed within past social relations.
Barbara Klinger[75]

In reaction to the often conscious ahistoricism of poststructuralism, a renewed interest in film history has given fresh attention to neglected questions of reception, audience, and movie exhibition. Along with neoformalism, this work distanced itself from psychoanalysis by its interest in the *conscious* activities of both audience members and industry practitioners. Its dual authorities were cognitive psychology and the archival, historical record of the motion picture industry itself. Paralleling the development of New Historicism and reader-response criticism in literary studies in the 1980s, what became known as **reception studies** operated with a variety of scales of reference; from consideration of the individual reader or viewer to the group audience, defined either by particular traits of their subjectivity such as race or gender, or by a shared historical setting. Most of this work acknowledged a debt to neoformalism's confident break with psychoanalysis, and also made use of the insights of cognitive psychology.

In her account of the "return" of the reader to the agenda of literary criticism, Elizabeth Freund explains that aesthetic reception theory assumes that perception involves an act of interpretation, and that the idea of the "text-in-itself" is an empty one, because a poem or a movie cannot be understood in isolation from the act of its interpretation.[76] Reader-response criticism had its foundations in the branch of philosophy called phenomenology, which concerns itself with the relationship between a perceiving individual and the world that might be perceived. Phenomenology understands this relationship not as one between "two separate realms connected only by the passive sensory mechanisms of the individual," but rather as "inextricably linked aspects of the process by which we know anything."[77] Phenomenology describes that process as one of "intention," a concept which refers to the conscious direction of sense-making faculties toward the surrounding world.

The subject exercises intention and makes sense of the world in perceiving, and is committed to "consistency building" and the fabrication of rational explanation. The movies, argued phenomenologist Maurice Merleau-Ponty, "are particularly suited to make manifest the union of mind and body, mind and the world, and the expression of one in the other."[78] A study in the aesthetics of reception might therefore be a matter of studying the ways in which a movie stimulates and regulates an "intending" viewer.

These issues have been implicit in most of my discussions of individual movies in this book. In the Hollywood movie, "intention" is largely stimulated by the creation of quite deliberate lacks in the viewer's knowledge, opening gaps or "indeterminacies" for the viewer to fill by constructing hypotheses about the presence of latent relationships and meanings. The account of controlled indeterminacy in *Casablanca* (1942) in chapter 16 would be an instance of this at work. Studies in the aesthetic reception of Hollywood seek to establish the systematic bases on which indeterminacy might be structured to produce viewer participation. In *The Role of the Reader*, Umberto Eco stresses that a reader's experience of conventions enables him or her to resolve indeterminacies with some confidence. As a result, the author "has to foresee a model of the possible reader (hereafter Model Reader) supposedly able to deal interpretively with the expressions in the same way as the author deals generatively with them."[79] Similarly, in deciding how a storyline should be plotted, a movie's producers can and do presume a level of competence on the part of their audience. This stress on the active participation of the conscious subject places aesthetic reception studies in stark contrast to psychoanalytically based models which see the "constitution" of the viewer as the basic effect of a text or the cinematic apparatus itself.

Identifying a pattern of indeterminacy is one thing, but not all viewers exhibit "model" characteristics or share the same levels of competence. Interpretations are, therefore, always acts of negotiation on the part of the viewer. When the possibility of generalizing "interpretive strategies" to cover shared response to literary texts began to be considered by Stanley Fish and others, it soon became clear that this work could be applied to the role of audiences in the overall system of Hollywood cinema.[80] Among others, Janet Staiger has used historical studies of reception to reconstruct a movie as an *event*, rather than to identify its meaning as an object. For Staiger, the event to be analyzed is "a set of interpretations or affective experiences produced by individuals from an encounter with a text or set of texts within a social situation." Her work seeks to delineate the boundaries – or what Hans Robert Jauss terms the "horizons" – within which a movie has been interpreted. "It is not an analysis of the text except in so far as to consider what textually might be facilitating the reading."[81] At this level the basic questions being asked are those of relativity (what were the range of interpretations?), constraint (what governed the limits to interpretation?), and appropriateness (at what points did interpretation shade into something resembling a misreading?). Far from narrowing or distilling a movie's meaning, this critical activity recognizes its capacity to generate a spectrum of interpretations. It is, indeed, prepared to appropriate whatever methods of poststructuralist and ideological textual analysis best suit its immediate project, on the understanding that "the connections and difference among the frameworks and perspectives must be theorized."[82] Typically, historical reception studies examines the relationships between a movie and the contexts of its reception: publicity, censorship, exhibition practice and reviews:"Such contextual analysis hopes to reveal the intimate impact of discursive and social situations on cinematic meaning, while elaborating the particularities of cinema's existence under different historical regimes."[83]

As an example, Staiger has charted the shifting reception of *The Birth of a Nation* (1915) across its always controversial re-exhibitions. Her account shows how its reception in the late 1930s contrasted sharply with the response to its initial release, and suggests reasons for that shift in interpretation. Controversy originally centered on its racist depiction of African-Americans, with charges of its potentially provocative effects being countered by its producers in terms of its technical expertise, historical accuracy, and balance. In the late 1930s, however, Communist party journalist David Platt argued that the movie was part of a Hollywood conspiracy to divide African-Americans and white Americans against their shared class interests. In its defense, liberal critic Seymour Stern invoked contemporary historical events to support an allegorical reading blind to the race issue. "By paralleling northern carpetbagger politics to fascist totalitarianism and, eventually, to Stalinism, Stern made *The Birth of a Nation* express liberal, democratic values."[84] Staiger traces the movie's subsequent critical history, in which it became a counter in aesthetic debates about whether subject matter and narrational procedures could be separated, and political arguments about the desirability of limits to free speech. She concludes that the contexts of pre-war isolationism and postwar anti-Communism framed responses to *The Birth of a Nation* which remain as extratextual "encrustations" to be negotiated by present-day viewers of the movie. Rather than exhausting the meaning of the movie, this accumulation of response expands the boundaries of the textuality to which the critic must now respond:

> Historicizing the reception of *The Birth of a Nation* transforms the text's polysemy, for the political foundation underlying some of the historical debates becomes more apparent. In the film's later reception, racial attitudes are not autonomous effects; they relate to the political agendas of the debaters, causing strange alliances in which a former progressive defends the film using much of the rhetoric and the arguments of 1915 radical conservatives.[85]

One of the paradoxes of reception studies is that despite their refocusing critical attention from the text to the viewer, they nevertheless operate with a model of the text as their generative point of reference. Most studies of reception turn around "case studies."[86] As literary theorist Terry Eagleton comments, "For an interpretation to be an interpretation of *this* text and not of some other, it must in some sense be logically constrained by the text itself. The work, in other words, exercises a degree of determinacy over readers' responses to it, otherwise criticism would seem to fall into total anarchy."[87] But the sense of textuality at work in reception studies is a revised one. A movie is seen not as a set of structures but as a network of incentives awaiting activation through the response of competent moviegoers reading particular cues against the background knowledge that provides the conditions for the movie's intelligibility. The concern of historical reception studies may then be summarized as the desire to detail the probable sense-making practices of viewers confronted by the network of cues and triggers composing the movie in projection. Such histories do not, as Barbara Klinger notes, tell us how individual spectators reacted, since such responses have seldom been recorded. Instead, they may provide "a sense of what the historical prospects were for viewing at a given time by illuminating the meanings made available within that moment."[88]

In their various guises, reception studies are largely differentiated by the degree of determinacy they are willing to recognize in the text, and indeed by their degree of willingness to accept some independent existence of the text beyond particular interpretations or "concretizations" of it. Anxiety around the potentially infinitely "open" text has taken different forms since the mid-1980s. On the one hand neo-formalist criticism has sought to identify the objective, irreducible features of the textual schemata, in an attempt to restore the solidity of the text in the face of reader power. On the other hand, the new historiography has increasingly turned away from texts to a consideration of their discursive and material contexts, looking at "the instabilities of the historical moment, its assembly of conflicting voices," attempting "to depict the many ideological interests that intersect with a film during its public circulation and to engage as fully as possible the range of its social meanings within its historical moment."[89]

The desire to account for the experience of movie audiences has increasingly drawn movie analysis away from the totalizing theories of Metz and Mulvey toward a plurality of methods with less grandiose ambitions. It has also led to work on smaller-scale and more local accounts of moviegoing. Robert Allen and Douglas Gomery begin their study of movie historiography with a refusal of "superhistory," an account that "could be written if only this or that 'correct' perspective were taken and all the 'facts' of film history uncovered . . . this is a futile task, since the domain of 'all the facts' is infinite."[90] Nöel Carroll calls for a similar shift at the level of theory, calling for "theorizing that is 'piece-meal' and 'bottom up' . . . with no presumption that these small-scale theories will add up to one big picture."[91] Carroll and Bordwell have identified this more modest theoretical trend as producing "local theories" through "middle-level research," which "asks questions that have both empirical and theoretical import."[92] Carroll's call to avoid the "extravagant ambiguity and vacuous abstraction" of semiotic and psychoanalytic theory is echoed in Robert Stam's suggestion that "semiotics has become diasporic, scattered and dispersed among a plurality of movements."[93] Theory is now, Stam suggests, "a little less grand, a little more pragmatic, a little less ethnocentric, masculinist, and heterosexist, and a little less inclined toward overarching system, drawing on a plurality of theoretical paradigms."[94]

It is, however, a sustained commitment to the historical study of Hollywood cinema through its empirical traces that seems likely to provide the most effective restraint on the wilder excesses of poststructuralist invention. A glance through any recent historical account of Hollywood will quickly indicate a commitment to archival research, factual accuracy, and verifiable evidence that was utterly absent from the largely anecdotal and personal histories of earlier periods. As if in flagrant refutation of the "unprovability" of symptomatic criticism, the accumulation of "hard evidence" usually now precedes even the most tentative assertion of historical interpretation.[95] Instead of attempting to understand movies in terms of psychic/transhistorical dreams and wishes, the new historiography aims to chart Hollywood in relation to rather more material and contingent desires, finding form and expression in concrete institutional circumstances.

As you will be aware, this book is not itself a work of theory, but not surprisingly, it ends by describing the theoretical position which most closely reflects its concerns. My principal aim has been to argue that Hollywood cinema must be understood through the specific historical conditions of its circulation as a commercial commodity. From this central proposition, I have suggested that critics of Hollywood must engage with its commercial aesthetic, and I have illustrated the various ways in which this perspective differs from those of a number of positions usually understood as theoretical. My position is not, however, exclusive; since I argue that Hollywood produces movies for multiple forms of consumption, I would contradict myself if it were. Movies are, in my understanding of them, promiscuously available to be appropriated by their viewers, for whatever purpose – even including theoretical discourse – gives them pleasure. The relatively short history of film theory has witnessed an increasing recognition of the movies' malleability. The totalizing, determinist theories of the 1970s do now seem hopelessly misplaced, while a conversation among critics, theorists, and historians has also led away from the wilder excesses of cultural studies' celebration of consumption. Consumption, however, remains the process to be analyzed; above all, movies are products for consumption. Their polyvalence, their indeterminancy, their malleability, their capacity to absorb interpretation unscathed, are properties of their commodity status, and it is through a thoroughgoing acknowledgement of their commercial existence, not a denial of it, that their complexity can be most fully examined.

Summary

- The body of work we know as "film theory" emerged from the interaction of three intellectual traditions – structuralism, Marxism, and psychoanalysis – in France in the 1960s. The development of film theory was instrumental in legitimating the academic study of cinema through its insistence on the intellectual complexity of its own activity.
- Semiology promised a structuralist methodology potentially able to take account of cinema's complex orchestration of verbal and non-verbal signals. Cine-semiology failed to deliver on its most grandiose promises because its fundamental proposition, that cinema is constituted like a language, proved

unusable. Nevertheless, the proposition that a movie should be understood as a "textual system," a matrix of codes and conventional structures, substantially influenced the subsequent direction of the critical study of cinema.

- After the events of 1968, there was a call for politically oriented criticism, seeking evidence of a text's ideological underpinnings. Ideological analysis encouraged viewers and critics to read "obliquely" or symptomatically. Such ideological analysis provided the motivating force behind the development of psychoanalytic and feminist film theory of the 1970s.

- Psychoanalytic theory was applied to cinema as a development from the idea that viewing could be considered analogous to dreaming. This led to the proposition that analysis could reveal a movie's unconscious by uncovering the repressed material that surfaced in the details of its narrative, form, or style.

- From psychoanalysis arose a theory of film spectatorship, in which the experience of each spectator could be considered to be essentially identical, since the subject position that is "the spectator" was constructed by the cinematic apparatus.

- Feminist criticism suggested that within mainstream cinema the gaze of the camera, and the position of the spectator, were inherently masculine. By orchestrating the "three looks" of spectator, camera, and character, the cinematic apparatus adopted a masculine gaze in the service of patriarchal ideology, leaving the female spectator without a gaze of her own. Subsequent feminist theorists have suggested that women's discourses are expressed in fragmented or "subtextual" ways.

- "Reading against the grain" of a Classical Hollywood movie became a widely adopted and productive strategy for textual analysis. Movies could be examined for their gaps and ellisions, in which the workings of ideology were exposed. This approach gave theoretical support to the practice of interpreting films subversively or ironically.

- Neoformalism is an aesthetic theory informed by branches of psychology concerned with perception and cognition, rather than with the unconscious. It regards itself as a "modest approach," seeking only to explain the realm of the aesthetic and its relation to the world.

- Historical reception studies have attempted to understand movies as *events*, rather than trying to uncover their meanings as objects. This approach examines the relationships between a movie and the contexts of its reception: publicity, censorship, exhibition practice, and reviews.

- The desire to account for the experience of actual movie audiences has increasingly drawn movie analysis away from totalizing "Grand Theory" toward a plurality of methods with less grandiose ambitions.

- The principal aim of this book has been to argue that Hollywood cinema must be understood through the specific historical conditions of its circulation as a commercial commodity. Above all, movies are products for consumption, and it is through a thoroughgoing acknowledgement of their commercial existence, not a denial of it, that their complexity can be most fully examined.

Further Reading

Overviews and anthologies

Dudley Andrew, *Concepts in Film Theory* (New York: Oxford University Press, 1984), provides a concise thematic introduction to the main issues which have preoccupied film theory since the 1960s. Robert Stam, *Film Theory: An Introduction* (Malden, MA: Blackwell, 2000), is the best recent overview of the whole field of film theory from its antecedents to new media. Its companion volume, *A Companion to Film Theory*, eds Toby Miller and Robert Stam (Malden, MA: Blackwell, 1999), has a series of essays surveying the history and current state of scholarship in a range of theoretical fields, which provide useful entry-points into discussion of topics from authorship to spectatorship and cognitivism.

A more critical overview of much of the theory discussed in this chapter is provided by Nöel Carroll's *Mystifying Movies: Fads and Fallacies in Contemporary Film Theory* (New York: Columbia University Press, 1988), which declares that "the purpose of this book is to oppose that which I take to be wrong in the area of contemporary film theory" (p. 7). Carroll explains the theory he dislikes with admirable clarity, but it would be charitable to suggest that Carroll's tone toward his opponents is uncharitable. Robert Stam, Robert Burgoyne, and Sandy Flitterman-Lewis, *New Vocabularies in Film Semiotics: Structuralism, Post-Structuralism and Beyond* (London: Routledge, 1992), provides a more dispassionate treatment, but does not always overcome the intense user-unfriendliness of much film theoretical writing.

Most of the essays discussed in this chapter are included in one or more anthologies of film theory: Bill Nichols, ed., *Movies and Methods* (Berkeley, CA: University of California Press, 1976); Bill Nichols, ed., *Movies and Methods. Vol. II* (Berkeley, CA: University of California Press, 1985); John Ellis, ed., *Screen Reader 1* (London: Society for Education in Film and Television, 1977); Philip Rosen, ed., *Narrative, Apparatus, Ideology: A Film Theory Reader* (New York: Columbia University Press, 1986); Gerald Mast, Marshall Cohen, and Leo Braudy, eds, *Film Theory and Criticism: Introductory Readings* (New York: Oxford University Press, 1992); Simon During, ed., *The Cultural Studies Reader* (London: Routledge, 1993); Robert Stam and Toby Miller, eds, *Film and Theory: An Anthology* (Malden, MA: Blackwell, 2000); Joanne Hollows, Peter Hutchings, and Mark Jancovich, eds, *The Film Studies Reader* (London: Arnold, 2000).

Christine Gledhill and Linda Williams, eds, *Reinventing Film Studies* (London: Arnold, 2000), has several essays examining previous debates in film theory with the aim of identifying what might constitute "really useful knowledge" for the second century of cinema. The essays in Jim Collins, Hilary Radner, and Ava Preacher Collins, eds, *Film Theory Goes to the Movies* (New York: Routledge, 1993), apply a range of theoretical approaches to Hollywood movies of the 1980s and 1990s.

Semiology, psychoanalysis, and feminist theory

Sylvia Harvey, *May '68 and Film Culture* (London: British Film Institute, 1978), provides the best account of the relationship between radical politics and the development of film theory. The work of Roland Barthes can be sampled in two collections, *Mythologies* (London: Paladin, 1973) and *Image Music Text*, trans. Stephen Heath (London: Fontana, 1977). Christian Metz's two most influential books are *Film Language: A Semiotics of the Cinema*, trans. Michael Taylor (New York: Oxford University Press, 1974), and *The Imaginary Signifier: Psychoanalysis and the Cinema*, trans. Celia Britton, Annwyl Williams, Ben Brewster, and Alfred Guzzetti (Bloomington: Indiana University Press, 1982). More recent semiological studies are presented in Warren Buckland, ed., *The Film Spectator: From Sign to Mind* (Amsterdam: Amsterdam University Press, 1995). For sympathetic accounts of the relationship between cinema and psychoanalysis, see Janet Bergstrom, ed., *Endless Night: Cinema and Psychoanalysis, Parallel Histories* (Berkeley, CA: University of California Press, 1999). Richard Allen provides a more critical analysis in *Projecting Illusion: Film Spectatorship and the Impression of Reality* (Cambridge: Cambridge University Press, 1995).

Laura Mulvey's writings are collected in *Visual and Other Pleasures* (Bloomington: Indiana University Press, 1989) and *Fetishism and Curiosity*

(London: British Film Institute, 1996). See also Mary Ann Doane, Patricia Mellencamp, and Linda Williams, eds, *Re-Visions: Essays in Feminist Film Criticism* (Frederick, MD: University Publications of America, 1984).

Neoformalism and cognitivism

Kristin Thompson provides a concise introduction to the neoformalist approach in *Breaking the Glass Armor: Neoformalist Film Analysis* (Princeton, NJ: Princeton University Press, 1988). David Bordwell's critique of other approaches is put forward at length in *Making Meaning: Inference and Rhetoric in the Interpretation of Cinema* (Cambridge, MA: Harvard University Press, 1989). Some responses to these arguments can be found in Jane Gaines, ed., *Classical Hollywood Narrative: The Paradigm Wars* (Durham, NC: Duke University Press, 1992), and, from a different perspective, in V. F. Perkins, "Must We Say What They Mean? Film Criticism and Interpretation," *MOVIE* 34/5 (Winter 1990), pp. 1–6, and Douglas Pye, "Bordwell and Hollywood," *MOVIE* 33 (Winter 1989), pp. 46–52. Bordwell and Nöel Carroll advance their argument for "local theory" in their introductory essays in *Post-Theory: Reconstructing Film Studies*, eds David Bordwell and Nöel Carroll (Madison: University of Wisconsin Press, 1996).

For other cognitive approaches to cinema, see Murray Smith, *Engaging Characters: Fiction, Emotion, and the Cinema* (Oxford: Oxford University Press, 1995); Torben Grodal, *Moving Pictures: A New Theory of Film Genres, Feelings, and Cognition* (Oxford: Oxford University Press, 1997); Carl Plantinga and Greg M. Smith, eds, *Passionate Views: Film, Cognition, and Emotion* (Baltimore, MD: Johns Hopkins University Press, 1999); and Richard Allen and Murray Smith, eds, *Film Theory and Philosophy* (Oxford: Oxford University Press, 1997).

History and reception studies

In 1985, Robert C. Allen and Douglas Gomery's *Film History: Theory and Practice* (New York: Knopf, 1985) both summarized the then-current state of film historiography and outlined a range of potential developments. Barbara Klinger's article "Film History Terminable and Interminable: Recovering the Past in Reception Studies," *Screen* 38:2 (Summer 1997), has a useful overview of more recent developments in this field. Janet Staiger provides a clear theoretical and methodological grounding for historical studies of reception in *Interpreting Films: Studies in the Historical Reception of American Cinema* (Princeton, NJ: Princeton University Press, 1992).

Chronology

This chronology includes the release dates of American movies discussed in the text, together with other movies that were either commercially successful or significant in the history of American cinema. Information on the box-office popularity of stars comes from polls among exhibitors.

1891   Thomas Edison files a patent application on a moving picture camera (Kinetograph) and film.

1892   Edison's patents rejected.

1893   Edison copyrights the first moving pictures ~ first public demonstration of the Kinetoscope.

1894   Edison Manufacturing Company established ~ the first Kinetoscope parlors open.

1895   William K. Dickson, principal inventor of the Kinetoscope, leaves Edison and helps found the American Mutoscope Company ~ the Latham's Eidoloscope in New York, Thomas Armat's Phantascope in Atlanta and the Lumières' Cinématographe in Paris show the first public projection of moving pictures.

1896   The first public performance of the Edison Vitascope pictures ~ J. Stuart Blackton founds the Vitagraph Company of America ~ William Selig forms the Selig Polyscope Company.
Rough Sea at Dover.

1897   Edison is granted a patent for his camera and film, and begins legal actions for patent infringement against other companies ~ the Lubin Manufacturing Company is formed ~ the Eden-Musee in New York is the first exhibition venue devoted to the full-time exhibition of moving pictures.

1898 "Actualities" of the Spanish–American war are immensely popular as a pictorial news service, shown in "legitimate" and vaudeville theaters, in amusement parks and by traveling exhibitors.
The Passion Play.

1899 American Mutoscope becomes the American Mutoscope and Biograph Company (Biograph).

1900 Biograph produces some of the first multiple-shot fiction pictures, including *The Downward Path* and *A Career in Crime*, but most pictures are actualities, re-enactments, or single-shot comedies.

1901 A strike of vaudeville performers encourages the use of moving pictures in vaudeville theaters ~ many install permanent projection equipment ~ Edison brings a patent suit against Biograph.

1902 Edison loses his patent case against Biograph ~ his patents are declared invalid, but then reissued ~ the Electric Theater, Los Angeles, is the first purpose-built cinema ~ the Biograph catalog offers 2,500 titles.

1903 Legal battles over patents leave the American industry disorganized and reliant on European product.
The Great Train Robbery ~ Life of an American Fireman.

1904 Story films begin to replace actualities as the dominant form of product ~ William Fox opens his first theater in New York ~ Adolph Zukor and Mitchell H. Mark form the Automatic Vaudeville Company.

1905 As the storefront theater becomes the dominant site of exhibition, the term "nickelodeon" is coined in Pittsburgh ~ the first "Hale's Tour" opens in Kansas City ~ *Variety* is first published ~ the first film exchanges appear in Chicago.

1906 Vitagraph becomes the leading American producer, but imports from French companies Pathé and Gaumont continue to provide a large share of the American market ~ Kinemacolor is the first color photography system ~ *Humorous Phases of Funny Faces* is the first cartoon.

1907 Edison and Biograph's patents are deemed valid, and Edison initiates new lawsuits against rivals ~ the Kalem Film Company and the Essanay Film Manufacturing Company are formed, and the industry's first trade association, the United Film Protective Service Association, is established ~ Chicago enacts the first motion picture censorship ordinance ~ *Moving Picture World* begins publication ~ in response to the nickelodeon boom, a network of film exchanges now covers the US.

1908 The nickelodeon boom reaches its height ~ moving pictures are covered by copyright laws ~ Edison licenses the use of his patents to Lubin, Selig Polyscope, Vitagraph, Kalem, Essanay, and importers Méliès and Pathé, the largest supplier of pictures for the American market ~ negotiations with Biograph lead to the establishment of the Motion Picture Patents Company (MPPC), the first attempt to establish a monopoly over the industry ~ the first safety film is introduced by

Eastman Kodak ~ the Cameraphone, combining sound with pictures, plays in vaudeville.

1909 Rival production companies, including Thanhouser, Rex, and Carl Laemmle's Independent Motion Picture Company (IMP), are established to contest the MPPC's attempted monopoly ~ the industry establishes the National Board of Censorship to vet movie content ~ Chicago has 400 picture houses ~ Vitagraph begins sending out prepared music scores with its "films de luxe," and releases the first American feature film, *Les Misérables* ~ Kalem is the first production company to put actors' names on posters.

1910 The MPPC forms the General Film Company (GFC) to control national distribution ~ Laemmle establishes the Motion Picture Distributing and Sales Company (MPDSC) as a rival to the GFC ~ access to the American market becomes increasingly difficult for foreign companies ~ Marcus Loew founds Loew's Consolidated Enterprises, with Joseph and Nicholas Schenck ~ Edison demonstrates the Kinetophone, with simultaneous sound ~ D. W. Griffith takes a Biograph film crew to Los Angeles ~ Essanay, Lubin, Kalem, and Nestor also send production units there ~ every major production company except Biograph publicizes their "picture personalities," among them Florence Lawrence and King Baggot.

1911 Los Angeles becomes the second most important production center in the US, after New York ~ Nestor builds the first studio located in Hollywood ~ Selig, Pathé, Biograph, Kalem, and Essanay also build permanent studios in the Los Angeles area ~ Pennsylvania is the first state to establish a board of censorship for moving pictures ~ the first fan magazines, *Motion Picture Story Magazine* and *Photoplay*, are published ~ the Bell and Howell camera is invented ~ Pathé's Weekly is the first American newsreel ~ "picture personalities," including Florence Turner, Mary Pickford, and Francis X. Bushman, become famous.

1912 The US government brings an anti-trust suit against the MPPC and General Film, which controls about 60 percent of the US market ~ the Majestic Film Company leaves MPDSC and forms Mutual Film ~ Carl Leammle forms the Universal Film Manufacturing Company, and builds a studio in Hollywood ~ Adolph Zukor founds Famous Players and distributes *Queen Elizabeth*, starring Sarah Bernhardt ~ Mack Sennett establishes the Keystone Company ~ Edison and Keith Albee launch the American Talking Picture Company ~ the first American Kinemacolor production, *La Tosca*, is released ~ US Congress bans pictures of prizefights after Jack Johnson's 1910 defeat of Jim Jeffries makes him the first black heavyweight champion.
From the Manger to the Cross.

1913 The Jesse L. Lasky Feature Play Company is formed ~ Ohio and Kansas establish state censorship ~ 3,000 movie theaters are in operation, and larger and more elaborate movie theaters are built in many American cities ~ Warner's Features Inc. is organized, with Albert Warner as its head ~ Maurice Costello and Alice Joyce are popular stars ~ Selig releases the first serial, *The Adventures of Kathlyn*.
Judith of Bethulia ~ *Traffic in Souls.*

1914 Paramount distribution company is formed by W. W. Hodkinson to distribute multiple-reel features ~ William Fox establishes the Box Office Attractions Film Rental Company, renamed the Fox Film Corporation in 1916 ~ US Senate hearings consider federal regulation of the industry ~ Earl Williams and Clara Kimball Young are among the most popular stars ~ Pearl White stars in Pathé's serial *The Perils of Pauline*.

1915   The US Supreme Court rules Ohio state censorship is constitutional, and denies movies First Amendment protection ~ protests against the racism of *The Birth of a Nation* do not affect its huge commercial success, but the National Board of Censorship loses credibility for passing the movie ~ Universal City opens for production in Hollywood ~ the US district court finds against the MPPC in its anti-trust suit ~ Vitagraph, Lubin, Selig, and Essanay form V-L-S-E to distribute their features ~ after leaving Mutual, Harry Aitken forms Triangle with Griffith, Sennett, and Thomas Ince, in an early attempt at vertical integration ~ Metro Pictures is formed as a distribution company ~ the Technicolor Corporation is founded ~ the Los Angeles Chamber of Commerce claims 80 percent of American films are produced there ~ William S. Hart and Mabel Normand are popular stars ~ the Fox Film Corporation begins production, making "vamp" Theda Bara a star in *A Fool There Was*.
The Cheat.

1916   Famous Players merges with the Jesse L. Lasky Feature Play Company to become Famous Players-Lasky (FPL), and takes over Paramount: Zukor is president, Lasky in charge of production ~ Samuel Goldfish leaves to form Goldwyn Pictures ~ the National Association of the Motion Picture Industry (NAMPI) is formed ~ New York replaces London as the center of worldwide movie distribution after the British impose tariffs on foreign film trade ~ exports of American movies benefit from the wartime disruption of European industries, and American companies open distribution offices in Latin America, Australia, South Africa, and the Far East as well as Europe ~ average theater seating capacity is 502 seats ~ the Society of Motion Picture Engineers (SMPE) is established ~ *The Gulf Between* is the first two-strip Technicolor picture.
Intolerance.

1917   In cooperation with the government's Committee on Public Information (CPI), NAMPI organizes the industry's contribution to the war effort, through propaganda speeches in theaters and drives to sell Liberty Bonds ~ after Triangle collapses, FPL absorbs Triangle's talent and reorganizes ~ in resistance to FPL's insistence that exhibitors block-book pictures, the First National Exhibitors' Circuit is formed, and signs up Chaplin ~ Metro Pictures enters production ~ Fox's Hollywood studio opens ~ Balaban and Katz's Central Park Theater, Chicago, is the first to have air-conditioning ~ Douglas Fairbanks is the top box-office star.

1918   The War Industries Board declares motion pictures an essential industry ~ MPPC is dissolved ~ American control of the world film market has increased enormously during the war ~ Robertson-Cole Company is formed ~ FPL distributes 220 pictures ~ Mary Pickford and D. W. Griffith join First National ~ Pickford, Marguerite Clark, and Douglas Fairbanks are the most popular stars.
Old Wives for New.

1919   United Artists (UA) is formed by Douglas Fairbanks, Mary Pickford, Charlie Chaplin, and D. W. Griffith ~ there are over 2,500 US theaters with more than 1,000 seats ~ financed by Wall Street capital, Zukor begins buying theaters, establishing FPL as the first vertically integrated motion picture company ~ General

Electric establishes the Radio Corporation of America (RCA) ~ the American Society of Cinematographers (ASC) is founded ~ *Film Daily Yearbook* is first published ~ Wallace Reid is the top box-office draw.
Male and Female ~ True Heart Susie.

1920 American movies earn one third of their gross income from the foreign market ~ Loew's, Inc., acquires Metro Pictures ~ CBC Sales Company (later to become Columbia) is formed ~ Irving Thalberg becomes head of production at Universal ~ tinting is used on 80–90 percent of pictures.
The Penalty ~ Under Crimson Skies ~ Way Down East ~ Why Change Your Wife?

1921 The Federal Trade Commission begins an investigation into industry trade practices, and institutes an anti-trust suit against FPL, which now owns over 300 theaters ~ First National merges with Associated Producers to become Associated First National ~ economic recession causes a box-office slump ~ in response to campaigns for state motion picture censorship, NAMPI proposes a code of self-regulation (the Thirteen Points), but New York establishes state censorship ~ *The Four Horsemen of the Apocalypse* launches Rudolph Valentino's career, followed by *The Sheik*.
The Conquering Power ~ The Three Musketeers.

1922 The Motion Picture Producers and Distributors of America, Inc. (MPPDA), is formed to replace NAMPI as the major companies' trade association, with former postmaster-general Will H. Hays as its president ~ Massachusetts state censorship is defeated in referendum ~ in protest at Hollywood's representation of Mexicans, the government of Mexico bans American movies ~ First National builds a studio at Burbank ~ Robertson-Cole is reorganized as Film Booking Offices of America (FBO) ~ average weekly attendance is 40 million ~ 84 percent of American movie production takes place in Hollywood ~ *The Toll of the Sea* is the first feature to use subtractive Technicolor.
Blood and Sand ~ Foolish Wives ~ Orphans of the Storm ~ Robin Hood ~ Tess of the Storm Country.

1923 Warner Bros. Pictures (WB) is incorporated: Harry Warner is president, Jack Warner in charge of production ~ *The Covered Wagon* and Cecil B. deMille's *The Ten Commandments* are the year's most successful movies ~ the HOLLYWOODLAND sign is erected ~ Walt Disney releases his first cartoon, *Alice in Cartoonland* ~ Thomas Meigham is the top box-office star.
The Hunchback of Notre Dame ~ Safety Last.

1924 Through "the Formula," the MPPDA prohibits its member companies from adapting the most dangerous and censorable books and plays ~ CBC Sales Company becomes Columbia Pictures, with Harry Cohn as head of production ~ Loew's, Inc., acquires Goldwyn Pictures and establishes Metro-Goldwyn-Mayer (MGM) as its production company: Louis B. Mayer is head of studio, Irving Thalberg head of production ~ the Association of Motion Picture Producers (AMPP) is formed as the Hollywood subsidiary of MPPDA ~ Joseph Schenck reorganizes UA after D. W. Griffith leaves ~ average weekly attendance is 45 million ~ Harold Lloyd is the most popular box-office draw ~ Norma Talmadge is the highest-paid star.
Greed ~ The Iron Horse ~ Merton of the Movies ~ The Navigator ~ The Sea Hawk ~ The Thief of Bagdad.

1925 FPL becomes Paramount-Famous-Lasky, buys a controlling interest in Chicago's Balaban and Katz theater chain, and merges its theater interests into Publix Theaters ~ WB takes over Vitagraph ~ Germany imposes a quota on American movie imports ~ Samuel Goldwyn joins UA ~ Fox begins an expansion program, buying West Coast Theaters ~ WB and Western Electric begin sound movie experiments.
The Big Parade ~ The Freshman ~ The Gold Rush ~ The Phantom of the Opera.

1926 AMPP establishes the Studio Relations Committee, and the Central Casting Corporation to regulate employment of extras ~ the Studio Basic Agreement recognizes five major unions ~ Western Electric grants WB exclusive license to the Vitaphone sound process ~ WB's *Don Juan* is the first feature with soundtrack synchronized on discs, with sound effects and recorded music ~ Western Electric forms Electrical Research Products Inc. (ERPI) ~ Fox-Case Corporation is formed to develop sound newsreels ~ Columbia begins distribution ~ Joseph Schenck takes control of UA ~ Joseph Kennedy buys production and distribution company FBO ~ average weekly attendance is 50 million ~ Publix Theaters employs more musicians than any other organization in the world ~ the major companies produce 449 pictures ~ Rudolph Valentino dies.
Beau Geste ~ Ben-Hur ~ The Black Pirate ~ The Son of the Sheik ~ What Price Glory?

1927 WB's *The Jazz Singer* is the first "talkie," Fox's Movietone the first sound newsreel ~ the Federal Trade Commission orders FPL to cease block-booking, then oversees an industry-wide agreement on trade practices ~ MPPDA establishes a code of "Don'ts and Be Carefuls" covering material liable to censorship in domestic and foreign markets ~ the Department of Commerce establishes a Motion Picture Department to assist the industry's foreign distribution, on the ground that "trade follows the films" ~ in an attempt to prevent the unionization of the production industry, the Academy of Motion Picture Arts and Sciences (AMPAS) is founded to "improve the artistic quality of the film medium, provide a common forum for the various branches and crafts of the industry, [and] foster cooperation in technical research and cultural progress" ~ Marcus Loew dies, Nicholas M. Schenck becomes president of Loew's, Inc. ~ New York's Roxy Theater opens ~ Tom Mix is a top box-office draw.
Chang ~ Flesh and the Devil ~ The General ~ It ~ The King of Kings ~ The Road to Glory ~ Seventh Heaven ~ Sunrise ~ The Unknown ~ The Way of All Flesh ~ Wings.

1928 Paramount, Loew's, and UA adopt Western Electric sound system ~ RCA finances the creation of a new vertically integrated company to exploit its rival Photophone system, and merges FBO with the Keith-Albee-Orpheum theater chain to form Radio-Keith-Orpheum (RKO), with RCA's David Sarnoff as president and William LeBaron in charge of production ~ Fox attempts a take-over of Loew's, to create the largest company in the industry ~ Darryl Zanuck becomes head of production at WB, which buys Stanley Theaters ~ Britain imposes a quota on American film imports, which make up 80 percent of the features shown ~ the first Academy Awards ceremony is held ~ average weekly attendance is 65 million ~ *Lights of New York* is the first all-talking feature ~ Walt Disney releases the first cartoon featuring Mickey Mouse, *Steamboat Willie.*
The Singing Fool ~ Steamboat Bill, Jr.

1929 WB takes over First National ~ Universal buys theaters ~ Paramount acquires half of the Columbia Broadcasting System (CBS) ~ Paramount and WB negotiate a merger, to create Paramount-Vitaphone, but are prevented by threats of government anti-trust action ~ the US Justice Department brings an anti-trust suit to dismantle Fox-Loew's merger ~ $24 million is spent on refurbishing theaters for sound ~ Fox experiments with the Grandeur widescreen process ~ Mascot Pictures is established ~ MPPDA suggests that 75 percent of the audience are women ~ *International Motion Picture Almanac* is first published ~ the majors produce 393 pictures.
Broadway ~ Broadway Melody ~ Hallelujah! ~ Sunny Side Up.

1930 The MPPDA's Production Code is written, and begins to be administered by the Studio Relations Committee ~ William Fox loses control of the Fox Film Corporation ~ Paramount-Famous-Lasky becomes Paramount-Publix and extends its theater ownership ~ the Academy Research Council is created to coordinate the studios' technical research and encourage technological standardization ~ attendance reaches a peak at 80 million a week ~ Monogram Pictures is established ~ *Hollywood Reporter* begins publication ~ Paramount introduces commercials to cinemas ~ Joan Crawford is a top box-office star ~ *Anna Christie* is Greta Garbo's first sound movie.
All Quiet on the Western Front ~ The Divorcee ~ Dracula ~ Hell's Angels ~ Little Caesar ~ Min and Bill ~ Morocco.

1931 The Depression begins to affect the industry as theater attendance falls to 70 million a week ~ burdened by their debts from theater purchases, the majors institute production cutbacks ~ Fox divests itself of its shares in Loew's ~ Publix Pictures is the largest movie circuit ever, with 1,200 theaters ~ RKO completes purchase of Pathé, and David O. Selznick takes charge of RKO production ~ Universal inaugurates a horror cycle with *Dracula* and *Frankenstein* ~ double bills become increasingly common ~ the majors produce 324 pictures.
Alias the Doctor ~ Back Street ~ Cimarron ~ City Lights ~ A Connecticut Yankee in King Arthur's Court ~ The Public Enemy ~ The Smiling Lieutenant.

1932 Attendance falls to 55 million a week ~ 4,000 theaters have closed ~ Paramount cuts production budgets by 33 percent, and sells its interest in CBS ~ Jesse Lasky leaves Paramount ~ Sidney Kent leaves Paramount and becomes president of Fox ~ Fox loses $11.5 million ~ RKO opens Radio City Music Hall ~ MGM's weekly payroll is estimated at $250,000 ~ Disney's *Flowers and Trees* is the first to use three-strip Technicolor ~ top stars are Marie Dressler and Janet Gaynor.
The Champ ~ Grand Hotel ~ I Am a Fugitive from a Chain Gang ~ The Mummy ~ Scarface ~ Scarlet Dawn ~ Trouble in Paradise ~ What Price Hollywood?

1933 Worst recorded year ~ Paramount's deficit of $20 million prompts its entry into receivership ~ Universal disposes of its theaters ~ both it and RKO are in receivership, Universal until 1936, RKO until 1940 ~ Darryl Zanuck leaves WB, and forms Twentieth Century Pictures with Joseph Schenck, distributing through UA ~ Hal B. Wallis becomes WB head of production ~ the Screen Writers Guild is formed ~ the motion picture industry's National Recovery Administration (NRA) Code of Fair Competition sanctions the Big Five's distribution practices ~ Joe Breen becomes head of the Studio Relations Committee ~ the Screen Actors Guild is formed ~ Joseph Walker receives a patent for the zoom lens ~ the Payne Fund

Studies into the effects of motion pictures on youth intensify calls for federal regulation of the industry ~ the majors produce 338 pictures ~ Mae West is the top box-office attraction.

42nd Street ~ Cavalcade ~ King Kong ~ Little Women ~ She Done Him Wrong ~ State Fair.

1934 Attendance, and box-office takings, begin to recover ~ the Legion of Decency is organized by the Catholic church to protest immoral movies ~ the Studio Relations Committee is renamed the Production Code Administration (PCA) and given greater authority to enforce self-regulation in production ~ Will Rogers and Clark Gable are the most popular box-office stars ~ *It Happened One Night* is the first movie to win Academy Awards in the four major categories, and is Columbia's biggest hit to date.

The Barretts of Wimpole Street ~ Of Human Bondage ~ Imitation of Life ~ A Modern Hero ~ One Night of Love ~ Roman Scandals ~ The Thin Man.

1935 Paramount is reorganized, becoming Paramount Pictures, Inc. ~ Twentieth Century merges with Fox to become Twentieth Century-Fox (TCF), with Joseph Schenck as chairman of the board and Darryl Zanuck as head of production ~ Ernst Lubitsch briefly becomes head of production at Paramount ~ David O. Selznick leaves MGM to form Selznick International Pictures, distributing through UA ~ Time Inc. launches *The March of Time* newsreel series ~ Floyd Odlum of Atlas Corporation buys a minority interest in RKO ~ Herbert J. Yates merges Monogram and Mascot to form Republic Pictures ~ the majors produce 356 pictures ~ Shirley Temple becomes the top box-office star ~ *Becky Sharpe* is the first three-strip Technicolor feature.

Bordertown ~ The Call of the Wild ~ Captain Blood ~ Dangerous ~ G-Men ~ Lives of a Bengal Lancer ~ A Midsummer Night's Dream ~ Mutiny on the Bounty ~ Top Hat.

1936 Loew's makes a profit of $10.6 million and buys one fifth of Gaumont-British Corporation ~ Irving Thalberg dies ~ Barney Balaban becomes president of Paramount, with Zukor as chairman of the board ~ Carl Laemmle sells Universal to J. Cheever Cowdin's Standard Capital Corporation ~ W. Ray Johnston leaves Republic to reform Monogram ~ the Hollywood Anti-Nazi League is formed ~ James Cagney wins a breach of contract case against WB ~ Deanna Durbin, the economic savior of Universal, first appears in *Three Smart Girls.*

Bullets or Ballots ~ The Charge of the Light Brigade ~ Fury ~ The Green Pastures ~ Mr Deeds Goes to Town ~ Modern Times ~ My Man Godfrey ~ Rose Marie ~ San Francisco ~ The Story of Louis Pasteur.

1937 World attendance is 215 million a week ~ movies account for 75 percent of the money Americans spend on amusements ~ Nathan J. Blumberg becomes president of Universal, Cliff Work head of production ~ studio craft unions strike for recognition, and the Screen Actors Guild is recognized by studios ~ the Screen Directors Guild is formed ~ the majors produce 408 pictures ~ *Snow White and the Seven Dwarfs* is Disney's first feature-length animated movie ~ *A Family Affair* is the first of MGM's Andy Hardy pictures, starring Mickey Rooney.

Black Legion ~ Dead End ~ The Good Earth ~ The Hurricane ~ The Life of Emile Zola ~ Lost Horizon ~ Marked Woman ~ A Star is Born ~ Stella Dallas ~ They Won't Forget.

1938 The Department of Justice begins an anti-trust suit (the Paramount suit) against the eight majors ~ the Screen Writers and Screen Directors Guilds are recognized by studios ~ Y. Frank Freeman becomes head of production at Paramount ~ many smaller neighborhood theaters install air-conditioning, and sales of popcorn and candy become an increasingly important source of profit for small exhibitors ~ Shirley Temple, Clark Gable, and ice-skater Sonja Henie are the most popular stars.
The Adventures of Robin Hood ~ *Angels with Dirty Faces* ~ *Blockade* ~ *Boy Meets Girl* ~ *Boys Town* ~ *Bringing Up Baby* ~ *In Old Chicago* ~ *You Can't Take It With You*.

1939 "Hollywood's greatest year" ~ the industry employs 177,420 people, 33,687 of them in production ~ $187 million is spent on production ~ average weekly attendance is 85 million ~ the majors produce 388 pictures ~ Bette Davis becomes top female star, in *The Private Lives of Elizabeth and Essex*, *The Old Maid*, and *Dark Victory*.
Confessions of a Nazi Spy ~ *Drums Along the Mohawk* ~ *Dust Be My Destiny* ~ *Gone with the Wind* ~ *Jesse James* ~ *Juárez* ~ *Mr Smith Goes to Washington* ~ *Ninotchka* ~ *Only Angels Have Wings* ~ *The Rains Came* ~ *The Roaring Twenties* ~ *Stagecoach* ~ *The Story of Alexander Graham Bell* ~ *The Wizard of Oz* ~ *Young Mr Lincoln*.

1940 The Paramount suit is temporarily settled by a consent decree, in which the majors agree to restrict the size of the block of movies they require exhibitors to buy ~ investment in the industry exceeds $2 billion ~ the House Committee on Un-American Activities (HUAC) conducts its first brief investigation of Hollywood ~ the Producers Releasing Corporation (PRC) is established ~ *Rebecca* is director Alfred Hitchcock's first American movie, for David O. Selznick ~ Bob Hope and Bing Crosby are teamed with Dorothy Lamour in *Road to Singapore*, the first of a successful series for Paramount ~ WB's *Santa Fe Trail* and *Four Wives* are the first American pictures in stereophonic sound ~ MGM releases the first *Tom and Jerry* cartoon.
Abe Lincoln in Illinois ~ *The Blue Bird* ~ *Escape* ~ *Fantasia* ~ *The Grapes of Wrath* ~ *The Great Dictator* ~ *Kitty Foyle* ~ *The Letter* ~ *The Long Voyage Home* ~ *The Mortal Storm* ~ *Our Town* ~ *The Philadelphia Story*.

1941 US Senate hearings investigating allegations that Hollywood is producing propaganda in favor of American entry into the war are curtailed by Pearl Harbor ~ President Roosevelt declares that movies should not be subject to war censorship ~ the industry organizes a War Activities Committee ~ Spyros Skouras becomes president of TCF ~ WB buys one quarter of the Associated British Picture Corporation ~ the Conference of Studio Unions is organized after a strike at the Disney Studios ~ the majors produce 379 pictures ~ Betty Grable begins her career at TCF in *Down Argentine Way* ~ Abbott and Costello begin their series of successful comedies for Universal with *Buck Privates*.
Back Street ~ *Citizen Kane* ~ *The Great Lie* ~ *The Little Foxes* ~ *The Maltese Falcon* ~ *Meet John Doe* ~ *Sergeant York* ~ *Sullivan's Travels* ~ *A Yank in the R.A.F.*

1942 The Bureau of Motion Pictures is established as part of the government's Office of War Information (OWI), to direct the industry's representation of the war ~ one in four pictures' theme relates to the war effort ~ wartime audiences of 84 million double the previous year's profits ~ the *Why We Fight* propaganda series of documentaries begins ~ Floyd Odlum buys a controlling interest in RKO and appoints Charles M. Koerner as head of production ~ wartime taxes encourage stars and producers to set up independent production companies ~ Abbott and Costello are top box-office draws.

Casablanca ~ *For Me and My Gal* ~ *Mrs Miniver* ~ *Now Voyager* ~ *The Palm Beach Story* ~ *Yankee Doodle Dandy.*

1943 Movie theaters participate in the sale of war bonds, scrap collections, and other war work ~ Hollywood's contributions to the war effort include pro-Russian movies *Mission to Moscow, North Star,* and *Song of Russia* ~ Disney makes *Victory through Air Power* ~ Olivia de Havilland wins an important legal victory against WB over players' contracts ~ the majors produce 289 pictures ~ Betty Grable and Bob Hope are top box-office stars.

Air Force ~ *Cabin in the Sky* ~ *Destination Tokyo* ~ *Destroyer* ~ *Dubarry was a Lady* ~ *For Whom the Bell Tolls* ~ *Madame Curie* ~ *The Ox-Bow Incident* ~ *This is the Army* ~ *This is the Navy* ~ *Watch on the Rhine.*

1944 The Department of Justice reactivates the Paramount suit ~ Hal Wallis resigns as head of production at WB to become an independent producer ~ the Motion Picture Alliance for the Preservation of American Ideals is founded ~ top stars are Bing Crosby and Gary Cooper.

Double Indemnity ~ *Going My Way* ~ *Hollywood Canteen* ~ *The Mask of Dimitrios* ~ *Meet Me in St Louis* ~ *Pin Up Girl* ~ *Since You Went Away* ~ *Up in Arms* ~ *Wilson.*

1945 Will Hays retires as president of the MPPDA ~ his replacement, Eric Johnston, changes the name of the industry trade association to the Motion Picture Association of America (MPAA), and establishes its foreign department as the Motion Picture Export Association (MPEA) ~ a strike by the Conference of Studio Unions lasts for 30 weeks ~ the Screen Extras Guild is organized ~ the majors produce 234 pictures ~ Humphrey Bogart and Lauren Bacall appear in *To Have and Have Not.*

Anchors Aweigh ~ *The Bells of St Mary's* ~ *Mildred Pierce* ~ *Objective Burma* ~ *Pride of the Marines* ~ *Spellbound* ~ *The Story of GI Joe* ~ *They Were Expendable.*

1946 The industry's most profitable year, in which it generates 1.5 percent of US corporate profit, and $232 million in domestic rentals ~ 600 American movies flood the postwar Italian market ~ Universal merges with William Goetz's International Pictures to become Universal-International, with Goetz as head of production ~ the studio's policy concentrates on independent production ~ RKO Theaters is formed ~ producer Howard Hughes is ordered to return the PCA seal after releasing an unauthorized version of *The Outlaw* ~ Bing Crosby and Ingrid Bergman are leading box-office stars.

The Best Years of Our Lives ~ *The Big Sleep* ~ *Duel in the Sun* ~ *Gilda* ~ *It Happened in Springfield* ~ *It's a Wonderful Life* ~ *The Jolson Story* ~ *The Lady in the Lake* ~ *My Darling Clementine* ~ *Night and Day* ~ *Notorious* ~ *The Postman Always Rings Twice* ~ *Terror by Night.*

1947 HUAC resumes its investigations of "Communist infiltration of the motion picture industry" ~ the Hollywood Ten are charged with contempt of Congress, and dismissed by their studios ~ the federal government files an anti-trust suit against

Technicolor ~ 90 percent of theaters sell popcorn, 66 percent show double bills ~ 742 actors are under studio contract ~ Britain briefly imposes an embargo on American films ~ WB buys RKO-Pathé newsreel ~ Dore Schary becomes head of production at RKO ~ there is a sharp fall in MGM profits.
Body and Soul ~ Crossfire ~ Dark Passage ~ Forever Amber ~ Gentleman's Agreement ~ Out of the Past.

1948 The Paramount case reaches the Supreme Court, which decides that industry practices are in breach of the anti-trust laws, and approves a consent decree that will divorce the majors' theaters from their production and distribution operations ~ Howard Hughes buys RKO ~ Dore Schary leaves RKO to become head of production under Mayer at MGM ~ Eagle-Lion absorbs PRC ~ "theater television" is initiated ~ 18,000 theaters in the US, but weekly audiences fall to 66 million ~ Burt Lancaster is one of several stars to establish his own production company, Hecht-Lancaster.
All the King's Men ~ The Beautiful Blonde from Bashful Bend ~ Easter Parade ~ Letter from an Unknown Woman ~ The Pirate ~ Red River ~ Rope ~ The Treasure of the Sierra Madre.

1949 Paramount and RKO enter into consent decrees to divorce their theater holdings from production~distribution ~ 20 percent of movies released by the majors are independent productions ~ one million American homes have television ~ Eastman Kodak introduces single-strip color stock ~ the majors produce 234 pictures, 46 in Technicolor ~ Bob Hope is the top box-office draw ~ Republic Studios has its biggest ever success with *The Sands of Iwo Jima*.
Adam's Rib ~ Champion ~ A Connecticut Yankee in King Arthur's Court ~ Home of the Brave ~ I Married a Communist ~ Intruder in the Dust ~ I Was a Male War Bride ~ Lost Boundaries ~ On the Town ~ Pinky ~ Samson and Delilah ~ The Secret Garden ~ She Wore a Yellow Ribbon ~ The Snake Pit ~ Twelve O'Clock High.

1950 The Hollywood Ten are jailed ~ the American Cinema Editors (ACE) organization is founded ~ John Wayne is the top box-office star.
All About Eve ~ The Asphalt Jungle ~ Battleground ~ Broken Arrow ~ Father of the Bride ~ The Gunfighter ~ No Way Out ~ Stage Fright ~ Sunset Boulevard ~ White Heat ~ Winchester '73.

1951 TCF and WB sign consent decrees ~ Louis B. Mayer resigns from MGM, and Dore Schary becomes head of the studio ~ Arthur Krim and Robert Benjamin take over UA ~ Krim's Eagle-Lion is absorbed into UA ~ the HUAC "mass hearings" begin ~ Columbia establishes a subsidiary, Screen Gems, to produce telefilms ~ Monogram releases the rights of 300 features to television ~ the Screen Actors Guild demands royalties for showings of all post-1948 movies on television ~ the majors release 320 pictures.
Ace in the Hole ~ An American in Paris ~ David and Bathsheba ~ Showboat ~ Storm Warning ~ A Streetcar Named Desire.

1952 The Supreme Court decision in *The Miracle* case establishes that motion pictures are protected by the First Amendment, making state censorship unconstitutional ~ TCF sells its theaters to National Theaters, Inc. ~ Decca Records buys Universal ~ UA releases the first 3-D movie, *Bwana Devil* ~ Cinerama is launched in

New York with *This is Cinerama* ~ Dean Martin and Jerry Lewis become the top box-office draw.
The African Queen ~ *The Bad and the Beautiful* ~ *The Greatest Show on Earth* ~ *High Noon* ~ *Quo Vadis?* ~ *The Road to Bali* ~ *Singin' in the Rain*.

1953 TCF releases the first movie in CinemaScope (*The Robe*) ~ 24 3-D movies are released ~ box-office returns improve for the first time since 1946, but only 32 percent of theaters make profits on admission income, and attendance is half that of 1946 ~ 46 percent of American families own a television ~ United Paramount Theaters merges with the American Broadcasting Corporation (ABC) ~ Disney forms its own distribution company, Buena Vista ~ Monogram Pictures is reorganized as Allied Artists ~ WB sells its theaters to the Stanley Warner Corporation ~ the majors release 301 pictures ~ Gary Cooper is the top box-office star ~ UA releases *The Moon is Blue* without a PCA seal, and the movie is a commercial success.
From Here to Eternity ~ *Gentlemen Prefer Blondes* ~ *How to Marry a Millionaire* ~ *Mogambo* ~ *Shane*.

1954 Major companies abandon production of 3-D movies ~ the Screen Writers Guild becomes the Writers Guild of America ~ Samuel Z. Arkoff and James Nicholson form the American Releasing Corporation (ARC) ~ 3,000 movie theaters have closed since 1948, but 3,000 drive-ins have opened ~ the majors' production drops to 225 pictures ~ Paramount releases *White Christmas* in VistaVision.
The Bridges at Toko-Ri ~ *Johnny Guitar* ~ *On the Waterfront* ~ *Rear Window* ~ *A Star is Born* ~ *Them!* ~ *The Wild One*.

1955 Of all movies released 62 percent are in color, 38 percent in widescreen ~ the Todd-AO process debuts with *Oklahoma!* ~ Howard Hughes sells RKO to General Telluride, a subsidiary of the General Tire and Rubber Company ~ *On the Waterfront* wins eight Oscars, including Best Actor for Marlon Brando ~ WB begins producing television programming ~ Nicholas Schenck retires as president of Loew's, Inc. ~ the majors are producing 20 percent of prime-time television programming, but their production of features drops to 215 pictures ~ John Wayne forms Batjac Productions, Kirk Douglas forms Bryna Productions, Randolph Scott forms Ranown Productions ~ James Stewart and Grace Kelly are top box-office stars.
All That Heaven Allows ~ *Bad Day at Black Rock* ~ *Blackboard Jungle* ~ *East of Eden* ~ *The Man with the Golden Arm* ~ *Marty* ~ *Rebel Without a Cause* ~ *Running Wild* ~ *The Seven Year Itch* ~ *Teenage Crime Wave*.

1956 The Production Code is revised to permit references to prostitution and drugs ~ Darryl Zanuck resigns as head of production at TCF, replaced by Buddy Adler ~ Harry and Albert Warner sell their interest in WB and retire ~ WB sells television rights to its library of pre-1948 movies ~ 229 actors are under studio contract ~ the last Hollywood serial is produced (*Blazing the Overland Trail*) ~ Dore Schary leaves MGM ~ ARC is reorganized as American-International Pictures (AIP) ~ William Holden and John Wayne are top box-office attractions.
Around the World in Eighty Days ~ *Baby Doll* ~ *Bandido* ~ *Bigger Than Life* ~ *The Big Knife* ~ *Guys and Dolls* ~ *Hot Rod Girl* ~ *Invasion of the Body Snatchers* ~ *The King and I* ~ *Rock Around the Clock* ~ *The Searchers* ~ *Tea and Sympathy* ~ *The Ten Commandments* ~ *Written on the Wind*.

1957 Production of movies in color declines to 34 percent of the total ~ RKO ceases movie production ~ 58 percent of the movies released by the majors are independent productions ~ UA acquires distribution rights to WB's pre-1948 film library, and is floated on the stock market ~ the majors release 268 pictures ~ 52 percent of the audience is under 20, 72 percent under 29 ~ Rock Hudson is the top box-office star.
The Bridge on the River Kwai ~ *I Was a Teenage Werewolf* ~ *Jailhouse Rock* ~ *The Long Hot Summer* ~ *No Down Payment* ~ *Peyton Place* ~ *Silk Stockings* ~ *Untamed Youth.*

1958 The RKO studio is bought by Desilu Productions, producers of the *I Love Lucy* television show ~ RKO's theaters merge with Stanley Warner ~ Republic Pictures closes ~ 4,700 drive-in theaters in the US, accounting for 20 percent of movie rentals ~ MCA buys Paramount's film library ~ Glenn Ford and Elizabeth Taylor are top box-office stars.
Cat on a Hot Tin Roof ~ *The Defiant Ones* ~ *High School Confidential* ~ *High School Hellcats* ~ *South Pacific* ~ *Touch of Evil* ~ *Vertigo* ~ *Young and Wild.*

1959 Loew's is the last major company to complete the divorcement of exhibition from production–distribution ~ Decca and MCA merge ~ Y. Frank Freeman retires as Paramount head of production ~ the majors release 189 pictures ~ Rock Hudson and Cary Grant are top box-office stars ~ *Behind the Great Wall* is the first movie in AromaRama.
Anatomy of a Murder ~ *Ben-Hur* ~ *Imitation of Life* ~ *North by Northwest* ~ *Pillow Talk* ~ *Rio Bravo* ~ *Some Like It Hot.*

1960 The Screen Actors Guild refuses to merge with the American Federation of Radio and Television Artists (AFRTA) ~ *Scent of Mystery* is the first movie in Smell-o-Vision ~ Dalton Trumbo is the first of the Hollywood Ten to receive screen credit, as writer on *Exodus* and *Spartacus* ~ Doris Day and Rock Hudson are top box-office stars.
The Alamo ~ *The Apartment* ~ *Comanche Station* ~ *The Magnificent Seven* ~ *Ocean's 11* ~ *Psycho* ~ *Strangers When We Meet* ~ *The Sundowners.*

1961 Average production costs $1.5 million ~ half of Hollywood's rental revenues come from the foreign market ~ NBC launches "NBC Saturday Night at the Movies," the first prime-time series of post-1948 movies on television ~ the TCF studio site is sold to Aluminum Corporation of America (ALCOA), and redeveloped as Century City ~ the majors release 167 pictures ~ Elizabeth Taylor is the top box-office star.
The Absent-Minded Professor ~ *The Guns of Navarone* ~ *West Side Story.*

1962 Talent agency Music Corporation of America (MCA) completes its take-over of Universal, and Lew Wasserman becomes president ~ Darryl Zanuck returns to TCF as president with Richard Zanuck in charge of production after the studio reports losses of $40 million ~ Doris Day is the top box-office star ~ MGM's *The Wonderful World of the Brothers Grimm* is the first full-length Cinerama feature.
Advise and Consent ~ *The Courtship of Eddie's Father* ~ *Lawrence of Arabia* ~ *The Longest Day* ~ *The Manchurian Candidate* ~ *The Man Who Shot Liberty Valance* ~ *Mutiny on the Bounty.*

Alan Hirschfield and David Begelman take over management at Columbia ~ a bill to limit runaway production is introduced to Congress ~ the majors release 132 pictures.

American Graffiti ~ Deep Throat ~ Devil in Miss Jones ~ The Exorcist ~ The Friends of Eddie Coyle ~ High Plains Drifter ~ The Long Goodbye ~ The Sting ~ Soylent Green.

1974 Box-office grosses increase by $150 million ~ 100 new screens open ~ weekly attendance is 18 million ~ Robert Redford is the top box-office star ~ *Earthquake* is the first movie in Sensurround.

Alice Doesn't Live Here Anymore ~ Blazing Saddles ~ California Split ~ Chinatown ~ The Conversation ~ Death Wish ~ The Eiger Sanction ~ The Godfather Part II ~ The Great Gatsby ~ The Longest Yard.

1975 Average admission price $2 ~ there are 10,000 indoor theaters in the US, and a total of 14,000 screens ~ an estimated 10 percent of production effort is applied to making sequels ~ Home Box Office (HBO) begins satellite transmission to its cable television networks ~ Industrial Light and Magic is established to develop special effects for *Star Wars* ~ the majors release 97 movies ~ Robert Redford and Barbra Streisand are top box-office stars ~ *The Towering Inferno* is the first co-production by two major studios, TCF and WCI.

At Long Last Love ~ Dog Day Afternoon ~ Jaws ~ Nashville ~ Night Moves ~ One Flew Over the Cuckoo's Nest ~ Rollerball ~ Shampoo.

1976 VHS and Betamax video-recording systems introduced ~ MCA and Disney bring suit against Sony, charging that video-recorders infringe copyright ~ the US Congress abolishes tax shelter schemes for financing movies, drastically reducing the volume of independent production ~ HBO wins its challenge against the Federal Communication Commission's protection of broadcast television.

All the President's Men ~ Bound for Glory ~ Carrie ~ Network ~ The Omen ~ Rocky ~ The Shootist ~ A Star is Born ~ Taxi Driver.

1977 Average production costs $7.5 million ~ CARA is reorganized as the Classification and Rating Administration, and abandons the practice of vetting scripts ~ MCA and Paramount form Cinema International Corporation (CIC) to distribute theatrical pictures outside the US ~ after a dispute with Transamerica corporate managers, Krim and Benjamin resign as UA's management team ~ TCF diversifies by buying a ski resort and a Coca-Cola bottling plant ~ Steadicam is developed ~ MPAA establishes the Office of Film Security to combat piracy ~ TCF releases 50 features to Sony for distribution on video ~ the majors release 78 movies ~ Sylvester Stallone becomes top box-office draw ~ *Star Wars* becomes the highest-grossing movie.

Annie Hall ~ Close Encounters of the Third Kind ~ The Hills Have Eyes ~ I Spit on Your Grave ~ New York, New York ~ Saturday Night Fever ~ Smokey and the Bandit ~ Sorcerer.

1978 Krim and Benjamin form Orion Pictures with Mike Madavoy ~ a Washington task force concludes that anti-trust decrees had little effect upon the majors' oligopoly power ~ David Begelman quits as head of Columbia following a financial scandal ~ Burt Reynolds is the most profitable star.

Coming Home ~ The Deer Hunter ~ Grease ~ Halloween ~ Jaws 2 ~ National Lampoon's Animal House ~ Piranha.

1979 The average movie earns 80 percent of its receipts from theatrical release, 20 percent from video and television ~ Cannon Pictures taken over by Menachem Golan and Yoram Globus ~ *Variety* claims business has doubled since 1971 ~ MGM resumes distribution ~ Cineplex Odeon opens its 18-screen multiplex cinema in Toronto ~ average production costs $6 million.
Alien ~ Apocalypse Now ~ The China Syndrome ~ Every Which Way But Loose ~ The Jerk ~ Kramer vs Kramer ~ Manhattan ~ Nocturna ~ Norma Rae ~ Star Trek ~ Superman.

1980 Average production cost rises to $10 million ~ *Heaven's Gate* records a box-office loss of $40 million, leading Transamerica to withdraw from the industry and sell UA ~ Sherry Lansing becomes president of Twentieth Century-Fox, the first woman to head a major Hollywood company ~ ten-week actors' strike ~ video-cassette sales account for 15 percent of domestic revenue ~ the American Film Marketing Association (AFMA) is formed as the trade association for smaller producers and distributors ~ Clint Eastwood is the top box-office draw.
American Gigolo ~ Dressed to Kill ~ The Empire Strikes Back ~ Friday the 13th ~ Ordinary People ~ Popeye ~ Raging Bull ~ The Shining.

1981 TCF is bought by oil tycoon Marvin Davis ~ Kirk Kerkorian buys UA from Transamerica and forms the MGM/UA Entertainment Company ~ MGM/UA joins CIC to form United International Pictures (UIP) to distribute their movies abroad ~ average features costs $11 million ~ the majors release 112 movies.
Body Heat ~ Hell Night ~ On Golden Pond ~ Outland ~ Raiders of the Lost Ark ~ Southern Comfort ~ Stir Crazy ~ Superman II.

1982 Coca-Cola purchases Columbia ~ Tri-Star Pictures is formed by Columbia, HBO, and CBS ~ drive-ins decline as their sites become valuable as real estate ~ *E.T. ~ The Extra-Terrestrial* becomes the highest-grossing movie of all time.
Blade Runner ~ Evil Under the Sun ~ Gandhi ~ An Officer and a Gentleman ~ Reds ~ Tender Mercies ~ The Thing ~ Tootsie.

1983 WCI abandons its involvement in video-games after large losses, and restructures to concentrate on movie and television production and distribution, recorded music and publishing ~ Cannon, now a "mini-major," is California's fastest-growing corporation ~ average weekly audience is 23 million ~ Frank Mancuso becomes president of Paramount ~ the majors release 106 movies ~ Clint Eastwood is top box-office star.
Flashdance ~ O. C. and Stiggs ~ Return of the Jedi ~ Terms of Endearment ~ Trading Places ~ Wargames ~ Zelig.

1984 The Supreme Court decides in favor of Sony in video-tape copyright suit ~ Michael Eisner and Jeffrey Katzenberg take over management at Disney, and establish Touchstone Pictures to make movies for adult audiences ~ after a dispute with producer-director Steven Spielberg over the rating for *Indiana Jones and the Temple of Doom*, CARA introduces a new classification of PG-13 ~ 85 percent of the audience is under 40 ~ Japan becomes the largest importer of American movies ~ the growth of multiplexes increases the number of screens to 22,000 ~ box-office gross reaches $4.2 billion.

Amadeus ~ Beverly Hills Cop ~ Ghostbusters ~ Gremlins ~ Indiana Jones and the Temple of Doom ~ Once Upon a Time in America ~ Police Academy ~ The Purple Rose of Cairo ~ Romancing the Stone ~ The Terminator.

1985   The legal decision that had required the major companies to sell their theaters after 1948 is reversed, and the majors begin buying theater chains ~ media mogul Rupert Murdoch's News International buys Twentieth Century-Fox, with Barry Diller in charge of production ~ TV magnate Ted Turner buys MGM/UA ~ average ticket price is $3.50 ~ home video business generates more revenue than theatrical rentals ($2.1 billion) ~ Dino de Laurentis forms De Laurentis Entertainment and buys Embassy Pictures ~ Cineplex Odeon takes over the Plitt Theater chain and becomes one of the four largest theater chains in the US ~ the majors release 116 movies ~ Sylvester Stallone is the top box-office star.
Back to the Future ~ Cocoon ~ Desperately Seeking Susan ~ Out of Africa ~ Rambo: First Blood Part II ~ Rocky IV ~ Witness.

1986   Ted Turner sells MGM/UA back to Kerkorian, but keeps its film and television library ~ British producer David Putnam briefly becomes chairman of Columbia ~ there are 30,000 video stores in the US ~ MCA buys half of Cineplex Odeon ~ Cannon acquires foreign production and distribution facilities, then collapses after a Securities and Exchange Commission investigation ~ admissions of over-40s rise ~ the majors release 102 pictures, compared to 131 released by independents.
Aliens ~ Blue Velvet ~ The Color Purple ~ Hannah and Her Sisters ~ Peggy Sue Got Married ~ Platoon ~ She's Gotta Have It ~ Top Gun.

1987   Coca-Cola merges Columbia with Tri-Star to form Columbia Pictures Entertainment ~ Universal has 50 percent equity in Cineplex Odeon cinemas ~ Paramount and Orion have the largest shares of the domestic box-office ~ independents release 25 percent of the top 100 pictures ~ Eddie Murphy is the top box-office star.
Angel Heart ~ Beverly Hills Cop II ~ Fatal Attraction ~ Robocop ~ School Daze ~ Three Men and a Baby ~ Wall Street.

1988   Disney has 20 percent of the domestic market ~ 50 percent of US households own VCRs ~ sales of *E.T.* on video generate $150 million for MCA ~ De Laurentis Entertainment folds ~ writers' strike in Hollywood ~ Tom Cruise is the top box-office star.
Beetlejuice ~ Big ~ Coming to America ~ Cop ~ Die Hard ~ Mississippi Burning ~ Rain Man ~ Who Framed Roger Rabbit ~ Willow.

1989   Record box-office takings of $5.03 billion ~ Columbia is bought by Sony Corporation for $3.4 billion in preparation for a convergence of technologies around high definition television ~ Gulf and Western becomes Paramount Communications Inc., and attempts to take over WCI ~ instead, WCI merges with Time Inc. to create Time-Warner, the world's largest media conglomerate ~ Joe Roth takes charge of production for TCF ~ Disney forms Hollywood Pictures.
Back to the Future Part II ~ Batman ~ Born on the Fourth of July ~ Do the Right Thing ~ Driving Miss Daisy ~ Field of Dreams ~ Lethal Weapon 2 ~ The Little Mermaid ~ sex, lies and videotape.

1990 Controversy over the content of *Henry and June* causes CARA to introduce the NC-17 category, replacing X ~ Pathé Corporation acquires MGM/UA ~ MCA opens Universal Studios in Orlando, Florida ~ the Matsushita Corporation buys MCA for $6.6 billion in the largest ever Japanese take-over in the US ~ average production cost rises to $24 million ~ 24 percent of the audience is now over 40 ~ Arnold Schwarzenegger is the top box-office star.
Dances with Wolves ~ Days of Thunder ~ Dick Tracy ~ Die Hard 2 ~ Ghost ~ Godfather Part III ~ Goodfellas ~ Guilty by Suspicion ~ Home Alone ~ The Hunt for Red October ~ Kindergarten Cop ~ Pretty Woman ~ Teenage Mutant Ninja Turtles ~ Total Recall.

1991 Thirty-one percent of the audience is 12–20, 25 percent is 21–9, 44 percent over 30 ~ Sony renames Columbia as Sony Pictures Entertainment ~ Kevin Costner is the top box-office star ~ computer "morphing" special effects are used in *Terminator 2: Judgment Day*.
The Addams Family ~ Arachnophobia ~ Barton Fink ~ Beauty and the Beast ~ Boyz N The Hood ~ Bugsy ~ Cape Fear ~ City Slickers ~ Father of the Bride ~ Grand Canyon ~ Hook ~ JFK ~ Jungle Fever ~ The Last of the Mohicans ~ Naked Gun 2½ ~ The Prince of Tides ~ Robin Hood, Prince of Thieves ~ The Silence of the Lambs ~ Slacker ~ Thelma and Louise.

1992 Time Warner forms alliance with Toshiba Corp and C. Itochu & Co. ~ despite a succession of box-office successes, Orion Pictures files for bankruptcy ~ stars' salaries are cut because of the recession ~ EuroDisney opens in Paris ~ videos are issued in widescreen format ~ Dolby digital six-channel stereo sound system launched ~ Tom Cruise is the top box-office star.
Aladdin ~ Alien 3 ~ Basic Instinct ~ Batman Returns ~ Bob Roberts ~ The Bodyguard ~ A Few Good Men ~ Home Alone 2: Lost in New York ~ Malcolm X ~ The Player ~ Sister Act ~ Unforgiven ~ Wayne's World.

1993 American theatrical exhibition accounts for only 20 percent of the average movie's earnings, foreign theatrical exhibition 15 percent, video and television sales the remainder ~ Disney buys Miramax Pictures ~ Ted Turner buys New Line and Castle Rock ~ GATT trade negotiations stall over American access to overseas movie and television markets ~ *Jurassic Park* becomes the highest-grossing movie ever.
The Age of Innocence ~ Cliffhanger ~ Dave ~ Falling Down ~ The Firm ~ The Fugitive ~ Groundhog Day ~ Indecent Proposal ~ The Last Action Hero ~ Mrs. Doubtfire ~ Philadelphia ~ Schindler's List ~ Sleepless in Seattle.

1994 Viacom acquires Paramount Communications and merges with Blockbuster Entertainment Corp., the largest retailer of video in the US ~ Oliver Stone's *Natural Born Killers* is embroiled in controversy for allegedly inciting real-life violence ~ Steven Spielberg, David Geffen, and Jeffrey Katzenberg form Dreamworks, the first new major Hollywood studio in 60 years ~ *The Lion King* is the highest-grossing movie of the year, taking $301 million.
Clear and Present Danger ~ Dumb and Dumber ~ Forrest Gump ~ Legends of the Fall ~ The Mask ~ Pulp Fiction ~ Quiz Show ~ Reality Bites ~ The Shawshank Redemption ~ Speed ~ True Lies ~ Wyatt Earp.

1995 Less than 20 percent of total movie revenues now come from the domestic US box-office ~ Disney acquires Capital Cities/ABC, with the ABC television network

~ Seagram's buys MCA and Universal from Matsushita ~ Carolco Pictures files for bankruptcy, selling most of its major assets to 20th Century-Fox ~ average production cost for a major release rises to $36.4 million, with a further $17.73 spent on marketing ~ *Batman Forever* is the highest-grossing movie of the year, taking $184 million.

12 Monkeys ~ Ace Ventura: When Nature Calls ~ The American President ~ Apollo 13 ~ Braveheart ~ The Bridges of Madison County ~ Casino ~ Clueless ~ Dead Man Walking ~ Die Hard with a Vengeance ~ Heat ~ Jumanji ~ Leaving Las Vegas ~ Nixon ~ Pocahontas ~ Se7en ~ Showgirls ~ Toy Story ~ The Usual Suspects ~ Waterworld.

1996 Telecommunications Act permits telephone companies to provide programming content, encouraging that industry's convergence with the entertainment industries ~ Time-Warner takes over Turner Broadcasting and New Line ~ Kirk Kerkorian incorporates MGM/UA into Tracinda Corporation ~ Disney signs a ten-year, $100-million-per-year licensing agreement with McDonald's ~ *Independence Day* is the highest-grossing movie of the year, taking $306 million.

Crash ~ The English Patient ~ Eraser ~ Fargo ~ The Hunchback of Notre Dame ~ Jerry Maguire ~ Mission: Impossible ~ The Nutty Professor ~ Ransom ~ The Rock ~ Scream ~ Sling Blade ~ Twister.

1997 After production difficulties and massive budget over-runs, *Titanic* becomes the highest-grossing film of all time, eventually taking $432 million ~ Universal acquires the last significant independent distributor, October Films ~ Dreamworks becomes the first studio to offer profit-share deals to screen-writers and technical crew members ~ *Men In Black* is the highest-grossing movie of the year, taking $250 million.

Air Force One ~ Amistad ~ The Apostle ~ As Good As It Gets ~ Boogie Nights ~ Contact ~ Face/Off ~ Good Will Hunting ~ Jackie Brown ~ LA Confidential ~ Liar Liar ~ The Lost World: Jurassic Park ~ My Best Friend's Wedding ~ Wag the Dog.

1998 Although moderately successful at the box-office, *Godzilla* fails to launch a "franchise" for Sony, leading to cutbacks in the production of high-budget special effects movies ~ the Sonny Bono Act extends the period of US copyright protection, just in time to preserve Disney's copyright of Mickey Mouse ~ Internet communications traffic is estimated to be doubling every 100 days ~ Seagram's acquires European music and movie industry company Polygram.

American History X ~ Armageddon ~ A Bug's Life ~ Bulworth ~ Doctor Dolittle ~ Gods and Monsters ~ Hard Rain ~ Lethal Weapon 4 ~ The Mask of Zorro ~ Primary Colors ~ Rush Hour ~ Saving Private Ryan ~ Shakespeare in Love ~ There's Something About Mary ~ The Thin Red Line ~ The Truman Show ~ The Waterboy.

1999 Converged entertainment industries generate $79.65 billion in overseas sales and exports ~ total retail value of the licensed product market is $70 billion ~ *The Blair Witch Project*, produced for $35,000 and notable for its Internet-based pre-release "mythologizing", becomes the most financially successful low-budget film in history ~ *Star Wars: Episode 1 ~ The Phantom Menace* is the highest-grossing movie of the year, taking $431 million.

American Beauty ~ Austin Powers: The Spy Who Shagged Me ~ Being John Malkovich ~ Bicentennial Man ~ Boys Don't Cry ~ The Cider House Rules ~ Eyes

Wide Shut ~ Fight Club ~ The Green Mile ~ The Hurricane ~ The Insider ~ Magnolia ~ The Matrix ~ The Mummy ~ The Sixth Sense ~ South Park: Bigger, Longer and Uncut ~ Three Kings ~ Toy Story 2.

2000 America Online merges with Time-Warner to form the world's largest entertainment conglomerate ~ French utilities company Vivendi takes over Seagram's and Universal to form Vivendi Universal ~ computer-generated images in *The Matrix* create hitherto impossible-to-stage special effects sequences ~ Tom Cruise collects an after-release salary of $75 million (including a profit share), the largest salary to that date, for *Mission: Impossible* ~ average production cost for a major release has risen to $54.8 million, with $27.3 million spent on marketing ~ *Dr. Seuss' How the Grinch Stole Christmas* is the highest-grossing movie of the year, taking $255 million.

Almost Famous ~ Book of Shadows: Blair Witch 2 ~ Cast Away ~ Erin Brockovich ~ Gladiator ~ Memento ~ O Brother, Where Art Thou? ~ The Perfect Storm ~ Thirteen Days ~ Traffic ~ What Lies Beneath ~ X-Men ~ You Can Count on Me.

2001 Digital cinema projection becomes commercially available, and sales of movies on DVD increase rapidly, but online distribution of movies is not yet a commercial reality ~ runaway production, particularly to Canada, becomes increasingly common ~ *Harry Potter and the Sorcerer's Stone* (elsewhere called *Harry Potter and the Philosopher's Stone*) achieves the highest opening-weekend gross in history ($90.3 million), just beating the amount taken by *Jurassic Park*'s sequel *The Lost World*, and becomes the highest-grossing movie of the year, taking $294 million.

AI: Artificial Intelligence ~ A Beautiful Mind ~ Black Hawk Down ~ Driven ~ Final Fantasy: The Spirits Within ~ Gosford Park ~ Hannibal ~ Jason X ~ Jurassic Park III ~ Lara Croft: Tomb Raider ~ Lord of the Rings: The Fellowship of the Ring ~ Monster's Ball ~ Monsters, Inc. ~ Moulin Rouge ~ Mulholland Drive ~ The Mummy Returns ~ Pearl Harbor ~ Rush Hour 2 ~ Shrek ~ Training Day.

blockbuster After **divorcement**, the major companies concentrated on producing more lavish and spectacular features which were expected to perform equally spectacularly at the box-office, on the theory that this strategy was more profitable than **Classical Hollywood**'s mass production studio system. The blockbusters of the 1950s and 1960s were epics or musicals. The economic logic of the blockbuster phenomenon was demonstrated by the success of *The Sound of Music* in 1965, and the pattern established in the late 1960s, whereby a handful of blockbuster movies make very large profits while the majority of movies produced fail to recoup their costs, persisted until video established a more solid second-release system in the 1980s. During the 1970s, the blockbuster evolved into the **event movie**. P. 160.

blocking The physical placement of characters in a scene. P. 339.

Brechtian German playwright Bertolt Brecht developed a theory and practice of political theater, the central principle of which was that the audience should always be aware that they were watching a representation of reality, rather than becoming caught up in an illusion of reality. "Brechtian" identifies the various techniques used to remind the audience that they are witnessing a constructed performance, and distance or alienate them from the illusion. P. 105.

CARA The Code and Rating Administration, later the Classification and Rating System, set up by the industry's trade association, the Motion Picture Association of America (**MPAA**), to administer the **rating system**. P. 23.

center line See **180-degree rule**.

"cinema of attractions" Term coined by film historian Tom Gunning to describe early cinema's address to the viewer, soliciting "spectator attention, inciting visual curiosity, and supplying pleasure through an exciting spectacle . . . emphasizing the direct stimulation of shock or surprise at the expense of unfolding a **story** or creating a **diegetic** universe." P. 372.

cinematic apparatus A term used in contemporary **film theory** to refer to both the techno-

logical and economic components of the cinema and the psychological operation of cinema's impression of reality on its spectators. In this context, the term "apparatus" adopts Louis Althusser's usage in his analysis of "ideological state apparatuses." In this book, I use the term **apparatus of cinema** to refer specifically to the technological components of cinema. P. 534.

cine-psychoanalysis In this book, the name given to a disparate body of critical writing about cinema, which takes its theoretical principles from a combination of Marxism, **semiology**, and psychoanalysis. Often called "psychoanalytic **film theory**," it has often also been identified as a "second semiology" or a "second-phase" semiotics. It is more or less synonymous with the term "contemporary film theory." P. 535.

Classical Hollywood In this book, Classical Hollywood cinema is taken to be a period of Hollywood's history, and refers to the style, the mode of production, and the industrial organization under which movies were made from the early 1920s to the late 1950s. P. 15.

clearance A trade practice by which the major, vertically integrated companies (see **vertical integration**) determined which **movies** were shown in which theaters, by allotting every movie theater in America a position on a scale of priorities that determined how long after its initial release a given theater could show a picture. In any given area or **zone**, a movie would play in a first-run theater for a period, before becoming available to second-run theaters, and then on down the scale until it eventually reached the neighborhood theaters in America's small towns and rural areas several months after its New York premiere. The system was designed to encourage patrons to pay the highest prices to see a movie at a first-run house, which was in any case most likely to be owned by one of the Big Five companies. P. 121.

close shot See **shot scale**.

close-up (CU) See **shot scale**.

commercial aesthetic In this book, the term used to describe Hollywood's aesthetic system, driven as it is by the existence of entertainment as a commercial commodity.

From this perspective, Hollywood's most profound significance lies in its ability to turn pleasure into a product we can buy. An understanding of Hollywood's commercial aesthetic requires a consideration of both the formal conventions of Hollywood movies and the external social and cultural pressures that regulate movies as products of a system of mass production and **distribution**. P. 14.

compositional motivation See **motivation**.

confrontation See **resolution**.

continuity system Hollywood's system of spatial construction, in which action unfolds as a smooth and continuous flow across shots. Within this system the camera remains relatively unobtrusive, seldom drawing attention to its mediating presence. Continuity editing keeps the position, movement, and screen direction of objects within the frame consistent between shots, ensuring audience comprehension of the action. P. 312.

continuous present The tense in which movies take place. Unlike writing, movies do not have a range of tenses at their disposal, because of the physical characteristics through which **film** produces the illusion of movement. At whatever point in a movie's **story** an event takes place, the audience always experiences it as being in the here and now of a continuous present. P. 432.

coverage The procedure by which the whole action of a scene is filmed in one shot (the master shot), and then filmed in smaller sections from a variety of camera positions, to provide the **editor** with enough material to construct the scene as he or she, or the **producer**, sees fit. P. 332.

crane shot The camera is mounted on the arm of a purpose-designed crane, allowing it to move up and down, as well as forward and back and from side to side. P. 242. A camera crane appears on p. 245.

cross-cutting Editing between two scenes taking place in separate spaces, to suggest the simultaneity of the action occurring in both scenes. P. 245.

cultural verisimilitude See **verisimilitude**.

cut-away A brief shot inserted into a longer **take**, showing either a detail of the scene, the reaction of another character to the action in the main shot, or another scene. P. 244.

dailies The first printing from the day's exposed negative stock, made to be examined before the next day's shooting begins. P. 137.

depth of field The range of distances from the camera that are in focus. P. 321. Depth of field is illustrated on p. 321.

dialectic The process of reasoning by argument and counter-argument: a thesis provokes an antithesis which contradicts it, and the two are reconciled in a synthesis. More generally, dialectical reasoning attempts to juxtapose and resolve contradictory ideas. P. 369.

diegesis See **mimesis**.

diegetic Film criticism uses the terms **diegetic** and **non-diegetic** to distinguish between what is included within the imaginary world of the **story**, whether it is visible onscreen or not, and what is outside it. The terms are often used to identify the source of sounds. The background music that sets the emotional tone of a scene is non-diegetic (sometimes the term **extradiegetic** is used to mean the same thing), unless we know that it is coming from an orchestra playing in the ballroom the characters are dancing in, or a radio in the room. Other non-diegetic elements in a movie include its credits and other titles. Extradiegetic background music had, of course, always accompanied silent movies, setting the mood of each scene. P. 246.

diffusion See **innovation**.

digital See **analogical/digital**.

director In **Classical Hollywood**, the person responsible for the shooting of the movie, and in effective control of this stage of the project. A director might also expect to have some influence over the final stages of writing and the early stages of editing. Some directors exercised significantly more authority over their productions than this, and most directors in post-Classical Hollywood have a longer involvement in the project, often from initial conception to final cut. Conventional critical practice identifies the director as the primary creative force and governing intelligence behind the movie. P. 139.

director of photography The person responsible for lighting and filming the movie; the supervisor of the camera crew. P. 141.

dissolve An optical transition between two shots, in which the second shot is gradually superimposed on the first. In **Classical Hollywood**, a dissolve most commonly implied a relatively short time lapse between the two scenes shown, while a **fade** suggested a longer interval. P. 242.

distribution The branch of the motion picture industry responsible for the circulation of movies to their **exhibition** venues. Economic power in the industry has in practice always resided in the distribution sector, where a small number of large companies can between them effectively control both movie producers' access to exhibition sites, and exhibitors' access to pictures. P. 117.

divorcement The result of the 1948 US Supreme Court decision in the **Paramount case** that the trade practices of the vertically integrated major companies (see **vertical integration**) constituted a monopoly. The court decided that the production and **distribution** branches of the major companies should be separated, or divorced, from their **exhibition** branches. P. 129.

dominant Formalist criticism (see **Formalism**) defines the dominant as the focusing component of a work of art; the dominant, which might be rhythm or **plot** or character, guarantees the integrity of the work's structure. P. 453.

editor The person responsible for assembling the movie into its final form. P. 141.

establishing shot The opening long shot in a scene, which shows the setting in which the scene will take place, and orients the viewer to the spatial relations between the objects and figures in the scene. See **shot scale**. P. 244.

event movie In the 1970s, the **blockbuster** evolved into the "event movie" such as *Star Wars* (1977), in which as much commercial importance was attached to the merchandizing of ancillary goods – toys, games, books, clothing, bubble-gum – as to the movie's performance at the box-office. This merchandizing extended the life of the product and guaranteed the success of its sequels. P. 184.

excess A Formalist concept (see **Formalism**) referring to the material in a movie that is not motivated, and which may distract viewers from their involvement with a movie's story. P. 376.

exclusive engagement An **exhibition** pattern used following the decision in the **Paramount case**. In it, a **movie** would be shown in continuous performances in a limited number of theaters, and usually only in one theater in any market, before it went into "general release." Subsequently known as **platform release**. P. 166.

exhibition The branch of the motion picture industry concerned with showing movies to paying audiences. Developments in domestic technology such as television, the video-recorder, and the digital video disk (DVD) have meant that exhibition has become no longer the exclusive preserve of specially constructed buildings – movie theaters or cinemas – and that the home has become an increasingly important exhibition site. P. 117.

ex machina A Latin phrase, usually *deus ex machina*, meaning literally "the god from the machine," referring to a supernatural or improbable intervention at the climax of a play or other **story**, which brings the **plot** to an unlikely happy **resolution**. P. 153.

exploitation The promotion of a movie through advertising, publicity, stunts, commercial tie-ins, and licensing. Before the 1950s, "exploitation picture" referred to movies presenting subjects prohibited by the **Production Code**, such as sex hygiene, prostitution, and drug use, in a style that combined sensationalism, a purportedly "educational" manner, and a very low budget. From the 1950s it was used to describe independently produced movies aimed at specific audiences, such as teenagers. P. 168.

expressive space Space endowed with meaning beyond the literal, **represented space** in an image. P. 314.

extradiegetic See **diegetic**.

eyeline matching A convention governing the direction of a character's gaze. When a character looks offscreen in one shot, we expect the next shot to show us what the character is looking at. Following characters' eyelines allows us to connect the spaces in separate shots together across a cut. Manuals of continuity editing (see **continuity system**) observe that "the most natural cut is the cut on the look," because "the eyes are the most powerful direction pointer that a human being has to attract or to direct interest." P. 337.

fabula See **story**.

fade In a **fade-out**, the screen is gradually darkened to black. This is followed by a **fade-in**, in which the screen gradually brightens on a new scene. In **Classical Hollywood**, a fade generally implied a longer time lapse between two scenes than was suggested by a **dissolve**. P. 242.

fade-in See **fade**.

fade-out See **fade**.

film Throughout this book, I distinguish between film and **movie**, using film to mean the physical, celluloid material on which images are registered and a soundtrack recorded. Thus, **film time** refers to the amount of time it takes to project a movie, and is a matter of fixed duration, determined by the length of the film and the set speed at which it passes through the projector. The distinction I make between film and movie is broadly comparable to the distinction between print and literature: the material and the experiential forms have different properties. Most other critics, however, use the two terms film and movie as if they were interchangeable. P. 7.

film time See **film**.

flashback A scene set in the past of the **story**, occurring out of chronological order in the **plot**. Flashbacks are most often staged as the memories of characters, or during scenes in which one character explains past events to another. P. 432.

focal length Technically, the distance between the center of the lens and the plane of the **film** in the camera, when the lens is focused at infinity. The focal length of a lens identifies its angle of view: a long focal length lens (or telephoto lens) has a narrow angle of view, and a short focal length lens is also called a wide angle lens. P. 321.

Formalism The name given to the work of a group of Russian literary critics of the 1920s, and to criticism which has made use of the theoretical premises (see **theory**) of their work. In **film** studies, **neoformalism** has combined these premises with an understanding of viewing activity informed by the branches of psychology concerned with perception and cognition, in contrast to psychoanalysis. Neoformalism defines the viewer as an active figure, responding to cues within the movie and forming hypotheses about its progress on the basis of previous experience. P. 546.

four-walling See **roadshow**.

framing The composition of an image, which takes place in relation first of all to the borders of its frame. P. 316.

franchise A phenomenon of Hollywood after 1980, in which a movie launches not only a series of sequels, but also an extensive lines of ancillary products, including toys, games, and clothing. Successful franchise movies like *Batman* (1989) established brand identities for the company producing them that lasted for over a decade. P. 191.

full shot See **shot scale**.

gauge The width of the **film** stock, normally 35 mm. P. 254.

genre The type or kind of **movie**, as determined either by a recurrent setting or **plot**, such as Westerns or romances, or by the affect the movie produces in its audience, such as thrillers or "weepies." Although critics have devoted much energy to debating where the boundaries between genres are located, genre is an incoherent and inconsistent system of classification, and this book argues that rather than seeing Hollywood as a cinema of distinct genres, it is more fruitful to understand it as a generic cinema, in which convention operates at multiple levels in any given movie. P. 74.

gross The box-office gross is the total amount of money taken at the box-office during a movie's theatrical release, before any deductions have been made. **Gross receipts** are the total income received by the distributor from all sources, including television, video, and ancillary rights, as well as **gross rental**

583

receipts. Publicly reported figures, such as those in the trade press, are often exaggerated, but more reliable figures are seldom available. P. 210.

gross receipts See **gross**.

gross rental receipts See **gross**.

high concept First used in the 1970s to describe made-for-television movies which needed stories that could be summarized in a 30-second television spot, "high concept" is an industry term for a movie with a straightforward, easily pitched, and easily comprehended story. Visual style, soundtrack music, and opportunities for marketing **tie-ins** are as important to the high-concept package as its minimal narrative. High-concept movies do not necessarily have high budgets, but the term is most often used to describe expensive action-adventure movies using previously tested and reliable ingredients, aimed at the global market. P. 218.

iconography A system of recurring visual motifs, which provides the knowledgeable viewer with a means of gleaning information about characters and situation from the appearance of characters and settings. **Genre** criticism often uses iconography as a way of distinguishing between genres. P. 86.

identification Cine-psychoanalysis argues that, in watching a movie, the spectator's primary identification is not with the characters or performers, but with the camera (we have to look where the camera looks; the camera is the eye/I). It then suggests that in **Classical Hollywood** cinema, the look of the spectator is passed through the camera onto the character, encouraging spectators to make a range of secondary identifications within the fiction. P. 347.

"impact" edit A cut that produces a violent disruption of spatial continuity, designed to have a shock effect on the audience. P. 360.

innovation Technological change is brought about in three stages. **Invention** requires only a limited financial commitment to fund experimentation and the development of a prototype. In the second stage, innovation, the invention is adapted to meet the requirements of a market. This involves much greater expenditure than the first. The final stage, dif-

fusion, occurs when the product is adopted as an industry standard, so that the whole industry invests in its exploitation. P. 255.

integrated performance An acting performance organized in order to further the movie's story, rather than to draw attention to itself as a performance. P. 381.

intertextuality A **movie**'s inheritance from, resemblance to, and relationship with other similarly styled aesthetic objects. P. 60.

intertextual motivation See **motivation**.

intertitle Widely used in silent movies to present characters' dialog or commentary on the action, where they were cut into the action of a scene, intertitles are used (much less frequently) in sound movies to indicate the time and place of the scene or to provide other similar information. P. 407.

invention See **innovation**.

legitimate theater "Legitimate" theater originally described plays with spoken dialog, distinguishing them from melodramas in which the dialog was accompanied by music. During the nineteenth century, the term gradually acquired overtones of identifying those plays deemed to have poetic quality or literary worth, and by the beginning of the twentieth century it distinguished drama from slapstick and acrobatics, which had by then become separate entertainment forms in vaudeville and burlesque. P. 378.

line of action See **180-degree rule**.

long shot (LS) See **shot scale**.

long take A shot that continues uncut for an unusually long time – a minute or more. P. 332.

medium long shot See **shot scale**.

medium shot (MS) See **shot scale**.

mimesis Imitation. The classical Greek philosopher Plato made a distinction between mimesis, in which the poet "makes a speech pretending to be someone else," and **diegesis**, in which "the poet speaks in his own person"; a distinction, that is, between a performance and a report. (This use of the term "diegesis" should be distinguished from the use defined in the entry on "diegetic" above.) **Analogical** forms of representation, such as photography and cinema, are conventionally considered more mimetic than **digital** forms such as writing. Within a movie, an action or situation can be considered mimetic if it provides a recognizable imitation of behavior that we might encounter outside the cinema. P. 231.

mise-en-scène The arrangement of screen space as a meaningful organization of elements: literally, the "putting into a scene" or staging of a fiction. It is through mise-en-scène that **represented space** becomes **expressive**. **Classical Hollywood** mise-en-scène balances and fills the frame, avoiding both distracting detail and empty spots in the composition, and using conventional compositional principles to focus attention on the main line of action. Some film **theories** draw a distinction between mise-en-scène and editing (montage), on the basis that mise-en-scène takes place on the set, and editing afterwards. However, in practice, **Classical Hollywood** mise-en-scène and continuity editing (see **continuity system**) are closely interrelated. P. 328.

mise-en-temps In this book, the term used to describe the process of constructing a coherent sequence of plot events as **movie time**. Mise-en-temps uses temporal conventions similar to those by which Hollywood constructs its spatial framework. Like **mise-en-scène**, these conventions are both obvious and virtually invisible to us. P. 429.

monocular perspective The perspective produced when viewing the world through a single lens. This mode of representing the world dominates the central tradition of western European art from the Renaissance until the early twentieth century, and is inherent in the optical arrangement of still and movie cameras. P. 320.

motivation The justification given for the inclusion of an object or other element within a scene or movie. **Formalism** distinguishes between four kinds of motivation. **Compositional motivation** explains the presence of an element in terms of its necessity for **story** comprehension. **Realistic motivation** justifies the presence of a device on the grounds that it makes the movie seem more authentic or plausible. **Intertextual motivation** appeals directly to the audience's familiarity with generic convention. **Artistic motivation** jus-

tifies the presence of a device on the grounds of the movie's stylistic pattern. Usually these kinds of motivation operate collaboratively. P. 466.

movie Throughout this book, I distinguish between **film** and movie, using "movie" to refer to the stream of images that we consume as both **narrative** and spectacle when the material is projected. Thus, **movie time** refers to the time represented within the fiction, and is much more flexible than **film time**, involving **flashbacks**, ellipses, and other conventional devices of temporal construction. The distinction I make between film and movie is broadly comparable to the distinction between print and literature: the material and the experiential forms have different properties. Most other critics, however, use the two terms "film" and "movie" as if they were interchangeable. P. 7.

movie time See **movie**.

MPA The Motion Picture Association, the international trade association for the American motion picture industry, previously known (until 1994) as the Motion Picture Export Association (**MPEA**), and before that as the Foreign Department of the Motion Picture Producers and Distributors of America, Inc. (**MPPDA**). Because of its close cooperation with the federal government, it was and is also frequently called "the little State Department."

MPEA See **MPA**.

MPAA The Motion Picture Association of America, the industry trade association from 1945 to the present. The MPAA defines its function as being "to serve as the voice and advocate of the American motion picture, home video and television industries, domestically through the MPAA and internationally through the **MPA** . . . to serve as leader and advocate for major producers and distributors of entertainment programming for television, cable, home video, and future delivery system not yet imagined." P. 23.

MPPDA The Motion Picture Producers and Distributors of America, Inc., the industry trade association from its founding in 1922 to 1945, when it became the Motion Picture Association of America (**MPAA**). P. 125.

myth Criticism has extended the common usage of myth as a form of folklore to refer to a society's widely held beliefs about its origin, common features, attitudes, and practices, usually as expressed in the stories it often tells itself. Anthropologist Claude Lévi-Strauss argued that myth could be analyzed as a structure, and subsequent literary and cultural theorists (see **theory**) have identified myth as one of the ways in which the particular power relationships within a society come to be seen by its members as natural and commonsensical. P. 84.

narration The process by which a **plot** is arranged to permit the telling of a **story**. As Edward Branigan describes it, "narration is the overall regulation and distribution of knowledge which determines *how* and when the spectator acquires knowledge." Where plot and story can both be understood as objects – sequences of events – narration is a process. One part of this process is undertaken by the movie's **producers**, when they arrange the sequence of events and actions within the plot. The procedures of **mise-en-scène** and editing become the means by which viewers are guided through the plot. While the devices of narration are constructed on the sound stage and in the editing room, the process of narration is only completed in the movie theater, when viewers use their knowledge of convention and the plot information provided for them to construct the story in their own minds. P. 462.

narrative An ambiguous term, often used as a synonym for **plot**, **story**, and **narration**, and having different connotations as a noun and an adjective. The ambiguous senses of the term "narrative" become useful if we understand it as identifying the play between senses of plot, story, and narration in our experience of viewing a **movie**. P. 462.

narratology The general study of **narrative**. P. 454.

NATO The National Association of Theater Owners, the principal trade association for the major **exhibition** companies, which shares responsibility with the **MPAA** for the administration of the **rating system**. P. 177.

naturalism As a critical term, "naturalism" has

a history almost as complex as that of "**realism**". Its most common contemporary sense is in describing representations or performances concerned to produce an accurate imitation of external appearances. A naturalistic acting performance, for instance, will be **integrated** into the **narrative**, and will not draw attention to itself as a performance (see **autonomous performance**). This "invisible" style of acting tries to imitate the expressions and emotions of the everyday world, since its aim is to create a sense of character for the audience without making them consciously aware of how that sense is created. P. 382.

negative cost The total cost of a movie up to the editing of the original negative, including overheads, interest, and other costs not included in the production budget (see **above the line costs** and **below the line costs**), but not including any of the costs of **distribution**. In contemporary Hollywood, a movie's negative cost may be between one-and-a-half and two times its production budget. P. 198.

negative pickup The purchase of an already completed **movie** for **distribution** by a major company.

neoformalism See **Formalism**.

non-diegetic See **diegetic**.

oligopoly Monopoly power exercised by a small group, such as **Classical Hollywood**'s major, vertically integrated companies (see **vertical integration**). P. 118.

ostensiveness The degree to which a performance (see **autonomous performance**) is visibly marked out as a performance for its audience by its expressive features. Different acting styles display different degrees of ostensiveness: styles considered to be naturalistic (see **naturalism**) are less ostensive than others, and Hollywood has usually required supporting players, ethnic minorities, and women to be more broadly expressive than white male stars. P. 389.

pan Pivoting movement of the camera from left to right or right to left. P. 242.

Paramount case See **divorcement**.

persistence of vision A **theory** explaining the perception of the illusion of movement, formalized in 1824 by Peter Mark Roget. He suggested that every time we look at something, a brief residual image is stored on the retina of the eye, so that in watching sequences of still images, each individual image is retained until the next one appears to replace it. More recent research into the psychology of perception, however, suggests that the process is much more complicated, and that seeing and hearing are positive mental activities, not involuntary physical processes. Rather than the illusion of movement being created by a deception of the eye, the brain constructs a continuous image from the sequence of stills, filling in the missing parts. This is known as the phi phenomenon. P. 420.

pickup An agreement between a distributor and an independent **producer** guaranteeing **distribution**, and used by the producer as a basis for gaining financing. The most common form of these agreements is the **negative pickup**. In these agreements, the distributor commits no resources to the movie until it is completed, effectively transferring most of the risk to the producer and other financiers. P. 220.

plan Americain See **shot scale**.

platform release A pattern of **exhibition** in which the movie is initially shown in a few key theaters in the hope of receiving good critical and word-of-mouth comment, before it is shown much more widely. Previously known as **exclusive engagement**, platform release was the best way of exhibiting a **sleeper**, which builds its reputation and earnings on audience word-of-mouth. Since the early 1990s, as **wide release** has increasingly become the dominant **distribution** practice, the platform a movie is allowed has grown steadily shorter. P. 166.

plot The order in which events are represented in the movie, for which the **Formalists** used the word **syuzhet**, defined as "the structured set of all causal events as we see and hear them presented." P. 462.

plot point An event or incident in a **plot** that turns the story in a new direction. P. 416.

point of view A shot taken from the approximate **viewpoint** of a character and showing what the character can see is usually called a point-of-view shot. In this book, I distinguish

between the literal viewpoint – a position in space, determined by its angle, level, height, and distance from its subject – and a point of view, which I use to describe a position of knowledge in relation to the fiction. A character's **narrative** point of view is a matter of the character's relative subjectivity or omniscience. P. 347.

poststructuralism A critical movement best understood as a reaction to **structuralism**'s attempts to establish broad, incorporative theoretical procedures. Rather than being a **theory** in itself, poststructuralism proposed a mode of inquiry concerned with what had been left out of, or repressed by, structuralism's totalizing systems. Instead, it argued for a "decentering" of the attention paid to the structures of a text, and a deconstruction of textual meaning. Although poststructuralism involved a rejection of the structuralist claim to scientific status, it also evolved out of structuralism's concerns and shared several of its fundamental assumptions. **Cine-psychoanalysis** is in large part a poststructuralist theory. P. 543.

producer The person with overall responsibility for the production of a movie, usually particularly concerned with the financial and administrative elements of production. In accounts of Hollywood which seek to emphasize the creative achievements of writers or **director**s, producers are most often cast as the villains, but in both **Classical Hollywood** and post-Classical, it is a role that many creative personnel aspire to, since the producer is the person most likely to oversee and control the whole production, integrating the contributions of other personnel and balancing creative and financial considerations. P. 139.

Production Code A set of guidelines stipulating what was and was not permissible in **Classical Hollywood**'s field of representation, particularly with regard to sexual and criminal subject matter. Written in early 1930 by a group of Hollywood executives and officials and administered by the **MPPDA**, the Code's main purpose was to enable movies with controversial subject matter to be brought to the screen in a form that would not encounter

587

censorship problems at home or abroad. It also served the important function of protecting the industry from attacks by powerful sections of the community, such as church or social welfare groups and politicians. Often incorrectly thought to have been ignored by the production industry until 1934, it governed the content of Hollywood cinema from its implementation in 1930 until it was rewritten in 1966 and abandoned for a **rating system** in 1968. It is reproduced here as appendix 1. Pp. 17, 471.

production designer See **art director**.

production season Before the introduction of air-conditioning from the 1930s, attendance was lowest in the summer months, and Hollywood's production seasons ran from September to September. P. 78.

production values Those elements of a movie designed to appeal to an audience independently of the story: the sets, the costumes, the star performances, the "quality" of the product visible on the screen. Production values represent areas of pleasure offered to the viewer incidental to, and separate from, the plausibility of the fiction. P. 42.

product placement The practice of inserting brand-name goods into movies for advertising purposes. See also **tie-ins**. P. 146.

pro-filmic A critical term used to describe any of the elements placed in front of the camera to be filmed, such as sets and actors. Prior to the use of computer-generated images in special effects technology, even fantastic objects had to be realized in some physical form before the camera could record them. P. 237.

pro-filmic space The physical material of the scene prior to the act of filming.

public fantasy See **safe space**.

rating system The classification system introduced by the **MPAA** in 1968 to indicate whether **movies** were suitable for all audiences or only for audiences above a certain age. The MPAA system, administered by the Classification and Rating Administration (**CARA**), is a form of industry self-regulation, with no legal force in itself, as was the **Production Code** which it replaced. Pp. 23, 612. The 1968 Code and Rating system is

described in appendix 2, and current MPAA classifications are described in appendix 3.

realism A term with a complex history and a multiplicity of meanings. In our everyday use of the term "realistic," we invoke realism to evaluate the extent to which a representation or a **narrative** is like some previously established reality – or, in a commonly used critical phrase, the extent of its "adequacy to the real." Many critical propositions about realism in cinema derive from the commonly held assumption that **analogical** media such as photography are inherently more "realist" than other, less mimetic media (see **mimesis**). Literary critic Raymond Williams has suggested that the purpose of realism in art is "to show things as they really are." John Ellis points out that beneath this tautology lie several other tautologies dealing with different ways in which "realism" can be "realistic": it "should have a surface accuracy; it should conform to notions of what we expect to happen; it should explain itself adequately to us as audience; it should conform to particular notions of psychology and character **motivation**." But no account of realism progresses very far before it recognizes that realism, like all other approaches to art, relies on a system of conventions of representation. P. 231.

realistic motivation See **motivation**.

reception studies A critical approach which concentrates its attention on the audience, viewer, or reader of a work, rather than on the work as a text. P. 549.

rentals The proportion of **gross** box-office revenues paid by exhibitors to the distributor to rent the movie. A movie's gross rental therefore excludes the exhibitor's percentage of the box-office (up to 35 percent, but often as little as 10 percent for a major distributor's **blockbuster**), and the "house nut" or operating cost of the theater. Gross rentals in contemporary Hollywood are approximately half the box-office gross of a movie. P. 161.

represented space The area that exists in front of the camera lens and is recorded by it. It is the recognizable space in which actors stand, in which props are placed, and in which things happen. P. 313.

resolution Contemporary screenwriting manuals declare that "proper structure occurs when the right events occur in the right sequence to elicit maximum emotional involvement in the . . . audience . . . good **plot** structure means that the right thing is happening at the right time." To this end, they suggest that a movie screenplay should have three acts. Act 1, the **setup**, establishes the plot situation in the first quarter of the movie. Act 2, the **confrontation**, builds it during the next half. Act 3, the resolution, brings the story to its conclusion in the final quarter. P. 416.

reverse-angle See **shot/reverse shot**.

roadshow Pattern of **exhibition** used in **Classical Hollywood** and more extensively between 1950 and 1975, in which a movie was released only to selected theaters at higher admission prices and with reserved seating. In some versions of roadshow exhibition, known as **"four-walling,"** the distributor would rent the theater from the exhibitor for a flat fee, pay all advertising and other expenses associated with the exhibition, and take all the box-office income as receipts. P. 165.

rough cut The first assembly of a movie, usually prepared by the **editor** while shooting continues. P. 141.

runaway production The practice of producing American-financed movies abroad, either to meet quota regulations, or to enhance the movies' appeal to the international market, or to take advantage of cheaper production costs outside the US. "Runaway" production reached its height during the late 1960s, when nearly half of the features made by American companies were produced abroad. P. 127.

rushes See **dailies**.

safe action area An area marked in the viewfinders of widescreen cameras to identify the dimensions of the television frame, so that cinematographers could ensure that the essential object in each shot was inside the part of the composition that would appear on the television screen. P. 254.

safe space In this book, safe space identifies an interrelated set of concepts around the presentation of a **movie**. The physical environment of the movie theater operates as a safe space for the audience's engagement in **public fantasy**, the public expression of ideas and actions we must each individually repress in our everyday behavior. The price of admission to this everyday place of refuge from the everyday is our knowledge that what happens inside the movie theater has nothing to do with what happens outside, but takes place only in the trivialized safe space of entertainment. Within the movie, the **continuity system**'s devices of invisible editing, **eyeline matches**, and **shot/reverse shot** patterns secure the viewer's mapping of a movie's spatial topography. By guaranteeing the secure placement of the audience in relation to the fictional world of the movie, safe space allows viewers to enjoy the pleasures of spectacle and **narrative**, and to engage emotionally with the characters, confident that the movie's image stream will avoid any sudden shocks that might abruptly disrupt our involvement in the action. P. 35.

saturation booking A pattern of **exhibition** in which a movie is simultaneously released to a large number of theaters within the same area, usually with a substantial advertising campaign. Prior to 1960, saturation booking was seldom used by the major companies, and widely assumed to be an exhibition strategy designed to maximize income from a poor picture, before audience word-of-mouth discouraged attendance. Television advertising made saturation booking a more attractive strategy, and under the name of **wide release**, it has been the dominant exhibition strategy in Hollywood since the mid-1980s. Although there were earlier examples of saturation booking being used in conjunction with television advertising, the simultaneous opening of *Jaws* (1975) in over 400 theaters is commonly taken to be the most influential use of this exhibition strategy, which now dominates the industry. From the mid-1990s, movies have commonly opened simultaneously on 2,000–3,000 screens. P. 182.

scopophilia Pleasure, particularly sexual pleasure, in looking. Scopophilia is distinguished from **voyeurism** in that it identifies a general pleasure in looking, while voyeurism is usually understood as a perversion. Scopophilia is a central idea in the account of the **cinematic apparatus** proposed by **cine-psychoanalysis**. P. 471.

semiology The study of signs, sign systems, and their meanings. In his *Course in General Linguistics*, Ferdinand de Saussure described semiology as a science that would show what constitutes signs, and what laws govern them. He understood linguistics to be part of the general science of semiology. Semiology, sometimes also called semiotics, has been central to structuralist studies of cinema (see **structuralism**), but its claim to scientific status has never been established. P. 503.

set-up One positioning of the camera and accompanying lighting arrangement. One set-up may yield more than one shot in the final picture: the **close-ups** of one player in a scene may well all be photographed from the same set-up, for instance. P. 332.

setup See **resolution**.

shot/reverse shot One of Hollywood's most frequent formal figures, in which two consecutive shots depict complementary spaces. The most common instance of this figure occurs in dialog scenes presented in over-the-shoulder close **medium shots**, where the looks of the characters at each other and the graphic similarity between the shots help the viewer infer that the spaces in the two shots are contiguous. **Apparatus theory** describes this operation as a process of "suturing," by which the viewer perceives gaps in the space represented, only to have these gaps filled in a process which binds the spectator into the coherence of the fiction. Through the suture, the Hollywood movie masks both its formal and its ideological operations. P. 344. Shot/reverse shot construction is illustrated on p. 345.

shot scale The range of different shots used in a movie, usually established in terms of the most commonly represented object, the human body. In a **long shot (LS)**, people fill half or three-quarters of the height of the screen. In a **full shot**, the height of the frame is filled with the human figure, while a **medium long shot** covers the body from mid-calf or knees up. This shot is sometimes

called a **plan Americain** or "Hollywood shot," because of the frequency of its use in Hollywood. A **medium shot (MS)** cuts characters off at the waist, a **close shot** takes in the character from the chest up, and a **close-up (CU)** is a shot of the face. P. 334. Shot scale is illustrated on p. 336.

sleeper A picture initially assumed to have limited appeal which gains a much larger audience through word-of-mouth recommendation. P. 203.

slow motion Slow-motion effects are produced by passing the **film** through the camera at a faster rate than normal, so that the film takes longer to project than the duration of the action it records. P. 420.

story The reconstruction of **plot** events in their chronological order, through which we can establish the chain of causality which links them. **Formalist** criticism designates the story the **fabula**. P. 462.

storyboard A series of sketches representing individual shots used to plan production, particularly of complex scenes involving stuntwork or special effects. P. 332.

structuralism As an intellectual movement, structuralism originated in the proposition, made by anthropologist Claude Lévi-Strauss, that kinship relations and primitive myths were structured like language, and could be studied according to the principles of linguistic analysis. Structuralism maintained that the elements within a structure did not possess meaning as independent units, but gained their meaning through their relations to other elements. Meaning is, for instance, often constructed through binary oppositions: "good" means something only in relation to "bad"; "raw" and "cooked" signify opposing states. Applications of the structuralist approach proliferated in European thought in the 1960s, and cultural theorists such as Roland Barthes and Umberto Eco argued that cultural events could be understood by examining the structure that underlay them as if it were a language. P. 503.

suturing See **shot/reverse shot**.

syuzhet See **plot**.

take The term used to describe each version of any given shot. Generally, the film crew will shoot several takes of each shot in a **set-up**, selecting the take with the best acting and technical performance for printing. A **long take** refers to the temporal duration of the shot.

theory The word "theory" has its origins in a Greek root, *thea*, meaning sight. It shares a linguistic point of origin with "theater" and a point of derivation with ideas of both spectacle and speculation. To formulate a theory is thus to articulate a **point of view**. Theory, however, often makes rhetorical claims to a degree of objectivity that it denies to other forms of criticism, and it also commonly lays claim to a broader scope than other critical practices. Dudley Andrew, for example, distinguishes between theory and criticism by suggesting that while criticism concentrates on individual movies or groups of movies, theory is concerned with the properties of cinema as a whole, or what he calls "the cinematic capability." P. 496.

tie-in Promotional campaigns for commercial products that are coordinated with a movie's release. These campaigns often also involve **product placement**. P. 146.

track, tracking shot A shot in which the camera physically moves through space. Often the camera will be mounted on a platform that runs on tracks laid on the ground like railroad tracks. A shot in which the camera moves toward the object it is photographing is called a **track-in**, and one in which it moves away is a **track-out**. P. 242.

track-in See **track**.

track-out See **track**.

transparency A quality of Hollywood's **commercial aesthetic**, often understood as contributing substantially to the particular kind of **realism** that Hollywood offers. Although acting, for instance, can draw attention to itself and function as a separate spectacle (see **autonomous performance**), it more routinely aspires to transparency (see **integrated performance**), in the same way as the **continuity system**'s codes of editing and camerawork seek to render themselves "invisible" by working according to what André Bazin called "the material or dramatic logic of a scene." P. 313.

turnaround A point in the development of a screenplay at which a studio or other purchaser of a script has decided not to proceed further with a project, so that the rights to the script revert to the **producer**. A script "in turnaround" is in search of a major company to agree to distribute it, or of other sources of finance.

unsafe space Post-**Classical Hollywood** cinema has frequently disrupted the audience's sense of the screen as a **safe space** to look at. The unsafe space of post-*Psycho* "nightmare movies" is actively malign, seeking to catch the viewer unawares and stab screen space when the audience least expects it. Movies may assault their audiences physically, stabbing them in the eye with flashes of light, rapid, disjointed cutting, or sudden movement. The frame can be violently penetrated by a murderous implement, at any moment and from any angle. Typically, unsafe space empowers malign characters, capable of moving through screen space in a manner incomprehensible or invisible to the audience, and threatening both sympathetic characters and viewers with their sudden, unpredictable appearance. In such movies, the audience is associated with the fictional victims, even when the camera's **viewpoint** is that of the monster as it attacks. Unsafe space disorients the viewer, emphasizing the power of a movie's image track to control the viewer's look. P. 354.

verisimilitude In a general sense "verisimilitude" means truthfulness, and although its meaning overlaps with that of **realism**, in the context in which it is used in this book it implies something that is probable, plausible, or appropriate, rather than realistic. Verisimilitude is also a matter of conventions, and sometimes generic conventions (see **genre**) transgress broader social or cultural regimes of verisimilitude: as, for instance, when a character bursts into song while walking down a street. P. 76.

vertical integration A vertically integrated company is involved in all three branches of its business: manufacture, wholesaling, and retailing; and this position gives it a much greater degree of control over its terms of trade than a company involved in only one branch of the business can exercise. A small number of vertically integrated companies, all pursuing the same business strategies, can between them dominate an industry. The history of American business since the start of the twentieth century has been predominantly a history of the growth of vertically integrated corporations, and with it the growth of **oligopoly** control. P. 118.

viewpoint See **point of view**.

voice-over A narrator's voice when the narrator is not seen. P. 433.

voyeurism See **scopophilia**.

wide release The most common form of theatrical release since the 1980s, formerly known as **saturation booking**, involving the simultaneous **exhibition** of a movie on multiple screens across a notional market. By the early 1990s, showing a movie on 2,000 screens was not uncommon. P. 203.

wipe A transition between shots in which a line moves across the screen, with the image changing behind it from one scene to the next. In **Classical Hollywood**, a wipe usually implied a transition between scenes occurring in different locations in continuous time. P. 242.

zone See **clearance**.

APPENDIX 1

The Motion Picture Production Code (as Published 31 March, 1930)

A CODE TO MAINTAIN SOCIAL AND COMMUNITY VALUES IN THE PRODUCTION OF SILENT, SYNCHRONIZED AND TALKING MOTION PICTURES

Adopted by Association of Motion Picture Producers, Inc., at Hollywood, Calif., and ratified by the Board of Directors of Motion Picture Producers and Distributors of America, Inc., March 31, 1930.

Reasons for the New Code

The advent of sound on the motion picture screen brought new problems of self-discipline and regulation to the motion picture industry. Sound unlocked a vast amount of dramatic material which for the first time could be effectively presented on the screen. It brought the dramatist to Hollywood, to supplement the work of the scenario writer. It brought stars from the legitimate stage and the variety stage to the talking motion picture screen. It brought spoken dialogue, which had to be adapted to the requirements of film presentation. It brought new "extras," many of whom were given spoken lines.

To meet this new situation it became necessary to reaffirm the standards under which silent films had been produced since 1922, and to revise, amplify and add to those principles in the light of responsible opinion, so that all engaged in the making of sound pictures might have a commonly understandable and commonly acceptable guide in the maintenance of social and community values in pictures.

The task undertaken by the Motion Picture Producers and Distributors of America, cooperating with educators, dramatists, church authorities and leaders in the field of child education and social welfare work, has now resulted in the adoption of a new Code by the Association of Motion Picture Producers.

The new Code has been accepted and subscribed to individually by such prominent producers in the motion picture industry as: Art Cinema Corporation (United Artists); Christie Film Company, Inc.; Columbia Pictures Corporation; Cecil B. de Mille Productions, Inc.; Educational Studios, Inc.; First National Pictures, Inc.; Fox Film Corporation; Gloria Productions, Inc.; Samuel Goldwyn, Inc.; Inspiration Pictures, Inc.; Harold Lloyd Corporation; Metro-Goldwyn-Mayer Studios, Inc.; Paramount Famous Lasky Corporation; Pathé Studios, Inc.; RKO Productions, Inc.; Hal Roach Studios, Inc.; Mack Sennett Studio; Tiffany Productions, Inc.; Universal Pictures Corporation; and Warner Bros. Pictures, Inc.

Principles Underlying the Code

1   Motion picture producers recognize the high trust and confidence which have been placed in them by the people of the world, and they recognize their responsibility to the public because of this trust.
2   Theatrical motion pictures . . . are primarily to be regarded as entertainment. Mankind has always regarded the importance of entertainment and its value in rebuilding the bodies and souls of human beings.
3   It is recognized that there is entertainment which tends to improve the race (or at least to re-create and rebuild human beings exhausted with the realities of life), and entertainment which tends to harm human beings, or to lower their standards of life and living.
4   Motion pictures are an important form of art expression. Art enters intimately into the lives of human beings. The art of motion pictures has the same object as the other arts – the presentation of human thought, emotion, and experience, in terms of an appeal to the soul through the senses.
5   In consequence of the foregoing facts the following general principles are adopted:

No picture shall be produced which will lower the moral standards of those who see it. Hence the sympathy of the audience should never be thrown to the side of crime, wrongdoing, evil or sin.

Correct standards of life shall be presented on the screen, subject only to necessary dramatic contrasts.

Law, natural or human, should not be ridiculed, nor shall sympathy be created for its violation.

Particular Applications

Crimes against the law

These shall never be presented in such a way as to throw sympathy with the crime as against law and justice or to inspire others with a desire for imitation.

1   *Murder*
   a   The technique of murder must be presented in a way that will not inspire imitation.

b   Brutal killings are not to be presented in detail.

c   Revenge in modern times shall not be justified.

2   *Methods of crime* should not be explicitly presented.

a   Theft, robbery, safe-cracking, and dynamiting of trains, mines, buildings, etc., should not be detailed in method.

b   Arson must be subject to the same safeguards.

c   The use of firearms should be restricted to essentials.

d   Methods of smuggling should not be presented.

3   *Illegal drug traffic* must never be presented.

4   *The use of liquor* in American life, when not required by the plot or for proper characterization, will not be shown.

Sex

The sanctity of the institution of marriage and the home shall be upheld. Pictures shall not infer that low forms of sex relationship are the accepted or common thing.

1   *Adultery,* sometimes necessary plot material, must not be explicitly treated, or justified, or presented attractively.

2   *Scenes of passion* should not be introduced when not essential to the plot. In general, excessive passion should so be treated that these scenes do not stimulate the lower and baser element.

3   *Seduction or rape*

a   They should never be more than suggested, and only when essential for the plot, and even then never shown by explicit method.

b   They are never the proper subject for comedy.

4   *Sex perversion* or any inference to it is forbidden.

5   *White-slavery* shall not be treated.

6   *Miscegenation* is forbidden.

7   *Sex hygiene* and venereal diseases are not subjects for motion pictures.

8   Scenes of *actual child birth*, in fact or in silhouette, are never to be presented.

9   *Children's sex organs* are never to be exposed.

Vulgarity

The treatment of low, disgusting, unpleasant, though not necessarily evil subjects, should be subject always to the dictates of good taste and a regard for the sensibilities of the audience.

Obscenity

Obscenity in word, gesture, reference, song, joke, or by suggestion, is forbidden.

Dances

Dances which emphasize indecent movements are to be regarded as obscene.

Profanity

Pointed profanity or vulgar expressions, however used, are forbidden.

Costume

1 **Complete nudity** is never permitted. This includes nudity in fact or in silhouette, or any lecherous or licentious notice thereof by other characters in the picture.
2 **Dancing costumes** intended to permit undue exposure or indecent movements in the dance are forbidden.

Religion

1 No film or episode may throw ridicule on any religious faith.
2 Ministers of religion in their character as such, should not be used as comic characters or as villains.
3 Ceremonies of any definite religion should be carefully and respectfully handled.

National feelings

1 The use of the Flag shall be consistently respectful.
2 The history, institutions, prominent people and citizenry of other nations shall be represented fairly.

Titles

Salacious, indecent, or obscene titles shall not be used.

Repellent subjects

The following subjects must be treated within the careful limits of good taste:

1 Actual hangings, or electrocutions as legal punishments for crime.
2 Third Degree methods.
3 Brutality and possible gruesomeness.
4 Branding of people or animals.
5 Apparent cruelty to children or animals.
6 Surgical operations.

Uniform Interpretation of the Code

That there may be no doubt about a uniform interpretation of the code by the different producers, machinery has been set up that makes available for every producer the knowledge and experience of the entire industry, aided by the cooperation available from socially-minded groups and public leaders in the selection of the material for screen use and in the treatments of such material.

We believe in and pledge our support to these deep and fundamental values in a democratic society:

Freedom of choice . . .

The right of creative man to achieve artistic excellence . . .

The importance of the role of the parent as the guide of the family's comfort . . .

Standards for Production

In furtherance of the objectives of the Code to accord with the mores, the culture, and the moral sense of our society, the principles stated above and the following standards shall govern the Administrator in his consideration of motion pictures submitted for Code approval:

- The basic dignity and value of human life shall be respected and upheld. Restraint shall be exercised in portraying the taking of life.
- Evil, sin, crime and wrong-doing shall not be justified.
- Special restraint shall be exercised in portraying criminal or anti-social activities in which minors participate or are involved. Detailed and protracted acts of brutality, cruelty, physical violence, torture and abuse shall not be presented.
- Indecent or undue exposure of the human body shall not be presented.
- Illicit sex relationships shall not be justified. Intimate sex scenes violating common standards of decency shall not be portrayed.
- Restraint and care shall be exercised in presentations dealing with sex aberrations.
- Obscene speech, gestures or movements shall not be presented. Undue profanity shall not be permitted.
- Religion shall not be demeaned.
- Words or symbols contemptuous of racial, religious or national groups shall not be used so as to incite bigotry or hatred.
- Excessive cruelty to animals shall not be portrayed and animals shall not be treated inhumanely.

APPENDIX 3
The Classification and Rating System: "What the Ratings Mean" (as Published January 2002)

G: General Audiences – All Ages Admitted

This is a film which contains nothing in theme, language, nudity and sex, violence, etc. which would, in the view of the Rating Board, be offensive to parents whose younger children view the film. The G rating is not a "certificate of approval," nor does it signify a children's film. Some snippets of language may go beyond polite conversation but they are common everyday expressions. No stronger words are present in G-rated films. The violence is at a minimum. Nudity and sex scenes are not present; nor is there any drug use content.

PG: Parental Guidance Suggested. Some Material May Not Be Suitable For Children

This is a film which clearly needs to be examined or inquired into by parents before they let their children attend. The label PG plainly states that parents may consider some material unsuitable for their children, but the parent must make the decision. The theme of a PG-rated film may itself call for parental guidance. There may be some profanity in these films. There may be some violence or brief nudity. But these elements are not deemed so intense as to require that parents be strongly cautioned beyond the suggestion of parental guidance. There is no drug use content in a PG-rated film.

PG-13: Parents Strongly Cautioned. Some Material May Be Inappropriate For Children Under 13

PG-13 is a sterner warning to parents to determine for themselves the attendance in particular of their younger children as they might consider some material not suited for them. A PG-13 film is one which, in the view of the Rating Board, leaps beyond the boundaries of the PG rating in theme, violence, nudity, sensuality, language, or other contents, but does not quite fit within the restricted R category. Any drug use content will initially require at least a PG-13 rating. In effect, the PG-13 cautions parents with more stringency than usual to give special attention to this film before they allow their 12-year olds and younger to attend. If nudity is sexually oriented, the film will generally not be found in the PG-13 category. If violence is too rough or persistent, the film goes into the R (restricted) rating. A film's single use of one of the harsher sexually-derived words, though only as an expletive, shall initially require the Rating Board to issue that film at least a PG-13 rating. More than one such expletive must lead the Rating Board to issue a film an R rating, as must even one of these words used in a sexual context. These films can be rated less severely, however, if by a special vote, the Rating Board feels that a lesser rating would more responsibly reflect the opinion of American parents.

R: Restricted, Under 17 Requires Accompanying Parent Or Adult Guardian

In the opinion of the Rating Board, this film definitely contains some adult material. Parents are strongly urged to find out more about this film before they allow their children to accompany them. An R-rated film may include hard language, or tough violence, or nudity within sensual scenes, or drug abuse or other elements, or a combination of some of the above, so that parents are counseled, in advance, to take this advisory rating very seriously. Parents must find out more about an R-rated movie before they allow their teenagers to view it.

NC-17: No One 17 And Under Admitted

This rating declares that the Rating Board believes that this is a film that most parents will consider patently too adult for their youngsters under 17. No children will be admitted. The reasons for the application of an NC-17 rating can be violence or sex or aberrational behavior or drug abuse or any other elements which, when present, most parents would consider too strong and therefore off-limits for viewing by their children.

Notes

Chapter 1   Taking Hollywood Seriously

1   F. Scott Fitzgerald, *The Last Tycoon* (Harmondsworth: Penguin, 1974), pp. 5–6.

2   Description of Hollywood in the opening sequence of *A Star is Born* (1937).

3   Rachel Field, *To See Ourselves*, quoted in Carey McWilliams, *Southern California: An Island on the Land*, 1st pub. 1946 (Santa Barbara: Peregrine Smith, 1973), p. 330.

4   Raymond Chandler, *The Little Sister*, 1st pub. 1949 (Harmondsworth: Penguin, 1973), p. 109.

5   "Hooray for Hollywood," composed by Richard Whiting and Johnny Mercer, from *Hollywood Hotel* (1937); Caitlin Moran, "The Day We Spent Granny's Lolly," *Observer* (July 26, 1992), p. 47.

6   Jack Valenti, "Hollywood, the Rating System and the Movie-Going Public," *USA Today* magazine, 122:2580 (September 1993), p. 87.

7   Pauline Kael, "Trash, Art, and the Movies," in *Going Steady* (Boston: Little, Brown, 1970), pp. 93, 104–5, 113–14.

8   Hortense Powdermaker, *Hollywood the Dream Factory: An Anthropologist Looks at the Movie-Makers* (Boston: Little, Brown, 1950), pp. 285, 313, 169, 16, 27, 142–3, 166.

9   Steven Bach, *Final Cut: Dreams and Disaster in the Making of Heaven's Gate* (London: Faber, 1986), pp. 195, 338, 416.

10   Frances Marion, *How to Write and Sell Film Stories* (New York: Covici Friede, 1937), pp. 26–7.

11   Quoted in Peter Krämer, "Women First: *Titanic* (1997), Action-Adventure Films and Hollywood's Female Audience," *Historical Journal of Film, Radio and Television* 18:4 (1998), p. 116.

12   Justin Wyatt and Katherine Vlesmas, "The Drama of Recoupment: On the Mass Media Negotiation of *Titanic*," in *Titanic: Anatomy of a Blockbuster*, eds Kevin S. Sandler and Gaylyn Studlar (New Brunswick, NJ: Rutgers University Press, 1999), p. 42.

13   David Sterritt, *Christian Science Monitor*, quoted in Matthew Bernstein, "'Floating Triumphantly': The American Critics on *Titanic*," in Sandler and Studlar, p. 15.

14 Katha Pollitt, "Women and Children First," *Nation*, 30 March 1998, p. 9.

15 Melanie Nash and Martti Lahti, "'Almost Ashamed to Say I Am One of Those Girls': *Titanic*, Leonardo DiCaprio, and the Paradoxes of Girls' Fandom," in Sandler and Studlar, p. 64.

16 Krämer, p. 130 n.42.

17 David M. Lubin, *Titanic* (London: British Film Institute, 1999), p. 69.

18 Tom Gunning, "An Aesthetic of Astonishment: Early Film and the (In)credulous Spectator," *Art and Text* 34 (Spring 1989), p. 31.

19 Quoted in John Kasson, *Amusing the Million: Coney Island at the Turn of the Century* (New York: Hill and Wang, 1978), pp. 63, 66.

20 Tom Gunning, "The Cinema of Attractions: Early Film, its Spectator and the Avant-Garde," in *Early Cinema: Space, Frame, Narrative*, ed. Thomas Elsaesser (London: British Film Institute, 1990), pp. 58–9.

21 David Bordwell, *The Cinema of Eisenstein* (Cambridge, MA: Harvard University Press, 1993), p. 6.

22 Sergei Eisenstein, quoted in Bordwell, pp. 115–16.

23 Quoted in Peter Wollen, *Signs and Meaning in the Cinema* (London: Secker and Warburg, 1972), p. 32.

24 Quoted in Laurie Oullette, "Ship of Dreams: Cross-Class Romance and the Cultural Fantasy of *Titanic*," in Sandler and Studlar, p. 169.

25 Quoted in Vivan Sobchack, "Bathos and Bathysphere: On Submersion, Longing and History in *Titanic*," in Sandler and Studlar, p. 202.

26 Lamar Trotti, "The Motion Picture as a Business," delivered as a speech by Carl E. Milliken, April 1928. Motion Picture Association Archive, New York.

27 Harold B. Franklin, *Motion Picture Theatre Management* (New York: Doran, 1927), p. 246.

28 Ezra Goodman, *The Fifty-Year Decline of Hollywood* (New York: Simon and Schuster, 1961); Richard Dyer McCann, *Hollywood in Transition* (Boston: Houghton Mifflin, 1962); Jim Hillier, *The New Hollywood* (London: Studio Vista, 1993); Jerzy Toeplitz, *Hollywood and After: The Changing Face of Movies in America* (London: Allen and Unwin, 1974).

29 André Bazin, "La Politique des Auteurs," in *The New Wave*, ed. Peter Graham (London: Secker and Warburg, 1968), pp. 143–4, 154.

30 David Bordwell, Janet Staiger, and Kristin Thompson, *The Classical Hollywood Cinema: Film Style and Mode of Production to 1960* (London: Routledge and Kegan Paul, 1985), p. 4.

31 Bordwell et al., p. 367.

32 Bordwell et al., p. 3.

33 Bordwell et al., p. xiv.

34 Kael, p. 101.

35 David Bordwell, *Narration in the Fiction Film* (London: Methuen, 1985), p. 159.

36 Rick Altman, "Dickens, Griffith, and Film Theory Today," in *Classical Hollywood Narrative: The Paradigm Wars*, ed. Jane Gaines (Durham, NC: Duke University Press, 1992), p. 32.

37 H. Kent Webster, "Little Stories of Great Films," *Nickelodeon* 3:1 (January 1, 1910), p. 13, quoted in Bordwell et al., p. 195.

38 Quoted in Hillier, p. 44.

39 Bordwell et al., p. 10.

40 Bordwell et al., p. 373.

41 Kristin Thompson, *Storytelling in the New Hollywood: Understanding the Classical Narrative Technique* (Cambridge, MA: Harvard University Press, 1999), pp. ix, 8, 336.

42 Thompson, p. 336.

43 Douglas Gomery, "The Coming of Sound: Technological Change in the American Film Industry," in *The American Film Industry*, ed. Tino Balio, 1st edn 1976, revised edn (Madison: University of Wisconsin Press, 1985), pp. 229–51.

44 Quoted in Hillier, p. 41.

45 Quoted in Kathryn Hughes, "Crocodile Tears from Hollywood," *Observer* (September 5, 1993), p. 43.

46 Bruce A. Austin, *Immediate Seating: A Look at Movie Audiences* (Belmont, CA: Wadsworth, 1989), pp. 44, 90.

47 2000 Motion Picture Attendance Survey, Motion Picture Association, www.mpaa.org.

48 Melvyn Stokes, "Female Audiences of the 1920s and Early 1930s," in *Identifying Hollywood's Audiences: Cultural Identity and the Movies*, eds Melvyn Stokes and Richard

Maltby (London: British Film Institute, 1999), pp. 43–5.

49 Margaret Thorp, *America at the Movies* (London: Faber, 1946), p. 17.

50 Kathryn H. Fuller, *At the Picture Show: Small Town Audiences and the Creation of Movie Fan Culture* (Washington, DC: Smithsonian Institution Press, 1996), pp. 144, 148.

51 Terry Ramsaye, "'Highbrow' Productions – and Tillie," *Motion Picture Herald*, 28 May 1932.

52 Review of *Taxi*, *Variety*, 12 January 1931; review of *Delicious*, *Variety*, 29 December 1931.

53 Bordwell et al., p. 16.

54 William R. Weaver, "AIP Heads Set Sight on Teenage Patron," *Motion Picture Herald* (May 25, 1957), p. 20, quoted in Thomas Doherty, *Teenagers and Teenpics: The Juvenilization of American Movies in the 1950s* (Boston: Unwin Hyman, 1988), p. 156.

55 Robin Bean and David Austen, "U.S.A. Confidential," *Films and Filming*, 215 (November 1968), pp. 21–2, quoted in Doherty, p. 157.

56 "Old 4-Hanky 'Women's Market' Pix, Far, Far From 1972 'Year of Woman,'" *Variety*, 30 August 1972, p. 5.

57 Jib Fowles, *StarStruck: Celebrity Performers and the American Public* (Washington, DC: Smithsonian Institution Press, 1992), p. 73.

58 Aljean Harmetz, "Rating the Ratings," in *Rolling Breaks and Other Movie Business* (New York: Knopf, 1983), p. 96; Georgia Jeffries, "The Problem with G," *American Film* (June 1978), p. 51.

59 Bruce A. Austin, Mark J. Nicolich, and Thomas Simonet, "MPAA Ratings and the Box Office: Some Tantalizing Statistics," *Film Quarterly* 35:2 (Winter 1981–2).

60 Quoted in Hillier, p. 31.

61 David Marc, *Demographic Vistas: Television in American Culture* (Philadelphia: University of Pennsylvania Press, 1984).

62 MPAA 2000 Motion Picture Attendance Survey.

63 Robert Allen, "Home Alone Together: Hollywood and the 'Family Film,'" in Stokes and Maltby, p. 118.

64 From 1913, the British Board of Film Censors categorized movies as being suitable either for exhibition to adult audiences, or "for universal exhibition."

65 Rick Altman, *The American Film Musical* (Bloomington: Indiana University Press, 1987), p. 340.

66 Altman, *American Film Musical*, p. 340.

67 David Morley and Kevin Robins, "Spaces of Identity: Communications Technologies and the Reconfiguration of Europe," *Screen* 30:4 (Autumn 1989), p. 21.

68 James True, *Printer's Ink* (February 4, 1926), quoted in Charles Eckert, "The Carole Lombard in Macy's Window," *Quarterly Review of Film Studies* 3 (Winter 1978), pp. 4–5.

69 "Certain Factors and Considerations Affecting the European Market," internal MPPDA memo, October 25, 1928, Motion Picture Association Archive, New York.

70 Quoted in Jeffrey Richards, *The Age of the Dream Palace: Cinema and Society in Britain, 1930–1939* (London: Routledge and Kegan Paul, 1984), p. 63.

Chapter 2   Entertainment 1

1 V. F. Perkins, *Film as Film: Understanding and Judging Movies* (Harmondsworth: Penguin, 1972), pp. 156–7.

2 Harold L. Vogel, *Entertainment Industry Economics: A Guide for Financial Analysis*, 5th edn (Cambridge: Cambridge University Press, 2001), pp. xvii–xviii.

3 Anonymous moviegoer (D. H.), quoted in Jackie Stacey, "Feminine Fascinations: Forms of Identification in Star–Audience Relations," in *Stardom: Industry of Desire*, ed. Christine Gledhill (London: Routledge, 1991), p. 141.

4 Reproduced in Russell C. Sweeney, *Coming Next Week: A Pictorial History of Film Advertising* (New York: Barnes, 1973), p. 17.

5 *Chambers Twentieth Century Dictionary* (Edinburgh: Chambers, 1977), p. 435. The *Oxford English Dictionary* offers "the act of occupying a person's attention agreeably; interesting employment; amusement . . . that which affords interest or amusement . . . a public performance or exhibition intended to interest or amuse" (*Compact Edition*, vol. 1 (1971), p. 871).

6 Quoted in Joanna Coles, "Eastern Promise for . . . Recession-hit Movies," *Guardian* (May 17, 1992).

7 Richard Dyer, "Introduction," in his *Only Entertainment* (London: Routledge, 1992), p. 3.

8 Father Daniel A. Lord, SJ, Reporter's Transcript, board meeting, Association of Motion Picture Producers (AMPP), February 10, 1930, p. 11, Motion Picture Association of America Archive, New York, 1930 AMPP Code file (hereafter MPA).

9 Jack Alicoate, "The Romance of the Roxy," reprinted in Ben M. Hall, *The Best Remaining Seats: The Golden Age of the Movie Palace* (New York: DaCapo, 1988), p. 82.

10 Advertisement in the *Saturday Evening Post*, quoted in Robert S. Lynd and Helen Merrill Lynd, *Middletown: A Study in Modern American Culture* (New York: Harcourt, Brace, and World, 1929), p. 265.

11 Richard Dyer, "Entertainment and Utopia," *MOVIE* 24 (1977), p. 8.

12 Martha Wolfenstein and Nathan Leites, *Movies: A Psychological Study* (Glencoe, IL: Free Press, 1950), pp. 11–12.

13 Wolfenstein and Leites, pp. 103, 193, 109, 87, 300, 24.

14 Wolfenstein and Leites, pp. 98, 178. Their sample group of 26 French films may have been somewhat less representative than the much larger sample of American movies.

15 Hortense Powdermaker, *Hollywood the Dream Factory: An Anthropologist Looks at the Movie-Makers* (Boston: Little, Brown, 1950), pp. 71–2.

16 Quoted in Mike Bygrave, "Jaglom and the Women," *Guardian* (December 12, 1991).

17 Theodor Adorno and Max Horkheimer, "Enlightenment as Mass Deception," in *Mass Communication and Society*, eds James Curran, Michael Gurevich, and Janet Woolacott (London: Edward Arnold, 1977), pp. 361–2.

18 Clement Greenberg, "Avant-Garde and Kitsch," in *Mass Culture: The Popular Arts in America*, eds Bernard Rosenberg and David Manning White (New York: Free Press, 1957), pp. 105–6.

19 Quoted in Robert Leedham, "Low, Low, Quick, Quick, Low," *Guardian* (October 3, 1991), p. 28.

20 F. Scott Fitzgerald, *The Last Tycoon* (Harmondsworth: Penguin, 1974), p. 5.

21 Robert Allen, *Speaking of Soap Opera* (Chapel Hill: University of North Carolina Press, 1985), p. 16.

22 Peter Wollen, *Signs and Meaning in the Cinema*, 1st pub. 1968 (London: Secker and Warburg, 1972), p. 10.

23 David A. Cook, *A History of Narrative Film*, 2nd edn (New York: Norton, 1990), p. 653.

24 Ronald Lightbown, *Sandro Botticelli. Volume 1: Life and Work* (London: Paul Elek, 1978), p. 86.

25 In 1815, *The Birth of Venus* was moved from the grand-ducal wardrobe of the Medici villa at Castello to the Uffizi gallery. Gabriele Mandel, *The Complete Paintings of Botticelli* (London: Weidenfeld and Nicolson, 1970), p. 97.

26 Umberto Eco, *The Role of the Reader: Explorations in the Semiotics of Texts* (Bloomington: University of Indiana Press, 1979), p. 7.

27 Dwight MacDonald, "A Theory of Mass Culture," in Rosenberg and White, pp. 60, 62, 72.

28 Walter Benjamin, "The Work of Art in the Age of Mechanical Reproduction," in his *Illuminations* (London: Cape, 1970), p. 223.

29 Jack Valenti, "Traveling that Sweet Road that Leads to Success," speech to ShoWest, Las Vegas, Nevada, 6 March, 2001. www.mpaa.org/jack/2001/2001_03_06b.htm.

30 Jan and Cora Gordon, *Stardust in Hollywood* (London: Harrap, 1930), pp. 79, 161.

31 Andrew Sarris, *The American Cinema: Directors and Directions, 1929–1968* (New York: Dutton, 1968), p. 31.

32 André Bazin, "La Politique des Auteurs," in *The New Wave*, ed. Peter Graham (London: Secker and Warburg, 1968), pp. 143–4, 154.

33 Quoted in Aljean Harmetz, *Round Up the Usual Suspects: The Making of Casablanca – Bogart, Bergman, and World War II* (New York: Hyperion, 1992), p. 64.

34 William R. Meyer, *Warner Brothers Directors: The Hard-Boiled, the Comic, and the Weepers* (New Rochelle, NY: Arlington House, 1978), p. 75.

35 Sarris, pp. 175–6.

36 Alfred Starr, "The 'Lost Audience' Is Still Lost," *Variety* (January 16, 1954), p. 61,

Notes to pp. 48–61

quoted in Tino Balio, ed., *Hollywood in the Age of Television* (Boston: Unwin Hyman, 1990), p. 7.

37 Quoted in Nicholas Kent, *Naked Hollywood: Money, Power and the Movies* (London: BBC Books, 1991), p. 182.

38 Barbara Klinger, "Digressions at the Cinema: Reception and Mass Culture," *Cinema Journal* 28:4 (Summer 1989), p. 12.

39 As part of contract negotiations in 2001, the Writers' Guild of America attempted to eliminate what it called "wholesale use of the possessory credit" – "a film by" – by directors, on the grounds that it derogated the writer's role in the creative process. Brian Lowry, "Power Play: Credit the Writer or the Director?," *Los Angeles Times*, 28 February 2001.

40 Thomas Schatz, *The Genius of the System: Hollywood Filmmaking in the Studio Era* (New York: Pantheon, 1988), p. 5.

41 Robert Parrish, *Growing Up in Hollywood* (London: Bodley Head, 1976), p. 209.

42 In 2000, Joel and Ethan Coen produced a movie called *O Brother, Where Art Thou?*, which borrowed randomly from *Sullivan's Travels'* settings, but came closer to fulfilling Hadrian's desire for "a nice musical" than Sullivan's ambitions for a drama of social consequence.

43 Kristin Thompson, *Storytelling in the New Hollywood: Understanding the Classical Narrative Technique* (Cambridge, MA: Harvard University Press, 1999), p. 11.

44 Robert Stam, *Reflexivity in Film and Literature: From Don Quixote to Jean-Luc Godard* (New York: Columbia University Press, 1992), p. 85.

Chapter 3   Entertainment 2

1 Quoted in Richard Maltby, ed., *Dreams for Sale: Popular Culture in the Twentieth Century* (London: Harrap, 1989), p. 19.

2 Robin Baker, "Computer Technology and Special Effects in Contemporary Cinema," in *Future Visions: New Technologies of the Screen*, eds Philip Hayward and Tana Wollen (London: British Film Institute, 1993), p. 38.

3 Susan Ohmer, "The Science of Pleasure: George Gallup and Audience Research in

Hollywood," in *Identifying Hollywood's Audiences: Cultural Identity and the Movies*, eds Melvyn Stokes and Richard Maltby (London: British Film Institute, 1999), pp. 61–80.

4 Thomas Elsaesser, "Why Hollywood?," *Monogram* 1 (1971), p. 7.

5 Michael Hauge, *Writing Screenplays that Sell* (New York: McGraw-Hill, 1988), p. 3.

6 Quoted in Douglas Gomery, *Shared Pleasures: A History of Movie Presentation in the United States* (London: British Film Institute, 1992), p. 58.

7 Judith Amory, quoted in Tom Stempel, *American Audiences on Movies and Moviegoing* (Lexington: University Press of Kentucky, 2001), p. 213.

8 Ronald Haver, *David O. Selznick's Hollywood* (New York: Knopf, 1980), p. 309; Stephen Rebello, *Alfred Hitchcock and the Making of Psycho* (New York: Dembner Books, 1990), p. 149.

9 Herbert Blumer, *Movies and Conduct* (New York: Macmillan, 1933), pp. 48, 115.

10 Marion Levine, in Stempel, p. 70.

11 Kenneth Roberts, *Leisure* (London: Longman, 1970), p. 6. See also Chris Rojek, *Capitalism and Leisure Theory* (London: Tavistock, 1985).

12 Gore Vidal, *Screening History* (London: Abacus, 1993), p. 18.

13 Robert Warshow, "Movie Chronicle: The Westerner," in *Film Theory and Criticism*, eds Gerald Mast and Marshall Cohen, 3rd edn (New York: Oxford University Press, 1985), p. 444.

14 Steve Neale, "Questions of Genre," *Screen* 31:1 (Spring 1990), p. 64.

15 *Mutual Film Corp. v. Ohio Industrial Commission*, 236 US, 230 US Supreme Court, 1915, reprinted in *The Movies in Our Midst: Documents in the Cultural History of Film in America*, ed. Gerald Mast (Chicago: University of Chicago Press, 1982), p. 142.

16 Will Hays, draft of 1932 Annual Report of the MPPDA, Will H. Hays Archive, Department of Special Collections, Indiana State Library, Indianapolis.

17 Will H. Hays, "Motion Pictures and the Public," an address before the Women's City Club of Philadelphia, April 20, 1925 (New York: MPPDA, 1925), p. 3.

18 "General Principles to Govern the Preparation of a Revised Code of Ethics for Talking Pictures." Reporter's Transcript, board meeting, Association of Motion Picture Producers (AMPP), February 10, 1930, Motion Picture Association of America Archive, New York, 1930 AMPP Code file, pp. 138–9.

19 Lea Jacobs, "Industry Self-Regulation and the Problem of Textual Determination," *Velvet Light Trap* 23 (Spring 1989), p. 9.

20 Ruth Vasey, *The World According to Hollywood, 1918–1939* (Exeter: University of Exeter Press, 1997), p. 107.

21 Joy to James Wingate, February 5, 1931. Production Code Administration Case file, *Little Caesar*, Department of Special Collections, Margaret Herrick Library of the Academy of Motion Picture Arts and Sciences, Los Angeles.

22 Martha Wolfenstein and Nathan Leites, *Movies: A Psychological Study* (Glencoe, IL: Free Press, 1950), p. 189.

23 Wolfenstein and Leites, p. 301.

24 Vidal, p. 26.

25 Jane Feuer, *The Hollywood Musical* (London: British Film Institute, 1982), p. 84.

Chapter 4   Genre

1 Jorge Luis Borges, "The Analytical Language of John Wilkins," in *Other Inquisitions 1937–1952* (London: Souvenir Press, 1973), p. 103. Michel Foucault cites this passage, and "the wonderment of this taxonomy," as the starting point for his work, *The Order of Things: An Archaeology of the Human Sciences* (London: Tavistock, 1974).

2 Andrew Tudor, "Genre," in *Film Genre Reader*, ed. Barry Keith Grant (Austin: University of Texas Press, 1986), p. 7.

3 Andrew Tudor, *Monsters and Mad Scientists: A Cultural History of the Horror Movie* (Oxford: Blackwell, 1989), pp. 5, 213.

4 J. P. Mayer, *British Cinemas and their Audiences: Sociological Studies* (London: Dobson, 1948), p. 217.

5 Steve Neale, *Genre* (London: British Film Institute, 1980), pp. 22–3.

6 Steve Neale, "Questions of Genre," *Screen* 31:1 (Spring 1990), pp. 46–7.

7 Douglas Pye, "Genre and Movies," *MOVIE* 20 (Spring 1975), p. 32.

8 Dallas W. Smythe, John R. Gregory, Alvin Ostrin, Oliver P. Colvin, and William Moroney, "Portrait of a First-Run Audience," *Quarterly Review of Film, Radio and Television* 9 (Summer 1955), p. 398; Paul F. Lazarsfeld, "Audience Research in the Movie Field," *Annals of the American Academy of Political and Social Science* 254 (November 1947), p. 166; both quoted in Bruce Austin, *Immediate Seating: A Look at Movie Audiences* (Belmont, CA: Wadsworth, 1989), p. 75.

9 Leo A. Handel, *Hollywood Looks at its Audience: A Report of Film Audience Research* (Urbana: University of Illinois Press, 1950), pp. 119–20.

10 Kleine Optical Company, *Complete Illustrated Catalog* (1905), quoted in Neale, "Questions of Genre," p. 55.

11 Tudor acknowledges, however, that other, less immediately obvious patterns of commercial, cultural, and social factors overlay this crude commercial Darwinism. Tudor, *Monsters and Mad Scientists*, p. 23.

12 Barbara Klinger, "'Local' Genres: The Hollywood Adult Film in the 1950s," paper presented at the BFI Melodrama Conference, London, July 1992.

13 David A. Cook, *A History of Narrative Film*, 2nd edn (New York: Norton, 1990), p. 293; Colin MacArthur, *Underworld USA* (London: Secker and Warburg, 1972), p. 34. For an extended discussion of this case, see Richard Maltby, "The Spectacle of Criminality," in *Violence and American Cinema*, ed. J. David Slocum, (New York: Routledge, 2001), pp. 117–52.

14 Tino Balio, *Grand Design: Hollywood as a Modern Business Enterprise, 1930–1939* (New York: Scribner's, 1993), p. 179.

15 Barry R. Litman, "Decision-Making in the Film Industry: The Influence of the TV Market," *Journal of Communication* 32:3 (Summer 1982), pp. 44–5, quoted in John Izod, *Hollywood and the Box Office 1895–1986* (London: Macmillan, 1988), p. 183.

16 Andrew Britton, "Blissing Out: The Politics of Reaganite Entertainment," *MOVIE* 31/2 (Winter 1986), pp. 2–3. The tendency of

horror-movie audiences to engage with the movie in this fashion has often brought down the moral or political disapproval Britton exhibits here. Rather than indicating a vicarious and sadistic participation in the acts of mayhem, it may indicate, as Carol Clover and Marco Starr have suggested, a more complex act of self-defense by viewers identifying not with the killer but with his victims. It is also worth noting that vocal audience engagement was a normal feature of theatrical audience behavior until fairly late in the nineteenth century, and remained an element in movie-going until the introduction of sound. Marco Starr, "J. Hills is Alive: A Defence of *I Spit on Your Grave*," in *The Video Nasties: Freedom and Censorship in the Media*, ed. Martin Barker (London: Pluto Press, 1984), p. 54; Carol J. Clover, *Men, Women and Chainsaws: Gender in the Modern Horror Film* (London: British Film Institute, 1992), pp. 118–19; Bruce A. McConachie, "Pacifying American Theatrical Audiences, 1820–1900," in *For Fun and Profit: The Transformation of Leisure into Consumption*, ed. Richard Butsch (Philadelphia: Temple University Press, 1990); Lawrence W. Levine, *Highbrow/Lowbrow: The Emergence of Cultural Hierarchy in America* (Cambridge, MA: Harvard University Press, 1988).

17 Carol Clover comes up with an alternative formulation, in which the movie's exhibition becomes "a cat-and-mouse" game in which the movie tries to catch the audience by surprise. She also understands the vocal responses of audiences in these terms. Clover, p. 202.

18 Seymour Stern, "Feature Length Films, 1944, 1945, 1946," *Hollywood Quarterly* 2:3 (April 1947).

19 Ring Lardner Jr tells a version of this story in Aljean Harmetz, *Round Up the Usual Suspects: The Making of Casablanca – Bogart, Bergman, and World War II* (New York: Hyperion, 1992), p. 107.

20 Quoted in Clover, p. 10.

21 Neale, "Questions of Genre," p. 56.

22 Barry R. Litman, *The Motion Picture Mega-Industry* (Boston: Allyn and Bacon, 1998).

23 Klinger's analysis of the "progressive/subversive" genre as an object manufactured by a particular critical practice (much like two of her instances, film noir and melodrama) is acute, as is her critique of that criticism's practice of "textual isolationism." Rather than attribute an immutable politics to a text by its possession of this or that narrative, thematic, or stylistic feature, Klinger sees generic variation as a form of regulated difference and an essential functioning element of the overall Hollywood system. Barbara Klinger, " 'Cinema/Ideology/Criticism' Revisited: The Progressive Genre," in Grant, pp. 74–5, 88–9.

24 Tudor, *Monsters and Mad Scientists*, p. 211.

25 James Twitchell, *Dreadful Pleasures: An Anatomy of Modern Horror* (New York: Oxford University Press, 1985), p. 84.

26 Clover, p. 11.

27 Robert Warshow, "Movie Chronicle: The Westerner," in *Film Theory and Criticism*, eds Gerald Mast and Marshall Cohen, 3rd edn (New York: Oxford University Press, 1985), pp. 449–50.

28 Will Wright, *Sixguns and Society: A Structural Study of the Western* (Berkeley, CA: University of California Press, 1975), p. 15; Claude Lévi-Strauss, "The Structural Study of Myth," *Journal of American Folklore* 68:270 (1955), pp. 428–44; Vladimir Propp, *Morphology of the Folktale*, trans. Laurence Scott (Austin: University of Texas Press, 1968). Vera Dika's analysis of the "stalker film," discussed later in this chapter, provides an example of the structuralist approach to movie narrative.

29 Although we could, if we were distinguishing among devices that could be used for storing liquids. The quotation from Jorge Luis Borges at the beginning of this chapter is both funny and provocative, because its system of generic classification is nonsensical, but it might make us wonder if our own systems are any more coherent or appropriate.

30 Pye, p. 31.

31 Thomas Sobchack, "Genre Film: A Classical Experience," in Grant, p. 103.

32 See, for example, Barry Keith Grant, who identifies *Casablanca* (1942) as a "non-genre film." Barry Keith Grant, "Experience and Meaning in Genre Films," in Grant, p. 117.

33 In *Genre and Hollywood*, Steve Neale identifies and discusses 14 genres: the action-adventure film, the biopic, comedy, the crime film

(where he distinguishes between detective films, gangster films, and suspense thrillers), the epic, the horror movie, the musical, the science fiction film, the social problem film, the teenpic, the war film, and the Western. Steve Neale, *Genre and Hollywood* (London: Routledge, 2000, pp. 51–150.

34 Thomas Schatz, *Hollywood Genres: Formulas, Filmmaking, and the Studio System* (New York: Random House, 1981), p. 38.

35 Alan Williams, "Is a Radical Genre Criticism Possible?," *Quarterly Review of Film Studies* 9:2 (Spring 1984), pp. 123–4; Tag Gallagher, "Shoot-Out at the Genre Corral: Problems in the 'Evolution' of the Western," in Grant, pp. 202–16.

36 Paul Schrader, "Notes on Film Noir," in Grant, p. 169.

37 For discussions of film noir as a critical construction, see Neale, *Genre and Hollywood*, pp. 151–78, and James Naremore, *More than Night: Film Noir in its Contexts* (Berkeley, CA: University of California Press, 1998), pp. 9–48.

38 Charles Musser, "The Travel Genre in 1903–04: Moving Toward Fictional Narratives," *Iris* 2:1 (1984), p. 57; Neale, "Questions of Genre," p. 54.

39 Thomas Elsaesser refers to this as a "phatic" process, by which the movie is greeting the audience, and letting them know what kind of experience they may expect. Thomas Elsaesser, "Narrative Cinema and Audience-Oriented Aesthetics," in *Popular Television and Film*, eds Tony Bennett, Susan Boyd-Bowman, Colin Mercer, and Janet Woollacott (London: British Film Institute, 1981), p. 271.

40 Vera Dika, "The Stalker Film, 1978–81," in *American Horrors: Essays on the Modern American Horror Film*, ed. Gregory A. Waller (Urbana: University of Illinois Press, 1987), pp. 93–4.

41 Rick Altman, "A Semantic/Syntactic Approach to Film Genre," in Grant, p. 30.

42 John Cawelti, *The Six-Gun Mystique* (Bowling Green, KY: Bowling Green Popular University Press, 1970).

43 Jim Kitses, *Horizons West: Anthony Mann, Budd Boetticher, Sam Peckinpah: Studies of Authorship within the Western* (London: Thames and Hudson, 1969), p. 11.

44 Brian Henderson, "*The Searchers*: An American Dilemma," in *Movies and Methods. Vol. II*, ed. Bill Nichols (Berkeley, CA: University of California Press, 1985), p. 444.

45 Neale, *Genre and Hollywood*, p. 77.

46 Warshow, pp. 438, 439, 449.

47 Jon Tuska, *The American West in Film: Critical Approaches to the Western* (Westport, CT: Greenwood, 1985), p. 263.

48 Edward Buscombe, ed., *The BFI Companion to the Western* (London: André Deutsch, 1988), p. 35.

49 Robert Ray, *A Certain Tendency of the Hollywood Cinema, 1930–1980* (Princeton, NJ: Princeton University Press, 1985), pp. 75, 84, 69.

50 Pye, pp. 34, 36.

51 I once witnessed a critical exchange in which one speaker's insistence that the cutting between shots of the feet of the protagonists during the build-up to the climax of a spaghetti Western deliberately confused their identities was greeted with the contemptuous assertion by one listener that if the speaker could not tell a Mexican boot from an American one, he had no business expressing an opinion about Westerns. In *Pat Garrett and Billy the Kid* Billy also tells a story in which a mistake in etiquette over a pair of boots leads to a fatal gunfight.

52 Producer Darryl Zanuck removed 30 minutes from John Ford's director's cut of *My Darling Clementine*, "deleting some humor and 'sentimentality,' " and allegedly strengthening "the storyline and pace." To Ford's chagrin but on the basis of preview reactions, his preferred ending was changed so that instead of shaking hands with Clementine before he rides off, Wyatt kisses her. Tag Gallagher, *John Ford: The Man and his Films* (Berkeley, CA: University of California Press, 1986), p. 233.

53 Philip French, in his introduction to a BBC television screening of the version released in 1989.

54 The acrimony surrounding the movie's production and editing is detailed in David Weddle, *Sam Peckinpah: "If They Move . . . Kill 'Em"* (London: Faber, 1996), pp. 445–91; Paul Seydor, *Peckinpah: The Western Films: A Reconsideration* (Urbana: University of Chicago Press, 1980), pp. 183–211;

Garner Simmons, *Peckinpah: A Portrait in Montage* (Austin: University of Texas Press, 1976), pp. 169–88; and Marshall Fine, *Bloody Sam: The Life and Films of Sam Peckinpah* (New York: Primus, 1991), pp. 240–60. Michael Bliss discusses the differences between the two versions, and suggests that the 1989 release version was an early, unfinished cut, in *Justified Lives: Morality and Narrative in the Films of Sam Peckinpah* (Carbondale: Southern Illinois University Press, 1993), pp. 217–18, 327–8. In its first year of release the movie grossed almost exactly its negative cost of $4.6 million dollars, eventually turning a small profit for the studio. David A. Cook, *Lost Illusions: American Cinema in the Shadow of Watergate and Vietnam, 1970–1979* (New York: Scribner's, 2000), p. 85.

55 Buscombe, p. 289.

56 The opposition between "official" and "outlaw" heroes is explored in Ray, pp. 59–66.

57 Gallagher, "Shoot-Out," pp. 209–10.

58 André Bazin, "The Western: Or the American Film Par Excellence," in his *What is Cinema? Vol. 2*, trans. Hugh Gray (Berkeley, CA: University of California Press, 1971), p. 147.

59 Warshow, p. 438.

60 Warshow, pp. 439–40.

61 Budd Boetticher, quoted in Laura Mulvey, "Visual Pleasure and Narrative Cinema," in *Visual and Other Pleasures* (Bloomington: Indiana University Press, 1989), p. 19.

62 Terence Butler, *Crucified Heroes: The Films of Sam Peckinpah* (London: Gordon Fraser, 1979), pp. 90–1.

63 Warshow, p. 449.

64 Stephen Prince, *Savage Cinema: Sam Peckinpah and the Rise of Ultraviolent Movies* (Austin: University of Texas Press, 1998), p. 141.

65 Prince, pp. 141, 145.

66 Clover, p. 163.

67 Clover, p. 168.

68 Bazin, "The Evolution of the Western," in his *What is Cinema? Vol. 2*, p. 149.

69 Christine Gledhill, "The Melodramatic Field: An Investigation," in *Home Is Where the Heart Is: Studies in Melodrama and the Woman's Film*, ed. Christine Gledhill (London: British Film Institute, 1987), p. 11.

70 Jackie Byars, *All That Hollywood Allows: Re-Reading Gender in 1950s Melodrama* (Chapel Hill: University of North Carolina Press, 1991), p. 14.

71 Linda Williams, "Melodrama Revised," in *Refiguring American Film Genres: Theory and History*, ed. Nick Browne (Berkeley, CA: University of California Press, 1998), p. 50.

72 Williams, pp. 49, 57, 59.

73 Frederic Taber Cooper, "The Taint of Melodrama and Some Recent Books," *Bookman* (February 1906), pp. 630–5, quoted in Ben Singer, "Female Power in the Serial-Queen Melodrama: The Etiology of an Anomaly," *Camera Obscura* 22 (January 1990), p. 95.

74 Montrose J. Moses, "Concerning Melodrama," *The Book News Monthly* (July 1908), p. 846, quoted in Singer, p. 95.

75 Steve Neale, "Melo Talk: On the Meaning and Use of the Term 'Melodrama' in the American Trade Press," *Velvet Light Trap* 22 (Fall 1993), pp. 70, 75.

76 Neale, "Melo Talk," p. 72.

77 Balio, p. 235.

78 Carol J. Clover notes that video stores are more likely to classify a plot as "horror" when it is low-budget and "drama" or "suspense" when it is high-budget. Clover, p. 5.

79 *Halliwell's Film Guide* describes *The Prince of Tides* as "a lushly romantic melodrama." Leslie Halliwell, *Halliwell's Film and Video Guide 2000*, ed. John Walker, 15th edn (London: HarperCollins, 1999), p. 662.

80 Andreas Huyssen, "Mass Culture as Woman: Modernism's Other," in *Studies in Entertainment: Critical Approaches to Mass Culture*, ed. Tania Modleski (Bloomington: Indiana University Press, 1987), p. 191. Tania Modleski and Dana Polan also engage these issues in their essays in this book.

81 Roger D. McNiven, "The Middle-Class American Home of the Fifties: The Use of Architecture in Nicholas Ray's *Bigger Than Life* and Douglas Sirk's *All That Heaven Allows*," *Cinema Journal* 22:2 (Summer 1983), p. 55. A number of influential essays first appeared in a special issue of *Screen* 12:2 (Summer 1971).

82 "Irony doesn't go down well with the Amer-

ican public. This is not meant as a reproach, but merely that in general this public is too simple and too naïve – in the best sense of these terms – to be susceptible to irony. It requires clearly delineated positions, for and against." Sirk, quoted in Paul Willemen, "Distanciation and Douglas Sirk," in *Douglas Sirk*, eds Laura Mulvey and John Halliday (Edinburgh: Edinburgh Film Festival, 1972), p. 26.

83 John Halliday, *Sirk on Sirk* (London: Secker and Warburg, 1971), pp. 116, 119.

84 Gledhill, p. 11.

85 Willemen, p. 26.

86 Jean-Loup Bourget, "Sirk and the Critics," *Bright Lights* 6 (Winter 1977–8), p. 8.

87 Brandon French, *On the Verge of Revolt: Women in American Films of the Fifties* (New York: Ungar, 1978), p. 102.

88 Laura Mulvey, "Notes on Sirk and Melodrama," *MOVIE* 25 (Winter 1977–8), pp. 53–6.

89 Rainer Werner Fassbinder suggested that the audience weeps during *Imitation of Life* (1959) because it understands why the movie's characters must be in conflict, and how that conflict is inevitably produced by social forces: "The cruelty is that we can understand them both [Annie and Sarah Jane], both are right and no one will be able to help them. Unless we change the world. At this point all of us in the cinema cried. Because changing the world is so difficult." Rainer Werner Fassbinder, "Six Films by Douglas Sirk," in Mulvey and Halliday, p. 106.

90 Barbara Klinger, "Much Ado About Excess: Genre, Mise-en-Scène and the Woman in *Written on the Wind*," *Wide Angle* 11:4 (1989), p. 11.

91 Quoted in Klinger, " 'Local' Genres," p. 10.

92 Quoted in Klinger, "Much Ado," p. 12.

93 Klinger, "Much Ado," p. 15.

Chapter 5   Industry 1: To 1948

1 Alfred D. Chandler, Jr, *The Visible Hand: The Managerial Revolution in American Business* (Cambridge, MA: Harvard University Press, 1977), p. 285.

2 Marcus Loew, quoted in Richard Koszarski, *An Evening's Entertainment: The Age of the Silent Feature Picture, 1915–1928* (New York: Scribners, 1990), p. 9.

3 Mae D. Huettig, *Economic Control of the Motion Picture Industry: A Study in Industrial Organization* (Philadelphia: University of Pennsylvania Press, 1944), p. 57.

4 Douglas Gomery, *The Hollywood Studio System* (London: Macmillan, 1986), pp. 7–8.

5 *The Film in National Life* (London: Allen and Unwin, 1932), p. 42.

6 Joel W. Finler, *The Hollywood Story: Everything You Always Wanted to Know about the American Movie Business but Didn't Know Where to Look* (London: Octopus Books, 1988); MPAA 2000 US Economic Review.

7 *The Golden Harvest of the Silver Screen, Compiled from Reliable Sources as a Basis for Evaluating Motion Picture Securities* (Los Angeles: Hunter, Dulin & Co., 1927).

8 Adolph Zukor, quoted in Richard Maltby, ed., *Dreams for Sale: Popular Culture in the Twentieth Century* (London: Harrap, 1989), p. 86.

9 *International Motion Picture Almanac, 1945–1946*.

10 Gomery, p. 13.

11 *International Motion Picture Almanac, 1951–1952*.

12 Harold B. Franklin, *Motion Picture Theater Management* (New York: Doran, 1927).

13 Carlie Beach Roney, "Show Lady," *Saturday Evening Post* 211 (February 18, 1939), reprinted in Gregory A. Waller, ed., *Moviegoing in America* (Malden, MA: Blackwell, 2001), pp. 198–9.

14 "Seeing Film from Start Important," *Motion Picture Herald*, August 25, 1934, p. 25, quoted in Thomas Doherty, "This Is Where We Came In: The Audible Screen and the Voluble Audience of Early Sound Cinema," in *American Movie Audiences: From the Turn of the Century to the Early Sound Era*, eds Melvyn Stokes and Richard Maltby (London: British Film Institute, 1999), p. 146.

15 Will Hays, president of the MPPDA, quoted in Huettig, p. 55.

16 By-laws of the MPPDA, quoted in Raymond Moley, *The Hays Office* (Indianapolis: Bobbs-Merrill, 1945), p. 227.

17 Gomery, p. 14.

18 Michael Nielsen, "Towards a Workers' History of the US Film Industry," in *The*

Media Reader, eds Manuel Alvarado and John O. Thompson (London: British Film Institute, 1990), pp. 166–80.

19   Quoted in Maltby, p. 11.

20   Kristin Thompson, *Exporting Entertainment: America in the World Film Market, 1907–1934* (London: British Film Institute, 1985), p. 50.

21   Ruth Vasey, *The World According to Hollywood, 1918–1939* (Exeter: University of Exeter Press, 1997), p. 7.

22   "Trade Follows the Motion Pictures," *Commerce Reports*, April 24, 1922, p. 191.

23   "Certain Factors and Considerations Affecting the European Market," internal MPPDA memo, October 25, 1928, Motion Picture Association Archive, New York.

24   James True, *Printer's Ink* (February 4, 1926), quoted in Charles Eckert, "The Carole Lombard in Macy's Window," *Quarterly Review of Film Studies* 3 (Winter 1978), pp. 4–5.

25   Jeffrey Richards, *The Age of the Dream Palace: Cinema and Society in Britain, 1930–1939* (London: Routledge and Kegan Paul, 1984), p. 27.

26   Quoted in Richards, p. 64.

27   That figure does, however, mask a number of shifts within the foreign market: for instance, the steady decline in the importance of the British market in the 1960s and 1970s, and the growth of the Japanese market until, in 1984, it became the largest single importer of American movies.

28   Thomas Guback, "Hollywood's International Market," in *The American Film Industry*, ed. Tino Balio, 1st edn 1976, revised edn (Madison: University of Wisconsin Press, 1985), pp. 477–80.

29   Sam Morris to Jack Warner, November 12, 1937, JLW Correspondence, Box 59 Folder 8, Warner Bros. Archive, Department of Special Collections, University of Southern California.

30   Nicholas Kent, *Naked Hollywood: Money, Power and the Movies* (London: BBC Books, 1991), pp. 101, 108.

31   MPAA 2000 US Economic Review.

32   Finler, p. 280.

33   MPAA 2000 US Economic Review.

34   Tino Balio, "Introduction to Part I," in *Hollywood in the Age of Television*, ed.

Tino Balio (Boston: Unwin Hyman, 1990), p. 37.

35   Quoted in Kent, p. 121.

36   Carey McWilliams, *Southern California: An Island on the Land*, 1st pub. 1946 (Santa Barbara: Peregrine Smith, 1973), pp. 339–40.

37   Leo Rosten, *Hollywood: The Movie Colony, the Movie Makers* (New York: Harcourt, Brace, 1941), pp. 41–2.

38   Joel Finler argues that the major production companies never fully recovered from the effects of the Great Depression in the early 1930s, and that the decline in the movies' share of the entertainment dollar really began in the mid-1930s, not the late 1940s. Finler, pp. 33–4.

39   Chandler, p. 363.

40   John Sedgwick and Michael Pokorny, "'The Risk Environment of Film Making: Warner Bros in the Inter-War Years'," *Explorations in Economic History* 35 (1998), p. 197.

41   John Sedgwick, "Cinemagoing Preferences in Britain in the 1930s," in *The Unknown 1930s: An Alternative History of the British Cinema, 1929–1939*, ed. Jeffrey Richards (London: Tauris, 1998), p. 6.

42   Sedgwick and Pokorny, p. 205.

43   Rosten, pp. 82–5.

44   "Metro-Goldwyn-Mayer," *Fortune* 6 (December 1932), p. 51. Reprinted in Balio, *The American Film Industry*, p. 311.

45   Rosten, pp. 242–3.

46   Quoted in Rosten, p. 240.

47   Gerald Horne, *Class Struggle in Hollywood, 1930–1950: Moguls, Mobsters, Stars, Reds and Trade Unionists* (Austin: University of Texas Press, 2001), p. 124.

48   Jesse Lasky, "The Producer Makes a Plan," in *We Make the Movies*, ed. Nancy Naumberg (New York: Norton, 1937), pp. 1–5. Quoted in Rosten, p. 239.

49   F. Scott Fitzgerald, "The Crack-Up," in his *The Crack-Up and Other Pieces and Stories* (Harmondsworth: Penguin, 1965), p. 39.

50   Economist Campbell MacCulloch, "The Real Boss of the Pictures," *Motion Picture Classic*, February 1931, pp. 28–9, 94.

51   F. Scott Fitzgerald, *The Last Tycoon* (Harmondsworth: Penguin, 1974), pp. 36–76.

52   Frank Capra, letter to the *New York Times* (April 2, 1939). Quoted in Richard Glatzer

and John Raeburn, eds, *Frank Capra: The Man and his Films* (Ann Arbor: University of Michigan Press, 1975), p. 15.

53 "An Analysis of the Motion Picture Industry by the Screen Directors Guild, Inc.," pp. 1–2, 4–5. Quoted in Rosten, p. 240.

54 Rudy Behlmer, ed., *Inside Warner Bros. (1935–1951)* (London, Weidenfeld and Nicolson, 1986).

55 Capra, letter to the *New York Times* (April 2, 1939), quoted in Margaret Thorp, *America at the Movies* (London: Faber, 1946), p. 92.

56 Ronald Haver, *David O. Selznick's Hollywood* (New York: Knopf, 1980), p. 267.

57 Art directors in contemporary Hollywood are normally referred to by the more grandiose title of production designer.

58 Whitney Stine, *Mother Goddam* (New York: Hawthorne Books, 1974), p. 79.

59 Thorp, pp. 49, 52.

60 Rosten, pp. 112–14.

61 *Photoplay* (February 1935). Reprinted in Richard Griffith, ed., *The Talkies: Articles and Illustrations from a Great Fan Magazine, 1928–1940* (New York: Dover, 1971), p. 196.

62 Thorp, p. 17.

63 Quoted in Martin Levin, ed., *Hollywood and the Great Fan Magazines* (London: Ian Allen, 1970), pp. 142, 214.

64 "How to Hold Him When You've Hooked Him, by Myrna Loy," *Picturegoer Famous Films Supplement* for *Double Wedding* (February 12, 1938), p. 11.

65 *Photoplay*, quoted in Levin, p. 145.

66 J. P. Mayer, *British Cinemas and their Audiences: Sociological Studies* (London: Dobson, 1948), p. 104.

67 Frank D. McConnell, *The Spoken Seen: Film and the Romantic Imagination* (Baltimore, MD: Johns Hopkins University Press, 1975), p. 171.

68 Malcolm Vance, *The Movie Ad Book* (Minneapolis: Control Data Publishing, 1981), p. 77.

69 Christine Frederick, *Selling Mrs Consumer* (New York: Business Bourse, 1929), pp. 4–5.

70 Irving Thalberg, "The Modern Photoplay," lecture at the University of Southern California, March 20, 1929, in *Introduction to the Photoplay*, ed. John C. Tibbetts (Shawnee Mission, KS: National Film Society, 1977), pp. 119–20.

71 Eckert, p. 10.

72 *Modern Screen* (September 1933), reprinted in Mark Bego, ed., *The Best of Modern Screen* (London: Columbus Books, 1986), p. 23.

73 Eckert, p. 3.

74 James Goldstone, "Deals on Reels," *Observer* (May 5, 1991), p. 32. Science fiction movies may appear less convincing predictions of the future if the products placed in them cease to exist: Pan Am, for instance, is shown running space flights in both *2001: A Space Odyssey* (1968) and *Blade Runner* (1982, set in 2019), but the airline filed for bankruptcy in 1991.

75 Blaise Cendrars, *Hollywood, Mecca of the Movies* (Berkeley, CA: University of California Press, 1995), pp. 83, 86.

76 Marquis Busby, "The Price they Pay for Fame," quoted in Levin, p. 94.

77 Busby, quoted in Levin, p. 94.

78 Rosten, p. 85.

79 Danae Clark, *Negotiating Hollywood: The Cultural Politics of Actors' Labor* (Minneapolis: University of Minnesota Press, 1995), p. 60.

80 Rosten, p. 382.

81 Rosten, pp. 31–2.

82 Clark, p. 20.

83 Screen Actors Guild report, quoted in Clark, p. 99.

84 "Are Extras People?," *Screen Guilds Magazine*, November 1935, p. 3, quoted in Clark, pp. 114–15.

85 Jane Gaines, *Contested Culture: The Image, the Voice, and the Law* (London: British Film Institute, 1992), pp. 160–1.

86 Milton Sperling, quoted in Leonard Moseley, *Zanuck* (New York: McGraw-Hill, 1984), p. 109.

87 Thorp, pp. 68–9.

88 Caroline Somers Holt, "It's Ruby's Turn Now...!," *Modern Screen*, reprinted in Levin, pp. 50–1.

89 Gladys Hall, "Are Women Stars the Home Wreckers of Hollywood?," *Motion Picture Magazine* (August 1932), pp. 44–5, 96.

90 The process is described in W. Robert La Vine, *In a Glamorous Fashion: The Fabulous Years of Hollywood Costume Design* (New York: Scribner's, 1980), p. 27.

91 Haver, p. 191.

Chapter 6 Industry 2: 1948–80

1 Harold L. Vogel, quoted in Tino Balio, "Adjusting to the New Global Economy: Hollywood in the 1990s," in *Film Policy: International, National and Regional Perspectives*, ed. Albert Moran (London: Routledge, 1996), p. 27.

2 Lee Beaupre, "Hits Few: Beasts of Burden: Analysis of 1971 Boom–Bust Biz," *Variety*, 30 November 1972, pp. 5–6.

3 Tino Balio, *United Artists: The Company that Changed the Film Industry* (Madison: University of Wisconsin Press, 1987), p. 88.

4 "Studio O'Head: What to Do?," *Variety*, March 12, 1958, p. 5, quoted in Balio, p. 91.

5 Joseph Satin, ed., *The 1950s: America's Placid Decade* (Boston: Houghton Mifflin, 1960), quoted in Wini Breines, *Young, White and Miserable: Growing Up Female in the Fifties* (Boston: Beacon Press, 1992), p. 3.

6 Taylor, p. 247.

7 Mary Morley Cohen, "Forgotten Audiences in the Passion Pits: Drive-in Theatres and Changing Spectator Practices in Post-War America," *Film History* 6 (1994), p. 473.

8 Cohen, pp. 482, 470.

9 Frank J. Taylor, "Big Boom in Outdoor Movies," *Saturday Evening Post* 229 (September 15, 1956), p. 31, reprinted in *Moviegoing in America*, ed. Gregory A. Waller (Malden, MA: Blackwell, 2002), p. 247.

10 Thomas Schatz, *Boom and Bust: American Cinema in the 1940s* (New York: Scribner's, 1997), p. 294.

11 Schatz, p. 393.

12 Tino Balio, "Introduction to Part I," in *Hollywood in the Age of Television*, ed. Tino Balio (Boston: Unwin Hyman, 1990), p. 28.

13 Balio, *United Artists*, pp. 128, 163–77.

14 Hollis Alpert, "Strictly for the Art Houses," *Saturday Review of Literature*, 28 April 1951, p. 27, quoted in Barbara Wilinsky, "'A Thinly Disguised Art Veneer Covering a Filthy Sex Picture': Discourses on Art Houses in the 1950s," *Film History* 8:2 (1996), p. 152.

15 Kenneth P. Adler, "Art Films and Eggheads," *Studies in Public Communication No. 2* (Summer 1959), p. 10, quoted in Janet Staiger, *Interpreting Films: Studies in the Historical Reception of American Cinema* (Princeton, NJ: Princeton University Press,

1992), p. 185; Gilbert Seldes, *The Great Audience* (New York: Viking, 1950), p. 13.

16 Seldes, pp. 12–13.

17 Thomas Doherty, *Teenagers and Teenpics: The Juvenilization of American Movies in the 1950s* (Boston: Unwin Hyman, 1988), p. 54.

18 Hy Hollinger, "'Lost Audience': Grass vs. Class," *Variety*, December 5, 1956, p. 86.

19 William R. Weaver, "AIP Heads Set Sight on Teenage Patron," *Motion Picture Herald*, May 25, 1957, p. 20.

20 "Wald Slams Exploitation Films, Told 'Peyton Place' Pretty Lurid," *Variety*, October 29, 1958, p. 7.

21 Irving Rubine, "Boys Meet Ghouls, Make Money," *New York Times*, March 16, 1958, section 2, p. 7, quoted in Doherty, p. 160.

22 Richard Dyer McCann, "Independence with a Vengeance," *Film Quarterly* 15 (Summer 1962), p. 14.

23 Balio, *United Artists*, p. 6.

24 Joan Didion, *The White Album* (Harmondsworth: Penguin, 1981), p. 162.

25 Douglas Gomery, "Failed Opportunities: The Integration of the US Motion Picture and Television Industries," *Quarterly Review of Film Studies* 9: 3 (Summer 1984), p. 227.

26 By 1955, at least ten times as much film was being generated in Hollywood for television as for theatrical exhibition. Robert Vianello, "The Rise of the Telefilm and the Networks' Hegemony Over the Motion Picture Industry," *Quarterly Review of Film Studies* 9:3 (Summer 1984), p. 213.

27 Michelle Hilmes, *Hollywood and Broadcasting: From Radio to Cable* (Urbana: University of Illinois Press, 1990), p. 165.

28 Christopher Anderson, *Hollywood TV: The Studio System in the Fifties* (Austin: University of Texas Press, 1994), p. 12; Lynn Spigel and Michael Curtin, "Introduction," in *The Revolution Wasn't Televised: Sixties Television and Social Conflict*, eds Lynn Spigel and Michael Curtin (London: Routledge, 1997), p. 3.

29 Mark Alvey, "The Independents: Rethinking the Television Studio System," in Spigel and Curtin, p. 139.

30 "Hollywood in a Television Boom," *Broadcasting*, October 26, 1959, pp. 88–90, quoted in Alvey, p. 141.

31 Quoted in Hilmes, p. 122.

32 Hilmes, p. 163. Quotations from David

Sarnoff, *Business Week*, March 3, 1956, p. 115.

33 Douglas Gomery, *Shared Pleasures: A History of Movie Presentation in the United States* (London: British Film Institute, 1992), p. 250.

34 Gomery, *Shared Pleasures*, p. 252.

35 "Pix Must 'Broaden Market'," *Variety*, March 20, 1968, p. 78, quoted in Doherty, p. 231.

36 Quoted in Balio, *United Artists*, p. 310.

37 Kim Newman, "Exploitation and the Mainstream," in *The Oxford History of World Cinema*, ed. Geoffrey Nowell-Smith (Oxford: Oxford University Press, 1996), p. 514.

38 Arthur B. Krim to John Beckett, February 12, 1971, quoted in Balio, *United Artists*, p. 313.

39 David A. Cook, *Lost Illusions: American Cinema in the Shadow of Watergate and Vietnam, 1970–1979* (New York: Scribner's, 2000), p. xv.

40 Stephen Farber, *The Movie Rating Game* (Washington, DC: Public Affairs Press, 1972), p. 47.

41 Charles Champlin, quoted in Farber, p. 48; Dougherty, quoted in Farber, p. 51.

42 Farber, p. 50.

43 Linda Williams, "'Sex and Sensation,'" in Nowell-Smith, p. 493.

44 Jon Lewis, *Hollywood vs Hard Core: How the Struggle over Censorship Saved the Modern Film Industry* (New York: New York University Press, 2000), p. 150.

45 Cook, p. 157.

46 Balio, *United Artists*, p. 261.

47 Michael J. Wolf, *The Entertainment Economy: How Mega-Media Forces Are Transforming Our Lives* (London: Penguin, 1999), p. 186.

48 Arthur De Vany and W. David Walls, "Bose–Einstein Dynamics and Adaptive Contracting: The Motion Picture Industry", *Economic Journal* 106 (November 1996), p. 1493.

49 Suzanne Mary Donahue, *American Film Distribution: The Changing Marketplace* (Ann Arbor: UMI Research Press, 1987), p. 179.

50 Cook, p. 1.

51 Martin Dale, *The Movie Game: The Film Business in Britain, Europe and America* (London: Cassell, 1997), p. 22.

52 Between 1965 and 1970, the number of shopping malls increased from 1,500 to 12,500, and to 22,500 in 1980. Thomas Schatz, "The New Hollywood," in *Film Theory Goes to the Movies*, eds Jim Collins, Hilary Radner, and Ava Preacher Collins (New York: Routledge, 1993), p. 17.

53 Gomery, *Shared Pleasures*, p. 105.

Chapter 7 Industry 3: Since 1980

1 Michael J. Wolf, *The Entertainment Economy: How Mega-Media Forces Are Transforming Our Lives* (London: Penguin, 1999), pp. 228, 230.

2 Janet Wasko, *Hollywood in the Information Age: Beyond the Silver Screen* (London: Polity, 1994), p. 250.

3 Martin Dale, *The Movie Game: The Film Business in Britain, Europe and America* (London: Cassell, 1997), p. 5.

4 Michele Hilmes, *Hollywood and Broadcasting: From Radio to Cable* (Urbana: University of Illinois Press, 1990), p. 141.

5 Robert Allen, "Home Alone Together: Hollywood and the Family Film," in *Identifying Hollywood's Audiences: Cultural Identity and the Movies*, eds Melvyn Stokes and Richard Maltby (London: British Film Institute, 1999), p. 121.

6 Robert Shaye, Chair of New Line Pictures, quoted in Toby Miller, "The Crime of Monsieur Lang," in *Film Policy: International, National and Regional Perspectives*, ed. Albert Moran (London: Routledge, 1996), p. 75.

7 Warner Communications Inc. 1981 Annual Report, p. 25. Quoted in Robert Gustavson, " 'What's Happening to Our Pix Biz?' From Warner Bros. to Warner Communications Inc.," in *Hollywood in the Age of Television*, ed. Tino Balio (Boston: Unwin Hyman, 1990), p. 584.

8 Tino Balio, "Introduction to Part II," in Balio, *Hollywood in the Age of Television*, pp. 277–82.

9 Bruce Austin, "Home Video: The Second-Run 'Theater' of the 1990s," in Balio, p. 321.

10 Quoted in Balio, "Introduction to Part II," in Balio, *Hollywood in the Age of Television*, p. 245.

11 Nicholas Kent, *Naked Hollywood: Money,*

Power and the Movies (London: BBC Books, 1991), p. 59.

12 Stephen Prince, *A New Pot of Gold: Hollywood under the Electronic Rainbow, 1980–1989* (New York: Scribner's, 2000), p. 95.

13 *Wall Street Journal*, March 7, 1989, p. B1, quoted in Michelle Hilmes, "Pay Television: Breaking the Broadcast Bottleneck," in Balio, *Hollywood in the Age of Television*, p. 315.

14 "Vivendi Universal: Who We Are," http://www.vivendiuniversal.com/vu2/en/who_we_are/who_we_are.cfm, accessed on May 10, 2002.

15 Axel Madsen, *The New Hollywood* (New York: Crowell, 1975), p. 94.

16 Harold L. Vogel, *Entertainment Industry Economics*, 2nd edn and 5th edn (Cambridge: Cambridge University Press, 1990, 2001), 2nd edn, p. 52, 5th edn, p. 62.

17 Kent, p. 60.

18 William Paul, "The K-Mart Audience at the Mall Movies," *Film History* 6:4 (Winter 1994), p. 497.

19 Parts of Katzenberg's memo were published as "The Teachings of Chairman Jeff," in *Variety*, February 4, 1991, p. 24.

20 Prince p. xxi.

21 Internet Movie Database.

22 John Sedgwick and Michael Pokorny, "The Risk Environment of Film Making: Warner Bros in the Inter-War Years," *Explorations in Economic History* 35 (1998), p. 197.

23 Arthur De Vany and W. David Walls, "Bose–Einstein Dynamics and Adaptive Contracting: The Motion Picture Industry," *Economic Journal* 106 (November 1996), p. 1513.

24 De Vany and Walls, p. 1493.

25 De Vany and Walls, p. 1493.

26 De Vany and Walls, p. 1501

27 Vogel, 5th edn, pp. 50–1.

28 Internet Movie Database.

29 Dale, p. 32.

30 Quoted in Peter Bart, *The Gross: The Hits, the Flops – the Summer that Ate Hollywood* (New York: St Martin's Press, 1999), p. 171.

31 Dale, p. 25.

32 Quoted in Allen, p. 121.

33 William Goldman, *Adventures in the Screen Trade: A Personal View of Hollywood and Screenwriting* (New York: Warner Books, 1983), p. 39.

34 Internet Movie Database.

35 Gary Cross, *Kids' Stuff: Toys and the Changing World of American Childhood* (Cambridge, MA: Harvard University Press, 1997), pp. 197–8.

36 Quoted in James Twitchell, *Carnival Culture: The Trashing of Taste in America* (New York: Columbia University Press, 1992), p. 142.

37 Wolf, p. 228.

38 Quoted in Prince, p. 139.

39 Patrick Denin, quoted in Wasko, pp. 190, 197. Domino's product placement in the movie did not inhibit Pizza Hut from a tie-in arrangement that included a commercial and coupon offer with the video-cassette release of *Teenage Mutant Ninja Turtles*. The movie was, however, a commercial failure in Japan, allegedly because of the absence of any tie-in toys to support it.

40 Allen, pp. 121–2.

41 Allen, p. 122.

42 Bart, p. 202.

43 Disney Annual Report, 1995, quoted in Barry R. Litman, *The Motion Picture Mega-Industry* (Boston: Allyn and Bacon, 1998), p. 128.

44 Wolf, pp. 25, 230.

45 MPAA Worldwide Market Research, 2000 US Economic Review. www.mpaa.org.

46 Wolf, p. 228.

47 Vogel, 5th edn, p. 130.

48 Wolf, p. 25.

49 Richard E. Caves, *Creative Industries: Contracts Between Art and Commerce* (Cambridge, MA: Harvard University Press, 2000), p. 327.

50 Caves, p. 328.

51 Wolf, pp. 186, 196, 204.

52 Philip McCarthy, "The Outsourcing of Tinseltown," *Age*, February 20, 2002. http://www.theage.com.au/entertainment/2002/02/20/FFXKNJOKUXC.html, accessed February 26, 2002.

53 John Ptak, Creative Artists Agency of Hollywood, quoted in Miller, p. 77.

54 Quoted in Wasko, p. 236.

55 Wasko, p. 236.

56 Jesse Heinstand, "Report: 18,000 Jobs lost in Biz," *Backstage.com*, http://www.backstage.com/backstage/news/article_display.jsp?vnu_content_id=1449332, accessed April 6, 2002.

57 Quoted in Wasko, p. 49.
58 Dale, p. 19.
59 Dale, p. 173.
60 Dale, pp. 166, 168.
61 Toby Miller, Nitin Govil, John McMurria, and Richard Maxwell, *Global Hollywood* (London: British Film Institute, 2001), p. 46.
62 Miller et al., p. 98.
63 Miller et al., p. 98.
64 Dale, p. 71.
65 Wolf, p. 291.
66 Quoted in Emanuel Levy, *Cinema of Outsiders: The Rise of American Independent Film* (New York: New York University Press, 1999), p. 1.
67 Quoted in Levy, p. 2.
68 Quoted in Kent, p. 121.
69 Douglas Gomery, *Shared Pleasures: A History of Movie Presentation in the United States* (London: British Film Institute, 1992), p. 257.
70 Prince, p. 159.
71 Greg Merritt, *Celluloid Mavericks: A History of American Independent Film* (New York: Thunder's Mouth Press, 2000).
72 Jon Lewis, *Hollywood vs Hardcore: How the Struggle over Censorship Saved the Modern Film Industry* (New York: New York University Press, 2000), p. 224.
73 Justin Wyatt, "The Formation of the 'Major Independent': Miramax, New Line and the New Hollywood," in *Contemporary Hollywood Cinema*, eds Steve Neale and Murray Smith (London: Routledge, 1998), p. 76.
74 Peter Bart, "Mouse Gears for Mass Prod'n," *Variety*, July 19, 1993, p. 5.
75 Wyatt, p. 84.
76 James Schamus, "To the Rear of the Back End: The Economics of Independent Cinema," in Neale and Smith, pp. 103–4.
77 Dale, p. 56.
78 Chuck Kleinhans, "Independent Features: Hopes and Dreams," in *The New American Cinema*, ed. Jon Lewis (Durham, NC: Duke University Press, 1998), p. 317.
79 Kleinhans, p. 324.
80 James Ulmer, *James Ulmer's Hollywood Hot List: The Complete Guide to Star Ranking* (New York: St Martin's Press, 2000), p. 210.
81 *The Economist* (July 30, 1983), p. 73, quoted in Hilmes, "Pay Television," pp. 315–16.

Chapter 8   Technology

1 Constant Coquelin, "Art and the Actor" (1st pub. in French, 1880, trans. Abby Langdon Alger, 1881), in *Papers on Acting*, ed. Brander Matthews (New York: Hill and Wang, 1958), p. 31.
2 Syd Silverman, "Entertainment in the Satellite Era," *Variety*, October 26, 1983, p. 13.
3 Philip Hayward and Tana Wollen, "Introduction: Surpassing the Real," in *Future Visions: New Technologies of the Screen*, eds Philip Hayward and Tana Wollen (London: British Film Institute, 1993), p. 3.
4 Barry Salt, *Film Style and Technology: History and Analysis* 1st edn 1983, 2nd edn (London: Starword, 1992); 1st edn, pp. 257, 288.
5 Rick Altman, "The Material Heterogeneity of Recorded Sound," in *Sound Theory, Sound Practice*, ed. Rick Altman (New York: Routledge, 1992), pp. 27–8.
6 Jean-Louis Comolli, "Machines of the Visible," in *The Cinematic Apparatus*, eds Teresa de Lauretis and Stephen Heath (London: Macmillan, 1980), pp. 121–42. Dickson, quoted in Richard Maltby, ed., *Dreams for Sale: Popular Culture in the Twentieth Century* (London: Harrap, 1989), p. 36.
7 Roy Armes, "Entendre, C'est Comprendre: In Defence of Sound Reproduction," *Screen* 29:2 (Spring 1988), p. 11.
8 André Bazin, "The Myth of Total Cinema," in *What is Cinema? Vol. 1*, trans. Hugh Gray (Berkeley, CA: University of California Press, 1967), p. 21.
9 Bazin, p. 20.
10 André Bazin, "Will CinemaScope Save the Cinema?," trans. Catherine Jones and Richard Neupert, *Velvet Light Trap* 21 (Summer 1985), p. 13.
11 André Bazin, "An Aesthetic of Reality," in *What is Cinema? Vol. 2*, trans. Hugh Gray (Berkeley, CA: University of California Press, 1971), p. 26.
12 Bazin, "Will CinemaScope Save the Cinema?," p. 13.
13 Bazin, "An Aesthetic of Reality," p. 26.
14 This is by no means the simple statement that

it may first appear, and Williams places this summary definition by observing that "it does not end, but only begins a controversy in art and literature when it is said that the purpose is 'to show things as they really are.'" A realism "of the surface," he says, "can miss important realities." Raymond Williams, *Keywords: A Vocabulary of Culture and Society* (London: Fontana, 1976), pp. 218–19.

15 John Ellis, *Visible Fictions* (London: Routledge and Kegan Paul, 1982), pp. 6–7.

16 Terry Lovell, *Pictures of Reality* (London: British Film Institute, 1980), p. 79.

17 Christian Metz, "Aural Objects," quoted in James Lastra, "Reading, Writing, and Representing Sound," in Altman, *Sound Theory, Sound Practice*, p. 65.

18 Imagine two photographs taken by the same camera in the same setting with the same lighting. One photograph is of an antique table, the other is of a reproduction antique table – that is, a close copy of the original. In all likelihood, we could not tell the representation of the reproduction apart from the representation of the original; only a close inspection of the objects themselves would allow us to do that. The point here is not to do with tables or even photographs, but with linguistic conventions. To talk of photographic reproduction is to use a conventional shorthand that chooses to ignore the conventions of photographic representation, to look through the photograph and see the object represented in it – just as talking about how realistic a representation is employs a similar shorthand.

19 Lovell, pp. 79–80.

20 Lastra, pp. 68, 81.

21 John Belton, "Technology and Aesthetics of Film Sound," in *Film Sound: Theory and Practice*, eds Elizabeth Weis and John Belton (New York: Columbia University Press, 1985), p. 70.

22 Amy Lawrence, *Echo and Narcissus: Women's Voices in Classical Hollywood Cinema* (Berkeley, CA: University of California Press, 1991), pp. 21–2.

23 Bazin, "The Ontology of the Photographic Image," in *What is Cinema? Vol. 1*, pp. 12, 14.

24 Bazin, "The Evolution of the Language of Cinema," in *What is Cinema? Vol. 1*, pp. 24, 28.

25 Bazin, "Evolution," p. 37.

26 Dudley Andrew, *The Major Film Theories: An Introduction* (New York: Oxford University Press, 1976), p. 163.

27 Andrew, p. 162.

28 Bazin, "Evolution," p. 40.

29 Andrew, p. 163.

30 Quoted in Edward Lowery, "Edwin J. Hadley: Travelling Film Exhibitor," *Journal of the University Film Association* 28:3 (Summer 1976), p. 6.

31 Fred Glass notes that discussions of the movie among teenagers "mostly revolved around the question of whether or not the entire movie was a dream," and considers the extent to which the movie's raising the possibility that it was a dream permits it to avoid resolving the thematic and ideological conflicts it raises. Fred Glass, "Totally Recalling Arnold: Sex and Violence in the New Bad Future," *Film Quarterly* 44:1 (Fall 1990), pp. 2–13.

32 Quoted in John Belton, "1950s Magnetic Sound: The Frozen Revolution," in Altman, *Sound Theory, Sound Practice*, p. 159.

33 Quoted in John Belton, "CinemaScope and Historical Methodology," *Cinema Journal* 28:1 (Fall 1988), pp. 33–4.

34 Richard Kohler and Walter Lassally, "The Big Screens," *Sight and Sound* 24:3 (January–March 1955), p. 120.

35 John Belton, *Widescreen Cinema* (Cambridge, MA: Harvard University Press, 1992), p. 202.

36 Philip Hayward has referred to this use of new technology to produce novel image effects as "impact aesthetics." Philip Hayward, "Industrial Light and Magic: Style, Technology and Special Effects in the Music Video and Music Television," in *Culture, Technology and Creativity*, ed. Philip Hayward (London: John Libbey, 1990).

37 Bazin, "The Ontology of the Photographic Image," in *What is Cinema? Vol. 1*, p. 13.

38 W. J. T. Mitchell, "The Pictorial Turn," *Art Forum* 30:3 (1992), p. 94.

39 Henry Jenkins, "The Work of Theory in the Age of Digital Transformation," in *A Companion to Film Theory*, eds Toby Miller and Robert Stam (Malden, MA: Blackwell, 1999), p. 253.

40 Robin Baker, "Computer Technology and Special Effects in Contemporary Cinema," in Hayward and Wollen, p. 42.

41 Michelle Pierson, "CGI Effects in Hollywood Science-Fiction Cinema 1989–95: The Wonder Years," *Screen* 40:2 (Summer 1999), p. 172.

42 Q. David Bowers, *Nickelodeon Theatres and their Music* (New York: Vestal Press, 1986), p. 129.

43 Ben M. Hall, *The Best Remaining Seats: The Golden Age of the Movie Palace* (New York: DaCapo, 1988), p. 192.

44 Mary Carbine, " 'The Finest Outside the Loop': Motion Picture Exhibition in Chicago's Black Metropolis, 1905–1928," *Camera Obscura* 23 (May 1990), p. 31.

45 Aubrey Solomon, *Twentieth Century-Fox: A Corporate and Financial History* (Metuchen, NJ: Scarecrow, 1988), p. 10.

46 Grandeur was a 70-mm wide-film process innovated by William Fox in the late 1920s. Although it offered the possibility of projecting a much larger image than the picture palaces' surprisingly small screens, none of the other major companies displayed much enthusiasm for absorbing the costs of conversion, and Grandeur became a victim of the collapse of Fox's business empire in late 1929. According to Upton Sinclair, *Sunny Side Up* was filmed in Grandeur, but it may well have been released before any theaters were equipped to show it in its 70-mm version. Sequences of the movie were filmed in Multicolor, a two-color bipack process. Belton, *Widescreen Cinema*, pp. 36, 48, 56; Upton Sinclair, *Upton Sinclair Presents William Fox* (Los Angeles: Upton Sinclair, 1933), p. 66; James L. Limbacher, *Four Aspects of the Film: A History of the Development of Color, Sound, 3-D and Widescreen Films and their Contribution to the Art of the Motion Picture* (New York: Brussel and Brussel, 1968), pp. 41, 270.

47 The first real camera crane was used on the Universal musical *Broadway* in 1929. Salt, 1st edn, p. 228.

48 John L. Cass, "The Illusion of Sound and Picture," *Journal of the Society of Motion Picture Engineers* 14 (March 1930), p. 325, quoted in Rick Altman, "Sound Space," in Altman, *Sound Theory, Sound Practice*, p. 49.

49 Rick Altman traces the development of these practices through the 1930s in "Sound Space," in Altman, pp. 49–62; and in more technical detail in "The Technology of the Voice," *Iris* 3:1 (1985), pp. 3–20.

50 Robert Ray, *A Certain Tendency of the Hollywood Cinema, 1930–1980* (Princeton, NJ: Princeton University Press, 1985), p. 29.

51 Ruth Vasey, *The World According to Hollywood, 1918–1939* (Exeter: University of Exeter Press, 1997), p. 68.

52 "General Principles to Govern the Preparation of a Revised Code of Ethics for Talking Pictures," Reporter's Transcript, board meeting, Association of Motion Picture Producers (AMPP), February 10, 1930, Motion Picture Association of America Archive, New York, 1930 AMPP Code file, pp. 138–9; Carl Milliken to Hays, October 9, 1929, PCA *Applause* file.

53 Quoted in Jeffrey Richards, *The Age of the Dream Palace: Cinema and Society in Britain, 1930–1939* (London: Routledge and Kegan Paul, 1984), pp. 63–4.

54 For many European audiences, neither spoke with his own voice, but with the dubbed voice of another actor.

55 George Orwell, *The English People* (London: Collins, 1947), p. 36.

56 R. T. Ryan, *A History of Motion Picture Colour Photography* (London: Focal Press, 1977), p. 77. In *Practical Motion Picture Photography*, Russell Campbell quotes surveys of American audiences that have suggested particular associations between colors and moods: blue is tender, cyan leisurely, green playful, yellow gay, red exciting or vigorous, magenta sad or solemn. He suggests that these associations "may perhaps explain why the American public appears to prefer prints with an overall reddish balance; in India, on the other hand, a greenish bias finds favor." Although Campbell is skeptical that these associations can be established by any form of systematic analysis, he concludes that "a cold (bluish) print has a distancing effect, while a warm (yellowish or reddish) balance tends towards audience involvement." Russell Campbell, *Practical Motion Picture Photography* (London: Zwemmer, 1970), p. 89. Perhaps the absence of system explains why Eastman Kodak's tinted film stocks bore such

descriptive names as Firelight, Sunshine, Nocturne, and Aqua Green.

57 *Elements of Color in Professional Motion Pictures* (1957), quoted in Edward Buscombe, "Sound and Color," *Jump Cut* 17 (1978), p. 24.

58 Quoted in Fred E. Barsten, *Glorious Technicolor* (London: A. S. Barnes, 1980), p. 71.

59 Steve Neale, *Cinema and Technology: Image, Sound, Colour* (London: Macmillan, 1985), p. 152.

60 Quoted in Neale, p. 147.

61 Natalie Kalmus, "Colour," in *Behind the Screen*, ed. Stephen Watts (London: Arthur Barker, 1938), p. 116, quoted in Neale, p. 150.

62 Quoted in Ronald Haver, *David O. Selznick's Hollywood* (New York: Knopf, 1980), p. 196.

63 "Faster Color Film Cuts Light in Half," *American Cinematographer* (August 1939), p. 356, quoted in Edward Braningan, "Color and Cinema: Problems in the Writing of History," in *The Hollywood Film Industry*, ed. Paul Kerr (London: Routledge and Kegan Paul, 1986), p. 139.

64 *The Wizard of Oz* was one of several movies to motivate a transition to color in the movement from reality to fantasy. In *The Blue Bird* (1940), a poor woodcutter (Nigel Bruce) tells fairy stories in black-and-white, while the stories themselves are in color. In *The Secret Garden* (1949), Margaret O'Brien discovers a magical, Technicolor garden in an otherwise black-and-white Victorian Yorkshire.

65 Eastman Kodak had cooperated in Technicolor's maintenance of its monopoly, but government anti-trust action against Technicolor as part of the Paramount suit encouraged it to develop an alternative, a spin-off from its development of color film for the domestic market.

66 Bosley Crowther, *New York Times* (October 5, 1952), quoted in Belton, *Widescreen Cinema*, p. 94.

67 Belton, "CinemaScope and Historical Methodology," pp. 28–30.

68 *Motion Picture Herald* (December 19, 1953), p. 14, quoted in Richard Hincha, "Selling CinemaScope: 1953–1956," *Velvet Light Trap* 21 (Summer 1985), p. 46.

69 Bazin, "Will CinemaScope Save the Cinema?," p. 12.

70 *Hollywood Reporter* (June 28, 1954), quoted in James Spellerberg, "CinemaScope and Ideology," *Velvet Light Trap* 21 (Summer 1985), p. 30.

71 Tana Wollen, "The Bigger the Better: From CinemaScope to IMAX," in Hayward and Wollen, p. 13.

72 Spellerberg, pp. 30–1.

73 Widescreen movies were initially prepared for television screening by a system known as "pan and scan," which allowed the technician preparing the television print to reframe a shot or cut from one side of the widescreen frame to the other. The end result often produced unbalanced compositions. Alternatively, the top and bottom of an Academy frame picture can be masked out for widescreen projection, and the whole image used for the television version. All these variations raise questions about the idea of an "original" version of a Hollywood movie. Belton, *Widescreen Cinema*, pp. 216–25.

74 The first "letterbox" video, *Manhattan*, was released in 1985 because director Woody Allen's contract with United Artists gave him control over the video versions of his work. Belton, *Widescreen Cinema*, p. 226.

75 The industry's early standardization on a film width of 35-mm gauge and an aspect ratio of 4:3 (1.33:1) had less to do with either engineering or aesthetics than it did with the exploitation of patents in pursuit of monopoly by the Edison and Eastman Kodak companies. Belton, *Widescreen Cinema*, pp. 22–8.

76 This model of the economics of technological change was adapted from business histories by Douglas Gomery in his work on the introduction of sound. J. Douglas Gomery, "The Coming of the Talkies: Invention, Innovation, and Diffusion," in *The American Film Industry*, ed. Tino Balio, 1st edn (Madison: University of Wisconsin Press, 1976), p. 211. See also Belton, *Widescreen Cinema*, p. 239.

77 Peter Wollen, "Cinema and Technology: A Historical Overview," in his *Readings and Writings: Semiotic Counter-Strategies* (London: Verso, 1982), p. 171.

78 Wollen, p. 171.

79 Patrick J. Ogle, "Technological and Aesthetic Influences upon the Development of Deep Focus Cinematography in the United States,"

in *Screen Reader 1: Cinema/Ideology/Politics* (London: Society for Education in Film and Television, 1977), pp. 81–108.

80 Patricia Zimmermann has pointed out, however, that the hardware of "amateur" film has always registered its difference from Hollywood and "encouraged the idolatry of technical wizardry" to which only Hollywood or television "professionals" have access. It is hardly accidental that the role broadcast television has found for amateur video is in the recording of domestic accidents in a comedy of domestic cruelty; the moments that are edited out of professional production are the only ones left in the shows of amateurs. Patricia R. Zimmermann, "Trading Down: Amateur Film Technology in Fifties America," *Screen* 29:2 (Spring 1988), p. 42.

81 These changes are discussed more fully in chapter 7.

82 Barry Salt uses the average shot length (ASL) of a movie as a means of comparing the frequency of cuts. This involves counting the number of separate shots in a movie, and dividing that by its running time. Salt suggests that ASLs fell steadily during the silent period to as low as 5 seconds, and then more than doubled with the coming of sound. After dropping to about 8 seconds in the mid-1930s, ASLs rose slightly through the 1940s and 1950s to about 11 seconds, and then fell during the 1960s to 7.5 seconds. There was, however, considerable variation between individual movies. Some studios and some filmmakers also cut faster than others. Salt, 1st edn, p. 282.

83 Robert Stam, *Film Theory: An Introduction* (Malden, MA: Blackwell, 2000), pp. 317–18.

84 James Verini, "New Movie Tycoon Philip Anschutz Wants to Make Celluloid Obsolete," *New York Observer*, March 27, 2001, p. 1.

85 Simon Turner, quoted in Peter Dean and Mark Kermode, "Windup," *Sight and Sound* 3:3 (NS, March 1993), p. 63.

86 Barbara Klinger, "The Contemporary Cinephile: Film Collecting in the Post-Video Era," in *Hollywood Spectatorship: Changing Perceptions of Cinema Audiences*, eds Melvyn Stokes and Richard Maltby (London: British Film Institute, 2001), pp. 140, 132.

87 Declan McCullagh, "High-Tech: U.S. Out of Hollywood," *Wired News*, February 27, 2002. http://www.wired.com/news/politics/0,1283,50716,00.html, accessed 5 March 2002.

88 Klinger, p. 134.

89 Robert Stam and Ella Habiba Shohat, "Film Theory and Spectatorship in the Age of the 'Posts,'" in *Reinventing Film Studies*, eds Christine Gledhill and Linda Williams (London: Arnold, 2000), p. 394.

90 Stam, *Film Theory*, p. 322.

Chapter 9 Politics

1 Ronald Brownstein, *The Power and the Glitter: The Hollywood–Washington Connection* (New York: Pantheon, 1990), p. 391.

2 Peter Biskind, *Seeing is Believing: How Hollywood Taught Us to Stop Worrying and Love the Fifties* (London: Pluto Press, 1983), p. 5.

3 Michael Wood, *America in the Movies; or, "Santa Maria, It Had Slipped My Mind!"* (New York: Basic Books, 1975), pp. 17–18.

4 Advertising tagline for *Air Force One*.

5 Wood, pp. 15–16, 190–3.

6 Wim Wenders, "The American Dream," in his *Emotion Pictures*, trans. Shaun Whiteside and Michael Hoffman (London: Faber, 1989), pp. 140–1.

7 Quoted in Margaret Thorp, *America at the Movies* (London: Faber, 1946), p. 161.

8 US Senate, 77th Congress, 1st Sess., Propaganda in Motion Pictures, Hearing before a Subcommittee on Interstate Commerce, on S. Res. 152, September 9–26, 1941 (Washington, DC: Government Printing Office, 1941), p. 1.

9 *Motion Picture Herald*, February 22, 1936, p. 16.

10 Ian Hamilton, *Writers in Hollywood* (London: Heinemann, 1990), p. 127; Leo Ribuffo, *Right, Center, Left: Essays in American History* (New Brunswick, NJ: Rutgers University Press, 1992), pp. 187–8.

11 "Whose Business is the Motion Picture," *Motion Picture Herald*, February 22, 1936, pp. 15–16.

12 Ned McIntosh, *Atlanta Constitution*, December 7, 1915, quoted in Fred Silva, ed., *Focus on The Birth of a Nation* (Englewood Cliffs, NJ: Prentice-Hall, 1971), pp. 34–5; Dorothy Dix, quoted in Richard Schickel,

D. W. Griffith and the Birth of Film (London: Pavilion, 1984), pp. 278–9. Dix, a journalist and reformer, urged her readers to see the movie because "it will make a better American of you."

13 Quoted in Schickel, p. 283.

14 Jason Joy to Will Hays, February 26, 1932; Joy to Irving Thalberg and Darryl Zanuck, February 26, 1932; Joy to Zanuck, July 26, 1932. Production Code Administration (hereafter PCA) case file, *I Am a Fugitive from a Chain Gang*; Thomas Cripps, *Making Movies Black: The Hollywood Message Movie from World War II to the Civil Rights Era* (New York: Oxford University Press, 1993), p. 5.

15 *Mutual Film Corp.* v. *Industrial Commission of Ohio*, United States Supreme Court, quoted in Gerald Mast, ed., *The Movies in Our Midst: Documents in the Cultural History of Film in America* (Chicago: University of Chicago Press, 1982), p. 142.

16 Lois Higgins, Director of the Chicago Crime Prevention Bureau, quoted in James Gilbert, *A Cycle of Outrage: America's Reaction to the Juvenile Delinquent in the 1950s* (New York: Oxford University Press, 1986), p. 75.

17 Stephen Prince, *A New Pot of Gold: Hollywood under the Electronic Rainbow, 1980–1989* (New York: Scribner's, 2000), p. 364.

18 http://www.family.org/pplace/pi/films/A0007941.html.

19 "Certificate of Incorporation of Motion Picture Producers and Distributors of America, Inc.," March 10, 1922, quoted in Raymond Moley, *The Hays Office* (Indianapolis: Bobbs-Merrill, 1945), p. 226.

20 Thorp, p. 160.

21 *Motion Picture Herald*, February 15, 1936, p. 24.

22 Quigley to Hays, July 11, 1938, 1939 Production Code File, Motion Picture Association of America Archive, New York (hereafter MPA).

23 Cripps, p. 204.

24 Zanuck to Joy, January 6, 1931, PCA case file, *Public Enemy.*

25 Joy, October 7, 1932, PCA case file, *I Am a Fugitive from a Chain Gang.*

26 Jack L. Warner, with Dean Jennings, *My First*

Hundred Years in Hollywood (New York: Random House, 1964), p. 218.

27 Nick Roddick, *A New Deal in Entertainment: Warner Brothers in the 1930s* (London: British Film Institute, 1983), p. 126.

28 *Time*, July 21, 1941, p. 73, quoted in Leo Rosten, *Hollywood: The Movie Colony, the Movie Makers* (New York: Harcourt, Brace, 1941), p. 327.

29 Advertising taglines for *Falling Down.*

30 Terry Christensen, *Reel Politics: American Political Movies from Birth of a Nation to Platoon* (New York: Blackwell, 1987), p. 212.

31 Breen, letter to John Hammel at Paramount, and to Louis B. Mayer at MGM, January 19, 1938. PCA case file, *Mr Smith Goes to Washington.*

32 In *Fury* (1936), the victim of mob violence is Spencer Tracy, playing a man falsely accused of murder. Joseph Breen, letter to Will Hays, June 22, 1938. 1939 Production Code file, MPA.

33 Ray Norr to Francis Harmon, January 1, 1939. 1939 Production Code file, MPA.

34 Charles Wolfe, "*Mr Smith Goes to Washington*: Democratic Forums and Representational Forms," in *Close Viewings: An Anthology of New Film Criticism*, ed. Peter Lehman (Tallahassee: Florida State University Press, 1990), pp. 310–11.

35 *Los Angeles Times*, October 22, 1939.

36 Donald J. Stirling to Hays, December 5, 1939. PCA case file, *Mr Smith Goes to Washington.*

37 Darryl Zanuck, Address to the Writers' Congress in Los Angeles, October 1943, quoted in Roger Manvell, *Films and the Second World War* (New York: Dell, 1974), p. 203.

38 On *No Way Out* (1950), quoted in Brian Neve, *Film and Politics in America: A Social Tradition* (London: Routledge, 1992), p. 104.

39 Humphrey Bogart, "Hollywood Strikes Back," radio broadcast by the Committee for the First Amendment, October 26, 1947, quoted in Robert Sklar, *City Boys: Cagney, Bogart, Garfield* (Princeton, NJ: Princeton University Press, 1992), p. 195.

40 Larry Ceplair and Steven Englund, *The Inquisition in Hollywood: Politics in the Film Community, 1930–1960* (Berkeley, CA: University of California Press, 1983), p. 92.

41 Carey McWilliams, *Southern California: An Island on the Land*, 1st pub. 1946 (Santa Barbara: Peregrine Smith, 1973), pp. 274, 293.

42 Ceplair and Englund, pp. 98–100; Brownstein, p. 49.

43 Sidney Buchman, the writer of a number of screwball comedies who became a producer at Columbia in the early 1940s, testified to his own membership of the Communist party at a hearing of the House Committee on Un-American Activities in 1951, but refused to inform on others. He was found guilty of contempt of Congress, and blacklisted. He worked again in the 1960s as a screenwriter and producer.

44 Gore Vidal, *Screening History* (London: Abacus, 1993), p. 29.

45 Harry M. Warner, *Christian Science Monitor*, April 1939, quoted in Mark Crispin Miller, "Introduction: The Big Picture," in *Seeing Through Movies*, ed. Mark Crispin Miller (New York: Pantheon, 1990), pp. 3–4.

46 Quoted in Rudy Behlmer, *Behind the Scenes* (New York: Samuel French, 1982), p. 191.

47 US Senate, pp. 19–20.

48 Darryl Zanuck, speech to the American Legion, September 1941, quoted in Mel Gussow, *Don't Say Yes Until I've Finished Talking* (New York: Doubleday, 1971), p. 105.

49 K. R. M. Short, "Note on Government Information Manual for the Motion Picture Industry," *Historical Journal of Film, Radio and Television* 3:2 (October 1983), p. 171.

50 Government Information Manual for the Motion Picture Industry, quoted in Clayton R. Koppes and Gregory D. Black, *Hollywood Goes to War: How Politics, Profits and Propaganda Shaped World War II Movies* (New York: Macmillan, 1987), pp. 66–7.

51 Koppes and Black, p. 184.

52 Cripps, p. ix.

53 Elmer Davis to Byron Price, January 27, 1943, quoted in Koppes and Black, p. 64.

54 Cripps, pp. 27, 65.

55 Jack L. Warner, testimony to HUAC, October 1947, quoted in Gordon Kahn, *Hollywood on Trial: The Story of the Ten who were Indicted* (New York: Boni and Gaer, 1948), p. 22.

56 RKO letter to Adrian Scott and Edward Dmytryk, November 26, 1947, quoted in Kahn, p. 191.

57 In 1947 President Truman had created a Federal Employee Loyalty Program, authorizing the security services to draw up a list of organizations deemed "subversive," and to examine the political affiliations of federal government employees. Any suspicion of "disloyalty" could provide grounds for dismissal. By the early 1950s, the program had spread, so that perhaps one out of every five working people – federal and state employees, teachers, members of professional associations, and industrial workers – had to swear a loyalty oath or receive "clearance" as a condition of employment. William H. Chafe, *The Unfinished Journey: America Since World War II* (New York: Oxford University Press, 1986), p. 99; David Caute, *The Great Fear: The Anti-Communist Purge under Truman and Eisenhower* (London: Secker and Warburg, 1978), p. 270.

58 *On the Waterfront* had begun as a collaboration between its director, Elia Kazan, and playwright Arthur Miller. Kazan, who had directed Miller's plays *All My Sons* (1947) and *Death of a Salesman* (1949) on Broadway, was among the most notorious of those who named names to HUAC because of the self-serving justification he produced for his actions – Victor Navasky calls him "the quintessential informer." Miller, who refused to cooperate with the Committee and broke with Kazan over his testimony, wrote two plays that directly addressed the politics of the period, *The Crucible* (1953) and *A View from the Bridge* (1955). A story is told that Miller sent Kazan a copy of *A View from the Bridge*, and Kazan replied saying he would be honored to direct it. "You don't understand," Miller told him. "I didn't send it to you because I wanted you to direct it. I sent it to you because I wanted you to know what I think about stool pigeons." Victor S. Navasky, *Naming Names* (New York: Viking Press, 1980), p. 199.

59 Brownstein, pp. 119, 176.

60 Cripps, pp. 220–1, 250.

61 Brownstein, p. 174.

62 Quoted in Brownstein, p. 274.

63 After his election as governor of California in 1966, liberal director William Wyler said rue-

fully to Charlton Heston, "You know, if we had given Reagan a couple of good parts, he'd never be in Sacramento now." Brownstein, p. 278.

64 Brownstein, p. 279.

65 Neal Gabler, "Have Script, Will Stand," *Sydney Morning Herald*, December 24, 1999, p. 6s.

66 Alan Nadel, *Flatlining on the Field of Dreams: Cultural Narratives in the Films of President Reagan's America* (New Brunswick, NJ: Rutgers University Press, 1997), p. 4.

67 Stephen Powers, David J. Rothman, and Stanley Rothman, *Hollywood's America: Social and Political Themes in Motion Pictures* (Boulder, CO: Westview Press, 1996), pp. 2–3, 5.

68 Fonda had played a similar role two years previously, in *Advise and Consent* (1962); Robertson had played the young John F. Kennedy in *PT 109* (1963).

69 The only issues raised in the movie itself are the bi-partisan questions of anti-Communism and civil rights, and the discussion of both of them is heavily conditioned by the caricatured images the movie presents of Cantwell and T. T. Claypool (John Henry Faulk).

70 James Monaco suggests that several of the movie's characters are recognizable caricatures of political campaign organizers. James Monaco, *American Film Now: The People, the Power, the Money, the Movies* (New York: New American Library, 1979), p. 361.

71 Charles Affron, *Cinema and Sentiment* (Chicago: University of Chicago Press, 1982), p. 119.

72 Brownstein, p. 267.

73 Tim Robbins, director and star of *Bob Roberts*, quoted in Martin Walker, "A Downhome Demagogue on the Stump," *Guardian*, July 29, 1992, p. 36.

74 Christensen, pp. 211–15.

75 Brownstein, pp. 136, 273, 391.

76 *Wag the Dog*'s source novel was Larry Beinhart, *American Hero* (New York: Ballantine Books, 1993).

77 James Castonguay, "Hollywood Goes to Washington: Scandal, Politics, and Contemporary Media Culture," in *Headline Hollywood: A Century of Film Scandal*, eds Adrienne L. McClean and David A. Cook

(New Brunswick, NJ: Rutgers University Press, 2001), p. 287.

78 Larry Beinhart, "Book, Movie, War, Reality," *New York Times*, May 18, 1999, p. A23.

79 Richard Goldstein, "That's Entertainment," *Village Voice*, September 19–25, 2001.

80 "Feds Enlist Hollywood for Theories," *Variety*, October 8, 2001.

81 On *Pinky* (1950), quoted in Cripps, p. 232.

82 Quoted in Beverly Walker, "Hackman: The Last Honest Man in America," *Film Comment* 24:6 (December 1988), p. 23.

83 Gavin Smith, "'Mississippi' Gambler," *Film Comment* 24:6 (November/December 1988), p. 30.

84 Quoted in Neve, p. 26.

85 As a setting, the South fulfills this function in a number of exploitation horror movies such as *I Spit on Your Grave* (1977). In mainstream cinema, this version of a contemporary Gothic South, which *Mississippi Burning* evokes in its imagery of burning churches, occurs in *Deliverance* (1972) and *Southern Comfort* (1981). Carol J. Clover, *Men, Women and Chainsaws: Gender in the Modern Horror Film* (London: British Film Institute, 1992), p. 163. The other frequent generic home for Hollywood dystopias is in science fiction movies: for instance, *Soylent Green* (1973), *Rollerball* (1975), *Outland* (1981), *Blade Runner* (1982). They, too, take place in a setting that "ain't America," yet.

86 Alan Parker, "Notes on the Making of the Film," *Mississippi Burning* press kit production notes, p. 1.

87 Andrew Britton, "Blissing Out: The Politics of Reaganite Entertainment," *MOVIE* 31/2 (Winter 1986), pp. 1–42.

88 Quoted in Joan Goodman, "Taking Flak for Fiction," *Guardian*, May 4, 1989.

89 Quoted in Goodman.

90 Robert Stam, "Bakhtin, Polyphony, and Ethnic/Racial Representation," in *Unspeakable Images: Ethnicity and the American Cinema*, ed. Lester Friedman (Urbana: University of Illinois Press, 1991), p. 253.

91 Smith, p. 29.

92 Quoted in Goodman.

93 Parker shunned any "based on a true story" credit because placing such a credit on *Midnight Express* (1978) "got me into far too much trouble." Quoted in Smith, p. 29.

94 Roddick, p. 126.

95 This generic context was recognized by *Mississippi Burning*'s writer, Chris Gerolmo, whose initial premise was "say, Clint Eastwood and Bill Hurt in those roles . . . a working-through of a Western-type conflict like *The Man Who Shot Liberty Valance*, where the rule of law needs the rule of force." Quoted in Smith, p. 28.

96 Nadel, pp. 132–3.

97 Goodman.

98 Robert Ray, *A Certain Tendency of the Hollywood Cinema, 1930–1980* (Princeton, NJ: Princeton University Press, 1985), pp. 296–325.

99 Parker, p. 5.

100 "General Principles to Govern the Preparation of a Revised Code of Ethics for Talking Pictures." Reporter's Transcript, board meeting, Association of Motion Picture Producers (AMPP), February 10, 1930, Motion Picture Association of America Archive, New York, 1930 AMPP Code file, pp. 138–9.

101 Parker's "Production Notes" remark, "March 10. Another church to be burned . . . March 14. Began a week of night church burnings and also the burning of Vertis Williams' farm." *Mississippi Burning* was nominated for five Academy Awards, including Best Film, but won only one. Parker felt that the controversy surrounding the movie damaged its chances of winning others.

102 Edward Branigan, "Color and Cinema: Problems in the Writing of History," in *The Hollywood Film Industry*, ed. Paul Kerr (London: Routledge and Kegan Paul, 1986), p. 135.

103 Wenders, p. 139.

104 Richard Dyer, "Entertainment and Utopia," *MOVIE* 24 (1977), pp. 6–8.

105 Daniel Bell, *The End of Ideology* (New York: Collier Books, 1960), p. 373.

106 Catherine Belsey, *Critical Practice* (London: Methuen, 1980), p. 5.

107 Belsey, p. 5.

108 Louis Althusser, "Marxism and Humanism," in his *For Marx* (London: NLB, 1977), p. 233; Louis Althusser, "Ideology and Ideological State Apparatuses: Notes towards an Investigation," in his *Lenin and Philosophy and Other Essays* (London: NLB, 1971), p. 169.

109 Belsey, pp. 57–8.

110 Belsey, p. 58.

111 Terry Eagleton, *Ideology: An Introduction* (London: Verso, 1991), p. xiii.

112 Frank Nugent, *New York Times*, October 29, 1939, quoted in Wolfe, p. 311; Richard Griffith, *New Movies*, November 1939, quoted in Wolfe, p. 301. Wolfe suggests that analyses of the movie that emphasize "the capacity of director Frank Capra to articulate a social vision for his audience" can be traced back to Griffith's review.

113 See, for instance, the discussion of *School Daze* (1987) in Ella Shohat, "Ethnicities in Relation: Toward a Multicultural Reading of American Cinema," and in Robert Stam, "Bakhtin, Polyphony, and Ethnic/Racial Representation," both in Friedman, pp. 215–50, 251–76.

114 "The how of racism . . . makes good cinematic spectacle. But what is never explained is the much more political why of racism." Ed Guerrero, "Spike Lee and the Fever in the Racial Jungle," in *Film Theory Goes to the Movies*, eds Jim Collins, Hilary Radner, and Ava Preacher Collins (New York: Routledge, 1993), p. 178.

115 Mark A. Reid, *Redefining Black Film* (Berkeley, CA: University of California Press, 1993), pp. 106–7; Malcolm Turvey, "Black Film-Making in the USA: The Case of Malcolm X," *Wasafiri* 18 (Autumn 1983), pp. 54–6.

Chapter 10   Space 1

1 David Bordwell and Kristin Thompson, *Film Art: An Introduction*, 6th edn (New York: McGraw-Hill, 2001), p. 141.

2 This debate is often presented as being staged between André Bazin and Jean Mitry. André Bazin, "Theatre and Cinema: Part 2," in *What is Cinema? Vol. 1*, trans. Hugh Gray (Berkeley, CA: University of California Press, 1967), pp. 95–124; Jean Mitry, *Esthétique et Psychologie du Cinéma*, 2 vols (Paris: Editions Universitaires, 1963, 1965); English trans. as *The Aesthetics and Psychology of the Cinema*, trans. Christopher King (Bloomington: Indiana University Press, 1997).

3 David Bordwell, Janet Staiger, and Kristin Thompson, *The Classical Hollywood Cinema: Film Style and Mode of Production to 1960*

(London: Routledge and Kegan Paul, 1985), p. 51.

4 Steve Neale, *Cinema and Technology: Image, Sound, Colour* (London: Macmillan, 1985), pp. 21–2.

5 Quoted in Stephen Rebello, *Alfred Hitchcock and the Making of Psycho* (New York: Dembner Books, 1990), p. 93.

6 J. A. Place and L. S. Peterson, "Some Visual Motifs of *Film Noir*," in *Movies and Methods*, ed. Bill Nichols (Berkeley, CA: University of California Press, 1976), pp. 325–38.

7 Elie Faure, "The Art of Cineplastics," in *Film: An Anthology*, ed. Daniel Talbot (Berkeley, CA: University of California Press, 1969), p. 6.

8 Occasionally a comparable aesthetic argument still appears in criticism of Hollywood. Barry Salt, for instance, has argued that, in the movies directed by Josef von Sternberg starring Marlene Dietrich, there is a "kinetic use of light and dark" that has no significant expressive function in the movies' narratives. Barry Salt, "Sternberg's Heart Beats in Black and White," in *Sternberg*, ed. Peter Baxter (London: British Film Institute, 1980), pp. 103–18.

9 Cinerama publicity, quoted in John Belton, *Widescreen Cinema* (Cambridge, MA: Harvard University Press, 1992), pp. 188–9.

10 Will Wright, *Sixguns and Society: A Structural Study of the Western* (Berkeley, CA: University of California Press, 1975), p. 193.

11 Roger D. McNiven, "The Middle-Class American Home of the Fifties: The Use of Architecture in Nicholas Ray's *Bigger Than Life* and Douglas Sirk's *All That Heaven Allows*," *Cinema Journal* 22:2 (Summer 1983), p. 38.

12 Daniel Arijon, *Grammar of the Film Language* (Los Angeles: Silman-James Press, 1976), pp. 4, 6, 20, 22, 528.

13 Jan-Christopher Horak, "G. W. Pabst in Hollywood or Every Modern Hero Deserves a Mother," *Film History* 1:1 (1987), p. 57.

14 Thomas Schatz, *The Genius of the System: Hollywood Filmmaking in the Studio Era* (New York: Pantheon, 1988), pp. 140–5, 225–6.

15 "Cutting Notes, *Angels with Dirty Faces*, August 24, 1938," *Angels with Dirty Faces* Production file, Warner Bros. Archive, Department of Special Collections, Doheney Library, University of Southern California, Los Angeles.

16 Bazin, "The Evolution of the Language of Cinema," in his *What is Cinema? Vol. 1*, pp. 24, 32.

17 Arijon, p. 32; Steven D. Katz, *Film Directing Shot by Shot: Visualizing from Concept to Screen* (Los Angeles: Michael Wiese Productions, 1991), p. 123.

Chapter 11 Space 2

1 James Clifford, *The Predicament of Culture* (Cambridge, MA: Harvard University Press, 1988), p. 34.

2 Reporter's Transcript, board meeting, Association of Motion Picture Producers (AMPP), February 10, 1930, Motion Picture Association of America Archive, New York, 1930 AMPP Code file, p. 14.

3 Daniel Dayan, "The Tutor-Code of Classical Cinema," in *Movies and Methods*, ed. Bill Nichols (Berkeley, CA: University of California Press, 1976), pp. 445–6, 448–9.

4 Patrick Tucker, *Secrets of Screen Acting* (London: Routledge, 1994), p. 53.

5 Bruce Block, *The Visual Story: Seeing the Structure of Film, TV, and New Media* (Boston: Focal Press, 2001), p. 145.

6 William Rothman, "Against 'the System of the Suture,'" in Nichols, pp. 451–9.

7 David Bordwell, *Narration in the Fiction Film* (London: Methuen, 1985), p. 161.

8 In a more recent instance, the audience's understanding of on-screen events in *Memento* (2000) is obscured by the presence of a first-person narrator suffering from short-term memory loss, and complicated by the narrative's pattern of flashbacks and ellipses.

9 Bordwell, p. 31.

10 Martha Wolfenstein and Nathan Leites, *Movies: A Psychological Study* (Glencoe, IL: Free Press, 1950), pp. 248, 250.

11 Laura Mulvey, "Notes on Sirk and Melodrama," *MOVIE* 25 (Winter 1977–8), pp. 53–6.

12 David Bordwell, Janet Staiger, and Kristin Thompson, *The Classical Hollywood Cinema: Film Style and Mode of Production to 1960* (London: Routledge and Kegan Paul, 1985), pp. 372, 375.

13 Bordwell et al., pp. 9, 375.

14 Paul Schrader, "Notes on Film Noir," *Film Comment* 8:1 (January 1974). Reprinted in *Film Genre Reader*, ed. Barry Keith Grant (Austin: University of Texas Press, 1986), p. 175.

15 Quoted in Donald Spoto, *The Life of Alfred Hitchcock: The Dark Side of Genius* (London: Collins, 1983), p. 419.

16 Robin Wood, *Hitchcock's Films Revisited* (New York: Columbia University Press, 1989), p. 146.

17 William Pechter, *Twenty-Four Times a Second* (New York: Harper and Row, 1971), quoted in Stephen Rebello, *Alfred Hitchcock and the Making of Psycho* (New York: Dembner Books, 1990), p. 162.

18 Quoted in Rebello, pp. 174, 169. Hitchcock also insisted on 30 seconds of darkness in the theater after the end-titles, so that the effect of the movie's ending would be "indelibly engraved in the mind of the audience, later to be discussed among gaping friends and relations. You will then bring up house lights of a greenish hue, and shine spotlights of this ominous hue across the faces of your departing patrons." Quoted in Rebello, pp. 150–1.

19 Quoted in Spoto, p. 406.

20 Carol J. Clover, *Men, Women and Chainsaws: Gender in the Modern Horror Film* (London: British Film Institute, 1992), p. 203.

21 Andrew Britton, "Blissing Out: The Politics of Reaganite Entertainment," *MOVIE* 31/2 (Winter 1986), pp. 2–3.

22 Clover, p. 202.

23 Clover, pp. 6–7.

24 Tania Modleski, *The Women Who Knew Too Much: Hitchcock and Feminist Theory* (London: Methuen, 1988), p. 107.

25 Clover, pp. 23, 27, 43–4, 229.

26 Robert E. Kapsis, *Hitchcock: The Making of a Reputation* (Chicago: University of Chicago Press, 1992), pp. 60–1.

27 Redford, in interview on *The South Bank Show: Melvyn Bragg Talks to Robert Redford about "Ordinary People"* (London Weekend Television, 1981).

28 Michael Ryan and Douglas Kellner, *Camera Politica: The Politics and Ideology of the Contemporary Hollywood Film* (Bloomington: Indiana University Press, 1988), p. 160.

29 Britton, p. 24.

30 Robin Wood, *Hollywood from Vietnam to Reagan* (New York: Columbia University Press, 1986), pp. 173–4.

31 Significantly, Alvin Sargent's screenplay informs us about Buck's death much more quickly than the novel by Judith Guest from which it is derived.

32 *Ordinary People* invokes the horror movie earlier, when a group of children come to the Jarretts' house trick-or-treating on Halloween.

Chapter 12   Performance 1

1 James Naremore, *Acting in the Cinema* (Berkeley, CA: University of California Press, 1988), p. 70.

2 Peter Brook, *The Empty Space* (Harmondsworth: Pelican, 1972), p. 55.

3 Vsevolod Pudovkin, "On Film Technique," in *Film Technique and Film Acting: The Cinema Writings of V. I. Pudovkin*, trans. Ivor Montagu (New York: Bonanza, 1949), p. 140.

4 Pudovkin, p. xiv.

5 Pudovkin, p. 54.

6 Lev Kuleshov, "Art of the Cinema," in *Kuleshov on Film: Writings by Lev Kuleshov*, ed. and trans. Ronald Levaco (Berkeley, CA: University of California Press, 1974), p. 54.

7 Frank D. McConnell, *The Spoken Seen: Film and the Romantic Imagination* (Baltimore, MD: Johns Hopkins University Press, 1975), pp. 177, 182.

8 Foster Hirsch describing Bette Davis in *The Little Foxes* (1941): Foster Hirsch, *Acting Hollywood Style* (New York: Abrams, 1991), p. 47.

9 Richard Dyer, *Stars* (London: British Film Institute, 1979), p. 166.

10 Naremore, p. 2.

11 Pudovkin, pp. 26, 67, 70.

12 Stephen Rebello, *Alfred Hitchcock and the Making of Psycho* (New York: Dembner Books, 1990), pp. 113, 123, 131–5.

13 McConnell, p. 175.

14 David Mayer, "Acting in Silent Film," in *Screen Acting*, eds Alan Lovell and Peter Krämer (London: Routledge, 1999), p. 17.

15 Dziga Vertov, "The Cine-Eyes. A Revolution," *Lef* 3 (June–July 1923), trans. and reprinted in *The Film Factory: Russian and*

Soviet Cinema in Documents, 1896–1939, eds Richard Taylor and Ian Christie (London: Routledge and Kegan Paul, 1988), pp. 91–3.

16   *New York Journal*, April 4, 1896, p. 9, quoted in Charles Musser, *Before the Nickelodeon: Edwin S. Porter and the Edison Manufacturing Company* (Berkeley, CA: University of California Press, 1991), p. 60.

17   *New York Herald*, April 24, 1896, p. 11, quoted in Musser, p. 63. Musser adds that "patrons in the front rows were disconcerted and inclined to leave their seats as the wave crashed on the beach and seemed about to flood the theater," a similar account of the behavior of early cinema audiences to that often reproduced about the Lumières' *L'Arrivée d'un Train en Gare de la Ciotat* (1895).

18   Tom Gunning, "The Cinema of Attractions: Early Film, its Spectators and the Avant-Garde," in *Early Cinema: Space, Frame, Narrative*, ed. Thomas Elsaesser (London: British Film Institute, 1990), p. 57. The largest chain of theaters exclusively showing films before 1906 was Hale's Tours, showing "Tours and Scenes of the World" at amusement parks across America. As one advertisement described the "panoramic effect" of this "ride," "The person wishing to make the tour enters what has every appearance of a regular [train] coach. A colored porter is at the door and the seats are arranged inside the same as in a regular tourist car.... By a splendid arrangement which is an elaboration on the moving picture scheme the passengers can without effort imagine that they are traveling on a train and viewing the scenery. There is a slight rocking to the car as it takes the curves, and in addition there is the shrill whistle of the locomotive and the ringing bell at intervals to carry out further the illusion." Charles Musser, *The Emergence of Cinema: The American Screen to 1907* (New York: Scribner's, 1990), p. 437. See also Raymond Fielding, "Hale's Tours: Ultrarealism in the Pre-1910 Motion Picture," in *Film Before Griffith*, ed. John L. Fell (Berkeley, CA: University of California Press, 1983), pp. 116–30. Rides like Disneyland's Star Tours are contemporary versions of these attractions.

19   Steven D. Katz, *Film Directing Shot by Shot: Visualizing from Concept to Screen* (Los Angeles: Michael Wiese Productions, 1991), p. 147.

20   Katz, p. 280.

21   André Bazin, "The Evolution of the Language of Cinema," in his *What is Cinema? Vol. 1*, trans. Hugh Gray (Berkeley, CA: University of California Press, 1967), p. 24.

22   Following its release on DVD, this "restored" version is more readily available than the studio release version.

23   Quoted in Doug McClelland, ed., *Starspeak: Hollywood on Everything* (London: Faber, 1987), pp. 9–10.

24   Robert Sklar, *City Boys: Cagney, Bogart, Garfield* (Princeton, NJ: Princeton University Press, 1992), p. 112.

25   Theodore Noose, *Hollywood Film Acting* (New York: Barnes, 1979), p. 11; Lillian Albertson, *Motion Picture Acting* (New York: Funk and Wagnalls, 1947), p. 10. With equal vagueness, one American acting school teaches that "to act is to do or to live truthfully under imaginary circumstances." Quoted in Steve Vineberg, *Method Actors: Three Generations of an American Acting Style* (New York: Macmillan, 1991), p. 109.

26   Patrick Tucker, *Secrets of Screen Acting* (London: Routledge, 1994), p. 98.

27   Bronson Howard, "Our Schools for the Stage," *Century*, November 1900, quoted in Brander Matthews, ed., *Papers on Acting* (New York: Hill and Wang, 1958), p. 281.

28   Mayer, p. 10.

29   Tucker, pp. 103, 46.

30   Quoted in Dyer, pp. 148–9.

31   Naremore notes that "different performing methods or styles of blocking can make acting seem more or less presentational, depending on the emotional tone of the players, their movements in relation to the camera, and the degree to which they mimic well-known forms of behavior." Naremore, pp. 30, 36.

32   McConnell, pp. 79, 87.

33   Vineberg, p. 112.

34   Vineberg, p. 110.

35   Inez Klumph and Helen Klumph, *Screen Acting: Its Requirements and Rewards* (New York: Falk, 1922), p. 141.

36   Hirsch, p. 155.

37   Klumph and Klumph, p. 181.

38   Albertson, pp. 65, 75.

39   Constant Coquelin, "Actors and Acting,"

Harper's Monthly, May 1887, reprinted in Matthews, pp. 163, 173.

40 Naremore, p. 5.

41 This example is discussed more fully in Richard deCordova, "Genre and Performance: An Overview," in *Film Genre Reader*, ed. Barry Keith Grant (Austin: University of Texas Press, 1986), p. 135.

42 Quoted in Nicholas Kent, *Naked Hollywood: Money, Power and the Movies* (London: BBC Books, 1991), p. 79.

43 Naremore, pp. 18, 102. Edward Wagenknecht, *The Movies in the Age of Innocence* (Norman: University of Oklahoma Press, 1962), pp. 249–50.

44 "Acting on the screen is not acting, it is *being*. It is getting into a character, fitting it as a hand fits into a glove, and then letting the public see what that character does under a given set of circumstances." Klumph and Klumph, p. 103.

45 For instance, early in the movie's production planning, *Photoplay* magazine declared that "to our mind there is but one Rhett – Clark Gable. . . . We like all the other handsome actors mentioned as Rhett – only we don't want them as Rhett." In the casting of Scarlett O'Hara, the magazine proposed, "the prime requisite" was that "Scarlett must be in Gable's arms." Gable himself, however, later claimed that he had not wanted the part: "Miss [Margaret] Mitchell had etched Rhett into the minds of millions of people . . . it would be impossible to satisfy them all. . . . The public interest in my playing Rhett puzzled me. . . . I was the only one, apparently, who didn't take it for granted that I was going to play the part." Ronald Haver, *David O. Selznick's Hollywood* (New York: Knopf, 1980), pp. 242, 251.

46 Philip French, "Faust Goes to Memphis," *Observer*, September 12, 1993, p. 48.

47 Barbara Klinger, *Melodrama and Meaning: History, Culture, and the Films of Douglas Sirk* (Bloomington: Indiana University Press, 1994), p. 100.

48 Cathy Klaprat, "The Star as Market Strategy: Bette Davis in Another Light," in *The American Film Industry*, ed. Tino Balio, 1st edn 1976, revised edn (Madison: University of Wisconsin Press, 1985), p. 363.

49 Klaprat, pp. 355, 363, 372, 375.

50 Quoted in Tucker, p. 84.

51 In *Out of Africa* (1985), Meryl Streep's Danish accent stands out against the movie's other voices, not because it is Danish or because it is in itself unsuccessful, but because her adoption of an accent separates the register of her performance from that of her co-star, Redford, who just sounds like Robert Redford.

52 Naremore, p. 22.

Chapter 13   Performance 2

1 Genevieve Stebbins, *Delsarte's System of Expression* (New York: Edgar S. Werner, 1902; reprinted New York: Dance Horizons, 1977), p. 76.

2 Quoted in Richard Schickel, *Brando: A Life in Our Times* (London: Pavilion, 1991), p. 126.

3 Schickel, p. 15.

4 Steve Vineberg, *Method Actors: Three Generations of an American Acting Style* (New York: Macmillan, 1991), p. 6.

5 Toby Cole and Helen Kritch Chinoy, eds, *Actors on Acting* (New York: Crown, 1970), p. 623, quoted in James Naremore, *Acting in the Cinema* (Berkeley, CA: University of California Press, 1988), p. 18.

6 "Affective memory is the conscious creation of remembered emotions which have occurred in the actor's *own* past life and then their application to the character being portrayed." Edward Dwight Easty, *On Method Acting*, 1st edn 1966 (New York: Ballantine, 1989), p. 44.

7 Lillian Albertson, *Motion Picture Acting* (New York: Funk and Wagnalls, 1947), p. 65.

8 Cynthia Baron, "Crafting Film Performances: Acting in the Hollywood Studio Era," in *Screen Acting*, eds Alan Lovell and Peter Krämer (London: Routledge, 1999), p. 40.

9 Albertson, p. 61.

10 Foster Hirsch, *Acting Hollywood Style* (New York: Abrams, 1991), p. 64.

11 Quoted in Michel Ciment, *Kazan on Kazan* (London: Secker and Warburg, 1973), p. 38.

12 Quoted in Bob Thomas, *Brando: Portrait of the Rebel as an Artist* (London: W. H. Allen, 1973), p. 74.

13 James F. Scott, *Film: The Medium and the*

Maker (New York: Holt, Rinehart, and Winston, 1975), p. 249.

14 Maureen Stapleton, in Lewis Funke and John E. Booth, eds, *Actors Talk About Acting: Fourteen Interviews with Stars of the Theatre* (New York: Random House, 1961), pp. 170–1. Quoted in Vineberg, p. 223.

15 Vineberg, p. 7.

16 Thomas R. Atkins, "Troubled Sexuality in the Popular Hollywood Feature," in *Sexuality in the Movies*, ed. Thomas R. Atkins (Bloomington: Indiana University Press, 1975), p. 114.

17 Vineberg, p. 91.

18 Richard Dyer, *Stars* (London: British Film Institute, 1979), p. 161.

19 Naremore, p. 201.

20 Easty, p. 67. This is Rod Steiger describing his own performance in *The Pawnbroker* (1965): "The last moment of *The Pawnbroker* when the boy is dead and I come out of the shop and I dipped my hand in the blood . . . I imagined it was my daughter. I was an emotional wreck before I started it. Then I remembered that Picasso picture of the bombing of Guernica, with the pointed tongues and the horses and the women shouting the loudest screams you have ever heard. Then I said to myself scream, but don't make a sound. That was one of my best moments." Stuart Jeffries, "A Method that No Longer Fits the Bill," *Guardian*, August 20, 1992, p. 21.

21 Patrick Tucker, *Secrets of Screen Acting* (London: Routledge, 1994), p. 59.

22 Inez Klumph and Helen Klumph, *Screen Acting: Its Requirements and Rewards* (New York: Falk, 1922), p. 125.

23 For instance, Gustave Garcia, *The Actor's Art: A Practical Treatise on Stage Declamation, Public Speaking and Deportment, for the Use of Artists, Students and Amateurs* (London: Pettitt, 1882), pp. 41, 62–3.

24 While Saussure asserts that the relationship between signifier and signified (between a word and the thing the word stands for) is arbitrary, Delsarte's "semeiotics" studied organic relationships, which he called correspondences. "Correspondence," he held, "is no arbitrary relationship like metaphor or figure, but one founded alike on the inward and outward nature of the things by which we are surrounded." Delsarte's "semeiotics" are, therefore, analogical, while Saussure's semiology is digital. Stebbins, pp. 135–42.

25 Stebbins, p. 142.

26 Benjamin McArthur, *Actors and American Culture, 1880–1920* (Philadelphia: Temple University Press, 1984), pp. 100, 182–3.

27 Quoted in Richard A. Blum, *American Film Acting: The Stanislavski Heritage* (Ann Arbor: UMI Research Press, 1984), p. 52.

28 Reproduced in Russell C. Sweeney, *Coming Next Week: A Pictorial History of Film Advertising* (New York: Barnes, 1973), p. 95.

29 Edmund K. Chambers, *The Elizabethan Stage*, vol. 4 (Oxford: Clarendon Press, 1923), p. 324.

30 Arthur Hornblow, *A History of the Theatre in America*, vol. 1 (New York: Benjamin Bloom, 1919), p. 24.

31 Mendel Kohansky, *The Disreputable Profession: The Actor in Society* (Westport, CT: Greenwood Press, 1984), p. 9.

32 McArthur, pp. 164–5.

33 Kohansky, p. 162.

34 Richard deCordova, *Picture Personalities: The Emergence of the Star System in America* (Urbana: University of Illinois Press, 1990), pp. 84–92.

35 Miriam Hansen, "Pleasure, Ambivalence, Identification: Valentino and Female Spectatorship," *Cinema Journal* 25:4 (Summer 1986), reprinted in *Stardom: Industry of Desire*, ed. Christine Gledhill (London: Routledge, 1991), p. 269.

36 Miriam Hansen, *Babel and Babylon: Spectatorship in American Silent Film* (Cambridge, MA: Harvard University Press, 1991), p. 262.

37 Lurine Pruette, "Should Men Be Protected?," *Nation* 125 (August 31, 1927), p. 200, quoted in Gaylyn Studlar, "The Perils of Pleasure? Fan Magazine Discourse as Women's Commodified Culture in the 1920s," *Wide Angle* 13:1 (January 1991), p. 25.

38 E. A. Ross, "What the Films are Doing to Young America," *World Drift* (New York: Century, 1928), quoted in Studlar, p. 16.

39 Adela Rogers St John, "What Kind of Men Attract Women Most?," *Photoplay* 21:5 (April

1924), p. 110, quoted in Hansen, *Babel and Babylon*, p. 257.

40   "Letters to the Editor," *Photoplay* 22 (July 1922), p. 115, and *Photoplay* 23 (September 1922), p. 113, both quoted in Studlar, p. 26.

41   Hirsch, p. 91.

42   Hansen, *Babel and Babylon*, p. 294. See also Studlar, pp. 6–34, and Studlar, "Discourses of Gender and Ethnicity: The Construction and De(con)struction of Rudolph Valentino as Other," *Film Criticism* 13:2 (1989), pp. 18–35.

43   Naremore, p. 4.

44   Gaylyn Studlar has argued that this scene appears as a "highly stylized balletic interpretation of rape," in which the "dance-like movement and repose" prevent it being understood as a realistic depiction of sexual assault. Studlar, "Valentino, 'Optic Intoxication,' and Dance Madness," in *Screening the Male: Exploring Masculinities in Hollywood Cinema*, eds Steven Cohan and Ina Rae Hark (London: Routledge, 1993), p. 35.

45   Dyer, pp. 133–5.

Chapter 14   Time

1   Joseph P. Kennedy, "Preface," in *The Story of the Films*, ed. Joseph P. Kennedy (Chicago: A. W. Shaw, 1927), p. vi.

2   Michael Hauge, *Writing Screenplays that Sell* (New York: McGraw-Hill, 1988), p. 82.

3   Syd Field, *Screenplay: The Foundations of Screenwriting* (New York: Dell, 1979), pp. 8–9. Field regards *Chinatown* as "the best American screenplay written during the 1970s." Field, p. 70.

4   Field, p. 116.

5   Robert McKee, *Story: Substance, Structure, Style and the Principles of Screenwriting* (London: Methuen, 1998), p. 218.

6   Kristin Thompson, *Storytelling in the New Hollywood: Understanding the Classical Narrative Technique* (Cambridge, MA: Harvard University Press, 1999), pp. 27–42.

7   Field, p. 53.

8   The story is told, for instance, in Peter Bogdanovich, *Fritz Lang in America* (London: Studio Vista, 1969), p. 88, and in Philip French, *The Movie Moguls: An Informal History of the Hollywood Tycoons* (Harmondsworth: Penguin, 1969), p. 78. A slightly different version (there are doubtless many others) is in Jack Vizzard, *See No Evil: Life Inside a Hollywood Censor* (New York: Simon and Schuster, 1970), p. 74.

9   Clifford Geertz, *The Interpretation of Cultures* (New York: Basic Books, 1973), p. 445.

10   Since silent movie cameras were hand-cranked, there were often significant minor variations in the speed at which they were shot, and one of the skills required of silent cinema archivists is the ability to judge the correct projection speed. Silent movies were also often projected at speeds slightly faster than those at which they had been shot. More recently, some large-screen formats have used higher frame speeds than 24 frames a second to improve their image quality.

11   More detailed accounts of these mental processes can be found in David Bordwell, *Narration in the Fiction Film* (London: Methuen, 1985), pp. 30–3, and Susan J. Lederman and Bill Nichols, "Flicker and Motion in Film," in Bill Nichols, *Ideology and the Image: Social Representation in the Cinema and Other Media* (Bloomington: Indiana University Press, 1981), pp. 297–8.

12   See, for example, James Monaco, *How to Read a Film: The Art, Technology, Language, History and Theory of Film and Media* (New York: Oxford University Press, 1977). David Bordwell has argued cogently against the analogy implied by this usage; see in particular chapter 11, "Why Not to Read a Film," in his *Making Meaning: Inference and Rhetoric in the Interpretation of Cinema* (Cambridge, MA: Harvard University Press, 1989), pp. 249–74.

13   During periods of product shortage, movies might be re-released several years after their initial exhibition, usually to make up the balance of double-feature programs. Before sales to television, however, this was a relatively unimportant and minor element in the major companies' finances.

14   Harold B. Franklin, *Motion Picture Theatre Management* (New York: Doran, 1927), p. 246.

15   Kevin Brownlow, "Burning Memories," *Sight and Sound London Film Festival Supplement*, October 1992, p. 13.

16   Both the freezing of the action on the urn,

and the act of placing the urn in a museum, are actions that celebrate the interruption of the historical continuum to preserve an activity and an object in a fixed aesthetic attitude. Although this is not the place to dwell on the pervasive Eurocentric assumptions about "culture" and "universal values" expressed in the poem, or to discuss how and why the British Museum acquired the urn, we might note that the poem expresses no concern with what Greeks actually used urns for. Its original purpose has come to have no bearing on the use to which the urn is now put as a repository of transhistorical and cross-cultural values, a use that it has only acquired through the process of its being put into a museum.

17 Eugene Vale, *The Technique of Screenplay Writing*, 1st pub. 1944 (New York: Grosset and Dunlap, 1973), p. 63.

18 American cinema manager, 1907, quoted by John L. Fell, *Film and the Narrative Tradition* (Berkeley, CA: University of California Press, 1986), p. 206.

19 Field, p. 92.

20 Field, p. 196.

21 David Bordwell, Janet Staiger, and Kristin Thompson, *The Classical Hollywood Cinema: Film Style and Mode of Production to 1960* (London: Routledge and Kegan Paul, 1985), p. 28.

22 Lewis Herman, *A Practical Manual of Screen Playwriting for Theater and Television Films* (New York: New English Library, 1974), p. 37.

23 Formalist criticism refers to this causal coherence as compositional motivation. Motivation (discussed in more detail in chapter 11) is the process by which a narrative justifies its story material; the elements of the story that must be present in order for it to proceed – as opposed to realistically or generically motivated factors – are its compositional elements. David Bordwell provides a Formalist account of motivation in Bordwell et al., pp. 19–21.

24 Vale, p. 154.

25 A few Hollywood movies have always attracted repeat business, and television and video release have also provided a form of repeat viewing. Only in the 1980s did the blockbuster syndrome reach such proportions that the expectation of repeat attendances became part of a movie's financial planning

and advertising. *Halliwell's Film Guide*'s review of *Raiders of the Lost Ark*, for instance, describes the pleasures and drawbacks of a repeat viewing: "Second time round, one can better enjoy the ingenious detail of the hero's exploits and ignore the insistence on unpleasantness; still, there are boring bits in between and the story doesn't make a lot of sense." *Halliwell's Film and Video Guide 2000*, ed. John Walker, 15th edn (London: Harper-Collins, 1999), p. 678. Several weeks after its opening, *Jurassic Park* (1993) ran advertisements announcing that "If you've only seen it once, you haven't seen it all yet." Secondary markets for video and even more obviously for DVD create the expectation that movies will be viewed more than once, and viewed in different manners. The DVD formats of *Se7en* (1995), for example, with multiple simultaneous commentaries, additional scenes, and alternative endings, are in themselves imitations of computer games, in which the player follows a similar but not identical narrative track each time he or she plays, and finds pleasure in both the repetition and the variation of event along the way.

26 François Truffaut, *Hitchcock*, revised edn (London: Paladin, 1986), p. 381.

27 Novels and other published literary forms are inevitably structured like this. The book must already be produced as a material object before its consumption can begin, and the ending of the book is already present before a reader starts reading. Thus the writing of the book always appears to have taken place in the past of its reading, and it might be argued that the conventional use of the perfect tense in the narration of realist fiction is a response to this temporal order of events.

28 Truffaut, p. 91.

29 Irving Thalberg, "The Modern Photoplay," in *Introduction to the Photoplay*, ed. John C. Tibbets (Shawnee Mission, KS: National Film Society, 1977), p. 131.

30 David Herlihy, "Am I a Camera? Other Reflections on Films and History," *American Historical Review* 93:5 (December 1988), p. 1188.

31 Critics have not resisted the desire to think about the complexities of temporal organization in time travel movies as successfully as Sarah Connor. See, for example, Constance

31 Thompson, p. 39. Thompson has argued for the retention of the terms "syuzhet" and "fabula" for the distinctions between plot and story being made here, pointing out that "the English terms also carry the burden of all the other senses in which non-Formalist critics have used them, while fabula and syuzhet relate only to the Russian Formalists' definitions" (p. 38). My preference, here as elsewhere, is to aim for a greater precision in the use of a non-specialist, everyday critical vocabulary.

32 Branigan, p. 76.

33 Gaines, p. 1.

34 Bordwell et al., p. 17. Quotations from Francis Taylor Patterson, *Cinema Craftsmanship* (New York: Harcourt, Brace, and Howe, 1920).

35 Bordwell et al., p. 18. Quotation from Barrett C. Kiesling, *Talking Pictures* (Richmond, VA: Johnson Publishing, 1937), p. 2.

36 Lewis Herman, *A Practical Manual of Screen Playwriting for Theater and Television Films* (New York: New American Library, 1974), pp. 87–8. Bordwell quotes the latter part of this passage, p. 18.

37 Quoted in Aljean Harmetz, *Round Up the Usual Suspects: The Making of Casablanca – Bogart, Bergman, and World War II* (New York: Hyperion, 1992), p. 267.

38 Barbara Klinger, "Digressions at the Cinema: Reception and Mass Culture," *Cinema Journal* 28:4 (Summer 1989), pp. 10, 14, 16.

39 Thompson, p. 70.

40 Quoted in Rudy Behlmer, ed., *Memo from: David O. Selznick*, 1st pub. 1972 (New York: Avon, 1973), p. 394.

41 Branigan, p. 190.

42 Richard Dyer, *Heavenly Bodies: Film Stars and Society* (London: Macmillan, 1987), p. 11.

43 Steve Seidman, *Comedian Comedy: A Tradition in Hollywood Film* (Ann Arbor: UMI Research Press, 1981), pp. 19–57; Steve Neale and Frank Krutnik, *Popular Film and Television Comedy* (London: Routledge, 1990), p. 104.

44 Stanley Cavell, *Pursuits of Happiness: The Hollywood Comedy of Remarriage* (Cambridge, MA: Harvard University Press, 1981), p. 113.

45 George Segal has exactly the same problem with Elliott Gould in *California Split* (1974).

Chapter 16   Narrative 2

1 "A Code to Maintain Social and Community Values in the Production of Silent, Synchronized and Talking Motion Pictures," Motion Picture Producers and Distributors of America, Inc. (hereafter MPPDA), 1930, reprinted in appendix 1.

2 "The Reasons Supporting Preamble of Code," in Raymond Moley, *The Hays Office* (Indianapolis: Bobbs-Merrill, 1945), p. 245.

3 Recent examples of these arguments are Neil Postman, *Amusing Ourselves to Death: Public Discourse in the Age of Show Business* (London: Heinemann, 1986), and Michael Medved, *Hollywood vs. America: Popular Culture and the War on Traditional Values* (New York: HarperCollins, 1992).

4 Umberto Eco, *The Role of the Reader: Explorations in the Semiotics of Texts* (Bloomington: University of Indiana Press, 1979), p. 9.

5 Ruth Vasey, *The World According to Hollywood, 1918–1939* (Exeter: University of Exeter Press, 1997), p. 76.

6 Lamar Trotti to Hays, February 2, 1931. Production Code Administration Archive, Margaret Herrick Library, Academy of Motion Picture Arts and Sciences, Los Angeles (hereafter PCA), *The Smiling Lieutenant* file.

7 "Mr Zanuck's Suggestions on Proposed Treatment of 'Environment,'" September 18, 1931. Warner Bros. *Alias the Doctor* Production File, University of Southern California.

8 Joy to Zanuck, November 23, 1931; Zanuck to Joy, November 24, 1931; Joy to Zanuck, November 24, 1931; Zanuck to Joy, November 30, 1931. PCA *Alias the Doctor*.

9 Stanley Cavell, *Pursuits of Happiness: The Hollywood Comedy of Remarriage* (Cambridge, MA: Harvard University Press, 1981), pp. 116–17.

10 Harold J. Salemson, *The Screen Writer*, April, 1946, quoted in Ruth Inglis, *Freedom of the Movies: A Report on Self-Regulation from the Commission on Freedom of the Press* (Chicago: University of Chicago Press, 1947), pp. 183–4.

11 Elliott Paul and Luis Quintanilla, *With a Hays Nonny Nonny* (New York: Random House, 1942), pp. 63–4.

12 Richard Maltby, "'To Prevent the Prevalent Type of Book': Censorship and Adaptation in Hollywood, 1924–1934," *American Quarterly* 44:4 (1992), pp. 554–83.

13 Edward Branigan, *Narrative Comprehension and Film* (London: Routledge, 1992), pp. 30–1.

14 Umberto Eco, "*Casablanca*: Cult Movies and Intertextual Collage," in his *Travels in Hyperreality* (London: Picador, 1987), pp. 197–8.

15 Entry on *Casablanca*, in *Cinemania Interactive Movie Guide* (Microsoft, 1992); Eco, "*Casablanca*," p. 208.

16 Branigan, p. 98.

17 Branigan, p. 149.

18 François Truffaut, *Hitchcock*, revised edn (London: Paladin, 1986), pp. 191–2.

19 Richard Raskin, "*Casablanca* and United States Foreign Policy," *Film History* 4:2 (1990), p. 161.

20 The published script, which does not give its source, describes the action at this moment in the following terms: "Rick has taken Ilsa in his arms. He presses her tight to him and kisses her passionately. She is lost in his embrace. Sometime later, Rick watches the revolving beacon at the airport from his window. There is a bottle of champagne on the table and two half-filled glasses. Ilsa is talking. Rick is listening intently." Howard Koch, *Casablanca: Script and Legend* (Woodstock: Overlook Press, 1973), p. 156.

21 For the prurient, such instances abound, even in movies well worked over by critics. In correspondence with me, Lea Jacobs has pointed out another elliptical Bogartian indiscretion, in his encounter with Dorothy Malone in the antiquarian bookstore in *The Big Sleep* (1946).

22 Lea Jacobs, "Industry Self-regulation and the Problem of Textual Determination," *Velvet Light Trap* 23 (Spring 1989), p. 9; Jacobs's argument is enlarged in *The Wages of Sin: Censorship and the Fallen Woman Film, 1928–1942* (Madison: University of Wisconsin Press, 1991).

23 Breen to Wallis, June 5, 1942; Breen to Warner, June 18, 1942. Quoted in Gerald Gardiner, *The Censorship Papers: Movie Censorship Letters from the Hays Office 1934 to 1968* (New York: Dodd, Mead, 1987), p. 3.

24 Robert B. Ray, *A Certain Tendency of the Hollywood Cinema, 1930–1980* (Princeton, NJ: Princeton University Press, 1985), p. 90. See also Richard Maltby, *Harmless Entertainment: Hollywood and the Ideology of Consensus* (Metuchen, NJ: Scarecrow, 1983), pp. 193–210.

25 Frank Miller, *Casablanca: As Time Goes By* (London: Virgin Books, 1993), p. 140. See also Rudy Behlmer, *Behind the Scenes* (New York: Samuel French, 1982), p. 170; Harlan Lebo, *Casablanca: Behind the Scenes* (New York: Simon and Schuster, 1992), p. 77; Aljean Harmetz, *Round Up the Usual Suspects: The Making of Casablanca – Bogart, Bergman, and World War II* (New York: Hyperion, 1992), pp. 228, 232.

26 "Virtue in Cans," *Nation*, April 16, 1930, p. 441.

27 David Bordwell, Janet Staiger, and Kristin Thompson, *The Classical Hollywood Cinema: Film Style and Mode of Production to 1960* (London: Routledge and Kegan Paul, 1985), p. 17.

28 Richard deCordova, *Picture Personalities: The Emergence of the Star System in America* (Urbana: University of Illinois Press, 1990), p. 13.

29 Oliver Eyquen, Michael Henry, and Jacques Saada, "Interview with Raoul Walsh," in *Raoul Walsh*, ed. Phil Hardy (Edinburgh: Edinburgh Film Festival, 1974), p. 43.

30 Thomas Elsaesser, "Narrative Cinema and Audience-Oriented Aesthetics," in *Popular Television and Film*, eds Tony Bennett, Susan Boyd-Bowman, Colin Mercer, and Janet Woollacott (London: British Film Institute, 1981), pp. 270–82. This is an abridged version of a British Film Institute Occasional Paper, first published in 1969.

31 Elsaesser, p. 271.

32 Other movies, including *The Ipcress File* (1965), have also used the apparatus of cinema as an instrument of torture.

33 Elsaesser, p. 272.

34 Otto Friedrich, *City of Nets: A Portrait of Hollywood in the 1940s* (London: Headline, 1987), p. 137. A different version of the

same anecdote appears in Harmetz, p. 185.

35 Lucy Fischer provides a valuable contextualization of the movie's psychology in "Mama's Boy: Male Hysteria in *White Heat*," in *Screening the Male: Exploring Masculinities in Hollywood Cinema*, eds Steven Cohan and Ina Rae Hark (London: Routledge, 1993), pp. 70–84.

36 Elsaesser, pp. 275–6.

37 Elsaesser, pp. 274–5.

Chapter 17   Criticism

1 David Bordwell, *Making Meaning: Inference and Rhetoric in the Interpretation of Cinema* (Cambridge, MA: Harvard University Press, 1989), p. xii.

2 Jerry Lewis, *The Total Film-Maker* (London: Vision Press, 1971), p. 157.

3 Pam Cook, ed., *The Cinema Book* (London: British Film Institute, 1985), p. v.

4 Frances Taylor Patterson, *Cinema Craftsmanship: A Book for Photoplaywrights* (New York: Harcourt, Brace, and Howe, 1920), p. 150.

5 Leslie Halliwell, *Halliwell's Film Guide*, 7th edn (London: Paladin, 1990), p. 267.

6 Donald C. Willis, *The Films of Howard Hawks* (Metuchen, NJ: Scarecrow, 1975), p. 178.

7 Michael Church, "Two Reel Women," *Observer*, December 8, 1991.

8 Halliwell, pp. 1161–7.

9 Alistair Cooke, ed., *Garbo and the Night Watchmen*, 1st pub. 1937 (London: Secker and Warburg, 1971).

10 See, for instance, the technical discourse on deep-focus photography in *American Cinematographer*, published by the American Society of Cinematographers, between 1932 and 1947. Cited in Patrick L. Ogle, "Technological and Aesthetic Influences upon the Development of Deep Focus Cinematography in the United States," in *Screen Reader 1: Cinema/Ideology/Politics*, ed. John Ellis (London: Society for Education in Film and Television, 1977), pp. 81–108.

11 Martin Quigley, "Dr Dale and Martin Quigley Debate Screen and Education," *Motion Picture Herald*, April 2, 1938. Behind Quigley's argument in this particular case was a specific concern with the cultural reputation

of Emile Zola. Several of Zola's novels, including *Nana*, were then on the Roman Catholic Index of Forbidden Books; hence Quigley's reference to Zola as a pornographer. Quigley, a prominent lay Catholic, was also therefore disapproving of Warner Bros.' idealization of the novelist.

12 Patterson, p. 150.

13 Slavko Vorkapich, "Cinematics: Some Principles Underlying Effective Cinematography," in *Cinematic Annual*, ed. Hal Hall, 1930. Reprinted in *Hollywood Directors 1914–1940*, ed. Richard Koszarski (New York: Oxford University Press, 1976), pp. 253–9. Koszarski notes that Vorkapich himself did not use the word "montage" in his own writings.

14 Parker Tyler, *The Hollywood Hallucination* (New York: Simon and Schuster, 1944), p. 237.

15 Patterson, p. 150.

16 Dudley Andrew, *The Major Film Theories: An Introduction* (New York: Oxford University Press, 1976), pp. 4–5.

17 Claude Lévi-Strauss, *Structural Anthropology*, trans. Claire Jacobson and Brooke Grundfest Schoepf (Garden City, NY: Doubleday, 1967).

18 Peter Wollen, *Signs and Meaning in the Cinema*, 1st pub. 1968 (London: Secker and Warburg, 1972), p. 168.

19 Wollen, p. 104.

20 The convoluted conclusion to the *Cahiers du Cinéma* analysis of "John Ford's *Young Mr Lincoln*" would serve as an example. In Ellis, pp. 147–52.

21 Wollen, p. 104.

22 James Naremore, "Authorship and the Cultural Politics of Film Criticism," *Film Quarterly* 44:1 (Fall 1990), p. 20.

23 Examples are from Jeffrey Sconce, "Spectacles of Death: Identification, Reflexivity, and Contemporary Horror," and Susan Jeffords, "The Big Switch: Hollywood Masculinity in the Nineties," both in *Film Theory Goes to the Movies*, eds Jim Collins, Hilary Radner, and Ava Preacher Collins (New York: Routledge, 1993), pp. 105, 197.

24 Robert Stam, "The Author," in *Film and Theory: An Anthology*, eds Robert Stam and Toby Miller (Malden, MA: Blackwell, 2000), p. 6.

25 Timothy Corrigan, *A Cinema without Walls:*

Movies and Culture after Vietnam (London: Routledge, 1991), p. 101.

26 Gerald Mast, A Short History of the Movies, 3rd edn (Oxford: Oxford University Press, 1981), p. 424.

27 Justin Wyatt, High Concept: Movies and Marketing in Hollywood (Austin: University of Texas Press, 1994), pp. 190–4.

28 Timothy Corrigan, "Auteurs and the New Hollywood," in The New American Cinema, ed. Jon Lewis (Durham, NC: Duke University Press, 1998), pp. 40, 50.

29 Michael Budd, "Authorship as a Commodity," Wide Angle 6:1 (1984), p. 16; James Naremore, "Authorship," in A Companion to Film Theory, eds Toby Miller and Robert Stam (Malden, MA: Blackwell, 1999), p. 21.

30 Stam, p. 6; Naremore, "Authorship," p. 23.

31 Robert Stam, Robert Burgoyne, and Sandy Flitterman-Lewis, New Vocabularies in Film Semiotics: Structuralism, Post-Structuralism and Beyond (London: Routledge, 1992), p. 191.

32 Tania Modleski, The Women Who Knew Too Much: Hitchcock and Feminist Theory (London: Methuen, 1988), p. 3.

33 Modleski, pp. 97, 100.

34 Virginia Wright Wexman, "The Critic as Consumer: Film Study in the University, Vertigo, and the Film Canon," Film Quarterly 39:3 (Spring 1986), p. 33.

35 Slavoj Žižek, "Introduction: Alfred Hitchcock, or, the Form and its Historical Mediation," in Everything You Always Wanted to Know about Lacan (But Were Afraid to Ask Hitchcock), ed. Slavoj Žižek (London: Verso, 1992), p. 10.

36 William Rothman, "Vertigo: The Unknown Woman in Hitchcock," in his The "I" of the Camera: Essays in Film Criticism, History and Aesthetics (Cambridge: Cambridge University Press, 1988), p. 173.

37 Modleski, pp. 120–1. Janet Staiger remarks of canonic texts that, "As ideal fathers, these select films are given homage or rebelled against." Janet Staiger, "The Politics of Film Canons," Cinema Journal 24:2 (Spring 1985), p. 4.

38 Katie Trumpener, "Fragments of the Mirror: Self-Reference, Mise-en-abîme, Vertigo," in Hitchcock's Rereleased Films: From Rope to Vertigo, eds Walter Raubicheck and Walter Srebnick (Detroit: Wayne State University Press, 1991), p. 175.

39 Ann West, "The Concept of the Fantastic in Vertigo," in Raubicheck and Srebnick, p. 171.

40 Corrigan, A Cinema without Walls, p. 104. The conscious marketing of Hitchcock's persona is the subject of Robert E. Kapsis, Hitchcock: The Making of a Reputation (Chicago: University of Chicago Press, 1992).

41 Ann Cvetkovich, "Postmodern Vertigo: The Sexual Politics of Allusion in De Palma's Body Double," in Raubicheck and Srebnick, p. 149.

42 Wexman, p. 36.

43 Sharon Willis, "Hardware and Hardbodies, What Do Women Want?: A Reading of Thelma and Louise," in Collins et al., p. 126.

44 Žižek, Everything You Always Wanted to Know, p. 5.

45 Frederic Jameson, "Spatial Systems in North by Northwest," in Žižek, Everything You Always Wanted to Know, p. 64.

46 Lucretia Knapp, "The Queer Voice in Marnie," Cinema Journal 32:4 (Summer 1993), pp. 7, 11, 13; Raymond Bellour, "Hitchcock the Enunciator," trans. Bertrand Augst and Hilary Radner, Camera Obscura 2 (1981), pp. 66–91.

47 Bordwell, p. 95. See also Barry Barnes, T. S. Kuhn and Social Science (New York: Columbia University Press, 1982), pp. 45–6.

48 Paul Willemen, "For Information: Cinéaction," Framework 32/3 (1986), p. 227.

49 Žižek, "Introduction," p. 2.

50 Eric Rohmer, quoted in Bordwell, p. 47.

51 Kristin Thompson, Breaking the Glass Armor: Neoformalist Film Analysis (Princeton, NJ: Princeton University Press, 1988), p. 34.

52 Howard Hawks, "A Discussion with the Audience of the 1970 Chicago Film Festival," in Focus on Howard Hawks, ed. Joseph McBride (Englewood Cliffs, NJ: Prentice-Hall, 1972), p. 18.

53 Robert Sklar, City Boys: Cagney, Bogart, Garfield (Princeton, NJ: Princeton University Press, 1992), p. 37.

54 Jacques Rivette, "The Genius of Howard Hawks," Cahiers du Cinéma, May 1953, reprinted in McBride, pp. 73, 76.

55 Peter John Dyer, "Sling the Lamps Low," Sight and Sound, Summer 1962, reprinted in McBride, p. 85.

56 Umberto Eco: "*Casablanca*: Cult Movies and Intertextual Collage," in his *Travels in Hyperreality* (London: Picador, 1987), p. 209.

57 Manny Farber, "Howard Hawks," in *Negative Space: Manny Farber on the Movies* (London: Studio Vista, 1971), pp. 27, 30; 1st pub. in *Artforum*, April 1969.

58 Andrew Sarris, "The World of Howard Hawks," *New York Film Bulletin* (1961), reprinted in McBride, pp. 48, 52.

59 Robin Wood, *Howard Hawks*, 2nd edn (London: British Film Institute, 1981), p. 17.

60 Wood, pp. 17–18.

61 Wood, p. 21.

62 Wood, p. 24.

63 Wood, p. 56.

64 Wood, p. 10.

65 Wollen, pp. 91–3.

66 Wollen, p. 90.

67 Robin Wood, "Hawks De-Wollenized," in his *Personal Views: Explorations in Film* (London: Gordon Fraser, 1976), p. 201.

68 V. F. Perkins, "Must We Say What They Mean? Film Criticism and Interpretation," *MOVIE* 34/5 (Winter 1990), p. 5.

69 Molly Haskell, *From Reverence to Rape: The Treatment of Women in the Movies* (Chicago: University of Chicago Press, 1973), p. 209.

70 Haskell, p. 209.

71 Haskell, p. 210.

72 Richard Dyer, *Stars* (London: British Film Institute, 1979), pp. 64, 178.

73 John Belton, "Hawks & Co.," *Cinema* (1971), reprinted in McBride, pp. 107–8.

74 Gerald Mast, *Howard Hawks, Storyteller* (New York: Oxford University Press, 1982), p. 68.

75 Leland Poague, *Howard Hawks* (Boston: Twayne, 1982), pp. 30–43.

76 Peter Wollen, "Introduction," in *Howard Hawks: American Artist*, eds Jim Hillier and Peter Wollen (London: British Film Institute, 1996), p. 1; Robin Wood, "Retrospect," in his *Howard Hawks*, pp. 176, 182, 187.

77 Willis, *The Films of Howard Hawks*, p. 81.

78 Robert Ray, *A Certain Tendency of the Hollywood Cinema, 1930–1980* (Princeton, NJ: Princeton University Press,1985), pp. 114–15.

79 Ray, pp. 119, 114.

80 Ruth Vasey, *The World According to Holly-wood, 1919–1939* (Exeter: University of Exeter Press, 1997), p. 215.

81 Wood, *Howard Hawks*, p. 17. In a parallel instance, when sociologist Edgar Dale analyzed the content of motion pictures in 1935, he distinguished those pictures set in "foreign locales" from those set in "imaginary" settings. In the "foreign" category he included a "quite adequate presentation of Orambo, a little, hot, dreary town some place on the coast of South America." Edgar Dale, *The Content of Motion Pictures* (New York: Macmillan, 1935), p. 30.

82 Todd McCarthy, *Howard Hawks: The Grey Fox of Hollywood* (New York: Grove Press, 1997), p. 269.

83 Vasey, p. 216.

84 The writer, Agnes Specht from Cleveland, Ohio, described the fan magazines as "the medium through which Hollywood phantoms become our next-door neighbors ... Through them we learn that all these glamorous people are just simple human beings like ourselves and that they have ambitions, struggles, heartaches and hopes. And through this knowledge we understand them better and are apt to be less critical of them or envious of their success." *Motion Picture*, August 1936, quoted in Martin Levin, ed., *Hollywood and the Great Fan Magazines* (London: Ian Allen, 1970), p. 7.

Chapter 18 Theories

1 Nöel Carroll, "Prospects for Film Theory: A Personal Assessment," in *Post-Theory: Reconstructing Film Studies*, eds David Bordwell and Nöel Carroll (Madison: University of Wisconsin Press, 1996), p. 41.

2 Robert Stam, *Film Theory: An Introduction* (Malden, MA: Blackwell, 2000), p. 194.

3 Toby Miller, "(How) Does Film Theory Work?," *Continuum* 6:1 (1992), p. 199.

4 Dudley Andrew, *The Major Film Theories: An Introduction* (New York: Oxford University Press, 1976), p. 4.

5 Jean Mitry, *Ésthétique et Psychologie du Cinéma*, 2 vols (Paris: Editions Universitaires, 1963, 1965). An abridged version of Mitry's work was translated into English in 1998, as *Aesthetics and Psychology of Cinema*, trans. Christopher King (Bloomington: Indiana

University Press, 1997). See also Andrew, p. 188.

6 Dudley Andrew, *Concepts in Film Theory* (New York: Oxford University Press, 1984), p. 6.

7 Henry Louis Gates Jr, "Whose Canon Is It Anyway?," *New York Times Book Review*, February 2, 1989, p. 44.

8 Christian Metz, *Film Language: A Semiotics of the Cinema*, trans. Michael Taylor (New York: Oxford University Press, 1974), p. 69.

9 Theodor Adorno, *Prisms*, trans. Samuel and Shierry Weber (Cambridge, MA: MIT Press, 1981), p. 34.

10 Ferdinand de Saussure, *Course in General Linguistics* (London: Fontana, 1974), p. 16.

11 However, as many critics have pointed out, Peirce's more complex account of iconic and indexical signs almost certainly offers a more fruitful basis for explaining visual sign systems than Saussure's linguistically derived assertion of the arbitrary nature of the sign. See, for instance, Peter Wollen, *Signs and Meaning in the Cinema*, 1st pub. 1968, revised edn (London: Secker and Warburg, 1972), pp. 120–5.

12 Roland Barthes, *Mythologies* (London: Paladin, 1973).

13 A summary and critique of this position can be found in James Spellerberg, "Technology and Ideology in the Cinema," in *Film Theory and Criticism: Introductory Readings*, eds Gerald Mast and Marshall Cohen, 3rd edn (New York: Oxford University Press, 1985), pp. 761–75.

14 Stam, p. 186.

15 Stam, p. 133.

16 Louis Althusser, "Marxism and Humanism," in *For Marx*, trans. Ben Brewster (London: NLB, 1977), p. 332.

17 Jean-Louis Comolli and Jean Narboni, "Cinema/Ideology/Criticism (1)," trans. Susan Bennett, in *Screen Reader 1*, ed. John Ellis (London: Society for Education in Film and Television, 1977), p. 4. 1st pub. in *Cahiers du Cinéma* (October–November 1969); 1st pub. in English in *Screen* 12:1 (1971).

18 Comolli and Narboni, p. 3.

19 Comolli and Narboni, p. 7.

20 Roland Barthes, "The Death of the Author," in his *Image Music Text*, trans. Stephen Heath

(London: Fontana, 1977), p. 146; Barthes, "From Work to Text," in *Image Music Text*, p. 157.

21 Barthes, "From Work to Text," p. 163.

22 Andrew, *Concepts in Film Theory*, p. 15.

23 Comolli and Narboni, p. 7.

24 Richard Dyer, *Only Entertainment* (London: Routledge, 1992), p. 4.

25 "John Ford's *Young Mr Lincoln*, a Collective Text by the Editors of Cahiers du Cinéma," originally pub. in *Cahiers du Cinéma* 223 (August 1970), trans. Helen Lackner and Diana Mathias, *Screen* 13:3 (Autumn 1972), p. 8.

26 Louis Althusser, "Ideology and Ideological State Apparatuses: Notes towards an Investigation," in his *Lenin and Philosophy and Other Essays* (London: NLB, 1971), p. 169.

27 Jean-Louis Baudry, "Ideological Effects of the Basic Cinematic Apparatus," in *Movies and Methods. Vol. II*, ed. Bill Nichols (Berkeley, CA: University of California Press, 1985), p. 537.

28 Stam, p. 137.

29 Jean-Louis Baudry, "The Apparatus," in *Apparatus*, ed. Theresa Hak Kyung Cha (New York: Tanam Press, 1981), p. 54.

30 Edward Said, *The World, the Text, and the Critic* (Cambridge, MA: Harvard University Press, 1983), p. 53.

31 Nöel Carroll also uses the term "psychosemiology" to refer to what I have called "cinepsychoanalysis." Christian Metz referred to it as the "semio-psychoanalysis of the cinema." Nöel Carroll, *Mystifying Movies: Fads and Fallacies in Contemporary Film Theory* (New York: Columbia University Press, 1988), p. 9.

32 Theodore Price, *Hitchcock and Homosexuality: His 50-Year Obsession with Jack the Ripper and the Superbitch Prostitute* (Metuchen, NJ: Scarecrow, 1991).

33 See, for example, Raymond Bellour, "Hitchcock the Enunciator," *Camera Obscura* 2 (Fall 1977), pp. 66–91; Thierry Kuntzel, "The Film Work 2," *Camera Obscura* 5 (Spring 1980), pp. 6–69.

34 Christian Metz, *The Imaginary Signifier: Psychoanalysis and the Cinema*, trans. Celia Britton, Annwyl Williams, Ben Brewster, and Alfred Guzzetti (Bloomington: Indiana University Press, 1982), pp. 125, 127–8.

35 Metz, *Imaginary Signifier*, p. 8.

36 Sandy Flitterman-Lewis, "Psychoanalysis," in Robert Stam, Robert Burgoyne, and Sandy Flitterman-Lewis, *New Vocabularies in Film Semiotics: Structuralism, Post-Structuralism and Beyond* (London: Routledge, 1992), pp. 146–7.

37 For Lacan, the child's primary identification in the mirror stage is also a misapprehension, since the image the child identifies with is not the child himself or herself, but an image.

38 Metz, *Imaginary Signifier*, p. 51.

39 Metz, *Imaginary Signifier*, p. 96.

40 Charles F. Altman, "Psychoanalysis and Cinema: The Imaginary Discourse," *Quarterly Review of Film Studies* 2:3 (August 1977), pp. 257–72; Barbara Klinger, "In Retrospect: Film Studies Today," *Yale Journal of Criticism* 2:1 (1988), pp. 133–4.

41 Carroll, p. 194.

42 Richard Allen, "Psychoanalytic Film Theory," in *A Companion to Film Theory*, eds Toby Miller and Robert Stam (Malden, MA: Blackwell 1999), p. 128.

43 Daniel Dayan, "The Tutor-Code of Classical Cinema," in *Movies and Methods*, ed. Bill Nichols (Berkeley, CA: University of California Press, 1976), p. 445.

44 Laura Mulvey, "Visual Pleasure and Narrative Cinema," *Screen* 16:3 (Autumn 1975), pp. 13, 17.

45 Mulvey, p. 6.

46 Mulvey, pp. 19, 20, 22.

47 See, for instance, Claire Johnston, "Towards a Feminist Film Practice: Some Theses," and B. Ruby Rich, "In the Name of Feminist Film Criticism," both anthologized in Nichols, pp. 315–27, 340–58.

48 B. Ruby Rich, in Michell Citron, Julia Lesage, Judith Mayne, B. Ruby Rich, and Anna Maria Taylor, "Women and Film: A Discussion of Feminist Aesthetics," *New German Critique* 13 (Winter 1978), p. 87.

49 Mary Ann Doane, "Misrecognition and Identity," *Cine-tracts* 11 (Fall 1980), p. 31.

50 Mary Ann Doane, Patricia Mellencamp, and Linda Williams, "Feminist Film Criticism: An Introduction," in *Re-Visions: Essays in Feminist Film Criticism*, eds Mary Ann Doane, Patricia Mellencamp, and Linda Williams (Frederick, MD: University Publications of America, 1984), p. 8.

51 Susan White, "Split Skins: Female Agency and Bodily Mutilation in *The Little Mermaid*," in *Film Theory Goes to the Movies*, eds Jim Collins, Hilary Radner, and Ava Preacher Collins (New York: Routledge, 1993), pp. 182–3. In the same collection, see also Hilary Radner, "Pretty Is as Pretty Does: Free Enterprise and the Marriage Plot," p. 69.

52 David Bordwell, *Making Meaning: Inference and Rhetoric in the Interpretation of Cinema* (Cambridge, MA: Harvard University Press, 1989), p. 245.

53 J. A. Miller, quoted in "*Young Mr Lincoln*, a Collective Text," p. 9.

54 Bordwell, p. 84.

55 "*Young Mr Lincoln*, a Collective Text," p. 9.

56 Charles Eckert, "The Anatomy of a Proletarian Film: Warner's Marked Woman," *Film Quarterly* 27:2 (Winter 1973–4), reprinted in Nichols, pp. 424–5.

57 Barbara Klinger, "'Cinema/Ideology/Criticism' Revisited: The Progressive Genre," in *Film Genre Reader*, ed. Barry Keith Grant (Austin: University of Texas Press, 1986), pp. 74–90.

58 Klinger, "'Cinema/Ideology/Criticism' Revisited," pp. 77, 87.

59 Deborah Linderman, "The Mise-en-abîme in Hitchcock's *Vertigo*," *Cinema Journal* 30:4 (Summer 1991), p. 53.

60 Gramsci's concept of hegemony is articulated in *A Gramsci Reader*, ed. David Forgacs (London: Lawrence and Wishart, 1988), pp. 189–221.

61 Foucault's conception of power as productive is developed in Michel Foucault, *Power/Knowledge: Selected Interviews and Other Writings*, eds Colin Gordon, Leo Marshall, John Meplam, and Kate Soper (Brighton: Harvester, 1980), and explicated in Michel Foucault, *The History of Sexuality. Volume 1: An Introduction*, trans. Robert Hurley (Harmondsworth: Penguin, 1981).

62 Stuart Hall, "Encoding, Decoding," in *The Cultural Studies Reader*, ed. Simon During (London: Routledge, 1993), pp. 90–103.

63 Kristin Thompson, *Breaking the Glass Armor: Neoformalist Film Analysis* (Princeton, NJ: Princeton University Press, 1988), p. 33.

64 Thompson, p. 29.

65 Thompson, pp. 3–47.

66 David Bordwell, *Narration in the Fiction Film* (London: Methuen, 1985), p. 335.

67 Bill Nichols, "Form Wars: The Political Unconscious of Formalist Theory," in *Clevssical Hollywood Narrative: The Paradigm Wars*, ed. Jane Gaines (Durham, NC: Duke University Press, 1992), p. 75.

68 V. F. Perkins, "Must We Say What They Mean? Film Criticism and Interpretation," *MOVIE* 34/5 (Winter 1990), p. 5. See also Douglas Pye, "Bordwell and Hollywood," *MOVIE* 33 (Winter 1989), pp. 46–52.

69 Thompson, p. 9.

70 Klinger, "In Retrospect: Film Studies Today," p. 148.

71 David Bordwell and Nöel Carroll, "Introduction," in Bordwell and Carroll, p. xvi.

72 Bill Nichols, "Film Theory and the Revolt against Master Narratives," in *Reinventing Film Studies*, eds Christine Gledhill and Linda Williams (London: Arnold, 2000), p. 42.

73 *Post-Theory: Reconstructing Film Studies*, Nick Browne, ed., *Refiguring American Film Genres: Theory and History* (Berkeley, CA: University of California Press, 1998); *Reinventing Film Studies*.

74 Carroll, p. 39.

75 Barbara Klinger, "Film History Terminable and Interminable: Recovering the Past in Reception Studies," *Screen* 38:2 (Summer 1997), p. 110.

76 Robert C. Allen, "Reader-Oriented Criticism and Television," in his *Channels of Discourse* (London: Methuen, 1987), p. 76.

77 Maurice Merleau-Ponty, "The Film and the New Psychology," in his *Sense and Non-Sense*, trans. Hubert L Dreyfuss and Patricia A. Dreyfuss (Evanston: Northwestern University Press, 1964), pp. 58-9.

78 Elizabeth Freund, *The Return of the Reader: Reader-Response Criticism* (London: Methuen, 1987), p. 10.

79 Umberto Eco, *The Role of the Reader: Explorations in the Semiotics of Texts* (Bloomington: University of Indiana Press, 1979), p. 7.

80 Stanley Fish, *Is There a Text in this Class?: The Authority of Interpretive Communities* (Cambridge, MA: Harvard University Press, 1980).

81 Janet Staiger, "Taboos and Totems: Cultural Meanings of *The Silence of the Lambs*," in Collins et al., p. 144; Hans Robert Jauss, *Toward an Aesthetic of Reception*, trans. Timothy Bahti (Minneapolis: University of Minnesota Press, 1982).

82 Staiger, p. 144.

83 Klinger, "Film History," p. 108.

84 Janet Staiger, *Interpreting Films: Studies in the Historical Reception of American Cinema* (Princeton, NJ: Princeton University Press, 1992), p. 150.

85 Staiger, *Interpreting Films*, p. 152.

86 Tony Bennett, "Text and Social Process: The Case of James Bond," *Screen Education* 41 (Winter/Spring 1982), pp. 3–14.

87 Terry Eagleton, *Literary Theory: An Introduction* (Oxford: Blackwell, 1983), p. 85.

88 Klinger, "Film History," p. 114.

89 Klinger, "Film History," p. 122.

90 Robert C. Allen and Douglas Gomery, *Film History: Theory and Practice* (New York: Knopf, 1985), p. iv.

91 Carroll, p. 8.

92 Carroll, p. 39; David Bordwell, "Contemporary Film Studies and the Vicissitudes of Grand Theory," in Bordwell and Carroll, p. 27.

93 Stam et al., p. 220.

94 Stam, p. 330.

95 As an example, see David M. Lugowski, "Queering the New Deal: Lesbian and Gay Representation and the Depression-Era Cultural Politics of Hollywood's Production Code," *Cinema Journal* 38:2 (Winter 1999), pp. 3–35.

Bibliography

Abel, Richard, *The Red Rooster Scare: Making Cinema American, 1900–1910* (Berkeley, CA: University of California Press, 1999).

Adair, Gilbert, ed., *Movies* (Harmondsworth: Penguin, 1998).

Addams, Jane, *The Spirit of Youth and the City Streets* (New York: Macmillan, 1909).

Adler, Mortimer, *Art and Prudence: A Study in Practical Philosophy* (New York: Longman, 1937).

Adorno, Theodor, *Prisms*, trans. Samuel and Shierry Weber (Cambridge, MA: MIT Press, 1981).

Adorno, Theodor, and Max Horkheimer, *Dialectic of Enlightenment* (London: Verso, 1979).

Affron, Charles, *Star Acting: Gish, Garbo, Davies* (New York: Dutton, 1977).

Affron, Charles, *Cinema and Sentiment* (Chicago: University of Chicago Press, 1982).

Affron, Charles, and Mirella Jona Affron, *Sets in Motion: Art Direction and Film Narrative* (New Brunswick, NJ: Rutgers University Press, 1995).

Agee, James, *Agee on Film* (New York: Beacon, 1958).

Albertson, Lillian, *Motion Picture Acting* (New York: Funk and Wagnalls, 1947).

Albrecht, Donald, *Designing Dreams: Modern Architecture in the Movies* (London: Thames and Hudson, 1986).

Allen, Jeanne, "The Film Viewer as Consumer," *Quarterly Review of Film Studies* 5:4 (Fall 1980), pp. 481–97.

Allen, Richard, *Projecting Illusion: Film Spectatorship and the Impression of Reality* (Cambridge: Cambridge University Press, 1995).

Allen, Richard, and Murray Smith, eds, *Film Theory and Philosophy* (Oxford: Oxford University Press, 1997).

Allen, Robert C., *Speaking of Soap Opera* (Chapel Hill: University of North Carolina Press, 1985).

Allen, Robert C., *Channels of Discourse* (London: Methuen, 1987).

Allen, Robert C., and Douglas Gomery, *Film History: Theory and Practice* (New York: Knopf, 1985).

Althusser, Louis, *Lenin and Philosophy and Other Essays* (London: NLB, 1971).

Althusser, Louis, *For Marx* (London: NLB, 1977).

Altman, Charles F., "Psychoanalysis and Cinema: The Imaginary Discourse," *Quarterly Review of Film Studies* 2:3 (August 1977), pp. 257–72.

Altman, Rick, ed., *Genre: The Musical* (London: Routledge and Kegan Paul, 1981).

Altman, Rick, *The American Film Musical* (Bloomington: Indiana University Press, 1987).

Altman, Rick, ed., *Sound Theory, Sound Practice* (New York: Routledge, 1992).

Altman, Rick, *Film/Genre* (London: British Film Institute, 1999).

Alton, John, *Painting with Light*, 1st edn 1949, reprint edn (Berkeley, CA: University of California Press, 1995).

Alvarado, Manuel, and John O. Thompson, eds, *The Media Reader* (London: British Film Institute, 1990).

Anderson, Christopher, *Hollywood TV: The Studio System in the Fifties* (Austin: University of Texas Press, 1994).

Andrew, Dudley, *The Major Film Theories: An Introduction* (New York: Oxford University Press, 1976).

Andrew, Dudley, *Concepts in Film Theory* (New York: Oxford University Press, 1984).

Andrew, Geoff, *Stranger than Paradise: Maverick Film-Makers in Recent American Cinema* (London: Prion, 1998).

Anger, Kenneth, *Hollywood Babylon* (San Francisco, CA: Straight Arrow, 1975).

Anger, Kenneth, *Hollywood Babylon II* (London: Arrow, 1984).

Arijon, Daniel, *Grammar of the Film Language* (Los Angeles: Silman-James Press, 1976).

Armes, Roy, "Entendre, C'est Comprendre: In Defence of Sound Reproduction," *Screen* 29:2 (Spring 1988), pp. 8–22.

Armes, Roy, *On Video* (London: Routledge, 1989).

Armes, Roy, *Action and Image: Dramatic Structure in Cinema* (Manchester: Manchester University Press, 1994).

Arnheim, Rudolf, *Film as Art* (Berkeley, CA: University of California Press, 1957).

Arnheim, Rudolf, *Film Essays and Criticism*, trans. Brenda Benthien (Madison: University of Wisconsin Press, 1997).

Arroyo, José, ed., *Action/Spectacle Cinema: A Sight and Sound Reader* (London: British Film Institute, 2000).

Atkins, Thomas R., ed., *Sexuality in the Movies* (Bloomington: Indiana University Press, 1975).

Austin, Bruce A., *Immediate Seating: A Look at Movie Audiences* (Belmont, CA: Wadsworth, 1989).

Austin, Thomas, *Hollywood, Hype and Audiences* (Manchester: Manchester University Press, 2002).

Bach, Steven, *Final Cut: Dreams and Disaster in the Making of Heaven's Gate* (London: Faber, 1986).

Balio, Tino, *United Artists: The Company Built by the Stars* (Madison: University of Wisconsin Press, 1976).

Balio, Tino, ed., *The American Film Industry*, 1st edn 1976, revised edn (Madison: University of Wisconsin Press, 1985).

Balio, Tino, *United Artists: The Company that Changed the Film Industry* (Madison: University of Wisconsin Press, 1987).

Balio, Tino, ed., *Hollywood in the Age of Television* (Boston: Unwin Hyman, 1990).

Balio, Tino, *Grand Design: Hollywood as a Modern Business Enterprise, 1930–1939* (New York: Scribner's, 1993).

Barker, Martin, ed., *The Video Nasties: Freedom and Censorship in the Media* (London: Pluto Press, 1984).

Barker, Martin, with Thomas Austin, *From Antz to Titanic: Reinventing Film Analysis* (London: Pluto Press, 2000).

Barker, Martin, and Kate Brooks, *Knowing Audiences: Judge Dredd, its Friends, Foes and Fans* (Luton: University of Luton Press, 1998).

Barnes, Barry, *T. S. Kuhn and Social Science* (New York: Columbia University Press, 1982).

Barsacq, Léon, *Caligari's Children and Other Grand Illusions: A History of Film Design* (New York: New American Library, 1976).

Barsten, Fred E., *Glorious Technicolor* (London: A. S. Barnes, 1980).

Bart, Peter, *The Gross: The Hits, the Flops – the Summer that Ate Hollywood* (New York: St Martin's Press, 1999).

Barthes, Roland, *Mythologies* (London: Paladin, 1973).

Barthes, Roland, *Image Music Text*, trans. Stephen Heath (London: Fontana, 1977).

Basinger, Jeanine, *Silent Stars* (Hanover, NH: Wesleyan University Press, 2000).

Baxter, Peter, ed., *Sternberg* (London: British Film Institute, 1980).

Bazin, André, *What is Cinema? Vol. 1*, trans. Hugh Gray (Berkeley, CA: University of California Press, 1967).

Bazin, André, *What is Cinema? Vol. 2*, trans. Hugh Gray (Berkeley, CA: University of California Press, 1971).

Bazin, André, "Will CinemaScope Save the Cinema?," trans. Catherine Jones and Richard Neupert, *Velvet Light Trap* 21 (Summer 1985), pp. 9–14.

Beauchamp, Cari, *Without Lying Down: Frances Marion and the Powerful Women of Early Hollywood* (Berkeley, CA: University of California Press, 1997).

Bego, Mark, ed., *The Best of Modern Screen* (London: Columbus Books, 1986).

Behlmer, Rudy, ed., *Memo from: David O. Selznick*, 1st pub. 1972 (New York: Avon, 1973).

Behlmer, Rudy, *Behind the Scenes* (New York: Samuel French, 1982).

Behlmer, Rudy, ed., *Inside Warner Bros. (1935–1951)* (London: Weidenfeld and Nicolson, 1986).

Bell, Daniel, *The End of Ideology* (New York: Collier Books, 1960).

Bellour, Raymond, "Hitchcock the Enunciator," *Camera Obscura* 2 (Fall 1977), pp. 66–91.

Belsey, Catherine, *Critical Practice* (London: Methuen, 1980).

Belton, John, "CinemaScope: The Economics of Technology," *Velvet Light Trap* 21 (Summer 1985), pp. 35–43.

Belton, John, "CinemaScope and Historical Methodology," *Cinema Journal* 28:1 (Fall 1988), pp. 22–44.

Belton, John, *Widescreen Cinema* (Cambridge, MA: Harvard University Press, 1992).

Benjamin, Walter, "The Work of Art in the Age of Mechanical Reproduction," in *Illuminations* (London: Cape, 1970), pp. 219–53.

Bennett, Tony, Susan Boyd-Bowman, Colin Mercer, and Janet Woollacott, eds, *Popular Television and Film* (London: British Film Institute, 1981).

Berenstein, Rhona J., *Attack of the Leading Ladies: Gender, Sexuality, and Spectatorship in Classic Horror Cinema* (New York: Columbia University Press, 1996).

Bergstrom, Janet, ed., *Endless Night: Cinema and Psychoanalysis, Parallel Histories* (Berkeley, CA: University of California Press, 1999).

Bernardi, Daniel, *The Birth of Whiteness: Race and the Emergence of US Cinema* (New Brunswick, NJ: Rutgers University Press, 1996).

Bernardi, Daniel, *Classic Hollywood, Classic Whiteness* (Minneapolis: University of Minnesota Press, 2001).

Bernstein, Matthew, *Walter Wagner: Hollywood Independent* (Berkeley, CA: University of California Press, 1994).

Bernstein, Matthew, ed., *Controlling Hollywood: Censorship and Regulation in the Studio Era* (New Brunswick, NJ: Rutgers University Press, 1999).

Bernstein, Matthew, and Gaylyn Studlar, eds, *Visions of the East: Orientalism in Film* (London: Tauris, 1997).

Berry, Sarah, *Screen Style: Fashion and Femininity in 1930s Hollywood* (Minneapolis: University of Minnesota Press, 2000).

Bingham, Dennis, *Acting Male: Masculinities in the Films of James Stewart, Jack Nicholson and Clint Eastwood* (New Brunswick, NJ: Rutgers University Press, 1994).

Birdwill, Michael E., *Celluloid Soldiers: Warner Bros.'s Campaign Against Nazism* (New York: New York University Press, 1999).

Biskind, Peter, *Seeing is Believing: How Hollywood Taught Us to Stop Worrying and Love the Fifties* (London: Pluto Press, 1983).

Biskind, Peter, *Easy Riders, Raging Bulls: How the Sex-Drugs-and-Rock 'n' Roll Generation Saved Hollywood* (New York: Simon and Schuster, 1998).

Black, Gregory D., *Hollywood Censored: Morality Codes, Catholics, and the Movies* (Cambridge: Cambridge University Press, 1994).

Black, Gregory D., *The Catholic Crusade Against the Movies, 1940–1970* (Cambridge: Cambridge University Press, 1997).

Bliss, Michael, *Justified Lives: Morality and Narrative in the Films of Sam Peckinpah* (Carbondale: Southern Illinois University Press, 1993).

Bliss, Michael, ed., *Doing It Right: The Best Criticism on Sam Peckinpah's The Wild Bunch* (Carbondale: Southern Illinois University Press, 1994).

Block, Bruce, *The Visual Story: Seeing the Structure of Film, TV, and New Media* (Boston: Focal Press, 2001).

Blum, Richard A., *American Film Acting: The Stanislavski Heritage* (Ann Arbor: UMI Research Press, 1984).

Blumer, Herbert, *Movies and Conduct* (New York: Macmillan, 1933).

Bogdanovich, Peter, *Fritz Lang in America* (London: Studio Vista, 1969).

Bogle, Donald, *Toms, Coons, Mulattoes, Mammies and Bucks: An Interpretive History of Blacks in American Films* (New York: Bantam, 1974).

Bordwell, David, *Narration in the Fiction Film* (London: Methuen, 1985).

Bordwell, David, *Making Meaning: Inference and Rhetoric in the Interpretation of Cinema*

(Cambridge, MA: Harvard University Press, 1989).

Bordwell, David, *The Cinema of Eisenstein* (Cambridge, MA: Harvard University Press, 1993).

Bordwell, David, *On the History of Film Style* (Cambridge, MA: Harvard University Press, 1997).

Bordwell, David, and Nöel Carroll, eds, *Post-Theory: Reconstructing Film Studies* (Madison: University of Wisconsin Press, 1996).

Bordwell, David, and Kristin Thompson, *Film Art: An Introduction*, 6th edn (New York: McGraw-Hill, 2001).

Bordwell, David, Janet Staiger, and Kristin Thompson, *The Classical Hollywood Cinema: Film Style and Mode of Production to 1960* (London: Routledge and Kegan Paul, 1985).

Borges, Jorge Luis, *Other Inquisitions 1937–1952* (London: Souvenir Press, 1973).

Bowers, Q. David, *Nickelodeon Theatres and their Music* (New York: Vestal Press, 1986).

Bowser, Eileen, *The Transformation of Cinema: 1907–1915* (New York: Scribner's, 1990).

Branigan, Edward, *Point of View in the Cinema: A Theory of Narration and Subjectivity in Classical Film* (New York: Mouton, 1984).

Branigan, Edward, *Narrative Comprehension and Film* (London: Routledge, 1992).

Brantlinger, Patrick, *Bread and Circuses: Theories of Mass Culture as Social Decay* (Ithaca, NY: Cornell University Press, 1983).

Breines, Wini, *Young, White and Miserable:Growing Up Female in the Fifties* (Boston: Beacon Press, 1992).

Brewster, Ben, and Lea Jacobs, *Theatre to Cinema: Stage Pictorialism and the Early Feature Film* (Oxford: Oxford University Press, 1997).

Britton, Andrew, "Blissing Out: The Politics of Reaganite Entertainment," *MOVIE* 31/2 (Winter 1986), pp. 1–42.

Brown, Royal S., *Overtones and Undertones: Reading Film Music* (Berkeley, CA: University of California Press, 1994).

Browne, Nick, *The Rhetoric of Filmic Narration* (Ann Arbor: University of Michigan Press, 1982).

Browne, Nick, ed., *Refiguring American Film Genres: Theory and History* (Berkeley, CA: University of California Press, 1998).

Brownlow, Kevin, *Behind the Mask of Innocence* (London: Cape, 1990).

Brownstein, Ronald, *The Power and the Glitter: The Hollywood–Washington Connection* (New York: Pantheon, 1990).

Bruzzi, Stella, *Undressing Cinema: Clothing and Identity in the Movies* (London: Routledge, 1997).

Buckland, Warren, ed., *The Film Spectator: From Sign to Mind* (Amsterdam: Amsterdam University Press, 1995).

Buhle, Paul, and Dave Wagner, *A Very Dangerous Citizen: Abraham Lincoln Polansky and the Hollywood Left* (Berkeley, CA: University of California Press, 2001).

Buhle, Paul, and Dave Wagner, *Radical Hollywood: The Untold Story behind America's Favorite Movies* (New York: New Press, 2002).

Burgoyne, Robert, *Film Nation: Hollywood Looks at US History* (Minneapolis: University of Minnesota Press, 1997).

Buscombe, Edward, ed., *The BFI Companion to the Western* (London: André Deutsch, 1988).

Buscombe, Edward, and Roberta E. Pearson, eds, *Back in the Saddle Again: New Essays on the Western* (London: British Film Institute, 1998).

Butler, Jeremy G., ed., *Star Texts: Image and Performance in Film and Television* (Detroit: Wayne State University Press, 1991).

Butler, Terence, *Crucified Heroes: The Films of Sam Peckinpah* (London: Gordon Fraser, 1979).

Butsch, Richard, ed., *For Fun and Profit: The Transformation of Leisure into Consumption* (Philadelphia: Temple University Press, 1990).

Byars, Jackie, *All That Hollywood Allows: Re-Reading Gender in 1950s Melodrama* (Chapel Hill: University of North Carolina Press, 1991).

Cameron, Ian, ed., *The Movie Book of Film Noir* (London: Studio Vista, 1992).

Cameron, Ian, and Douglas Pye, eds, *The Movie Book of the Western* (London: Studio Vista, 1996).

Campbell, Russell, *Practical Motion Picture Photography* (London: Zwemmer, 1970).

Carbine, Mary, "'The Finest Outside the Loop': Motion Picture Exhibition in Chicago's Black Metropolis, 1905–1928," *Camera Obscura* 23 (May 1990), pp. 9–41.

Carnes, Mark C., ed., *Past Imperfect: History According to the Movies* (London: Cassell, 1996).

Carr, Steven, *Hollywood and Anti-Semitism: A Cultural History* (Cambridge: Cambridge University Press, 2001).

Carringer, Robert L., *The Making of Citizen Kane* (Berkeley, CA: University of California Press, 1985).

Carroll, Noël, *Mystifying Movies: Fads and Fallacies in Contemporary Film Theory* (New York: Columbia University Press, 1988).

Carroll, Noël, *The Philosophy of Horror, or Paradoxes of the Heart* (London: Routledge, 1990).

Carroll, Noël, *Theorizing the Moving Image* (Cambridge: Cambridge University Press, 1996).

Carroll, Noël, *A Philosophy of Mass Art* (Oxford: Oxford University Press, 1998).

Casetti, Francesco, *Inside the Gaze: The Fiction Film and its Spectator*, trans. Nell Andrew with Charles O'Brien (Urbana: Indiana University Press, 1998).

Casetti, Francesco, *Theories of Cinema 1945–1995*, trans. Francesca Chiostri and Elizabeth Gard Bartolini-Salimbeni (Austin: University of Texas Press, 1999).

Caughie, John, ed., *Theories of Authorship* (London: British Film Institute, 1981).

Caute, David, *The Great Fear: The Anti-Communist Purge under Truman and Eisenhower* (London: Secker and Warburg, 1978).

Cavell, Stanley, *The World Viewed: Reflections on the Ontology of Film* (New York: Viking, 1971).

Cavell, Stanley, *Pursuits of Happiness: The Hollywood Comedy of Remarriage* (Cambridge, MA: Harvard University Press, 1981).

Cavell, Stanley, *Contesting Tears: The Hollywood Melodrama of the Unknown Woman* (Chicago: University of Chicago Press, 1996).

Caves, Richard E., *Creative Industries: Contracts Between Art and Commerce* (Cambridge, MA: Harvard University Press, 2000).

Cawelti, John, *The Six-Gun Mystique* (Bowling Green, KY: Bowling Green University Popular Press, 1970).

Cendrars, Blaise, *Hollywood, Mecca of the Movies* (Berkeley, CA: University of California Press, 1995).

Ceplair, Larry, and Steven Englund, *The Inquisition in Hollywood: Politics in the Film Community, 1930–1960* (Berkeley, CA: University of California Press, 1983).

Cha, Theresa Hak Kyung, ed., *Apparatus* (New York: Tanam Press, 1981).

Chafe, William, H., *The Unfinished Journey: America Since World War II* (New York: Oxford University Press, 1986).

Chandler, Alfred D., Jr, *The Visible Hand: The Managerial Revolution in American Business* (Cambridge, MA: Harvard University Press, 1977).

Chandler, Raymond, *The Little Sister*, 1st pub. 1949 (Harmondsworth: Penguin, 1973).

Charney, Leo, and Vanessa R. Schwartz, eds, *Cinema and the Invention of Modern Life* (Berkeley, CA: University of California Press, 1995).

Charyn, Jerome, *Movieland: Hollywood and the Great American Dream Culture* (New York: New York University Press, 1989).

Chatman, Seymour, *Story and Discourse: Narrative Structure in Fiction and Film* (Ithaca, NY: Cornell University Press, 1978).

Chatman, Seymour, *Coming to Terms: The Rhetoric of Narrative in Fiction and Film* (Ithaca, NY: Cornell University Press, 1990).

Chion, Michel, *Audio-Vision: Sound on Screen*, trans. Claudia Gorbman (New York: Columbia University Press, 1994).

Christensen, Terry, *Reel Politics: American Political Movies from Birth of a Nation to Platoon* (New York: Blackwell, 1987).

Ciment, Michel, *Kazan on Kazan* (London: Secker and Warburg, 1973).

Clark, Danae, *Negotiating Hollywood: The Cultural Politics of Actors' Labor* (Minneapolis: University of Minnesota Press, 1995).

Clifford, James, *The Predicament of Culture* (Cambridge, MA: Harvard University Press, 1988).

Clover, Carol J., *Men, Women and Chainsaws: Gender in the Modern Horror Film* (London: British Film Institute, 1992).

Cohan, Steven, *Masked Men: Masculinity and the Movies in the Fifties* (Bloomington: Indiana University Press, 1997).

Cohan, Steven, and Ina Rae Hark, eds, *Screening the Male: Exploring Masculinities in Hollywood Cinema* (London: Routledge, 1993).

Cohan, Steven, and Ina Rae Hark, eds, *The Road Movie Book* (London: Routledge, 1997).

Cohan, Steven, and Linda M. Shires, *Telling Stories: A Theoretical Analysis of Narrative Fiction* (London: Routledge, 1988).

Collins, Jim, Hilary Radner, and Ava Preacher Collins, eds, *Film Theory Goes to the Movies* (New York: Routledge, 1993).

Combs, James, ed., *Movies and Politics: The Dynamic Relationship* (New York: Garland, 1993).

Comolli, Jean-Louis, and Jean Narboni, "Cinema/Ideology/Criticism (1)," trans. Susan Bennett, in John Ellis, ed., *Screen Reader 1* (London: Society for Education in Film and Television, 1977), pp. 2–11; 1st pub. in *Cahiers du Cinéma* (October–November 1969); 1st pub. in English in *Screen* 12:1 (1971).

Cones, John W., *Film Finance and Distribution: A Dictionary of Terms* (Los Angeles: Silman-James Press, 1992).

Cook, David A., *A History of Narrative Film*, 2nd edn (New York: Norton, 1990).

Cook, David A., *Lost Illusions: American Cinema in the Shadow of Watergate and Vietnam, 1970–1979* (New York: Scribner's, 2000).

Cook, Jim, Jacky Bratton, and Christine Gledhill, eds, *Melodrama: Stage, Picture, Screen* (London: British Film Institute, 1994).

Cook, Pam, ed., *The Cinema Book* (London: British Film Institute, 1985).

Cooke, Alistair, ed., *Garbo and the Night Watchmen*, 1st pub. 1937 (London: Secker and Warburg, 1971).

Copjec, Joan, ed., *Shades of Noir* (London: Verso, 1993).

Corrigan, Timothy, *A Cinema Without Walls: Movies and Culture after Vietnam* (London: Routledge, 1991).

Corrigan, Timothy, *The New American Cinema* (Durham, NC: Duke University Press, 1998).

Corrigan, Timothy, *A Short Guide to Writing about Film*, 3rd edn (New York: Longman, 1998).

Couvares, Frank, ed., *Movie Censorship and American Culture* (Washington, DC: Smithsonian Institution Press, 1996).

Crafton, Donald, *The Talkies: American Cinema's Transition to Sound, 1926–1931* (New York: Scribner's, 1997).

Crane, Jonathan Lake, *Terror and Everyday Life: Singular Moments in the History of the Horror Film* (Thousand Oaks, CA: Sage, 1994).

Craven, Ian, "Alternatives to Narrative in the American Cinema: A Study of Comic Performance," PhD dissertation, University of Exeter, 1982.

Cripps, Thomas, *Slow Fade to Black: The Negro in American Film, 1900–1942* (New York: Oxford University Press, 1977).

Cripps, Thomas, *Making Movies Black: The Hollywood Message Movie from World War II to the Civil Rights Era* (New York: Oxford University Press, 1993).

Cripps, Thomas, *Hollywood's High Noon: Moviemaking and Society before Television* (Baltimore, MD: Johns Hopkins University Press, 1997).

Cross, Gary, *Kids' Stuff: Toys and the Changing World of American Childhood* (Cambridge, MA: Harvard University Press, 1997).

Curran, James, Michael Gurevich, and Janet Woolacott, eds, *Mass Communication and Society* (London: Edward Arnold, 1977).

Custen, George F., *Bio/Pics: How Hollywood Constructed Public Fiction* (New Brunswick, NJ: Rutgers University Press, 1992).

Custen, George F., *Twentieth Century's Fox: Darryl F. Zanuck and the Culture of Hollywood* (New York: Basic Books, 1997).

Czitrom, Daniel, *Media and the American Mind: From Morse to McLuhan* (Chapel Hill: University of North Carolina Press, 1982).

Dale, Alan, *Comedy Is a Man in Trouble: Slapstick in American Movies* (Minneapolis: University of Minnesota Press, 2000).

Dale, Edgar, *The Content of Motion Pictures* (New York: Macmillan, 1935).

Dale, Martin, *The Movie Game: The Film Business in Britain, Europe and America* (London: Cassell, 1997).

Dance, Robert, and Bruce Robertson, *Ruth Harriet Louise and Hollywood Glamour Photography* (Berkeley, CA: University of California Press, 2002).

Dancynger, Ken, *The Technique of Film and Video Editing* (Boston: Focal Press, 1993).

Daniels, Bill, David Leedy, and Steven D. Sills, *Movie Money: Understanding Hollywood's (Creative) Accounting Practices* (Los Angeles: Silman-James Press, 1998).

Danto, Arthur C., *Narration and Knowledge* (New York: Columbia University Press, 1985).

Dardis, Tom, *Some Time in the Sun: The Hollywood Years of Fitzgerald, Faulkner, Nathanael West, Aldous Huxley, and James Agee* (London: André Deutsch, 1976).

Davies, Philip, and Brian Neve, eds, *Cinema, Politics and Society in America* (Manchester: Manchester University Press, 1981).

DeBauche, Leslie Midkiff, *Reel Patriotism: Movies and World War I* (Madison: University of Wisconsin Press, 1997).

deCordova, Richard, *Picture Personalities: The Emergence of the Star System in America* (Urbana: University of Illinois Press, 1990).

de Lauretis, Teresa, *Alice Doesn't: Feminism, Semiotics, Cinema* (Bloomington: Indiana University Press, 1984).

de Lauretis, Teresa, *Technologies of Gender: Essays on Theory, Film, and Fiction* (London: Macmillan, 1987).

de Lauretis, Teresa, and Stephen Heath, eds, *The Cinematic Apparatus* (London: Macmillan, 1980).

Deming, Barbara, *Running Away from Myself: A Dream Portrait of America Drawn from the Films of the Forties* (New York: Grossman, 1969).

de Saussure, Ferdinand, *Course in General Linguistics* (London: Fontana, 1974).

Desser, David, and Garth S. Jowett, eds, *Hollywood Goes Shopping* (Minneapolis: University of Minnesota Press, 2000).

Deutelbaum, Marshall, and Leland Poague, eds, *A Hitchcock Reader* (Ames: Iowa State University Press, 1986).

Dick, Bernard F., *The Merchant Prince of Poverty Row: Harry Cohn of Columbia Pictures* (Lexington: University Press of Kentucky, 1993).

Dick, Bernard F., *City of Dreams: The Making and Remaking of Universal Pictures* (Lexington: University Press of Kentucky, 1997).

Dick, Bernard F., *Engulfed: The Death of Paramount Pictures and the Birth of Corporate Hollywood* (Lexington: University Press of Kentucky, 2001).

Didion, Joan, *The White Album* (Harmondsworth: Penguin, 1981).

Doane, Mary Ann, *The Desire to Desire: The Woman's Film of the 1940s* (London: Macmillan, 1987).

Doane, Mary Ann, *Femmes Fatales: Feminism, Film Theory, Psychoanalysis* (London: Routledge, 1991).

Doane, Mary Ann, Patricia Mellencamp, and Linda Williams, eds, *Re-Visions: Essays in Feminist Film Criticism* (Frederick, MD: University Publications of America, 1984).

Doherty, Thomas, *Teenagers and Teenpics: The Juvenilization of American Movies in the 1950s* (Boston: Unwin Hyman, 1988).

Doherty, Thomas, *Projections of War: Hollywood, American Culture and World War II* (New York: Columbia University Press, 1993).

Donahue, Suzanne Mary, *American Film Distribution: The Changing Marketplace* (Ann Arbor: UMI Research Press, 1987).

Duclos, Denis, *The Werewolf Complex: America's Fascination with Violence* (Oxford: Berg, 1998).

Dukore, Bernard F., *Sam Peckinpah's Feature Films* (Urbana: University of Illinois Press, 1999).

During, Simon, ed., *The Cultural Studies Reader* (London: Routledge, 1993).

Dyer, Richard, "Entertainment and Utopia," *MOVIE* 24 (1977), pp. 2–13.

Dyer, Richard, *Stars* (London: British Film Institute, 1979).

Dyer, Richard, *Heavenly Bodies: Film Stars and Society* (London: Macmillan, 1987).

Dyer, Richard, *Only Entertainment* (London: Routledge, 1992).

Dyer, Richard, *White* (London: Routledge, 1997).

Eagleton, Terry, *Literary Theory: An Introduction* (Oxford: Blackwell, 1983).

Eagleton, Terry, *Ideology: An Introduction* (London: Verso, 1991).

Easty, Edward Dwight, *On Method Acting*, 1st edn 1966 (New York: Ballantine, 1989).

Eckert, Charles, "The Carole Lombard in Macy's Window," *Quarterly Review of Film Studies* 3 (Winter 1978).

Eco, Umberto, *The Role of the Reader: Explorations in the Semiotics of Texts* (Bloomington: University of Indiana Press, 1979).

Eco, Umberto, *Travels in Hyperreality* (London: Picador, 1987).

Edwards, Christine, *The Stanislavsky Heritage: Its Contribution to the Russian and American Theatre* (New York: New York University Press, 1965).

Eisenschitz, Bernard, *Nicholas Ray: An American Journey*, trans. Tom Milne (London: Faber, 1993).

Ellis, John, ed., *Screen Reader 1: Cinema/ Ideology/Politics* (London: Society for Education in Film and Television, 1977).

Ellis, John, *Visible Fictions* (London: Routledge and Kegan Paul, 1982).

Ellwood, David W., and Rob Kroes, eds, *Hollywood in Europe: Experiences of a Cultural Hegemony* (Amsterdam: VU University Press, 1994).

Elsaesser, Thomas, "Why Hollywood?," *Monogram* 1 (1971), pp. 4–10.

Elsaesser, Thomas, ed., *Early Cinema: Space, Frame, Narrative* (London: British Film Institute, 1990).

Eyman, Scott, *The Speed of Sound: Hollywood and the Talkie Revolution* (New York: Simon and Schuster, 1997).

Farber, Manny, *Negative Space: Manny Farber on the Movies* (London: Studio Vista, 1971).

Farber, Stephen, *The Movie Rating Game* (Washington, DC: Public Affairs Press, 1972).

Fell, John L., ed., *Film Before Griffith* (Berkeley, CA: University of California Press, 1983).

Fell, John L., *Film and the Narrative Tradition* (Berkeley, CA: University of California Press, 1986).

Feuer, Jane, *The Hollywood Musical* (London: British Film Institute, 1982).

Field, Syd, *Screenplay: The Foundations of Screenwriting* (New York: Dell, 1979).

Film Daily Yearbook (New York: Jack Alicoate).

Finch, Christopher, *Special Effects: Creating Movie Magic* (New York: Abbeville, 1984).

Fine, Marshall, *Bloody Sam: The Life and Films of Sam Peckinpah* (New York: Primus, 1991).

Fine, Richard, *Hollywood and the Profession of Authorship* (Ann Arbor: University of Michigan Press, 1985).

Fine, Richard, *West of Eden: Writers in Hollywood, 1928–1940* (Washington, DC: Smithsonian Institution Press, 1993).

Finler, Joel W., *The Hollywood Story: Everything You Always Wanted to Know about the American Movie Business but Didn't Know Where to Look* (London: Octopus Books, 1988).

Fish, Stanley, *Is There a Text in this Class?: The Authority of Interpretive Communities* (Cambridge, MA: Harvard University Press, 1980).

Fitzgerald, F. Scott, *The Last Tycoon* (Harmondsworth: Penguin, 1974).

Flinn, Carol, *Strains of Utopia: Gender, Nostalgia and Hollywood Film Music* (Princeton, NJ: Princeton University Press, 1992).

Fordin, Hugh, *The World of Entertainment: Hollywood's Greatest Musicals* (New York: Avon, 1975).

Foucault, Michel, *The Order of Things: An Archaeology of the Human Sciences* (London: Tavistock, 1974).

Foucault, Michel, *Power/Knowledge: Selected Interviews and Other Writings*, eds Colin Gordon, Leo Marshall, John Meplam, and Kate Soper (Brighton: Harvester, 1980).

Foucault, Michel, *The History of Sexuality. Volume 1: An Introduction*, trans. Robert Hurley (Harmondsworth: Penguin, 1981).

Fowles, Jib, *StarStruck: Celebrity Performers and the American Public* (Washington, DC: Smithsonian Institution Press, 1992).

Francke, Lizzie, *Script Girls: Women Screenwriters in Hollywood* (London: British Film Institute, 1994).

Franklin, Harold B., *Motion Picture Theatre Management* (New York: Doran, 1927).

Frederick, Christine, *Selling Mrs Consumer* (New York: Business Bourse, 1929).

Freedman, Jonathan, and Richard Millington, eds, *Hitchcock's America* (New York: Oxford University Press, 1999).

French, Brandon, *On the Verge of Revolt: Women in American Films of the Fifties* (New York: Ungar, 1978).

French, Philip, *The Movie Moguls: An Informal History of the Hollywood Tycoons* (Harmondsworth: Penguin, 1969).

Freund, Elizabeth, *The Return of the Reader: Reader-Response Criticism* (London: Methuen, 1987).

Friedman, Lester, ed., *Unspeakable Images: Ethnicity and the American Cinema* (Urbana: University of Illinois Press, 1991).

Friedrich, Otto, *City of Nets: A Portrait of Hollywood in the 1940s* (London: Headline, 1987).

Fuller, Kathryn H., *At the Picture Show: Small Town Audiences and the Creation of Movie Fan Culture* (Washington, DC: Smithsonian Institution Press, 1996).

Gabler, Neal, *An Empire of Their Own: How the Jews Invented Hollywood* (New York: Crown, 1988).

Gaines, Jane, ed., *Classical Hollywood Narrative: The Paradigm Wars* (Durham, NC: Duke University Press, 1992).

Gaines, Jane, *Contested Culture: The Image, the Voice, and the Law* (London: British Film Institute, 1992).

Gaines, Jane, and Charlotte Herzog, eds, *Fabrications: Costume and the Female Body* (New York: Routledge, 1990).

Gallagher, Tag, *John Ford: The Man and his Films* (Berkeley, CA: University of California Press, 1986).

Gardiner, Gerald, *The Censorship Papers: Movie Censorship Letters from the Hays Office, 1934 to 1968* (New York: Dodd, Mead, 1987).

Geertz, Clifford, *The Interpretation of Cultures* (New York: Basic Books, 1973).

Gelder, Ken, ed., *The Horror Reader* (London: Routledge, 2000).

Genette, Gerard, *Narrative Discourse: An Essay in Method*, trans. Jane E. Lewin (Ithaca, NY: Cornell University Press, 1980).

Gilbert, James, *A Cycle of Outrage: America's Reaction to the Juvenile Delinquent in the 1950s* (New York: Oxford University Press, 1986).

Giovacchini, Saverio, *Hollywood Modernism: Film and Politics in the Age of the New Deal* (Philadelphia: Temple University Press, 2001).

Glatzer, Richard, and John Raeburn, eds, *Frank Capra: The Man and his Films* (Ann Arbor: University of Michigan Press, 1975).

Gledhill, Christine, ed., *Home Is Where the Heart Is: Studies in Melodrama and the Woman's Film* (London: British Film Institute, 1987).

Gledhill, Christine, ed., *Stardom: Industry of Desire* (London: Routledge, 1991).

Gledhill, Christine, and Linda Williams, eds, *Reinventing Film Studies* (London: Arnold, 2000).

Goldman, William, *Adventures in the Screen Trade: A Personal View of Hollywood and Screenwriting* (New York: Warner Books, 1983).

Goldman, William, *The Big Picture: Who Killed Hollywood? and Other Essays* (New York: Applause, 2000).

Goldman, William, *Which Lie Did I Tell?: More Adventures in the Screen Trade* (New York: Pantheon, 2000).

Goldstein, Laurence, and Ira Konigsberg, eds, *The Movies: Texts, Receptions, Exposures* (Ann Arbor: University of Michigan Press, 1996).

Gomery, Douglas, *The Hollywood Studio System* (London: Macmillan, 1986).

Gomery, Douglas, *Shared Pleasures: A History of Movie Presentation in the United States* (London: British Film Institute, 1992).

Goodman, Ezra, *The Fifty-Year Decline of Hollywood* (New York: Simon and Schuster, 1961).

Gorbman, Claudia, *Unheard Melodies: Narrative Film Music* (Bloomington: Indiana University Press, 1987).

Gordon, Jan and Cora, *Stardust in Hollywood* (London: Harrap, 1930).

Gorer, Geoffrey, *The Americans: A Study in National Character* (London: Cresset, 1948).

Graham, Peter, ed., *The New Wave* (London: Secker and Warburg, 1968).

Gramsci, Antonio, *A Gramsci Reader*, ed. David Forgacs (London: Lawrence and Wishart, 1988).

Grant, Barry Keith, ed., *Film Genre Reader* (Austin: University of Texas Press, 1986).

Gray, Lois S., and Ronald L. Seeber, eds, *Under the Stars: Essays on Labor Relations in Arts and Entertainment* (Ithaca, NY: Cornell University Press, 1996).

Green, Philip, *Cracks in the Pedestal: Ideology and Gender in Hollywood* (Amherst: University of Massachusetts Press, 1998).

Greene, Ray, *Hollywood Migraine: The Inside Story of a Decade in Film* (Dublin: Merlin, 2000).

Griffith, Richard, ed., *The Talkies: Articles and Illustrations from a Great Fan Magazine, 1928–1940* (New York: Dover, 1971).

Grodal, Torben, *Moving Pictures: A New Theory of Film Genres, Feelings, and Cognition* (Oxford: Oxford University Press, 1997).

Gunning, Tom, "An Aesthetic of Astonishment: Early Film and the (In)credulous Spectator," *Art and Text* 34 (Spring 1989), pp. 31–45.

Gunning, Tom, *The Films of Fritz Lang: Allegories of Vision and Modernity* (London: British Film Institute, 2000).

Gussow, Mel, *Don't Say Yes Until I've Finished Talking* (New York: Doubleday, 1971).

Haberski, Raymond L., Jr, *"It's Only a Movie": Films and Critics in American Culture* (Lexington: University Press of Kentucky, 2001).

Hall, Ben M., *The Best Remaining Seats: The Golden Age of the Movie Palace* (New York: DaCapo, 1988).

Halliday, John, *Sirk on Sirk* (London: Secker and Warburg, 1971).

Halliwell, Leslie, *Halliwell's Film Guide*, 7th edn (London: Paladin, 1990).

Halliwell, Leslie, *Halliwell's Film and Video Guide 2000*, ed. John Walker, 15th edn (London: HarperCollins, 1999).

Hamilton, Ian, *Writers in Hollywood* (London: Heinemann, 1990).

Handel, Leo A., *Hollywood Looks at its Audience: A Report of Film Audience Research* (Urbana: University of Illinois Press, 1950).

Hansen, Miriam, *Babel and Babylon: Spectatorship in American Silent Film* (Cambridge, MA: Harvard University Press, 1991).

Hardy, Phil, ed., *Raoul Walsh* (Edinburgh: Edinburgh Film Festival, 1974).

Hardy, Phil, ed., *The BFI Companion to Crime* (London: Cassell, 1997).

Harmetz, Aljean, *Rolling Breaks and Other Movie Business* (New York: Knopf, 1983).

Harmetz, Aljean, *Round Up the Usual Suspects: The Making of Casablanca – Bogart, Bergman, and World War II* (New York: Hyperion, 1992).

Harvey, James, *Romantic Comedy in Hollywood from Lubitsch to Sturges* (New York: DaCapo, 1998).

Harvey, Sylvia, *May '68 and Film Culture* (London: British Film Institute, 1978).

Harwood, Sarah, *Family Fictions: Representations of the Family in 1980s Hollywood Cinema* (London: Macmillan, 1997).

Haskell, Molly, *From Reverence to Rape: The Treatment of Women in the Movies* (Chicago: University of Chicago Press, 1973).

Hauge, Michael, *Writing Screenplays that Sell* (New York: McGraw-Hill, 1988).

Haver, Ronald, *David O. Selznick's Hollywood* (New York: Knopf, 1980).

Hayward, Philip, ed., *Culture, Technology and Creativity* (London: John Libbey, 1990).

Hayward, Philip, and Tana Wollen, eds, *Future Visions: New Technologies of the Screen* (London: British Film Institute, 1993).

Heath, Stephen, *Questions of Cinema* (London: Macmillan, 1981).

Heath, Stephen, and Patricia Mellencamp, eds, *Cinema and Language* (Frederick, MD: University Publications of America, 1983).

Herman, Lewis, *A Practical Manual of Screen Playwriting for Theater and Television Films* (New York: New English Library, 1974).

Higson, Andrew, and Richard Maltby, eds, *"Film Europe" and "Film America": Cinema, Commerce and Cultural Exchange, 1925–1939* (Exeter: University of Exeter Press, 1999).

Hill, John, and Pamela Church Gibson, eds, *The Oxford Guide to Film Studies* (Oxford: Oxford University Press, 1998).

Hillier, Jim, ed., *Cahiers du Cinéma: The 1950s* (Cambridge: Cambridge University Press, 1986).

Hillier, Jim, *The New Hollywood* (London: Studio Vista, 1993).

Hillier, Jim, ed., *American Independent Cinema: A Sight and Sound Reader* (London: British Film Institute, 2001).

Hillier, Jim, and Peter Wollen, eds, *Howard Hawks: American Artist* (London: British Film Institute, 1996).

Hilmes, Michelle, *Hollywood and Broadcasting: From Radio to Cable* (Urbana: University of Illinois Press, 1990).

Hincha, Richard, "Selling CinemaScope: 1953–1956," *Velvet Light Trap* 21 (Summer 1985), pp. 44–53.

Hirsch, Foster, *A Method to their Madness: The History of the Actors Studio* (New York: Norton, 1984).

Hirsch, Foster, *Acting Hollywood Style* (New York: Abrams, 1991).

Hochman, Stanley, ed., *From Quasimodo to Scarlett O'Hara: A National Board of Review Anthology, 1920–1940* (New York: Ungar, 1982).

Hollows, Joanne, Peter Hutchings, and Mark Jancovich, eds, *The Film Studies Reader* (London: Arnold, 2000).

Horne, Gerald, *Class Struggle in Hollywood, 1930–1950: Moguls, Mobsters, Stars, Reds and Trade Unionists* (Austin: University of Texas Press, 2001).

Horton, Andrew S., *Comedy/Cinema/Theory* (Berkeley, CA: University of California Press, 1991).

Houghton, Buck, *What a Producer Does: The Art of Moviemaking (Not the Business)* (Los Angeles: Silman-James Press, 1991).

Hozic, Aida, *Hollyworld: Space, Power, and Fantasy in the American Economy* (Ithaca, NY: Cornell University Press, 2001).

Huettig, Mae D., *Economic Control of the Motion Picture Industry: A Study in Industrial Organization* (Philadelphia: University of Pennsylvania Press, 1944).

Hugo, Chris, "The Economic Background," *MOVIE* 27/8 (1981), pp. 43–9.

Inglis, Ruth, *Freedom of the Movies: A Report on Self-Regulation from the Commission on Freedom of the Press* (Chicago: University of Chicago Press, 1947).

Ingram, David, *Green Screen: Environmentalism and Hollywood Cinema* (Exeter: University of Exeter Press, 2000).

International Motion Picture Almanac (New York: Quigley).

Izod, John, *Hollywood and the Box Office 1895–1986* (London: Macmillan, 1988).

Jacobs, Lea, "Industry Self-Regulation and the Problem of Textual Determination," *Velvet Light Trap* 23 (Spring 1989), pp. 4–15.

Jacobs, Lea, *The Wages of Sin: Censorship and the Fallen Woman Film, 1928–1942* (Madison: University of Wisconsin Press, 1991).

Jauss, Hans Robert, *Toward an Aesthetic of Reception*, trans. Timothy Bahti (Minneapolis: University of Minnesota Press, 1982).

Jowett, Garth, *Film: The Democratic Art* (Boston: Little, Brown, 1976).

Jowett, Garth, "'A Capacity for Evil': The 1915 Supreme Court *Mutual* Decision," *Historical Journal of Film, Radio and Television* 9:1 (1989), pp. 59–78.

Jowett, Garth, Ian C. Jarvie, and Kathryn H. Fuller, *Children and the Movies: Media Influence and the Payne Fund Controversy* (Cambridge: Cambridge University Press, 1996).

Kael, Pauline, *Going Steady* (Boston: Little, Brown, 1970).

Kahn, Gordon, *Hollywood on Trial: The Story of the Ten who were Indicted* (New York: Boni and Gaer, 1948).

Kanfer, Stefan, *Serious Business: The Art and Commerce of Animation in America from Betty Boop to Toy Story* (New York: Scribner's, 1997).

Kaplan, E. Ann, ed., *Women in Film Noir* (London: British Film Institute, 1978).

Kaplan, E. Ann, *Women and Film: Both Sides of the Camera* (New York: Methuen, 1983).

Kaplan, E. Ann, ed., *Psychoanalysis and Cinema* (New York: Routledge, 1990).

Kapsis, Robert E., *Hitchcock: The Making of a Reputation* (Chicago: University of Chicago Press, 1992).

Karnick, Kristine Brunovska, and Henry Jenkins, eds, *Classical Hollywood Comedy* (London: Routledge, 1995).

Kasson, John, *Amusing the Million: Coney Island at the Turn of the Century* (New York: Hill and Wang, 1978).

Katz, Steven D., *Film Directing Shot by Shot: Visualizing from Concept to Screen* (Los Angeles: Michael Wiese Productions, 1991).

Kauffman, Stanley, ed., *American Film Criticism from the Beginnings to Citizen Kane* (New York: Liveright, 1972).

Kawin, Bruce, *How Movies Work* (Berkeley, CA: University of California Press, 1992).

Kennedy, Joseph P., ed., *The Story of the Films* (Chicago: A. W. Shaw, 1927).

Kent, Nicholas, *Naked Hollywood: Money, Power and the Movies* (London: BBC Books, 1991).

Kerr, Paul, ed., *The Hollywood Film Industry* (London: Routledge and Kegan Paul, 1986).

Kiesling, Barrett C., *Talking Pictures* (Richmond, VA: Johnson Publishing, 1937).

Kinden, Gorham, ed., *The American Movie Industry: The Business of Motion Pictures* (Carbondale: Southern Illinois University Press, 1982).

King, Geoff, *Spectacular Narratives: Hollywood in the Age of the Blockbuster* (London: Tauris, 2000).

King, Neal, *Heroes in Hard Times: Cop Action Movies in the US* (Austin: University of Texas Press, 1999).

Kitses, Jim, *Horizons West: Anthony Mann, Budd Boetticher, Sam Peckinpah: Studies of Authorship within the Western* (London: Thames and Hudson, 1969).

Kitses, Jim, and Gregg Rickman, eds, *The Western Reader* (New York: Limelight, 1998).

Kline, Herbert, ed., *New Theatre and Film, 1934–1937* (New York: Harcourt Brace Jovanovich, 1985).

Klinger, Barbara, "Digressions at the Cinema: Reception and Mass Culture," *Cinema Journal* 28:4 (Summer 1989), pp. 3–19.

Klinger, Barbara, "Much Ado About Excess: Genre, Mise-en-Scène and the Woman in *Written on the Wind*," *Wide Angle* 11:4 (1989), pp. 4–21.

Klinger, Barbara, *Melodrama and Meaning: History, Culture, and the Films of Douglas Sirk* (Bloomington: University of Indiana Press, 1994).

Klumph, Inez, and Helen Klumph, *Screen Acting: Its Requirements and Rewards* (New York: Falk, 1922).

Koch, Howard, *Casablanca: Script and Legend* (Woodstock: Overlook Press, 1973).

Kohansky, Mendel, *The Disreputable Profession: The Actor in Society* (Westport, CT: Greenwood Press, 1984).

Kolker, Robert, *Film Form and Culture* (New York: McGraw-Hill, 1999).

Konigsberg, Ira, *The Complete Film Dictionary*, 2nd edn (New York: Penguin, 1997).

Koppes, Clayton R., and Gregory D. Black, *Hollywood Goes to War: How Politics, Profits and Propaganda Shaped World War II Movies* (New York: Macmillan, 1987).

Koszarski, Richard, ed., *Hollywood Directors 1914–1940* (New York: Oxford University Press, 1976).

Koszarski, Richard, *Hollywood Directors, 1941–1976* (New York: Oxford University Press, 1977).

Koszarski, Richard, *An Evening's Entertainment: The Age of the Silent Feature Picture, 1915–1928* (New York: Scribner's, 1990).

Kozloff, Sarah, *Invisible Storytellers: Voice-Over Narration in American Fiction Film* (Berkeley, CA: University of California Press, 1988).

Kozloff, Sarah, *Overhearing Film Dialogue* (Berkeley: University of California Press, 2000).

Kracauer, Siegfried, *From Caligari to Hitler: A Psychological History of the German Film* (Princeton, NJ: Princeton University Press, 1947).

Krämer, Peter, "Women First: *Titanic* (1997), Action-Adventure Films and Hollywood's Female Audience," *Historical Journal of Film, Radio and Television* 18:4 (1998), pp. 599–618.

Kuhn, Annette, *The Power of the Image: Essays on Representation and Sexuality* (London: Routledge and Kegan Paul, 1985).

Kuhn, Annette, ed., *Alien Zone: Cultural Theory and Contemporary Science Fiction* (London: Verso, 1990).

Kuleshov, Lev, *Kuleshov on Film: Writings by Lev Kuleshov*, ed. and trans. Ronald Levaco (Berkeley, CA: University of California Press, 1974).

Kuntzel, Thierry, "The Film Work 2," *Camera Obscura* 5 (Spring 1980), pp. 6–69.

Lack, Russell, *Twenty Four Frames Under: A Buried History of Film Music* (London: Quartet, 1997).

Lamster, Mark, ed., *Architecture and Film* (New York: Princeton Architectural Press, 2000).

Landy, Marcia, ed., *Imitations of Life: A Reader on Film and Television Melodrama* (Detroit: Wayne State University Press, 1991).

Lang, Robert, ed., *The Birth of a Nation* (New Brunswick, NJ: Rutgers University Press, 1994).

Lapsley, Robert, and Michael Westlake, *Film Theory: An Introduction* (Manchester: Manchester University Press, 1988).

Lastra, James, *Sound Technology and the American Cinema: Reception, Representation, Modernity* (New York: Columbia University Press, 2000).

La Vine, W. Robert, *In a Glamorous Fashion: The Fabulous Years of Hollywood Costume Design* (New York: Scribner's, 1980).

Lawrence, Amy, *Echo and Narcissus: Women's Voices in Classical Hollywood Cinema* (Berkeley, CA: University of California Press, 1991).

Lebo, Harlan, *Casablanca: Behind the Scenes* (New York: Simon and Schuster, 1992).

Leff, Leonard J., and Jerrold R. Simmons, *The Dame in the Kimono: Hollywood, Censorship, and the Production Code from the 1920s to the 1960s* (New York: Grove, Weidenfeld, 1990).

Lehman, Peter, ed., *Close Viewings: An Anthology of New Film Criticism* (Tallahassee: Florida State University Press, 1990).

Leibman, Nina C., *Living Room Lectures: The Fifties Family in Film and Television* (Austin: University of Texas Press, 1995).

Leitch, Thomas M., *Find the Director and Other Hitchcock Games* (Athens, GA: University of Georgia Press, 1991).

Lenihan, John L., *Showdown: Confronting Modern America in the Western Film* (Urbana: University of Illinois Press, 1980).

Levin, Martin, ed., *Hollywood and the Great Fan Magazines* (London: Ian Allen, 1970).

Levine, Lawrence W., *Highbrow/Lowbrow: The Emergence of Cultural Hierarchy in America* (Cambridge, MA: Harvard University Press, 1988).

Lévi-Strauss, Claude, "The Structural Study of Myth," *Journal of American Folklore* 68:270 (1955), pp. 428–44.

Lévi-Strauss, Claude, *Structural Anthropology*, trans. Claire Jacobson and Brooke Grundfest Schoepf (Garden City, NY: Doubleday, 1967).

Levy, Emanuel, *Small-Town America in Film: The Decline and Fall of Community* (New York: Continuum, 1991).

Levy, Emanuel, *Cinema of Outsiders: The Rise of American Independent Film* (New York: New York University Press, 1999).

Lewis, Howard T., *The Motion Picture Industry* (New York: Van Nostrand, 1933).

Lewis, Jerry, *The Total Film-Maker* (London: Vision Press, 1971).

Lewis, Jon, *Whom God Wishes to Destroy: Francis Coppola and the New Hollywood* (Durham, NC: Duke University Press, 1995).

Lewis, Jon, ed., *The New American Cinema* (Durham, NC: Duke University Press, 1998).

Lewis, Jon, *Hollywood vs Hardcore: How the Struggle over Censorship Saved the Modern Film Industry* (New York: New York University Press, 2000).

Lewis, Jon, ed., *The End of Cinema as We Know It: American Film in the Nineties* (New York: New York University Press, 2001).

Leyda, Jay, *Kino: A History of the Russian and Soviet Film*, 3rd edn (Princeton, NJ: Princeton University Press, 1983).

Limbacher, James L., *Four Aspects of the Film: A History of the Development of Color, Sound, 3-D and Widescreen Films and their Contribution to the Art of the Motion Picture* (New York: Brussel and Brussel, 1968).

Lindsay, Vachel, *The Art of the Moving Picture*, 1st pub. 1915 (New York: Liveright, 1970).

Lister, Martin, ed., *The Photographic Image in Digital Culture* (London: Routledge, 1995).

Litman, Barry R., *The Motion Picture Mega-Industry* (Boston: Allyn and Bacon, 1998).

Litwak, Mark, *Reel Power: The Struggle for Influence and Success in the New Hollywood* (London: Sidgwick and Jackson, 1987).

Lovell, Alan, and Peter Kramer, eds, *Screen Acting* (London: Routledge, 1999).

Lovell, Terry, *Pictures of Reality* (London: British Film Institute, 1980).

Lowery, Shearon, and Melvin L. DeFleur, *Milestones in Mass Communication Research: Media Effects* (New York: Longman, 1983).

Lubin, David M., *Titanic* (London: British Film Institute, 1999).

Lynd, Robert S., and Helen Merrill Lynd, *Middletown: A Study in Modern American Culture* (New York: Harcourt, Brace, and World, 1929).

McArthur, Benjamin, *Actors and American Culture, 1880–1920* (Philadelphia: Temple University Press, 1984).

MacArthur, Colin, *Underworld USA* (London: Secker and Warburg, 1972).

McBride, Joseph, ed., *Focus on Howard Hawks* (Englewood Cliffs, NJ: Prentice-Hall, 1972).

McBride, Joseph, *Frank Capra: The Catastrophe of Success* (London: Faber, 1992).

MacCabe, Colin, "Realism and the Cinema: Notes on Some Brechtian Theses," *Screen* 15:2 (Summer 1974), pp. 7–27.

McCann, Richard Dyer, *Hollywood in Transition* (Boston: Houghton Mifflin, 1962).

McCarthy, Todd, *Howard Hawks: The Grey Fox of Hollywood* (New York: Grove Press, 1997).

McClelland, Doug, ed., *Starspeak: Hollywood on Everything* (London: Faber, 1987).

McConnell, Frank D., *The Spoken Seen: Film and the Romantic Imagination* (Baltimore, MD: Johns Hopkins University Press, 1975).

McDougal, Dennis, *The Last Mogul: Lew Wasserman, MCA, and the Hidden History of Hollywood* (New York: Crown, 1998).

McGilligan, Patrick, and Paul Buhle, *Tender Comrades: A Backstory of the Hollywood Blacklist* (New York: St Martin's Press, 1997).

McKee, Robert, *Story: Substance, Structure, Style and the Principles of Screenwriting* (London: Methuen, 1998).

McLean, Adrienne L., and David A. Cook, eds, *Headline Hollywood: A Century of Film Scandal* (New Brunswick, NJ: Rutgers University Press, 2001).

McNiven, Roger D., "The Middle-Class American Home of the Fifties: The Use of Architecture in Nicholas Ray's *Bigger Than Life* and Douglas Sirk's *All That Heaven Allows*," *Cinema Journal* 22:2 (Summer 1983), pp. 38–57.

McWilliams, Carey, *Southern California: An Island on the Land*, 1st pub. 1946 (Santa Barbara: Peregrine Smith, 1973).

Madsen, Axel, *The New Hollywood* (New York: Crowell, 1975).

Maeder, Edward, ed., *Hollywood and History: Costume Design in Film* (London: Thames and Hudson, 1987).

Malossi, Giannino, ed., *Latin Lover: The Passionate South* (Milan: Edizioni Charta, 1996).

Maltby, Richard, *Harmless Entertainment: Hollywood and the Ideology of Consensus* (Metuchen, NJ: Scarecrow, 1983).

Maltby, Richard, "Film Noir: The Politics of the Maladjusted Text," *Journal of American Studies* 18:1 (1984), pp. 49–71.

Maltby, Richard, "American Media and the Denial of History," in Dennis Welland, ed., *The United States: A Companion to American Studies*, 2nd edn (London: Methuen, 1987), pp. 490–517.

Maltby, Richard, ed., *Dreams for Sale: Popular Culture in the Twentieth Century* (London: Harrap, 1989).

Maltby, Richard, "'To Prevent the Prevalent Type of Book': Censorship and Adaptation in Hollywood, 1924–1934," *American Quarterly* 44:4 (1992), pp. 554–83.

Maltby, Richard, "'The Problem of Interpretation . . .': Authorial and Institutional Intentions in and around *Kiss Me Deadly*," *Screening the Past* 10 (June 2000), www.latrobe.edu.au/ www/screeningthepast/firstrelease/fr0600/ rmfr10e.htm

Maltby, Richard, and Kate Bowles, "Hollywood: The Economics of Utopia," in Jeremy Mitchell and Richard Maidment, eds, *The United States in the Twentieth Century: Culture* (London: Hodder and Stoughton, 1994), pp. 99–134.

Manovich, Lev, *The Language of New Media* (Boston: MIT Press, 2001).

Manvell, Roger, *Films and the Second World War* (New York: Dell, 1974).

Marc, David, *Demographic Vistas: Television in American Culture* (Philadelphia: University of Pennsylvania Press, 1984).

Marchetti, Gina, *Romance and the "Yellow Peril": Race, Sex and Discursive Strategies in Hollywood Fiction* (Berkeley, CA: University of California Press, 1993).

Marion, Frances, *How to Write and Sell Film Stories* (New York: Covici Friede, 1937).

Marks, Martin Miller, *Music and the Silent Film: Contexts and Case Studies* (New York: Oxford University Press, 1997).

Marner, Terence St John, *Directing Motion Pictures* (London: Tantivy, 1972).

Massey, Anne, *Hollywood Beyond the Screen: Design and Material Culture* (Oxford: Berg, 2000).

Mast, Gerald, *A Short History of the Movies*, 3rd edn (Oxford: Oxford University Press, 1981).

Mast, Gerald, *Howard Hawks, Storyteller* (New York: Oxford University Press, 1982).

Mast, Gerald, ed., *The Movies in Our Midst: Documents in the Cultural History of Film in America* (Chicago: University of Chicago Press, 1982).

Mast, Gerald, and Marshall Cohen, eds, *Film Theory and Criticism*, 3rd edn (New York: Oxford University Press, 1985).

Mast, Gerald, Marshall Cohen, and Leo Braudy, eds, *Film Theory and Criticism: Introductory Readings* (New York: Oxford University Press, 1992).

Matthews, Brander, ed., *Papers on Acting* (New York: Hill and Wang, 1958).

May, Lary, *Screening Out the Past: The Birth of Mass Culture and the Motion Picture Industry* (New York: Oxford University Press, 1980).

May, Lary, *The Big Tomorrow: Hollywood and the Politics of the American Way* (Chicago: University of Chicago Press, 2000).

Mayer, J. P., *Sociology of Film: Studies and Documents* (London: Faber, 1946).

Mayer, J. P., *British Cinemas and their Audiences: Sociological Studies* (London: Dobson, 1948).

Medved, Michael, *Hollywood vs. America: Popular Culture and the War on Traditional Values* (New York: HarperCollins, 1992).

Mellencamp, Patricia, and Philip Rosen, eds, *Cinema Histories, Cinema Practices* (Frederick, MD: University Publications of America, 1984).

Merleau-Ponty, Maurice, *Sense and Non-Sense*, trans. Hubert L. Dreyfuss and Patricia A. Dreyfuss (Evanston: Northwestern University Press, 1964).

Merritt, Greg, *Celluloid Mavericks: A History of American Independent Film* (New York: Thunder's Mouth Press, 2000).

Metz, Christian, *Film Language: A Semiotics of the Cinema*, trans. Michael Taylor (New York: Oxford University Press, 1974).

Metz, Christian, *The Imaginary Signifier: Psychoanalysis and the Cinema*, trans. Celia Britton, Annwyl Williams, Ben Brewster, and Alfred Guzzetti (Bloomington: Indiana University Press, 1982).

Meyer, William R., *Warner Brothers Directors: The Hard-Boiled, the Comic, and the Weepers* (New Rochelle, NY: Arlington House, 1978).

Miller, Frank, *Casablanca: As Time Goes By* (London: Virgin Books, 1993).

Miller, Mark Crispin, ed., *Seeing Through Movies* (New York: Pantheon, 1990).

Miller, Toby, and Robert Stam, eds, *A Companion to Film Theory* (Malden, MA: Blackwell, 1999).

Miller, Toby, Nitin Govil, John McMurria, and Richard Maxwell, *Global Hollywood* (London: British Film Institute, 2001).

Mitry, Jean, *The Aesthetics and Psychology of the Cinema*, trans. Christopher King (Bloomington: Indiana University Press, 1997).

Modleski, Tania, ed., *Studies in Entertainment: Critical Approaches to Mass Culture* (Bloomington: Indiana University Press, 1987).

Modleski, Tania, *The Women Who Knew Too Much: Hitchcock and Feminist Theory* (London: Methuen, 1988).

Moley, Raymond, *Are We Movie Made?* (New York: Macy-Masius, 1938).

Moley, Raymond, *The Hays Office* (Indianapolis: Bobbs-Merrill, 1945).

Monaco, James, *How to Read a Film: The Art, Technology, Language, History and Theory of Film and Media* (New York: Oxford University Press, 1977).

Monaco, James, *American Film Now: The People, the Power, the Money, the Movies* (New York: New American Library, 1979).

Moore, Schulyer M., *The Biz: The Basic Business, Legal and Financial Aspects of the Film Industry* (Los Angeles: Silman-James Press, 2000).

Moran, Albert, ed., *Film Policy: International, National and Regional Perspectives* (London: Routledge, 1996).

Moseley, Leonard, *Zanuck* (New York: McGraw-Hill, 1984).

Motion Picture Almanac (New York: Quigley).

Mulvey, Laura, *Visual and Other Pleasures* (Bloomington: Indiana University Press, 1989).

Mulvey, Laura, *Fetishism and Curiosity* (London: British Film Institute, 1996).

Mulvey, Laura, and Jon Halliday, *Douglas Sirk* (Edinburgh: Edinburgh Film Festival, 1972).

Munby, Jonathan, *Public Enemies, Public Heroes: Screening the Gangster from Little Caesar to Touch of Evil* (Chicago: University of Chicago Press, 1999).

Münsterberg, Hugo, *The Photoplay: A Psychological Study*, 1st pub. 1916, reprint (New York: Dover, 1970).

Murch, Walter, *In the Blink of an Eye: A Perspective on Film Editing* (Los Angeles: Silman-James Press, 1995).

Murray, Edward, *Nine American Film Critics: A Study of Theory and Practice* (New York: Ungar, 1975).

Muscio, Giuliana, *Hollywood's New Deal* (Philadelphia: Temple University Press, 1997).

Musser, Charles, *The Emergence of Cinema: The American Screen to 1907* (New York: Scribner's, 1990).

Musser, Charles, *Before the Nickelodeon: Edwin S. Porter and the Edison Manufacturing Company* (Berkeley, CA: University of California Press, 1991).

Nadel, Alan, *Containment Culture: American Narratives, Postmodernism and the Atomic Age* (Durham, NC: Duke University Press, 1995).

Nadel, Alan, *Flatlining on the Field of Dreams: Cultural Narratives in the Films of President Reagan's America* (New Brunswick, NJ: Rutgers University Press, 1997).

Naremore, James, *Acting in the Cinema* (Berkeley, CA: University of California Press, 1988).

Naremore, James, *More than Night: Film Noir in its Contexts* (Berkeley, CA: University of California Press, 1998).

Naremore, James, ed., *Film Adaptation* (New Brunswick, NJ: Rutgers University Press, 2000).

Natoli, Joseph, *Speeding to the Millennium: Film and Culture 1993–1995* (Albany: State University of New York Press, 1997).

Navasky, Victor S., *Naming Names* (New York: Viking Press, 1980).

Neale, Steve, *Genre* (London: British Film Institute, 1980).

Neale, Steve, *Cinema and Technology: Image, Sound, Colour* (London: Macmillan, 1985).

Neale, Steve, "Questions of Genre," *Screen* 31:1 (Spring 1990), pp. 45–67.

Neale, Steve, "Melo Talk: On the Meaning and Use of the Term 'Melodrama' in the American Trade Press," *Velvet Light Trap* 22 (Fall 1993), pp. 66–89.

Neale, Steve, *Genre and Hollywood* (London: Routledge, 2000).

Neale, Steve, and Frank Krutnik, *Popular Film and Television Comedy* (London: Routledge, 1990).

Neale, Steve, and Murray Smith, eds, *Contemporary Hollywood Cinema* (London: Routledge, 1998).

Neve, Brian, *Film and Politics in America: A Social Tradition* (London: Routledge, 1992).

Nichols, Bill, ed., *Movies and Methods* (Berkeley, CA: University of California Press, 1976).

Nichols, Bill, *Ideology and the Image: Social Representation in the Cinema and Other Media* (Bloomington: Indiana University Press, 1981).

Nichols, Bill, ed., *Movies and Methods. Vol. II* (Berkeley, CA: University of California Press, 1985).

Nielsen, Mike, and Gene Mailes, *Hollywood's Other Blacklist: Union Struggles in the Studio System* (London: British Film Institute, 1995).

Noose, Theodore, *Hollywood Film Acting* (New York: Barnes, 1979).

Nowell-Smith, Geoffrey, ed., *The Oxford History of World Cinema* (Oxford: Oxford University Press, 1996).

Nowell-Smith, Geoffrey, and Stephen Ricci, eds, *Hollywood and Europe: Economics, Culture, National Identity, 1945–95* (London: British Film Institute, 1998).

O'Connor, John E., and Martin A. Jackson, eds, *American History/American Film: Interpreting the Hollywood Image* (New York: Ungar, 1980).

Ogle, Patrick J., "Technological and Aesthetic Influences upon the Development of Deep Focus Cinematography in the United States," in John Ellis, ed., *Screen Reader 1: Cinema/Ideology/Politics* (London: Society for Education in Film and Television, 1977), pp. 81–108.

Ohmer, Susan, "Measuring Desire: George Gallup and Audience Research in Hollywood," *Journal of Film and Video* 43:1–2 (Summer 1991), pp. 3–28.

Owen, Bruce M., *The Internet Challenge to Television* (Cambridge, MA: Harvard University Press, 1999).

Palmer, William J., *The Films of the Eighties: A Social History* (Carbondale: Southern Illinois University Press, 1993).

Parrish, Robert, *Growing Up in Hollywood* (London: Bodley Head, 1976).

Patterson, Frances Taylor, *Cinema Craftsmanship: A Book for Photoplaywrights* (New York: Harcourt, Brace, and Howe, 1920).

Paul, Elliott, and Luis Quintanilla, *With a Hays Nonny Nonny* (New York: Random House, 1942).

Paul, William, *Laughing Screaming: Modern Hollywood Horror and Comedy* (New York: Columbia University Press, 1994).

Penley, Constance, ed., *Feminism and Film Theory* (London: Routledge, 1988).

Perkins, V. F., *Film as Film: Understanding and Judging Movies* (Harmondsworth: Penguin, 1972).

Perkins, V. F., "Must We Say What They Mean? Film Criticism and Interpretation," *MOVIE* 34/5 (Winter 1990), pp. 1–6.

Phelan, J. J., *Motion Pictures as a Phase of Commercialized Amusement in Toledo, Ohio*, 1st pub. 1919, reprinted in *Film History* 13:3 (2001).

Phillips, Patrick, *Understanding Film Texts: Meaning and Experience* (London: British Film Institute, 2000).

Pierson, John, *Spike, Mike, Slackers and Dykes: A Guided Tour Across a Decade of Independent American Cinema* (London: Faber, 1996).

Pierson, Michele, *Special Effects: Still in Search of Wonder* (New York: Columbia University Press, 2002).

Pinedo, Isabel Cristina, *Recreational Terror: Women and the Pleasures of Horror Film Viewing* (Albany: State University of New York Press, 1997).

Pizzitola, Louis, *Hearst over Hollywood: Power, Passion and Propaganda in the Movies* (New York: Columbia University Press, 2002).

Plantinga, Carl, and Greg M. Smith, eds, *Passionate Views: Film, Cognition, and Emotion* (Baltimore, MD: Johns Hopkins University Press, 1999).

Poague, Leland, *Howard Hawks* (Boston: Twayne, 1982).

Postman, Neil, *Amusing Ourselves to Death: Public Discourse in the Age of Show Business* (London: Heinemann, 1986).

Potamkin, Harry Alan, *The Compound Cinema*, ed. Lewis Jacobs (New York: Teachers College Press, 1977).

Powdermaker, Hortense, *Hollywood the Dream Factory: An Anthropologist Looks at the Movie-Makers* (Boston: Little, Brown, 1950).

Powers, Stephen, David J. Rothman, and Stanley Rothman, *Hollywood's America: Social and Political Themes in Motion Pictures* (Boulder, CO: Westview Press, 1996).

Price, Theodore, *Hitchcock and Homosexuality: His 50-Year Obsession with Jack the Ripper and the Superbitch Prostitute* (Metuchen, NJ: Scarecrow, 1991).

Prince, Stephen, *Savage Cinema: Sam Peckinpah and the Rise of Ultraviolent Movies* (Austin: University of Texas Press, 1998).

Prince, Stephen, *A New Pot of Gold: Hollywood under the Electronic Rainbow, 1980–1989* (New York: Scribner's, 2000).

Prince, Stephen, ed., *Screening Violence* (New Brunswick, NJ: Rutgers University Press, 2000).

Prindle, David F., *The Politics of Glamour: Ideology and Democracy in the Screen Actors Guild* (Madison: University of Wisconsin Press, 1988).

Propp, Vladimir, *Morphology of the Folktale*, trans. Laurence Scott (Austin: University of Texas Press, 1968).

Pudovkin, Vsevolod, *Film Technique and Film Acting: The Cinema Writings of V. I. Pudovkin*, trans. Ivor Montagu (New York: Bonanza, 1949).

Pye, Douglas, "Genre and Movies," *MOVIE* 20 (Spring 1975), pp. 29–43.

Pye, Douglas, "Bordwell and Hollywood," *MOVIE* 33 (Winter 1989), pp. 46–52.

Pye, Michael, and Lynda Myles, *The Movie Brats: How the Film Generation Took Over Hollywood* (London: Faber, 1979).

Radner, Hilary, and Moya Luckett, eds, *Swinging Single: Representing Sexuality in the 1960s* (Minneapolis: University of Minnesota Press, 1996).

Ramsaye, Terry, *A Million and One Nights: A History of the Motion Picture through 1925* (New York: Simon and Schuster, 1926).

Raubicheck, Walter, and Walter Srebnick, eds, *Hitchcock's Rereleased Films: From Rope to Vertigo* (Detroit: Wayne State University Press, 1991).

Ray, Robert, *A Certain Tendency of the Hollywood Cinema, 1930–1980* (Princeton, NJ: Princeton University Press, 1985).

Rebello, Stephen, *Alfred Hitchcock and the Making of Psycho* (New York: Dembner Books, 1990).

Reid, Mark A., *Redefining Black Film* (Berkeley, CA: University of California Press, 1993).

Reisz, Karel, and Gavin Millar, *The Technique of Film Editing* (New York: Hastings, 1973).

Rhode, Eric, *A History of the Cinema from its Origins to 1970* (Harmondsworth: Penguin, 1978).

Ribuffo, Leo, *Right, Center, Left: Essays in American History* (New Brunswick, NJ: Rutgers University Press, 1992).

Richards, Jeffrey, *The Age of the Dream Palace: Cinema and Society in Britain, 1930–1939* (London: Routledge and Kegan Paul, 1984).

Richards, Jeffrey, ed., *The Unknown 1930s: An Alternative History of the British Cinema, 1929–1939* (London: Tauris, 1998).

Richetson, Frank H., *The Management of Motion Pictures* (New York: McGraw-Hill, 1938).

Riesman, David, *The Lonely Crowd: A Study of the Changing American Character* (New Haven: Yale University Press, 1950).

Rimmon-Kenan, Slomith, *Narrative Fiction: Contemporary Poetics* (London: Methuen, 1983).

Roberts, Kenneth, *Leisure* (London: Longman, 1970).

Roddick, Nick, *A New Deal in Entertainment: Warner Brothers in the 1930s* (London: British Film Institute, 1983).

Rogin, Michael, *Ronald Reagan, the Movie and Other Episodes in Political Demonology* (Berkeley, CA: University of California Press, 1987).

Rogin, Michael, *Blackface, White Noise: Jewish Immigrants in the Hollywood Melting Pot* (Berkeley, CA: University of California Press, 1996).

Rojek, Chris, *Capitalism and Leisure Theory* (London: Tavistock, 1985).

Rollins, Peter C., *Hollywood as Historian: American Film in a Cultural Context* (Lexington: University Press of Kentucky, 1983).

Rollins, Peter C., and John E. O'Connor, eds, *Hollywood's Indian: The Portrayal of the Native American in Film* (Lexington: University Press of Kentucky, 1998).

Romney, Jonathan, and Adrian Wooton, eds, *Celluloid Jukebox: Popular Music and the Movies Since the 50s* (London: British Film Institute, 1995).

Rosen, David, with Peter Hamilton, *Off-Hollywood: The Making and Marketing of Independent Films* (New York: Grove, Weidenfeld, 1990).

Rosen, Marjorie, *Popcorn Venus* (New York: Avon, 1973).

Rosen, Philip, ed., *Narrative, Apparatus, Ideology: A Film Theory Reader* (New York: Columbia University Press, 1986).

Rosen, Philip, *Change Mummified: Cinema, Historicity, Theory* (Minneapolis: University of Minnesota Press, 2001).

Rosenberg, Bernard, and David Manning White, eds, *Mass Culture: The Popular Arts in America* (New York: Free Press, 1957).

Rosenstone, Robert A., *Visions of the Past: The Challenge of Film to Our Idea of History* (Cambridge, MA: Harvard University Press, 1995).

Ross, Murray, *Stars and Strikes: Unionization of Hollywood* (New York: Columbia University Press, 1941).

Ross, Steven J., *Working-Class Hollywood: Silent Film and the Shaping of Class in America* (Princeton, NJ: Princeton University Press, 1998).

Rosten, Leo, *Hollywood: The Movie Colony, the Movie Makers* (New York: Harcourt, Brace, 1941).

Rothman, William, *The "I" of the Camera: Essays in Film Criticism, History and Aesthetics* (Cambridge: Cambridge University Press, 1988).

Ryan, Michael, and Douglas Kellner, *Camera Politica: The Politics and Ideology of the Contemporary Hollywood Film* (Bloomington: Indiana University Press, 1988).

Ryan, R. T., *A History of Motion Picture Colour Photography* (London: Focal Press, 1977).

Said, Edward, *The World, the Text, and the Critic* (Cambridge, MA: Harvard University Press, 1983).

Salt, Barry, *Film Style and Technology: History and Analysis*, 1st edn 1983, 2nd edn (London: Starword, 1992).

Sanders, Don, and Susan Sanders, *The American Drive-In Movie Theatre* (Osceola, WI: Motorbooks, 1997).

Sandler, Kevin S., ed., *Reading the Rabbit: Explorations in Warner Bros. Animation* (New Brunswick, NJ: Rutgers University Press, 1998).

Sandler, Kevin S., and Gaylyn Studlar, eds, *Titanic: Anatomy of a Blockbuster* (New Brunswick, NJ: Rutgers University Press, 1999).

Sante, Luc, and Melissa Holbrook Pierson, eds, *OK You Mugs: Writers on Movie Actors* (London: Granta, 2000).

Sarris, Andrew, *The American Cinema: Directors and Directions, 1929–1968* (New York: Dutton, 1968).

Sarris, Andrew, *You Ain't Heard Nothin' Yet: The American Talking Film, History and Memory, 1927–1949* (New York: Oxford University Press, 1998).

Schaefer, Eric, *"Bold! Daring! Shocking! True!": A History of Exploitation Films, 1919–1959* (Durham, NC: Duke University Press).

Schatz, Thomas, *Hollywood Genres: Formulas, Filmmaking, and the Studio System* (New York: Random House, 1981).

Schatz, Thomas, *The Genius of the System: Hollywood Filmmaking in the Studio Era* (New York: Pantheon, 1988).

Schatz, Thomas, *Boom and Bust: American Cinema in the 1940s* (New York: Scribner's, 1997).

Schickel, Richard, *D. W. Griffith and the Birth of Film* (London: Pavilion, 1984).

Schickel, Richard, *Brando: A Life in Our Times* (London: Pavilion, 1991).

Schwartz, Nancy Lynn, *The Hollywood Writers' Wars* (New York: Knopf, 1982).

Scott, James F., *Film: The Medium and the Maker* (New York: Holt, Rinehart, and Winston, 1975).

Sedgwick, John, *Popular Filmgoing in 1930s Britain: A Choice of Pleasures* (Exeter: Exeter University Press, 2000).

Seidman, Steve, *Comedian Comedy: A Tradition in Hollywood Film* (Ann Arbor: UMI Research Press, 1981).

Seldes, Gilbert, *The Seven Lively Arts* (New York: Sagamore Press, 1924).

Seldes, Gilbert, *The Great Audience* (New York: Viking, 1950).

Sennett, Robert S., *Hollywood Hoopla: Creating Stars and Selling Movies in the Golden Age of Hollywood* (New York: Billboard Books, 1998).

Seydor, Paul, *Peckinpah: The Western Films: A Reconsideration* (Urbana: University of Illinois Press, 1980).

Sikov, Ed, *Laughing Hysterically: American Screen Comedy of the 1950s* (New York: Columbia University Press, 1994).

Silva, Fred, ed., *Focus on The Birth of a Nation* (Englewood Cliffs, NJ: Prentice-Hall, 1971).

Silver, Alain, and James Ursini, eds, *Film Noir Reader* (New York: Limelight, 1996).

Silver, Alain, and James Ursini, eds, *Film Noir Reader 2* (New York: Limelight, 1999).

Silver, Alain, and James Ursini, *The Noir Style* (New York: Aurum, 1999).

Simmons, Garner, *Peckinpah: A Portrait in Montage* (Austin: University of Texas Press, 1976).

Sinclair, Upton, *Upton Sinclair Presents William Fox* (Los Angeles: Upton Sinclair, 1933).

Singer, Ben, "Female Power in the Serial-Queen Melodrama: The Etiology of an Anomaly," *Camera Obscura* 22 (January 1990), pp. 90–129.

Skal, David J., *The Monster Show: A Cultural History of Horror* (New York: Penguin, 1994).

Sklar, Robert, *Movie-Made America: A Cultural History of American Movies* (New York: Random House, 1975).

Sklar, Robert, *City Boys: Cagney, Bogart, Garfield* (Princeton, NJ: Princeton University Press, 1992).

Sklar, Robert, and Charles Musser, eds, *Resisting Images: Essays on Cinema and History* (Philadelphia: Temple University Press, 1990).

Sklar, Robert, and Vito Zagarrio, eds, *Frank Capra and Columbia Pictures: Authorship and the Studio System* (Philadelphia: Temple University Press, 1998).

Slide, Anthony, *The American Film Industry: A Historical Dictionary* (Westport, CT: Greenwood Press, 1986).

Slocum, J. David, ed., *Violence and American Cinema* (New York: Routledge, 2001).

Slotkin, Richard, *Gunfighter Nation: The Myth of the Frontier in Twentieth-Century America* (New York: Harper, 1992).

Smith, Murray, *Engaging Characters: Fiction, Emotion, and the Cinema* (Oxford: Oxford University Press, 1995).

Smoodin, Eric and Ann Martin, eds, *Hollywood Quarterly: Film Culture in Postwar America, 1945–1957* (Berkeley, CA: University of California Press, 2002).

Sobchack, Vivian, *Screening Space: The American Science Fiction Film* (New York: Ungar, 1991).

Sobchack, Vivian, *The Persistence of History: Cinema, Television and the Modern Event* (New York: Routledge, 1996).

Solomon, Aubrey, *Twentieth Century-Fox: A Corporate and Financial History* (Metuchen, NJ: Scarecrow, 1988).

Spellerberg, James, "CinemaScope and Ideology," *Velvet Light Trap* 21 (Summer 1985), pp. 26–34.

Spigel, Lynn, and Michael Curtin, eds, *The Revolution Wasn't Televised: Sixties Television and Social Conflict* (London: Routledge, 1997).

Spoto, Donald, *The Life of Alfred Hitchcock: The Dark Side of Genius* (London: Collins, 1983).

Squire, Jason E., ed., *The Movie Business Book*, 2nd edn (New York: Simon and Schuster, 1992).

Stacey, Jackie, *Star Gazing: Hollywood Cinema and Female Spectatorship* (London: Routledge, 1994).

Staiger, Janet, "The Politics of Film Canons," *Cinema Journal* 24:2 (Spring 1985), pp. 4–25.

Staiger, Janet, *Interpreting Films: Studies in the Historical Reception of American Cinema* (Princeton, NJ: Princeton University Press, 1992).

Staiger, Janet, ed., *The Studio System* (New Brunswick, NJ: Rutgers University Press, 1994).

Stam, Robert, *Reflexivity in Film and Literature: From Don Quixote to Jean-Luc Godard* (New York: Columbia University Press, 1992).

Stam, Robert, *Film Theory: An Introduction* (Malden, MA: Blackwell, 2000).

Stam, Robert, and Toby Miller, eds, *Film and Theory: An Anthology* (Malden, MA: Blackwell, 2000).

Stam, Robert, Robert Burgoyne, and Sandy Flitterman-Lewis, *New Vocabularies in Film Semiotics: Structuralism, Post-Structuralism and Beyond* (London: Routledge, 1992).

Stamp, Shelley, *Movie-Struck Girls: Women and Motion Picture Culture after the Nickelodeon* (Princeton, NJ: Princeton University Press, 2000).

Stanfield, Peter, *Hollywood, Westerns and the 1930s: The Lost Trail* (Exeter: Exeter University Press, 2001).

Stanfield, Peter, *Horse Opera: The Strange History of the 1930s Singing Cowboy* (Urbana: University of Illinois Press, 2002).

Stanislavski, Constantin, *An Actor Prepares*, trans. Elizabeth Reynolds Hapgood, 1st pub. 1936 (London: Methuen, 1988).

Stanislavski, Constantin, *Building a Character* trans. Elizabeth Reynolds Hapgood, 1st pub. 1949 (London: Methuen, 1988).

Stanislavski, Constantin, *Creating a Role*, trans. Elizabeth Reynolds Hapgood, 1st pub. 1961 (London: Methuen, 1988).

Stebbins, Genevieve, *Delsarte's System of Expression* (New York: Edgar S. Werner, 1902; reprinted New York: Dance Horizons, 1977).

Stempel, Tom, *American Audiences on Movies and Moviegoing* (Lexington: University Press of Kentucky, 2001).

Stine, Whitney, *Mother Goddam* (New York: Hawthorne Books, 1974).

Stokes, Melvyn, and Richard Maltby, eds, *American Movie Audiences: From the Turn of the Century to the Early Sound Era* (London: British Film Institute, 1999).

Stokes, Melvyn, and Richard Maltby, eds, *Identifying Hollywood's Audiences: Cultural Identity and the Movies* (London: British Film Institute, 1999).

Stokes, Melvyn, and Richard Maltby, eds, *Hollywood Spectatorship: Changing Perceptions of Cinema Audiences* (London: British Film Institute, 2001).

Strasberg, Lee, *A Dream of Passion: The Development of the Method* (Boston: Little, 1987).

Studlar, Gaylyn, "Discourses of Gender and Ethnicity: The Construction and De(con)struction of Rudolph Valentino as Other," *Film Criticism* 13:2 (1989), pp. 18–35.

Studlar, Gaylyn, "The Perils of Pleasure? Fan Magazine Discourse as Women's Commodified Culture in the 1920s," *Wide Angle* 13:1 (January 1991), pp. 6–33.

Studlar, Gaylyn, *This Mad Masquerade: Stardom and Masculinity in the Jazz Age* (New York: Columbia University Press, 1996).

Studlar, Gaylyn, and Matthew Bernstein, eds, *John Ford Made Westerns: Filming the Legend in the Sound Era* (Bloomington: Indiana University Press, 2001).

Sutcliffe, Thomas, *Watching: Reflections on the Movies* (London: Faber, 2000).

Sweeney, Russell C., *Coming Next Week: A Pictorial History of Film Advertising* (New York: Barnes, 1973).

Talbot, Daniel, ed., *Film: An Anthology* (Berkeley, CA: University of California Press, 1969).

Tasker, Yvonne, *Spectacular Bodies: Gender, Genre and the Action Cinema* (London: Routledge, 1993).

Tasker, Yvonne, *Working Girls: Gender and Sexuality in Popular Cinema* (London: Routledge, 1998).

Taves, Brian, *The Romance of Adventure: The Genre of Historical Adventure Movies* (Jackson: University Press of Mississippi, 1993).

Taylor, Greg, *Artists in the Audience: Cults, Camp, and American Film Criticism* (Princeton, NJ: Princeton University Press, 1999).

Taylor, Richard, and Ian Christie, eds, *The Film Factory: Russian and Soviet Cinema in Documents, 1896–1939* (London: Routledge and Kegan Paul, 1988).

Thomas, Bob, *Brando: Portrait of the Rebel as an Artist* (London: W. H. Allen, 1973).

Thompson, Kristin, *Exporting Entertainment: America in the World Film Market, 1907–1934* (London: British Film Institute, 1985).

Thompson, Kristin, *Breaking the Glass Armor: Neoformalist Film Analysis* (Princeton, NJ: Princeton University Press, 1988).

Thompson, Kristin, *Storytelling in the New Hollywood: Understanding the Classical Narrative Technique* (Cambridge, MA: Harvard University Press, 1999).

Thorp, Margaret, *America at the Movies* (London: Faber, 1946).

Tibbetts, John C., ed., *Introduction to the Photoplay* (Shawnee Mission, KS: National Film Society, 1977).

Toeplitz, Jerzy, *Hollywood and After: The Changing Face of Movies in America* (London: Allen and Unwin, 1974).

Tolkin, Michael, *The Player* (London: Faber, 1988).

Toplin, Robert Brent, *History by Hollywood: The Use and Abuse of the American Past* (Urbana: University of Illinois Press, 1996).

Traube, Elizabeth G., *Dreaming Identities: Class, Gender and Generation in 1980s Hollywood Movies* (Boulder, CO: Westview Press, 1992).

Truffaut, François, *Hitchcock*, revised edn (London: Paladin, 1986).

Tucker, Patrick, *Secrets of Screen Acting* (New York: Routledge, 1994).

Tudor, Andrew, *Theories of Film* (London: Secker and Warburg, 1974).

Tudor, Andrew, *Monsters and Mad Scientists: A Cultural History of the Horror Movie* (Oxford: Blackwell, 1989).

Turim, Maureen, *Flashbacks in Film: Memory and History* (New York: Routledge, 1989).

Turner, Graeme, *Film as Social Practice* (London: Routledge, 1988).

Tuska, Jon, *The American West in Film: Critical Approaches to the Western* (Westport, CT: Greenwood Press, 1985).

Twitchell, James, *Dreadful Pleasures: An Anatomy of Modern Horror* (New York: Oxford University Press, 1985).

Twitchell, James, *Carnival Culture: The Trashing of Taste in America* (New York: Columbia University Press, 1992).

Tyler, Parker, *The Hollywood Hallucination* (New York: Simon and Schuster, 1944).

Tyler, Parker, *Magic and Myth of the Movies* (New York: Simon and Schuster, 1947).

Ulmer, James, *James Ulmer's Hollywood Hot List: The Complete Guide to Star Ranking* (New York: St Martin's Press, 2000).

Vale, Eugene, *The Technique of Screenplay Writing*, 1st pub. 1944 (New York: Grosset and Dunlap, 1973).

Valentine, Maggie, *The Show Starts on the Sidewalk: An Architectural History of the Movie Theatre* (New Haven: Yale University Press, 1994).

Vance, Malcolm, *The Movie Ad Book* (Minneapolis: Control Data Publishing, 1981).

Vanderwood, Paul J., ed., *Juárez* (Madison: University of Wisconsin Press, 1983).

Vasey, Ruth, "Foreign Parts: Hollywood's Global Distribution and the Representation of Ethnicity," *American Quarterly* 44:4 (December 1992), pp. 617–42.

Vasey, Ruth, "The Media," in Mick Gidley, ed., *Modern American Culture: An Introduction* (London: Longman, 1993), pp. 213–38.

Vasey, Ruth, *The World According to Hollywood, 1918–1939* (Exeter: University of Exeter Press, 1997).

Vaughn, Stephen, *Ronald Reagan in Hollywood: Movies and Politics* (Cambridge: Cambridge University Press, 1994).

Vaz, Mark Cotta, and Patricia Rose Duignan, *Industrial Light + Magic: Into the Digital Realm* (New York: Ballantine, 1996).

Vertrees, Alan David, *Selznick's Vision: Gone with the Wind and Hollywood Filmmaking* (Austin: University of Texas Press, 1997).

Vidal, Gore, *Screening History* (London: Abacus, 1993).

Vineberg, Steve, *Method Actors: Three Generations of an American Acting Style* (New York: Macmillan, 1991).

Vizzard, Jack, *See No Evil: Life Inside a Hollywood Censor* (New York: Simon and Schuster, 1970).

Vogel, Harold L., *Entertainment Industry Economics: A Guide for Financial Analysis*, 5th edn (Cambridge: Cambridge University Press, 2001).

Wagenknecht, Edward, *The Movies in the Age of Innocence* (Norman: University of Oklahoma Press, 1962).

Walker, John, ed., *Halliwell's Film Guide*, 8th edn (London: Grafton, 1992).

Waller, Gregory A., ed., *American Horrors: Essays on the Modern American Horror Film* (Urbana: University of Illinois Press, 1987).

Waller, Gregory A., *Main Street Amusements: Movies and Commercial Entertainment in a Southern City, 1896–1930* (Washington, DC: Smithsonian Institution Press, 1995).

Waller, Gregory A., ed., *Moviegoing in America* (Malden, MA: Blackwell, 2002).

Walsh, Andrea S., *Women's Film and Female Experience, 1940–1950* (New York: Praeger, 1984).

Warner, Jack L., with Dean Jennings, *My First Hundred Years in Hollywood* (New York: Random House, 1964).

Wasko, Janet, *Hollywood in the Information Age: Beyond the Silver Screen* (London: Polity, 1994).

Wasko, Janet, *Understanding Disney* (Cambridge: Polity, 2001).

Wasko, Janet, Mark Phillips, and Eileen R. Meehan, eds, *Dazzled by Disney? The Global Disney Audiences Project* (London: Leicester University Press, 2001).

Wasser, Frederick, *Veni, Vidi, Video: The Hollywood Empire and the VCR* (Austin: University of Texas Press, 2001).

Weales, Gerald, *Canned Goods as Caviar* (Chicago: University of Chicago Press, 1985).

Weddle, David, *Sam Peckinpah: "If They Move . . . Kill 'Em"* (London: Faber, 1996).

Weis, Elizabeth, and John Belton, eds, *Film Sound: Theory and Practice* (New York: Columbia University Press, 1985).

Wenders, Wim, *Emotion Pictures*, trans. Shaun Whiteside and Michael Hoffman (London: Faber, 1989).

Wexman, Virginia Wright, "The Critic as Consumer: Film Study in the University, *Vertigo*, and the Film Canon," *Film Quarterly* 39:3 (Spring 1986), pp. 32–41.

Wexman, Virginia Wright, *Creating the Couple: Love, Marriage, and Hollywood Performance* (Princeton, NJ: Princeton University Press, 1993).

Williams, Alan, "Is a Radical Genre Criticism Possible?," *Quarterly Review of Film Studies* 9:2 (Spring 1984), pp. 123–4.

Williams, Linda, *Playing the Race Card: Melodramas of Black and White from Uncle Tom to OJ Simpson* (Princeton, NJ: Princeton University Press, 2001).

Williams, Raymond, *Keywords: A Vocabulary of Culture and Society* (London: Fontana, 1976).

Williams, Raymond, *The Sociology of Culture* (New York: Schocken, 1982).

Willis, Donald C., *The Films of Howard Hawks* (Metuchen, NJ: Scarecrow, 1975).

Wills, Sharon, *High Contrast: Race and Gender in Contemporary Hollywood Film* (Durham, NC: Duke University Press, 1997).

Wilson, George M., *Narration in Light: Studies in Cinematic Point of View* (Baltimore, MD: Johns Hopkins University Press, 1986).

Winokur, Mark, *American Laughter: Immigrants, Ethnicity, and 1930s Hollywood Film Comedy* (London: Macmillan, 1996).

Winston, Brian, *Media Technology and Society: A History from the Telegraph to the Internet* (London: Routledge, 1998).

Wolf, Michael J., *The Entertainment Economy: How Mega-Media Forces Are Transforming Our Lives* (London: Penguin, 1999).

Wolfenstein, Martha, and Nathan Leites, *Movies: A Psychological Study* (Glencoe, IL: Free Press, 1950).

Wollen, Peter, *Signs and Meaning in the Cinema*, 1st pub. 1968, revised edn (London: Secker and Warburg, 1972).

Wollen, Peter, *Readings and Writings: Semiotic Counter-Strategies* (London: Verso, 1982).

Wollen, Peter, *Singin' in the Rain* (London: British Film Institute, 1992).

Wood, Michael, *America in the Movies; or, "Santa Maria, It Had Slipped My Mind!"* (New York: Basic Books, 1975).

Wood, Robin, *Personal Views: Explorations in Film* (London: Gordon Fraser, 1976).

Wood, Robin, *Howard Hawks*, 2nd edn (London: British Film Institute, 1981).

Wood, Robin, *Hollywood from Vietnam to Reagan* (New York: Columbia University Press, 1986).

Wood, Robin, *Hitchcock's Films Revisited* (New York: Columbia University Press, 1989).

Wood, Robin, *Sexual Politics and Narrative Cinema: Hollywood and Beyond* (New York: Columbia University Press, 1998).

Wright, Will, *Sixguns and Society: A Structural Study of the Western* (Berkeley, CA: University of California Press, 1975).

Wyatt, Justin, *High Concept: Movies and Marketing in Hollywood* (Austin: University of Texas Press, 1994).

Žižek, Slavoj, ed., *Everything You Always Wanted to Know about Lacan (But Were Afraid to Ask Hitchcock)* (London: Verso, 1992).

Zucker, Carole, ed., *Making Visible the Invisible: An Anthology of Original Essays on Film Acting* (Metuchen, NJ: Scarecrow, 1990).

Index

180 degree rule 337, 340–1, 360, 364, 410, 578, 580, 584 *see also* line of action
2001: A Space Odyssey 146, 424, 570, 614n.74
3-D 70, 231, 235, 251, 264, 266, 498, 567, 568

Abbott and Costello 566
ABC *see* American Broadcasting Company
Abe Lincoln in Illinois 276, 565
Academy Awards 12, 99, 150–1, 171, 207, 213, 221, 274, 284, 299, 358–9, 378, 394, 410, 438, 440, 562, 564, 568, 571, 580, 626n.101
Academy of Motion Picture Arts and Sciences (AMPAS) 125, 252, 562
Academy ratio 25–7, 320–1, 579, 621n.73
acting 154, 299, 368, 370–1, 378–9, 381–3, 385, 387, 389–92, 394–6, 398–401, 403, 405, 407, 409–12, 563, 564, 567, 569, 630n.44 *see also* blocking; Method acting; performance
acting manuals 382, 395, 402
action movies 12, 21, 75, 77, 103, 108, 216, 218, 259, 269, 419, 428, 430, 453, 486
action sequences 139, 180, 332, 371–2, 378, 407, 409, 411, 451
actors *see* stars
    character 148, 158

    extras 148, 158
Actors Studio 394, 401, 412 *see also* Method acting
actualities 385, 558
adaptations 106, 197, 425, 446, 475
Addams, Jane 272, 523
Adler, Buddy 568
Adler, Stella 393
Adorno, Theodor 39, 44–5, 53, 415, 524, 529
"adult" movies 106, 169, 177
Adventures of Robin Hood, The 47, 565
advertising 78, 82, 88, 90, 123, 141, 145, 149, 163, 177, 182–4, 190, 198, 203, 210–18, 272, 422, 443, 582, 588, 589, 590
Advise and Consent 625n.68
African Queen, The 568
African-Americans 120, 272, 278, 282, 296, 308, 441, 551
"against the grain" viewing 59, 304, 484, 542–3, 554
agents 171, 182, 187, 198
Agony and the Ecstasy, The 380, 570

Aherne, Brian 143
AIP *see* American-International Pictures
Air Force One 269, 576
air-conditioning *see* theaters
Airport 571
Albertson, Lillian 383, 395
Algren, Nelson 106
Alias the Doctor 473, 563
Alice Doesn't Live Here Anymore 572
Alien 183, 356, 573
Alien 3 356, 575
Aliens 100, 291, 574
All Quiet on the Western Front 563
All That Heaven Allows 102, 106, 311, 315–16, 326, 329–30, 352, 359, 362, 364, 568
All the King's Men 49
All the President's Men 297, 387–8, 572
Allen, Karen 356
Allen, Robert 27, 41, 191, 205–6, 225, 468, 470, 520, 552, 560
Allen, Woody 461, 468, 490, 621n.74
Allied Artists 167, 186, 568
Althusser, Louis 302–4, 530–1, 533, 545, 580
Altman, Rick 16, 29, 73, 90, 91, 108–9, 266, 470
Altman, Robert 180, 325, 571
ambiguity 62–3, 96, 234, 236–7, 246, 473, 476, 481, 489, 542
America, Hollywood's representation of 29–30, 520
America Online (AOL) 190, 195, 577
American Beauty 207, 274, 576
American Broadcasting Company (ABC) 195, 568, 570
American Cinematographer 461, 495
American Film Institute 571
American Gigolo 573
American Graffiti 572
American in Paris, An 567
American Multi-Cinema 183
American President, The 576
American Society of Cinematographers 561
American Zoetrope 176, 571
American-International Pictures (AIP) 21, 169–70, 179, 186, 568
Americanization 29–30, 271
AMPAS *see* Academy of Motion Picture Arts and Sciences
AMPP *see* Association of Motion Picture Producers
analogical systems of representation 370, 390, 530, 578, 568, 571, 572 *see also* semiology

anamorphic lens 251
ancillary markets for movies 182, 190–2, 195–6, 198, 209, 224, 225
Anderson, Christopher 172, 188
Andrew, Dudley 32, 53, 109, 234, 460, 501, 523, 527, 532, 555, 591
Andrews, Julie 167
Angel Heart 23, 574
Angels with Dirty Faces 332–3, 565
angle of view 321
animation 28, 122, 161, 206, 209, 237
Annie Hall 468, 572
Antheil, George 461
antitrust laws 125 *see also* legislation; monopoly; oligopoly; Paramount antitrust case; vertical integration
AOL *see* America Online
AOL-Time Warner 190 *see also* America Online
Apartment, The 167, 569
Apocalypse Now 180, 232, 573
Apollo 13 576
apparatus of cinema *see* cinematic apparatus
apparatus theory 534–5, 541, 543, 545, 579, 590
Arachnophobia 75, 575
Arbuckle, Roscoe 404
Argentina 126
ARI *see* Audience Research Institute
Arijon, Daniel 330–1, 341
Aristotle 456, 458, 513
Arkoff, Samuel Z. 169, 568
Armes, Roy 470
Armstrong, R. G. 97–8
Arnheim, Rudolf 498, 523
AromaRama 569
Around the World in Eighty Days 568
art cinema 7, 17, 180, 500 *see also* European cinema
art directors 141, 248, 579, 588
Arthur, Jean 246, 514, 516, 518, 520
artistic motivation *see* motivation, artistic
Arzner, Dorothy 542
Ashby, Hal 180
Ashley, Ted 176, 571
ASL *see* Average Shot Length
aspect ratio 251–2, 254, 579 *see also* Academy ratio; CinemaScope; Panavision
assistant directors 141, 150
Association of Motion Picture Producers (AMPP) 561, 593, 594
Astaire, Fred 40, 58, 474
At Long Last Love 180, 572

attendance 19, 124, 158, 183, 203 *see also* moviegoing
Aubrey, James T. 94, 176
audience *see* audiences; viewers
audience research 524
Audience Research Institute 21
audiences 1, 10–11, 13–14, 16, 18–23, 25–6, 28, 30, 32, 35–9, 44–5, 54–6, 58–60, 63–4, 66–7, 69–72, 76–7, 81, 83, 85–6, 92, 93–5, 101, 104, 106–7, 115–16, 119, 121–3, 138, 142–3, 145, 148, 151, 154–5, 160–1, 168–9, 171–2, 174–5, 177–8, 180–2, 184, 186, 190, 202, 203, 205, 215, 221, 223–5, 235, 238, 241, 250–1, 253, 259, 261, 264, 275, 277, 286–7, 295, 300, 302, 304, 306–7, 311, 327, 329, 344, 346, 358–9, 375, 377, 386, 390, 400, 419, 428, 435, 449, 456, 464, 465, 467–8, 475, 482, 489, 499, 509, 521, 537, 539, 545, 549–50, 552, 553–4, 565, 567, 571, 573, 575, 582, 583, 584, 585, 586, 587, 588, 589, 590, 591, 609n.17, 609n.18
    African-American 121, 156, 239
    children 26, 32, 274
    couples 56
    demographics 25–6, 28, 32, 116, 158, 168, 208, 223 *see also* baby boom; echo boom
    family 20, 23, 27, 81, 163–4, 205, 219, 225, 237, 178, 184, 188
    female 12, 20, 22, 25, 103, 107, 353
    foreign 29
    industry classification of 19–20, 30
    industry perception of 19
    international 28, 30, 180, 246–7 *see also* foreign markets
    juvenilization of 21, 168
    "lost" 47, 162, 168, 251
    male 21, 25, 102
    mass 168
    middle-class 239
    niche 226
    previews 55
    seduction of 57
    tastes 20, 47, 61, 205
    teenage 11, 21, 26, 32, 56, 82, 162, 168–9, 176, 186–8, 207, 257, 357, 583 *see also* juvenile delinquency
    undifferentiated 19, 22, 61, 63, 501
    word-of-mouth recommendations 202, 230
Austen, Jane 455
auteur theory 46–7, 53, 502–3, 506–7, 579

auteurism 46–9, 51, 53, 83, 85, 106, 108, 180, 501–2, 504–7, 513, 521–2, 524, 529, 543, 579 *see also* authorship
    as marketing strategy 506, 509, 522
auteur-structuralism 503–5, 507, 579
authorship 43, 46, 49, 63, 84, 138, 467, 501–2, 506–7, 524, 559 *see also* auteurism
Automatic Dialog Replacement 233
autonomous performance *see* performance
autonomous spectacle *see* spectacle
avant-garde film 7, 254, 327
average shot length (ASL) 622n.82
Ayres, Agnes 406–7

baby boom 22, 25–7, 127, 162–3 *see also* audience demographics; echo boom
Baby Doll 106, 568
Bacall, Lauren 64, 76, 566
Bach, Steven 10, 31, 55
Back Street 103, 563, 565
Back to the Future 436, 437, 591, 634n.32
Back to the Future Part II 146, 423, 437, 574
back-projection 432
Bad and the Beautiful, The 149, 568
Bad Day at Black Rock 294, 568
Badham, John 49
Balaban, Barney 172, 560, 564, 570
Balio, Tino 31, 72, 81, 156, 161, 170, 187–8, 392
Bandido 379, 568
Banky, Vilma 406, 408
Barthes, Roland 501, 503, 506, 529–30, 532–3, 559, 590
Basic Instinct 39, 380, 575
Batman 14, 190, 192, 211, 212, 265, 574, 575, 576, 583
Baudry, Jean-Louis 534, 539, 579
Baxter, Warner 144
Bazin, André 15–16, 47, 53, 95, 229, 231, 233–4, 236–7, 253, 255, 264–5, 319, 327, 337, 341, 360, 375, 498, 501, 539, 591
Beatty, Warren 276, 286, 289, 318–19
Beautiful Blonde from Bashful Bend, The 59, 567
Beckett, John R. 174
Beckett, Samuel 41
Beery, Noah Jr, 519, 520
Begelman, David 176, 572
Bell, Daniel 301
Bellour, Raymond 510
Belsey, Catherine 301, 303
Belton, John 233, 236, 266, 517
Ben-Hur 165, 380, 562, 569

Bender, Lawrence 223
Benjamin, Robert 170, 567
Benjamin, Walter 45, 53, 170, 256, 501, 531, 572
Bergman, Ingmar 41, 179
Bergman, Ingrid 302, 376, 432, 476–7, 479–80, 482, 566
Berman, Pandro 49
Best Man, The 287–8, 291, 297–8, 303–4, 570
Betamax video format 192, 195, 572
Beyond the Valley of the Dolls 177, 571
B-features 81, 121–2, 129, 132–4, 163, 169, 172, 416, 544 *see also* double bills; Poverty Row; programmers
Bicentennial Man 386, 576
Bicycle Thief, The 167
Biehn, Michael 436
Big 574, 613n.32
Big Five 118 *see also* antitrust laws; major companies; oligopoly; vertical integration
Big Knife, The 147, 568
Big Parade, The 421, 562
Big Sleep, The 39, 64, 428, 566, 637n.21
Bigger Than Life 330, 568
Biograph Company 558, 559
biopics 438–9, 579
Birnbaum, Roger 25
Birth of a Nation, The 272, 308, 551, 560
Birth of Venus, The 42–3, 45, 606n.25
Bischoff, Sam 48, 444
Biskind, Peter 188, 268, 308
Black Legion, The 446, 564
Black Pirate, The 36, 562
Blackboard Jungle, The 168, 286, 568
blacklisting 125, 283–4, 624n.43, 624n.57 *see also* Hollywood, alleged Communist influence in; Hollywood Ten; House Committee on Un-American Activities
Blade Runner 55, 237, 573, 614n.74, 625n.85
Blair Witch Project, The 200, 576
Blanke, Henry 446, 448
"blaxploitation" 571
Blockade 275, 307, 565
block-booking 123, 270, 279, 562, 579 *see also* trade practices
Blockbuster video rental chain 422
blockbusters 10, 106, 132, 160–1, 165, 167, 171, 173, 176, 178–9, 181–2, 184, 187, 198, 200, 207, 209, 214, 219, 570, 580, 582, 589
blocking 339, 580, 629n.31
Blow-Up 177

Blue Bird, The 565, 621n.64
B-movies *see* B-features
Bob Roberts 289, 293, 575
Body and Soul 103, 566
Boetticher, Budd 97
Bogart, Humphrey 87–8, 280, 302, 381, 383, 392, 428, 432, 475–9, 482–3, 566
Bogdanovich, Peter 179–80
Bond, James, series 180, 183, 419
Bonnie and Clyde 56, 176, 223, 446, 570
Book of Shadows: Blair Witch 2 200–1, 577
Bordertown 386, 564
Bordwell, David 15, 17–18, 31, 265–6, 316, 341, 347, 349, 353, 366, 450, 453, 458–9, 461–3, 465, 470, 484, 489, 493, 510, 542–3, 545–8, 552, 556, 635n.23
Borges, Jorge Luis 74, 609n.29
Born on the Fourth of July 451, 574
Boston 116, 121
Botticelli, Sandro 42
Bound for Glory 180, 572
Bourget, Jean-Loup 104–5
boutique cinema 507
Bow, Clara 20, 146
box-office
    grosses 134, 203, 214, 230
    seasons 181, 184 *see also* exhibition
Boys in the Band, The 177, 585
Brando, Marlon 284, 346, 393, 396–7, 399, 401, 410, 568
Branigan, Edward 266, 300, 366, 451, 454, 462, 465, 470, 475–6, 586
Brecht, Bertoldt 105, 580
Breen, Joseph 278–9, 294, 297, 304, 473, 481, 571
Brent, George 144
Brewer, Roy 125
Bridge on the River Kwai, The 569
Bridges at Toko-Ri, The 77, 568
Bringing Up Baby 468, 474, 480, 565
Britain 126, 219, 221, 271, 443, 502, 528, 567, 613n.26
British Board of Film Censors 605n.64
Britton, Andrew 82, 295, 354, 359–61, 364, 366, 559
Broadcasting magazine 172
Broadway 19, 21, 247, 253, 396
Broadway 563, 620n.47
Broccoli, Cubby 180
Brook, Peter 368–9
Brooks, Louise 73

Brownstein, Ronald 268, 289, 307
Buchanan, Patrick 441
Buchman, Sidney 624n.43
Bullets or Ballots 87–9, 564
Bullitt 373, 570
burlesque 67, 378, 584
Burr, Raymond 350
Buscombe, Edward 109
Bush, George 274, 289–91
Bushman, Francis X. 403, 559
Butch Cassidy and the Sundance Kid 460, 571
Butler, Terence 98, 385
Bwana Devil 579
Byars, Jackie 102, 109

Cabaret 586
Cable News Network (CNN) 290
Cage, Nicholas 437
Cagney, James 21, 103, 149, 246–7, 333–8, 381, 392, 440, 486, 564
Cahiers du Cinéma 46, 501, 511–12, 524, 531, 543, 579
Cain, James M. 434
California 118, 130, 136, 212–13, 280, 354, 573
California Split 572, 636n.45
Call of the Wild 438–9, 564
camera movement 242, 351, 373–6, 406, 409, 410
camera obscura 320
camera placement 140, 245, 328, 337, 409, 411
  see also composition; framing
camera speed 420
Cameraphone 229, 559
Cameron, James 10, 14, 109, 367, 506
Canada 75, 126, 167, 577
Candidate, The 288–9, 291, 293, 304, 571
Cannon 191, 223, 573, 574
capitalism 38–9, 42, 44–5, 58, 97, 114, 217, 300–1, 415, 472, 487
Capra, Frank 137–8, 277, 279, 336, 525, 626n.112
Captain Blood 564
CARA *see* Classification and Rating Administration
Carné, Michel 513
Carolco 198, 216, 218, 576
Carpenter, John 82
Carrey, Jim 221
Carrie 179, 572
Carroll, John 519
Carroll, Nancy 276

Carroll, Nöel 109, 366, 489, 526, 538, 546, 548–9, 552, 559–60
Carter, Jimmy 286, 290
cartoons *see* animation
Caruso, Enrico 233
Casablanca 47, 134, 139, 302–3, 338, 413, 428, 432, 456, 464, 475–83, 486–90, 513, 554, 566, 637n.20
Casino 576
Cast Away 146, 577
Castle Rock 223, 575
causality 102, 435, 462–4, 467, 469, 485, 590
  see also narrative causality
Cavalcade 378, 564
Cavell, Stanley 109, 468, 475, 480
Caves, Richard 215
Cawelti, John 90, 108
CBS *see* Columbia Broadcasting System
celluloid 7, 227, 369, 415, 421, 485, 583
censorship 47, 60, 62, 125, 167, 246, 271–6, 275, 306, 403, 473–4, 488, 499, 520, 523, 551, 554, 558, 559, 561, 562, 567, 570, 588 *see also* Classification and Rating Administration; Production Code Administration; self-regulation
  federal 270
  political 275, 278–3
  state and local (US) 60, 178, 247, 285
center line *see* 178 degree rule; line of action
Central Casting Corporation 150
CGI *see* computer-generated images
Chabrol, Claude 502
chameleon narrative *see* narrative
Champion 168, 567
Chandler, Alfred D. 113
Chandler, Raymond 6, 349
Chaney, Lon 382
Chang 14, 562
Chaplin, Charlie 121, 381, 498, 560
character movement 242, 376 *see also* composition
Charge of the Light Brigade 48, 443–6, 564
Charisse, Cyd 54, 58, 67, 72
Chase, The 298, 570
Chatman, Seymour 454, 470
Chekhov, Anton 400
Chicago 116, 121, 272, 298, 358, 360, 439, 525, 558, 559, 560
Chinatown 180, 416, 587
choreography 67, 88
Christensen, Terry 277, 289, 308
Cimarron 100, 563

Cimino, Michael 10–11, 180, 506
cinema
  as social institution 6
  invention of 288
  of attractions 13, 372, 390–5, 409, 455, 486, 580
CinemaScope 166, 235, 251, 253–4, 265–6, 354, 398, 568 *see also* widescreen
cinematic apparatus 57, 71, 210, 229, 233, 236, 264, 340, 381, 421, 527, 530, 533–37, 541–5, 544–5, 550, 554, 579, 580, 590, 637n.32
Cinématographe 557
Cineplex Odeon 184, 573, 574, 591 *see also* theaters, multiplex
cine-psychoanalysis 535–40, 542–3, 545–7, 558, 580, 584, 588, 590, 641n.31 *see also* poststructuralism, psychoanalytic criticism
Cinerama 235, 251–3, 264, 320, 327, 567, 569 *see also* widescreen
cine-semiology 530
circus 56, 378
Citizen Kane 256–7, 266, 565
City Slickers 506, 575
Civil Rights 295–6, 308, 441
Clark, Susan 427
class, Hollywood's representation of 11, 14, 100, 247, 270, 278, 295, 300, 306, 359, 543
Classical Hollywood *see* Hollywood, Classical
classification 23, 80, 83, 103, 134, 570, 572, 584, 588
  generic 75, 77, 81, 85, 103
Classification and Rating Administration (CARA) 23–5, 177, 489, 570, 571, 572, 575, 580, 588, 599, 600, 601 *see also* ratings; self-regulation
clearance 121, 123, 171, 194, 196, 580, 591 *see also* distribution; trade practices
Cleopatra 192, 570
Cliffhanger 409, 575
Clifford, James 343–4
Clift, Montgomery 87, 394
Clinton, Bill 291, 441
Clockwork Orange, A 485, 571
Close Encounters of the Third Kind 572
close shot 334–5, 362, 364, 580, 590 *see also* shot scale
close-up 242, 244, 258, 318, 324, 331, 334–5, 337, 364, 368–9, 376, 379, 408–9, 433, 455, 479, 482, 580, 590 *see also* shot scale
closure *see* narrative closure

Clover, Carol 84, 100–1, 110, 356–7, 367, 609n.17, 609n.18, 611n.78
Clueless 218, 576
CNN *see* Cable News Network
Cobb, Lee J. 346, 394
Coburn, James 74, 95, 97–8
Coca-Cola 146, 191, 217, 572, 573, 574, 592
Code and Rating Administration (CARA) *see* Classification and Rating Administration
Coen, Joel and Ethan 607n.42
cognitivism 493, 546–9, 559–60
Cohan, Steven 73, 111, 412, 458–9
Cohen, Arthur 203
Cohn, Harry 49–50, 121, 128, 131, 136, 419, 561
coincidence 12, 38, 150, 232, 291, 416, 423, 425, 428, 435, 464, 478, 484, 486, 489
Colbert, Claudette 336
Cold War 65, 282–3, 285, 448
Colman, Ronald 143
color 105, 228, 236, 241, 248–50, 254, 264, 266, 326–7, 342, 361, 398, 498, 558, 567, 568, 569, 571, 620n.56
  coordination 249–50
  photography 231, 249
  tinting 248–9, 561, 620n.56
Color Purple, The 574
Columbia Broadcasting System (CBS) 570
Columbia Pictures 49, 121, 134–5, 172, 175, 179, 182, 185, 191, 195, 279, 419, 514, 520, 561, 562, 563, 564, 567, 570, 571, 572, 573, 574, 575, *see also* Sony-Columbia
Comanche Station 569
comedy 38, 63, 65, 75, 78–9, 81, 83, 85, 110, 175, 246, 274, 291, 304, 372, 374, 389, 431–2, 438, 456, 467
  screwball 50, 269, 379, 468, 474
  slapstick 51, 77, 584
comic onlooker 349
Coming Home 572
commercial aesthetic 2, 14–16, 30, 42, 45–6, 51–3, 55, 57, 59–60, 63, 71–2, 107, 113, 130, 171, 229, 271, 311, 332, 357, 377, 381, 387, 391, 409, 417, 425, 430, 445, 449, 472, 557, 580, 591
communism 125, 275, 280, 283–4, 287, 301, 551, 566 *see also* Hollywood, alleged Communist influence in
Comolli, Jean 531–2, 540, 542, 544
composition 25, 105, 254, 314, 316–18, 326, 328–30, 334, 340–1, 354, 361, 364, 371,

composition *cont'd*
  375, 377, 583, 585, 589 *see also* camera
    movement; character movement; framing;
    frontality
  conventions of 15
compositional motivation *see* motivation,
    compositional
computer-generated images (CGI) 237, 314,
    588
Coney Island 13
Conference of Studio Unions (CSU) 125, 576
Confessions of a Nazi Spy 276, 281, 446, 565
conglomerates 173–4, 182, 186–7, 192, 195–6,
    211, 228, 241
Congress, US 270, 279, 283, 559, 572
Connecticut Yankee in King Arthur's Court, A
    437, 563, 567
Conquering Power, The 455, 561
Conrad, Joseph 513, 520
conscience-liberalism 282, 286, 296, 299, 304,
    306–7
consumption 36, 56, 59, 71, 130, 150, 154, 202,
    217, 257, 414–15, 421, 468, 488–9, 497,
    500, 502, 514, 522, 532, 546, 557–8
contemporary film theory 535, 547, 559, 580
  see also film theory
continuity editing *see* editing
continuity script 15
continuity system 312, 331, 339–40, 347,
    349–50, 353, 375, 581, 583, 585, 589, 591
continuous performance 55, 133, 165–6, 582
  see also exhibition; time
continuous present 432–3, 435, 437–8, 449,
    455, 463, 466, 469, 581 *see also* tense;
    time
conventions
  generic 76, 100, 104, 106, 297, 311, 319,
    339, 438, 507, 591
  narrative 311, 438, 476
  performance 69, 311, 383, 389, 396
  of representation 63, 95, 232, 390, 463, 589
  of spatial representation 311, 324, 339, 341,
    353–4, 361, 364–5, 431
  temporal 449–50, 465, 585
Conversation, The 180, 572
Cook, David 41, 180
Cook, Pam 493
Cooper, Gary 60, 144, 246, 374, 386, 401, 467,
    566, 568
Cop 574
Coppola, Francis Ford 48, 176, 179–80, 188, 571
copyright 28, 192, 206, 217, 558, 572, 573

industries 190, 195, 217
  protection 260–2, 287, 576
Coquelin, Constant 227, 383
Corman, Roger 19, 179, 571
Corrigan, Timothy 506
Costello, Maurice 403, 559
Costner, Kevin 575
costume 94, 192, 249, 342, 437, 443–4, 446,
    448
couple, the 16, 64, 67, 71, 105, 314, 479, 482
Courtship of Eddie's Father, The 54, 569
coverage 332, 581
crab dolly 257
crane 376, 581 *see also* camera movement
Crash 226, 576
Crawford, Joan 6, 103, 149, 250, 563
crime movies 29, 63, 77–9, 82, 85–8, 91, 109,
    275, 284, 349 *see also* gangster movies
Cripps, Thomas 31, 272, 282, 285, 308
criticism 2, 18, 35, 40–3, 46–7, 52–3, 56, 100,
    103–5, 136, 178, 233, 304–5, 325, 343,
    366, 370–1, 390, 400, 421, 443, 462–3,
    469, 493–8, 501–3, 505–7, 509–11, 513,
    515–18, 520–4, 526, 529–30, 532–3, 535,
    537, 540, 542, 544–6, 549, 551–2, 554,
    581, 583, 591
  auteurist 49, 52, 83, 93, 103, 377 *see also*
    auteur theory; auteurism
  cultural 500
  formalist *see* formalism; neoformalism
  ideological 502, 531–2, 543–4, 558
  reviewing 48, 55, 83, 494–6, 513, 523
  symptomatic 535, 539, 542, 553
  textual 43, 509
Crosby, Bing 438, 468, 565, 566
cross-cutting 245, 581 *see also* editing
Crossfire 283, 285, 567
Crown International 191
Cruise, Tom 36, 49, 574, 575, 577
CSU *see* Conference of Studio Unions
Cukor, George 139
Culkin, Macauley 28
cultural studies 53, 528, 542, 545, 553
cultural verisimilitude 76, 233, 249, 581
culture industry 44, 53, 507, 518, 522
Cunningham, Sean 506
Curtis, Tony 445
Curtiz, Michael 47–8, 138, 486
Custen, George 157, 438–9, 451
cutting on action 375 *see also* editing
cycles 81, 106 *see also* genres
Cyrano de Bergerac 383

Dafoe, Willem 294–5, 298
dailies 69, 137, 141, 589
Dale, Martin 182, 205, 215–16, 225, 520
Daley, Robert 466
Dali, Salvador 67
Damon, Matt 222
Dances with Wolves 99, 422, 575
Dane, Karl 406
Dangerous 386, 564
Dark Passage 567
Dark Victory 145, 565
Darnell, Linda 97
Dave 290–1, 304, 575
David and Bathsheba 165, 567
Davis, Bette 76, 145, 149, 379, 385–7, 392,
    565
Davis, Elmer 282
Day, Doris 467, 569
Dayan, Daniel 341, 346, 539
Days of Thunder 208, 373, 575
De Laurentis, Dino 191, 216, 574
De Niro, Robert 23, 87, 142, 291–2
De Palma, Brian 49
De Vany, Arthur 181, 202, 225
de Wilde, Brandon 96
Dead End 564
"dead media" 263
deadlines 425–7, 433, 435, 449, 487
Dean, James 168, 396, 398–9
Death Wish 298, 572
deCordova, Richard 157, 484
Deep Throat 178, 572
deep-focus cinematography 231, 234, 253,
    256–7, 264, 266, 341, 344, 498
Deer Hunter, The 572
Defiant Ones, The 285, 569
Del Toro, Benico 459
Delaroche, Paul 320
Deliverance 294, 571, 625n.85
Delsarte, François 400, 412, 631n.24
deMille, Cecil B. 146, 165, 561
Deming, Barbara 500, 524
Demme, Jonathan 179
Democratic Party 136, 280, 285–6, 289, 293
deniability, principle of 63, 221, 481
Depardieu, Gerard 216
Department of Justice, US 279, 565, 566
Depression, the 115, 122, 124, 241, 248, 269,
    279–80, 294, 498, 563, 613n.38
depth of field 321–2, 581
Desperately Seeking Susan 494, 574
Destination Tokyo 566

Destroyer 78, 566
detective stories 269, 297
deus ex machina 105, 153, 582
Devil in Miss Jones, The 178, 572
Devine, Andy 86, 150
DiCaprio, Leonardo 11, 12
Dick Tracy 575
Dickinson, Angie 345
Dickson, William K. 228, 561
Diderot, Denis 399
Didion, Joan 130, 171
Die Hard 486, 574, 575
Die Hard with a Vengeance 576
diegesis 371, 456–7, 581, 585
diegetic theories of narration 458–60
Dieterle, William 446
Dietrich, Marlene 251, 541, 627n.8
digital distribution 190, 260, 262–3, 265, 598
    see also e-cinema
digital projection 260, 262, 265
digital systems of representation 261, 370, 390,
    575, 581, 585 *see also* semiology
digital technology *see* technology, digital
Digital Video Disks (DVDs) 190, 194, 228,
    260–3, 414–15, 422, 465, 577, 582,
    633n.25
digressions 426, 449, 464–5
Dika, Vera 89, 356
Diorama 238
directors 9, 39, 46–2, 129–30, 132, 137–8, 155,
    171, 176, 179, 198, 260, 325, 332, 393,
    422, 431, 465, 467, 473, 503, 506–7, 513,
    570, 579, 581, 588 *see also* auteurism;
    authorship
director's cut 261, 415
directors of photography 140, 581
Dirty Dozen, The 570
Dirty Harry 218, 298, 351, 384, 571
disaster movie 11, 14, 292
Disney Company 28, 175, 191–2, 195, 198, 206,
    208–9, 221, 563, 564, 565, 568, 571, 573,
    574, 575, 576
  Disney-ABC 190
Disney, Walt 312, 498, 561, 562
Disneyland 312
dissolve 334, 354, 430–1, 482, 582, 583
distribution 19–20, 22, 60, 62, 80, 83, 113–14,
    116–18, 121, 123–5, 127, 130–2, 136, 145,
    155–6, 159–61, 163, 165, 167, 170–6,
    181–3, 186–7, 190–2, 195–6, 198, 202,
    213–15, 223–8, 230, 238, 259–63, 414, 421,
    545, 559, 560, 562, 563, 567, 568, 569,

distribution *cont'd*
571, 572, 573, 574, 576, 577, 580, 581,
582, 586, 587 *see also* digital distribution;
film exchanges; film rentals; general release;
major companies; saturation release; sleepers;
"tentpole" movies; wide release
zone 121, 123, 580, 592
divorcement 128, 130, 161, 186, 191, 582,
580, 582, 587 *see also* Paramount antitrust
case
Djola, Badja 298
Do the Right Thing 269, 305, 574
Doane, Mary Ann 542, 560
documentary 7, 288, 299, 341, 391, 415, 440,
461, 531
Dog Day Afternoon 425, 572
Doherty, Thomas 187
Dolby 586, 594
Dolby sound systems 233
Don Juan 562
double bills 121–2, 133, 169, 563, 567, 632n.13
see also B-features
double entendre 474–5, 481, 488
Double Indemnity 314–15, 433–5, 459, 566
Dougherty, Eugene 177
Douglas, Kirk 36, 445, 568
Douglas, Michael 295, 380
"drop-off" movies 81
Dr Strangelove 570
Dr Zhivago 570
Dracula 258, 563
drama 75, 77–9, 103, 395, 458, 461, 510, 584
see also genres
drama of false appearances 63, 65, 72
Dreamworks 575, 576
Dressed to Kill 23, 573
Dressler, Marie 563
drive-ins *see* theaters
Driven 373, 486, 577
Driving Miss Daisy 203, 223, 574
Drums Along the Mohawk 438, 565
Dubarry was a Lady 69, 566
dubbing 18, 67, 73
Duel in the Sun 566
Dumb and Dumber 218, 575
Dunaway, Faye 56, 416
Dunn, Michael 428
duration 57, 242, 247, 346, 374, 416, 419–20,
423–4, 449–50, 486, 583, 591 *see also* film
time; movie time
plot 425, 427
story 425, 450

Durbin, Deanna 564
Dust Be My Destiny 293, 565
Duvall, Robert 394
DVD *see* Digital Video Disks
Dyer, Peter John 513–14, 518
Dyer, Richard 37–8, 53, 157, 300, 303, 392,
398, 410, 467, 516–17, 533
Dylan, Bob 94

E.T. 573
Eagleton, Terry 303, 551
early cinema 13, 31, 251, 372–3, 390, 423, 486,
580
Earthquake 236, 572
East of Eden 398, 568
Eastman Kodak 248, 250, 254, 559, 567,
621n.65, 621n.75
Eastmancolor 250, 254
Eastwood, Clint 86, 100, 142, 384, 392, 466–7,
571, 573
Easty, Edward D. 399, 412, 630n.6
Easy Rider 176, 218–19, 360, 571
Eat My Dust 19
Ebert, Roger 55
echo boom 27–8, 205 *see also* audience
demographics; baby boom
e-cinema 260 *see also* digital distribution
Eckert, Charles 543–4
Eco, Umberto 43, 472, 476, 489, 503, 513,
529–30, 550, 590
Edison, Thomas 229, 238, 372, 557, 558, 559,
621n.75
editing 139, 141, 234, 237, 246, 258, 325,
331–2, 334–5, 337, 339–41, 346, 349, 358,
360, 362, 369–71, 373–5, 377–8, 390, 406,
409–11, 430, 459, 462, 465, 467, 469, 512,
530, 536, 586 *see also* suture
continuity 313, 337, 341, 355, 410, 581, 583,
585, 589, 591
editors 62, 141, 261, 333, 581, 582, 589
Eiger Sanction, The 384, 572
Eisenstein, Sergei 13–14, 41, 451, 497
Eisner, Michael 205, 209, 573
El Dorado 570
Elam, Jack 86, 96
Electrical Research Products Inc. (ERPI) 562
Eliot, T. S. 41
Ellis, John 232, 266, 555
Elsaesser, Thomas 31, 55, 340, 391, 485–7, 497,
534, 610n.39
Emmerich, Roland 217
Empire Strikes Back, The 573

entertainment 2, 6, 8, 10, 13–14, 18–19, 30, 33–7, 42, 44, 51–2, 55–9, 61–2, 65–6, 69–72, 82, 106, 124, 132, 136, 155, 159–61, 162–3, 174, 178, 181, 190, 195, 205, 209, 211, 263, 269–70, 272, 275–76, 280–2, 286, 292–3, 295, 297, 300–3, 305–7, 343, 409, 414–15, 424, 435, 443, 449, 453, 469, 472, 479, 487, 494–496, 521, 528, 535, 581, 584, 589, 605n.5
    as apolitical 274, 304
    "correct" entertainment 71
    entertainment industry 8, 35, 191–92, 209, 211, 215, 217, 224–5, 274, 287
    entertainment market 128, 195, 211
    entertainment value 429, 495, 522
Ephron, Nora 19
epics 11, 81, 165–6, 192, 253, 416, 580
Erin Brockovich 577
Ermey, Lee 294
ERPI *see* Electrical Research Products Inc.
Escape 276, 565
escapism 2, 33, 37, 39, 52
establishing shot 244, 324
ethnicity, Hollywood's representation of 302, 308
    see also race
Euripides 104
European cinema 215–16, 223 *see also* art cinema
event movies 184, 202–3, 215, 218, 580, 582
Evil Under the Sun 461, 573
excess 54, 106, 120, 154, 236, 243, 326, 398, 407, 460, 465, 506, 539, 544, 582
    stylistic 376
exchange rates 217
exclusive engagements 166, 171 *see also* exhibition
exhibition 19, 29, 32, 116–18, 122, 126–7, 132–3, 136, 155–6, 159, 161, 163–6, 169–2, 176–8, 181–4, 186, 188, 190–2, 196, 202, 205, 208, 215, 221, 223, 238–9, 253, 260–1, 263, 419, 421–3, 468, 495, 509, 549, 551, 554, 558, 575, 582, 586, 587, 589, 590, 591, 592 *see also* double bills; platform release; presentation cinema; roadshow presentation; theaters, first-run; theaters, multiplex; theaters, neighborhood
    independent 124, 163
Exorcist, The 176, 179, 572
exploitation movies 21, 110, 168–9, 179, 182, 225, 464, 544, 582
expressive space *see* space, expressive
extras 148, 158 *see also* actors

eyeline matching 337, 340, 355, 360, 582, 589
    see also composition; conventions of representation; framing
Eyes Wide Shut 489

fabula 450, 462, 469, 583, 591, 636n.31 *see also* story
fade 431, 473, 482, 583
Fairbanks, Douglas 36, 121, 276, 404, 560
Fairbanks, Douglas Jr 276
Falling Down 276, 308, 428, 575
family movies 27, 205
family, Hollywood's representation of 77, 92, 101, 104, 125, 151, 276, 295, 302, 353, 358–9, 364, 367, 441, 544
Famous Players-Lasky (FPL) 116, 394, 560, 561
fan culture 21
fan magazines 18–20, 67, 70, 142–4, 146, 149–51, 386–7, 444, 482, 495, 520, 559, 640n.84
Fantasia 498, 565
fantasy 58 *see also* public fantasy
Faraday, Michael 229
Farber, Manny 513–14, 518, 523
Fargo 576
Farrell, Charles 21, 241, 243
fashion 14, 59, 126, 145–6, 446
Fassbinder, Rainer Werner 612n.89
Fatal Attraction 39, 55, 574
Father Knows Best 130
Father of the Bride 567, 575
Faulkner, William 140, 157
Faure, Elie 327, 344
Fawcett, George 406
FCC *see* Federal Communications Commission
Federal Communication Commission (FCC) 172, 572
Federal Trade Commission (FTC) 274, 561, 562
femininity, Hollywood's representation of 92, 399, 401, 516, 518, 520–1, 541–2
feminist criticism 100, 110, 359, 366, 391, 441, 507–8, 516, 528, 533, 540–3, 545, 554
    see also cine-psychoanalysis, poststructuralism
Feuer, Jane 71, 73, 109
Fiddler on the Roof 571
Field of Dreams 574
Field, Syd 416–17, 419, 425, 450–1
Fight Club 577
film
    as material 6–7
    gauge 254, 583, 621n.75
Film Daily 156, 474, 561

film exchanges 118, 558
film industry *see* entertainment industry, motion picture industry
film noir 83, 85, 91, 102, 109, 326, 354, 367, 500, 541, 544, 609n.23
film rentals 119, 121, 161 *see also* distribution
film studies 7, 15, 35, 53, 122, 453, 495, 501, 505–6, 511, 513, 518, 530, 540, 543, 545, 583
film theory 347, 497–9, 503, 521, 523, 526–9, 532–3, 535, 537, 541, 543, 545, 548, 553–9, 580, 591 *see also* contemporary film theory
film time 420, 422–5, 427–8, 430, 433, 436, 449–50, 583, 585, 632n.10 *see also* duration, long takes
Final Fantasy: The Spirits Within 237, 577
First Amendment, US Constitution 60, 168, 272, 285, 306, 560, 567
First National Pictures 118, 594
first-run theaters *see* theaters, first-run; exhibition
Fish, Stanley 550
Fitzgerald, F. Scott 31, 40, 136–7, 140, 157, 359, 450
flashbacks 361, 362, 420, 424, 432, 461, 583, 585
Flashdance 25, 573
Fleischer, Richard 379
Flesh and the Devil 72, 562
Flitterman-Lewis, Sandy 470, 537, 555
focal length 321, 337, 583
folk culture 57
folklore 84, 96, 586
Fonda, Henry 95, 287, 303, 318, 386, 426, 487
Fonda, Jane 289, 386, 460
Fonda, Peter 224
Fool There Was, A 560
Foolish Wives 561
For Me and My Gal 268, 566
Ford, Glenn 54, 569
Ford, Harrison 269, 356, 385, 419
Ford, John 41, 84, 95, 102, 176, 179, 332, 385, 498, 503, 610n.52
foreign markets 32, 126–7, 155, 194, 214, 219, 225, 246, 271, 285, 566, 568, 582, 613n.26 *see also* audience, international, international markets
formalism 84–5, 434, 450, 462, 465–7, 469–70, 485, 501–2, 537, 546, 582, 583, 585, 587, 591, 633n.23, 636n.31 *see also* neoformalism

Forrest Gump 440–3, 448, 451, 461, 575
Forster, E. M. 455
Fortune magazine 134, 442
Foucault, Michel 506, 545, 608n.1
Four Horsemen of the Apocalypse, The 422, 561
Fox Film Corporation 118, 144, 241, 520, 559, 560, 562, 563, 564, 565, 567, 568, 569, 574, 594 *see also* News Corporation/Fox
Fox, Michael J. 437
Fox, William 120, 558, 559, 562, 620n.46
Foy, Bryan 82
FPL *see* Famous Players-Lasky *see also* Paramount Pictures
frame cutting 375 *see also* editing
framing 57, 243, 316–18, 330, 334, 340, 459, 461, 467, 583 *see also* composition
France 216, 271
franchises 181, 205, 211–12, 218, 583, 597
Frankfurt School 39, 45, 500
Frederick, Christine 145
Freeman, Y. Frank 565, 569
French Connection, The 298, 571
Freud, Sigmund 101, 528, 533, 535–6, 548
Freudianism 107
Freund, Elizabeth 549
Friday the 13th 82, 357, 506, 573
Friends of Eddie Coyle, The 510, 572
From Here to Eternity 568
frontality 316, 409 *see also* composition
Fugitive, The 575
full shot 335, 364, 583, 590
Fuller, Sam 103
Funny Girl 175, 571
Furthman, Jules 141
Fury 278, 294, 297, 564, 623n.32

Gable, Clark 144, 149, 162, 336, 385, 438–9, 564, 565, 630n.45
Gaines, Jane 453, 470, 555
Gallagher, Tag 85, 95
Gallup, George 21, 276
Gandhi 291, 573
gangster movies 21, 73, 77, 81, 85, 87, 102, 108, 179, 440, 543 *see also* crime movies
Garbo, Greta 72, 151, 217, 392, 563
Garcia, Gustave 402
Gardner, Ava 162
Garfield, John 392, 434
Garland, Judy 8, 147, 268, 437, 456
Garson, Greer 145
Gates, Henry Louis Jr 528
Gaumont Company 558

Gaynor, Janet 8, 21, 143, 146–7, 149–50, 241, 243, 246, 249, 250, 386, 563
Geertz, Clifford 419
gender roles 302–3, 403, 516, 535, 540–2
General Cinema 183
General Electric Company 146, 174, 560–1
General Film Company (GFC) 559
General Motors 132, 138, 146, 212
general release 166, 171, 582 see also distribution
Generation X 222
Generation Y 25, 205 see also echo boom
General Agreement on Tariffs and Trade (GATT) 575
Genette, Gerard 365
genres 74–6, 81–2, 83–9, 91–5, 98–102, 103–9, 142, 179, 228, 423, 438, 443, 583, 609n.23, 609n.33
genre criticism 83, 84, 85, 86, 89, 91, 101, 102, 104, 107, 108, 501, 505, 584
genre recognition 86
genre studies 503
generic classification see classification, generic
generic conventions see conventions, generic
Gentleman's Agreement 283, 567
Gentlemen Prefer Blondes 386, 418, 568
German Expressionism 17
Germany 216, 271
gesture 105, 389, 399–400, 406, 408, 410 see also acting
GFC see General Film Company
Ghost 25, 575
Ghostbusters 574
Gibson, Mel 208, 212
Gilbert, John 69, 72, 168
Gilda 64, 566
Gish, Lillian 384, 392
Gladiator 207, 577
glamour 142
Gledhill, Christine 73, 102, 105, 109, 157, 367, 392, 412, 555
globalization 219–21
G-Men 258, 564
Godard, Jean-Luc 311, 501
Godfather, The 176, 179, 394, 425, 571, 572, 575
Godzilla 208, 212, 576
Gold Rush, The 562
Golden Section 316–17
Goldfinger 180, 570
Goldman, William 31, 188, 205, 454
Goldwyn, Samuel 121, 135, 560, 562, 594

Gomery, Douglas 114, 125, 156, 187, 223, 552, 556
Gone with the Wind 56, 139–40, 165, 385, 565, 630n.45
Good Will Hunting 223, 576
good-bad girl 64
Goodfellas 575
Gordon, Jan and Cora 46
Gorer, Geoffrey 500, 524
gossip 83, 143–4, 152, 495, 523
gossip columnists 65, 142, 147, 387, 495
Gould, Elliot 324–9, 636n.45
Grable, Betty 43, 145, 566
Graduate, The 175–6, 218, 570
Gramercy 220
gramophone 36
Gramsci, Antonio 545
Grand Canyon 254, 276, 575
Grand Hotel 563
Grand Prix 373, 570
Grandeur process 620n.46
Grant, Cary 431, 468, 514, 516, 518–20, 569
Grapes of Wrath, The 565
Grease 572
Great Escape, The 167, 570
Great Gatsby, The 387, 572
Great Lie, The 387, 565
Great Train Robbery, The 86, 558
Greed 561
Green, Richard 144
Greenberg, Clement 40
Greenstreet, Sidney 477
Griffith, D. W. 121, 272, 455, 470, 559, 560, 561
grosses see box-office grosses
Groundhog Day 308, 436, 575
Group Theater 393, 401
Guardino, Harry 426
Guess Who's Coming to Dinner 285, 570
Guilty by Suspicion 276, 575
Gulf and Western 173, 186, 191, 195, 570, 574
Gulf War 291
Gunfighter, The 567
Gunning, Tom 13, 31, 340, 372, 374, 390–1, 525, 580
Gunsmoke 130
Guys and Dolls 568

Hackford, Taylor 49
Hackman, Gene 293–5, 298–9, 304
Hagen, Jean 67, 70, 73
Hale's Tours 562, 629n.18

Hall, Jon 143
Hall, Porter 50
Hall, Stuart 545
Haller, Ernest 249
Halliwell, Leslie 438, 494, 523
Halloween 82, 356, 572
Hamilton, Linda 436
Handel, Leo 77, 524
Hanks, Tom 440, 442
Hannah and Her Sisters 574
Hannibal 75, 422, 577
happy endings 11–12, 16–17, 35, 37–8, 59, 65, 71, 104, 246, 291, 460, 582
Hard Day's Night, A 183
Hard Rain 216, 576
Harding, Warren 274
hardware 173, 192, 195, 211, 214, 223, 261, 263
Hardy, Oliver 122
Harlow, Jean 144, 146
Harry Potter and the Sorcerer's Stone 211, 577
Hart, Gary 286
Hart, William S. 560
Haskell, Molly 516–17
Hauge, Michael 55
Haver, Ronald 154
Hawks, Howard 87, 324–5, 414, 418, 511–13, 515–18, 520, 525
Hawn, Goldie 318–9
Hays, Will H. 60–1, 72, 125–6, 270, 274–5, 293, 473, 496, 561, 566
Hayward, Philip 288, 266
Hayworth, Rita 64, 145, 516
HBO *see* Home Box Office
heads of production 10, 47, 61, 135–6, 141, 157, 247, 331, 333, 419, 444, 473, 561, 563, 564, 566, 569, 570 *see also* studio heads
Heat 87, 576
Heath, Stephen 533, 559
Heaven's Gate 31, 100, 192, 215, 506, 573
Hecht, Ben 140
Hell Night 82, 89, 356, 573
Hell's Angels 563
Henderson, Brian 91
Henie, Sonja 143, 565
Henreid, Paul 476, 477
Henry and June 575
Hepburn, Katherine 151, 246, 468
Herman, Lewis 464, 486
heroism, Hollywood's representation of 34, 38, 92, 95–6, 98–9, 281, 296, 302, 305, 487, 513, 518, 521

Heston, Charlton 376, 380–1, 625n.63
high concept movies 17, 218, 584
"high" culture 44–5
High Noon 31, 374, 568
High Plains Drifter 466–7, 572
High School Confidential 169, 569
High School Hellcats 169, 569
Hills Have Eyes, The 100, 572
Hilmes, Michelle 172, 188, 190
Hirsch, Foster 382, 392, 396, 412
Hirsch, Judd 358
historical pictures 436–48
Hitchcock, Alfred 103, 322, 332, 350, 354–5, 357, 376–7, 414, 424, 429, 431, 435, 461, 478, 486, 503–4, 507–9, 511, 517, 524, 536, 539, 565, 628n.18
Hitler, Adolf 276, 448, 461
Hoffman, Dustin 291–2, 377, 382, 388
Holbrook, Hal 388
Holden, Lansing C. 249
Holden, William 140, 435, 568
Holland 216
Hollywood *see also* Los Angeles; motion picture industry
accounting 210, 225
alleged Communist influence in 125, 283, 306 *see also* blacklisting; Hollywood Ten; House Committee on Un-American Activities
as "art industry" 44
as commercial institution 1, 264
as Utopian 12, 29–30, 35, 37–8, 52–3, 70, 152, 154, 247, 267, 269, 294, 300, 303, 312, 339, 437, 520
Classical 15–18, 20–2, 25, 28, 30–2, 62, 72, 102–4, 107, 109, 122, 128, 132, 147–8, 155–60, 164, 184, 187, 190, 192, 196, 212, 220, 259, 265, 316, 328, 331, 335, 341, 347, 349, 353, 357–8, 365–7, 385, 391, 395–396, 399, 407, 411, 421, 424, 429, 431, 449, 453, 465, 470, 484, 488–9, 507–8, 518, 523, 525, 542, 544, 546, 554, 556, 579, 580, 581, 582, 583, 584, 585, 587, 588, 589, 591, 592 *see also* studio system
multiple logics of 46, 49, 51, 171, 255, 276, 285, 328, 467, 553
New 14, 17, 53, 173, 176, 187–8, 192, 228, 230, 339, 366, 416, 451, 506, 524
post-Classical 25, 220
sociological studies of 499
Hollywood Anti-Nazi League 280, 564

Hollywood Renaissance 48, 161, 176, 178, 187, 358, 571
Hollywood Reporter 495, 563
Hollywood shot 335, 590
Hollywood sign 5, 31, 561
Hollywood Ten 283, 566–7, 569 *see also* blacklisting; Hollywood, alleged communist influence in; House Committee on Un-American Activities
Home Alone 27–8, 575
Home Box Office (HBO) 195, 572
home cinema 6, 37 *see also* video
Home of the Brave 168, 285, 567
Hook 575
Hope, Bob 468, 574–5, 567
Hopkins, Anthony 212, 355, 556
Hopper, Dennis 219
Hopper, Hedda 495
Horkheimer, Max 39, 44–5, 53, 415, 524
Hornblow, Arthur 144
horror movies 75, 77, 79, 81, 83–5, 88, 100–1, 108, 110, 169, 179, 251, 340, 356–8, 364, 366–7, 563, 609n.17, 611n.78, 628n.32
Hot Rod Girl 169, 568
House Committee on Un-American Activities (HUAC) 283–4, 286, 307, 539, 565, 566, 567, 624n.43 *see also* blacklisting; Hollywood, alleged communist influence in; Hollywood Ten
Houston, Penelope 355
How to Marry a Millionaire 163, 253, 568
Howard, Bronson 379
Howard, Leslie 144
Howard, Ron 506
HUAC *see* House Committee on Un-American Activities
Hudson, Rock 102, 106, 316, 352, 569
Hughes, Howard 118, 162, 567, 568
Humanophone 238
Hunchback of Notre Dame, The 561
Hunter, Kim 396
Hurricane 143, 564, 577
Hutton, Betty 145, 358
Huxley, Aldous 140, 157
Huyssen, Andreas 104

I Am a Fugitive from a Chain Gang 272, 275, 294, 297, 563
I Married a Communist 567
I Spit on Your Grave 100, 572, 625n.85
I Was a Teenage Werewolf 22, 569

IATSE *see* International Alliance of Theatrical and Stage Employees
IBM 261
Ibsen, Henrik 400
iconography 28, 86–7, 89, 94, 108, 206, 423, 584
identification 102, 347, 357, 360, 365–6, 368, 485, 538, 584
ideological criticism *see* criticism, ideological
ideology 16, 45, 99, 268, 287, 300–4, 307, 320, 362, 364, 446, 348, 502, 516–17, 520–1, 530–3, 535, 539, 541–5, 547, 554
Ihnat, Steve 426
illusion of movement 371, 420, 432, 455, 581, 587 *see also* perception; persistence of vision
Imitation of Life 103, 315–16, 330, 564, 569, 612n.89
"impact" edit 360, 584
In Old Chicago 438, 565
In the Heat of the Night 294, 298, 570
Independence Day 576
Independent Motion Picture Company 559 *see also* Universal
independent production *see* production, independent
Indiana Jones and the Temple of Doom 574
innovation 179, 584
integrated performance *see* performance, integrated
Intel 261
interchangeability 59–60, 145
International Alliance of Theatrical and Stage Employees (IATSE) 125
international audience *see* audiences, international
international market 165, 194, 214, 216–17, 223–5, 589 *see also* foreign markets
Internet Movie Database 451
Internet, the 190, 195, 211, 256, 261–3, 267, 451, 576
intertextual motivation *see* motivation, intertextual
intertextuality 60, 206, 584
intertitles 242, 246, 407, 409–10, 431, 455–6, 460, 584
Intruder in the Dust 285, 567
Invasion of the Body Snatchers 463, 568
Ipcress File, The 637n.32
Irma La Douce 167, 570
Iron Horse, The 86, 561
It Can't Happen Here 271
It Happened in Springfield 275, 566
It Happened One Night 336, 418, 564

It's a Wonderful Life 437, 566
Italy 216, 271, 286, 566

Jackson, Samuel L. 223
Jacobs, Lea 62, 72, 341, 489, 637n.21
Jaglom, Henry 39
Jameson, Frederic 510
Japan 216, 573, 613n.26, 619n.36
Jason X 82, 577
Jauss, Hans Robert 550
Jaws 178, 183, 356, 572
Jaws 2 572
Jazz Singer, The 239, 562
Jenkins, Henry 110, 237, 271
Jerry Maguire 576
JFK 276, 290, 451, 575
Johnny Guitar 568
Johnson, Lyndon 286, 295, 442
Johnson, Van 76
Johnston, Eric 566, 570
Jolson, Al 49, 151, 239, 566
Jolson Story, The 49, 566
Jones, Shirley 54
Joslyn, Allyn 520
journalists 141, 282
Jowett, Garth 72, 524
Joy, Jason 63, 272, 474
Juárez 276, 281, 443, 446–2, 565
Jungle Fever 305, 575
Jurado, Katy 375
Jurassic Park 190, 206, 211, 212, 373, 488, 575, 576, 577, 633n.25
juvenile delinquency 164, 168–9, 272, 286
   see also audiences, teenage

Kael, Pauline 7, 496
Kafka, Franz 41
Kalmus, Natalie 249–50
Kaplan, Jonathan 179
Kapsis, Robert 357
Katz, Steven D. 341, 375, 560
Katzenberg, Jeffrey 198, 209, 573, 577
Katzman, Sam 168–9
Kazan, Elia 396, 624n.58
Keaton, Buster 381
Keaton, Diane 276, 490
Keats, John 422–3, 455
Keeler, Ruby 151
Kefauver, Estes 277
Kellner, Douglas 359
Kelly, Gene 58, 66–7, 69–70, 73, 268, 313–15
Kelly, Grace 162, 452, 510, 568

Kennedy, John F. 286, 290, 295, 442, 625n.68
Kennedy, Robert 531
Kennedy, Joseph P. 413, 562
Kent, Sidney 127, 563
Kerkorian, Kirk 570, 573, 574, 576
Kershner, Irving 179
Keystone Company 559
Kinetophone 238, 559
Kinetoscope 228–9, 557
King Kong 564
King of Kings, The 562
King, Martin Luther 286, 531
Kingsley, Ben 291
Kinney National 174, 570
kitsch 40, 44
Kitses, Jim 90–2, 100, 109
Klaprat, Cathy 386, 392
Kleine Optical Company 78
Kline, Kevin 290
Klinger, Barbara 49, 81, 83, 106–7, 109, 262, 340, 386, 464–5, 470, 544, 548–9, 552, 556
Klumph, Inez and Helen 383, 399
Klute 460–1, 571, 635n.23
Knapp, Lucretia 510
Korean war 77
Koszarski, Richard 31, 156
Kozloff, Sarah 266, 455, 461, 470
Krämer, Peter 392
Kracauer, Siegfried 500, 524
Krämer, Peter 31, 109
Kramer, Stanley 168, 285
Kramer vs Kramer 359, 573
Krim, Arthur 170, 175, 286, 567, 572
Kristofferson, Kris 96–8
Ku Klux Klan 272, 294, 298
Kuhn, Thomas 510
Kuleshov, Lev 368–70, 391

labor relations *see* motion picture industry; unions
Lacan, Jacques 503, 530, 533, 535–7, 543
Ladd, Alan 96
Ladd, Diane 416
Lady in the Lake 349, 566
Laemmle, Carl 137, 559, 564
Lake, Veronica 52
Lancaster, Burt 567
Lang, Fritz 103, 525
Langella, Frank 291
Lansing, Sherry 573
Lara Croft: Tomb Raider 211, 577
Larner, Jeremy 289
laser disks 415

Lasky, Jesse 136, 559, 560, 562, 563
Last Action Hero, The 269, 575
Last of the Mohicans, The 100, 575
Last Picture Show, The 571
Last Tango in Paris 178
Last Tycoon, The 31, 137, 157
Lastra, James 232, 266
Laurel, Stanley 122
Lawrence, Amy 233
Lawrence, Florence 559
Lawrence, Martin 223
Le Grice, Malcolm 327
LeBeau, Madeleine 477
Lee, Spike 305, 346
Legion of Decency 412, 564, 570
legislation 23, 127, 180, 218, 261, 270, 274, 287, 306, 499 *see also* antitrust laws
"legitimate" theater 378, 584
Lehman, Ernest 355
Leigh, Janet 354, 376
Leigh, Vivien 396
Leighton, Margaret 287
leisure 20–1, 35, 39, 57, 160, 163, 414–15, 449
    leisure industries 57, 71
Leites, Nathan 38, 53, 63, 65, 349, 500, 524
Lemmon, Jack 445, 570
LeRoy, Mervyn 332
Lethal Weapon 2 429, 574
Lethal Weapon 4 212, 576
Lévi-Strauss, Claude 84, 503, 505, 515, 529, 586, 591
Levinson, Barry 292
Lewis, Jerry 389, 428, 493, 568
Lewis, Jon 32, 178, 188, 225, 489, 524
Lewis, Sinclair 271
Life of Emile Zola, The 446, 496, 564
lighting 85, 88, 140, 248–9, 256, 313, 326, 328, 354, 361, 400, 459, 513, 544, 582, 590
Linderman, Deborah 545
Lindsay, Vachel 497, 523
line of action 328, 337, 567, 584, 571 *see also* 180-degree rule
Lion King, The 575
lip-synchronization 68, 239 *see also* sound
Little Caesar 81, 87, 109, 563
Little Mermaid, The 206, 542, 574
Little Three 121 *see also* major companies; oligopoly
Little Women 564
Lloyd, Harold 355, 561, 594

Lloyd, Christopher 423, 437
Loew, Marcus 113, 559, 561, 562, 563, 564, 568
Loew's, Inc. 118, 121, 569 *see also* Metro-Goldwyn-Mayer
Long Goodbye, The 159, 324–5, 572
Long Hot Summer, The 294, 569
long shot 317, 334–5, 375–6, 379, 409, 411, 582, 584, 585, 590 *see also* shot scale
long takes 332, 346, 374, 377, 585, 591 *see also* duration; film time
Long Voyage Home, The 276, 565
Longest Yard, The 424, 572
look, the 344, 346, 351, 366, 540–1, 583, 584, 590
Lord of the Rings, The: The Fellowship of the Ring 237, 577
Lord, Daniel A. 62, 343, 472
Lorre, Peter 476
Los Angeles 5, 8–9, 114, 118, 121, 126, 130, 172, 203, 213, 214, 224, 264, 280, 416, 559, 560
Lost Boundaries 285, 567
Lost Horizon 49, 520, 564
Lost World, The 206, 576, 597
Love Bug, The 175, 571
love stories 70, 77, 276, 439, 476 *see also* romance
Love Story 176, 571
Love, Montague 406–7
Lovell, Terry 232, 265
Loy, Myrna 144
Lubitsch, Ernst 213, 572
Lucas, Paul 49, 198
Lucas, George 259
Lucasfilms 208
Lumière, Louis and Auguste 340, 629n.17

M*A*S*H 177, 571
MacArthur, Charles 108, 140
MacCabe, Colin 455, 460, 635n.23
McConnell, Frank 145, 369–71, 379, 381, 392
McCrea, Joel 50
MacDonald, Dwight 44, 46, 53
MacDonald, Jeanette 439
McDonald's 206, 576
McDormand, Frances 297
MacDowell, Andie 436
McDowell, Malcolm 485
McGovern, Elizabeth 358
McGovern, George 286

"MacGuffin," the 478–9
McKee, Robert 416, 450
MacMurray, Fred 314, 433
McQueen, Steve 373
McWilliams, Carey 131, 280
Madame Curie 145, 566
Madigan 425–8, 570
Maeder, Edward 342, 444
Magnificent Seven, The 167, 183, 569
major companies 18, 20–1, 23, 25, 32, 114,
    117–18, 121, 123–34, 157–6, 159–61,
    163, 165, 169–77, 179, 181–2, 185–9,
    191, 193–4, 196, 203, 208–9, 211, 213,
    215–17, 220–4, 241, 248, 252, 260, 262,
    274, 446, 506, 561, 563, 564, 565, 566,
    567, 568, 569, 570, 571, 572, 573, 574,
    580, 582, 590 *see also* Big Five; Little
    Three; mini majors; oligopoly;
    vertical integration
Malcolm X 305, 575
Malden, Karl 53, 294, 394
Male and Female 561
Malone, Dorothy 331, 637n.21
Malpaso Company 142
Maltese Falcon, The 383, 565
Man Who Shot Liberty Valance, The 95, 297, 569,
    626n.95
Man with the Golden Arm, The 106, 171, 568
Manchurian Candidate, The 569
Manhattan 573, 621n.74
March, Frederic 150
Marion, Frances 10, 149, 157
Marked Woman 543, 564
marketing 20, 25, 28, 36, 83, 126, 132, 160–1,
    169, 174, 178, 180–2, 187, 189, 192, 198,
    207, 207–9, 217, 220–1, 261, 263, 272,
    357, 387, 410, 415, 445, 506–7, 595, 598,
    584
    costs 160
Marnie 510, 570
Martin, Dean 386, 389, 568
Martin, Steve 428
Marty 168, 171, 568
Marx Brothers 69, 246, 428
Marx, Karl 528, 548
Marxism 14, 45, 302, 500, 528, 530, 533, 535,
    553, 580
Mary Poppins 584
masculinity, Hollywood's representation of 287,
    401, 404, 516–18, 520
Mask of Dimitrios, The 39, 566
masochism 404

mass culture 28, 30, 35, 40, 44, 104, 272, 415,
    500
Mast, Gerald 53, 72, 109, 506, 517, 524–5, 559
matinee idols 403
Matisse, Henri 47
Matrix, The 236, 414, 424, 428, 577
Matsushita Company 195, 211, 215, 575, 576
Mature, Victor 97
Max Factor 249
Mayer, J. P. 75, 77
Mayer, Louis B. 133–6, 152, 185, 379, 561,
    578
MCA *see* Music Corporation of America
meanings
    dialectical 369
    "subversive" 488, 544
    unstable 63
mechanical reproduction 45, 229, 233, 320
    see also technology
medium shot 317, 324, 335, 346, 352, 585, 590
Medved, Michael 307
Meet John Doe 386, 575
Meet Me in St Louis 576
Mekas, Jonas 327
melodrama 39, 78, 83, 101–3, 105–6, 108, 150,
    284, 361, 364, 398–400, 407, 510, 513,
    519, 544, 609n.23 *see also* genres
Memento 627n.8
Men In Black 576
Menjou, Adolphe 150, 154
merchandising 27, 168, 174
mergers 118, 175, 194–5, 209–10, 212, 226,
    563
Merleau-Ponty, Maurice 550
Metalious, Grace 106
Method acting 377, 393–401, 409–12, 630n.6,
    631n.20 *see also* acting; Actors Studio
Metro-Goldwyn-Mayer (MGM) 49, 61, 93, 118,
    121–2, 134–5, 138, 139, 143, 146, 148,
    162, 167, 177, 180, 182, 185, 288, 247,
    271, 278, 406, 561, 563, 564, 565, 567,
    568, 569, 573, 574, 575, 576 *see also*
    MGM/UA
MGM/UA 191, 574, 575, 576
Metz, Christian 366, 451, 527–30, 536–9, 552,
    555, 579
MGM *see* Metro-Goldwyn-Mayer
Microsoft 261
Midnight Cowboy 571
Midsummer Night's Dream, A 564
Milchan, Arnon 212
Mildred Pierce 47, 566

Miller, Arthur 53, 146, 156–9, 624n.58
Milliken, Carl 14
mimesis 456–8, 570, 571
mimetic theories of narration 458, 571
mimetic properties of cinema 231–2
mini-majors 191, 223 *see also* major companies
Miracle, The 168, 285, 567
Miramax 224–5, 575
mise-en-scène 328–30, 332, 340–2, 360–1, 364, 371, 375, 390, 406, 409–11, 426, 429, 431, 444, 449, 462, 464, 471, 502, 517, 536, 585, 586
mise-en-temps 429, 431–2, 435, 449, 585
Mission: Impossible 576, 577
Mission: Impossible II 36
Mission to Moscow 282, 575
Mississippi Burning 269, 293–299, 304–6, 574, 626n.95, 626n.101
Mitchell, Millard 67
Mitchum, Robert 326, 378–9, 510
Mitry, Jean 527
Modern Hero, A 332, 564
Modern Screen magazine 142, 146
Modernism 327, 500
Modleski, Tania 357, 507, 545
Mogambo 162, 568
moguls 136–7, 157, 176, 280, 286, 293
Moholy-Nagy 327
monocular perspective *see* perspective, monocular
Monogram Pictures 121, 563, 564, 568
monopoly 118, 127, 134, 155, 161, 248, 279, 559, 582, 621n.75 *see also* antitrust laws; major companies; oligopoly; Paramount antitrust case
Monroe, Marilyn 386–7, 418, 445, 541
montage 13, 234, 294, 369, 391, 536, 585
montage sequence 152, 294, 440, 497
Soviet 17, 497
Montgomery, Robert 349, 383–4
Monthly Film Bulletin 75
Moon is Blue, The 171, 568
Moore, Mary Tyler 358, 360
Morgan Creek 218
Morley, David 29
Morocco 7, 533, 541, 563
morphing 236–7, 593
Mortal Storm, The 276, 565
Mosjoukine, Ivan 368–9
Motion Picture Alliance for the Preservation of American Ideals 566
Motion Picture Artists' Committee 280

Motion Picture Association (MPA) 585
Motion Picture Association of America (MPAA) 23, 27, 32, 78, 177, 187, 210, 225, 285–6, 566, 570, 572, 580, 586, 588, 608
see also Motion Picture Producers and Distributors of America, Inc.
Motion Picture Democratic Committee 280
Motion Picture Export Association (MPEA) 127, 566, 585, 586
Motion Picture Herald 20, 169, 271, 275, 495, 496
motion picture industry 18, 20, 29, 45, 49, 60, 77, 86, 93, 114–16, 125–6, 131, 134, 136, 155, 165, 172, 190, 192, 219, 255, 259, 261, 271, 274, 278, 283, 311, 387, 495, 522, 539, 549, 563, 582, 585, 593, 594, 613n.38
"major independent" companies 226
alleged Jewish dominance of 136, 157
alleged Communist influence in *see* Hollywood, alleged Communist influence in
consolidation 192
convergence 190, 263
deregulation 215, 286
diversification 160, 174, 186, 191–2
financing 220
horizontal integration 192
investment in 114–15, 179, 219
labor relations in 125 *see also* unions
ownership of 115
pickup deals 225
tax shelter financing 179, 219, 572
vertical integration of 118, *see also* major companies; vertical integration
workforce 114, 130
Motion Picture magazine 520
Motion Picture Patents Company (MPPC) 117, 558, 559, 560
Motion Picture Producers and Distributors of America, Inc. (MPPDA) 62, 116, 125, 127, 155, 274, 276, 285, 306, 524, 561, 562, 566, 585, 586, 593 *see also* Motion Picture Association of America
Motion Picture Research Bureau 77
motivation 76, 429, 438, 460, 466–9, 475, 579, 581, 584, 585, 589
artistic 467, 579, 585
character 232
compositional 466, 468, 581, 585, 633n.25
intertextual 467, 471, 584, 585
narrative 413
realistic 361, 467, 585, 589

Moulin Rouge 261, 577
MOVIE 31, 53, 365, 502, 547, 556
Movie Brats 188
movie theaters *see* theaters
movie time 420, 423–5, 427, 429–30, 435–6,
  449–50, 585 *see also* film time
moviegoing 55, 126, 159, 165, 179, 183, 192,
  208, 251, 253, 472, 499, 536 *see also*
  attendance
movies
  as culturally affirmative 61
  as experience 7
  as software 414
  emotional effect of 54–5
  sociological studies of 499
Moving Picture World 558
Moviola 258
MPAA *see* Motion Picture Association of
  America
MPEA *see* Motion Picture Export Association
MPPC *see* Motion Picture Patents Company
MPPDA *see* Motion Picture Producers and
  Distributors of America, Inc.
Mr Deeds Goes to Town 49
Mr Smith Goes to Washington 245, 277, 279, 281,
  289–90, 300, 303, 308, 565
Mrs Miniver 566
Mulvey, Laura 105, 353, 366, 540–2, 552, 555
Mummy, The 59, 563, 577
Mummy Returns, The 200, 230, 577
Muni, Paul 294, 446
Münsterberg, Hugo 497, 523
Murch, Walter 232, 341
Murdoch, Rupert 195, 574
Murphy, Eddie 384, 574
Murray, Bill 436
music
  narrative role of 461
  non-diegetic 371, 431, 581
Music Corporation of America (MCA) 171,
  173–5, 191, 195, 211, 286, 569, 572, 574,
  575, 576
music video 334, 376
musicals 21, 29, 44, 50–1, 58, 65–71, 73, 75,
  77, 79, 81, 83, 84–5, 88, 110, 133, 145,
  147, 166, 175, 239, 241, 250, 264, 268–9,
  314, 372–3, 377–8, 407, 429, 435, 438,
  440, 449, 453, 461, 469, 474, 532, 579,
  580
  backstage 68–9, 468
Mussolini, Benito 135, 448
Mutiny on the Bounty 167, 438–9, 564, 569

Mutual Film 221, 560
My Darling Clementine 92, 96, 98, 317–18, 487,
  610n.52
My Man Godfrey 269, 564
Myra Breckinridge 177, 571
mystery movies 77–9, 461, 465
myth 84, 98, 99, 108, 505, 519, 529, 586
mythical kingdoms 519
mythology 84, 91–3, 96, 99, 147, 500

NAMPI *see* National Association of the Motion
  Picture Industry
Napster 262
Narboni, Jean 531–3, 540, 542, 544
Naremore, James 53, 109, 367–8, 370, 381,
  384, 389, 392, 399, 406, 507, 524,
  629n.31
narration 313, 324, 327, 331, 339, 347, 349–50,
  352, 360, 381, 395, 401, 410–11, 416, 425,
  428, 433–4, 437, 449, 454–6, 458–9,
  461–2, 465–6, 468–71, 475, 478, 482,
  488–9, 547, 586
narrative 7, 13, 15–17, 30, 56, 61, 84–5, 88,
  100–1, 102, 242, 259, 328–9, 366, 372,
  375–6, 388, 409, 416, 423–4, 428, 431,
  449–10, 452–74, 476–8, 482–89, 502, 530,
  534, 537, 541, 547, 558, 579, 585, 586,
  596
  causality 453, 455
  chameleon 476, 479
  closure 297, 426, 453, 478, 483, 486–7, 489,
    544
  conventions *see* conventions, narrative
  omniscience 347, 455, 461, 469, 587
  motivation *see* motivation, narrative
  theory 456, 458
narratology 454, 470, 586
Nash, Ogden 137
Nashville 180, 375, 572
National Association for the Advancement of
  Colored People 285
National Association of the Motion Picture
  Industry (NAMPI) 560
National Association of Theater Owners (NATO)
  177, 296, 586, 600
National Board of Censorship 559–60 *see also*
  censorship; self-regulation
NATO *see* National Association of Theater
  Owners
Natural Born Killers 575
naturalism 248, 382, 394, 396, 399, 401, 407–8,
  410–11, 498, 586, 587

Neale, Steve 59, 72, 76, 83, 91, 109, 225, 249, 265–66, 320, 609n.33
negative cost 196, 210, 586
negative pickup 587
Negri, Pola 73
neighborhood theaters *see* theaters, neighborhood; *see also* exhibition
neoformalism 462, 470, 516, 546–9, 558, 583, 587 *see also* formalism
neo-realism 41
Network 588
New Deal 281–3, 307
New Historicism 549
New Hollywood *see* Hollywood, New
New Line Films 191, 225–6, 292, 575, 576
New Theatre and Film 497, 523
New Wave 41, 502, 524
New World Pictures 179, 571
New York 20, 36, 72, 117, 121, 130–1, 137, 168, 172, 174, 178, 191, 203, 242, 246, 276, 285, 341, 372, 392–3, 412, 428, 460, 483, 489, 520, 543, 557, 558, 560, 561, 568, 580
New York, New York 180, 572
Newman, Paul 571
News Corporation 190, 195
newsreels 122, 161, 190, 280, 442, 562
Nichols, Bill 341, 366, 547, 555
Nicholson, Jack 179, 224, 392, 416
Nicholson, James H. 169, 568
Nickelodeon magazine 16
nickelodeons 118, 558
Night and Day 439, 566
Night Moves 180, 572
Night Must Fall 383
Nightmare on Elm Street 221
Ninotchka 59, 65, 565
Niven, David 143
Nixon 576
Nixon, Richard 179, 286, 442
No Down Payment 169, 569
No Way Out 285, 567
Nocturna 75, 573
non-diegetic music *see* music, non-diegetic
"non-drop-off" movies 28, 81
North by Northwest 384, 430–1, 510, 569
North Star 566
North, Sheree 427
Notorious 376, 566
Novak, Kim 512
novelty 70, 76, 82, 83, 107, 145, 202, 236, 253, 258, 265, 417, 423

Now Voyager 385, 392, 566
Nugent, Frank 303

O Brother, Where Art Thou? 204, 230, 577, 607n.42
O. C. and Stiggs 180, 590
O'Brien, Margaret 621n.64
O'Brien, Pat 333
O'Connor, Donald 58, 67, 69–70, 373–4, 378, 381, 393, 459
Objective Burma 566
obsolescence 263
Ocean's 11 250, 569
October Films 221, 576
Odlum, Floyd 293, 564, 566
Of Human Bondage 386, 564
offcasting 387
Office of War Information (OWI) 282, 303, 565
Officer and a Gentleman, An 359, 573
Ogle, Patrick J. 256, 266
Oklahoma! 75, 568
Old Wives for New 560
oligopoly 118, 155, 159, 173, 274, 588, 587, 592 *see also* antitrust laws; major companies; monopoly; Paramount antitrust case
Olivier, Laurence 377, 382
Omen, The 179, 572
On Golden Pond 359, 573
On the Town 567
On the Waterfront 284, 294, 346, 394, 410, 568, 624n.58
Once Upon a Time in America 420, 574
One Flew Over the Cuckoo's Nest 180, 572
O'Neill, Eugene 513
Only Angels Have Wings 511–21, 565
Ordinary People 358–1, 364, 573
Orion 191, 223, 572, 574, 575
Orphans of the Storm 561
Orwell, George 247
Oscars *see* Academy Awards
ostensiveness 389, 407, 409, 411, 587
Our Gang series 122
Our Town 276, 565
Out of Africa 83, 574, 630n.51
Out of the Past 326, 567
Outland 625n.85
Outlaw, The 566
OWI *see* Office of War Information

Pabst, G. W. 213, 331–2
Pacino, Al 87, 394

packaging 19, 171, 173–4, 187, 216–17 *see also* agents
Page, Joy 302, 479
Palm Beach Story 425, 566
Paltrow, Gwynneth 60
Panavision 252, 254, 265, 354
panning 337, 360, 362, 373–5, 587 *see also* camera movement
pantomime 378, 400
Paramount 36, 55, 116, 121, 125, 135, 172–4, 181–2, 187, 191, 195, 203, 278, 559, 560, 562, 563, 564, 565, 566, 567, 569, 570, 572, 573, 574, 575, 594 *see also* Famous Players-Lasky; Publix theaters
    Paramount Stock Company School 394
    Viacom/Paramount 190
Paramount antitrust case 128–9, 132, 155, 159–61, 163, 165, 172, 187, 285, 565, 567, 570, 582, 587, 621n.65
Parker, Alan 294–6, 299, 305
parody 105, 408, 461, 520
Parrish, Robert 49
Parsons, Louella 495
Pat Garrett and Billy the Kid 74, 93–100, 108, 375, 460, 571, 610n.51, 610n.54
Pathé 558, 559, 563, 567, 575
Pathé, Charles 229
patriarchy 300, 353, 359, 516, 528, 541–2
Patterson, Frances Taylor 494, 496, 501
Paul, Elliott 475
Paul, R. W. 372
Pawnbroker, The 570, 631n.20
Payne Fund Studies 499, 524, 563
PCA *see* Production Code Administration
Pearl Harbor 201, 230, 577
Pearson, Roberta 108
Peckinpah, Sam 93–4, 99, 109, 180, 610n.54
Peggy Sue Got Married 436, 574
Peirce, Charles Sanders 529, 641n.11
Penalty, The 382, 561
perception, psychology of 29, 421, 587
performance 56, 58, 67–8, 70, 95, 145, 207, 289, 298, 329, 369–71, 373–4, 377–84, 386–7, 389–1, 393–401, 403, 406–10, 418, 427, 441, 449, 453, 456, 458, 464, 468, 474, 483, 517, 580, 586, 587, 591
    autonomous 381, 389–90, 478, 579, 586, 587, 591
    conventions *see* conventions, performance
    idiolect 406–7

integrated 381–2, 389, 584, 574
Perkins, V. F. 33, 341, 391, 502, 516, 547, 560
persistence of vision 420, 587 *see also* illusion of movement
Persona 41–2
perspective 319, 325, 341
    monocular 320, 585
    sound perspective *see* sound
"Peter Pan Syndrome" 22, 357
Petersen, Wolfgang 217
Peyton Place 106, 169, 569
PFD *see* production-finance-distribution deal
Phantasmagoria 238
Phantom of the Opera, The 562
phenomenology 549
Philadelphia 575
phonograph 229, 232, 241
photographic representation 619n.18
photographic reproduction 619n.18
photography 45, 234, 236–7, 264, 316, 320, 562, 585, 588
Photophone 241, 569
Photoplay magazine 142, 559, 630n.45
Photoplay study guide 444
photoplays 10, 146, 149, 494, 496, 497
Pickens, Slim 86, 94, 375
Pickford, Mary 121, 403, 559, 560
picture palaces *see* theaters
Picturegoer magazine 75
Pidgeon, Walter 145
Pierson, Michelle 237
Pillow Talk 569
Pinky 285, 567
piracy *see* video piracy
Piranha 16, 572
Pirate, The 456, 459, 461, 567
platform release 166, 203, 204, 582, 587
Plato 456, 458, 585
Platoon 295, 308, 574
Platt, Louise 349
Play It Again, Sam 490, 571
Playboy magazine 64, 181, 490
Player, The 31, 59, 83, 575
Plitt Theaters 184
plot 17, 21, 70, 86, 89, 235, 359, 364, 374, 405, 425–9, 431, 433, 437, 446, 450, 454, 461–5, 467–9, 475–85, 487–9, 583, 586, 587, 591, 636n.31 *see also* syuzhet
plot point 416–7, 425, 449–50, 587
point of view 242, 347, 349–50, 352, 362,